THE OXFORD HANDBOOK OF

THE WORD

OXFORD HANDBOOKS IN LINGUISTICS

Recently published

THE OXFORD HANDBOOK OF THE HISTORY OF ENGLISH
Edited by Terttu Nevalainen and Elizabeth Closs Traugott

THE OXFORD HANDBOOK OF SOCIOLINGUISTICS
Edited by Robert Bayley, Richard Cameron, and Ceil Lucas

THE OXFORD HANDBOOK OF JAPANESE LINGUISTICS
Edited by Shigeru Miyagawa and Mamoru Saito

THE OXFORD HANDBOOK OF THE HISTORY OF LINGUISTICS
Edited by Keith Allan

THE OXFORD HANDBOOK OF LINGUISTIC TYPOLOGY
Edited by Jae Jung Song

THE OXFORD HANDBOOK OF CONSTRUCTION GRAMMAR
Edited by Thomas Hoffman and Graeme Trousdale

THE OXFORD HANDBOOK OF LANGUAGE EVOLUTION
Edited by Maggie Tallerman and Kathleen Gibson

THE OXFORD HANDBOOK OF ARABIC LINGUISTICS
Edited by Jonathan Owens

THE OXFORD HANDBOOK OF CORPUS PHONOLOGY
Edited by Jacques Durand, Ulrike Gut, and Gjert Kristoffersen

THE OXFORD HANDBOOK OF LINGUISTIC FIELDWORK
Edited by Nicholas Thieberger

THE OXFORD HANDBOOK OF DERIVATIONAL MORPHOLOGY
Edited by Rochelle Lieber and Pavol Štekauer

THE OXFORD HANDBOOK OF HISTORICAL PHONOLOGY
Edited by Patrick Honeybone and Joseph Salmons

THE OXFORD HANDBOOK OF LINGUISTIC ANALYSIS
Second Edition
Edited by Bernd Heine and Heiko Narrog

THE OXFORD HANDBOOK OF THE WORD
Edited by John R. Taylor

THE OXFORD HANDBOOK OF INFLECTION
Edited by Matthew Baerman

For a complete list of Oxford Handbooks in Linguistics please see pp. 865–866.

THE OXFORD HANDBOOK OF

THE WORD

Edited by

JOHN R. TAYLOR

OXFORD
UNIVERSITY PRESS

Great Clarendon Street, Oxford, OX2 6DP,
United Kingdom

Oxford University Press is a department of the University of Oxford.
It furthers the University's objective of excellence in research, scholarship,
and education by publishing worldwide. Oxford is a registered trade mark of
Oxford University Press in the UK and in certain other countries

First published 2015
First published in paperback 2017

Published in the United States of America by Oxford University Press
198 Madison Avenue, New York, NY 10016, United States of America

British Library Cataloguing in Publication Data
Data available

Library of Congress Cataloging in Publication Data
Data available

ISBN 978-0-19-964160-4 (Hbk.)
ISBN 978-0-19-880863-3 (Pbk.)

Contents

PART II WORDS AND LINGUISTIC THEORY

PART III MEANINGS, REFERENTS, AND CONCEPTS

PART IV WORDS IN TIME AND SPACE

PART V WORDS IN THE MIND

PART VI WORDS IN ACQUISITION AND LEARNING

PART VII NAMES

PART VIII FUN WITH WORDS

A FINAL WORD

List of Abbreviations

A	Agent
ABS	Absolutive case
ACC	Accusative case
ADJ	Adjective
ADV	Adverb
AFF	Affix
ANIM	Animate
ART	Article
ASP	Aspectual marker
ASS	Associative case
C	Consonant
CAUS	Causative
COND	Conditional
DEF	Definite article
DEM	Demonstrative
DET	Determiner
EMPH	Emphasis
EP	Epenthetic
ERG	Ergative case
ESS	Essive case
F	Feminine
FACT	Factive
GEN	Genitive case
HAB	Habitual
IDPH	Ideophone
IMPF	Imperfect
IND	Indicative
M	Masculine (gender)
MA	Marker
MEDIOPASS	Mediopassive
N	Noun
NCM	Noun class marker
NEG	Negative
NEUT	Neuter

NF	Non-finite
NM	Nominalizer
NP	Noun phrase
NPST	Non-past
O	Object
P	Patient argument
PASS	Passive
PC	Predicational constituent
PERF	Perfect
Pl	Plural
PLUPF	Pluperfect
POSS	Possessive
PP	Prepositional phrase
PRES	Present
PRO	Pronoun
PRT	Particle
PST	Past tense
PTC	Participle
PUNC	Punctual
PX	Possessive suffix
REMP	Remote past
REP	Reported
S	Subject
SBJV	Subjunctive
Sg	Singular
SRFL	Semireflexive
ST	Stative
SUFF	Suffix
TNS	Tense
TR	Transitive
V	Verb; Vowel
1	First person
2	Second person
3	Third person

List of Contributors

Marc Alexander is Senior Lecturer in Semantics and Lexicology at the University of Glasgow, and his work primarily focuses on digital humanities and the study of meaning in English, with a focus on lexicology, semantics, and stylistics through cognitive and corpus linguistics. He is Director of the Historical Thesaurus of English, and works mainly on applications of the Thesaurus in digital humanities, most recently through the AHRC/ESRC-funded SAMUELS and Mapping Metaphor projects. He has published, on his JISC-funded Hansard Corpus 1803–2003, a 2+ billion word corpus of political discourse over the past two centuries, and is working on enhancements to the Early English Books Online corpus. He is also Director of the STELLA Digital Humanities lab at Glasgow.

John M. Anderson is Emeritus Professor of English Language at the University of Edinburgh, where his entire university career was spent, apart from visiting posts at other European universities. He is interested in linguistic theory, particularly in relation to English and its history. He is mainly associated with the development of dependency-based approaches to linguistic structure and of localist case grammar and notional grammar.

Benjamin Blount is a retired anthropologist who received his Ph.D. in 1969 (University of California, Berkeley) and who taught at the University of Texas Austin, the University of Georgia, and the University of Texas San Antonio. He specializes in information systems, including human cognitive models. He was the inaugural editor of the *Journal of Linguistic Anthropology* and a former Editor-in-Chief of the *American Anthropologist*. His recent publications are on the history of cognition in anthropology, cultural models of knowledge in natural resource communities, and cognition in ethnographic research.

Frank Boers' initial research areas were lexicology and semantics (e.g., studies of polysemy and metaphor from a Cognitive Linguistics perspective). His more recent research interests were sparked by his experience as a language teacher and teacher trainer. He now publishes mostly on matters of instructed second or foreign language acquisition, with a particular focus on vocabulary and phraseology. He is co-editor of the journal *Language Teaching Research*.

Geert E. Booij obtained his Ph.D. degree in 1977 at the University of Amsterdam. From 1981 to 2005, he taught linguistics at the Vrije Universiteit Amsterdam. From 2005 to 2012, he was professor of linguistics at the University of Leiden. He is founder and editor of the book series *Yearbook of Morphology* and its successor, the journal *Morphology*. He is the author of *The Phonology of Dutch* (1995), *The Morphology of Dutch* (2002), *The Grammar of Words* (2005), and *Construction Morphology* (2010), all published by Oxford University Press, and of linguistic articles in major Dutch and international journals.

Kate Burridge is Professor of Linguistics in the School of Languages, Cultures and Linguistics, Monash University. Her research focuses on grammatical change in Germanic languages, the Pennsylvania German spoken by Amish/Mennonite communities in North America, the notion of linguistic taboo, and the structure and history of English. Recent books include *Forbidden Words: Taboo and the Censoring of Language* (with Keith Allan, 2006), *Introducing English Grammar* (with Kersti Börjars, 2010), and *Gift of the Gob: Morsels of English Language History* (2010).

G. **Tucker Childs** is Professor in Applied Linguistics at Portland State University in Oregon. Over the past fifteen years he has focused on documenting endangered languages spoken on the coasts of Guinea and Sierra Leone. Childs has worked on many non-core linguistic topics such as sound symbolism, which is particularly robust in the African word class known as ideophones, as well as on pidgins and urban slangs, and language variation in general. He is editor of *Studies in African Linguistics* and begins work on the Sherbro language of Sierra Leone in 2015.

Eve V. Clark is the Richard Lyman Professor in Humanities and Professor of Linguistics at Stanford University. She has done extensive cross-linguistic research, both experimental and observational, on children's acquisition of a first language, with particular emphasis on semantic and pragmatic development. She has also worked on the acquisition of word formation, again cross-linguistically, and on the kind of information adults provide in conversation that licenses child inferences about new word meanings. Her books include *Psychology and Language* (1977, with H. H. Clark), *The Ontogenesis of Meaning* (1979), *The Lexicon in Acquisition* (1993), and *First Language Acquisition* (2nd edn, 2009).

David Crystal is Honorary Professor of Linguistics at the University of Bangor, and works from his home in Holyhead, North Wales, as a writer, editor, lecturer, and broadcaster on linguistic topics. His main interests relate to the history and development of English, as illustrated by such works as *The Cambridge Encyclopedia of the English Language* (2nd edn 2003), *The Stories of English* (2004), *Spell It Out: The Singular Story of English Spelling* (2012), and (with Hilary Crystal) *Wordsmiths and Warriors: The English-Language Tourist's Guide to Britain* (2013).

Simon De Deyne obtained a master's degree in theoretical and experimental psychology at the University of Ghent in 2000 and received his Ph.D. in psychology on the topic of semantic vector spaces from the University of Leuven in 2008. From 2014 he has been a research associate at the University of Adelaide. His research uses a computational approach to uncover structure and dynamics in the representation of word meaning in the mental lexicon. He also coordinates the small world of words project, a cross-disciplinary effort to map the associative structure of the mental lexicon in various languages.

Philip Durkin is Deputy Chief Editor of the *Oxford English Dictionary*, and has led the dictionary's team of specialists in etymology for the past fifteen years. His publications include *The Oxford Guide to Etymology* (2009) and *Borrowed Words: A History of Loanwords in English* (2014), and he is currently editing a handbook of lexicography for OUP. His main research interests are in etymology, language contact (especially loanwords), polysemy, homonymy, and the history of the English language.

Christiane Fellbaum is a Senior Research Scientist at Princeton University, where she earned her Ph.D. in linguistics. Her work focuses on lexical semantics, computational linguistics, the syntax–semantics interface and multi-word expressions. She is one of the original developers of the WordNet lexical database and currently directs the WordNet project, for which she was awarded, together with the late George A. Miller, the 2006 Antonio Zampolli Prize. She is a co-founder and co-President of the Global WordNet Association, and supports the developments of cross-lingual lexical databases.

Dirk Geeraerts is Professor of Linguistics at the University of Leuven and founder of the research group Quantitative Lexicology and Variational Linguistics. He is the author of *The Structure of Lexical Variation* (1994), *Diachronic Prototype Semantics* (1997), *Words and Other Wonders* (2006), and *Theories of Lexical Semantics* (2010), and the editor, along with Hubert Cuyckens, of *The Oxford Handbook of Cognitive Linguistics* (2007).

Nikolas Gisborne is Professor of Linguistics in the School of Philosophy, Psychology and Language Sciences at the University of Edinburgh. He is interested in syntax and semantics, with a research focus on the interaction of subsystems in the grammar. He is the author of *The Event Structure of Perception Verbs*, published by Oxford University Press in 2010.

Cliff Goddard is Professor of Linguistics at Griffith University, Australia. He is a leading proponent of the Natural Semantic Metalanguage approach to semantics and its sister theory, the cultural scripts approach to ethnopragmatics. His major publications include the edited volumes *Ethnopragmatics* (2006, Mouton de Gruyter), *Cross-Linguistic Semantics* (2008, John Benjamins), and *Semantics and/in Social Cognition* (2013, special issue of *Australian Journal of Linguistics*), the textbook *Semantic Analysis* (2nd edn, 2011, Oxford University Press), and *Words and Meanings: Lexical Semantics Across Domains, Languages and Cultures* (co-authored with Anna Wierzbicka; Oxford University Press, 2014). He is a Fellow of the Australian Academy of Humanities.

Katharine Graf Estes is a member of the Psychology Department at the University of California, Davis. She received her Ph.D. in developmental psychology from the University of Wisconsin-Madison in 2007. Her research investigates the processes underlying early language acquisition. She has received funding from the National Institutes of Health and the National Science Foundation.

Anthony P. Grant is Professor of Historical Linguistics and Language Contact at Edge Hill University, Ormskirk. Having studied at York under Robert Le Page, he continued work on creolistics; his Ph.D. (Bradford, 1995) explored issues in agglutinated nominals in Creole French, and he has published over fifty articles and chapters on Native North American languages, Romani, Austronesian historical linguistics, pidgins, creoles, mixed languages, English dialectology and etymology, and lexicostatistical methods.

Peter Grzybek works at the Slavic Department of Graz University in Austria. After his MA thesis on 'Neurosemiotics of Verbal Communication' (1984) and his Ph.D. dissertation on 'The Notion of Sign in Soviet Semiotics', he qualified as a professor in 1994 with his 'Slavistic Studies on the Semiotics of Folklore'. His major research fields are linguistics and semiotics, literary and cultural theory, phraseology and paremiology. In his study of text and language, his particular focus is on exact and quantitative methods, attempting to apply statistical methods to the modelling of text structures and processes.

Reese M. Heitner teaches applied linguistics at Drexel University in Philadelphia. His interest in the developmental bootstrapping relationship between basic-level object categorization and phonemic word categorization and the experiment outlined in his chapter were inspired by Roger Brown's 'Original Word Game' approach to word learning.

Kristine A. Hildebrandt received her Ph.D. in Linguistics at the University of California Santa Barbara in 2003. She is currently an Associate Professor in the department of English Language and Literature at Southern Illinois University Edwardsville. Her research interests include phonetics–phonology interfaces, prosodic domains, the phonetic dimensions of tone, and language documentation and description.

Andrew Hippisley is Professor of Linguistics and Director of the Linguistics Program at the University of Kentucky, where he also serves as Chair of University Senate Council. He is author of *Network Morphology: A Defaults-Based Approach to Word Structure* (Cambridge University Press, 2012; with Dunstan Brown) and has published numerous articles on morphology in such outlets as *Yearbook of Morphology, Linguistics, Studies in Language, Natural Language Engineering* as well as chapters in books such as *Variation and Change in Morphology* (Benjamins, 2010), and *Handbook of Natural Language Processing* (Taylor & Francis, 2010). He is co-editor of *Deponency and Morphological Mismatches* (Oxford University Press, 2007), *Cambridge Handbook of Morphology* (2016), and *Defaults in Morphological Theory* (Oxford University Press, forthcoming).

Michael Hoey is a Pro-Vice Chancellor and Emeritus Professor of English Language at the University of Liverpool, with interests in discourse analysis, lexicography, and corpus linguistics. His book *Patterns of Lexis in Text* won the English Speaking Union Duke of Edinburgh Award for best book in applied linguistics 1991, and his book *Lexical Priming* was short-listed for the BAAL Award for best book in applied linguistics 2005. He was chief consultant to Macmillan for their award-winning *Macmillan English Dictionary*, aimed at advanced learners of English. He is an academician of the Academy of Social Sciences.

Carole Hough is Professor of Onomastics at the University of Glasgow, where she has worked since 1995. She is President of the International Council of Onomastic Sciences, President of the International Society of Anglo-Saxonists, and Vice-President of the Society for Name Studies in Britain and Ireland. Her research interests focus particularly on the interaction between names and other areas of language, and she has published extensively on Anglo-Saxon studies, historical and cognitive linguistics, and onomastics.

Christian Kay is an Honorary Professorial Research Fellow at the University of Glasgow. She was an editor of the *Historical Thesaurus of the Oxford English Dictionary* (Oxford University Press, 2009) and founded the Scottish Corpus of Texts and Speech (SCOTS). She has written on historical semantics and lexicography and is currently working on two projects: 'Mapping Metaphor with the Historical Thesaurus of English' and 'SAMUELS (Semantic Annotation and Mark-Up for Enhancing Lexical Searches)'.

Robert Kennedy is a Continuing Lecturer at University of California, Santa Barbara. His research interests include phonology, phonetics, reduplication, accents of English, naming practices, and the linguistics of sports.

Adam Kilgarriff is Director of Lexical Computing Ltd. He has led the development of the Sketch Engine, a leading tool for corpus research used for dictionary-making at Oxford University Press, Cambridge University Press, and by many universities and publishers worldwide. Following a Ph.D. on polysemy from Sussex University, he worked at Longman Dictionaries, Oxford University Press, and the University of Brighton prior to starting the company in 2003.

Marie-Claude L'Homme is Professor in the Department of Linguistics and Translation of the University of Montreal, where she teaches terminology. She is also the director of the Observatoire de linguistique sens-texte (OLST), a research group investigating various theoretical, methodological, and applied aspects related to the lexicon (general and specialized). Her main research interests are lexical semantics and corpus linguistics applied to terminology. She develops, along with researchers in linguistics, terminology, and computer science, lexical resources in the fields of computing and the environment.

Barbara C. Malt is a Professor of Psychology at Lehigh University. Her research focuses on thought, language, and the relation between the two. She is especially interested in how objects and actions are mentally represented, how monolingual and bilingual children and adults talk about these objects and actions using the tools available in their language(s), and what influence, if any, the different ways of talking have on non-linguistic representations. She is an associate editor for *Journal of Experimental Psychology: Learning, Memory, and Cognition*.

Asifa Majid is Professor of Language, Communication, and Cultural Cognition at the Centre for Language Studies at Radboud University Nijmegen. Her work is interdisciplinary, combining standardized psychological methodology, in-depth linguistic studies, and ethnographically-informed description. This coordinated approach has been used to study domains such as space, event representation, and more recently the language of perception.

Rosamund Moon is a Senior Lecturer in the Department of English at the University of Birmingham. She was previously a lexicographer, working on the Cobuild Dictionary Project at Birmingham (1981–90, 1993–9), and also at Oxford University Press (1979–81, 1990–93). Her main research areas are lexis and phraseology, lexicography, figurative language, and corpus linguistics; her publications include *Fixed Expressions and Idioms in English: A Corpus-Based Approach* (1998, Oxford University Press), and (with Murray Knowles) *Introducing Metaphor* (2006, Routledge).

Paul Nation is Emeritus Professor of Applied Linguistics in the School of Linguistics and Applied Language Studies at Victoria University of Wellington, New Zealand. His books on vocabulary include *Teaching and Learning Vocabulary* (1990) and *Researching and Analysing Vocabulary* (2011) (with Stuart Webb) both from Heinle Cengage Learning. His latest book on vocabulary is *Learning Vocabulary in Another Language* (2nd edn, Cambridge University Press, 2013). Two books strongly directed towards teachers appeared in 2013 from Compass Media in Seoul: *What Should Every ESL Teacher Know?* and *What Should Every EFL Teacher Know?* He is also co-author, with Casey Malarcher, of *Reading for Speed and Fluency* (Seoul: Compass Publishing, 2007).

Victor Raskin the founder of the dominant linguistic theory of humour, is a theoretical and computational semanticist who earned his degrees in mathematical, structural, and computational linguistics from Moscow State University, USSR (Ph.D., 1970). Besides his alma mater, he taught at the Hebrew University of Jerusalem (full time) and Tel Aviv University (part time) in 1973–8. At Purdue University since 1978, he is now Distinguished Professor of English and Linguistics, with courtesy affiliations in Computer Science and Computer and Information Technology. He is the Founding Editor-in-Chief (1987–99) of *Humor: International Journal of Humor Research*, now into its 27th volume, the author of a grossly overrated and over-cited *Semantic Mechanisms of Humor* (1985, Reidel), a charter Board member of the International Society of Humor Studies, and its first elected academic President in 2000.

Nick Riemer works on lexical semantics and the history and philosophy of linguistics at the University of Sydney, Australia, and at the Laboratoire d'histoire des théories linguistiques, Université Paris-Diderot, France.

Niels O. Schiller is a professor of psycho- and neurolinguistics. He is interested in the cognitive system underlying language processing and its neural substrate. In particular, he investigates syntactic, morphological, and phonological processes in language production and reading aloud. Furthermore, he is interested in articulatory-motor processes during speech production, language processing in neurologically impaired patients (aphasia), and forensic phonetics. Schiller makes use of behavioural as well as neurophysiological (EEG/ERP) and neuroimaging (fMRI) methods. He has published widely in international peer-reviewed journals in his field.

Mark C. Smith is currently a lecturer in the Department of Psychology at the Open University. He obtained his Ph.D. in experimental psychology at the University of Birmingham. He has published on a wide variety of topics including linguistics, psychology, and art history. At present, his main topic of research is the problem of propositional unity.

Joseph Sorell holds a Ph.D. in Applied Linguistics from Victoria University of Wellington, New Zealand, and an MA in TESOL from Michigan State University. His research interests are in vocabulary learning, corpus linguistics, and cross-cultural communication. He has taught EFL, literature, linguistics, and computer literacy in Taiwan, Saudi Arabia, and Abu Dhabi and has worked or studied in Germany, Israel, the UK, and the USA.

Gert Storms obtained a master's degree in social and clinical psychology in 1983 and received his Ph.D. in mathematical psychology from the University of Leuven in 1990. He is currently a full professor at the laboratory for experimental psychology at the University of Leuven. Using both modelling and correlational and experimental procedures, he has been doing research in the areas of category learning, concept representation, psychosemantics, and psychological scaling.

Dennis Tay is Assistant Professor at the Department of English, Hong Kong Polytechnic University. He has been working on the application of cognitive linguistic theory to the analysis of discourse, particularly in mental health contexts. He has authored a monograph, *Metaphor in Psychotherapy: A Descriptive and Prescriptive Analysis* (John Benjamins, 2013), published articles in discourse analysis and counselling journals, and co-edited a volume (with Masataka Yamaguchi and Benjamin Blount), *Approaches to Language, Discourse, and Cognition* (Palgrave, 2014).

John R. Taylor obtained his Ph.D. in 1979. He is the author of *Possessives in English* (1996), *Cognitive Grammar* (2002), *Linguistic Categorization* (3rd edn, 2003), and *The Mental Corpus* (2012), all published by Oxford University Press, and co-editor of the *Bloomsbury Companion to Cognitive Linguistics* (2014). He is a managing editor for the series *Cognitive Linguistics Research* (Mouton de Gruyter) and an Associate Editor of the journal *Cognitive Linguistics*.

Rinus G. Verdonschot is currently a JSPS post-doctoral fellow at Nagoya University, Japan. His research uses behavioural and neuro-correlational methods, and focuses on language production, language comprehension, bilingualism, and music cognition.

Henk J. Verkuyl is Emeritus Professor of Linguistics at Utrecht University. His main research interest has been the semantics of tense and aspect resulting in work including *On the Compositional Nature of the Aspects* (1972), *A Theory of Aspectuality* (1993), and *Binary Tense* (2008). He also hides behind the pseudonym 'Dr. Verschuyl' (quite literally, 'Dr. Hyde', because the Dutch verb *verschuilen* = *hide* in English) with his *Cryptogrammatica* (Cryptogrammar), a book about the linguistic principles behind the

Dutch crossword puzzle (7th edn, 2005). In 2014 his most recent work under this pseudonym, a crossword dictionary, appeared as *Groot Puzzelwoordenboek* (1,399 pages).

Cynthia Whissell teaches psychology at Laurentian University (Ontario, Canada) with a focus on psycholinguistics, emotion, statistics, and research methodology. She teaches methodology in an interdisciplinary doctoral programme involving both the Humanities and the Social Sciences. Most of her research addresses the quantification of emotion expressed in the words and sounds of the English language. This gives her the excuse to study entertaining works of literature as well as trends in onomastics.

John N. Williams is Reader in Applied Psycholinguistics at the University of Cambridge. He is co-editor of *Statistical Learning and Language Acquisition* (Mouton de Gruyter, 2012) and area editor for the cognitive section of the *Encyclopedia of Applied Linguistics* (Blackwell, 2012). His research on cognitive aspects of second language learning and processing has appeared in *Studies in Second Language Acquisition, Language Learning, Second Language Research, Applied Psycholinguistics, Bilingualism: Language and Cognition*, and *Lingua*.

Margaret E. Winters is Professor of French and Linguistics in the Department of Classical and Modern Languages, Literatures, and Cultures at Wayne State University, where she is currently Provost and Senior Vice President for Academic Affairs. Her research interests are in historical semantics and the history of the Romance languages, both within the framework of Cognitive Linguistics. She has published in these fields in a variety of scholarly journals in North America and Europe and in volumes of collected papers. She has also published two editions of Old French courtly romances and has co-edited two volumes, one of papers in applied linguistics with Geoffrey Nathan, also at Wayne State University, and the other a co-edited book of papers on semantic change. She is working currently on a textbook of historical linguistics and papers both on semantics and the history of linguistic theory.

Alison Wray is a Research Professor in Language and Communication at Cardiff University. She gained a BA (1st class) from the University of York, UK, in linguistics with German and Hindi, and a D.Phil. in psycholinguistics from the same institution. After a postdoctoral position and a lectureship in York, she became Assistant Director of the Wales Applied Language Research Unit, University of Swansea, before being appointed senior research fellow at Cardiff University in 1999. Since 2004 she has been Director of Research for Cardiff's School of English, Communication and Philosophy. Her main research area is theoretical explanations for formulaic language (recurrent patterns in language output), extending across adult native speaker language, first and second language acquisition, the evolutionary origins of language, and language disorders, particularly attrition and compensation in the language of people with dementia. She has also contributed to researcher development agendas by means of textbooks, training materials, and research coaching.

INTRODUCTION

JOHN R. TAYLOR

1 INTRODUCTION

WORDS are the most basic of all linguistic units, and the ones which speakers of a language are most likely to be aware of and to talk about. Newspapers carry articles listing the new words which have made it into the dictionaries; parents identify the onset of speech by their child's first words; improving proficiency in one's own language is often thought of as a matter of increasing one's vocabulary; learning a foreign language is associated, above all, with learning the words; important aspects of a culture can be encapsulated in key words; languages are perceived to be related on the basis of similarities between words; prior to the 20th century, with its focus on syntax, linguistic description was mainly an account of words, their meaning, their pronunciation, their history, their structure, and the relations they contract with each other. One of the most striking facts about words—and one which is often overlooked, probably because it is so obvious—is their sheer number; for Carstairs-McCarthy (1999: 10–12) the abundance of words is one of the features which distinguish human languages from all animal communication systems. Practically all the major subdivisions of linguistic study have something to say about words. In the case of morphology and syntax this is self-evident, but it is no less true of phonology, historical linguistics, sociolinguistics, psycholinguistics, and language acquisition research.

What, though, are words, how is 'word' to be defined, and how do we identify the words in the language around us? Before approaching these questions, we need to clear up some ambiguities in the use of the term.

A first distinction is between **word token** and **word type**. The word count facility on your word processing package counts the number of word tokens, usually defined, for this purpose, as anything that occurs between spaces and/or punctuation marks (though apostrophes and hyphens are typically ignored; *mother-in-law's*, on the programme I am currently using, is counted as one word). When a publisher specifies that a manuscript should come in at a certain number of words (800, 8000, 150,000, or whatever), it is word tokens that are at issue. Even here, though, we encounter some problems of definition and identification. A word processing package might identity such things as numerals, bullet points, listing devices such as '(a)' and 'i.', and even dashes (if surrounded by spaces) as words. These kinds of elements are not normally thought of as words, and authors submitting an 800-word article would not be expected to include them in the word count.

In any text (barring the very shortest), some word tokens, however they are identified, will occur more than once. These tokens are instances of the same word type. Inevitably, then, the number of word types in a text is going to be smaller (or, at least, cannot be greater) than the number of word tokens. It is word types that we have in mind when we speak of some words being more frequent in the language than others. Word types are also at issue when we enquire into vocabulary size. How many words did Shakespeare use? How many words does an average 10-year-old know? How many words do you need to know to get the gist of a newspaper article, a scientific paper, or a weather report? What are the most frequent words in English? Does English have more words than French?

The notion of word type hides some further distinctions. *Catch, catches, catching* are three different **word forms**. Yet if we were interested in stating the size of a person's vocabulary, we would probably want to regard the three forms as instances of the same word, or **lexeme**. The rationale for this is simple: the three word forms do not have to be individually learned. Once you have learned any one of the three forms (and provided that you know the rules for inflecting the verb and the conditions for the use of the different forms), you automatically have access to the other two forms. For this reason, a dictionary would list only one form, in this case, the 'basic' uninflected form *catch*. For English the matter is relatively trivial; regularly inflected verbs have four distinct forms: *talk, talks, talking, talked*, while nouns have only two: *dog, dogs*. For languages with more complex inflectional systems, the number of distinct forms can be quite large. For regularly inflecting verbs in Italian, Spanish, and Latin, the number of distinct forms can approach the high double digits, while nouns and adjectives in languages such as Russian and (again) Latin can have up to a dozen different forms. An Italian or Spanish speaker who learns a new (regular) verb has immediate access to (i.e. can produce and can understand) several score word forms. For heavily inflecting languages there is also the question of what the 'basic' form might be, i.e. the one that is to be listed in a dictionary and from which all others can be created. (The listed form is sometimes referred to as a **lemma**.) Often, more than one basic form is required. For example, Latin nouns, even those which are fully regular, are usually listed in dictionaries in both the nominative singular and the genitive singular forms.

The picture is complicated by the existence of irregular forms. Past tense *caught*, being irregular, does have to be learned. Even so, *caught* would (probably) not be regarded as a distinct lexeme, additional to *catch*, and (probably) would not be taken into consideration in statements of vocabulary size. It is important, however, to distinguish between word forms that *have to be* learned (irregular past tenses and irregular plurals are cases in point) and those which *have been* learned, and which are stored as such in the speaker's mental grammar. There is psycholinguistic evidence that perfectly regular forms, such as English plurals, may indeed be stored as such, alongside their base forms, especially when the plurals are of high frequency vis-à-vis the singulars. One source of evidence is performance on lexical decision tasks. Here, you are shown a string of letters on a screen and must decide as quickly as possible whether the string constitutes a word or not. One factor which influences the speed of your response is the frequency of the word form in the language. High-frequency plurals tend to elicit shorter response times than the corresponding lower-frequency singulars, suggesting that language users have registered the plural forms in their mental grammar (see e.g. Sereno and Jongman 1997).

Not all word forms need to be learned, of course, and many are surely not learned. English speakers will have no hesitation in declaring *portcullises* to be an English word, even though few will ever have had occasion to speak of more than one portcullis. Consider the case raised by George Miller:

> For several days I carried in my pocket a small white card on which was typed UNDERSTANDER; on suitable occasions I would hand it to someone. 'How do you pronounce this?' I asked.
> He pronounced it.
> 'Is it an English word?'
> He hesitated. 'I haven't seen it used very much. I'm not sure.'
> 'Do you know what it means?'
> 'I suppose it means "one who understands."'
>
> (Miller 1967: 77–78)

Is *understander* an English word? No instances are recorded in the 100-million-word British National Corpus (BNC: Davies 2004–), though five tokens are found in the 450-million-word Corpus of Contemporary American English (COCA: Davies 2008–).[1] An example like the following, from the 1.9-billion-word Corpus of Global Web-based English (GloWbE: Davies 2013) is unlikely to raise any eyebrows:

> I'm no great understander of women.

The case of *understander* is crucially different from the case of *portcullises*. *Portcullises* is an inflected form of a familiar, if somewhat infrequent word. In general, inflectional processes have the property of not allowing 'gaps' in their paradigms; every singular noun has a plural form (even if irregular, as with *ox~oxen* and *sheep~sheep*), which we are able to create should the need arise, and every present-tense verb form has a corresponding past-tense form (even if irregular, as with *catch~caught* and *put~put*). *Understander*, in contrast, is a derived form. Whereas inflection creates variants of a word (lexeme), derivation creates new words, often of a different lexical category (part of speech), and

[1] How does 100 million words relate to a person's linguistic experience? Obviously individuals differ enormously with respect to the amount of language (spoken and written) that they are exposed to (and attend to). Assuming, however, an average speaking rate of 120 words per minute, at ten hours per day without breaks, it would take a person almost 4 years to read out loud the total content of the BNC (Taylor 2012: 16). It seems fair to conclude that 100 million words corresponds to a substantial chunk of a person's lifelong linguistic experience.

with sometimes specialized or unpredictable meanings. Derivational processes tend to be less than fully productive and subject to all kinds of restrictions—semantic, phonological, or simply idiosyncratic. We have *length*, not *longness; goodness*, not *goodth; ethnicity*, rather than *ethnicness; childhood* is a common word, while *infanthood, babyhood*, and *teeenagehood* are not. This is not to say that *infanthood* etc. are not English words; like *understander*, they are readily understood if encountered, but unlikely to be listed in a dictionary, and unlikely to be found in any but the largest of corpora.

A second distinction is between **actual** words and the **potential** words in a language. Actual words are those that have been attested; potential words are those which have not been attested but which could be created by one of the word-formation processes operative in the language and which could, therefore, become part of a language's vocabulary.

The notion of actual word, however, is far from unproblematic. Enumerating the existing words of a language looks straightforward enough and, one might suppose, could be accomplished on the basis of a very large and representative corpus of texts. Even so, no corpus is able to deliver a complete, definitive list of all the words of a language. Increasing the size of even a very large corpus will result in ever more potential words making their appearance; we saw this in the example of *understander* (this word is absent from a 100-million-word corpus, but is attested in a corpus four and a half times larger). Neither would it be possible to enumerate the potential (but not yet actualized) words of a language. To take just one example. How many potential words are there which take the suffix *-hood*? There are about a dozen words in *-hood* in common use, and a further couple of dozen which are somewhat rare but still understandable in their context. Linguists might talk of wordhood, and even sentencehood, texthood, and phonemehood.[2] But to make a list of all the not-yet-existing words in *-hood* would be an impossible task.

The question of potential words becomes especially acute when we consider two further processes of word creation, in addition to derivation, namely, compounding and blending. Compounding is an extremely productive process in English. In principle, just about any two randomly selected nouns can come together in a noun–noun compound; the process is also recursive, in that a compound can be built out of already existing compounds. Is *airport* one word or two? The orthography suggests that it is one word, as does the phonology (the compound has only one primary stress) and the semantics (an airport is not really a kind of port). But what about *seaport*? *Bus route*? *Airport bus route*? *Airport bus route management company*? Since nominal compounding is recursive, the number of noun–noun compounds in English is truly open-ended, and any attempt to list all the not-yet-actualized compounds would be futile.

Blending is another word-formation process with open-ended outputs. Blends are created by combining the first part of one word with the second part of another word (where 'part', in the limiting case, can comprise the whole word). Often-cited examples

[2] In my first draft of this paragraph, I used *texthood* and *phonemehood* as examples of non-existing potential words in *-hood*. A subsequent Google search showed that these words were indeed attested in linguistics texts.

include *brunch* (*br*eakfast + l*unch*) and *smog* (*sm*oke + f*og*). Many blends are, in fact, compressed syntagms and are subject only to the ingenuity and creativity of speakers (which is not to deny that phonological and other constraints may not be relevant: see Kelly 1998 and Gries 2006). Readers may be familiar with the term *Brexit*—referring to the possibility (or desirability) of a *Br*itish *exit* from the European Union. A couple of decades or so ago, when the concept of Brexit had not yet crystallized, the word would not even have been deemed to be potential.

2 Identifying words

Identifying the words in an utterance might seem a trivial matter (even given the distinctions discussed above). In most cases, it is easy. But sometimes it is not. It is to these problematic cases that we now turn.

To illustrate some of the issues, consider the tag question below. How many words are there in the following, and what are they?

Isn't it?

One answer would be 'two', separated by a blank space. On the other hand, one might argue that *isn't* is a shortened form of two words, *is* and *not*. This is the analysis supported by the Corpus of Contemporary American English. If you search the corpus for the form *isn't*, you will be instructed to insert a word space before contracted *n't*; that is, *isn't* is taken to be *is* + *n't*. Similarly with *wasn't, aren't*, and *don't*. This procedure guarantees that occurrences of the forms *isn't, aren't*, and *don't* contribute to the frequency count of the word forms *is, are*, and *do*. There are, however, a number of problems. First, *Is not it?* is not a usual sequence. If the 'component words' of *isn't it* are spelled out in full, the accepted form would be *Is it not?* Second, application of the procedure to the forms *won't, can't*, and *shan't* attributes word status to *wo, ca*, and *sha*. In fact, these 'words' will turn out to have quite a high frequency of occurrence in the language. We might want to say that *wo, ca*, and *sha* are forms of the lexemes WILL, CAN, and SHALL. How, then, do we handle the form *ain't*? This can be a contracted form of *am/is/are not*, as well as of *has/have not*. Then there is the question of how to deal with the orthographic rendering of *isn't it* as *innit*, sometimes written as *ennit*. Is this one word (no internal spaces), two words (if so, what are they?), or a contracted form of three words?

The question of word identity also arises in connection with the following example (Lakoff 1987: 562):

There's a man been shot.

Suppose we say that *there's* is a contracted form of two words. What is the second of the two words? *Is* or *has*? Note that *There is a man been shot* and *There has a man been shot* are both of dubious acceptability. The choice of a tag might suggest that the contracted item should be construed as *has*.

There's a man been shot, hasn't there? /*isn't there?

But try putting the sentence into the plural:

?There've two men been shot.
There's two men been shot.

The second example seems preferable, suggesting that *there's*, pronounced [ðəz], is a unique word form, specific to the presentational construction. This supposition is supported by the following examples (sourced from the Internet), where the form *there's* appears to be insensitive to possible paraphrases with *is/are/has/have*:

There's lots of people been saying it's dangerous.
There's someone been looking for scapegoats.
But there's some people been waiting two hours.
There's some people been here longer than you.
There's someone been on my mind lately.
There's somebody been asking around about you.

Decisions on these matters are of vital importance to anyone studying the statistical properties of words in text, such as their frequency or their length. How we handle a relatively frequent form such as *isn't* will impact on frequency measures for *is* and *not*. If *isn't* is treated as one word, the frequency profile of *is* (and of the lexeme BE) will be lowered. A similar situation arises in connection with conventions for the use of the word space. Older texts—the novels of Charles Dickens are an example—have *some where, some one, every one*, whereas the modern practice is to join up the two components: *somewhere, someone, everyone*. We write *indeed* (one word) but *in fact* (two words), *perchance* but *by chance*. *Of course* distributes in the language as if it were a single word (cf. German *sicher, natürlich, selbstverständlich*; French *naturellement*); treating it as two words increases the frequency count for *of* and for *course*. The consequences are not insignificant. A search of the BNC shows that of the 48,654 occurrences of the noun *course*, 29,429—about 60 per cent—are in the phrase *of course*. Treating *of course* as two words more than doubles the frequency count for the noun *course* in the language.

There is a common theme here. The dubious cases nearly all concern high-frequency items and 'small words', such as parts of *be, have, do*, and markers of negation. It is worth noting that word-frequency distributions (see Sorell's chapter) tend to become somewhat erratic when the highly frequent words are considered. It would seem that when we get down to the most frequently occurring bits of a language, the notion of 'word' begins to dissolve.

3 Approaches to 'the word'

The above remarks notwithstanding, the reader may well be objecting that the notion of what constitutes a word is in most cases rather clear-cut. *Dog* and *cat* are words, as are *run* and *sesquipedalian*. The existence of clear-cut cases, alongside more problematic cases, points to the word as a prototype category. Prototypical words share a number of distinctive properties: orthographic, phonological, syntactic, and semantic. The problematic cases we have been considering constitute marginal words, in that they fail to exhibit the full range of characteristic properties.

Let us consider the properties in turn, taking as our reference point examples of prototypical words, with an eye on less prototypical, more marginal examples.

(a) Orthography. Orthographically, a word is separated by spaces or punctuation marks (though what counts as a punctuation mark can be open to question). Obviously, the criterion cannot be universally applicable, since some writing systems do not make use of the word-space convention (neither, of course, is it relevant to speakers who are not literate in their language). For literate English speakers, though, and for speakers of other European languages, the word-space criterion is paramount; it is also the criterion preferred by workers in computer language processing. It must be borne in mind, however, that word-space conventions are just that—conventions, which have emerged over the course of time and presumably in response to non-orthographic principles of wordhood. Even today, the conventions are not fully settled. One sometimes finds *nevertheless* and *nonetheless* written out as three words. Then there is the case of compounds. These, if conventionalized, are often written without a space or, variably, with a hyphen; otherwise, the components are separated by spaces. The conventions are different in German and Dutch; here, even nonce compounds are joined up; cf. Verkuyl's 'Word Puzzles' (this volume) example of *zuurstoftententententoonstelling* 'oxygen tent exhibition'.

(b) Phonology. A second criterion relates to pronunciation. A number of aspects are relevant. First, a phonological word must have one, and only one, main accent (or primary stress—the terminology is fluid). The number of primary stresses in an utterance is therefore a marker of the number of words (though the incidence of stresses does not indicate the location of the word boundaries.) This is why *airport* and *bus route* would be considered to constitute single words, whereas *busy port* and *direct route* would consist of two words. On this criterion, many of the 'little' words, such as articles, prepositions, and parts of *be, do*, and *have*, would not constitute words; lacking stress, they must attach to an adjacent item. Thus, *fish and chips* would consist of two phonological words: [fish and] [chips], with unstressed *and* [n̩] attaching as a clitic to the preceding stressed word, reflecting the predominately trochaic foot structure of English. Of course, the little words can, on occasion, be spoken with stress, for contrastive emphasis, for example.

A second criterion is that of being able to be preceded and followed by pauses. (One recalls Bloomfield's 1933: 178 definition of word as a minimal free form.) *And*, on this criterion, would count as a word. It can be utterance-initial and can be followed by a hesitation pause. Dixon and Aikhenvald (2002a: 12) propose, as a useful heuristic, the pauses that a native speaker makes when repeating an utterance 'word for word', as when giving dictation. *Fish and chips* is likely to be dictated as three words, with *and* being spoken with the full [æ] vowel.

A third phonological criterion is more subtle, and relates to the fact that some phonological generalizations (or 'rules') may be restricted to words and their internal structure, whereas others apply only across word boundaries. For example, double (or geminate) consonants are not allowed within English words. The spelling notwithstanding, *adder* is pronounced with a single 'd'; compare Italian *freddo*, which contains a lengthened 'd', spread over two syllables. Double consonants can occur in English, however, but only over word boundaries: *good dog, black cat, big girl, love Vera, his sister*, etc. The occurrence of a geminate can thus be seen as a marker of a word boundary. An interesting case is provided by examples like *non-native* and *unnatural*, which may be pronounced with a lengthened 'n', suggesting that *non-* and *un-* are (phonological) words. In contrast, there is no lengthened 'n' in *innate, innumerable*, or *innocence*, indicating that the prefix *in-* lacks the status of a phonological word.

In considering the phonological criteria for wordhood, we need to bear in mind that pronunciation—even more than writing—is variable. *Fish and chips* can be spoken, variably, with two or three main accents. *Unnatural* does not have to be spoken with a geminate 'n'. This means that the status of prefixed *un-* as a (phonological) word is also variable.

(c) Syntax. A third criterion is syntactic, or, less contentiously, distributional, having to do with the kinds of things a linguistic unit can, or must, or may not, occur next to. Here a distinction needs to be made between a word's **internal syntax** and its **external syntax**.

Internally, a word permits no variation, pauses, or insertions. Essentially, then, a word has no internal syntax. That is why compound *blackboard* (the thing to write on) is considered to be one word, whereas *black board* (referring to a board which is black) is two words. The latter can accept intrusions—*a black and white board, a blackish board*, etc.—the former cannot (at least, not if its status as a compound is to be preserved). One well-known caveat pertains to the phenomenon of expletive insertion: *abso-bloody-lutely*. The insertion is possible between two (typically trochaic) feet, each with a stressed syllable (McCarthy 1982).

Even so, there are cases which are less than clear-cut. Suppose we want to refer to a collection of blackboards and whiteboards (both single-word compounds, by most criteria). The conjunction *black- and whiteboards* (spoken with two main accents) seems entirely plausible. Or take the case of *mother-in-law*. Is this one word or three (or two)? One relevant consideration would be what the plural form is: do we say *mother-in-laws* (suggesting that we are dealing with only one word, permitting no internal intrusions) or *mothers-in-law* (suggesting a word division between *mother* and *in-law*). According to the COCA corpus, the former is more frequent by a factor of about 5:1; a similar bias exists for other *in-law* expressions. The odds, therefore, are in favour of regarding *mother-in-law* as one word (though the very fact of variation is surely of interest, showing that the word status of *mother-in-law* is not fully fixed). Note that by the no-intrusion criterion, *in-law* would have to count as one word; indeed, it functions as a regular count noun, with a predictable plural form: cf. *my in-laws*.

Another interesting case is *mum and dad*, and its plural. We would expect *mums and dads*, and this indeed is the preferred form. However, consider the following (from the GloWbE corpus):

If the markets can't pick interest rates how can the *mum and dads* pick interest rates?

Here, *mum and dad* appears to be functioning as a single semantic unit (as a single lexeme, in fact); it does not refer to a collective consisting of a mum and a dad, but is roughly equivalent to 'typical retail investor'.

External syntax has to do with the items that a word can occur next to. There are very few restrictions on the neighbours of a (prototypical) word. Certainly, (attributive) adjectives tend to occur immediately before nouns, predicative adjectives immediately after *be, become, seem*, etc. But these are tendencies, not absolutes; for example, an adverb can easily be inserted between *be* and a predicative adjective. Compare the situation with that of a bound affix such as *-ness*. This can only occur (indeed, must occur) as an affix to an adjectival stem, with no intrusions allowed between stem and affix.

In terms of its external syntax, possessive *'s* is a word. The morpheme attaches to whatever happens to occur last in a possessor nominal. Mostly, of course, the possessive morpheme ends up attaching the possessor noun (*the man's hat*); in principle, however, the morpheme can attach to practically any kind of word (*the man I was speaking to's hat*); see Hildebrandt's chapter. The possessive morpheme would not count as a prototypical word, of course, because it is phonologically dependent and cannot occur between pauses. Its status, rather, is that of a clitic.

(d) Semantics. A prototypical word associates a stable phonological/orthographic form with a coherent semantic category, with its distribution in the language being determined by the syntax. *Dog* and *cat, airport* and *sesquipedalian*, obviously qualify for word status on this criterion—though the case of articles, parts of *be* and *do*, some prepositions such as *of*, and the possessive morpheme, is less clear. Homonymy and polysemy also muddy the picture—polysemy, in that a word form may be associated with a range of semantic values, and homonymy, in that the semantic values may be so disparate that it may be more appropriate to speak of two or more words which happen to share the same form. Nevertheless, it is clearly the semantics which motivates the word status of *mum and dad* and *mother-in-law* (discussed above).

4 Word as prototype

As the preceding remarks will have shown, the various criteria for wordhood do not always coincide. The situation indicates a prototype approach to words; there are 'good examples' of the category (where all the criteria coincide), and more marginal examples, where only some of the criteria apply. Thus, a prototypical word will

- have a stable phonological form, intolerant of interruptions and internal variation;
- be associated with a reasonably stable semantic content (or array of related contents, in case the word is polysemous);
- be separated in writing by spaces;
- have one main stress and be pronounceable on its own, surrounded by pauses;
- be relatively free with regard to the items to which it can be adjacent.

These criteria are particularly useful when we try to differentiate words from competing categories, such as word vs. phrase, word vs. bound morpheme, word vs. clitic. The dividing line between these categories is not always clearly drawn. The definite article *the* (when unstressed) has clitic-like properties, adjective+noun combinations may waver in their status as phrases or compounds, affixes can sometimes get detached from their hosts and function as full-fledged words (*anti, pro, ism*, etc.) (Taylor 2003). This kind of fuzziness is just what one would expect on a prototype view of 'word'.

5 Are these words?

To see how a prototype-based approach might be applied, consider the various vocalizations which interlard our speech; these are represented orthographically as *oh, ah, um, er, hm, erm*, etc. Are these words? Let us go through the features:

(a) These vocalizations, if written, are separated by spaces. This makes them words. On the other hand, their 'spelling' is somewhat variable, and we would not expect to find them listed in a dictionary. This speaks against their word status.
(b) The vocalizations are phonologically autonomous in that they may bear primary stress, they do not need to lean on adjacent elements, and they may be surrounded by pauses. From this point of view, they are undoubtedly words.

(c) They are relatively free to occur at any point in an utterance and are not required to attach to items of a specified syntactic category. In this, they are like words. They differ from prototypical words in that they do not contract syntactic relations with neighbouring items; instead, they have the character of parenthetical intrusions.

(d) They are not associated with a fixed semantic content; their function is discoursal and attitudinal, signifying such things as hesitation, uncertainty, and prevarication. Yet they are not somatic noises, whether voluntary or involuntary (like coughs and yawns). They are, on the contrary, language-specific; mostly, these vocalizations are made up of phonetic segments characteristic of the language in question. English speakers do not hesitate and prevaricate in the same way as French or Russian speakers do.

In brief, the vocalizations exhibit a number of properties of typical words, yet they would by no means be considered full-fledged words; they are marginal words par excellence. Indeed, many people would not consider them to be words at all. They are typically absent from the word inventories that we find in dictionaries and the word lists that are derived from corpus analysis. And if they are taken into consideration in corpus studies, they are likely to cause all manner of problems (see Sorell's chapter).

6 Exhaustive analysis, no residues

A different approach would be to question the view that utterances can be exhaustively analysed into words.

The idea of exhaustive analysis is a common assumption in linguistic description. We divide texts up into sentences, sentences into words, words into morphemes, and all of these ultimately into phonemes. In all cases, the expectation is that once the dividing-up has been done, nothing will be left over. Now, in the case of the word–morpheme relation, 'residues' are in fact not at all uncommon. Sometimes, the residue is accorded the status of a 'cranberry morpheme', named after the *cran-* of *cranberry*. Even this ruse to save the exhaustive-analysis approach, however, quite often fails. Take the case of the names of many of the consonants; these terminate in [iː]: *B* [biː], *C* [siː], *D* [diː], etc. The strength of this association is manifest in the name of the final letter, *Z*, often pronounced [ziː] rather than [zɛd]. But if we recognize [iː] as a morpheme (with roughly the semantic value of 'name of a consonant'), what are we to say about the initial segments [b], [s], [d], etc.? To refer to these as morphemes, even as cranberry morphemes, with the semantic value of, respectively, the consonants *B*, *C*, and *D*, seems a bit outlandish. The proper approach, it seems to me, is to recognize that while bits of a word might have a function across several words in the lexicon, we are under no obligation to accord comparable status to all of the remaining bits.

The idea that words and utterances can be exhaustively analysed into phonemes (or, less contentiously, phones, or phonetic segments) is much more entrenched, and counterexamples are rarely entertained or discussed. Few linguists would want to quibble with Chomsky's assumption that 'each utterance of any language can be uniquely represented as a sequence of phones' (Chomsky 1964: 78). Yet there are all manner of noises that people make as they speak—coughs, laughs, giggles, grunts, smacking of lips, inhalations, sucking on teeth, and so on. These are going to be filtered out of any linguistic (phonological) analysis (though they may be of interest in a study of the communicative act in progress). On what basis they are to be ignored is, however, rarely addressed; a notable exception is Zellig Harris: see Harris (1951: 18–19) on why coughs should be overlooked in phonemic analysis.

(On a personal note: I first became aware of the problematic nature of these non-speech noises when working with some colleagues in the Information Science department on a system of phoneme—and ultimately, it was hoped, word—recognition. The problem was that the system interpreted the sound of inhalation variously as [h], [f], and [θ] and the clanking of furniture as voiceless plosives. Adjusting the sensitivity of the system did not solve the problem. This simply resulted in genuine cases of [h], [f], and [θ] being missed.)

Occasionally, the status of a noise as a linguistic or non-linguistic element is far from clear. One of the texts in Crystal and Davy (1975) consists of a lengthy deadpan monologue narrating the attempts of an accident-prone driver to reverse her car. The listener responds with an utterance transcribed by Crystal and Davy as follows:

|HM̀| –t |oh BLÌMEY|

The authors inform us (p. 46) that the 't' represents an alveolar click [!], expressive of the speaker's sympathetic appreciation. Is this sound part of the sound system of English, or is it extraneous to the system, comparable, perhaps, to a noisy inhalation of breath, or even (to take a non-acoustic example) a shake of the head? Listening to the recording which accompanies the volume suggests that the click is functioning as a consonantal onset of the word (is it a word?) *oh*. On the other hand the listener could have responded simply with the click (perhaps accompanied by a shake of the head and with raised eyebrows). At best, the click is a (very) marginal phonetic segment of English.

The relevance of this to our main topic is as follows. We can easily recognize the words in an utterance. Sometimes, though, there are bits left over which fail to achieve word status on the usual criteria. We might regard these as 'marginal' words, which fail to exhibit the full range of word-defining properties. An alternative approach, suggested by Wray (this volume), would be to acknowledge that utterances are not composed only of words; once the words have been identified, there may be bits and pieces left over which cannot easily be assimilated to the word category. As Wray puts it, words are the bits that fall off of an utterance when you shake it (p. 750). To borrow an image from Kilgarriff's chapter, what is left is like the stuff found at the bottom of a schoolboy's pocket: 'very small pieces of a wide variety of substances, often unsavoury, all mixed together, often unidentifiable' (p. 33).

7 Overview of the volume

With quotations from over thirty writers, **David Crystal** documents the fascination of poets, novelists, and critics with words, and reflects on the various viewpoints that have been expressed in literature and linguistics about the form and function of words and their relationship to thoughts, actions, and culture. He touches on a number of topics which are dealt with in subsequent chapters, such as historical change, word innovation, and the impossibility of quantifying the size of the lexicon.

Adam Kilgarriff takes up the question of how many words there are in a given language. Dictionaries (and their users) persist in the fiction that a definitive answer is possible—if it's 'not in the dictionary', then it's not a word; conversely, if it is a word, then it has to be in the dictionary. There are many reasons why a definitive listing is not possible. Word-formation processes are productive, to a greater or lesser extent, which means that a language's vocabulary is essentially open-ended. Second, all manner of specialized interests and activities, from chemistry to cooking, have their own vocabulary, and many branches of knowledge have the means for creating their own words as needed. Then there is the question of how to handle foreign borrowings, variant spellings and pronunciations, misspellings (and mispronunciations), and dialectal forms. A more fruitful line of enquiry would concern the words that a person needs in order to function in a given context—the topic of Paul Nation's chapter.

The chapters by **Marc Alexander** and **Christian Kay** deal, respectively, with dictionaries and thesauri. A dictionary lists the words, and for each word describes its meaning. A thesaurus does the reverse—it lists the concepts, and for each concept gives the words which can express it. Both kinds of resource have a venerable history, and both are undergoing rapid developments in our digital age. Alexander addresses the sometimes conflicting concerns of scholars, users, and publishers in the design and presentation of dictionaries, while Kay raises the question of whether a universal system of concepts is possible, or whether conceptual classification should be allowed to emerge from language usage itself.

There follow two chapters dealing with quantitative aspects of the words of a language—their frequency and their length. George Zipf (1949) pioneered work on these topics, pointing to a linear relation between the logarithm of word frequencies and the logarithm of their frequency ranking, also noting that word length tends to correlate inversely with frequency. **Joseph Sorell** presents updates on the Zipfian frequency distribution, nuanced with respect to text types and genres. He also speculates that the distribution may be motivated by functional considerations, having to do, specifically, with the accessing of words stored in small world networks. **Peter Gryzbek** addresses the length of words—again building on the Zipfian thesis that the more frequently a word is used, the shorter it tends to be. His research explores the dynamics of word length—within texts, within genres, within languages, and over time. He argues that the study of word length involves much more than just the length of words. Word length stands at the intersection of numerous language systems, and impinges on such matters as polysemy, a language's phonological inventory, and syntactic and textual organization.

The next two chapters go beyond the word, narrowly construed. **Rosamund Moon** writes about multi-word units—groups of words which have quasi-unitary status, and which need to be learned as such. Quite a lot comes under the scope of Moon's topic—from fixed idioms and proverbs to recurring phrases and preferred collocations; indeed, a significant proportion of any text will comprise formulaic material of different kinds. Of special interest are phrasal patterns which permit some degree of variation, sometimes with humorous effect.

Michael Hoey pursues the matter on the detailed analysis of a short text fragment. Speakers, he argues, subconsciously note the collocations that a word makes with other words, as well as the collocations that the combination has with other words or word combinations. Speakers also note the syntactic environments of words and word combinations (i.e. their colligations) and their association with words of particular semantic sets. Parts of words also participate in these kinds of relations. Thus, a word can be said to prime the contexts of its previous uses. These primings influence the way we interpret a word in context as well as our future uses of the word. The chapter also shows how collocation contributes to textual cohesion. The relation of a word to its neighbours thus lies at the very core of language as stored in the mind and in its use.

The next group of chapters address word structure and the status of words in linguistic theory. **Geert Booij** overviews the internal structure of words (morphology) and processes for word creation—inflection, derivation, compounding, blending, and univerbation (the process whereby groups of words acquire the status of single words). Complex words may acquire pronunciations and meanings which are not fully predictable from their parts, thereby obscuring a word's internal structure.

The notion of part of speech is a familiar one. However, as **Mark Smith** shows, the setting up of categories, and determining their membership, are subject to decisions which are ultimately arbitrary. Some words are 'quirky', and do not readily fit into any of the recognized categories; in a sense, they belong to categories with a membership of one. And even for the better-established categories, such as noun or verb, it is rarely the case that their members share the same range of properties.

Nikolas Gisborne argues for the lexicalist hypothesis, according to which words are 'atoms' whose combination is sanctioned by the syntax. Essentially, this boils down to the claim that the syntax does not need to 'look into' the internal structure of words. Gisborne defends the claim by addressing a number of controversial examples, including the use of the passive participle in English, pronominal clitics in French, and noun incorporation in Mohawk.

Kristine Hildebrandt discusses the word as a phonological unit, i.e. a unit around which language-specific phonological generalizations may be made. Mostly, the phonological word coincides with the grammatical word as discussed by Gisborne, but often it does not. Moreover, different languages draw on different sets of phonological criteria. Rather than seek a universal definition, phonological words emerge on the back of phonological processes of a given language.

Andrew Hippisley turns to the question whether the word has universal status—whether, that is, all languages have items that we want to call words. Words are, he argues, the basic symbolic resources of a language, uniting a pronunciation (and spelling), a meaning, and a syntactic status. This neat association is often upset, most obviously by homonymy and synonymy, as well as by such phenomena as incorporation; at best, then, words are universals of a fairly plastic kind. Hippisley also considers the question whether words are unique to human languages—whether, that is, animal communication systems have 'words'. He argues that they do not; animal signs are tied to specific external phenomena, whereas words designate 'mind-dependent' concepts. Hippisley proposes that cross-language variation in the properties of words results from different solutions to the problem of how complex conceptual information is channelled into a one-dimensional stream of sounds.

Kate Burridge's chapter addresses word taboo. When a word denotes something unpleasant, forbidden, or emotionally sensitive, people behave as if the very sound of the word equates to what it denotes. The word itself becomes unpleasant, and should be avoided. Even words that sound similar to the taboo word may be shunned. The feelings are so intense that they may affect expressions recruited as euphemism. Taboo is therefore a potent source of lexical renewal and semantic change.

Word taboo challenges a basic tenet of Saussure's (1916) theory of the arbitrariness of the link between sound and meaning. The thesis of arbitrariness also needs to be nuanced by the widespread phenomenon of sound symbolism. The less-than-arbitrary association of sound and meaning is the topic of **Tucker Childs**' chapter. Some of these associations—such as between high front vowels and the idea of smallness—would appear to be universal, while others emerge by association within the language and can affect significant portions of a language's lexicon.

The next group of chapters deal with semantic issues. Prefacing his chapter with a warning that 'word meaning' is a theoretical notion, whose legitimacy derives from its usefulness in explaining language use, and noting that some languages do not even have a term for this supposed property of words, **Nick Riemer** discusses two major approaches to word meaning. One is based on reference, and studies the kinds of things and situations that a word may refer to. While a referential approach has the appeal of 'objectivity', it is clear that many words lack referents (*ghost* and *Martian*, presumably); the approach is also unable to capture the affective connotations of words. The other approach appeals to shared concepts; indeed, it is because of the concepts that they link to that words are able to refer to the outside world at all. A third approach—which Riemer briefly touches on—proposes that word meaning can be explicated in terms of relations amongst words themselves—a topic developed in Christiane Fellbaum's chapter.

Barbara Malt discusses the referential use of words, specially, the factors which motivate a speaker's choice in the designation of objects, events, relations, properties of things, etc. These do not usually come associated with a name which intrinsically belongs to them and which uniquely identifies them. Even for those entities which have been assigned a proper name, a speaker is still at liberty to refer by means of a pronoun or a descriptive phrase. A speaker's choice is motivated by many factors—the options made available by the language, the ones that the speaker has learned and which are available at the moment of speaking, as well as the speaker's assessment of the knowledge base of the addressee.

Naming is also the topic of **Marie-Claude L'Homme**'s chapter on terminology. Experts in all fields of knowledge, from scientists and engineers to bureaucrats and hobby enthusiasts, have developed systems of terms for the naming and classification of concepts, with the aim of facilitating communication amongst specialists and avoiding ambiguity and misunderstandings. The chapter draws attention to the dynamic nature of terminologies and their dependence on features of the communicative situation, including the supposed degree of expertise of the addressee.

Christiane Fellbaum discusses the semantic relations amongst words in a language. She makes the distinction between relations between words and relations between concepts. Antonymy (the relation of 'opposites') is a relation between specific words (*big, little; large, small*), as are collocational preferences (*strong* collocates with *tea; powerful*, a near synonym of *strong*, does not). Taxonomic and meronymic (whole–part) relations are relations between concepts (*vehicle, car; car, wheel*). Relations (lexical and semantic) are the basis of the WordNet project, a large electronic database of about 155,000 words, incorporating properties of both a conventional dictionary and a thesaurus, organized around relations of various kinds. It is hypothesized that it is just this kind of network which underlies speakers' ready and effortless access to the contents of their lexicon.

As every language learner knows, a word in one language rarely has an exact translation equivalent in another. **Asifa Majid** examines two semantic domains—perception and the human body—in order to illustrate similarities and differences across a wide range of languages in the way in which these areas of human knowledge are structured and lexicalized. She discusses the possible sources of the variation—the environment, the ecological niche where the language is spoken, cultural practices, and historical development.

Cliff Goddard's chapter reviews different ways in which words can be carriers of culture-related meaning. Culture-laden words are untranslatable, by normal means, into other languages. The chapter reviews examples from various abstract and concrete domains, stressing that cultural themes are often conveyed by a suite of related, mutually reinforcing words. The chapter demonstrates how the Natural Semantic Metalanguage (NSM) approach is able to capture subtleties of meaning, while counteracting the danger of conceptual Anglocentrism creeping into the definitions.

Philip Durkin and **Dirk Geeraerts** discuss historical matters. Durkin takes the broader perspective of etymological research, presenting the methodology of tracing (or reconstructing) the historical past and the relationship between the words of different languages. He highlights cases where the line of descent from an earlier to a later form is blurred by mergers and blendings. Geeraerts zooms in on processes of semantic change, the emergence of new meanings, and the loss of older ones.

All languages borrow items from other languages, some extensively. This is the topic of **Anthony Grant**'s chapter. Some borrowings are for naming previously unknown concepts; others replace (or coexist with) native terms. While nouns are particularly subject to borrowing, there do not appear to be any absolute restrictions on what can be borrowed. Borrowings can be an important pointer to the history of a language, and can function as a conduit for the introduction of new phonemes and new inflectional and derivational morphemes into a language.

Margaret Winters writes on the results of borrowing on language/vocabulary structure. While English, to take one of her examples, is 'basically' a Germanic language, a large number of words (and syntactic constructions) have been borrowed from French. In some cases, the two strands have been homogenized, with only an expert being able to disentangle the influences. Often, however, the borrowed items may constitute a sub-component of the vocabulary, with its own phonological, morphological, semantic, stylistic, and even syntactic and orthographic identity, and recognized by speakers as different from the core lexicon of the language.

The next group of chapters address the mental representation and mental access of words. The topic of the chapter by **Simon De Deyne** and **Gert Storms** is research on word associations. The word association paradigm is a familiar one: given a word (such as *bread*), what is the first word that comes to mind? (Answer, for most people, *butter*.) The association paradigm provides insights into the links which exist in the mental lexicon, and is a valuable accessory to findings from usage data. The authors propose that the mental lexicon can be viewed as a large association network, whose properties facilitate lexical search and retrieval.

The accessing of words from the mental lexicon is the topic of the chapter by **Niels Schiller** and **Rinus Verdonschot**. Lexical access is a crucial component in the process of transforming thoughts into speech; a widely used paradigm requires subjects to name pictured objects, often against various kinds of distraction. The chapter reviews a number of models for lexical access. Also addressed is the storage and access of morphologically complex words, including compounds.

John Williams addresses the storage and access of words in bilingual speakers. Do bilinguals keep their two languages distinct, or do the representations overlap and interact in usage situations? Does the relation between the languages change as a function of level of proficiency and context of acquisition? Williams reviews extensive research showing that, when performing tasks in one language, bilinguals and proficient second-language learners cannot avoid activating orthographic, phonological, lexical, and semantic representations in their other language(s), suggesting that representations in a bilingual's different languages continuously compete with each other for selection. Bilinguals rely on domain-general executive control mechanisms to manage the activation levels of their different languages.

Dennis Tay writes on words and psychological disorders. He approaches the matter from two perspectives. On the one hand, the disorder manifests itself in the patient's inability to access words, or to use them appropriately. Disorders of this nature feed into models of lexical storage and access. The second perspective is to regard words, particularly the metaphorical use of words in therapeutic discourse, as pointers to psychological disorders which are not in themselves inherently linguistic, such as psychogenic seizures and delusional thought. Tay proposes some possible directions for metaphor and corpus research in mental health discourse.

The next three chapters deal with child acquisition. Early word acquisition is the topic of **Eve Clark**'s chapter. Children normally start to talk in their second year and build their vocabulary to around 14,000 words by age 6. However, vocabulary size varies considerably with the amount of direct adult–child interaction children get to participate in before age 3. Clark discusses the factors which facilitate the process of word learning, such as joint attention with adult speakers, the presumed contrast of new words with words already known, and adults' reformulations of the child's errors.

The topic of **Katharine Graf Estes'** chapter is the strategies that infants use to identify the words of the ambient language. While the written language may demarcate its words by means of spaces, the spoken language does not (usually) demarcate words by means of pauses. However, already by one year of age, children are paying attention to cues for word boundaries, such as phonotactic constraints and patterns of lexical stress. Indeed, the ability to extract words from continuous speech may be an important driver of lexical acquisition.

Reese Heitner draws attention to what he calls the 'inherent duality' of word learning. To be sure, the learner needs to recognize that a great variety of creatures, of different shapes, sizes, colours, and temperaments, can all be called 'dog'. But the learner also has to recognize that a great variety of pronunciations can be regarded as instances of the phonological form /dɒg/. Languages differ not only in the way they categorize the environment, but also in the way they categorize speech sounds. Heitner proposes that each process is able to bootstrap the other, in a kind of virtuous circle.

Paul Nation and **Frank Boers** address vocabulary from a pedagogical point of view—Nation on the words that a learner needs, and Boers on the strategies of teaching and learning words. Given the Zipfian distribution of word frequencies, a smallish number of word types make up a largish portion of the word tokens in a text. From one point of view, the most frequent words are the most useful, in that they guarantee coverage of a large amount of a text. On the other hand, frequent words—precisely because of their frequency—are the least informative. Nation discusses the criteria for drawing up lists of words which are likely to guarantee optimal understanding of different kinds of text. With emphasis on second- and foreign-language pedagogy, Boers warns against teaching strategies which might actually impede the learning of words, while extending the discussion to the learning of multi-word phrases and idioms.

The next topic is names. Names are special kinds of words, for a number of reasons. **John Anderson** discusses their status in the linguistic system. Do proper names have a meaning? Although some philosophers have argued that they do not—names attach 'directly' to their referents, without an intervening 'concept'—the prevailing view amongst linguists is, probably, 'yes'. Concerning their syntactic status, the prevailing view is that they are a kind of noun. Anderson points out that names do not have a uniform grammar. Overall, however, their syntactic properties overlap more with those of pronouns than with (common) nouns, as befits their use for definite reference to individuals.

Mostly, a speaker has to abide by the sound–meaning conventions of the ambient language, following the Saussurean doctrine of the arbitrariness of the sign. Especially when it comes to the naming of infants, however, people are able to establish new labels (usually from a given name pool, and respecting the prevailing cultural conventions), which they perceive to be 'appropriate' to their referent, in one way or another. Naming practices around the world are the topic of **Benjamin Blount**'s chapter. He draws attention to the equation, prevalent in many societies, of the name with the individual. Hence, the use of names may be socially restricted, and after the death of the individual the name may become taboo (its mention conjuring up the deceased), thus necessitating the invention of alternative descriptive names. Even words phonetically similar to the deceased's name may be affected—a major factor in lexical renewal, in some societies.

Carole Hough introduces the field of onomasiology—the study of names, with special reference to place names, man-made structures, and features of the natural environment. In view of their conservative nature, these kinds of names are of special interest for the light they shed on settlement patterns. Hough concludes with some suggestive remarks on the sociolinguistic dimension of naming, for example, in the construction of community identity.

Word creation is also the topic of **Robert Kennedy**'s chapter on nicknames, their form, content, and function. Nicknames range from forms internally derived from formal names to items coined via more creative processes. In function, they can be used for reference or for address. Nicknames for males and females tend to have different patterns of phonemic structure, coinage, and semantic content. Like Hough, Kennedy draws attention to the sociolinguistic dimension of nicknaming, in that, for example, nickname coinage may reflect the relative power of coiners over recipients.

Cynthia Whissell addresses the factors which may influence the choice of a name—usually for a child, but also for pets, and even a novelist's choice of names for his or her protagonists. Her research shows, once again, that names are not arbitrary strings of sounds but can be felt to be appropriate to their subjects. She explores, amongst other things, the emotive associations of the sounds in a name and, related to this, the phonological differentiation of male and female names and changes in naming fashions over time.

Victor Raskin writes on verbal humour. He notes that words as such are not funny—the only exception, perhaps, being names (here again, the special status of names vis-à-vis other words is worth noting). But it is the words, in their appropriate combination, which make up verbal humour. Defending his theory that humour arises through conflicting scripts, he notes that jokes depend on the possibility of words and expressions being compatible with more than one script, a punchline making the ambiguity evident.

People's fascination with words finds its expression in all manner of word games, from Scrabble to palindromes and anagrams, and, of course, crosswords, especially the 'cryptic' crosswords so popular in Anglophone (and Dutch) cultures. **Henk Verkuyl** offers a linguistic analysis, both erudite and entertaining, of word puzzling in English and Dutch.

Alison Wray sums up with remarks on the paradox of words. We think we know what they are, we believe that they exist, yet find it extraordinarily difficult to define them precisely and efficiently. It is not just that there are conflicting understandings of 'word' (word form, lexeme, lemma) and different (and not always consistent) definitions of word (phonological, orthographic, semantic, grammatical). The situation suggests a prototype account. Wray offers an alternative. Words, she says, in a striking image, are the bits that fall off when you shake an utterance. What this means is that we can certainly pick out words in an utterance—these are mostly the high-content nouns, verbs, adjectives, and adverbs. But then we are left with a residue of bits and pieces which can be assigned word status only with difficulty or by relaxing our notion of what a word is.

PART I

WORDS: GENERAL ASPECTS

CHAPTER 1

THE LURE OF WORDS

DAVID CRYSTAL

I have never met anyone who has not at some time been lured by words. The word is one of those concepts that seem to accompany us from the cradle to the grave. Parents are excited by (and never forget) the emergence of their child's 'first word'. At the opposite end of life, we pay special attention to 'last words'—and if their owners are famous, collect them into books. In between, we find 'words' entering idiomatically into virtually every kind of daily activity. We 'have words' when we argue. We 'give people our word' when we promise. We can eat words, bandy them, mark them, weigh them, hang upon them, and not mince them. People can take words out of one mouth, and put words into another.

Words operate within parameters of linguistic extremes. One such parameter is length. At one end, we see words as single strings of sounds separated by pauses, or of letters separated by spaces. They are the entities we identify when we do crosswords or play word games. At the other end, we make words equivalent to entire sentences or discourses. We talk about news travelling 'by word of mouth', and when we say 'a word in your ear', or we 'put in a good word' for someone, the utterances might be any length.

Another parameter is meaning. At one end we pay scrupulous attention to the meaning words convey, and many books have been written attempting to explicate what is involved when we say a word 'has meaning'. At the other end, there are contexts where the meaning is totally irrelevant. In a game such as Scrabble, the critical thing is to find a word that fits into the grid and is allowed by the official dictionary, rather than to know what it means. Most people have little clue about the meaning of some of the two-letter words they look up in the word lists, such as *en*, *qi*, and *ka*. The important thing is that they help the player to score well.

A third parameter is scope: 'words' can be equivalent to 'language', and then they evoke another contrast of responses, ranging from positive to negative. The proverbs of the world express both attitudes. On the one hand, we have the Arabic maxim 'Words draw the nails from the heart', the Bulgarian 'A gentle word opens an iron gate', and the Chinese 'A kind word warms for three winters'. On the other hand, we hear that 'Fair words butter no parsnips' (or 'cabbage', as it is in parts of south-east Europe), that 'Words don't season soup' in Brazil, and that in Germany 'Words are good, but hens lay eggs'.

The contrast here is variously expressed: between words and things, words and deeds, words and thoughts, words and ideas. Writers throughout history have pondered the relationship between these pairings. Two broad trends are apparent. One is to see words as inadequate representations of thoughts, poor replacements for actions, or a dangerous distraction from experiential realities. The other is to see them as indispensable for the expression of thoughts, a valuable alternative to actions, or a means of finding order in inchoate realities.

We see the first position at work when words are described as 'the small change of thought' (by French novelist Jules Renard in his *Journal*, 1988) or 'merely stepping stones for thought' (by Arthur Koestler in *The Act of Creation*, 1964) or 'the great foes of reality' (by Joseph Conrad in *Under Western Eyes*, 1911). Francis Bacon is in no doubt: 'Here therefore is the first distemper [abuse] of learning, when men study words and not matter' (1605, *The Advancement of Learning*).

On the other hand, for British poet and novelist Osbert Sitwell, 'A word is the carving and colouring of a thought, and gives it permanence' (*Laughter in the Next Room*, 1949); for American longshoreman philosopher Eric Hoffer, 'Action can give us the feeling of being useful, but only words can give us a sense of weight and purpose' (*The Passionate State of Mind*, 1954); and for science-fiction author Philip K. Dick, 'The basic tool for the manipulation of reality is the manipulation of words' (*I Hope I Shall Arrive Soon*, 1986). The writer of the Book of Proverbs is in no doubt: 'Deep waters, such are the words of man: a swelling torrent, a fountain of life' (18:4, *Jerusalem Bible* translation).

Several writers search for a middle way, stressing the interdependence of words and thoughts. This is German philologist Max Müller's view: 'Words without thought are dead sounds; thoughts without words are nothing. To think is to speak low; to speak is to think aloud. The word is the thought incarnate' (*Lectures on the Science of Language*, 1861). English poet Samuel Butler gives the relationship poetic form: 'Words are but pictures, true or false, design'd / To draw the lines and features of the mind' (*Satire upon the Imperfection and Abuse of Human Learning*, 1670s). And Bronislaw Malinowski provides an anthropological perspective, observing the way different languages express different visions of the world: 'The mastery over reality, both technical and social, grows side by side with the knowledge of how to use words' (*Coral Gardens and Their Magic*, 1935).

The metaphors increase and multiply, as writers struggle to find ways of expressing the relationship between words, on the one hand, and thoughts, deeds, and things, on the other. American historian Henry Adams: 'No one means all he says, and yet very few say all they mean, for words are slippery and thought is viscous' (*The Education of Henry Adams*, 1907). British novelist Aldous Huxley: 'Words form the thread on which we string our experiences' (*The Olive Tree*, 1937). An Indian proverb, much loved by Samuel Johnson: 'Words are the daughters of Earth, and things are the sons of Heaven.'

Some writers focus on what words actually do. Malinowski emphasizes their dynamic and pragmatic force: 'Words are part of action and they are equivalents to actions' (*ibid.*), and makes his point with some convincing examples: 'In all communities, certain words are accepted as potentially creative of acts. You utter a vow or you forge a signature and you may find yourself bound for life to a monastery, a woman or a prison'. German novelist Thomas Mann adopts a social perspective, thinking of individuals: 'The word, even the most contradictious word, preserves contact—it is silence which isolates' (*The Magic Mountain*, 1924). British management educator Charles Handy also thinks socially, but on a grander scale: 'Words are the bugles of social change' (*The Age of Unreason*, 1991). Lord Byron gives words a mind-changing power: 'But words are things, and a small drop of ink, / Falling like dew upon a thought, produces / That which makes thousands, perhaps millions, think' (*Don Juan*, 1819–24). American columnist Peggy Noonan captures their emotional force: 'words, like children, have the power to make dance the dullest beanbag of a heart' (*What I Saw at the Revolution*, 1990).

It is the tension between the two perspectives that some writers see as critical, for it generates a creative impulse. American novelist Julien Green puts it like this: 'Thought flies and words go on foot. Therein lies all the drama of a writer' (*Journal*, 1943). For Ralph Waldo Emerson, 'Every word was once a poem. Every new relation is a new word' (*Essays*, 1844). T. S. Eliot describes the tension as an 'intolerable wrestle / With words and meanings' ('East Coker', in *Four Quartets*, 1944). It's the challenge that provides the lure, evidently, especially for the poets. For Thomas Hood, 'A moment's thinking, is an hour in words' (*Hero and Leander*, 1827). For American poet laureate Richard Wilbur, writing is 'waiting for the word that may not be there until next Tuesday' (in *Los Angeles Times*, 1987). And Lord Tennyson expresses the quandary thus: 'I sometimes hold it half a sin / To put in words the grief I feel; / For words, like Nature, half reveal / And half conceal the Soul within' (*In Memoriam A.H.H.*, 1850).

The whole situation is made more fascinating by language variation and change. Words and their meanings do not stand still, and perpetually offer new possibilities to the creative user. 'For last year's words belong to last year's language / And next year's words await another voice' (T. S. Eliot, 1944, 'Little Gidding', in *Four Quartets*). 'A word is dead / When it is said, / Some say. / I say it just / Begins to live / That day' (Emily Dickinson, *Complete Poems*, c.1862–86). And creativity extends to going beyond the existing wordstock. One of the most popular competitions I ever ran in my BBC radio series *English Now*, back in the 1980s, was the challenge to invent a word that the language needs. I received thousands of entries. The winner was the word we need when we are waiting by an airport carousel for our luggage, and everyone else's bags appear except yours. We are *bagonizing* (see Crystal 2006).

Word competitions are held every day, in some newspapers. How many words can you form from a string of letters? Which is the most beautiful word in the language? What is the longest word? What is the longest isogram (a word in which every letter appears the same number of times)? Can you make a humorous anagram out of the letters in the name of the prime minister? Can you write a poem in which every word contains the same vowel (a *univocalic*)? Can you write a text that doesn't make use of a particular letter of the alphabet (a *lipogram*)? Some people spend huge amounts of time on such tasks. Ernest Wright's novel *Gadsby* (1939), which uses no letter *e*, has 50 000 words. There seems to be a very fine dividing line between allurement and addiction (see Crystal 1998).

Exploring the history of words provides a further dimension. 'The etymologist finds the deadest word to have been once a brilliant picture', says Ralph Waldo Emerson (*Essays*, 1844), concluding that 'Language is fossil poetry'. The etymological lure is undoubtedly one of the strongest. I never cease to be amazed at the way word-books attract interest. Mark Forsyth's *The Etymologicon* topped the best-seller Christmas list in 2011. I have had more online reaction to my own *The Story of English in 100 Words* than to any other of my books: making a personal selection of words seems to encourage others to talk about their own favourites. Any listing of obsolescent words generates a nostalgia which can turn into a call for resurrection. A word can be given a new lease of life through online social networking—or a good PR campaign.

When in 2008 Collins decided to prune a couple of dozen old words from its dictionary—such as *agrestic*, *apodeictic*, *compossible*, *embrangle*, *niddering*, *skirr*, and *fubsy*—a cleverly managed campaign generated huge publicity for the next edition. Collins agreed to monitor public reaction, and to retain words that obtained real support. *The Times* took up the campaign (Adams, 2008). Celebrities agreed to sponsor the words: British poet laureate Andrew Motion, for example, adopted *skirr* (the sound made by a bird's wings in flight); British television personality Stephen Fry adopted *fubsy* (short and stout) and used it on his BBC panel/quiz show QI (i.e. Quite Interesting). A 'savefubsy' petition was launched online. An art exhibition featuring the words ran at the German Gallery in London. The result: both *fubsy* and *skirr* were reprieved, along with a few others, and all of the endangered words were retained in the online version of the dictionary.

Why do words get this kind of response? Henry Thoreau provides one answer (*Walden*, 1854):

> A written word is the choicest of relics. It is something at once more intimate with us and more universal than any other work of art. It is the work of art nearest to life itself. It may be translated into every language, and not only be read but actually breathed from all human lips;—not to be represented on canvas or in marble only, but be carved out of the breath of life itself. The symbol of an ancient man's thought becomes a modern man's speech.

Oscar Wilde provides another (*Intentions*, 1891):

> Words have not merely music as sweet as that of viol and lute, colour as rich and vivid as any that makes lovely for us the canvas of the Venetian or the Spaniard, and plastic form no less sure and certain than that which reveals itself in marble or in bronze but thought and passion and spirituality are theirs also, are theirs indeed alone.

I take these responses from the literary canon, and that is how it should be, for, as Ezra Pound affirms, talking about the writing of *Ulysses*, 'We are governed by words, the laws are graven in words, and literature is the sole means of keeping these words living and accurate' (quoted by George Steiner in *Language and Silence*, 1967). But the lure of words extends well beyond literature in its canonical form.

Perhaps it is the sheer number of words that provides the attraction. The size of a language's vocabulary is such that there are always new lexical words to explore. When learning a language, the task of mastering the pronunciation, orthography, and grammar is a finite task. There are only so many sounds and symbols, and only so many ways of constructing a sentence. But there is no limit to the words. I have elsewhere called vocabulary 'the Everest of language learning', to capture the challenge learners face; but even that metaphor is misleading, for vocabulary has no summit or end-point. To count the words of a language is an impossible task, and estimates of the number of words in, say, English, are always wide of the mark. Great publicity surrounded the claim made by an American agency, Gobal Language Monitor, in 2009 that the millionth word had entered the English language (Payack 2008). All they had done, of course, was devise an algorithm which was able to count up to a million. The English language has long had more than a million words.

The reason that the task is impossible is partly empirical, partly methodological, and will be discussed in detail later in this book. It is empirical because the English language is now used worldwide, and thousands of fresh words—and fresh meanings of words—are being introduced by the 'new Englishes' that have evolved. Dictionaries and word lists of Jamaican, South African, Indian, Singaporean, and over fifty other global varieties of English show the extent to which the emerging identities of recently independent countries is reflected in lexical innovation (see Crystal 2003). There are 15 000 words listed in a dictionary of Jamaican English, for example—that is, words used in Jamaica that aren't known globally. Many of them are colloquial or slang expressions, unlikely to appear in print, but that does not rob them of their status as words. Many of these words come and go like the tides. It is impossible to keep track of all of them.

The word-counting task is also complicated by methodological considerations. For what counts as a word? Are *cat* and *cats* one word or two? How many words are there in *flower pot* or *flower-pot* or *flowerpot*? Does an abbreviation count as a word? Do proper names count as words? Normally, we exclude names (such as *David* and *London*) from a word-count, assigning them to an encyclopedia rather than a dictionary; but we include them when they take on an extended meaning (as in 'The White House has spoken'), and there are many cases where we need to take a view ('That's a Renoir'). We need to be alert to these issues, to avoid making false claims. How many 'different words' does Shakespeare use? If we count *go, goes, going, goeth, gone*, etc. as separate words, the total is around 30 000 (it can never be a precise figure because of uncertainties over editions and what counts as part of the canon); if we count them as variants of a single 'word', *GO*, then the figure falls to less than 20 000. It is the need to clarify which motivated linguists to introduce a new term into the literature: *lexical item*, or *lexeme*. *Go, goes*, etc. are said to be variant forms of the lexeme *GO*.

The other counting task is more feasible: how many words do you, the reader of this book, know? If you have the time, all you have to do is go through a medium-sized dictionary and make a note of them. (Most people don't have the time, so they base their estimate on a sampling of a small percentage of the pages.) This would be only a first approximation, because not all the words you know will be in that dictionary—especially if you are a scientist and have a large specialized vocabulary—but it will not be too far away from the truth. An English desk dictionary of 1500 pages is likely to contain around 75 000 boldface headwords. Most people find they have a passive vocabulary (i.e. the words they know) of around 50 000; their active vocabulary total (i.e. the words they use) is significantly less. Authors and word-buffs might have a vocabulary that is double this figure (Crystal 1987). One can nonetheless do a great deal with a relatively small active vocabulary, as the Shakespeare total illustrates—or the 8000 or so different words (excluding proper names) that are in the King James Bible.

Using this perspective, we now can quantify the lure of words. For if there are over a million English words waiting in the wings, and the best of us knows perhaps a tenth of these, there is an unimaginable lexical world waiting to be explored—unimaginable also because the vast majority of these words has more than one meaning. And they are all waiting in dictionaries to be used in new contexts. British novelist Anthony Burgess found a vehicular metaphor apposite: 'A word in a dictionary is very much like a car in a mammoth motorshow—full of potential but temporarily inactive' (*A Mouthful of Air*, 1992). American physician and essayist Oliver Wendell Holmes, Sr used a gustatory one: 'Every word fresh from the dictionary brings with it a certain succulence' (*The Autocrat of the Breakfast Table*, 1858).

Once again, looking to the poets helps us identify what it is that makes people talk about the 'magic' of words. Dylan Thomas, in his *Poetic Manifesto* (1961), picks up on the theme of quantity when he describes his first experience of reading:

> I could never have dreamt that there were such goings-on in the world between the covers of books, such sand-storms and ice-blasts of words, such slashing of humbug, and humbug too, and staggering peace, such enormous laughter, such and so many blinding bright lights breaking across the just-awaking wits and splashing all over the pages in a million bits and pieces all of which were words, words, words, and each of which was alive forever in its own delight and glory and oddity and light.

Sylvia Plath (in *Ariel*, 1965) describes the consequences of word choice. For her, words are 'Axes / After whose stroke the wood rings, / And the echoes! / Echoes travelling / Off from the centre like horses'.

So who should have the last word on *lurement* (first recorded usage, 1592, and marked 'rare' in the *Oxford English Dictionary*)? Or is it *luresomeness* (no attestation, yet, though there is a single record of *luresome* in 1889)? Perhaps we need a reality check from Samuel Johnson (in Boswell's *Life*, 1791): 'This is one of the disadvantages of wine, it makes a man mistake words for thoughts'. Or from Thomas Kyd (in *The Spanish Tragedy*, *c*.1589): 'Where words prevail not, violence prevails; / But gold doth more than either of them both'. Given the range of enthusiasms evident in the following pages, I opt for Evelyn Waugh, in a *New York Times* article in 1950: 'Words should be an intense pleasure, just as leather should be to a shoemaker'. Clearly, in this book, they are.

CHAPTER 2

HOW MANY WORDS ARE THERE?

ADAM KILGARRIFF

2.1 Introduction

WORDS are like songs. The ditty a mother makes up to help her baby sleep, the number the would-be Rolling Stones belt out in their garage, the fragment in a strange dialect recalled by the octogenarian, these are all songs. The more you look, the more you find.

The dictionary, as an institution, is misleading. The big fat book has an aura of authority to it, carefully cultivated by its publishers. On the back covers of the dictionaries on my shelf we have: 'Full and completely up-to-date coverage of the general, scientific, literary, and technical vocabulary', 'No other single-volume dictionary provides such authoritative and comprehensive coverage of today's English', 'The new authority on the world's language', 'The most comprehensive and up-to-date picture of today's English'. This is sales talk. They want to give their potential purchasers the impression that they have all the words in them (and more than their competitors). They also have numbers—always a bone of contention between the editorial department and the marketing department:

MARKETING:	How many words are there, for the press release?
EDITOR:	Well, there are 57,000 full entries.
MARKETING:	That's no good, Chambers and Websters both have far more.
EDITOR:	Well, we could count run-on items, the embedded compounds, phrasal verbs and phrases, that gets us up to 76,000.
MARKETING:	Still not enough, I'm sure you can do better, what about these bolded bits in examples?
EDITOR:	But they're just common expressions, they are not even defined.
MARKETING:	Are you forgetting who pays your salary? We need to sell!

There is even something strange about the syntax. We don't say 'Is it in a dictionary?', always 'Is it in the dictionary'. This is a triumph of marketing. Another word that works like that is *bible*. In the case of *bible*, it is reasonable to say that, at source, there is just one, and that all editions, in all languages, are just versions of that. The use of *the* for *dictionary* suggests some Platonic ideal that any published item is a more or less true version of.

Dictionaries have a variety of uses. Consider Scrabble. The simple role of the dictionary in Scrabble is to say if a string of letters is a word. It can only do that by having all the words in it. Alongside word games, there is resolving family arguments. A dictionary that does not allow a protagonist to say 'I told you so, it's not in the dictionary' is not worth the paper it is written on.

The impulse to document a language has much to do with comprehensiveness. 'Today's lesson is about glaciation. Let's start with gelifluction and move on to polynas,' says a character in a cartoon in the 'Horrible Geography' series (Ganeri 2002: 7). There are, indeed, a lot of words. All sorts of nooks and crannies of human activity have their own terms, not known to the general public but nonetheless, straightforwardly and unequivocally, words of English. *Gelifluction* does not have an entry in the largest dictionary I had available to check, the *Oxford English Dictionary*, although it does occur (apparently misspelt *gelifiuction*) in an example sentence for the related word *solifluction*. *Polynya* (note the difference of spelling) does have an entry. *Gelifluction* occurs just four times in a database of 12 billion words of text crawled from the web, *polynya/s* occurs 328 times, mostly with the second 'y', sometimes without it.

All this makes it hard to give a number. The primary reason is the sheer number of nooks and crannies of human activity that there are: how might we cover all of them? There are other reasons:

(a) Rules for making new words up. This is the province of derivational morphology and word formation rules (see Booij, this volume). Some specialisms even have their own rules for generating an unlimited number of specialist words (see l'Homme, this volume). The *Nomenclature of Inorganic Chemistry: IUPAC Recommendations* (Connelly 2005) is a collection of rules for naming inorganic compounds. If the rules are followed, then different chemists working independently will give the same name to a new compound according to its chemical composition, thereby reducing ambiguity and confusion. The rules sometimes give rise to terms with spaces in, sometimes to terms containing hyphens, brackets, numbers (Arabic and Roman), Greek letters, the + and – signs, and sometimes to long strings with none of the above. Examples (from Wikipedia) include *ethanidohydridoberyllium*, *bis(η^5-cyclopentadienido)magnesium*, *pentaamminechloridocobalt(2+) chloride*, *di-μ-chlorido-tetrachlorido-1κ^2Cl,2κ^2Cl-dialuminium*, and *Decacarbonyldihydridotriosmium*.

(b) Homonymy. Where there are two different meanings, when do we want to say we have two different words? Some cases are clear, e.g. *file* 'type of tool' and 'collection of documents', others less so (see Durkin, this volume).

(c) Multi-words. Do we allow in words written with spaces, like *all right*? When does a sequence of words turn into a single word, and *vice versa*? (See Wray, this volume, and Moon, this volume.)
(d) Imports. There can be uncertainty about the language that a word belongs to; when do words borrowed from other languages start to count? (See Grant, this volume, and Sorell, this volume.)
(e) Variation: when do two different spellings, or pronunciations, start to count as two different words?

First, we present a little data, and then we say some more about imports and variation.

2.2 A LITTLE DATA

The question 'How many words are there?' may be asked of any language. All the aspects discussed here relate to any language, though sometimes in different ways. Here, we mainly discuss English, with occasional reference to how different considerations play out differently in other languages.

enTenTen12 (Jakubíček et al. 2013) is a database of 12 billion words of English gathered from the web in 2012. The 12 billion is the number of tokens, not types: that means that the 547 million occurrences of *the* count as 547 million, not as just one, as they would if I was counting types. To put it another way, how many words are there in *dog eats dog*? There are two possible answers: three, if I am counting tokens, but two, if I am counting types. The question 'How many words are there?' clearly relates to types, not tokens.

Another ambiguity to draw attention to is between inflected forms of words and lemmas. Do *invade, invading, invades, invaded* count as forms of the same word, or as different words? If we say 'forms of the same word', we are talking about lemmas, or dictionary headwords. If we say 'four different words' we are talking about word forms. For English, the difference between the two is not so great, since very few lemmas are associated with more than four forms (the standard number for verbs, like *invade*), with nouns having just two (singular and plural). For many languages, the numbers are higher, sometimes running into hundreds. In this section all discussions are of word forms, largely because they are easier to count.

There are 6.8 million different types in enTenTen12 (including only items comprising exclusively lower-case letters, separated by spaces and punctuation). Their distribution is Zipfian: the commonest items occur far, far more often than most, and very many occur only once (see Sorell, this volume). Here there are 1,096 words that occur over 1 million times, and 3,745,668 words occurring just once. The distribution is broken down in Table 2.1.

At the 1,000,000 point (capturing words which occur more than 1,000,000 times) we have mainstream, core vocabulary words.

Table 2.1 Selected words from 9 frequency bands in the 12-billion-word corpus enTenTen12

Frequency band	No. of words	Random sample from lower edge of frequency band
1,000,000+	1096	active expensive floor homes prior proper responsible round shown title
1,000–999,999	60,789	ankh attunements diatom dithered limoncello mobilisations sassafras seemeth softgel uremic
100–999	109,362	alledge dwellin faceing finacee frackers neurogenetic sacralized shl symbole vigesimal
10–99	511,714	abbut arquebusses bundas carcer devilries feace hotu petronel taphophiles theaw
5–9	611,146	athambia dowter hazardscape humanracenow kernelled noatble producest stancher sullens trattles
4	307,309	boarwalk intercousre layertennis locutory meritest nonhumanistic pitiyankees scapularies starbeams uitrekenen
3	483,720	rokas faraa cuftucson cremosas topboard brahmanam samuebo messenblokken regenica
2	941,181	androgynized bolibourgeoisie lascomadres lowspot neoliberialism nonmorbid oapmaking projectst salesm whatsoevery
1	3,745,668	cirumscriptions digatel dramturgy figurability frelks inactivazed mixtore shunjusha teires wrider

At the 1,000 point we have:

(a) words from specialist domains, found in large dictionaries:
- An *ankh* is an Egyptian symbol usually meaning 'life' or 'soul'.
- A *diatom* is a single-cell alga.
- *Sassafras* is a species of tree with aromatic leaves and bark, and the extract drawn from it.
- *Limoncello* is an Italian alcoholic drink made from lemons. Also note that *limoncello* is on the margins of being a name, and in addition to 1,000 lower-case occurrences, there are 729 capitalized. On the borderline between regular words and names, see Anderson (this volume); also see restaurants section below.
- A *softgel* is an oral dosage form for medicine similar to capsules.

(b) inflected forms for familiar, if not specially common, words: *attunements, dithered, mobilisations*; also *seemeth*, an archaic inflected form of a common word; and *uremic* (relating to the disease *uremia*).

At the 100 point we have

- *vigesimal*, a number system based on twenty, present in the larger dictionaries.
- One simple spelling error, *faceing* (the target form was *facing* in all cases that I checked).
- *finacee*, target form: *fiancé, fiance, fiancée, fiancee*, depending on gender and the tricky business of how accented characters in imported words relate to English spelling. One thing is clear: the *a* should be before the *n*.
- Spelling errors mixed with old or other non-standard forms: *alledge, dwellin*. A mixture is a case where some of the instances are of one kind, e.g. spelling errors:

  If you hear or read anyone in the United States assert or *alledge* that we have a democracy, a representative democracy or anything short of a kleptocracy

  while others are of another kind, e.g. an old form:

  That the Debts either by Purchase, Sale, Revenues, or by what other name they may be call'd, if they have been violently extorted by one of the Partys in War, and if the Debtors *alledge* and offer to prove there has been a real Payment, they shall be no more prosecuted, before these Exceptions be first adjusted.

- A spelling error mixed with a foreign word: *symbole*.
- Inflected forms of derived forms of words: *frackers* is plural of *fracker*, 'someone who fracks', where fracking is a process of extracting gas from underground reserves, currently a politically and environmentally contentious topic; *sacralized*, past tense of 'made sacred' or 'treated as sacred'.
- A prefixed form: *neurogenetic* (where *neuro* is a mid- to low-frequency prefix).
- *shl*: a mixture of programming language command, url-parts, shortened *shall*, abbreviations.

At the 10 point, *abbut, arquebusses, devilries*, and *taphophiles* are recognizably words of English, albeit obscure and/or misspelt and/or inflected/derived forms, while the remaining six are not even that, and so it is as we carry on down to the items occurring just once. These are like the residue at the bottom of a schoolboy's pocket: very small pieces of a wide variety of substances, often unsavoury, all mixed together, often unidentifiable. One would rather not have to look into them too closely.

In sum, at the top of the list—at least the top 1,000—we have core vocabulary. By the time we have reached 60,000 we have obscure vocabulary and marginal forms. Another 100,000 items, and dictionary words are thin on the ground, though we still often have their inflected and derived forms, and their misspellings. After a further half million, half the items no longer even look like English words, but are compounded from obscure forms, typos, words glued together, and other junk, and so on down to *bolibourgeoisie, whatsoevery*, and *frelks*.

2.3 Imports

2.3.1 Restaurant English

As explained by Douglas Adams in *The Hitchhiker's Guide to the Galaxy*, a distinct form of mathematics takes over in restaurants at that moment when it comes to working out each person's contribution to the bill. Likewise, a distinct form of English. Let us make a linguistic visit to the grandest of our local vegetarian restaurants, Terre a Terre. A sample of their menu:

> Red onion, mustard seed, cumin crumpets with coconut curry leaf and lime sabayon, ginger root chilli jam and a fresh coriander, mint salsa sas. Served with thakkali rasam of tamarind and tomato, nimbu bhat cardamom brown onion lemon saffron baked basmati rice with our confit brinjal pickle.

The peculiar thing about this form of English is that, while the language is English, most of the nouns don't seem to be. They form a subtext to the history of the population itself, with:

- indigenous: *onion, mustard, seed, crumpet, leaf, root, jam, mint, pickle*
- fully naturalized: *cumin, coconut, curry, lime, ginger, coriander, tamarind, tomato, cardamom, saffron, rice*
- recent (within my lifetime): *salsa, bhat, basmati, confit, brinjal*
- novel: *sabayon, sas, thakali, rasam, nimbu*

A restaurant like Terre a Terre is at the leading edge of both culinary and linguistic multiculturalism. All sorts of other areas have their borrowings too: wherever we share artefacts or ideas or practices with another culture, we import associated vocabulary, for example in music (*bhangra, didgeridoo*), clothes (*pashmina, lederhosen*), or religion (*stupa, muezzin*). The question 'But is this word English?' feels narrow-minded and unhelpful. To give a number to the words of English, we would need to be narrow-minded and unhelpful.

2.3.2 Naturalization

A side-effect of importing words is: how much naturalization do we do?

There are assorted reasons—some good, some bad, most contentious—for having immigration policies and controlling which people are allowed into a country, and those policies are then strenuously policed. For words, some countries (famously France, with its Académie française) have, or have had, policies, and we may argue about the reasoning behind those policies being good or bad. They are also hard to police. English does not have such a tradition. We welcome all sorts of words—but are often not sure how to say them or how to write them. The Nepalese staple lentil soup, in enTenTen12, is found as *dal baht, dal bat, dahl bat, dahl baht, dahl baat.* If the source language does not use the Latin alphabet, the imports will suffer vagaries depending on the source-language writing system and transliteration schemes. The *dal baht* case suggests a problematic mapping for the /aː/ sound between Nepali (usually written in Devanagari script) and English (written in Latin). Arabic usually does not write vowels, which is a main reason why there are so many options for how *Mohammed* is spelt in English. *Mohammed, Mohammad, Mohamed, Mahmoud, Muhammed, Mehmet, Mahmud, Mahmood, Mohamad, Mahomet*, and *Mehmood* all occur more than 1,000 times in the enTenTen12 corpus.

English can be seen as an imperialist language, currently the world's pre-eminent imperialist language, with its words marching into other cultures and taking over. English speakers, at least so far as their language is concerned, have no anxieties about being taken over and fading out. But the situation looks quite different from the other side. All over the world, languages are threatened and are dying, usually where, more and more often, bilingual speakers choose the alternative over their indigenous language (Crystal 2000). One part of this process is at the level of vocabulary, with speakers, even when speaking the indigenous language, using imports more and more often, either in preference to a local term or because there is no well-established local term. Many languages have government-supported terminology committees, charged with identifying, or creating, local language terms where as yet there is nothing well-established in the local language. Most often the non-local term is an English one.

The question 'Do we include this word in the count for *our* language?' is an interesting one for English—but for many languages it is also a political one, closely related to the very survival of the language.

2.3.3 Variants

Most English words have a single standard spelling; if the word is spelt in any other way, it is a spelling error. We all learnt that at school. We are troubled by the few exceptions: does *judg(e)ment* have an *e* in the middle? Answer: it can. There are also the transatlantic variants, including the *or/our* group (*colo(u)r, favo(u)r, hono(u)r*, etc.) and the *ise/ize* group. In our count of the words of the language, do we treat variants as different words?

Many languages have far less stabilized spelling than English, in particular languages which do not have a long written tradition.

There is interplay between standardization, pronunciation, and dialects. How far can a word stray and still be the same word? When I first came across *eejit*, when working with Glaswegians, I was puzzled as I felt I did not know the word. It was some months before I discovered it was a variant of *idiot.*

2.4 Conclusion

'How many words are there?' begs a set of further questions about what a word is: across time, across languages, across variation in meaning and spelling and spaces-between-words, across morphological structure. There is also the question of whether we are talking about the core of the language, or about the whole language including all the specialist corners where some small groups of people have developed their own terms and usages.

Dictionaries are no help. They have pragmatic solutions to the question that they face, namely, 'How many words shall we include?', and the answer varies from dictionary to dictionary. Whatever they say on the back cover is to be treated with the greatest scepticism.

'How many words are there?' is not a good question. A better question is 'How many words do various different speakers of a language (of various levels of education, etc.) typically know?' or, moving on from a purely academic perspective to one where the answer has practical implications, 'How many words do you need?' For that, we pass you on to the chapter by Paul Nation (this volume).

CHAPTER 3

WORDS AND DICTIONARIES

MARC ALEXANDER

3.1 Words and dictionaries

Dictionaries seek to be a core reference guide to words, presenting knowledge about a word as separate facts, such as its meaning, its pronunciation, or its history. They are some of the oldest forms of reference ever produced, with modern dictionaries tracing their bilingual roots to Sumerian-Akkadian word lists assembled a few millennia BCE (Snell-Hornby 1986: 208), with the first monolingual dictionary, the *Erya* or *Ready Guide*, being a Chinese collection of word glosses around 300 BCE (Yong and Peng 2008: 3). Their evolution has mirrored changes in world culture and technology across the ages, from being individualistic—and idiosyncratic—manuscripts to some of the first printed materials produced, then to centrally planned nationally authoritative tomes, to research outputs based on empirical scientific methodologies, and now to interactive and dynamic electronic databases. At each stage in this development, each change inherits, modifies, and develops the techniques of the past—taking always as their core the necessity for delimiting, cataloguing, and explaining words to a reader, but shifting often in approach, execution, and evidence.

Modern dictionaries, as the inheritors of this tradition, are born at the confluence of three contradictions: they are both scholarly and commercial, both judicious and impartial, and both artificial and yet grounded in natural language. These three contradictions explain much of what we need to know about both dictionaries themselves and their relationship with the words they contain: they are produced by expert scholars, but most often at the behest of publishers concerned with sales; they often strive to be descriptive and neutral, but users often require them to act as arbiters; they are unnatural things, but they are rooted in the natural use of words. These intersections explain why dictionaries are the unusual contraptions that they are, and each contradiction is examined in turn below, following an overview of dictionary history and structure.

3.2 A BRIEF HISTORY OF DICTIONARIES

The study of dictionaries, formally called *lexicography*,[1] requires, for much of dictionary history, the study of their compilers; because for many years the vast undertaking of dictionary compilation was undertaken by a single individual, so the judgements, biases, enthusiasms, and—in some cases—the personality of the compiler were irrevocably bound together with their work. Perhaps the most famous example of this is the 1755 *Dictionary of the English Language* by Samuel Johnson (now often referred to simply as *Johnson's Dictionary*, or just as *Johnson*). Although sensible and thorough in the main, Johnson's *Dictionary* contains a range of idiosyncratic choices, omissions, and definitions—he defines, for example, a *lexicographer* as 'a writer of dictionaries; a harmless drudge, that busies himself in tracing the original, and detailing the signification of words'. Johnson is somewhat exceptional in so forcefully displaying his personality and humour in his dictionary, although the history of lexicography is filled with biases, unfortunate choices, and unusual omissions.

Early dictionaries are very far from the modern conception of what a dictionary should be. Primarily taking the form of glosses and word lists, providing bilingual translations or explanations of difficult words, their sole shared characteristic is a focus on the word as a unit and in giving information about that word. Many consist of collections of manuscript glosses, where a reader or scribe would annotate the margins or line-spaces of an existing manuscript with word meanings or translations (Sauer 2009). This phenomenon represents a key aspect of the formation of dictionaries; the conceptual jump from annotating a word in context with a meaning to formally decontexualizing this word and treating it as an atomistic unit which can be defined separately is one which should not be underestimated from a modern point of view. Similarly, what we now call an early dictionary could also be easily categorized as a thesaurus (see Kay, this volume); although dictionaries are thought of nowadays as being characterized by their alphabetical order, many pre-modern works do not even countenance this sort of structure, instead preferring to list words thematically. Johannes Balbus, in his Latin dictionary of 1286, was sufficiently concerned with what he thought of as the innovation of alphabetical ordering to explain it in great detail, ending: 'I beg of you, therefore, good reader, do not scorn this great labor of mine and this order as something worthless' (Daly 1967: 73). Such ordering is counterproductive in many ways—it places unrelated items next to each other, refuses a user the opportunity to make connections between words close in meaning, and blocks easy browsing on one particular theme or topic—but it has one enormous advantage, that of a previously unprecedented ease of lookup. These two

[1] While *lexicography* generally refers to the creation and analysis of dictionaries, its companion term *lexicology* is somewhat broader, referring to the scholarly and linguistic study of words, such as that found in this Handbook. The distinction is somewhat blurred; lexicology often uses dictionaries as a source of evidence for the investigation of the lexicon of a language, and the lexicographical process of analysing words in order to create a dictionary can be easily seen as a process of lexicology.

innovations—abstraction from context and alphabetical order—primarily describe all dictionaries as we know them today; containers of facts about words, assembled according to alphabetical order.

Dictionaries began to homogenize in the Early Modern period, starting with the 16th century growth in bilingual dictionaries between European languages. In Paris, Robert Estienne produced his *Dictionarium, seu Latinæ Linguæ Thesaurus* in 1543, which was intended to be a monolingual Latin dictionary but whose first edition contained many definitions in French. The *Dictionarium* remains a significant work of Latin lexicography, and was reprinted and revised by later hands, often without the author's consent (Greswell 1833: 199–200). The classical languages dominated the beginning of this bilingual period; Sir Thomas Elyot's 1538 Latin–English dictionary, for example, was considered a major work of scholarship at the time, and most bilingual dictionaries linked a European language with either Latin or Greek.

Later English monolingual lexicography grew out of a 'hard words' tradition, beginning with what is usually recognized to be the first English dictionary, Robert Cawdrey's 1604 *A Table Alphabeticall*, which contained a list of 'difficult' or rare words each with a very brief English gloss. This sparked a long chain of plagiarism of English dictionaries over the next few hundred years, where authors took Cawdrey's work (itself based on earlier sources), added and changed some material, and then published their own dictionary, which in turn would be plagiarized by later authors (this rather endearing story of repeated and brazen theft is told briefly in Landau 2001: 48ff, and in more detail in Green 1996 and Considine 2008). By the time of Nathan Bailey's 1721 *Universal Etymological English Dictionary*, English had a dictionary containing not only hard words but also some of the core vocabulary of the language, alongside some etymologies and occasional invented examples of usage. There was some dissatisfaction with the state of these dictionaries, however, as they were highly uneven in quality and accuracy; following the publication of a large and authoritative French dictionary, an awareness grew in Britain that a better dictionary was required for the English language, which Samuel Johnson supplied in 1755.

The rapid evolution of English dictionaries can be seen by comparing some of their entries: *abash*, Cawdrey's second entry in 1604, was defined by him simply as 'blush', while Bailey in 1721 gives an etymology plus the definition 'to make ashamed or confound', and Johnson gives 'To put into confusion; to make ashamed. It generally implies a sudden impression of shame', alongside its part of speech, a cross-reference, a note on its use as a phrasal verb (*abashed at, abashed of*), and five illustrative quotations (in all, the entry totals 201 words, and is fairly short by Johnson's standards). The use of illustrations particularly marks out Johnson's work, with entries furnished with a range of quotations chosen from authors in high regard (usually from the 16th century, and frequently mistranscribed); this marks lexicography's move towards a respect for natural language, rather than invented examples and editorial guesswork.

The 17th and later centuries therefore saw the formation of major, rigorous national dictionaries, either officially sanctioned or considered generally authoritative by users: as well as Samuel Johnson's 1755 *Dictionary*, this period saw the publication of the 1612 Italian *Vocabolario Degli Accademici della Crusca*, the 1694 *Dictionnaire de l'Académie française*, the 1780 Spanish *Diccionario de la lengua española*, and the 1880 German *Vollständiges orthographisches Wörterbuch der deutschen Sprache*, generally known as the *Duden* after its author. The New World was also represented here, with Noah Webster's 1828 *An American Dictionary of the English Language* following his 1783 *The American Spelling Book* (which deliberately introduced many spellings now considered characteristic of American English, such as *color, traveled, honor*, and *center*).

More ambitious multigenerational scholarly projects began later in the 19th century, their completion taking decades or even over a century, including the Grimm brothers' 1838–1961 *Deutsches Wörterbuch*, the Dutch 1863–1998 *Woordenboek der Nederlandsche Taal*, the (still in progress) Latin 1894–2050 *Thesaurus Linguae Latinae*, and the English 1884–1928/1933 *Oxford English Dictionary* (*OED*), originally titled the *New English Dictionary on Historical Principles*. None of these, as is common to dictionary projects since the age of Samuel Johnson, was ever predicted to take as long to complete as it eventually did (the *OED* was originally intended to take only a decade). To continue the example above, the *OED* uses 628 words to define and exemplify *abash*, including four sub-senses, 94 words of etymology, 14 spelling variants, and 394 words of quotations spanning five centuries.

Few new dictionaries of the same scope have been founded to match these projects, with later work instead focused on the updating and revision of existing multi-volume works; the *OED*, for example, currently has a third edition in preparation, its first full revision since its original publication, and the Académie française is working on a ninth edition of their *Dictionnaire*. More recent dictionary innovations rely on technological advances to reformulate their structure, style, or evidence base, although apart from the use of computers for editing and assembling sample citations, the same process is followed now as in the 19th century: assemble uses of a word, analyse and classify them, and then describe them. This process is explored further in the following section.

3.3 Types of dictionary and word facts

The process of analysing words depends, primarily, on what style of dictionary the analysis is necessitated by. Dictionary types vary along six main dimensions: their languages, variety, audience, timespan, format, and specialization.

3.3.1 Languages

A dictionary can be *monolingual, bilingual*, or the semi-intermediate category of a *learner's dictionary*—one which is monolingual but aimed at non-native speakers. While the normal market for non-native learners of a language is a bilingual dictionary (where each word meaning in the first language is given an appropriately chosen alternative in the second language), a learner's dictionary is monolingual, but aims to define and give facts about a word using a restricted and simplified vocabulary alongside a detailed explanatory style. They are therefore appropriate for students of a language who are ready for a monolingual dictionary, but require more explicit assistance with words, and an avoidance of overly technical or difficult terminology in the definition. These dictionaries are often the source of many present-day innovations in dictionary-making, such as full-sentence definitions and more assistance with usage (for example, the *Collins COBUILD English Language Dictionary* defines *abashed* as 'If you are abashed, you feel embarrassed and ashamed', and notes that it is mostly found only in written texts).

3.3.2 Variety

Monolingual dictionaries can vary depending on which variety of the language they choose to represent; most choose the standardized form of the language, but some represent regional uses (such as dictionaries of Australian, New Zealand, Indian, or Canadian English, or the comprehensive *English Dialect Dictionary* and the *Dictionary of American Regional English*). On occasion, one dictionary can be adapted for an alternative variety, such as the British *New Oxford Dictionary of English*, later adapted to become the *New Oxford American Dictionary*.

3.3.3 Audience

Dictionaries can be aimed either at a scholarly or a commercial audience; if they are scholarly, then they are generally given more freedom to change their form to fit the data they describe, whereas commercial dictionaries tend to impose external restrictions on the size, scope, and other features of the dictionary (see section 3.4).

3.3.4 Timespan

A dictionary can be either *synchronic* (covering only one point in time) or *diachronic* (covering a span of time). The majority of commercial dictionaries sold are synchronic dictionaries focusing on the present day, while diachronic dictionaries tend to be aimed at scholars. These include the large multigenerational projects described in section 3.2, as well as such examples as the period dictionaries of Scots and English: the (in progress) *Dictionary of Old English* (600–1150); the *Dictionary of Middle English* (1100–1500), completed in 2001; the *Dictionary of Early Modern English* (1475–1700), begun and then abandoned, with its data folded into the revisions for the *OED*; and the complete *Dictionary of the Scots Language*, made up of the *Dictionary of the Older Scots Tongue* (early Middle Ages to 1700) and the *Scottish National Dictionary* (1700 to the present).

3.3.5 Format

A modern dictionary can be *print, print and electronic*, or *electronic-only*. Fewer dictionaries are now sold in hardcopy and more are sold as computer programs, online services, and smartphone apps. It is unlikely that a new major dictionary will now appear and not be available online; it is fairly likely that the majority of dictionaries will begin to move to electronic-only distribution.

3.3.6 Specialization

Not all dictionaries cover the general language; some specialize in their subject coverage. These include dictionaries of names, of medical or legal language, of abbreviations, or of other specialist areas, often aimed at expert practitioners needing a reference guide to obscure terminology in their professional area (such as *Black's Law Dictionary* or *Brewer's Dictionary of Phrase and Fable*). Many standard dictionaries contain frequently occurring specialist terms such as these, but very few will claim to be comprehensive in these areas. Some dictionaries take normal features of a standard dictionary and expand on them, such as the *Oxford Dictionary of English Etymology*, giving the derivations of words but no other information, or specialist pronunciation dictionaries, which are often aimed at learners or, in one notable case (the *Oxford BBC Guide to Pronunciation*), newsreaders.

These six features serve to mark each dictionary as separate from the others, and dictate its form, size, budget, and selection principles. Variation within these categories is usually comparatively minor, and consists of the ways in which various publishers and dictionaries distinguish themselves in the marketplace. It is therefore on the grounds of these features that the dictionary will allocate its resources and so decide the likely size and budget (and then determine how much of the dictionary can be revised from earlier editions, how much can be original, and how much has to be imported without alteration).

These final decisions then aid in the selection principles of the dictionary, those guidelines which determine which words should be included and which should not. These are not trivial matters; even Samuel Johnson, in his 1747 'Plan' for his dictionary, was anguished at how it was 'not easy to determine by what rule of distinction the words of this dictionary were to be chosen', concluding that such a rigid and inflexible rule was unworkable, because 'in lexicography, as in other arts, naked science is too delicate for the purposes of life' (2008: 20). As a result, selection principles tend to be guidelines rather than regulations, and the base principle followed by all modern dictionaries is that a candidate word for inclusion should both have definitively entered the language in question and have some currency amongst its speakers. Oxford University Press's modern English dictionaries, for example, have amongst their selection principles that a word must be found in a variety of different sources by different writers, must not be limited in its usage to one group of users, and should both have a fairly long history of use and be likely to be used in future. This last principle is notoriously difficult to predict but is nonetheless essential; dictionaries do not record every minor neologism which is not likely to enter common currency, as otherwise they would be packed with useless 'nonce words'. This term was coined by James Murray, first editor of the *OED*, to describe words which are invented purely on the spur of the moment and used as one-offs, such as the verb *forficulate*, meaning to feel a creeping sensation, 'as if a forficula or earwig were crawling over one's skin' (*OED*), recorded only in use once but nonetheless included in the dictionary by Murray and marked as a nonce word. This is not the only principle that can be often broken; Oxford's criterion of not including a word limited to a single group of users is almost always violated in the case of technical vocabulary or slang which is characteristically used by one particular group—such as chemical engineers or teenagers—but with which the general public may well come into contact. Drawing a line in the sand to indicate where a word is said to be definitely 'in' the language is therefore somewhat superfluous, with some general rules discussed in a dictionary's front matter to give a broad sense of principle, but with editors normally given broad leeway to include whatever words they see fit.

Beyond deciding what new words to include, one of the major issues for a new dictionary is to what extent it will cover the core of the language—not all dictionaries give equal coverage both to basic, frequent words and to rare, difficult words. The core of English, for example, includes such very frequent words as *the, and, into, was*, and *of*, and these words are rarely looked up by native speakers as they are too basic for a user who is already competent in the language. These users will instead prefer a dictionary in the 'hard words' tradition, which will define and elucidate the periphery of the language in order to assist with composition, spelling, and comprehension on the one hand and, on the other, leisure activities such as crossword puzzles and word games (such as Scrabble) (see Verkuyl, this volume). Learners of English, by contrast, frequently find the very common and highly polysemous words of a language challenging, and therefore their dictionaries require significant resources to be devoted to explaining these words, with a corresponding lack of attention on rarer and more specialized words. Both types of user may benefit from the inclusion of encyclopedic content (such as that often found in US English dictionaries), but again a line must be drawn. Most British dictionaries reject encyclopedic content and only define generic words, such as *king* or *country*, and so assign the task of providing information about particular countries or kings to an encyclopedia; the *OED* has no entry for *Bhutan*, for example, while the *New Oxford American Dictionary* gives its location, population, capital, and official languages. The *OED* does, however, have an entry for *0898 number*, a British term for a premium-rate phone line, generally sexual, while neither dictionary has an entry for the *M25*, London's orbital motorway which is used frequently as a shorthand for the boundaries of the city.[2]

[2] The M25 is a good example of an entity which might not normally be considered a natural candidate for inclusion in a dictionary, and yet it is used frequently in the UK Parliament's *Communications Act 2003* (which stipulates that in the UK 'an appropriate range and proportion of programmes [must be] made outside the M25 area' in order to assist economic growth outside of London). There is therefore a strong case for considering this term enough a part of the language that it should be included in a dictionary. (I owe this example to John R. Taylor.)

Once coverage has been decided, the creators of a dictionary must turn to what goes into each individual word entry. Such entries contain, at a minimum, a word and a corresponding definition. Many contain more, including separate sub-definitions for different meanings of the same word, alongside pronunciations, parts of speech, lists of variant spellings, example sentences, usage labels, and word origins and etymologies. With regards to these elements, dictionaries inherit all the issues addressed in this Handbook, and from the outset, lexicographers have to engage with each problem that languages throw at them. One issue is a base form of a word, what dictionaries call a *headword* or *citation form*, and linguists call a *lexeme* (Lyons 1977: 18ff.). This headword is intended to collapse multiple forms of a word, such as *play, playing, plays, played*, into a single lookup item for ease of reference (in this English example, the unmarked *play*).

This collapse may be straightforward in a language like English, with its relatively straightforward prefix and suffix structure, but is rather more difficult in a non-alphabetical language or one where words have a complex internal structure. For example, monolingual Chinese dictionaries, such as the 1993 *Hanyu Da Cidian*, arrange their entries by *radicals* or *bùshǒu*, the meaning-bearing components of a character, while those marketed to foreigners are arranged alphabetically based on a transliteration of each component into the Roman alphabet. A Chinese arrangement by radical (or the provision of an index of radicals) involves ordering the radical list based on how many strokes the character takes to write—for example, two strokes for 人 'man/person', seventeen for 龠 'flute'. Each further character (made up of a radical with other elements) is then listed according to the remaining number of strokes, so that 人 has listed underneath it 介 'to lie between', requiring two additional strokes, and 企 'to plan a project' has the radical plus four strokes. Other arrangements, such as phonetic order, are also possible. Similarly, Arabic and other Semitic dictionaries use as their headword the *consonantal root*, the basic sequence of consonants which combine with other features to form a word. Languages with highly complex word structure, such as Turkish, Eskimo, and some Mesoamerican languages, generally structure their dictionaries around *morphemes*, or meaning-carrying units smaller than a word (for example, the English morphemes inside *novelization* are *novel, -ize, -ate*, and *-ion*, each with its own meaning; see Booij, this volume). Further elements are arranged under these roots in an intricate grammatical ordering. Beyond this, the system in Romance/Germanic languages of using the least-modified infinitive form of a verb, such as *play* or *achever*, does not apply in other languages, where the least-marked simplest form can be in another form—in Greek, for example, this is the present indicative 1st person singular. Some semantic units are not words at all, but rather opaque idiomatic phrases (such as *raining cats and dogs*), which must be given their own entry as their meaning cannot be reduced to that of their component words (see Moon, this volume).

Similar issues arise when choosing a pronunciation of a word (in countries with an accepted 'standard' or 'reference' pronunciation, there is often an issue as to how well this fits actual widespread usage); when dealing with exceptional word forms (so that, for example, the adjectival form *imperial* may not be best placed under its parent noun *empire*, even when this sort of placement is normal practice for a dictionary); when choosing a part of speech for an entry (which requires the choice of a particular grammatical model); arranging the order of an entry (historical dictionaries tend to order senses by date, while modern dictionaries order by frequency or other criteria); and more. Even the style of phonetic transcription is a major consideration, with the majority of dictionaries using the standard academic IPA system (in which *late* is /leɪt/ and *far* is /fɑː/),[3] but many others, particularly US monolingual dictionaries, preferring instead a simplified 'respelling' system using standard alphabetical characters with various diacritics (so in *The New Oxford American Dictionary* of 2001, *late* is given as /lāt/ and *far* is /fär/, with footnotes on each page indicating that /ä/ is the sound in *car* and /ā/ in *rate*; this is simpler for native speakers but all but useless for early-stage learners who may not know the pronunciation of the reference words). In all these cases, the lexicographers working on the dictionary must aim to carefully resolve each of the issues which arise, based on the best of evidence, and in accordance with established dictionary policies, publisher policies, and the large number of considerations listed above.

With all this in mind, it is an amazing feat for any dictionary to be produced at all. But these are not the only issues which face dictionaries and their makers.

3.4 Scholarly but commercial

Almost all lexicographers must work with the tension between scholarly and commercial aims at the front of their mind.

Dictionaries are ultimately commercial because they are produced at the behest of publishers in order to sell to a public. Not every dictionary is entirely commercial; in the past, some were produced under the patronage of rich individuals (although patronage only goes so far—Johnson's *Dictionary* of 1755 had a patron but was mainly funded by a consortium of booksellers, as the patron contributed very little to the finances of the work; Johnson's feelings on the matter were clear both from his letters and his definition of *patron* as, in part, 'a wretch who supports with insolence, and is paid with flattery'). Many wholly scholarly dictionaries of modern times are funded by national academies, university presses, charities, or public research funders, who pay for the work on the grounds that the end result will be of significant public and scholarly benefit. But such funding is comparatively rare; large, multi-generational projects which take up significant resources over long periods are normally not attractive projects to funders, whose resources are often constrained and who have an uncertain ability to commit to future spending for decades to come. Scholarly dictionary projects instead often rely on patchy

[3] IPA stands for the International Phonetic Alphabet, overseen by the International Phonetic Association (also IPA); their homepage, with details of the Alphabet, can be found at http://www.langsci.ucl.ac.uk/ipa/.

portfolios of funding, seeking small grants for limited times from a range of funding bodies and charities, always with the uncertainty that future resources may not be forthcoming. The majority of new dictionaries produced are therefore commercial projects, funded by publishers on the expectation of future sales, usually with a firm budget and a tight scope. Such dictionaries are often commercially very successful, particularly in the lucrative non-native learners market.

However, the instincts of a well-schooled lexicographer are scholarly; they are experts who puzzle over large amounts of data regarding a word, and who take pride in setting themselves the task of teasing apart the fine variations of meaning that the word can realize, and in so doing create a well-turned explanation of the nature, structure, meaning, history, and usage of the word which they are examining. This expertise is hard-won, and the complexity of language does not lend itself easily to quick investigation (academics can often write whole articles or even books concerned with the meaning and usage of a single word, particularly if it is a culturally significant, contested, or semantically complex term). This does not always sit well with the commercial need for rapid turnover and efficient progress towards a publication date, and the tension between the scholarly and commercial needs of lexicography is often revealed in the occasionally fractious interactions between dictionary editors and their publishers or sponsors.

It is also notable that a publisher's budget will dictate to what extent a dictionary is wholly new and to what extent it is a reprint or reuse of existing material alongside additions and updates. It is very rare for dictionaries to be written from scratch; following the constant plagiarism of early dictionaries, in modern years almost all publishers with an existing dictionary will update their data rather than begin again wholesale. Those rare exceptions are where entirely new projects are undertaken in order to address shortcomings in existing dictionaries, such as the *OED*, or the 1987 *COBUILD* dictionary (see chapter 5 of Béjoint 2010 for more on this). Tight budgets often result in an increased tolerance for a lack of revision between dictionary editions, meaning that most new editions of a dictionary for the general market are now marketed on the basis of a much-trumpeted short list of very recent famous words, often those words which are seen to be part of the general cultural zeitgeist of recent years. This is the means by which an existing dictionary can highlight its new revision in order to establish itself as a sufficiently up-to-date reference source, and, in some cases, a justifiable purchase for owners of a previous edition. However, inclusion of such words can also easily date a dictionary, and often those entries which are inserted for the sake of a marketing push are themselves removed from later editions as they no longer meet the notability requirements many dictionaries place on their entries. The American Dialect Society's 2006 Word of the Year, the verb *to Pluto* (meaning to demote something, as was done to the former planet Pluto), was added to some dictionaries in that year and included on their marketing material—but eight years later is not to be found in recent editions of any major modern dictionary. This habit of featuring zeitgeist terms which violate a dictionary's standard inclusion policy is one notable example of commercial needs overriding a lexicographer's guidelines.

Scholarly and commercial interests also sit uncomfortably alongside each other when it comes to the inclusion of taboo words. A neutral linguist, examining the language, will say that all words are worthy of interest, and that swear words are generally of more interest than others (see Burridge, this volume); however, a publisher may be wary of including examinations of such words in a dictionary intended for general readership. This was a key concern in the mid-20th century: the 1961 *Webster's Third New International Dictionary* was intended to include an entry on *fuck*, but the publisher vetoed this and a reviewer later criticized its 'residual prudishness'; the 1966 *Random House Dictionary of the English Language* did not include the word, and so the *New York Times* review of the book discussed its 'stupid prudery [...] in a dictionary of this scope and ambition the omission seems dumb and irresponsible' (Sheidlower 2009: xxx–xxxi). By contrast, the scholarly *Dictionary of Middle English* included *cunte* in 1961, although not all scholarly dictionaries followed the urge for maximal inclusion; the *OED* editor C. T. Onions supported the omission of *fuck* and other strong taboo terms from the first edition of the *OED* in the early 20th century, but it appeared along with a range of other taboo terms in the later 1972 *Supplement* (see also Burchfield 1972). Such omission was not universal, however. Onions argued for the 1933 *OED Supplement* to include *lesbianism*, which he described in a letter as 'a very disagreeable thing, but the word is in regular use and no serious Supplement to our work should omit it' (Brewer 2007: 49).

One final area for commercial interests to be prioritized by a dictionary is in the protection of a modern work's copyright. It is fairly easy to plagiarize dictionaries, given that they assemble facts about words in common use and are generally available in electronic form. It is therefore somewhat common in reference sources to insert a fake item, sometimes called a *copyright trap* or a *Mountweazel*, after a well-known trap entry in a 1975 encyclopedia; should this fake entry be found in another reference work, it could only have been taken directly from the inventing source rather than be the result of independent work. The most famous word of this sort is *esquivalience*, an entry inserted in 2001 in the *New Oxford American Dictionary*; the non-word was later found without attribution on the online *dictionary.com* resource, and then taken down from that site (Alford 2005). There are now, interestingly, some natural uses online of *esquivalience* (meaning the wilful avoidance of one's official responsibilities)—a consequence, explored in the following section, of the popular view of a dictionary as an absolute authority.

3.5 Impartial but judicious

The second contradiction is that dictionaries are both judicious and impartial. Expert lexicographers generally wish to act as other exploratory scientists do—like biologists, catching butterflies and examining their provenance, or cartographers, exploring new vistas and charting their extent. Lexicographers of this type are not concerned with value judgements, just as biologists do not speculate on whether a butterfly is morally dubious and cartographers do not solely chart those areas of which only the well-bred approve. However, one of the primary uses of a dictionary is to assist users in finding words which are appropriate for a purpose, and in some cases to avoid words which are considered by other speakers to be offensive or otherwise inappropriate. This tension is frequently problematic, as a core tenet of modern descriptive language study is that it is concerned with describing all aspects of a language within its natural habitat, free of value judgements.

Nonetheless, many dictionary users wish a dictionary to be judicious and to act as an authority, describing what is and is not considered part of 'the language'. This perhaps arises from the privileged position of a dictionary in the educational system; dictionaries are often purchased by or for students in order to assist them with language learning and as an aid in composition (the sales categories for dictionaries, such as *Collegiate*, *Student*, or *School*, reinforce this). As Kilgarriff points out in this volume, dictionaries are usually referred to with the definite article; people say that things should be checked in *the* dictionary, not *a* dictionary. This 'implicit belief that the dictionary is one's linguistic bible' (Quirk 1982: 87) has become so entrenched that judges often use dictionaries in court cases to establish 'natural' meaning (Solan 1993). This desire is, on occasion, explicitly fulfilled; the modern prescriptive dictionary par excellence is that of the Académie française, which acts as the canonical authority on the use and vocabulary of French—but these works are rare.

The desire for prescription relies on the assumption that a dictionary can be more of an authority than is actually possible; dictionaries are necessarily imperfect because they are created through many compromises, by people working on often-imperfect data within a tight timescale, and often have problems with regards to the constant struggle to be up-to-date. Nonetheless, dictionaries are given an unusual privilege amongst reference materials. Should a person look up their location on a map and find features to be missing, they would believe the map to be incorrect; if they were to hear of a country and search fruitlessly for it in an encyclopedia, they will consider the encyclopedia out of date; however, if they were to look to a dictionary for a word they have just heard and find that the word is not in the dictionary, there is a significant chance that the user may conclude that the word is itself improper, to be avoided, or even that it isn't a 'real' word at all, rather than the more natural conclusion that the dictionary is flawed or out of date.

When dictionaries break away from this tradition, they may find themselves following the desires of lexicographers and of linguists, but acting against the wishes of users. This is particularly evident in the United States, where the 1961 publication of *Webster's Third New International Dictionary* was the source of much controversy when it adopted an impartial, descriptive approach to the language, including many slang words in common use but not generally approved of by prescriptive authors (the most famous being the contraction *ain't*). This resulted in virulent displeasure from many writers who desired a more judicious dictionary; the *New Yorker* published an unrestrained and full-throated attack on descriptivism in response, arguing against this 'trend toward permissiveness, in the name of democracy, that is debasing our language' and concluding, quoting *Troilus and Cressida*, that *Webster's Third* had 'untuned the string, made a sop of the solid structure of English, and encouraged the language to eat up himself'

(Macdonald 1962: 166ff.). *Life* magazine's review further complained that the dictionary had 'abandoned any effort to distinguish between good and bad usage—between the King's English, say, and the fishwife's' (quoted in Skinner 2012: 246–7, who with Morton 1995 presents a detailed account of this controversy). The wholly descriptive account was not, it became clear, what many users desired from their dictionary.

One frequent strategy to appease both the descriptive urge and the prescriptive desire is to describe word usages neutrally in the dictionary text itself, and then to include separate usage notes (often in a box or in a separate font in order to highlight their different status). *The American Heritage Dictionary of the English Language* (currently in its 5th edition, 2011) is well known for its usage notes, with a large panel of eminent writers forming its 'usage panel' (including, in its first edition, a number of the most vehement critics of *Webster's Third*). For words such as *epicenter*, the note states what the term 'properly' means and then supplies a figure for what percentage of the usage panel approves of various types of figurative extensions (for example, only 50% per cent of the panel 'accept' figurative uses of this word outside of its earthquake or explosive meaning—such as 'New York City is the epicenter of European immigration'). This is now the standard means of giving prescriptive judgements in a dictionary, but doing so at arm's length; lexicographers can avoid having to say, from their position as impartial experts, what is 'correct' and 'incorrect', or 'good' or 'bad', but rather can give evidence that, should words be used in certain ways in certain situations, that use may be judged inauspicious by some readers.

3.6 Artificial but natural

The final contradiction at the heart of dictionaries is that they are highly artificial but must be entirely rooted in natural language.

They are artificial because a dictionary by its nature unnaturally separates a word from its context. Words derive their meaning from their context and from their usage; a dictionary, however, must remove words from their linguistic situation and present them alphabetically, separated even from words in the same semantic field. This artificiality occurs throughout every part of the dictionary entry: words change their pronunciation depending on where they are in a sentence, yet a reference form must be given; they alter their meaning depending on the context of their use, yet dictionaries must strip away contextual influence while, in some cases, pointing out its influence. It is perhaps a sign of the naturalization of dictionaries, and of their significance within modern culture, that they are not more often viewed as the extreme oddities which they are.

This artifice must then sit alongside the need for dictionaries to reflect natural language, as far as the prescriptive/descriptive balance can allow. Importantly, a dictionary's evidence source should always be rooted in samples of natural language, as the dictionary seeks to represent either the word-stock of a language or of a well-defined subset of this (such as modern German words of a certain level of currency, or all

Middle Scots words in written use). This inventory is impossible to gather without linguistic evidence. Originally, this was accomplished by means of a reading programme, where employees or volunteers read through books, journals, newspapers, and other texts and transcribed examples of words in context onto paper slips. Enough of these slips, once assembled and collected by word, would then be given to a lexicographer, whose job it would then be to identify and define all the meanings found in the slips; their task would be complete when they had accounted for every meaning and every sense represented by the collection of evidence for each word. A reading programme is a very expensive and time-consuming undertaking, however, and can be unconsciously biased. Henry Bradley, an editor of the *OED*, once discovered that there were no citations for the word *glass*, used as the name of articles made of that substance, presumably because it was not exotic enough to be noted by readers (Mugglestone 2005: 41). Similarly, Jürgen Schäfer has noted the reliance of the *OED* citations on 'great literature, a fact which has proved a boon for the literary scholar [...] however, this policy leads to distortion' (1980: 13).

Preferable is the modern method of using an electronic corpus (usually shortened to just *corpus*), 'a collection of pieces of language text in electronic form, selected according to external criteria to represent, as far as possible, a language or language variety as a source of data for linguistic research' (Sinclair 2005: 16). These resources can contain huge amounts of language data, and are used by all modern dictionaries in order to provide the evidence from which their lexicographers draw conclusions about words. The choice of electronic texts to go into a corpus has now become a key concern of lexicography. While a corpus's creators must balance it to best represent what is being analysed, there will always be questions of both quality and inclusion: should internet sources be treated as valid standard language use, for example, or should *Jerry Springer* transcripts, soap opera scripts, and articles from the sensationalist US *National Enquirer* be included, to the detriment of literary novels and financial newspapers?

It is unfortunately not sufficient simply to take as much data as possible and trust that issues of quality and representativeness even themselves out. Corpora have grown enormously across the years; one of the first corpora of English was the Brown Corpus, a 1960/70s collection of 1 million words of American English, followed by the 20-million-word Birmingham Collection of English Text in the 1980s (later renamed the Bank of English, and used for the *COBUILD* dictionary), the 100-million-word British National Corpus in the 1990s, the billion-word Oxford English Corpus in the 2000s (used by Oxford University Press for their dictionaries), and the 155-billion-word Google Books corpus in the 2010s. As corpus size increases, the issue for lexicographers is no longer how to get enough raw examples of word use to create dictionaries, but rather how best to deal with the overwhelming number of examples which can be found. A search in the Brown Corpus for *inside* has 178 example results, a reasonable number to analyse, whereas the British National Corpus gives 13,449 results, and the Google Books corpus 10,057,203. Modern lexicographers must then take random samples from these corpora instead of aiming, as was once the practice, to account for all meanings found in a search; software is also used to automate some of the process of working out what is happening with a word's context, its usage, and its common collocates. Corpus selection and design are therefore still of high importance.

The contradiction here lies in the unusual situation of seeking to remove words from their natural context while gathering as many samples of natural context as possible. The way in which these two, in practice, act in harmony with each other is perhaps the greatest art of the lexicographer; many recent advances in the quality and usability of dictionaries' treatment of words, particularly for non-native language learners, have arisen from digital techniques applied to corpora to assemble as much word data as possible.

3.7 The future

Where next? The likely future directions of dictionaries are predictably expected to rely on electronic formats; developments in this area have led to new lexicographic projects challenging every orthodoxy established over the past few centuries, with varying degrees of success. Perhaps most unusually, it has been hypothesized that corpora can replace dictionaries for most users—a dictionary entry may not need a carefully written definition, but can instead consist simply of a set of well-chosen sample sentences which themselves do the job of providing that definition. This has already been done on occasion by many older dictionaries, including large scholarly works such as the *OED*, where an editor has chosen to let an example stand as the entry's definition (see e.g. the *OED2* entries for *calicle* or *reel-bird*); the corresponding modern extension is that, provided with a sufficiently large corpus and the ability to automatically search for text patterns which characterize pre-existing definitions in texts, details of the meaning of any given word could theoretically be retrieved from the corpus automatically and dynamically (Hearst 1992 describes some of these definitional patterns). There is an attraction to this idea—after all, words are frequently defined in text, and when it comes to rare and unusual recent coinages, it is usually possible to find their original definition in an electronic copy of the text in which they were coined. The online resource *Wordnik* (http://www.wordnik.com) does this; a search for *decimate*, for example, finds example sentences with patterns like 'the word decimate' or *decimate* in inverted commas, which are more likely to give definitions than randomly chosen samples.

But lexicographers are not so easily replaced. As large amounts of raw data become more and more widely available, there is a corresponding increase in the desire of users to be guided appropriately through the overwhelming amount of variable information at hand. The same desire that causes users to ask for prescription and guidance through the thicket of words also requires expert intervention in the face of a wall of sample text—a well-tended and comprehensive set of clear, accurate definitions is preferable to something as easily confusing as natural language. A lexicographer, in this view, is not a stern and prescriptive schoolmaster but rather a curator of data; much as a museum curator is valued for their expert ability to present their exhibits for best comprehension, the value of a modern dictionary is in the expert summations which a lexicographer can provide for the language user. While the surface form of dictionaries will inevitably change, usually to the advantage of users, the underlying function of the dictionary—that of having an expert examine language use and provide an authoritative encapsulation of facts about any given word—will probably not be lost.

Dictionaries also have a new lease of life in their use in digital and online applications. There is an increased desire to have computers *understand* texts as best they can, rather than simply search for words as they do now; it is in the comprehension of the meaning of texts that computers can extract useful information from vast data sources, including the web. Words are used by corpus linguists, computer programmers, and others as *search proxies*, simple means of hunting through texts for information about culture, history, language, literature, and the human experience. It is, however, rare that the word is of interest in its own right, rather than the meaning behind it; in this way a word is used as a proxy for its meaning, and in enhancing this proxy with dictionary data computers can begin to deal with information about meaning rather than just word forms. As computing grows beyond its infancy in this field, and as computers become able to tag and extract word meanings from texts, new prospects open up with regards to the aggregation and investigation of culture using semantic techniques, and it is through dictionaries and thesauri that this becomes possible. Here, the dictionary and the thesaurus have finally returned to their roots as not simply august reference volumes for the aid of the curious, but as comprehensive inventories of meanings, of words, and of the relationship between the two.

CHAPTER 4

WORDS AND THESAURI

CHRISTIAN KAY

4.1 What is a thesaurus?

The English word *thesaurus* derives from a Greek word meaning a store or treasure, and also refers metonymically to the place in which these things were kept, a storehouse or treasury. According to the *Oxford English Dictionary* (*OED*), it appeared in English in the Latin titles of reference books from 1565, and in English titles from 1736 (*OED* sense 2a).[1] Its first recorded use specifically to describe a thematically organized collection of words is in the title of probably the most famous thesaurus of all, Roget's *Thesaurus of English Words and Phrases* (*Roget*), first published in 1852. In modern use, the word can also be applied to an alphabetically organized dictionary of synonyms and antonyms, and to a classified list of terms used in various technical applications, such as indexing and information retrieval (*OED* senses 2b and 2c).The primary focus in this chapter will be on the thematically organized type of thesaurus exemplified by *Roget* and on the issues raised by attempting to present the diverse and expanding lexicon of English within a structure based not on the straightforward progression of the alphabet but on the much more unwieldy and controversial concept of a classification based on meaning.

4.2 Historical overview

In discussing the development of thesauri, scholars are hugely indebted to the work of the late Werner Hüllen, and especially to his monumental *English Dictionaries 800–1700. The Topical Tradition* (1999). So used are we in western societies to the dominance of the

[1] The online *OED* is under revision; dates or other information may have changed by the time this chapter is read.

alphabetical tradition, that it may come as a surprise to learn that the topical or thematic tradition is much older. Indeed, Robert Cawdrey, author of what is generally agreed to be the first English-English alphabetical dictionary, *A Table Alphabeticall, Conteyning and Teaching the True Writing, and Understanding of Hard Usuall English Words* (1604), felt obliged to explain this novel system in laborious detail to his readers, writing in his preface:

> If thou be desirous (gentle Reader) rightly and readily to vnderstand, and to profit by this Table, and such like, then thou must learne the Alphabet, to wit, the order of the Letters as they stand, perfecty [sic] without booke, and where euery Letter standeth: as *b* neere the beginning, *n* about the middest, and *t* toward the end. Nowe if the word, which thou art desirous to finde, begin with *a* then looke in the beginning of this Table, but if with *v* looke towards the end. Againe, if thy word beginne with *ca* looke in the beginning of the letter *c* but if with *cu* then looke toward the end of that letter. And so of all the rest. &c.

Modern dictionary users, being entirely attuned to the alphabet, might find such a level of instruction more appropriate when attempting to understand the mysteries of a semantic classification such as Roget's.

Hüllen (1999: 30–1) traces the existence of topical word lists as far back as the ancient civilizations of Egypt and China. These early compilations focused on the natural world and on the conditions and objects of everyday life, including plants and animals, buildings, kinship terms, and so on. Their purpose was to record knowledge and to pass it on to others. The chosen topics remind us of the close relationship between language and ethnography: much can be revealed about a culture by examining the concepts it chooses to lexicalize and record in writing. Hüllen comments that the Egyptian lists were 'lists of entities rather than lists of words', thus raising a fundamental issue in semantics—the relationship between objects in the material world and the words by which we name or classify them. Whether words should be regarded as names for things, or as signs representing the more abstract notion of mental concepts, has been much discussed in philosophy and linguistics over the years (see Riemer, this volume).

In Europe, the practice of glossing difficult words in texts, such as foreign or dialectal words or archaisms, can be traced back to ancient Greece (Hüllen 1999: 44). As time went on, such glosses were gathered together into wordlists or glossaries for ease of reference, at first related to particular texts, then as more generally useful independent lists divorced from the texts. In England, Latin texts with marginal or interlinear glosses in Old English (OE) are found from the 8th century onwards. Their primary purpose, as in other parts of Europe, was the study and teaching of Latin. Frequently compiled lists included such useful topics as the body and its parts, precious stones, medicinal herbs, and natural kinds such as animals, birds, fish, and plants. The practice of compiling glossaries continued during the Middle English period (1150–1500), when we also find glosses in Anglo-Norman and Old French, the languages of vernacular literacy at the time. Perhaps because of the disruption and development of society during this period, increasing attention was paid to civil domains such as the church, society, arts and crafts, and the home.

In the 15th century, social changes such as the introduction of printing, and increased literacy and mobility among the population, created a demand for materials for learning vernacular European languages. These materials often consisted of multilingual thematic lists, with words from up to eight languages appearing in parallel. English, however, was a low-prestige language at the time, and was rarely included (Hüllen 1999: 105). The Renaissance period also saw the appearance of many new or translated works on technical subjects such as warfare, navigation, and horticulture, some of which were accompanied by thematic glossaries. As Hüllen notes (1999: 54), 'The beginnings of English lexicography, and indeed of the lexicography of other European languages, lie in glosses.'

From the 17th century onwards, the lexicographical focus in the English-speaking world has been very much on the ever-increasing size and sophistication of alphabetical dictionaries, with some notable exceptions, including John Wilkins' *An Essay towards a Real Character, and a Philosophical Language* (1668), and Peter Mark Roget's *Thesaurus of English Words and Phrases* (1852), which acknowledges a considerable debt to the earlier work. More recent thesauri, such as the *Historical Thesaurus of the Oxford English Dictionary* (*HTOED*, 2009), have followed somewhat different pathways in devising their classifications.[2] Various aspects of these works will be dealt with below.

4.3 What are we classifying, and why?

Words and their meanings are notoriously hard to pin down. Some word forms are polysemous, i.e. they have more than one meaning—sometimes considerably more; the verb *set*, for example, is divided into 126 main categories of meaning in the *OED*, not counting subcategories and phrases. In the opposite case, we may have several words, synonyms, which appear to refer to the same concept, but which on closer examination are subtly different, depending on where and when they are used. Issues like these can often be resolved by examining the words in context, but in the case of thesauri, words are usually removed from their contexts and treated as independent entities. We may thus find *beautiful, handsome*, and *pretty* grouped together as words referring to pleasing appearance, although a finer-grained analysis would show that we rarely, if ever, talk about *handsome babies* or *pretty sausages*. It is, of course, on the basis of collocations which *do* occur, such as *pretty baby* or *handsome man*, that dictionary definitions are formulated.

[2] Further details about *HTOED* and the procedures used in its classification can be found in its *Introduction* (2009: xiii–xx), and in Kay (2010; 2012).

Such problems were of concern to scholars in the 17th century for a variety of reasons. As a result of the explosion of knowledge during the Renaissance, and increased contact with modern languages, the vocabulary of English had expanded rapidly, leaving many people feeling insecure about their ability to use it. Learned words derived from Latin presented particular problems to the less well educated, and it was their needs that early dictionaries were designed to address. In the title page of his *Table Alphabeticall* of 1604 (see section 4.2), Cawdrey announced that his aim was to tackle these difficult words 'with the interpretation thereof by plaine English words, gathered for the benefit & helpe of Ladies, Gentlewomen, or any other unskilfull persons'. However, it was not only 'unskilfull persons' who were facing linguistic problems. At the same time as these Latinate words were entering English, Latin itself was losing the place it had held throughout the medieval period as the lingua franca of European scholarship. Academic works were increasingly written in vernacular languages, including English, and scholars struggling to develop a suitable style for these works had to confront problems such as the ambiguity and vagueness of words in natural language.[3] Scholars in the rapidly developing field of science, especially the biological sciences, were particularly exercised by such issues. They also engaged in discussion about the relationship between words and the things they designate in the external world, and about what goes on in our heads when we connect the two.

4.3.1 John Wilkins and universal languages

The most draconian solution to the inadequacy of natural language is simply to replace it with an artificial language, rather in the manner in which words for basic relationships are replaced by signs in symbolic logic. Theoretically at least, the inventor of such a language can control the situation by ensuring that each sign designates one, and only one, meaning; polysemy and synonymy are outlawed. Discussion and implementation of artificial languages with such an aim occupied a good deal of scholarly time in the 17th century.

Although the first person to attempt an artificial language in England was Francis Bacon, the most influential scholar in the field, and the one who took his plans furthest, was John Wilkins, a botanist whose primary interest lay in the classification of plants.[4] His work culminated in *An Essay towards a Real Character, and a Philosophical Language*, published in 1668. In his title, *character* means a set of written symbols, while *real* is used in *OED* sense 4b, 'Of written characters: representing things instead

[3] For a discussion of how such issues, and others raised in this chapter, have affected the development of specialist terminologies in more recent times, see L'Homme in this volume.

[4] A full account of Wilkins' work in the context of his time is given in Slaughter (1982). For a detailed account of his work on classification, see Hüllen (1999: 244–301, the sample tables in pp. 459–67, and 2004).

of sounds; ideographic'. Several of the *OED* citations refer to the Chinese writing system, knowledge of which had recently reached England. The language projectors, as they are sometimes called (because they had a project), realized the potential of such a system: just as it enabled speakers of mutually unintelligible languages like Mandarin and Cantonese to communicate in writing, so it could be used in a much grander way to enable communication among speakers of all languages, thus diluting the effects of the tower of Babel. The projectors, however, wanted to go beyond a universal language where signs represented words and to create one based on the 'things and notions' which occurred in nature; that is, a 'philosophical language'. As Slaughter writes, they aspired to a system that

> ... directly referred not to words but to things or to notions of things, just as 2 refers to the quantity two and not the word *two, deux, duo*, etc. To say that one will invent a common language of ideographic signs presupposes, however, that there is a common set of notions which the ideographic signs are to represent. While these common notions are obvious in the indisputable case of numbers they become more problematical once we go beyond numbers. The language projectors, since many were also scientists, soon made it their business to set out or to discover precisely what those universal notions were.
>
> (Slaughter 1982: 1–2)

The second part of this quotation identifies one of the problems that beset any attempt at creating a universal language. Notions which seem to be so basic that they must be common to all humankind often appear to be less than universal on closer examination. Much 20th-century linguistic research on the world's languages, in areas such as colour or kinship terminology, proves just this point: what is meant by such apparently straightforward concepts as 'red' or 'sister' can vary widely across languages and cultures.

It is impossible in a few paragraphs to do justice to Wilkins or to the many contemporary scholars and fellow members of the Royal Society who shared his interests, such as Christopher Wren, John Ray, Isaac Newton, and Gottfried Leibnitz. Like his colleagues, Wilkins was concerned with finding order and structure in the apparent chaos of the external world. As a foundation for his philosophical language, therefore, he set about experimenting with a classification of plants, which involved identifying their distinguishing characteristics and organizing them into classes on that basis. From these basic units he built up a taxonomy, a hierarchical classification in which each level was related by a distinctive feature to those above and below. From these relationships, definitions of the classified things and notions could be constructed. To modern readers, used to elaborate scientific taxonomies such as the Linnaean classification of plants, such an arrangement may not seem particularly novel, but it was revolutionary in its day. Until the 17th century, such taxonomies as existed were essentially folk classifications, based on popular knowledge, such as whether plants were edible, or poisonous, or useful in medicine.

By the time his book was published, Wilkins had gone far beyond the domain of plants and devised a taxonomy that encompassed, in varying degrees of detail, all phenomena capable of observation. Robins observes:

> The Essay, which runs to 454 pages ... sets out what purports to be a complete schematization of human knowledge, including abstract relations, actions, processes, and logical concepts, natural genera and species of things animate and inanimate, and the physical and institutionalized relations between human beings in the family and in society.
>
> (Robins 1967: 114)

Wilkins himself acknowledged that information was deficient in many areas, but defended his decision to publish on the grounds that he wanted to show the potential of taxonomically organized data.

Once the taxonomic tables had been established, the next stage was to assign symbols to them, rather in the manner of headings in a thesaurus such as *Roget*, but avoiding the ambiguity of natural language. Thus the letter <g> indicates the superordinate category 'Plants', and is followed by subordinate categories such as <ga> 'plants classed by flowers' and <ge> 'plants classed by seed vessels'. Three letters indicate a further subdivision, as in <gab> 'plant, herb/flower, stamineous', and so on for a further fifteen levels. These elements constitute the primitives or root words of the system, unambiguous units denoting a single idea out of which more complex units might be constructed (Slaughter 1982: 168–70). The final stage in the process is to assign to each primitive and composite form a symbol that will fix its meaning for all times and all natural languages. For composite forms, these utilize repeated signs, such as a semi-circle above the middle of a character indicating 'male' or a short vertical line on the left indicating metaphorical use (Robins 1967: 115).

4.3.2 After Wilkins

Interest in philosophical languages had virtually disappeared by the end of the 17th century, although universal languages such as Esperanto, usually based on existing languages, are a recurrent phenomenon, as is the search for components of meaning which can be combined to form the words of natural languages. Much of this kind of work has been done by anthropological linguists, who find it useful when analysing areas like kinship terminology to employ components such as plus or minus [MALE], [SAME GENERATION AS EGO], and [MATRILINEAL]. Componential analysis, as this process is usually called, assumes structured lexical fields, where words can be defined in terms of one another. It can be applied to specific languages or to a renewed search for deep structure features common to all languages. The former objective informs the thesaurus of New Testament Greek compiled by Eugene Nida and described in Nida (1975). Here a total of some 5,000 words yields around 15,000 different meanings, classified under approximately 275 semantic domains tailored to the cultural context of the time. Another thesaurus-related use aimed at a particular language was the setting up of the twenty-six major categories of *HTOED*, based on the extraction of components from *OED* definitions of key words (Kay and Samuels 1975). A form of componential analysis also played a part in the development of generative semantics, as in Katz and Fodor's influential paper of 1967, 'Recent issues in semantic theory'. In this project, the aim was to formalize the components that distinguish the various meanings of a word such as *bachelor*, with a view to supplying a dictionary as part of the base component of a generative grammar. An ongoing universalist approach is represented by the work of Anna Wierzbicka, initially published in *Semantic Primitives* (1972), the first step in the development of her Natural Semantic Metalanguage, which offers a set of indefinable meaning units by means of which more complex terms in any language can be defined (Goddard, this volume).

Although Wilkins' work never passed into popular use, its very existence contributed to future endeavours. Roget, in the 1852 introduction to his own thesaurus, praised 'the immense labour and ingenuity' expended in the construction of Wilkins' tables, but considered the work 'far too abstruse and recondite for practical application' (2002: xxx, note 2). Ironically, this comment foreshadowed some of the reaction to his own work when it first appeared. A reviewer of the first edition of *Roget* in *The Critic* wrote:

> This is at least a curious book, novel in its design, most laboriously wrought, but, we fear, not likely to be so practically useful as the care, and toil, and thought bestowed upon it might have deserved.
>
> (cited in Emblen 1970: 272)

In fact, *Roget* did not really become a best-seller until a craze for crossword puzzles swept North America and Britain in the 1920s. During this period, his publisher, Longmans, was reprinting a run of up to 10,000 copies at least once a year (Emblen 1970: 278–81).

Roget nevertheless shared many of Wilkins' objectives and insights, noting that 'classification of ideas is the true basis on which words, which are their symbols, should be classified', and pointing out the advantages for improved communication among speakers of different languages of constructing a 'polyglot lexicon' using the *Roget* framework (2002: xxx). As Hüllen says, Wilkins did great service not only to science and theories of classification, but also to his native language by introducing 'the idea of a comprehensive and monoglot onomasiological dictionary of the language into lexicography (possibly without being aware of it)' (1999: 271–2).

Nor have scientists lost their interest in the classification of ideas through words. One of the most original volumes of recent years is Henry Burger's *Wordtree* (1984), described on its title page as

> A Transitive Cladistic for Solving Physical and Social problems. The dictionary that analyzes a quarter-million word-listings by their processes, branches them binarily

> to pinpoint the concepts, thus sequentially tracing causes to their effects, to produce a handbook of physical and social engineering.

Having found existing dictionaries 'overly humanistic', the editor turned to the language of technology, 'an increasingly important part of the mapping of any culture seeking to control its environment'. Over a period of twenty-seven years, he collected transitive verbs, analysed them into binary semantic primitives, and combined them to form a multiply cross-referenced hierarchy of lexical items, where each word is defined by a word from the level above, plus a differentiating component (*Wordtree*: 13–14). This is a book like no other, yet Burger's comment 'Each scientific revolution produces a somewhat different grammar and world-view' reminds us both of the relationship between thesauri and culture, and of the role that scholars from different disciplines can play in their development.

4.4 Synonymy

A somewhat less draconian approach to the problem of synonymy is the development of the synonym dictionary, a hybrid form, which combines the convenience of alphabetical order with the opportunity to consider a range of possibilities for expression in particular contexts. Despite their lack of theoretical interest for aficionados of thesauri, such works continue to be popular nowadays and appear on many publishers' lists, often with the word *thesaurus* in their titles. Full-scale thematic thesauri, on the other hand, are often daunting to users unfamiliar with their structures—an observation confirmed by the fact that thesauri from Wilkins onwards have included an alphabetical index for ease of reference.

The development of synonym dictionaries filled the gap between Wilkins and Roget, although the primary focus in the period was the production of ever larger and more comprehensive monolingual dictionaries, culminating in the beginning of publication of the *OED* in 1884. The purpose of these synonym dictionaries is not to unravel the intricacies of nature, but to offer opportunities for stylistic, and possibly social, improvement. In this they have something in common with the early monolingual dictionaries, as indicated by Robert Cawdrey's reference on his title page to 'ladies and unskilfull persons' (see section 4.3). Hester Lynch Piozzi, one of the early compilers of a synonym dictionary, and one of the first women to appear in the annals of lexicography, perhaps had a similarly delimited audience in mind when she compiled *British Synonymy; or, An Attempt at Regulating the Choice of Words in Familiar Conversation* (1794). As Hüllen points out:

> In the preface, Piozzi conforms to the limited role that the eighteenth century allowed a woman, even one of her panache. It is a woman's work, she writes, to direct the choice of phrases in familiar talk, whereas it is a man's work to prescribe grammar

> and logic. Synonymy, her topic, has more to do with the former than the latter, with the elegance of parlour conversation rather than with truth.
>
> (2004: 224)

Having married an Italian and lived in Italy, Piozzi also had a concern with the problems of foreign learners faced with stylistic choice. Rather than simply offer lists of words, she put them into articles establishing their collocations, as in the group containing *abandon, forsake, relinquish*, etc., where she writes:

> ... a man *forsakes* his mistress, *abandons* all hope of regaining her lost esteem, *relinquishes* his pretensions in favour of another; *gives up* a place of trust he held under the government, *deserts* his party, *leaves* his parents in affliction, and *quits* the kingdom for ever.
>
> (cited in Hüllen 2004: 226–7)

One can imagine the parlour gossip which might have given rise to that scenario.

A similar model is followed in a later work, George Crabb's *English Synonymes Explained, in alphabetical order with copious illustrations and examples drawn from the best writers* (1816). This was a popular and influential book, running through many editions until the final one in 1953, and aspired to cover all the synonyms in the language in alphabetical order (Hüllen 2004: 254). As with other synonym dictionaries, such ambition entailed a good deal of cross-reference. The inclusion of quotations from the 'best writers', such as Addison, Dryden, Johnson, Milton, and Pope, was a practice that had been developing steadily in alphabetical dictionaries since the 17th century, and is, of course, a cornerstone of the *OED*. An example of Crabb's style is his article for *Dispel, disperse*:

> *Dispel*, from the Latin *pellere*, to drive, signifies to drive away. *Disperse* comes from Latin *dis*, apart, and *spargere*, to scatter, and means to scatter in all directions.
>
> *Dispel* is a more forcible action than to *disperse*: we destroy the existence of a thing by *dispelling* it; we merely destroy the junction or cohesion of a body by *dispersing* it; the sun *dispels* the clouds and darkness; the wind *disperses* the clouds or a surgeon *disperses* a tumour.
>
> (1916: 276)

Entries of this kind go some way towards dispelling (or dispersing) the criticism often levied against thesauri, that they give the user no means of discriminating amongst the words on offer. Such criticism was anticipated by Roget, whose thesaurus simply listed words under headings and, sometimes, subheadings. Addressing those who are 'painfully groping their way and struggling with the difficulties of composition', he assured them that their 'instinctive tact will rarely fail to lead [them] to a proper choice'

(2002: xx). As anyone will testify who has read a student essay that relied heavily on *Roget* for elegant variation of style, such an assumption may be over-optimistic. On the other hand, Roget's category 621 *Relinquishment* in the most recent edition (2002: 338) contains over a hundred verbs, comparing favourably in quantity at least with the much smaller number offered by Piozzi or Crabb.

Discrimination among lists of synonyms is a particular problem for foreign learners of a language. Roget's work is clearly aimed at native English speakers, even if their discriminatory powers are not as finely tuned as he suggests. Modern thesauri intended for learners, such as Tom McArthur's pioneering *Longman Lexicon of Contemporary English* (1981), give examples of usage as well as supplementary information, for instance about grammatical patterns. The *Oxford Learner's Thesaurus* (2008), despite its title, is a dictionary of 17,000 synonyms and antonyms, and includes short definitions as well as collocations and usage notes. Thus the entry for *beautiful* is divided into 1. a beautiful woman, and 2. a beautiful place. Synonyms for the former, based on frequency of occurrence in a corpus, are *beautiful, pretty, handsome, attractive, lovely, cute, good-looking, gorgeous, stunning, striking.* A usage note under *pretty* tells us that it 'is used most often to talk about girls. When it is used to talk about a woman, it usually suggests that she is like a girl, with small, delicate features' (53). *Plain* is given as the antonym for *pretty*, whereas that for *beautiful* is *ugly*. Overall, the learner is offered a good deal of assistance in making appropriate choices. Interestingly, right at the back of the book, there is a topic index, grouping the dictionary entries under thirty headings such as *the arts, conflict*, and *health* (903-12). The difference between a thesaurus and a dictionary is to some extent relative.

4.4.1 What is a synonym?

Dictionaries like those discussed above draw attention to the problems involved in discriminating amongst synonyms. Underlying such problems is the superficially straightforward question, 'What is a synonym?', to which the superficially straightforward answer would be that it is a word which 'means the same' as another word or words. This is a particularly pertinent question for English, which has accumulated large numbers of synonyms or near-synonyms as a result of its long history of absorbing words from other languages, and coining new ones from its own resources. Two key periods here are Middle English, where French was the predominant source language for borrowings, and the Renaissance, which saw an influx of words from Latin.

During much of the twentieth century, when structural linguistics was the dominant paradigm in many parts of Europe and America, the question of what constituted synonymy was widely debated. John Lyons, for example, proposed a distinction between a strict interpretation of the term, where synonyms enter into the same set of sense relationships, and a loose one, which covers the sorts of lists found in *Roget*, where some, but by no means all, meaning is shared (1968: 446–53). In fact, language has a natural tendency to differentiate words that may originally have been synonymous, often by narrowing the meaning of one of them; there is no particular advantage, other than elegant variation of style, in having two or more words that mean exactly the same thing. In theory at least, it is possible to say everything in Wilkins' philosophical language, with its exclusion of synonyms, that one can say in a much larger and more unwieldy language like modern English.

Within cognitive semantics, defining synonymy is no longer such an issue. On the one hand, building on the notion of a fuzzy set, prototype theory allows for categories that contain both good and less good examples, as in a *Roget* list. On the other hand, individual meanings of words are defined within a framework of knowledge, rather than solely in terms of their relationships to one another. As Geeraerts writes:

> Cognitive semantics . . . takes a maximalist perspective on meaning, one in which differences between semantic and encyclopedic knowledge, or more generally, between semantics and pragmatics, are not taken as a point of departure. Giving up the distinction is relevant for the description of separate lexical items: it implies that it is no longer necessary to draw the borderline between strictly definitional and merely descriptive features.
>
> (2010: 222)

Exclusion of real-world knowledge is in fact an impossible position for anyone attempting to construct a thematic thesaurus (see further section 4.5). Information deduced from the words often has to be supplemented by information about the things or notions they designate. It would, for example, be difficult, if not impossible, to attempt a classification of Old English words for agricultural implements and their parts without any knowledge of what a plough or a mattock was like.

In passing, it may be noted that polysemy is not an issue for thesauri. If a word has ten different meanings, then they will appear in ten thesaurus categories as independent entities, related only through the alphabetical index.

4.5 The bigger picture

Some of the points in section 4.4.1 can be illustrated from *Roget* category 252 *Rotundity*:

> N. *rotundity*, rondure, roundness, orbicularity 250 *circularity*; sphericity, sphericality, spheroidicity; globularity, globosity, cylindricity, cylindricality, gibbosity, gibbousness 253 *convexity*.
>
> *sphere*, globe, spheroid, prolate s., oblate s., ellipsoid, globoid, geoid; hollow sphere, bladder; balloon 276 *airship*; soap bubble 355 *bubble*; ball, football, pelota, wood (bowls), billiard ball, marble, ally, taw; crystal ball; cannon ball, bullet, shot, pellet; bead, pearl, pill, pea, boll, oakapple, puffball, spherule, globule; drop,

> droplet, dewdrop, inkdrop, blot; vesicle, bulb, onion, knob, pommel 253 *swelling*; boulder, rolling stone; hemisphere, hump, mushroom 253 *dome*; round head, bullet h., turnip h.[5]
>
> (2002: 132)

Pairs like *sphericity/sphericality* or *rotundity/roundness* might be accepted as synonyms, but in the second pair there is a difference of register, with *rotundity* more likely to be used in formal or humorous contexts. *Gibbosity* and *gibbousness* are now mostly in technical use, and for many speakers would occur only in collocations such as *gibbous moon.* In the second set, *sphere* and *globe* might be considered synonyms, but *spheroid, prolate s[pheroid], oblate s., ellipsoid, globoid,* and *geoid* are not synonyms but hyponyms of *sphere* in that they refer to a particular sub-type. Thereafter, the classification wanders off into a miscellaneous collection of words referring to objects that just happen to be round—in Aristotelian terms, 'roundness' is an accidental property of such objects rather than an essential one. If people are asked where they would expect to find such words, they are likely to allocate *pea, onion,* and *mushroom* to a category of *Vegetables, football* to *Sport,* and *bullet* to *Armaments;* that is to lexical fields representing domains of use in the external world. In current *Rogets,* many words appear in both types of categories.

To some extent, *Roget* categories of the kind represented by 252 *Rotundity* are a historical accident. Early editions of his work focus on abstract vocabulary areas, which are more likely to attract synonyms than words with material referents. (*Pea,* for example, according to *HTOED,* has had only one synonym in its long history, and that was *roly-poly,* recorded twice from a single colloquial source in 1784.) Subsequent editors have added in large amounts of vocabulary for material objects, generally using the existing categories rather than, as might have been preferable, setting up new ones. Thus, because of both its original plan and its subsequent history, many people find Roget's classification less easy to use than he claimed in the passage from his *Introduction* below:

> In constructing the following system of classification of the ideas which are expressible by language, my chief aim has been to obtain the greatest amount of practical utility. I have accordingly adopted such principles of arrangement as appeared to me to be the simplest and most natural, and which would not require, either for their comprehension or application, any disciplined acumen, or depth of metaphysical or antiquarian lore (2002: xxii).

This statement draws attention to one of the many issues confronting anyone rash enough to embark on compiling a thesaurus from scratch: do you start with an *a priori* scheme of classification into which words can be slotted, or do you build up the

[5] In *Roget*'s layout, semi-colons separate minor divisions of meaning. Numbers with italicized headings, as in 250 *Circularity,* are cross-references to related categories. In cognitive semantic terms, these indicate the peripheral members of the category, as opposed to the clear members at its core.

classification from an examination of the lexical materials? The first of these approaches was favoured by Wilkins and Roget, both of whom, as we have seen, had a desire to establish order in the world before embarking on lexical analysis. Indeed, Roget's most recent biographer suggests that his desire for order was an attempt to compensate for an insecure childhood, spent wandering around England with his over-anxious widowed mother (Kendall 2008). The *a priori* approach was also favoured by the major alternative to their systems proposed in the 20th century, Rudolph Hallig and Walther von Wartburg's *Begriffssystem als Grundlage für die Lexikographie: Versuch eines Ordnungsschemas* (1952). Although the scheme of classification and some sample entries are given in French, this is not a thesaurus of a particular language but a taxonomy of concepts into which, they claim, the lexicon of any language could be inserted, thereby enabling comparative lexical and cultural studies. Ullmann reports that the work caused considerable interest when it was revealed at the Seventh International Congress of Linguists in 1952 (1957: 314–15; see also Hüllen 1999: 18–21), but there is no record of its being used in its totality or of it having much effect on practical lexicography.

Schemes such as these perpetuate the idea that a universal system of concepts is discoverable (see section 4.3.2). In fact, such an objective is unlikely to be accomplished. As Lyons writes of Hallig and von Wartburg:

> It is difficult to justify, for English at least, even the highest-level tripartite division of the vocabulary into lexemes relating to the universe, to man, and to man and the universe; as it is difficult to justify, in terms of hyponymy and quasi-hyponymy, Roget's six main classes of lexemes, (i) abstract relations; (ii) space; (iii) matter; (iv) intellect; (v) volition; (vi) sentient and moral powers.
>
> (1977: 300–1).

In the case of Hallig and von Wartburg, the decision to place 'man' at the centre of the universe is sociopolitical, rather than linguistic. Humans and other living creatures have a great deal in common when it comes to the processes of physical existence: living, breathing, eating, sleeping, and so on. A thesaurus of English based on their separation would lead to huge amounts of duplication in listing the vocabulary for these processes.

It is often a sorrow for thesaurus-makers, and an argument against the universality of human conceptual structures, that one person's self-evident system of classification will be largely mysterious to others. Robert Chapman, for example, editor of the fifth edition of the American *Roget's International Thesaurus* (1992), made some radical changes to Roget's framework, re-organizing the highest level of the taxonomy into fifteen categories, starting with *The Body and the Senses*. He claimed that Roget's scheme:

> ... does not coincide with the way most people now apprehend the universe. Casting about for a more fitting arrangement, I chose what I call a 'developmental-existential' scheme ... The notion has been to make the arrangement analogous

> with the development of the human individual and the human race ... This seems to me 'the simplest and most natural' array in the mind of our own time.
>
> (quoted in Fischer 2004: 43; see also Hüllen 2009: 44).

Thesaurus-makers are nothing if not ambitious, but one is tempted to ask who 'most people' are, and on what grounds the editor speaks for them.

A more modest approach is taken in Buck's *A Dictionary of Selected Synonyms in the Principal Indo-European Languages* (1949). After criticizing *Roget* for its large groupings and consequent 'lack of coherence', he says that his own classification is by 'semantically congeneric groups', and continues:

> The particular order and classification adopted is not copied from others, but no remarkable merit is claimed for it ... There will be much that is frankly arbitrary, both in the classification and in the selection of synonyms to be included.
>
> (1988: xiii)

His 'congeneric groups' are somewhat similar to lexical fields, starting with The Physical World in its Larger Aspects, with subcategories at three levels of delicacy, and concluding with Chapter 22, Religion and Superstition. Despite the fact that there is 'some recourse to Miscellaneous' as a category (1988: xiii), the classification is relatively easy to navigate.

More recent thesauri, such as *A Shakespeare Thesaurus* (1993), *A Thesaurus of Old English* (*TOE*) (1995), and the *Historical Thesaurus of the Oxford English Dictionary* (2009), have taken the second approach noted above and started from the lexical data. In so doing, they aim to construct the world-view from the lexicon, and to postpone the identification of things and, especially, notions until the words have been analysed. As the editors of *HTOED* explain:

> It was acknowledged from the start that each section should be allowed to develop its own structure. Within the general taxonomic framework [the 26 major categories], classifiers were given a free hand, being told simply to 'sort, sort, and sort again' until an acceptable structure emerged; in other words, the classification was 'bottom up' from the data rather than imposed 'top down'.
>
> (2009: xviii)

A similar procedure had already been followed for *TOE*, which served as a pilot study for the larger work. The editors go on to remark that the most successful classifiers were often people who combined linguistic and philological skills with some knowledge of the subject being classified, especially in the sections dealing with the external and social worlds. In this they show some affinity with the tenets of the *Wörter und Sachen* (words and objects) movement in early 20th-century Germany, of which Geeraerts writes: 'The principal idea is that the study of words, whether etymological, historical, or purely variational, needs to incorporate the study of the objects denoted by these words'

(2010: 24). Given the ethnographic nature of their interests, it is not surprising that this group concentrated on the vocabulary of the material universe and its culture. One of the challenges for the *HTOED* team was to extend this system to abstract concepts, where boundaries of both meanings and categories are less clear-cut, and the taxonomy tends to be much flatter (Kay and Wotherspoon 2005).

It is perhaps no coincidence that all three of the works mentioned above are historical thesauri, covering particular periods in English in the case of the first two, and the complete recorded history of English in the case of *HTOED*. World-views change with the passage of time, as well as with synchronic variational factors, making it impossible in both theory and practice to devise a classification where one size fits all.

Abbreviations

HTOED	*Historical Thesaurus of the Oxford English Dictionary*
OE	*Old English*
OED	*Oxford English Dictionary*
Roget	*Roget's Thesaurus of English Words and Phrases*
TOE	*A Thesaurus of Old English*

CHAPTER 5

WORD FREQUENCIES

JOSEPH SORELL

5.1 Introduction

SCIENCE fiction authors and filmmakers have long faced an inconvenient linguistic problem. How does one write realistic dialogue for extraterrestrials? C. S. Lewis in his *Space Trilogy* took into account that not all *hnau* (the term for 'sentient species' in Lewis's interplanetary lingua franca, Old Solar) necessarily share the same vocal apparatus as homo sapiens. The makers of *Star Trek* commissioned a linguist, Marc Okrand, to create deliberately non-human-like languages, rather than ask viewers to suspend disbelief as Klingons converse with each other in American English. This raises the question of how we would even recognize a transmission from E.T. as meaningful. The answer lies, surprisingly, not in understanding the meaning of the message, but in analysing the word frequencies.

The story behind this solution begins over a century ago with an astute observation by a French stenographer. Jean-Baptiste Estoup (1916) noticed that some words were not just more frequent than others; they towered far above the average by a factor of thousands. Harvard professor George Kingsley Zipf (1949) made the same observation and wrote extensively on this pattern of word frequencies. Today, this frequency distribution is known generally as Zipf's law.

The statistical tools for gauging the central tendency in a normal distribution turn out to be of little use when dealing with word frequencies in naturally produced texts. The vast majority of word types (the words in the vocabulary of the text) are less frequent than the mean (or average). In H. G. Wells's *The First Men in the Moon*, the novel that inspired Lewis's trilogy, the mean frequency is 9.7. Of the 7,179 word types in the novel, 89 per cent are less frequent than the mean. Rather than being near to the mean, the median frequency (the frequency of the type at the mid-point of the distribution, i.e. type number 3,589 or 3,590) is only 2.0. The mode (the most common frequency) for naturally produced texts is always 1.0. In *The First Men in the Moon*, 54 per cent of the word types are hapax legomena (types that occur only once in the text).

What makes this distribution of words interesting, though, is not just that there are a few oddly frequent words. Estoup and Zipf found that this highly skewed pattern of frequencies followed a markedly consistent pattern. The second most frequent word in a text occurred roughly half as many times as the most frequent word. The third most frequent word occurred around one-third as often as the most frequent word, and so on. To put it another way, if one lists the words in a text in descending order of frequency and then multiplies a word's frequency (*f*) by its rank (*r*), the product remains approximately constant (*C*).

$$r * f \approx C$$

As can be seen in Table 5.1, the first two types do not fit the pattern very well. This is actually typical and a potentially significant phenomenon that will be discussed later in

Table 5.1 Sample of word types and frequencies from H. G. Wells's *The First Men in the Moon*

Word type	Frequency (*f*)	Rank (*r*)	Product (*C*)
the	3759	1	3759
and	2680	2	5360
of	2396	3	7188
I	2193	4	8772
a	1796	5	8980
was	928	10	9280
on	407	20	8140
our	304	30	9120
an	232	40	9280
or	195	50	9750
through	96	100	9600
life	41	200	8200
anything	25	300	7500
feeling	19	400	7600
held	15	500	7500
master	7	1000	7000
clumsy	3	2000	6000
halfway	2	3000	6000
bedroom	1	4000	4000
zuzzoing	1	7179	7179

the chapter. At the bottom of the table, also notice that each type has been assigned an individual rank. One could argue that all types with the same frequency should have the same rank. One could assign each of the types at a given frequency the highest rank among that group or the lowest or an average. This would be logical, since *bedroom* and *zuzzoing* were assigned their particular rank in the table only because the list was also alphabetized after sorting for frequency.

In Table 5.1, ranks have been shown in even increments for clarity, but choosing the highest rank among each group of types with the same frequency would have given even more consistent results. In Fig. 5.2, words with the same frequency show up as a horizontal line of overlapping circles. The point furthest to the right, i.e. the highest rank in that frequency group, is typically a better fit to the expected distribution.

A chart of word frequencies is usually shown on a double-logarithmic graph, i.e. the first increment on both the x and the y axes is 1, the second 10, the third 100, etc. A non-logarithmic graph (Fig. 5.1) looks like a large letter L with a few very high-frequency words lined up tight against the y-axis and the rest of the words spread out along the x-axis. If the logarithm of each type's frequency is plotted instead, the points line up at a roughly 45° decline (Fig. 5.2).

This type of distribution is referred to as a power law in mathematics, and Zipf's law is the best-known example. This mathematical insight allowed Estoup to improve French stenography by choosing simpler and shorter symbols for the most common items. Zipf, a linguist, also found this frequency pattern in the words, and even the morphology, of Chinese, Dakota, Gothic, High German, Plains Cree, Yiddish, and many

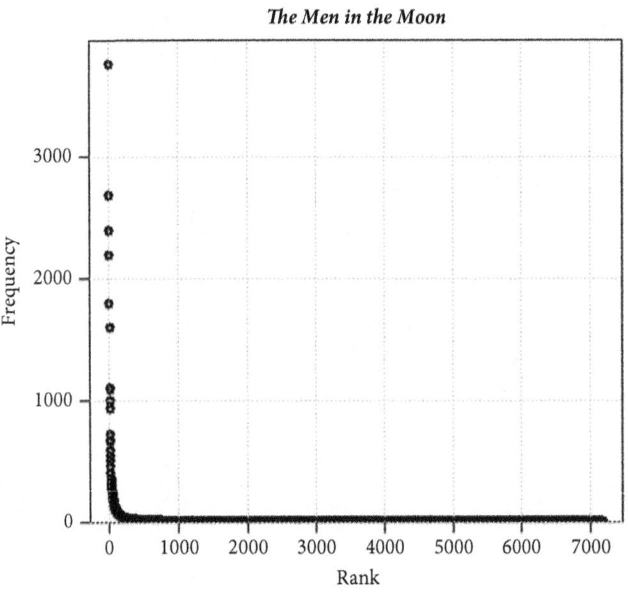

FIG. 5.1 Non-logarithmic Zipf graph of H. G. Wells's *The First Men in the Moon.*

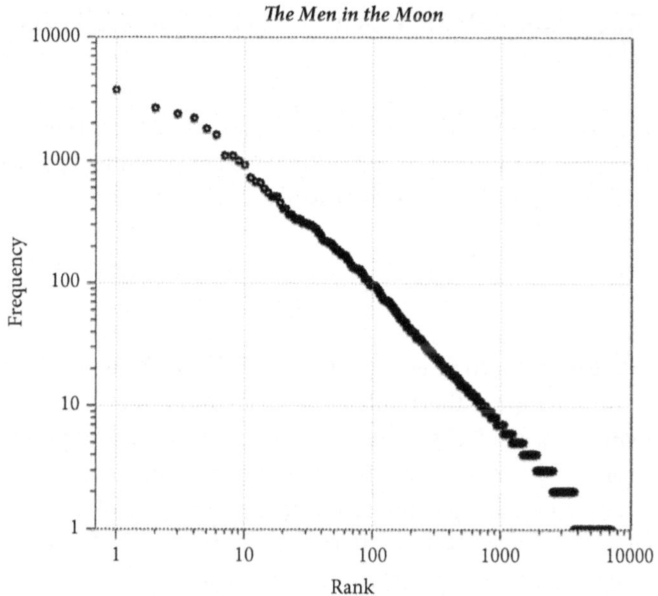

FIG. 5.2 Double-logarithmic Zipf graph of H. G. Wells' *The First Men in the Moon.*

other languages (Zipf 1949). He argued that this curious and apparently universal pattern arose as a compromise between speakers and hearers (1949: 20–21), each of whom wished to expend the least effort possible.

After Zipf published his *Human Behavior and the Principle of Least Effort* (1949), a young mathematician, Benoît Mandelbrot, was looking for something to read on the Paris Métro. He retrieved a review of the book from his uncle's wastebasket (Mandelbrot 1982: 346). His uncle, Szolem Mandelbrojt, was professor of mathematics at the Collège de France. The young Mandelbrot was inspired, and wrote his first academic paper on the connection between Zipf's law and thermodynamics (1982: 345). He envisioned himself becoming the Isaac Newton of linguistics, but he later concluded that Zipf's law 'is linguistically very shallow' (1982: 346; see also Ferrer-i-Cancho and Elevåg 2010; Li 1992; Miller 1957). This fateful encounter eventually led to Mandelbrot's famous work in fractal geometry, and though he described his work on Zipf's law as a 'self-terminating enterprise', some of his insights into Zipf's law have yet to be fully explored.

Mandelbrot (1953, 1982: 347) realized there was an important connection between Zipf's law, thermodynamics, and the recent work of Claude Shannon on information theory (1948). Understanding the efficient communication of information is a good first step towards understanding the mechanics behind Zipf's law. Efficient communication is, in fact, the common denominator that links better systems of stenography, the vocabularies of the world's languages, and spotting a potentially meaningful transmission from another world.

5.2 Entropy and information

Shannon, building on the work of two of his colleagues at Bell Labs, Hartley and Nyquist, devised a measure for quantifying information. Hartley (1928) had earlier suggested a measure of the information (*H*) in a transmission:

$$H = n \log s$$

This formulation turned out to be essentially identical to Boltzmann's formula which is the basis for the second law of thermodynamics (Shannon 1948). Boltzmann's formula calculated the entropy of an ideal gas. The variable *s* corresponds to Boltzmann's variable for the number of possible microstates in which the molecules of gas could find themselves, i.e. how many possible positions and velocities each molecule could have in a particular situation (Mitchell 2009: 49). In Hartley's formula, *s* is the number of symbols in the code and *n* is the number of elements in the transmission.

Entropy in information theory can be thought of as the amount of surprise one encounters in a message (Mitchell 2009: 54). This is partly based on the number of elements in the code. If the message were the results of a fair coin toss, there would be two equally probable elements: heads and tails. Whether the received message is heads or tails will not cause a great deal of surprise. Either result has a probability of 0.5. Rolling a dice would have six possible outcomes, so any of these results would be slightly more surprising than the result of a coin toss. If the code were the English alphabet, there would be 26 possible outcomes (27 if the space is counted). A problem soon becomes evident, however. Information content cannot grow as a simple multiple of the number of elements in the code. If that were true, a single Chinese character would have to convey a massive amount of information. Of course, a single Chinese character does typically communicate more information than a single Latin letter. However, there needs to be a way to temper the quantity of symbols, while still recognizing the effect of the code's size on the information content. Hartley's (1928) 'practical measure'—a logarithm—turned out to be a brilliant solution.

A logarithm can be thought of as a bank—a very generous bank that gives 100 per cent interest per annum on all deposits (Azad 2007). Shannon chose the base 2 logarithm for his equations (instead of base 10 that was used above for the Zipf graph), since the bit (from *binary digit*) is the most basic quantity of information, 1 or 0, a switch that is on or off. For that reason, the following examples will all use a base 2 logarithm.

If we want to know the logarithm of 6 (the number of possible outcomes from rolling a single dice), we deposit $1 in the bank and then ask how long we will have to wait until we will have $6. After one year, we will have $2, after two, $4. The balance will reach $6 after a little more than two and a half years—2.58 years, since interest is added in a steadily rising curve, not a straight line (see Fig. 5.3). That means that the result from the roll of a single dice would have an entropy of 2.58. The above formula

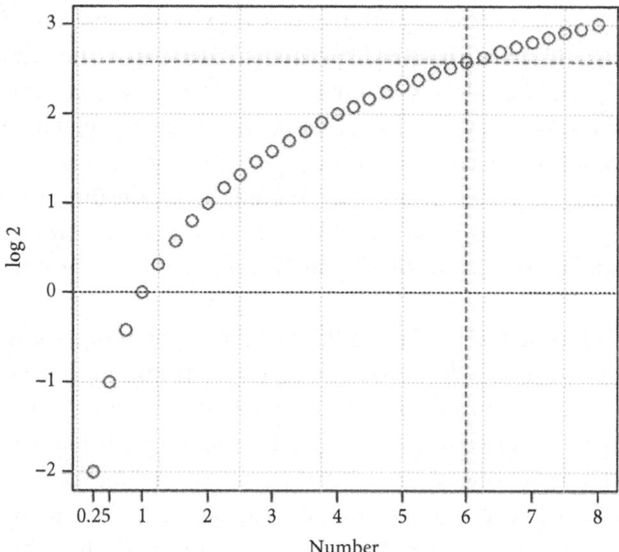

FIG. 5.3 Values for the base 2 logarithm from 0.25 to 3.0 in increments of 0.25. Dashed lines indicate the base 2 logarithm of 6.

would estimate the information in such a message as 2.58 times the number of results reported.

The entropy for a letter in the standard English alphabet would be 4.7 if we ignore case and spaces and assume all letters are equally probable. The latter assumption is of course ridiculous. Words and the letters that compose them are far from random. Samuel Morse realized this when designing his telegraphic code. He estimated the frequency of letters in English based on how many pieces of movable type there were for each letter at a local newspaper (Gleick 2011: 21).

Shannon's (1948) formula for entropy allows the elements in the code to have differing probabilities:

$$H = -\sum_{i=1}^{n} p_i \log_2 p_i$$

To understand how this formula works, imagine a communication code that has a vocabulary of only three words, *green*, *yellow*, and *red*, like the signals of a traffic light. In the record of these signals, we find that *green* is transmitted 50 per cent of the time, while *yellow* and *red* are each recorded 25 per cent of the time. We first calculate the entropy for each of the words by multiplying that word's probability by the logarithm of its probability. The probability for *green* is 0.5. The logarithm of 0.5 is −1, since at 100 per cent interest, we would already have had \$0.50 six months before we deposited the dollar (see Fig. 5.3). The negative sign in front of the symbol for sum Σ indicates that we should sum these quantities by subtracting them from each other. This cancels out the negative from the logarithm, since all probabilities less than 100 per cent will be negative. Multiplying the probability 0.5 by the logarithm 1 gives the entropy for *green* as 0.5. The logarithm of 0.25 is −2 by the same logic, since at 100 per cent interest we would already have had that amount two years earlier. Thus the values for the words *yellow* and *red* are also 0.5. Summing these three values gives a total entropy of 1.5 for words in this vocabulary. Of course, a transmission system cannot have fractional bits, so a 2-bit code would be needed to carry a message of this type (see Fig. 5.4).

The 2-digit binary sequences *10, 01,* and *00* could encode the three words of this code. The remaining possibility, *11*, could be used as the space between words. This example code is too small, however, to allow us to see any difference between frequent and less frequent items.

Table 5.2 is a frequency table of an artificial text of 100 running words (tokens) and a vocabulary of 48 types that follow a roughly Zipfian distribution. The vocabulary of this text would have a Shannon entropy of 4.81 and so would require a 5-bit code. The most frequent word type has a frequency of 20 and, therefore, a probability of 0.2. This type's entropy at 0.464 represents 9.65 per cent of the total entropy for the text. So, each of the 20 tokens of this word type accounts for only 0.48 per cent of the total entropy. At the other end of the distribution, there are 35 hapax legomena. Each of these single words accounts for 1.3 per cent of the total entropy. Rare words are more surprising, and therefore convey more information than frequent words.

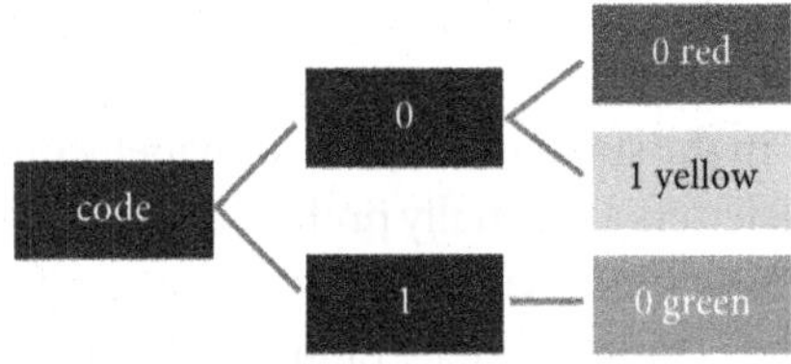

FIG. 5.4 Huffman code for the 'traffic light' system.

Table 5.2 Shannon entropy calculated for an artificial Zipfian distribution

Rank	Frequency	p_i	$\log_2$	$p_i \log_2 p_i$
1	20	0.20	−2.322	0.464
2	10	0.10	−3.322	0.332
3	7	0.07	−3.837	0.269
4	5	0.05	−4.322	0.216
5	4	0.04	−4.644	0.186
6~8	3	0.03	−5.059	0.152
9~13	2	0.02	−5.644	0.113
14~48	1	0.01	−6.644	0.066
Total	100	**1.00**		**4.81**

If rarer, technical words carry a greater amount of information, why should speakers bother using the more general, low-information-content words? Would it not be more efficient to skip directly to more specialized vocabulary? The answer to these questions is a practical one with a surprisingly consistent mathematical outcome.

In natural language, messages are composed of items retrieved from memory and translated into motor-neural gestures that produce sounds, written symbols, or manual signs, depending on the discourse medium. These need to be perceived and deciphered, and often a message needs to be composed in response. In conversation, this needs to happen in real time. If the mental lexicon were a random collection of many thousands of words or a strictly arranged hierarchical grid, accessing a particular word would be either very unreliable or very time-consuming. The power–law distribution of vocabulary items that Zipf and Estoup noticed was an important first clue that the mental lexicon fits neither of these patterns.

In 1950, Mandelbrot sensed that Zipf's law is related to 'some underlying scaling property' (1982: 345). He would later realize that a fractal object, what he called 'a lexicographical tree', was behind this pattern of word frequencies.

5.3 The Zipf–Mandelbrot model

In the graph of word frequencies for Wells's novel, there were noticeable deviations from a −1 (45°) slope among both the highest and lowest frequency words (see Figs. 5.2 and 5.5). In larger collections of texts, these deviations become even more pronounced. Understanding what causes these deviations will help in understanding the connection between a Zipfian word distribution and its underlying structures.

Mandelbrot added two parameters to Zipf's original formula; these shape the expected line of word frequencies to better fit the highest- and lowest-frequency regions:

$$f = \frac{C}{(r+\beta)^{\alpha}}$$

The variable β has the effect of lowering the expected constant by adding to the value for rank. This has a substantial effect on the high-frequency types, but it does little to the low-frequency items that already have very large values for rank. If the constant C were 7,500, increasing the rank for the most frequent word *the* by 1 would lower its expected frequency to 3,750, which is approximately correct. The hapax legomenon with the lowest rank in Wells's novel is *abandon* at rank 3,744. Dividing 7,500 by its rank plus 1 gives an expected frequency of 2, only slightly higher than its actual frequency.

The variable α shapes the curve by factoring the sum of each word's rank plus β by an exponent of less than one. For this novel, $\alpha = 0.809$, which would reduce the expected frequency of *abandon* calculated above from 2 to 1.6. Of course, α would also lower the expected frequency for *the* below where it actually is, as can be seen in Fig. 5.5. The above

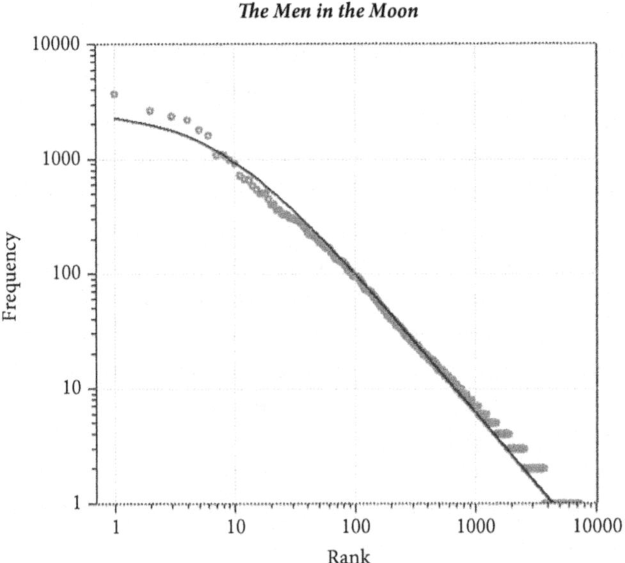

FIG. 5.5 Zipf graph of H. G. Wells's *The First Men in the Moon* showing the expected curve using a finite Zipf–Mandelbrot model.

calculations are crude and only for the purpose of illustration. The variables must be chosen in conjunction, not independently of each other. The constant *C* must also be modified, since α and β have altered the expected number of words in the text. Baroni and Evert's (2006) ZipfR package is useful for determining these parameters and exploring the Zipfian distribution of texts.

Mandelbrot's α variable was specifically designed to fit the long tail of rare words in the vocabulary of a text, and for single texts this modification is an adequate solution. Though they represent a significant number of the types in the vocabulary of a text, rare words make up only a small percentage of the actual tokens. In a larger collection or corpus, however, the percentage of low-frequency tokens may remain low, but the number of types grows steadily as the size of the corpus is increased. That is not to say that the lexicon of any speaker or language is infinite. Over time, however, new words are added to the language and others fade. For a discussion of individual vocabulary growth over the lifespan of an individual, see Nation (2001: 9; also this volume, 6.2) and Schrauf (2009: 259–62). The projected Zipf–Mandelbrot line in Fig. 5.5 was plotted using a finite model which does not anticipate any additional types.

5.4 A DOUBLE DISTRIBUTION

In the late 20th century, corpora of many millions of words became available, and the deviation from the expected –1 slope in these corpora is much less manageable for the Zipf–Mandelbrot formula. Ferrer-i-Cancho and Solé (2001a) and Montemurro (2001) have argued that the difficulty in trying to fit the curve of natural language frequencies is due to the fact that there are really two distributions. Ferrer-i-Cancho and Solé used the 100,000,000-word British National Corpus (BNC), and Montemurro compiled a 183,000,000-word collection of books available from gutenberg.com. In each study, they found 5,000–6,000 words aligned in the classic −1 distribution that Estoup and Zipf observed. The rarer words then formed a second steeper slope of around −2. Montemurro's findings seem to indicate that an even larger corpus would approach −3. The words in this second distribution are the high-entropy items that have been sifted out and collected from the many individual texts of the corpus. They represent the cumulative experience of many texts, many interactions, and many individual language users.

The BNC used in Ferrer-i-Cancho and Solé's study is composed of 90 per cent written and 10 per cent spoken texts, and Montemurro's study was exclusively of written texts. In a multi-dimensional analysis of a corpus of spoken and written texts compiled at US universities, Biber et al. (2002) found that 'spoken registers are fundamentally different from written ones in university contexts, regardless of purpose' (p. 9). Similar differences had been observed in multi-dimensional analyses of spoken and written text types in English, Somali, Korean, and Nukulaelae Tuvaluan (Biber 1995). Therefore, separate spoken and written corpora should be examined to see if they show a similar pattern.

To represent spoken language, an approximately 7,000,000-word corpus of face-to-face conversation was compiled using the demographically sampled spoken data from the BNC, conversational portions of the Santa Barbara Corpus of American English, the Vienna Oxford International Corpus of English, and the Wellington Corpus of Spoken New Zealand English, as well as the International Corpus of English (ICE) from Canada, East Africa, Great Britain, Hong Kong, India, Ireland, Jamaica, New Zealand, Philippines, and Singapore (Sorell 2013). Face-to-face conversation was chosen, since it is 'the most basic register of human language' (Biber and Conrad 2009: 86) and 'the primary type of language use from which all others spring' (Larsen-Freeman and Cameron 2008: 164).

In Biber's (1995) study, the text type with the largest cluster of texts was 'General Reported Exposition'. A corpus of approximately 47,650,000 tokens that matched those in Biber's study was compiled using the Popular Writing, Reportage, Instructional Writing, and Persuasive Writing sections of the ICE (listed above) and similar sections from the BNC, the Brown University Corpus of American English, the Freiburg–Brown Corpus of American English, the Lancaster–Oslo/Bergen Corpus of British English, the Freiburg–LOB Corpus of British English, the Kolhapur Corpus of Indian English, and the Wellington Corpus of Written New Zealand English (Sorell, 2013).

Separate examinations of spoken and written corpora at least partially confirm the findings of Montemurro, Ferrer-i-Cancho, and Solé. Natural language, thus, evidences not one but two interlinked power–law distributions. Measuring the decline of the primary slope (Fig. 5.6) from rank 176 to 6,000, the general writing corpus has a slope of −0.99, and an angle of −1.97 from rank 6,000 to the end. The angle of each slope closely matches the findings by Montemurro, Ferrer-i-Cancho, and Solé. The two distributions, however, seem to blend into each other in a gentle arching transition.

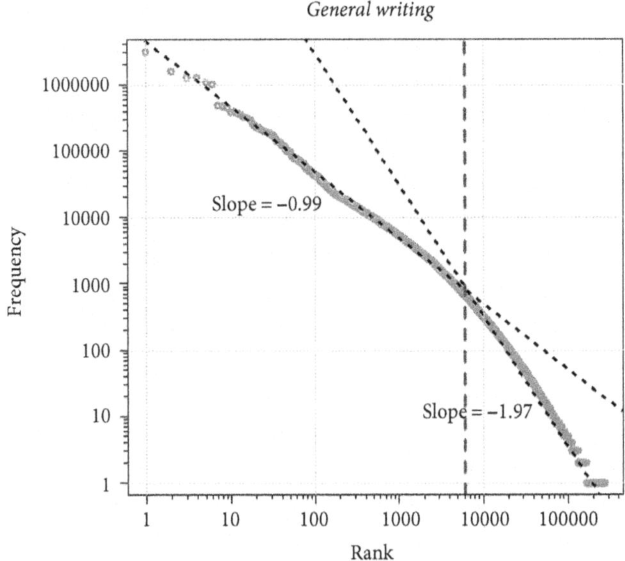

FIG. 5.6 Zipf graph of a corpus of general writing (approximately 47,650,000 tokens) showing two power-law distributions. Dotted lines show the angle of each slope. A dashed vertical line marks rank 6,000, the approximate point of transition from general to more specialized vocabulary.

For conversation, the primary slope is considerably steeper at −1.45, measuring from rank 66 to 6,000. The second angle, from rank 6,000 to the end, is −2.03. It was suspected that the steeper than expected slope may have been due to the transcription of interrupted words, so Paul Nation's BNC Range program was used to isolate any words not already seen in the BNC (Nation and Heatly 2002).

In all, there are only 110 additional types not on Nation's BNC lists among the most frequent 6,000 words in the conversation corpus. Some of the most frequent items are, indeed, word fragments, such as *wha*^{2969}, *ca*^{3670}, and *whe*^{4421}, *wi*^{5553}, which are often partial pronunciations of *what, whatever, can, when, wherever*, or *with*, respectively. (The rank for each type is shown in superscript.) Many of the frequent types are additional proper nouns, e.g. *Cantonese*^{1808}, *UWI*^{3282} (*the University of the West Indies*), *Daren*^{4010}, *Mysore*^{4050}, *Kowloon*^{4882}, and *Macau*^{5289}. There are also several regular nouns, e.g. *Internet*^{4218}, *email*^{5109}, and *sushi*^{5829}, which would no doubt be among the more frequent types in a new BNC were it compiled today.

Nation's BNC lists already contained many variant spellings of vocalized pauses, minimal responses, back channelling, interjections, etc. This broader conversation corpus contained many more among the most frequent types: *uhm*^{55}, *mhh*^{651}, *na*^{949}, *uhn*^{1050}, *uhu*^{1211}, *ta*^{1253}, *tt*^{1309}, *hh*^{1493}, *mhhm*^{1908}, *unhunh*^{2274}, *ahn*^{2291}, *hunh*^{2552}, *nuh*^{3643}, *aiyah*^{3573}, *sshh*^{3836}, *uhum*^{4259}, and others. Some of the most frequent types were onomatopoeic transcriptions, e.g. *da*^{562}, *doo*^{1030}, *ee*^{1171}, *di*^{1454}, *bom*^{2259}. The corpus also contained additional nonstandard pronunciations or expressions not usually found in written English: *int*^{850} (*isn't*), *anyways*^{2823}, *yuck*^{3925}, *youse*^{4312} (plural *you*), *im*^{4675} (*him*), *sorta*^{5109}, *ish*^{5458} (as in *nine ish*).

The network of words in a language is, of course, not isolated from other lexical networks speakers may be part of. Many corpora of spoken English naturally include frequent switches to other languages. Often these are individual borrowings that are commonplace in that variety of English, or they may be true code switches of several turns in length. Filtering out all the words tagged as 'indigenous' would result in a bizarre situation where a word like *chapati* is considered English in London but excluded in East Africa. As a compromise, where three or more contiguous words were tagged as 'indigenous', those words were not included in the frequency count.

Some of the types among the most frequent 6,000 types in conversation are good examples of how International English continues to intersect with other lexical networks. The type *oo*[1968] is sometimes onomatopoeic, but in many instances it is the Tagalog word for *yes*. *Oo* is often used as a minimal response in conversations in Philippine English. The Tagalog words *ano*[2757] (*what*) and *sa*[4175] (*in*) are also very frequent. Hindi and Urdu contribute *haan*[1790] (*yes*) and *yaar*[2588] (*mate*) in Indian English. The Māori definite article *te*[3309] is part of many Māori terms in New Zealand English. The term *Marae*[4485], a traditional Māori meeting house, is also among the most frequent types. The most frequent example of this type of lexical enrichment of spoken English is the originally Chinese verbal particle *lah*[472] from the Singapore corpus, which also contributes *lor*[2574] from Cantonese and *leh*[5937] from Hokkien. The voices of some other species with whom we share our lives were also heard among the most frequent types: *woof*[3214] and *meow*[5028].

This corpus is still a very limited representation of English as an International Language (cf. Kirkpatrick 2007), but it already demonstrates that internationally face-to-face conversation shows significantly greater lexical variety than general published writing. This variation is seen among the most frequent types, not just in the tail of low-frequency vocabulary, which in this case is much smaller given the smaller size of the conversation corpus.

5.5 Small worlds

Researchers also discovered power–law distributions when trying to discern the structure of the Internet and the World Wide Web that it hosts. Both the physical connections of the Internet and the software links of the World Wide Web have evolved organically over the years. When teams of researchers examined the hard- and software connections, they independently discovered that each network has a power–law distribution of links (Albert, Jeong, and Barabási 1999; Faloutsos, Faloutsos, and Faloutsos 1999; Kumar et al. 1999). This means they are not random networks, in which each node or webpage has a few statistically random connections to others in the network, nor do they resemble a regular lattice shape like that of a city street map. In both networks, 'just a few nodes have so many links that 80 to 90 per cent of the network's total number of links feed into just a small fraction of the nodes' (Buchanan 2002: 84). This frequency pattern has important implications for surfing the Internet and for using the lexicon of a language.

This configuration, in which most nodes have a handful of connections but a few serve as hubs connecting a vast number of nodes, is an important species of what is known as

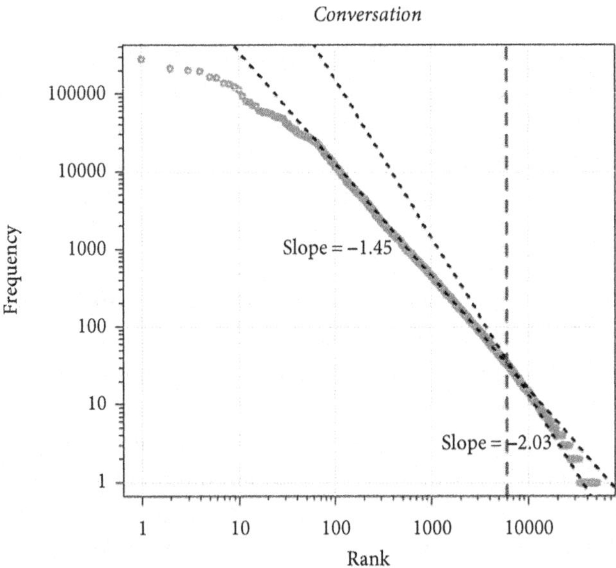

FIG. 5.7 Zipf graph of a corpus of conversation (7,050,000 tokens) showing two power-law distributions. Dotted lines show the angle of each slope. A (dashed) vertical line marks rank 6,000, the approximate point of transition from general to more specialized vocabulary.

a small world network. Small world networks combine reliability with efficiency since they have a high clustering coefficient, i.e. nodes are well connected to a smaller local group, while at the same time, each node's distance to other nodes in the network is relatively small. A few hyperconnected hubs radically reduce the overall distance between these groups (Barabási 2003: 64). Without these hubs, the network would likely be fragmented, or traversing it would require a very large number of jumps. It would be the World Wide Web without Google, Yahoo, or other similarly popular sites. In 1999, one could jump from one randomly chosen page on the web to another randomly chosen page in an average of 19 clicks (Albert et al. 1999). Though the web is much larger today, the number of clicks necessary to span its diameter will not have increased too dramatically, since the separation between pages is 'proportional to the logarithm of the number of nodes in the network' (Barabási 2003: 32).

Seeing the power-law distribution of Zipf's law, Ferrer-i-Cancho and Solé suspected a similar network pattern in the human lexicon. In a second study (2001b), they investigated the links between words by counting which words were found one or two words away from other words. They uncovered a network in which the most frequent 5,000–6,000 words had the vast majority of in-links from each other and from the rarer words. Amazingly, they found that any two words in the lexicon of the BNC could be linked to each other by 'less than three intermediate words on average' (2001b: 4).

These 5,000–6,000 words in the core vocabulary link to the less frequent words in the network and allow for both robust and rapid communication. Low-frequency items are not typically shared by all speakers of the language, but this need not cause irreparable breakdowns in communication since the core items can be used to clarify and provide contextual cues to understanding.

5.6 A WEB WITH MANY SPIDERS

How is it that the World Wide Web and the lexicons of human languages share a similar network structure? One of the forces that creates the hubs that are so vital to such a network is preferential attachment (Barabási and Albert 1999; Simon 1955). The explosive growth of a website like Facebook is a good example. Part of the site's popularity is its functionality, but most of its value is in the number of people already using it. Therefore, Internet users looking for a way to connect to family and friends are currently much more likely to sign up for a Facebook account than to seek out a competing site. This will only add to the site's attractiveness.

But on the Internet and in the lexicon, there are other forces at work as well. An example from the world of physics will help to visualize the dynamics involved. Imagine an hourglass with grains of sand slowly falling from the upper bulb and accumulating as a pile in the lower bulb. The falling sand is similar to the effect of preferential attachment. The sand at the bottom forms a conical pile. The highest point is always directly under the aperture that connects the two bulbs. Gravity is causing the slow trickle of sand from above but continues to pull downward on all the grains of sand. If the sand were replaced with water, the surface in the lower bulb would be level. The reason the sand does not form a level surface is the friction between the grains of sand. Despite the fact that this system continues to change, the angle of the slope is maintained within very tight parameters by these two opposing forces: gravity and friction. When an excess of sand builds up to the point where the mass of the grains in a particular region is greater than the friction holding them back, an avalanche occurs. The sand on the slope is thus permanently on the verge of collapse. The next grain of sand could lodge in a small gap on the slope or it could trigger an avalanche that covers most of the slope. After that, the next large avalanche will likely not occur for some time until the spaces along the slope have been filled in again (Bak 1996).

Like the opposing forces of gravity and friction, the frequency distribution of vocabulary is balanced between information content and the carrying capacity of the communication channel. A network of vocabulary items arranged according to a power–law distribution allows a signal to be quickly modulated up or down, i.e. the transmission rate (the quantity of information per word) can be adjusted according to the audience, as will be seen below.

Rather than being in opposition, as Zipf argued, speaker and hearer are cooperatively negotiating meaning (Grice 1975)—interactively in conversation or in a delayed manner when reading or writing. In their mental lexical networks, they can efficiently move across the core of relatively low-information items to particular information-heavy items when necessary. Not coincidentally, high-frequency (especially function) words are articulated more rapidly in natural speech, whereas low-frequency items are pronounced more slowly and carefully (Bell et al. 2009). One could say that the power at each octave of the lexicon is balanced. The top of the distribution has a few fast, lightweight types, but many tokens. The long tail has many types, but most represent a single heavyweight token.

A text or interaction, however, is the product of multiple lexical cascades. Like one grain of sand bumping into another and sending it and other grains tumbling, each word and utterance influences the subsequent word choices to a greater or lesser degree. The lexical network's small world structure gives it remarkable robustness and flexibility. A momentary flash of confusion on the face of a conversation partner can lead one to add an elaboration or quickly divert to a less technical term than one might normally have chosen. Zipf's law and Shannon entropy are really two related perspectives on the same fractal object: the network of words.

5.7 Graded texts and entropy

Comparing an original text with a graded version of the same text will illustrate how the entropy of a text can be modulated through the choice of more frequently used words. This comparison (inspired by Claridge 2005) uses Bible translations, since the translators of both texts strove to maintain the same information content despite restricting the vocabulary in the graded version (Sorell, 2013). The New International Version is a widely used Bible translation, while the New International Reader's Version is intended for children or ESL readers.

1 Corinthians 13:1–10
(New International Version)

[1] If I speak in the tongues of men or of angels, but do not have love, I am only a
resounding gong or a clanging cymbal. [2] If I have the gift of prophecy and can fathom
all mysteries and all knowledge, and if I have a faith that can move mountains, but
do not have love, I am nothing. [3] If I give all I possess to the poor and give over my
body to hardship that I may boast, but do not have love, I gain nothing. [4] Love is
patient, love is kind. It does not envy, it does not boast, it is not proud. [5] It does not
dishonor others, it is not self-seeking, it is not easily angered, it keeps no record of
wrongs. [6] Love does not delight in evil but rejoices with the truth. [7] It always protects,
always trusts, always hopes, always perseveres. [8] Love never fails. But where there are
prophecies, they will cease; where there are tongues, they will be stilled; where there
is knowledge, it will pass away. [9] For we know in part and we prophesy in part, [10] but
when completeness comes, what is in part disappears. [191 words]

(New International Reader's Version)

[1] Suppose I speak in the languages of human beings and of angels. If I don't have
love, I am only a loud gong or a noisy cymbal. [2] Suppose I have the gift of prophecy.
Suppose I can understand all the secret things of God and know everything about
him. And suppose I have enough faith to move mountains. If I don't have love, I am
nothing at all. [3] Suppose I give everything I have to poor people. And suppose I give
my body to be burned. If I don't have love, I get nothing at all. [4] Love is patient. Love

> is kind. It does not want what belongs to others. It does not brag. It is not proud. 5 It is
> not rude. It does not look out for its own interests. It does not easily become angry. It
> does not keep track of other people's wrongs. 6 Love is not happy with evil. But it is full
> of joy when the truth is spoken. 7 It always protects. It always trusts. It always hopes. It
> never gives up. 8 Love never fails. But prophecy will pass away. Speaking in languages
> that had not been known before will end. And knowledge will pass away. 9 What we
> know now is not complete. What we prophesy now is not perfect. 10 But when what is
> perfect comes, the things that are not perfect will pass away. [229 words]

Each word type in the two translated texts was assigned a rank based on the conversation corpus described above. Where a type was missing from the conversation corpus, the type's rank from the corpus of general writing was substituted. The ranks were then plotted for each text in the order in which they occurred (see Fig. 5.8).

The types with the lowest frequencies in the graded translation are *cymbal*, *prophecy*, and *prophesy*. As can be seen, the number of low-frequency items has been greatly reduced, and they are framed by an even greater number of high-frequency items. One consequence of maintaining the information content while restricting the vocabulary is a longer text and, therefore, a longer transmission time.

5.8 Higher orders of entropy

Speaking and writing are, of course, not simply a matter of mixing words at the appropriate frequencies. Shannon's entropy formula is useful for examining the structure of language at the microscopic level of phonemes and graphemes or at the macroscopic level of multi-word units. If first-order entropy is based on the probabilities for

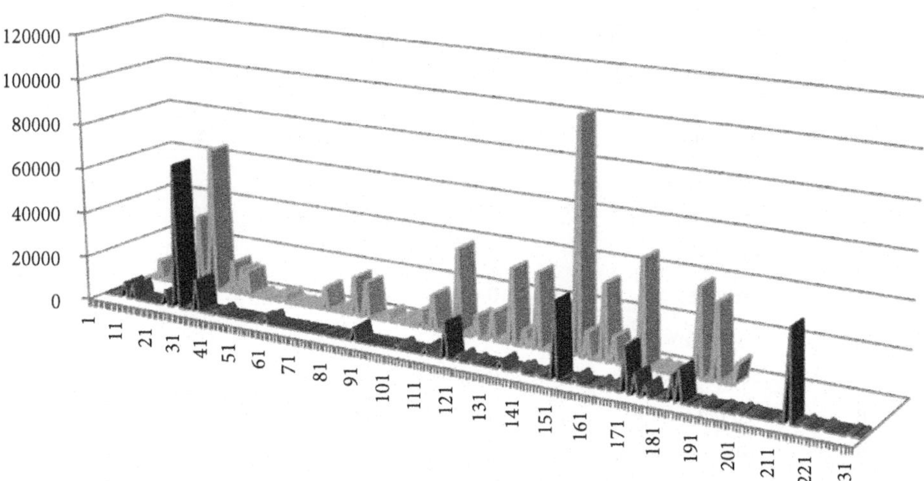

FIG. 5.8 A comparison of 1 Cor. 13:1–10 in a standard (rear, grey) and a graded translation (front, black.)

individual words, second-order entropy would calculate the number of bits necessary to encode all the possible pairs of words. In the traffic light example above, it was found that a code of two bits per word would suffice to transmit messages from this source. Since there are three words in the code, there could be at most nine possible pairings. If each pair is equally likely, each pair would have a probability of 0.11. The $\log_2$ of 0.11 is 0.352. The total entropy for all nine pairs is 3.17, so a 4-digit binary code would be needed to encode messages from this source, if the words are grouped in pairs.

However, if this source follows the pattern *green, green, yellow, red, green,* etc. (above *green* had twice the probability of *yellow* or *red*), then the probability of each pair would be as shown in Table 5.3. This would mean that signals from this source could be encoded in a 2-bit binary code, even when the message is grouped in pairs. When entropy is calculated for pairs of words a message's entropy is expected to increase if the word choices are random, but here it has not. This is evidence of patterning in the signal.

An assessment of higher orders of Shannon entropy looks for larger patterns in a text, i.e. collocations or multi-word units of 2, 3, 4, or more words. Shannon estimated at least 8 orders of entropy for printed English (Shannon 1951: 54). In other words, choosing one word has a discernible influence on the choice of the next 7 words. McCowan, Hanser, and Doyle (1999) found that the whistles of bottlenose dolphins show at least 3 orders of entropy, and possibly more. Data is hard to come by, unfortunately, since dolphins do not publish.

Using the n-gram and collocation functions of Laurence Anthony's Antconc concordancer, the most frequent word sequences were extracted from the conversational sections of the ICE (Sorell 2013). There were no 8-word sequences with a frequency greater than 5 that were not simply recapitulation or back-channelling. Table 5.4 lists the 7-word sequences that occurred more than 5 times. (The

Table 5.3 Calculation of second order entropy for the 'traffic light' code

	Pair	p_i	$\log_2$	$p_i\log_2 p_i$
1	green green	0.25	−2	0.5
2	green yellow	0.25	−2	0.5
3	yellow red	0.25	−2	0.5
4	red green	0.25	−2	0.5
5	green red	0	0	0
6	red yellow	0	0	0
7	yellow green	0	0	0
8	red red	0	0	0
9	yellow yellow	0	0	0
Total				2.0

apostrophes in contractions such as *isn't* and *don't* are counted as word boundaries.) Fig. 5.9 shows a branching graph of many of the most frequent sequences, as well as other branches for comparison. The frequency for each sequence up to that point is given under each word. Therefore, the 5-word n-gram *I don't know about that* has a frequency of 14.

Exploring the statistical features of dolphin communication appears to be a good test case for determining if a transmission from outer space could be an intelligent message. Hanser et al. (2004) suggest that after detecting a Zipfian distribution in an extraterrestrial transmission, SETI Institute (search for extraterrestrial intelligence) researchers should look for the number of orders of entropy that can be discerned in the message. One might rightly ask how one would know where to look for the word divisions. Then again, infants face the same problem when learning their first language(s). Elman (2005: 113) found that word boundaries could be predicted at points where the probability of the next sound is low. For example, a small child whose mother speaks American English could reasonably predict that the next sound after the sounds [mɑm] will likely be the [i] in *Mommy*. However, the sound after that would be less predictable. This drop in entropy provides a possible key to one of the first steps in language acquisition (see Graf Estes, this volume).

Table 5.4 Seven-word n-grams for the conversational portions of the ICE

Frequency	7-word n-gram
17	I don t know if it s
12	I don t know how to say
11	I don t know what it is
10	I don t know what it s
10	I don t know what to do
9	I don t know if that s
8	So what are you going to do
7	at the end of the day I
7	at the end of the day you
7	I don t know what kind of
6	at the University of the West Indies
6	I don t know if it was
6	I don t want to talk about
6	I think it s going to be

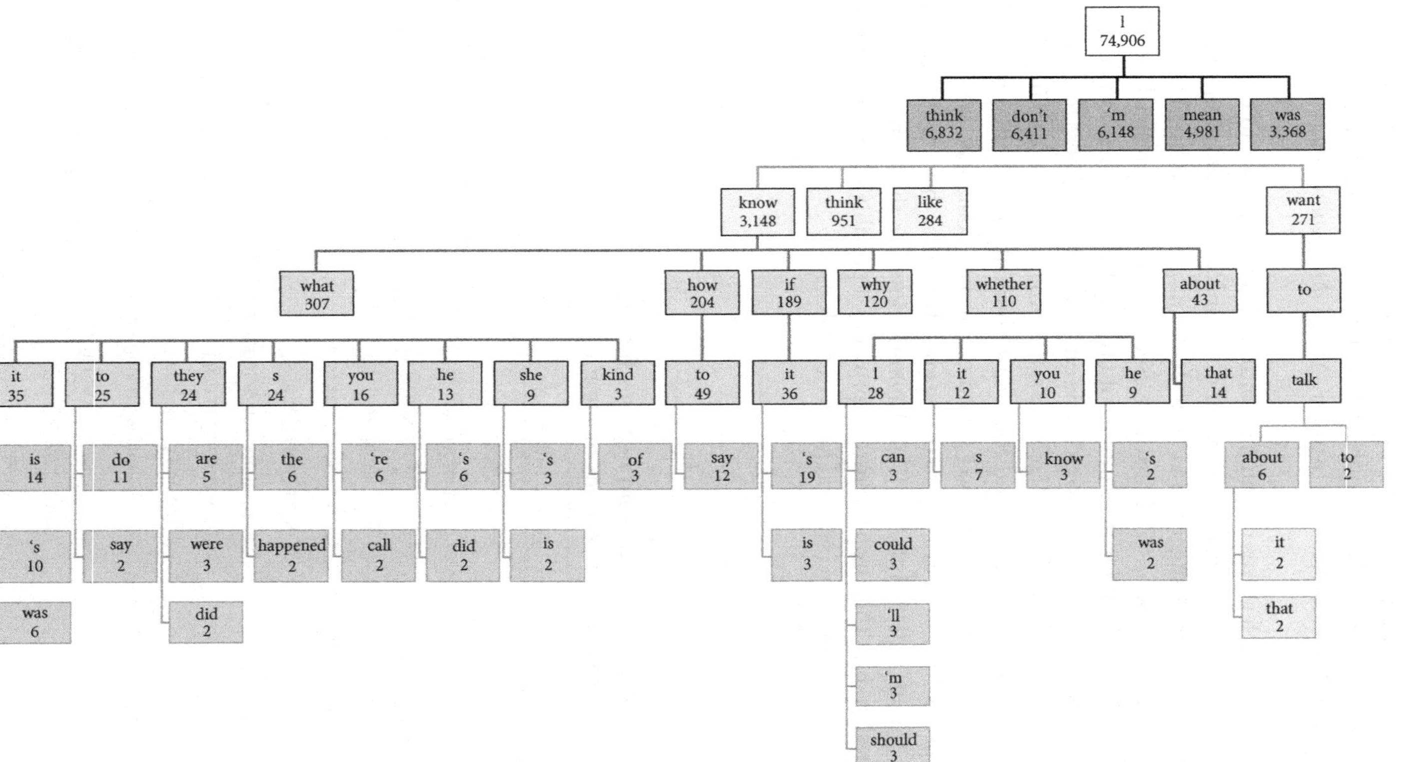

FIG. 5.9 A branching graph of many of the most frequent n-grams in the conversational sections of the ICE. Additional items have been added for comparison.

5.9 Grammar and N-grams

Erman and Warren (2000) found that prefabricated multi-word sequences make up 55 per cent of spoken and written English. An even higher proportion was found for spoken (65%) and written (58%) Russian (Stukova 2011: 105). Bybee (2007: 313–35) argues that the structures observed in language have grown out of highly frequent sequential word patterns. Each time a sequence of words is accessed, its associated pathways are reinforced, making subsequent access even easier. High-frequency patterns can then form the basis of more general morphosyntactic abstractions, or, as she put it, '[s]chemas emerge from the network' (Bybee 2007: 325; see also Langacker 1987: 370).

Zipf's law has similar implications for first language acquisition. Ninio (2006a) examined the verbs in the child-directed speech of Hebrew-speaking mothers with children 10–32 months old. The verbs, not surprisingly, showed a Zipfian distribution. More interesting is the relationship between the frequent and infrequent verbs. Ninio examined all the utterances that contained verbs followed by an indirect object prefixed with the preposition *le-*. The indirect object was optionally preceded by an adjective. This construction is semantically diverse, but she found that 'each slice of the syntactic pattern is covered by one or more … frequently used, generic verb of its own' (Ninio 2006b: 430). In other words, the high-frequency verbs in the mothers' speech could serve as exemplars for low-frequency verbs in the same semantic category.

The verbs used by children in this [verb (adjective) preposition indirect object] pattern also followed a Zipfian distribution. However, the most frequent verbs used by the children showed more individual diversity. More than 60 per cent of the children's frequent verbs were not among the mothers' most frequent verbs. The children joined the network of language, but they made their own pragmatic choices (Ninio 2006a: 140).

5.10 Journey to the Centre of the Core

In the discussion of the Zipf–Mandelbrot formula above, a deviation was noted among the most frequent items (Figs. 5.5, 5.6, and 5.7). This region of the lexical network in some ways is like the core of a planet. Words in this region are used in a number of frequent word sequences, and their habitual use can melt the phonological boundaries in the sequence and cause words to fuse together to become new lexical items. Other types are split as some of their tokens are absorbed by other items. This process is visible in the formation of the new forms *gonna, gotta*, and *hafta*. New types have been formed, while the frequency of some types has been effectively reduced since some of the tokens of *going, got, have*, and *to* have been lost to their original types. The same is true for contracted forms like *n't, 've, 're, 'll*, and *'m*; these are among the most common types in conversation.

The above metaphor is easy to visualize, but it is thermodynamically backwards. Rather than being the hottest region of the network, the centre of the core is actually the coldest.

Words of the highest frequency have the lowest entropy. The hottest portion of the network is the region of low-frequency words. This is counterintuitive unless we imagine the core as a peak jutting up into the clouds. The core is reminiscent of super-cooled condensed matter where structures are breaking apart due to the extreme cold rather than heat. This also explains frozen irregular forms and archaic structures that survive in the core even though they have vanished elsewhere, e.g. *ate, broke, wrote*, or the subject–verb inversion still used to form interrogatives with modals (Bybee 2007: 351–4).

This blurring of the lines between morpheme, word, and multi-word unit is as old as the network of language. Many of the words in this uppermost region were formed by this process. The three-letter word *not* was once the Old English phrase *ná wiht* 'not a thing' (Aitchison 2000: 116). The most frequent word in written texts, *the*, comes from *that*. The indefinite articles, *a* and *an*, are from *one*. Articles like *a* and *the* have also been described as clitics. A clitic is phonologically somewhere between an affix and a 'proper' word. Many affixes can be traced back to once frequent lexical words as well. The suffix *-ly* in *only* and *really* is from a now extinct word for 'body' (see Booij 11.8 in this volume).

Historical linguists have also described a phenomenon called semantic bleaching in which high-frequency words participate in so many different meaning contexts that they become essentially meaningless. They reach a state of near-zero entropy. It is not an oxymoron to describe *give, go, have, make*, and *take* as 'delexical' verbs, at least in some of their uses, e.g. *have a bath, take a walk*. These ongoing processes, known as grammaticization, explain the irregularity of the frequencies at the centre of the core (Bybee 2007: 336ff.).

5.11 Network upon network

A small world network for the lexicon is almost certainly more than a visual metaphor, since neuroscientists have found a similar structure in the neurons of the cerebral cortex (Buchanan 2002: 61–72; Scannell 1997), and power-law distributions have been observed in the sizes of neuronal avalanches (Klaus, Shan, and Plenz 2011; Shew et al. 2011). One could visualize each utterance as a series of sequential nerve firings that flicker across connections on the network, racing across high-frequency nodes to other, possibly less common ones.

This conception of spreading activation across the lexical network fits well with findings of cascading effects during the selection of lexical items (Dell 1986; Dell, Oppenheim, and Kittredge 2008; Janssen and Caramazza 2009; Jescheniak and Schriefers 2001; Morsella and Miozzo 2002; Peterson and Savoy 1998; Rapp and Samuel 2002).

A curious pattern in the frequency of words has led to the discovery of the fractal nature of reality. It is not surprising that a web of words should reside in millions of neural networks and be mirrored in human social networks and the systems we build to support them.

CHAPTER 6

WORD LENGTH

PETER GRZYBEK

6.1 Introduction: Length in linguistics

Studying the word, as well as other linguistic units, requires quantitative as well as qualitative approaches. Taking language to be a system of rules, or of structures and functions, one might be tempted to assume, erroneously, that we are concerned not with quantities but with qualities, and that we could arrive at a theory of language by way of qualitative methods only; one might also object that language does not (or at least not in all of its aspects) lend itself to quantification. Such objections are, however, but transfers from epistemology to ontology, falsely assuming that qualities and quantities 'naturally' exist as such, in and by themselves. In fact, both quantitative and qualitative categories are but abstractions of the mind with which we attempt to grasp the external world; ultimately, we do not quantify external phenomena, but our models thereof (Altmann 1978, 1993).

Length is a quantitative category; it is a property which we can ascribe to a linguistic (or any other physical) object and which can in principle be measured by reference to the dimensions of time and/or space. With regard to word length, it may be useful terminologically and conceptually to distinguish 'length' from the closely related concepts 'duration' and 'complexity', reserving 'duration' for the temporal quantification of an event's unfolding.

Whereas duration is the result of measuring the time course of an event, length and complexity imply spatial measures. Measuring an object's length involves a spatial perspective along one (horizontal) dimension, length being measured in terms of the number of equivalent components in sequential order which make up the object and serve as its measuring units. In comparison, a linguistic object's density, or complexity, concerns the number of its elements, their relations to each other, as well as the functions of these relations, not taking account of horizontal extension or sequential order. In practice, measuring the length of a linguistic unit implies the counting of its constituent components, in sequential order, which presupposes the identification of these discrete (linguistic) units; moreover, all components in this context should be structurally equivalent, i.e. they should belong to one and the same structural level.

With these definitions, the categories of duration, length, and complexity are likely to play different roles in the analysis of spoken vs. written forms of language(s). Given the interaction between written and spoken language, however, complex as they may be for different languages, it becomes obvious that the decision in favour of any one of these concepts is rather a matter of research interest.

Against the background of these introductory remarks, this chapter will be organized as follows. First, some basic definitions are addressed (section 6.2) concerning the word and the constituent components that serve as measuring units. Next, a number of relevant distinctions are made as to the concrete material serving as a basis of word-length studies; at issue here are distinctions of texts (of different kinds) vs. corpora vs. dictionary material, of word forms vs. lemmata, of types vs. tokens (section 6.3). Then follow some basic statistical descriptive characteristics of word length (section 6.4). The major part of the chapter concentrates on theoretical issues, concerning models for word-length frequencies, sequential and positional aspects, and relations of word length to other linguistic phenomena (section 6.5). Finally, section 6.6 addresses practical aspects of word length studies, such as the contribution of word length to author identification and to text readability.

6.2 Definitional aspects: The word and its measuring units

As is well known since Saussurean times, there are no positive facts in language: the categories applied in linguistics, far from being God-given truths, are the results of authoritative decision or common agreement. From a theoretical perspective, any such definition functions as an axiom, and any result obtained depends on the initial settings. Although the situation is not much different in other disciplines, there is a tendency in linguistics to adhere to specific definitions once they have been made, and to ignore their relative arbitrariness. As a consequence, in word-length studies we should be aware that there is more than one definition of word, as well as of possible measuring units of word length, such as letter, grapheme, syllable, mora, and morpheme.

6.2.1 What is a word?

No binding definition of the word, valid for more than one language or even type(s) of language, with possibly different writing systems, can be offered *en passant* in this contribution; for detailed discussions, see Dixon and Aikhenwald (2002b) and Wray (this volume). With regard to word-studies, at least for European languages, three operational definitions have been predominantly applied:

a. graphemic/graphematic;
b. phonological (accent group);
c. phonetic–orthographic.

6.2.1.1

A *graphemic definition* is based on a word's written form, a word being marked by two separators, usually blank spaces or a punctuation mark, occasionally a hyphen. Although this definition is quite practical, particularly for computer-based analyses, a number of problems arise. Irrespective of the fact that there are languages without a written tradition, the definition works only for letter-based (or grapheme-based) scripts, thus excluding languages with other writing systems as well as orthographies without separators, such as Chinese or Thai. Moreover, a graphemic definition is dependent on diachronic developments and changes in orthographic norms (concerning, among other matters, the writing of compounds or the treatment of clitics). Nevertheless, due to its simplicity, a graphemic definition is often favoured by workers in computer and information sciences. In these approaches, it is a matter of speculation how to deal with hyphenated words (e.g. English: *mother-in-law*) or apostrophied words (English: *that's, isn't, man's*; French: *Jeanne d'Arc*). In any case, it would be consistent with a graphemic definition to measure word length in terms of linguistic units which are realized in written form, such as letters or graphemes. The result will be, of course, an analysis of written language, which, on account of language-specific orthographic rules and specific relations between written and spoken language, may deviate substantially from analyses based on other definitions of the word, the more so since no intermediate constituting levels (such as syllables or morphemes) are taken into consideration. More importantly, a graphemic definition may give contradictory results if word length is measured in units other than written ones, such as morphemes or syllables—one problem being zero-syllable words, such as the vowel-less prepositions in Slavic languages (e.g. 'к', 'с', 'в' in Russian), which would be counted as words in their own right.

6.2.1.2

The existence of zero-syllable words and similar problems are avoided in definitions which refer to the phonetic, phonological, or prosodic criteria of spoken language, integrating and emphasizing performance factors of pronunciation. *Phonological word definitions* thus refer to a string of phones or phonemes (or, in related approaches, to their written equivalents) which behave as units for phonetic/phonological processes, particularly the location of (lexical) stress or accent. A basic axiom in these approaches is that a phonological word carries only one (primary) stress. Since English prepositions such as *for* and the definite and indefinite articles *the* and *a(n)* usually are not (though, for pragmatic reasons, may occasionally be) stressed, the sentence *I came for the milk*—consisting of five graphemically defined words—would probably be composed of fewer phonological words, with *I came* and *the milk* each forming one unit, the preposition *for* being attached to the latter expression; also, the treatment of compounds (as separate words or word fusions, with or without hyphenation) presents no major problems in this approach: cf. English *bottle opener* vs. *homeowner* vs. *man-eater*.

6.2.1.3

Phonetic-orthographic word definitions attempt to combine and balance the technical simplicity of a graphemic approach with linguistic (i.e. phonetic/phonological and morphological) criteria. In this framework, graphemically defined zero-syllable words (see 6.2.1.1) are interpreted as clitics, with proclitics being merged to the following, and enclitics to the preceding graphemically defined word. This procedure covers at least some of the orthographic inconsistencies in languages and their writing systems, which, more often than not, are the result of diachronic developments (e.g. Russian *v kratsu* vs. *vkratse*, both variants meaning practically the same: 'in brief', 'briefly').

Not surprisingly, linguistic definitions of the word influence the analysis of word length. A quantitative approach must take account of such influences, and it would seem reasonable to systematically compare the effect of different definitions, which may vary across languages or even within a language, depending e.g., among others, on text type effects. Similar problems are likely to concern measuring units, as will be discussed in the next section.

6.2.2 Definition of measuring units

Word-length measurements will differ depending on which measuring units are chosen; these, in turn, may depend on how the word is defined.

Letters or graphemes might be regarded as adequate measuring units in a graphemic approach. Measuring word length by the number of letters or graphemes is (seemingly) straightforward. The approach is additionally supported by the fact that letters and graphemes are not chaotically distributed, but have their own frequency profile (cf. Grzybek 2007; Grzybek et al. 2009), thus fulfilling a major postulate in quantitative linguistics: that the constituents of a higher-level unit must have their own regular frequency organization.

However, definitional aspects cannot be ignored on this level either. An English word like *shoe* may be considered to consist of four letters; it might also be possible to speak of two graphemes, with the two letters <s+h> counting as one grapheme representing the phoneme [ʃ] and the combination <o+e> representing the phoneme [uː]. Whereas here the components of a grapheme also occur as individual letters in the given alphabet, this need not be the case in other languages. Different definitions are possible in the case of letters containing diacritical characters, such as ä, å, á, ä, ç, õ; these may be considered either as letters in their own right or as combinations of basic characters plus diacritics.

While some of these problems might be solved by measuring word length in terms of phones or phonemes—whether on the basis of a phonetic/phonological transcription or if graphical units are taken to be semiotic representations of spoken language—other problems are likely to arise. After all, it is a matter of linguistic definition what is to be considered a phone, or phoneme; with regard to the analysis of (transcribed) spoken language, additional differences may come into play depending on whether slow, careful, or more casual pronunciation, with elisions and coalescences, is taken as the norm.

More importantly, neither letters/graphemes nor phones/phonemes are direct constituents of the word: in a traditional structuralist framework, they would be regarded as low-level units, forming syllables or morphemes on the next level, which in turn are then taken to be direct constituents of the word. When linguistics, in contradistinction to information and computer science-based approaches, favours the measurement of word length in terms of the number of direct constituents, there is more than one reason to do so: (a) measurements in terms of indirect constituents are likely to result in a greater amount of variation, thus possibly concealing underlying tendencies; (b) measurement fluctuations or inaccuracies, due to definitional aspects, are likely to come into play and to be multiplied the more levels of analysis are at stake; and (c) given that there are control mechanisms which regulate length relations between units of neighbouring levels (see below), the leapfrogging of an intermediate level is likely to obscure (or even disturb) these self-regulating processes.

As a result, measuring word length in terms of the number of syllables or morphemes per word would turn out to be the most appropriate approach, notwithstanding additional problems in defining these units.[1] In any case, although syllables and morphemes measure word length along different scales, there is increasing evidence showing correlations between the results of syllable-based and morpheme-based analyses, at least for the languages studied thus far.

Yet another alternative for measuring word length concerns the number of morae[2] per word. In the context of word-length studies, morae have been used for the analysis of languages like Japanese, not least because here the mora-based approach represents a compromise between the phonetics and the writing system. Given the definitions above, and taking into account that in the context of prosody studies a mora serves a measure

[1] With regard to the initial definition of length given above, one may argue against Altmann's (2013) recent suggestion to consider measuring word length on the basis of morphemes as a measure of complexity rather than of length; such different views may be related, however, to the treatment of morphemes, e.g., the - *s* morpheme in the English verb form 'runs', either as one morpheme, or as a complex of four morpheme functions (3rd person, singular, indicative, present tense).

[2] The concept of mora originates in classical verse theory, where it is understood as the smallest time unit with regard to verse and syllable duration. In modern linguistics, it is defined as a psycho-physiologically perceptible measure, primarily in the fields of phonetics/phonology and prosody research as a measure of syllable weight. The definitions in this field are not cross-linguistically unified. Generally speaking, the following rules hold: a syllable onset (i.e., the first consonant/s of a syllable) is not considered to represent a mora; a syllable nucleus with a short vowel, or a short vowel with maximally one following consonant, constitutes one mora (such syllables being termed 'monomoraic' or 'light'); and syllables with a long vowel or with one short vowel and more than one consonant are counted as two morae and termed 'bimoraic' or 'heavy'. In some languages (e.g., Japanese), the coda (i.e., the consonant/s of a syllable which follow the nucleus) represents one mora, in others not, and for some the state of affairs is unclear. In English, for example, the final consonant of a stressed syllable may be considered to constitute a separate mora; thus the word *cat*, if stressed, would be bimoraic, whereas the identical unstressed syllable in *tomcat* would be monomoraic.

for syllable-time units, one may rather consider mora-based word-length studies as a mixture of approaches studying duration and length.

6.3 Material: Sample vs. text vs. corpus, word form vs. lemma, type vs. token

Once we measure the length, not of a single word but of more than one word, we are able to construct some kind of word-length frequency distribution; this becomes the basis for the derivation of various statistical characteristics (section 6.4), as well as for the study of theoretical frequency models (section 6.5). The distribution is likely to vary depending on empirical and methodological factors: on the one hand, the kind of material chosen for analysis will, to one degree or another, influence the results; on the other, the manner of analysis, depending on initial decisions, will modify the outcome.

As to differences concerning the material chosen, one must make a basic distinction between (a) random samples, i.e. randomly chosen parts of texts, (b) complete individual texts, and (c) text combinations, or corpora, composed of different samples and/or texts.

In this context, one must distinguish between the notion of randomness on a linguistic vs. probabilistic understanding of the term. On a linguistic understanding, randomness refers to an arbitrarily chosen text selection. In contrast, a random sample on a statistical (or rather probabilistic) understanding is any selection of a subset of individuals from within a statistical population, made in order to estimate characteristics of the whole population, i.e. to indicate the probability of an item being from the entire population.

An arbitrary text selection can be conceived of as a random sample in statistical terms as well as a complete individual text or some combination of texts or text selections; the crucial question is if the (intended) statistical description of the linguistic material concerns only the material under study, or if conclusions are (to be) made beyond the material observed. The distinction is between descriptive statistics, which confines itself to the material under study, and inferential statistics, which aims at more general statements, based on inferential procedures.

The choice of material is particularly relevant in an inferential framework, where a decision must be made as to what kind of sample material allows for what kind of conclusions. If no conclusions beyond the material under study are intended, choice and control of the material is less relevant and is motivated only by an interest in the given material. As soon as the conclusions to be drawn turn out to be more ambitious and strive to generalize beyond the material under study, attention must be paid to a number of methodological caveats. Any random sample, taken to be representative of some more encompassing population, denies the existence of intralingual differences, and as soon as such differences are proven to exist, the choice would result in a violation of the assumption of data homogeneity and the ceteris paribus condition. The same holds true for corpus analyses which have long been taken to represent a given language as a whole, since any corpus is but a mixture of heterogeneous texts, or text elements.

In actual practice, it has often been assumed that a given sample, provided that it is 'large enough' (whatever this means in practice and however it may be theoretically based), is characteristic (i.e. 'representative') of a given language as a whole, and can thus serve to establish specific 'norms'; this assumption was particularly prevalent in early corpus linguistics with its 'the more the better' conviction. In less extreme forms, assumptions have been made with regard to some kind of domain-specific, author-specific, or other kind of representativeness, as for example when a sample is considered to be characteristic of individual author styles, text types, chronological periods of a given language, and so on. In this case, the sample-population assumption is related to the assumption of homogeneous sub-groups within the total population.

Methodologically speaking, the assumption of data homogeneity is manifested by the desire to control all independent variables other than the one(s) under study, so that the effect of the independent variable(s) under observation can be isolated; in other words, all other relevant factors are (assumed to be kept) constant, and all remaining features, which are regarded as possibly affecting the data, are considered to be external factors, conceived of as being constant for the sample, at least over the period of observation.

In reality, homogeneous data are rare, and this is of specific concern in linguistics. Indeed, a crucial question is whether homogeneity can ever be assumed to exist in language, be that with regard to (a given) language as a whole or to possible (intralingual) subgroups; not only is any combination of texts (a corpus) a fusion of heterogeneous elements (it is no accident that a corpus as a mixture of texts has been termed a 'pseudo text': Orlov 1982), each text also differs from any other text, and even within one and the same text the presence of heterogeneous elements is the rule. As a consequence, in order to forestall inadequate generalizations in word-length studies, due attention must be paid to the existence of such intratextual and intralingual heterogeneities. We may note that the genre of letters has long been assumed to be an adequate prototype for a given language's structures (cf. Best 2005), especially since this is a genre on the borderline between spontaneous speech and written language and usually the result of homogeneous acts of text production, less subject to stylistic variation and a posteriori manipulation. Systematic studies have shown, however, that the genre of letters is far from being homogeneous (Grzybek 2013c; Grzybek and Kelih 2006), and different kinds of letter (private letters, open letters, letters to the editor, letters from epistolary novels) are clearly characterized by different word lengths, not necessarily resulting in different theoretical models of word-length distribution (see below).

Not only is the material's quality a crucial factor in the analytical process, so also is its linguistic preparation. Analysing (whatever kind of) text or corpus material necessarily implies the notion of frequency; not all words occur with equal frequency, and given that not all words are of equal length, it is important to decide whether word frequency is taken into account or not. If each lexical appearance is analysed, an individual word's frequency of occurrence plays a major role; if the material is (or has previously been) transformed into word lists, or into dictionaries containing each occurring entity only once, the frequency aspect is deleted. Frequency lists, or frequency dictionaries, represent a special case. A decision on this point can of course not be 'correct' or 'incorrect'; rather, it is a matter of research interest and perspective.

The decision whether or not to take frequency of occurrence into consideration relates to the distinction between types and tokens. In this respect, some important caveats are necessary. First and foremost, it is important to note that the type/token distinction, introduced into scientific discourse by Charles Peirce in the 19th century, is of a rather general kind and concerns not only the lexical level of language, as has often been assumed, but any kind of semiotic entity, lexical items being but one instance. It would therefore be incorrect to identify word forms with tokens and lemmas with types; rather, these are distinctions along two different dimensions. One may be concerned with word-form types or word-form lemmas, as well as with lemma types and lemma tokens, and decisions on this point will influence word-length measures.

6.4 Descriptive characteristics: Object-related

Within a descriptive approach, statistical measures are derived from a given frequency distribution, in order to characterize it quantitatively. Figs. 6.1a and 6.1b represent in graphic form the word-length frequency distribution, or 'spectrum', of an English text, the novel *The Portrait of a Lady* by Henry James from 1881. Fig. 6.1a is based on letter counts per word, Fig. 6.1b on syllable counts.

It is evident that under both conditions the distribution is not symmetrical, but left-skewed; this is typical for linguistic phenomena in general, not only for word length. It is also clear that the distributions differ in their profiles: not only are there fewer classes under the syllable condition, but the frequencies are monotonously decreasing,

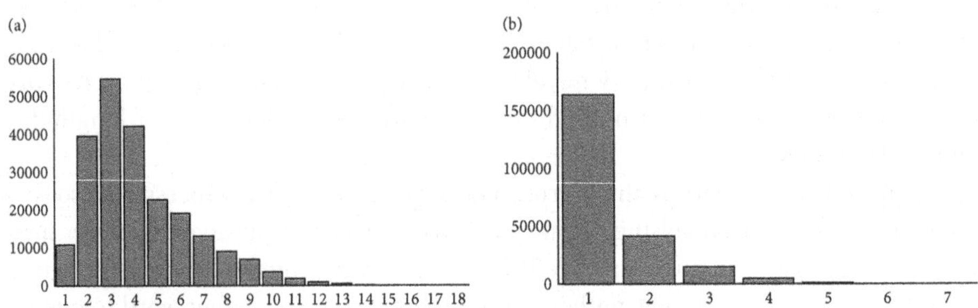

FIG. 6.1 Word-length frequency distribution of *The Portrait of a Lady*.

whereas there is an initial increase up to a peak of 3-letter words under the letter condition before the remaining frequencies decrease. This aspect is particularly relevant for model-theoretic approaches (see below).

On the basis of empirically observed frequencies, descriptive statistics (or summary statistics) provide specific information about the given distribution in maximally condensed form. They provide measures of location (or central tendency), of dispersion (or variation), and of the shape of the distribution; if more than one variable is analysed, measures of statistical dependence are available. Only the most common characteristics are presented here, using the syllable-based results reported above by way of an example.

Given the absolute frequency f_j of j-syllable words, the total sum of words (N) in a given sample is represented as $\Sigma_{j=1}^{K} f_j = N$; in our case, $N = 225{,}234$ words. On this basis, the relative frequencies h_j of j-syllable words can be computed as $h_j = f_j/N$, the sum of which, ranging from the first element $j = 1$ to the last element $j = K$, equals 1: $\Sigma_{j=1}^{K} h_j = 1$. Since there are 163,622 one-syllable words, we have $h_1 = 163622 / 225234 = 0.7261$, which corresponds to 72.61 per cent of all words. On the basis of these frequencies, the arithmetic mean $\bar{x}$, often favoured for characterizing a frequency distribution, can easily be calculated as $\bar{x} = \frac{1}{N} \Sigma_{i=1}^{N} x_i$. In the case of James's novel, we have an average word length of $\bar{x} = 1.3969$. As a minimum of information, any descriptive approach should also give the standard deviation $s = \sqrt{\frac{1}{N} \cdot \Sigma_{j=1}^{N} (x_i - \bar{x})^2}$ (the square root of the variance s^2) as an essential characteristic of the given sample's measure of variation around the mean value.

Further statistical characteristics can be computed from given frequency data, such as the median, the central moments, the coefficient of variation, the dispersion index, skewness, kurtosis, Ord's criteria, absolute and relative entropy, repeat rate and redundancy. All these measures, in isolation or in specific combinations, may be useful for methods like clustering, discrimination, or post hoc comparisons, when the identification of homogeneous subgroups is at stake.

Compared to such measures, attempts to model word-length frequency distributions as a whole represent a crucial step from descriptive approaches to hypothesis formation and testing, thus building a bridge to theory-oriented approaches.

6.5 Model-related and theory-oriented approaches

The scope of descriptive approaches is to characterize the linguistic material under study as a given product. In comparison, theoretical approaches attempt to provide models which claim relevance not only for the concrete material under study but beyond, and which are thus necessarily based on the formulation of testable hypotheses.

As Altmann (2013: 28), in a synoptic reflection on word-length studies (see also Popescu et al. 2013) has pointed out, three major conditions must be fulfilled if word length is to contribute to, or be integrated into, a theory of language. These conditions are that

1. word length is not an isolated property;
2. word length underlies language evolution and diversification;
3. word length frequencies are not arbitrary, but abide by laws.

Laws, or law-like regularities, are thus expected to exist with regard to each of these three aspects, with word length as an integral ingredient of a theory of the word within a theory of language.

6.5.1 From word-length spectra to theoretical frequency-distribution models

The idea of analysing word-length spectra goes back to the beginnings of word-length studies in the 19th century.[3] After the English logician Augustus De Morgan, in a private letter of 1851 which was published only in 1882, had suggested that questions of authorship might be settled by determining whether one text deals in longer words than another, it was Thomas C. Mendenhall (1887) who initiated systematic word-length studies. As a mathematician, he was familiar with contemporary spectral analysis in physics, and in analogy to this he proposed to go beyond mere averages of word length and to analyse a text by creating what he suggested might be called a 'word-spectrum', or 'characteristic curve', by which he meant a graphic representation of an arrangement of words according to their length and to the relative frequency of their occurrence. Mendenhall (1887: 239) was convinced that

> [...] personal peculiarities [...] will, *in the long-run*, recur with such regularity that short words, long words, and words of medium length, will occur with definite relative frequencies, so that for him, his approach turned out to be rather an 'application of the doctrine of chance'.

Whereas these early works remained on a merely empirical level, based on intuitive comparisons of visual/graphical impressions, first attempts to develop theoretical models were undertaken in the 1940s and 1950s.

In principle, there are continuous and discrete-frequency models, and it is a matter of philosophy and data structure which kind of approach is favoured, especially since both kinds of model can usually be translated into each other. With regard to word

[3] For the history of word-length studies in general, see Grzybek (2006); for the importance of word length in 19th stylistics, see Grzybek (2013b).

length, discrete models have often been favoured, which is reasonable, since word length is measured in discrete units. The idea of such approaches is to find a mathematical model which, on the basis of observed frequencies, yields theoretical frequencies; these models may have a different number of parameters, and depending on the concrete parameter values—which are estimated by specific methods on the basis of the given empirical data—the final results may vary for one and the same model. The differences between expected and observed values are then submitted to statistical testing. For evaluating the goodness of fit, it is common to apply the χ^2 test; since the χ^2 value increases with increasing sample size, and the test is therefore increasingly prone to declare differences to be significant, approaches in quantitative linguistics (usually concerned with large sample sizes) prefer to use the standardized determination coefficient $C = \chi^2/N$.

With regard to word length, the search for theoretical models started in the late 1940s. As far as English is concerned, Elderton's (1949) study deserves mention, in which he suggested the geometric distribution in its 1-shifted form $P_x = p \cdot q^{x-1}$, $x = 1,2,3,\ldots$ as an appropriate model. Here, P_x is the probability of a given (word-length) class, p is a parameter to be estimated (with $q = 1 - p$). For parameter value $p = 0.7123$ and $q = 1 - p = 0.2877$, the theoretical frequencies P_x—represented by white bars in Fig. 6.2a, alongside the grey bars for the observed frequencies—can be obtained for the above mentioned results of *The Portrait of a Lady*.

However, the geometric model, with its monotonously decreasing theoretical values, would not be adequate for other languages, as a comparison with Chekhov's short story 'Dama s sobachkoi' [The Lady with the Dog] shows (see Fig. 6.2b). Here, the theoretical values are based on the Poisson distribution, first discussed by Russian military doctor S. G. Chebanov (1947), who analysed word-length data from various languages and argued in favour of this model. Like the German physicist Wilhelm Fucks, who later, in a series of works from the 1950s (cf. Fucks 1956), Chebanov was convinced that he had found a universal model. Both Chebanov and Fucks took the 1-parameter Poisson distribution $P_x = \dfrac{e^{-a} \cdot a^x}{x!}$, $x = 0,1,2,\ldots$ (with parameter a to be estimated) as their starting

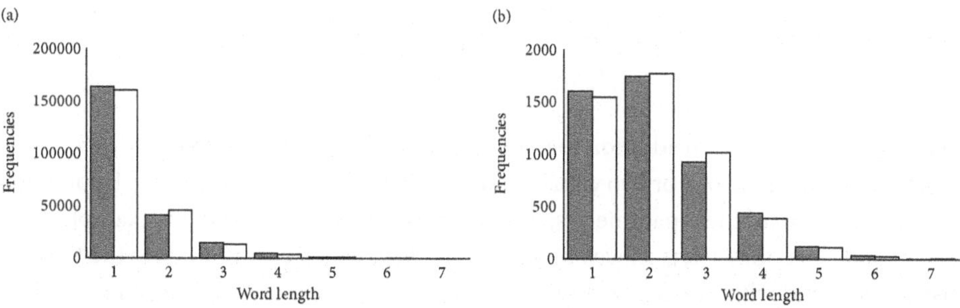

FIG. 6.2 Observed (grey bars) and theoretical (white bars) word length distributions (syllables per word) in two texts.

point, displacing it by one since, according to the definition, there were no zero-syllable words, thus obtaining the 1-displaced Poisson distribution $P_x = \frac{e^{-a} \cdot a^{x-1}}{(x-1)!}$, $x = 1, 2, 3, \ldots$

As can be seen, the fit is very good in both cases, with $C = 0.0054$ and $C = 0.0038$, respectively. Neither model can claim universal relevance for all languages, although early attempts in this field hoped to offer such a perspective; this holds true also for Fucks who used a specific weighted modification of the Poisson distribution, of which the above mentioned 1-displaced model is only a special case (cf. Antić et al. 2005).

In the late 1950s and early 1960s there were some attempts to use the lognormal distribution. Given the characteristic left-skewness of linguistic data (see above), these are assumed to be normally distributed after logarithmic transformation, though such approaches have been mostly abandoned today for theoretical reasons. An important step in the history of word-length modelling, however, was Grotjahn's (1982) suggestion of taking the negative binomial distribution as a standard model which, under specific conditions, converges on the geometric or the Poisson distribution (which thus turn out to be special cases of a more general model). The major impact of this suggestion is not so much the introduction of one more model into the discussion of word length; its importance has instead to be seen in the proposal to concentrate on a variety of distributions which are able to represent a valid 'law of word formation from syllables' (Grotjahn 1982: 73), instead of looking for one general (universal) model.

This idea was subsequently taken up by Grotjahn and Altmann (1993) and elaborated by Wimmer et al. (1994) and Wimmer and Altmann (1996). The basic idea pursued in these papers is that the frequency, or probability, of a given class of x-syllable words (P_x) is determined by the class preceding it (P_{x-1}), thus resulting in the proportionality relation $P_x \sim P_{x-1}$. Further assuming that this relation is characterized by a specific proportionality function $f(x)$, one obtains $P_x = f(x)P_{x-1}$.

Later these ideas, which initially concentrated on word length only, were integrated into Wimmer and Altmann's (2005; 2006) 'Unified derivation of some linguistic laws'. It would lead us too far here to discuss this approach in detail; in short, for a discrete variable X, this general approach leads to recurrence formula (1):

$$P_x = \left(1 + a_0 + \frac{a_1}{x} + \frac{a_2}{x^2} + \cdots\right) P_{x-1}. \qquad (1)$$

In function (1) we have, in addition to a constant ($1 + a_0$), specific variables (a_i, $i = 1,2, \ldots$); usually, not more than one or two variables are needed in linguistic modelling. Depending on the exact form of these parameters, different models can be derived: for example, with $a_0 = -1$ and $a_i = 0$ for $i = 2,3, \ldots$ we obtain $P_x = a/x\, P_{x-1}$, which corresponds to the Poisson distribution, and with $-1 < a_0 < 0$ and $a_i = 0$ for $i = 1,2, \ldots$, one obtains the geometric distribution; similarly, most distribution models relevant for linguistics can be derived from this function.

Over the last decades, much empirical evidence has been gathered corroborating hypotheses deduced from this approach. The approach provides a basis for deductive reasoning in quantitative linguistics, and it allows for the derivation of most frequency distributions known in the field of linguistics, word spectra being but one.[4]

With regard to function (1), it can be considered to be a matter of boundary conditions how many and which parameters are needed in a specific research situation. In this respect, individual languages, authorship and personal style, genre, or other factors may be interpreted to represent specific boundary conditions of a general law. In any case, there will not only be cross-linguistic (interlingual) differences; one will always be concerned with intralingual and intertextual (e.g. author or genre specific) differences, too. Even single texts can be shown to be composed of different registers (e.g. narrative or descriptive passages vs. dialogue) ultimately being characterized by intratextual heterogeneities (Grzybek 2013a).

In practice, it may be a matter of research interest and data situation if models are searched for each individual data set, or if a single model is searched to cover heterogeneous (sub)sets under a common theoretical roof. In this context, it may be appropriate to use mixtures of two distributions, to introduce local modifications (e.g. separate modelling of one-syllable words), or to work with generalizations (against which the individual models converge, or of which they are special cases, under specific circumstances), the more so since there could well be linguistic reasons and justification for such procedures.

From what we know today, word length depends on both intratextual and intralingual factors, and it is a matter of academic decision to focus on existing sub-populations as specific sets in their own right, or as variations from a more general, language-specific profile. In any case, individual author-specific factors seem to play only a minor, subordinate role. By way of an example, Fig. 6.3 shows the result of discrimination analyses, based on 190 Russian texts, a balanced set of letters and poems by three Russian authors (Anna Akhmatova, Daniil Kharms, and Aleksandr Pushkin). Whereas a classification based on authorship yields a poor 38 per cent of correctly discriminated texts (Fig. 6.3a), a genre-based discrimination improves to 89.5 per cent (Fig. 6.3b). Obviously, individual variation is relatively limited within genre norms (Kelih et al. 2005).

In summary, it is text type which is a decisive factor influencing word length; as soon as an author enters some textual space, word length is predominantly influenced by basic discourse types, rather than by author-specific factors. The discourse types are not to be identified with functional styles or registers, but are of a more general kind, along distinctions such as dialogical vs. narrative, private vs. official, or oral vs. written. As shown by discrimination analyses of 398 Slovenian and 613 Russian texts from different text types, the best results (92.7 per cent) were obtained for three

[4] From the equivalent continuous approach, many continuous functions, the relevance of which for linguistics has repeatedly been proven over the years, can likewise be derived.

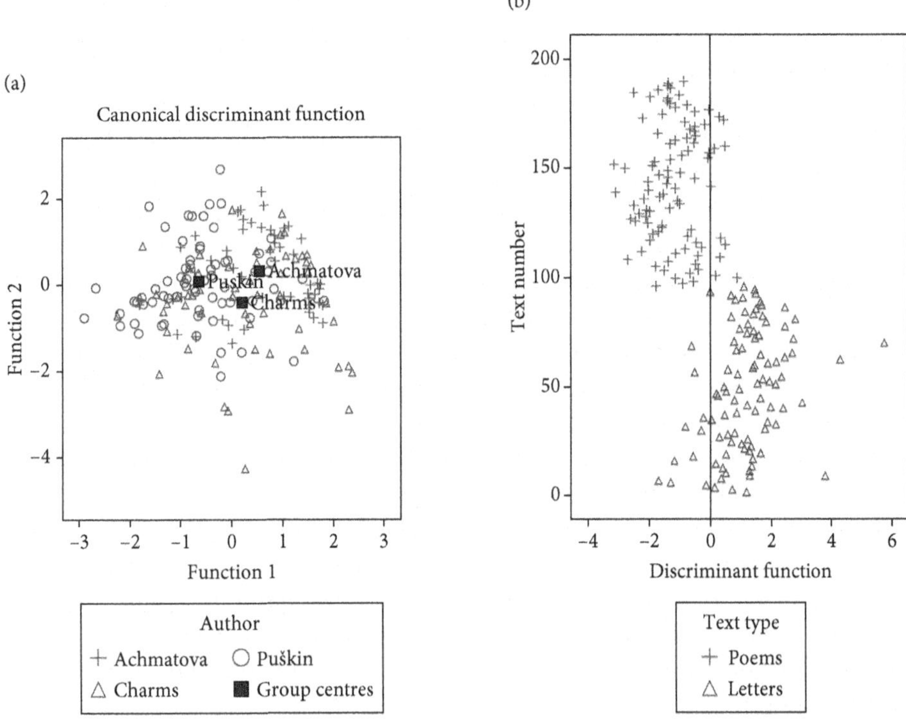

FIG. 6.3 Discrimination analyses for 190 letters and poems by three Russian authors.

discourse types: private/oral, public/written, and poetic (Friedl 2006; Grzybek and Kelih 2006).

Across languages, word length of course depends on other linguistic factors too, such as phoneme inventory size, syllable and morphological structure, and degree of analyticity/syntheticity. Some of these factors represent a kind of starting condition, others can be considered to play a crucial role in the given language's processes of self-regulation.

6.5.2 Word-length relations

In the previous section word length was treated in a self-contained manner, the textual environment being considered as a kind of global boundary condition. A different perspective is offered when the length of a word is analysed in its direct or indirect relation to other linguistic entities. After all, a word and its length are not isolated phenomena, and any word-length frequency distribution is the product of words' dynamic interactions with other entities in the process of speech generation. In this respect, the following kinds of approach may be distinguished:

a. *Sequential analyses.* In the simplest case, the length of a word is related to the length of neighbouring words; issues include the distances between words of the same length, word-length *n*-grams, and *L*-motifs (discussed below).

b. *Positional analyses.* A related though essentially different approach concerns positional aspects of word length in the course of longer text passages, starting from (parts of) sentences up to whole texts.
c. *Horizontal* or *collateral relations.* This perspective takes into consideration the relation of word length to other properties of the word, such as frequency, polysemy, and polytextuality.
d. *Vertical* or *hierarchical* relations. A fourth approach refers to linguistic entities from other structural levels.

6.5.3 Sequential analyses

Whereas descriptive characteristics—offering global summarizing measures—and distributional approaches—attempting to describe and model a given sample as a whole—both focus on the linguistic material as a given product, various methods try to take account of procedural aspects, analysing the linguistic data not as some given totality, but—understanding text as a linear sequence of events—in the course of their appearance within the text. These dynamic approaches are here termed 'sequential analyses'.

6.5.3.1 *Word-length distances*

Zörnig (2013a; 2013b) studied the regularity of distances between words of equal length. Defining a real text as a sequence $S = (s_1, \ldots, s_n)$ of length n, consisting of elements chosen from the set $\{1, \ldots, m\}$, where the element r occurs exactly k_r times for $r = 1, \ldots, m (k_1 + \cdots + k_m = n)$, the distance between two consecutive elements of type r is defined as the number of elements $\neq r$ lying between them. Based on the number of occurrences of the distance d between two consecutive elements of type r, a frequency

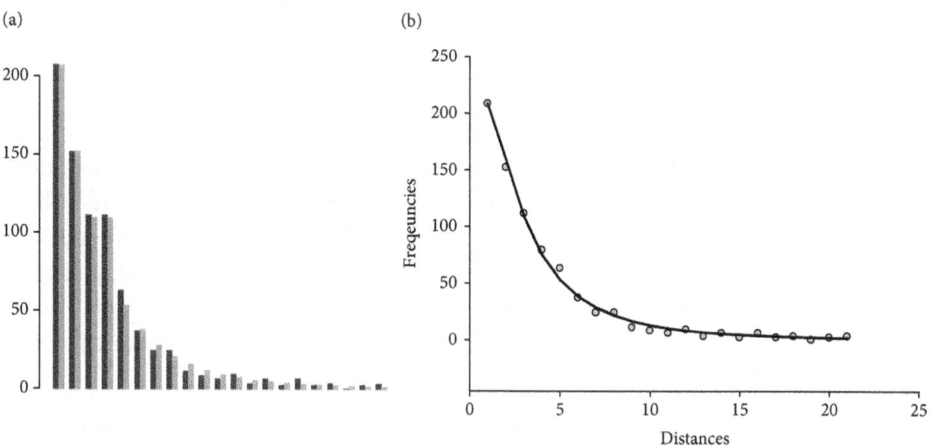

FIG. 6.4 Fitting the Zipf–Alekseev model to word-length distances.

distribution is obtained, for which Zörnig (2013a) suggests a discrete model or, alternatively, a continuous function (2013b). Among the texts that Zörnig tested was Nikolai Ostrovsky's 1932 novel *Kak zakalialas' stal'* [How the Steel was Tempered]. As Fig. 6.4 (with distances on the *x*-axis and their frequencies on the *y*-axis) shows, the Zipf–Alekseev model (cf. Wimmer and Altmann 1999: 665f.) fits both the discrete ($C = 0.17$) and continuous modelling ($R^2 > 0.99$).

6.5.3.2 *Word-length n-grams*

The concept of *n*-grams, widely used in the fields of computational linguistics and probability, are contiguous sequence of *n* items from a given text; items usually analysed are letters, phonemes, syllables, or words: an *n*-gram of size 1 is referred to as a 'unigram', size 2 is a 'bigram', size 3 is a 'trigram', etc.

Applying this concept to word-length studies, Grzybek and Kelih (2005) analysed the frequency of word-length bigrams: given a sequence 1-3-4-2-5-3-4-1-3-4, for example, we can identify nine pairs 1-3, 3-4, 4-2, 2-5, 5-3, 3-4, 4-1, 1-3, 3-4, of which one (1-3) occurs twice, and another (3-4) three times. For a given text one thus obtains a frequency distribution of length bigrams, which may be rearranged in decreasing order to obtain a rank frequency distribution for which a theoretical distribution model may be searched.

Again, linguistic decisions must be made, such as whether to take sentence boundaries into account; thus far, no systematic studies are available on this matter. As a starting point, in Grzybek and Kelih's (2005) study, ten texts by the Russian author Viktor Pelevin were first submitted to unigram analyses, as described above: for this condition, excellent results were obtained, showing the hyper-Poisson distribution, well-known in quantitative linguistics in general and in word-length studies in particular. Subsequent analysis of the bigram rank frequency distributions showed that they seem to follow a clearly regulated organization, the (right-truncated) negative binomial distribution proving an adequate model in this regard.

Fig. 6.5 represents the results for one of the texts, the novel *Chapaev i pustota* [Chapayev and Void[5]]; the observed frequencies are presented in grey, the theoretical values in white.

6.5.3.3 *Word-length motifs*

Yet another kind of sequential analysis has been suggested by Köhler (2006; 2008) and Köhler and Naumann (2008), who studied groups of word lengths which they term 'motifs'. Köhler defines a length motif (*L*-motif) as the longest continuous series of units (e.g. morphs, words, sentences) of equal or increasing length. In terms of word length measured in syllables, the sentence *Word length studies are almost exclusively devoted to the study of distributions* gives a sequence of five

[5] This novel, first published in 1996, is also known in the US as *Buddha's Little Finger*, and in the UK as *Clay Machine Gun*.

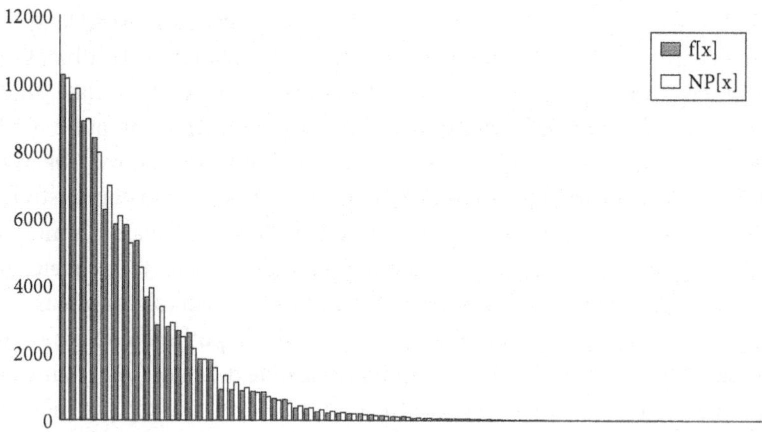

FIG. 6.5 Word length bigrams in a Russian text, with observed (grey, f_x) and theoretical (white, NP_x) frequencies.

L-motifs: (1-1-2)(1-2-4)(3)(1-1-2)(1-4). Second-order *LL*-motifs can be derived. In the above example, there are two *L*-motifs of length 3, followed by one of length 1, etc., resulting in the *LL*-motif sequence (3-3)(1-3)(2). As Köhler shows, the frequency of these motifs can be modelled with distributions well-known in linguistics, such as the Zipf–Mandelbrot or the hyper-Pascal distributions (Wimmer and Altmann 1999: 279ff., 666)

6.5.4 Positional analyses

6.5.4.1 *Word-length dynamics in running sentences*

Words of a given length are not equally distributed within a sentence; instead, average length tends to increase from beginning to end (Fan et al. 2010; Niemikorpi 1991; 1997; Uhlířová 1997a; 1997b). A reasonable explanation of this phenomenon refers to information theory and theme–rheme (or topic–comment) approaches, implying that in the course of a sentence, new information follows (references to) known information; this explanation would be in line with the well-established fact that longer (and more rarely occurring) words contain more information. A still outstanding question is whether this tendency applies to the intermediate level of clauses and phrases, and, eventually, to the position of a clause within a sentence.

6.5.4.2 *Word-length dynamics in running text*

Given the hypothesized increase of information in the course of text segments such as sentences, it is reasonable to assume that the same tendency will characterize larger text segments, or even texts as a whole. (Note that this question makes no sense with regard to text mixtures, or corpora.) In order to test the hypothesis, mean word length must be calculated separately for each sentence (or paragraph, chapter, or text blocks of equal size), and then studied progressively over the course of the text. To date, there is not much empirical evidence concerning these questions. Mention might be made, however, of Kelih's (2012) study of a Russian text (Mikhail Bulgakov's novel *The Master and Margarita*) and its Bulgarian translation, which was indeed able to demonstrate regular tendencies between text and word length. Word length was calculated cumulatively for all 33 chapters, starting with chapter 1, then for chapters 1+2, 1 ... 3, 1 ... 4, etc., up to the whole novel. Analysing both word-form types and word-form tokens (measured either in the number of graphemes or syllables per word), the hypothesis could be confirmed, the increase of word length (*WoL*) with an increase of text length (*TeL*) being modelled by the simple regression function $WoL = a \cdot TeL^b$. However, the regular increase could only be observed when text length was measured in the number of word-form types, not of word-form tokens.

6.5.5 Interim summary

The above list of approaches is not exhaustive; regularities in the organization of word length may be approached in many other ways. In any case, static and dynamic approaches, as outlined above, are not mutually exclusive but complementary: descriptive statistics are simply focused perspectives on a given frequency distribution, and theoretical frequency models not only provide evidence that frequency behaviour as a whole is regularly organized, but also predict the probability of an element of that distribution to occur in the given material, without making prognoses as to when exactly (i.e. at which position) this element is likely to occur. Dynamic approaches, in comparison, provide evidence that sequential order is not randomly organized, but follows particular rules, too. We are still far from understanding the mechanisms in detail; it is however noteworthy that Köhler's results on motifs are strikingly similar to quantitative analyses of syntactic structures, which show a comparable frequency behaviour (Köhler 2012). Similarly, recent research on prose rhythm, concentrating on the distribution of accent and stress in running texts, seems to indicate convergences between word length and rhythmic patterns, insofar as the frequency distribution of distances between stressed/accented syllables appears to be related to the frequency distribution of word-length classes, depending again on the definition of word that is applied, the phonological word being of particular relevance in this context (Grzybek 2013d; 2013e).

6.5.6 Horizontal/collateral relations

Collateral or *horizontal* relations concern relations of word length to other properties of the word, such as frequency, polysemy, or polytextuality.

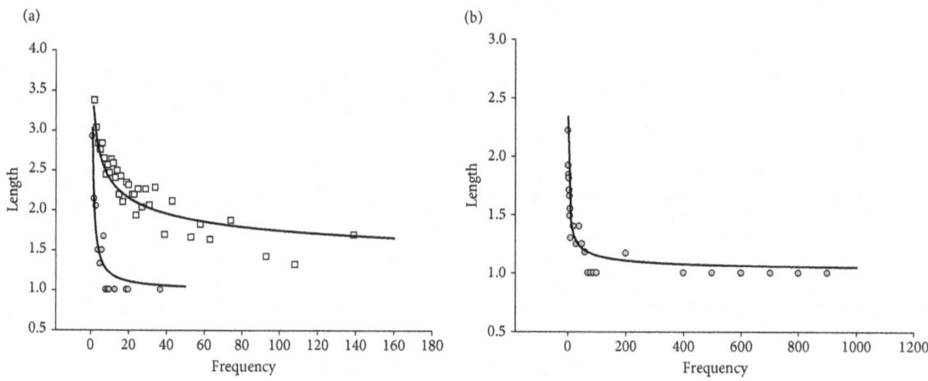

FIG. 6.6 Dependence of word (forms) length on frequency.

6.5.6.1 *Word frequency ⇔ Word length*

The relation between word length and word frequency is well known, and has been redundantly corroborated since G. K. Zipf (1935) formulated the corresponding hypothesis (cf. Grzybek and Altmann 2002). Although many details still remain a matter of discussion, it is generally agreed that the more frequently a word is used, the shorter it tends to be; here, too, it is important whether lemmas or word forms are analysed. This is not the place for an extensive discussion of word-frequency issues (for a recent survey of methods, see Popescu et al. 2009); suffice it to say that different word classes (and, as a consequence, their length) may be differently affected by frequency, the distinction between synsemantic and autosemantic (function and content) words being of special importance.

Paying special attention to the factors of sample size (or text length) and data homogeneity, Strauss et al. (2006), in their analysis of texts from various languages, found the relation between word length (*WoL*) and frequency (*WoF*) to follow the potency function $WoL = a \cdot WoF^{-b} + 1$. Fig. 6.6a shows the results for Tolstoy's *Anna Karenina*, both for the first chapter (represented by circles) and for all 34 chapters of the first book (squares); Fig. 6.6b shows the results for *The Portrait of a Lady*. On the *x*-axis we see the absolute frequency of occurrence in the given text, on the *y*-axis the corresponding word length (in syllables). In both cases, data have been pooled to show the trend more clearly.[6]

6.5.6.2 *Polysemy ⇔ Word length*

The relation between polysemy and word length is a repeatedly discussed issue in quantitative linguistics. The direction of dependence has been controversial, both directions in principle being open to testing. Since word prolongation (by affixation, compounding,

[6] There are different methods of data pooling, which are usually used in case of sparse data. Pooling procedures require careful processing: on the one hand, they serve to make initially hidden structures more clearly visible, on the other hand, pooling must retain exactly these structures and not destroy them.

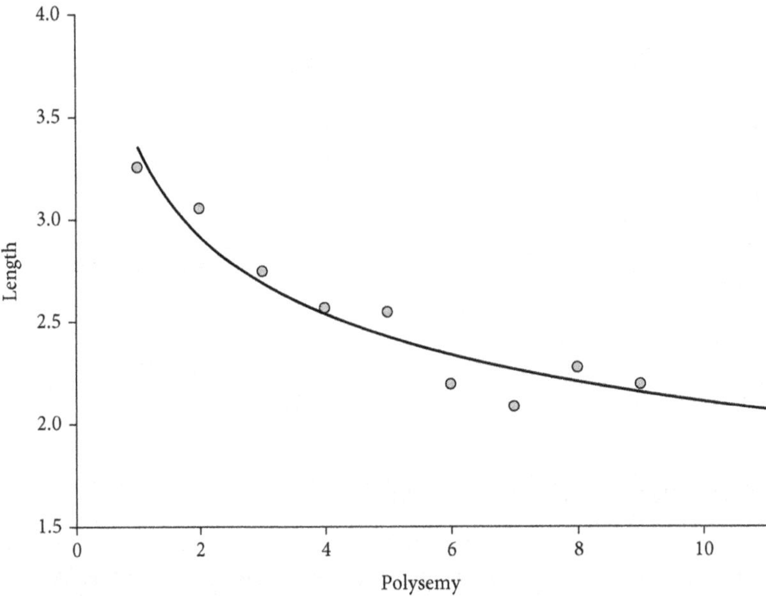

FIG. 6.7 Word length and polysemy.

reduplication, etc.) results from semantic needs (specification or diversification of meaning), one might consider polysemy to be the independent and length the dependent variable; this would result in the assumption that the fewer meanings a word has, the longer it should be, and the more meanings it has the shorter it should be. If, however, shortening is considered to be primarily a result of increased frequency, it seems rather that polysemy should be considered a function of length, shorter words being more likely to be polysemous than longer words. It seems reasonable to side with Köhler (1999), for whom increase of length and decrease of polysemy are simultaneous results of one and the same process. Fig. 6.7 represents Köhler's results for Māori (based on the analysis of lexematic dictionary material), with length (measured in the number of syllables per lexeme) as the dependent variable.

6.5.6.3 *Polytextuality ⇔ Word frequency*

There is a lawful relationship between the number different environments (or environment types) in which a word occurs (i.e. its polytextuality) and the overall frequency of the word (Köhler 1986; 2006). Since polytextuality—usually measured in terms of the number of different texts in a corpus which contain at least one token of the given word—is related to frequency, and frequency to length, we have an indirect relation between polytextuality and length. Fig. 6.8 shows the results presented by Köhler (1986), based on an analysis of the German LIMAS corpus:[7] on the *x*-axis we see the number of different texts in which a given

[7] The LIMAS corpus (cf. http://korpora.zim.uni-duisburg-essen.de/Limas/index.htm) consists of 500 texts and text passages, each of ca. 2000 word lengths, thus summing up to 1 million words.

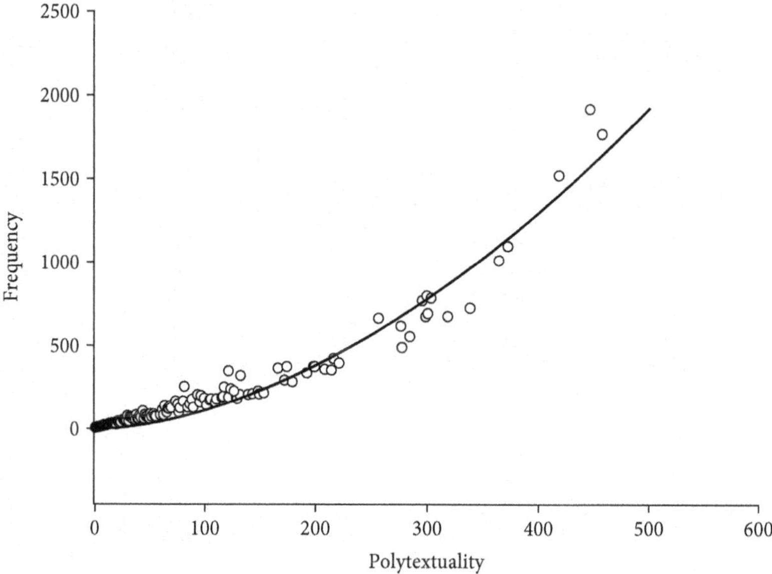

FIG. 6.8 Word frequency and polytextuality.

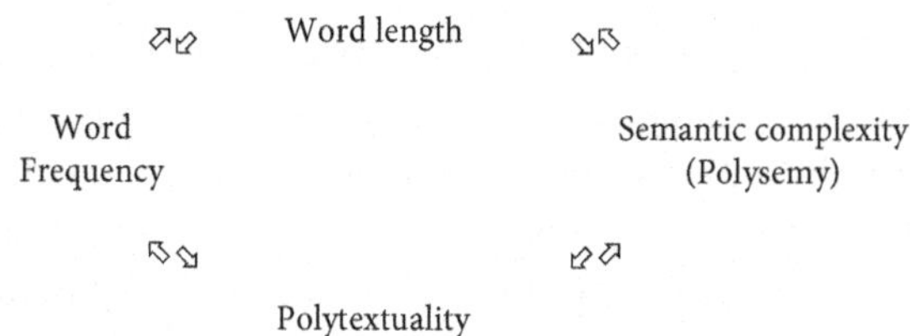

FIG. 6.9 Collateral relations.

word (form) occurs (i.e. its polytextuality), pooled for a given class, on the *y*-axis their frequency of occurrence.

6.5.6.4 *Synergetics: Word length and collateral relations*

On the basis of the factors discussed above which directly or indirectly influence word length, we obtain the following logical chain of reasoning. Frequently used words tend to be shortened; shorter words tend to be polysemous which in turn are likely to be used in more different (con)texts and thus used more frequently. As a result, a system of collateral interrelations emerges, which can be represented in the form of a simplified control cycle (Fig. 6.9).

The cycle in Fig. 6.9 can be regarded as a small component of a complex synergetic system of linguistic self-regulation (Köhler 2005). Concentrating on the needs of a given system (and, ultimately, its users), synergetics is function- and process-oriented,

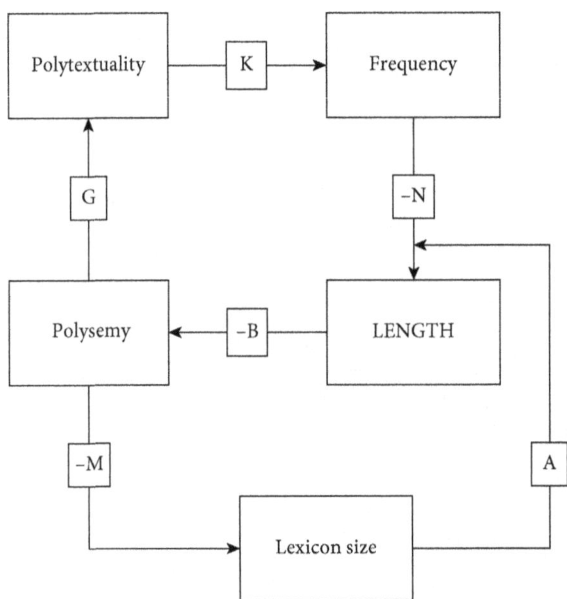

FIG. 6.10 Partial synergetic model of word length relations.

aiming at functional explanations of dynamic systems through studying processes of self-organization and self-regulation. Synergetic linguistics thus deals with needs and requirements like minimization of production effort (*minP*), memory effort (*minM*), and decoding effort (*minD*), amongst others; since at least some of these are antagonistic by nature—minimal effort for a producer, for example, implies maximal effort for the recipient—the system is in a permanent process of change and dynamic balance, guaranteeing the system's functioning (and, in the successful case, its efficiency and survival).

The relations depicted in Fig. 6.10 represent a part of the lexical subsystem of a synergetic model of language. In this schema, rectangles represent system variables (state and control variables), squares represent operators, and arrows stand for effects or bonds; the squares contain symbols for operator types, in our case proportionality operators, with '+' or '–' for their values. For an interpretation of this diagram, one must bear in mind that the original hypotheses have been linearized by way of a logarithmic transformation; that is, in order to interpret the schema, one must use the anti-logarithm along with rules of operator algebra and graph theory. The schema in Fig. 6.10 thus graphically presents the following hypotheses:[8]

[8] As a matter of fact, the schema and the equations derived from it are gross simplifications, concentrating on those system components discussed above, and omitting additional system requirements and interactions between them, as well as further components to be integrated.

$LS = PS^{-M}$	Lexicon size (LS) is a function of mean polysemy (PS). 'The more polysemous words there are, the smaller the lexicon.'
$WoL = LSAFrq^{-N}$	Word length (WoL) is a function of lexicon size (LS) and frequency (Frq). 'The more words are needed, the longer they are on average; the more frequently a word is used, the shorter it tends to be.'
$PS = WoL^{-B}$	Polysemy (PS) is a function of word length (WoL). 'The longer a word, the less its polysemy.'
$PT = PSG$	Polytextuality (PT) is a function of polysemy (PS). 'Words with high polysemy occur in more different (con)texts.'
$WoF = PTK$	The frequency of a lexical item (WoF) is a function of polytextuality. 'A word is more frequent when it occurs in more different (con)texts.'

6.5.7 Vertical/hierarchical relations and the Menzerath–Altmann law

Hierarchical or *vertical* relations concern relations of word length to properties of linguistic entities from other structural levels. Levels, here, are conceived of in classical structuralist terms. On the one hand, we have 'downward' relations of a word to 'lower-level' units such as phone(me)s, letters, or graphemes, these in turn being the constituents of syllables or morphemes; on the other we have 'upward' relations to clauses or phrases, then to sentences, paragraphs, chapters, etc. These levels, and the entities they represent, are of course a matter of linguistic definition. Additional levels may be recognized, depending on text types, e.g. verses or stanzas in poetic texts, sections and books in longer novels. Importantly, all these entities are supposed to have their own regularities, be that with regard to frequency, length, or other properties.

Hierarchical relations can be traced through all structural levels. These relations hold primarily for units of strictly adjacent levels; analyses which leapfrog units from an intervening level are likely to result, not only in an increased degree of variation, but also in more complex, and perhaps even distorted or reverse relations.

In this context, the Menzerath–Altmann Law is of utmost relevance. Generalizing previous findings by Paul Menzerath (1928; 1954) on the relation between word and syllable length, Gabriel Altmann (1980) claimed that, generally, a constituent's length decreases with an increase in the length of the construct; thus, for example, the longer a word, the shorter the syllables which make up the word. This tendency concerns relations between adjacent levels only: the relation between entities from indirectly related levels (e.g. between sentences and words, leapfrogging the intermediate level of clauses or phrases) is expected to show different or even reverse tendencies.

As for intratextual relations, the Menzerath–Altmann Law concerns, first and foremost, the relation of a construct to its immediate constituents. Accordingly, these relations have frequently been modelled with the simple two-parameter function $y = K \cdot x^b$, where *y* represents the construct as the dependent variable, *x* the constituent as the independent variable, *K* some constant, and *b* (for $b < 0$) the steepness of the decrease. This function has long been interpreted as a special case of the more complex function $y = K \cdot x^b \cdot e^{cx}$ (for $c = 0$), as well as $y = K \cdot e^{cx}$ (for $b = 0$). More recently, they have all been derived analogically from the more complex function $y = K \cdot e^{ax} \cdot x^b \cdot e^{-c/x}$, which is the continuous equivalent of equation (1), and from which other relevant functions may also be derived. This extension might eventually lead to a partial re-interpretation of previous attempts to find adequate models.

6.5.7.1 *Word length ⇔ Syllable/morpheme length*

With respect to 'downward' relations of word length, we are concerned with syllable and morpheme structures, these being the direct constituents of the word. In terms of the Menzerath–Altmann Law, syllable/morpheme length is expected to decrease with an increase of word length (measured in the number of syllables, or morphemes, per word). Much empirical corroboration has been gathered in this respect over the last decades. Fig. 6.11 shows two selected examples from German. Fig. 6.11a displays data for the word–syllable relation, taken from Menzerath (1954); Fig. 6.11b illustrates data for the word–morpheme relation from Gerlach (1982); for further illustrations see Altmann and Schwibbe (1989) and Cramer (2005). To model the relation, instead of the potency function $SyL = K \cdot WoL^{-b}$ the exponential function $SyL = K \cdot e^{-c/WoL}$ has been taken here, with $R^2 > 0.99$ in both cases (with $K = 2.11$, $c = 0.60$, and $K = 2.33$, $c = 0.66$, respectively).

6.5.7.2 *Word length ⇔ Phoneme inventory size*

On the next level we are concerned with phonemes, or phonological segments, and related elements. Studies analysing the relation between a language's phoneme

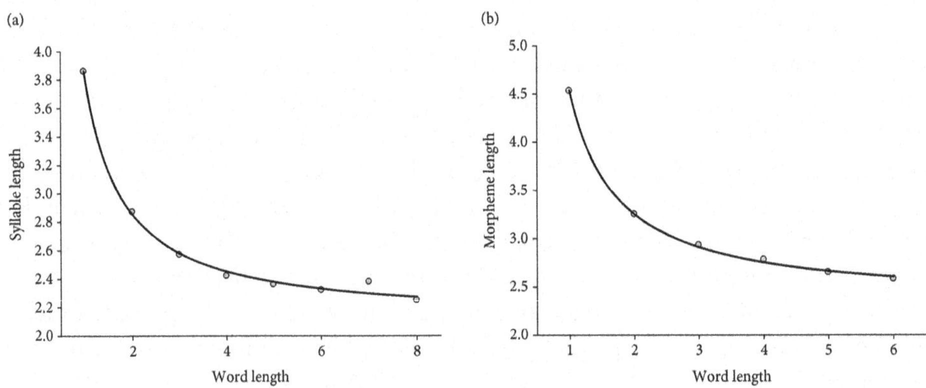

FIG. 6.11 Relation between word length and syllable/morpheme length (based on Menzerath 1954 and Gerlach 1982).

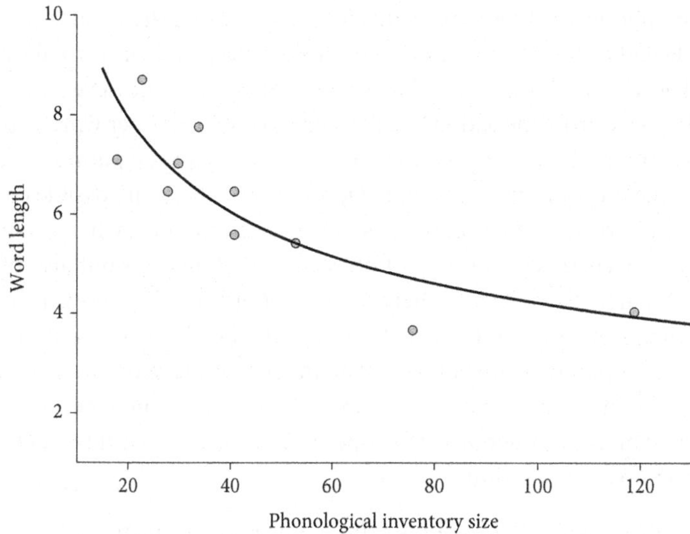

FIG. 6.12 Relation between phonological inventory size and word length (in phonological segments). Based on Nettle (1995).

inventory size (IS_P) and average word length deserve special mention. Nettle (1995) analysed 50 randomly chosen dictionary entries from ten languages. Referring to Köhler's (1986) theoretical discussions of phonological inventory size as an important factor in the self-regulating processes of language, Nettle concluded that word length is inversely related to the size of phonological inventories, the latter being defined as the number of phonological segments available, with tones being multiplied by the number of vowels.

Nettle's (1995) results are shown in Fig. 6.12; included in the figure is the theoretical curve, based on the function $WoL = a \cdot IS_P{}^{-b}$, as used by Nettle. Nettle's (1995) study was extended by Nettle's (1998) analysis of twelve West African languages, and has recently been placed on a wider language basis by Wichmann et al. (2011).

As Fig. 6.12 shows, the results appear to be convincing; with parameter values $a = 26$ and $b = 0.40$, the fit is $R^2 = 0.72$. The results should, however, be interpreted with caution, because of a number of open questions, some of which have not yet been systematically taken into account in approaches to the length–inventory issue (cf. Kelih 2008; 2010; 2012). Apart from definitional problems (such as the definition of phoneme, or phonological segment, the treatment of tones, or the notion of word analysed in terms of lemmatized dictionary entries), the most problematic issue from a theoretical perspective concerns the presumed direct relation between inventory size and word length. First, word length has been measured in the number of phonemes (or phonological segments), thus leapfrogging the intermediate level of syllables or morphemes. Second, not only phonological but also phonotactic issues must be taken into consideration, as well as questions of syllable and morpheme structure. For example, it is evident that the more phonemes there are available in a language, the greater the number of different syllable types that can be formed on their basis; this in turn allows for more variation, likely to result in shorter syllables. Shorter syllables, however, are likely to correlate with longer words (measured in the number of syllables per word), following the Menzerath–Altmann Law. The situation is even more complex if phonotactics are taken into account; the more phonemes a language has, the fewer of all possible combinations are actually realised. The situation becomes even more complex when account is taken of frequency of occurrence, not only of phoneme combinations but also of individual phonemes. Of particular relevance here is the proportion of vowels (in their essential syllable-forming function) in the inventory. Despite the disputed assumption that languages with larger phoneme inventories contain relatively fewer vowels, languages with relatively more consonants tend to form more complex syllables, resulting in shorter words (in terms of the number of syllables per word), particularly if frequency of occurrence is taken into consideration.

6.5.7.3 *Word length ⇔ Clause length ⇔ Sentence length*

Following the assumption that the Menzerath–Altmann Law also regulates the relationship between the lexical and the sentence level, one might be tempted to expect a decrease of word length with an increase of sentence length. However, this hypothesis would not take into account the intermediate level of clauses, or phrases,[9] which has repeatedly been shown to play an important role in the syntactic processes of self-regulation. In fact, there is abundant evidence proving a regular relation between sentence length and clause length, an increase of sentence length accompanying a decrease of clause length, the latter being measured in the number of words per clause. One should therefore expect an increase of word length with a decrease of clause length and, as a logical consequence, an increase of word length with an increase of sentence length (accompanied by a large portion of variation, due to leapfrogging one analytical level).

Surprisingly, however, the word–clause relation has not to date been empirically studied (Cramer 2005: 672)—a research gap soon to be filled (Grzybek and Rovenchak 2014). What are available, however, are studies on the relation between word length and sentence length, from which eventually indirect evidence can be derived, given the considerations outlined above. However, in this respect, due attention must be paid to the distinction between intratextual and intertextual word–sentence relations.

The intertextual perspective concerns the study of a sample of texts. For each text, mean word length and average sentence length is calculated separately, the resulting vector of means then being submitted to analysis. Based on results on excerpts from 117 German literary prose texts provided by Arens (1965), Altmann (1983) formulated the Arens–Altmann Law, according to which this vector can be grasped in analogy to

[9] Again, what counts as a clause is of course a matter of definition, which may change for different languages. Other units, such as phrases, may also be appropriate for this intermediate level between word and sentence.

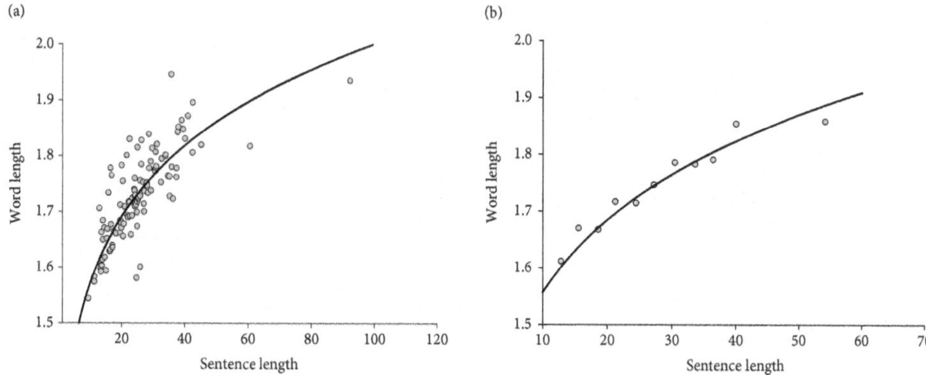

FIG. 6.13 Intertextual relation between sentence length (in words) and word length (in syllables).

the Menzerath–Altmann Law (cf. Grzybek 2013c), which had originally been designed for intratextual relations. Fig. 6.13a shows the results of fitting to the original data, while Fig. 6.13b shows the results for pooling sentences in intervals of 3, yielding a significantly better fit.

Recent research has yielded evidence, however, that the state of affairs may be more complex and less clear than hitherto assumed. Separately analysing the relation in homogeneous text types (private letters, dialogues from dramas, short stories, etc.), Grzybek et al. (2007) and Grzybek and Stadlober (2007) found that within each of these genres there is much less variation of word length as compared to sentence length, resulting in a lack of the predicted tendency; in contrast, literary texts, especially novels, seem to be composed of heterogeneous elements, each with its own regulating regime, the overall picture being more the reflex of these different regimes than of a general rule. As a consequence, the Arens–Altmann Law might turn out to be predominantly valid for the characterization of heterogeneous texts, or text types.

Compared to this, the intratextual relation between sentence length and word length has been studied to a lesser degree, for both theoretical and empirical reasons: calculating sentence length in the number of words per sentence leapfrogs the intermediate level of clauses, and measuring in terms of 'indirect units' should not only be avoided in principle, but has also led to results which turned out to be too complex to be grasped by one of the original three versions of the Menzerath–Altmann Law. It was only recently that the sentence–word relation has been modelled for Tolstoy's *Anna Karenina* with the complex function $y = K \cdot e^{ax} \cdot x^{b} \cdot e^{-c/x}$ mentioned above, resulting in a very good $R^2 = 0.92$. Taking into account that this complex novel consists of heterogeneous text passages (descriptive, narrative, dialogical), and that the immediate sentence–clause relation is leapfrogged, the need for a four-parameter model instead of the less complex potency function seems fully reasonable. Fig. 6.14a shows the curve for pooled data up to sentence length 30. By way of a comparison, Fig. 6.14b shows equivalent results

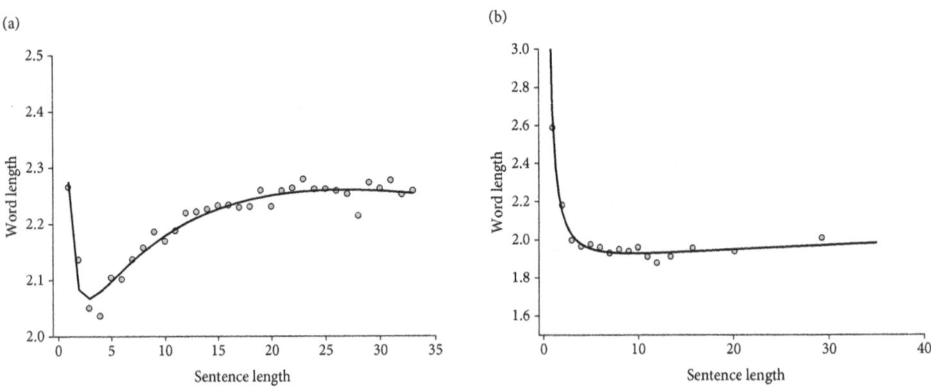

FIG. 6.14 Relation between sentence length (in words) and word length (in syllables) in a Russian and a Slovene text.

for a 1991 Slovene novel, *Zbiralci nasmehov*, by Marijan Pušavec. As can be seen, the trend is also regular, but less complex and in the opposite direction; it seems likely that this reverse tendency is due less to genre factors that to syntactic specifics of Slovene—a hitherto unsolved question requiring systematic study.[10]

6.5.8 Word length in an evolutionary perspective

Language, as a dynamic system, undergoes evolution, a fact which has long been ignored in linguistics due to the dominating Saussurian dichotomy of synchrony vs. diachrony. Any synchronic cut in a language's history is but an abstract temporal model of the language, and the same is true for any diachronic perspective, which is also but a momentary snapshot at a given historical point of time. And no matter how many snapshots are piled on one another, the result will always be an additive compilation of layers; only modelling the evolving transitions between diachronic cuts, each static by nature, can provide a dynamic understanding of language as an evolving system.

Word length is but one aspect in an overall evolutionary process. The foregoing discussion will have shown that word length, far from being an isolated category in a language or text, is closely interrelated with other linguistic units and levels and forms part of a complex system of interrelations and control cycles. It is evident, therefore, that changes in word length will be related to other changes in the linguistic system. Either

[10] In further pursuing such intra-textual (self)regulatory mechanisms, one should be aware of the fact that sentence length, too, is not a 'given' unit; rather, there seem to be rule-like relations (again following the Menzerath-Altmann law) between sentence length and supra-sentential units like paragraphs, or chapters, depending on the text type studied (cf. Grzybek 2011, 2013). Taking into account that relating word length to such supra-sentential units is leapfrogging more than one level, no straightforward results should be expected, however.

change in word length will lead to changes in other elements or it is likely to be the result of other changes.

On an evolutionary perspective on word length, we are concerned with a dynamic (sub)system which, by definition, is subject to change and variability, part of this variability being likely to include processes of diversification. Depending on the perspective taken, diversification may be understood either as a process or as a result of a process. A frequency distribution, for example, may be interpreted as the diachronic result of a previous diversification process (given e.g. an evolutionary process from one-syllable to multi-syllable words), or it may be related to other (simultaneously existing) frequency distributions, which in sum represent an ongoing diversification process (whether stylistic, dialectal, sociolectal, etc.).

Given the complex synergetic embedding of word length in a language's complex dynamic system, it is clear why relevant studies to date have yielded either weak evidence of clear trends, or even contradictory results. Whereas for English, Liberman (2011) observed only a minor decrease in word length in the public speeches of American presidents over a period of about 200 years, Bochkarev et al. (2012) observed an increase over the same period for British and American texts, as well as for Russian, although with specific fluctuations over the given time period. Whereas these studies were based on letter-counts, Ammermann's (2001) analysis of German letters over a 500-year period was syllable-based. Yet he too found no clear trend, but rather wave-like fluctuations. However, none of these studies controlled relations to other linguistic units which may have locally influenced word length—not only changes in patterns of word formation (derivation, compounding, etc.), but also genre-specific developments, involving changes in sentence length and related factors. As a result, word-length data presently available provide only localized insights into evolutionary questions, and more systematically designed studies in this direction are needed for the theoretical modelling of evolutionary processes of word length.

6.6 Practical aspects

One of the earliest practical applications of word-length studies was in the sphere of authorship attribution. Indeed, at the very beginning of word-length studies, Mendenhall (see above) addressed the question of unknown or uncertain authorship. It soon turned out, however, that word length, or rather word length alone, is not an appropriate factor for solving authorship issues. Nevertheless, word length continues to be one factor which is taken into account in authorship studies still today, although, more often than not, with insufficient attention to interfering factors such as text typology and other factors like those discussed above.

In fact, word length has traditionally played a particular role for text typological issues, assuming that different text types are characterized by different word length. It is important, of course, what kind of text typology is used (or searched for): since word length covers only a relatively restricted range of variation, within a given language, no typology comprising some 4,000 text sorts (cf. Adamczik 1995) may be expected to find its correlate in word-length differences. Concentrating on rather general types (or registers), one can show that word-length differences concern basic discourse types (along distinctions such as 'public/private', 'oral/written', 'narrative/descriptive/dialogical'), rather than traditional functional styles (cf. Grzybek and Kelih 2006, Grzybek et al. 2005).

Another field where word length has played a crucial role is the measurement of text readability, or reading difficulty. Starting from the 1920s, dozens of readability formulae have been developed, a particularly relevant topic for schoolbook and text-book compilations. Based on statistical correlations between readers' (intuitive) estimations and text-linguistic criteria, various measures of text difficulty have been suggested. In the early days of readability research, as many linguistic variables as possible were taken into consideration. It soon became clear, however, that an increased number of variables does not necessarily yield better results, since many of the variables turned out to be interrelated, ultimately measuring one and the same dimension. The subsequent strategy of reducing the number of variables was additionally fostered by the desire to derive formulae which can be handled with maximum ease in everyday practice. In this context, word length and sentence length have always been major criteria; due to its manifold relations to other linguistic categories, word length contains much more information than on length alone.

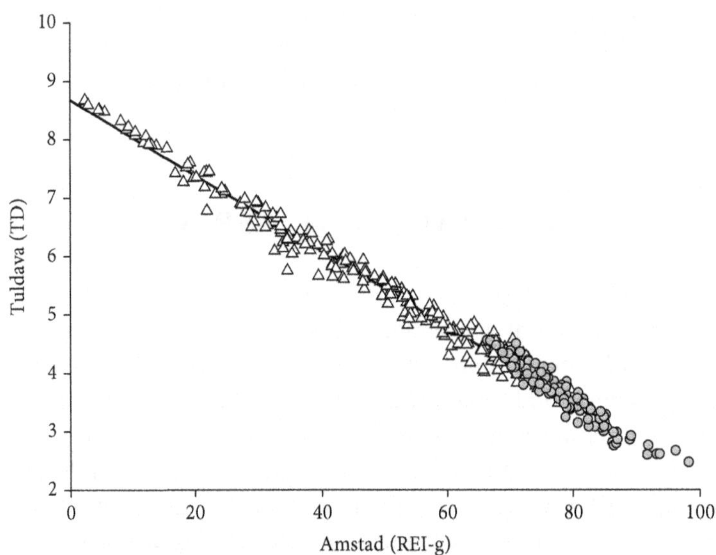

FIG. 6.15 Comparison of Amstad's (1978) German *REI* (Reading Ease Index) with Tuldava's (1993a; 1993b) TD (Text Difficulty) measure, for technical (white triangles) and literary (grey circles) texts (cf. Grzybek 2010: 66).

One of the best known formulae, still widely used, is Flesch's (1948) Reading Ease Index (REI) from the 1940s. This is a linear function, combining a constant with language-specifically weighted sentence length (*SeL*) and word length (*WoL*): $REI_E = 206.835 - 84.6 \cdot WoL - 1.015 \cdot SeL$. This formula applies to English texts only and must be adapted for other languages. For German, Amstad (1978) has suggested the modification $REI_G = 180 - 58.5 \cdot WoL - SeL$: there are similar adaptations for other languages. These adaptations are language-specific, virtually ruling out the possibility of interlingual comparisons (cf. Grzybek 2010).

In this respect, Tuldava's (1993a; 1993b) alternative suggestion for measuring text difficulty (*TD*) might turn out to be useful. His formula is based on the simple multiplication of word length (*WoL*) measured by the number of syllables per word and the logarithm of sentence length (*SeL*) measured by the number of words per sentence: $TD = WoL \cdot \ln(SeL)$. Its language-independence renders this formula appropriate for both intra- and interlingual comparisons. A comparison with the German Flesch adaptation has shown a highly significant correlation, proving its obvious efficiency. Fig. 6.15 shows the results for 240 German texts, separately for literary and technical texts; comparisons with other languages are presently ongoing.

6.7 Conclusion

It has been a major concern of this chapter to show that word-length behaviour, far from being chaotic or irregular, displays systematic and regular properties. Moreover, word length is not a peripheral or incidental property of the word or indeed of language in general; rather, at least from a quantitative linguistics point of view, word length stands at the intersection of structural levels and functional dimensions. Word length, with its manifold interrelations with other linguistic units, levels, and structures, provides information that goes well beyond word length alone. For this reason, word length needs to be incorporated into a general theory of language.

CHAPTER 7

MULTI-WORD ITEMS

ROSAMUND MOON

7.1 Introduction

This chapter on phraseology deals specifically with the phenomenon of multi-word items: that is, lexical items which consist of more than one 'word' and have some kind of unitary meaning or pragmatic function. While the existence of idiomatic, irregular, or unpredictable combinations of words seems universal in natural languages, there are marked differences in morphological and semantic types amongst different languages, and so, to avoid generalization, this chapter focuses primarily on multi-word items in English, adopting a largely synchronic and descriptive approach.

The following subsection discusses terms, then section 7.2 discusses general criteria for multi-word items and section 7.3 gives a short overview of descriptive and theoretical approaches. Section 7.4 looks at idioms; section 7.5 at proverbs and some other types of multi-word item; and section 7.6 at formulae, frames, and prefabs. Finally, section 7.7 comments briefly on cross-linguistic aspects.

7.1.1 Terminology

As many have pointed out, the study of multi-word items is complicated not just by the range of types of item and the unclear boundaries between types, but also by the range of terms in use, often in conflicting ways. The problem arises because different methodological approaches, theoretical departure points or end purposes, have led to different systems of classification, which, however internally consistent and satisfactory, do not fit well together. Consequently, new terms are introduced while existing terms are redefined and applied to categories with divergent characteristics. (For discussion of this problem, see Howarth 1996; Moon 1998; Wray 2002.) For the sake of clarity, I will keep to relatively standard categories, using central terms as follows.

'Multi-word item' (MWI) is used as a superordinate term for the more specific types described below: idioms, formulae, and so on. Other general terms in use include 'fixed expression',[1] 'fixed phrase', 'lexical phrase', 'multi-word unit', 'phrasal lexeme', 'phraseme', and 'phraseological unit'. Recurrent sequences of words, including complex forms of verbs (*has been standing, to be considered*) and freely-formed collocations (*hot weather, walk slowly*), cannot be considered MWIs, nor are quotations unless associated with additional meanings or functions (as with, for example, *an eye for an eye* and *thereby hangs a tale*). Also excluded are compound nouns, verbs, and adjectives, where multi-wordedness is a matter of orthography, with open forms often in free variation with hyphenated or solid forms; consider examples like *textbook, text book, text-book* and the slight but increasing tendency for prefixes to be written as separate words (*the anti war demonstrators, non existent*).

The term 'idiom' is particularly confusing since there are multiple established uses. I will adopt a middle position here, and use 'idiom' to designate MWIs which are problematic because of their semantics: potentially ambiguous, often figurative, and also often evaluative or connotative. Canonical examples are *bury the hatchet, follow in someone's footsteps, move heaven and earth, out on a limb, rain cats and dogs, a skeleton in the cupboard/closet, spill the beans, with all guns blazing*. Broader uses in the phraseology literature include non-transparent compounds (*nosedive, paperback*), and some grammatically anomalous items (*at all, by and large*) or other fossilized sequences (*thank you, needless to say*), which I will instead classify as formulae. *Idiom* is sometimes extended still more broadly to constructions such as *neither ... nor* or *prefer X to Y*: I exclude these altogether. In contrast, the narrowest uses limit 'idiom' to opaque polysemous phrases with a viable literal meaning: thus *bury the hatchet* and *spill the beans* are considered idioms, but transparent items like *follow in someone's footsteps* and hyperboles like *move heaven and earth* are not. This does not seem a helpful distinction to me, as literal interpretations are usually precluded by context, and all need some kind of explanation.

Formula is used here to label a subset of MWIs characterized by their pragmatic functions: greetings, discourse markers, and other situation- or text-bound items. Some are agrammatical, some well-formed, and examples include *how do you do?, many happy returns, thank you, mind the gap!, by the way, in fact, needless to say, and so on*, etc. See further in section 7.6.

7.2 Criteria: The Phraseology Continuum

There are no hard-and-fast rules for distinguishing MWIs from other recurring word sequences, nor are there clear-cut divisions between MWIs and non-MWIs. Instead, it is generally agreed that there is a phraseology continuum and that several factors need to

[1] Including by myself, as in Moon (1998).

be taken into account: in particular, the institutionalization of a sequence; its fixedness or frozenness; and its degree of semantic or pragmatic compositionality.

'Institutionalization' as a criterion refers to the extent to which a string of words recurs. This can be measured by inspecting, say, corpus evidence, though some MWIs are comparatively infrequent, or restricted to certain kinds of language.[2] Some would add that for a string to be considered an MWI it must be recognized as a holistic sequence in the lexicon in order to exclude very frequent freely-formed strings such as *in the middle of* or *it is possible to*. As a criterion, this is more subjective and imprecise, though it can be partially assessed through informant testing or checking dictionary inclusion.

'Fixedness' refers to the extent to which a string of words is fossilized, either paradigmatically (other words cannot be substituted or added, component words cannot be omitted) or syntagmatically (with restrictions on sequencing and/or regular grammatical operations such as inflection, passivization, and negation). This too can be checked with corpus evidence. Variability is discussed further in section 7.2.1.

'Non-compositionality' refers to the extent to which a string of words has a unitary meaning that cannot be derived by decoding, literally, each component word. Sometimes unitary meanings are obscure and impossible to retrieve synchronically (as with *rain cats and dogs* = 'rain heavily'[3]). Others are more amenable to interpretation (*alarm bells ring*) or have specialized pragmatic functions (*happy birthday*).

These three criteria are variables: idioms like *kick the bucket* are institutionalized (at least in the folk lexicon), fixed, and non-compositional, as are anomalous formulae like the emphasizer *at all* following a negative or *any*. *Live and let live, change horses in midstream* are institutionalized and relatively fixed, but partly compositional. *Miss the bus/boat* varies without significant change of meaning; *break the ice* permits a wide range of grammatical operations. Sequences such as *at the same time* are semantically compositional but fill discourse roles in argumentation.

Further criteria used to distinguish English MWIs from ordinary sequences include some kind of syntactic unity (e.g. functioning as a prepositional phrase, noun phrase, verb+complement, clause, etc.) and, in spoken discourse, phonology and intonation. To these can be added some notion of non-productivity, since there can be no rules for MWI formation beyond the usual grammatical and semantic resources of a language and, sometimes, a process of analogy. At the same time, some MWIs are particularly susceptible to creative manipulations, and there are also some very productive phraseological frames (see section 7.6.3).

[2] To give some idea of idiom etc. (in)frequencies: according to evidence in the Bank of English corpus (see footnote 8), *bury the hatchet* and *spill the beans* occur roughly 5–6 times per 10 million words; *kick the bucket, kith and kin, rain cats and dogs* occur roughly once per 10 million words; *bag and baggage, cupboard love, one man's meat is another man's poison* occur less than once per 20 million words.

[3] There are several theories about the historical meaning of *rain cats and dogs*, including the drowning of small animals in floods following torrential rain, and a possible derivation from Greek *katádoupoi* 'cataracts'.

7.2.1 A note on variation

Statements about the incidence and nature of MWI fixedness reflect different approaches to lexical variability. One approach—a lexical approach[4]—is to consider each lexically unique item as independent: thus *throw in the towel, chuck in the towel,* and *burn one's boats, burn one's bridges* constitute pairs of idioms rather than variant forms. A second or lexicographical approach would consider each pair as a single idiom with institutionalized variations: in a conventional dictionary, these are likely to be defined together under a stable lexical element (e.g. *towel, burn*—if necessary, with comments where variations represent British/American distinctions, as with *flog/beat a dead horse*).[5] Neither approach deals well with the phenomenon of extreme and multiple variations, as with these clusters:

shake/quake/quiver in one's shoes
shake/quake/quiver in one's boots
shake/quake/quiver in one's loafers/sandals/wellies/size nines (etc.)

fan the fire/fires/flames (of something)
add fuel to the fire/flame/flames
fuel the fire/fires/flame/flames (of something)

A single metaphor underlies each cluster, with the component lexis selected from restricted sets, but nothing except *in* and *the* is fixed. A conceptual approach might therefore consider them as single idioms. In my terms, they are 'idiom schemas' (1998: 161ff.). See also Nunberg et al. (1994: 504ff.), who term them 'idiom families', and discussion of sets of variants in Taylor (2012: 77ff.).

7.3 Multi-word items in theory and practice

This section looks briefly at different kinds of approach to the study and description of MWIs, and provides a short selection of references. As already mentioned, it is this diversity of approach which has led to conflicts in terminology and indeed in taxonomic description, irrespective of other differences arising from the different languages being examined.

At the most descriptive end of the range are lexicographical approaches, where MWIs are identified as fixed and semi-fixed items needing to be defined or explained in dictionaries (this is essentially the approach I adopted in Moon 1998, from which I draw

4 See Moon (2008) for discussion of these approaches in relation to *as*-similes.

5 Different dictionaries adopt different policies for their listing of multi-word items, particularly idioms and other phrases; some list them under the first lexical element, some under a component noun.

heavily in the following discussions of types of MWI). Mainstream lexicography generally seeks to be consistent and clear, rather than conforming tightly to theoretical models, and uses a restricted range of typological labels—sometimes only *phrase* and *phrasal verb, proverb, saying*. But lexicography also has the discipline of dealing non-selectively with a whole lexicon, pair of lexicons, or substratum of a lexicon, thus treating several thousand items from across the phraseology continuum, not just best-case exemplars or the much-discussed few such as *bury the hatchet, spill the beans, kick the bucket, kith and kin*.[6] Sometimes linked to the lexicographical are lexicalist approaches, which segment the phraseology continuum into major categories reflecting degrees of collocational frozenness as well as semantic opacity: see, for example, the work of the Russian lexicalists, including Melčuk, Vinogradov, and Amosova as in Cowie's account (1998: 4ff., 209ff.). See too discussion by Howarth (1996), where he describes 'four major phraseological categories': 'free collocations' (*blow a trumpet*), 'restricted collocations' (*blow a fuse* in the literal sense), 'figurative idioms' (*blow your own trumpet*), and 'pure idioms' (*blow the gaff*) (1996: 33 and *passim*). Similar segmentations of the phraseology continuum have been widely adopted.

Corpus approaches, also descriptive, are driven by a concern with the phraseological patterning observed in the target language. Since many subtypes of MWI are relatively infrequent, the focus of corpus approaches tends to be on collocation and recurrent strings, which may be entirely compositional. Sinclair's work with collocation led to his model of language structure as composed of both an Open-Choice Principle and Idiom Principle,[7] with phraseologies often of 'indeterminate extent' (his example is *set eyes on*, which tends to co-occur with *never* or temporal expressions) and allowing internal variation: see Sinclair (1991: 109ff. and *passim*); later, his corpus-driven work on meaning led to his view that 'units of meaning are expected to be largely phrasal' (2004: 30). Biber et al.'s corpus work on grammar led to identification of 'lexical bundles', which they explain as 'recurrent expressions, regardless of their idiomaticity, and regardless of their structural status' that are three or more words in length (1999: 990ff.): amongst their four-word examples are *I don't know (what), have a look at, the nature of the, as a result of, are likely to be*. These two approaches typify a very productive field: special interests include co-textual constraints; what amount to prefabricated sequences; and implications for the study and teaching of MWIs.

With pedagogically oriented approaches, concerns relate to teaching language learners about MWIs in their target language, including recognition of multi-word sequences as idiomatic units and asymmetries between first and foreign language: for English, phrasal verbs are a particular problem area. However, these approaches are also concerned more broadly with idiomaticity and phraseology, since these are essential for fluency in speech and writing. Issues include, in particular, collocations (e.g. Howarth 1996; Nesselhauf 2005), formulae, and general phraseological phenomena, as with

[6] I exclude logophiliac dictionaries of lexical curiosities, which are driven by a very different set of non-linguistic principles.

[7] 'Idiom' approximates here with idiomaticity.

prefabricated sequences, routines, lexical phrases (e.g. Nattinger and De Carrico 1992), or lexicalized sentence stems (Pawley and Syder 1983). See also discussions in collections edited by Schmitt (2004) and Meunier and Granger (2008). Cognitive approaches, for example Kövecses and Szábo (1996) and Boers (2011), have contributed insights to the teaching of more figurative MWIs by drawing attention to the conceptual metaphors and other patterns which underlie sets of idioms and other MWIs; Wulff (2008) combines cognitive and corpus approaches in her exploration of the nature of idiomaticity.

Partly linked to these are psycholinguistic approaches, including the pioneering work of Wray on the formulaic nature of language (2002, 2008): her 'heteromorphic lexicon model ... permits multiple part-mappings of the same information in the lexicon' such that phraseologies can be stored both holistically and decomposed into 'subparts' (2008: 14–15), thus allowing for routine, idiomaticity, and creativity. A further important strand of psycholinguistic research relates to the processing of MWIs, in particular whether idioms and similar non-compositional items are processed as gestalts or first processed word-by-word (reaction times support the first): classic studies here include many by Gibbs (1985, 1986, 1995, 2007) and work reported in Cacciari and Tabossi (1993).

Lastly, a significant and dominant strand in MWI theory has developed from syntactic work: since MWIs are gestalts and often ill-formed grammatically, they cannot be accommodated within standard generative or rule-governed models of language, and have to be accounted for elsewhere, for example via a look-up list of exceptions. Important discussions of this include those by Katz and Postal (1963), Katz (1973), Weinreich (1969), and, partly revisionist, Jackendoff (1995) and Nunberg et al. (1994); see also Fraser's work (1970) on degrees of fixedness and grammatical defectiveness in MWIs.

7.4 Idioms

Even adopting a constrained definition of 'idiom', this is a very diffuse category in English in terms of grammatical behaviour and degrees of fixedness, institutionalization, and non-compositionality (and frequency or infrequency of occurrence). First and foremost, however, these items are characterized by semantic peculiarities; examples include:

between a rock and a hard place
bury the hatchet
cut corners
get along like a house on fire
give someone the cold shoulder
once in a blue moon
a piece of cake
pull someone's leg
smell a rat
pigs might fly/when pigs fly

Amongst these, *cut corners* is relatively transparent, as is *smell a rat*, where its meaning, 'be suspicious about something', could just about be retrieved from the conventional negative connotations of *rat* in English (untrustworthiness, dishonesty, etc.), leaving aside the more obvious interpretation of a dead and decomposing rat. More opaque is *get along like a house on fire*, where a common-sense interpretation via literal meaning may not produce the appropriate idiomatic meaning, but instead suggest 'destructively' rather than 'extremely well'. For items like *a piece of cake*, the idiomatic meaning might be guessed from context, but might not; it could be interpreted as 'something pleasant or indulgent' rather than 'something easy'. Thus non-compositionality is subjective, depending on individuals' linguistic and metaphorical competence and their decoding of component words.

Since idioms have non-literal meanings they are potentially ambiguous, and this ambiguity is interesting from theoretical perspectives. In practice, however, ambiguity is less of an issue, partly because context excludes literal readings, and partly because data suggests that idiomatic meanings are privileged over literal. For example, the 450-million word Bank of English corpus (BoE)[8] has 145 examples of *smell a rat*, 226 of *bury the hatchet*, and 50 of *kick the bucket*: in each case just one example is literal. This tendency is further supported by psycholinguistic evidence, which suggests that informants process idiomatic meanings faster than literal uses: that is, the collocational sequence predisposes receivers to expect the idiomatic meaning. There are, however, a few genuinely ambiguous idioms, including some body language idioms, such as *shake hands* (on a deal, in reconciliation) or *raise one's eyebrows* (expressing surprise or doubt), which may or may not imply a physical action alongside agreement or reaction. Even where literal equivalents of idioms almost never occur, literal meanings may still be partly retained and exploited in puns or acknowledged in some other way, as in ... *there are times when I fancy I smell if not a rat, then a pretty sinister mouse* (from BoE); some further examples are given below.

While the origins of some idioms are uncertain or idiosyncratic, there are others which correspond to conceptual metaphors (Lakoff and Johnson 1980), and have been used in the literature to explore those metaphors. For example, idioms such as *hot under the collar, hot and bothered, see red, one's blood boils* realize the metaphor ANGER IS HEAT (Lakoff 1983: 380ff., drawing on joint work with Kövecses). Similarly with clusters of metonymic idioms, such as those containing *hand* which refer to actions carried out by those hands (*lend a hand, turn one's hand to, get one's hands dirty*), or *eye*, referring to understanding or observation (*see eye to eye, keep one's eye(s) on, turn a blind eye*). For further discussion and examples, see Kövecses (2000, 2002) and Goatly (1997, 2007); also Moon (1998: 202ff.).

An important aspect of idiom meaning is evaluative orientation. While, for example, *a piece of cake* and *get along like a house on fire* evaluate a task or friendship positively,

[8] The Bank of English corpus was created by COBUILD at the University of Birmingham. All extended/contextualized examples are drawn from this corpus.

between a rock and a hard place and *give someone the cold shoulder* evaluate negatively. Evaluations are sometimes predictable, as with *smell a rat*, and sometimes not, as with *cut corners*, which evaluates negatively but where the metaphor might imply efficiency and so evaluate positively. See Moon (1998: 215–308) for discussion of the discoursal roles of idioms, including evaluative and cohesive functions; Fernando (1996) also gives special focus to the functions and evaluations of idioms in text.

7.4.1 Grammatical aspects

Idioms are often noted for grammatical peculiarities, such as transformational deficiencies or inflectional defectiveness. It is difficult to establish these fully except by considering items individually, and the following draws on BoE for information (see also discussion in Moon 1998: 94ff.). Inflectional issues relate particularly to whether component nouns inflect. For example, *leg* in *pull someone's leg* mostly pluralizes consistently with the number of persons being teased. However, *shoulder* in *give someone the cold shoulder* usually remains singular; with *lend a hand, turn a blind eye to*, the component nouns conventionally but illogically remain singular (cf. Sinclair 2004: 30ff., who comments that that singular *eye* is typically associated with figurative and idiomatic usage rather than literal). Occasionally, items such as *collective* are inserted to mitigate singular/plural mismatches. Some examples of these:

> *I am quite interested in what Damien Hirst does, even though a good deal of it* ***is pulling our legs.***
>
> *They say* ***banks gave them the cold shoulder*** *because their only real collateral was books, which are hard to liquidate at a good price.*
>
> *...* ***we need to all pitch in, lend a hand*** *and do our part to help forge a brighter future for this country.*
>
> ***They have chosen to turn a blind eye to*** *the fact that most of their pledges are undeliverable at Westminster.*
>
> *... its parliamentarians seemed ready* ***to toss the Commission out on its collective ear*** *for failing to deal with long-running fraud and corruption.*

Where idioms include transitive verbs they should in principle be passivizable; however, some such idioms passivize freely, some only infrequently, and some not at all. *Pull someone's leg* occurs both as *someone's leg was pulled* and *have one's leg pulled*, though active uses are more common. While *give someone the cold shoulder* sometimes passivizes, with the indirect object becoming subject (BoE: *She was given the cold shoulder by the staff there*), more frequent is the lexicalized alternative *get the cold shoulder*. Very few ditransitive idioms have double passivization: a rare example is *pay lip service to someone/something*, where *lip service is paid (to)* and *be paid lip service* are both found. *Kick the bucket* does not passivize at all—logically, since its meaning 'die' is essentially intransitive. *Smell a rat* also seems not to passivize, though this is less easily explained.

Some idioms are canonically negative, as in *not lift a finger, not put a foot wrong*; idioms such as *pull one's weight* and *up to scratch* are more often found with negatives than without. Polarity may also be expressed lexically through antonymous pairs of idioms, as in *keep track of something, lose track of something; in one's element, out of one's element; go up in the world, come down in the world*. Noun groups in idioms are rarely pronominalized, since the idiomatic meaning produced through the noun group would be lost or concealed, though compare institutionalized *on the one hand ... on the other*; also *pull the other one*, used independently of *pull someone's leg*. A more frequent phenomenon is the number of idioms which generate nominal or adjectival derivatives, often involving inversion of elements: for example, *leg-pull, corner-cutting*; from *blaze a trail, trail-blazing, trail-blazer*; from *break the ice, ice-breaking, ice-breaker*. Compare too the verb *to cold-shoulder* and adjectival forms as in *a once-in-a-blue-moon treat*.

The above comments relate to the internal grammatical workings of idioms. In context, many idioms are further associated with particular structures or selection restrictions. For example, *rock the boat* typically follows a modal or negative expression; *pour cold water on something* needs a human subject, and 'something' is typically realized by an idea or suggestion.

> *We are just going to have to accept their decision because we* ***don't want to rock the boat.***
>
> *Strategists spent the conference* ***pouring cold water on*** *optimistic forecasts.*

7.4.2 Variation

A number of idioms have regular lexical variations, with little or no change in idiomatic meaning, as in the following:

lower/drop one's guard, let down one's guard
bend/stretch the rules
make one's blood run cold, make one's blood freeze
a skeleton in the closet/cupboard
from head to foot/toe
throw someone to the wolves/lions
a bad/rotten apple
bleed someone dry/white
by/in leaps and bounds
out of/from thin air

At the same time, a few pairs of idioms which might look like simple variations actually have distinct meanings, as in

get one's hands dirty (get involved)
have dirty hands (be guilty)
fill one's boots (get something valuable)
fill someone's boots/shoes (replace someone)

In another type of variation, forms represent different grammatical relationships, as with possession, causation, or aspect:

have/get/develop cold feet
have no/an axe to grind, with/without an axe to grind
cross one's fingers, keep one's fingers crossed
come to a head, bring something to a head
get/have the wind up, put the wind up someone
one's hackles rise, raise someone's hackles
let the cat out of the bag, the cat is out of the bag
open the floodgates, the floodgates are open

In lexical manipulations of idioms, items are inserted to emphasize, add focus or humour, or signal idiomaticity or metaphoricity, as in these from BoE:

But later, when the Goss Government decided on corporatisation, the Queensland Opposition ***smelt an ideological rat.***
Beating arch rivals Dublin was ***the icing on the league cake.***
Hong Kong banks are ***weathering the economic storm*** *better than their regional counterparts.*
There have been numerous new electronic gadgets which claim to convert the front room into the front stalls–and it need not ***cost a sofa-arm and chair-leg.*** *All home cinema systems are based on* [etc.].
Some of the world's best wine regions are ***literally on your doorstep*** *and close enough for you to visit on a one to two day trip.*
Indeed they ***got along like the proverbial house on fire.***

Compare too items such as *hang up one's boots* ('retire'), which has a large number of variations with *boots* replaced by another contextually appropriate, metonymic noun:

But he was forced to ***hang up his boots*** *last month because of a knee injury, after making only 30 Saints appearances.*
The housewives' favourite is ***hanging up his microphone*** *after 26 years as Ireland's most popular broadcaster.*
Now Dowell is ***hanging up his dancing shoes.***

Lastly, exploitations: these are idiosyncratic but interesting stylistically and for ways in which idioms remain sufficiently intact for meanings to be retrieved:

She who pays the undertaker calls the tune. [sc. *pay the piper*]
Will the prisoner be about to spill the enchiladas on Joe when he is suddenly spirited away and will Joe barely escape with his life? [sc. *spill the beans*]
Journalism's job is to tell truth to power. That happens once in an avocado moon. [sc. *once in a blue moon*]
But although the merry Duffield looks like Santa in disguise (if the hood fits, wear it), his generosity may not always be what it seems. [sc. *if the cap/shoe fits*]

7.5 Proverbs, phrasal verbs, binomials, and similes

This section looks in turn at some types of MWI which have traditionally been picked out as special categories of item for formal or pragmatic reasons.

7.5.1 Proverbs and proverbial sayings

Proverbs are generally characterized as traditional maxims or sayings with didactic meanings, typically offering advice or reflections on life and human nature, social relations, or the natural world. Because many are old and have cognates in other languages and because they express social practices and/or beliefs, they are historically and culturally very interesting, generating a substantial paremiological literature: Mieder (2004) provides an extended discussion. Of the following English examples, some have parallels or sources in classical writers and the Bible:

absence makes the heart grow fonder
a bird in the hand is worth two in the bush
first come, first served
a friend in need is a friend indeed
if in doubt, do nothing/nowt
a leopard does not change its spots
live and let live
a penny saved is a penny earned
one swallow does not make a summer (sometimes as *does not a summer make)*
they that sow the wind shall reap the whirlwind
you can take a horse to water but you cannot make him drink
don't judge a book by its cover

Some proverbs are literal, some figurative; however, the non-compositionality of proverbs lies particularly in their illocutionary and perlocutionary roles.

Canonically, proverbs take the form of complete utterances—simple-present statements presenting universal truths, imperatives, quasi-conditionals—though structures may be adapted to a grammatical context (cf. *you cannot have your cake and eat it* and 'he's trying to have his cake and eat it'). Formally, proverbs may pattern internally, for example with paired noun groups, clauses, repeated items, and alliteration, reinforcing their rhetorical effect. Many proverbs contain archaisms; others have changed over time, as with *don't spoil the ship for a ha'porth of tar*, where *ship* was previously *sheep*. Some proverbs have standard lexical variations (*many hands make light work/labour*, or antonymous *familiarity breeds content/contempt*). In context, proverbs may be truncated and used allusively or manipulated:

In fact every time she saw Flo she threw her out. Muttered something about ***two's company****—there's no point in quoting the rest.*

Well, the compromise was found and it is a very traditional compromise. It's what you call ***half a loaf****.*

The problem comes, of course, with that large area in which ***one person's*** *experimental* ***meat is another person's*** *moral* ***poison****, where so much is a matter of personal opinion.*

Occasionally reduced forms of proverbs exist as independent MWIs, as with these:

call the tune; he who pays the piper calls the tune
last/final straw; it's the (last) straw that breaks the camel's back
make hay; make hay while the sun shines
rolling stone, gather no moss; it's a rolling stone that gathers no moss
silver lining; every cloud has a silver lining

(The last also has a recurrent variation/reversal, *every silver lining has a cloud*.)

7.5.2 Phrasal verbs

Phrasal verbs are combinations of verbs and adverbial or prepositional particles (e.g. *in, on, up*), which are associated with meanings that cannot necessarily be derived or predicted from ordinary meanings of those component verbs and particles. Examples include:

break down
chicken out
get back
give up
go off
let on
make up
put down
set in
take out

Many combinations are highly polysemous and frequent. As an MWI subtype, they are particularly associated with English and northern Germanic languages such as Dutch, Danish, and Swedish: cf. the phenomenon of separable verbs in German and Old English. Amongst the most prolific contributing verbs in English are *come, get, give, go, hold, lay, put, run, set, take*, etc., while the most prolific particles are *down, in, off, on, out*, and especially *up* (of the 60 possible combinations of these items alone, no fewer than 58 are found as phrasal verbs). Phrasal verbs are sometimes marginalized as informal and most have single-word synonyms, often Latinate; however, phrasal verbs are often less marked as choices. Compare *give up, stick out, draw up* vs. more formal *desist, protrude, formulate*. See Bolinger (1971) for a classic study of phrasal verbs; Biber et al. (1999: 407 ff.) for distributional statistics and corpus-informed discussion.

One reason why English phrasal verbs attract attention is that they are particularly problematic for language learners, who not only need to recognize them as special combinations in text but understand how to manipulate them grammatically: whether they passivize, and where particles are placed in relation to grammatical objects. This requires identifying whether the particle is adverbial or prepositional. For transitive uses of adverb combinations, pronouns and shorter objects are typically placed between active verb and particle, but longer or foregrounded objects are placed after the particle: hence *they set up a new organization, they set it up, they set the organization up*. When passive, the adverb follows: *the organization was set up*. In active prepositional combinations, the prepositional object/complement must follow the particle: *they went over the problem, they referred (us) to the rules, they put thought into the matter*. Some combinations of apparently intransitive verbs and prepositions passivize, others do not: *the problem was looked at* but not normally **they were sided against*. By the same token, a few combinations of apparently transitive verbs and adverbs do not passivize (**she was got down by her problems*).

Phrasal verbs are sometimes described as arbitrary combinations, and many are semantically non-compositional, not least where verbs are non-literal or semantically depleted: qualities of takeness, getness, giveness, may be difficult to explain. However, there are some distinct patterns in combinations, where particles are associated with recurrent uses or meanings, and this leads to a measure of productivity. For example, *up, out*, and *away* have completive functions, where combinations describe actions done fully, to the maximum extent or point of disappearance (*burn up, fold up, die out, stretch out, fade away*, etc.); *off* occurs in combinations describing separation or blocking (*cordon off, divide off, wall off*); *on* in combinations indicating perseverance or continuation (*go on, push on, soldier on*). *Up* is associated with intensification or improvement, as in *brighten up, speed up, whip up* and combinations such as *wise up, glam up, man up*; a completive use of *out*, to the point of exhaustion, occurs not just in *tire(d) out, wear/worn out* but in *shopped out, partied out*, even ad hoc *business-conferenced out*. While not all combinations are susceptible to rationalization, many fall neatly into semantic sets linked by some regularity of meaning, and this is particularly interesting for cognitive linguists investigating the conceptual metaphors inherent in notions of up and down, in and out (Lindner 1981), also for teachers of English as a foreign/second language—see Kövecses and Szábo (1996), Boers (2000), and Lindstromberg (2010)—and lexicographers producing phrasal verb dictionaries for learners of English.[9]

A number of phrasal verbs have derived adjectives and nouns, sometimes with inversion of the verb/particle sequence: for example, *rundown, throwaway, downcast, uplifting; leftover(s), takeup, outpouring, overspill*. Compare too single-word verbs such as *input, outgrow, overturn* which correspond with phrasal verb senses for *put in, grow out (of), turn over*.

[9] For example, dictionaries of phrasal verbs edited by Sinclair and Moon (1989) for Collins Cobuild, and by Rundell (2005) for Macmillan, both draw attention to regularities in particle meaning.

7.5.3 Binomials and trinomials

English binomials and trinomials are institutionalized pairs or triples of words, often linked by *and, or, but*, or *to* and occurring in a fixed order: for example,

back and forth
bloody but unbowed
come and go
head to foot
high and dry
hit and/or miss
lock, stock, and barrel
loud and clear
sink or swim
whys and wherefores
wrack/rack and ruin

Some are alliterative or assonantal; some fossilize (near-)obsolete words, which survive as unique items in these MWIs (*wrack* and *wherefore* above; also *to and fro, spic(k) and span*—phraseological fossils are discussed in section 7.6.2). While most pairs or triples are irreversible, there are some exceptions, such as *day and night, night and day*, also institutionalized exploitations, such as *poacher turned gamekeeper* and *gamekeeper turned poacher*. Most of the items listed above emphasize or indicate repetition or completeness, and there also seem to be other patterns underlying the frozen sequences, for example logicality (*born and bred, cut and dried*) or speaker orientation (*come and go, now and then*).[10]

7.5.4 Similes

These conventionalized comparisons also emphasize. Items with *like* include a range of grammatical types and degrees of compositionality, some of which can equally be classified as idioms:

know something like the back of one's hand
like a bolt from the blue
like clockwork
get along like a house on fire

[10] Cf. Lakoff and Johnson's discussion of a 'me-first' orientation in such sequences (1980: 132f), reporting Cooper and Ross's (1975) observations. Other factors in sequencing include the relative length of words (shorter is often first) and as John Taylor points out (personal communication), the relative frequencies of words (the more frequent word tends to come first: Fenk-Oczlon 1989) and the sequencing of the stressed vowels (vowels with a lower second formant tend to follow vowels with a higher second formant: Oakeshott-Taylor 1984).

Much more restricted syntagmatically is the *as*-simile frame, for example

as clean as a whistle
as cool as a cucumber
as dry as a bone
as fit as a fiddle
as hard as nails
as quick as a flash
as solid as a rock
as white as a sheet

Initial *as* is frequently omitted. All emphasize the adjective, which may be non-literal: *cool* above refers to behaviour, *white* to pallor caused by illness or shock. Some similes have single-word adjectival derivatives (*bone-dry, rock-solid*) and the frame itself is very productive: candidates for MWIs are simply those that recur. A variation on the frame, *about as ADJECTIVE as NOUN GROUP*, is especially creative and used ironically (cf. Sinclair 2003):

about as alluring as a wet sock
about as reliable as an election promise
about as useful as a chocolate parasol

See Moon (2008) for discussion of *as*-similes.

7.6 Formulae and formulaic items

This section groups together recurrent idiomatic sequences of different kinds: some are compositional, some not, and many are associated with pragmatic functions. While from cultural or logophiliac perspectives, they can seem less interesting than idioms, proverbs, and the like, from the perspectives of psycholinguistics, applied linguistics, and general phraseology, they are not only interesting but crucially important in relation to the production of language.

7.6.1 Formulae

Many MWIs could be placed under this vague heading: what links them is their association with specific functions or meanings. One subgroup consists of ritual or conventionalized formulae used in greeting, well-wishing, thanking, responses, conversational gambits, text structuring, modalizing, and so on:

come to think of it
excuse me
for example/instance
good luck
good morning

happy birthday
(it's) needless to say
no comment
see you (later), (I'll) be seeing you
thank you
well done
you're welcome

There are many other items with such strong pragmatic functions or force that they must be considered MWIs, even if compositional:

above all
as a matter of fact
at best, at worst
for a start
in effect
in fact
in other words
no doubt
not exactly
talking of—
to all intents and purposes
to say the least

To these can be added conversational fillers such as *you know, you never know, I see, I mean, I guess*: perfectly understandable, yet so frequent that they may receive treatment as MWIs in reference and teaching materials for language learners. There is no fixed or stable set of such items, nor can there be, since their MWI-ness is a matter of interpretation and convention. Moreover, the process whereby phraseologies acquire pragmatic functions is a productive one; some items are long institutionalized, others are transient.

Other kinds of institutionalized formulae include catchphrases, slogans, and some quotations, for example *the best thing since sliced bread, you can't take it with you, I'll have what she's having, diamonds are a girl's best friend, because you're worth it, —doesn't get any better than this, tomorrow is another day*. These are sometimes labelled as sayings, but while 'saying' is widely used to refer to some kind of colloquialism, recurrent formula, or platitude, it is scarcely a definable linguistic category. In the following BoE examples, it is simply a metalinguistic comment on a choice of words:

He was, as the saying went, 'a good mixer.'
But as the saying goes, 'You see what you want to see.'
He is a great believer in the saying that too many cooks spoil the broth.

7.6.2 Defective phraseologies

A subset of formulae consists of anomalous items, uninterpretable either because it is difficult to work out the syntactic relations between elements, or else because component items are too semantically depleted for holistic meanings to be retrieved (in any case, many are associated with pragmatic functions). There are many degrees and types of anomaly, and examples include:

at all
by and by
by and large
hard done by
how do you do?
in case
of course
so long
to do with
to hand

Some are partially decomposable (in the cases of *by and large* and *of course* only through reference to their historical origins). In the following, component words are used in atypical grammatical roles:

all of a sudden
go for broke
in the know
on the make
on the up and up
the dos and don'ts

Items like these result from diachronic processes, though are not productive in the usual sense: some are fossilized relics of more coherent structures, some contain non-standard grammatical uses (e.g. *no can do, come what may*). Another type of phraseological fossil is where MWIs contain words which are otherwise obsolete, thus making the sequence non-compositional: Makkai (1972) refers to such words as 'cranberry morphs'. Examples include:

by dint of
(days) of yore
in cahoots (with)
kith and kin
out of/off kilter
put the kibosh (on)[11]
run/go amok
short shrift

In a few cases, the unique item is more or less restricted to the MWI, though occasionally occurs in other, freer, structures, perhaps with allusion to the MWI: examples here

[11] *Kibosh* is occasionally found as an independent verb (BoE: 'The net effect is invariably to kibosh the Conservative Party').

are *dudgeon, fettle, grist, umbrage, wend* which are mainly associated with *in high dudgeon, in fine/good fettle, grist to one's mill, take umbrage, wend one's way*. In other cases, unique items are homonymic with words in ordinary distribution (*hue and cry, leave someone in the lurch, to boot*), while some MWIs include obsolete or peculiar senses of polysemous words (*beg the question, forlorn hope, toe the line*).

7.6.3 Phraseological frames

Following on from these is the phenomenon of productive phraseological frames, where a slot can be filled by any of a set of items and where there is some consistency of meaning. Several such frames consist of prepositions and nouns, as in

beyond + belief, description, doubt, question, recognition, repair
in + a fix, hole, mess, spot
on + the alert, boil, bubble, fly, hoof, hop, march, run
under + consideration, discussion, examination, observation, scrutiny

While some of these combinations are non-compositional, there are clearly conventionalized patterns of meaning and usage, not least in the metaphorical meanings of the prepositions (at the same time, some would consider these simple collocations). Frames can be compared to clusters of idiom-like phraseologies, such as these metonymic items formed with the verb *hit* (cf. discussion in Ruhl 1979; Moon 1998: 148):

hit the books/bottle/deck/road/sack (etc.)

They seem related to semantically depleted uses of *take, make, give*, etc. in strings such as *take a look, make a comment, give a smile*, but that model of periphrastic construction is really too broad and general to be considered an MWI frame. Compare too the existence of what Fillmore et al. term 'formal idioms' (1988): that is, idiomatic syntactic frames, sometimes clausal or above the level of the clause, such as *the X-er, the Y-er* (e.g. *the more the merrier*) and *X, let alone Y*. See also Taylor's discussion of such frames (2012: 84ff.).

A few phraseological frames are particularly associated with creative uses, typically humorous: cf. the ironic *about* subtype of simile discussed in section 7.5.4. Some have recurrent realizations, but in many cases the point of using them is to be inventive and entertain, as with these:

a few beers short of a six-pack (= inadequate, stupid)
a few ice floes short of a Titanic
two sandwiches short of a picnic
two thumb-screws short of a torture chamber

busier than a three-legged horse in a dog-food factory (= very busy)
busier than a one-armed juggler
busier than a two-dollar hooker

not the sharpest pencil in the box (= stupid)
not the sharpest tool in the shed
not the sharpest knife in the drawer
not the brightest crayon in the box
not the brightest bulb in the chandelier

and drawing from Veale (2012: 65f.):

Tungsten is the Cleopatra of the elements
The Manhattan is the Cary Grant of cocktails
Pac Man is the King Lear of the 1980's 8-bit videogame revolution

See Veale (2012) for a book-length account of creativity and the patterns underlying creative formulations like these.

7.6.4 Prefabs

Last are 'prefabs', or prefabricated sequences: a useful label to encompass a range of idiomatic phraseological phenomena, not necessarily MWIs, and so scarcely fitting into the remit for this chapter: they lie at the very edge of MWI-ness. What characterizes them is that they recur and seem preferred ways of construction and/or articulation: they may be two-word sequences, complete sentences, or something in between (or longer). The following extract of unscripted dialogue from the BoE contains a variety of phraseological items:

A *and erm I was almost hoping the children would do something a little bit sort of* <laughs> *not bad*
B *Yeah that's right.*
A *but they were so good and everyone was saying such nice things about them I and I was always a bit of a goody two shoes and I did all the things that mums and dads want you to do you know went to university all this stayed at home with my* < ... > *children I've always done the right things and erm*
B *Paragons of virtue.*
A *you know all these children* < ... > *the* < ... > *the children I mean cos they're obviously* < ... > n+ < ... > *not better than not brilliant at home but I mean they did pull the stops out last weekend I'm happy to say.*
B *Oh that's good.*

At the idiom end of the spectrum are *goody two shoes* and *pull (all) the stops out*; binomial-like *mums and dads* is over 60 times as frequent as its reversal; *paragons of virtue* is a restricted or recurrent collocation which accounts for 10 per cent of BoE occurrences of *paragon*. Further units include *a little bit, a bit of, at home*, and speech formulae/fillers *you know, I mean, sort of*. But there is evidence here of plenty more chunks of language—not just pragmatically oriented *that's right/good* and *I'm happy to say*, but prefabricated sequences such as *saying (such) nice things about, went to university, stay at home (with my children), done the right things*; also *I was (almost) hoping* and *I was always a*, which have narrative-building functions. While there are different ways of considering such strings descriptively and theoretically, they are further evidence of the phraseological nature of lexis and point towards phraseological models for the lexicon rather than atomistic ones.

7.7 Cross-linguistic aspects

This chapter has looked only at English MWIs, their structures and types. There are closely parallel phenomena in many other languages, though equally some languages differ markedly from English, for example in the morphology of non-compositional units (Chinese is a case in point), or in the anisomorphism of items which may be multi-word sequences in one language but simplex words in another. This presents problems for language teaching and learning, for the creation of bilingual dictionaries, and for translation: also, of course, for language engineering.

But cross-linguistic comparisons foreground many interesting features. Some proverbs and other items recur in almost identical forms in different languages, showing cross-cultural influences or common cultural origins. The first of the following can be traced back to medieval Latin, the second to Greek (which has 'spring', like the French equivalent, rather than 'summer'):

all roads lead to Rome
French: *tous les chemins mènent à Rome*
German: *viele Wege führen nach Rom*

one swallow does not make a summer
French: *une hirondelle ne fait pas le printemps*
German: *eine Schwalbe macht noch keinen Sommer*

Proverbs with loose parallels in non-European languages/cultures reflect the universality of their messages:

once bitten, twice shy
Chinese: *'once bitten by a snake, he is scared all his life at the sight of a rope'*

birds of a feather flock together
Malay: *'hornbills are like hornbills, sparrows like sparrows'*

don't teach your grandmother to suck eggs
Congolese: *'You do not teach the paths of the forest to an old gorilla'*

There are also individual conceptual metaphors which recur in MWIs in different languages. For example, Kövecses (2002: 163ff. and 95ff.) discusses metaphors for anger in Hungarian, Japanese, Chinese, Polish, and isiZulu: these parallel English MWIs where anger is conceptualized in terms of pressure in a container (*blow one's top/stack, blow a fuse/gasket, blow up, bottle up (one's anger), go through the roof, hit the roof/ceiling, be steamed up*), and heat (see examples in section 7.4). In other cases, idioms etc. have similar meanings or even structures in different languages, but are realized through different metaphors:

English: *kill two birds with one stone*
Dutch: *twee vliegen in één klap slaan* ('kill two flies with one blow')
French: *faire d'une pierre deux coups* ('make two shots with one stone')
Italian: *prendere due piccioni con una fava* ('catch two pigeons with one bean')
Portuguese: *matar dois coelhos de uma cajadada só* ('kill two rabbits with a single stick')

See Piirainen (2012) for an extensive cross-linguistic study of idioms, including 74 European languages and 17 non-European.

CHAPTER 8

WORDS AND THEIR NEIGHBOURS

MICHAEL HOEY

TRADITIONAL theories of language used to separate grammatical descriptions from the descriptions of the lexicon, regarding the former as complex and the latter as essentially simple (albeit cumbersome). Such was true, for example, of the earliest versions of transformational-generative grammar. A consequence of this divide was not, as might appear from a superficial inspection of the literature, the neglect of lexis; the 20th century was a golden era for lexical study, from the completion of the *Oxford English Dictionary* in the first quarter of the century to the appearance in the last quarter of the corpus-driven Collins *COBUILD Advanced Learners' Dictionary* and its successors. But this way of describing lexis inevitably meant that for much of that century discoveries about vocabulary were presented in essentially granular, list-like fashion.

Amongst descriptive and theoretical linguists it is probably no longer necessary to argue the case for a more integrated theory, but the separation of grammar and lexis is still widespread in language-teaching programmes, and most of the traditional terms used to describe the ways the lexicon is organized assume a particularity and separateness to our vocabulary. Antonymy, co-hyponymy, and meronymy are all paradigmatic relationships: it is hot as opposed to cold, it is a spaniel rather than a Chihuahua, it is a toe not a foot. Hyponymy and synonymy also draw on paradigms, though with awareness of context. It is sweltering, it is scorching; it is a dog, in fact it is a spaniel. Corpus linguistic work has overturned that opposition, showing that the evidence points to a lexicon that is greatly more complex than previously allowed for and, in the view of some at least (Hoey 2005; Hoey et al. 2007: ch. 2; Hunston and Francis 2000), a grammar that is simpler or at the very least less coherent. Above all else, the findings of corpus linguistics show that we have viewed words too long as particles and as belonging to fields, and it is time to look at them as belonging also to waves (Halliday 1982; Pike 1959); this wave-like function is particularly focused on in Sinclair's (2004) discussion of the lexical item. This chapter seeks to show some of the features of a word's context that contribute to the waves that words are part of and to which they contribute.

A sentence such as *I must have dozed straight off* (uttered by my wife, 16.6.13, but hardly original) illustrates the problems of treating lexis as uncontextualized. The *off* may hint at a light switch but it is not in opposition to *on. Dozed* might be replaced by *drifted* (though not by *slept*), but if *drifted* is used, *straight* ceases to be a natural option as a modifier of *off. Straight* here is used grammatically in a manner similar to the usage in *straight ahead* and *straight up* but has no close meaning association with either. Finally, the modal choice *must have* has no parallel in, say, *I must have just woken up*. The lexical choices in the sentence are much more readily explicable in contextualized terms, that is, in terms of the effect they have on each other.

To show how necessary it is to look at a word's neighbours, and to help identify the different ways in which a word's neighbours may influence our understanding of any particular word, I want to start with a handful of sentences that ought not to be intelligible together because they contain a significant lexical 'mistake', and yet are in fact so immediately intelligible that the mis-selection is characteristically overlooked. The text of which they are a part was found in the travel supplement for a Sunday newspaper; the sentences in question are as follows:

> In the village of Chilling there were more lessons, this time in metalwork. From out of this tiny mud-hut hamlet comes the most beautiful beaten bronze, copper and silver, found cladding traditional kitchen stoves across Ladakh. Smoke from the crude forgeries rose over the village as I picked my way carefully down the mountain between twisted trunks of willow trees. (*The Independent on Sunday*, 2 November 2008, p. 69)

The mis-selection is the choice of *forgeries* (= fraudulent copies) rather than *forges* (= places for working on molten metal) in the third sentence, and the question I want to address as a way of looking at how words relate to their neighbours is why the choice of *forgeries* was not detected by the author, the editor, or any of the readers to whom I have shown the passage. (I only noticed it because I was reading the text aloud.) In the process of answering this question, I will sketch out some of the ways in which a word's neighbours affect (or are affected by) the choice and interpretation of that word.

The first and most obvious feature of the neighbourhood of any particular word (or, as we shall see, any phrase or part of a word) is that of collocation. The term can be traced at least as far back as Dr Samuel Johnson's friend and companion, Sir William Jones (to whom is usually attributed the notion of language families); his use of the term is cited in *Webster's New International Dictionary*, 1928 edition. The concept was reintroduced into linguistic theory by Firth (1957), but actually the credit for discovering that collocation is a ubiquitous and fundamental characteristic of the lexicon properly belongs to Sinclair and his COBUILD team, much in the way that the Higgs-Bosun particle was postulated by Higgs but its discovery was the work of the combined research forces of CERN.

Collocation may be defined both statistically and psychologically. A statistical definition might be that a collocation is the co-occurrence of two words within a defined close proximity where the frequency of the co-occurrence is demonstrably greater than can be explained in terms of random juxtaposition. A psychological definition would draw on experimentation with word associations, and would note that the language user more readily associates one of the words with the neighbour(s) in question than with any randomly selected item. An example of collocation (defined either way) is indeed that of *crude* with *forgeries*, as inappropriately illustrated in the passage above. This is the strongest lexical collocation of *forgeries* in the *Guardian* corpus,[1] accounting for 4 per cent of the 99 occurrences of *forgeries*. Since, though, these data are sparse, I undertook a Google search on *crude forgeries* which resulted (on 28.6.13) in approximately 18,900 hits, corresponding to marginally over 1 per cent of the hits for *forgeries* (1,790,000). The same picture applied to *crude forgery*, where a Google search resulted in 40,500 hits, corresponding to slightly under 0.5 per cent of hits for *forgery*. These data suggest that the collocation with *crude* is robust for both *forgeries* and *forgery*.

A word's relationships with its neighbours also include its colligations, i.e. the grammatical patterns it participates in or the grammatical relationships it forms (Sinclair 2004; Hoey 2005). In the case of *crude* and *forgeries*, the relationship is dominantly that of [adj + N], rather than (for example) [the N BE adj]. In the first 100 hits from a Google search for *crude* and *forger**, there were 72 instances of *crude forger** and 28 instances of all other combinations.

On the other hand, *crude* does not collocate with *forge*. Instead, an example of collocation with the word *forge* is *blacksmith's*. There were 29 instances of the nominal use of *forge* in the *Guardian* corpus (eliminating addresses, places, and company names, where there was no reference to the function of a forge), and four of these occur with *blacksmith's*, in the phrase *blacksmith's forge*. The fact that we have only 29 instances of *forge* in five years of news tells us that manual crafts such as forging are rarely newsworthy. If, however, one Googles the words *blacksmith's* and *forge*, one gets (approximately) 304,000 hits, suggesting again that the words are a robust collocation rather than an accident of the sparse data from the *Guardian*.

The first important observation about these facts, which is generally true for collocation, is that each collocation holds only for the grammatical form quoted; *blacksmith's* does not collocate with *forges* (at least, in the phrase *blacksmith's forges*). *Fraud* collocates with *forgery* in my *Guardian* corpus but not with *forgeries*. Renouf (1986) and Sinclair (1991) have both noted that collocation is a property of the word form, not the lemma. So the collocational contexts of each grammatical form of a word need to be separately described.

The second important observation is that the neighbours of a word may strongly affect the sense of the word in question. Thus the strongest collocations of *crude* in my *Guardian* data are with *oil* and *price*, where *crude* means 'unprocessed' in the first case and in the second functions as a noun, denoting 'unprocessed oil'. The third strongest collocation of *crude* is *attempt* as in *a crude attempt to* or *a crude attempt at*, where *crude* means 'unsubtle'. Its sense in *crude forgeries* is closely related to this last sense but also picks up the idea of 'poorly crafted'. Thus a word's relationships with its different neighbours results in different senses or shades of meaning for the word.

[1] The data used here and subsequently are taken from a corpus of the *Guardian* 1990-5, by their kind permission; here and elsewhere the software used is WordSmith 6.0 (Scott 2013).

The third observation is that slight differences in the way the same two words collocate may connote significant communicational differences. In other words, not only do a word's different neighbours affect the word's likely sense but the different ways in which the same neighbour is used may do the same. Thus in the first 100 Google hits for the search on *blacksmith's* and *forge*, we have 37 instances of *blacksmith's forge* (occasionally separated by a modifier or classifier), 15 instances of *blacksmith forge* (with, again, an occasional intervening pre-modifier), and 48 instances of *blacksmith* + *forge* where the words occur in the same immediate text but not as part of a single nominal group. The first of these combinations behaves differently from the others in that 20 of the 37 instances (54 per cent) make reference to history, with the remainder referring either to the craft of forging metal (14 instances) or to fantasy games of the sword and sorcery kind (3). This contrasts markedly with the behaviour of the other two types of combination, where historical reference is the exception, accounting for just three (20 per cent) of the combination *blacksmith forge* and two (4 per cent) of *blacksmith* + *forge*. By contrast, 11 of the 15 instances (73 per cent) of the second combination (*blacksmith forge*) and 43 out of the 48 instances of the third (90 per cent) refer to the craft of forging, which is true of only 38 per cent of instances of *blacksmith's forge*.

The statistical definition of collocation treats collocates as occurring with higher than random frequency within a span of five words (or fewer) on either side of the node word. But a word may be affected by its less close neighbours as well. To investigate this possibility, I created a mini-corpus of *forge* by searching on the word using Google, first eliminating uses of *forge* where the word was serving as a verb and then taking the first page of each website that referred to the craft of forging out of the first 300 sites listed (plus two advertising sites offered by Google but set apart from the list). When a corpus was created in this way (between 28.6.13 and 30.6.13), 69 of the sites listed (23 per cent) matched the criteria given.[2] The mini-corpus so created contained 5,345 words and the average length of the 'texts' was 77 words. Within this tiny corpus of tiny texts, there were 198 instances of *forge*, and *traditional* occurred six times within the conventional five word environment. (It did not appear as a collocate of *forge* in the *Guardian* corpus.) However, examination of the word list for the mini-corpus taken in its (small) entirety showed there were a further 22 instances of *traditional* in the mini-texts, which means that 26 instances of *traditional* occur in 5,345 words (slightly under one occurrence every 200 words). It is theoretically possible that almost 41 per cent of the 69 mini-texts of my corpus contain both the word *forge* and the word *traditional*, though the likelihood is that the proportion is a little lower, given the possibility of the words occurring more than once in a mini-text.

[2] The other sites used *forge* in three ways without remainder. They incorporated *forge* into a name but made no other reference to the craft that might once have been associated with the name; they referred to a technical software service; or they were associated with swords and sorceries gaming in a range of ways. Only one site was hard to classify, with both gaming and real metalworking associations.

Collocations are frequently evidence of a more general relationship that a word might have with its context, namely that of semantic preference (Sinclair 1999; 2004) or semantic association (Hoey 2005); I shall use the latter term here, but there is very little difference between the concepts. A semantic association occurs whenever we find, within a defined close proximity of a particular word (or phrase, or part of word), a lexical choice drawn from a recognizable semantic set or field. In addition to the six instances of *traditional* occurring within five words of *forge*, we also have *old* (one instance, excluding non-temporal uses), *modern* (3), *historic* (2), *historical* (2), and *steeped in history* (2) occurring within the immediate vicinity of *forge*. From this we can conclude that *forge* has a semantic association with POSITIONING IN TIME. It seems generally to be the case (though I am not aware that it has been tested whether it is always the case) that at least one member of the semantic set forming a semantic association with the node word will also be a collocation with the node word. Where such is the case, it is probable that we are initially primed to associate the node word with its collocate(s) and then extrapolate from this relationship to the more general relationship of semantic association on the basis of further encounters with the word in the company of words semantically related to the originally noted collocate(s). Our recognition of the collocate(s) in effect serves as a bridge to our identifying the semantic association and then subsequently as a reminder of its existence. In the case of the semantic association of *forge* with POSITIONING IN TIME, it is *traditional* that forms the bridge between collocation and semantic association, as to a weaker extent does *modern*.

Parallel to this, we noted above that *forgery* collocates with *fraud* in the *Guardian* corpus, the latter word occurring 24 times in L2 position with respect to the node word (i.e. two places prior to *forgery*), characteristically in the phrase *fraud and forgery*. But we also find in the same position the following words: *theft* (12 occurrences), *deception* (5), *bribery* (3), *blackmail, burglary, counterfeiting*, and *murder*, indicating that *forgery* has a semantic association with CRIMINAL ACTIVITY. So, in this case, there are two collocates—*fraud* and *theft*—that build the bridge to the semantic association with CRIMINAL ACTIVITY and pave the way for recognition and acceptance of other members of the set.

Both collocation and semantic association have a wider and less recognized dimension than the one just described. The collocations and semantic associations we have been describing all make use of the five-word environment to the left and right of the node word. But there are reasons to believe that a word's relationship with its neighbours is not exhausted by this narrow span.

Returning to *forge*, this word has a further (relatively unsurprising) semantic association with METAL. In the *Guardian* corpus, the data are too sparse to permit this to be observed, though *iron* appears as a collocation and *aluminium* and *metallurgist* both occur once within the conventional five-word environment. When, however, we turn to the *forge* mini-corpus created from the web, we find that both *iron* and *metal* are collocates of *forges*, *iron* occurring 7 times and *metal* 6 times in the 198-line concordance, accounting between them for 6.6 per cent of the instances of *forge*. In addition, still within the five-word environment to left and right of the node word, we find two instances each of the words *ironwork* and *ironworks* and one of *metalwork*. So far, then, we have done no more than give another example of collocation and semantic association, with *iron* and *metal* as the bridge words between the two. However, a glance at the outer ends of the concordance lines beyond the five-word limit suggests that there are other members of the METAL semantic association seven or eight words away from the node word, as well as further instances of the words already mentioned. In short, the glance suggests that words within the five-word boundary are the tip of a metallic iceberg in the larger environment of the node word. This is confirmed by an examination of the word list for the 5,345-word mini-corpus, which reveals that 241 of the words of this mini-corpus are members of, or relate to, the semantic set of METAL (see Table 8.1). This means that 4.5 per cent of the vocabulary of the *forge* mini-corpus is METAL-related, or, put another way, that 1 in 22 of the words contained in the corpus is a member of the METAL semantic set or can be paraphrased in such a way that the paraphrase includes a member of the set.

In many respects this should not be surprising. It is part of our knowledge of forges that they are used to work metal, and my mini-corpus was, after all, constructed out of websites that referred to forges. But it is striking how the statistics we have traditionally used to identify collocation have characteristically denied collocational status to words in the local but not immediate environment of the word under investigation. We are reminded that Halliday and Hasan (1976) originally listed collocation as one of the cohesive strategies available to language users, and were thinking of lexical relationships that crossed sentential boundaries, not of relationships formed by items in close proximity to each other.

It may therefore be helpful to distinguish *immediate collocation* (collocation as characteristically defined by corpus linguists, occurring within a narrow span of the node

Table 8.1 METAL-related words in the web-derived mini-corpus of texts retrieved with the search-term *forge* (after the removal of verbal forms, names, and addresses)

steel	52	*metallurgical*	5	*aluminium*	1
iron	45	*bronze*	4	*pewter*	1
metal	35	*copper*	4	*silver*	1
ironwork	33	*ironmongery*	3	*gold*	1
alloy	16	*alloys*	2	*iron-masters*	1
metalwork	11	*ironmasters*	2	*metallurgically*	1
metals	10	*irons*	2	*metallurgist*	1
ironworks	7	*magnesium*	1	*metalworking*	1
steelwork	7	*nickel*	1	*nickel-plated*	1
brass	5	*tinmill*	1	*wrought-iron*	1

Table 8.2 FUEL-related words in the web-derived mini-corpus of texts retrieved with the search-term *forge* (after the removal of verbal forms, names, and addresses)

fuel	13	*charcoal*	4	*woodburning*	1
coal	12	*firewood*	2	*coals*	1
coke	11	*kindling*	2	*diesel*	1
wood	9	*log*	2	*multifuel*	1
gas	9	*oil*	2	*multi-fuel*	1

word) and *cohesive collocation* (words that occur in the local textual environment of the word under investigation but beyond the five-word span). Both, I would argue, are essential to our interpretation of the word. Indeed, it is the presence and importance of the latter type of collocation that partly accounts for the near-universal failure of readers to notice the mistaken use of *crude forgeries* in the passage with which this chapter started, and the corresponding and apparently universal success of these readers in interpreting the passage in the way it must be assumed the writer intended.

The interpretation of *forgeries* as *forges* is further reinforced, albeit less strongly, by the fact that in the *forge* mini-corpus, *forge* collocates (in the immediate sense) with *coal* (7 occurrences in 198 concordance lines), *gas* (7), and *fire* (6). Two of these belong to, and build a bridge to, a semantic association with FUEL, with *charcoal* (2) and *wood* (1) occurring in the immediate environment of *forge* in the mini-corpus and *charcoal, oil, electricity*, and *wood* (again), each occurring once in the *Guardian* corpus in the immediate environment of *forge*. This semantic association is greatly strengthened if we take into account cohesive collocation. The word list for the *forge* mini-corpus reveals the cohesive collocates listed in Table 8.2.

The combination of the FUEL semantic association, marked both in the immediate and less immediate environments, and the collocation of *forge* with *fire* (which occurs 5 times as immediate collocation and 42 times as cohesive collocation) is liable to make the reader interpret *smoke* in the phrase *smoke from the crude forgeries* as referring to the use of fuels in the forge rather than to the destruction of illegal copies by fire.

Finally, of course, the passage we have been examining contains the most common manifestation of the POSITIONING IN TIME association—*traditional*—though again beyond the five-word boundary. I repeat the passage below with the METAL, FUEL, and POSITIONING IN TIME items marked in bold. It will be noted that the first emboldened word, *metalwork*, occurs 11 times in the *forge* mini-corpus. Although it may not qualify as an immediate collocate, it would appear to be a strong cohesive collocate.

> In the village of Chilling there were more lessons, this time in **metalwork**. From out of this tiny mud-hut hamlet comes the most beautiful beaten **bronze, copper** and

> **silver**, found cladding **traditional** kitchen stoves across Ladakh. **Smoke** from the crude forgeries rose over the village as I picked my way carefully down the mountain between twisted trunks of willow trees

In short, words are assigned their meanings by users on the basis of their immediate collocations and semantic associations and on the basis of their cohesive collocations. In the case of the passage we have been considering, it would appear that the cohesive collocations and semantic associations—METAL, FUEL, POSITIONING IN TIME—override the expectations of CRIMINAL ACTIVITY associated with *crude forgeries*. Or, perhaps more plausibly, it is the presence of words from these semantic sets that sets up the expectation of mention of *forges* and results in readers ignoring the fact that *forgeries* has been used in its place; Emmott (1997) shows how a frame might be set up in a narrative in such a way as to control interpretation of subsequent language that is encountered.

I have tried so far to demonstrate how the different kinds of neighbour a word may have (and the different kinds of relationships it may have with these neighbours) help explain the interpretive process in at least one, otherwise inexplicable, textual encounter. But I have only done part of the work. I have shown how the relationships that *forge* characteristically has with its neighbours enable readers to recognize that *forge* is intended. I have not shown why we overlook the mistake. For this, we must make reference to two other claims about the ways words relate to, and gain significance from their relationships with, their neighbours.

The first of these claims is that once a relationship is formed between a word and its neighbour, the combination takes on a life of its own, such that it too may form collocations, colligations, and semantic associations. These need not be the same as those that the separate words might form.

To investigate, I created a second mini-corpus from the web by searching for *crude forgeries* and extracting each sentence that contained the search phrase. A total of 106 instances were collected and then concordanced in the normal way. The following characteristics were identified for the word combination. First, it has a strong colligational tendency to occur as the complement of BE clauses. Slightly over half the occurrences in my data (55 out of 106) occurred in this pattern. It is unsafe to compare these results with those for the 96 instances of *forgeries* (excluding *crude forgeries*) collected from the *Guardian* corpus because of the different ways in which these corpora were created, but it is interesting to note that only a quarter of the latter (23 out of 96) occurred as complement with BE.

Secondly, one of the immediate collocations of *crude forgeries* is *documents* (7 out of 106—accounting for 6.6 per cent of cases). The proportion is very much higher if cohesive collocation is included (and here we are only talking of instances visible in the KWIC format but outside the five-word limit): including these there are 28 instances of *documents* (accounting for over a quarter of the data). The collocation is even stronger with the combination *BE crude forgeries*. Of the 28 instances of *documents* just mentioned, 23 occur to the left of *BE crude forgeries*, accounting for almost exactly half of the cases of the combination (50.9 per cent).

Thirdly, the word *documents* itself serves as a bridge into two semantic associations that heavily overlap with each other—PAPER OR ELECTRONIC DOCUMENTS and PAPER ARTEFACTS. The former occurs in 62 of the concordance lines (58.5 per cent); the latter occurs in a further 11 lines. Taken together, the semantic associations are manifested in 68.9 per cent of the data.

Fourthly, the combination *crude forgeries* has a semantic association with EXPOSURE. This is manifested as *shown* (4 instances), *revealed* (3), *exposed* (3), *turned out to be* (3), *identify* (2), *proved* (2), and *detected* (2) in the immediate environment, accounting for 17.8 per cent of the data; as before, there are considerably more instances if we take account of instances falling just outside the five word boundary.

As before, the association is more precise than it first appears. EXPOSURE is particularly associated with the nested combination PAPER OR ELECTRONIC DOCUMENTS/PAPER ARTEFACTS *BE crude forgeries* (of which there are 55—the discrepancy with the figure quoted above is explained by reference to the fact that there are a handful of cases where *BE* is not present). There are 25 instances of semantic association with EXPOSURE to be found among the 55 cases of the above combination, the great majority making use of the reporting structure. A further 11 cases colligate with reporting verbs of CLAIM. Altogether there are 36 cases of PAPER OR ELECTRONIC DOCUMENTS/PAPER ARTEFACTS *BE crude forgeries* (65.5 per cent of the data) that are either associated with claims of forgery or with claims of evidence of forgery.

These kinds of interconnecting phenomena were described by Sinclair (2004) in his account of the lexical item, and are key to the way that lexical priming theory seeks to account for the complexities of the language we use and interpret. Of course the account given here is incomplete. There is a collocation of *crude forgeries* with *as*, for example, in which *as* functions as a stand-in for BE and immediately follows either EXPOSURE or CLAIM. There is also an association with COLLECTIBLES, especially stamps, notes, and coins. Even so, very few of the instances of *crude forgeries* escape all of the features that have been discussed so far in this chapter, and this explains why the reader overlooks the substitution of *forgeries* for *forges*. On the one hand, the larger textual environment offered by our chosen passage conforms wholly to our primings for *forge*; on the other hand, the same textual environment conforms to none of our primings for *forgeries*. It is no wonder that when we read the passage we ignore *forgeries* and think that we have read *forges* (or that *forgeries* is another word for *forges*).

The different kinds of relationship that a word has with its neighbours—collocations, colligations, semantic associations, and a number of other relationships not discussed here (see Hoey 2005 for a fuller account)—amount to a corpus-driven account of interpretation, in which the key facts are lexical in nature rather than grammatical, and are specific to the item rather than widely generalizable across the language (though of course the types of relationship posited by corpus linguists are themselves a kind of generalization). It is not necessary to accept any underlying theory of language to admit the explanatory value of the features described in this chapter. Nevertheless, though the study of corpora has led to the discovery of these features, they are arguably best understood as psycholinguistic phenomena rather than purely corpus-linguistic phenomena.

Since the 1970s, psycholinguistic research has been demonstrating that exposure to certain words may accelerate recognition of certain other words (semantic priming), the inference being that the words in question are stored in close proximity (Meyer and Schvanefeldt 1976; Neely 1976; 1977). Other psycholinguistic research, also of 35 years' standing, has shown that earlier exposure to a particular combination of words will result, in some cases after a considerable time, in accelerated recognition of the second word after the first word has been shown, even where the combination originally shown was highly likely to have been a unique occurrence (repetition priming) (Scarborough et al. 1977). The conclusion to be drawn is that each encounter with any piece of language (contra Pinker 1994) is stored as received (though of course it may also be processed in the ways Pinker and others suggest), and that this store is capable of being accessed on subsequent linguistic encounters (see Pace-Sigge 2013 for a far more thorough account of this literature). The ability to recognize literary allusion (and, more wretchedly, plagiarism) in part depends on this access to the original wordings that are being borrowed.

Lexical priming theory (Hoey 2005) seeks to integrate this psycholinguistic research (which because it has its origins in psychological concerns has, as far as I can see, been little accessed by linguists) with the findings of corpus linguists. It argues that every encounter we have with language, whether spoken or written, results in what we have heard or read being stored. The mental store, as it accumulates data about any piece of language, primes us to expect that piece of language to collocate with particular other pieces of language because the store shows that they have been encountered repeatedly. As we encounter linguistic expressions that only partly conform to our expectations, though, we modify those expectations and become primed to associate the piece of language in question with members of a particular semantic set, to which the collocations originally identified belong. At the same time, our increasing collection of instances of this piece of language will prime us to associate that piece of language with certain grammatical functions, grammatical structures, and, most fundamentally, grammatical categories. The grammar of a language, according to this view, is the cumulative and inconsistent product of the local colligational primings of innumerable words.

As noted above, acceptance of the observable kinds of relationship that a word may form with its neighbours does not entail acceptance of any particular theory that might attempt to account for those observations. But if the theory just outlined were to be taken seriously (and there is still a need to account for the psychological reality of the collocations even if it is not), then it places the relationships that a word forms with its neighbours at the very core of what it is to be a linguistic being. An essay that is ostensibly about the reasons why a linguistic mistake is ignored and a text correctly interpreted is in reality an essay about how we make and find meaning.

The discourse conventions of academic writing ought to have meant that the previous sentence was the final one of this chapter. It is after all a broad generalization derived from the previous analyses and discussion, and it attempts to assign significance to the argument of the chapter. But it is not the final sentence and it should not be. The reason is that in the previous four paragraphs there has been linguistic sleight of hand. The title of this chapter is 'Words and Their Neighbours' and the previous paragraph, as well as my brief account of the psycholinguistic research into semantic and repetition priming, also talks of words. But the intervening account of lexical priming talks vaguely of 'pieces of language'. The reason of course is that the word does not have hallowed status as a category. Corpus linguists of languages that employ alphabetic systems tend to make use of words because they appear to be orthographically distinct, but they are markedly less so in a language such as Chinese, where combinations of characters may in the view of Chinese speakers result in collocations, phrases, or single words. Young learners, whatever language they are primed in and for, cannot during early encounters with the speech of those around them have any thoughts about which pieces of the sound stream are words and which are combinations or constituents of words. A child's first primings (and an adult's L2 primings where learning is solely by immersion) must be the primings that associate certain pieces of the sound stream with certain meanings or speech acts.

The reason I raise these issues is that I want to argue that our correct interpretation of the *crude forgeries* passage is contingent upon a further factor in the wording that comes from an unexpected quarter. So far we have looked at a word's relationships with its neighbours at the level of the word and word combination; now we must look at the rank below that of the word, or what might misleadingly be referred to as the level of morphology. A word's relationships to the surrounding text are partly affected by the relationship of its sub-components to the surrounding text.

The difference between *forges* and *forgeries* lies in the piece of language *-eries*. I therefore examined the ways that *-eries* is used in English, as represented in my corpora. In the combined corpora of the *Guardian* and the BNC, there were 118,932 tokens of words ending in *-eries*. Excluding *series* and *queries*, there were 142 separate types making use of the ending, and these types could be grouped according to their membership of a small number of distinct and unequal semantic sets. Two of these we need not dwell on. The first group consists of *Tuileries, shrubberies, rockeries, palmeries, orangeries*, and *nurseries* (in one of its senses) and appears to comprise gardens of various kinds; these make up 4.2 per cent of the types. (*Nurseries* is the outlier of this group, in that nurseries prepare plants for gardens rather than being gardens themselves.) The other group is made up (somewhat curiously) of *monasteries, menageries, nurseries* (in another sense), *presbyteries, piggeries, nunneries, deaneries, catteries, chancelleries, chanceries*, and *fisheries*. This group seems to consist of the residences of animals and the religious, with *nurseries* again the outlier, babies being neither bestial nor saintly. They account for 11 (7.7 per cent) of the types ending in *-eries*.

The remaining groups are directly relevant to the way we interpret our *crude forgeries* example. The first is concerned with sins and crimes. In the list are *adulteries, trickeries, treacheries, mockeries, snobberies, ruderies, bitcheries, skulduggeries, savageries, debaucheries, robberies, quackeries, pruderies, lecheries, butcheries, enslaveries, chicaneries, flatteries*, and of course *forgeries*. These items account for 14.1 per cent, or 1 in 7, of the types ending in *-eries*. To these might be added a heterogeneous set of words that, while not crimes or sins, seem to be used to express repugnance, unhappiness, or disapproval: *snotteries, splatteries, miseries, sludgeries, misdeliveries, slickeries, grotesqueries,* *gaucheries, camperies, flummeries*, and *dysenteries*. If these are added to the tighter earlier list, they together comprise 21.8 per cent, or 1 in 5, of the types found in my corpora. So we are characteristically primed to associate the ending of *forgeries* with crimes, sins, and unpleasantness.

However, there is an even more important (for this argument) *-eries* group. Consider the following group of types:

wineries	*potteries*	*tanneries*
surgeries	*saddleries*	*rotisseries*
refineries	*perfumeries*	*patisseries*
ouzeries	*noodleries*	*bakeries*
meaderies	*smokeries*	*hatcheries*
haberdasheries	*fisheries*	*distilleries*
creameries	*collieries*	*canneries*
breweries	*butteries*	*fromageries*
boulangeries	*piggeries*	*orangeries*
creperies	*nurseries*	

All of these 29 items, a couple of which were included in earlier groupings, are concerned with the production of something—food, drink, products—and they constitute 20.4 per cent, or 1 in 5, of the list of types generated by my corpora. To them might be added another group concerned with the provision of food and drink: *boozeries, fast-fooderies, hostelries, nosheries, kebaberies, chocolateries*, and *carveries*. (Indeed *noodleries, brasseries*, and *creperies* belong in both groups.) The two groups combined, all concerned with the provision or production of some purchasable product, constitute 25.3 per cent, or 1 in 4, of all the types. The implication is that we are primed to associate *-eries* with products. In the light of this, consider again, for the last time, the passage we have been using as the peg for our discussion of the ways words relate to their neighbours:

> In the village of Chilling there were more lessons, this time in metalwork. From out of this tiny mud-hut hamlet comes the most beautiful beaten bronze, copper and silver, found cladding traditional kitchen stoves across Ladakh. Smoke from the crude forgeries rose over the village as I picked my way carefully down the mountain between twisted trunks of willow trees

We saw that the *-eries* of *forgeries* has a semantic association with products, and here we find that the passage speaks of products—*the most beautiful beaten bronze, copper and* *silver*—and talks of where the products are used. It is no wonder that *forgeries* are (correctly) understood to mean *forges*.

To sum up, then, words relate to their neighbours in a variety of ways and at a variety of levels of detail. When we construct our own utterances or interpret those of others, we subconsciously note the collocations that the word on its own makes with other words; we also note the collocations that the combination has with other words or combinations of words. The same goes for the colligations that we note for the word or word combination, and for the semantic associations that we make in our minds between the word or word combination and particular semantic sets. There are other kinds of association that a word or a combination of words may contract, which we have not touched upon, such as pragmatic association, textual collocation, textual semantic association, or textual colligation (Hoey 2005), as well as referential association, orthographic association, and punctuation association (Salim 2012).

Furthermore, as we have seen above, there are grounds for investigating whether the sub-components of words also regularly participate in all these kinds of relationship, and here of course we need to take account of phonetics and phonology. To the 'sins and crimes' list of *-eries* could be added *burglaries* if the sound image rather than the spelling is accessed, and to the 'provision and products' list could be added *factories* and *foundries*. As I said above, near the false first ending of this chapter, the relationships that a word forms with its neighbours are at the very core of what it is to be a linguistic being; it is therefore unsurprising that an investigation of these relationships should ultimately incorporate all levels, ranks, and types of language description.

PART II

WORDS AND LINGUISTIC THEORY

CHAPTER 9

THE STRUCTURE OF WORDS

GEERT E. BOOIJ

9.1 Introduction

Words may have an internal structure. For instance, the English word *singer* can be divided into two constituents, *sing* and *-er*. Both constituents contribute to the meaning of the word as a whole. These constituents are referred to as morphemes, the minimal meaning-bearing units of a language. The word *singer* is therefore a complex word, as opposed to the word *sing*, which has no internal morphological structure and is therefore a simplex word. The morpheme *sing* is a lexical morpheme, as it can also occur as a word of its own, whereas the morpheme *-er*, which expresses the meaning 'agent of the action', is a bound morpheme.

How do we know that *singer* is a complex word, whereas other words that also end in *-er* are not considered complex, such as *border, father*, and *order*? The reason is that for a word to be considered complex we expect a systematic correspondence between its form and meaning. The internal structure of the noun *singer* is determined on the basis of a comparison of sets of words such as the following:

(1)	*verb*	*agent noun in* -er
	bake	baker
	speak	speaker
	dance	dancer
	use	user

The two sets of words stand in a systematic form–meaning relationship, and on the basis of this relationship we can assign an internal morphological structure to nouns in *-er* with a verbal subconstituent. We call these nouns deverbal, as they are derived from base words that are verbs. In the case of *border, father*, and *order* there is no base word to be found and there is no agentive meaning; hence we consider these words as simplex.

This also makes it clear why we want to assign internal morphological structure to words like *singer*: the meaning of this word is not completely arbitrary, but motivated, namely, by its constituents and their arrangement.

A second example of complex words are the following plural nouns in English: *apples, books, pages*, which all end in the plural morpheme *-s*. These words are also complex since they show a systematic form–meaning correspondence with the words *apple, book*, and *page*. The difference with the agent nouns is that this is not a case of word formation, but of inflection. Whereas *sing* and *singer* are two different words, with their own entry in a dictionary, this is not the case for *apples*, which is an inflectional form of the lexeme APPLE, as is the singular form *apple*. A lexeme is the abstract unit that stands for the set of inflectional forms, and is usually represented with small capitals.

The two basic functions of morphological operations that create complex words are word formation and inflection. Word formation processes create new lexemes and hence expand the lexicon of a language. Once the speaker of English has discovered the pattern exemplified in (1), (s)he may hit on a word formation schema which we can characterize, informally, as follows:

(2) $[[x]_V\ er]_N$ 'one who Vs'

The speaker may then use this schema to create new words with the appropriate form and meaning, such as *skyper*, derived from the verb *(to) skype*, or *texter*, derived from the verb *(to) text*. The new words may not only have the meaning predicted by the schema, but also additional idiosyncratic properties. For instance, the *Urban Dictionary*[1] defines a *texter* as 'a person who prefers to send text messages instead of picking up the phone'.

Inflection is the grammatical subsystem that deals with the proper form of lexemes, often in relation to specific syntactic contexts. In Dutch, for instance, the verb *werk* 'to work' has five different finite forms. The selection of a present or past form depends on the information the speaker wants to convey, and this is called inherent inflection. The choice of a particular present or past form depends on the number and person of the subject of the clause in which the verb occurs, and this is called contextual inflection since the choice of a form depends on the syntactic context:

(3)
werk	present 1st person singular
werk-t	present 2nd/3rd person singular
werk-en	present 1st/2nd/3rd person plural
werk-te	past 1st/2nd/3rd person singular
werk-te-n	past 1st/2nd/3rd person plural

[1] [http://www.urbandictionary.com/]

We consider these five forms as forms of the same lexeme. Thus, Dutch has a lexeme WERK. The stem form of this lexeme is *werk*, and the different inflectional affixes are added to this stem. The Dutch word *werker* 'worker' is a different lexeme than the word *werk* 'to work' (so Dutch has the lexemes WERK and WERKER). The plural form of this noun *werkers* 'workers' has the following morphological structure:

(4) werk -er -s
work -AGENT -PLURAL
'workers'

This is a simple example of the morphological analysis of a complex word, and presented in a form that follows the conventions of interlinear morphemic glossing (Lehmann 2004). The first line presents the internal constituency of the complex word. The second line provides a morpheme by morpheme glossing, and the third line gives a paraphrase of the meaning of the linguistic unit.

Cross-linguistically, the most common form of word formation is compounding, the combination of two or more lexemes into a complex word, such as the English word *songbook* composed of the nouns *song* and *book*. Many languages also make use of derivation, the process in which bound morphemes (affixes) such as *-er* are attached to a base word. These two mechanisms are instances of concatenative morphology, in which complex words are created by means of the concatenation, or stringing together, of morphemes.

However, these are not the only means of making complex words. In reduplication, a complete or partial copy of a word is added to that base word. Thus, reduplication may be seen as a specific form of compounding (total reduplication) or affixation (partial reduplication). Here are some examples from the Austronesian language Begak spoken in Malaysia (Goudswaard 2005: 52–6):

(5) *total reduplication*

suran 'story'	suran-suran 'many stories'
puti 'white'	puti-puti 'very white'
panow 'to go'	panow-panow 'to go a little bit'
partial reduplication	
bua 'fruit'	bə-bua 'various types of fruit'
bunu 'to kill'	bə-bunu' 'to kill each other'
satu 'one'	sə-satu 'only one'

In the case of partial reduplication, a copy of the first consonant forms a prefix together with a fixed vowel [ə].

Other, non-concatenative, mechanisms are the use of specific vowel and/or consonantal patterns (as in *sing-sang, bring-brought*), and tonal patterns. The use of vowel alternations is a characteristic of Indo-European languages. The Semitic languages are well known for their system of creating related verbal lexemes by combining a consonantal root with a specific pattern of C and V positions and a vowel melody. In addition, prefixes may be used. This type of morphology is called root-and-pattern morphology. A set of verbal lexemes with the same morphological pattern is called a *binyan* ('building', plural *binyanim*). The root *qtl* 'to kill' as used in Biblical Hebrew has the following five binyan forms with active meaning (Aronoff 1994: 124), of which the 3SG.MASC.PERF forms are illustrated in (6):[2]

(6)	*Binyan*	3SG.M.PF	CV-PATTERN	V-PATTERN	*gloss*
	Qal	qâtal	CVCVC	â-a	to kill
	Nif'al	ni-qtal	ni-CCVC	a	to kill oneself
	Pi'el	qittel	CVC_iC_iVC	i-e	to massacre
	Hif'il	hi-qtil	hi-CCVC	i	to cause to kill
	Hitpa'el	hit-qattel	hit-CVC_iC_iVC	a-e	to kill oneself

In addition to these five binyanim, there are two binyanim with a passive meaning, the Pu'al as a passive variant of the Pi'el, and the Hof'al as the passive of the Hif'il.

The use of a tone pattern as a morphological marker can be found in many tone languages. Here is an example from Ngiti, a central-Sudanic language of Congo (Kutsch Lojenga 1994: 135):

(7)	*singular*	*plural*	
	àba-du	abá-du	my father(s)
	abhu-du	abhú-du	my grandfather(s)
	akpà-du	akpá-di	my husband(s)
	andà-du	andá-du	my uncle(s)

In the plural possessive form, the prefinal syllable always carries high tone (indicated by the acute accent on the vowel letter, e.g. *á*), whereas the other syllables carry mid tone (indicated by the lack of an accent symbol). In the singular, some vowels carry low tone (indicated as *à*). Thus, plurality is systematically marked by a specific tone pattern.

Finally, there are operations like blending (*smog* < *smoke* + *fog*), the formation of acronyms (*N.A.T.O*, spoken as [neɪtəʊ] < *North Atlantic Treaty Organization*), clippings (*mike* < *microphone*), and truncations (*commie* < *communist, Becky* < *Rebecca*), in which only parts of words appear in the derived word.

In the domain of concatenative morphology, the structure of a complex word can be represented by means of labelled bracketing of a string of morphemes. For instance, the

[2] The apostrophe ' indicates a glottal stop, and the symbol *â* stands for an open /o/; C_iC_i stands for two identical consonants.

English compound *songbook*, the derived word *singer*, and the plural noun *books* can be represented as follows:

(8) $[[\text{song}]_N [\text{book}]_N]_N$

$[[\text{sing}]_V \text{er}]_N$

$[[\text{book}]_N \text{s}]_N$

It is obvious that in the case of non-concatenative morphology it is not possible to represent the structure of a word in terms of a sequence of morphemes. For instance, the structure of *smog* can be represented linearly as *sm-og*, but these two constituents are not morphemes. The structure of this word can be represented by a non-linear representation of the following type:

```
(9)  s  məu k
     |  |
     C C V C
         | |
       f o g
```

This representation indicates how the abstract CCVC skeleton of the word *smog* is 'fleshed out' by sound segments of the words *smoke* and *fog*.

9.2 Morphological classification

Languages may be classified according to the role and nature of their morphology (Comrie 1981; Haspelmath 2009). A first dimension is the index of synthesis: languages that do not make use of morphology are called analytic or isolating, languages with a lot of morphology are called synthetic. Languages may be ranked on an index of synthesis. Traditionally, Chinese is referred to as an isolating language because it has no, or almost no inflection. However, there is no doubt that word formation, in particular compounding, is very productive in this language (Packard 2000). Hence, Chinese is not analytic in an absolute sense.

The second index on which languages can be ranked is that of polysynthesis: some languages allow the incorporation of lexical morphemes, leading to relatively complex words, as illustrated by the following one-word-sentence of Central Alaskan Yup'ik in which the lexical morpheme *tuntu* 'moose' is incorporated in the verb *te* 'to catch' (Mithun 2000: 923):

(10) tuntutuq=gguq

tuntu-te-u-q=gguq

moose-catch-INDICATIVE.INTRANSITIVE-3SINGULAR=HEARSAY

'He got a moose'

In this example, the complex word is followed by a clitic morpheme ('=' is the symbol for the link between a host word and a clitic) of evidentiality that indicates the nature of the information source.

The third dimension of classification is the index of fusion. In fusional languages, one morpheme may express more than one grammatical feature. Dutch is an example of such a language. For instance, in (3), the inflectional suffix *-te* expresses both 'past tense' and 'singular number'. Fusional languages differ from agglutinating languages in which each bound morpheme corresponds with one grammatical feature. Turkish is the textbook example of an agglutinating language. For instance, case and number in Turkish are expressed by different suffixes:

(11) çocuk-lar-ın
child-PLURAL-GENITIVE
'of the children'

These three indices of morphological complexity are useful in giving a global characterization of the morphology of a language. One should be aware, however, that languages are not homogeneous with respect to these indices. For instance, many Indo-European languages are fusional in their inflectional system but agglutinating in their derivational morphology. Chinese also illustrates this point since it is synthetic as far as word formation is concerned but analytic with regard to inflection, since the language has no inflection.

9.3 Morpheme order and hierarchical structure

A basic question in the analysis of the structure of complex words is what determines the order of its constituent morphemes.

A first principle is that the order of morphemes reflects the order of morphological derivation and its semantics. In the word *acceptability*, the suffix *-ity* is at the right edge because this word means 'the property of being acceptable'. This suffix takes adjectives as base words and forms nouns from them. In its turn, *acceptable* is formed by adding the suffix *-able* to *accept*, with the meaning 'can be accepted'. The suffix *-able* takes verbs as bases to create adjectives. Thus, the following hierarchical word structure can be proposed, which also implies a specific linear order of the morphemes involved:

(12) $[[[\text{accept}]_V\ \text{able}]_A\ \text{ity}]_N$

At the same time, this hierarchical structure will determine the way in which this complex word is assigned its meaning.

A second principle that governs the order of morphemes is that inflectional morphemes are usually peripheral to derivational morphemes, this being one of the universals proposed by Greenberg (1963). This is exemplified by the word *workers*, in which the derivational morpheme *-er* precedes the plural suffix *-s*.

Within the domain of inflection there are also principles for the order of morphemes. Consider the following inflected form of the Italian verb *temere* 'to fear'

(13) tem-e-va-no 'they feared'

In this verb form the stem *tem* 'to fear' is followed by a so-called thematic vowel *-e-*, then by the suffix *-va-* which expresses past imperfective, and finally by the suffix *-no* which expresses third person plural. This form conforms to the following general schema:

(14) [base—thematic vowel]$_{\text{stem}}$—inherent inflection—contextual inflection

The stem of a word is what remains of a word after removal of the inflectional elements. Contextual inflection is the type of inflection dictated by syntax, such as case marking on nouns and adjectives in specific syntactic configurations, and person and number marking on verbs in languages with subject–verb agreement. In example (13), the morpheme *-va-* expresses inherent inflection (past imperfective) while the morpheme *-no* is a case of contextual inflection, as it may be required by the presence of a third person plural subject. The base may consist of a root followed by a thematic vowel, as is the case in *temevano*, but it may also be complex itself. That is, the stem may contain derivational prefixes and/or suffixes.

The schema in (14) is an instantiation of the more general tendency of contextual inflection to be peripheral to inherent inflection (Booij 1996). This applies to nouns. For instance, in inflected nouns case marking (a case of contextual inflection) is peripheral to plural marking (a case of inherent inflection), as in the inflected Turkish noun in (11) where the plural suffix indeed precedes the case suffix.

Languages may also exhibit 'position class morphology'. This means that they have complex words in which the order of the morphemes is determined by a template with a number of slots. Morphemes are then specified for their ability to appear in a particular slot. For instance, in Nimboran, a Papuan language of New Guinea, each finite verb contains a number of morphemes, including the root. There are eight positions, with the root appearing in position 0. The morpheme for 'plural subject' has to appear in slot 1, immediately after the root (slot 0), whereas the morpheme for 'person of subject' has to appear in slot 8, preceded by the morpheme for tense in slot 7 (Inkelas 1993).

In Kimatuumbi, a Bantu language spoken in Tanzania, the verb may be assigned a hierarchical structure of the following type (Odden 1996: 71), where the positions for specific morphemes are specified.

(15) [(relative) [subject [object [[root—suffix]$_{\text{derivational stem}}$ final vowel]$_{\text{inflected stem}}$]]]

This structure is exemplified by the following verb form:

(16) cha-ba-nį-telek-ey-a
what-they-me-cook-CAUSATIVE-FINAL VOWEL
'what they make me cook'

In compounds the order of the lexemes depends on which lexeme is the head, if there is one (these are so-called endocentric compounds). In Germanic languages, the head of a compound is its rightmost constituent, a regularity often referred to as the Right-hand Head Rule (Williams 1981). It is this constituent that determines word class and subclasses such as gender, etc. Compare the following minimal pairs of compounds in Dutch:

(17) a. koor 'choir, neuter gender', zang 'song, common gender'
koor-zang 'lit. choir-song, choral singing' (common gender)
zang-koor 'lit. song-choir, choir' (neuter gender)
b. water 'water, neuter gender', tafel 'table, common gender'
water-tafel 'water table, common gender'
tafel-water 'table-water, neuter gender'

These data show that in these Dutch compounds the head is on the right. *Tafel-water* is a type of water, not a type of table, and it has neuter gender, just like its right constituent word *water*.

In compound schemas, the order of the elements is part of the definition of the schema, and thus defines the order of the compound's constituents. For instance, Romance languages such as Italian have compounds for agents and instruments in which the verb (V) precedes the noun (N):

(18) lava-piatti 'lit. wash-dishes, dish washer'
spazza-camino 'lit. sweep-chimney, chimney sweeper'

It is the order V–N that is essential for evoking this agent/instrument interpretation.

9.4 Meaningless elements in word structure

Complex words may contain building blocks that do not contribute to the meaning of the complex words but are just there for creating a particular morphological form. An example is the occurrence of thematic vowels in verbal forms, exemplified in (9) above. The thematic vowel *e* of the verb *temere* 'to fear' has no meaning contribution of its own.

It does, though, define a conjugation class, as not all verbs of Italian have the same thematic vowel. Most verbs have *a*, others have *e* or *i*.

In compounds, the constituents may be linked by an element without a meaning of its own. For instance, Greek compounds have a linking element *-o-*:

(19) gloss-o-logos 'language-LINK-student, linguist'
pag-o-vuno 'ice-LINK-mountain, iceberg'

Such linking elements are also referred to as empty morphs or interfixes. The Slavic language Polish makes use of such interfixes both in compounding and derivation. In compounds, the default linking element is the vowel *o*, as in the following.

(20) gwiazd-o-zbiór 'star-LINK-collection, star constellation'
star-o-druk 'old-LINK-print, antique book'

In the domain of derivation, the suffix *-ski* that is used to derive adjectives from nouns (*student* 'student'—*student-ski* 'student-like'), is often preceded by an interfix *-ow-*, as in the following denominal adjectives with the meaning 'related to N' (Szymanek 2010: 253):

(21) kat 'hangman' kat-ow-ski
szpieg 'spy' szpieg-ow-ski
tchórz 'coward' tchórz-ow-ski

These data show that word structure may comprise building blocks with a purely formal role.

Words may also show an internal formal structure without a correlating semantic structure. English has many prefixed verbs with a Latinate root, such as:

(22) con-ceive, de-ceive, per-ceive, re-ceive,
de-duce, in-duce, re-duce, se-duce

The roots *ceive* and *duce* do not have a meaning of their own. Yet these roots have specific properties. In particular, the nominalized form of all verbs in *-ceive* ends in *-ception*, and the nominalized form of all verbs in *-duce* ends in *-duction*. These generalizations can only be made if the formal internal structure of these verbs is recognized.

Complex words may lose their internal semantic structure due to the loss of the base word. For instance, Dutch has many verbs with a prefix followed by a root that once was a verb but has since disappeared as a verb on its own:

(23) *prefixed verb* *past participle*
be-gin 'to begin' be-gonnen / *ge-be-gonn-en
ge-niet 'to enjoy' ge-noten / *ge-ge-not-en
ont-beer 'to miss' ont-beer-d / *ge-ont-beer-d
ver-geet 'to forget' ver-get-en / *ge-ver-get-en

We have to assign internal morphological structure to these Dutch verbs since they behave as prefixed verbs. In Dutch, past participles are formed from the stem by means of prefixation with *ge-* and simultaneous suffixation with *-t/-d* or *-en*, as in *ge-werk-t* 'worked' and *ge-slap-en* 'slept'. However, when the verb is prefixed, the prefix *ge-* has to be omitted:

(24)	*simplex verb*	*participle*	*prefixed verb*	*participle*
	slaap 'sleep'	ge-slap-en	be-slaap 'sleep on'	be-slap-en
			ver-slaap 'oversleep'	ver-slap-en
	neem 'take'	ge-nom-en	ont-neem 'take away'	ont-nom-en
			ver-neem 'hear'	ver-nomen

These facts also show that word-internal morphological structure may be relevant for the application of morphological rules. If the syllable *ver-* is a prefix, there is no prefix *ge-* in the past participle, but if *ver-* is just a syllable, as in the Dutch verb *verbaliseer* 'to fine', the past participle is *ge-verbaliseer-d*, not **verbaliseer-d*.

In the case of verbs such as those listed in (22–23) we speak of 'formally complex words'. Words may also be partially motivated from a semantic point of view. In the English word *cranberry* we recognize the word *berry*, but we do not know what *cran* means. However, because a cranberry is a type of berry, we have to consider *cranberry* a compound. Many words end in a recognizable suffix but the part before the suffix has no meaning of its own. This applies to many words in *-ism*:

(25) altru-ism, aut-ism, bapt-ism, pacif-ism, solips-ism

There are no base words *altru, aut, bapt, pacif,* and *solips*. However, we can tell from the fact that the words in (25) end in *-ism* that they are nouns with meanings such as 'predisposition, activity, ideology'. This internal structure can also be seen when we derive corresponding person-denoting nouns in *-ist* denoting. Here, *-ism* is replaced with the suffix *-ist*:

(26) altru-ist, aut-ist, bapt-ist, pacif-ist, solips-ist

These facts show that words may exhibit a formal internal structure without a completely corresponding semantic structure.

9.5 Word structure and semantic interpretation

The classic principle of compositionality states that the meaning of a complex linguistic expression is a compositional function of the meaning of its constituent words and the manner of their combination. The interpretation of the word *acceptability* mentioned in Section 9.3, 'the property of being acceptable', is a clear illustration of this principle. In the case of the right-headed compounds of Dutch, also discussed in Section 9.3, we saw the role of hierarchical structure: it is the head that determines primarily which concept is denoted by the compound as a whole.

The Italian VN compounds in (18) are called exocentric, because they do not have a head. The constituent lexemes contribute to the meaning, but the agent or instrument meaning is not expressed by a morpheme. This meaning component is a property of the morphological construction as a whole.

Holistic properties of complex words can also be observed for the class of so-called co-compounds, in which two words are coordinated into a compound. In some cases, the meaning of the compound is a hyperonym of the meanings of the constituent lexemes. Here are some examples from Lezgian (Haspelmath 1993: 108):

(27) biba-dide 'father-mother, parents'
xeb-mal 'sheep-cattle, domestic animals'

It is the coordination construction that evokes the hyperonym interpretation.

Reduplication is interesting from the semantic point of view because it is the prototypical example of the role of iconicity (meaning as a direct reflection of form) at the level of the word: the formal repetition of the base word may indicate a repetition of its meaning, that is 'increase'. Hence, a reduplicated noun may indicate plurality, a reduplicated verb that the action denoted by the base verb takes place intensively or iteratively, and a reduplicated adjective may indicate a high degree of the property expressed by the base adjective (see the examples in (5)). This illustrates once more that meaning components of complex words may arise from the morphological construction as such. Note, however, that the meaning of reduplication is not always that of plurality or intensity. In the reduplicated form of the Begak verb *panow* 'to go', the verb *panow-panow* 'to go a little bit' in (5), the meaning contribution of the reduplication pattern is that of diminishment. Hence, other types of meaning than 'increase' may be linked to the reduplication construction.

A second challenge for the compositionality principle as the sole principle for constructing the meanings of complex words is the phenomenon of conversion, the change of words to another word class without the addition of overt morphological material. In English, nouns can be converted to verbs without adding an affix, as is illustrated by the following sentences in which the recently coined verbs *to virus, to transition*, and *to friend* are used:

(28) I keep getting a message saying my computer is virused.
He is transitioning to a new job.
Do you get offended when someone won't friend you on Facebook?

Although it is easy to reconstruct the meaning of these verbs on the basis of the meaning of the corresponding nouns, there is an additional meaning component 'to perform an action related to the base noun' which is not marked by a morpheme, but only by the change of word class. Moreover, the exact nature of the relation between the noun and the kind of action has to be determined on the basis of context or conceptual knowledge. Conversion may be qualified as a type of paradigmatic word formation, since the meaning of the verb is to be defined with reference to the meaning of the corresponding noun (the term 'paradigm' is used to denote systematic relationships between words in the lexicon of a language). One may 'translate' this paradigmatic relation into a syntagmatic structure, by assuming conversion constructions such as the following for English (Booij 2010):

(29) $[[x]_{Ni}]_{Vj}$ 'action V_j related to N_i'

In other cases of paradigmatic word formation, such a structural interpretation is not available; we then have to make explicit reference to the paradigmatic relationship between the two sets of words in order to express the relationship between form and meaning. Consider the following Dutch word pairs (Booij 2010: 34):

(30)

verb	*noun*
alloc-eer 'to allocate'	alloc-atie 'allocation'
communic-eer 'to communicate'	communic-atie 'communication'
reden-eer 'to reason'	reden-atie 'reasoning'
stabil-is-eer 'to stabilize'	stabilis-atie 'stabilization'

The nouns in *-atie* '-ation' are semantically the nominalizations of the verbs on the left, just like their English counterparts. Yet, the part before *-atie* is not identical to the corresponding verb, which has an additional morpheme *-eer*. This mismatch between form and meaning is due to the historical fact that the inflectional ending *-er* of French infinitives has been reinterpreted in Dutch as a derivational suffix *-eer*. In combination with the massive borrowing of the corresponding nouns in *-atie*, this led to the following productive paradigmatic pattern, where the symbol ≈ stands for 'paradigmatically related to', the angled brackets demarcate a morphological schema, and the double arrow stands for the relationship between form and meaning (SEM):

(31) $< [x\text{-eer}]_{Vi} \leftrightarrow [SEM]_i > \approx < [x\text{-atie}]_{Nj} \leftrightarrow [\text{action of } SEM_i]_j >$

New Dutch nouns in *-atie* can readily be formed on the basis of verbs in *-eer*. For instance, now that the verb *implement-eer* 'to implement' has been coined, the corresponding noun *implement-atie* 'implementation' is the derived nominal.

Mismatch between form and meaning may also be due to the fact that a constituent of a complex word has a different semantic scope from what we would expect given its structure. This is illustrated by the following complex adjectives of Dutch

(32)	a.	tak 'branch'	ge-tak-t 'branched'
		spits 'point'	ge-spits-t 'pointed'
	b.	rok 'skirt'	kort-ge-rok-t 'short-skirted'
		jas 'coat'	wit-ge-jas-t 'white-coated'
		schouder 'shoulder'	breed-ge-schouder-d 'broad-shouldered'

Denominal adjectives can be formed with a prefix *-ge* and the simultaneous attachment of the suffix *t/d*, as shown in (32a). These complex adjectives can function as the head of an adjectival compound of the type Adjective + Adjective. However, the modifier adjective does not modify its adjectival head as a whole, but only its nominal base part. For instance, *kortgerokt* does not mean 'skirted in a short manner' but 'dressed in a short skirt'. Hence, the semantic scope of the modifier is more restricted than the structure of the AA-compounds would lead us to expect. This restricted semantic scope is a property of this type of AA-compounds as a whole. Similar examples from English are the lexical units *criminal lawyer* and *atomic physicist*, where the adjectives do not modify the meaning of the whole noun, but only of a subpart if it. Thus, a criminal lawyer is one who practises criminal law, rather than a lawyer who commits crimes.

In sum, even though the structure of complex words is necessary for computing their meaning, there are a number of complications in the relationship between the morphological structure and the semantic structure of complex words, which require us to specify holistic semantic properties of complex words.

9.6 Word structure and the interface with phonology

The structure of complex words is not only important for computing their meaning, but also for computing their phonological structure and properties. The systematic relationship between two different levels of linguistic structure is referred to as an interface. Whereas Section 9.5 discussed the interface between morphological form and semantic structure, this section focuses on the way that morphological structure determines the way in which the constituent morphemes of a complex word are realized phonetically. This type of interface is an important topic of research in phonology.

A first illustration of this interface is the assignment of stress patterns to complex words. In Dutch compounds, main stress falls on the first constituent, while secondary stress falls on the second constituent:

(33) a. kóor-zàng 'lit. choir-song, choral singing'
záng-kòor 'lit. song-choir, choir
b. wáter-tàfel 'water table'
táfel-wàter 'table-water'

A similar rule applies to English (the so-called Compound Stress Rule), but in some types of English compounds the second constituent carries main stress: compare *Bráttle Street* with *Massachusetts Ávenue.* In the words in (33a), two consecutive syllables carry stress, thus creating a so-called stress clash; simplex words in Dutch, on the other hand, exhibit a regular rhythmic alternation between stressed and unstressed syllables. The stress clash is due to the fact that each compound constituent is a phonological word of its own (cf. Chapter 7) and hence a separate domain of stress assignment. In other words, the presence of morphological structure is essential in explaining why two consecutive syllables of a word can be stressed.

Affixes may also play a crucial role in computing the location of the main stress of a word. For instance, English nouns in *-ity* require the main stress of the word to fall on the last syllable before the suffix:

(34) superfícial superficiálity
fúnctional functionálity

Languages differ in the extent to which morphological structure plays a role in stress assignment. For instance, in Polish the presence of suffixes has no influence on the location of the main stress: both simplex and suffixed words carry main stress on the penultimate syllable. On the other hand, in Polish compound words, each part functions as a separate stress domain.

Word structure also plays a role in the way in which a word is divided into syllables. In Germanic languages, the morphological boundary between the constituents of a compound usually coincides with a syllable boundary, because each of these constituents corresponds with a separate phonological word. On the other hand, the morphological boundary before vowel-initial suffixes is ignored in syllabification. The contrast is illustrated by the syllabification of the suffixed words *walker* and *walking* versus the compound word *walk-in* (as in *walk-in wardrobe*) (where σ denotes a syllable):

(35) walk-er (wɔː)$_{\sigma}$(kər)$_{\sigma}$
walk-ing (wɔː)$_{\sigma}$(kɪŋ)$_{\sigma}$
walk-in (wɔːk)$_{\sigma}$(ɪn)$_{\sigma}$

In this respect, prefixes often differ from suffixes. In English, the morphological boundary after *un-* coincides with a syllable boundary. For instance, in *un-able*, the syllabification in careful speech is $(un)_\sigma(a)_\sigma(ble)_\sigma$ rather than $(u)_\sigma(na)_\sigma(ble)_\sigma$, even though in simplex words the C in a VCV sequence always forms a syllable with the following V. In *un-natural* the prefix *un-* also preserves word-like properties in that *unnatural* may be spoken with a lengthened, geminate [nː], which we do not find in simplex words.

A third domain of phonology where word structure plays a role is that of allomorphy: morphemes may have different phonetic shapes co-varying with their appearance as independent words or as parts of complex words. Consider the following set of related words:

(36)	sane	sanity
	opaque	opacity

The letter *a* stands for the tense vowel [eɪ] in the adjectives and for the lax vowel [æ] in the corresponding de-adjectival nouns. This kind of alternation does not apply, however, to all words with this suffix; witness a noun like *obesity* where the vowel of the second syllable is the tense vowel [iː] rather than the short vowel [ɛ] (compare the vowel qualities in *serene* and *serenity*).

Allomorphy may be triggered by specific morphemes. In English, the nasal consonant of the Latinate prefixes *in-* and *con-* may change according to the sound at the beginning of the following morpheme.

(37) in-adequate, im-potent, in-tact, i[ŋ]-competent, il-logical, ir-rational
com-petent, con-tact, co[ŋ]-gress, col-league, cor-relation

This assimilation process does not apply to other morphemes ending in /n/. For instance, the nasal consonant of *un-* in *unless* is not pronounced as [l].

A different type of allomorphy is the alternation between voiced and voiceless stops and fricatives at the end of morphemes in Dutch and German. The rule is that these consonants are realized as voiceless at the end of a syllable. Here are some examples from German (the dot indicates a syllable boundary):

(38)	Bund [bunt] 'union'	Bund-e [bundə] 'unions'	syllables: bun.də
	Sarg [sɑrk] 'coffin'	Särg-e [sɛrgə] 'coffins'	syllables: sɛr.gə

In this case, morphological structure has an indirect effect only. Due to the addition of the plural morpheme *-e* [ə] the final consonant of the stem morpheme appears in the onset of the second syllable. Hence, it is no longer syllable-final and will therefore not be devoiced.

9.7 Loss of word-internal structure

Complex words, once formed and stored in lexical memory, may lose their semantic transparency, because the meaning of the word as a whole has become idiosyncratic and is no longer fully derivable from the meanings of its constituents. This may also lead to phonological change. Classic examples are the faded compounds *lord* and *lady* that derive historically from the old English compounds *hlāf-weard* 'bread-warden' and *hlāf-dige* 'bread-kneader'.

One cause of this loss of motivation is that one of the constituent parts is no longer a word by itself. This can be seen in the names of the days such as *Tuesday* and *Wednesday*, where only the part *day* is recognizable. *Tues-* derives from *Tiwes*, the genitive form of *Tiw*, the name of a god of war and law, and *Wednes-* derives from the genitive form of the Germanic god *Wodan*. And a *holi-day* is no longer a *holy-day*. In the Dutch word *barn-steen* and its German equivalent *Bern-stein*, both meaning 'amber', the second part is recognized as the regular word for 'stone', but there is no recognizable morpheme *barn/bern*. This constituent derives historically from the verb *bern* 'to burn' which no longer exists in these languages.

The phonological form of a demotivated compound may change into the canonical form of a simplex word. For instance, *gospel* (< *god-spell* 'good message') has lost the /d/, since /ds/ is not a regular word-medial consonant cluster in English simplex words, while the canonical vowel in the second syllable of a simplex word is [ə]. In certain varieties of Dutch, the still existing standard Dutch compound *boom-gaard* 'lit. tree-garden, orchard' has acquired the canonical phonetic form of a simplex word (two syllables, the first stressed, the second with [ə]). Hence the word *boomgaard* [bóːmɣàːrt] has changed into *bongerd* [bɔ́ərt].

Loss of transparency can also be seen in the way in which a word is syllabified. For instance, although Dutch still has the words *voort* 'forth' and *aan* 'on', the compound *voortaan* has the meaning 'from now on', in which the two constituents are no longer recognized. Hence, this word is syllabified as (voːr)$_{\sigma}$ (taːn)$_{\sigma}$, not as (voːrt)$_{\sigma}$ (aːn)$_{\sigma}$, as would be expected if it were still recognized as a compound.

In sum, complex words, once formed, may be subject to a process of demotivation and lose their morphological structure. The cause of this loss is semantic in origin, but it may have effects on phonological form as well, since demotivation moves the phonetic forms of words in the direction of the canonical phonological forms of simplex words.

9.8 Univerbation and grammaticalization

Morphological processes such as compounding and derivation are the main sources of complex words in a language. However, there is a second source, the historical process by which a sequence of words, often a phrase, becomes tighter, and behaves (and is usually written) as one word. This process is referred to as univerbation. An example from English is the word *notwithstanding*, which derives historically from the word *not* and the participle *withstanding*. In modern English it counts as a single word, namely, as a preposition, as in the prepositional phrase *notwithstanding his request* (compare the ungrammatical *withstanding his request*). Further examples are the conjunction *because* from Middle-English *bi* + *cause* 'by cause of', parallel to French *par cause* 'by cause of', and the compound *handful* from *hand* + *full*, as in *a handful of eggs*, in which *handful* refers to a quantity, not to what is (literally) contained in a hand.

When a univerbated word sequence becomes the model for a class of words, univerbation leads to the rise of a morphological process. A famous example is the rise of the adverbial suffix *-ment(e)* in various Romance languages. It derives from the ablative form of the Latin noun *mens* 'mind'. For instance, *clara mente* (two words) meant 'with a clear mind'; interpreted as one word, it became the adverb *claramente* 'in a clear manner'. This and similar words could then function as models for new deadjectival adverbs in *-mente*. The historical origin can still be observed in the fact that *-mente* takes the feminine form of adjectives as stem form since Latin *mens* is a feminine noun, as in Italian *chiar-a-mente* and French *clair-e-ment* in which the stem forms *chiar-a* and *clair-e* have a feminine ending.

An important difference between word formation and univerbation is that the output words of word formation always belong to the class of lexical words: nouns, verbs, adjectives, and adverbs, whereas univerbation may lead to the expansion of classes of grammatical (or function) words. For instance, *notwithstanding* is a preposition and *because* is a conjunction.

A second source of grammatical words with word-internal structure is the process of grammaticalization. This is the process in which words of lexical classes become grammatical words within specific syntactic constructions, or grammatical words develop into even more grammatical words (Hopper and Traugott 2003). An example is the reinterpretation of past participles in participial clauses as prepositions, as illustrated by the use of *given* in *given this situation*. Dutch has many prepositions with the form of present or past participles that now function as prepositions:

(39) *present participles > prepositions*
ge-dur-end-e 'lit. lasting, during'
staan-d-e 'lit. standing, during'
niet-tegen-staan-de 'not-with-stand-ing

past participles > prepositions
ge-gev-en 'given'
ge-zien 'lit. seen, because of'
uit-ge-zonder-d 'out-PREF-separate-SUFF, with the exception of'

In conclusion, univerbation may lead to new complex words, including words belonging to grammatical classes. The process of grammaticalization may lead to the expansion of sets of grammatical words with word-internal structure. Therefore, we should not conceive of morphological processes as the only source of complex words.

9.9 Suggestions for further reading

Recent introductions to the study of word structure are Booij (2012) and Haspelmath and Sims (2010). Handbooks of morphology are Booij et al. (2000, 2004) and Spencer and Zwicky (1998). A handbook on compounding is Lieber and Štekauer (2009) and a typological survey of word formation can be found in Štekauer et al. (2012).

Information on the morphology of the world's languages is provided in Haspelmath et al. (2005), which can also be consulted on line: [http://wals.info/]. The standard glossing rules for word-internal structure, the Leipzig glossing rules, are available at [http://www.eva.mpg.de/lingua/resources/glossing-rules.php].

The interface between morphology and phonology is the topic of Volume 4 of Van Oostendorp et al. (2011).

The lexicalization and grammaticalization of complex words are discussed in Hopper and Traugott (2003), Brinton and Traugott (2005), and in Narrog and Heine (2011).

CHAPTER 10

WORD CATEGORIES

MARK C. SMITH

10.1 Introduction

Words are often grouped into lexical categories ('parts of speech') on the basis of the types of entities that they denote. Thus, words may be grouped into a category of nouns if they denote things (e.g. *tomato, basket, piano*), a category of verbs if they denote events (e.g. *sing, run, eat*), a category of adjectives if they denote properties of things denoted by nouns (e.g. *red, hairy, loud*), and so on. In the Western linguistic tradition, this view of lexical categories has its roots in the Latin grammars of Priscian and Donatus and, ultimately, in the philosophy of Plato and Aristotle (Harris and Taylor 1997; Seuren 1998). However, modern linguists have repeatedly challenged this view. In particular, they have observed that any given lexical category is liable to contain members that fail to denote the type of entity associated with the category (Baker 2003; Carstairs-McCarthy 1999). While many nouns do denote things (e.g. *basket*), some denote events (e.g. *explosion*), and some denote properties (e.g. *goodness*). In other cases, the matter is unclear. In the following examples, the adjectives *impossible* and *normal* have been used as nouns.

(1) a. There's no point trying to achieve the impossible.
    b. Is economic stagnation the new normal?

It is by no means obvious whether these words denote things or properties, some combination of the two, or something else entirely.

The difficulty is compounded by the fact that some words don't seem to denote anything at all. In example (2), *that* is a type of word commonly termed a complementizer.

(2) John remembered that the plants needed watering.

As with other complementizers, such as *if* and *whether, that* has the grammatical function of marking out a subordinate clause (*the plants needed watering*) and signalling that it forms a part of the main clause (*John remembered*). The word *the* in this sentence is a type of word known as a determiner. Like *that*, it can hardly be said to denote anything at all. Instead, like other determiners (*a, this, some*, etc.), it indicates whether the object denoted by the following noun is definite or not. Thus, in (2), *the* suggests that John is thinking about a definite or specific set of plants in contrast to the following example which suggests that he is thinking about plants in general:

(3) John remembered that plants needed watering.

As a final example, consider the following sentences:

(4) a. Mike's a hell of a cook!
b. What the hell is Dave doing that for?

Here, the noun *hell* does not denote hell. Rather, it combines with a determiner to form a noun phrase that conveys the attitude of the speaker. Thus, *a hell (of)* in (4a) suggests the speaker's admiration for Mike's ability as a cook, while *the hell* in (4b) indicates the speaker's contempt for Dave's behaviour. While some words, then, can be defined in terms of the types of entity that they denote, other words do not denote entities at all and must be defined in other terms, such as their grammatical function, abstract features such as definiteness, and the attitude of the speaker.

As well as grouping words into lexical categories, linguists often group the words within a given lexical category into a number of subcategories. Typically, the words within one subcategory will exhibit properties that are to some extent distinct from the properties of the words in other subcategories. Consider, for instance, interjections in English. According to Huddleston et al. (2002: 1361), the interjection category consists of 'words that do not combine with other words in integrated syntactic constructions'. This lack of syntactic integration is most clearly demonstrated when interjections occur on their own as single word utterances (*Damn!, Ouch!, Oops!, Shh!*). Even when they occur as part of a longer utterance, they tend to precede a sentence rather than forming an integral part of it, or they are quoted in the form of distinct one-word utterances:

(5) a. Damn! We've missed the bus again!
b. 'Oi!' yelled the police officer.
c. They all went 'Shh'.

In English, the interjection category contains a subcategory of ideophones. These are words such as *splash* and *bang* whose sound directly symbolizes their meaning (see Childs, this volume). The interjection category also contains a subcategory of expletive words such as *blast* and *damn*. These are typically derived from verbs and, as a result, they can occur with noun phrases in syntactically integrated utterances just as verbs can (Huddleston et al. 2002: 1361):

(6) Damn these mosquitoes!

Other interjections cannot be grouped into either of these subcategories (*ugh, oh, wow, oops, hey, ah, eh*, etc.). However, they resemble the interjections in the two subcategories insofar as they primarily function to express the mood of the speaker and often occur as syntactically unintegrated, one-word utterances.

Words can also be grouped into so-called mixed categories. These generally contain words that cannot easily be accommodated in standard lexical categories because they exhibit properties associated with two or more categories. In example (7):

(7) an amusing anecdote

the word *amusing* is like an adjective both because it denotes a property of an object denoted by a noun and because it immediately precedes a noun. At the same time, it is verb-like in that it is derived from the verb *amuse* and has the *-ing* suffix commonly found with verbs. As such, *amusing* is a typical member of the participle category whose members exhibit a mixture of adjectival and verbal properties.

Linguists also make use of ad hoc categories in order to capture the fact that particular words from different lexical categories have certain idiosyncratic properties in common. Consider the italicized words in the following example:

(8) a. What *ever* did you do that for? (adverb)
b. What *the hell* did you do that for? (noun phrase)
c. What *on earth* did you do that for? (prepositional phrase)

In these sentences, the italicized words modify the interrogative pronoun *what* and express the angry or incredulous mood of the speaker. Because they have these properties in common, Huddleston (2002: 916) groups them together into a lexical category he terms 'emotive modifiers'. At the same time, he recognizes that they can also be described as belonging to a wide range of other categories, such as adverb, noun phrase, and prepositional phrase. Similarly, Pullum and Huddleston (2002a: 823–8) postulate an ad hoc category they term 'negatively-oriented polarity-sensitive items' (or NPIs for short). The members of this category all prefer to occur in sentences with a negative meaning. For instance, Sinclair (2004) analysed the thirty occurrences of the verb *budge* in a corpus of 20 million words and found that the word always occurs in sentences denoting a failure to move, as in the following:

(9) a. But Mr Volcker has yet to budge ...
b. ... but he refuses to budge on design principles he knows to be ...
c. I determined not to budge from it until closing time.

There were no examples such as the following in Sinclair's corpus:

(10) I pushed it and it budged.

Similarly, Taylor (2012: 60) observes that the NPI (and quantifying phrase) *much of* can only occur in negative sentences when it functions to evaluate the object denoted by the following noun:

(11) a. I'm not much of a cook.
b. *I'm much of a cook.
c. They don't think I'm much of a cook.
d. *They think I'm much of a cook.

The NPI category is a typical ad hoc category in that it groups together words and phrases from a wide range of different lexical categories all of which exhibit an idiosyncratic property not associated with other lexical categories.

It is also the case that lexical categories can be grouped into larger supercategories. For instance, a distinction is often made between content word categories (e.g. nouns, verbs, adjectives, adverbs), whose members denote types of entities, and function word categories (e.g. determiners, complementizers, prepositions), whose members have a primarily grammatical rather than semantic function. However, there are a number of problematic examples which suggest that it is difficult to draw a clear distinction between the two supercategories. It has often been observed that some content word categories contain function words. Consider the following sentences from Leech and Li (1995: 190):

(12) a. ... the question would seem to be a legitimate *one* ...
b. He looked a mournful *man*.
c. 'I became a political *being* for the first time in my life,' she said.

The italicized nouns provide little new semantic information. Instead, the semantic information is given primarily by the adjective modifying the noun. Rather than having a semantic function, the noun's role is mainly grammatical—it supplies the obligatory head noun required by noun phrases in English. In this way, 'dummy nouns' are examples of function words that belong in a content word category, namely the noun category. A further problem is that some function word categories contain content words. The preposition category is often regarded as a function word category (see e.g. Chomsky, 1995) but most of its members are clearly semantic insofar as they can denote temporal and spatial relations (e.g. *during, after, between*). Moreover, certain prepositions are content words in some contexts and function words in others (Hudson 2000). In (13a), *by* has a spatial meaning, comparable to that of phrases such as *next to* or *in proximity to*. In contrast, in (13b), *by* has the grammatical function of marking the attacker as the agent of the activity.

(13) a. Dave stood by the fire.
b. Sue was being pursued by her attacker.

Such observations cast doubt over whether a clear distinction can be maintained between content word categories and function word categories.

In contemporary linguistics, lexical categories underpin a view of language that has been variously labelled the 'slot and filler model' (Sinclair 1991: 109) and the 'dictionary plus grammar model' (Taylor 2012: 44). According to this view, lexical categories enable words to be combined into phrases and sentences on the basis of a set of grammatical rules. A grammatical rule might stipulate that a determiner (e.g. *the*), an adjective (e.g. *sleepy*), and a noun (e.g. *cat*) can be combined together into a noun phrase (*the sleepy cat*). Another rule might stipulate that a noun phrase (e.g. *the sleepy cat*) and a verb phrase (e.g. *yawned*) can be combined together into a sentence (*The sleepy cat yawned*). Basing grammatical rules around lexical categories in this way allows the number of grammatical rules that make up a grammar to be greatly reduced. If English words can be grouped into eight or nine lexical categories, as proposed by e.g. Aarts (2007) and Huddleston and Pullum (1984), this implies that a grammar of English need only comprise eight or nine sets of rules, one for each category, in order to be able to describe the grammatical behaviour of all of the words in all of its lexical categories. If, however, English words cannot be grouped into lexical categories, then the grammar would need to comprise a distinct set of rules for each of the hundreds of thousands of words in the language in order to be able to describe their grammatical behaviour. In this way, lexical categories make possible a simple and elegant description of how words combine into phrases and sentences. Without lexical categories, grammar would become hopelessly complex and chaotic.

Yet while lexical categories are of fundamental importance in grammar, much recent work has argued that they are highly problematic. In particular, these studies have suggested that the grammatical behaviour of words is far too complex to be captured by the properties associated with lexical categories (Croft 2001; Crystal 1967/2004; Culicover 1999; Francis 1993; Gross 1994; Sinclair 1991, 2004; Taylor 2012). They have also argued that determining the lexical categories of a language and the properties associated with them is inevitably a highly arbitrary process (Croft 2001; Plank 1984; Smith 2010, 2011). The remainder of this chapter gives an overview of this recent critical work. It concludes that there are a number of deep and intractable problems associated with lexical categories, and that lexical categories fail to provide an adequate description of the grammatical behaviour of words.

10.2 Subsective and intersective gradience in categories

It is rarely the case that all the words in a lexical category will exhibit all the properties associated with that category. Indeed, it is rarely the case that all the words within a category will share even a single property. Consider, for instance, adjectives in English. Properties associated with the category include the ability to occur in prenominal and predicative positions, the ability to take the prefix *un-*, and the ability to be intensified and graded (Aarts 2007).

(14) a. a happy woman (prenominal position)
b. She is happy (predicative position)
c. very happy (intensification)
d. happy/happier/happiest (gradedness)
e. unhappy (*un*-prefixation)

Many adjectives are unlike *happy* in that they do not exhibit all of these properties. Table 10.1 is adapted from Aarts (2007: table 8.2).

In Table 10.1, there is no single property which is exhibited by all six adjectives. Moreover, even a word such as *happy*, which displays all five of the listed properties, does not exhibit all the properties associated with English adjectives. For example, as Ferris (1993) notes, *happy* generally does not occur postnominally (e.g. **the winner happy*) in contrast to adjectives such as *galore* which do (e.g. *restaurants galore*; also *for reasons unknown, the body beautiful*). This tendency for the words within a lexical category to exhibit some but not all the properties associated with that category is known as subsective gradience (Aarts 2007). Subsective gradience can be linked to the notion of prototypicality (Rosch 1978). Specifically, some words will be better, more prototypical examples of their category than other words because they exhibit more of the properties associated with it. *Happy* is a prototypical adjective because it exhibits so many adjectival properties. In contrast, *utter* is not a prototypical adjective because it exhibits so few adjectival categories.

As a further example of subsective gradience, consider nouns in English. A key characteristic of nouns is their ability to occur either as the subject of a verb (e.g. *professor* in the following example) or as the object of a verb (e.g. *students*):

(15) The professor thanked the students.

However, a number of nouns only occur inside prepositional phrases (e.g. *sake* in *for the sake of, accordance* in *in accordance with, dint* in *by dint of*), and while most nouns

Table 10.1 Adjective criteria

	Prenominal	Predicate	Intensification	Gradedness	*un*-prefix
happy	+	+	+	+	+
thin	+	+	+	+	–
afraid	–	+	+	+	+
alive	–	+	+	?	–
utter	+	–	–	–	–
galore	–	–	–	–	–

can be marked as plurals (e.g. *students* in the above example), many nouns cannot (e.g. *hydrogen, machinery, furniture*). Further evidence of subsective gradience is provided by the category of English determiners. Culicover (1999) analysed the behaviour of eighteen determiners (e.g. *every, this, each, our*) in terms of six different properties. He observed that none of the determiners exhibits all six properties even though each property is exhibited by at least one of them. For instance, some determiners such as *this* can appear without an overt head whereas others such as *every* cannot (Culicover 1999: 62):

(16) a. I'll take this.
b. *I'll take every.

Some determiners such as *all* can shift to the right whereas others such as *our* cannot:

(17) a. All the women have gone.
b. The women have all gone.
c. Our women have gone.
d. *Women have our gone.

Some determiners such as *many* can occur between a determiner and a noun just like an adjective, whereas other determiners such as *both* cannot.

(18) a. Water conditioning is just one of the many uses of salt.
b. *I thought the both entries were very impressive.

The English adjective, noun, and determiner categories are not unusual in exhibiting subsective gradience. Instead, most lexical categories in most languages exhibit such variation to some extent (Aarts 2007; Bhat 1994; Croft 2001; Crystal 1967/2004; Culicover 1999; Hunston and Francis 2000; Plank 1984; Smith 2011).

Moreover, the words within a given lexical category are liable to vary not only in terms of subsective gradience but also in terms of intersective gradience. Intersective gradience concerns the propensity of the words within a given lexical category to exhibit properties associated with other lexical categories. Consider, again, the adjectival properties listed in Table 10.1. Like adjectives, nouns can also occupy a prenominal position (e.g. *apple* in *apple pie*). Similarly, nouns often occur predicatively (e.g. *teacher* as in *John is a teacher*) and can be modified by *very*, as the following example from the British National Corpus demonstrates:

(19) Indeed, the very notion of student access implies curricular foundations.

Moreover, adverbs can be modified by *very* (e.g. *quickly* as in *very quickly*) and can be graded as the following example from the British National Corpus demonstrates:

(20) Familiarity increased most quickly, and is now highest, with well-educated people.

Finally, many verbs can take an *un*-prefix (e.g. *do* as in *to undo*). Moreover, adjectives often exhibit properties associated with other categories. Thus, determiner marking is typically regarded as a nominal property (although pronouns, proper names, and some common nouns such as *accordance* and *fatherhood* typically occur without a determiner). Nevertheless, adjectives often occur with determiners as the following examples from Ferris (1993) demonstrate:

(21) a. The older a violin is, the more valuable it is supposed to be.
b. Martin is now the thinnest he's ever been.
c. Father came back $500 the poorer.

Moreover, some adjectives can take noun phrase complements (e.g. *worth* in *It was worth a hundred pounds* or *like* in *She is so like her brother*), even though this is a property which is typically associated with prepositions and verbs.

While the words of a given lexical category will often be able to display properties associated with other lexical categories, there will typically be a range of other properties that they cannot display without being converted into a different lexical category. For the adjective *kind* to occur like a noun as the subject of a verb, the category converting suffix -*ness* must be added to it to indicate that it is now functioning as a noun:

(22) Your kindness touched me deeply.

Similarly, for the verb *develop* to occur like a noun as the object of a verb, the category converting suffix -*ment* must be added to indicate that it is now functioning as a noun:

(23) The entire organization requires substantial development.

Nevertheless, certain words seem not to respect the limits of intersectively gradient behaviour associated with their category. In particular, they seem to be able to display an extremely wide range of properties without having a category converting suffix added to them. Consider the word *spare*. It can occur as an adjective, a verb, or a noun without the addition of a category converting suffix:

(24) a. They couldn't even spare me a dime. (verb)
b. Have you got a spare cigarette? (adjective)
c. There is a garage nearby that can sell you spares. (noun)

Note that the -*s* suffix in (24c) is not a category-converting suffix; its function is to mark *spare* as plural rather than to signal that it has been converted into a noun. Moreover, this lack of category converting suffixes can even render the lexical category of *spare* ambiguous, as the following examples demonstrate:

(25) a. Have you got a spare?
b. Have you got a spare one?
c. Have you got any spares?

It can be argued that *spare* in (25a) is an adjective modifying an ellipsed noun, as suggested by the possibility of adding the dummy noun *one* (25b). However, it can also be argued that *spare* in (25a) is a head noun in a noun phrase, as suggested by the possibility of adding the plural marker *-s* (25c). One conclusion might be that *spare* is so intersectively gradient that it straddles different categories and blurs the boundaries between them.

Subsective and intersective gradience suggest that we cannot restrict membership of a lexical category to those words exhibiting all and only the properties associated with the lexical category. Restricting membership in this way would exclude a large proportion of the words typically included in a given category. As a result, it is necessary to take a more flexible approach to category membership. In much recent work, this has been achieved by means of the Best Fit Principle. This states that we should assign a word to whichever category it possesses the most properties of (Aarts 2007; Crystal 1967/2004; Plank 1984). If *utter* exhibits a single adjectival property and no properties associated with other categories, then it will be assigned to the adjective category. If a word exhibits some properties associated with the verb category, then it still might be assigned to the noun category if it exhibits more noun properties than verb properties. Consider the following example (from Huddleston 1984: 307):

(26) These killings must stop.

The gerund *killings* exhibits two verb properties: it is derived from the verb *kill* and contains the suffix *-ing* typically associated with verbs. At the same time, it exhibits three noun properties; it occurs as the subject of a verb, contains the plural marking suffix *-s*, and is marked by the determiner *these*. Consequently, *killings* would be assigned to the noun category on the basis of the Best Fit Principle. In this way, then, the Best Fit Principle allows lexical categories to accommodate intersectively gradient words.

The Best Fit Principle is problematic in a number of respects (Smith 2011). Because the principle is so tolerant of subsective and intersective gradience, it can sanction lexical categories like the English adverb category which contains such a miscellaneous set of members that it risks becoming incoherent. While adverbs are often defined as words that modify verbs and adjectives, the English category contains words such as *too* that modify adjectives and adverbs but not verbs, and words such as *upstairs* that modify verbs and nouns but not adjectives or adverbs:

(27) a. It was too *silly* to contemplate. (adjective)
b. Sara had eaten her food too *quickly*. (adverb)

(28) a. They *ran* upstairs as fast as they could. (verb)
b. The *room* upstairs is no longer vacant. (noun)

Moreover, adverbs such as *almost* can modify an astonishing range of different kinds of words and phrases (Pullum and Huddleston 2002b: 562):

(29) a. They almost *suffocated.* (verb)
b. The article was almost *incomprehensible.* (adjective)
c. She almost *always* gets it right. (adverb)
d. Almost *all* the candidates failed. (determiner)
e. They are almost *without equal.* (prepositional phrase)
f. She read almost *the whole book* in one day. (noun phrase)

Given this bewildering variety of grammatical behaviour, it is difficult to pinpoint exactly what kind of word an adverb is. Nevertheless, because the Best Fit Principle allows for such variation, it is able to generate this kind of ragbag category.

The Best Fit Principle gives rise to a number of other problems. For instance, the principle would assign a gerund that exhibited five noun properties and six verb properties to the verb category. In so doing, however, it would fail to reflect the fact that the gerund is almost as strongly associated with the noun category as it is with the verb category, and the fact that it may exhibit more nominal properties than many words categorized as nouns. A model employing the Best Fit Principle would also assume that all the properties associated with a category are equally diagnostic of that category. In many instances, such an assumption is contentious. Aarts's model assumes that the ability to take a nominal suffix and the ability to occur as a subject are equally diagnostic of nounhood. However, nouns lacking nominal suffixes are often highly prototypical (e.g. *shoe, boat*) while nouns that cannot occur as subjects are not at all prototypical (e.g. *dint, sake, accordance*).

The Best Fit Principle also assumes that any given property will be associated with only a single category. But why, for instance, should we regard the ability to occur in predicate or prenominal position as exclusively adjectival properties and not also as nominal properties, given that nouns also occur in these positions?

(30) a. John is a teacher
b. a piano factory

Similarly, why should we regard the ability to occur with a determiner as a nominal property when adjectives can also occur with determiners, as (21) above demonstrates? Moreover, it is often unclear whether a given word should be regarded as exhibiting a particular property or not. For instance, it is natural to assume that pronouns lack the ability to occur with determiners because pronouns and determiners so rarely co-occur. Nevertheless, an internet search will return perfectly legitimate instances of pronouns occurring with determiners, as in the following:

(31) What's inside can make all the difference in the you you turn out to be.

Should we regard this example as evidence that pronouns can occur with determiners? If we do, we overlook the important fact that determiners regularly occur with common nouns but only rarely with pronouns. But to assume that pronouns do not occur with determiners leaves us unable to account for examples such as (31). While, then, the Best Fit Principle does enable lexical categories to accommodate subsectively and intersectively gradient words, it does so only at the cost of simplifying and distorting the complex grammatical behaviour of words.

10.3 Quirky properties

Many of the grammatical properties exhibited by words cannot be explained in terms of properties associated with lexical categories. These 'quirky' properties are exhibited by only a handful of words or even by a single word. For instance, *at* can occur with *night* and *night-time* but not with *day* and *daytime* (Taylor 2012: 97–8):

(32) a. at night
b. at night-time
c. *at day
d. *at daytime

This contrast cannot be explained in terms of lexical category differences because *night, night-time, day*, and *daytime* are all nouns. It is simply a quirky property of *at* that it occurs with certain words but not others. Similarly, while *burning* can occur with *ambition*, it cannot occur with *row*. The reverse is true for *blazing*:

(33) a. a blazing/*burning row
b. a burning/*blazing ambition

This contrast cannot be explained in terms of differences in lexical category because *blazing* and *burning* are both participles and *row* and *ambition* are both nouns. It is simply a quirky property of *row* and *ambition* that they combine with certain participles but not others.

There can also be quirky restrictions on the kinds of words that occur in a particular grammatical structure. Consider the following examples:

(34) a. my love of strawberries
b. my hatred of strawberries
c. *my hate of strawberries

Love and *hatred* can occur in a grammatical structure comprising a noun modified by a possessive pronoun (*my*) and an *of* phrase (*of strawberries*). In contrast, *hate* cannot occur in this structure even though it is a noun like *love* and *hatred*. As a result, (34c) cannot be explained in terms of lexical category differences. It is simply a quirky property of *hate* that it is barred from a grammatical structure that other semantically similar nouns can occur in. A further example of quirky restrictions was observed by Francis (1993) in an analysis of the occurrences of the adjective *possible* in the Bank of English corpus. This demonstrated that *possible* can occur between a superlative adjective and a head noun, and following a superlative adjective and head noun:

(35) a. I have the *strongest possible* belief in him …
b. … in the *best way possible* by beating them.

The only other adjective to occupy such positions in the corpus is *imaginable*. Francis also observes that *possible* can occur in the rightmost gap of *as* … *as* … structures.

(36) a. She tried to visit as little as possible.
b. Try to stay as relaxed as possible.

A wide range of adjectives, adverbs, and quantifiers can occur in the leftmost gap of *as* … *as* … structures (e.g. *soon, quick*). However, it is difficult to substitute any other adjectives for *possible*. Examples such as the following are not attested in the corpus:

(37) She tried to visit as little as??feasible/??imaginable/??plausible/??likely.

Other environments in which *possible* is commonly found, but where other adjectives hardly ever occur, include adjunct phrases such as *where/wherever possible, when/whenever possible*, and *if possible*. Clearly, the distinctive behaviour of *possible* cannot be explained in terms of its lexical category because other adjectives cannot occupy the same grammatical positions. It is simply a quirky property of *possible* that it can occur in a number of grammatical structures from which other adjectives are barred.

A word can also exhibit its own quirky restrictions on the properties associated with lexical categories. The word *go*, for instance, typically occurs as a verb but it can exhibit nominal properties when it occurs as an argument of *have* and other light verbs:

(38) a. How many goes did you take then?
b. They were so beautiful that I decided to have a go at growing them.
c. She just knew she could make a go of it!
d. Phoebe decided to give it a go.

As these examples (from the British National Corpus) illustrate, *go* can exhibit various nominal properties such as plural marking and occurring in argument positions with quantifiers and determiners. Crucially, when *go* occurs as an argument of *have* and other light verbs, its nominal properties are highly restricted. For instance, it can occur with the indefinite article but not with the definite article:

(39) *I decided to have the go at growing them.

When it combines with light verbs such as *have*, it can occur in a direct object phrase but not as subject of a passive verb:

(40) *A go was had at the referee by the players.

Nominal *go* is quirky insofar as it typically occurs as the argument of a restricted set of light verbs. Even when it occurs in this construction, there are quirky restrictions on the nominal properties that it exhibits. These restrictions cannot be explained in terms of the fact that nominal *go* is a noun since other nouns typically do not exhibit such restrictions.

While we cannot explain quirky properties in terms of lexical categories, a number of studies have suggested that they may be subject to semantic restrictions. For instance, Stubbs (2002) analysed approximately 40,000 occurrences of *cause* as both a noun and verb in the Bank of English corpus. He found that all fifty of the words that co-occurred most frequently with *cause* had unpleasant connotations (*cancer, pain, trouble*). Stubbs also analysed 400 occurrences of *undergo* from the Cobuild corpus and found that most of the twenty words that co-occurred most frequently with it were either medical in nature (*heart, medical, surgery*) or denoted the serious or involuntary nature of events (*major, forced, required*). Yet while some quirky properties can be explained in semantic terms, it is clear that others cannot. The contrast between *my hatred of strawberries* and *my hate of strawberries* cannot be motivated semantically, because *hate* and *hatred* are synonymous. Gross (1994: 250–51) makes a similar point with regard to quirky properties in French. He observes the following contrast between *concerner* and *regarder*:

(41) a. Cette affaire concerne Max.
b. Cette affaire regarde Max.
c. Max est concerné par cette affaire.
d. *Max est regardé par cette affaire.

It is difficult to motivate this contrast semantically because *concerner* and *regarder* have similar meanings. Both (41a) and (41b), for instance, can be translated as 'This affair concerns Max'.

Like subsective and intersective gradience, quirky properties suggest that the behaviour of a word can only be partially captured by the set of properties associated with lexical categories. While subsective gradience shows that a word may not exhibit all of the properties associated with its category, and intersective gradience shows that a word may exhibit some of the properties associated with a different category from its own, quirky properties demonstrate that a word may exhibit properties not associated with any category at all. In each case, the net effect is the same—the three phenomena all imply that lexical categories and their associated properties are only partially successful in capturing the behaviour of words. While some of the behaviour of words such as *possible* and *go* can be captured in terms of the properties associated with their lexical categories, large parts of their behaviour cannot be. As a result, any comprehensive description of their behaviour must specify not only the set of properties associated with their lexical category but also how they are subsectively and intersectively gradient and what quirky properties they exhibit. Words such as *possible* and *go* are not unusual in this respect. In fact, when we study actual language usage, it can be difficult to find a word which does not exhibit some subsective or intersective gradience or some quirky properties (Gross 1994; Partington 1998; Sinclair 1991, 2004; Stubbs 2002; Taylor 2012). Francis summarizes the situation as follows:

> If we take any one of a huge range of the more frequent words in English, and examine its citations en masse, it will emerge that it, too, has a unique grammatical profile, which certainly cannot be encapsulated by calling the word in question an adjective or a noun or a preposition.
>
> (Francis 1993: 147–8)

10.4 Lumping and splitting categories

Words within a lexical category do not vary at random. Instead, within any category, groups of words can often be discerned which cluster together insofar as they exhibit similar patterns of properties. As noted in section 10.1, these groups are often referred to as subcategories. Nouns in English, for instance, are often divided into four subcategories: common nouns, pronouns, proper names, and gerunds, each of which is associated with a distinct set of properties. For instance, common nouns often occur with determiners and adjectives (*a happy child*) but are not marked for case, while pronouns rarely occur with determiners and adjectives but can exhibit case marking (*he* vs. *him*). Moreover, groups of words exhibiting distinct sets of properties can also be discerned within each of the subcategories. The pronoun category can be split into possessive (e.g. *your*), demonstrative (e.g. *these*), personal (e.g. *him*), and reflexive (e.g. *himself*) categories. While possessive and demonstrative pronouns can occur before a noun, personal and reflexive pronouns tend not to. These categories can then be split even further. The personal pronoun category can be split into personal pronouns that occur only as subjects (e.g. *I*), those that occur only as objects (e.g. *him*), and those that occur both as subjects and objects (e.g. *you*).

In this way, then, categories can be split into ever smaller categories each of which exhibits its own distinctive set of properties. If a very wide range of properties are considered, then splitting can continue until a large open-class category has been split into hundreds of distinct categories each containing only one or two words. Gross (1994) analysed 12,000 French verbs in terms of a set of 300 properties. He observed that only about seventy French verbs enter into the construction N V à N where the second noun denotes a human, as in the following:

(42) a. Max obéit à Bob.
     b. Max pense à Bob.

Of these seventy verbs, only around twenty allow the second noun to be converted into a pronoun occurring before the verb:

(43) a. Max lui obéit.
     b. *Max lui pense.

Using a set of 300 properties such as these, Gross (1994) split the 12,000 into 9,000 distinct categories each exhibiting a unique combination of properties. Very few of these categories contained more than two verbs. Gross predicted that if the number of properties had been increased still further, no two verbs would have exhibited exactly the same set of properties; consequently, no two verbs would have belonged to the same category. Each category would have had only one member.

Splitting increases the number of categories and decreases the number of words in each category. As splitting renders categories progressively smaller, the members of those categories become increasingly homogeneous in terms of the properties that they exhibit. As a result, the set of properties associated with each category would provide an increasingly precise description of the grammatical behaviour of its members (Croft 2001; Plank 1984). Yet while splitting would result in a precise description of word behaviour, it would also result in a complex and uneconomical model of the grammar, one which would lack information about any categories larger than the smallest subcategories. It would fail to capture the fact that words within larger categories, such as nouns, do tend to share some common properties.

A model that featured a small number of large categories (categories such as nouns, verbs, and adjectives) would clearly be simpler and more economical. However, since each category would contain an extremely heterogeneous collection of words (e.g. the noun category would lump together common nouns, pronouns, gerunds, and proper names), the set of properties associated with that category would provide only a very imprecise description of the grammatical behaviour of its members (Crystal 1967/2004; Plank 1984). Moreover, the set of properties would fail to capture the similarities in grammatical behaviour between members of smaller subcategories. Thus, the single set of properties associated with the noun category would fail to capture the fact that words within smaller categories such as gerunds tend to share a distinct set of properties.

There is also the danger that lumping, like splitting, can be carried to extremes. As noted in section 10.2, if a model of lexical categories employs a flexible approach to category membership, as sanctioned by the Best Fit Principle, it can allow categories to include subsectively and intersectively gradient words. Thus, Aarts's (2007) model can lump common nouns, pronouns, proper names, and gerunds into a single noun category, even though these words exhibit contrasting sets of properties. However, because Aarts's model is so tolerant of subsective and intersective gradience, it can also lump nouns, verbs, and adjectives into a single supercategory, by simply attaching all the properties associated with nouns, verbs, and adjectives to the supercategory. Because any noun, verb, or adjective would be likely to display more of the properties associated with this supercategory than any other category, they would be assigned to this supercategory on the basis of the Best Fit Principle. Aarts (2007: 436–7) attempts to guard against this danger by stipulating that categories should not be 'too heterogeneous'. However, any attempt to specify exactly how much heterogeneity is acceptable is bound to be arbitrary and subjective (Smith 2011). For instance, we may feel that a supercategory that lumped together nouns and adjectives would be far too heterogeneous. Yet Donatus's grammar of Latin did precisely this and was the most widely accepted and influential grammar until the 11th century (Seuren 1998). At least according to medieval tastes, such a supercategory would not be too heterogeneous.

The grammatical behaviour of the words in a language can be described using either a small set of large categories or a large set of small categories. The former yields an economical but imprecise model of the grammatical behaviour of words, but fails to capture generalizations regarding smaller categories. In contrast, the latter approach yields an uneconomical but precise model of the grammatical behaviour of words, but fails to capture generalizations regarding larger categories. Because both approaches are successful in capturing some aspects of the data but flawed insofar as they fail to capture other aspects, it is difficult to see how either approach can be regarded as 'correct' or even better than the other. Each approach has its different strengths and weaknesses.

10.5 Arbitrary and Inconsistent Categories

We have seen that no approach to categorizing the words in a language can be regarded as inherently correct. This raises the concern that any choice between different approaches will be little more than an arbitrary matter of taste. Croft (2001) makes the point that in many perennial linguistic debates, such as whether Japanese has one or two adjective categories, or whether North American languages such as Nootka distinguish nouns and verbs, each side inevitably presents a model which succeeds in capturing some aspects of the data but fails to capture other aspects. In order to present their model as empirically correct, each side emphasizes the importance of the data that their model gets right while dismissing the relevance of the data that it fails to capture. As an example of this problem consider the word *piano* in the phrase *a piano factory*. There has been a long-running debate over whether such a word should be categorized as an adjective or a noun (Smith

2010). That *piano* occurs before a noun and modifies its meaning both suggest that it is an adjective, as does the fact that it cannot support plural marking (e.g. **a pianos factory*). However, the fact that it denotes an object and the fact that it has the same form as a word that typically occurs as a noun (e.g. *piano*) both suggest that it is a noun. Consequently, in order to argue that it is an adjective, it is necessary to emphasize the importance of its adjectival properties while dismissing the relevance of its nominal properties. Conversely, in order to argue that it is a noun, it is necessary to emphasize the importance of its nominal properties while dismissing the relevance of its adjectival properties. Both sides misrepresent their own model as the only empirically correct one when in fact both are empirically correct in certain respects and empirically flawed in other respects. While the choice between the two is presented by each side as a choice between an empirically correct model and an empirically incorrect model, the choice cannot be decided on empirical grounds but is ultimately, as Croft notes, little more than a matter of personal taste.

Croft (2001) also raises the concern that many of the decisions that inform models of lexical categories are not only arbitrary but also inconsistent. Suppose, for instance, that we have arbitrarily chosen to regard *piano* in *a piano factory* as a noun rather than an adjective on the basis that it denotes a kind of object. If we choose to privilege such a semantic criterion over other criteria in this way, then we should at least apply this criterion consistently when we come to make other decisions about other lexical categories. We should decide that *examination* in *the examination of the patient* is a verb rather than a noun on the basis that it denotes an event rather than a thing. In fact, linguists are rarely consistent in this way because such consistency would typically lead to odd and counterintuitive categorizations (Croft 2001, 2007). Instead, linguists typically apply certain sets of criteria in deciding the category of certain words and different sets of criteria in deciding the category of other words. Thus, one might argue that *piano* in *a piano factory* is a noun because of its semantic properties while simultaneously arguing that *examination* in *the examination of the patient* is a noun because of its grammatical properties. Models of lexical categories, then, are typically a product of a series of decisions that are both arbitrary and inconsistent.

Croft's (2001) own model of nouns, verbs, and adjectives avoids such inconsistency because it consistently defines these categories in terms of a combination of semantic and pragmatic properties. Specifically, the model stipulates that a prototypical noun exhibits the semantic property of denoting an object and the pragmatic function of reference, a prototypical verb exhibits the semantic property of denoting an action and the pragmatic function of predication (i.e. saying something about the object denoted by a noun phrase), and a prototypical adjective exhibits the semantic property of denoting a property and the pragmatic function of modification (i.e. specifying the meaning of the object denoted by a noun). Words which exhibit a different combination of semantic properties and pragmatic functions are left uncategorized by Croft's approach. Consider again *piano* in *a piano factory*. This word combines the semantic property of denoting an object with the pragmatic function of modification. As such, it does not qualify for inclusion in any of Croft's categories. What is more, Croft is not able to state what category it does belong to (Croft 2010; Smith 2010). We could, for instance, categorize the word as a non-prototypical noun on the basis that it exhibits the semantic property of denoting an object—a property associated with nouns—but the pragmatic function of modification—a property associated with adjectives. However, doing this would involve the arbitrary decision that it is the semantic property of a word rather than its pragmatic function which determines its category. Such a decision might commit us to the view that *examination* in *the examination of the patient* is a verb rather than a noun on the basis that it exhibits the semantic property of denoting an action associated with verbs. Alternatively, we could decide that *examination* is a noun on the basis that it exhibits the pragmatic function of reference that is associated with nouns. However, this would be inconsistent with our prior decision to define nouns in terms of semantic properties and consequently to categorize *piano* in *a piano factory* as a noun. In this way, then, attempting to categorize words that do not belong to the prototypical noun, verb, and adjective categories necessitates arbitrary and inconsistent decisions. These, however, are precisely the kinds of decision that Croft is determined to avoid. Unfortunately, by avoiding these decisions, Croft's approach is incapable of categorizing all those words (prenominal nouns, gerunds, action nominals, infinitives, participles, etc.) that do not belong in his prototypical categories (Smith 2010). In effect, Croft deals with subsectively and intersectively gradient words by simply excluding them from his model of lexical categories.

10.6 Categories from a cross-linguistic perspective

Just as the properties associated with particular lexical categories vary within languages, so too they vary between languages. A given property might be subsectively variant across languages insofar as the property is exhibited by words in a particular category in some languages but not by the words in a particular category in other languages. In many languages, for instance, nouns exhibit number, gender, and case marking. Vietnamese, however, lacks these features (Croft 2001), so these properties are irrelevant for Vietnamese. Similarly, nouns in many languages take determiners, but this property is irrelevant to Latin, since Latin lacks determiner marking. The following example is from Blake (2001: 9):

(44) *Mīlitēs vident urbem*
'The troops see the city'

While verbs in a wide variety of languages exhibit tense marking, verbs in some languages do not. An example is Mandarin Chinese. The following is from Tiee (1986: 97):

(45) *Zuótiān* *tā* *xiě* *zì*
yesterday he write word
'He wrote yesterday'

Intersective variance can also be observed across languages insofar as a property might be exhibited by words in a different category from the category it is typically associated with in other languages. Tense marking is exhibited by verbs in a wide variety of languages. However, in certain languages it is also exhibited by nouns. In the following example from the Amazonian language Tariana (Nordlinger and Sadler 2004: 780), a marker of future tense is attached to the noun *unyane*:

(46)	*kayu-maka*	*hi*	*waſipeſe*	*unyane-pena*
	SO-AFF	DEM:ANIM	Walipere	flood-fut
	di-kakwa=pidana			
	3SG.NF-plan=REMPREP			
	'Thus Walipere was planning the future flood'			

Similarly, determiner marking is typically associated with nouns, but in certain languages, verbs may also be determiner marked. Croft (2001: 252) provides the following Palauan example:

(47)	a	ngalęk	a	męnga	ęr	a	ngikęl
	DET	child	DET	eat	OBJ	DET	fish
	'The child is eating the fish'						

Properties may also be cross-linguistically quirky insofar as they are exhibited by words in only one or very few languages. In a wide variety of languages, nouns are divided up into idiosyncratic semantic categories. In the Alaskan language Ahtna the noun class marker *d* denotes enclosed liquids and units of time, while the marker *n* denotes round objects, string-like objects, and liquids (Rice 2000: 326). Noun-class markers in the African language Kivunjo divide nouns up into sixteen semantically distinct subcategories, including body-parts, instruments, abstract qualities, and objects that come in pairs or clusters (Pinker 1994).

Such cross-linguistic variation makes it difficult to compare categories across languages; cross-linguistic generalizations about categories are also put in doubt. If a given category in one language exhibits a different set of properties from the corresponding category in a different language, how can we be sure that they are the same category and that it is valid to equate them? German adjectives exhibit a number of properties, such as case marking, that English adjectives do not. For Croft (2007: 417), this means that 'we have no syntactic basis for assuming that the English Adjective class is the same as the German Adjective class'. Rather, he maintains: 'English Adjective and German Adjective are just language-specific categories, defined within each language, with no theoretical connection to each other.' While we may not be able to compare English and German adjectives in terms of properties that they do not have in common, there is still the possibility that we might compare them in terms of properties that they do have in common. One difficulty with this suggestion is that there are very few properties that a category of a given type is likely to exhibit across all languages. It would be wrong, for example, to assume that verbs across all languages exhibit tense marking, or that nouns in all languages exhibit determiner marking, as the above examples from Mandarin Chinese and Latin demonstrate. Nevertheless, it has often been argued that while there is no single grammatical property that a category will share across all languages, categories across languages might share common semantic properties. In particular, it has been maintained that in all languages nouns denote objects, verbs denote events, and adjectives denote properties (Croft 2001). However, it is clearly not the case that all nouns, verbs, and adjectives in all languages exhibit these semantic properties. There are many nouns in English that denote events rather than objects (e.g. *kiss, explosion, party*), and if we were to define categories in terms of semantic properties we would run the risk of misclassifying such nouns as verbs. Overall, then, it is difficult to determine what properties can be used to define lexical categories cross-linguistically.

There may also be cross-linguistic variation in the types of category exhibited by languages. For instance, adjectives and verbs can be clearly distinguished in English because they tend to exhibit a number of different properties. However, it is much harder to separate adjectives and verbs in, for example, the West African language Wolof because they tend to exhibit almost identical sets of properties. As a result, it is debatable whether such a language has a separate adjective category at all (McGlaughlin 2004). Similarly, in languages such as Mundari and Straits Salish, nouns, verbs, and adjectives exhibit such a similar set of properties that it can be argued that they form a single super-category rather than three distinct categories (Bhat 1994). Moreover, cross-linguistic variation may arise not only because certain languages fail to exhibit common categories such as nouns, verbs, and adjectives, but also because they exhibit uncommon categories. A number of Australian languages, for instance, exhibit a category of words known as coverbs. Typically, a coverb does not inflect for tense, mood, or agreement but co-occurs with a finite verb that does. Consider the following example from Marra (Baker and Harvey 2010: 14).

(48) rang=ng-anyi Ø-manuga
hit=1sg.S/3sg.O-TAKE.PC MA-rock
'I hit a rock'

Here, the coverb *rang* 'hit' combines with an inflected finite verb *nganyi* 'take'. If it were to be used without an accompanying coverb, *nganyi* would mean 'I was taking it'. However, when combined with a coverb such as *rang*, it functions as a light verb which conveys tense, aspect, mood, and agreement but little in the way of predicational meaning. Whereas verbs can occur independently of coverbs in Marra, coverbs cannot occur without an accompanying verb. Moreover, as Baker and Harvey (2010) emphasize, verbs in Marra form a small, closed class with fewer than forty members, whereas coverbs form a large, open class. For all of these reasons, then, it is necessary to postulate a category of coverbs in languages such as Marra which is distinct from the category of verbs. Such differences in the categories that different languages exhibit, however, only exacerbate the problem of equating categories across languages. Should we equate the Marra verb category with the English verb category, or with the subcategory of light verbs such as *have* and *give* in English? Perhaps, instead, we should equate the English verb category with the set of Marra coverbs or even a combination of verbs and coverbs. Clearly, any such choice is liable to result in an imperfect match between the categories of Marra and English, since the two categories will inevitably exhibit radically different properties. It would be difficult to avoid Croft's (2007: 417) pessimistic conclusion that such categories 'are just language-specific categories, defined within each language, with no theoretical connection to each other'.

10.7 Conclusion

In contemporary linguistics, it is generally assumed that the grammatical behaviour of the words in a language can be adequately described in terms of a small set of lexical categories and the grammatical properties associated with them. Numerous studies, however, have shown that the behaviour of words is so complex and disorderly that it cannot be reduced to the grammatical properties associated with the lexical categories. As Taylor (2012: 280–81) has stated, 'The allocation of a word to one of the standardly recognized lexical categories, such as noun, verb, or adjective (or even to sub-categories of these, such as count noun, transitive verb, or predicative adjective) is grossly inadequate as a guide to the word's use in the language.' Nevertheless, many linguists have persisted in attempts to force words into lexical categories. Ultimately, all such attempts are inevitably arbitrary. Because there is never a good fit between lexical categories and the words that are forced into them, any choice of a set of lexical categories will be arbitrary. Similarly, this lack of fit also renders arbitrary any decision to assign a particular word to a given category or to associate a particular set of grammatical properties with a given category. In short, because lexical categories deny the complexity of word behaviour, any analysis of word behaviour that is based upon them is condemned to be arbitrary.

CHAPTER 11

THE WORD AND SYNTAX

NIKOLAS GISBORNE

11.1 Introduction

Most modern theories of syntax, including Generalized Phrase Structure Grammar (GPSG: Gazdar et al. 1985), Head-driven Phrase Structure Grammar (HPSG: Pollard and Sag 1994), Lexical-Functional Grammar (LFG: Bresnan 2001), and Minimalism (Chomsky 1995), as well as less familiar theories such as Word Grammar (WG: Hudson 2007), are lexicalist. Lexicalist theories treat words as the atoms of syntax, so they adopt what has been called the 'strong lexicalist hypothesis' (Di Sciullo and Williams 1987; Halle 1973; Lapointe 1980). This hypothesis states that the job of syntax is to combine words, or to state well-formedness constraints on combinations of words. The creation of inflected words or new words through derivation or compounding belongs elsewhere, in morphology. There is a weaker theory (the 'weak lexicalist hypothesis': Anderson 1982; Aronoff 1976) which holds that compounding and derivation belong in morphology, but that inflection is syntactic. Among modern theories of grammar, one major school rejects lexicalism: Distributed Morphology (Embick and Marantz 2008; Embick and Noyer 2007; Halle and Marantz 1993). The lexicalist turn in syntax follows Chomsky (1970). In this chapter, I address what it means to assert that the word is a 'syntactic atom' (Ackema and Neeleman 2002).

In any discussion of the word and its relationship to syntax, there are potential ambiguities in the terminology. For example, some authors talk of inflection and derivation being 'in the lexicon', and the combination of words into phrases being 'in the syntax'. This follows from a temporal metaphor which assumes a procedural architecture of grammar where syntax is derivational, and where morphology 'takes place' in the lexicon before a word enters the syntax and potentially participates in derivational processes. I find the terminology unhelpful, because it often leads to a conflation of morphology with the lexicon, and because theories such as HPSG, LFG, and WG reject derivations in favour of constraint satisfaction.

The lexicon includes information about words that is not relevant to the issue of whether words or subparts of words are the atoms of syntax: their meanings, for example. In addressing the question of what it means for a theory to be lexicalist, we need to understand that the debate is just this: does syntax need to look at subparts of words or not? What is at stake is whether the better (simpler, more psychologically plausible) theory is one where the same system creates new words, inflected words, phrases, clauses, and sentences, or whether it is one where there are discrete systems for creating words and for combining them.

In terms of linguistic theorizing, a lot hangs on this debate. There are two main reasons. One is in the nature of the complexity of the data: a substantial degree of the complexity of natural language belongs at the interfaces between subsystems, and the main task of the linguist is to find the regularities and generalizations. Phenomena such as 'clitics' and Noun Incorporation, discussed in section 11.3, present significant descriptive problems posing major challenges for linguistic theories.[1] The other main reason is that natural language is a complex system, and therefore so too are the theories that set out to describe it. There are consequences to adopting a particular position on the modularity or contiguity of syntax with respect to morphology. For example, Baker (1988, 1996) treats Noun Incorporation (NI) as syntactic, and his work presents the original arguments for the theory of head movement. If NI turns out not to be syntactic, and therefore not to involve head movement, how much motivation is left for the theory of head movement?

In this chapter I focus on three topics, presenting and defending the lexicalist position in each case. The first case study (section 11.2) looks at inflection—the passive participle. Section 11.3 looks at two phenomena at the boundary of syntax and morphology: French pronominal affixes (typically treated as clitics) and the phenomenon of 'clitic climbing', and Noun Incorporation, especially the Mohawk data, which has been generally taken to be particularly problematic for the lexicalist position. In section 11.4, I conclude and explore some wider perspectives on the atoms of syntax.[2]

11.2 Evidence from the passive participle

There are two kinds of evidence from the passive participle. One is to do with its relationship to word formation, the other with its distribution. Both concern the relationship of passive participles to other kinds of participle. It is possible for a participle of any subtype to be converted into an adjective. Although there are historically lexicalized forms, such as CHARMING and INTERESTING, there are also nonce conversions.

[1] I have 'clitics' in scare quotes because this is a descriptive term capturing a range of phenomena which are not amenable to a single formal treatment. See Zwicky (1977, 1995).

[2] This chapter takes a syntactic view of lexicalism. There is a substantial morphological literature which looks at the same general question, but from the point of view of morphology. Lieber and Scalise (2007) review the history of the lexical integrity hypothesis and explore various morphological phenomena which pose challenges to it, including, for example, phrasal compounds in various Germanic languages.

11.2.1 Passive participles and word formation

Chomsky (1957) presented a syntactic treatment of passivization which involved deriving the passive participle in the syntax—a syntactic approach to inflection. Subsequent developments led to the passive participle being treated as morphological. The weak lexicalist position is that derivation is morphological, but inflection is syntactic. But what if inflected forms are the input to a word formation process? If that were the case, then both inflection and word formation must be morphological, and neither could be syntactic. Bresnan (1978, 1982) has argued just this; her arguments are summarized in Bresnan (2001: 30–9). The claim is that passive participles have two distributions, as non-finite verbs and as adjectives; the adjectival passive participles are derived from the verbal; the verbal passive participles are an inflected form of the verb; therefore inflection comes before derivation, and both must take place in the same domain of the grammar: morphology.

First, she shows that participles in general convert to adjectives. The examples in (1) are Bresnan's (2001: 31) example (10).

(1) a. *present participles*: a smiling child, a breathing woman, the boring story;
b. *perfect participles*: a fallen leaf, an escaped convict, wilted lettuce;
c. *passives*: a considered statement, the spared prisoners, an opened can.

These converted participles have the properties of adjectives: it is possible to have negative (rather than reversive) *un*-prefixation; they are gradable; and they can head concessive relatives beginning with HOWEVER.

(2) an unconsidered statement, a very considered statement, however considered her statement might have been.

The full range of passive participial forms count for conversion to adjectives, as in (3). The examples are Bresnan's (2001: 31) example (12).

(3)	*Verb*	*Participle*	*Adjectival participle*
	sing	sung	an unsung hero
	fight	fought	hard-fought battles
	write	written	a well-written novel
	give	given	a recently given talk
	consider	considered	an unconsidered action
	inhabit	inhabited	an uninhabited island
	break	broken	my broken heart
	split	split	split wood

These examples show that the same form occurs as verbal passive participle and as adjectival passive participle. Therefore, adjectival passives must have verbal passives as their input, otherwise there is no way to account for the morphological parallels.

Another argument comes from prepositional passives: it is possible to have adjectival versions of prepositional passives, as in (4), and where it is not possible to have a verbal prepositional passive the adjectival passive is likewise ruled out (5 and 6). The examples come from Bresnan (2001: 31–2).

(4) a. After the tornado, the fields had a *marched through* look.
b. Each *unpaid for* item will be returned.
c. You can ignore any recently *gone over* accounts.
d. His was not a *well-looked on* profession.
e. They shared an *unspoken, unheard of* passion for chocolates.
f. Filled with candy wrappers and crumpled bills, her bag always had a *rummaged around in* appearance.

The next two pairs of examples show that if a verb cannot have a prepositional passive, then neither can there be an adjective derived from it which permits a prepositional passive.

(5) a. *The twin is looked like by his brother.
b. *a looked like twin [cf. 'like-minded']

(6) a. *No reason was left for.
b. *the left-for reason [cf. 'each unpaid-for item']

Given the data above, the simplest story is that the verbal passive participle is an input to adjective formation. It makes far less sense to say that there is a separate process of passive adjective formation which runs parallel to a mechanism that derives the passive construction. For these reasons, Bresnan (1978; 1982) argued that passive was a morphological and not a syntactic rule: passive participles, and the adjectives derived from them, are formed in the lexicon.

Bresnan has shown that both kinds of passive have to be lexical, while treating the verbal passive as inflection and the adjectival passive as word formation—which in turn provides evidence for the strong lexicalist hypothesis, or Zwicky's (1992: 354–5) Principle of Morphology Free Syntax (see also Brown and Hippisley 2012).[3]

[3] Bresnan dealt a significant blow to Wasow's (1977) claim that adjectival passives had a different derivation from verbal passives, as well as demonstrating alongside Wasow the incorrectness of Friedin's (1975) claim that all passive participles were adjectives.

But there are still some loose ends. First, how do we account for prepositional passives such as *These woods were walked in by Anne Boleyn* in a lexicalist theory? Secondly, what about verbs which apparently have objects but which do not figure in the passive construction and which appear not to have passive participles, such as RESEMBLE, FIT, INVOLVE, WEIGH? I return to these in section 11.2.3. In the next section, I present a distributional argument in favour of the strong lexicalist position: that the behaviour of verbal passive participles argues in favour of the lexicalist position.

11.2.2 The distribution of passive participles and other inflected elements

I am not aware of any published work that argues for a lexical account of passive participles from their distribution—though Hudson (1990: 339) has pointed out that passive participles and the *-ing* participle have the same distribution. It seems to me, however, that one of the major arguments in favour of the lexicalist position is the distribution of lexical items, including passive participles. Passive participles can be found in a number of different environments. But before we discuss their distribution we need first to agree on terms. The distributional argument requires one additional premise: that forms realize cells in a paradigm.[4] I take the view that passive participles are exponents of a feature bundle which includes information such as the verb's name, the fact that it is a verb, and the fact that the verb has passive voice which is realized as VERB-*ed*. Because of the general property of syncretism, we can (and need to) distinguish between the passive participle and the other verbal morphosyntactic form which is realized as VERB-*ed*, the perfect participle. This common form is a syncretism, the phenomenon where one form occurs in more than one cell in a paradigm (Matthews 1991: 202).

We have to distinguish passive participles from perfect participles because they have different feature specifications. The form *broken* is ambiguous in three ways: it could be the passive participle (*my glasses were broken by some idiot*); the perfect participle (*you have broken my glasses*); or the adjective (*my glasses seemed broken*). The passive participle has the same distribution as the active participle ending in *ing*, while the perfect participle is more restricted, typically occurring as the predicative complement of HAVE. Neither the active nor the passive participle occurs in that position. I show the basic distributions in (7); the other contexts that passive participles occur in are discussed below.

[4] It is possible for a theory to be lexicalist and morphemic or lexicalist and realizational (see Stump 2001: 1–3). The argument developed in this section requires us to adopt a theory which is both lexicalist and realizational.

(7) a. The walls were *repainted* yesterday afternoon (by the new builders). [Passive]

b. The children were *running* in the 3-legged race yesterday afternoon. [Active]

c. The children have *broken* their ankles. [Perfect]

Note that neither the passive not the active participle can occur as the predicative complement of HAVE. Note too that the perfect participle cannot occur as the predicative complement of BE.

(8) a. *The walls have repainted yesterday afternoon by the new builders.

b. *The children have running in the three-legged race yesterday afternoon.

c. *The children are broken their ankles.

I have kept the voice features stable in (8a) and (8c): *repainted* has its patient argument as its subject and its agent is expressed in the phrase *by the builders*; likewise, *broken* has a direct object: *their ankles*. From this, we have to conclude that the passive and the perfect participles are distributionally different as well as having different feature specifications. Their formal similarity is just a syncretism.

We can now turn to the range of distributions of the passive participle. I take the view that the passive participle itself is what has the distribution, not passive clauses headed by that participle; but nothing much hinges on the distinction in the argument that follows. We can start with the GET passive in (9a,b), which looks very like the prototypical passive in (7a). The example in (9c) is not like a typical passive clause, because here the subject of *broken* is *your neck*, which is not the subject of *get*.

(9) a. His leg got broken in the car accident.

b. He finally got kissed by the girl he fancied.

c. Try not to get your neck broken when you're climbing that mountain.

As I said above, *broken* is three-ways ambiguous, and I used SEEM as a diagnostic of an adjective. Verbs like SEEM are not like BE and GET. The example in (10a) is adjectival not verbal, as (10b,c) show: SEEM is not a copular verb and cannot have a verbal predicative complement, although it can take an adjective (10d).

(10) a. We'd better not move him: his leg seems broken.

b. *His leg seemed broken by the lorry's wheel.

c. *The child seemed running fast.

d. The child seemed happy.

The use of the BY-phrase forces a long passive interpretation, and (10b) is ungrammatical. In (10c), we see that SEEM cannot have an active participle as its predicative complement either, so the generalization is that SEEM is one of the verbs which does not select for participle predicative complements.

However, we do see passive verbs as the predicative complements of those other non-copular verbs which do permit verbal elements as their predicative complements. For example, passive participles can occur as the complement of causative and experiential HAVE and SEE.

(11) a. The drug-lord$_i$ had his enemy's$_j$ legs broken (by his*i* thugs).
 b. She had her car stolen from her driveway last week.
 c. We saw the city destroyed by enemy troops.

And there are constructions with COME and GO which also occur with passive clauses. These examples are from Pullum (2011).

(12) a. The problems with the building went unnoticed by the owners for weeks.
 b. This software comes pre-installed by the manufacturers.

There is a construction with NEED which shows dialectal variation—in standard English, (13a) is the usual form; in Irish and Scottish English, it is (13b). The point of the example in (13a) is that in one particular construction, the property of having passive voice is exceptionally realized by the *-ing* participle rather than the *-ed* one.

(13) a. The windows need washing. (='to be washed')
 b. The windows need washed.
 c. He likes counselling.

The example in (13c) is ambiguous: it can either be interpreted as 'he likes being counselled', or as 'he likes counselling others'. I take it that this speaks to the potential ambiguity of the *-ing* form.

Two further distributions are relevant to the issue of where participles are created: they occur as the adjuncts of nouns, in participial relatives (14) and as clause-initial adjuncts (15). In (14), the bracketed elements are Noun Phrases with participial relatives modifying the noun.

(14) a. [The student attacked by the police] successfully sued.
 b. [The speaker acclaimed by the senator] was a dreadful drunk.

(15) a. Attacked by wolves, the cat raced up the tree.
 b. Running home, the boy tripped over.

The clausal adjuncts in (15a) and (15b) are both participial constructions; the example in (15a) involves a verbal passive participle. It is not adjectival.

The first point to be established is that each of the environments where a passive participle can occur is also an environment where the active participle in *-ing* can occur. Therefore, not only is there no separate transformational rule for each of the different possible passive constructions, but the distribution of passive participles does not even need to be stated as a constraint on **passives**: it is a constraint on **participles**. I return below to what that means for an account of the lexicalist hypothesis; but first let us go through some examples.

We have seen that both active and passive participles can occur as the complement of BE. It is sometimes argued—in fact it is a very common textbook position—that there must be different auxiliary verbs BE, one which selects the passive participle and one which selects the active one. This claim is unwarranted, but it is argued for on the basis of auxiliary order in (16).

(16) He may have been being beaten.

Here, *have* selects the perfect participle *been*, which in turn selects the active participle *being*, which selects the passive participle *beaten*. However, that sequence of selection patterns is no reason to assume that there are two auxiliary verbs BE. In the case of auxiliary BE, all we have to say is that it selects a participle. Everything else follows. When the active participle is itself an instance of BE, then—because it's BE—it selects a participle. BE cannot have a passive participle because it does not have an object. And there are no constructional semantics: the semantics of VERB-*ing* follow compositionally, as do the semantics of VERB-*ed*.

The next case to be discussed is the complementation of GET. The examples in (17) show GET with VERB-*ing* structures, both with and without an object.

(17) a. He got cooking as soon as he arrived at home.
b. Try to get your children cooking early in life, so that they can look after themselves.

These patterns match those in (9). I have already shown that SEEM does not allow participle complements in (10), so I move on to causal and experiential HAVE and SEE.

(18) a. She had his heart racing whenever she came into the room.
b. He had his heart racing after five minutes on the treadmill.
c. We saw the dog running across the road.

In (18), the present participles could each be replaced by a passive participle and the distribution is just the same as in (11).

In the case of COME and GO, the interpretation is depictive, as it is with passive participles, and the structures admit active participles just as well as passive ones.

(19) a. The children went running past all afternoon.
b. I inherited an old Persian carpet; it came crawling with bugs.

Just for now, I am putting the examples with NEED to one side—they feature at a later stage in the argument. The next distributional pattern is the participial relative, and here too we can have active participles just as well as passive ones.

(20) a. [The student attacking the police] was a Trot.
b. [The speaker droning on] bored even his fans.

And finally, we see active participles as clause-initial adjuncts.

(21) a. Running home, I tripped and fell.
b. Advancing on the enemy, he died in the first skirmish.

The first task is to establish the right generalization, which is that active and passive participles share their distribution. Therefore, we do not want to discuss the distribution of passive participles as a separate phenomenon. More to the point, although this has long since been decided, there can be no passive transformation and passive clauses are not derived from active clauses.

However, the shared distribution does not necessarily get us to a lexicalist story. It could be argued that the distribution is shared by *-ing* and *-ed*$_1$ (where the subscript '1' distinguishes this *-ed* from the other one found in the perfect verb form). On such a theory, the ending is the head of the word, and the grammar can look 'inside' the word to see what its distribution is: parts of words are the terminal nodes of syntactic trees or dependencies.

There are two arguments against this position: the behaviour in (13) with NEED, and suppletion. In (13a), passive voice is expressed by a participle ending in *-ing*. How are we to understand this? According to the model I have been arguing for in this section, I would say that *washing* is an unanalysed whole, and that it is the contextually determined form which realizes the passive of WASH. If, on the other hand, we were to argue that there was a form, *-ing*, which had its own lexical entry, stating that it was a head, that its morphological root was its syntactic dependent, and that it was active voice, we would need a new *-ing* to capture the facts in (13a). This would cause us to set up two distinct lexical entries, active voice *-ing*$_1$ and passive voice *-ing*$_2$. It is certainly possible to do that, and I own that there are people who might want to make such a move, but I think that the alternative position is better.

The alternative position is the realizational argument I offered at the beginning of this section. According to this position, the *-ing* form in (13a) is just a lexically conditioned realization of the passive participle. This analysis has some properties which are simpler than the alternative one, with multiple entries in the lexicon for *-ing* and *-ed*, as well as an entry for *-en* which we would also need to capture for examples such as *broken*. First of all, it reduces the number of forms-with-meanings in the lexicon: realizations do not have meanings themselves; the paradigm cells they realize do. Secondly, it means that the dialectal fact, where in one variety *-ing* can realize either the active or the passive participle, is just a local irregularity in one of the cells of a paradigm. No new word needs to be set up to capture that fact, and we know from other dialects of English that there can be quite a lot of variation in the realizational facts of English verb morphology. For example, there are northern English varieties that have *were* as the past tense of BE through the system, singular and plural. Likewise, there are varieties from the south west of England that have *be*.

Why might it be better to locate this variation in a theory of realizations rather than a theory that says there are different word entries across the different dialects? One reason is that we should expect word entries to be more stable than realizations, because word entries are linked to more information. They are related to the word class of the form, and also to its meaning. A realization, on the other hand, is related to the cell in the paradigm that it realizes. The cell in the paradigm does the work of relating the word, its class, and its meaning together. So in a realizational theory, parts of words are not themselves meaningful. Matthews (1991: 180) presents a clear case of the difficulty of a morphemic analysis, and working out what means what, in his treatment of Ancient Greek *elelýkete*; he also points out that the boundaries of morphological forms can be hard to establish (1991: 203). But there is a simpler argument.

When he was aged between 4 and 5, my younger son came out with the utterance in (22).

(22) I wish I didn't hadded a big brother. I wish I hadded a dog.

What is important about this example is that the semantics is really difficult: my son had to know that under a verb like WISH he's expressing irrealis semantics. He also had to know that in subordinate clauses, irrealis semantics is expressed by a past tense verb. In the example, these two things are perfectly expressed. What he didn't know was how to express past tense. The irrealis semantics is right; the use of past tense is right; but the realization of past tense is a complete mess: he's got triple tense marking in the first clause, and double in the second. What does this mean? It must be an argument against a direct relationship between morphological forms and their meanings. If the forms were directly related to the meanings, then my son could not have got the semantics right while getting the morphology wrong.

And what of suppletion? This too is an argument for a lexicalist and realizational approach. There are suppletive forms for the passive participle which would make it impossible to build a morphemic analysis around *-ed*, and there are also forms replacing the *-ing* form. Both examples are non-standard, with (23b) perhaps being dialectal; (23c), however, taken from an SMS/text message, is naturally occurring.

(23) a. The train has already gone.
b. It was broke when I got there.
c. I am sat on the bench in front of the station.

In (23a), *gone* is the lexically specific suppletive form of the perfect participle of GO. It's monomorphemic, so it is clearly not built around any of the common morphological parts.[5] In (23b), *broke* realizes the passive voice of the verb BREAK. These kinds of suppletion are very common in non-standard Englishes. For example, where I live in Scotland, I often hear *The train has went* for *The train has gone* where the suppletive form is syncretic with the past tense form. The final example in (23c) is not passive but progressive, and means the same as *I am sitting on the bench in front of the station.* Although it is 'non-standard', it is common enough in the speech of speakers of Standard British English. Suppletion is straightforward to negotiate in a realizational theory: the realization of a given cell in a paradigm is not the default form. Rules which are more specific than defaults override defaults, and so the suppletive form is the realization of that cell across the grammars of a number of speakers.

So much for participles. What about the other forms of verbs? In brief, the same arguments apply, as I suggested when I discussed the dialectal forms of BE above. I take the view that the category 'verb' does not supply any distributional information. It is the inflected forms of verbs that have distributions, which applies to tensed verbs every bit as much as to the participles. It is heads that select their dependents, so finite verbs may be dependents only of those predicates that select them. Otherwise, they are the matrix verb in main predications; the lack of categorial distributional information on verbs is what allows gerunds to have the distribution of a noun and the complementation of a verb in a mixed-category analysis (Hudson 2003; Malouf 2000), although Hudson claims that it is 'non-finite verbs' that lack distributional information.

11.2.3 Prepositional passives and lexicalism

I now address the problems posed for the lexicalist account of passivization by cases such as prepositional passives, as in (24).

(24) a. This bridge has been flown under.
 b. This paper has been written on both sides of.
 c. The roof has been walked on.

There is an argument that asks how examples like (24) can be reconciled with a non-transformational account of passive: if the words FLY and UNDER are not stored together in the lexicon, how is a string like (24a) possible (Bruening 2012: 9; McCawley 1998: 85–94)? Bresnan's lexical approach (1982) assumes reanalysis, with the passive participle and the preposition making a new complex predicate (see also Levin and Rappaport 1986). This reanalysis is assumed to be morphological, in that it creates a new item in the lexicon and is a kind of incorporation.[6]

[5] Historically, it is {go}+{en} but I take it that it is monomorphemic in the contemporary native speaker's mental lexicon.

[6] In an alternative lexicalist account, Hudson (1990) analyses different subtypes of prepositional passive using a novel dependency-type, 'passive-link'. If dependencies are constructions (Gisborne 2008), then this is a kind of constructional analysis; it is certainly *ad constructionem*.

However, Postal (1985), Baltin and Postal (1996), and Lødrup (1991) all find problems with Bresnan's analysis, summarized in Alsina (2009), which argues instead for structure sharing. The main problem for the lexical analysis that Postal (1996) and Baltin and Postal (1996) find is that the Verb+Preposition sequence does not behave like a word, but like a syntactic sequence. Alsina's proposal addresses the criticism by taking the relationship between the passive participle and the preposition to be syntagmatic and related to the phenomena of subject-to-subject raising and extraction.

As Huddleston and Pullum (2002: 1444) point out, there are discourse, semantic, and pragmatic constraints on passives. One of the discourse constraints is that the passive subject has to be discourse old, at least relative to the content of the passive BY-phrase. Hypothetically, any verb could have a passive participle, irrespective of whether it is transitive or not, just as any verb can have an *-ing* participle whether it is stative or not. For a passive participle to be used grammatically, either the subject of that participle must be in the semantic relation normally associated with its active voice object, or it must denote some entity which is affected by the action denoted by the verb, and which is present in the grammatical structure. Thus the grammaticality of the examples in (24)—we can treat flying under a bridge as affecting it in some way; likewise writing on both sides of a piece of paper. Any treatment, lexicalist or not, has to be sensitive to these discourse and semantic facts.

However, some verbs patently do not have passive participles; for a subset, this is because they do not have semantic arguments which map to their subjects, and so do not license the basic requirement of a passive participle, which is that the semantic argument mapping to Subject in the active voice is delinked from the Subject in the passive voice. Such examples would include SEEM and WEIGH, where SEEM is a raising verb which does not collocate with prepositions at all, and WEIGH is a verb which takes a nominal predicative complement, with the meaning 'is, by weight'.

It is now possible to account for the adjectival passive of examples such as (24): the verb has a passive participle; therefore the passive participle is available for conversion into an adjective. The converted adjective retains the collocational possibilities of the verb it derives from because both verbs and adjectives can collocate with prepositions. When a verb has a PP complement, the derived adjective simply inherits that PP complement.

11.2.4 Evaluating the facts about passive

I have drawn on three different sets of data in this section. The first two, the derivation of adjectival passives and the distribution of passive participles, offer clear arguments in favour of a lexical treatment of passive participles. In particular, when there are clearly passive structures which are not derivable from active clauses, it is axiomatic that passive participles are formed in the morphology and that passive constructions work by simple pattern matching. It follows that inflection is lexical.

There are adequate lexicalist accounts of the more complex data surrounding prepositional passives, so there is no need to invoke a derivational approach to account for them. One of the main points that follows from the discussion is that it is specific proposals that need to be evaluated, not the general research strategy.

The main remaining issue is whether there need be any direct relation between active and passive clauses. I have argued that there does not—the main reason being that there are so many subtypes of passive clause that it makes no sense to privilege a particular case, although the mapping between active and passive voice motivates Collins (2005).

11.3 The boundaries of grammar

So far, I have argued that it is both possible and desirable to take a lexicalist stance on verb inflection, and have shown that this is necessary from the point of view of modern lexicalist theories of syntax. In developing the argument, particularly the distributional argument for the lexicalist position on the English passive, I argued for a realizational theory of morphology. Now I turn to two further sets of data which have been claimed to be problematic for the lexicalist position. The first problem is the behaviour of clitics, in particular clitic climbing. The second is Noun Incorporation. In both cases, it has been shown that it is possible to handle these data without recourse to syntactic solutions, including 'mixed' analyses, which treat certain kinds of phenomenon as partly in one system and partly in another.

Clitics are a general research problem. As Zwicky (1977, 1995) pointed out, backed up in more depth by Miller (1992), Anderson (2005), and Spencer and Luis (2012), several different phenomena have been identified as 'clitics', and they are not amenable to a single analysis. Crudely speaking, clitics are elements that have the form of an affix, but the syntax of a word. They are therefore a problem for lexicalism, because they appear to be on both sides of the syntax/morphology boundary. One particular problem is the case of the pronominal affixes which I address in section 11.3.1. These look very much like affixes, but they also display the properties of clitic climbing, where a pronominal form is realized on a higher verb than the one whose argument structure it belongs to. To explore the issues, I discuss a particular case study: Miller and Sag (1997).

Noun Incorporation (NI) is a kind of compounding, which has been subject to both lexicalist and syntactic analyses. On the face of it, compounding should be a simple matter of morphology, but there are complications in some of the data. In particular, Mohawk has been subject to syntactic analysis by Baker (1988, 1996) because it has the property of incorporating an argument which is definite and discourse-referential. It is widely assumed that only words can have these semantic properties, and consequently NI has become a general testbed for lexicalist and syntacticist accounts. Mithun (1984, 1986), Rosen (1989), and DiSciullo and Williams (1987) all take a lexicalist approach; Sadock (1991) and Baker (1988, 1996) take a syntactic one.[7]

[7] One complication in the NI literature is whether the phenomenon in West Greenlandic discussed by Sadock is the same as the phenomenon discussed by Mithun, Rosen, and Baker. Noun Incorporation is arguably a sub-species of compounding; the West Greenlandic facts are more like derivational morphology.

11.3.1 French pronominal affixes

French pronominal affixes include examples such as those in (25) from Miller and Sag (1997)—their example (1). In the literature, these are usually called clitics; in fact, they are one of the subtypes of "Zwicky's (1977) 'special' clitics, discussed at length in Anderson (2005), but following Miller and Sag's analysis I refer to them as 'pronominal affixes.'"

(25) a. Marie le voit. 'Marie sees him.'

b. *Marie le voit Jean. 'Marie sees Jean.'[8]

c. Marie voit Jean. 'Marie sees Jean.'

These examples show that a pronominal formative, such as *le* in (25a), reduces the valency of the verb, which is why (25b) is ungrammatical. It is also possible to have combinations of pronominal formatives as in (26)—Miller and Sag's (2)—and for pronominal formatives to reduce more than one complementation property.

(26) a. Marie lui donne le livre. 'Marie gives her the book.'

b. Marie le lui donne. 'Marie gives it to her.'

c. *Marie lui donne un livre à Anne. 'Marie gives a book to Anne.'

d. *Marie le lui donne le livre. 'Marie gives her the book.'

As Miller and Sag (1997) point out, these cases have been analysed in various ways. Some scholars have argued for analyses involving movement from an argument position (Kayne 1969, 1975, 1991; Perlmutter 1970), others for base-generated analyses (Jaeggli 1982; Rivas 1977), which Sportiche (1996) has criticized on the basis of examples such as those in (27), which are Miller and Sag's (3). Here, the pronominal affixes are realized on an auxiliary verb rather than on the main verb whose valency they reduce—a phenomenon known as clitic climbing.

(27)	a. Mari l'a vu.	'Marie has seen him.' [*l'*: argument of *vu*]
	b. Le livre lui a été donné.	'The book has been given to him.' [*lui*: argument of *donné*]
	d. Pierre lui reste fidèle.	'Pierre remains faithful to him.' [*lui*: argument of *fidèle*]
	e. Marie en connaît la fin.	'Marie knows the end of it.' [*en*: argument of *fin*]
	f. Marie le fait lire à Paul.	'Marie is making Paul read it.' [*le*: argument of *lire*]

[8] Miller and Sag (1997: 574, fn 2) point out that examples such as (25b) 'are grammatical with a pause before the final element (*Jean*), which we take to be indicative of a right dislocated (unbounded dependency) structure'.

The question posed by the examples in (27) is how it is possible to have a base-generated account of the affixes when they are dislocated from the verbal heads whose argument arrays they satisfy. The dislocated pronominals look as though they violate the lexicalist hypothesis, because they behave like clitics which have moved. A further set of issues is spelled out by Bonami and Boyé: because there are particular constraints on the co-occurrence of French pronominal elements, it is widely held that they can be best analysed in a templatic structure assuming seven position classes (Bonami and Boyé 2007: 293). This makes the situation worse, because if the pronouns in (27) have moved, it would mean that there are both morphological constraints and syntactic movement.

Following Miller (1992), Miller and Sag (1997) demonstrate that it is a straightforward matter to analyse French pronominal clitics lexically while at the same time capturing the facts in (27). They analyse the pronominal elements as lexically attached inflections, not as postlexical clitics. Their criteria for treating the pronouns as inflectional affixes draw on Zwicky and Pullum's (1983) arguments that English *n't* is an affix. It is also important to note that Miller and Sag (1997: 576) assume that the pronominal affixes really are pronouns. They state that 'agreement marker vs. pronoun status and affix vs. word status are two independent parameters', so the bound pronouns are 'affixal (or "incorporated") pronouns. The evidence for this is the absence of systematic doubling.'

This is a challenging position to adopt, because it keeps a number of theoretical consequences and decisions in play. First, though, it requires us to keep a number of factors clearly separate. In Miller and Sag's (1997) theory, what is at stake is the relationship between morphology and syntax: as far as the syntax is concerned, these pronominal elements do not exist. The combinatorics of the sentence only involve the larger words, which include the words which themselves include the pronouns. As far as the morphology is concerned, however, these pronominal elements do exist and are part of word structure. What is not at stake, on the other hand, is the relationship between syntax and semantics, or morphology and semantics. These pronominal elements are fully referential, and therefore for Miller and Sag (1997) can refer independently. This is significant, because it tells us where their theory locates complexity.

Crudely speaking, complexity can be found at the interfaces. A simple illustration involves the raising/control distinction, although this is about the syntax–semantics and syntax–phonology interfaces and does not strictly involve morphology. The difference between *I expected her to go* and *I persuaded her to go* is that with *expected, her* is not a semantic argument of the matrix verb, whereas with *persuaded*, it is. If reducing complexity at the syntax–semantics interface is what matters, the solution is to posit that there is an additional, phonologically unrealized word (PRO) which is the subject of *to go* when the non-finite clause complements *persuaded*. If, on the other hand, what matters is minimizing complexity between morphology and phonology, then a theory will allow *her* under *persuaded* to serve syntactically in both clauses, reducing the complexity in terms of having elements which are phonologically unrealized, but increasing the complexity in terms of the relationship between syntax and semantics, by allowing an item to receive more than one semantic role. The theory presented by Miller and Sag (1997) puts the complexity at the syntax–semantics interface, in order to minimize complexity between syntax and morphology.

Miller and Sag (1997) exploit seven criteria, presented in (28), to establish that the pronominal elements are affixes. The first three are taken directly from Zwicky and Pullum (1983: 503–504).

(28) a. Degree of selection with respect to the host: clitics can exhibit a low degree of selection with respect to their hosts, while affixes exhibit a high degree of selection with respect to their stems.

b. Arbitrary gaps in the set of combinations, more characteristic of affixed words than of clitic groups.

c. Morphophonological idiosyncrasies which are more characteristic of affixed words than of clitic groups.

d. Rigid and idiosyncratic ordering which is 'typical of affixation rather than of cliticization. For instance, the ordering of dative and accusative pronominal affixes in standard French depends on the persons of the affixes involved' (Miller and Sag 1997: 579).

e. Pronominal affixes undergo lexical phonological rules: 'affix+stem units undergo lexical phonological rules, such as obligatory liaison of nasal consonants' (Miller and Sag 1997: 579).

f. Object affixes cannot have wide scope over coordination. **Pierre les voit et écoute*, which would mean something like 'Pierre sees and hears them', is ungrammatical, and Miller (1992) argues that this is strong evidence for the lexically attached status of these elements (Miller and Sag 1997: 579–80).

g. Syntactic explanations for clitic ordering have failed. Miller and Sag cite a literature which has shown that it is not possible to provide a principled syntactic account of pronominal affix ordering.

All of these diagnostics are concerned with morphosyntactic diagnostics for the word boundary. This is even true of (f) which means that object affixes can only be construed as the object of the verb that they are attached to, and not the 'understood' object of another verb in a coordination. Miller and Sag (1997) are therefore focused on establishing the limits of syntax with respect to word boundaries. Their theory does not elaborate a wider notion of the word, perhaps with respect to a theory of signs, or with respect to a larger 'constructicon'. This point will be important in section 11.4.

Once they have made their empirical arguments about the nature of pronominal affixes, the crucial task for Miller and Sag is to account for the data in (27), especially the non-canonical placement of these affixes. Miller and Sag set themselves a particular challenge in that, having demonstrated that French pronominal affixes are affixes, their realization on an auxiliary has to be accounted for.

Miller and Sag's solution exploits the logic of default inheritance and the possibility of multiple inheritance, as expressed in the architecture of HPSG. They argue

(1997: 586) that there are two types of verbal realization: verbs can be realized as plain words, whose arguments are phrases, and cliticized words, which are verbs that have at least one argument that is realized affixally. They elaborate a theory that assumes that French auxiliaries and main verbs enter into a flat structure rather than a hierarchical one, with constituency tests confirming the analysis. This allows them to assume a lexical entry for the tense auxiliary verbs where the elements of the Argument Structure list of the participial complement are also arguments of the auxiliary. As a result, 'the argument structure of the participle determines that of the auxiliary verb's lexeme, and hence the valence of words formed from that auxiliary' (Miller and Sag 1997: 601). Therefore, they provide an argument-sharing analysis which 'interacts with the analysis of pronominal affixation [...] so as to predict a wide range of nonlocal pronominal affixation phenomena'. As a result, 'what appears to be "climbing" of clitic elements follows immediately from lexical principles and local syntactic combination, without the introduction of any further devices' (p. 603).

In the next section, I show that the property of being independently referential has been criterial in some aspects of theorizing about incorporation. Miller and Sag, however, simply establish an affix type (either 'a-aff' for an anaphoric affixal pronoun, or 'p-aff' for a personal affixal pronoun) in their SYNSEM feature matrix. Miller and Sag's (1997) proposal gets the relevant grammaticality differences of the examples in (29).

(29) a. Jean$_i$ sait que Paul$_j$ s'aime. 'Jean$_i$ knows that Paul$_j$ loves himself$_{j,*i}$'
b. Jean$_i$ sait que Paul$_j$ l'aime. 'Jean knows that Paul$_j$ loves him$_{i,*j}$.'

As a result, the full referentiality of the pronominal affix is not an issue for them.

Miller and Sag's (1997) theory has a number of consequences for the theory of grammar. As we shall see in the next section, many have argued for a lexicalist theory of incorporation which similarly has broad consequences for the theory of grammar. Miller and Sag (1997: 633) raise doubts about the Head Movement Constraint, as Anderson (2000) does, and they also argue that the Mirror Principle—which holds that the ordering of morphemes mirrors that of the hierarchy of functional projection—is untenable. Ackema and Neeleman (2004) point out that in derivational syntax it is possible to create complex heads which have different properties from compounds in the same languages. See also Ackema and Neeleman (2010: 23).

11.3.2 Noun incorporation

Noun Incorporation (NI) presents similar problems to French pronominal affixes. In NI, which is a type of compounding (Di Sciullo and Williams 1987; Giegerich 2009; Mithun 1984; Rosen 1989), an argument of the verb is realized within a morphologically complex verb as a nominal root; there are different types of NI, but in at least one subtype the incorporation of the nominal root reduces the verb's valency so that if the incorporated nominal root corresponds to the verb's direct object it is not possible for there to be a discrete Noun Phrase direct object. The alternative analysis is that NI involves movement from the direct object position to the incorporation site/landing site within the complex verb (Baker 1988, 1996). NI is therefore a classic testbed for questions of wordhood and theories of the word. Baker (1988, 1996) presents the main arguments for a syntactic treatment of NI; Anderson (2000, 2001, 2005: 257–87) usefully summarizes and presents a number of arguments for the lexicalist position.

The examples in (30) and (31) below are from Rosen (1989: 295), and are her examples (1) and (2).

(30) Onondaga (Woodbury 1975: 10)

a. *wa ʔhahninúʔ* *neʔ* *oyɛ́kwaʔ.*

TNS.3SG.3N.BUY.ASP ART 3.N.tobacco.NM

'He bought the tobacco'

b. *wa ʔha y ɛ ʔkwahní:nuʔ.*

TNS.3SG.3N.tobacco.buy.ASP

'He bought tobacco'

(31) Niuean (Seiter 1980: 69)

a. *Takafaga* *tu:mau* *ni:* *e* *ia* *e* *tau* *ika.*

hunt always EMPH ERG he ABS PL fish

'He's always hunting fish' (= He's always fishing)

b. *Takafaga* *ika* *tu:mau ni:* *ni:* *a* *ia.*

hunt fish always EMPH ABS he

'He's always fish-hunting' (= He's always fishing)

There are different kinds of NI languages. In the Niuean example, the incorporated noun is non-specific and indefinite or generic. But in Mohawk, it is possible for the incorporated noun to be referentially definite and specific—just as the French pronominal affixes could be. In the example below, the morph corresponding to the meaning 'bed' is referred to by an anaphoric element which is part of the third word in (32); as Baker (1996: 288) points out, the initial use of *-nakt-* is indefinite (and specific), but the incorporated pronoun *-ye-* is definite.

(32) Mohawk (Baker 1996: 288)

Thet´ʌre' wa'-ke-nakt-a-hnínu-'. Í-k-her-e' Uwári

Yesterday FACT-1SG.S-bed-o-buy-PUNC o-1SG.S-think-IMPF Mary

ʌ-ye-núhwe'-ne'

FUT-F.SG.S-like-PUNC

'I bought a bed yesterday. I think Mary will like it (the bed)'

Baker (1996: 307) takes definite reference as criterial alongside the observation that incorporated nouns 'can be modified by elements that appear outside the verb'. For him, these phenomena argue against a lexicalist treatment of NI. However, we have seen that for Miller and Sag (1997), the ability to be independently referential is not criterial in establishing wordhood.

Baker (1996) states that NI is one of the central areas for investigating the lexicalist hypothesis, and he sets up a comparison of a version of a lexicalist theory against his own syntactic theory of the facts, which assumes Head Movement from the canonical argument position after the verb.[9] We can take the semantic argument first. I think that this is a non-argument: it is not at all clear that discourse reference is relevant to wordhood. There is a substantial literature which looks at how sub-events in word meanings can be modified (Levin 1993; Parsons 1990; Pustejovsky 1991). Gisborne (2010: 33) offers this example: *The submarine immediately sank for three hours.* Here, the argument goes, there is no temporal conflict between *immediately* and *for three hours* so there must be two events in the meaning of *sank*, where each event is separately modified, one by *immediately* and one by *for three hours*. These events could be a 'going under' event and a 'staying under' event. An example of how a sub-part of a word's meaning can be relevant to discourse reference would be *I reject the Thatcher$_i$ite view because she$_i$ didn't believe in society.*

Discourse reference is necessarily conceptual. If a verb's meanings can interact with modifiers decompositionally, there is no reason to privilege discourse reference as a property of words. The research question is not, 'How is it that some languages can have definite reference and discourse referents built into their verbs' meanings?' but 'Why does English not include definite reference and discourse referents among the subparts of verbs' meanings that are independently accessible to the grammar?' Anderson (2000, 2001), in a reply which differs from Baker's, suggests (following Rosen 1989; Di Sciullo and Williams 1987) that the verb with NI might well still be transitive, but that the argument is realized by a *pro* which is anaphoric to the incorporated nominal root. However it is entirely compatible with Miller and Sag's (1997) treatment of French pronominal affixes.

Anderson (2001) offers two independent arguments in favour of the lexicalist position. The first is that there is often non-systematic variation between the free form and the incorporated form (see also Osborne 1974). Quoting Mithun (1986: 876), he points out that in Mohawk '*-nahskw-* "domestic animal" only appears incorporated while a semantically equivalent stem *-tshenv* appears only as an independent N[oun]'.

The second is that the semantics of incorporated roots can be subject to lexical drift. This is particularly evident when the NI construction has a meaning which is different from its unincorporated analogue.

(33) Mohawk (Baker 1996; cited in Anderson 2000)

a. tu-s-a-yu-[a]t-háh-a-hkw-e'

DUP-ITER-FACT-FSG.S-SRFL-road-pick.up-PUNC

'She started her journey.' (lit.: 'picked up the road')

[9] Ackema and Neeleman (2007) point out differences between Head Movement in NI, and more straightforward syntactic cases.

b. #tu-s-a-yú-([a]te)-hkwe-e' ne oháha
DUP-ITER-FACT-FSG.S-SRFL-pick.up-PUNC art road
'She picked up the road.' (literal reading only)

The semantic arguments, then, are either irrelevant to an account of wordhood (as in the argument from discourse reference) or provide evidence in favour of the lexicalist approach. What about Baker's claim about apparently stranded modifiers? Anderson (2000) simply asserts that the material modifies the *pro* in the argument position. His difference from Baker (1996) is in his inventory of empty categories. Anderson (2000) also points out, that '[i]n Mohawk, as in most languages, there is no overt correspondent of English *one*, so the object phrase in *I want a new one* consists of just the Adjective *new*'.

However, although there is no inherent lexicalist reason to reject empty categories, the theories I mentioned at the beginning of this chapter all do. I reject empty categories because they are unlearnable, and make no sense unless you adopt nativist assumptions about language acquisition. But no empty category is needed: the apparently stranded modifiers modify a subpart of the conceptual structure associated with the incorporated word, just as in my SINK example earlier. This is not very different from *He drinks his coffee black*, where the adjunct of the Verb modifies an argument of the verb.

What, then, are the diagnostics which will decide whether NI is syntactic or morphological? The issue is important because a lot hangs on it. The debate goes back to Kroeber (1909) and Sapir (1911), with Kroeber arguing that there was no such thing as NI and Sapir providing a lexicalist analysis. More recently, Sadock (1980, 1985) has provided a syntactic account of incorporation phenomena in West Greenlandic, and Baker (1988, 1996) has developed a syntactic approach which in turn provides a substantial part of the empirical and theoretical underpinnings of the theory of Head Movement.[10, 11] On the other hand, Sapir (1911), Mithun (1986, 2000), Anderson (1992, 2000, 2001), Asudeh and Mikkelsen (2000), and others have argued that NI is built by morphological processes which are not part of syntax.

Baker (1996: 314–29) claims that there are three main arguments in favour of a syntactic solution to the problem of NI. First, he observes that the incorporated nominal element cannot be co-referential with the subject of the NI verb form, and argues that this is due to a Condition C binding effect—a referring expression cannot be locally bound—and that this follows from the incorporated nominal being extracted from the object position of the verb, and leaving behind a trace. However, Spencer (1995)

[10] The phenomena Sadock (1980, 1985) discusses are arguably more like derivation than compounding (but see Spencer 1995) and some scholars such as Rosen (1989) have argued that they should not be included in discussions of incorporation. On the other hand, Sadock's approach brings the West Greenlandic phenomena in line with NI.

[11] Baker (2009) maintains that NI requires Head Movement despite other non-lexicalist theorists (Massam 2001; Van Geenhoven 2002) arguing that it is not necessary.

extensively shows that this claim does not follow for other languages with NI, such as Chukchi, which also show discourse reference effects with respect to the incorporated noun, and so are very similar to the Mohawk case. Moreover, Spencer shows that Baker's claim that adjuncts cannot incorporate does not apply to Chukchi, and effectively reduces Baker's theory to a set of parochial claims about Mohawk. It is also worth noting that the binding theory is itself subject to a number of theoretical challenges (Pollard and Sag 1992), and does not constitute a reliable diagnostic or analytic tool for other distributional facts.

Second, Baker shows that there are restrictions on questions: an interrogative form corresponding to WHO or WHAT cannot be extracted from object position when there is incorporation, which he accounts for by the argument that something else (the incorporated element) has already been extracted from object position. This argument does not wash in the terms of Principles and Parameters theory itself: Head Movement has a head position as its landing site; the landing site for WH operators in that theory is Spec,C. Moreover, we know that there are languages which permit the filling of both Spec,C and C, according to the literature on 'Doubly-Filled Comps' in languages such as Belfast English (Henry 1995).

But Baker argues that his most important claim centres on the observation that there is no agreement with the incorporated (syntactic) argument in Noun Incorporation. As Anderson (2000) points out, this puts him in direct conflict with Postal (1979), who argues that there is agreement, but the absence of agreement is essential to Baker's position because he claims that it is not possible to have agreement with a trace, and his theory of NI requires there to be movement from the object position.

According to Baker (1996), the absence of agreement in NI structures is consistent with his claim that there is movement of a nominal element from the object position of the verb to the incorporated position. Baker (1996: 314–20) compares the structure in (34a) with that in (34b).

(34) a. The syntactic analysis of Baker (1988): [N_i—V t_i]
b. A lexicalist analysis with *pro*: [N—V *pro*]

The argument is that the syntactic account involves movement, leaving a trace behind, whereas the lexicalist account involves *pro*. Traces do not trigger agreement, so no agreement would be expected according to Baker's theory, whereas *pro* occupies the ordinary object slot, and so agreement would be expected according to the lexicalist account. Baker is not merely putting up a straw man: Rosen's lexicalist account calls for *pro*-drop to account for the stranding facts (1989: 316), although the same is not true of Mithun (1984, 1986) and Mithun and Corbett (1999).

There is a complication. As Baker (1996: 315) points out, 'Mohawk has no overt agreement morpheme for neuter objects.' This is a particularly awkward wrinkle, because '[M]ost natural and spontaneous instances of NI in Mohawk generally involve neuter nouns [... which] has led to some confusion in the literature about whether I[ncorporated] N[ouns] are agreed with or not.' Before I come to these points, I should make it clear that my own approach, with no empty categories, also predicts that there will be no agreement.

Once we reject empty categories, and if we at the same time treat NI as a straightforward case of compounding, there is nothing in the structure to trigger agreement. Therefore, if Baker is right, the absence of agreement is not evidence in favour of his movement-based approach. It is evidence against an approach which has the empty category *pro* as part of its analysis. As I said above, none of the lexicalist theories of syntax I mentioned in the introduction assumes empty categories, so the argument against a lexicalist theory that adopts *pro* is a strangely parochial argument.

Mohawk does occasionally incorporate animate nominal roots, and when it does they are also typically not accompanied by an agreement marker. I would have thought that the analysis was simple: it is not possible for a nominal root to be incorporated with its agreement markers in place, because we do not find inflection within words, and NI is a kind of compounding. But Baker (1996: 318) says that this argument will not work, because of data like those in (35), where there is an incorporated element and there is also doubling, in that it appears that the Object is simultaneously present with the incorporated nominal stem.

(35) Ra-wir-a-núhwe'-s thíkʌ (owirá'a)
MSG.S-baby-o-like-HAB that baby
'He likes that baby.'

Baker (1996: 318) claims that this is the most important example in his book, because 'it shows that verbs with incorporated nouns have a unique syntax [. . .]' and 'If the verb in (75) [=35, NG] were truly intransitive, then there would be no argument position to licence the external NP in this sentence [. . .] if the verb were a simple transitive, then it would have to agree with its object.' The external NP in this case is the apparent object *thíkʌ (owirá'a)*, which Baker analyses as an adjunct. It is true that such data are difficult for the lexicalist analysis, because this means that the lexicalist account is obliged to have a theory of doubling which accounts for the absence of agreement in examples such as (35). One possibility of course is simply that (35) involves a structure such as *I like it, that baby.* Given the next item of evidence, it is certainly not enough to hang a whole theory off an example such as (35).

Baker (1996: 319) presents the examples in (36) as problematic for his theory. As he says, in these examples either an agreeing or a non-agreeing form is acceptable.

(36) a. Uwári ye(-ruwa)-kstʌ-hser-ʹʌhaw-e' ne rake-'níha
Mary FSG.S(/MSG.O)-old.person-NOM-carry-IMPF PRT my-father
'Mary is holding my father.'

b. Wa'-ke (-hi)-kstʌ-hser-áhset-e'
FACT-1SG.S(/MSG.O)-old.person-NOM-hide-PUNC
'I hid the old person (the old man).'

Baker writes, 'I would like to suggest that the material [...] shows that *both* the lexical compounding analysis and the syntactic incorporation analysis are valid after all. The two structures often exist side by side in Mohawk.' I am not sure how to address these facts. There is more relevant data, however. Noun stems such as *-wir-* 'baby' can be incorporated, even though babies are not inanimate. In the example given, when *-wir-* is incorporated, there is no agreement. The examples are Baker's (1996: 316) examples (69) and (70).

(37) a. Shako-núhwe'-s (ne owirá'a)
MSG.S/3PL.O-like-HAB NE baby
'He likes them (babies).'

b. *Ra-núhwe'-s (ne owirá'a)
MSG.S-like-HAB NE baby
'He likes them (babies).'

(38) a. *?Shako-wir-a-núhwe'-s
MSG.S/3PL.O-baby-o-like-HAB
'He likes babies.'

b. Ra-wir-a-núhwe'-s
MSG.S-baby-o-like-HAB
'He likes babies.'

Baker's argument hinges on examples like (37) and (38): the examples in (37) show that with the 'ordinary transitive verb, feminine or masculine agreement is required when the direct object is understood to be a baby; null/neuter agreement is considered inappropriate.' However the judgements are reversed in (38) when the noun is incorporated. This, Baker (1996: 316) claims, is what is predicted by the theory in (34a), and it disconfirms the theory in (34b). But of course it is also entirely compatible with treating Mohawk incorporation as being a form of compounding with no empty category in the canonical object position.

11.4 The theoretical stance

In the three case studies I have discussed, I have argued for a lexicalist take on the relationship between the word and syntax, while pointing at a literature which often takes a very different position. The theoretical proposal about the word and syntax has been discussed in the context of a larger theoretical package. We cannot just compare a generally lexicalist with a generally syntactic proposal: we need to discuss a specific syntactic proposal and compare it with an equally well-worked-out lexicalist proposal. The lexicalist position has turned out to be highly focused: for example, Miller and Sag's (1997) account of French pronominal affixes is concerned with the question of what the terminal node in a syntactic string is—and Miller and Sag argue that the terminal node is the word, not some sub-part of a word. Therefore, they also take the view that sub-parts of words do not participate in syntax.

And this is the debate: are words, or sub-word elements (morphs, or morphemes), the primitives of syntax? My three case studies have been concerned with evaluating the evidence and exploring different proposals about this particular question: I have not been led to questions about the relationship between words and constructions, or words and their meanings. This last point has been particularly important in looking at pronominal affixes in section 11.2 and the incorporation facts in section 11.3. These assertions mean, of course, that I am not assuming that it is necessary (for the purposes of linguistic theory) to define 'The Word' across a range of parameters, which is one of the objectives of Dixon and Aikhenvald (2002b) and several of the chapters therein.

This last point is important, because there are authors, such as Haspelmath (2011), who argue that the notion of the word should be dispensed with because it is too hard to define so that it is cross-linguistically valid, and there is no simple convergent set of criteria for wordhood. In a sense there is also a general question about whether the word is the basic unit of analysis or whether the utterance is. Even this question has consequences for the theoretical status of the word. And so to the most important point: the word—the syntactic word in the case of this chapter—is a theoretical construct. Prototypical words might well exist in the wild, but when it comes to complex data involving boundaries between sub-parts of grammar, what a word is will depend on a host of intellectual choices made by the theorist. Hippisley (this volume) addresses similar issues.

There are three theoretical issues. What are the bounds on abstractness? What are the bounds on complexity? And where is the mess? I will take the last first. Mismatch is a kind of mess—arguably, most syntactic theorizing is about working out the limits on mismatch. A theory like Baker's (1996) reduces the mismatch, and therefore the mess, between syntax and semantics. His incorporated nominal stems can be in a one-to-one relationship with discourse referents. Baker puts the mess at the syntax–morphology interface: for Baker, what looks like a word is a syntagm. A theory like Miller and Sag's, on the other hand, locates the mess at the morphosyntax–semantics interface: an affixal part of a word can have an independent discourse referent, but their theory reduces the complexity at the morphology–syntax interface: the combinatorial units of syntax are words, and the problems of pronominal affixes being subject to affix ordering restrictions and being able to undergo 'clitic climbing' go away.

Abstractness is another issue. My account of the distribution of the passive participle in section 11.2 relied on an abstract approach to morphology: I treated morphs as realizations of abstract feature clusters, so they do not have meaning in their own right, and argued that this was the approach which best handled facts such as suppletion. A less abstract theory of morphology would have morphemes—meaningful morphs which are not abstract realizations. But this would arguably add complexity, because it would mean that the lexicon would have to store a large number of homophonous morphemes. So, we might make a theory less abstract with a particular strategy, but that same strategy could make it more complex. Likewise, the decision about where the mess goes will have consequences for how abstract a theory is, and how complex. Baker's theory introduces the complexity of head movement. That of Miller and Sag has the complexity of a mismatch between the word and discourse referents. Head movement gives us the abstractness of functional heads. Miller and Sag work with the abstractness of default inheritance and default overriding.

There are other dimensions of abstractness that I have not addressed. The version of a lexicalist analysis of NI presented by both Baker (1996) and Anderson (2000, 2001) involves an unrealized pronoun, *pro*. Both Baker and Anderson assume that the debate about how to tackle NI reduces to a question of what the relevant empty category should be. While the debate can be framed in those terms, it is not obvious that it should be. After all, the theory proposed by Miller and Sag (1997) has no recourse to empty categories at all, and it manages to account for apparent 'clitic climbing' without clitics and without climbing.

CHAPTER 12

THE PROSODIC WORD[1]

KRISTINE A. HILDEBRANDT

12.1 Introduction

In languages like English, with long orthographic and literary (and prescriptive) traditions, the notion of a 'word' has centred around a written unit bounded by spaces, or which may be uttered alone, carrying its own meaningful content (cf. Bloomfield 1933's 'Minimal Free Forms'; Bolinger 1963: 113 on the word as 'prime'; Lyons 1968 on the word as a core unit of traditional grammatical theory). However, it does not take long to identify units across languages that are problematic under a singular definition of word, but that still somehow manifest word-like properties to some extent, based on different criteria.

Words are typically defined on a combination of orthographic, grammatical, phonological, and semantic/conceptual criteria. At times these criteria neatly align to converge on a notion of word that embodies all of these senses at once, but at other times they do not. In English, for example, a word is typically thought of as having independent content meaning, as being a syntactic head or terminal node, able to be uttered in isolation as an independent whole (typically with pauses both before and after), and as being represented orthographically with flanking typographic spaces. These diagnostics converge on units like lexical nouns and verbs, and also on adjectives and adverbs (*cat, walk, beautiful*, etc.).

But even with these seemingly clear-cut criteria, there are complications. For example, orthographic conventions can interfere with phonological understanding of word constituents and boundaries (a kind of orthographic–phonological misalignment), as has been demonstrated in studies of literate children who struggle to process the phonemic equality in words with different spellings. For example, children are liable to conceptualize

[1] This chapter emerges from research done within the *Word Domains* project, supported by the Deutsche Forschungsgemeinschaft (Grant No. BI 799/2-3). I wish to thank Balthasar Bickel and John Taylor for helpful comments. All errors are my own.

the affricate segment /t͡ʃ/ differently in words like *rich* /ɹɪt͡ʃ/ and *pitch* /pɪt͡ʃ/ because of their different spellings (Ehri and Wilce 1980).

English function words such as prepositions (*on, of, by*), conjunctions (*and, but*), and discourse markers (*um, so*) represent another kind of mis-match between prototypical word criteria, as these may carry a main stress, are minimally mono- or disyllabic (and thus phonologically word-like), yet they have little content (lexical) meaning but instead perform syntactic and pragmatic functions of grammatical linkage and transition.

The English possessive marker *'s* is also problematic for a singular notion of word hood (Hudson 2001). Orthographically, it looks more like an affix than a word. Prosodically, it is smaller than a minimal free unit (being sub-syllabic in size), and like suffixes in English it coheres phonologically with a constituent of greater phonological bulk (as evidenced by voicing assimilation: *the dog'*[z] *food* vs. *the cat'*[s] *food*). However, its prosodic host may be a variety of lexical classes, as shown in (1)

(1) (a) Host to a NP: [The man]'s dog
(b) Host to a nested NP: [The house of a friend of mine]'s roof blew off. (Halliday 2005: 230)
(c) Host to a relative clause: [The man I was speaking to]'s dog
(d) Host to another possessive phrase: [John's brother]'s radio

These examples illustrate that the scope of possession is phrasal or clausal, which sets the possessive marker apart from suffixes like the plural in English, which must cohere to each syntactic head in a larger phrase (e.g. *several cat<u>s</u> and dog<u>s</u>* vs. *several *cat and dog<u>s</u>*). The English possessive marker is thus classified as an (en)clitic: a unit that is not a word in a prototypical sense, but with fewer selectional restrictions than a grammatical affix. So it is not an affix either. The idiosyncratic phonological and distributional patterns of clitics have been considered in detail within formal models of prosodic words (cf. Nespor and Vogel 2007; Vogel 1990, 2009), and I return to these in section 12.4.

These examples also suggest that more may be revealed about the patterns and manifestations of word-like units across languages by separating out the criteria and considering them from different perspectives. This chapter treats words as they are defined in a phonological sense.

As will be detailed in section 12.2, a prosodic word is a linguistic unit around which language-specific phonological generalizations may be made. A phonological treatment of words has a number of advantages. Following Pike (1947), a recognition of prosodic words (or p-words) allows for a distinction between grammatical units (and the patterns that define these) and units defined by phonemic, phonotactic, stress, rhythm, and intonational patterns. In English, this distinction may be illustrated with the sentence in (2).[2]

[2] Selkirk (1996) distinguishes between 'free clitic' vs. 'affixal clitic' instantiations for English function words like auxiliaries, prepositions, demonstratives, and object pronouns.

(2) English uncontracted auxiliary
((He)GW)PW ((will)GW)PW ((go)GW)PW

In its uncontracted form, the auxiliary *will* is a separate grammatical word (GW) (as evidenced by its independent front ward movement in a yes–no question: *Will he go?*), a separate orthographic word, and a separate prosodic word (PW) (as it carries its own main stress). When the auxiliary attaches to the subject pronoun *he*, it merges prosodically with that subject pronoun; the pronoun vowel centralizes, the auxiliary reduces, and there is now a single main stress for the entire contracted form (*he'll* → [ˈhɪɫ]). The two grammatical words align as a single prosodic (and orthographic) word, as illustrated in (3)

(3) ((He)GW('ll)GW)PW ((go)GW)PW

Here, it makes sense to think of one prosodic word-like unit (*he'll*) comprising two grammatical words (the subject pronoun and the auxiliary).

This recognition of prosodic words is also handy for delineating domains for languages like Turkish, where suffix vowels alternate in their backness features (and where high vowels also alternate in rounding) in stem–suffix combinations (Crothers and Shibatani 1977; Waterson 1956). This is shown with noun-plus-genitive suffixes in (4) and (5).

(4) Bare noun stem

ev	'house'	(–high, -back, -rounded)
göl	'lake'	(–high, -back, +rounded)
kɨz	'girl'	(+high, +back, -rounded)
kutu	'box'	(+high, +back, +rounded)

(5) Turkish stem plus genitive suffix

ev-in	'of the house'	(backness harmony)
göl-ün	'of the lake'	(backness harmony)
kɨz-ɨn	'of the girl'	(backness and rounding harmony)
kutu-un	'of the box'	(backness and rounding harmony)

In contrast to stem–suffix combinations, compounds, which may also be thought of as a single grammatical word, do not participate in vowel harmony, as shown in (6).

(6) Turkish compound
kurk + ayak 'forty' + 'foot' 'centipede'

In (6), the vowels of the stems do not show backness or rounding harmony. With the examples in (4) and (5) in mind, a grammatical word in Turkish may be (for example) a stem with or without inflectional suffixes, while a prosodic word in Turkish for the purposes of vowel harmony includes only a single inflected noun stem, as illustrated in the schema in (7).

(7) Grammatical words and prosodic word alignment in Turkish
((stem-suffix)GW)PW
((stem)PW + (stem)PW)GW

The rest of this chapter will turn to definitions and generalizations regarding prosodic words and examples of prosodic word diagnostics in a range of languages (sections 12.2 and 12.3). It will also cover (section 12.4) issues and debates surrounding the treatment of prosodic words in different theoretical frameworks, and will close (section 12.5) with some commentary on current and future trends in the scholarship of prosodic words.

12.2 Prosodic words: preliminaries and treatments

The term 'prosodic word' was first used by Dixon (1977a, 1977b), and shortly thereafter by Selkirk (1978, 1980a, 1980b), and has subsequently been adopted by numerous scholars (e.g. Booij 1999; Downing 1999; Raffelsiefen 1999; Schiering et al. 2010; and in this chapter). While it appears to be the most commonly used term, other frequently observed (and synonymic) variants include 'phonological word' (Dixon and Aikhenvald 2002a; Hall 1999a; Nespor and Vogel 2007), while the contributions in Hall et al. (2008) vary from one author to the next. Hall (1999a) and numerous others also make use of short-hand versions, including 'p-word' (adopted below), 'pword', 'PW', 'pw', and the Greek character small omega ω (also used below).

As illustrated in the introduction, the prosodic word is distinguished in some languages from the grammatical word, which is defined by Dixon and Aikhenvald (2002b: 18–19) as a grammatical element fulfilling criteria of (morphosyntactic) cohesiveness, fixed ordering, and conventionalized meaning. As they note, the difference between the types is not always made explicit in reference grammars (even those with otherwise comprehensive phonetic, phonological, and morphophonological descriptions) because of the (implicit) observation or assumption that the two domains coincide. This appears to be the case in languages like Yokuts (Yokutsan; Newman 1967), and to a more limited extent, Moses-Columbia Salish (Salishan; Czaykowska-Higgins 1998). In many more cases, however, prosodic words and grammatical words do not align neatly, either with prosodic words containing more than one grammatical word (often observed with the behaviour of clitics) or with grammatical words containing more than one prosodic word (typically observed with compounds). These cases will be elaborated on in sections 12.3 and 12.4.

Dixon's grammars of Dyirbal and Yidiny (Pama-Nyungan, Australia) are amongst the earliest published works containing sections devoted to the analysis of words in both grammatical and phonological senses (1972, 1977a, 1977b).

Regardless of the specific theoretical framework appealed to, most scholars define the prosodic word as a unit greater than a syllable (or a phonological foot) that is the domain for various phonological generalizations, typically categorized into:

a. domains for phonological rules;
b. domains for phonotactic generalizations;
c. domains for prosodic minimality constraints.

The Turkish example in section 12.1 illustrates domain type (a). Evidence for type (b) has been historically harder to come by, as phonotactic generalizations are typically assumed to be syllable-based only and are not frequently examined in the context of p-words. However, close analysis of the distribution of phonotactic patterns and constraints in Germanic languages has revealed some of these to be p-word-based. For example, Hall (1999b) demonstrates that in German, short, lax, non-low vowels [ɪ, ʏ, ɛ, œ, ʊ, ɔ], while found in open syllables word-medially, as in (haʀ.ˈmoː.nɪ.ka)ω 'harmonica', are not found in open syllables in p-word-final position. As for the third criterion, a number of languages impose restrictions on the minimal size of prosodically free units. For example, prosodic words are minimally disyllabic in Yidiny (Dixon 1977a, 1977b). In Burmese, minor (toneless, reduced vowel, and prosodically unfooted) syllables do not occur in isolation, and are prosodically licensed at the level of the p-word in combination with full (tonal, full vowel, footed) syllables (Green 1995: 78–9). This is illustrated in the schema for the word *zəbwɛ̀*: 'table' in (8).

(8) Syllable, foot, and word in Burmese
((zə)σ((bwɛ̀ː)σ)ϕ)ω

The initial syllable is subminimal and is not parsed as a prosodically independent unit (as schwa is not a full vowel). The initial syllable is licensed prosodically in combination with the final syllable. As such, the minimal p-word in Burmese is a stressed syllable, containing a full vowel, that can be a tone-bearing unit.

Contemporaneously with other non-linear alternatives emerging in the field in the 1970s and 1980s (e.g. Goldsmith 1976), both Selkirk (1978, 1980a) and Nespor and Vogel (2007) argued within a framework of prosodic phonology for a hierarchical representation of phonological units, defined on the basis of phonological mapping rules that reference information from different grammatical components (e.g. syllables, morphological structure, phrasal structure). These approaches recognized that the phonological component of the grammar interacts non-trivially with other grammatical subsystems.

As a result of these developments, it is now common practice to define and represent the prosodic word in relation to other prosodic units with which it aligns in the larger hierarchy (the 'Prosodic Hierarchy'). The representation of the Prosodic Hierarchy, including the prosodic word (ω), is presented in (9), adapted from Hall (1999a: 9).

(9) The Prosodic Hierarchy[3]

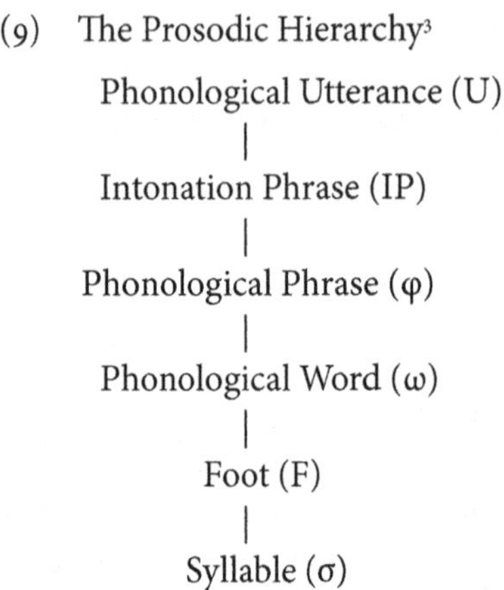

As modelled in the Prosodic Hierarchy Hypothesis (PHH), the p-word is defined as the lowest constituent in the hierarchy to make substantial use of non-phonological information. It is largely, but not necessarily, coextensive with the grammatical word, and as such represents a significant interaction between morphology and phonology (Nespor and Vogel 2007: 109). The syllable and foot are claimed to reference purely phonological information, while the phonological phrase, intonational phrase, and phonological utterance reference syntactic information and are assumed to consist of multiple grammatical words (see Nespor and Vogel 2007 for a full treatment of all proposed domains).

At the heart of Prosodic Phonology are sets of predictions regarding the relationship of p-words within the larger hierarchy. One central methodological assumption, discussed by Nespor and Vogel (p. 18) and termed by Schiering et al. (2010) the 'Generality Assumption,' is that the hypothesis only holds for processes and patterns that apply generally across the lexicon of a given language (i.e. processes that are lexically specified are exempt from consideration within the theory). An example of a lexically specified process is trisyllabic shortening in English, where some words show a vowel quality change in the initial vowel when in a derived environment with two following syllables, the first of which is unstressed (e.g. n[ej]tion → n[æ]tional, div[ai]n → div[ɪ]nity). But this occurs

[3] There is some variation in the symbols used for these constituents. The Phonological Utterance is variably represented as U (Hall 1999a; Nespor and Vogel 2007) or as Utt (Selkirk 1978). The Intonation Phrase is variably represented as I (Nespor and Vogel 2007) or IP (Hall 1999a; Selkirk 1978). The phonological phrase is variably represented as P (Hall 1999a; Schiering et al. 2010), as φ (Nespor and Vogel 2007), or as PhP (Selkirk 1978). The Prosodic Word is variably represented as ω (Hall 1999a; Nespor and Vogel 2007; Schiering et al. 2010) or as PWd (Selkirk 1978). The Foot is variably represented as Ft (Selkirk 1978), as F (Hall 1999a), as Σ (Nespor and Vogel 2007), or as φ (Schiering et al. 2010).

only in certain morphological environments, and with exceptions (e.g. sens[ej]tion → *sens[æ]tional). Such processes are immune from consideration within the PHH.

While this delineation appears to avoid unnecessary complications and complexities with the model, it should be noted that there are cases of languages that appear to have very few (if any) lexically general phonological processes and patterns; see, for example, Matisoff's (1973) grammar of Lahu, a Tibeto-Burman language in which the vast majority of (mainly syllable-referencing) phonological processes are lexically specified.

Another central principle of Prosodic Phonology and the PHH is that of 'Clustering', which predicts a single and universally present set of domains—as represented in (6)—that phonological processes and patterns map to (Inkelas and Zec 1995: 547f.; Nespor and Vogel 2007: 11). In other words, the Hierarchy is a universal, as are the domains that build up the Hierarchy. As such, p-words are said to be universally present in all natural human languages. However, despite a multitude of published literature on p-word diagnostics and indicators across a wide range of families (surveyed in section 12.3), there are (as will be seen in section 12.4) some languages that defy diagnostics for prosodic words; it is therefore questionable whether p-words are relevant at all in a phonological description of these languages.

Another important principle of the PHH is formulated as a set of interrelating principles that predict how the different domains of the hierarchy will align. These principles are frequently referred to in unison as the 'Strict Layer Hypothesis' (Hall 1999a; Selkirk 1984), and as a group they predict against skipping and against recursivity (or replication) of domains. The 'no skipping' dimension is referred to variably as 'Strict Succession', and has been reformulated slightly to predict that any given prosodic domain *n* will be properly headed by an immediately dominant category *n+1* (Ito and Mester 1992). In this prediction, the p-word immediately dominates at least one foot, and is itself immediately dominated by one prosodic phrase.

As noted by Inkelas and Zec (1995: 548) and as surveyed typologically in Bickel et al. (2009) and Schiering et al. (2010), these predictions and generalizations are largely accepted in several contemporary accounts and approaches, although they have been reformulated in a general sense in the form of violable constraints in Optimality Theory (Selkirk 1996). At the same time, they have been variably challenged and reformulated in a variety of language-specific accounts. A summary of some of these challenges and the responses are further elaborated on in section 12.4. Before that, section 12.3 contains a more detailed survey of prosodic word diagnostics and types across a diverse sample of languages.

12.3 Prosodic words: diagnostics and types

12.3.1 Preliminary considerations

The theoretical architecture of the Prosodic Hierarchy has motivated different large-scale typological inquiries on how words and other constituents may be identified and how they align with each other. *Stresstyp* (http://st2.ullet.net) charts the metrical systems of over 500 languages (Goedemans et al. 1996; Hulst 1999; Hulst et al. 2010). The Word Domains Project, part of the *Autotyp* research programme (http://www.spw.uzh.ch/autotyp/projects/), charts the range of diversity in how languages define prosodic words. As a result, there is a growing database of comprehensive p-word profiles (as well as syllable- and foot-level) across a range of languages from different genealogical affiliations and geographical regions. This section revisits the main diagnostics for p-words as they are evidenced across a range of languages (phonological rules, phonotactic generalizations, and minimality requirements), and includes further discussion of stress as a p-word diagnostic. It should be noted, however, that it can be tricky to separate these diagnostics from each other, as they interrelate and overlap in many languages. In Yidiny, for example, a verb root may be (minimally) disyllabic or trisyllabic, but inflected trisyllabic p-words are subject to syllable reduction or deletion, as illustrated in (10a,b).

(10) Yidiny P-word maximality and reduction (Dixon 1977a: 90)
  a. /milba-ŋal-ɲu/ clever-CAUS-PST → [milbaŋalɲu]ω 'made clever'
  b. /guma:ɽi-ŋal-ɲu/ red-CAUS-PST → [gumaɽiŋa:l]ω 'made red'

In (10a) with the disyllabic verb root the suffixes surface in unreduced phonetic form, while in (10b) with the trisyllabic verb root there is deletion with compensatory lengthening. This constraint also applies to those grammatical affixes that are disyllabic. So while the reduction in Yidiny is triggered by a general size restriction, the process (or reconciliation) is uniquely a prosodic word diagnostic in this language.

As another example of this overlap, in Dagbani (Gur, Ghana), ATR ('Advanced Tongue Root') vowel harmony optionally applies across monosyllabic roots and suffixes, but does not apply across polysyllabic roots and suffixes (either when the root is underlyingly polysyllabic or in cases of schwa-epenthesis), or across compounds (Olawsky 2002: 209–11). This represents an intersection of maximality constraints with a phonological rule or process (which variably applies or fails to apply, depending on other prosodic properties of the domain).

12.3.2 Phonological rules

A wide range of phonological rules, processes, and alternations are employed as diagnostics for prosodic words across languages. Example (10) in section 12.3.1 demonstrated that vowel reduction and deletion are p-word diagnostics in Yidiny. Bickel et al. (2009) classify these rules into different subtypes, including allomorphy and allophony, assimilations, dissimilations and harmonies (by far the most common), insertions and deletions, fortitions and lenitions, tone alternations, and a category of other assorted processes (e.g. specific kinds of resyllabification).

The examples of vowel harmony in Turkish in (4) and (5) demonstrate the prosodic word as constituting root morphemes, variably including suffixes. Vowel harmony does not apply across roots plus prefixes, or across stems in a compound. In Eastern/Central Arrernte (Pama-Nyungan, Australia), the plural suffix *-errir* has an allomorph *-ewarr* based on the phonological structure of a preceding morpheme within a specific prosodic domain, resembling a kind of vowel harmony (Henderson 2002: 117). But within a grammatical word, the suffix is now prosodically separated from its harmony trigger, as in (11).

(11) Failure of application of allomorphy in Arrernte
(akwaketye)ω+(ak-errir-eme)ω (*ewarr-eme)
put.arm.around$_1$+put.arm.around$_2$-PL-PRES
'more than two put arms around (someone)'

In (11), while *-ewarr* is expected based on the prosodic properties of the first stem piece, it is in fact *-errir* that surfaces. So unlike Turkish, where suffixes are included in a p-word domain for one type of allophony (vowel harmony), in Arrernte suffixes are potentially excluded from a p-word domain for the type of allophony at play in this language (namely e~a alternations). This example shows that prosodic words are identified by language-specific processes, and that their alignment with particular morphological domains is also language-specific, a trend that is repeated throughout this account.

In addition to allophony, prosodic words may be identified via a variety of other constraints and processes. For example, Hohenberger's (2008) account of the prosodic word in signed German includes minimality/maximality constraints, as well as what is termed a 'symmetry constraint' in two-handed signs that demands that the hands move with symmetry within the prosodic word (p. 261). In typologically and genealogically quite different languages, tone processes, alternations, or domains of application align with prosodic words. This is true for Tamangic, Tibeto-Burman languages (Tamang, Nar-Phu, Manange), where the tone of the entire p-word is determined by the underlying tone of a lexeme (Mazaudon 2004, 2012; Hildebrandt 2005). In these languages, all grammatical (non-lexical) morphemes are atonal, and all words, whether monosyllabic or polysyllabic, whether morphologically simple or complex, carry one of four tones. As such, in Tamang, a mid-level (tone /2/) verb like /tha:/ *cut* phonetically displays the same mid-level pitch properties (manifested through fundamental frequency) on the monosyllabic root as it does across a trisyllabic inflected stem (e.g. [˧tha:-˧sa-˧mi] cut-COND-TAM *if he cuts*) (Mazaudon 2004: 6–7). The prosodic word-as-tone-bearing unit is a typological rarity, but it is not unattested; see Donohue (2003, 2008) for Skou (Austronesian) and Post (2009) for Galo (Tibeto-Burman).

Galo also makes use of regressive consonant voicing (for stops) and place (for nasals) assimilation, which is obligatory and productive word-internally and optional across words. This is illustrated in (12).

(12) Prosodic-word medial assimilations in Galo (Post 2009: 949)
/gók-boolo/ 'call-COND' → [gogbooló]
/ɲóm-káa/ 'swallow-PF' → [ɲoŋkáa]

We can see from these examples that phonological processes may identify and delineate prosodic words as much by their presence (their application) as by their absence (or failure to apply) in particular morphological domains.

12.3.3 Phonotactic generalizations

Dutch is a language in which phonotactic generalizations (combined with other evidence) identify p-words that may or may not align with a single grammatical word. Prosodic words that align with content words must contain minimally one full vowel (not schwa), and they cannot be schwa-initial. With these criteria, function words such as articles are not p-words (e.g. *een* 'a' /ən/), and this is independently supported by their failure to carry a main stress (another diagnostic for p-words in Dutch) (Booij 1999: 47, 99). Prosodic words also have restrictions on consonant clusters. The syllable template for Dutch is as follows, where 'X' represents any segment and (S) is the fricative /s/.

(13) Dutch syllable template (Booij 1999: 29)

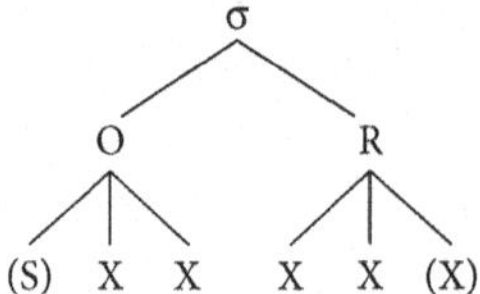

Syllable rhymes in Dutch are always heavy, and onset and rhyme positions can have consonant clusters (which obey the Sonority Sequencing Generalization: Clements 1990; Zec 1988). However clusters of four consonants (in which one of the segments is the coronal fricative /s/) are found only at the right edge of a p-word (e.g. *bedaardst* 'calmest'), while word-initial and medial (onset and coda) clusters are limited to three (or fewer) consecutive consonants (p. 27). With these criteria in mind, prepositions, also classed as function words (e.g. *naast* 'besides'), and certain suffixes (e.g. *-achtig* 'like') form their own prosodic words, as they contain one full vowel, carry an independent main stress, and may have final sC clusters (p. 47). Booij represents the prosodic word in Dutch schematically as in (14), where the p-word is of one syllable or greater, and where the rhyme ('appendix') comprises three or fewer non-sonorant, coronal consonants.

(14) Dutch prosodic word template (Booij 1999: 29)

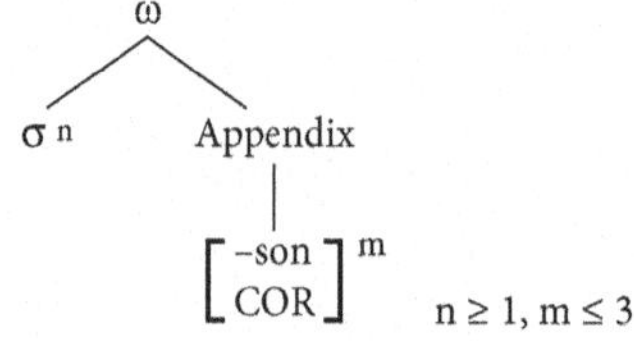

Unlike Dutch, Dagbani has a simpler syllable template of (C)V(ː)(C). Words are frequently disyllabic (about 76 per cent of the lexicon) and rarely trisyllabic (Olawsky 2002: 206). In word-medial position, a variety of coda consonants may be present: [m, n, ŋ, l, r, b, ɣ]. In word-final position only the bilabial and velar nasals [m, ŋ] are observed. This is in a sense the mirror opposite of Dutch: word-medial position in Dagbani licenses a greater range of phonotactic options than does word-final position.

Phonotactic constraints in Dagbani also interact with the word-stress system. In most words, a penultimate stress is observed (in both morphologically simple, suffixed, and in compound words). There is a subset of words with final stress, and when these words are suffixed, the surfacing phonetic form appears to be in line with the dominant penultimate pattern, as shown without and with the plural suffix and its allomorphs (which also trigger resyllabification) in (15).

(15) Words with final stress in Dagbani (Olawsky 2002: 207)
nəŋ.ˈg͡buŋ 'body' → nəŋ.ˈg͡bu-na 'body-PL'
kun.ˈdun 'hyena' → kun.ˈdu-na 'hyena-PL'
da.ˈtɕeː 'playmate' → da.ˈtɕɛ-hi 'playmate-PL'

Olawsky observes that it is only a subset of disyllabic nouns that end in /n/ or /ŋ/ or a long vowel that show this pattern. He analyses these disyllabic, final-stressed words as a shortened version of the underlying trisyllabic form /CVC.CVC.X/ or /CVC.CVː.X/, where 'X' is an invisible (catalectic) prosodic unit (i.e. a syllable), which forms the prosodic structure for an actual penultimate stress (p. 207). As such, both p-word maximality (a dispreference for words greater than disyllabic) and p-word-final phonotactic patterns both play a role in the stress placement in this sub-set of words.

12.3.4 Minimality and maximality

As noted in section 12.3.1, syllable reduction and deletion processes are resolutions to minimality and maximality constraints at work in Yidiny. Modern Greek, on the other hand, does not demonstrate an abundance of p-word-defining diagnostics; however, one interesting phenomenon is that inflected stem-words (e.g. inflected verbs and pronouns) undergo a final vowel epenthesis ('euphonic e'), as in (16) (Philippaki-Warburton and Spyropoulos 1999: 54).

(16) Euphonic-e in inflected stems (data from Joseph 2002: 255)

/milún/	→	[milúne] 'They speak.'
/ton/	→	[tone] 'him'

Joseph notes that this insertion does not apply to morphologically simple roots (e.g. **betón<u>e</u>* 'cement'). This appears to be a minimality requirement in Modern Greek, applying only to morphologically inflected words, providing them with an additional, (open) syllable.

A parallel may be observed in other languages, for example in Belhare (Tibeto-Burman, Nepal), where inflected stem words must be minimally disyllabic (Bickel 1998: 7). This is automatically satisfied in the language, as almost all affixes are minimally one syllable (creating a disyllabic inflected word). However, for those few affixes that are sub-syllabic (e.g. *-t* NPST), there is a syllabic allomorph (*-yu*) that is chosen just in case the disyllabic minimality constraint would be violated, e.g. *tai-t-i* come-NPST-1PI 'we will come' vs. *ta-yu* 's/he comes' (3rd person is zero-marked). This minimality-motivated epenthesis, even when a fully syllabic prefix is present, further highlights prefixes as non-cohering to a prosodic word (and therefore not contributing to word minimality in Belhare), as in (*mai-*)(*lu-yu*) 1SG.P-tell-NPST 's/he tells me'. As such, the p-word for inflected verbs in Belhare, for the purpose of minimality constraints, is prefix-(stem-suffix)ω.

Prosodic analyses of sign languages typically claim that the optimal size of a prosodic word is one syllable, and the maximal size is the disyllable (Hohenberger 2008; Sandler 1999; Zeshan 2002). The prosodic features of sign languages can be subgrouped into manual (movement) and non-manual gestures (e.g. facial expressions, mouthings, body positions) (Brentari 1998). It is the non-manual tier that is claimed to align with p-words, while g-words and other prosodic units align with the manual tier (Hohenberger 2008: 271). Hohenberger, with a focus on Signed German, demonstrates that non-manual gestures (particularly mouthings) are isomorphic with manual gestures, expanding and shortening to align with these gestures. The shortenings in particular concatenate larger grammatical structures to fit in with a maximally disyllabic (dual orientation-movement combination). Following Haspelmath (1999), Hohenberger speculates that maximality in Signed German is mediated by the complex prosodic and grammatical frame of the upper torso, arms/hands/fingers, and the face/head movement, in which signing takes place. A 'no greater than two syllables' constraint emerges in such languages as an optimal domain for this complex oscillation interplay.

12.3.5 Stress, rhythm, and prosodic words

Stress and rhythm have been traditionally treated as foot-level phenomena. But in some accounts, stress is variably invoked as going hand-in-hand with (or further bolstering) the phonotactic generalizations and phonological rules that also identify p-words.

One example of this may be found in English, where there is an observed asymmetry between the types and sizes of consonant cluster that are tolerated in word-medial position versus at word edges (Raffelsiefen 1999). This coexists with another observation in English that prefixes fall into two classes: those that are prosodically cohering within the larger p-word (e.g. *in-*) and those that are prosodically non-cohering (e.g. *un-*) (Szpyra 1989). Non-cohering prefixes may be parsed as their own p-word, and as such the left edge of the verb or adjective stem is also the left edge of a separate p-word (and therefore subject to greater restrictions on consonant clusters).

This asymmetry in English consonant clusters is further bolstered in historically (now semantically opaque) prefixed verbs and adjectives that tolerate increased consonant cluster size and complexity (in terms of sonority and voicing), as well as carrying a single iambic stress (uninfluenced by the presence of the prefix), as in (17) (adapted from Raffelsiefen 1999: 155).

(17) Historically prefixed, semantically non-compositional English p-words

(di[sgɹ]úntle)ω (tra[nsgɹ]éss)ω

(a[bstɹ]áct)ω (su[btɹ]áct)ω

These historical prefix–stem combinations are parsed as single prosodic words, permitting consonant cluster types in medial position (e.g. *sgr* and *bstr*) that are not observed in initial position.

In some languages, stress is treated as its own phonological rule or process, such that cases of stress application, stress deletion, or stress shift define or delineate p-word boundaries. In Finnish, some monomoraic case and possessive suffixes optionally attract a secondary stress to preceding syllables, creating an unusual sequence of two word-internal unstressed syllables, as in (18) (Elenbaas 1999; Hanson and Kiparsky 1996).

(18) Optional stress shift in Finnish
(ópettajà-si)ω 'teacher-PX.2SG'
(kálevalà-na)ω 'Kalevala-ESS'

The p-word domain for this particular stress pattern in Finnish is stem-plus-suffix.

The foot is typically defined by stress and rhythm properties as constrained by rhyme or moraic structure, but stress is also invoked as a constraint that delineates prosodic word boundaries. The Word Domains Project database includes 51 languages (of a total of 76 languages catalogued) that have a constraint of 'single main stress.'[4] In Yimas (Lower Sepik), certain (adjectival verb) stem–suffix combinations create a separate domain in which secondary stress applies (Foley 1991). In Dutch, p-words carry a single main stress that aligns variably according to word origin (Booij 1999: 99–100).

It is also commonly the case in Germanic languages (and beyond) that grammatical affixes may or may not integrate into a (content-meaning carrying) prosodic word for main stress application. Some affixes are simply prosodically non-cohering, while others are their own domain for main stress assignment; this is the case in Dutch, for example with the derivational suffix *-achtig* (-ˈʔɑx.təɣ/) '-ish' (p. 112).

[4] The project description, and the Word Domains database may be accessed at http://www.spw.uzh.ch/autotyp/projects/wd_dom/wd_dom.html

12.4 Some contemporary issues and debates

As introduced in section 12.2, the prosodic word is generally recognized as a prosodic constituent that aligns with morphological material (prototypically a morphological stem or root-word, with or without morphologically bound elements). This alignment is articulated by Nespor and Vogel (2007: 109) in their definition of the p-word as 'the lowest constituent of the prosodic hierarchy which is constructed on the basis of mapping rules that make substantial use of non-phonological notions' (where mora, syllable, and foot reference purely phonological material). But the specific ways in which prosodic words do and do not map to particular types of morphological information has been the focus of a number of language-particular and cross-linguistic studies, discussions, and debates. These debates also have consequences for the viability of the Prosodic Hierarchy Hypothesis as a whole (also introduced in section 12.2). As noted by Vogel (2009: 19–22), there is a danger in both over-predicting (over-generating) and under-predicting (under-generating) the constituents of the Hierarchy and their relationship to each other, particularly if evidence for such constituents is not empirically observable in languages, or if languages display repeated 'deviations' of particular predictions (as in the case of the relationship of clitics to prosodic words and prosodic phrases). This section considers some of these ongoing issues and debates in more detail.

12.4.1 Prosodic words, grammatical words, and non-isomorphism

A common generalization about p-words is that they align with morphological boundaries, although this alignment is deliberately non-specific. However, some restrictions are noted. Nespor and Vogel (2007) view the p-word as containing fewer than two grammatical words, while other accounts are more specific in holding that a p-word cannot contain more than one grammatical word. A grammatical word in such scenarios is defined as a unit to which morphological generalizations apply, particularly:

- elements that always co-occur or show grammatical cohesion;
- elements that occur in a fixed order;
- elements that have an independent, conventionalized coherence and meaning, whereas the individual morphemes that contribute to the word may not carry such meaning to speakers (Bloomfield 1933; Lyons 1968; itemized and commented on in Dixon and Aikhenvald 2002b).

One commonly observed phenomenon within this context is that of 'non-isomorphy', in which prosodic words and grammatical words misalign in various ways. These observations are of generally two types: prosodic words that are smaller than a grammatical word in its traditional sense, and prosodic words that are larger than (or contain two grammatical words). These cases are visualized in the schematics in (19).

(19) Two types of non-isomorphism

a.	[GRAMMATICAL WORD]	b.	[GW] [GW]
	[PW] [PW]		[PROSODIC WORD]

The most commonly discussed cases of prosodic words aligning with more than one grammatical word involve compounds and clitics (discussed in more detail in section 12.4.2).

As shown in section 12.3.1 (example 10), in Yidiny, a disyllabic suffix is always parsed as a case of a grammatical word containing two prosodic words (type (a) above), evidenced through minimality and maximality constraints and by vowel lengthening and vowel deletion restrictions and processes (Dixon 1977a, 1977b). Certain derivational prefixes in English (e.g. *in-* and *un-*) are also parsed as separate p-words (another case of type (a) above) because the stress attracted to the prefixes is unattested in other morphologically complex forms (Raffelsiefen 1999). As such, words like *impolite* and *unaware* are represented prosodically as in (20):

(20) English prefixes parsed as separate p-words
(ɪm)ω (pəlait)ω 'impolite'
(ʊn)ω (əwɛɹ)ω 'unaware'

Example (3) at the beginning of this chapter, with the contracted pronoun plus auxiliary, is a case of type (b).

The Kyirong variety of Tibetan presents a more extreme case of non-isomorphism in that only one suffix (the nominalizer *-ba*), in an inventory of approximately 31 inflectional and derivational suffixes, is prosodically cohering with the root (Hall and Hildebrandt 2008). Additionally, a subset of these suffixes are not prosodically cohering with the root, but they themselves are also not parsed as independent p-words (they do not participate in word-delineating tone contour and onset aspiration rules). Yet another subset may be parsed as separate p-words because they display onset aspiration, present only at the left edge of a prosodic word in Kyirong (p. 232).

Another Tibeto-Burman language, Chintang, demonstrates a striking phenomenon known as permutation, where prefixes (including agreement and negative markers) may be scrambled, without any resulting meaning change to the morphologically complex word form. This is shown in (21).

(21) Prefix ordering in Chintang (Bickel et al. 2007: 44)
a. a-ma-im-yokt-e
2-NEG-sleep-NEG-PST

b. ma-a-im-yokt-e
NEG-2-sleep-NEG-PST
Both: 'You didn't sleep.'

This permutation is possible because prefixes in Chintang (and a closely related language Bantawa) are parsed as individual prosodic words. Evidence for prefixes as separate p-words in Chintang comes from two types of process. One is glottal-stop insertion to provide an onset to a vowel-initial syllable; glottal insertion applies to the left edge of a prefix, and between a prefix and stem morpheme, but never between a stem and suffix. As such, glottal insertion is a left-edge defining cue to prosodic words in Chintang, where prefixes are parsed as independent p-words. Word-internally, different types of vowel coalescence are observed (p. 57). Another process demarcating prefixes as separate p-words is the location of the focus clitic *=ta*. This clitic may attach to a prefix (breaking up a prefix–stem combination), but it never breaks up a stem-suffix combination (p. 58). Interestingly, for stress assignment, prefix–stem(–suffix) combinations are parsed as a single prosodic word. As such, a grammatical word may contain more than one p-word in Chintang, and one or more smaller prosodic words is contained within a larger one (the domain for stress assignment). The prosodic representation of morphologically complex words in this language is therefore represented as in (22).

(22) Prosodic and grammatical word alignment in Chintang
[((prefix)ω -(stem-suffix)ω)ω2]GW

In light of these types of non-isomorphism, it is important to note that the PHH does not post explicit predictions about the relationship of prosodic structure and morphological structure; in fact, non-isomorphism is a strong argument in favour of the existence of two separate sets of hierarchies: syntactic and prosodic (Nespor and Vogel 2007: 110). Attempts to predict more specifically the behaviour of different affix types across languages have included proposals of affix classes (e.g. Siegel 1974; Szpyra 1989 for English) or have appealed to diachronic forces in the varying degrees of phonologization in contexts of grammaticalization (cf. Hopper and Traugott 2003).

12.4.2 Recursivity of prosodic domains and clitics

One persistent issue alluded to in section 12.2 is that of the Strict Layer Hypothesis (SLH), part of the Prosodic Hierarchy Hypothesis (PHH). The SLH predicts an optimal layering of prosodic constituencies (i.e. no recursive application of identical prosodic domains and no skipping of domains). So, representations like those in (23a,b) are predicted against in the SLH.

(23) Prosodic alignments predicted against in the Strict Layer Hypothesis

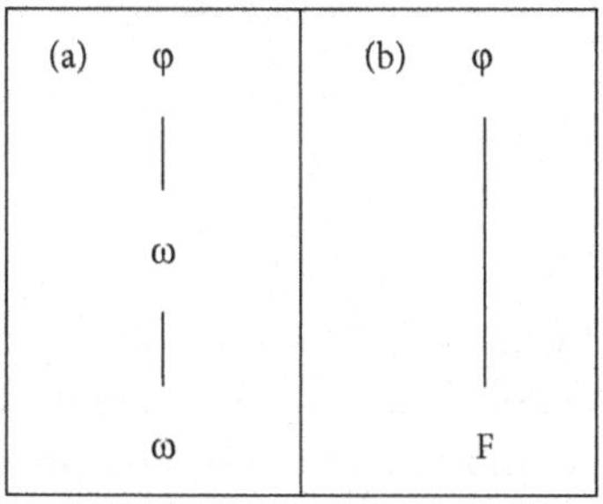

(a) φ | ω | ω	(b) φ | F

Despite these predictions, recursion, also known as 'prosodic adjunction' (in 23a), is rather commonly observed in prosodic words in compounding in many languages, for example in particular types of Turkish noun–noun, noun-incorporation, and light-verb compounds, as in (24) (Kabak and Revithiadou 2009: 117).

(24) Turkish compounds
(kɯrk)ω (ayak)ω 'forty' + 'foot' 'centipede'
(red)ω (et)ω 'reject' + 'do' 'reject'
(kitap)ω (oku)ω 'book' + 'read' 'read a book'

Each prosodic word in the larger structure is a distinct domain for phonological processes like vowel harmony. The larger compounded structure is also the domain for other word-level (non-phrasal) processes like lexical stress assignment and phonotactic generalizations.

Because of these phenomena, the predictions contained in the SLH have been adjusted and recast as 'prosodic adjunction' in the Weak Layering hypothesis (Ito and Mester 1992, 2003, 2009), which allows for multiple levels of identical prosodic structure. Kabak and Revithiadou (2009), in a slightly different take, argue that prosodic word (and clitic) recursion is in fact a by-product of language-particular prosodic and morphosyntactic alignment mandates.

Still other considerations of recursion are more language- (or family-) specific. In Bantu, the issue does not concern recursion of prosodic words that themselves align with lexical words (as in Turkish), but rather prosodic recursion observed within polysynthetic verb words. In languages like SiSwati (Swaziland), an inflected verb stem demonstrates two non-isomorphic and presumably recursive prosodic alignments. The prosodic word (comprising a stem with or without prefixes) is a domain for three processes or constraints: disyllabic minimality requirements (with syllable epenthesis as resolution), onset phonotactic requirements, and a rightward high tone shift (Downing 1999: 76–8). The prosodic stem, on the other hand, contains the prosodic word, along with suffixes, and is a separate domain for vowel epenthesis as a separate response to other minimality requirements (pp. 80–81). This recursive structure of word-plus-prosodic stem is usually co-terminous with the inflected verb stem as a grammatical word, but misalignments are tolerated for the sake of other prosodic well-formedness requirements at work in SiSwati and related languages. This special type of recursion is illustrated in (25).

(25) Prosodic recursion in SiSwati
$((\text{prefixes-}\Sigma)_{P\omega}\text{-suffixes})_{PSTEM}$

As noted, many discussions on recursion focus on the prosodic incorporation of clitics, a hybrid and widely defined class of small, function (vs. content), or 'weak' words. Across a wide range of languages, the idiosyncratic prosodic properties of clitic-like elements have been considered in relation to those defining prosodic words (see Aikhenvald 2002b for the varied properties of clitics in Tariana (Arawak, Colombia)).

Italian and Hungarian, with their abundant inventories of clitics and their hybrid prosodic behaviours, have been the subject of extensive discussion and debate regarding recursion. Nespor and Vogel (2007) and Vogel (1990, 2009) have argued that the variable inclusion of clitics in word-level processes in such languages motivates an additional constituent to the Prosodic Hierarchy: the Clitic Group (later recast as the Composite Group/CG).

In Hungarian, main stress is leftward/initial on prosodic words which are also co-terminous with grammatical words (shown with diacritic): *égyetem* 'university'. Determiners (analysed by Vogel as clitics) do not carry their own main stress, and as such do not fulfil minimality requirements for prosodic word-hood in Hungarian. Furthermore, when they are present, they shun main stress such that it does not fall on the initial syllable, but rather on the first syllable of the lexical noun: *a égyetem* 'the university' (Vogel 1990: 451). The determiner clitic adjoins to the p-word at the level of the CG, as shown in (26):

(26) Representation of the Clitic Group for Hungarian

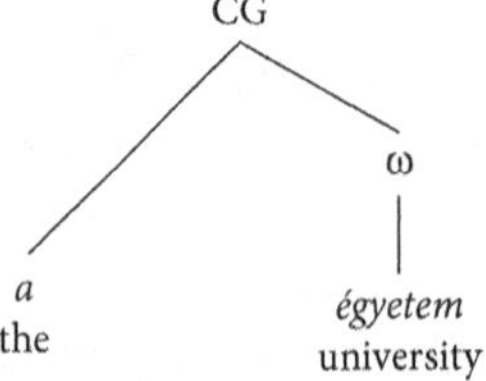

Peperkamp (1996), on the other hand, has argued that stress assignment in the Neopolitan variety of Italian (NI) in fact motivates p-word domain recursivity. NI has a rule of stress placement which puts stress on the rightmost trochaic foot (symbolized by ϕ) in a prosodic word, with a recursive application of this rule on all qualifying domains, regardless of grammatical word status. In (27) both the host *conta* 'tell' and the following clitic cluster *tennə* 'you.of.it' constitute separate (stressed) trochaic feet (Peperkamp 1996: 113).

(27) Recursive stress application
((cónta)w (ténnə)ϕ)w

As (27) shows, the stress placement rule in NI applies both to the word domain, which consists of the prosodic word corresponding with a grammatical word, and to the clitic cluster with foot status. The phonology–morphology mapping will grant the host prosodic word status, and since this word consists of one foot only, it will take trochaic stress. The clitic cluster constitutes a foot and is adjoined to the preceding phonological word. The stress placement rule now applies again (recursively) to the word domain consisting of the prosodic word and the clitic cluster with foot status. According to the stress rule, which applies recursively on this second word domain, the rightmost foot of the prosodic word receives stress and the clitic cluster surfaces with a primary stress on its first syllable.

Unstressed (monosyllabic) enclitics in NI do not have foot status and are thus unstressed, even when in right-most position, as shown in (28).

(28) Representation of monosyllabic enclitics in Neapolitan Italian
(((cónta)ϕ)w" (tə)σ)w)

Additionally, the same preposed clitic clusters in NI, regardless of foot structure, do not carry stress, because they are not the rightmost foot in a prosodic word, illustrated in (29).

(29) Representation of preposed clitics in Neapolitan Italian
((tənə)ϕ ((cóntə)w)w)
((tə)σ ((cóntə)ϕ)w)w

It is the iterative application of the *same* stress assignment rule that identifies a recursive projection of the same identical domain (prosodic word) in NI, rather than a separate, dominating domain (like CG).

12.4.3 Challenges to the prosodic hierarchy hypothesis

As discussed in section 12.2, the PHH predicts a finite set of structures that phonological constraints, processes, and generalizations will indirectly reference, with further predictions articulated in the forms of 'clustering' and 'strict succession' predictions. Clustering predicts that phonological patterns and constraints reference only the constituents proposed in the hierarchy, and strict succession predicts that constituents are not skipped (i.e. each prosodic constituent is dominated by a constituent *n+1* and itself dominates a constituent *n–1*).

Because of the accumulation of language-specific reports that address issues and complications with these predictions (several of which are illustrated in this chapter), Bickel et al. (2009) and Schiering et al. (2010) have attempted a comprehensive account of these challenges, with the ultimate claim that, with the exception of a stress-defining domain, the notion of 'word' has no privileged or universal status in phonology. Rather, p-word (or prosodic domain-defining) processes should be charted on language-specific and cross-linguistic bases and factors such that these domains can be systematically compared to test for family and areal signals to types and trends. This section summarizes the challenges from two languages examined in Schiering et al. (2010) that most profoundly illustrate these challenges and recommendations.

Limbu is a polysynthetic Tibeto-Burman language of Nepal in which at least two distinct and non-aligning prosodic word domains emerge when the standard criteria as covered in section 12.3 are applied. The grammatical word in Limbu is represented as in (30), based on data and descriptions from van Driem (1987), Hildebrandt (2007), and Schiering et al. (2010: 681–684).[5]

(30) The g-word in Limbu
(prefix–circumfix$_a$-Σ–circumfix$_b$-suffix=enclitic)GW

Two types of p-word are described by Schiering et al.: the major p-word and the minor p-word. The major p-word is defined by a single main stress constraint and by a process of regressive coronal-labial place assimilation, both applying at the left edge of the stem (including prefixes) of the grammatical word. These processes are illustrated in a prefix–stem–suffix environment in (31a) and in a stem–enclitic environment in (31b), with data from Schiering et al. (2010: 686–687).

(31) Stress and assimilation in the Limbu major p-word

(a) /mɛ-**n-mɛt-**paŋ/ → [mɛ**m**ˈ**mɛpp**aŋ]
NSA-NEG-tell-1S>3.PST 'I did not tell him.'

(b) /myaŋluŋ=phɛlle hɛ**n=ph**ɛlle/ → [ˈmjaŋluŋbhɛlle ˈhɛ**mb**hɛlle]
Myaŋluŋ=SUB what=SUB 'What does *Myaŋluŋ* mean?'

The minor p-word excludes the prefix, and is defined by /l/ ~ [r] allophony (where [r] surfaces intervocalically). This is illustrated in (32a) in a stem–suffix environment, in (32b) in a stem–enclitic environment. Example (32c) shows that this process is blocked in a prefix–stem environment.

[5] Limbu also has a stem-class type known as bipartite stems, represented as: pfx-Σ_1-pfx-Σ_2-sfx=enclitic. These stem types are elaborated on in Hildebrandt (2007).

(32) /l/ ~ [r] Allophony in the minor p-word (Schiering et al. 2010: 689)

(a)	[pha-**re** siŋ]	vs.	[mik-**le** raŋ]
	bamboo-GEN wood		eye-GEN colour
(b)	[pe:g-i=**ro**:]	vs.	[pe:g-aŋ=**lo**:]
	go-P=ASS		go-1SPST=ASS
	'Come on, let's go!'		'I'm on my way!'
(c)	[kɛ-**l**ɔʔ]	and	[mɛ-l-**l**ɛ-baŋ]
	2-say		NEG-NEG-know-1S>3.PST
	'you say'		'I didn't know [it].'

As shown with Chintang in section 12.4.1, the minor p-word in Limbu is also defined by glottal-stop insertion to resolve V–V hiatus across morpheme boundaries, as shown in (33). As (33c) shows, glottal-stop insertion applies iteratively in Limbu both before a vowel-initial prefix and between a prefix and stem (intervocalically).

(33) Glottal stop insertion in the minor p-word (Schiering et al. 2010: 690)

(a)	/iŋghɔŋ/	→	[ʔiŋghɔŋ]	'message'
(b)	/ku-iŋghɔŋ/	→	[kuʔiŋghɔŋ]	
	3POSS-message			'his news'
(c)	/a-i:r-ɛ/	→	[ʔaʔi:rɛ]	
	1-wander-PST			'We (plural, inclusive) wandered.'

This insertion does not occur in a stem–suffix environment. Other solutions to V–V hiatus are observed instead (e.g. diphthongization). Both of these processes apply at the left edge of the morphological stem, but crucially, they exclude prefixed material. These two non-isomorphic prosodic word types in Limbu (and in Chintang, with up to three non-isomorphic p-word domains) are similar to phenomena observed in Bantu languages. In these languages, multiple non-aligning prosodic words are also highlighted via a variety of phonological processes and restrictions. Some of these processes highlight in particular the prosodic saliency of stems to the exclusion of other morphologically-defined domains. As such, the 'prosodic stem' has been successfully invoked in Bantu as an active prosodic domain (Downing 1999; Hyman 2008; Hyman and Katamba 1987).

Based on these two non-aligning p-word types, Schiering et al. provide two prosodic representations in (34) for Limbu using the structure /a-oŋ-e:/→ [ʔaˈʔoŋˌŋe:] 'My brother in-law!'

(34) Two prosodic word representations for Limbu

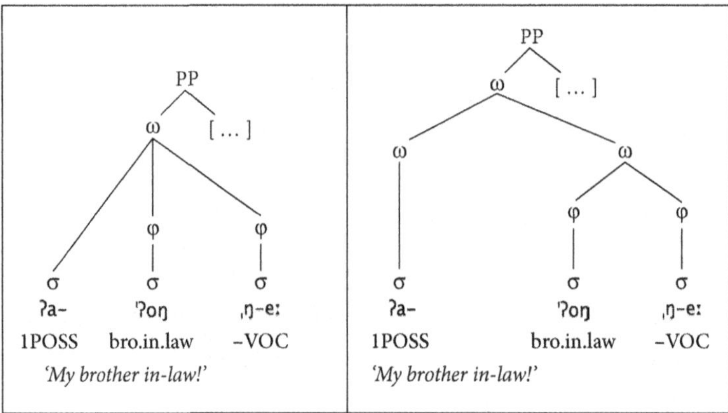

Each of these representations presents its own problem to the PHH.[6] The representation on the left adheres to 'clustering' in that the predicted constituents are present, although a violation of 'strict succession' is evidenced in that the prefix is dominated by a p-word and not a foot. However, a bigger problem for the left-hand representation is that it undergenerates structure that would otherwise account for the two non-aligned p-words. The representation on the right side recognizes both types of p-word, but this is problematic for both 'clustering' and 'strict succession' predictions of the PHH due to recursive proliferations of the p-word constituent.

While Limbu, with recursive prosodic words, presents one type of challenge to the architecture of the Prosodic Hierarchy, Vietnamese presents a different type of challenge in that there is no clear evidence for p-words based on any lexically general phonological processes or constraints in the language. The lack of positive evidence for prosodic words in Vietnamese was observed by Thomas (1962: 521): 'There is no significant unit in Vietnamese intermediate between the syllable and the phonological phrase.'

Grammatical words in Vietnamese may be identified on the basis of their occurrence in isolation with a conventionalized meaning, although g-words in the language are still somewhat problematic for criteria of fusion/cohesiveness and ordering, as word-like units may be interrupted and variably ordered without any required change in meaning, as in (35a,b), from Schiering et al. (2010: 666).

(35) Interruptability and variable word order in Vietnamese g-words

a.	cà-phê 'coffee'	vs.	cà voi phê	'coffee and the like'
b.	com-rom còm-ròm	vs.	còm-ròm com-rom	'be emaciated'

The prosodic profile of Vietnamese is determined based largely on phonotactic, stress-assignment, and tonal patterns. None of these characteristics positively

[6] Evidence for the relevance of the phonological phrase in Limbu is presented in Schiering et al. (2010: 692–693).

identifies a unit like the prosodic word (or the prosodic foot). Main stress is computed irrespective of word vs. phrasal structures, and the syllable canon in Vietnamese (C(w)V(C)) is identical in grammatical word and phrasal environments (Schiering et al. 2010: 673). The tone-bearing unit in Vietnamese is the syllable. There are no sandhi rules at phrase levels, nor are there lexically general rules of tonal harmony applying in reduplicated or compounded forms. As an illustration of this lack of rules in larger structures, the Vietnamese form *hoa hồng* may have two different descriptive meanings depending entirely on the context in which it occurs, with no phonetic or phonological changes that would otherwise differentiate between the two meanings. In a single-word (lexicalized) context, it means 'rose', and in a phrasal context, it means 'pink flower', with identical phonetics and phonology in both cases (e.g. identical stress placement and phonotactics) (Thompson 1965: 126ff.; Nhàn 1984: 101).

So, while a prosodic representation for Vietnamese as illustrated in (36) (replicated from Schiering et al. 2010: 677) respects clustering in that all prosodic constituents are included, it over-generates structure at the word-level.

(36) Prosodic representation for Vietnamese

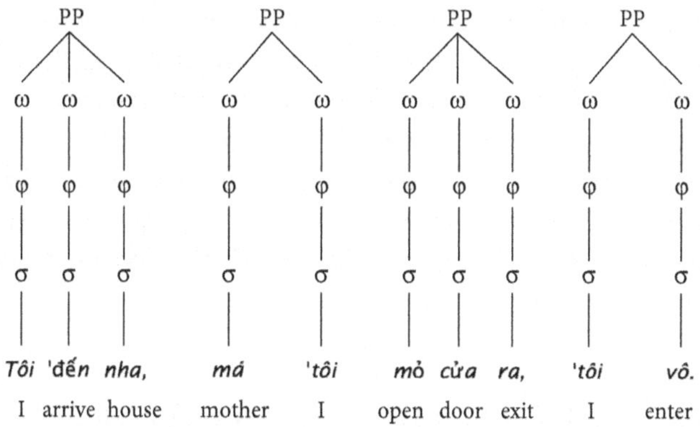

'I arrived at the house, my mother opened the door, and I went in.'

An alternative representation, shown in (37) (replicated from Schiering et al. 2010: 678) violates Strict Succession in that the prosodic word is not included.

(37) Alternate prosodic representation for Vietnamese

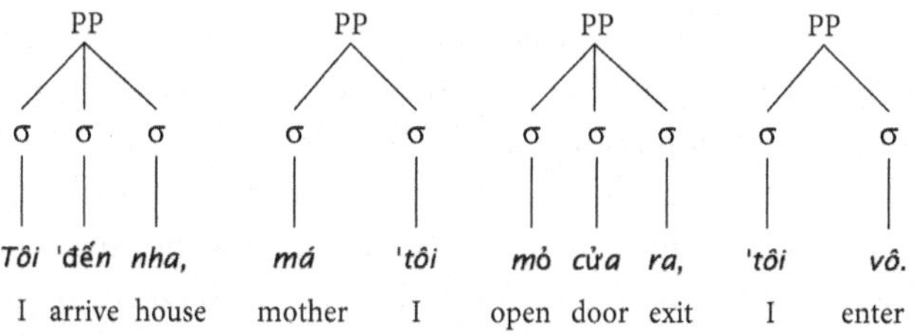

'I arrived at the house, my mother opened the door, and I went in.'

In summary, a PHH-based account of Limbu prosodic phenomena undergenerates domains, while in Vietnamese it over-generates them. With these case studies in mind, a number of solutions have been proposed to salvage the predictive power of the PHH, including a co-phonologies approach in which prosodic subcategorization is sensitive to morphological properties (Inkelas 1989); but Schiering et al. (2010: 695) also note that these are not the only languages in the *Word Domains* database that present these types of complication. Another alternative is to propose a new way of asking about words. Instead of reducing observed diversity in such languages to a single universal model (with repeated adjustments to account for the exceptions), it is a more fruitful exercise to observe and measure the actual distribution of word-level domains across languages, controlling for genealogy and areality, noting cross-linguistic trends, and then to search for universal principles to account for these trends (and deviations).

This approach, using prosodic domain data from a subset of languages from three families (Indo-European, Sino-Tibetan, Austroasiatic) reveals only that stress-defining p-word types converge on larger grammatical structures, while other p-word types show variation across families and geographic space. The point emphasized, though, is that the absence of absolute universals does not mean that the nature and distribution of prosodic domains is random. Rather, the notion of a (prosodic) word is an emergent one: it is the unit type most frequently (although not necessarily uniquely) referenced by the available phonological processes in a given language. In this sense, Schiering et al. argue that 'the prosodic word can thus be redefined as a language-particular category which emerges through frequent reference to the prosodic system' (2010: 703). This makes languages like Limbu prosodically quite different from Vietnamese, for example; whereas in Limbu the bounty of processes and generalizations converge on two larger, non-aligning, morphologically complex structures, in Vietnamese they converge on smaller syllable- and foot-type environments.

12.5 Directions for future research

Despite the seemingly incompatible conclusions arrived at regarding the predictions contained in the Prosodic Hierarchy Hypothesis, the debates and the detailed language-specific and cross-linguistic comparisons generated by these ongoing questions have opened the door to a wide range of studies that continue to shed new light on this topic, and will undoubtedly keep the field active for some time.

One quickly emerging avenue of research on prosodic words concerns children's acquisition of phonology. This chapter has covered prosodic words wholly from the perspective of studies of and assumptions about the phonologies of adults (equivalent to a synchronic approach). However, emerging research on children's speech disorders can also shed new light on how such domains are acquired and how they may be vulnerable to change. Echols (1993, 1996), Echols and Newport (1992), Lleó (2003, 2006), and Lleó and Arias (2009) focus on the acquisition of lower constituents like syllable, rhyme, mora, and foot, while Demuth (2006), Demuth et al. (2006), Prieto (2006), and Vigario et al. (2006) focus on the prosodic word. These studies have demonstrated that what were commonly assumed to be developmental limitations, or else the earlier emergence of typologically 'unmarked' structures, in fact reflect employment of high-frequency syllable and prosodic word structures that are language specific.

Similarly, recent studies of childhood apraxia (intra-word inconsistencies in the repeated production of the same word by the same individual) have shown that these inconsistencies affect segmental and syllabic tiers (via segment substitutions and onset or code deletions) more so than the prosodic word tier, indicated by a lower frequency of abnormal stress shifts or deletion of polysyllabic units (Tabul-Lavy 2012). One hypothesis regarding this asymmetry is that word forms as whole units are retrieved earlier and more regularly in the acquisition schedule, and are thus resistant to these disfluencies (Levelt 1992).

CHAPTER 13

THE WORD AS A UNIVERSAL CATEGORY

ANDREW HIPPISLEY

13.1 Introduction

THE standard view of grammar is of a complex system made up of several major interfacing subsystems, principally semantics, syntax, and phonology. How the subsystems, or modules, interface is an important aspect of how the grammar, as a sign-based system, works.

Words play a crucial role as the ultimate interfacers that sew together the three modules. This makes them the ultimate signs. This is because knowledge about a word includes knowledge about its meaning (semantics interface), its syntactic distribution including part of speech (syntax interface), and its form (phonology interface). This view of the word as a unit that straddles the interfaces of the grammar is best captured by the notion *lexeme*, and in this chapter we will imply the notion of lexeme when we talk about the word.

A lexeme is a unit of syntactic, semantic, and phonological properties that make one word distinct from another. These properties can be thought of as predefined instructions for operations in the environments of the three modules. The syntactic instructions determine what phrase-level configurations the unit can appear in; the semantic instructions constrain the space of possible interpretations and meaning uses of the unit, which entails combination possibilities too; and the phonological instructions regulate the unit's formal expression.

As an illustration, consider the lexemic representation of the word *friend* in (1).

(1) FRIEND

Noun	*syntactic level*
'person known well to another and regarded with affection'	*semantic level*
/fɹɜnd/	*phonological level*

We could extend the syntactic information in (1) for instructions on how to vary the standard shape of the lexeme to distinguish its use in different syntactic settings. For example, when it shows up in a plural setting, the lexeme will take the form /fɹɜndz/. Encoding morphosyntactic features such as Number makes a word the domain of morphological operations, and enriches its interface with syntax. We will use the term *paradigm* for the set of a lexeme's phonological shapes that correlate with morphosyntactic features, such as Number. We can think of the lexeme when associated with a particular set of morphosyntactic features, such as Number, as a *grammatical word*. The formal expression of a grammatical word is a *morphological word*, a member of the lexeme's paradigm.

Words, as lexemes, are ultimate signs because of the crucial role they play in the double articulation, or duality of patterning, of language. At the *primary* level of articulation they are the source of combination into higher level, phrasal units. This is where they interface with syntax. Simultaneously they are the natural target for combinations of *secondary* articulators, phonemes. This is where they interface with phonology. They are thus the (main) product of secondary articulation and the (main) unit of primary articulation. They are therefore the (main) domains of the mapping between form and meaning, and this is where they interface with semantics to serve as ultimate signs. Moreover, they can be both sources and targets of combination at the same level. The compound word *desktop computer* is the product of combining the two words *desktop* and *computer*, the former being a combination of the words *desk* and *top*.

It is therefore not surprising that words are a cross-linguistic as well as a cross-modality phenomenon. Spoken as well as sign languages deal in the currency of words, called 'signs' in sign language. They also extend beyond human communication, and are feasible units in animal communication. Primates have been trained to acquire and successfully exploit lexical items in communication acts; see Savage-Rumbough and Lewin (1994) for their account of lexical training of Kanzi, the bonobo ape. Here words are closer to signs in sign language, as the visual-gestural is a more practical modality than the audio-acoustic for attempts at language training. This is far from saying that primates *naturally* acquire words, and we'll get onto the communicative things they naturally do outside the laboratory in section 13.5.3, but the *feasibility* of words in their communication is the important point here. Do these ubiquitous, highly versatile, highly valuable vehicles of sign-based communication, then, constitute a universal category?

To answer this question we will begin with a brief survey of how words can be quite unreliable signs and interfacers. Connected to this is the wide variation we see in the design and function of words across languages. This kind of inconsistency may call into question their universality, and for some linguists this knocks on the head the whole idea of the universal word (e.g. Haspelmath 2011). In the sections that follow we explore in more detail the issues that are raised, looking at variation in word design across languages, what we could think of as morphological typology (section 13.3), and variations in the success with which words interface with syntax, illustrating primarily with a limiting case, deponency, where the interface is best described as a mismatch of what the word is saying and what the syntax is doing (section 13.4).

Another problem with words as universals of language is that they appear to be too ubiquitous, extending beyond human language to animal communication systems (ACS). This begs the question of what exactly we mean by a language universal. If universals are meant to be the *sine qua non* of language as human language, then are words in or out of the set of universals? They can only be universals if we can demonstrate that they are unique to *our* communication system. Words seem to be directly linked to concepts, and we could argue that the ability to lexicalize concepts is evidence that primates have concepts, though perhaps their conceptual structure is much more limited than ours. But having concepts is not the same as having words. With regard to the language faculty, conceptual structure is, in evolutionary terms, *primitive*; the lexicalization of that structure—at any rate the propensity to lexicalize—is *derived*. Acquisition and use of lexeme-type objects with phonological and syntactic levels of description is restricted to humans. Part of the answer to the question of whether or not words are universals will be found in answers to questions about language origins, and we address this in section 13.5. There we conduct a more detailed discussion of what is meant by *universal*, a notion that means different things to different people, and explore how words fit into such a landscape.

13.2 The problem with words: A brief survey

Before jumping to the perhaps obvious conclusion that words must be universal, we should briefly mention some rather un-word-like behaviours that languages can display. We develop these points in section 13.3.

One problem is that words can be bad signs. That is to say, they can be unreliable domains for the mapping of meaning to form. *Bank* has multiple meanings, including (a) financial institution, (b) mound of earth, and (c) the action of tipping laterally along the longitudinal axis (*OED* definition). We could argue that (a–c) are actually three distinct lexemes, each with the kind of lexemic representation shown in (1). Lexeme (c) is a verb, (a, b) are nouns, but (a–c) all happen to share identical phonological level information, the stem pronounced [bæ̃ŋk]. What makes them bad signs, then, is a lack of originality in the way they interface with phonology. There are other ways in which words can be bad signs. When two words combine to form a third word, the meaning of one of the combining words may change, or be obscured. When *black* combines with *board* to form *blackboard*, the word *black* no longer necessarily means 'black', since the compound can refer to any colour of board which requires chalk; usually a shade of green, in fact.

This failure to deliver on the basic form-to-meaning mapping makes a word a bad sign, but we could also say that it makes a word a bad interfacer, here between semantics and phonology. Words can also be bad interfacers with syntax. In many languages a word's use in a particular syntactic context is phonologically encoded. In Russian, when the word for 'book' heads an NP that is the subject of a clause, it is nominative case-marked and appears as *kniga*; when it heads an object NP it is accusative case-marked and appears as *knigu*. The difference, /a/ or /u/, correlating with a syntactic difference, is said to be *morphosyntactic* where a language's morphology is responsible for such encodings. And it is in this context that a word can also be unreliable. Still on Russian, the word *soldat* 'soldier' appears as *soldata* when it heads an object NP, but also when it heads a possessor NP, i.e. accusative and genitive case marking are the same. Two different syntactic distributions map onto a single morphosyntactic encoding. The form, specifically the morphology, has let down the syntax (Baerman et al. 2005: 1).

As well as such inconsistencies in function, cross-linguistically words seem to vary substantially in overall design, which to some degree undermines claims for universal status, or at least makes it a very plastic notion. This is most apparent in the way words map morphosyntactic functions to forms. In the Russian example above, *kniga* expresses the lexeme KNIGA in a syntactic configuration that requires nominative case marking. The marking simultaneously expresses an additional syntactic relationship, one where the subject NP and the verb agree in number, that is singular. So one piece of the word is expressing two morphosyntactically relevant things about the word. The interface with the syntax is happening twice through one piece of form, as it were. Nouns in Archi, a Lezgic Nakh-Daghestanian language spoken in the Caucasus, are designed differently. In a configuration requiring the genitive case and a context requiring the plural, the lexeme AˁRI 'military division' appears as *aˁrit:en* where the /t:e/ piece performs the mapping to plural morphosyntax and, quite separately, the /n/ piece the mapping to genitive morphosyntax. We will look more closely at this type of inconsistency in word design vis-à-vis Russian and Archi in the next section, where we will see quite a wide range of discrepancies.

Another kind of variation concerns the kind of meaning associated with words. In the Russian and Archi examples, the words have an inherent 'lexical' meaning together with extra morphosyntactic information, in these examples Case and Number. But a language like Vietnamese has two kinds of words, one with only inherent lexical meaning and another which contains only morphosyntactic information. For the sentence 'I met Mr Smith' in (2) we see a word-for-word translation into Vietnamese, *except* Vietnamese has an extra word for the morphosyntactic feature Past, *có*.

(2) Vietnamese

tôi	có	găp	ông	Smith
I	PST	meet	Mr.	Smith

'I met Mr. Smith'

At the opposite extreme, a language like Mohawk, an Iroquoian language of North America, has words which encode far more than do the familiar Russian and

Archi instances. Example (3) gives the word for 'I've planted flowers' (Mithun and Corbett 1999).

(3) Mohawk
wak-tsi'tsi-a-ientho-on
1SG.P-flower-EP-plant-ST
'I've planted flowers'

The word encodes not only the expected morphosyntactic information, such as Person, Number, and Aspect, but also the object grammatical relation, here the piece of the word that corresponds to 'flower' *tsi'tsi*. This makes the word more than just an interfacer with syntax but itself a kind of syntactic configuration. It can be used in place of the syntactic equivalent in (4).

(4) Mohawk, syntactic equivalent

o-tsi'tsi-a'	wak-ientho-on
N-flower-N.SUFF	1SG.P-plant-ST

'I've planted flowers'

Words, then, can be inconsistent linguistic objects. This, we could argue, makes them unreliable universals. In the next section we look more carefully at their unreliability as ultimate signs, an important topic when considering whether words are universals.

13.3 Words as unreliable signs

Languages differ in word design, as we showed above. But it is worth asking what the ideal design would look like for a word as the ultimate sign. According to Peirce (1935), a semiotic event includes the signified (or meaning), the signifying (or form), and how to interpret the relation between the two. The relation can be *iconic, indexical*, or *symbolic*. One design principle, which we discuss below, is that a word is primarily a symbolic sign. Another principle concerns the integration of morphosyntactic meaning with lexical meaning within the domain of the lexeme. Vietnamese words don't integrate both kinds of meaning, as our example showed: words either have lexical or morphosyntactic meanings but not both. But our Archi, Russian, and English examples appear to abide by this principle. We will give examples where such integration is a matter of degree: from tighter to looser, where Vietnamese marks the limiting case. Finally, a rather obvious principle which ought to underpin any word is that there be a one-to-one mapping between signified and signifying, between meaning and form. When morphosyntax is integrated into the word, this principle is not always adhered to. While in Archi it is a fairly simple matter to pick out the form corresponding to Number and the form corresponding to Case, and to distinguish those from the lexeme's stem, Russian is less straightforward. If *knigu* denotes the accusative singular of KNIGA, then /u/ is one form mapping onto two different morphosyntactic meanings, suggesting that Russian does not (always) adhere to the one-meaning-to-one-form principle. It turns out that languages vary in the extent to which they adhere to these three design principles; moreover, a single language may be less than consistent with its own words. Below, we look at this kind of variation by treating each principle in turn.

13.3.1 Words as symbols

An instance of signification, according to Peirce, requires a sign, an object (or referent), and an interpretation of how the sign and object relationship is regulated. The interpretation can be iconic: here the sign shares properties with the object it refers to. This is the signification found in ACS, such as a mocking bird's mimicry, where what is shared by the sign is the song that characterizes a particular bird species. Another possibility is *indexical*: here the sign bears some connection with the object. The connection could be causal. An oft-cited example is a weather vane whose orientation bears a causal connection to the wind's direction. Indexical signs are also prominent in ACS. Different vervet monkey calls are directly connected to different kinds of threat, such as a nearby snake, eagle, or leopard. These calls are indexes because they are generated in direct response to the sighting of the threat, and interpreted through the connection between the threat and the response it provokes. Unlike indexes and icons, a *symbolic* relationship between sign and object is indirect. The sign shares no properties with the object, i.e. is arbitrary with respect to the object. Linguistically, the phoneme stream that defines a linguistic sign is uninformative about the object except by convention, which has to be learnt. So the symbolic sign allows for *displacement*: the object need not be present. And this in turn allows the sign to map, not onto a single referent in the world, but onto a class that names properties shared by some set of referents. For example /bʊk/ as a sign does not require the presence of a book, and by convention names a set of properties associated with books. With symbolic signs comes the possibility of lexicalizing concepts, here the concept 'book'. Such concepts can be rather abstract, like 'past time'. This introduces the possibility of lexicalizing functional categories such as Tense. The use of symbolic signs is an important distinguisher between ACS and language.

Of course we can find instances of words being used less symbolically and more indexically or iconically. Plenty of languages have plenty of examples of sound symbolism, where the phoneme stream that defines the formal level of the lexeme shares properties with the object: *cuckoo* in English. Childs (this volume) suggests that non-arbitrary mapping of sound and meaning is much more common in language than we might think, and even manifests itself in universal patterns. Childs gives examples of an entire lexical category devoted to sound symbolism, the *ideophone*, found for instance in many of the languages of South America.

But these are still symbols because they are nonetheless conventionalized—you can't guess at the referent—and they name a class of properties rather than a specific object in the world. The sign can therefore be used without the referent being present, so displacement is maintained. Languages also provide for indexical reference through deictic elements such as demonstrative pronouns which make an explicit connection between an object and its symbolic sign: not just any book but *this* book. So words may have iconic and indexical degrees of interpretation. According to Deacon (2003), indexicalization delimits, or anchors in reality, the instance of the symbol, for example *book*, in a particular situation. Linguistically, this is seen in predication. The symbols of language are not isolated from their context in a given proposition. So in an utterance about 'book', the symbol must be anchored: this book, that book, the book I was referring to before, etc. This is expressed as predication (e.g. through demonstratives), where the argument anchors the symbol, thus connecting it to its referent. The symbol therefore is really a symbol–index pair: book(my friend), i.e. 'my friend's book'. Tense anchors an event in time.

13.3.2 Words as domains integrating lexical and morphosyntactic meaning

As an interfacer with semantics and syntax, a word-as-lexeme would be expected to phonologically encode invariable lexical semantics along with variable morphosyntactic information, as the word varies in syntactic configurations. A lexeme's paradigm is a collection of both such encodings, as we outlined above. Example (5) is the full paradigm of the Archi noun lexeme Aˤʀɪ 'military division' (Kibrik 1977: 251, 254, 256).

(5)

	sg	pl
Absolutive	aˤri	aˤritːu
Ergative	aˤrili	aˤritːaj
Genitive	aˤrilin	aˤritːe-n
Dative	aˤrilis	aˤritːe-s
Comitative	aˤriliɬːu	aˤritːe-ɬːu
Comparative	aˤriliχur	aˤritːe-χur
Permatitve	aˤrilikɬ'əna	aˤritːe-kɬ'əna
Partitive	aˤriliqˤiš	aˤritːe-qˤiš
Superlative	aˤrilitːik	aˤritːe-tːik
Sublative	aˤrilikɬ'ak	aˤritːe-kɬ'ak

Each cell is filled with a single word form that expresses the meaning 'military division' and different combinations of values for Case and Number. Thus *aˤritːes* is the realization of the combination {NUMBER: PL, CASE: DATIVE} whereas phonologically distinct *aˤrilin* is the realization of a different combination {NUMBER: SG, CASE: GENITIVE}. For each cell we can identify a phonologically constant substring, the root, that correlates with the invariable lexical semantics of the lexeme, namely *aˤri-*; the remainder of the string varies as the feature set varies. Thus a single word form operates as a sign that integrates both lexical and morphosyntactic semantic information.

Slippage from this ideal is possible, and not uncommon. We already saw how in Vietnamese, lexical and morphosyntactic/grammatical information was expressed as a multi-word expression, with lexical entries dedicated as signs for the grammatical information. We could think of Vietnamese as marking an extreme deviation from the integration principle, where integration is at its loosest. There are also situations where integration is tighter than Vietnamese but not as tight as the principle implies. In Ancient Greek sub-parts of a verb's paradigm look like Archi, and sub-parts look like Vietnamese. In (6) we see two sub-paradigms of the lexeme LY:O: 'loose', both part of the larger mediopassive subjunctive paradigm, taken from Smyth (1956: 117).

(6) LY:O: 'loose' mediopassive subjunctive

	Aorist	*Perfect*
Singular 1	ly:so:mai	lɛlymɛnos o:
Singular 2	ly:sɛ:	lɛlymɛnos ɛ:s
Singular 3	ly:sɛ:tai	lɛlymɛnos ɛ:
Dual 2	ly:sɛ:st^{h}on	lɛlymɛno: ɛ:ton
Dual 3	ly:sɛ:st^{h}on	lɛlymɛno: ɛ:ton
Plural 1	ly:so:mɛt^{h}a	lɛlymɛnoi o:mɛn
Plural 2	ly:saist^{h}ɛ	lɛlymɛnoi ɛ:tɛ
Plural 3	ly:sainto	lɛlymɛnoi o:si

In the Aorist we see full integration of grammatical and semantic information into a single word form. But the Perfect makes use of a multi-word expression. The 3rd person plural Aorist is the single word *ly:sainto*, while the 3rd person plural Perfect is the combination of word$_1$ *lɛlymɛnoi* and word$_2$ *o:si*. However, the situation differs from Vietnamese. Unlike the Vietnamese example, the burden of the grammatical exponents is borne by *both* word$_1$ and word$_2$, making for a tighter integration of grammatical and lexical information, though not as tight as when the grammatical exponents show up exclusively on a single word. (7) shows how the values of the features in the set {Voice, Tense, Mood, Person, Number} are distributed over word$_1$ and word$_2$ as exponents. Bold marks the phonologically invariable parts of word$_1$ and word$_2$, i.e. the respective stems of LY:O: 'loose' and the auxiliary E:MI 'be'.

(7) lɛlymɛnoi o:si

lɛ-**ly**-mɛn-oi	**o:**-si
PERF-**loose**-PERF.PTC.MEDIOPASS-PL.NOM.M	**be**.SBJV.PRES-3PL
word$_1$	word$_2$
{Tense:Perfect, Voice:Mediopassive, Number:Plural}	{Mood:Subjunctive, Person:3, Number:Plural}
{Voice, Tense, Number}	{Mood, Person, Number}

From the last row we see that the five features are shared evenly across the two word forms: word$_1$ is the location of exponents for Voice, Tense, and Number; and word$_2$ for Mood, Number, and Person. This underlines the *paradigmatic* nature of the Greek multi-word expressions in (6). In the Perfect sub-paradigm we are dealing with the intersection of the same features as in the Aorist sub-paradigm: so the 'paradigmatic space' of the language is being filled out both by single and by multi-word expressions—the hallmark of *periphrasis* as opposed to the kind of multi-word expressions found in languages like Vietnamese, as argued in Brown et al. (2012: 246). This makes periphrasis the domain of the morphology, i.e. the multi-word expressions in (6) are the output of morphological rules, in the same way as the single word expressions in (6) are: this is Ackerman and Stump's Periphrastic Realization Hypothesis (Ackerman and Stump 2004; Ackerman et al. 2011). Their point is that syntax is responsible for what we see in Vietnamese, but it is morphology that regulates what we see in cases like Greek perfect mediopassives, making for a tighter integration of grammatical features with a lexeme. In some cases of periphrasis the morphology has extra work to do. In (7) we see that 'extra' features of Case (nominative) and Gender (masculine) are being expressed on word$_1$ that don't play a part in the synthetic sub-paradigm in (6).

Another kind of slippage from full integration is represented by cases where grammatical features are expressed as forms that are not phonologically bound to the lexeme's stem, but bound to some other element in the clause. We can think of such *clitic* forms as floating affixes. Verbs in Shughni, an Eastern Iranian language, have synthetic sub-paradigms as well as sub-paradigms involving clitics. The present forms of the verb lexeme WIFTOW 'knit' are given in (8).

(8) WIFTOW 'knit'

	Present	*Pluperfect* (subj pronoun + clitic)	
SG			
1	wāf-um	wuz=um	wīfč-at
2	wāf-i	tu=t	wīfč-at
3	wāf-t	yu-yi	wīfč-at

PL			
1	wāf-am	māš=am	wīfč-at
2	wāf-et	tama=yet	wīfč-at
3	wāf-en	wāδ=en	wīfč-at

For the Pluperfect subparadigm, we include the subject pronoun to show how the forms /um/, /t/, /yi/, etc., which are exponents of values of the intersecting features {Number, Person}, attach to the right edge of the first element, whatever that happens to be. The first element may be multiple words away from the verbal element, as shown in (9).

(9) Wuzum ar dam gůl parwos wīx̌čat

wuz=**um**	ar	dam	gůl	parwos	wīx̌č-at
I=**1sg**	in	this	pool	last.year	swim-PLUPF

'I had swum in this pool last year'

Cliticization thus represents another way in which integration of exponents of grammatical features falls outside the domain of the word; but unlike Vietnamese the alternative is not free isolated words but expressions phonologically dependent on other words.

13.3.2.1 *What gets integrated*

The integration of the grammatical features is scalar: synthetic morphology the tightest integration, the situation in Vietnamese the loosest, and periphrasis and cliticization somewhere in between. We also need to consider what we should expect to be integrated. Our original design point was that the word as a sign should convey simultaneously both lexical-semantic and syntactic information. This would suggest that integratable features must be relevant to syntax. In the Greek example in (5) the features were {Voice, Tense, Mood, Person, Number}. Some of these are more relevant to syntax than others. We can distinguish as purely morphosyntactic features those 'distributed according to syntactic constraints', such as agreement and government (Corbett 2012: 49). These would include Person and Number, whose values are determined by a constraint of feature agreement with the controlling element, normally the subject. Also included would be Case in the Archi paradigm in (5). Excluded would be Voice, Mood, and Tense, whose choice of value is not syntactically determined and whose role is more semantic: these might be termed *morphosemantic* (Corbett 2012: 49). This feature partition goes back at least as far as Sapir's (1921) 'pure relational concepts' (roughly morphosyntactic features) and 'concrete relational concepts' (roughly morphosemantic features); see discussion in Anderson (19921: 330). The two groups have elsewhere been termed *contextual* and *inherent* features respectively

(Booij 1996).[1] Though morphosemantic features are not relevant to syntax in the same way as morphosyntactic ones, they still have relevance, albeit indirectly.

There are, however, situations where what is integrated is not just relevant to syntax but where integration results in the word performing what is usually viewed as a syntactic function. Recall the Mohawk example in (4), where the morphologically complex word expresses a proposition, which is normally conveyed in syntax by a clause: 'I've planted flowers'. In such examples the domain of the word seems to be being stretched beyond its original design. In function it is climbing too far up into syntax. The Central Alaskan Yup'ik example in (10) presents an extreme case of syntactic work being done by a word; here the domain of the word stretches over the equivalent of a bi-clausal sentence in syntax (example from Mithun 1999, discussed in Spencer 2006).

(10) ayallrunillruat
ayag-llru-ni-llru-a-at
go-PST-say-PST-IND.TR-3PL/3SG
'they said he had left'

An alternative view of such words is that they are really the result of syntactic processes that operate over free *and* bound morphemes as minimal signs. In the Mohawk incorporation example (4), the head of an object NP, the morpheme *tsi-tsi*, is moved from its position to the VP node headed by 'plant'; incorporation is therefore the result of a head-to-head movement (Baker 1988). There are a number of arguments against such a syntax-based analysis. One important one is that head-to-head movement would prohibit modifiers of a phrase being incorporated. Yet such examples exist. (11) is an example of an incorporated expression in Chukchi and its syntactic equivalent, from Spencer (2000: 315). The adjunct 'quickly' has been incorporated.

(11a)	*Incorporated expression*	(11b)	*Syntactic equivalent*	
	jəq-amecat-gʔe		nə-jeq-ʔew	amecat-gʔe
	quick-hide-2.SG		ADV-quick-ADV	hide-2.SG
	'you hid quickly'		'you hid quickly'	

Similar arguments based on inconsistencies with 'real' head-to-head movement, such as stranding effects and extraction constraints, can be found in Ackema and Neeleman (2007); arguments that incorporation is more consistent with what is found in 'normal' morphology are set forth in Mithun and Corbett (1999). For a summary of both kinds of argument see Brown and Hippisley (2012: 26–9).

[1] A feature can fall into different categories depending on part of speech. Number is contextual for verbs but inherent for nouns. For Corbett it is morphosyntactic because it can be contextual; for Sapir it is concrete-relational because it can be morphosemantic.

13.3.3 Words as unambiguous signs

Our first design principle was that words are symbolic signs. Whereas indexical and iconic signs relate directly to real-world entities, a word as a symbol is at one level removed from a real-world referent since it a generalization over some set of entities, or more precisely their relevant qualities. Thus words are really labels for concepts; the referent is a *mind-dependent* thing, occupying a mental space with other such referents (Chomsky 2007). Concepts may be broken down into further sub-concepts, where generalization is pitched at a lower level and the sub-concept could receive a label: *animal* vs. *cat*, for example. The indexical and iconic signs of ACS, on the other hand, map onto *mind-independent* referents. This situation inevitably means that words are less precise than other kinds of signal. We mentioned above the need for predication, i.e. the presence of other words to take reference from the general to the specific: 'that loud boy' as opposed to the much less precise 'boy'. According to Givón (2010), syntax is the adaptive response to the displacement entailed by symbols. Pinker and Bloom argue that recursion was the evolutionary solution to this kind of semiotic-entailed ambiguity, since with it you can 'specify reference to an object to an arbitrarily fine level of precision' (Pinker and Bloom 1990: 27). But there is another way in which word as symbol is at least potentially ambiguous. The class (or concept) named by the word could be a set of different generalizations depending on who the speaker is: two different language users mean in theory two different perspectives. Pinker and Bloom make the point that, for the sake of communication, individual preferences for what goes into the class must cede to the conventionalized perspective shared by the speech community. Word learning entails learning the conventionalized perspective. As Deacon (2003: 120) puts it, symbolic communication places a 'large demand on antecedent preparation' of the precise interpretation of the mapping of symbol to referent. In sum, the precision you lose from using symbolic signs can be regained to an extent through predication and acquisition of conventionalized class content. Of course, not all the intentions of the speaker get registered, even when symbols are anchored in this way. Interpretive gaps are filled by inference; *pragmatics*—'the study of the intention of utterances in context' (Sperber and Orr 2010)—follows directly from signs as symbols (see Sperber and Orr for the importance of pragmatics in the evolution of language). In the context of this potential semiotic-based ambiguity, one might assume that the actual mapping between signaller and signified, i.e. form of the word and the class it refers to, would be as watertight as possible, and hence one of the design features of words. What we find, however, is that words are not always unambiguous signs.

13.3.3.1 Exponent-base ambiguities

If a well-designed word integrates grammatical features as part of its job as interfacer with syntax, then a further design principle is that such an integration be interpretable. A morphologically complex word should signal both its lexical and grammatical meaning unequivocally through a one-to-one mapping of lexical meaning to form on the one hand and a one-to-one mapping of grammatical meaning to form on the other. This is what we saw for Archi in (5): one piece of the word signalled its invariant lexical semantics, and other pieces were exponents of feature values, specifically of Case and Number. What we actually find is that both kinds of mapping are often *not* one-to-one. The result is words that are less than perfect signs with respect to ambiguity of reference.

We start by looking at deviations from one-to-one mapping between a grammatical feature and its exponent. In Archi (5), we can compare the Partitive Singular with the Partitive Plural of Aˤri 'military division': *aˤriliqˤiš* (Partitive Singular), *aˤrit:e-qˤiš* (Partitive Plural). From this comparison, we can identify the *-li-* piece with the Number feature and the *-qˤiš-* piece with the Case feature. (12) shows deviations from the Archi situation where grammatical meaning and exponent is a one-to-one mapping (based on Spencer 2004).

(12) *Deviations from one to one mapping, exponent-based*

	Meaning(s)	*Form(s)*	*Phenomenon*
1	one (or more)	zero	*zero morphs*
2	zero	one	*meaningless morphs*
3	many	one	*cumulation*
4	one	many	*extended exponence*

The Shughni paradigm in (8) exemplifies the type 3 deviation, cumulation, where more than one grammatical meaning, i.e. feature, is associated with a single form. The 2nd person singular of wiftow 'knit' is *wāf-i* and the 2nd person plural is *wāf-et*, so the interpretation of the *-et-* formative must involve two features: Number (plural) and Person (second). These two features share a single exponent in all the cells of this paradigm. A more extreme example of cumulation is represented by the Greek synthetic sub-paradigm in (6) where multiple features appear to map onto a single exponent: if the *-s-* formative is the exponent of Aorist, then in the 1st person singular the formative *-o:mai-* must be expressing Voice, Mood, Person, and Number feature values. (6) also illustrates type 4 deviation, where a single feature has multiple exponents. In the periphrastic sub-paradigm, the periphrasis construction itself expresses Perfect as opposed to Aorist; but Perfect is also expressed by the reduplication of the stem transforming *ly:-* to *lɛly-*; we could add that the shortening of the stem vowel is yet another exponent of Perfect. For type 1 deviation we need look no further than Archi. The Absolutive singular is simply the lexeme's stem without any additional material: thus both Number and Case map onto zero forms. This leaves us type 2, meaningless morphs, where we have 'extra' material in the word form that carries no grammatical meaning. We leave Greek and turn to Latin to illustrate the meaningless morph phenomenon. (13) gives the active and passive infinitive forms of four different Latin verbs.

(13)

Conj. I		Conj. II		Conj. III		Conj. IV	
amō 'love'		*moneō* 'advise'		*regō* 'rule'		*audiō* 'hear'	
ACTIVE	PASSIVE	ACTIVE	PASSIVE	ACTIVE	PASSIVE	ACTIVE	PASSIVE
am-ā-re	*am-ā-rī*	*mon-ē-re*	*mon-ē-rī*	*reg-e-re*	*regī*	*aud-ī-re*	*aud-ī-rī*

We can identify *-re* and *-(r)i* with the Active and Passive respectively, while the four roots are analysable as *am-*, *mon-*, *reg-*, and *aud-*. This leaves each word form with an extra meaningless formative, highlighted in (13): in the case of *amāre* and *amārī* it is *-ā-*.

13.3.3.2 *Stem-based ambiguities*

As we observed, the root of the Archi lexeme remains constant throughout its paradigm of inflections. The one-to-one mapping of lexical semantics and the form it takes is stable. Such stability is, however, often not maintained across cells in a paradigm, resulting in a one-to-many mapping. We observed that in Greek the root's onset and nucleus is reduplicated in the perfect; the nuclear vowel is also shortened. This results in two different versions of the root, i.e. two different stems, one for the aorist and one for the perfect sub-paradigm. Shughni displays the same kind of disparity between versions of the root of the same lexeme: for WIFTOW 'knit' *wāf-* is used for Present cells and *wīf-* for Pluperfect cells. Some changes in root shape may be the result of phonetic assimilation processes whose triggers are or were present in that particular environment, an example being, in the Greek case, the shortening of the root vowel in the context of a short vowel. In other cases, differing root shape can be purely morphological. The Latin verbs have (typically) three root versions, or stems, distributed across a stable set of paradigmatic cells. For *am(ō)* 'love' these are *amā-*, *amāv-*, and *amāt-*, used respectively for Imperfect cells, Perfect cells, and a specific combination of Perfect, Past, Future, and Supine cells. Though the one-to-one mapping is not perfect, in all these cases it is partially left intact. In cases of suppletion, however, the paradigm is partitioned by phonologically dissociated stems, e.g. English *go* (Present) and *went* (Past). The three stems of *am(ō)* correspond to the three suppletive stems of the verb *ferō* 'carry': *fer-*, *tul-*, *lat-*. We could think of such cases of suppletion as the extreme breakdown in the one-to-one mapping of lexical meaning and its corresponding form. Yet suppletion is quite widespread in the world's languages. In a genetically diverse study of thirty languages reported in Hippisley et al. (2004), instances of some kind of suppletion were found in all but four.

Grammatical feature integration leads to a complex sign, demanding an interpretation that parses out the formal components of the sign. We end with the observation that the boundary between lexical semantic and grammatical component can be blurred. Plungian (2001) cites the example of Russian infinitives in *-t′*, as in *dela(t′)* 'do'. But in the case of the verb 'be able', whose root is *mog-*, the infinitive form obscures the root ending and the affix: *moč′*. Such examples abound in the world's languages. Given such a situation, the worst kind of word sign is one where the lexical semantic-to-form mapping is fully obscured, as is the boundary between stem and exponent. Such cases are termed 'suppletion with fused exponence' by Corbett (2007: 15), who classifies paradigms containing these as the most non-canonical. The example he gives is *bad* ~ *worse*, a worse example than *good* ~ *better* since in the latter the Comparative exponent is still available for parsing.

13.4 Words as unreliable interfacers

In section 13.1.1 I made the point that words are fundamental to the grammar, since they are the principal interfacers between the grammar's various components. In the previous section I showed different ways in which a word can be an unreliable sign; we could think of each of these as really being an interface problem, specifically the interface with semantics (lexical and grammatical). In this section we focus on words as interfacers with the syntactic component, and show how things can go wrong here too. The example given in section 13.2 was the syncretism of the accusative and genitive singular of Russian masculine animate nouns: the word form *soldata*, expressing genitive singular, is delivered to syntax for contexts requiring accusative singular word forms. Syncretism should be viewed as a dissociation between the syntactic information carried by a lexeme and its formal (morphological) expression. The word is not being a reliable interfacer with the syntax. In the Greek periphrasis example in (7) something similar is going on: the auxiliary *o:si* expresses Present Indicative yet the meaning of the entire periphrastic construction is Perfect Subjunctive—there is a separate sub-paradigm for Mediopassive Present Subjunctive.

(14) lɛ-**ly**-mɛn-oi **o:**-si
PERF-**loose**-PERF.PTC.MEDIOPASS-PL.NOM.M **be**.SBJV.PRS-3PL

The leads to an expression that is non-compositional, i.e. you cannot compute the overall meaning by reference to all the meanings expressed. And in fact non-compositionality is claimed to be a hallmark of periphrasis (Ackerman and Stump 2004; Ackerman et al. 2011; for an opposing view see Brown et al. 2012). Both syncretism and non-compositional periphrasis can be thought of as essentially miscommunication of syntax and phonology through the word, i.e. a *morphological mismatch* of syntactic function and (word) form. To illustrate the word as an unreliable interfacer in the sense of morphological mismatch, we consider deponent verbs in Latin.

Latin has a class of verbs that miscommunicates Passive form to the syntax; though morphologically Passive, they are used actively. The word for 'encourage' belongs to this class, as shown in (15), from the playwright Plautus' *The Merchant*.

(15) sed coqu-os... ita horta-batur
But cook-PL.ACC so encourage-PASS.IMPF.3SG
'but he encouraged the cooks in the same way'

We can compare the Imperfective Active and Passive sub-paradigms of the regular verb *amō* 'love' with those of *hortor* 'encourage'. The latter's Active forms are identical to the regular verb's Passive forms. At the same time there is a gap in the paradigm for Passive use.

(16)

	active	*passive*	*active*	*passive*
Sg				
1	amābam	amābar	hortābar	–
2	amābās	amābāris	hortābāris	–
3	amābat	amābātur	hortābātur	–
Pl				
1	amābāmus	amābāmur	hortābāmur	–
2	amābātis	amābāminī	hortābāminī	–
3	amābant	amābantur	hortābantur	–

The mismatch between morphology and syntax that occurs with Latin nouns can be schematized as in (17), where the Roman character is a stem variable and the Greek character an exponent variable.

(17)

lexeme 1		*lexeme n*		*hortor*	
ACTIVE	PASSIVE	ACTIVE	PASSIVE	ACTIVE	PASSIVE
X–α	X–β	Y–α	Y–β	Z–β	–

This kind of mismatch where the 'wrong' exponent gets used is not rare in the world's languages, as shown in Baerman et al. (2007) (see also the Cross-linguistic Database for Deponency for over 100 language case studies examining extended deponence). Some Archi nouns are examples of extended deponence. For example, *c̓aj* 'goat' patterns like the Plural sub-paradigm of AˁRI 'military division' when used in syntactically singular contexts: so Ergative and Genitive singular are respectively *c̓ajt:aj* and *c̓ajt:en*. The Ergative and Genitive *plural* cells in the *aˁri* paradigm (5) are *aˁrit:aj* and *aˁrit:en* (Brown and Hippisley 2012: 215).

In sum, words are fairly inconsistent in performing their primary function as ultimate signs and interfacers between syntax, semantics, and phonology. And the latitude between what they should be doing and what they are actually seen doing can be pretty large. If they are a universal, the universal is very plastic, at the least.

13.5 Words and Language Universals

Evans and Levinson (2009) draw attention to the fact that, unlike communication systems in other species, the human communication system has *variety*—indeed very great variety, in almost every way possible, from phonological inventories to basic word order or no word order, from constituency to complete absence of constituency, even from the use of recursive rules for syntax to an absence of such rules (for the latter, see

Everett 2005 on Pirahã). In previous sections we saw that word design is very much part of that variety. Evans and Levinson conclude that such variety presents overwhelming evidence that there simply are no language universals. On the basis of cross-linguistic inconsistencies in what is meant by word, Haspelmath (2011) goes as far as eliminating the word from serious linguistics analysis, claiming it to be a notion anchored in the space-delimited units of (mainly) Western writing systems. He radically suggests there really is no need to posit a system dedicated to the creation and regulation of words, i.e. a distinct role for morphology. In the context of such a plastic notion of word, we need to take such anti-universal claims seriously, and ask how fundamental words actually are. A useful starting point will be to clarify what exactly is meant by universal.

13.5.1 Language universal, different views

A language universal suggests something that is found in every language, and by implication whose presence in the system is essential. One conclusion would be that such properties are always there because they are innate, along the lines of Cartesian innate ideas (see Miral and Gil 2006 for the philosophical roots of the notion of language universals); they are part of a Universal Grammar, the language acquiring cognitive capacity that all people are born with.

Universals are discoverable in one of two ways: through deduction or induction. Induction seems the most obvious: compare many languages and the distilled commonalities are suggestive of universal properties. The tool for such an analysis is classical Greenbergian typology. Deductive-driven discovery, on the other hand, follows from hypothesis generating and the testing and refining of principles that govern a particular language; the tool is the scientific method combined with introspective experimentation. The resulting set of principles for one language is by default the very same for all languages, and therefore represents evidence for the properties of a universal grammar. Methodological differences aside, the premise and goal of deductive and inductive approaches are the same: there are innate language universals, find them.

At the same time, the difference in methodology has led to different outcomes. Cross-linguistic observation has been less successful in discovering 'absolute unrestricted' universals, and instead has focused on correlations of variables, so-called restricted or conditioned universals. Examples of unrestricted universals would be that all languages have vowels, or that all languages distinguish verbs and nouns. An example of a restricted universal is that languages with a mechanism for expressing dual number also have a morphological marker for plural number, but not the other way round (Corbett 2000). Another example is that languages whose default word order places object before verb have postpositions, whereas VO languages have prepositions. Most of Greenberg's universals are of this kind. The implicational relationship between two variables accounts for the kind of empirical patterning schematized in (18).

(18) Where a given language has *q* it will also have *p*

1. *p* and *q*
2. *p* and not *q*
3. not *p* and *q*
4. not *p* and not *q*

Universals are more relations between variables than variables themselves. The relationship could be one of markedness: dual is more 'marked' than plural because it is more specific in the information it conveys. If a language is going to be so specific that it distinguishes two of something, then it will at least convey the less specific 'more of something (though not how many more)'. Or the relationship could be a function of a more general principle of harmony: the value of headedness in one part of the grammar is the same in all parts of the grammar. OV displays right headedness, as does NP P. In (18), type 1 is a language with the implying as well as the implied property: a language which morphologically expresses plural (*p*) and dual (*q*). Types 2 and 4 are also possible through the implicational relation: having a plural but no dual, like English; having neither a plural nor a dual, like most of Mandarin. But type 3 is predicted never to occur.

In fact most typological investigations result in 'exceptions' to these kinds of correlations. Shughni is an OV language with postpositions, but it also has prepositions. Rather than being abandoned for the sake of a minority of cases, the correlations are preserved as statistical hypotheses, testable through regression models (Bickell 2011). So it is mostly the case that if you find *p* you also find *q*. Not only should Shughni be in the minority, but within Shughni you should find more constructions with postpositions than prepositions. In a markedness relation, like plural and dual, in a type 1 language (18) the frequency of *p* should be expected to be significantly higher than the frequency of *q*. Such tendencies are strong enough to warrant some kind of explanation. But the explanation does not have to be based on the idea that there is an innate universal grammar.

These tendencies may be a function of a range of factors external to a language faculty: 'stable engineering solutions satisfying multiple design constraints' (Evans and Levinson 2009: 429). They could be due to general cognitive abilities: many principles based on locality constraints, e.g. subjacency, could be due to the limits of working memory. Or the tendencies could be the result of the influence of other languages, genetically or geographically related: the high incidence of polysynthesis in native American languages points to this kind of external influence (Mithun 1999). They could have a purely cultural explanation: implicational animacy hierarchies used to regulate *p* and *q* patterns, for example in the availability of number (Smith-Stark 1974), may have slots that are culturally derived (e.g. Enfield 2002: 23–7). History can also provide an alternative explanation for what looks like a restricted universal. Anderson (1977) gives the example of split ergative systems, where ergative case may be found in Perfect/Past and Accusative in Imperfect/Present but never the other way around. But this synchronic pattern is simply the result of a reanalysis of the passive past participle construction as active. This yields oblique marked agent subjects (Ergative), and direct marked patient objects (Absolutive). (The Iranian and Indic languages both followed such a path, completely independent of one another.) An interesting proposal by Bybee (2006), elaborating on Greenberg (1969, 1978), is that such statistically significant patterns are synchronic epiphenomena of universal constraints on how languages change. Through a universal set of mechanisms of change, a language moves from state S to state S+1. What you find at S+1 can be explained by the path to this state that is constrained by such mechanisms. The occurrence and character of a Perfect construction, for example, is the result of collocation frequency, lexical form reduction, and automatization, resulting in the transformation into morphological markers of a particular construction (see Gisborne, this volume). In general, the claim is that explanation for recurrent patterns is to be sought not in an innate language faculty but rather in the processes that are invoked for *using* languages (though for an alternate view that these mechanisms reflect innate universals, see Kiparsky 2008).

13.5.2 Words are special

Whether common linguistic patterns are evidence of innate universals or the reflection of a complex interaction of factors that get dragged into the practical usage of language, words seem to be axiomatic, a priori 'givens' of anything that could be claimed to be a language. In a contribution to a volume outlining the state of the art on determining universals, Hockett (1963) proposes the comparative method in evolution to pinpoint the properties of human communication that are not shared by other animals, and then using the findings as evidence for a universal property. The result is a list of human language design features, including semanticity, arbitrariness, discreteness, displacement, and openness. All these features are active at the level of the word-as-lexeme, as we have shown. Greenberg (1963) makes it clear that properties that are universal by definition—the *sine qua non* of natural languages—fall outside the typologists' interest in a cross-linguistic inductive pursuit of universals (Evans and Levinson 2009). If this is the case, then we could view words as anterior to the debate over what is and is not a universal, and whether there are universals or not.

In the deductive, generative tradition where universals are essential properties of the language faculty, a distinction is drawn between formal properties and substantive properties. The formal group are reminiscent of Hockett's design features. For example, Jackendoff (2002a) outlines as formal universals, or architectural givens, the levels of representation shown in (1), the rules that regulate how elements are combined at these levels, and how the levels interface with one another. Substantive universals, on the other hand, include linguistic principles such as the binding principles, the Object Constraint, and constraints on extraction, i.e. deductively worked out and confirmed hypotheses (see Carnie 2013 for a textbook treatment of these principles). They also include the building blocks that fill out the architecture as well as the targets for combination: phonemes at the phonological level, phrases at the syntactic level, parts of speech at the interface of the syntactic and semantic levels. However, the *architecture* of these elements should probably be viewed as a part of the formal group; similarly, for phonemes, assumptions about binary features and autosegmental tiers (Nevins 2009).

Where do words fit in? It could be argued that words are part of the architectural type: as discussed above, words are the ultimate interfacers. But they could also be part of the substantive set of universals: they are members of an open class that are the product of combinatorial rules that take phonemes as their input. And they are targets for syntactic combinatorial rules, i.e. objects of syntax. However, Haspelmath's argument for dismissing words as universal categories is that precisely as interface rules, products of (morpho)phonological combination, and objects of syntax, cross-linguistic investigation reveals just how far short they can fall from the roles assigned to them. We saw in section 13.3 how wide the variation can be in architectural design, yielding a range of morphological types. Even the relatively straightforward notion of POS (part of speech) that a lexeme is associated with, fundamental to a lexeme for its interface with syntax, is called into question. Evans and Levinson claim that POS is not universal, citing languages without adjectives, e.g. Lao, and languages even without a verb/noun distinction, assumed to be an absolute universal, e.g. Straits Salish (Evans and Levinson 2009: 434).

One response to all of this is that a universal occupies a space inhabited by the prototypical as well as the less prototypical. Prototypically, words are the ultimate interface rules between the semantic, phonological, and syntactic subsystems of language. But sometimes elements larger than the word can act as the interface rule: syntactic phrase idioms such as 'kick the bucket' instead of the word 'die', and the lexicalized abstract constructions studied in Construction Grammar, for example 'go PP while V[produce sound]ing', which serves as the template for a family of phrases such as 'the trolley squealed round the corner', 'the bullet whistled by my ear' (Jackendoff 2010: 18). Elements stored in the lexicon are not necessarily words, and objects larger than words serving as interface rules should be possible even if not prototypical. Even within a single language, POS can be less than prototypical. Malouf (2000) is a careful study of mixed categories in English, such as verbal gerunds, that share properties with more than one POS; prototypical properties are expressed as defaults, and mixed categories inherit from multiple prototypical sources. Fruitful typological research conducted by Corbett and collaborators conceive of variation of this sort as degrees of distance from a location in space occupied by the *canonical* situation. This location is 'discovered' as the convergence of a set of dimensions all of whose values are canonical (see Brown and Chumakina 2012 for a helpful outline of canonical typology). The canonical word, in this approach, we would suppose to have canonical values for architectural design: this would correspond typologically to what is found in an agglutinating language. It would also be canonical with respect to interfacing properties, with a one-to-one relation to syntax and semantics, and a sign would be symbolic. These aspects are implied in Corbett (2007), who looks at paradigms containing suppletion and syncretism as departures from canonical inflectional classes.

If we think of (at least some) universals as having a kind of plasticity, as expressed by the prototype or canonical approach to typology, then words could be allowed to stay within the domain of universals. A different kind of evidence for words as universals comes from looking at language as the result of an evolutionary process; this perspective also appears to account for the plasticity of words.

13.5.3 Words and the origins of language

Hockett's design principles *qua* universals flow from a comparison between language and ACS. For words to be a universal category of human language, we should not expect to find them in the communication system of any other species; they are 'derivative' rather than 'primitive' in evolutionary terms, with no known homologue. Contributors to the debate on the origins of language disagree on various points: whether language evolved gradually or suddenly; whether it was a target for natural selection or arose for non-adaptive reasons (Gould and Lewontin 1979; Pinker and Bloom 1990: 708–10); if adaptive, what it was an adaption for, etc. But there seems to be a general consensus that although conceptual structure itself is primitive, albeit with humans having 'extra' concepts, the *propensity* to lexicalize concepts is derivative, i.e. uniquely human. Hence, the lexicalization of concepts as symbolic signs is a major distinguisher between ACS and language. In fact the signals in ACS are less encodings of concepts such as 'leopard' but more triggered vocal articulations of appropriate *behaviour* in the presence of the actual present danger of a leopard. They are therefore indexical rather than symbolic (see section 13.3.1). At the same time they are encodings of *categories* of stimuli plus best response rather than concepts, a distinction made by Bickerton (2009: 206–7). An ACS-based category is a class in which to place mind-independent, i.e. real-world, external stimuli, such as multiple instances of the appearance of leopards, and an associated behavioural response (Bickerton 2009: 206).

The information conveyed by ACS signals is limited and closed, exhausted by a small number of communicative functions such as foraging, mating, territorial control, social rank, and rearing of young (Bickerton 2009: 16; Givón 2010). In contrast, words as lexicalized concepts do not pick out mind-independent objects and events; as symbols they are 'the product of cognoscitive powers that provide us with the means to refer to the outside world from intricate perspectives' (Berwick and Chomsky 2011: 30). Important here is that the encoding of concepts is derivative. The concepts themselves, or at least a subset of them, are viewed as being primitive. Evidence for a fairly complex conceptual structure in vervet monkeys is provided by their ability to keep track of kinship relations both with respect to themselves as well as outside themselves: if its kin is attacked, an individual will attack kin of the aggressor—see Jackendoff (2011: 606), who cites Cheney and Seyforth (1990); see also Tomasello (2000b) for non-human cognition. Subsequently, uniquely human concepts are built on top of a homologous (shared) substrate (Pinker and Jackendoff 2005: 206). Suggestions for primitive concepts that are at a higher level of abstraction than, say, 'leopard' are found in Jackendoff (2010: 10–15), and include Thing, Event, State, Action, Place, Property, etc., the semantic prototypes for POS. One view is that a prior stage in the evolution of language was the evolution of protolanguage which consisted purely of utterances containing lexicalized concepts, i.e. 'protolexemes', which lack the syntactic and morphological levels of representation shown in (1), since there is no syntax for a lexeme to plug into. These levels only begin to be necessary when full language with semantic, phonological, and morphosyntactic components evolves at a later stage.

(19) PROTOLEXEME

- [no syntactic level of description]
- Semantic level: via conceptual structure
- Phonological level: combination of proto-phonological units

The inventory of phonological units, possibly syllables initially (e.g. MacNeilage 1998; discussed in Jackendoff 2002a: 244), are units of computation that yield an infinite number of signs, making protolanguage an open system in contrast to ACS. One view is that phonological words evolved from the generalization of ACS calls, and gradually replaced holistic signals with analytical word-like signals (Wray 2002a). Syllable-based words give way to digital units of sound—phonemes—yielding the important double articulation characteristic of language and greatly increasing the number of concepts than can be lexicalized. The human vocal tract is a mixture of primitive (the larynx) and derivative (the filter); the latter makes differentiation at the phonemic level possible (Hauser and Fitch 2003: 162).

It should be noted that a different kind of protolexeme is envisaged by adherents of the biolinguistic approach to language evolution (Chomsky 2007; Di Sciullo and Boeckx 2011; Hauser et al. 2002). In this approach the communicative aspect of language is viewed as secondary; language really evolved as a tool for thought, and the essential ingredient was a new capacity to perform, recursively, computational operations over word-like atoms that could interface with the conceptual world of the mind. Syntax comes early on. Words are the discrete objects of a simple syntactic computation[2] 'Merge'. So a protolexeme has a syntactic level, at least a POS that acts as the license for its combinatorial possibilities. Lexicalization makes concepts 'sticky' so they can participate in Merge, i.e. it makes them mergeable. This allows for the creation of thoughts that are made up of concepts from different domains; the concepts are now 'uprootable': '[Now] Man seems to have the ability to transcend the boundaries of modular thought and engage in cross-modular concept formation' (Boeckx 2011: 58–59). The phonological level is therefore missing from the protolexeme. It arrives when language is externalized in communication, a secondary function made possible by a second interface with the sensorimotor system. There is no protolanguage stage, rather an evolutionary leap from no language to grammatical language, minus its externalization as communication. From a biolinguistic perspective,

> The evolution of language will reduce to the operation Merge, the evolution of conceptual atoms of the lexicon, the linkage to conceptual systems, and the mode of externalization.
>
> (Berwick and Chomsky 2011: 30)

[2] Merge is the process whereby two elements combine to form a third element: 'eat' plus 'apples' yields 'eat apples'; see Chomsky (2007: 21) for this and other examples.

Though there is sharp disagreement about the exact trajectory from non-language hominids to where we are now, the central place of lexicalized concepts, or 'conceptual atoms of the lexicon', i.e. words, is undisputed.

Propositional information about unique events, states, and objects (Givón 2010) can be fully represented only by means of syntax (and morphology), which either is already there (the biolinguistic view) or evolves from the word strings of protolanguage. But the externalization of propositional information, through speech or signing, comes at a cost. Externalization really amounts to 'trying to express multi-dimensional mental representations on one dimensional sequences of sounds' (Hurford 2002: 314). The complexity and diversity in languages is the result of the problem thrown up by 'dimension squashing', to use Hurford's term, as there are many different ways of solving this problem.

Evidence of this can be found in language change. Time expressions using adverbs such as 'yesterday' can give way to grammatical features such as tense, which can move from being expressed as function words ('will' in English for future tense) to bound morphemes, i.e. inflectional features such as the synthetic future in French (Comrie and Kuteva 2005). Grammaticalization theory models these kinds of trajectories (see the papers in Norde et al. 2013, a special issue of *Language Sciences* devoted to recent research on grammaticalization). The result is languages with morphological complexity, languages whose words have a morphological dimension. Comrie and Kuteva make the point that historical changes of this sort, which can be observed through historical records, reverberate in evolution of language itself, from protolanguage to complex system. A kind of fossil of the evolution of complexity can be seen in child language acquisition and its mirror image in individual language attrition and large-scale language death (Comrie 1992: 207). A different kind of evidence is young languages, creoles, which have grammatical structure but are lacking in morphology (Bickerton 2009; McWhorter 2011)—though for the view that some creoles are morphologically complex, see Henri (2010) for Mauritian Creole, and that sign languages, also young languages, by default have morphology, see Aronoff et al. (2005). The diversity of word design, discussed in section 13.3, is really, then, a kind of diversity in staging posts along the grammaticalization path: isolating languages, absence of morphology; agglutinating languages, recent morphology; fusional morphology, 'older' morphology (Comrie 1992: 208). Older morphology correlating with fusional systems can be explained by increasing phonological tightness of inflectional markers with the stem. There are two constraints to be satisfied, and they pull in opposite directions. In Optimality Theory terms (Prince and Smolensky 1993), 'faithfulness' guarantees that the phonological representations of the pieces that make up the morphologically complex word do not alter. And 'markedness' guarantees that juxtaposing two phonological strings will not disrupt default phonotactics. In the agglutinating situation, the first constraint is prioritized; and in the fusional situation, it is the second constraint. In evolutionary terms, Carstairs-McCarthy (2005) blames the relatively low-level motor control of articulators for the markedness constraint: what is easier to pronounce wins, even if it obscures the morphological boundaries of a word.

13.6 Concluding remarks

When considering a fragment of a given language, we might ask: 'what's that word doing exactly?' We might expect the answer to be more or less the same regardless of language and regardless of language fragment. The word *should* be functioning as the ultimate symbolic sign within a symbolic sign system. And it *should* be a coalescence of syntactic, semantic, and phonologic properties as the ultimate interfacer between the chief components of the grammar. What words *should* do we can view as the canonical situation. But the slipperiness of the notion of word presented in Dixon and Aikhenvald (2002b) and our discussion here show that actual and canonical are not always the same. What we could say is that the canonical situation has evolutionary roots, with words as lexicalized concepts that evolved into mediators across levels of an increasingly more complex system. And that various factors come into play that nudge words off their canonical spot: symbolic communication through a one-dimensional serial channel (motor-sensory) with associated loss of information; reanalysis over time of meaning, form, and formal boundaries based on frequency effects through language use; and blurring of structural lines due to the relative weakness of motor control. The result is an expansion of possible design from original design of the word, rather than the loss of the word itself. As an integral part of the language system, words must be viewed as universal. But as a point of comparison between languages, and across diachronic stages of a particular language, words present good observation posts for variation. The upshot is that if words are universals, they are universals of a fairly plastic kind.

CHAPTER 14

TABOO WORDS

KATE BURRIDGE

14.1 INTRODUCTION

> When dinner came on table not one of my guests would sit down or eat a bit of any thing that was there. Every one was Tabu, a word of very comprehensive meaning but in general signifies forbidden.
>
> (Logbook of Captain Cook of his third voyage, 1776–9: Cook 1967]

THE word *taboo* (or *tabu*) entered English from Tongan during the 18th century, originally in reference to forbidden behaviour that was believed to be dangerous to certain individuals or to society as a whole. It included bans on naming dangerous animals, food restrictions, prohibitions on touching or talking to members of high social classes, and injunctions to do with aspects of birth, death, and menstruation. Such things were avoided because they were thought to be ominous or evil or somehow offensive to supernatural powers. To violate a taboo automatically caused harm (even death) to the violator and perhaps to his or her fellows. In this context, the use of avoidance language, or euphemism (Greek *eu* 'good, well' and *phēmē* 'speaking'), could be quite literally a matter of life or death (Allan and Burridge 2006: ch. 1).[1]

Traditionally, much was made of the difference between conditional and unconditional (or absolute) taboo. Taboos Polynesian-style were said to be absolute—a 24-hour-a-day, round-the-clock affair. However, in reality no taboo holds for all people, times, and contexts. Moreover, Old Polynesia had evidence of the sorts of taboo on bad manners with which readers of this book will be more familiar—in other words, sanctions placed on behaviour regarded as distasteful or at least impolite within a given social

[1] A neutral orthophemism (Greek *ortho* 'proper, straight, normal', cf. *orthodox*) is also a word or phrase used as an alternative to a taboo word; it is typically more direct or more formal than the corresponding euphemism.

context. Taboos Western-style are linked to social organization and traditions of etiquette; they are defined by culturally sensitive social parameters such as age, sex, education, social status, and the like. A taboo word in today's English is avoided (i.e. censored out of use on a particular occasion), not because of any fear that physical or metaphysical harm may befall either the speaker or the audience (though for some people harm is still a possibility if religious sensibilities are transgressed), but lest the speaker lose face by offending the sensibilities of the audience. Whether one speaks of *micturating, powdering [one's] nose, going to the washroom, taking a leak, a piss*, or *a pee*, the choice is a matter of appropriate style. Some speakers would even claim that to utter taboo terms offends their own sensibilities, because of the obnoxious nature of the terms themselves; but while these taboos may be observed in private, they will always be strongest in the public domain. In this context, euphemism is the polite thing, and offensive language, or dysphemism (Greek *dys* 'bad, unfavourable' and *phēmē* 'speaking'), is little more than the breaking of a social convention. It is the untimeliness that causes the offence.

From the earliest periods in history, and in all human societies, themes such as 'private parts', bodily functions, sex, lust, anger, notions of social status, hate, dishonesty, drunkenness, madness, disease, death, dangerous animals, fear, and God have inspired taboos and inhibitions, such that there has been considerable impact on languages from censoring discussion of them. These taboos will often persist even when speakers are unaware of the reasons leading to their establishment; original motivations become lost to unthinking ritual, distaste replaces fear, and routine ensures that linguistic sanctions endure. As with other social practices, what one group cherishes, another comes to spurn; hence taboos also strengthen group identity and social fabric through feelings of distinctiveness. The rites and rituals that accompany tabooing routines also provide a sense of control in a chaotic environment. When old taboos are jettisoned, people grow anxious that disorder is setting in. As Douglas (1966) argues, the distinction between cleanliness and filth stems from the basic human need to structure the world and render it understandable.

Taboo is dynamic, and notions about what is forbidden will change, sometimes dramatically, across cultures and across time. In the English-speaking world, the Bowdlerites of the 19th century targeted profanity and sexual explicitness and this triggered the progressive sanitizing (or 'bowdlerizing') of a range of works, including the Bible. *Damned* became *undone; whoremaster* became *misleader*; even *belly* was transformed via euphemistic magic to *stomach, viscera*, and *embryo* (the publisher of Trollope's *Barchester Towers* changed *fat stomach* to *deep chest*).[2] Their activities seem excessive according to today's sensitivities, and yet, from a modern perspective, works of this period also appear remarkably uninhibited. The police-court reports of Charles

[2] Dr Thomas Bowdler is best known for his expurgated edition of Shakespeare's works. Together with his sister, Henrietta Maria, he produced *The Family Shakspeare* (1818), from which, as he announced on the title page, 'those words and expressions are omitted which cannot with propriety be read aloud in a family'.

Adam Corbyn from the 1850s, for example, abound in descriptions of local residents that make a modern reader's toes curl: Mr Ninivian Stewart is portrayed as 'a long-nosed, lank-jawed, hypocritical-looking shoemaker'; Robert Tindal 'a hen-pecked old man'; Leah Harris 'a handsome Jewess'; Miss Mary Anne Walsh 'a middling aged spinster'; Mrs Elizabeth Hilton 'a tall, powerful woman, whose face outvies in colours those of a round of spiced beef'; Donald M'Kenzie (or Darkey Ken) 'an ogre-like Negro, of the dirtiest black colour imaginable'. Since the 1980s, gender, sexuality, disability, and race have become so highly charged that English speakers will shun anything that may be interpreted as discriminatory or pejorative. These new taboos make sexist, racist, ageist, religionist, etc. language not only contextually dysphemistic but also legally so. Such '-ist' taboos have surpassed in significance irreligious profanity, blasphemy, and sexual obscenity, against which laws have been relaxed. Perrin (1992) presents a history of expurgated works in both Britain and America, with a chapter on the targets of contemporary bowdlerism, notably dictionaries and literature classics. He shows that, though censoring on religious and sexual grounds has diminished, the increase in racial and ethnic expurgation has been striking. Ravitch (2004), in a more recent publication on the sanitizing of textbooks and state education testing services in the USA, shows this transition even more strikingly.[3]

An illustration of evolving sensitivities is provided by changes to the expression *pot calling kettle black arse* > *pot calling kettle black* > *pot calling kettle* (the saying which is used to claim that someone is guilty of that of which they accuse another). Societal queasiness around the Victorian era saw *arse* disappear from the end of the phrase; more recently speakers have been dropping *black*.[4] The dynamic nature of taboo is reflected in dictionary-making conventions of different eras, in particular the pressures put on lexicographers to alter definitions or even to omit entries entirely. Early dictionary-makers included religious and racial swearwords (the obscenities of more modern times), but were reluctant to admit sexually obscene words. In contrast, the 20th century saw mounting pressure on editors to change or omit the racial and political definition of words. It is now religion, race, and disability that create a linguistic minefield for lexicographers. Robert Burchfield (1989) recounts the fierce debates in the early 1970s while he was editor of the *Oxford English Dictionary* over the inclusion in the dictionary of opprobrious senses of the word *Jew*, while Lakoff (2000) details the 1990s dispute between the publishers of the *Merriam-Webster's Collegiate Dictionary* (10th edn) and members of the African-American community over the definition of *nigger* (see Perrin 1992: ch. 7 and Hughes 1991: ch. 11 for accounts of various crusades over the years).

A British report provides qualitative and quantitative evidence for the linguistic fallout from the new taboos (Millwood-Hargrave 2000). Research carried out jointly

[3] Some readers may recall that an episode of the BBC's classic comedy *Fawlty Towers* shown on 20 January 2013 was edited to remove racist language, specifically Major Gowen's reference to *niggers* and *wogs*.

[4] For an internet discussion of the racist nature of the idiom, see Goldberg's 'Racist pot calls kettle a bigot' on http://www.nationalreview.com

by the Advertising Standards Authority, the British Broadcasting Corporation, the Broadcasting Standards Commission, and the Independent Television Commission tested people's attitudes to swearing and offensive language. In the first part of the study, participants were asked to respond to the perceived 'strength' of swearwords with no context suggested. Though there were gender and age biases, participants were clear about the relative severity of the twenty-eight words. Least offensive was verbal play, such as 'baby-talk' *poo* and *bum* or rhyming slang like *berk* (which almost no one links to *cunt*). Ranked slightly more offensive were such profanities as *God* and *Jesus Christ*, followed by sexually/physically based expressions (expletives such as *shit* and *fucking hell* and sexual references such as *shag* and *pussy*). Towards the top of the scale of severity was derogatory language towards minority groups, including people with disabilities, those from different religious faiths, homosexual men and women, and ethnic minorities. Most severe of all was racial abuse.

14.2 Violating taboos

> Whether they are referred to as swearing, cursing, cussing, profanity, obscenity, vulgarity, blasphemy, expletives, oaths, or epithets; as dirty, four-letter, or taboo words; or as bad, coarse, crude, foul, salty, earthy, raunchy, or off-color language, these expressions raise many puzzles for anyone interested in language as a window into human nature.
>
> (Pinker 2007: 267)

There can be significant differences between societies, and between individuals within those societies, with respect to the degree of tolerance shown towards taboo-defying behaviour. Much will depend on the values and belief systems of the period. It was not so very long ago that some transgressions against Western taboos were severely punished, by such as imprisonment, hanging, or burning at the stake. In Britain up until the end of the 17th century, blasphemy was punishable by burning. There are still people who would take such biblical commandments as Leviticus 24:16 literally: 'He that blasphemeth the name of the Lord, he shall surely be put to death, and all the congregation shall certainly stone him.' And even though few in this technically advanced and (for many) secular 21st century would admit to the sort of fear and superstition they associate with the taboos of exotic and unenlightened peoples, there are many in it who believe in lucky and unlucky numbers, carry talismans, knock on wood, cross fingers, walk around ladders, avoid black cats, and believe in the magic of names. Words can be curative (the placebo effect); conversely, they can harm a person's health (the nocebo effect).[5]

[5] The power of words to positively or negatively affect health outcomes is something many in the medical profession are now taking seriously, especially when it comes to breaking bad news to patients; see Cordella (2004).

There will also be times when speakers deliberately defy taboos and their purifying impetus. Taboo words come with considerable sociocultural and psychological benefits in the form of the ready-made material for speakers to let off steam, to abuse and offend, to signal a dysphemistic attitude or degree of feeling, or simply to intensify what is being said. These words provide off-the-shelf expletives, as exclamatory interjections with a highly expressive function (*Bugger!, Shit!*). They are uttered in intense emotional situations, as when a speaker is angry and frustrated, under pressure, in sudden pain, or confronted by something unexpected and usually (though not necessarily) undesirable. The taboo quality of the expressions provides the catharsis the speaker seeks in order to cope with the situation that provoked the expletive in the first place; the breaking of the taboo triggers a release of energy.[6] Abusive language with taboo words adds extra insult to injury; swearwords provide that bonus layer of emotional intensity and added capacity to offend in curses, name-calling, any sort of derogatory or contemptuous comments to intentionally slight or offend. On the other hand, swearwords can act as in-group solidarity markers within a shared colloquial style. Like the 'incorrect' language of non-standard grammar, these words fall outside what is good and proper, and help to define the gang. They can be a cultural indicator, a sign of endearment, a part of steamy pillow talk, and, in many societies, an important component of humour.

Since taboos furnish languages with their preferred terms of opprobrium, patterns of swearing will change over time. As Hughes (1991, 2006) nicely outlines, the history of 'foul' language in English has seen the sweeping transition from the religious to the secular. When blasphemous and religiously profane language was no longer considered offensive (at least by a majority of speakers), what stepped in to fill the gap were the more physically and sexually based modes of expression. The terms *bastard* and *bugger* were the first of these to be pressed into maledictory service (the 18th century) and risqué body parts and bodily functions followed later (the 20th century). However, the potency of profanity relating to sexual and bodily functions has more recently diminished. True, emotional expressions always lose their sting with frequent use, but it is also true that sex and bodily functions are no longer tabooed as they were in the 19th and early 20th centuries. While some people still complain about hearing such words in the public arena, what is now perceived as truly obscene are racial and ethnic slurs, the use of which may provoke legal consequences. For instance, in Australia, sports players are occasionally 'sin-binned' but never charged for foul language on the field, unless the complaint involves race discrimination or vilification. When a footballer

[6] Studies over the years have shown that at times of extreme stress, swearing will typically diminish. Writing of the use of *fuck* by British soldiers in the First World War, Brophy and Partridge (1931) report that to omit the word was an effective way of indicating emergency and danger (p. 16f.); Ross (1960) examined swearing among a group of 5 male and 3 female British zoologists in the Norwegian Arctic and reported that 'under conditions of serious stress, there was silence' (p. 480); in his analysis of swearing by psychiatric ward personnel at staff meetings over a 6-month period, Gallahorn (1971) reported expletive usage reduced when ward tension was intense.

was disciplined for calling Aboriginal player Michael Long 'black cunt' during an Australian Rules match, the reports and re-reports of the incident made no reference to the use of *cunt*. It was the racial abuse that triggered the uproar, and the incident gave rise to a new code of conduct against racial vilification both on and off the sporting oval (Scutt 2002).

14.3 Strategies for circumventing taboo

Ten anderen can desen Meester helpen ende ghenesen alle secrete ghebreken van mannen ende vrouwen, hoe desolaet die selfde persoonen syn, die hier niet en dienen verhaalt te zyne om der eerbaerheyt wille.

[Furthermore, this Master can help and cure all secret illnesses of men and women, however devastated they are, which here cannot serve to be repeated for decency's sake.]

(16th-century Antwerp quack pamphlet: Hüsken 1987)

Euphemisms have many functions, but primarily they act as a verbal escape hatch in response to taboos. Very broadly, they are the sweet-sounding, or at least inoffensive, alternatives that speakers or writers create when they are faced with the difficult problem of how to talk about things that for one reason or another they would prefer not to speak of unrestrainedly in the prevailing context.

No matter what population group you look at, past or present, there will be euphemism, and examples are wide-ranging. In classical times, blunt verbs such as 'die' and 'kill' were avoided; instead people 'curled up', 'fell', 'went to sleep' or 'went on a journey', or they were described as simply 'having lived' (Griffin 1985). Medieval Dutch physicians used to write of *vernoy smans/swijfs* 'irritation of the man's/woman's' where the name for the sexual organs is simply omitted (Burridge 1993). *The monosyllable* was one of many invisible words in Victorian times; its equivalent today is *the C-word*. Some people still say *crumbs* instead of *Christ*; many newspapers still print *c**** and *f****; politicians speak of *community charges, levies*, or even *voluntary contributions* rather than of *taxes* or *tolls*; the push for non-sexist usage has rendered words like *chairman* and *actress* taboo for some people; and so on. Clearly, not all euphemisms are in response to taboo. In their ability to place whatever it is they designate in a favourable light, many are simply alternatives for expressions speakers prefer not to use on a given occasion. They might be used to enhance whatever is being referred to, perhaps even to amuse, and they have no real taboo counterparts; *potholes* are simply upgraded to *pavement deficiencies, cheese on toast* becomes *Welsh rarebit*.

The many different linguistic strategies used in the formation of euphemisms fall into three overarching mechanisms: analogy (generalization of forms to new situations), borrowing (incorporation of forms from elsewhere), and distortion (modification of forms). Which of these strategies is used often depends on the function of a euphemism (Burridge 2012).

Of the broadly analogical processes, the most common involves the semantic extension of non-taboo terms; the taboo topic is paired up with a pleasurable notion, sometimes establishing chains of figurativeness, almost in the manner of an overarching megametaphor (e.g. *at a ripe old age, in riper years, mellow, mature*, etc. for 'old'). Many euphemistic substitutions refer to something that is conceptually linked somehow with the tabooed sense; typically they have more pleasing connotations, as a way to dress up the reality (e.g. *venerable* and *respected* carry lofty associations that emphasize some of the positive aspects of the ageing process). Typically the replacements involve a high level of abstraction; consider linguistic subterfuges such as *doing it* for 'sexual intercourse', where very general words are used in place of more explicit terms (see Allan and Burridge 2006: ch. 4, on various kinds of whole-for-part and part-for-whole substitution).

Substitution can also involve a type of internal borrowing from sub-varieties (such as jargon and slang) within the same language. Learned or technical terms provide ready-made euphemisms (e.g. *spirochaetal/treponemal/luetic disease* in preference to *syphilis*). The antithetical strategy is to use a colloquial rather than a learned term; here the levity of the slang makes the reality easier to bear (*cupid's measles*). Effective euphemisms are also lexical exotics based on words or morphemes borrowed from another language. Latin and French have been providing English with fig leaves, smokescreens, and dress-ups for centuries (*perspire* instead of *sweat, defecate* and *faeces* instead of *shit*).

Another common strategy for fashioning euphemism involves modifying the offensive expression in some way. This can involve some form of shortening, such as end-clipping (*jeeze* 'Jesus'), abbreviations (also with regard to a word's spelling: *pee* 'piss', *S.O.B.* 'son-of-a-bitch', *f**** 'fuck', *the C-word*), and ellipsis (as in *pot calling kettle* ——). An antithetical modifying strategy is circumlocution (or long-windedness). This reconfigures the original expression via a process akin to componential analysis; the senses of a taboo concept are unpacked and listed, and the resulting periphrasis functions as a euphemism (*urine* becomes *excrementitious human kidney fluid; faeces* becomes *solid human waste matter*). Many types of verbal play can effectively renovate an offensive word, such as phonological remodelling that adjusts the pronunciation of words (*eld* 'old age', *heck* < *hell*); affixation (*oldie* and *oldster)*; blending (*zoomer* 'the aging baby boomer' < *boomer* + *zip*); reduplication (*jeepers creepers* 'Jesus Christ'); rhyming (slang) and alliteration/assonance (*dentured dandy* 'old man'; *brown bread* 'dead').

14.4 Taboo words raise gooseflesh

> There is something very terrible in an oath torn from its proper home and suddenly implanted in the wrong social atmosphere. In these circumstances the alien form is endowed by the hearers with mysterious and uncanny meanings; it chills the blood and raises gooseflesh.
>
> (Wyld 1920: 387)

Words are symbolic. Despite the fact that every language has some vocabulary based on sound symbolism (e.g. *clang, jangle, woosh*), the correlation between the form and the meaning of language expressions is arbitrary; individual sounds such as /e/, /p/, /n/ do not have meaning. However, over time this arbitrariness can fall away as speakers create a meaningful connection between the sound of a word and what is being referred to. Thus, meanings sometimes shift because of the way a word sounds (e.g. for many, *flagrant* describes 'the way flowers smell') and words change their shape to fall in line with others related in meaning (e.g. *grine* becomes *groin* to be more like *loin)*. In the case of taboo words, the link made between sound and sense is particularly strong. Speakers really do behave as if somehow the form of the expression communicates the essential nature of what it denotes (*'Cunt' is such a horrible word!*).

More generally the belief in the potency of words has been dubbed the 'naturalist hypothesis'; in Sir James Frazer's words (1911: 318): 'the link between a name and the person or thing denominated by it is not a mere arbitrary and ideal association, but a real and substantial bond which unites the two' (see Allan 1986: ch. 2.8), and this is what forms the basis for the distinction between the mentionable euphemism and an unmentionable taboo alternative: *vagina* and *excrement* versus *cunt* and *shit*. It is as if the obscenity lurks in the words themselves rather than in what they denote. Speakers even describe these words as 'unpleasant', 'ugly-sounding', 'dirty', etc. They are felt to be intrinsically nasty, and this makes them disturbing and powerful.

Such is the potency of taboo terms that innocent vocabulary may also be affected through spurious association. *Regina* makes some people feel uncomfortable because of its phonetic similarity to *vagina*, and they avoid it. *Coney* (rhymes with *honey*) 'rabbit' dropped out of use because of its anatomical significance (though it still exists in the distorted form *bunny*, and with a change of vowel in place names like *Coney Island*). Gender, sexuality, disability, and especially race are now so highly charged that speakers will shun anything that may be interpreted as discriminatory or pejorative—and this includes blameless bystanders that get in the way. The word *niggardly* has no etymological connections with the taboo term *nigger*, yet many Americans now censor the expression. The effects of taboo commonly cross language boundaries, too. Thais are apprehensive about using the Thai word *fuk* 'gourd, pumpkin' in the hearing of English speakers; they also avoid the English word *yet* because of its phonetic resemblance to the offensive colloquial Thai verb 'fuck'. Many other peoples practise similar self-censoring under multilingual conditions.

The English words *titivate* and *titillate* illustrate another effect of taboo. The two similar-sounding words are currently in the process of colliding.[7] *Titivate* originally meant 'to tidy up', but some dictionaries give the additional meaning (usually labelled 'incorrect') 'tickle, excite agreeably'. *Titivate* is taking on the meaning of similar-sounding *titillate* 'to excite pleasantly' (with strong association to lust). The fact that the word begins with *tit* may also play a part. We should not be surprised that

[7] For further examples of lexical collisions, see Durkin (this volume).

titillate wins out over *titivate*; risqué meanings will always come to dominate. Economics has Gresham's Law: 'Bad money drives out good.' Sociology has Knight's Law: 'Bad talk drives out good.' Linguistics has the Allan–Burridge Law of Semantic Change: 'Bad connotations drive out good.'

The effect of this law is that many euphemisms become tainted over time as the negative associations reassert themselves and undermine the euphemistic quality of the word. Such is the stigma surrounding mental illness that any euphemism for the condition will quickly degenerate into dysphemism. The word *insanity* derives from Latin *in* 'not' + *sanus* 'healthy'. Now confined to 'mentally unsound', it originally had a much broader domain encompassing all bodily organs and their functions. Today even the word *sane* has narrowed under the influence of *insane* to designate a mental condition only. The pejoration can be rapid. As society's prejudiced perceptions foment, the euphemistic value is diluted and the negative connotations quickly reattach themselves, requiring the formation a new euphemism. True, some euphemisms are simply so fleeting that they never linger long enough to become unfit for use (e.g. expressions for 'old age' such as *ultra-mature, dynamic maturity, seasoned, golden ager* were short-lived), but generally taboo areas of the lexicon generate narrowing and deterioration of meaning: Steven Pinker's (1997) 'euphemistic treadmill'; Allan and Burridge's (2006) 'X-phemism mill'. The result of this chronic contagion is a flourishing of vocabulary as people seek less offensive words to speak the unspeakable: *latrine* > *water closet* (*WC*) > *toilet* > *bathroom/washroom*. The image is that of an ever-grinding lexical mill. The more severe the taboo, the longer the chain of euphemistic substitutions it churns out.

Few euphemisms that have degraded in this way come back from the abyss, even after they have lost their taboo sense. Only occasionally will an expression not only resist contamination but also retain its euphemistic qualities, even over long periods: *to sleep with* 'have sexual intercourse' has been in use since the 10th century; *to lose* 'be deprived (of someone) by death' since the 12th century; *pass away/pass* since the 14th century; *deceased, departed*, and *no longer with us* 'dead' since the 15th century; and *ageing* since the early 18th century. So familiarity does not always breed contempt. These expressions have in common that they allude to taboo topics in a very remote way; their association lacks any sort of precision, perhaps allowing them to remain unobtrusive and sneak through the discourse unscathed. Nonetheless, the longevity of these euphemisms remains something of an anomaly, in the manner of those atypical slang expressions that manage somehow to retain their original energy, sometimes over centuries (Burridge 2012). As Jespersen (1905/1962: 230) describes, 'the usual destiny of euphemisms' is that the 'innocent word' becomes 'just as objectionable as the word it has ousted and now is rejected in its turn'. Taboo senses seem to have a saliency that will dominate and eventually kill off all other senses belonging to any language expression recruited as euphemism. Even across languages these words seem able to contaminate other words, bringing down innocent expressions that just happen to sound similar. Psychological, physiological, and neurological studies also corroborate that forbidden words are more arousing, more shocking, more memorable, and more evocative than all other language stimuli.

In 1957 Charles Osgood and his colleagues provided psycholinguistic support for deteriorating euphemism. People were asked to evaluate numerous words and phrases on a series of seven-point bipolar rating scales. The aim was to locate a concept in semantic space within three dimensions of attitude: evaluation (is the word good or bad?); activity (is the word active or passive?); potency (is the word strong or weak?). Their research confirmed what we know from the behaviour of words over time: that there is a general tendency for any derogatory or unfavourable denotation or connotation within a language expression to dominate, whatever the context.

Another notable group of experiments using a technique known as electrodermal monitoring lends scientific confirmation to Wyld's (1920: 387) account of taboo words given at the start of this section. Participants are hooked up to fingertip electrodes that measure their emotional responses to a range of taboo words. It is akin to polygraph testing and records what are known as 'galvanic skin responses' (GSRs). These are changes in the skin's ability to conduct electricity and are triggered by changes in emotional stimulus (pleasant or unpleasant) involving fright, anger, shock, sexual feelings, and such like. Research supports overwhelmingly what every native speaker knows: taboo words compared to other words evoke stronger GSRs—the feeling that non-specialists report as a 'creeping' or 'raising of the flesh'.

Over the years this research has also looked into the effects of arousal on memory (e.g. MacWhinney, Keenan, and Reinke 1982). The findings are always the same: taboo words are more stimulating than non-taboo words and are stored differently in memory. A 2004 report by MacKay and colleagues describes the effects of emotion on memory and attention using what is known as a Stroop task. Taboo words were displayed in a salient colour, and participants were asked to name the colour and ignore the word. There were three significant effects. Participants were slower in naming the colour of the taboo words compared to the colour of the neutral words (presumably distracted by the disturbing nature of taboo words). This effect diminished with word repetition; this is consistent with the fact that the affective power of frequently encountered words gradually wears out. The second effect was superior recall of taboo words in surprise memory tests following colour naming. The third effect was better recognition memory for those colours consistently associated with taboo words rather than with neutral words. Other experiments have demonstrated that taboo words impair immediate recall of the preceding and succeeding words in rapidly presented lists. All these findings are consistent with the strong emotional reactions triggered by culturally potent taboo expressions.

A slightly different perspective is provided by experiments that examine the emotional responsiveness of bilingual speakers. A study reported by Harris and colleagues of 32 English–Turkish bilinguals used fingertip electrodes to measure the emotional responses of participants to taboo and other kinds of highly charged words. Researchers found that the greatest emotional reactivity was to taboo words in both languages. Consistent with earlier studies using only monolingual speakers, taboo words (curses, sexual terms, etc.) generated far stronger responses measured by amplitude of skin conductance than other kinds of emotional words such as reprimands (*Don't do that!*), aversive words (*cancer, kill*), positive words (*bride, joy*), and neutral words. In fact, the amplitude was almost double that of neutral words. The responses were even stronger for the speakers' first language. These findings support what second language speakers have often reported anecdotally, namely, that they find it easier to utter taboo words in their second language than their first. This study also recorded that the auditory stimuli elicited greater emotional arousal than the visual stimuli in the first but not in the second language. In other words, the sound of taboo words was found to be more disturbing than their appearance in print, once more confirming the subjective reports of language users generally: taboo words sound awful and are much harder to say than to write.

The reason taboo words elicit stronger physiological responses when learned earlier in life can be explained by the childhood experience. Children acquire the emotive components of the meaning of these words early on, well before they have knowledge of the social and cultural pressures that require us to censor them. Taboo words come with social rewards (maximum attention) and penalties (reprimands, banishments), so are coded with the equivalent of a linguistic health warning: DANGEROUS—USE ONLY WITH EXTREME CAUTION. As our brain systems mature and we develop discretion about what we say, we learn to censor taboo words via the usual neurological processes of inhibition. Taboo words and phrases acquired by late bilinguals lack the cultural imprint of the forbidden and have different neurological representations. In fact, a number of participants in the Harris et al. experiment, during the debriefing sessions, reported that they 'felt nothing' when they heard or even uttered the taboo expressions in their second language.

Neurological and psychiatric disorders shed additional light on the neural architecture that underpins the production and control of taboo expressions. People with certain kinds of dementia and/or aphasia lose all language ability except the ability to produce dirty words (Jay 2000). The technical term for the involuntary utterance of obscene language is *coprolalia* (from Greek *kopros* 'dung' and *lalia* 'talk'). It is related to the variety of highly emotional language that we automatically produce when we are angry and frustrated, under pressure, or in sudden pain. People who manifest this kind of disorder curse profusely, producing what sound like exclamatory interjections as an emotional reaction. However, if called upon to repeat the performance, they are unable to do so because they have lost the capacity to construct ordinary language. There may not yet be any laboratory or neuro-imaging studies that have conclusively identified the exact neuroanatomical sites where taboo expressions are stored or that have evaluated specifically the neurological processing of obscenities, but the evidence seems overwhelming: taboo language is rooted deeply in human neural anatomy; the sociocultural setting then provides the expression. 'Society shapes the noise that is made', to quote the mother of a young child, whose Tourette's Syndrome manifested coprolalia (Allan and Burridge 2006: 248).

14.5 Names and taboo words

> In ancient Egyptian mythology, Isis gained power over the sun god Ra because she persuaded him to divulge his name. In the European folktales about the evil character variously called Rumpelstiltskin (Germany, parts of England), Terry Top (Cornwall), Tom Tit Tot (Suffolk), Trit-a-Trot (Ireland), Whuppity Stoorie (Scotland), and Ricdin-Ricdon (France), the discovery of the villain's name destroyed his power. In some societies it seems to have been acceptable to know a personal name provided the name was never spoken.
>
> (Allan and Burridge 1991: 45)

Throughout history people have attributed supernatural powers to names, and naming forms a special case of word taboo (Allan and Burridge 2006: ch. 9). Both in the past and in certain contemporary societies, people may substitute the original name of feared powers with some sort of euphemistic appellation in the hopes of somehow being able to appease such powers and win their favour. The elves and fairies of folklore used once to be referred to as *good neighbours*; the ancient Greeks called the *Furies* the *Eumenides* 'the well-minded ones'. There are also naming taboos observed by people undertaking hazardous pursuits such as mining, hunting, and fishing, and they involve, for example, taboos on the names of dangerous animals. These practices are motivated by fears comparable with those relating to death and disease, and people use similar strategies to avoid calling down malfeasance upon themselves. Many languages have equivalents to the English proverb *Speak of the devil and he comes running*.

Not surprisingly, personal names (i.e. true names) have been or still are taboo among peoples in many parts of the world (see Blount, this volume). This is another fear-based taboo. Sorcerers can do harm to a person if they are in possession of that person's true name. A name is regarded as a proper part of the name-bearer, not just a symbol but the verbal expression of his or her personality. Thus in many languages, a name is an inalienable possession and is assumed to be an inseparable part of the body. Other properties of personal representation such as mind, spirit, soul, shadow, and reflection, are often treated in the same way and this can have repercussions for the grammar (Chappell and McGregor 1996). Because true names are so closely associated with their name-bearer as to be a proper part of him/her, in some societies true names are often secret, rendering euphemistic names necessary for public naming and addressing. In many places, names of the dead are (or were until recently) taboo. Sometimes the ban extends to those personal names that the dead person may have given to others. Violations of such taboos are believed to cause misfortune, sickness, and death; they may also cause offence to living descendants.

Naming taboos can have major effects on the ordinary vocabulary of some languages, because the personal names are common words or derive from common words. In this way, naming taboos can be extended to become word taboo. Simons (1982) describes how, of a sample of 50 Austronesian languages which are known to have some sort of naming taboo, 25 of these have a name taboo that extends into a common word taboo. A further 18 have a taboo whereby words even resembling the tabooed names are taboo themselves. On Santa Cruz (part of the Solomon Islands), where there is a taboo against using the name of certain affines, names consist of a common word, normally with a gender-marking prefix. Thus if a man's mother-in-law is called *ikio* (*i*=prefix to female's name, *kio* 'bird'), he cannot use the common word *kio* to refer to birds. The effect of this is that something like 46 per cent of the everyday vocabulary is potentially taboo for some people on Santa Cruz; on the island of Malaita, this figure is as high as 59 per cent.

Euphemisms are thus created via the methods outlined earlier: semantic shifts of existing words, circumlocution, and phonological modification. As a result, sounds turn up in odd places and mutate unexpectedly. Words are often funny-looking. (Here you might compare the situation where the urge to swear in polite company drives an English speaker to spontaneously change *fuck* to *fudge*.) There is also a high rate of borrowing, even among core vocabulary items that that are not generally borrowed. It is precisely these established common-usage words that historical linguists trust when it comes to establishing genetic relationships and reconstructing lost stages of languages. Yet in this context even basic vocabulary of this kind cannot be relied on to remain stable. Extensive borrowing and taboo-induced remodelling make it difficult to determine the chronology of linguistic changes that have occurred. Irregular sound shifts have the effect of accelerating vocabulary differentiation between genetically related languages and can create a false impression of long divergences, in some cases even hiding genetic connections.

Aboriginal Australia offers another perspective on the effects of naming taboo on vocabulary. In many traditional Australian Aboriginal communities, any kind of vocabulary item, including grammatical words, can be proscribed if it is the same as, or phonetically similar to, the name of a recently deceased person. Replacement vocabulary is created by using synonyms from the language's own repertoire (or from an auxiliary repertoire of respect language), by semantic shifts of existing words, compounding, circumlocution, borrowing from a neighbouring language, and in some cases by use of a hand sign or gesture. Some languages have special vocabulary items to be used in place of proscribed words, sometimes a kind of 'whatsitsname/whatchamacallut' word, or one that is reserved especially for the purpose of name avoidance. For example, in some Kimberley languages in the north of Western Australia, those whose personal names have been tabooed are addressed as *nyapurr* 'no name' (William McGregor, pers. comm.). Striking illustration of this involves the changes to the first person pronoun in some dialects of the Western Desert. On the death of a man named *Ngayunya*, these languages replaced the pronoun *ngayu* 'I/me' with *nganku*. Subsequently, this term was itself tabooed and replaced by either English *mi* or by *ngayu* borrowed back into the language from dialects where it had never been tabooed (Dixon 1980: 29). This shows that the taboo on a word may cease after some years have passed, allowing it to come back into use. This recycling is one of the very few ways in which a former tabooed item can itself become a euphemism, and is another dent in the notion of absolute taboo. Alpher and Nash (1999) claim that, where the history is clear, such cases of death-tabooing have always proved to be temporary. The taboo on a word may cease after some months, or after one or two years have passed, allowing the word to come back into use. Moreover, it appears that there is no absolute prohibition on mentioning the name of a dead person. Vocabulary is taboo for only those people who stand in a certain relationship with the dead person. Locals can continue to use the taboo forms out of earshot of the bereaved family.

Given the experience of Aboriginal Australia, we have to allow for the fact that the effects of taboo on vocabulary might occasionally be overstated. Understandably, in the fieldwork context it would be natural, the polite thing to do, for an informant to provide the outside fieldworker with the avoidance terms. This could well give an exaggerated impression of the severity of the taboo and the extent of the vocabulary replacement rate. There might even be some embellishment on the part of the fieldworker (exotification of the other) and perhaps also on the part of the informant seeking to make a deeper impression on the naïve onlooker. However, even allowing for exaggerated accounts, it is clear from the endeavours of historical linguists that this kind of naming taboo can have a profound effect on the vocabularies of these languages. Many researchers working on languages in Australasia and the Pacific have noted the difficulty of identifying regular sound correspondences between cognate (or related) forms (see Dyen 1963; Holzknecht 1988; Keesing and Fifi'i 1969; Ray 1926; Wurm 1970). But of course, these speech communities are not closed to innovation either, and they are certainly not closed to importing cultural elements from the outside. As earlier described, taboos and attitudes towards taboo violation do change over time and many of these old taboos are now disappearing, having been affected by the spread of Western ideas.

CHAPTER 15

SOUND SYMBOLISM

G. TUCKER CHILDS

15.1 Introduction

In beginning linguistics classes, students are told that the association between words and meanings is arbitrary: there is no necessary or obvious relation between the form of a word (the signifier) and that which it represents (the signified).[1] Charles Hockett differentiated human language from animal communication systems by means of 'design features', one of which was 'arbitrariness', a central concern of this chapter and one dating back as a tenet of linguists to at least de Saussure (1948[1916]).[2] Hockett restated arbitrariness as 'the duality of patterning', the efficient use of a small number of units (individual sounds, or 'phonemes', meaningless in themselves) which are combined to form meaningful units—morphemes—the smallest phonological unit capable of conveying meaning (Hockett 1982[1960]).

Despite the title of this volume, it is necessary here to analyse the word into smaller components than is usually done. The smallest standard unit of meaning by definition is the morpheme. For example, the word *symbolism* has two morphemes, the stem *symbol* and the suffix *-ism*. Sound symbolism, as its name suggests, takes as its significant unit sequences smaller than the word or morpheme—the individual sound or sound sequence.

For example, given three contrastive sounds (phonemes) such as /t/, /æ/, and /k/, it is possible to order them in several ways to make different (and unrelated) words. No one segment in itself has meaning. Allowable combinations consist of the words *tack* [tæk], *cat* [kæt], *act* [ækt] (Hockett 1982[1960]), as well as a subset of those

[1] My thanks to Mark Dingemanse for many references and much conversation, and to Laura Downing for access to a recently published article (Downing and Stiebels 2012).

[2] As soon as his *Cours* was published in 1916, Saussure's expansive claim for arbitrariness was criticized as too strong in Jespersen (1922b) (Jakobson and Waugh 1979:186). This criticism illustrates something of the early and ongoing controversy.

permutations, *at* [æt] and perhaps *ack* [æk] (an expresssion of disgust in American English). Note that not all possible sets and subsets are possible: there are no English words consisting of just one consonant or containing impermissible consonant clusters as in [tkæ]. Such restrictions on permissible sequences (a language's phonotactics) represent one way in which a language limits possible words. Nonetheless, the general point of linguistic orthodoxy is clear: independent patternings exist at the level of both sound and meaning, linked together by an arbitrary mapping between the two.

This chapter challenges this belief by identifying mapping that is not arbitrary. Individual sounds and sound sequences smaller than the morpheme will be shown to have established meanings and sets of associations which, if not pervading the language, certainly represent a significant portion of the mapping between sound and meaning.[3] The distinction between arbitrary and non-arbitrary associations, however, is not a discrete one but rather represents a continuum, of which few speakers are aware. Everyday speakers of a language may see all mappings as identical and thus may not make the same distinction linguists do.[4]

15.2 Sound symbolism defined

'Cock-a-doodle-do!', as speakers of English know, is what roosters do, and since roosters crow in pretty much the same way around the world, it is not surprising that the word used to represent the crowing of a rooster in unrelated languages is pretty much the same. (Directly imitating sounds in nature is known as 'onomatopoeia'). Familiar examples other than the crowing of the rooster are the *hissing* of a snake, the *croaking* of a frog, or the *tick-tock* of a clock (an old-fashioned analogue one as opposed to a silent digital one, of course). The association between sound and meaning is direct; the correspondence is iconic. Many such words in a language imitate sounds in nature, but onomatopoeia is, of necessity, restricted to entities that actually emit sound. However, since it displays many features found in other sound symbolic forms, a consideration of onomatopoeia allows for the beginnings of a definition of sound symbolism.

Because human beings are neither frogs nor roosters and cannot replicate these animals' vocalizations, the human renditions will be at best a pale approximation, as filtered through a language and probably affected by the language's phoneme inventory and its

[3] Klamer (2002) presents a revealing analysis of (non-)arbitrariness in the lexicons of Dutch and Kambera (Malayo-Polynesian; Indonesia).

[4] On the other hand, the widespread incidence of sound symbolism, and its invasion into large tranches of a language's vocabulary, may well contribute to speakers' feeling that quite a few words are somehow 'appropriate' for the concepts which they designate. Doesn't the phonetic make-up of the words *twirl*, *clump*, and *flap* somehow match their meanings? (Reasons for this intuition are discussed later in this chapter.) (ed.)

Table 15.1 Animal sounds illustrating onomatopoeia

	Dog	Rooster	cat	cow	laugh	sneeze
Arabic	ʕaw-ʕaw	kukuriku	maw-maw	ʕuu	qah-qah	ʕats
English	*bow-wow*	*cock-a-doodle-do*	*meow*	*moo*	*ha-ha*	*achoo*
French	wah-wah	kokoriko	miaw	mœ	ha-ha	a-cum
German	vaw-vaw	kikeriki	miaw	mu	ha-ha	hatschi
Hebrew	haw-haw	kukuriku	miaw	mu	ha-ha	hapci
Japanese	wa-wa	kokekoko	niaw/nyaa	moomoo	ha-ha-ha	hakʃu
Mandarin	waw-waw	kuku	meaw	m̂	ha-ha	hakʃu
Polish	haw-haw	kukiriku	miau	muu	ha-ha	apshik
Spanish	waw-waw	kokoroko	miaw	mu	xa-xa	acu
Venda	hwuu-hwuu	kókókó-dî-kò	ŋáù	mɔ̰mɔ̰	hɛhɛhɛ	atsʲa
Zulu	khowu-khowu	ki-ki-li-gi-gi	nyawu	mu-mu	ga-ga-ga	wethí

Columns 2–5 refer to the sounds animals make; the last two reference human (non-linguistic) sounds.

Sources: Akita et al. (2011), Childs (2011), and Kunene (2011)

phonotactic constraints. Some of the sounds are more cross-linguistically common than others, as seen in Table 15.1.

Sound symbolism is a more extensive phenomenon than onomatopoeia and perhaps qualitatively different. Note that onomatopoeia represents only a small fraction of what most would consider sound symbolic forms, although it may, in some sense, be basic to all sound symbolism. As will be seen, 'sound symbolism' is a more inclusive term and more integrated into language proper. A common misperception, probably fostered by literary studies (cf. Crystal 2010: 176), is that all sound symbolism is onomatopoeia, but sound symbolism often has few ties to sounds in nature.

One difference has to do with the relationship between signified and signifier. Onomatopoeia *directly* imitates sounds in nature. The iconic link between sound and meaning is obvious and transparent, as seen in Table 15.1. Sound symbolism, on the other hand, can involve any meaning (not just sound), and there is no direct imitation. That the association is extensive, i.e. found in many forms, is also significant. Thus, a consideration of sound symbolism leads us to the conclusion that the relationship between sound and meaning is not arbitrary for all words, but rather that there are parts of language where sound and meaning have some degree of correspondence; in virtue of these correspondences, words can position themselves in a network of 'verbal affinities' (Bolinger 1940).[5]

[5] Bolinger notes that the phenomenon had already been 'perceived and explained' in Jespersen (1922a).

Sound symbolism is here defined as an extensive correspondence between sound and meaning, at a level below that of the morpheme. One name given to such units is 'phonaestheme' (Householder 1946; Bolinger 1950b).[6] Sound symbolism represents a recurrent and remarkable singularity of meaning and form correspondence not unlike more grammatical phenomena such as the non-concatenated partials found in Semitic triliterals (McCarthy 1985), where discontinuous sequences have meaning. For example, the sequence k-t-b, depending on what other sequence it is concatenated with, can mean 'book', 'letter', 'write', etc. Sound symbolism may involve individual sounds, such as the high front vowels [i] and [ɪ] denoting 'small' as in the compound words *teeny-weeny* and *itsy-bitsy*.[7] Note that partial and even full reduplication is often found in many words employing sound symbolism. Even features of individual sounds can be used: voicing modes (Sicoli 2010) or sounds characterized by the feature [grave][8] (Jakobson, Fant, and Halle 1952).

Such associations are illustrated by the Zulu examples in (1). Increasingly more powerful action is conveyed as one moves through the ejective series [p'-t'-k'] (represented orthographically by initial p-t-k), the aspirated series of stops (ph-th-kh), and the breathy-voiced or plain voiced stops (gh-d-g). All of the examples are full verbs.

(1) Consonantal sound symbolism in Zulu verbs (Van Rooyen, Taljaard, and Davey 1976: 38)

paku	'slap lightly'	phaku	'flutter'	bhaku	'be excited'
taphu	'touch something soft'	thaphu	'take something'	daphu	'grab'
kete	'chatter'	khete	'babble'	gede	'chatter loudly'

In Japanese mimetics, similar associations obtain.

(2) Consonantal sound symbolism in Japanese mimetics (Imai et al. 2008: 55)

Mimetics	Meaning	Mimetics	Meaning
goro	'heavy object rolling'	koro	'a light object rolling'
guru	'a heavy object rotating around an axis'	kuru	'a light object rotating around an axis'

[6] In a series of papers (Bolinger 1940, 1948, 1950a, b), Bolinger articulated the notion of a sub-morphemic unit, a notion expanded in Rhodes (1994) and Rhodes and Lawler (1981).

[7] Whissell (this volume) contains a discussion of the criteria used to choose a name, many of which depend on sound symbolic associations.

[8] The feature [grave] is characterized by a concentration of sound in the lower frequency regions; labial and velar consonants, and back vowels, have this feature. In terms of articulation, grave sounds are produced in the peripheral regions of the vocal tract, that is, front or back.

bota	'thick/much liquid hitting a solid surface'	pota	'thin/little liquid hitting a solid surface'
		potapota	'thin/little liquid hitting a solid surface repeatedly'

In addition to exploiting such segmental features as voicing, sound symbolism may involve suprasegmentals or prosodic features, i.e. those which are a secondary or overlaid property of segments. Lexical tone is one such property, for its phonetic substance involves the manipulation of an inherent property of segments, i.e. pitch or fundamental frequency. Tonal iconicity in Bini is shown in (3) below and is found in other West African languages (Wescott 1973).

(3) Tonal iconicity in Bini (Nigeria)

'tall' (with uniform high tone)		'short' (with uniform low tone)	
gadagbaa	'long and lanky'	bɛtɛɛ	'short and fat'
gisigbii	'big and high'	giɛghɛgiɛghɛ	'short'
gbokoo	'tall and portly'	giɛɛnriɛn	'small'
gbɔhuun	'tall and fat'	giɛgiɛɛgiɛ	'tiny'
gegeege	'lofty'	kpɛkurlu	'short'
geletee	'towering'	kpukurlu	'cringing'

Similar tonal iconicity has been demonstrated in Gbaya (Central African Republic) and Ewe (Ghana) (Samarin 1965), and in the two Nigerian languages Yoruba (Courtenay 1976) and Igbo (Maduka 1983–84). A comparable use of tone is found in the formation of two-word expressives in White Hmong, a language spoken in Southeast Asia (Ratliff 1992).

Vowel quality may also carry symbolic value. For example, the concepts of 'more' or 'larger' take the High set of vowels in Diola (Greenberg and Sapir 1978). Vowels have been found to have even more extensive associations in Kaluli relating to place and direction (Feld 1982). The size–sound association is found with Semai vowels as well (Diffloth 1994), albeit in an unexpected pattern. There are thus a great many resources available for sound symbolism, both at the segmental and at the suprasegmental level. Sound symbolism has been shown to be a resource in a wide variety of languages: Navajo (Webster 2012), in several Central African languages (Noss 1975), Russian (Lahti 2012), and in the Mayan language K'iche' (Barrett 2012).

This chapter will not treat symptomatic forms, i.e. those forms that directly indicate the physical, emotional, or psychological state of a speaker. In an influential study of sound symbolism, such associations have been referred to as 'corporeal sound symbolism' (Hinton, Nichols, and Ohala 1994a: 2). This can include expressions of pain, *Ouch!*, or pleasure, *M-m-m*, or of disgust, *Eww!*, and interjections such as *Zounds!* or *Great Caesar's ghost!* As can be seen by the spelling, some are more normalized in their written representation than others.[9] Many are language-particular and highly conventionalized in their form. For example, *Whoops!* (also *Oops*) as an expression of surprise at inadvertently dropping something, is likely unique to English. The discussion of such forms, however, will not form part of the discussion here.

Sound symbolism has been dismissed as unimportant or insignificant by major scholars from de Saussure (1948[1916]) to Newmeyer (1993), yet its interest to linguists and others has persisted over time. The study of sound symbolism has engaged not only linguists but also psychologists, anthropologists, cognitivists, philosophers, and others.

One reason for the interest is the pervasiveness of sound symbolism, often within a language but more generally across languages both areally (geographically: it is found throughout Sub-Saharan Africa: Childs 1994) and genetically, as within related Mayan languages (Durbin 1973). Sound symbolism is found throughout the world, from Tofa(lar) and Tuvan in southern Siberia (Harrison 2004) to Polish (Kwiatkowski 1992).

When sound symbolism is restricted to a single word category, that word category can be quite large, for example, *giongo/gitaigo* in Japanese (Amanuma 1974). Imai et al. (2008) report that mimetics constitute a large class of words in Japanese, and new words can be easily created: one mid-sized dictionary of mimetics (Atoda and Hoshino 1995) lists 1,700 entries. A similar word category is ideophones in African languages, which number 8,000–9,000 in Gbaya (Central African Republic) (Samarin 1979: 55) and over 3,000 in Zulu (von Staden 1977). Another part of a language where sound symbolism is often found is in animal names and in systems of ethnobiological classification (Berlin 1994, 2004).

Psycholinguists have also shown an interest in sound symbolism. Several recent studies have identified the facilitative nature of sound symbolism in language learning (Monaghan and Christiansen 2006) and specifically word learning (Monaghan, Mattock, and Walker 2012). Others state:

> ... sound symbolism is not a peripheral or trivial phenomenon in language, as sound symbolism facilitates one of the most important tasks for children in language development, namely, the learning of novel verbs. Furthermore, the investigation of the neural and psychological mechanisms underlying sound symbolism leads to important questions about the nature and origin of language, including how language is linked to non-linguistic visual, auditory, tactile, and motion perceptions, and how iconicity in multi-sensory mappings bootstraps children to break the initial barrier for language learning (Maurer and Mondloch 2006; Ramachandran and Hubbard 2001).
>
> (Imai et al. 2008: 63)

[9] Bolinger (1940: 65) identifies a process he calls 'onomatopoeia in reverse'. It is when such expressions are pronounced as they are spelled, originally a poor representation of how they were pronounced. An example is the dental click [ǀ], used in English as an expression of disapproval, spelled 'tsk' and pronounced [tɪsk]. The sound is also represented as *tut-tut*, and pronounced accordingly: 'He tut-tutted to himself.'

The association of gesture with mimetics has also been a fruitful field of research, providing insights into cognition (Kita 1997). Sound symbolism also has interest for those looking at language change (Kaufman 1994; Lanham 1960; McGregor 1996; Mithun 1982). In literary circles, sound symbolism is of great interest (Nänny and Fischer 1999), especially ideophones as a literary device (Dingemanse 2011a; Noss 1975). Sound symbolism has been said to appeal more directly to the reader or listener, particularly in performance, and thus has relevance for theories of aesthetics and poetics (Tsur 1992, 2012). The study of sound symbolism is also important for ethnopoetics, culture and knowledge systems, and cognitive theory (Nuckolls 1999: 244f.)

In fact, sound symbolism is of interest to anyone who studies language. In their introduction, Hinton et al. (1994a: 11) identify the categories that feature in sound-symbolic vocabulary. Their conclusion on presenting this list is that '[t]hese six areas may be seen as encompassing most of language'. Thus, anyone interested in language, particularly in its cognitive and functional aspects, cannot ignore sound symbolism.

The next subsection introduces the literature on sound symbolism, a rather extensive one with some history. Because there have been a number of reviews, this section will be relatively short but will reference a few of them where relevant.[10]

15.2.1 Studies of sound symbolism

The literature on sound symbolism has seen little integration of different perspectives until relatively recently. A thorough assessment can be found in Nuckolls (1999), which references the oft-quoted distinction made by Peirce between icon, index, and symbol. Her definition of sound symbolism serves as the basis for the definition used here.

> The term sound symbolism is used when a sound unit such as a phoneme, syllable, feature, or tone is said to go beyond its linguistic function as a contrastive non-meaning-bearing unit, to directly express... meaning. Discussions of sound symbolism are indebted to the semiotic scheme outlined by Peirce 1955. A component of this scheme lays out three logically possible relations between symbols and their referents. These three logical distinctions, the icon, index, and symbol, are stock-in-trade terminology for semiotic analysis and are heuristically useful as long as one remembers that such clear-cut types are practically non-existent. When a unit such as a phoneme seems highly motivated or natural with respect to some articulatory or

[10] Dingemanse (2012) gives the following as offering typological reviews of ideophones: Childs (1994); Diffloth (1972); Güldemann (2008); Lamp (1979); Samarin (1971); de Saussure (1948 [1916]); Vydrin (1989, 2001). For sound symbolism and iconicity he gives: Hinton et al. (1994b); Jakobson and Waugh (1979); Nuckolls (1999); Vydrin (2002). Mok (1993) is a bibliography of sound symbolism that forms the background for a study of Chinese sound symbolism, Mok (2001). I would also include Brown (1958b) and a number of the papers collected in Bolinger (1965).

> acoustic criteria, it may be called an icon, which refers, denotes, or communicates by its resemblance to a sensation, feeling, or idea.... An ideal type of sound symbolism would seek to identify iconic and indexical relations, but all types of sound symbolism necessarily involve conventionally symbolic relations as well.
>
> (Nuckolls 1999: 228–9)

I would underscore Nuckolls' point that sound symbolism is rarely pure, and make an additional one—that speakers (non-linguists and perhaps non-poets) rarely make such distinctions between arbitrary and non-arbitrary associations, except perhaps in the case of onomatopoeia. Sound-symbolic associations are no different from any other ones, a point made repeatedly (Bolinger 1940; Hinton, Nichols, and Ohala 2006; Imai et al. 2008). Native speakers do not in general distinguish arbitrary and non-arbitrary mappings between form and meaning.

There is an extensive experimentalist literature on sound symbolism (Ciccotosto 1991), the early work assessing the psychological reality of sound symbolism (Köhler 1929), continuing on into such work as LaPolla (1994). Recently the research has looked at the value of sound symbolism in learnability (Kelly 1992; Monaghan and Christiansen 2006; Parault and Parkinson 2008; Parault and Schwanenflugel 2006). In all of these studies there is an interest in how sound symbolism helps children in learning. The work of Kita and his associates on Japanese mimetics and gesture (Kita 1997, 2003) complements this work in identifying the cognitive importance of sound symbolism.

To what extent sound symbolism is universal and to what extent it is language-particular is a vexed question. The answer is rather unsatisfying: all sound symbolism is language-particular, but there are shared patterns cross-linguistically, none of them shared universally. As many have remarked, true universals (as opposed to universal tendencies) are hard to come by (Downing and Stiebels 2012). Languages partake of both language-specific tendencies and universal ones. As a group of researchers on Japanese put it, 'sound symbolism in mimetics seems to involve both universally shared sound-meaning mappings and language specific components that are embedded in the language's phonological characteristics' (Imai et al. 2008: 56). Nonetheless, it should be remembered that onomatopoeia is imitative—sound symbolism generally is not. Without a doubt sound symbolism lies embedded within a particular language, for that is where it originates and prospers.

The rise of sound symbolism in a language is an organic process involving the gradual accretion or snowballing of instances of shared meaning about a sound–meaning correspondence. The accumulation of these correspondences through a yet unknown process is what leads to sound symbolism (Childs 1989). The partials that illustrate conventional sound symbolism may be segmental or prosodic, or even non-concatenative, as stated above. '[A]n "arbitrary" form once integrated into the system, assumes all the affective and associative privileges enjoyed by the most obvious onomatopoeia' (Bolinger 1965: 231). The parallel on the non-iconic side is just as powerful: sound-symbolic associations possess the strength of the arbitrary associations between form and meaning as well.

The Frequency Code (Ohala 1983, 1984, 1994) is one claim for the universality of sound-symbolic meaning. The phenomenon is the long-attested association between high front vowels, high formant frequency, etc., and small size (brightness and related concepts). A less powerful but nonetheless powerful association is between low back vowels and large size. Supporting such a claim are investigations of Zulu ideophones, where, for example, the ideophone *mbim-mbim-mbim* was judged to be the sound of a smaller quantity of water than *bho-bho-bho* or *bhu-bhu-bhu*. Although the Frequency Code explains many patterns cross-linguistically, it never accounts for all representations of size or related phenomena.

One of the most extensive mappings of sound-symbolic associations is reported for Semai, a Mon-Khmer language spoken in Malaysia. Semai has long been known for its rich sound-symbolic vocabulary expressed in a class of words known as expressives (Diffloth 1972, 1976), but recent work has extended our knowledge of how extensive that mapping is.

> Expressives display a diagrammatic iconic structure whereby related sensory experiences receive related linguistic forms... gradient relationships in the perceptual world receive gradient linguistic representations... a diagrammatic iconic structure within sensory vocabulary creates networks of relational sensory knowledge. Through analogy, speakers draw on this knowledge to comprehend sensory referents and create new unconventional forms, which are easily understood by other members of the community. Analogy-making such as this allows speakers to capture fine-grained differences between sensory events, and effectively guide each other through the Semai sensory landscape.
>
> (Tufvesson 2011)

What is significant in Semai is not only the quantity of the mapping but also the quality, the density of the relatedness network, and the gradient quality,[11] much as in a connectionist model.

African ideophones have proved another fertile area for the investigation of sound symbolism, primarily on the formal side (Awoyale 1988) but also recently on the cognitive and cultural side. Ideophones are the word category, equivalent to expressives and mimetics, robustly featuring sound symbolism. Dingemanse (2011b) has tied their use to performance and interaction, seeing ideophones as 'depicting' rather than merely representing an iconic relationship: 'Depiction foregrounds speaker intent and mode of signification, whereas iconicity focuses only on the putative resemblance between sign and object' (Dingemanse 2012: 657). Moreover, he sees ideophones as implicated in the grammar, encoding modal distinctions such as evidentiality. Their morphosyntax is often distinctive. Ideophones typically have little morphology and stand syntactically apart, often at a margin and set off phonologically by a pause. They will frequently be introduced by a dummy verb such as 'say', as in the first Mani example in (4a), or 'do' in (4b) (both Sesotho examples).

[11] Gradience indeed seems part of the picture of sound symbolism (Childs 1994). Bolinger (1950a) identifies 'a gradience among forms—degrees of similarity between wholes rather than the absolute identity of parts'.

(4) The syntax of African ideophones

a. Mani (Sierra Leone and Guinea)

mɛ́n cɛ̀ mà fɔ́ pɔ̀tɔ̀-pɔ̀tɔ̀ ...
mɛ́n ǹ-cɛ mà fɔ́ pɔ̀tɔ̀-pɔ̀tɔ̀ ...
water NCM-DEF PRO say glug-glug (IDPH)
'The water poured out glug-glug.' (jd 2/6/05)

dòmɔ̀ cɛ́ wɔ́í drè ↑yòrúŋ
dòmɔ̀ cɛ wɔ́ drɛ yòrúŋ
shirt DEF PRO red IDPH
'The shirt is really (bright?) red.' (jd 3/6/05) (Childs 2011: 98–99)

b. Sesotho (Lesotho, South Africa)

a mo re nyemo
a mo re nyemo
3SG to.him do give.dirty.look (IDPH)
'He gave him a dirty look.'

lehapu la re phatlo
lehapu la re phatlo
watermelon PRO do SPLIT! (IDPH)
'The watermelon cracked open.' (Kunene 2001)

Janice Nuckolls has worked on a similar category of words in Pastaza Quechua (Ecuador) and has identified a way that they, too, are implicated in the grammar. In this case ideophones encode aspectual distinctions, such as duration and punctuality (Alpher 1994; Nuckolls 1996). Thus we see once again how sound symbolism can be used in special ways in individual languages: rich and gradient semantic mappings as well as distinctions normally marked on verbs. All of these extensions to strictly iconic relationships underscore the importance of metaphor and analogy—explaining the unknown or unrepresented, extending the sensory or what we know by means of the familiar. The depth of these studies attests to the core importance of sound symbolism.

The next section exemplifies a number of cases of sound symbolism, briefly and selectively.

15.3 Sound symbolism cross-linguistically

The snapshots here of sound symbolism around the world are necessarily selective. The goal is to show both the areal and language-specific variety of sound symbolism but also the commonality. The latter feature, usually identified as universality, is a research focus of much psycholinguistic work on sound symbolism. A generalization about areal biases (cf. Dingemanse 2012) is the broad differences between sound symbolism in the Americas, Africa, and Asia. In the Americas the concepts encoded are sound and movement; in Africa there is reference to sound and image, but also to the other senses; in Asia there is reference to internal states. In Japanese, for example, sound symbolism is much more frequently used in expressing tactile sensation, emotion, and manner of motion than in expressing shape (Imai et al. 2008: 56; Oda 2000). Areality is definitely a factor in the distribution of sound symbolism, even at a more local level, as in the Pacific Northwest of the USA, as described in Nichols (1971).

Although it may be difficult to prove conclusively, it is likely that all languages partake of at least some sound symbolism. Marttila (2011) presents a claim as to its universality 'based on a genealogically stratified sample of 237 languages' using a survey of bird names.[12] The implicational hierarchy below (Dingemanse 2012: 664), intended to display the synchronic distribution of encoded meanings, probably displays a diachronic development sequence.

SOUND < MOVEMENT < VISUAL PATTERNS < OTHER SENSORY PERCEPTIONS < INNER FEELINGS AND COGNITIVE STATES

Using analogy and metaphor, speakers elaborate and extend sound symbolic systems from a basic onomatopoeic system to personal emotions and attitudes.

The following subsections characterize the variation by looking at how sound symbolism manifests itself cross-linguistically. The selective survey begins with English.

15.3.1 English

Some of the most important work on sound symbolism in English can be found in the work of Dwight Bolinger. The examples in (5) show the sub-morphemic partials introduced above.

(5) Some examples of sound symbolism in English (Bolinger 1940)[13]

having something to do with light: glance, glow, glare, gleam, glimmer, glitter, gloat, glower, gloom, glaze, glass, glimpse, glim[14]

general idea of 'neat' or 'trim': *sli-* or *sle-* words: *slender, slight, slim, sleazy* [*sic*], *sliver, slick, slip, slipper, slit*[15]

[12] The common cross-linguistic patterns have been seen as proof of universality (e.g. Givón 1984: 29–45, 1989; Haiman 1985). They have also been dismissed as 'merely ding-dongism' (Silverstein 1994: 41).

[13] Bolinger references Bloomfield (1933), Firth (1935), and Jespersen (1922a). See also Ciccotosto (1995: 135–139).

[14] In one account, 'roughly half of the common English words starting with *gl-* imply something visual' (Imai et al. 2008: 55).

[15] As the author of this chapter notes, *sleazy* seems out of place in Bolinger's list of 'neat' and 'trim' words. The word does, however, fit easily into another paradigm of *sl-* words, which Firth—citing about

'heavy masses or the movement of heavy masses': words ending with *-ump: dump, rump, hump, crump, lump, stump, slump, gump* (a heavy-witted person)

'breaking' or 'fragments' caused by a (destructive) force: words ending in *-ash: bash, clash, thrash, trash, slash, mash, dash*, etc.[16]

'a twisting or pinching motion' *tw-: twist, twirl, tweak*, and *tweeze* + 'circular or round movement or shape' *-irl: curl, furl, whirl*, and *swirl*. The word *twirl*, then, can be analysed as consisting of two phonaesthemes *tw-* and *-irl*.

These are likely to be the result of 'accretions': 'once a partnership is fixed between a sound and an idea, nothing more is needed to cause that sound to give the cast of its idea to many words, alike in sound, that previously symbolized something different' (Bolinger 1965: 194).

Building on the work of Bolinger, Rhodes and Lawler (1981) provide some less obvious examples, analysing English monosyllables such as *ring* into an 'assonance' (onset) and 'rime' (the terms come from Bolinger 1950a, as shown in (6a)). As with the above example of *twirl*, the meaning of *ring* turns out to be an almost compositional function of the meanings of its submorphemic partials, viz: 'non-abrupt onset of sound with an extended envelope'. The display in (6b) shows an entire paradigm.

(6) a. *r-* ' non-abrupt onset (of sounds)' (cf. *rumble, rattle, roar*, etc.)
cf. *kr-* as in *crack, creak* and *kl-* as in *click, clatter*, etc.
-ing 'BE/MAKE a sound with an extended envelope' (cf. *ding, ping, sing*).

b.

	Rimes			
Assonances	*-ump*	*-op*	*-ing*	*-ap*
Fl- [2D extended]	—	*flop*	*fling*	*flap*
st- [1D rigid]	*stump*	*stop*	*sting*	—
kl- [together]	*clump*	*[clop]*	*cling*	*clap*

I now turn to sound symbolism in other parts of the world.

40 examples including *slime, sloppy, slug, sludge, slipshod, sly, slither, sloth, slink, slovenly, slum, slump, slobber*, and *slur* — characterizes as 'in varying degrees pejorative' (Firth 1930: 184). Firth notes a similar sound symbolic association in other Germanic languages, citing numerous examples of pejorative *sl-* words from Dutch and Norwegian (pp. 191–192). (ed.)

[16] The psychological reality of this association 'has been confirmed through priming experiments (Bergen 2004)' (Monaghan and Christiansen 2006: 1838).

15.3.2 Asia

One of the earliest and most insightful writers on what are called 'expressives' is Gérard Diffloth (e.g. Diffloth 1972), whose early work on Semai paved the way for further researchers. Expressives is where much sound symbolism is found as is illustrated by Bahnar (a Mon-Khmer language of Vietnam): 'Bahnar expressives tend to cluster into small networks of semantically and phonologically related forms.' These clusterings are just what we have seen in other languages, when a language exploits a sound–meaning correspondence fostering other correspondences. The examples were chosen to illustrate the importance of sound-symbolic vowels for 'big' and 'small'. Somewhat contrarily to the usual pattern with size–sound symbolism, the 'big' vowels are /ii i uu u ee e oo o/ and the 'small' vowels /ɛɛ ɛ ɔɔ ɔ/. The examples show not only a language-specific sound symbolism but also a variable, non-concatenative partial representing 'flickering light', /bl-ŋ/ and /bl-l/, sometimes with reduplication, the quintessential pattern for sound symbolic words.

(7) flickering light and size–sound symbolism (Diffloth 1994: 109–11)

blooŋ-blooŋ	of numerous reflections caused by rays of light on a large object elongated in shape
blɔɔŋ-blɔɔŋ	id., small object
blooŋ-blɛɛw	of the numerous reflections caused by a single ray of light on a big, shiny object
blɔɔŋ-blɛɛw	id., small, shiny object
bleel-bleel	of large flames appearing intermittently but remaining vivid
blɛɛl-blɛɛl	id., small flames
bliil-ɲip	of a large scintillating fire, of the last flashes of a large fire about to die
blɛɛl-ɲɛp	id., small fire

Both Korean and Japanese have thousands of words employing sound symbolism, and study of them has been prolific. It has been said that ideophones are at least as important to the Japanese language as traditional classical art forms such as *kabuki* (dance theatre) and *bunraku* (puppet theatre) are to Japanese culture (Gomi 1989: 243–244). Indeed, there is a whole dictionary of Japanese ideophones: Kakehi, Tamori, and Schourup (1996), updating Amanuma (1974) and Ono (1984).

One special feature of both Japanese and Korean ideophones is their phonology. Mimetic vowel harmony (MVH) in Korean is distinct from the VH in its verbal morphology. As seen in (8), many Korean mimetics form a minimal pair based on the 'dark' vs. 'light' distinction, as symbolized by the exclusively 'dark' or 'light' vowels, separated by a line.

(8) MVH in Korean (Cho 1994: 439)

Dark:	i ü ɪ u	*tüluk*	*k'itək*	*əlluk*
	e ö ə o	*tölok*	*k'atak*	*allok*
Light:	æ a	'obese'	'nodding'	'mottled' (Akita et al. 2011: 2)

Just as MVH is special to the sound-symbolic part of the lexicon, so too is a phonological rule in Japanese: a rule of palatalization is found only in mimetics (Nuckolls 1999: 240).

In addition to the experimental studies mentioned above, Annamalai (1968) in an earlier paper looks at how widespread sound symbolism is in three Dravidian languages, Tamil, Malayalam, and Telugu and how it resists sound change (palatalization); Mok (2001) investigates the phonology of Chinese sound symbolism.

15.3.3 Australia and the Pacific

In the Pacific region, patterns identical to those identified elsewhere similarly obtain. In Ilocano, a Malayo-Polynesian language spoken in the Philippines, a set of sound symbolic associations is based on velars in syllable codas and the glottal stop, as shown in (9).

(9) Ilocano sound symbolism (Rubino 2001: 304–5)

-og 'thumping sounds, violent falls': *bitog* 'thump', *togtog* 'knock on the door', *paltog* 'gun'

-ak for high-pitched sounds 'breaking, splitting, or cracking': *litak* 'sound of splitting (dried bamboo), bursting sound', *pakpak* 'sound of a wooden club beating the laundry', *ripak* 'sound of a slammed door'

-ok for low-pitched sounds 'breaking, splitting, or cracking': *litok* 'sound of a cracking joint', *ritok* 'crackling sound of joints', *toktok* 'sound of knocking on something hard'

-ng [ŋ] 'buzzing, resonant, moaning': *areng-ng* 'muffled moaning sound of pain', *baeng* 'sneezing', *bariwengweng* 'sound of stone swishing in the air', *ing-ing* 'violin', *kiling* 'sound of bell', *kutibeng* 'sound of a guitar'

In addition, Ilocano has a number of affixes that have sound-symbolic values, often dealing with punctuality or durativity, as in Yir-Yoront (Australia) and Quechua.

Kaluli (Papua New Guinea) has a great number of sound-imitative words that fade into non-onomatopoeic representations, i.e. bird cries, movements, and other environmental phenomena. The examples in (10) illustrate vocalic contrasts which represent both sounds (in a non-onomatopoeic way) and location or direction.

(10) *gɔnɔ to* 'sound words'; sound symbolism, vocalic contrasts (Feld 1982: 145–148)

'height' contrast (1): [i] vs. [ɛ] 'hum, ambiguous source' vs. 'buzz, directional'

[i] 'generic for bush sounds whose direction or source is ambiguous, tree or bush rumbling, soughing of trees; sound of coucals, rain sprinkling or dripping'

[e] 'source of sound visible, sounds of flies, bees, or cicadas; puckering and sucking sounds of bats eating, shellfish claws snapping'

'height' contrast (2): [u] vs. [ɔ] 'swoop down, originate above, dissipate below' vs. 'swing out, radiate over horizontal distance or concentrically'

[u], whooping men, sounds of aeroplanes, sound of Harpy Eagle, thunder, waterfall

vs. [o] earth rumbling, grackle, insects and birds at daybreak, trilling kingfisher, panting, wind

'depth' contrast: [e] vs. [o] 'crackle, at ground, sharp and crisp' vs. 'pop, move with source, durative'; both observable and both stay at source of making

[e] crunching sounds of bush underfoot as one walks on forest paths, musical instruments
vs. [o] flying beetles that sound continuously through flight, white water making sound over rocks, pop sounds in cooking, farts

These examples of Kaluli sound symbolism do little justice to the richness of the description in Feld (1982), where birds and their songs and many more sounds in nature are structured, and extend metaphorically to represent reflections of humans and their behaviour. As an example of the richness, one can note how the mapping of the rich taxonomy of bird songs is used for characterizing weeping, a prominent expressive behaviour in the culture.

(11) bird-song-related weeping and mourning (Feld 1982: 88–93)

yɛlɛma (*yɛ* 'onomatopoeic' for weeping, bird name + *ɛlɛ* 'like this' + *ma* < *sama* 'speak')

(a) male weeping (emotional and volatile, spontaneous)
iligi-yɛlɛma 'shocked or startled weeping, high-pitched vocalizations' (English 'get choked up') (*iligi* 'be startled or shocked')
gana-yɛlɛma 'loud falsetto melodic weeping' (*gana*, generic 'onomatopoeic' for 'sound')
gana-gili-yɛlɛma 'loud wailing with body convulsing, quivering sometimes shrieking voice' (*gili* 'rumbling')

(b) female weeping (more controlled and prolonged, performed)
gese-yelema 'pitiful or sorrowful melodic weeping' (*gese* used in contexts of children, birds, and sound terminology) identical to sound of *muni*, a small fruit dove
sa-yɛlɛma 'melodic texted sung weeping' elaborate and ritual, 'closest sound to "being a bird" (*sa* 'waterfall')

A more grammaticalized case of sound symbolic words is found in Australia. In northern Australian languages, formerly sound-symbolic forms (ideophones) have been incorporated into the verbal morphology as 'uninflecting verbs', something like verbal particles (McGregor 2001), similarly to what has happened in Jaminjung (Schultze-Berndt 2001). The latter author provides some examples of 'multiplexity' and/or 'extension', e.g. contact with an extended surface (a–e), motion along a surface (f–j), and/or multiplicity of participants (d, e, i–l).

(12) The alveolar trill suggesting 'multiplexity' and/or 'extension' in Jaminjung (Australia) (Schultze-Berndt 2001)

a.	*dudurr*	(sit with) legs straight
b.	*jajurr*	stop, halt
c.	*bayirr*	on top of, supported
d.	*warrb*	be/sit together (cf. *waga* 'sit, of single entity')
e.	*murruny*	be heaped up
f.	*ngarrang*	stagger
g.	*warr*	scratch
h.	*yirrirrij*	slide
i.	*burrurrug*	scatter
j.	*bunburr*	take off, of many entities (cf. *gud* 'take off, of single entity')
k.	*thaburr*	smash up
l.	*garrb*	pick up, of multiple entities (cf. *durd* 'pick up, of single entities)

Schultze-Berndt notes that the correlations are not dissimilar to those found in Gooniyandi, another Australian language from the western part of the country (McGregor 1996).

Although the claim is that there is little sound symbolism in Yir-Yoront, another Australian language, Alpher does find some associations, including the correlation of perfectivity with final stops (Alpher 1994: 163), much like the aspectual distinctions found in Quechua (Nuckolls 1996). This contrasts with the situation in the distantly related Australian language Kuniyanti, where there is a strong and pervasive correlation between particular final consonants and 'action types' (McGregor 1986).

15.3.4 Africa

The literature on sound symbolism in African languages is expansive, particularly as instantiated in the word class of ideophones (Childs 1994; Dingemanse 2012; Voeltz and Kilian-Hatz 2001). Ideophones represent an expressive word category found throughout

Africa in all language phyla. Note that, as shown by the Zulu examples above in (1), sound symbolism is not restricted to ideophones, and not all ideophones contain sound symbolism. The general tendency, however, is for ideophones to feature more sound symbolism than other word categories (as do mimetics and expressives in other parts of the world).

The example below comes from Baka, an Adamawa-Ubangi language spoken in southeast Cameroon. It illustrates the sound symbolic association of 'the velar nasal [and] resonating metallic sounds' (Kilian-Hatz 2001: 158).

(13) Baka: *lang lang lang* 'beat a nut or hard fruit with a machete'

Examples above illustrated the importance of tone level (high vs. low) in conveying meaning. The examples in (14) illustrate how uneven patterns of tones may also convey meaning. Much more unusual than the level of tones is the iconic use of non-uniform tone (alternating high and low) to denote irregular shape or motion.

(14) Non-uniform tones in Bini (Nigeria) and irregular shape or motion

rhúrhùrhú	'staggering'
tíghítìghìtíghí	'twisted' (Wescott 1973: 201)

A common iconic relation is that observed in expressive lengthening or (unlimited) reduplication, as in Gbaya (Central African Republic). In each case the prolongation represents a lengthy or repeated action or state, in some cases standing in contrast with a non-prolonged form.

(15) Iconic lengthening and reduplication in Gbaya (Noss 1985: 242–243)

fɛɛ	'a breath of air'	fɛɛɛ	'a long breath of air'
dirr	'a rumble like thunder'	dirrr	'a long rolling rum ble like thunder or an earthquake'
kpuk	'a rap on a door'	kpuk-kpuk-kpuk	'insistent rapping on the door'
bit	'to miss once'	bít-bít-bít	'miss repeatedly'

Note how the sound symbolism can take the form of a prolonged vowel or consonant or the complete repetition of a word.

15.3.5 The Americas

Nuckolls (1999) contains an extensive survey, as mentioned above; she notes that '[m]agnitude sound symbolism ... is a widespread feature of Native American languages (Sherzer 1976), where alternations of consonants in roots function to express augmentative/diminutive contrasts' (Nuckolls 1999: 230). Six chapters in Hinton et al. (1994b; reissued as Hinton et al. 2006) are devoted to sound symbolism in Native American languages in Latin America and Mexico. Sound symbolism in the Pacific Northwest of the United States and northward into Canada has been particularly well researched: Nichols (1971) notes the areal nature of size–sound symbolism and identified the principles at work in conveying magnitude symbolism: (1) tonality (the raising of the second formant by articulating sounds more forward in the mouth) and (2) hardness (a more forceful manner of articulation, more tension and muscle activity).

Beck (2008) looks at ideophones, adverbs, and predicate qualification in Upper Necaxa Totonac (central Mexico), including the following sound symbolic forms.

(16) Sound symbolism in Upper Necaxa Totonac (UNT)

lam	'a bright light flashing, a fire flaring up'
lipli	'a diamond or piece of glass sparkling'
lipilip	'sun glinting off the water, a mirror, etc.'
limlim	'sun sparkling off flowing water'
slimslim	'something twinkling'

- *lam* expresses the most energetic, brightest phenomenon, as opposed to *liplip* and *limlim*
- the /m/ ~ /p/ alternation corresponds to longer vs. shorter, sharper phenomena (*lam* vs. *lip)* or punctual events (*lip, lipi*) vs. events with a continuous, static component (*lim, slim*)

Beck points out that UNT also uses consonantal alternations that correlate with relative size, intensity, or force, a pattern found in other Totonacan languages (Bishop 1984; Levy 1987; McQuown 1990; MacKay 1999; Smythe Kung 2005), and in other parts of the Americas (Aoki 1994; Nichols 1971; Nuckolls 1996), as noted above.

In contrast, UNT also has highly conventionalized, language-particular sound symbolism, not partaking of the usual associations noted in Nichols (1971). The examples in (17) show how the s~x~lh alternation is correlated with increasingly more energetic or forceful action, or with the size of an event/participant.

(17) Conventionalized sound symbolism in Upper Necaxa Totonac (Beck 2008)

(a)	lanks	'hand hitting something hard'
	lanhx	'a blow striking with great force'
	lanhlh	'something being kicked with great force'
(b)	spipispipi	'something small trembling'
	xpipixpipi	'something shivering or shaking slightly'
	lhpipilhpipi	'someone shaking, someone having convulsions'

Beck points out that the same pattern is found in a number of verbs and adjectives as well, thus representing an association that is relatively extensive in the language. Although size-sound symbolism is probably the most common sort of sound symbolism, other associations exist—at the least ones which build analogically or metaphorically on those basic associations.

15.3.6 Summary

This section has illustrated the formal variety of sound symbolism and its many functions. Any sound unit at a level below that of the morpheme or phonological word may convey meaning, and the sound symbolic unit may exist independently or be closely integrated into the grammar of the language. The final task of this chapter is to indicate some further areas of research.

15.4 Outstanding issues

A comprehensive and synthetic treatment of sound symbolism is still needed. Research has tended to restrict itself to rather focused views determined by the training, background, and intellectual orientation of the investigator. For a full understanding of the significance of sound symbolism, some integration is needed of at least the following fields: psycholinguistics, cognitive linguistics, phonetics and phonology, semantics, poetics and aesthetics in general, and ethnography.

One weakness in the research thus far is the relative absence of contributions from native speakers of languages where sound symbolism is used extensively. The Africanist literature is exceptional in this regard where much work has been conducted by native speakers (Ameka 2001; Awoyale 1983–84; 2000; Kunene 2001; Maduka 1988; Maduka-Durenze 2001).

A second major weakness is in methodology. Despite the fact that sound-symbolic forms flourish more in interaction and in performance-oriented genres, most studies have focused on data obtained in traditional linguist-consultant interviews or in a psycholinguistic lab. Studies such as Nuckolls (1996) and Dingemanse (2011b) are exceptional in this regard in being conducted *in situ*. The latter in particular has used intensive and innovative techniques for studying sound symbolism in real-world contexts.

A still-unanswered question concerns the extent to which sound symbolism is exploited grammatically. Recent experiments show that sound symbolism is of use in language learning and that it is put to use in grammatical contrasts, but where else is it exploited? The big and perhaps unanswerable question is: why do some languages use it more than others? What is the relationship between sound symbolism and gesture? Did sound symbolism play any role in language origin? These are all substantive questions that should stimulate the further study and theorizing of sound symbolism.

PART III

MEANINGS, REFERENTS, AND CONCEPTS

CHAPTER 16

WORD MEANINGS

NICK RIEMER

16.1 Meaning as a pretheoretical and cross-linguistic category

Few metalinguistic categories are appealed to as readily by ordinary speakers as the category of meaning. Not only do we often talk about word meanings explicitly, we also presuppose their existence in a wide range of commonplace situations involving talk about language, as when asking for synonyms, antonyms (opposites), or definitions, when correcting the misuse of an expression, clarifying the sense in which we intend an utterance, or drawing out a word's implications in a particular context. However, for all its centrality to our metalinguistic practices, meaning proves strikingly resistant to clear definition. In his philosophical dialogue *De quantitate animae*, written in the 4th century CE, Augustine of Hippo (Saint Augustine) likens meanings to the souls of words, a comparison that perfectly captures the elusive, ill-defined nature of meaning as a concept (*De quantitate animae* §66: Augustine 1950: 94). Closer to our own time, the English philosopher J. L. Austin claimed that 'the meaning of a word' is, 'in general, if not always, a dangerous nonsense-phrase' (Austin 1961: 24). Much 20th-century philosophy, along with some linguistics, has agreed with Austin: although 'word meanings' play a crucial role in our everyday talk about language, there may be no reason to assume that they will figure in our best theory of language structure and use. Many linguists and philosophers, however, have pursued far-reaching semantic investigations, though without the prospect of agreement on how word meanings are best defined, let alone on how they might be most revealingly studied, at least so far.

Before sketching some of the questions raised by the theoretical study of meaning, it is worth reflecting on the role that the term plays in ordinary discourse about language. The indispensability of our appeal to meaning makes it hard to envisage its absence from our metalinguistic vocabulary. Not infrequently in the world's languages, however, that is exactly the situation found. Just as languages often lack a precise equivalent for the term 'word' (Dixon and Aikhenvald 2002a), they also often lack a precise equivalent for the English term 'meaning', in the sense of a stable linguistic property of words (Riemer 2010: 9ff.).

This should provide food for thought. Speakers of languages without an exact equivalent for 'word meaning' are not, presumably, handicapped in their linguistic interactions or in their talk about language use. This raises the following question: what are the practical moves in ordinary conversation that the term 'meaning' makes possible in those languages that have it, which languages lacking it must achieve through different means?

The key to an answer is arguably provided by the concept of *repair strategy* (Schegloff et al. 1977). Like other human actions, language use is fallible and error-prone. Communication often fails. The chain linking utterance to utterance, or utterance to action, is fragile and we frequently fail to achieve the end for which we used words in the first place.

Situations of communicational breakdown can be repaired in a variety of ways. Imagine that a cooking class runs into difficulty because one of the participants does not know the meaning of the word *colander*. In that situation, the meaning can be conveyed quite easily: the instructor can simply point to a colander and the class can proceed. This way of repairing a breakdown is called *ostensive definition*. Often, however, ostensive definition is unavailable and some other means of restoring flow to the conversation is needed.

Here, we encounter something of a paradox. The paradox is that it is *language itself* that provides its own repair strategy. If a word or utterance poses a problem in conversation, we enlist other words and utterances that we could substitute for it and that provide an alternative route to the conversational purpose we want to achieve.

Imagine that cooking instructions were being given over the phone. Ostensive definition for *colander* would obviously be unavailable. Instead, the instructor could offer any one of the following *verbal* explanations:

'the perforated bowl for removing liquid from food'
'the thing you empty pasta into to drain off the water'
'a receptacle with holes in it you can pour the contents of saucepans into'.

These explanations are very different—they do not even use the same words. The only criterion of adequacy relevant to them is whether they resolve the addressee's problem with the term and allow the conversation to proceed. The vocabulary of English provides many options for the resolution of this sort of breakdown: the correct explanation of *colander* is whatever works in the particular situation in which the explanation is needed. Once the instructor's form of words allows the pupil to identify the correct piece of equipment, the explanation has proven itself to be adequate. The metalinguistic connections we make in order to explain what we understand by a word in one situation, to one addressee, will often be completely different from the ones we make in a different situation to a different addressee, even if what we think of as the *meaning* of the word concerned is the same.

In English and many other languages we have a particular folk-theory of the metalinguistic repair strategy just described: this activity is called *explaining* or *defining* meaning. We believe that meanings are things that words have (see Reddy 1993), and when communication fails it is because the meaning hasn't been conveyed. The availability of the term 'meaning' provides a shortcut to these explanations: we can say 'What does that word mean?' or 'What do you mean?', thereby signalling that a breakdown needs to be repaired. We do so in conformity with our folk 'theory of mind'—our basic presupposition that, like us, other people are motivated in their linguistic and other actions by underlying mental intentions, beliefs, and desires (Premack and Woodruff 1978).

As we have seen, however, there are many languages—one example would be Warlpiri, a member of the Pama-Nyungan family spoken in central Australia (Nash 1986)—which don't name anything like word or utterance meaning as a metalinguistic category, and which therefore don't frame metalinguistic problem-solving in these terms at all. Despite its unfamiliarity to an English speaker, there is nothing surprising or shocking in this. Just like English speakers, Warlpiri speakers can rephrase an utterance that has caused a breakdown. Their language does not, however, designate 'word meaning' as the factor responsible for communicative content. This allows us to relativize our own folk-picture of communication. When we resolve linguistic misunderstandings, we don't have to think that we're explaining things called meanings which words have. That's just one way of theorizing what happens when we rephrase an utterance in order to overcome a particular conversational breakdown.

The concept 'meaning', then, arguably arises as a particular theory or rationalization of the various situationally determined ways in which we use language to explain language. To say that a word means such and such is a shorthand way of saying that we might, in certain situations, effectively paraphrase it in such and such a way.

16.2 Internalist and externalist approaches

If the role of meaning in pretheoretical discourse about language is to label and thereby provide a shortcut to a repair strategy, what is its explanatory role in linguistic theory? The fact that not all languages have a term for 'meaning' does not invalidate the concept as a starting point for linguistic semantics. For the purposes of linguistic research, what matters is not whether a term like 'meaning' is universal, but whether it can be given a satisfying explanatory role in a theory of language and language use. Meaning, in other words, should not just be seen as the *object* of semantic investigation, it should also be seen as a *hypothesis*. We attribute meanings to words and other expressions in order to *explain* aspects of the way they function in language. The hypothesis might, of course, be mistaken. Perhaps it will turn out that words should not, on a theoretical level, be thought of as having meanings at all, and that the phenomena we currently describe through postulating them can be accounted for in some other way entirely.

The most important approach to meaning in linguistics before around 1970 was in the tradition of structuralism (Ducrot 1973; Saussure 1979 [1916]). Structuralists offered an account of meaning interestingly different from the one most semanticists assume today. Whereas contemporary theorists set out to describe and explain *all* of a word's semantic properties, structuralists are only interested in accounting for the respects in which words' meanings differ from each other. Instead of giving a comprehensive analysis of a noun like *colander*, of the kind that might be found in a definition, a typical structuralist account is only concerned with the semantic features that differentiate it from related words (*saucepan, bowl, pot, sieve*, etc.). This is exactly parallel to the situation in phonology. Phonology doesn't offer an exhaustive analysis of every aspect of pronunciation; that is the job of phonetics (Laver 1994). Phonology only aims to characterize the features that distinguish one sound from another.

Structuralism is now a minority current in semantics (for a discussion suggesting that it should by no means be seen as a spent force, see Rastier 2009). In current linguistics, there are two principal ways of giving meaning an explanatory role in a theory of language, which we can refer to as *externalist* and *internalist*. For externalists, the most important thing about a word's meaning is its reference (Stainton 2006). From this perspective, the study of meaning investigates the ways in which words refer to objects, situations, possibilities, and so on. For internalists, by contrast, the crucial explanatory target is a word's psychological or cognitive content—the conscious or unconscious cognitive or affective states that words convey (Jackendoff 1989, 1996; Riemer 2013). As we will see, there is a close link between the two perspectives. Nevertheless, they split the discipline of semantics.

16.3 Meaning and reference

Externalists take the principal semantic phenomenon to be reference, the connection between language and the world. The relationship of words to concepts and other internal psychological states—the subject matter of internalist semantics—is thought to be far too uncertain, changeable, and individual to serve as a possible object of principled investigation. Indeed, externalists point out that there is a real risk of circularity for any theory that simply assumes that meanings are concepts or other kinds of inner mental state. Without an independent account of what concepts *are*, we lack any way of substantiating their claimed identity with word meanings (Givón 1995: 17; Kamp and Reyle 1993; Murphy 1996). Investigating words' relationships with *things* seems a safer starting point for an objective study of meaning.

Obviously, however, not all words relate to things; not all words, that is, refer. Acts of ostensive reference, in which a word's referent is explicitly pointed to, are essentially only able to indicate *objects*: pointing to an athlete running on the track is most naturally interpreted as an ostension of the category RUNNER, or of the particular athlete present (Usain Bolt, say), but certainly not of RUNNING—though, as Wittgenstein (1953) noted, pointing is inherently ambiguous and open to a virtually limitless variety of interpretations. While nouns like *tree, computer, galaxy, kaleidoscope, fontanelle, catwalk*, and so on can—in the appropriate discourse and syntactic context—refer to particular objects and can therefore be involved in acts of ostensive reference, many other kinds of word are excluded from such acts. Verbs, adjectives, adverbs, prepositions, and interjections are inherently non-referential in this sense. Perhaps we might say that verbs refer to events or states, adjectives to properties, prepositions to relations, and declarative sentences to situations, but this seems an extension of the notion of reference beyond the fundamental word–thing relation that exists in the case of nouns. Moreover, abstract nouns like *justice*, nouns referring to unobservables like *belief* or *greed* or to non-existent entities like (presumably) Martians, are equally incapable of reference in this basic word–object sense. The only kinds of words capable of reference are nouns and pronouns, and even in the case of nouns (such as *colander*) it is strictly speaking the noun phrase (e.g. *the colander*) that refers, not the head noun *colander*.

Despite the fact that many vocabulary items do not have a possible referential function, reference has often been taken to be the principal dimension of meaning in linguistics. This is partly explained by the undoubted importance of language's referential role, partly by the pretheoretical salience of naming practices (acts of naming children, coinage of technical terms, nicknames, etc.), in which a link between a particular referent and a word is consciously established by speakers, and partly by certain trends of 20th-century intellectual history—beyond the scope of this chapter—which witnessed the development of formal logical tools well suited to an externalist, referential approach (Meyer 1982; Seuren 2009).

16.4 Descriptive and expressive meaning

Reference is not all there is to meaning, even for words that do have referents. It is an elementary aspect of our experience of language that words contract relations with our inner psychological states—ideas, memories, emotions, mental images. Reflecting on these psychological states, an intuitive distinction becomes obvious (Allan and Burridge 2006; Potts 2007). On the one hand, expressions like *go, run, woman, dinosaur, round*, etc., are naturally seen as having the role of communicating information of different kinds. Words like these serve to designate categories of objects, properties, and events (Taylor 2003): *dinosaur*, for instance, is a label that we apply to animals of a certain category only. Alpacas and sparrows aren't dinosaurs, a stegosaurus is. When we refer to something as a dinosaur, we are placing it in this category, implying that it shares crucial properties with other dinosaurs, such as being an extinct land animal.

The references and categorizations communicated by expressions of this kind supply information that listeners use to draw factual inferences about how things are or are imagined to be. If I tell you that *aspirin prevents cancer* or that *foxgloves are poisonous* you have been given information that allows you to draw various conclusions, which you may use to influence the courses of action you take.

On the other side, there are expressions like *hurray, yum, damn*, and *ouch*; these seem not to communicate information in the same way as the first class (Riemer 2013). A listener can certainly draw inferences from the fact that an expression like this has been uttered—if someone suddenly cries out *ouch!* we might conclude that they are in pain. But these inferences do not derive from the understanding of what we might call propositional or conceptual content. Crying out *ouch!* is more like an involuntary outburst than an act of information transmission.

Acts of reference and categorization accomplished by the first type of expression are naturally thought of as springing from fully cognitive psychological mechanisms, dealing with what we can variously think of as knowledge, propositions, categorization, information-processing, or judgement. In contrast, the second type appears to belong to a different domain of human psychology: affect or emotion (Ochs and Schieffelin 1989; Oller and Wiltshire 1997; Ortony et al. 1987).

As has long been acknowledged (e.g. Christophe 1988; Lepschy 1971: 133), the basis of the distinction between cognition and emotion is unclear. The validity of some kind of distinction along these lines is, however, widely acknowledged, and has often been articulated in the history of reflection on language. Expressions of the information-conveying kind are naturally spoken of as having a literal meaning, whereas expressions of the second, emotion-expressing kind, are not. Sincere utterances of *ouch* and *hurray* do not appear to communicate 'meanings' in the sense in which sincere utterances involving *galaxy* and *woman* do. For this reason, there seems something wrong about any attempt to paraphrase or describe their meaning (Potts 2007). It is possible to articulate the conditions in which such expressions are typically uttered (*ouch* at moments of (mild) physical pain, *hurray* at moments of jubilation), but these descriptions do not have the same status as the paraphrases or definitions that can be supplied for informational terms. It makes sense to think of the definitions of words like *galaxy* and *woman* as being psychologically represented and as playing a role in the production of utterances. But it does not seem right to think of expressions of the second type as having psychologically real definitions.

Reflecting this intuitive division, a standard working assumption of linguistic semantics has been that the lexicon can be broadly divided into two classes of expression: descriptives (*galaxy, woman*, etc.) and expressives (*ouch, hurray*, etc.) (Potts 2007). The meaning of descriptives is understood as cognitive content (Prinz 2002) and taken to be analysable in terms of concepts. It corresponds to stable informational content, which can be captured by metasemantic paraphrase (definition) and attributed to the linguistic knowledge of the language-user.

In contrast, expressive meaning is usually assumed not to be open to treatment in these terms; expressives do not communicate information, but express feelings. This division reflects the fact that (a) the two classes have a very different phenomenology (they feel different, for the speaker); and (b) expressives, unlike descriptives, are assumed to resist metasemantic decomposition or paraphrase.

The importance of non-cognitive, expressive factors in meaning has characteristically been downplayed, the assumption being that meaning in language is predominantly descriptive (a notable exception is Berkeley 1965 [1710]: 57, Introduction, §20). Complicating this question is the fact that it is not entirely clear how straightforward the classification of a word or an utterance as descriptive or expressive is in the first place. One school of 20th-century philosophy of language (Ayer 1971 [1946]; Stevenson 1937) has been inclined to analyse evaluative words—*good, bad*, and others that express the speaker's attitude to a referent—as *wholly* expressive. If adopted, this analysis would vastly expand the extent of expressive meaning in the lexicon, since *good* and *bad* are general terms whose meaning is present in many other words such as *excellent* ('extremely good') and *terrible* ('extremely bad'). The expressive analysis of these terms has not been widely adopted in linguistics, but it highlights the difficulty of adequately specifying the descriptive, informational content of these and related terms (Riemer 2013).

Finally, it is important to note that many words have both a descriptive and an expressive component. The latter is usually considered part of a word's *connotation*—the secondary 'penumbra' of meaning accompanying it (think of the different positive and negative connotations that attach to *stingy, thrifty, generous*, and *spendthrift*). Moreover, it is likely that the balance between descriptive and expressive meaning in a given word varies, at least partly, as a function of the extent to which speech is consciously planned. In many dimensions of linguistic structure, ordinary discourse is not homogeneous, but consists of 'a range of unselfconscious and more self-conscious varieties' (Schilling-Estes 2007: 174). Recently, psycholinguists have started to hypothesize that semantics is also influenced by this parameter (Sanford 2002).

This allows us to distinguish two contexts of language use: *planned* and *free*. Planned language use occurs in those contexts in which speakers are consciously paying attention to the communicative effectiveness of their words and where they are, as a result, more consciously aware of the normative constraints to which their language is subject (Verschueren 1999). Conversely, in free or unplanned contexts—for instance, a casual chat between friends—participants are *not* paying any particular attention to these factors: they are speaking spontaneously and without special care. We can speculate that as utterances become more spontaneous and less planned, the descriptive contribution to meaning is muted, and connotational, emotional, or 'expressive' content comes to the fore.

16.5 Meaning, communication, and the 'language of thought'

Internalist semantics assumes that there is something more to a word's descriptive meaning than its reference. This 'something more' is usually called *sense* (Frege 1986 [1892]). Indeed, it is sense, not reference, that most people have in mind when they talk about a word's meaning. Internalists assume that sense is a matter of concepts; the word *carrot* refers to one particular kind of vegetable and not some other kind because it is this kind that corresponds to speakers' mentally represented concept. Alongside all the phonetic, phonological, and syntactic information stored about the word *carrot*, speakers also have a concept CARROT which, like a mental definition, records basic information about carrots that allows speakers of English to apply the word to the correct type of object. We use the word *carrot* to refer to carrots, and not potatoes, since our concept CARROT records the information that carrots are long, orange, and tapered, not round, brown, and lumpy.

Why postulate the existence of concepts? As argued in Riemer (2013), since people use words to refer to, control, and change a common external environment, different speakers can only coordinate their linguistic action on the world successfully if they share a similar enough way of using words to refer to aspects of the environment, and if the factual knowledge they have about their environment and the things in it is basically congruent. Different individuals must not only have congruent internal knowledge of fire (the thing); they must use the word *fire* in highly similar patterns of reference and inference if it is to serve as a useful tool of coordinated action. The assertion *the house is on fire* will only serve its purpose if the thoughts it produces in the hearer are sufficiently similar to the thoughts that prompted it in the speaker. The possibilities of successful, coordinated action in the world require, in other words, an identity in 'language–world' relations between individuals (and, for similar reasons, within the same individual over time). On the level of delicacy at which they contribute to action and communication, then, the psychological structures evoked by environment-referring words must be invariant, because they must all represent their referents factually. These psychological structures are concepts (Riemer 2013).

Shared concepts explain both similarities in people's relation to perceptible features of the world (people do not try to cool themselves with fire, but they do try to heat themselves with it), and regularities of reference and inference that can be observed between different speakers in the use of words referring to those features (Fodor 1980). English speakers use *fire* to refer to a similar range of objects and include it in comparable chains of inferences—such as *if this is fire, then it is hot*, but not *if this is fire, then it is cold*—since they possess one invariant FIRE concept.

This reasoning justifies our strong pretheoretical conviction that meanings are things that two individuals can *share*. Without some level on which speakers of the same language share the same concepts, it is impossible to see how communication and mutual understanding happen. Concepts must be shared if there is to be communication and understanding in the normal sense of these terms (Rey 1998).

Exactly how is conceptual information recorded? As is often acknowledged by cognitive scientists and philosophers—and not acknowledged often enough by linguists—no one knows; indeed, the nature of conceptualization and cognition is shrouded in mystery (Prinz 2004: 41). For the purposes of the explanation of communication, however, to say that language communicates something conceptual or cognitive is a way of saying that language is a means of exchanging *knowledge* about the world, a way of coordinating (updating, revising, cancelling) the *representations* we store in our memory about the ways things are.

The traditional metaphor through which mental representations have been described is that of the 'language of thought'—a language-like mental format or code that serves as the support for our conceptualization, like the software codes running a computer (Fortis 1996). This language of thought is conceived of as the medium in which central mental processes unfold, neutral between the different perceptual channels that input to it. The neutrality of the language of thought—or, to give it its usual technical description, its amodality—has traditionally been one of its central properties. To see why, consider this basic fact about our mental lives. Once we have been given a linguistic description of a referent—an avalanche, let us say—we are able to make a link between the factual knowledge we have acquired and information deriving from our perceptual faculties. When we see an avalanche for the first time, our abstract knowledge of avalanches allows us to identify it as such, forging a link between the abstract facts we have learnt through language and the visual particularities of the real event. Similarly, if we are blindfolded and given an object to hold, we can make inferences about its likely appearance. The fact that these kinds of information exchanges are possible—that our different cognitive, motor, and perceptual channels can 'talk' to each other—is often thought to be explained by the availability of some central conceptual clearing-house or medium—the language of thought—to which they are all ultimately directed.

For decades now in some quarters, the idea that meanings are couched in an amodal format has been losing ground to the idea that meanings are *embodied*—that the 'situatedness' of our physical experience is central to the ways in which our cognitive faculties represent and store information. Linguistic research under the broad umbrella of *cognitive linguistics* has taken the embodiment of meaning particularly seriously (Evans and Green 2006; Lakoff 1987). We return to this idea below.

16.6 Three theories of concepts

Internalists posit a close relation between concepts and referents. It is in virtue of the concept a word conveys that it has the reference it has. What, though, are concepts like?

16.6.1 Concepts as definitions

Historically, there are three main contenders for a theory of concepts (Laurence and Margolis 1999). The earliest, derived from Aristotle, is the necessary and sufficient conditions theory (also called the definitional or classical theory). On this view, the mentally represented factual information constituting a concept takes the form of a list of conditions or features that are individually necessary and jointly sufficient to capture every object falling under it. The concept underlying the word *bird* might be a list of the features 'animal; has wings; has feathers; has beak; lays eggs; typically flies'. This is the kind of information likely to be found in a dictionary definition, such as that of the *Concise Oxford* (Soanes and Stevenson 2008): 'a warm-blooded egg-laying vertebrate animal of a class distinguished by the possession of feathers, wings, and a beak, typically able to fly'. These features are individually necessary to birdhood—if something doesn't have wings or feathers, it's not a bird—and, together, they are sufficient to delimit the category. They are the *only* criteria that something needs to meet in order to count as a bird.

Definitions like this raise numerous questions. One concerns their psychological reality. The necessary and sufficient conditions are stated in words—'animal', 'has', 'wings', and so on. This presupposes that English speakers who have the concept BIRD also understand the meaning of each of the terms used in the definition. Since meanings are, *ex hypothesi*, definitions, what speakers understand must be the *definitions* of each of the terms involved. In order to grasp the definition of *bird* as a particular kind of 'animal', speakers must understand the definition of *animal* as (roughly) 'a living organism which is typically distinguished from a plant by feeding on organic matter, having specialized sense organs and nervous system, and being able to move about and to respond rapidly to stimuli' (*Concise Oxford*: Soanes and Stevenson 2008). But, in order to understand the definition of *animal*, we need to understand the meanings—definitions—of each of the expressions—'living', 'organism', and so on—contained in it. And to do that, we need to understand the definition of each of the words figuring in the definitions of *them*. We have unleashed a regress from which there is no escape.

What is worse, we are bound sooner or later to enter a vicious circle, where the *same* word occurs on both sides of the definitional equation. With *bird*, the vicious circle arises almost immediately. As we have seen, the definition contains the term 'wing'. But when we consult the *Concise Oxford* entry for *wing*, we find the definition 'a modified forelimb or other appendage enabling a *bird*, bat, insect, or other creature to fly' (Soanes and Stevenson 2008; emphasis added). *Bird* functions both as the term whose definition is being sought (the *definiendum*) *and* a term that contributes to the definition (the *definiens*). This circularity vitiates the proposed definition.

The problem of definitional circularity has long been recognized. One solution has been to posit a finite set of *semantic primitives* that are used to define all other words but that are not themselves open to definition. This project was characteristic of early modern philosophy of language (Leibniz, Descartes: see Dascal 1987) but, with the exception of the 'Natural Semantic Metalanguage' school (Goddard and Wierzbicka 2002), no longer has many adherents. Not the least of its problems is that it inherently disqualifies all the primitive terms—words like *body*, *good*, and *think*—from semantic analysis, thereby leaving investigators entirely in the dark about the meanings of key parts of the vocabulary.

Another response is to claim that all meanings are primitive. This is Fodor's (1998) approach. From a linguist's point of view, this is equally unsatisfactory, given that the very aim of semantic analysis is to reveal the internal structure of meanings in a way that explains regularities in the way that words are used. We want to be able to say that the sentence *a bird is a kind of animal* is true, whereas *a bird is a kind of tree* is not, because the meaning of the word *bird* (i.e. the concept BIRD) contains—in some sense of 'contain'—the meaning of the word *animal* (the concept ANIMAL), and therefore licenses statements of this type, whereas it does not contain the meaning of the word *tree* (the concept TREE). But this explanation is unavailable if we adopt an atomistic picture of concepts along Fodorian lines.

Meanings, or concepts, are psychological, not linguistic, objects. They are not themselves words. No one supposes that whenever we entertain the concept BIRD (or use the word *bird*), the words of the dictionary definition ('an animal of a class distinguished by the possession of feathers, wings, and a beak, typically able to fly') 'flash up', as it were, in our minds. The words in definitions are simply labels for other concepts. Until we can isolate and define these concepts in some terms other than linguistic ones, we have failed to offer any deep account of meaning.

A striking feature of dictionary definitions is their variability. Lexicographers rarely agree about the best way of defining any given word (except, of course, when they have copied from each other!). This in itself is a strong reason to be sceptical of the definitional approach. If definitions really constitute meanings, specialists should be able to agree on what they are. Casting our minds back to the discussion of the role of meaning in pretheoretical discourse allows us to understand why definitions are so various. If 'explaining meaning' is, essentially, a rationalization we make of a particular metalinguistic repair strategy in cases of conversational breakdown, and if what functions as an appropriate repair strategy varies from one conversation to the next, then it is not surprising that it proves impossible to propose a single definition for any word on which all speakers can agree. The way we understand language is so deeply embedded in the particularities of individual and social variation that the means for creating a successful explanation of a word will vary from one situation to the next.

The theory of concepts based on necessary and sufficient conditions is open to further objections. One of the most powerful derives from the difficulty of formulating accurate definitions using it. Take *picnic*, defined by the *Concise Oxford* as 'a packed meal eaten outdoors' and 'an occasion when such a meal is eaten'. This definition certainly seems to capture some obvious features of picnics. However, picnics need not always be eaten outdoors (they might be eaten in a car or in a school hall, in the case of bad weather), and need not even involve any eating: it would be appropriate to describe something as a picnic at which food is served, but at which, for whatever reason, people only drink. Furthermore, there may be certain kinds of occasion in which we hesitate over whether the label *picnic* is appropriate. Could mountaineers be described as having a picnic when they eat an outdoor energy food breakfast in base camp before their assault on the summit? These kinds of cases are characteristic: words *mostly* show a set of referents of varying centrality, some of which are clearly good examples of the category in question, while others are ambiguous as to whether they belong or not. Category membership, in other words, is *graded*. Other examples of graded categories include BIKE (an ordinary pushbike vs. a unicycle), CITY (Paris vs. Pompeii or the Vatican), and LIE (an untruth told with the explicit intention of deceit vs. a 'white lie', told to preserve someone's feelings) (Coleman and Kay 1981).

16.6.2 Concepts as prototypes

The insight that category membership is often graded is at the heart of a second theory of concepts—*prototype theory*—developed by cognitive psychologists in the 1970s (Rosch 1978; Rosch and Mervis 1975) and extremely influential in linguistics (Lakoff 1987; Taylor 2003). According to prototype theorists, the categories that constitute natural language meanings are structured as weighted arrays of features. The category BIRD, for example, is defined through features such as 'with wings', 'with beak', 'flies', etc. Not all birds have all features—penguins don't fly, a bird that has lost its feathers is still a bird—but the ones we think of as the best or most representative examples of birds (pigeons or sparrows) possess all the features, and more peripheral examples (emus or penguins) possess fewer. On this view, categories need not have hard-and-fast boundaries, and it is not surprising that it proves hard to agree on a single definition for any given term. What ties together a category like BIKE, LIE, or CITY isn't any single set of features shared by every member of the category, but a *family resemblance* structure. There is a pool of features that are distributed among the category members in such a way that while the majority of members have many of the features, there is no guarantee that any two members will share exactly the same features or that a given feature will be exhibited by all members, just as the characteristics we think of as family resemblances can be unevenly distributed among relatives. This approach avoids some of the pitfalls of the classical theory. On the classical picture, either something is a member of a given category or it isn't, and there is no room for varying degrees of representativity.

16.6.3 Concepts as exemplars and simulations

Prototype theory seemed to hold considerable promise for understanding how meaning works in natural language and inspired a large amount of investigation in cognitive linguistics. Nevertheless, it is not the only theory of categorization—and hence of linguistic meaning—currently entertained in psychology. The main alternative is *exemplar* theory (Medin and Schaffer 1978; Nosofsky 1986; Storms et al. 2000). According to exemplar theory, categories are not structured around weighted abstract features, but around *actual examples* of the category, stored in memory. My concept BIKE, for instance, is constructed on the basis of the particular bikes I have encountered in the course of my experience, without any process of feature abstraction. Something is assigned to the BIKE category on the basis of its similarity to the stored exemplars (accordingly, the way similarity is calculated is a crucial explanatory challenge for such theories.) Exemplar theories have not yet had significant take-up in linguistics (see, however, Pierrehumbert 2001 for phonology), but in their rejection of feature abstraction as an element of categorization they are compatible with those theories that stress the embodied character of linguistic meanings.

Exemplar theory is related to an emerging alternative to conceptualist understandings of mental representation. According to some cognitive scientists, it is plausible that the cognitive system uses *simulations* as the basis for cognitive activity. Drawing on work in neurophysiology (Damasio 1994, 2000) and psychology (Barsalou 1999, 2008), Prinz (2002) rejects the amodality of conceptual representations, discussed above, arguing that '[c]oncepts are couched in representational codes that are specific to our perceptual systems' (2002: 119). There is no central language of thought that cognition draws on in the planning and control of action. Instead, concepts are couched in the perceptual modality appropriate to their referent—visual concepts visually, tactile ones tactually, and so on.

Recent research in brain science supports the contention that simulation underlies language comprehension. Pulvermüller (2005) found that 'action words are defined by abstract semantic links between language elements and motor programs' (2005: 577). During acquisition, synaptic connections between motor and language areas are strengthened as the child comes to associate various physical action routines with the words that refer to them. These connections have been demonstrated experimentally, suggesting that 'specific action representations are activated during action word understanding' (Pulvermüller 2005: 579). Exploration of these connections now constitutes an important research trajectory in neurolinguistics; results pointing in a similar direction to Pulvermüller's have been obtained by Buccino et al. (2005), Myung et al. (2006), and Hauk et al. (2008). Cognitive linguists have long stressed the centrality of embodied experience to the semantics of language. Jackendoff, too, has argued (1989, 2002) that semantic representations underlying words related to visual experience may link up to a 3D visual component, in order to capture the fine-grained distinctions between different perceptual contents, such as the difference between terms like *swan* and *duck*. Like the differences underlying colour terms, such as *aqua* and *royal blue*, these distinctions cannot be represented in any word-based metalanguage, because they are inherently visual. They are, in other words, 'simulations' of the perceptual experiences on which they are based. Kemmerer (2006) supplies neuroscientific support for modal representations in the meanings of action verbs like *bite*, *punch*, and *kick* with his claim that the same brain-regions activated during performance of the actions are also activated during production of the verbs referring to them.

16.7 Polysemy, Metaphor, and the Limits of Semantics

So far we have neglected the crucial fact that most words, perhaps all, have more than one meaning (think of the different senses of *party*, *application*, *mission*, and *smell*).

Polysemy is standard in the vocabularies of natural languages. However, the extent of a word's polysemy—the number of separate meanings it has—is often unclear. In simple cases, everyone will agree on the presence of two quite separate meanings: *quarry*, for instance, clearly means both 'site from which stone is extracted' and 'object of a search or hunt'. Many cases, however, are unclear. How many separate senses should we recognize in the noun *ring*? Three ('sound of something ringing; circle; round object')? Six ('sound of something ringing; phone call; circle; arena; piece of jewellery worn on finger; network (of spies), etc.)'? More? Fewer? The conversation could last all night. Since we are not sure how semantic information is mentally represented, it is no surprise that we are also in the dark on questions of meaning individuation. As demonstrated by Geeraerts (1993), the criteria typically used to settle the question are themselves contradictory. According to some semanticists, in fact, the extent of polysemy in the world's languages has been vastly overstated (Ruhl 1989). According to others, the very project of counting word meanings is ill-posed (Geeraerts 1993; Riemer 2005; Tuggy 1993).

Polysemy is a situation where a word appears to have a stable set of multiple meanings. A major challenge for any semantic theory is the process by which words gain—or lose—meanings in more occasional, context-specific ways. We frequently use words loosely, in ways that we would acknowledge not to match what we think of as their standard meanings. This is especially the case in 'free', unmonitored conversation, where we do not exercise a high degree of vigilance in our linguistic choices. At other times, the temporary departure from a word's ordinary use seems more regular: cases like these are referred to as *figurative*, and can be principally classed into *metaphors* and *metonymies*. The interest of figurative language for a theory of meaning is capital, since metaphorical and other uses represent systematic cases in which words are *not* used in accordance with their meanings. The utterance *it's hot in the sun*, for instance, when expressed by someone at the beach, is clearly not intended in its literal sense *it is hot in the interior of the sun*. *Sun* stands not for the sun itself—presumably its literal meaning—but instead refers to *sunlight* or to the *heat* of the sun. This is an example of metonymy, the substitution for a word's literal meaning of a meaning that is somehow related, in this case by the cause–effect relation, the sun being the cause of both sunlight and heat. Other kinds of metonymic relation include part for whole (*the cinema complex has seven screens*—seven *auditoriums*), place for institution (*The ambassador is responsible to Canberra*—the Australian government), and container for contents (*the kettle is boiling*—the *water* is boiling).

The other principal category of figurative language is *metaphor*. *My memory is a sieve* violates the ordinary sense of *sieve*, but we rationalize this by saying that the metaphor *compares* my memory to a sieve. Metaphor is traditionally understood to involve some kind of comparison, analogy, or 'mapping' between two kinds of concept. This is what distinguishes it from metonymy, which does not involve any kind of comparison between two notions: the sun is not *like* its own heat in the way in which my memory is *like* a sieve.

The *sieve* metaphor is somewhat conventionalized; it has been used before, and will be used again. Many metaphors, however, are novel, as all conventionalized metaphors once were. The exact nature of metaphor and other figurative language is one of the oldest and most perplexing topics in the study of meaning. Since the very *point* of the concept 'meaning' is to contribute to an explanation of language use—words are used as they are used *because of* the meanings they have—the existence of a systematic class of exceptions to this principle is a matter of some interest. Without some explanation of the way novel metaphor functions, we are left with a gaping hole in our account of language. Words have meanings; these meanings are shared; understanding someone amounts to extracting the meanings they have put into their words: so goes the received view. But if, as is the case with metaphors, we can identify a widespread and systematic set of cases where words' conventional meanings can be violated, and violated in ways that remain theoretically hard to explain satisfactorily, then it would seem that our basic theory of language, meaning, and communication is seriously wanting. To repair it, we will need some explanation of how, exactly, metaphor works. Sadly, the general lack of theoretical consensus over basic questions is even more a feature of the study of metaphor than it is of other aspects of meaning, with numerous different approaches being taken, none of which commands general agreement (see Cooper 1986 for still relevant discussion).

Researchers' inability to achieve an elementary degree of consensus over semantic questions does not just indicate the enormous complexity of meaning as an object of empirical investigation. It also highlights the extent to which semantic phenomena fit uneasily into the epistemological mould on which much other basic linguistic research is predicated—that of the objective, empirical investigation of a factual phenomenon, in principle able to be brought into relation with the psychological and biological sciences. In its subjective, interpersonal, and hermeneutic dimensions, meaning seems less readily absorbed into such a scientific—or, perhaps, scientistic—enterprise (Riemer 2005). A unified 'science' of word meaning that manages to achieve a consensus among the very different, balkanized trends in contemporary semantic research is certainly not likely to emerge any time soon. Whether it can *ever* emerge is a question to which the answer is far from clear, but which will be settled less through attention to aprioristic considerations than through the continued attempt to achieve deep, empirical models of linguistic phenomena with widening explanatory reach.

CHAPTER 17

WORDS AS NAMES FOR OBJECTS, ACTIONS, RELATIONS, AND PROPERTIES

BARBARA C. MALT

17.1 Words as names

A little brown bird with a bubbly song, its perky tail upright, is found in woods and gardens in the United States and Great Britain. What is its name? Casual observers may call it Jenny Wren. To birders in the US, it's House Wren. To birders in Britain, it's just plain Wren. But the situation is a little more complex. Jenny Wren is actually two different species. In the US, it's *Troglodytes aedon*. In Britain, it's *Troglodytes hiemalis*. In the US, both species occur, so American birders distinguish them as House Wren and Winter Wren. In Britain, only the second is found, so it is just plain Wren. Is the only right name for each of these birds the scientific name, then? The problem is that scientific names are always subject to revision. As knowledge of evolutionary relations advances, species are split or lumped, and even the genus assignment can change. There is no such thing as a final, fixed, correct scientific species name. This situation lends a certain irony to the quotation on the International Ornithologists' Union's list of preferred bird names: 'Wisdom begins with putting the right name on a thing.'

But, of course, people use names all the time. Imagine, for instance, that you spy a fledgling wren sitting in the dogwood tree, begging loudly for food from its parent, and you want to tell your grandmother about it. You must choose a word not only for the bird, but also for its begging action, for the strident property of its action, for its relation to the tree, and for the target of its action. If there are many possible names for each thing, how do you choose the words to convey all this information?

Olson (1970) provided a thought experiment for a simpler circumstance. Suppose a gold star is placed under a small, round, white, wooden block. There might also be a small, round, black block present. Alternatively, there could be a small, square, white block, or there could be several—a round black one, a square black one, and a square white one. How would you tell someone where the star is? In the first case, you might say that it is under *the white one*. In the second, you might say it is under *the square one*, and in the third, that it is under *the round, white one*. The gold star is under the same block each time, but the utterances differ. Olson concluded that words pick out an intended referent relative to the alternatives from which it must be differentiated. Words are chosen to reduce alternatives or uncertainty, not because they are the name for something.

So, returning to the wren, if you want to be understood, you must take into account the context in which you are talking. If you are talking to your grandmother, whose knowledge of birds is casual at best, the optimal name may be Jenny Wren. If you were to tell her that there's a *Troglodytes aedon* in the dogwood tree, her uncertainty about what you mean would not be reduced. On the other hand, if your grandmother is an ornithologist, then the opposite will be true. *Troglodytes aedon* is unambiguous. If you tell your ornithologist grandmother you saw a Jenny Wren, she will infer that your own knowledge of birds is casual at best and that you might even have seen some sparrow or finch instead of a wren.

The lesson is that objects, actions, relations, and properties do not each come with a name that intrinsically belongs to them and uniquely identifies them. A good name is one that successfully conveys what the speaker wanted to convey to his or her audience. A bad name is one that doesn't. In the rest of this discussion, we will consider two issues in detail: first, how speakers choose among different possibilities in light of their communication goals, and second, what determines the word options available to speakers when they make those choices.

17.2 Satisfying communication goals

17.2.1 What information does the speaker want to convey?

Brown (1958) provided what has become a classic discussion of how speakers choose words. He was interested in how adults name things for children. Short names may be viewed as suitable for young children, since they should be easiest for a child to remember or pronounce. Still, he noted, sometimes choices do not follow this bias: *pineapple, banana*, and *apple* are longer and harder than *fruit*, but an adult will still call the fruit by its longer name. Possibly the longer names are more frequent, but that just raises the question: why are they more frequent? Brown suggested that the names chosen anticipate the functional structure of the child's world. For a child who will interact with a particular dog as a family member, the dog will be called *Prince*. For a child who will interact with it only in passing as a member of a larger category, the dog will be called *dog*. More generally, names will be chosen to identify what the thing is equivalent to and distinct from in its typical use. A banana is not interchangeable with a pineapple or apple for most purposes; therefore, it won't do to call it *fruit*. On the other hand, one banana is about as good as the next, so there's no need to differentiate them further by name.

Brown's notion of naming at the 'level of usual utility' suggested that things will tend to have one preferred name among possibilities ranging from specific to general. Anthropologist Brent Berlin and colleagues studied members of traditional (non-industrialized) societies, such as those in some remote areas of central and south America, and they found that knowledge of plants and animals could be described as being organized in a hierarchical fashion (Berlin 1992). Members of these societies used labels that distinguished among species of oak trees, distinguished oaks as a group from maples or pines, distinguished trees from shrubs and vines, and so on. Despite knowledge of relations at these many levels, the things tended to be named at a middle level for most purposes. Psychologist Eleanor Rosch and colleagues (Rosch et al. 1976) studied American college students in a laboratory setting and showed further that names from the middle of a hierarchy (see Table 17.1) are special in several ways. Mid-level names (such as *chair*, as opposed to *kitchen chair* or *furniture*) pick out the most inclusive groupings of things that have similar visual properties and have many features in common, and that people interact with in physically similar ways. Going up a level (to *furniture*, for instance), things have few properties in common. Going down a level (to *rocking chair* vs. *kitchen chair*), things have much in common but are not very distinct from each other. Names at the middle level achieve a balance of within-category similarities and between-category differences. Rosch et al. dubbed this the 'basic level', and they found that students most often chose to name pictured objects at this level. That is, shown a kitchen chair, they were more likely to say *chair* than either *kitchen chair* or *furniture*. In Olson's terms, the basic level can be interpreted as the level that, for many circumstances, reduces alternatives just as much as needed but not more so. In Brown's terms, the middle level is the level of usual utility.

The idea that things are preferentially named at a middle level of abstraction has been highly influential, but it does need some qualification. For one thing, there are circumstances where it is desirable to reduce uncertainty further. For anyone wanting to talk about the wren that visited her garden or was seen on her bird walk, *wren* by itself is not good enough if she lives where more than one species is found; she must specify

Table 17.1 A naming hierarchy

Superordinate	Furniture								
Basic	Table			Chair			Lamp		
Subordinate	Kitchen table	Dining room table	Drafting table	Kitchen chair	Arm chair	Rocking chair	Desk lamp	Floor lamp	Lava lamp

House Wren or another species. Further, finding utility at any particular level depends on a certain degree of knowledge in the domain. Rosch et al. noted that not even *wren* or *oak* was the basic level for her urban American college students (much less *House Wren* or *Red Oak*). When shown pictures of birds or trees, they tended to say merely *bird* and *tree*. This contrasts with members of the traditional societies studied by the anthropologists. These groups live in close connection with the natural world, and their everyday, basic-level terms were at a level below that of the American students. When it comes to human-made objects, though, Western urbanites may be more likely to be able to go down one level (e.g. *sedan* or *convertible* instead of *car*). In any society, subsets of people may develop expertise in some domain that not only provides them with more word choices at a lower level but makes groupings at this level more distinct from one another (Rosch et al. 1976; Tanaka and Taylor 1991). The basic level and the level of usual utility are thus to some extent flexible, depending on situational needs and knowledge base.

But also consider Olson's gold star under the blocks. No matter how many blocks there are, the best you can do is say that it's under the big, white, round, wood, slightly rough-edged (etc.) one. There just are no more specific terms to choose from. Vocabulary for many common objects may be somewhat limited in that respect. Malt (2013) had people name common household objects under circumstances where each one had to be discriminated from either several dissimilar objects or else many very similar ones. This context manipulation altered the number of adjectives that were produced by participants (e.g. *jar* vs. *big blue jar; bottle* vs. *plastic juice bottle*), but the nouns they used were the same. Her participants had no other conventional subordinate names to use for these ordinary containers, so they used freely composed sets of modifiers. So would most likely all English speakers other than perhaps makers of laboratory glassware or curators of ancient Greek container collections.

There is another complication. Students shown a picture of a kitchen chair are more likely to say *chair* than either *kitchen chair* or *furniture*, but what if it were a rocking chair that they were shown, or a beanbag chair? The name *chair* is most closely associated with prototypical examples of chairs such as kitchen chairs or living room chairs. A beanbag or rocking chair is different enough from what the addressee would normally expect upon hearing *chair* that it seems insufficiently informative, maybe even deceptive, to just say that you saw a *chair*. Murphy and Brownell (1985) found that when presented pictures of objects and asked if a certain name applied to them, people were fastest to respond to basic-level names if the objects were typical of the name (e.g. when they verified a kitchen chair for *chair*). If the objects were atypical of the basic level name, people were actually faster to respond to a more specific name (e.g. faster to respond to *rocking chair* than *chair* when shown the rocking chair). Geeraerts (1994) observed a similar phenomenon in the names used for clothing items in Dutch language magazines. For many types of clothing worn on the legs or upper body, terms similar in meaning to English *pants* (in the US)/*trousers* (in the UK) or *shirt* were used. However, for blue jeans (a kind of pants/trousers), *jeans* was used most often, and for t-shirts (a kind of shirt), *t-shirt* was. If a basic-level word will call to mind examples different from what is meant, that word may not reduce uncertainty enough, so something that better specifies the intended referent is needed. In short, selection tends to take into account the typicality of the intended referent with respect to that name.

One might ask whether the notion of basic level applies outside of names for concrete objects. The case of the fledgling wren begging for food on a branch highlights that there is much more to be named—including actions, properties, and relations. Actions, like objects, are usually complexes of attributes. Properties like loudness or brownness, or relations such as being on rather than in or above a branch, may be conceptually simpler. Regardless, there is almost always more than one possible word the speaker could use in conveying information about what she has in mind. Colours seem somewhat similar to objects in hierarchical depth: there is the superordinate term *colour* and one can list *chestnut, chocolate, walnut, tan*, etc. as instances of *brown*. Some of the subordinate colour terms, though, tend to be restricted in their application to specific types of entity such as hair or furniture, which creates a new dimension to this hierarchy. As far as other elements of the sentence are concerned, the fledgling could be said to be begging, asking, chattering, or calling for food; the begging could be loud, strident, staccato, or persistent. However, in these cases the various alternatives may not necessarily arrange themselves in neat hierarchical relationships. The fledgling's noise could be framed more abstractly as *vocalizing*, but there do not seem to be subordinate terms to differentiate more finely among the forms. For the auditory quality of the vocalization, there may be neither superordinate nor subordinate words that are relevant to it.

There has been some consideration of this issue of hierarchical depth for verbs in particular. Dimitrova-Vulchanova and Martinez (2013) suggest that verbs for forms of locomotion (such as *walk* and *run*) do occur within a hierarchy. For instance, *go* and *move* can be considered superordinate to *walk* and *run*, and *strut* or *lope* could be considered subordinates. Majid et al. (2007a) studied the verbs available in different languages to describe 'acts of material destruction' such as slicing a carrot with a knife, cutting hair with scissors, and tearing cloth by hand. Looking at four Germanic languages (Majid et al. 2007b), they noted that English has a two-level hierarchy in which, for instance, snapping and smashing are considered forms of breaking. Swedish, in contrast, appears to be flat, having five separate verbs that are not subordinate to any more general verbs. Brown (2007) found that Tzeltal also had a flat structure, with many verbs for different forms of material destruction but none functioning as superordinate to others. Based on these pieces of evidence, names for actions may sometimes occur within hierarchies but they may tend to have less hierarchical depth than names for objects, and the depth may vary from language to language.

To whatever extent object hierarchies are deeper than others, the key division may not actually be between nouns and other parts of speech. Nouns that do not refer to concrete objects may also tend to lack hierarchical depth. For instance, consider events like parties or competitions. There are subordinate names for such events—*birthday party, bachelor party*, or *baby shower*, and *swim meet, canoe race*, or *ice dance competition*—but there may not be more abstract names that are parallel to *furniture* or *clothing*. *Event* may be the best that can be found, encompassing a much wider range of entities. Nouns that name abstractions such as truth and beauty may show even less depth. A lack of hierarchical depth may also occur for other types of term. English spatial terms such as *in, on, under, above, around,* and *next to* have no obvious subordinates or superordinates. Terms picking out individual properties such as *loud, soft, smooth, tall, blue,* and *green* likewise do not have obvious subordinate and superordinate names in the sense of conventional labels (although one can always construct ad hoc phrases such as *way far under* or *really soft* and *outrageously loud* to convey subordinate-level nuances).The shallower hierarchical depth for most of these cases may be tied to lesser property richness of the entities being labelled (how many properties can you list for hitting or cutting or for truth or loudness, compared to a cup or a dog?), which may in turn provide fewer bases for grouping at different levels. It is less clear, though, why names for complex events do not encourage a deeper hierarchy.

Despite fewer choices, it may be wrong to conclude that name selection is necessarily easier when hierarchies are shallow. Although choices among levels may be less necessary, generating a word for something lacking a rich set of features may be more difficult than generating one for concrete objects due to that very abstractness. Concrete words are learned earlier by children (Gleitman et al. 2005), and age of acquisition of words is known to influence speed of responding in tasks such as reading a word out loud or deciding if a letter string is a real word (Cortese and Khanna 2007). It is hard to test this prediction about relative difficulty, though, by its very nature. It is easy to show pictures of concrete objects and have people name them; much harder to depict abstract concepts.

All of these points so far assume that the speaker's goal in choosing words is mainly to pick out some entity (whether object, action, or relation) in a straightforward way. Choices can also be influenced by communicative goals. A desire to bring attention to some specific attributes of an object can shift the name selected. If someone folds a paper hat out of a newspaper, how it is named later will depend on what the goal at the time is. If the goal is to have fun with the hat, someone might say *Hand me the hat*; if it is to clean up the room by recycling stuff, the person might say *Hand me the newspaper* (Malt and Sloman 2007). Loftus and Palmer (1974) noted that when a car runs into another car, calling the action *bumping, hitting,* or *crashing* conveys different images of the event. And choice of object names can even imply an entirely different object function. A teapot can be used as a watering can, a Frisbee as a picnic plate (Matan and Carey 2001). Calling the object *watering can* or *picnic plate* signals the speaker's current perspective on the objects. The longer the object has been used by the speaker in the new role and the more its features are compatible with that role, the more likely it may be to consistently receive the new name (Malt and Sloman 2007). Sometimes the choice may also convey attitude or emotion, as, for instance, when choosing among *house, hut, dump, McMansion,* or *palace* to name a dwelling. And sometimes the choice of name can provide feedback. If one conversational partner has already introduced a name for an object, using that name in return signals understanding and acceptance of the partner's interpretation of the object (Brennan and Clark 1996).

This last example brings up a new dimension to the question of how names are chosen. So far, we have been looking at the issue mainly from the perspective of what the speaker wants to convey. But that choice has to take into account what the addressee will make of it. Next we consider this point more fully.

17.2.2 What is the addressee prepared to understand?

We have noted Olson's argument that words are chosen to reduce alternatives or uncertainty. The importance of implicit contrast sets was made more broadly by Clark (1991). He pointed out that *red* is used for the colour of not only blood and fire engines but also hair, skin, potatoes, wine, wood, and cabbage. The colour that these things actually are (that is, the wavelengths of light reflected back to the eye) varies substantially. The varied usages are not just because *red* covers a range of shades or has fuzzy boundaries. The colour of native American skin would be called *brown* if seen on a leaf. The colour of a sunburnt skin would be called *pink* if seen on a flower. Clark argued that the colour name used for an object depends on the range of possibilities for that object. This range will be mapped onto existing colour names, usually the most common ones, so that a potato at the reddish end of potato possibilities will be *red* rather than *mauve* or *salmon*. Speakers can use *red* in such cases because their choices, and the interpretation by the addressee, are always made against the conceptual possibilities for the particular domain. By the same token, several mountains may be fewer than several crumbs, and a large mouse can be smaller than a small elephant.

In these cases, the knowledge of how an addressee might interpret the name chosen is implicit, since for the most part people will use terms for object colours that they have learned as conventions. Brown's (1958) discussion illustrates how adults may more explicitly take into account the range of conceptual possibilities to a child at different ages. Adults may call all coins *money* when speaking to a small child, because at that age all coins are equivalent as objects not to be swallowed or dropped down the heating vent. For an older child, the adult will switch to *dime* vs. *nickel*, because the child's range of conceptual possibilities has become more differentiated. As Brown phrased it, parents 'anticipate the functional structure of the child's world'. Although the selection process in light of the projected functional structure may still not be a fully conscious one, it does require a dynamic assessment that allows the name to change as the child matures. In a related vein, Mervis (1987) noted that basic-level groupings for a child do not necessarily match those of adults. For instance, a child may apply *kitty* to lions and tigers as well as house cats, or *duck* to ducks, swans, and geese. Sometimes an adult may then provide corrective feedback, pointing out how lions, tigers, and house cats are different from one another. At times, though, the adult will choose to use a child-basic label in speech to a child (calling a tiger a *kitty*), presumably on an assessment that the child is not ready to learn more detailed discriminations.

These ways that speakers accommodate word choices to their addressees have been labeled 'audience design' (Clark and Carlson 1981). Audience design effects come in many forms. Accommodation based on the level of knowledge is not confined to adults speaking to children. Choosing Jenny Wren vs. *Troglodytes aedon* (or *House Wren*) depending on what your grandmother knows about birds would also be an example of accommodating to addressee knowledge. Knowledge that the speaker and addressee share can come from several sources (Clark and Marshall 1981). First is general world knowledge. Adults share some level of knowledge of many things such as foods, weather, animals, activities, and (depending on culture) business, politics, computers, and TV shows. Other shared knowledge derives from community membership. If you and your grandmother are both ornithologists, then you will share certain knowledge relevant to ornithology. If you are both baseball fans or from Boston, you will share other knowledge. Also, some knowledge is shared due to co-presence. If a speaker and addressee are both in a room with an object or have been talking together about an object, then their references to the object can proceed on the assumption that both already know what object is being referred to. If the Porsche but not the SUV has been under discussion, then the Porsche may be adequately picked out by the name *the car* because the addressee knows which car is of current interest and the speaker knows that the addressee knows it.

Experiments testing how speakers adjust word choice to their addressee use a 'referential communication' paradigm in which two people are each given cards with pictures on them. The two sets of pictures are the same, and the task of one person (the 'matcher') is to line up her cards in the order specified by the other (the 'director'). The challenge is that the director and matcher are separated so they cannot see each other's cards; they can only coordinate by talking about them. Clark and Wilkes-Gibbs (1986) tracked the referring expressions used by the partners when the pictures were complex geometric shapes having no conventional names. They found that partners went through a process of negotiating names for the pictures, beginning with elaborate phrases such as *looks like a person who's ice skating, except they're sticking two arms out in front* and converging in the end on much shorter ones such as *the ice skater. The ice skater* became a suitable name for the picture based on their mutual acceptance of it, but it would not have necessarily worked as an initial name to use with anyone else.

In fact, once a name is established between partners, they may tend to keep using the same name even when a shorter, simpler name could be used. Brennan and Clark (1996) showed this in a version of the task where the pictures were of ordinary objects such as shoes and cars. In initial trials, there were multiple instances of each category—say, several different shoes. To pin down which card was under discussion, the partners had to use names like *penny loafer* or *high heels* that distinguished among the shoes. In later trials, there was only one object per category on the cards, so *shoe* alone would pick out the right card. The partners continued to use the longer name previously established between them.

Despite this evidence for attention to addressee knowledge, speakers are not always as attentive to addressees as they might be. For example, even though a new partner would not know which card depicts the ice skater as described above, speakers will sometimes use the abbreviated referential terms developed with an earlier partner. Barr and Keysar (2002) suggest this means that speakers are more egocentric than past research has indicated. However, Horton and Gerrig (2005) argue that some of the seemingly contradictory evidence on how much speakers design word choices for their audiences depends on past experiences in particular tasks. In many situations, there is little by way of addressee-specific accommodation that needs to be made. If a book is sitting out in plain sight, talking about *the book* should work for just about any English-speaking addressee. It may not always be self-evident when a situation requires adjusting utterances to particular audiences. Gibbs and Van Orden (2012) note that studies favouring the egocentric view use more complex tasks where a speaker may be easily misled to think that certain information is shared when it is not.

17.3 What names are available to choose among?

17.3.1 Online memory processes and name choice

One might guess that whatever possible names a person has stored in memory, these names can all be equally well accessed and considered for use. Such a thing could be true if the human brain were a computer and could access all relevant words in parallel, instantaneously. The human brain is not a computer, though, and the options that become available for use and the order in which they do are influenced by memory retrieval processes.

In light of this fact, researchers have studied those retrieval processes. One major factor influencing speed of word retrieval (as measured by how fast a name can be produced to a picture of an object) is how frequent the word is (with frequency usually measured by how often the word appears in newspapers, books, and other written material.) Lower-frequency words are harder to produce, and it is within this lower range that frequency level matters most. That is, higher-frequency words are easy enough to retrieve that modest differences in frequency do not affect production much. Other variables also matter. As mentioned earlier, age of acquisition influences how easily a word can be retrieved. Age of acquisition is strongly correlated with word frequency, and the effects of both may reflect amount of experience with the words over the lifespan (Bock and Griffin 2000). Word-length effects are also part of this package, since short words tend to be high-frequency (Zipf 1935). For current purposes, though, our main interest is not in how fast people can produce a name for an object, but what name they choose. The results about speed of retrieval have implications for this choice. When several possible names for something have similar meaning but vary in retrieval ease, the name retrieved first is more likely to be the one produced. If a speaker wants to mention an object of a certain colour, she will be more likely to call it a *blue sofa* than an *azure divan*, even if she knows the words *azure* and *divan*. This phenomenon also most likely feeds into the bias toward naming at the basic level. The general utility of basic-level names results in their tending to be short words of high frequency, which will result in their being more easily retrieved than names at other levels, which in turn reinforces the pattern of being the most frequently used.

Another factor related to frequency is typicality. Here, the issue is how typical the object (or action, or property, or relation) is of words available. We noted before that for objects that are typical of a word (e.g. a robin for *bird* or a button-down shirt for *shirt*), people will tend to use the basic-level term, but if the object is atypical of the word (e.g. a penguin or a t-shirt), they tend to use a subordinate label (*penguin* or *t-shirt*). The explanation was that, for atypical examples, the basic-level name might not accurately enough convey what kind of thing is being referred to. But some of this usage tendency may also be related to the workings of memory, again in a self-reinforcing fashion. If penguins are most often heard being called *penguin* rather than *bird*, then *penguin* will be the name first retrieved and most easily produced. And of course, the more frequent retrieval and production perpetuates it being more frequently heard.

Memory retrieval processes most likely also figure in speakers' tendency to reuse names in conversation. Recently heard or used chunks of language tend to be reused. For instance, English has two different sentence structures available for describing selling something to someone: *The dealer sold the antique car to the collector* and *The dealer sold the collector the antique car*. Bock (1986) showed that after speakers produce the second type of structure, they are more likely to describe a new event in a similar way. For instance, after using the second to talk about selling the car, they are more likely to say *The girl handed the man the paintbrush* even though the topics are unrelated. Malt and Sloman (2004) found a similar tendency to re-use names recently heard. They adapted the standard referential communication task by having the first director of each matching session be a confederate who introduced one of two possible names for each object (e.g. *booklet* vs. *pamphlet*, or *bucket* vs. *pail*) into the conversation. The director role then rotated so that the original director departed, the original matcher became the director, and a new person became the matcher. In a final round, the new matcher became director. Whichever name was initially introduced by the confederate received increased use and had higher preference ratings in a post-test, even by participants who had not heard the name from the original director. Once a name is heard in association with an object, it is likely to become the most easily retrieved name for it, at least in the short term, and most likely to be used again.

The idea that name choice is influenced by retrievability from memory puts a different spin on some previously observed phenomena. The debate over whether the speaker's perspective is egocentric or addressee-centred in selecting names in conversation assumes that taking someone's perspective is part of the process. Perspective-taking may actually be less relevant than simple retrievability of words from memory. Speech happens quickly. English speakers produce about 150 words per minute in ordinary discourse (Levelt 1999), and there may be a strong tendency to go with whatever name becomes available first, regardless of whose perspective it reflects. Horton and Slaten (2012) have recently argued that even the selective use of names in conjunction with specific addressees can be a consequence of ordinary memory processes. Names become encoded in memory along with the conversational partners with whom they were used, and the partner then serves as a retrieval context that tends to cue the name that was used before. The correct interpretation of name choices that show an influence of prior conversational histories is likely to be an area of ongoing investigation.

These points about retrievability concern words considered individually—i.e. without taking into account how other words around them may influence production. Most of what adults say comes in phrases or sentences made up of multiple words. And words activate other words. Hundreds (maybe thousands) of studies by now have shown priming effects whereby activating one word facilitates processing of a related word. Seeing *doctor* allows people to respond faster to *nurse* (e.g. judge whether *nurse* is word or non-word) than seeing *chair* does (e.g. Neely 1991), presumably because processing *doctor* causes activation of *nurse* before *nurse* even appears. This phenomenon implies that the words needed for the early part of a sentence might influence the words retrieved and used later in a sentence. Consistent with this idea, the effects of word frequency on selection are reduced in sentence contexts (Griffin and Bock 1998). Words that are predictable or most coherent in the sentence context are more easily produced. For instance, following the sentence fragment *The farmer milked the. . . .*, the word *cow* can be produced faster to a picture of a cow than the word *dog* can be to a picture of a dog, even if *dog* is a higher frequency word. Applying this observation to how a name is chosen among the different possibilities available, the idea is that the name used may be influenced by words or phrases occurring shortly before. A sentence about relaxing with the TV and a bowl of popcorn may be more likely to evoke *couch*, whereas one about buying a new Oriental rug for the living room may more likely evoke *sofa*, even if it's the same object in both cases.

17.3.2 Language histories

The cognitive processes just discussed operate over whatever candidate words a person has stored in memory. Those options are not unlimited. Most obviously, the candidates are determined largely by the language that the person is using. A person speaking English will choose among English words, a person using Chinese will choose among Chinese words. (There can also be code-mixing in which bilinguals use some words of one language when speaking another; see Williams' chapter, this volume.)

Although it is trivial that the particular forms of words will differ across languages, what is less obvious is that the semantic contrasts available in a domain can vary by language. One of the best-known examples is colour. People all over the world can see essentially the same range of colours because the mechanics of colour vision are the same for everyone. Still, languages vary in the colour terms available. English has 11 basic colour terms (*red, blue, green*, and so on) and many more specific terms (*maroon, turquoise*, etc.). Some languages have only five or six basic terms (generally roughly equivalent to *black, white, red, yellow, green*, and *blue*) and some do no more than distinguish lighter from darker colours (Hardin and Maffi 1997). The same diversity in naming patterns exists for many other domains including household objects, body parts, spatial relations, causal relations, acts of cutting and breaking, and acts of carrying and holding. (For illustration of many of these domains, see Malt and Wolff 2010.) And languages

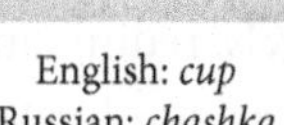
English: *cup*
Russian: *chashka*

English: *cup*
Russian: *stakan*

English: *glass*
Russian: *stakan*

FIG. 17.1 The English *cup-glass* distinction in contrast to the Russian *chashka-stakan* distinction.

don't just vary in how finely they divide up a domain by name. They can differ in how properties are used in creating lexical contrasts. For instance, for drinking vessels, English distinguishes *glass* from *cup* based heavily on the material, whereas Russian separates *stakan* (encompassing English glasses plus plastic and paper cups) from *chashka* (more restricted to traditional tea/coffee cups) based more heavily on shape (Pavlenko and Malt 2011) (see Fig. 17.1).

This phenomenon runs counter to an intuition that the world contains some inherently separate things that everyone sees and that all languages will name in parallel ways. The intuition is not entirely faulty. Languages do tend to make some shared lexical distinctions reflecting what everyone sees as distinct in the world. Languages tend to distinguish arms from hands and both from legs (Majid 2010), walking from running (Malt et al. 2008), and red from black (e.g. Kay et al. 1997). The range of colours that get subsumed under a single name is constrained by contiguity; languages don't have a term that covers red and yellow but excludes orange (Regier, Kay, and Khetarpal 2007). Still, many degrees of freedom remain. The set of names that each speaker has at any moment in time is not the result of people perceiving the world and dividing it up by name according to what they see as distinct at that moment. The names were acquired from the generation before, and theirs from the generation before that. So naming patterns reflect the evolutionary path of the language up to that point, developed over hundreds or thousands of years. Just as plants and animals have radiated out in many different directions from a shared origin, languages can follow different paths in the development of their lexicons depending on the influences on them along the way.

One such influence is cultural history. Cultures are exposed to new objects (and maybe new actions, such as forms of dance or interactions with technology—consider *web surfing* or *mouse over it*) at different times in their histories. Sometimes existing names are extended to cover the new experience, and sometimes new names are coined. Which one happens may depend on how close the new experience seems to an old one. In many English-speaking countries, dial telephones were widespread before similar phones with buttons came along. English speakers extended *dial* as the verb for entering a phone number to those phones and then carried it forward as new types of phone emerged, so that it is used with the cellphones of today. Each application of the word can be thought of as a link in a chain from the original use to its current use (Lakoff 1987;

Malt et al. 1999). In some developing countries, telephones were scarce until the arrival of the cellphone. In their languages, it is less likely that the verb for entering the phone number derives from a word for a dial.

Another influence is contact with other cultures and languages. New words can enter a language through contact with another. Sometimes these terms fill gaps in the lexicon, as when English adopted Yiddish *klutz* to label a clumsy person. (Consider also *schlock, schmooze*, and *mensch.*) Sometimes the added terms are largely redundant vis-à-vis existing terms, creating a situation of instability since languages tend to avoid synonymy. If the new term catches hold (as it is likely to do if it comes from a language high in prestige), then the old term may drop out of use, which doesn't produce any net change to how the domain is divided up. Sometimes both terms remain, though, in which case they may differentiate in meaning. In English, an animal and its flesh have the same name when it comes to chicken, fish, goat, buffalo, and some other animals, but the two are differentiated for cattle (*cow/beef*), sheep (*sheep/mutton*), and pigs (*pig/pork*) (e.g. Hock and Joseph 1996). The second of each term originated in the Romance influence on English after the Norman invasion. This differentiation is not necessarily paralleled in other languages lacking the imported lexical item.

More generally, the existence of one name in a semantic domain can exert an influence on the range of applicability of others, with either expansion or contraction of ranges possible. Even subtle differences between dialects of the same language can exist. For instance, in British English, all long outer garments for the legs can be called *trousers*, including casual ones and ones worn by women. *Pants*, on the other hand, is reserved for the undergarment. In American English, *trousers* is reserved for a more formal garment of a style usually worn by men. *Pants* covers all long outer garments for the legs including trousers; and the undergarment is *underpants*. It may be more the exception than the rule for languages to have set of words with exactly parallel meanings (see Malt and Majid 2013, and Majid's chapter, this book, for further discussion of variation across languages, and Geeraerts' chapter for more on change over time.)

17.3.3 Individual histories

There is also individual-person variation in naming within language communities. One source is age. Children naturally have fewer words in their vocabularies and so may choose different names than adults do for an object. As already noted, a small child may call a lion and tiger as well as a domestic cat *kitty*. Children also have lesser conceptual grasp of the differences among things in the world, which contributes to their misuse of words (Mervis 1987). Children may also have some biases about how words work that cause them to name things differently from adults. Believing that different words signal different types of thing can be useful for mapping words to things in the world, but it can also cause young children to refuse to apply more than one word to the same thing (Markman and Wachtel 1988). Two- to 3-year-old children who know *chair* or *bird* may deny that a chair is also *furniture* and a bird is also *animal*.

Even once a child grows beyond these early factors, she may still use words differently from adults. Ameel, Malt, and Storms (2008) studied the names that children aged 5 and above gave to common household objects such as bottles, jars, dishes, plates, and cups. By age 6, the children produced almost the same set of words as adults, but they still did not use them in the same way. Some of the names were applied too broadly and others too narrowly. It was not until age 14 that the children's choices of names for individual objects fully mirrored those of adults. In one sense it is surprising that it would take children so long to work out adult naming patterns for common words applied to simple objects. It is less surprising, though, in light of the language-specific nature of the naming patterns that exist. Children have to figure out the details of their own language's pattern, which is not obvious from simple observation of similarities among the objects.

In light of the different naming patterns across languages, and how long it takes for children to master the pattern of just one language, one might wonder how bilinguals handle learning two different ones. There is growing evidence that bilinguals may not acquire the equivalent of two monolingual patterns. Ameel et al. (2005) studied adult bilinguals who had grown up in Belgium with one parent who was a native speaker of Dutch and the other, French, and who had learned both languages from birth. They compared the bilingual naming patterns to those produced by monolingual speakers of Dutch and French in Belgium for the same household objects studied with children. The monolinguals had differences in their naming patterns for these objects. The bilinguals showed more correspondence between the naming patterns in their two languages than the monolinguals did. That is, the bilinguals partially merged the patterns of the two languages so that they were less distinct. At least for simultaneous acquisition, it may be difficult or impossible to completely separate the two. Other studies have shown that when one language is learned after another, the second language may even reshape naming patterns of the first (Malt et al., 2015; Pavlenko and Malt 2011), at least when the second language becomes the stronger one. Different conditions of learning and use may result in different outcomes for bilingual word use.

17.4 Conclusion

Objects, actions, relations, properties, and other elements of the world do not each come with a name that intrinsically belongs to them and uniquely identifies them. With every utterance, a speaker must select among possible names for each element of a thought that she wants to convey. This selection reflects both what the speaker wants to transmit and what the addressee is prepared to understand. Name choice is further constrained by the set of options retrieved from memory at the moment of the utterance. Those, in turn, are constrained by the full set available to that individual speaker, which is a function of both the historical development of the target language and the language-learning experiences of the speaker. For every thought to be conveyed through language, multiple interacting factors converge rapidly to determine word choice.

CHAPTER 18

TERMINOLOGIES AND TAXONOMIES

MARIE-CLAUDE L'HOMME

18.1 Two opposing forces

All fields of specialized knowledge have particular naming requirements.[1] Entities referred to by experts, such as a disease, a regulation, or a micro-organism, need to have names free of vagueness and ambiguity. In an ideal world, specialized communication should be clear and efficient and this should be reflected in the terms that are used. This is why, over the centuries, experts in many fields, such as biology, law, and medicine, have gone to great lengths to agree on and to establish rules for naming specialized entities or to develop criteria for standardizing existing terms. This is also an important focus of terminology. This discipline, whose origin can be situated around 1930, devised a series of theoretical principles that address these requirements. Until the 1990s, regulating the creation, form, and use of terms were its main foci. For, as Felber (1984: 99) put it, 'in terminology, the fair-play of language would lead to chaos'.

From Ancient Greece we know of preoccupations for giving suitable names to items of knowledge new to the world. Since the 18th century, however, naming and classifying new discoveries became a major concern. One thinks of Linnaeus and his Latin binomial classification of plants based on ancient Greek precedents, and Lavoisier's efforts to develop a chemical nomenclature which would be adaptable to the vernacular languages of learned societies of the time. With increasing industrialization and globalized commerce in the late 19th century, technical languages were needed which would serve a much wider community than that of the scientific fraternities of botany or chemistry. The International Electrotechnical Committee, created around the turn of the 20th century, was one of the very first truly international organizations which set itself the

[1] I express my warmest thanks to Juan C. Sager, who made extensive comments on a previous version of this contribution. I would also like to thank John Taylor for his numerous suggestions.

task of coordinating the essential vocabulary—and, of course, the appropriate units of measurement—of electricity for the major industrialized countries. Only in the 1930s were these various activities provided with a theoretical framework and given the name 'terminology', i.e. the science of terms. The creation of terminology as a special discipline is attributed to Wüster (1979). The principles presented below—which fall under the scope of the General Theory of Terminology (now often called 'traditional terminology')—result from Wüster's ideas and changes introduced in the years following his first proposal (in the thesis he defended in 1931) as well as reinterpretations made in translations of his writings.

Although establishing rules for naming specialized entities is necessary in specific situations, it is a fact that all knowledge is mainly conveyed by means of language, and specialized entities are expressed in the form of linguistic units (i.e. terms) that appear in sentences and as such comply with rules that apply to all linguistic units. Terms combine with other words and, like them, are subject to variation, vagueness, and ambiguity. As Sager points out:

> [The] origins [of terms] in texts of genuine natural language must, however, never be forgotten because terminologists use texts as their basic material and the dictionary tools they develop are intended to explicate natural language items or advise on the usage of terms in natural language contexts.
>
> (Sager 1990: 55)

Hence, while efforts are made to control linguistic phenomena that are considered to impede efficient communication in science and technology, an opposing force is exerted by natural language. This contribution examines how experts and terminologists have dealt with these two opposing forces and have suggested methods to find a balance between naming requirements on the one hand and the 'fair play of language' in different kinds of application on the other.

18.2 Terms as means for naming specialized entities

In the 1800s, biologists felt the need to solve the communication problem raised by the existence of various names or ad hoc naming conventions for species. In addition to having different names in different languages, a species could have more than one name in one and the same language. In zoology, for instance, a set of very strict rules were defined which experts had to follow to identify a new animal (the rules are regularly updated, and a provisional final version was released at the beginning of the 1960s).

In zoology, naming conventions rely on principles of classification (i.e. taxonomy) established in biology. According to these principles, species are organized in a hierarchical system based on their natural relations (shown in Fig. 18.1).

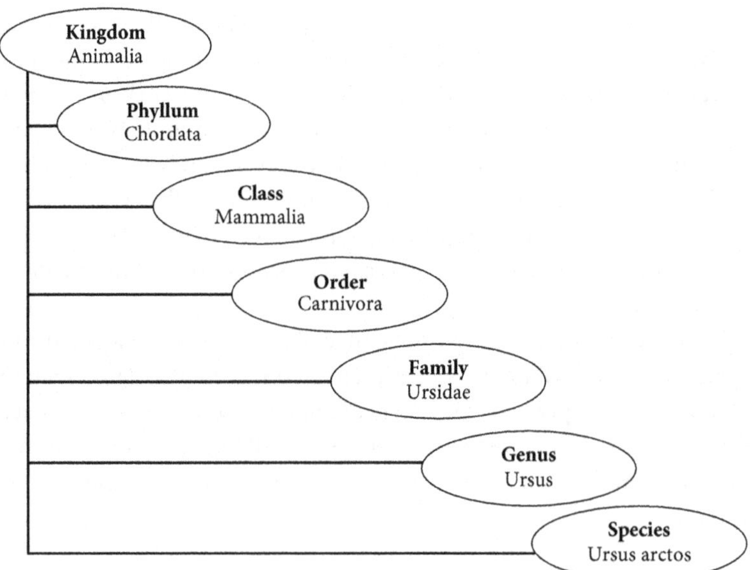

FIG. 18.1 Classification of *Ursus Arctos* (commonly known as *grizzly bear*).

The rules for naming animals are regulated by the International Commission on Zoological Nomenclature and can be found in the *International Code of Zoological Nomenclature* (International Commission on Zoological Nomenclature 2000), henceforth, the *Code*. The *Code* determines what names are valid for a taxon (an item in the taxonomy) at the family, genus, and species levels. Naming conventions are based on a set of six principles; three are presented below, since they are related to observations made in this chapter (other principles are meant as guidelines to deal with competing designations for the same taxon).

- Principle of binominal nomenclature. A species' name is a combination of a generic name and a specific name (*Ursus arctos*); a subspecies' name has three components (a generic, specific, and subspecific name); taxa's names at higher levels have one component (*Ursus; Ursidae*). Names are formed in grammatically correct Latin and are used internationally; the issue of translation therefore does not arise.
- Principle of coordination. Within the family group, genus group, or species group a name established for a taxon at any rank in the group is deemed to be simultaneously established with the same author and date as for taxa based on the same name-bearing type at other ranks in the group (*Code* 2000).
- Principle of homonymy. The name of each taxon must be unique.

For obvious reasons, very few fields of knowledge have such clear guidelines for classifying and naming entities, and the example of zoology can be considered to be exemplary in this respect. We can also mention chemistry, which resorts to symbols that reflect the composition of elements and compounds (CO_2 for carbon dioxide; *Ti* for titanium). To assist international comprehensibility, medical terminology favours Greek and Latin morphemes with specific meanings in the creation of terms (e.g. *-pathy* used to refer to a disease, as in *cardiomyopathy* for 'heart muscle disease'). However, scientific disciplines need to organize or classify the items of knowledge they manipulate in order to better understand them, and prefer to use names that label them unambiguously. These needs for classifying and conventionalizing names are partially reflected in terminology theory and in the methods developed to describe terms in dictionaries, as will be seen below.

In terminology, items of knowledge are called 'concepts'. These are defined as representations that are assumed to be generalizations over extralinguistic entities, i.e. the items of knowledge manipulated in science and technology (concrete objects such as 'computer', 'bear', representational entities such as 'data', animates such as 'criminal lawyer', activities such as 'surgical operation', etc.). Names for these concepts are called 'designations'. The combination of a concept with a designation is a 'term'.

Traditional terminology theory postulates that concepts are the starting point of the analysis of terms. This means that terminologists should start by identifying concepts and then find or assign designations for them. Example (1) illustrates the application of this onomasiological procedure.

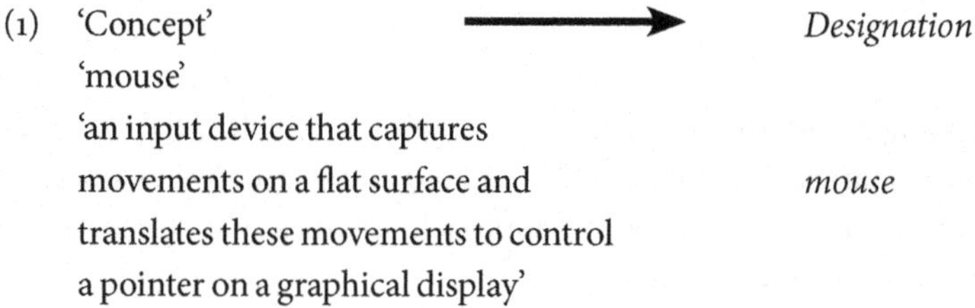

(1) 'Concept'
Designation
'mouse'
'an input device that captures movements on a flat surface and translates these movements to control a pointer on a graphical display'
mouse

Concepts are delineated by methods of classification (similar to those used in zoology). The representation of this classification in a subject field is called a 'conceptual structure'. For example, when defining the concept 'mouse' in the field of computing, terminologists must distinguish it from other neighbouring concepts. Fig. 18.2 shows that 'mouse' is related to a generic concept, i.e. 'input device'; that it shares a certain number of characteristics with 'keyboard', since it has the same superordinate concept; it also differs from 'keyboard' since they each have specific characteristics. 'Mouse' subsumes two specific concepts; they inherit all the characteristics attributed to the concept 'mouse' but have one or two additional characteristics. Finally, 'mouse' also shares a part–whole relation with 'button'.

This simple conceptual structure illustrates the two main types of relation dealt with in terminology (generic–specific and part–whole); however, as will be seen below, many more relations can be observed between concepts. When describing terms in

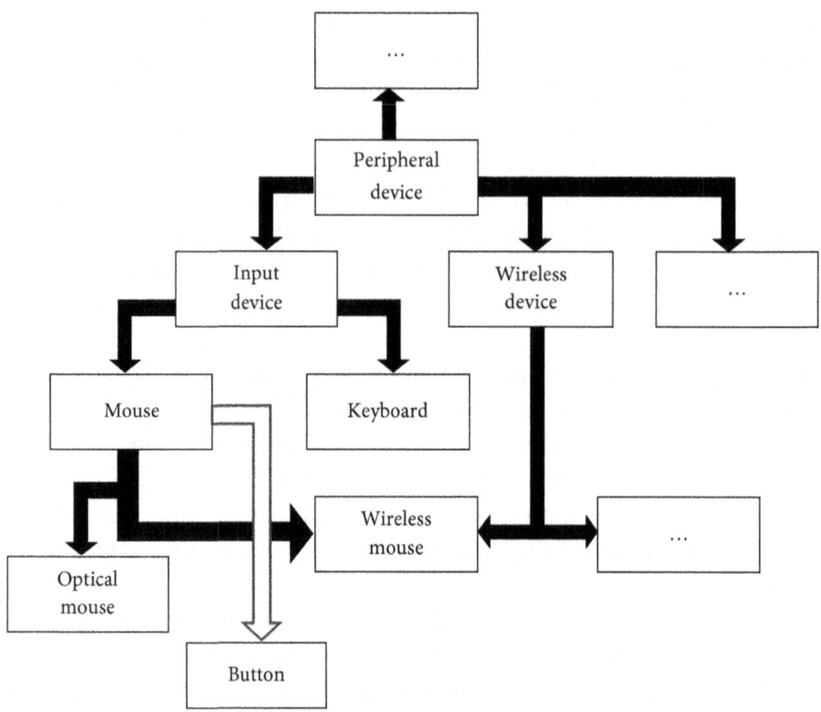

FIG. 18.2 'Mouse' and related concepts in a miniature conceptual structure

dictionaries, terminologists attempt to make these relations explicit.[2] Definitions written in specialized dictionaries aim to capture the shared and distinctive characteristics of concepts (Rey 1995). Of course, the entire approach assumes that concepts can be defined precisely, at least at a given point in time.

The methods for delineating concepts and gradually unveiling conceptual structures presented above are seldom applied systematically in everyday terminology work. Terminologists are not experts in the fields they are asked to explore, and hence are not in a position to precisely delineate the concepts. They usually apply an iterative analysis that consists in reading texts and acquiring knowledge to gradually build up a conceptual representation.

Another important principle in traditional terminology is that of biunivocity (Fr. *Biunivocité*). According to the biunivocity principle, a concept should have a single designation; conversely, a designation should be used to label a single concept. This means that synonyms and polysemous lexical items should be avoided. Of course, this

[2] Relations are also important in lexicographical work. Thesauri take into account relations that we mentioned in our 'mouse' example in addition to other kinds of less well-defined ones (such as 'associated with'). In traditional terminology, however, structures are built on the basis of concepts, whereas lexicographers attempt to identify relations between words or word senses.

ideal situation can seldom be observed, and terminologists must create rules similar to those used in zoology and adapt them to specific situations. For instance, the concept 'email' defined as 'an application that uses networks for exchanging messages in digital form' can be labelled with *email, electronic mail, email program, emailer*. Similarly, *email* can refer to: (1) the application (*I sent the file by email*), (2) a specific message in digital form (*I just read your email*), and (3) a collection of such messages (*Please check your email*). Situations where polysemy can be encountered are not as common as in general language, since terminologists concentrate on meanings within a special subject field; synonyms, on the other hand, are quite frequent.

Even though rules such as those applied in zoology exist in very few subject fields, some regularity can be observed in the terminologies of most fields of knowledge (Sager 1990). This is due in part to a willingness to use transparent (i.e. compositional) terms. Transparent terms facilitate the understanding of new concepts and probably contribute to the success of knowledge transfer. The forms of many terms reflect the concepts they denote by stating some of their characteristics, such as their function, one of their components, or their origin. For instance, *wireless* in *wireless mouse* or *wireless modem* means that the device is not connected to the computer with a cord. *Optical* in *optical mouse* refers to the way the peripheral captures movements (by means of an optical sensor). Morphemes can have the same function: *-ware* in *antispyware, adware, courseware, demoware, gameware*, etc. means that the term refers to a type of software program. (In French, *-ciel* is used in terms denoting software: *didacticiel, ludiciel, graphiciel*, etc.) Terms can also reflect the place of the concepts in a hierarchical structure. This is illustrated by the examples in (2).

(2) *Mouse > optical mouse > wireless optical mouse*
énergie > énergie éolienne > énergie éolienne marine (Eng. *energy, wind energy, offshore wind energy*)

Finally, the form of terms can instantiate a contrast between two concepts (e.g. *sustainable development ↔ unsustainable development; download ↔ upload*).

The principles described above are applied directly or can be adapted by terminologists, translators, or agencies responsible for recommending or standardizing terms. In most terminology projects, information collected on terms is recorded in a specialized dictionary, a glossary, a term bank, or another kind of online resource. Terminological entries differ from what can be found in general language dictionaries, since they adhere to the principles mentioned above. In a term bank (Fig. 18.3), a record is devoted to a single concept—associated with a specific subject field—and all terms (usually in more than one language) used to designate this concept are listed (a result of the onomasiological approach). A preferred term can be identified and others are labelled as synonyms, variants, or deprecated forms (a mild version of biunivocity). A subject label is used to distinguish concepts in specialized dictionaries containing terms related to different fields. The information given concentrates on the explanation of the concept (definition, subject field label). Linguistic information is often reduced to the indication of the part of speech.

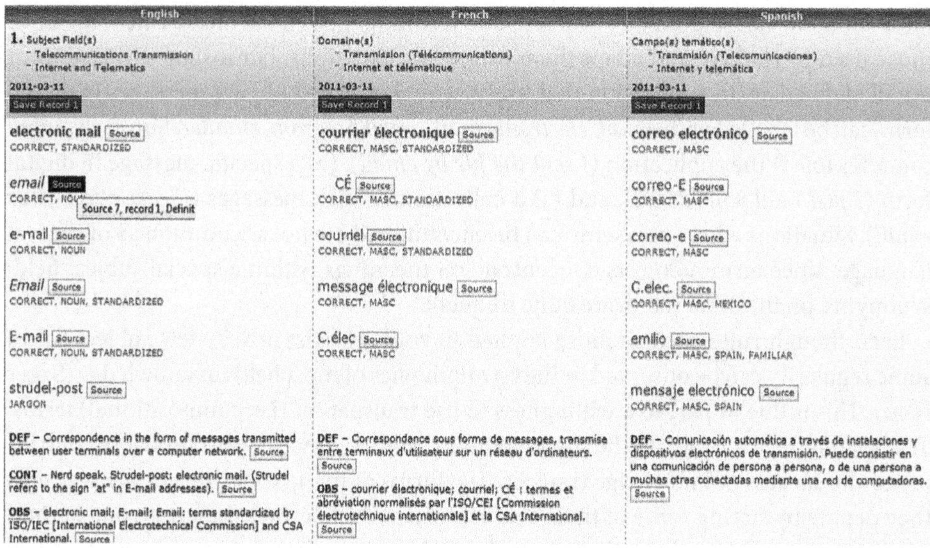

English	French	Spanish
1. Subject Field(s) – Telecommunications Transmission – Internet and Telematics 2011-03-11 Save Record 1	Domaine(s) – Transmission (Télécommunications) – Internet et télématique 2011-03-11 Save Record 1	Campo(s) temático(s) – Transmisión (Telecomunicaciones) – Internet y telemática 2011-03-11 Save Record 1
electronic mail Source CORRECT, STANDARDIZED	**courrier électronique** Source CORRECT, MASC, STANDARDIZED	**correo electrónico** Source CORRECT, MASC
email Source CORRECT, NOU[N] Source 7, record 1, Definit	CÉ Source CORRECT, MASC, STANDARDIZED	correo-E Source CORRECT, MASC
e-mail Source CORRECT, NOUN	courriel Source CORRECT, MASC, STANDARDIZED	correo-e Source CORRECT, MASC
Email Source CORRECT, NOUN, STANDARDIZED	message électronique Source CORRECT, MASC	C.elec. Source CORRECT, MASC, MEXICO
E-mail Source CORRECT, NOUN, STANDARDIZED	C.élec Source CORRECT, MASC	emilio Source CORRECT, MASC, SPAIN, FAMILIAR
strudel-post Source JARGON		mensaje electrónico Source CORRECT, MASC, SPAIN
DEF – Correspondence in the form of messages transmitted between user terminals over a computer network. Source **CONT** – Nerd speak. Strudel-post: electronic mail. (Strudel refers to the sign "at" in E-mail addresses). Source **OBS** – electronic mail; E-mail; Email: terms standardized by ISO/IEC [International Electrotechnical Commission] and CSA International. Source	**DEF** – Correspondance sous forme de messages, transmise entre terminaux d'utilisateur sur un réseau d'ordinateurs. Source **OBS** – courrier électronique; courriel; CÉ : termes et abréviation normalisés par l'ISO/CEI [Commission électrotechnique internationale] et la CSA International. Source	**DEF** – Comunicación automática a través de instalaciones y dispositivos electrónicos de transmisión. Puede consistir en una comunicación de persona a persona, o de una persona a muchas otras conectadas mediante una red de computadoras. Source

FIG. 18.3 Term record extracted from Termium Plus.

18.3 Terms as units of language

The principles applied in order to produce unambiguous naming conventions (presented briefly in the previous section) have a number of linguistic consequences:

- Terms are viewed as canonical labels isolated from text. In extreme cases such as zoology or chemistry, where the naming conventions aim at yielding systematic, official, and universal names, the result is a form of semi-artificial language that serves as a reference in specialized situations. Of course, most units manipulated by terminologists are not artificial and pertain to natural language; to be standardized, however, terms must be defined according to the way they refer to a concept (the concept itself being well-defined within a field) and not to the way they behave in the language at large.
- Terms are assumed to be linguistic labels that can be superimposed on knowledge configurations. Subject field experts or terminologists build consensual or ad hoc conceptual structures or taxonomies, such as those that appear in Figs. 18.1 and 18.2, and do this prior to reflecting on the linguistic forms used to express this knowledge. By doing so, scientists or terminologists need to create categories or concepts (and labels for them) that would not have been spontaneously proposed if only natural distinctions had been at play. For instance, the 'order' and 'family' categories in Fig. 18.1 or the 'wireless peripheral' category in Fig. 18.2 appeared as a result of modelling in zoology and computing.

- Most terms are nouns. This is a consequence of the focus of terminology on concepts (most of them denoting entities). Even in cases where activity concepts need to be taken into account (linguistically expressed by nouns or verbs), nouns are still preferred. This is why specialized discourse is said to be predominantly nominal in character.
- Designations tend to be complex (consisting of derivatives, compounds, or multiword units). This is the result of the preference for transparency and clarity in scientific communication.

In recent years, the perspective proposed by traditional terminology has been questioned from many different angles (Bourigault and Slodzian 1999; Cabré 2003; Gaudin 2003; Temmerman 2000). Most critics attack the implicit assumption that terms are analysed outside their linguistic context, and highlight the fact that terms appear in running text and behave like other linguistic units. The following subsections discuss recent terminology research that challenges the more traditional view of terms and the concepts they designate.

18.3.1 Terms are not the same for everyone

Terms are defined against the background of a special subject field, as had already been underlined in traditional terminology. However, it has been increasingly emphasized that they are also defined relative to the application that uses them. Terms are manipulated by experts in special subject fields (who view them as items that convey knowledge), by specialists involved in different forms of information management (for whom terms are descriptors of the content of documents), by translators (who need to find adequate equivalents of linguistic units that are unfamiliar), and, of course, by terminologists (who identify units that are likely to be recorded in specialized dictionaries). Recently, knowledge engineers have also reflected on terms and the way they should be represented in knowledge structures—more specifically, in ontologies (Montiel-Ponsada et al. 2010). Each category of experts has different needs triggered by specific applications, and this inevitably has an impact on the way the notion of 'relevant term' is defined.

Estopà (2001) showed the differences between the perspectives of experts, information managers (more specifically indexers), translators, and terminologists. The author demonstrated that, when asked to identify linguistic items that correspond to terms in a medical text, these different categories of experts compiled lists that varied both in length and content. Terminologists produced the longest lists; indexers, the shortest. Experts, translators, and terminologists identified terms that belonged to different parts of speech (although most were nouns); indexers focused exclusively on nouns and noun phrases.

These observations imply that a more flexible definition of *term* is needed which takes account of different applications (standardizing terms, the main application of traditional terminology and certain scientific disciplines, could be one of these applications, but not the only one). According to Bourigault and Slodzian (1999: 31):

> Le terme est un 'construit', c'est-à-dire qu'il résulte de l'analyse faite par le terminographe: cette analyse prend en compte la place occupée par le terme dans un corpus, une validation par des experts *et les objectifs visés par une description terminographique donnée* [emphasis added].[3]

18.3.2 Some concepts are envisaged from different perspectives

Concepts can be considered from different viewpoints and classified differently in different fields of knowledge. For instance, 'tomato' in biology belongs to the category of 'fruit' since it shares with other fruits the same natural characteristics (it starts as a flower, carries seed that can produce new plants, etc.). This classification, although it relies on sound scientific criteria, is not applicable in the food industry. The class 'fruit' exists but is defined in order to group other types of food that are sweet and often used in the preparation of desserts or for making jam. 'Tomato' is classified in a different class, that of 'vegetable', which has no status in biology and which comprises other types of food such as onions, carrots, cabbages, and cucumbers (another fruit for biologists).

The example of 'tomato' is by no means an exception. Many other concepts can be defined and classified differently. This implies that a single universal classification cannot be imposed in all areas. In knowledge modelling, more specifically in ontology development, these different perspectives are recognized as a fact and can lead to distinct conceptualizations, provided that each conceptualization is consensual (Guarino et al. 2009).

18.3.3 Concepts can change over time

Concepts are not always clear-cut entities which, when defined by a scientific discipline, remain the same once and for all. They can be further specified or completely redefined as knowledge in a scientific area evolves.

Consider the concept of 'atom', which until the 1800s was defined as an indivisible entity but which has evolved considerably since then. (The word *atom* derives from Greek *atomos* whose meaning is, precisely, 'indivisible'.) The atom was first broken down into three specific parts: electrons, protons, and neutrons. More recently, other elementary particles, i.e. quarks, were isolated and the structure of the atom could no longer be described in terms of three subatomic particles. Recent theories propose new elementary particles, such as types of bosons and lepton.

The changes in the conceptions of 'atom' are now recognized and well established. In addition, this is a case where scientists had to react rather quickly in order to adjust

[3] 'The term is a "construct", i.e. it results from the analysis carried out by the terminologist: this analysis takes into account the place of the term in a corpus, a validation by an expert, *and the objectives of a specific terminological description*' (my translation and emphasis).

a universal definition. In many other fields of knowledge, concepts and the linguistic expressions used to label them can go through considerable instability before experts agree on a definition. For instance, the series of phenomena affecting climate in the world were originally labelled as *global warming*. More recently, experts tend to agree on a more general designation, i.e. *climate change*. But 'climate change' has not yet been defined as clearly as atoms, and is still being debated in different circles.

The examples presented in this section, and many others, show that knowledge is construed gradually and undergoes change over time. Terminologists and organizations involved in the standardization of terms must adjust to changes that occur when new items of knowledge appear in a discipline. Changes must be taken into account in definitions and in the choice of designations. In addition, experts involved in knowledge modelling must accept that even a consensual conceptualization will probably be modified in the future.

Temmerman (2000) takes this issue a step further and argues that in the life sciences most concepts do not in fact lend themselves to a clear-cut and straightforward delimitation. She suggests adopting the notion of 'unit of understanding' rather than 'concept'. Units of understanding result from a cognitive process according to which we capture knowledge in a field, and are best defined in terms of prototype structure.

18.3.4 Relations between concepts are diversified and complex

Knowledge representations (conceptual structures or ontologies) illustrate how concepts are related to each other with explicit links. Figs. 18.1 and 18.2 show that taxa and peripheral devices are related in terms of generic-specific (taxonomic) relations. Peripheral devices can also share part–whole relations with other concepts ('button' vs. 'mouse'). These relations are those that naturally apply to entities (animals, machines, instruments, etc.) and frequently appear in conceptual structures. Some prioritize taxonomic relations (e.g. types of peripheral devices or vehicles); others favour part–whole relations (e.g. human or animal anatomy).

However, when other types of concept (processes, properties) are taken into account, many different relations emerge. The examples in (3), taken from Sager (1990: 34), illustrate this diversity. Fig. 18.4 shows that a single concept in the field of the environment can be related to other concepts in many different ways.

(3)	FALLOUT	is caused by	NUCLEAR EXPLOSION
	PAPER	is a product of	WOOD PULP
	COMPRESSIBILITY	is a property of	GAS
	TEMPERATURE	is a quantitative measure of	HEAT
	COMPUTER	is an instrument for	DATA PROCESSING
	INSECTICIDE	is a counteragent of	INSECT

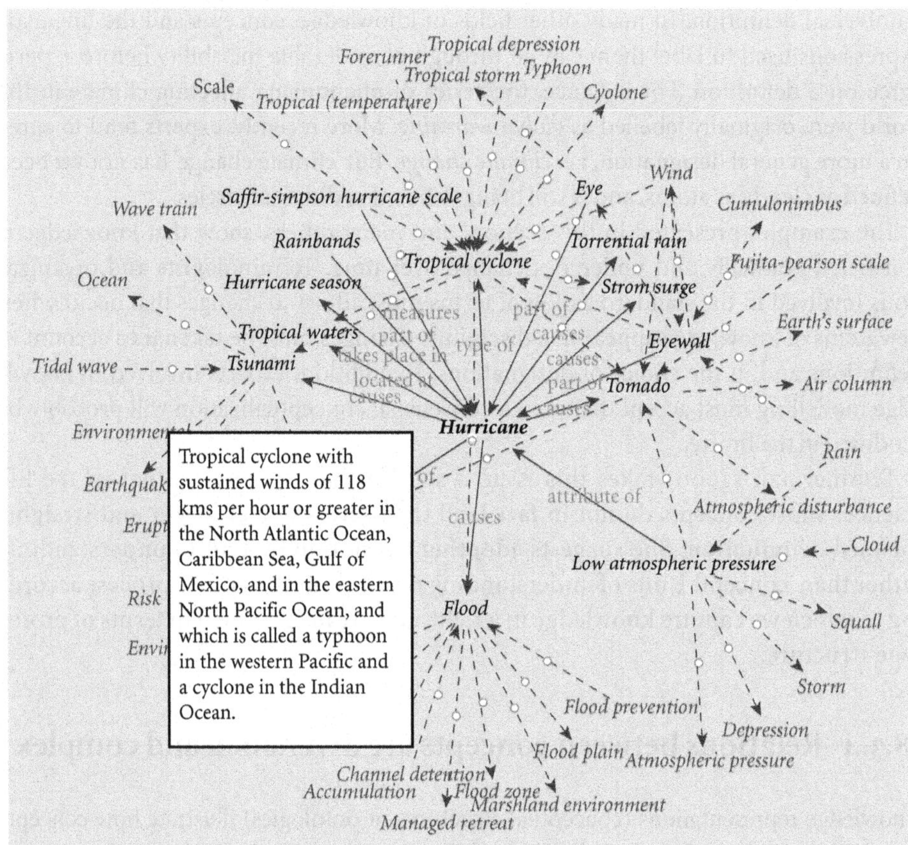

FIG. 18.4 Relations between 'hurricane' and other concepts in the field of the environment (Buendía and Faber 2012). Reproduced with permission.

The extent to which these relations are represented depends on the special subject field and the conceptualization it implements.

18.3.5 Variants do not occur accidentally

One of the main criticisms levelled at traditional terminology is that it considers the existence of synonyms or variants as something that is accidental and often undesirable. The existence of variants is quite common in all fields of knowledge, and may be caused by one or a combination of the following factors.

- Level of specialization: Specialized knowledge can be conveyed in many different forms (reports, peer-reviewed journals, lectures, conferences, etc.: Sager et al. 1980) and involves different kinds of participant (experts to experts; experts to laypeople: Pearson 1998). This diversity of forms, addressees, and producers inevitably results in different choices of terms. For instance, a medical doctor, while compelled to use *cardiopathy* in a scientific journal, may use *heart disease* or alternate between *cardiopathy* and *heart disease* if speaking to a wider audience. Even in extreme examples such as those given for zoology or chemistry, official names or symbols usually coexist with non-official ones (e.g. popular names for animals and plants) used in less formal situations. One of the first alternative approaches to traditional terminology, namely socioterminology (Gaudin 2003), highlighted that the same concept could be labelled differently according to the category of experts referring to it. For instance, in a manufacturing plant, engineers, technicians, and managers can refer to the same process with different designations. Socioterminology suggests that these different terms should be collected and better understood, rather than suppressed by imposing a single label for everyone.

- Regional differences: Differences may occur in the same language spoken in different parts of the world. This phenomenon, which has long been recognized in common language, also prevails in specialized languages. Speakers of French in France and Québec use different terms to refer to concepts in the field of computing: French *spam* vs. Québec *pourriel*. This also applies to usage in Spain and some South American countries: Spanish *ordenador* vs. Mexican *computadora* (for 'computer'). When recommending or standardizing terms, agencies—since many adopt regulations at the national level—can promote different terms as standards, since they focus on usage within their own jurisdictions.
- Historical evolution: Changes in science and technology mentioned in section 18.3.3 have repercussions on the designations used to label concepts. Dury (1999) discusses how the concept 'ecosystem' evolved since it was first created, and the different terms that have been used in English and French since the first half of the 20th century. In English, different competing terms were used by experts—*community, biotic community, biosystem*, etc. (some of them covering slightly different concepts)—before *ecosystem* was finally established. The instability accompanying new concepts can also be reflected in competing designations. When Internet chatting became a popular activity, different names were used in English (*chat, chatting, Web chat*, etc.) as well as in French (*chat, tchat, barvardage en ligne, cyberbavardarge, clavardage*).
- Attempts at differentiation: Experts can deliberately create new designations for existing concepts. They might also wish to introduce a new distinction and show that the concept to which they are referring differs somehow from an existing one. For example, *complementizer* was introduced in generative grammar to refer to what is called a *subordinating conjunction* in traditional grammar. Companies might want to create new terms for existing concepts in order to establish their own standard or promote a new product or process (several examples exist in the computer and pharmaceutical industries).
- An effort to vary phrasing in a text: Authors of specialized texts may want to vary the ways they refer to entities or phenomena. This can be to introduce a nuance

> or simply for stylistic purposes. For instance, in a French text on global warming, the following expressions may be found: *réchauffement climatique* (lit. *climatic warming*), *réchauffement du climat* (lit. *climate warming*), *réchauffement global* (lit. *global warming*), *réchauffement de la planète* (lit. *warming of the planet*), etc.

Variants are phenomena that must be described in all applications where terms are identified or produced in text. Translators, for instance, must be able to recognize that the same meaning can be conveyed by different forms. They can decide to standardize the target text by using a single equivalent for source-language variants or, conversely, use similar variants in the target language. Some variants—those recognized as true synonyms—are also listed by terminologists in term records (cf. Fig. 18.3) but often one of them is identified as preferred. In knowledge modelling, variants are also often taken into account. But here again, a standard form serves as the reference and others appear as other possible linguistic forms for the expression of the concept, as shown in Fig. 18.5.

Typologies of term variants are available in different languages. Variants are often classified into the following formal categories (some of which may not apply to all languages): orthography (*meter* vs. *metre; tool box* vs. *toolbox*); inflection (*entity* vs. *entities*; Fr. *changement climatique* vs. *changements climatiques*); permutation (*data processing* vs. *processing of data*); morphology (*climate change* vs. *climatic change*); surface syntax (*coffre à outils* vs. *coffre d'outils*, '*toolbox*'); and morphosyntax (*data processing* vs. *to process data*) (Daille et al. 1996). Different techniques have been developed to process variants automatically (Jacquemin 2001).

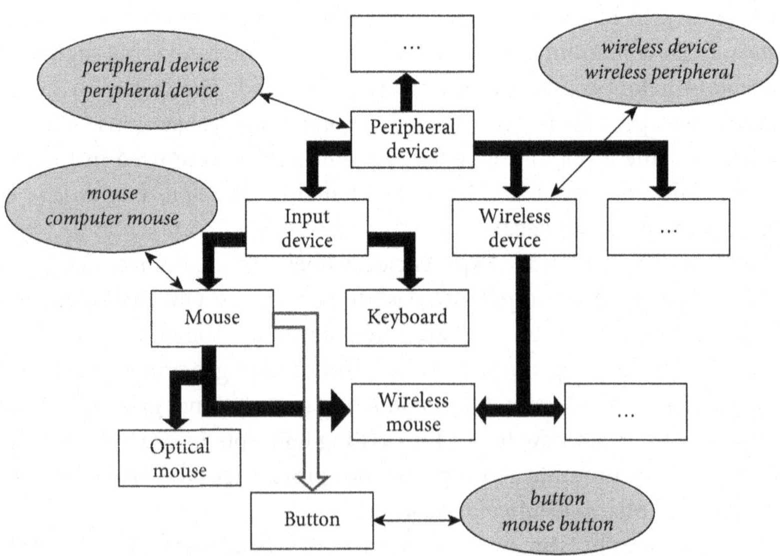

FIG. 18.5 Variants in a conceptual structure.

18.3.6 Knowledge is conveyed by different types of linguistic units

The emphasis placed on concepts and conceptual structures in terminology, but also in other endeavours concerned with knowledge modelling, tend to give more importance to entities linguistically expressed by nouns.

However, other concepts refer to activities and properties, and these are not prototypically expressed by nouns (although they can be). Events and processes can be expressed by verbs (e.g. *configure, constitutionalize, pollute*) and properties are often designated by adjectives (*sustainable, dynamic*). In knowledge modelling they are often considered as variants of nouns. For instance, if clicking is considered a relevant activity in computing, *to click* and *click* (as a noun) will be considered two linguistic variants that refer to the same concept.

However, Estopà (2001) noted that experts, translators, and terminologists identify other parts of speech as relevant terms (cf. section 18.3.1). The study does not state whether the units of other categories convey meanings that are otherwise expressed by nouns. In another small study (L'Homme 2012), it was shown that non-experts and experts, when asked to read sentences and decide whether verbs are specialized or not, unanimously classify some verbs as specialized and hesitate with others. Examples of such sentences are reproduced in (3).

(3) [Informatique] Avec ce type de connexion, vous pouvez **naviguer** rapidement dans Internet. ([Computing] With this kind of connection, you can **browse** the Internet rapidly.)

[Environnement] L'extraction ou la récolte de ces ressources peuvent également ***polluer*** le sol, l'eau et l'air. ([Environment] Extracting or harvesting these resources can also **pollute** the soil, water, and air.)

All respondents agree that *naviguer* is specialized whereas *polluer* is classified as a specialized verb by only half. These observations raise the issue of the role of verbs in knowledge communication. Some answers to these questions are provided in the literature, but there is no general agreement as to how verbs (or adjectives) should be processed in terminology.

Some authors have suggested factors according to which verbs may be considered more or less specialized (Condamines 1993; Lerat 2002; Lorente 2002). Some verbs can only be found in one special subject field (this would apply to the verb *download* in computing), while others acquire a new meaning (this applies to the French *naviguer* in computing; its original meaning is 'to sail').

Some work has focused on defining linguistic criteria for deciding which verbs should be included in specialized dictionaries (L'Homme 1998). One criterion takes into account the nature of arguments. If arguments are expressed by terms, then the verb is likely to be a term. For instance, the fact that the verb *install* combines with computing terms (as in *a user installs a program on his PC; the word processor can be installed on your laptop*), makes it a likely candidate for terminological status.

18.3.7 Polysemy and ambiguity

Some lexical items may have more than one meaning even when considered from a single subject field (cf. *email* in section 18.2). Examples can be found in many other fields of knowledge. *Aerosol* can refer to 'a suspension of solid or liquid particles in a gas' or 'a chemical substance that is dispersed in the air for different purposes'. *Law* can be defined as a discipline or a specific regulation. In specialized term banks and dictionaries, these meanings are usually described in different entries. In multilingual terminology work, meaning distinctions in one language can lead to the recording of different equivalents in the other.

Some polysemous terms can become ambiguous when used in text. In the field of computing, for example, *download* can convey an activity, i.e. 'the act of downloading', but also a result, i.e. 'a file that can be or has been downloaded'. In some sentences, each meaning can be clearly identified (e.g. *a download that never finishes; the download is an executable file*); in others, the distinctions cannot be made as easily (e.g. *The user sends back brief instructions and waits for the next download*).

Another form of ambiguity affects multi-word terms. This problem, called 'structural ambiguity', is caused by the fact that the syntactic and semantic relations between the components of a noun phrase cannot be properly identified without extralinguistic knowledge. For instance, to understand *main fuel system drain valve*, one needs to know that '*main* applies to *fuel system*, not to *fuel* or *drain valve*, and that … (the expression) refers to a valve whose function is to drain the main fuel system' (Lehrberger 2003: 213).

18.3.8 Terms do not reflect knowledge organization perfectly

Traditional terminology (as well as some applications of knowledge modelling) is based on an implicit and very strong assumption that there is a perfect correspondence between knowledge representations and terms. In other words, there should be a linguistic expression for each concept identified in specialized knowledge.

There are a number of indications to the contrary. First, scientific classifications or conceptual representations result from the application of criteria that take into account only part of the characteristics of the concepts involved. In zoology, for instance, birds are defined as animals that have feathers and lay eggs. Flying, a natural activity carried out by most birds, is not considered as a relevant characteristic from the point of view of classification. However, it will often be expressed in language. The same applies to whales, which live in water but are not classified as fish. Knowledge in a field is usually much more complex than can be captured in taxonomies or ontologies. In addition, some categories in knowledge representations are created solely for the purpose of classifying entities; linguistic labels are created afterwards.

Although it is assumed that both knowledge and language have an underlying structure, these structures obey different rules and are subject to different constraints (Hirst 2009). Hirst was referring to everyday language, but the differences also apply to terminologies. L'Homme and Bernier-Colborne (2012) compared the contents of two ontologies with that of a specialized dictionary, and found that only a few linguistic items could be found in both repositories.

18.4 Concluding remarks

This chapter first discussed the importance of defining naming conventions in specialized subject fields. Whilst these efforts are necessary in specific communication situations, they are also difficult to put into place. Any attempt at regulating the creation and the use of terms (even in very specific special subject fields) requires a great deal of effort. It also underlined the fact that advocates of these naming conventions (experts and terminologists) have probably underestimated or overlooked the linguistic properties of the terms they were regulating or replacing with more standard or universal names.

The theoretical models and methods first devised by terminology were clearly defined for the purpose of standardizing terms. It is now recognized that the principles were too inflexible and that they should be redefined (partially for some, completely for others) in order to take into account the linguistic expressiveness of terms and their behaviour in text.

As of today, no generally accepted model has imposed itself as a way of dealing with the two opposing forces at play in specialized knowledge communication. Some proposals, however, seem to point in that direction. Sager (1990) described terminology as a set of activities that can be considered from three different perspectives: cognitive (concepts and relations between concepts), linguistic (formation of terms and relations between designations and concepts), and communicative (the purpose for which terminology work is undertaken). The Communicative Theory of Terminology (Cabré 2003) proposes a model in which terms are viewed as polyhedrons and, as such, can lend themselves to different kinds of analysis (cognitive, linguistic, or communicative), each shedding a different light on the properties and functioning of terms.

CHAPTER 19

LEXICAL RELATIONS

CHRISTIANE FELLBAUM

19.1 Introduction

The lexicon is the inventory of the words of a language. Several properties distinguish it from other language components. First, the lexicon is huge: it has been estimated that speakers of American English with a high-school education have a passive knowledge of approximately 60,000 root words (Miller 1991). Knowing the phonological, morphological, collocational, syntactic, and semantic properties of tens of thousands of words seems a far greater feat than mastering the rules of syntax or the sounds of one's language. Second, speakers' acquisition of the lexicon is never completed. While the rules of phonology, syntax, and morphology are mostly acquired by around the age of 5, the lexicon keeps growing at an astonishing rate, though the learning curve flattens off around the age of 10 (Carey 1978, 1988). Finally, the lexicon is dynamic and changes at a much faster rate than other parts of a language; even linguistically naive speakers are aware of lexical innovation and obsolescence. New words appear daily while others fall into disuse, and words often change their connotative or denotative meaning.

These properties make the fact that speakers effortlessly and effectively access their lexicon when encoding and decoding messages all the more impressive. It seems safe to assume efficient, economic mechanisms for storing and retrieving lexical items and the associated knowledge, but a comprehensive theory of the lexicon that is able to fully account for all the above observations is still outstanding. It is highly likely that the lexicon is a structured rather than a random collection of words, and that lexicalization—the labelling of concepts with words—follows patterns that are accessible to speakers (though most are unaware of them and unable to articulate them).

Different properties of words—phonological, morphological, and syntactic—lend themselves to orthogonal organizations of the lexicon. Traditional paper dictionaries are organized orthographically to allow for straightforward searches. But spelling and phonology are merely formal aspects of words that, with few exceptions, have nothing to do with their meanings or with the way speakers use words to communicate. There is ample evidence that words in speakers' minds are largely organized by meaning (see section 19.8.1), though word association data and the 'tip-of-the-tongue' phenomenon (Brown and McNeill 1966) show that phonemic, prosodic, and rhyming similarities also connect words in the mental lexicon.

Levin (1993) offers an organization of the English verb lexicon based on shared syntactic privileges of verbs; for example, verbs of transfer (*give, sell, send*, etc.) are identified as a class by virtue of the fact that they participate in the so-called Dative Alternation (*I gave/sold/sent Charles my laptop; I gave/sold/sent my laptop to Charles*). Levin showed that the members of such syntactically based classes are also semantically similar and share sublexical meaning components such as MOVE and CAUSE. Semantic similarity among verbs allows speakers to unconsciously assign neologisms like *fax* and *tweet* to the class of transfer verbs and use them in sentences like *I faxed/tweeted the news to Bob* and *I faxed/tweeted Bob the news*.

The observable regularities of the lexicon also constrain its growth and allow a characterization of both 'possible' and 'impossible' words (Carter 1976; Levin 1993; Pinker 1989). For example, there are no simplex English verbs that mean 'go to X', where X is a location like *New York* or *the office*, nor are there verbs with multiple CAUSE meaning components, such as 'cause to kill' (cause to cause to be dead) (Carter 1976). Lexicalization patterns, which tend to vary across languages, are regular and productive because words bear specific relations to one another, transparent to speakers. Meaning relations can thus be considered a 'glue' that connects words and the concepts they express to one another.

In a relational model of the lexicon, the meaning of a word is constituted by its relations to other words, in particular its semantic relations. Such a model is supported by rich psycholinguistic data from child language acquisition (Keil 1989; Malt this volume), word association norms (De Deyne and Storms this volume) as well as by the co-occurrence preferences of words.

In the remainder of this chapter, we examine the nature of specific relations and their role in the lexicon.

19.2 Relations: lexical vs. conceptual-semantic

There are many ways to relate words to one another. One broad distinction is that between lexical relations, which hold among word forms, and conceptual-semantic relations, which hold among concepts. One lexical relation is synonymy, as between the word forms *car, auto, motor car*, and *automobile*. Another is antonymy, which holds between specific word pairs. Thus, *big* and *little* are in an antonymic relation, as are *large* and *small*. While *big* and *large*, and *little* and *small*, are synonyms, the strong relation among the word-specific pairs is reflected in textual co-occurrence (Justeson and Katz 1995) and association data (see section 19.8).

An example of a conceptual-semantic relation is meronymy, the part–whole relation. It applies equally to *wheel–car* and to *wheel–automobile*, as *car* and *automobile* are synonyms and thus express the same concept. Similarly, both *vehicle–car* and *vehicle–automobile* are related by hyponymy, the superordinate relation. Neither the part–whole relation nor hyponymy is sensitive to specific word forms.

Although we distinguish lexical and conceptual relations, a given lexical relation implies a semantic-conceptual relation. Thus, the fact that only *large* and *small* but not *large* and *little* share the same distributions and strongly evoke each other does not negate the fact that *large* and *little* (and *big* and *small*) are semantic opposites.

19.3 Two fundamental lexical relations among words

Two features of the lexicons of all natural languages represent a challenge to human learners and automatic language processing systems alike. These are polysemy and synonymy, which manifest the one-to-many mapping relations between word forms and word meanings.

19.3.1 Synonymy

When several different words all express (approximately) the same meaning, we have a case of synonymy. Example sets of roughly synonymous words ('synsets,' marked by curly brackets) are {*car, automobile, auto*}, {*shut, close*}, {*bright, intelligent*} and {*bright, shiny*}. There are arguably no absolute synonyms in English (or in any natural language). A more workable notion of synonymy is Cruse's (1986) 'cognitive' synonymy which applies to distinct word forms that denote that same concept and are interchangeable in some, but not all contexts. Cognitive synonymy could also include denotational differences in register (e.g. slang vs. formal) or dialectal variations (e.g. US vs. British English). Synonymy presents a speaker or writer with choices for expressing a given concept.

19.3.2 Polysemy

A single word form expressing several meanings is a case of polysemy. (We disregard the distinction between polysemy and homonymy here, as the boundary between related and unrelated word meanings is often fuzzy.) Highly polysemous words in English are *check, case*, and *line*. Some lexicographers restrict polysemy to words with multiple meanings from the same lexical class; others allow the term to cover words with distinct readings from several classes. The second kind of polysemy is frequent and regular in English, where many nouns can function as verbs (Clark and Clark 1979). An example is *bottle*, where a verb meaning 'to put into a bottle' was derived from the noun. Polysemy requires the reader or listener to identify the intended context-appropriate sense of the word form.

19.3.2.1 Regular polysemy

Some polysemy seems arbitrary, and is often due to sound or meaning shifts that modern speakers are unaware of. For example, the two meanings of *bank* ('financial institution' and 'slope by a body of water') ultimately go back to the same Germanic root **banki-* ('height'); both river banks (and sandbanks etc.) and the exchange table or bench, where moneylenders worked, are characterized by their elevation relative to the immediate surroundings. In other cases, distinct senses of a word form are transparently related, as in the case of *book* referring to the printed object and its contents. Such polysemy is often systematic and extends to all or most members of a class (Apresjan 1976). Thus, many words referring to publications (*newspaper, magazine, journal*) show the same two related meanings as *book*. Similarly, many nouns referring to fruit, vegetables, and animals have separate readings as biological entities and as food (*apple, eggplant, chicken*). Verbs of change of state or motion such as *break, crack*, and *roll, drop* show regular causative-inchoative readings (*The heat broke/cracked the plate/The plate broke/cracked; He rolled/dropped the ball/The ball rolled/dropped*). Verb-derived nominalizations like *destruction* and *examination* tend to have both process (activity) and result (product) readings (*The examination of the candidate took just a few minutes; The examination was stolen from the professor's office*).

A special case of regular polysemy is metonymy, where one reading of a polysemous word refers to the whole and the other to a part, as in the case of the 'tree–wood' readings of *beech, maple, oak*, etc., or one reading refers to an institution and the other to the people associated with it (*The White House denied the rumor of the President's affair with an intern*). Metonymy overlaps somewhat with the part–whole relation (see section 19.4.2).

Regular polysemy is productive, and speakers, when encountering a new word, readily encode and decode all its related meanings. Pustejovsky (1995) shows how the different readings of polysemous words are conditioned by their contexts. For example, the adjective *fast* means different things in phrases like *fast road, fast car, fast food*, and *fast typist*. Speakers have no trouble interpreting the meanings of the adjectives because they are constrained by the semantics of the nouns that they modify.

19.3.2.2 Less regular polysemy

In some cases, different meanings of polysemous words are in a paradigmatic relation to one another. Fellbaum (2000, 2002) collected and classified a number of English 'auto-relations'. For example, verbs like *cost* and *behave*, when occurring with a complement, have 'neutral' meanings; when occurring alone, a specific complement is implied:

The children behaved well/badly/appropriately for their age
The children behaved (= behaved well)

This trip is going to cost you $2,000
This trip is going to cost you! (= cost a lot of money)

Some word forms, like *sanction*, can refer to both members of an antonymous pair. Horn (1989) examined denominal verbs like *dust* and *milk*, which can systematically refer to either placing or removing a substance (*dust the crops/dust the furniture; milk your tea/milk the cow*).

19.3.2.3 *Metaphor*

Metaphors are less regular than metonymy, though within the domain of a 'conceptual metaphor' (Lakoff and Johnson 1980), entire nests of words can assume metaphoric readings. The sentences below illustrate the metaphoric use of verbs and adverbs in the 'time is money' metaphor:

I *spent/wasted* too much time with this student.
The student *invested* a lot of time in this project.
The professor is *generous/stingy* with his time.
She lives on *borrowed* time.
Let's *save* time by phoning instead of visiting.
This project *cost* me 4 months of my life.

Speakers easily assign the appropriate metaphoric meanings to words in such contexts.

19.3.3 The lexical matrix

Given synonymy and polysemy, one could plot the lexicon of a language as a huge matrix, where each row contains word forms referring to the same concept (i.e. synonyms), and each column contains one word form, different from those in all other columns; if the word is polysemous, it occupies several cells in that column. In this way, each cell is a unique mapping of word form and word meaning. Many columns have only one filled cell; this is the case for monosemous words. Polysemous words (columns) have as many cells filled as there are senses of the same word form. Most of the cells would be empty: too much polysemy would make disambiguation in communication difficult, and too many synonyms for expressing a given concept would pose an excessive burden on speakers' memory and would slow production. In the illustrative snippet of the lexical matrix shown in Table 19.1, the part of speech is indicated in a few places for clarity; all words in a row belong to the same lexical category.

Table 19.1 A lexical matrix

pitch (n)	tar					
pitch (n)		frequency				
pitch (v)			throw		toss	
	tar (v)			tarball		compress

Semantic-conceptual relations, which hold among multiples of groups of words expressing a given concept, link all the words in one row of the matrix to all words in one or more other rows of the matrix.

19.4 Semantic-conceptual relations: paradigmatic

Semantic-conceptual relations include paradigmatic relations, which link words from the same lexical category (or part of speech), and syntagmatic relations, which link words that tend to co-occur with one another (in a phrase) and are therefore members of different lexical categories. While paradigmatically related words can be substituted for one another in a syntactic configuration, syntagmatically related words cannot. Informally, one could think of paradigmatic relations as 'vertical' and syntagmatic relations as 'horizontal'.

19.4.1 Hyponymy

The relation that arguably interlinks most of the noun lexicon is the superordinate–subordinate relation (also called hyperonymy, hyponymy, or the ISA relation). It connects synsets referring to more general concepts like {*furniture, piece_of_furniture*} to increasingly specific ones like {*bed*} and {*bunkbed*}. Thus, a relational lexicon reflects the fact that the category *furniture* includes *bed*, which in turn includes *bunkbed*; conversely, concepts like *bed* and *bunkbed* make up the category *furniture*. Hyponymy generates hierarchies, or 'trees', in either direction, from general to specific or from specific to general concepts. The hyponymy relation is transitive: if an *armchair* is a kind of *chair*, and if a *chair* is a kind of *furniture*, then an *armchair* is a kind of *furniture*.

Hyponymy relations can be found as far back as Aristotle's *Categories*, and they have guided the hierarchical organization of Roget's thesaurus as well. Hyponymy is also reflected in traditional lexicography, where definitions often follow a classical pattern of referring to the superordinate and the distinguishing feature of the defined term (see L'Homme this volume; Malt this volume).

19.4.1.1 *Types, instances, and roles*

The diagnostic formula for hyponymy, *X is a Y*, hides in fact at least three different kinds of relation. One is the Type or Kind relation, which can be paraphrased with the formula *X is a type/kind of Y*. Thus, a *bunkbed* is a type/kind of *bed*, and a *bed* is a type/kind of *furniture*.

The Instance relation holds among general concepts, expressed by common nouns, and specific instances such as persons, countries, and geographic entities, expressed by proper nouns (or 'named entities'). Thus, while an *armchair* is a type or kind of *chair*,

Barack Obama is not a type or kind, but an instance of a president; similarly, *Zambia* is an instance of a country and the *Rhine* is an instance of a river. Instances are always leaf (terminal) nodes of a hierarchy—no instance can have a subordinate. Miller and Hristea (2006) report on their manual classification of instances in WordNet, showing that the type/instance distinction is not always clear-cut. For example, *Bible* can be seen both as an instance of *book* (the Christian Bible) but also as a type of book, with hyponyms like *King James Bible* and *Vulgate Bible*.

Another distinct relation encoded by the formula *X is a Y*, is that of role. Nouns like *president* and *chairman* encode roles rather than types. A hallmark of roles is that they are not time-independent: a person may bear a role such as chairman or president for only a limited time; by contrast, a person will always be a *type* of a biological creature. Types, but not roles, encode 'rigid' or necessary properties of an entity (Gangemi et al. 2002). Roles can be lexically encoded in word pairs that denote the related nouns. Such relational noun pairs include *parent–son/daughter* and *teacher–student*. (Note that biological relations such as *father–child* are rigid.) *Friend* implies at least two people in a friend-of relation to each other (a friendship-giving and a friendship-receiving person), though there is only one relational noun, *friend*, for both.

19.4.2 Meronymy

Another important bidirectional relation is meronymy, the part–whole relation. It holds between holonym synsets like {*chair*} and meronyms such as {*back, backrest*}, {*seat*}, and {*leg*}. Parts are inherited from their superordinates: if a *chair* has *legs*, then an *armchair* has *legs* as well. Parts are not inherited 'upward', as they may be characteristic only of specific kinds of things rather than the class as a whole. Thus, *chairs* and kinds of *chair* have legs, but not all kinds of *furniture* have legs. Entities that can be, but are not necessarily, parts of a whole present a particular difficulty; consider *freckles* or *embryo*, which are body parts only for some people or for a certain time period.

Meronymic relations can be distinguished with different degrees of granularity. For example, Winston, Chaffin, and Herrmann (1987) distinguish six kinds of meronymy, compared with WordNet's coarser classification of three types (Fellbaum 1998).

19.4.3 Antonymy, contrast, semantic opposition

Relations among contrasting words are intuitively accessible to speakers and require little reflection. *Hot* readily evokes *cold*, and *open–close* and *man–woman* seem like clearly contrasting pairs. Lyons (1995) distinguishes several contrast relations, including complementarity (*blue–red*), gradable antonymy (*long–short*), and a converse relation (*give–take*) (see also section 19.7.3).

19.5 Syntagmatic relations

Within a context, only one of multiple paradigmatically related words can appear in any given slot. By contrast, syntagmatic relations hold among words that are found in close proximity to one another within a context. Examinations of text corpora reveal systematic patterns of co-occurrences as well as the statistically measurable 'strength' of specific co-occurrences based on their frequency.

19.5.1 Selectional preferences and mutual information

Words that co-occur in close proximity of one another must necessarily be meaningfully related; otherwise, the message is unlikely to make sense. Noam Chomsky's famous sentence *colorless green ideas sleep furiously* is a classic example of a syntactically well-formed but semantically odd string. Put informally, the sentence does not agree with our world knowledge; linguistically, its oddity derives from the violation of selectional preference rules. The verb *sleep* does not select for an inanimate, abstract subject like *idea* nor an adverb like *furiously*. Selectional preferences can be stated in terms of the concepts that are compatible with one another in a given context; in addition, they are often lexically specific. Church and Hanks' (1990) classic example is the contrast between *powerful tea* vs. *strong tea* on the one hand and *powerful computer* vs. *strong computer* on the other hand. Both adjectives have approximately the same meaning, but the two nouns are selective with respect to which adjective they co-occur with: *strong tea* and *powerful computer* are the preferred pairings. Church and Hanks proposed pointwise mutual information (PMI) as a corpus-based statistical measure of the collocational properties of words, and noted that PMI is a predictor of human association norms (De Deyne and Storms, this volume). Collocational patterns could be viewed as relations between specific words, though they are preferences rather than absolutes.

19.6 Relations in lexical resources

Traditional dictionaries, besides their obvious spelling-based organization, in fact contain an implicit structure based on semantic relations. They strive to represent word meanings in terms of informative and unambiguous definitions, often accompanied by illustrative examples. Standardly, a word is defined in terms of its superordinate (more general) concept and salient properties that distinguish it from the superordinate as well as other concepts with which it shares that superordinate. The words in the definitions (the definiens) are necessarily related in meaning to the defined word (the definiendum). But there is no obvious (non-local) way in which the definiendum and the words in the definition fit into the larger lexicon; one would have to look up all the words in the definition, their definitions, and so forth to arrive at a coherent, more global picture of the lexicon. Efforts at parsing definitions (Byrd et al. 1987) have revealed the regularity of definitions at least for the noun lexicon.

A thesaurus is a particular kind of dictionary that serves language users who have a concept in mind and are looking for words to express it. The implicit assumption is that the user is familiar with the words and their meanings but is looking for the best 'fit' for a specific context. Thesauri therefore do not offer definitions, but present words that are semantically similar. Roget's thesaurus is composed of broad semantic classes that contain narrower divisions; these in turn are broken up into more fine-grained sections. The sections are clusters of words whose relations to one another are not spelled out, but inspection shows that they include relations like synonymy and antonymy.

19.7 WordNet: a lexicon based on relations

WordNet (Fellbaum 1998; Miller 1995; Miller and Fellbaum 1991; Miller et al. 1990), a manually constructed lexical database for English, can be thought of as a large electronic dictionary organized around relations.[1] It contains information about some 155,000 nouns, verbs, adjectives, and adverbs, including simplex words like *put*, phrasal verbs like *put up*, and idioms like *put out the dog*. Its digital format frees WordNet from the constraints of traditional paper dictionaries where entries are arranged according to their spelling. Instead, WordNet aims to inform users about word meanings, and words are organized in terms of their semantics. Specifically, words in WordNet that are similar in meaning are interlinked by means of labelled pointers that stand for semantic relations. Formally, WordNet is a semantic network, an acyclic graph in which automatic systems can 'travel' along the edges connecting related words and concepts and, on the basis of their distance to one another, quantify their semantic similarity.

The building blocks of WordNet are groups of synonyms (words that are interchangeable in many but not all contexts), dubbed 'synsets'. Polysemy is reflected in the different synsets that a given word form occurs in; membership in *n* synsets means that the word has *n* meanings, or is *n*-fold polysemous. In this way, each form–meaning pair in WordNet is unique.

Synsets were constructed for each major lexical category, nouns, verbs, adjectives, and adverbs. Because the semantic relations for each lexical category differ somewhat, WordNet in fact consists of four largely unconnected semantic networks.

[1] Users can browse the WordNet database by accessing the website wordnet.princeton.edu.

19.7.1 Relations among nouns in WordNet

The most frequently encoded relation among noun synsets is hyponymy, which creates hierarchical tree structures up to seventeen levels deep. All noun synsets have a single shared root, *entity*. WordNet distinguishes types and instances, as discussed in section 19.4.1, though roles have not been separately encoded. Three types of meronymy relations (proper parts, as in *leg–chair*), substances (*oxygen–water*), and members (*tree–forest*) are distinguished. There are only few antonym relations (*man–woman, love–hate*).

19.7.2 Relations among verbs in WordNet

Verbs refer to events and states that are anchored in time and space, and events necessarily involve participants that are expressed by the verbs' arguments. Verbs are thus arguably more complex concepts than nouns, and a relational approach to verb meanings is less straightforward. Fellbaum (1990) argues that verbs can be interrelated by means of a 'troponymy' relation, which resembles hyponymy but distinguishes verbs based on the 'manner' with which the action is performed. Troponymically related verb synsets can be arranged into hierarchies where verbs express increasingly specific manners characterizing an event. An example is {*move*}–{*run*}–{*jog*}. The specific manner expressed can elaborate the more general event along many different dimensions; speed-of-motion (as in {*move*}–{*run*}–{*jog*}), medium-of-motion (as in {*move*}–{*swim*}), or intensity-of-emotion (as in {*like*}–{*love*}–{*idolize*}).

Different languages show different patterns of such manner elaborations. A much-discussed typological distinction (Talmy 1985) is that between languages like French and Nez Percé that typically encode the fact of motion and direction in a single verb (*entrer, sortir*), whereas languages like English and Chinese prefer to conflate fact of motion and manner into a single lexeme (*float, run*).

Additional links among verb synsets encode the necessary entailment of different events. For example, {*listen*} entails {*hear*} in that every time that someone listens to a sound, he necessarily also hears the sound. A second kind of entailment holds among two events that follow in temporal order, such as *try–succeed*; in order to succeed, one must necessarily have tried. Finally, causation is expressed in the links among pairs like *give–have*. In each case, the entailment is unidirectional: the event expressed by the first verb necessarily entails that expressed by the second verb, but not vice versa (Fellbaum 1990).

19.7.3 Relations among adjectives in WordNet

Adjectives in WordNet are interlinked via the antonymy relation; this representation is strongly supported by psycholinguistic evidence (Gross, Fischer, and Miller 1989; K. Miller 1998). Pairs of 'direct' antonyms like *wet–dry* and *young–old* reflect the strong semantic contrast between the members. The intensity of this relation is shown in the fact that they bring each other to mind, as reflected in association norms. Additional textual support was provided by Justeson and Katz (1995), who demonstrated that direct antonyms co-occur in the same sentence with far greater frequency than chance. Each of WordNet's polar adjectives in turn is linked to a number of 'semantically similar' ones. For example, *dry* is linked to adjectives including *parched, arid, dessicated,* and *bone-dry.* These adjectives are dubbed 'indirect antonyms,' as their relation to both the polar adjectives (*wet*) and to its similar adjectives (*soggy, waterlogged,* etc.) seems less strong. Direct antonyms are characterized by higher frequency, greater polysemy, and consequently a greater range of nouns that they can modify: *soil, weather, dishes, clothes,* and *lips* can all be both *dry* and *wet*, while indirect antonyms are more specific in their meaning and hence more selective of their nouns (*soggy/*waterlogged bread, parched/*arid throats*).

Sheinman and Tokunaga (2009) and Sheinman et al. (2013) discuss an intensity relation among dimensional and evaluative adjectives that label different points on a scale. Such a relation would link adjectives like *good–great–fantastic.* Fellbaum and Mathieu (2011) extend the intensity relation to emotion verbs and nouns, such as *like–love–venerate.*

19.7.4 Morphosemantic relations

WordNet contains a syntagmatic relation, dubbed 'morphosemantic,' which links words and word families that are both semantically related and derived from a shared stem by regular morphological processes (Fellbaum and Miller 2003). For example, the members of the verb synset {*conduct, lead, direct*} and the derived nouns in the synset {*conductor, director, music_director*} share a core meaning. Another sense of *direct*, in the synset {*direct, manage*}, is linked to {*director, manager, managing_director*} and {*directorship*}. Traditional dictionaries often list the derivations as run-ons but do not distinguish their senses. The relation among many noun–verb pairs can be specified in terms of the semantic role that the noun plays in the event. Thus, {*sleeper, sleeping_car*} is the LOCATION for {*sleep*}, and {*painter*}is the AGENT of {*paint*}, while {*painting, picture*} is its RESULT (Fellbaum, Osherson, and Clark 2009). The kinds and number of these semantic relations depends on the grainedness of one's classification, but likely candidates include AGENT, CAUSE, INSTRUMENT, and LOCATION.

19.7.5 Automatic identification of related words in corpora

Cruse (1986) notes that semantically related words can be discovered with diagnostic tests in the form of lexical-semantic patterns. For example, *Xs and other Ys* is a pattern in which *X* is a hyponym (subordinate) of *Y*, as in *roses and other flowers.* The pattern *Ys such as X* similarly establishes *Y* as a hypernym (superordinate) of *X* (*flowers such as roses*). Hearst (1992) showed that the availability of searchable text corpora allows one to apply such patterns and detect correspondingly related words. Snow et al. (2006) automatically augment WordNet's noun hierarchy by means of this technique. Chlovsky and Pantel (2004) and Fellbaum (2013) show that lexical-semantic patterns can also be used to identify verbs related in a number of different ways. Sheinman and Tokunaga (2009) demonstrate the use of patterns to derive partial orderings among scalar adjectives that express different degrees of a shared attribute; in cases like *if not X then at least Y, Y* is the less intense adjective relative to *X* (*if not great then at least good*). New patterns can be discovered in a corpus by searching for a pre-classified word pair (Sheinman and Tokunaga 2009; Schulam and Fellbaum 2010 for German adjectives).

19.8 What is the evidence for relations?

An examination of the lexicon readily reveals systematic and productive lexicalization patterns that can be formulated in terms of relations such as hyponymy, meronymy, and antonymy, familiar to lexicographers for centuries. WordNet has identified and encoded some additional relations. But how many relations are there that can be said to indicate the way speakers label concepts, and is the number of relations finite? What is the evidence for relations, beyond lexicographic analysis?

19.8.1 Psycholinguistic evidence

Psychologists interested in the organization of the mental lexicon have long been aware of the importance of word associations. Given a stimulus word, participants are asked to respond with the first word that comes to mind. In many cases, the same response is given by a majority of the participants, showing that the associations are remarkably uniform and entrenched. Moreover, they are similar across different populations (age, gender, language) and stable across time. An inspection of the association norms that have been compiled (Moss and Older 1996; Palermo and Jenkins 1964) shows that stimulus and response words are often semantically related in a way that can be captured by paradigmatic or syntagmatic relations (Chaffin and Fellbaum 1990). A particularly robust, bidirectional association exists between lexically specific pairs of antonymous adjective such as *hot* and *cold, long* and *short*. The psychological reality of this association was explored in an experiment by Gross, Fischer, and Miller (1989), and inspired WordNet's treatment of this lexical category. Moreover, as noted in section 19.5.1, the statistical analysis of Church and Hanks (1990) proves to be a good predictor of association norms.

Hyponymy and meronymy in particular seem to lend themselves to an efficient organization for words, concepts, and knowledge about concepts. Collins and Quillian (1969) proposed and tested a semantic-network model of human memory that tried to explain how people can store and retrieve information about tens of thousands of concepts. Concepts and the words expressing them are organized into hierarchies.

A concept at a given level in the hierarchy inherits by default all the properties from its superordinate (more general) concept; only those properties that distinguish a concept from its superordinate are stored with the more specific concept. Thus, speakers know that a canary can fly because they know that a canary is a bird and that birds can fly; but the knowledge that a canary is yellow is linked to the concept canary itself rather than inherited.

19.8.2 Evocation

Many associations are syntagmatic, i.e., among words that speakers frequently use together, such as *blue* and *sky* and *sweater* and *knit*. Boyd-Graber et al. (2006) collected some 100,000 judgements from speakers about the degree with which one concept evokes another (both concepts were presented in the form of WordNet synsets so as to avoid ambiguity arising from polysemy). The synsets represented all four major lexical categories and the participants were not asked to specify the nature of the relations between them. The results showed that, in addition to the familiar paradigmatic relations, words that tend to be found within the same context strongly evoke one another. As expected, the degree of evocation was not the same for both directions: while *dollar* evokes *green*, *green* evokes *dollar* much less strongly. A systematic classification of all the relations among the synsets that were judged to evoke one another seems a difficult, if not impossible, undertaking despite their intuitive relatedness.

19.9 Relations in the lexicons of other languages

How universal are the kinds of relation discussed in this chapter? The creation of wordnets in dozens of other languages gives an indication. EuroWordNet (Vossen 1998) comprises eight European languages, including Estonian, Greek, and Basque, which are genetically and typologically unrelated. An important goal of EuroWordNet was to connect all wordnets to one another, so that equivalent words and meanings could easily be identified. EuroWordNet took the Princeton WordNet as its hub, to which each new wordnet was mapped.

Unsurprisingly, it was found that not all languages lexicalize the same concepts. Moreover, the lexicons of some languages encode relations not found in others. For example, many languages lexically distinguish male and female members of the same class more systematically than English, which has relatively few such pairs (*actor* and *actress*, as well as *masseur* and *masseuse*, borrowed from French). Slavic languages distinguish systematically among verbs denoting a completed event and those expressing an imperfective event. Such relations arguably cross the border between lexicon and morphology.

An interesting case is presented by Semitic languages like Arabic and Hebrew, which generate semantically related words from a common tri-consonantal root denoting a general concept via patterns associated with specific meanings; these meanings can be expressed and encoded by relations among the roots (which are not lexemes) and the derived words (Black et al. 2006). Another kind of challenge for a relational approach to the lexicon is posed by languages with semantic classifiers, such as Zulu and Xhosa (LeRoux, Bosch, and Fellbaum 2007). These classifiers label broad categories, such as person, animal, food, and they attach as bound morphemes to the words that are members of a given category. Classifiers could be seen as a kind of semantic relation among all words in a given class. But such a classification does not always agree with one based on canonical relations like hyponymy and meronymy. Thus, Lakoff (1987) reports that in Dyirbal, an Australian Native language, women and fire are classified together in the 'dangerous things' category. In the lexicon of Cree, an Algonquin language, hyponymy appears not to be represented at all (Marie-Odile Junker, p.c.). Thus, while many languages share core relations (Fellbaum and Vossen 2012), they are not universal.

19.10 Conclusions

WordNet has shown that is possible to construct a relational lexicon of English, where each word is connected to others by means of a handful of semantic relations and where the meaning of a word is represented in terms of its relations to others. Well-known, possibly near-universal relations like hyponymy, meronymy, and antonymy seem predominant in the lexicon. More fine-grained versions of these as well as completely different relations arguably exist, but a full inventory and understanding of relations in the lexicon remains a challenge for lexicologists, lexicographers, and theoretical and computational linguists.

Acknowledgements

The preparation of this chapter has been supported by grant CNS 0855157 from the U.S. National Science Foundation and a grant from the Tim Gill Foundation.

CHAPTER 20

COMPARING LEXICONS CROSS-LINGUISTICALLY

ASIFA MAJID

20.1 Introduction

The study of how meaning is packaged into words is simultaneously the most fascinating and vexing of topics. Best-selling books such as *The Meaning of Tingo and Other Extraordinary Words from Around the World* (de Boinod 2006) and *They Have a Word for It: A Lighthearted Lexicon of Untranslatable Words* (Rheingold 1988) are testament to the interest the public have for learning about curiosities in other languages. But this same popular interest can result in scholars viewing cross-linguistic meaning as merely that—a charming curiosity not worthy of serious attention. It turns out, however, that the lexicon is central to many broad questions that occupy psychologists, linguists, and anthropologists, such as: Where does meaning come from? How similar are the meanings of words across communities? How are language and thought connected?

Some suppose that the stock of concepts expressed in the lexicon is universal and innate. This is based (partly) on the 'venerable view' (Gleitman and Papafragou 2005: 634) that you must be able to entertain a concept in the first place in order to be able to acquire it, thus creating a conundrum for theories postulating that concepts are learned. In favour of the nativist view is the impressive body of work examining infant conceptual development (Spelke 1994), which shows that there is a rich repertoire of knowledge which we hold prior to any kind of linguistic experience. As Chomsky (2000: 120) states: 'The linkage of concept and sound can be acquired on minimal evidence ... the possible sounds are narrowly constrained, and the concepts may be virtually fixed.' We might therefore expect that lexicons across languages would be largely similar.

A very different view holds that the words and concepts in a language vary widely, since they are moulded to fit local preoccupations. Evidence of well-fittedness is abundant. Many pastoralist societies of East Africa, for example, have impressively large lexicons referring to cattle (Evans-Pritchard 1934; Turton 1980); the cultural preoccupation of seafaring peoples is reflected in their terminology for geographical features (Boas 1934; Burenhult and Levinson 2008); and, indeed, lexical elaboration can be seen in response to all manners of ecological and environmental interests. However, the relationship between lexicon and culture is not so straightforward that we can suppose that all cultural interests are directly elaborated in the lexicon, or that lexical elaboration always betokens heightened cultural significance. As Hymes (1964) points out, although the Yana Indians from California may have a heightened interest in baskets and acorns, as reflected in their many terms for these objects, it is unclear what to make of the fact that there is also considerable elaboration of terms to do with the eyes and vision. This, Hymes says, 'would not have been predicted and does not depend on the environment. The Yana are not reported to have had more eyes, or kinds of eyes, than other people' (p. 167).

Items in the lexicon have three components: the form; the syntactic properties of that form; and the meaning. It is this last aspect that is the focus of this chapter. Words, such as *dog, blue, run*, are typically considered the unit relevant to the lexicon, but there are both smaller and larger chunks that need to be taken into account. The smallest meaningful unit is the morpheme, such as *un-* and *-cover* in *uncover*. Some morphemes, like *cover*, can be used on their own as words. Others, like *un-*, are affixes; they are 'bound' and cannot occur independently. When comparing lexicons, sometimes meanings that appear in independent words in one language will appear in a bound morpheme in another. Likewise there can be phrases whose meanings are not predictable from the combination of the words and morphemes that appear in them. Consider *chew the fat* which means 'to discuss a matter'. The meaning of the phrase is not literal; it cannot be derived from simply combining the meanings of *chew, the*,[1] and *fat*. Rather, it is likely that the whole phrase is stored in the mental lexicon as a chunk. So, when comparing lexicons cross-linguistically it might be that we have to compare words in one language with morphemes or phrases in another.

Every term in a language is connected to a rich internal mental representation that is correspondingly activated on producing or comprehending a word. This internal representation, or concept, is multiplex, and there are many points of debate regarding some of the basic aspects of this representation (see Riemer, this volume).

One way to think about how word meanings are stored is to consider them as something like the entries in a mental dictionary, with ancillary information stored separately in a mental encyclopedia (Clark and Clark 1977). Depending on the viewpoint, entries in the mental dictionary could be formulated in an amodal, propositional system (e.g. Jackendoff 1983; Wierzbicka 1992), in sensorimotor primitives (e.g. Barsalou 1999; Prinz 2002), or maybe even represented in an entirely atomistic fashion (Fodor 1981, 1998). The mental dictionary analogy can be helpful, but not everyone subscribes to a strong distinction between the mental dictionary and the mental encyclopedia (e.g. Hagoort et al. 2004; Murphy 2004); instead, word meaning is taken by some to be much richer,

[1] On the 'meaning' of determiners such as *the*, see Smith (this volume).

and includes many aspects of what we know about things in the real world. However, regardless of which theory one subscribes to, the content of the internal representation must be such that it fixes the range of things that a word can refer to, i.e. the word's extension, otherwise language could not be used to talk about things in the world.

Words in the mental lexicon are not isolated entities but are related to each other through relations of hyponymy (e.g. *poodle* to *dog; burgundy* to *red; slice* to *cut*), synonymy (e.g. *fiddle* and *violin; monarch* and *sovereign; settee* and *sofa*), antonymy (e.g. *long* vs. *short; black* vs. *white; married* vs. *single*), and so forth (see Fellbaum, this volume). These are the paradigmatic relations between terms. At the same time, words can combine with other words only in certain ways, and this collocational information can also tell us something about their meanings; while *the big square* is an acceptable sequence, *the circular square* is not. The possibilities for terms to appear in certain contexts or collocations are the syntagmatic relations between units. According to structuralism, the meaning of a term is a function of its relationship to other terms within the same system (de Saussure 1916). Terms which stand in systematic paradigmatic or syntagmatic relations with other terms all belong to what came to be known as a lexical field, a notion developed by scholars such as the German linguist Jost Trier (1931):

> Fields are living realities intermediate between individual words and the totality of the vocabulary; as parts of the whole they share with words the property of being integrated in a larger structure (sich ergliedern) and with the vocabulary the property of being structured in terms of smaller units (sich ausgliedern).
>
> (Trier, quoted in Lyons 1977: 253)

In Trier's original formulation, lexical fields are internally well-structured and coherent, they cover one semantic field, and are clearly separated from other semantic fields. All terms fall into one, and only one, semantic field, and no word is left floating on its own. Decades of studies suggest a different picture, with much overlap and criss-crossing, as well as lexical gaps in many fields, as will be illustrated in the sections below.

The idea that the mental lexicon can be subdivided into subsets based on shared meaning has certainly played a critical role in the comparison of lexicons cross-linguistically. However, there is no real consensus on what constitutes a semantic field or semantic domain, nor how it can be identified. Here we encounter another set of conflicting views. Should we compare lexicons by beginning with an analysis of language-internal structures, or should we instead use a neutral non-linguistic space and then see how individual languages 'carve up' that conceptual domain? Different disciplines have ended up with different sets of semantic fields, based on different weightings of these criteria. Within the tradition of linguistic anthropology, scholars have studied domains such as kinship, numerals, and colour; linguists identify domains such as space, time, and cause; whereas neuropsychologists and neuroscientists tend to identify domains such as animals, plants, and tools. There is also the question of the granularity of a semantic field. Should it be identified at the level of colour, smell, and taste, or should it instead be broader, perhaps identified with 'perception'? One possibility is to think of the lexical fields as in a set of relations to one another so that it is possible to zoom in or out of a field depending on the particulars at hand.

Certain aspects of meaning are preferentially expressed in the lexicon rather than through grammar or prosody. While tense, aspect, and mood *can* be expressed lexically, they predominantly lend themselves cross-linguistically to grammatical expression. On the other hand, the domains of colour, smell, temperature, texture, and weight only appear to be expressed in the lexicon (Allan 1977; Evans 2011; Goldin-Meadow 2007), which makes these domains particularly attractive for further study. For those domains where meaning distinctions appear in both lexicon and grammar—which, aside from tense, aspect, and mood, include matters such as body parts, shape, and emotions—one particularly pertinent question becomes the division of labour between the two. For example, in P'urhepecha, an indigenous language of Mexico, body parts are coded in a set of independent nouns, as they are in English, but there is also another system of distinctions made in a closed set of (spatial) suffixes. Although some suffixes appear to refer to the same body part as those coded by independent nouns (e.g. the word *jak'i* 'hand' appears to denote the same body part as the suffix *-k'u*), other suffixes make different distinctions (e.g. *-rhu* refers to nose *and* forehead). The body-part suffixes can be used to determine the precise location of the ground object, as in the example *Mikua kapa-**rhu**-ku-s-ti mesa-rhu* (lit. cover container+upside down-**nose. forehead**-intr-perf-asser.3 table-loc 'The lid is upside-down **on the edge** of the table' (Mendoza 2007). In general, the meanings of these body-part suffixes are more schematic than those of the corresponding nouns, as grammatical forms are wont to be. The term *-rhu* 'nose, forehead', for example, also refers to point, tip, projection, end of object, edge, fruit, flow, seed, etc.

In the remainder of this chapter we look more closely at two broad domains, 'perception' and 'the body', in order to illustrate some of the points of debate briefly introduced above.

20.2 Perception

It is in the domain of perception that semantic distinctions perhaps seem most straightforward. Our eyes deliver information about form, motion, and colour; our ears pick out the loudness and pitch of sounds; our tongues distil the qualities of sweet, sour, and bitter, etc. According to John Locke (1690), 'If a child were kept in a place where he never saw any other [colour] but black and white til he were a man, he would have no more ideas of scarlet or green, than he that from his childhood never tasted an oyster or a pineapple has of those particular relishes.' Our perceptual organs and the environment to which they are sensitive are for the most part similar from person to person, and presumably, therefore, the resulting categories are too. But there is considerable variation in how languages carve up these sensory experiences for the purposes of language. Even the semantic categories coding the simple sensations of the tongue show substantial variation across languages. Leaving aside the combined sensation of 'flavour' which integrates smell, texture, and pleasure/pain signals with 'taste' proper, and focusing only on the qualities experienced by taste receptors, i.e. 'sweet', 'sour', 'salty', and 'bitter', variation abounds. Speakers of some languages conflate 'sweet' and 'salty' with a single word, while grouping 'bitter' and 'sour' together under a different label (e.g. in Aulua, an Austronesian language spoken in Vanuatu).[2] In other languages, however, 'salty' is conflated with 'sour' or with 'bitter'; while in yet others all three—'salty', 'sour', and 'bitter'—are conflated (apparently common in New Guinea, the New Hebrides, and most of Polynesia; see Chamberlain 1903 and Myers 1904). Even these discriminable, basic sensations do not straightforwardly require distinct words in all languages.

This notionally simple domain also illustrates some of the problems with identifying semantic domains for cross-linguistic comparison. For example, the British psychologist Myers in his study of taste vocabulary started with a non-linguistically defined space of the four taste qualities 'sweet', 'salty', 'sour', and 'bitter', and then examined how speakers of different languages referred to these qualities. In contrast, the North American anthropologist Chamberlain took as his starting point the lexical field of taste in Algonkian languages and came to a rather different set of qualities. Including the distinctions covered by Myers, there seemed to be additional terms covering the qualities of 'astringent', 'peppermint', 'pungent', and 'rancid'. In both cases considerable variation across languages was found, but it is clear that the mapping of lexical fields to semantic fields is a thorny matter.

Variation abounds in other perceptual domains too. Some languages elaborate on tactile expressions, with words labelling very many texture distinctions. Siwu (a language of eastern Ghana) is one such language, where there are many specific words for haptic sensations, as illustrated by *kpɔlɔkpɔlɔ* 'unpleasantly slippery (e.g. muddy road, mudfish)', *dɛkpɛrɛɛ* 'fine-grained (e.g. flour)', *safaraa* 'coarse-grained (e.g. sand)' (Dingemanse 2011; Dingemanse and Majid 2012). In Yukatek (spoken in Mexico) there is a productive derivational morphology that allows speakers to concisely express tactile sensations in single words such as *k'ixlemak* 'stinging (e.g. having a small piece of wood in the eye)' vs. *k'ixinak* 'stinging (e.g. rubbing the fur of wild boar)' (Le Guen 2011).[3] Other languages elaborate on smell qualities. The Aslian languages spoken in the Malay Peninsula shine here (Burenhult and Majid 2011; Tufvesson 2011; Wnuk and Majid 2012). For example, in Jahai around a dozen or so stative verbs categorize smell qualities whose connoisseurship eludes ordinary speakers of Indo-European languages. Sound qualities, such as loudness or pitch, are also treated differently cross-linguistically (Eitan and Timmers 2010). While English and other Germanic languages make use of

[2] If one were to paraphrase the relevant distinction, the words in question would appear to refer to pleasant vs. unpleasant tastes, though crucial data is are missing for us to be entirely sure that this is the underlying semantics. Salt is only pleasant in low concentrations, so if participants would still use the same term for sweet plus high concentrations salt, the gloss 'pleasant taste' would be less felicitous.

[3] Formed from the root *k'ix* 'thorn'.

a vertical spatial metaphor to talk about variation in pitch (*high* vs. *low*), languages like Farsi, Turkish, and Zapotec use a horizontal metaphor instead (*thick* vs. *thin*; Dolscheid et al. 2013; Shayan, Ozturk, and Sicoli 2011). 'Sounds' can also form the basis of words. In a number of languages many names for animals, such as birds, frogs, and insects, are derived from the sound typically made by that animal. The animal's call is translated into the phonological repertoire of the language, and this onomatopoeic form becomes conventionalized as that creature's name (Berlin and O'Neill 1981; Childs, this volume).

As with other sensory modalities, visual experiences can also be carved up in different ways (Saunders and Brakel 2002; Wierzbicka 2005). Beneath the rampant variation, recurring patterns can nevertheless be detected. In the domain of colour, for example, Berlin and Kay (1969) compared the colour lexicons of nearly 100 languages and concluded that there was a total universal inventory of exactly eleven basic colour categories and that all languages drew from this basic stock. The variation between languages was in how many colour words they had; on the other hand, in languages with the same number of terms, the terms had the same referential range, consistent with the tenets of semantic field theory. Moreover, they argued, there was systematicity in how colour lexicons grew. According to their analysis, all languages have terms for 'white' and 'black'; if there is to be a third colour word in a lexicon it will be 'red'; next comes either 'green' or 'yellow', and so on.

Berlin and Kay focused on the denotational or referential aspect of colours terms (i.e. their extensions). They presented speakers with a colour array consisting of over 300 standardized colour chips, and asked speakers to indicate the boundaries and best examples of colour words from their native language. Of course, speakers are able to refer to colours using a wide range of strategies. They can use dedicated, abstract terms, such as *red*, *green*, and *blue*; conventionalized source-based descriptions, such as *lilac* or *turquoise*; or even ad hoc phrasal expressions such as *shark-infested water blue* or *white if it had a wine spill on itself and let it dry for a few days and then tried to wash it but it just left it that awful colour*.[4] This fact alone might suggest substantial cross-linguistic variation in the expressibility of colour, since if source objects vary crossculturally (as they surely do), then descriptions will also vary. Rather than compare all possible strategies speakers might use to talk about colours, Berlin and Kay focused on 'core' or 'basic' vocabulary. Since even this restriction can result in an unwieldy number of terms, Berlin and Kay proposed a number of criteria which allowed them to identify core colour vocabulary, or in their parlance 'basic colour terms'. These terms are monolexemic (i.e. compounds or modified terms are excluded), are psychologically salient, and are without unusual distributional behaviour; they are not foreign borrowings or source descriptors (such as *gold* or *aubergine*) nor are they restricted to a narrow class of objects (such as *blond*); finally, their extension is not included in that of any other colour term. By using these criteria, Berlin and Kay were able to extrapolate the regularities in colour lexicon development described above.

[4] Actual colour descriptions from an on-line colour naming survey at http://blog.xkcd.com/2010/05/03/color-survey-results/.

There have been a number of revisions to Berlin and Kay's original theory (see Biggam 2012 for a summary of these developments) in response to various criticisms (e.g. Levinson 2000; Lucy 1997; Wierzbicka 2008). One point of criticism has been the use of English glosses. Glossing words as 'black' and 'white', for example, is misleading, argues Wierzbicka, because this suggests that terms taken from different lexicons have exactly the same meaning. This is especially problematic when we consider that the extension of a term glossed as 'black' in a language with only three colour terms will be vastly larger than a term glossed as 'black' in a language with eleven terms. Generally, the boundaries of colour terms shift as a function of the number of colour words within a lexicon.

A number of scholars have questioned whether colour is a coherent semantic domain cross-linguistically. Many terms that appear on the surface to encode colour in small-scale languages are in essence multimodal, including in their semantics information about such matters as texture and succulence (Conklin 1955; Roberson 2005). Syntagmatic and paradigmatic relations for colour words also suggest that it might not cohere as a lexical field. Even in English, the distributional properties of colour words differ; while we can *blacken, whiten*, or *redden* something, we cannot **yellow-en*, **green-en*, or **blue-en* it (Lucy 1997). These findings, amongst others, prompted many to worry whether colour was a coherent domain at all, and whether by limiting the field to the three dimensions of hue, saturation, and lightness, Berlin and Kay were excluding the very facts that would challenge their universalist claims. Other worries concerned the language sample that was the basis of their theory (the sample was biased towards languages with large populations of literate speakers) as well as the speaker sample (made up of bilingual speakers resident in the United States).

In response to these latter criticisms, the 'World Color Survey' was launched (Kay et al. 2009). This is the largest database of referential meaning ever collected. Within it are naming data for 330 different colour chips from 2,616 speakers of 110 small-scale non-literate communities, as well as judgements of the best examples of colours from each language. By applying various statistical models, Kay and Regier (2003) confirmed that the distribution of categories is not random but represents optimal partitions of colour space (Regier, Kay, and Khetarpal 2007). Moreover, best examples of colour categories cluster in colour space (Regier, Kay, and Cook 2005). This finding is interesting because it suggests that although boundaries between categories are influenced by which other colour words are present within a language, focal points are not, which in turn supports the hypothesis that focal colours may form the bedrock from which colour categories are formed (Kay and McDaniel 1978).

However, the story turns out not to be quite so straightforward. First, if focal colours are universally available and the basis for colour categories, then speakers of 'grue' languages (languages with a single word to cover both green and blue) should identify the best example for their 'grue' word as either focal green or focal blue, or perhaps as both (Regier and Kay 2004). However, around a third of speakers of grue languages choose a point mid-way between focal green and focal blue; this is inconsistent with the universal focal colours proposal but consistent with a proposal by Roberson and colleagues that people calculate focal points on the basis of the category boundaries within a particular language (Roberson, Davies, and Davidoff 2000). The universality of focal points has been questioned from a different perspective. Lindsey and Brown (2002) noticed that languages with a grue category are not distributed randomly around the world but tend, rather, to be found near the equator. Speakers living nearer the equator are exposed to higher levels of sunlight and thus high amounts of ultraviolet-B which, according to Lindsey and Brown, leads to changes to the lens of the eye. According to their account, then, (at least some) people speaking a grue language simply do not see 'blue' in the same way as speakers of a language that differentiates 'green' and 'blue'. If enough people within a community suffer from 'lens brunescence', this might bias speakers of the whole community not to use different words for green and blue, since the distinction would not be successfully communicated to all other speakers. The Lindsey–Brown hypothesis predicts that speakers of grue languages will not choose focal green or blue as best examples of the category, due to the 'warping' of the speakers' perceptual field. Other evidence is also consistent with the idea that visual experience can warp perceptual space. A recent study testing Norwegians born above the Arctic circle found that individuals were less sensitive to the yellow-green-blue spectrum and more sensitive to variation in the purple range than those born below the Arctic; Laeng and colleagues (2007) ascribe this to differences in light exposure. Although this study does not directly assess colour names, considered together with Lindsey and Brown's analyses it is suggestive of the experiential shaping of colour categories, a topic that is still relatively under-explored.

This brings us back to Locke's example cited at the beginning of this section, with blindness as an extreme form of variation in experience. Although missing the crucial qualia, does a blind person really have 'no ideas' about colour? A study by Shepard and Cooper (1992) is enlightening in this respect. They presented speakers who had normal vision, different kinds of colour-blindness, or complete absence of vision since birth, with colour chips or colour names (corresponding to those chips), and asked participants to sort each set according to their similarity. For participants with normal vision, sortings of colour chips corresponded to Newton's colour circle (see Fig. 20.1), and their sortings of names matched this same circular structure. Shepard and Cooper take this as evidence that internal representations mirror external structure, or in this case that the organization of the colour lexicon is isomorphic to colour perception. More intriguing are the results from colour-blind individuals. Those with red-green colour-blindness (deutans and protans in Fig. 20.1) sorted the colour chips consonant with their colour deficiency—the colour circle was collapsed so that red and green appear much closer together than for normally sighted people. But—and this is the fascinating part—when it came to sorting the names of colours, colour-blind individuals sorted more like normally-sighted individuals than their own perceptual colour space. There are two interesting things about this. First, colour-blind individuals have acquired considerable knowledge about the colour lexicon, presumably through their exposure to collocational information in the language. Second, the lexical fields for colour are substantially similar across groups (although not identical), demonstrating the potent ability of

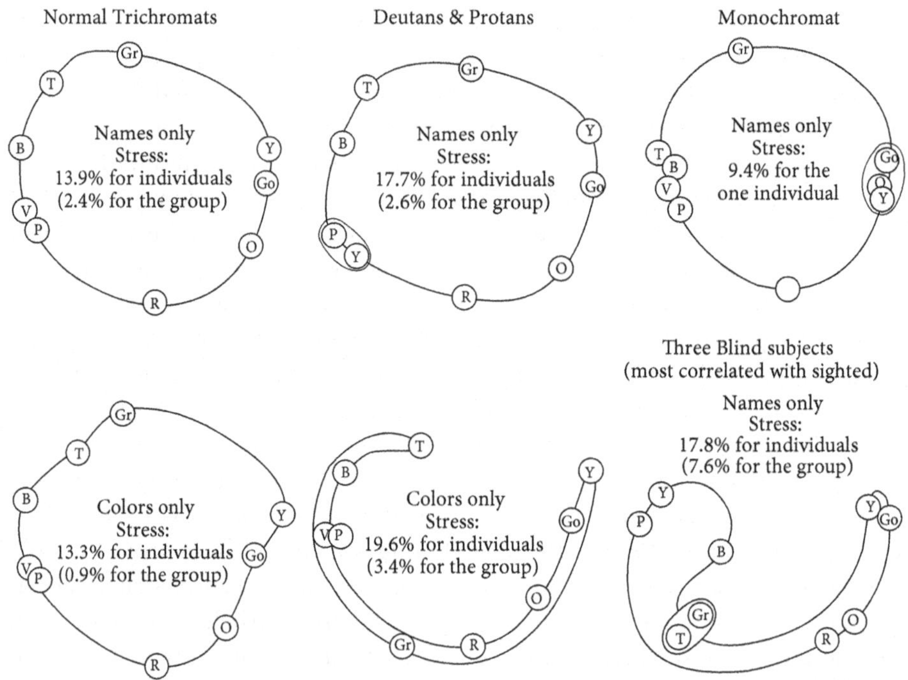

FIG. 20.1 Taken from Shepard and Cooper (1992: 100). Multidimensional scaling solutions for similarity data for colours and colour names collected from normally sighted, colour-blind, and completely blind individuals. Gr = green, Y = yellow, Go = gold, O = orange, R = red, P = purple, V = violet, B = blue, T = turquoise.

language to coordinate mental representations across individuals and thus bring them into alignment.[5]

Perceptual vocabularies across cultures illustrate the dual-shaping of meaning in the lexicon. On the one hand, words have to map onto the structure of the environment as perceived by our perceptual organs. Shepard and Cooper's study illustrates this point very nicely: colour word similarity mirrors perceived colour similarity in normally-sighted people. This parallelism of lexicon and perceptual psychophysics appears across sensory modalities (Dingemanse and Majid 2012; Wnuk and Majid 2012). On the other hand, words also reflect varying cultural forces. Languages vary in the size of their colour, smell, and taste lexicons and in the distinctions made therein, despite the fact that there are potentially universal environmental and physiological influences. Different cultural factors may account for this variation depending on the affordances of the domain. Dyeing technology is perhaps at the root of variation in colour terminologies (Berlin and Kay 1969; Conklin 1973); subsistence patterns may explain the

[5] Even people with no experience of colour—the monochromats and the three blind subjects in Fig. 20.1—nevertheless demonstrated considerable knowledge about the meanings of colour words, knowledge which can only have been derived from linguistic input.

existence of smell lexicons (Hombert 1992); while culinary traditions could shape taste lexicons (Enfield 2011). Or perhaps the differences are better accounted for by variation in the environment, such as varying light conditions across the globe (Laeng et al. 2007; Lindsey and Brown 2002), or by historical circumstances such as contact with other linguistic groups (Malt et al. 1999).

20.3 The body

The notion that the body is made up of parts, such as hands, arms, legs, and feet, seems obvious. Paul Bloom puts it thus:

> A psychologically natural part, while not bounded, will nonetheless move as an internally connected region. Hence fingers are natural parts and so are toes, but it is profoundly unnatural to think of the ring finger and the kneecap as a single body part (a fingerknee) because fingers and knees are unconnected. But connectedness isn't enough. A one-inch wide ribbon of skin running from the left hand, up the arm, over the shoulder, and ending at the middle of the lower back is connected (and also conforms to the principles of solidity and continuity), but it is not naturally seen as a body part... Something more is required.
>
> (Bloom 2000: 109)

The 'something more' could come from vision, as Hoffman and Richards (1984: 82) suggest. According to their account, parts can be discovered using general geometric principles, and they note that '[i]t is probably no accident that the parts defined by minima [their procedure for determining parts] are often easily assigned verbal labels'.

The idea that some kinds of parts are more 'natural', and therefore likely to be labelled in language, is widespread (e.g. Andersen 1978; Brown 1976), and various algorithms have been proposed to determine parts (Biederman 1987; Hoffman and Richards 1984; Marr 1982). It is often claimed that the body and some of its parts (such as face and back) universally serve as source domains for the conceptualization and expression of other aspects of the world, including spatial location (Heine 1997; Svorou 1994). So do these prelinguistically defined parts hold up to cross-linguistic scrutiny? One way to answer this question is to take an approach similar to that used for colour categories, namely, to examine the extension of words used to refer to the body and then to examine how much cross-linguistic correspondence there is (Majid 2010; Majid, Enfield, and van Staden 2006).

As with the colour domain, we first have to consider which terms should be compared across languages. As mentioned in section 20.1, an independent word in one language may correspond to a bound morpheme in another. And as with the colour vocabularies considered earlier, it is always possible to coin a new expression to refer to a specific bit of the body—*the back of the knee, the inside of the elbow, between the shoulder blades, the tip of my pinky*. No one would expect these ad hoc expressions to necessarily fit non-linguistic

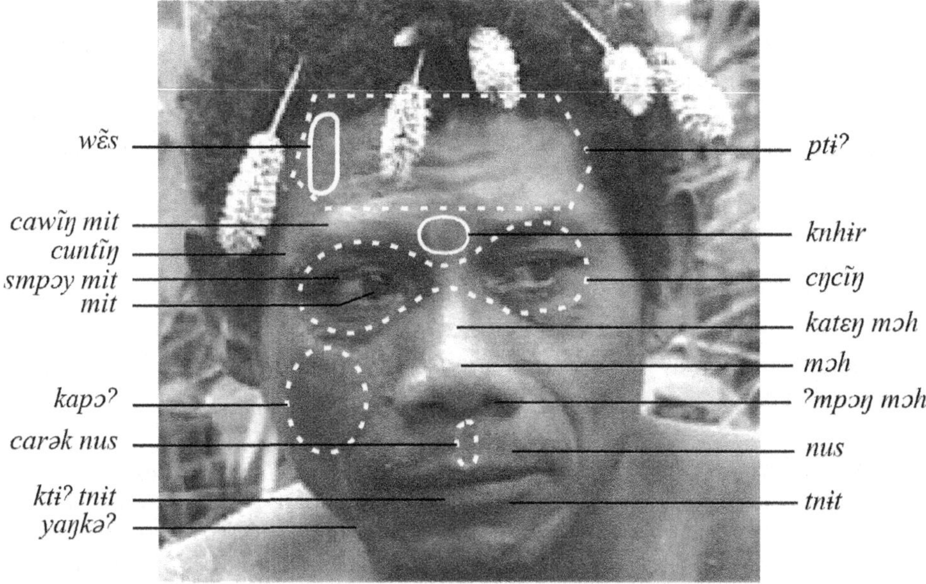

FIG. 20.2 This figure depicts the main words (and their extensions) used by Jahai speakers to refer to parts of the face. Reproduced with permission from Burenhult (2006).

segmentation principles. The claims about how parts are labelled in language only apply to 'basic' body-part terms. We will therefore restrict our attention to these.

Even when we restrict ourselves to this smaller set, however, it is clear that there is much more variation in this domain than might be expected. For example, in Jahai (mentioned earlier for its many smell words) there is no word that corresponds exactly to 'head' (Burenhult 2006). The closest term is *kuy*, which refers only to that part of the head that is covered in hair (i.e. 'crown'). This is even more surprising when we discover that there is also no word for 'face'. Jahai speakers appear instead to rely on many fine-grained distinctions when talking about the face and the body (see Fig. 20.2). For example, the word *cŋcĩŋ* is used for the area around the eyes and picks out a spectacle-shaped region; *wɛ̃s* refers to a prominent vertical ridge on the side of the forehead; *knhɨr* refers to the root of the nose/the wrinkles between the eyebrows; and *carək nus* (literally 'upper lip streambed') refers to the indent between the upper lip and nose (i.e. philtrum). Similarly detailed distinctions are evident when Jahai speakers talk about 'arms' and 'legs'; in fact, there are no such general terms. Instead, speakers refer to *klapəh* 'deltoid part of the shoulder', *bliŋ* 'the upper arm', *prbɛr* 'lower arm', *cyas* 'hand', *blɨʔ* 'upper leg', *gor* 'lower leg', and *can* 'foot'.[6]

[6] It is unclear whether in English *arm* and *leg* include in their reference 'hand' and 'foot'. When asked to colour in the *arm* or *leg* on a picture of the human body, around half of participants included the 'hand'/'foot' and half excluded these parts, just as Dutch speakers did (Majid 2010). Linguistic tests suggest a similar ambiguity. *He lost his arm in an accident* entails that he lost a hand too, but *She has a tattoo on her arm* does not entail that she also has it on her hand. Whether this really suggests two distinct meanings of *arm* or whether a secondary meaning is only inferred in context is not clear (Cruse 1979).

These fine-grained categories do not necessarily deviate from general visual parsing principles. The surprise is more in the fact that the default way to refer to body parts is more refined than in English or other Standard Average European languages.[7] It turns out, however, that there are also body-part terms that are more challenging to the proposal that body parts can be identified by general non-linguistic constraints. For example, Jahai *nus* 'upper lip' also includes the fleshy part between the mouth and the nose where a moustache might be located; *tnit* 'lower lip' includes the fleshy part between the mouth and chin. Note that there is no coverall term 'mouth'. Here, the salient boundaries of the lip, including protuberance and colour, are discarded, and the linguistic partitioning uses a different logic.

Jahai is not alone in having terms that violate general visual parsing principles. In Tidore, a Papuan language of North Moluccas, the term for leg, *yohu*, begins at the foot but finishes not at the hip but three-quarters of the way up the leg where there is no salient perceptual boundary (van Staden 2006). In Swedish, *nak* refers to the neck but also includes the back of the head (also Danish *nakke*), so a 'head rest' is a *nackstöd* (literally, 'neck support').[8] These examples also demonstrate how linguistic examples relying on collocational evidence reveal the same meaning components as extensional evidence; both sorts of data project from the same representation and should be viewed as complementary evidence revealing the underlying concept.

As Bloom suggested above, a 'natural' part should 'move as an internally connected region'; Swanson and Witkowski (1977) put it more strongly: 'Discontinuous categorising of body parts, for example, does not occur' (exempting the same term being used for the left and right sides). More specific statements of this general constraint can be found in two classic papers on the typology of body parts, according to which legs and arms should always receive distinct terms, as should hands and feet (Andersen 1978; Brown 1976). Here we also find counterexamples. In Lavukaleve, a Papuan language of the Solomon Islands, the term *tau* covers both legs and arms (Terrill 2006), while in Mawng, an Australian language, hand and foot are subsumed under a single term *yurnu* 'limb extremity' (reported in Evans 2011).

Some find this hard to credit. Wierzbicka (2007: 28), for example, states:

> human hands mediate to a very large extent, between the world and the human mind. The fact that 'hands' are fundamental in human thinking is reflected in the relative semantic simplicity of this concept: it appears that of all the body-part concepts this is the only one which can be explicated directly in universal semantic primes, and without any reference, direct or indirect, to any other parts of the body. 'Arms', 'legs' and arguably, 'head' require in their explications a reference to shape, and 'eyes', 'ears', 'nose' and 'mouth' appear to require a reference to 'head', but an explication of 'hands' can be couched exclusively in primes, without any use of shape concepts which are inherently semantically complex.
>
> (Wierzbicka 2007: 28)

[7] Standard Average European is used to refer to the Indo-European languages of Europe. These languages share a number of traits which are quite different from other languages of the world.

[8] Thanks to Carsten Levisen for pointing this out to me.

Wierzbicka offers a semantics of body parts not based on visual discontinuities, but in terms of paraphrase into 'semantic primes' such as I, YOU, GOOD, BAD, PART, ONE, TWO, and LIKE (see Goddard, this volume). She argues that '[s]ince the most reliable evidence for the presence of such a concept is the presence of a word, the question of whether all languages have a word for "hand" is of great importance to both cognitive anthropology and cognitive science' (Wierzbicka 2007: 29). It is not, however, necessary, according to Wierzbicka, that there is a separate word that only encodes the concept of 'hand'. What is critical, instead, is that there is a distinct 'word meaning' expressible in every language. That word meaning (given below in (a–g)) could be expressed polysemously by one term. This is the analysis she proposes for Polish *ręce* which extensionally covers the arm and hand. Wierzbicka claims that there are two distinct word meanings covered by *ręce*: *ręce*$_1$ has the meaning outlined in (a–g) (i.e. 'hand') but *ręce*$_2$ has a meaning closer to English *arm* (with some subtle differences).

hands

a. two parts of someone's body
b. they are on two sides of the body
c. these two parts of someone's body can move as this someone wants
d. these two parts of someone's body have many parts
e. if this someone wants it, all the parts on one side of one of these two parts can touch all the parts on one side of the other at the same time
f. because people's bodies have these two parts, people can do many things with many things as they want
g. because people's bodies have these two parts, people can touch many things as they want

Of around 600 languages sampled by Brown (2008), over one third (including Russian, Marathi spoken in India, Hausa from West Africa, and Seri from Mexico) do not distinguish between hand and arm with separate words, so Wierzbicka's arguments regarding Polish *ręce* has important implications for how we are to understand variation in the lexical field of body parts. According to Wierzbicka, there are two main arguments in favour of a polysemous analysis. First, she argues that the hand is a fundamental element in understanding many other concepts, including physical actions like *clap, slap, tear*, object concepts such as *gloves* and *handle*, and attributes like *hard, soft, long*, and *flat*. Because it is so fundamental, all speakers must have a distinct concept for hand. Second, she suggests that whereas other body parts have shape as an important component in their definition, hand does not rely on the notion of shape, and this lends further credence to the distinctness (and priority) of hand as a concept.

There are some problems with these arguments. First, Wierzbicka conflates concept and word meaning. It may well be that every speaker has a distinct non-linguistic concept of 'hand', but not all concepts are reflected directly in the lexicon. Murphy (2004: 389) gives some invented examples of concepts which we can all recognize: 'The actions of two people maneuvering for one armrest in a movie theatre or airplane seat' (which he dubs ELBONICS); 'The moist residue left on a window after a dog presses its nose to it' (dubbed PUPKUS). It is a postulate of Wierzbicka's Natural Semantic Metalanguage that a concept which is to be used in explicating the meaning of another term should have formal expression, but the postulation alone is not a reason to accept this. Second, the argument for polysemy is inconsistently applied. While Wierzbicka analyses *ręce* as polysemous, the corresponding term *nogi*, which covers legs and feet, is analysed as being monosemous; it is not entirely clear why the two could not be analysed in a similar way, apart from for theory-internal constraints (cf. Riemer 2006). The critical empirical data, either collocational or extensional, is conspicuously absent from her account.

Finally, some brief remarks on the organization of the lexical field of the body across lexicons. It has been suggested by Andersen (1978) and Brown (1976) that the body is organized into a hierarchical partonomy with no more than six hierarchical levels, and rarely more than five. The hierarchy is constructed by establishing whether native speakers accept the relationship of 'part of' between terms, e.g. *the arm is part of the body*. This was the approach followed by Stark (1969) in order to produce the hierarchy of the body in Quechua (Fig. 20.3). There are some strange elements in this figure: *maki* appears on three different levels as a simple term (and another two times in complex expressions), each time with a different gloss—'arm', 'finger-to-elbow', and 'hand'. These glosses Stark derives from their relation to other terms at the same level

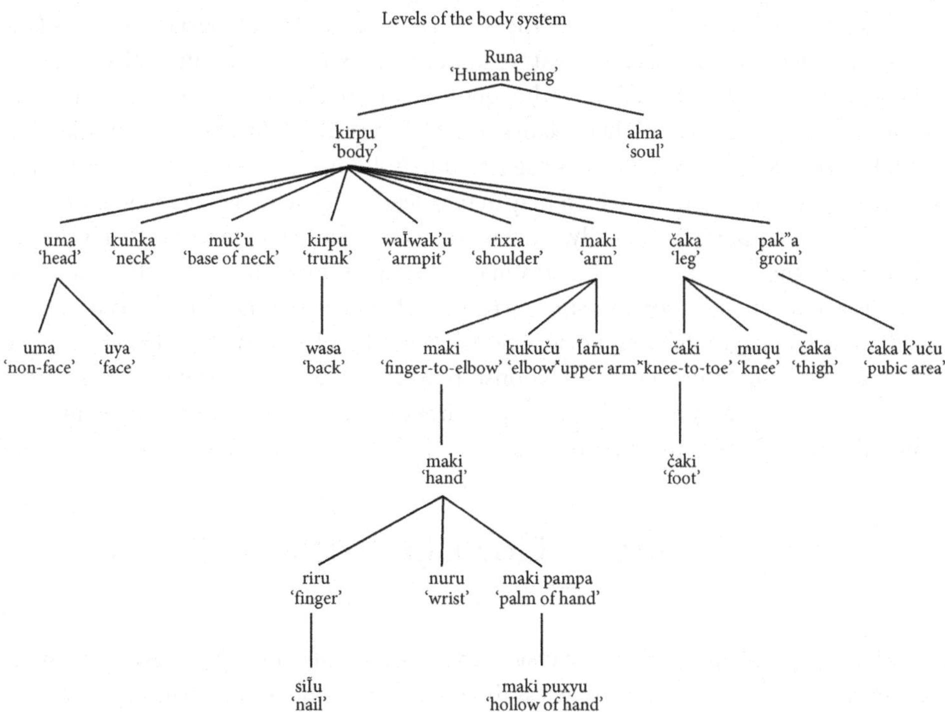

FIG. 20.3 The hierarchy of the body in Quechua, adapted from Stark (1969).

of the hierarchy: *maki* 'arm' stands in relation to 'leg' at level 3 in the hierarchy, but *maki* 'hand' stands in relation to 'foot' at level 5. But are these different senses really distinct representations in the minds of Quechua speakers? Do Quechua speakers really accept that a *maki* is a part of the *maki* which in turn is part of *maki*? It seems unlikely. One cannot help but sympathize with the sentiment of Swanson and Witkowski (1977: 324): 'It seems possible that some writers in the literature have been too eager in placing the anatomical domain into neat, cut and dried structures with the appropriate (and perhaps culturally and universally obvious) branching and nicely labelled levels.'

Cross-linguistically, the 'part of' relation is not always available as the necessary relation between body-part terms. In some languages the most natural relation is one of possession, e.g. *the face has eyes* (Swanson and Witkowski 1977; van Staden 2006) or spatial connectedness, e.g. *the fingernails are on the fingers* (Majid 2006; Palmer and Nicodemus 1985). In a recent collection of papers exploring the lexical field of the body across a wide array of languages, only half the languages showed evidence of any kind of partonomy. Take Jahai, which was introduced earlier in this section. The lexical field of the body in Jahai appears to avoid hierarchical organization; potential superordinates such as head, arm, and leg are conspicuously absent. In other languages, the partonomies that were discovered were neither exhaustive nor deep. Furthermore, it is not clear to what extent these relations are actually entailed or to what extent speakers merely derive these relations, when questioned, from a non-linguistic spatial schema of the body. Further careful analysis and argumentation is required in this area.

To summarize, the lexical field of the body shows considerable variation across languages. Explaining the variation that we find, however, is not easy; after all, bodies are the same across the globe (cf. the earlier quotation from Hymes). But perhaps there are other factors at play that might explain some of the variation. Brown (2008; Witkowski and Brown 1985), for example, has suggested that differences in climate might lead to different dress conventions, which may in turn lead to the hand being made more salient as a distinct part. Specifically, Brown argues that wearing gloves and long sleeves that end at the wrist in cold climates makes the hand prominent, resulting in a distinct name for it; and there is some correlational evidence in favour of this proposal, with more languages showing a distinction between hand and arm the further we move from the equator. However, this relationship may be a spurious result of the sampling of the languages (Majid and Dunn, in preparation), leaving it unclear why languages should vary in the way that they do.

20.4 Conclusions

Despite the problems and controversies which plague this area of research, researchers in recent decades have nonetheless discovered a number of fascinating generalizations and important facts about the lexicon across languages. In order to make further progress, additional in-depth studies of multiple languages using the same methods are required. Both fine-grained comparison of two or three languages and large-scale studies involving dozens of languages will provide crucial data regarding the similarities and differences in lexical fields. In addition, systematic investigations are required to explore whether the attested cross-linguistic variation can be explained by differences in environment, cultural practices, language history, or some other factors. As we saw earlier, it is possible that variations in the environment (temperature) affect body-part lexicons, while variation in culinary traditions affect taste words. There are many such plausible accounts for different lexical fields, but little or only weak demonstrable empirical support. Future studies are important for understanding the lexicon cross-linguistically and thus settling some of those fundamental questions at the heart of the cognitive and linguistic sciences.

Acknowledgements

Part of this chapter was written while the author was a fellow at the Swedish Collegium for Advanced Studies in Uppsala. This work was supported by a Vici grant from the Netherlands Organisation for Scientific Research (NWO).

CHAPTER 21

WORDS AS CARRIERS OF CULTURAL MEANING

CLIFF GODDARD

21.1 Introduction

21.1.1 Approaches and attitudes to cultural meaning

This chapter is about ways in which words, both as individual lexemes and in lexical subsystems or domains, can be 'carriers' of culture-related meaning. It must be said that this is not a topic that rates very highly on the agenda of most professional linguists. A commonly encountered attitude is: 'Yes, yes, everyone knows that there's cultural content in the lexicon, but it's not important for linguistics', i.e. it has little relevance to what is often seen as the core concern of linguistics, namely, understanding 'the grammar'. A related view is that to the extent that cultural aspects of meaning are significant, they are best left to the anthropological linguist or to the cultural historian. Both views presuppose that cultural aspects of meaning are easily visible without dedicated linguistic study—an assumption that derives, presumably, from thinking that cultural aspects of meaning are chiefly vested in content words for culturally distinctive kinds of food and drink, clothing, tools, weapons and other artefacts, social institutions, and the like. As we will see, cultural content in the lexicon may run much deeper than this and hold greater significance for our understanding of the lexicon.

Looking outside linguistics, one cannot help but be struck by a very stark contrast. The study of culture-laden words is of great and enduring interest to a raft of scholarly traditions in the humanities: not only cultural anthropology and cultural history, but also literary studies, hermeneutics, and translation studies. Works such as C. S. Lewis's (1960) *Studies in Words* and Raymond Williams' (1976) celebrated *Keywords* spring to mind, along with their descendants such as Bennett et al.'s (2005) *New Keywords* and Rosenthal's (2005) *Words and Values*. These studies tend to focus on English words that loom large in public discourse, such as *democracy, equality, opinion, system, reason, community, relationship*, and *environment*. Among cultural historians and scholars detailing the history of ideas, there have been a string of insightful book-length studies of English cultural philology, including McMahon (2006) and Potkay (2007) on *happiness* and *joy*, respectively, and Thomas Dixon's (2003, 2008) studies on *passions* and *emotions*, and on *altruism*. To give the flavour of these works, consider Wierzbicka's (2014a) summary of Dixon (2003), which documented the remarkable career of the word *emotions* over the past 300 years:

> ... the shift from *passions* to *emotions* represented a cultural and conceptual, and not only lexical, change. The direction of that change can be gleaned from the lexical and conceptual networks to which the two words belonged. The network to which *passions* belonged also included words such as *soul, conscience, sin* and *grace*, whereas the one to which *emotions* belonged included words such as *psychology, evolution, organism, brain, nerves, expression, behaviour* and *viscera*.

This quotation gives a sense of how words can act as carriers of cultural meaning, not only in isolation but in concert with a suite of related, mutually reinforcing, words.

Within ethnography and cognitive anthropology, emotion vocabulary has proved a rich vein of study. One thinks of brilliant inquiries by Clifford Geertz (1973) into *lek* 'stage fright' and *rasa* 'feeling, meaning' in Balinese, Catherine Lutz's (1988) study of the meaning and function of *fago* 'compassion, love, sadness' and *song* 'justifiable anger' among the Ifaluk people of Micronesia, and Michelle Rosaldo's (1980) inquiry into *liget* 'anger, passion, energy' among the Philippine Ilongot. In a different tradition, developing out of the ethnography of communication, Donal Carbaugh and colleagues have shown how Finnish key cultural expressions, such as *olla omissa oloissaan* 'being undisturbed in one's thoughts' and *mietiskellä* 'contemplative and thoughtful', defy easy translation into English while providing a key to understanding Finnish 'quietude' (Carbaugh 2006; Carbaugh et al. 2006). In recent years, there have been a number of important lexical-cultural studies in crossover disciplines such as cultural psychology (e.g. Shi-xu and Feng-Bing 2013; Shweder 2001, 2008; Shweder et al. 2004).

Compared with this body of work from other disciplines, relatively few lexical-cultural studies have come from linguists (with notable exceptions, of course). The reasons are connected with the ascendancy of syntax, especially as studied by Chomskyan generative linguistics. Before this, the study of languages was integrally connected with the humanistic tradition (think, for example, of the line of scholarship that leads through Herder and Humboldt to Boas and Sapir), but under the influence of Chomsky and generativism, linguistics, especially in North America, largely disavowed its links with the humanities and sought to define itself as part of cognitive psychology and, more recently, as a branch of biology (biolinguistics). Interest in cultural aspects of the lexicon was never completely extinguished, of course. It was maintained in anthropological linguistics and in the newer field of ethnography of communication, and in the last third of the 20th century two new trends emerged in lexicology and lexical semantics which promised to bring new rigour and systematicity to the study of the lexicon, as well as a revived interest in cultural semantics, namely: the Natural Semantic Metalanguage (NSM) approach originated by Anna Wierzbicka (Wierzbicka 1992, 1996, 1997, 2006a, 2010a, and other works; Goddard 2011a; Goddard and Wierzbicka 2002, 2014a, 2014b) and the Meaning–Text Theory (MTT) associated with Russian linguists such as Jurij Apresjan (2000) and Igor Mel'čuk (2012).

The bulk of this chapter will be illustrated from studies by NSM researchers, not only because this school has produced a large and internally consistent body of work on descriptive cultural semantics, but also because the approach sets out to provide the finest level of resolution of semantic detail (even greater than that sought by the MTT approach.[1] The point is that when approaching cultural aspects of meaning (or indeed, any aspect of meaning) what one sees—how much detail, how much accuracy—depends on the method of description that is being brought to bear. Without a sufficiently precise, high-resolution method of semantic analysis, one may simply not 'see' the culture-specificity of many ordinary-seeming word meanings in a given language. Likewise, one may not be able to discern enough semantic detail to recognize culturally relevant semantic themes that link words in one domain to those in another. These contentions will be illustrated shortly with examples from a variety of languages.

21.1.2 Methodological issues in cross-cultural semantics

In the contentious field of lexical semantics (see Riemer, this volume), one of the main fault lines is that which separates conceptualist/intensionalist approaches from referentialist/extensionalist approaches. The former aim to describe the concept or sense behind word meanings, while the latter aim to anchor meaning in references to a presumed real or objective world. Extensionalist approaches are of limited help in dealing with cultural aspects of meaning, many of which concern intangibles (values, attitudes, psychological constructs, spiritual beliefs, and the like) that lack external referents. We will therefore proceed using a conceptualist approach, and this can be most straightforwardly done by means of verbal definitions. The main principle when using verbal definitions is the reductive principle: avoid using in the definition any words which are semantically more complex than the word being defined. The reasons are obvious: first, the goal of clarifying meaning cannot be served if every definition introduces more obscurities, and second, using complex terms in definitions frequently leads to definitional circularity.

Although lexicographers often pay lip service to the reductive principle, in practice they usually fail to adhere to it and other professional 'explainers' of words, including

[1] The MTT linguists are sometimes known as the Moscow School. There is also a second Moscow School, which is more focussed on 'cultural semantics' (cf. Zalizniak et al. 2005; Shmelev 2012a, 2012b) but whose works are as yet available only in Russian.

semanticists, seldom adhere to it either. The exception is the NSM research community. They have worked for decades to isolate what they call semantic primes, i.e. the minimal inventory of semantically simple word meanings (see Table 21.1), and to show how complex lexical meanings can be resolved into text-like configurations, termed explications, of semantic primes. The significance for present purposes, as explained below, is that semantic primes can be used as a 'safe', relatively culture-neutral defining vocabulary for investigating lexical meaning across languages. NSM semantics also makes use of a small set of non-primitive lexical meanings (termed 'semantic molecules') that can be shown to function as building blocks, alongside semantic primes, in explications for many concepts. This has important implications for the cultural loading of the vocabulary, because some semantic molecules appear to be language-specific (see section 21.3.3).

When dealing with meanings across a cultural gulf, the choice of defining vocabulary has a special significance on account of the danger of conceptual and terminological

Table 21.1 Semantic primes (English exponents) (Goddard and Wierzbicka 2014a)

I~ME, YOU, SOMEONE, SOMETHING~THING, PEOPLE, BODY	Substantives
KIND, PART	Relational substantives
THIS, THE SAME, OTHER~ELSE	Determiners
ONE, TWO, MUCH~MANY, LITTLE~FEW, SOME, ALL	Quantifiers
GOOD, BAD	Evaluators
BIG, SMALL	Descriptors
THINK, KNOW, WANT, DON'T WANT, FEEL, SEE, HEAR	Mental predicates
SAY, WORDS, TRUE	Speech
DO, HAPPEN, MOVE, TOUCH	Actions, events, movement, contact
BE (SOMEWHERE), THERE IS, BE (SOMEONE/SOMETHING), (BE) MINE	Location, existence, specification, possession
LIVE, DIE	Life and death
WHEN~TIME, NOW, BEFORE, AFTER, A LONG TIME, A SHORT TIME, FOR SOME TIME, MOMENT	Time
WHERE~PLACE, HERE, ABOVE, BELOW, FAR, NEAR, SIDE, INSIDE	Space
NOT, MAYBE, CAN, BECAUSE, IF	Logical concepts
VERY, MORE	Augmentor, intensifier
LIKE	Similarity

Primes exist as the meanings of lexical units (not at the level of lexemes). Exponents of primes may be words, bound morphemes, or phrasemes. They can be formally, i.e. morphologically, complex. They can have combinatorial variants or allolexes (indicated with ~). Each prime has well-specified syntactic (combinatorial) properties.

ethnocentrism, more specifically, Anglocentrism, i.e. the possibility that our meaning analyses of non-English languages may be distorted and inauthentic if couched in words whose meanings do not have precise equivalents in the language being described and which therefore impose an Anglo cultural bias. Fortunately, as it appears from the available evidence (Goddard and Wierzbicka 1994, 2002; Goddard 2008; cf. Goddard 2001a), semantic primes are lexical universals in the sense that they can be expressed through lexical means (words, bound morphemes, or phrases) in all languages. More precisely, the claim is that semantic primes exist as discrete word-meanings, or, equivalently, as the meanings of lexical units (Cruse 1986; Mel'čuk 1989) in all languages. This claim is not, of course, uncontroversial but even if it should turn out not to be 100 per cent correct, it is surely indisputable that semantic primes and basic semantic molecules, that is, words like 'people', 'do', 'know', 'say', 'good', 'bad', and 'because' (examples of semantic primes) and 'man', 'woman', 'child', 'mouth', 'be born', 'long', and 'sharp' (examples of basic semantic molecules) are *relatively* more cross-translatable and relatively less prone to cultural bias than words like 'relationship', 'experience', 'communication', and 'control' (examples of highly English-specific meanings).

Space precludes an overview of the semantic primes here, but in view of the theme of this Handbook, the proposal that WORD(S) is a semantic prime deserves some elaboration, as is the related claim that the concept of WORD(S) is universally lexicalized (Goddard 2011b; Wierzbicka 1996). Integral to the first claim is its resistance to non-circular definition. Consider, for example, sentences such as 'He/she said one word' (which contrasts with 'He/she said one thing') and 'He/she said the same thing in other words'. These sentences show that there is a conceptual contrast between, roughly speaking, the content of what is said and the form (WORDS) in which it is said. On the NSM view, it is literally impossible to paraphrase the meaning of 'word(s)', as used in sentences like these, in a reductive, non-circular fashion.[2] As suggested by the representation WORD(S), the proposed semantic prime is intended to be indeterminate between singular and plural, i.e. to be capable of referring to a single word (when combined with ONE) and equally to be capable of referring to something that is multiple in character.

The claim that the concept of WORD(S) is universally lexicalized has often been contradicted (e.g. Dixon and Aikhenvald 2002a: 2): 'It appears that only some languages actually have a lexeme with the meaning "word"'.[3] Examined carefully, however, this counter-claim turns out to be based on a failure to properly take account of polysemy.

[2] Typical ordinary language definitions of *(a) word*, such as 'ultimate minimal unit of speech' (*OED*) and 'single unit of language' (Collins Cobuild), fail both on account of their obscurity and because the words 'speech' and 'language' themselves depend conceptually on 'words', thus making the definitions implicitly circular.

[3] Despite Dixon and Aikhenvald's (2002a) claim to the contrary, WORD(S) is well attested as a lexical meaning in Australian languages such as Arrernte, Warlpiri, Kayardild, and Bundjalung (Goddard 2011b: 51). Likewise, there seems to be no particular difficulty in locating exponents of WORD(S) in polysynthetic languages, despite the tremendous difference in the kinds of words that can be found in them (Goddard 2001a).

Exponents of semantic primes are often polysemous (a phenomenon which has been much studied by NSM linguists). Even in English, the word *word* has extended meanings that go beyond the semantically primitive meaning; for example, in fixed and semi-fixed expressions such as: *a word of warning, a kind word* (or *kind words*), *to have a word with someone, to have the last word, to put in a good word, to get/bring word of something, to give one's word*, not to mention biblical expressions such as *the word of God*. All these expressions refer to someone saying something (usually something brief) about something: they are not examples of WORD(S) in its semantically primitive sense. In cross-linguistic perspective, English is rather typical in this respect. In many languages the lexeme that can express the meaning WORD(S) can also express other, distinct, meanings such as 'talk', 'way of speaking', 'message', 'utterance', and 'what is said'.

To say that the concept of WORD(S) is apparently a pan-human concept is not to say that people everywhere have the same set of cultural beliefs and ideas about WORD(S). Obviously they do not; and to map out the patterns in word-related beliefs and practices across the world's cultures would be a fascinating project in linguistic anthropology. Three observations that can be made are: first, that WORD(S) are (presumably) universally implicated in religious/spiritual beliefs and practices, e.g. in rituals, prayers, chants, magical formulae, and the like; second, that variation in word use is (presumably) universally accorded social significance, e.g. taken to indicate identity, affiliation, status, and the like; and third, that the institution of writing inevitably introduces a complex of new, culturally variable ideas and ideologies about words (Ong 1982). The existence of variation in beliefs and practices involving WORD(S) is in no way inconsistent with the claim that WORD(S) is a universally lexicalized meaning. On the contrary, it is testimony to the importance of words to human beings, and to people's high level of awareness and attention to words.

Before proceeding, one additional analytical concept must be mentioned. This is what is variously referred to in the literature as cultural norms (norms of interaction, norms of interpretation), cultural rules, cultural assumptions, cultural scripts, etc. Despite the differences in terminology, all analysts agree that some constructs of this kind are important in cultural analysis. Such cultural norms or assumptions are different from word meanings: they are part of cultural pragmatics or ethnopragmatics, rather than semantics. At the same time, however, cultural assumptions are not unconnected with word meanings, just as pragmatics is not unconnected with semantics. As it happens, semantic primes can be used not only for descriptive semantics but also as a notation for writing cultural scripts (Goddard 2006; Goddard and Wierzbicka 2004). This enables hypotheses about shared cultural assumptions to be formulated in terms that are recognizable to the people concerned and can represent cognitively realistic 'insider perspectives'. It also facilitates an easy integration between lexical semantics and pragmatics, i.e. roughly, between meaning that is encoded or encapsulated in words and meaning that is 'brought in', so to speak, by contextual assumptions. The focus of this chapter, however, is lexical meanings.

21.2 Cultural key words

21.2.1 The 'key word' concept

The term 'cultural key words' refers to particularly culture-rich and translation-resistant words that occupy focal points in cultural ways of thinking, acting, feeling, and speaking. Wierzbicka (1997: 17) explains:

> A key word such as *duša* (roughly 'soul') or *sud'ba* (roughly 'fate') in Russian is like one loose end which we have managed to find in a tangled ball of wool: by pulling it, we may be able to unravel a whole tangled 'ball' of attitudes, values, and expectations, embodied not only in words, but also in common collocations, in set phrases, in grammatical constructions, in proverbs, and so on...

The concept of a cultural key word is a qualitative one and somewhat inexact in the sense that it is not always possible to draw a strict line between cultural key words, other culturally important words, and less important but still culture-related words. Nevertheless, the key word concept has an undoubted heuristic value in helping to focus attention on culturally prominent concepts. Sometimes certain key words rise to the attention of a speech community (usually by way of contrast with outsiders) and attain an iconic, and therefore frequently contested status, in national identity discourses, e.g. Danish *hygge* 'pleasant togetherness cosy sociality', Dutch *gezellig* 'convivial, cosy, fun', Australian English *fair go*. Other key words stay below the horizon of consciousness of most speakers.

Cultural key words may be found in different departments of the lexicon, sometimes in unexpected places. The following is a non-exhaustive listing of areas which are known, on the basis of existing work, to be natural homes, so to speak, for cultural key words, along with a sample of quality work on a range of languages. The use of double inverted commas is intended to indicate that the English "translations" are approximate and inaccurate, to a greater extent than usual.

Cultural values and ideals, e.g. English *fair, reasonable* (Wierzbicka 2006a), German *Pflicht* "duty" (Wierzbicka 2014b), Chinese *xiào* "filial piety", *ren* "perseverance" (Goddard 2011a: 84–6; Ye 2006), Malay *sabar* "patient", *setia* "loyal" (Goddard 2001b), Danish *tryghet* "security", *hygge* "cosy sociality" (Levisen 2012), French *méfiance* "wariness, mistrust" (Peeters 2013), Japanese *wa* "harmony, unity", *omoiyari* "empathy" (Wierzbicka 1997: 248–53, 275–8), Spanish *confianza* "trust", *calor humano* "human warmth" (Travis 2006).

"Sociality" concepts. This heading overlaps with the previous one, but it may be helpful in view of the new emphasis on sociality (Enfield and Levinson 2006). Examples include English *privacy* (Wierzbicka 2008), as well as the personal descriptors *rude* and *nice* (Waters 2012), French *s'engager* "being engaged, committed" (Peeters 2000), and *kastom* "traditional practices" in Melanesian Creoles (Levisen forthcoming).

Ethnophilosophical terms, including religious, metaphysical, epistemological, and cosmological terms: terms concerned with the nature of the world and people's position in it. Examples include: Russian *sud'ba* "fate, destiny" (Wierzbicka 1997), English *God, the devil* and their near-equivalents in Arabic and Hebrew (Habib 2011a, 2011b), English *evidence, commonsense* (Wierzbicka 2010a), Oceanic *mana* "spiritual power" (Goddard and Wierzbicka 2014b; cf. Keesing 1986).

Emotions. As mentioned, emotions have been a rich vein for studies in culture-related meaning. Examples include: English *happiness* and German *Angst* "fear, anxiety" (Wierzbicka 1999: ch. 3; 2014a), Malay *malu* "shame" and related social emptions (Goddard 1996b), German *Wut* "rage, anger" (Durst 2001), Ilonglot *liget* "anger, passion, energy" (Rosaldo 1980), Ifaluk *fago* "compassion, love, sadness", *song* "justifiable anger" (Lutz 1988), Japanese *amae* "trusting dependency" (Wierzbicka 1997: 238–43).

Ethnopsychological constructs. This term refers to nominal expressions designating non-physical parts of a person, akin to English *mind, heart, soul,* and *spirit.* Significant studies exist on Russian *duša* "soul" (Wierzbicka 1992, 2005; cf. Pesmen 2000), English *heart* (Goddard 2008), French *âme* and German *Seele* (Wierzbicka 1992: 55–9), Malay *hati* (Goddard 2001c, 2008), Korean *maum* and *kasum* (Yoon 2006), Chinese *xin* (Yu 2009), Japanese *kokoro* (Hasada 2000: 115–16), Persian *del* and *chesm* (Sharifian 2011).

Cross-cutting a number of these categories are cultural studies of figurative (especially, metaphorical) language; e.g. Sharifian et al. (2008); Idström and Piirainen (2012).

21.2.2 Sketches of two cultural key words (English, Chinese)

Space permits only quick sketches of two examples of cultural key words, and these fall far short of expounding their full cultural relevance. There is nothing surprising about this. These are cultural key words, after all: by definition, each one could sustain and reward extensive study.

Anglo English *fair*. Wierzbicka (2006a) argues that *fairness* is one of the key values in modern Anglo culture, and points out that the expressions *That's not fair!* and *It's not fair!* are commonly heard in daily life from both children and adults, and across registers from informal to formal (e.g. in scholarly works, government publications, public administration, business, trade, and law).[4] This is all the more remarkable given their non-translatability into other European languages, let alone non-European languages. *Fair* (and *fairness*) form part of an ensemble of related Anglo concepts, such as *right* and *wrong, reasonable*, and even *rules*. Explication [A] below, for the expression *That's*

[4] Some legal scholars, notably Rawls (2001), have attempted to re-think the concept of *justice* in terms of *fairness*. This can be seen as a natural move, from the point of view of those anchored in Anglo ways of thinking. Less commonly, some legal scholars, such as Fletcher (1996: 81), have recognized that '[r]emarkably, our concept of fairness does not readily translate into other languages.'

not fair, is based on that proposed in Wierzbicka (2006a).[5] Notable aspects include the relational character of *fairness* (one is *fair* or *unfair* **to** someone) but that *fairness* does not necessarily involve doing something to someone. It rather turns on the negative effect of an action on someone else ('being bad for someone else'). Equally importantly, *fairness* presupposes doing something **with** someone else: it implies having 'dealings', so to speak, with the affected person. In these respects, *fairness* differs markedly from, for example, *justice*; in English, one can easily describe a teacher, for example, as *fair* or *unfair*, but hardly as *just* or *unjust*. Likewise, *rules* can be *fair* or *unfair* (and *rules* apply in situations in which people want to do things together). The link between *fairness* and *rules* highlights the fact that *fairness* implies a certain consensus about what can and can't be done within the 'rules of the game', so to speak.

[A] *That's not fair.*

a. I say: 'people can't do things like this,
   if someone does something like this, he/she does something bad'
b. if other people know about it, they can't not say the same
c. when people want to do things of some kinds with other people, it is like this:
d.   they can do some things
e.   at the same time they can't do some other things,
     because if they do things like this, it is very bad for these other people
f. everyone knows this

Notice that although *fairness* is often used in contexts that imply equality of treatment, in expressions like *fair share*, this is not always or necessarily the case. For example, in the collocation *fair prices* the focus is not on prices being the same for everyone, but rather on prices being such that they could be judged, by the general consensus, as justifiable (in terms of what is 'reasonable' for both sellers and buyers). Consider also expressions like *fair comment* and *fair criticism*. What is common across the full range of uses, Wierzbicka argues, is the assumption of consensus about what range of behaviours one can and cannot adopt, and, consequently, the assumed 'right' to say to someone who is being seen as acting *unfairly* that 'you can't do things like this'.

Attempting to summarize, informally, the unconscious cultural assumptions underlying the concept of *fairness*, Wierzbicka (2006a: 152) puts it as follows:

> Human interaction, which is based largely on what people as individuals want to do, needs to be regulated, in everyone's interest, by certain rules. These rules cannot be all stated in advance—presumably, because life is too complex and varied for that. ... The rules are seen as general, the same for everyone ('democratic') and voluntary. The approach is pragmatic and flexible (the rules are not necessarily all stated in advance). It allows for free pursuit of one's wants (it is 'liberal'), but within limits.

[5] Though its key semantic content is retained, this explication differs in form from its predecessor in Wierzbicka (2006a). The revised version presented in [A] was devised jointly by Wierzbicka and the present author.

In these respects, Wierzbicka (2006a: 152) argues: 'the everyday word *fair* has crystallized in its meaning political and philosophical ideas which were developed in the seventeenth and eighteenth century by the thinkers of the British Enlightenment and which have become entrenched in modern Anglo consciousness'.

Chinese *xiào* 'filial piety'. The noun *xiào* represents an ancient and enduring Chinese virtue, and many people have located it at the very core of traditional Confucian values. As one traditional saying has it: *Băi shàn xiào wéi xiān* 'Of the hundred good deeds, *xiào* comes first'. *Xiào* is normally rendered into English by way of the curious expression 'filial piety', but this expression is a highly specialized one, and most ordinary speakers of English would have only a hazy idea of what it is supposed to convey. Djao (2003: 203) says that *xiào* implies 'love, respect, obedience, solicitude, devotion, care' and 'the utter sense of duty of the children towards the parents, with the implicit understanding that the children will look after the parents in their old age'. Confucius himself characterized *xiào* simply as: 'Give your father and mother no cause for anxiety other than illness.' At the core of *xiào* is the notion that a person owes a unique lifelong debt to his or her parents, though it can also be extended to grandparents and, especially for a woman, to parents-in-law. One's parents (*fùmŭ* 'father [and] mother') have given you life, raised you, educated you, and so on. *Fùmŭ eng bí shān gāo, bí hăi shēn* 'What our parents give us is higher than a mountain, deeper than the ocean.'

The meaning of *xiào* can be explicated as shown in [B]. The first batch of components, in (a), establishes the focus on one's father and mother and on their special role in bringing an individual into the world and sustaining his or her life, and indicates that the individual has a special emotional attitude towards them. The components in (b) state that a person should always keep one's parents in mind and maintain a deep concern for the parents' satisfaction and peace of mind, such that one feels compelled to do certain things to make them feel good, and to refrain from doing certain other things which could make them feel bad. The components in (c) specify that it is considered very good if a person puts this attitude into practice in a substantial way, and very bad if they do not.

[B] *xiào* 'filial piety'

a. people can think about some other people like this:
'one of these people is my father, one of these people is my mother
I live because these people did many good things for me for a long time after I was born
because of this, when I think about them, I feel something very good'
b. it is good if someone thinks about these people at all times
it is good if someone thinks about these people like this:
'I want these people to feel something very good at all times
because of this, I want to do many good things for them
I can't not do these things
I don't want these people to feel something bad at any time
because of this, I can't do some things
I don't want to do these things'
c. it is very good if so'meone does many things because this someone thinks like this it is very bad if someone does not do many things because this someone thinks like this

Notice that the explication does not indicate which particular kinds of action are to be pursued or avoided. These could vary from situation to situation, though obviously looking after the parents' material wellbeing and peace of mind would be a minimum expectation. As for their mental satisfaction, given broader Chinese cultural concerns, this would often include things like achieving success in business or scholarship, bringing honour to the family name, and so on. The explication does not specify that anything like 'obedience' as such is required, taking it for granted that going against one's parents' wishes on a serious matter is ruled out because of the distress this would cause them.

Emphasizing that the *xiào* concept has no real equivalent in non-Confucian cultures, Ho (1996: 155) goes so far as to assert: 'filial piety surpasses all other ethics in historical continuity, the proportion of humanity under its governance, and the encompassing and imperative nature of its precepts.'

21.2.3 Additional comments

Although we have presented cultural key words as characteristic of languages, it is worth pointing out that there is not necessarily a one-to-one alignment between key words and languages, for two reasons. First, different varieties of a single language can have some different key words (while sharing others). For example, comparing American English with Australian English, it can be argued that the words *freedom* and *dream* (in the sense of 'ambition') have a better claim to key word status in American English, while in Australia the concept of *the fair go* (which is not equivalent to 'equality of opportunity': Wierzbicka 1997a) would have sound claim to key word status. In English English, the (folk) concept of *(social) class* undoubtedly has key word status (Goddard 2012), which it lacks in Australian or American English.

Second, it is possible to broaden the key word concept to make it applicable to 'areal semantics' (Matisoff 2004; Ameka 2009). Concepts such as 'money', 'God', and 'country' would presumably be entitled to the status of pan-European cultural key words. But although they occur with identical or near-identical meanings across the European culture zone and therefore hardly attract attention from Europeans, they are in fact culturally very distinctive when set against, for example, the traditional Aboriginal languages of the Australian continent. Similarly, the Australian Aboriginal concept often represented in English as 'Dreamtime' or 'Dreaming' (Green 2012) is widespread across Australian Aboriginal languages (cf. Arrernte *altyerre*, Warlpiri *Jukurrpa*, Yankunytjatjara *tjukurpa*) and can equally be seen as an areal cultural key word.

21.3 Other culturally important words

Many words are not sufficiently prominent and distinctive to qualify for the epithet of 'key word', but are nonetheless culture-laden to a significant extent. In the first part of this section (21.3.1), we survey a number of lexical domains, as speech-act verbs, social-category words, and terms of address, which are known to be particularly sensitive to cultural loading. Then in section 21.3.2 we shall see examples from several areas, such as cognitive/epistemic verbs, which may not be such obvious candidates. In section 21.3.3, we examine another way in which culture-specific meanings can manifest themselves across the vocabulary, namely, the role of culture-specific semantic molecules.

21.3.1 Social and interactional words

Probably every language has some areas of 'lexical elaboration' (Majid, this volume). Though not an exact term, this expression designates the situation of a language having an impressively large number of words in a particular semantic domain, thereby providing the terminological scaffolding for fine conceptual differences. Usually lexical elaboration can be seen to serve some cultural and/or functional purpose, though in some cases the reasons may not immediately apparent.

This can be illustrated with the example of English **speech-act verbs**, i.e. words such as *ask, suggest, apologize, thank, promise, complain*, and *congratulate*. Speech-act verbs provide a 'catalogue' of salient kinds of verbal interactions recognized in a particular culture. There is great cross-linguistic variation in the number of speech-act verbs in particular languages and in their character; see Ameka (2009) on Ewe, Goddard (2004) on Malay, Wierzbicka (2003, 2012a) on English, Polish, and Russian, and Peeters (2013) on French.

English is unusual in having literally hundreds of speech-act verbs, outdoing all or most of the other languages of Europe in this respect, let alone most languages from other parts of the world. In other words, the English speech-act lexicon is an area of great lexical elaboration, with many fine-grained meaning differences; consider, for example, *suggest* vs. *recommend, promise* vs. *guarantee, praise* vs. *compliment, insult* vs. *abuse, refuse* vs. *decline* (Goddard and Wierzbicka 2014a. But why? Wierzbicka (2003, 2006a, 2012) has argued that lexical elaboration in this arena supports cultural attention to the dynamics of interpersonal causation, which in turn arises from the modern Anglo cultural ideal of personal autonomy. Going further, she argues that one English speech-act verb—*suggest*—stands out as the prime example of contemporary Anglo interactional style. Not only is English unique among European languages in possessing a speech-act verb with the precise semantics of *suggest*, but the English language has also developed a whole brace of 'suggestive' strategies and formulas (Wierzbicka 2006b).

Related to speech acts, words for **genres and speech events** (such as English *story, interview, lecture, joke)* represent a cultural inventory of recognized forms of extended verbal interaction. They are usually heavily culture embedded. Many studies in the ethnography of communication have focused attention on culturally revealing words of this kind (e.g. Katriel 1986 on Israeli *dugri* 'straight talk'; cf. Carbaugh 2005; Philipsen and Carbaugh 1986), but dedicated linguistic semantic studies are rare. Exceptions include Wierzbicka (1990) on Polish *kawal* 'conspirational joke' and *podanie* 'application, letter of request', Wierzbicka (2010b) on English *story* (which she regards as an

Anglo cultural key word), Goddard (1992) on the Yankunytjatjara indirect speech style *tjalpawangkanytja*.

Social categories, words for kinds of people. Examples include English *friend* (Wierzbicka 1997), Korean *noin* 'respected old people' (Yoon 2004), Russian *drug* 'close friend' and *rodnye* 'dear kin' (Wierzbicka 1997: 55–84; Gladkova 2013; Chinese *shúrén* 'old acquaintance' and *shēngrén* 'stranger', *zìjĭrén* 'insider, one of us', and *wàirén* 'outsider' (Ye 2004; 2013; Koromu (PNG) reciprocal terms *namuka* '(female) age-mate' and *waikohu* '(male) age-mate' (Priestley 2013); words for moieties in Australian Aboriginal societies (Wierzbicka 2013). An interesting dimension of such words in many languages are semantic components e.g. 'all these people are like one something, I am one of these people') that express someone's sense of belonging to a group, such as a family, moiety, clan, etc.

It is widely recognized that **terms of address** and address practices are indicative of local systems of social status, social distinction, and affiliation. Less often recognized is that address terms are not merely governed by pragmatic rules but have specifiable semantic content, which can be explicated to a high degree of accuracy. For a study of Australian English *mate*, see Wierzbicka (1997: 101–18). Wong (2006a, 2006b) deals with *auntie* and other kinship or quasi-kinship address terms in Singapore English.

Other culturally revealing areas include ethnomedical terminology, proverbs, and other traditional sayings (cf. Goddard 2009; Goddard and Wierzbicka 2014a), and conversational formulae and routines, including interjections (Ameka 1992, 1994, 2009; Bromhead 2009).

21.3.2 Cultural semantics in unexpected places

The domains treated in the previous section all plainly concern social interaction, and are therefore natural candidates for culture-related meaning. In this section, we look into several domains where culture-related meanings occur in unexpected places.

Cognitive verbs might seem an unlikely domain for social meaning, but when one considers that voicing one's thoughts and opinions often implies positioning them in relation to the thoughts and opinions of other people, the potential for socially oriented meaning to enter the picture becomes clearer. This can be illustrated with examples from English, Russian, and Danish. Compare the explications below for English *believe (that)* and Russian *sčitat'* 'firmly believe', respectively (Gladkova 2007: 75; Wierzbicka 2006a: 216–18). The *believe* explication applies to the meaning found in the grammatical frame with a *that*-complement, e.g. *I believe that they shouldn't have the vote*. Roughly speaking, it conveys a considered conviction, along with a certain gravitas, as shown by the fact that it can collocate with adverbs like *strongly*, e.g. *I strongly believe that* ... There is also acknowledgement of the possible existence of another point of view ('I know that someone else can think not like this'). Subsequent components express the speaker's apparent confidence that he or she can provide some kind of justification for thinking this way, almost as if the person is expecting to be asked to justify his or her belief. The semantic content of *believe* resonates with Anglo cultural values of openness to others' opinions and a 'reasonable' attitude.

[C] *I believe that* — —:

a. when I think about it, I think like this '— —'
b. I know that someone else can think not like this
c. I can say why I think like this
d. I can say why it is good if someone thinks like this

Comparing with explication [D] for Russian *sčitat'* (Gladkova 2007), we can see some similarities (the first and final components of the two explications are similar), but there are many differences. The Russian word presents a seriously considered position about which there is no longer any room for doubt. It does not allow for or envisage other credible options and opinions. The final components portray the subject's determination to uphold and stick to the position expressed. These components explain why *sčitat'* cannot be used with any of the words that can intensify opinions in Russian—*gluboko* 'deeply', *sil'no* 'strongly', or *tverdo* 'firmly' (sentences like **Ja gluboko sčitaju, čto…*, **Ja sil'no sčitaju, čto…*, and the like, are ungrammatical). Gladkova (2007) links the 'absoluteness' of *sčitat'* to the value Russians place on forcefully speaking one's mind and on *govorit' pravdu* 'telling the truth' for its own sake.

[D] *Ja sčitaju, čto* — —:

a. when I think about it, I think this '— —'
b. I thought about it for some time
c. I thought about things like this before
d. I want to think like this
e. I know why I want to think like this
f. I don't want to think about it in any other way
g. it is good to think about it like this

Levisen (2012) argues that several Danish verbs of cognition reflect characteristically Danish ways of thinking about thinking. *Synes*, for example, depicts an immediate and impressionistic response ('I think like this because I feel something now'). According to Levisen, willingness to share subjective impressions is valued in the Danish speech community, as is recognition that another person might think differently ('I know that someone else can think not like this'). The verb *mener* reflects another cognitive trend in the Danish speech community, anchored, as Levisen puts it, in 'co-cognition'. This is related to the value that is placed on being able to navigate one's way through a landscape of opinions: '*Mener* reflects a social reality which operates with "groupy" structures, and in which groups of like-minded people are thought to share opinions. At the same time, one's opinions are known to conflict with those of other groups' (Levisen 2012: 177). Levisen's explication includes the components: 'I know that some people can think the same, I know that some other people don't think the same.'

Related to cognitive verbs, but very different in terms of grammar, are epistemic adverbs, e.g. words such as English *probably, certainly, presumably*. Wierzbicka (2006a) argues that English exhibits lexical elaboration in this domain, motivated by the Anglo cultural value placed on epistemic caution and acknowledgement of other's opinions.

Ethnogeographical words. It is easy to assume that words like *mountain, river*, and *coast* simply designate places (or kinds of place) and thus lack cultural content, but in fact languages and cultures differ as to how they categorize the landscape (Bromhead 2011, 2013; Burenhult 2008; Mark and Turk 2003). This raises the possibility of culture-related aspects of meaning. For example, the meaning of English *desert* is largely constituted in terms of 'absences' and difficulties (Arthur 2003): lack of water, lack of people, the difficulty of living in hostile conditions. This construal reflects the perspective of outsiders, rather than the perspective of indigenous inhabitants, such as the Pitjantjatjara/Yankunytjatjara (P/Y) A̲nangu of Central Australia. The same stretch of country that an English speaker could see as *desert* could be described using a P/Y 'eco zone' word such as *pu̲ti* 'bush country' or *ta̲li* 'sandhill country'. Although this is not evident from the English glosses, Bromhead (2013) argues that these words incorporate a certain amount of ethnobiological and ethnozoological knowledge; for example, that kangaroos and small game can be found in *pu̲ti* and that many kinds of berries are found in the *ta̲li*. If this is correct, the P/Y words can be seen as partly analogous to English words like *meadow, field*, and *paddock*, because in both cases the meanings include some idea of the kind of human use or activity. Human use is even more evident in P/Y geographical terms like *tjukula* 'rockhole' and *tjintjir̲a* 'claypan', whose semantic content is motivated by their usefulness as water resources in the arid Central Australian landscape. As Lowe and Pike (1990: 11; Bromhead 2013) remark: 'Because water was so precious in the lives of desert people, they [Aboriginal people] paid particular attention to places where it could be found at different times of the year, and had special names for the various kinds of holes or cavities in which water might collect.' Bromhead (2011) argues, in part, that the semantics of the Australian English word *creek* has adapted to the dryness of the continent in allowing for there being a variable amount of flowing water.

21.3.3 Culture-specific semantic molecules

As mentioned, semantic molecules are non-primitive word meanings which function as building blocks in the meanings of many other words. Some semantic molecules are believed to be universal or near-universal, e.g. various body-part words (e.g. 'hands', 'mouth', 'eyes', 'ears', 'legs', 'teeth', 'blood'), environmental terms (e.g. 'sky', 'ground', 'sun', 'fire', 'water'), physical properties (e.g. 'hard', 'long', 'sharp', 'heavy'), and some social categories and family-related words (such as 'men', 'women', 'children', 'mother', 'father', and 'be born'). Semantic molecules can also be highly language-specific, e.g. for English, 'God', 'colour', and 'number', and these can have great relevance to cultural content in the lexicon. Some of the ways in which semantic molecules can enter into the meanings of other words are more or less obvious to the untutored semantic intuition, but some only come to light after careful semantic analysis. As an example of the former, presumably no-one would deny that the concept of 'God' is involved in the meanings of 'Christian' words such as *priest, church, sin, hymn, prayer, abbot, cloister, monastery*.

As for the concept of 'number', it may be well to remember that, as with 'colour', there are many languages and cultures that have no word for 'number' and lack elaborate systems of number words, and that in many cultures people do not engage in counting or similar practices, such as tallying (Goddard 2009). Arguably, the concept of 'number' enters into the meaning structure of a great many 'quantitative words' of one kind or another. For example, in English there are property-related abstract nouns, such *temperature, weight*, and *age* (Goddard and Wierzbicka 2014a), words for measuring devices and units of measurement (*clock, scales, speedometer; date, hour, minute, kilo, inch, kilometre*), words for types of numerical reckoning (*count, calculate, addition, subtraction*), and for numerical fields of study and practice (*maths, arithmetic*). It can be argued that the idea of precise and verifiable quantitative statements forms part of the concept of 'science' (cf. Wierzbicka 2011). More unexpected, perhaps, is the proposition that the concept of 'science' is implicated in the large register of English 'scientific' words, e.g. words like *hydrogen, electron, genome*, which can be regarded as part of everyday English but which still bear the semantic stamp, so to speak, of science.

21.4 Other culture-related words

As mentioned earlier, whether and to what extent we see the culture-connectedness of seemingly ordinary words depends to some extent on the method of semantic analysis. This applies even to words for items of material culture (artefacts, clothing, and the like). For example, anyone unfamiliar with Western Desert lifestyle will see at a glance that the words listed below (with definitions from the *Pitjantjatjara/Yankunytjatjara To English Dictionary*, Goddard 1996b) are linked to the lifestyle and culture of their speakers:

KIṮI: adhesive gum, made from the resin of spinifex or mulga. Used to plug holes or cracks in bowls, etc. and in making tools and weapons, such as spearthrower and hunting spears

PITI: large hemispherical wooden bowl, used to carry water

TJIRPIKA: a bed of leafy sprigs or small branches to put meat on, so it won't get covered in dirt

It may be much less obvious that a subtle and seemingly trivial difference, such as that between English *cup* and *mug*, could have any cultural relevance. On close analysis, however, it emerges that part of the meaning structure of *cup* is a 'use scenario' involving drinking a hot beverage, often while seated at a table (sometimes in association with a saucer) and typically picking it up and putting it down while drinking, while the scenario associated with *mug* involves holding the vessel in the hand for an extended period (Goddard 2011a: 225–32). At this micro-level of analysis, even small differences in the semantics of artefact words may be seen to have some culture-related content.

Likewise, it would be easy to assume that **words for natural kinds**, such as biological species, have little or no culture-related content, but this depends on the assumption that such words are simply labels for objective existing entities (or classes of entities) and nothing more. From a semantic point of view, it is more plausible that human perspectives of various kinds enter into the meanings of 'folk category' words; for example, that the meaning of English *tiger* includes the idea that they are fierce and dangerous, that the meaning of English *dog* and *cat* includes the idea that they are domestic animals (roughly, that they often live with people and can be useful); that the meanings of *cow* and *sheep* includes the idea that they are or can be 'farm animals' and that people get useful products, such as meat and wool, from them.

Attitudinal differences (or emotional stereotypes and associations) can also be part of the meanings of species words. The cultural associations of English *dog* and Malay *anjing* 'dog', for example, are significantly different because in the canonical Malay (Islamic) belief system *anjing* are unclean animals: one must ritually purify oneself after touching one, and the idea that they could live in one's house is quite repulsive. Similar observations apply to English *pig* vs. Malay *babi*; see also Levisen (2013) on Danish *svin* and *grise*. Examples like these could obviously be multiplied at length. In short, different cultural attitudes and different cultural utilizations may be embedded into word meanings.

Even the meanings of **physical-activity verbs** that may seem to correspond readily across languages may turn out, on closer examination, to differ in fine details in ways that make sense in cultural context. For example, Levinson (2007) argues that the peculiar semantics of 'cut/break' verbs in the Papuan language Yélî Dnye (e.g. *châpwo* 'sever across the grain' vs. *chaa* 'sever along the grain') reflect a traditional material culture based on splitting fibres with simple stone tools. In making canoes and houses '[c]utting across the grain was especially problematic, and wherever possible timber, vines and fibers were divided along the grain'. A contrastive semantic study is provided by Goddard and Wierzbicka (2009; Goddard 2011a: 285–95), who focus on 'chopping' verbs. English *chop*, Polish *rąbać*, and Japanese *kizamu* have very similar semantic structures and are normally listed as simple translation equivalents in bilingual dictionaries. They all involve a prototypical intention of transforming something into smaller pieces using an instrument with a sharp edge, by making repeated movements to raise the instrument and bring it down into contact with the object. Nonetheless, there are fine differences. Compared with *chop*, Polish *rąbać* depicts a larger and more forceful action, typically in relation to something very hard, such as wood and ice. The instrument is typically heavy, such as an axe or a heavy butcher's knife (not an ordinary kitchen knife, for example), and it is typically raised high above the object, before being brought down with force. Japanese *kizamu*, on the other hand, depicts small-scale and less forceful action than either *rąbać* or *chop*. The verb is prototypically used in relation to food preparation, where the desired outcome is very small pieces. Typically the instrument is smaller, lighter, and not raised high above the thing being affected. These differences can be linked with different cultural contexts and practices. In Poland there is a great need to chop wood in winter and to chop/cut openings (*przerębel*) in the ice of frozen lakes and ponds for fishing. The semantics of Japanese *kizamu* makes sense in terms of Japanese culinary traditions, which involve preparing small and delicate pieces of food which can be held daintily between finger and thumb or elegantly lifted to the mouth with chopsticks. (In the Japanese tradition, it was not common for wood to be chopped: firewood was typically gathered from fallen branches.)

21.5 Discussion

Emerging from the forest of detail, I would like to conclude with four broad points. First, almost any and every word can be seen as culture-bearing to some extent. From a practical point of view, this contention can readily be illustrated by the kind of examples reviewed in this chapter, but it also makes sense from a theoretical point of view. Though the number of genuine absolute semantic universals has not yet been established, it is almost certain that it cannot be more than 200 or so, given that there are 65 known semantic primes and only about 30–40 currently known or suspected universal semantic molecules (Goddard 2001a; Goddard and Wierzbicka 2014a, 2014b). This means that the vast bulk of the vocabulary of every language is subject to variability, and hence, potentially, to culture-related variation.

Second, the main contribution that linguistics can bring to the humanistic tradition of interest in cultural aspects of word meaning is the added discipline and rigour of linguistic analysis. To make good this promise, however, semantic analysis must be carried out reductively, i.e. from complex to simple, using minimal and standardized units of description which are as free as possible from ethnocentric bias. It remains a concern that many schools of linguistic analysis proceed without regard to these principles, producing analyses which are framed in an ever-proliferating maze of obscure and Anglocentric terms (Wierzbicka 2014).

Third, the culture-laden nature of most English words, including those invented or co-opted for the purposes of semantic analysis, has broader implications for linguistics as a discipline and community of practice in the 21st century. As an incipient global lingua franca, English is extending its functional reach and conceptual influence over other major national and international languages. Meanwhile, the world's minority languages are disappearing at an alarming rate. There is an urgent need for linguists to pay attention to the fact that English words too are carriers of cultural meaning, to help dispel the impression that the advance of global English is a purely functional, culture-neutral phenomenon, and to document ways in which even major national and international languages are changing under the semantic influence of English. This can happen via the adoption of loanwords (albeit often adapted in meaning as they enter the recipient language) or, more subtly, as Anglo cultural themes and values exert an influence on the semantics of indigenous vocabulary. Both phenomena can be illustrated by recent studies of Russian (Gladkova 2008; Zalizniak et al. 2005, 2012).

Fourth, there is the need for an improved standard of lexical-semantic documentation of endangered languages (Austin and Sallabank 2011; Evans 2010). Existing fieldwork manuals pay scant attention to the importance of locating and exploring culturally important words, or to the challenges involved in doing so (Goddard and Wierzbicka 2014b). Lexical-semantic analysis and documentation should be a priority for linguistics in the field, with cultural aspects of meaning at the forefront of attention.

We cannot understand the true nature of language without understanding words, and words are much more heavily, and more subtly, culture-laden than is usually recognized by linguists. Linguists need to engage more seriously with high-resolution approaches to lexical semantics and to be more open about the role of words as carriers of cultural meaning.

Acknowledgements

I am grateful to Anna Wierzbicka for helpful input to this chapter. Zhengdao Ye also made many useful suggestions.

PART IV

WORDS IN TIME AND SPACE

CHAPTER 22

ETYMOLOGY

PHILIP DURKIN

22.1 Introduction: Etymology and Words

A topic that is crucial to any study of words is how we decide whether we are dealing with two different words or with a single word. Essentially, this is a matter of distinguishing between homonymy and polysemy. For instance, do *file* 'type of metal tool' and *file* 'set of documents' show two meanings of a single word (i.e. polysemy) or two different words which happen to be identical in pronunciation and spelling (i.e. homonymy)? This question will be approached differently depending on whether we adopt a synchronic or a diachronic perspective. From a synchronic perspective, what matters is whether we perceive a semantic link between the two words. Psycholinguistic experiments may even be conducted in order to measure the degree of association felt by speakers. Such approaches are outside the scope of this chapter.[1] From a diachronic perspective, what we most want to know is whether these two words of identical form share a common history, and if not, whether any influence of one word upon the other can be traced. These questions are answered by the application of etymology. In this particular example, the answer is quite categorical: the two words are of entirely separate origin (one is a word of native Germanic origin, the other a loanword from French; see further section 22.2), and there is no reason to suspect that either has exercised any influence on the other.

This chapter will look to give an overview of the core methods of etymology, i.e. how it is that we establish the separate histories of *file* 'type of metal tool' and *file* 'set of documents'. It will also look closely at those areas where etymology can ask difficult questions about words as units in the diachronic study of the lexicon. Some words show a fairly simple linear progression from one stage in the history of a language to another, and

[1] For discussion of these issues see Koskela (2016), and also Klepousniotou (2002), Beretta et al. (2005).

there is no difficulty in saying that a word at one stage in the history of a language is the direct ancestor of a word in a later historical stage of the same language. In other cases things are much less simple. A single word in contemporary use may have resulted from multiple inputs from different sources, or a single word in an earlier stage in language history may have shown a process of historical split, giving rise ultimately to two quite distinct words in a later stage of the same language. Such phenomena, and the causes by which they arise, present many challenges for the assumption that we can always speak with confidence about 'the history of a word', and hence they will merit particular attention in this chapter.

22.2 A PRACTICAL INTRODUCTION TO THE CORE METHODS OF ETYMOLOGY, THROUGH TWO SHORT EXAMPLES

Section 22.1 introduced the examples of modern English *file* 'type of metal tool' and *file* 'set of documents', and stated that from a diachronic perspective they are definitely two quite separate words: the first is part of the inherited Germanic vocabulary of English, while the second reflects a borrowing from French in the 16th century. It can further be stated that there is definitely no relationship between the Germanic word and the French one, and there are no grounds for supposing that the two English words have had any influence on one another during their history in English. All of this is established by applying the core methods of etymology, which this section will introduce by looking briefly at the histories of these two words.[2]

Modern English *file* 'type of metal tool' has a well-documented and very simple history in English. The word existed already as *fīl* in the same meaning (though features of the referent may have changed, due to technological changes) in the earliest documented stage of the English language, Old English, and is also well attested in the Middle English period (*c.*1150–*c.*1500) and throughout the Modern English period (1500–). The word would have been pronounced /fiːl/ in Old English and Middle English; the modern diphthongal pronunciation /fʌɪl/ (with minor variation in different varieties of English) results from a regular sound change that affected /iː/ late in the Middle English period or very early in the Modern English period. This sound change is one of a series of changes in the pronunciation of vowels and diphthongs in English in this period, known collectively as the Great Vowel Shift (see further section 22.3).

[2] For fuller treatment of etymological methodology see Durkin (2009). For some different perspectives see (with examples drawn chiefly from German) Seebold (1981), (focussing purely on issues to do with the history and pre-history of English) Bammesberger (1984), (focussing particularly on Romance languages and their coverage in etymological dictionaries) Malkiel (1993), or (targeted at a more popular audience) Liberman (2005).

The history of Modern English *file* 'set of documents' is a little more complicated, because semantic change as well as change in word form is involved. The word is first recorded in English in the early 16th century. It shows a borrowing of Middle French *fil*. The modern pronunciation shows that it must have been borrowed early enough to participate in the same development from /fiːl/ to /fʌɪl/ that is shown by the homonym *file* 'type of metal tool'. The core meaning of the French word is 'thread' or sometimes 'wire'. The earliest use of the word in English that is recorded by the *Oxford English Dictionary* refers to a wire, but specifically one on which papers and documents are strung for preservation and reference; the earliest example, from 1525, reads 'Thapothecaries shall kepe the billis that they serue, vpon a fyle', i.e. the apothecaries are to keep on a length of wire written records of the prescriptions that they have administered. From this beginning in English, the meaning of *file* developed by a process of metonymy from the wire on which a collection of records was kept (in later use, especially legal ones), to the set of records itself. This also explains why documents are described as being kept *on file*, or in earlier use *upon (a) file*.

22.3 Teasing out core etymological methods from these examples

The examples of *file* 'type of metal tool' and *file* 'set of documents' show the two main concerns of etymology: detecting and explaining change in word form, and detecting and explaining change in meaning. The histories of both words that I have set out here are well documented, but it is important to note that the historical narrative only emerges from interplay between the historical documents and etymology.

The word *fīl* exists in Old English and Middle English with the same meaning that *file* has in Modern English. A large mass of comparative and historical data tells us that Old English and Middle English *fīl* was pronounced /fiːl/. Observation of hundreds if not thousands of similar word histories tells us that as a result of one of the collection of changes we know as the Great Vowel Shift, a word that has /iː/ in Middle English will have /ʌɪ/ in contemporary (British) English pronunciation. The Great Vowel Shift consisted of a number of interrelated changes in the vowel system of English which extended from roughly the 15th century to the 18th, and which can be represented schematically as in Fig. 22.1. (In fact, the modern quality of the diphthong in *file* probably results from later changes, but the initial diphthongization of /iː/ is a result of the Great Vowel Shift.)[3]

[3] On this and other sound changes discussed in this chapter see Durkin (2009) and further references given there. For a more detailed account of the Great Vowel Shift and an overview of the extensive literature on this topic see especially Lass (1999).

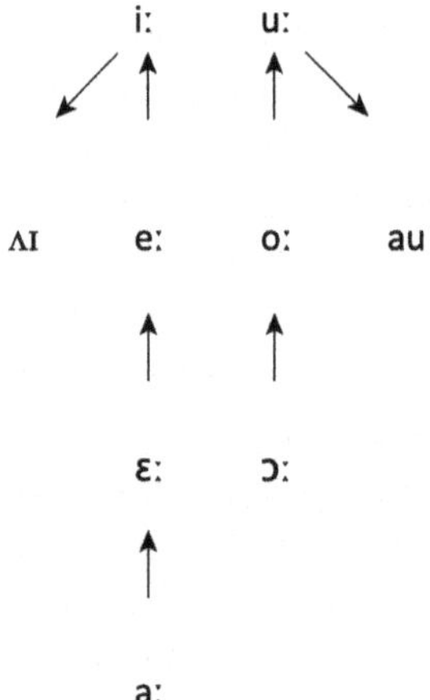

FIG. 22.1 The Great Vowel Shift (simplified).

Regular sound change of this type, affecting all sounds in a similar phonetic environment within a particular time period, is the most powerful explanatory tool available to an etymologist. Because of what we know about the history of English, based on etymological investigation of all of its lexis, we know that a word pronounced /fiːl/ in Old English and Middle English should be pronounced /fʌɪl/ in modern English. If it were not, we would have a problem with our historical account. Since it is, we do not. (See more on this issue below.)

As already explained, the same regular sound change that accounts for *file* 'type of metal tool' also accounts for the pronunciation history of *file* 'set of documents'. This word additionally shows a rather dramatic semantic change, from 'wire' to 'set of documents'. Because of our rich historical documentation for English, we can observe what has happened in detail. The explanation remains a hypothesis, but one about which there can be no reasonable doubt, because we can see all of the stages in the semantic history illustrated in contemporary documents, and because the semantic changes involved are well-known types:[4]

- semantic narrowing, from a wire to specifically a wire on which paper documents are strung;
- and then metonymy, from the wire on which a collection of records is kept, to the collection of records kept on the wire, and then semantic change mirroring technological change, as the records come to be stored by means other than hanging on a wire, and the word *file* comes to refer to any collection of paper documents;
- and then further semantic change mirroring technological change, as the meaning becomes extended to documents (or now more typically a single document) in electronic form.

[4] For types of semantic change, see Geeraerts, this volume.

Precisely the same explanatory methods are used in attempts to construct etymological hypotheses where we have less data, and also for hypotheses that attempt to bridge large gaps in the historical record, or to project word histories back beyond the limits of the historical record. Regular sound change is by far the strongest explanatory tool in the armoury of an etymologist, because it tells us that a particular change should have occurred in a particular language (or dialect) at a particular time. The question of just how much regularity is shown by regular sound changes is a central one in historical linguistics, and one that has profound implications for etymology. Normally, most etymologists work with the assumption that the less data is available about a particular word history, the more important it is to ensure that general rules and tendencies apply. It is very poor methodology to hypothesize that a single word history may have shown a number of undocumented exceptions to otherwise regular sound changes in order to get from stage A to stage B.

Change in meaning is rather more of a problem for etymological reconstruction. General tendencies, such as metaphor, metonymy, narrowing, broadening, pejoration, or amelioration can be traced in countless word histories. The problem is that these changes rarely affect groups of words together. Certainly, we do not have any regular, period-specific changes such as 'general late Middle English or Early Modern English semantic narrowing', analogous to 'late Middle English or Early Modern English diphthongization of /iː/' which we can assume will have affected all words in a particular class in a particular period. For this reason, hypothesizing semantic histories is generally much more difficult than hypothesizing the form histories of words. In the case of *file*, we can get easily from the meaning 'thread or wire' to 'set of documents' because known tendencies in semantic change explain what we can see reflected in the historical record. Without the intervening historical record, if we knew only that *fil* means 'thread or wire' in Middle French and that *file* means 'set of documents' in modern English, it would be a brave and daring step to hypothesize a borrowing followed by this set of changes in order to explain this word history.

22.4 Comparison and reconstruction

The examples discussed so far have all been restricted to the history of English, except that in the case of *file* 'set of documents' it is assumed that Middle French *fil* 'thread or wire' was borrowed into late Middle English or Early Modern English. In this case, we are dealing with borrowing between two well-attested languages. We can see that *fil* 'thread' extends back into Old French (and clearly shows the continuation of a word in the parent language, Latin), and we can see that there is no earlier history of *file* 'thread or wire' in English; we also know that French and English were in close contact in this period, and that many words were borrowed. The situation becomes rather different if we push the history of both *file* 'type of metal tool' and *file* 'set of documents' back a little further.[5]

As well as establishing word histories within languages, etymology can be employed to establish connections between words in different languages. These may be connections involving borrowing, as just illustrated, or they may be connections involving cognacy. This concept needs some explanation. One of the major findings of historical linguistics is that many present-day or historically documented languages can be identified as common descendants from earlier languages. Thus, French, Italian, Spanish, and the other Romance languages can all be traced as descendants from a common ancestor, Latin. Since Latin is amply attested in historical documents, the stages in the development can be traced in detail. The history of the Roman empire also gives us a crucial historical context in which to understand the circumstances of the wide geographical spread of Latin, and gives us some important hints about other languages that Latin was in contact with in different parts of the Empire. To focus on the level of an individual word, French *fil* can be seen to show the reflex, or direct linear development, of Latin *fīlum* 'thread'. The same is true of Italian *filo* and Spanish *hilo*, and thus these are said to be cognates of French *fil*, showing a common descent from Latin *fīlum*. By contrast, French *choisir* 'to choose' does not show the reflex of a Latin word, but rather reflects a direct borrowing into French (or perhaps into the ancestor form of Vulgar Latin spoken in Gaul) from a Germanic language, probably in the context of the Frankish invasions of Gaul; the word is ultimately related to English *choose*.

By the application of what is termed the historical comparative method, many other such relationships of common descent have been identified. For instance, English can be identified as showing common descent with Frisian, Dutch, Low German, and High German; collectively they form the West Germanic branch of the Germanic language family. The relationships between the major members of the Germanic family can be reconstructed as in Fig. 22.2. Proto-Germanic sits at the head of the Germanic languages, just as Latin sits at the head of the Romance languages. It is not directly attested, unlike Latin, but a great deal of its vocabulary, and of its phonology, morphology, and (to a lesser extent) its syntax can be reconstructed by comparison of its attested descendants. A great deal more information, and confirmation of much of what can be hypothesized from comparison within Germanic, comes from comparing the evidence of Germanic with the evidence for the much wider language family, Indo-European, to which it in turn belongs. Scholars working

[5] The etymologies presented in this chapter all draw on documentation from the standard etymological and historical dictionaries for each language involved. Listing all of the dictionaries concerned would be beyond the scope of this article. The etymological dictionary is one of the major outlets for etymological research; as well as advancing new ideas, etymological dictionaries typically summarize the main earlier hypotheses, taking note of data from the other major outlet for etymological research, articles in scholarly journals. On the typology and structure of etymological dictionaries see Buchi (2016) and Malkiel (1975, 1993).

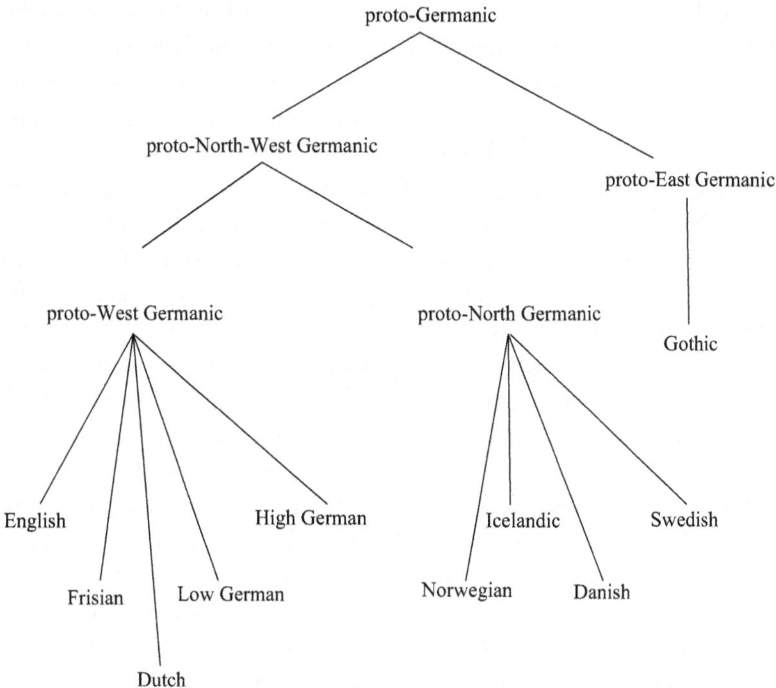

FIG. 22.2 The major Germanic languages.

on Indo-European are very lucky, in that many separate branches have been identified, and some of them include languages that have very early surviving documentation (especially Hittite and Luvian), while others (especially Sanskrit, Greek, and Latin) have recorded histories that both go back a long way and extend over a very long period, with copious historical records. However, there are still limitations to how much of the vocabulary of proto-Indo-European can be reconstructed, and with what degree of confidence.[6] (Attempts to link Indo-European with other language families, in order to establish a shared linguistic descent from a common ancestor, are highly controversial, and not regarded as successful by most linguists working today.)

To return to the example of *file* 'type of metal tool', there are direct cognates in other West Germanic languages. Two of them are Old High German *fīhala* (modern German *Feile*) and Old Saxon *fīla* in the same meaning; the common ancestor of these words can probably be reconstructed as **fīlō*. Old Icelandic *þél* in the same meaning is probably a North Germanic cognate, since a change from initial /f/ to /θ/ is plausible (if not expected). Here the trail becomes much more difficult to trace further. No reliable

[6] For an excellent introduction to the Indo-European languages see Fortson (2009). On the methodology for establishing the family see especially Clackson (2007). For a very useful overview of some of the core reconstructed vocabulary of Indo-European see Mallory and Adams (2006).

identification has been made of the same word in other branches of Indo-European. As a result of etymological research extending back into the 19th century, a great deal has been learnt about the typical morphological structures of Indo-European words, and in particular about the shape of the roots from which morphologically more complex words were typically formed by derivational processes. Many etymologists hypothesize, on the basis of comparison of words in other Indo-European languages and of what is known about the derivational processes in proto-Germanic and proto-Indo-European, that **fīlō* 'file' may have developed from an earlier Germanic form **finhlō* which it may be possible to explain ultimately as reflecting a derivative from a reconstructed Indo-European root **pei̯ḱ-* which probably lies behind Latin *pingere* 'to colour, paint', ancient Greek πικρός (*pikrós*) 'sharp, pointed, piercing, bitter, painful', and a number of other words in other branches of Indo-European. On the basis of comparison of all of these words, it is hypothesized that **pei̯ḱ-* may have meant something like 'stitch, paint'. Such hypotheses rest ultimately on the recognition of regular sound correspondences between languages. For instance, the assumption that Germanic **fīlō* will (if it goes back to Indo-European at all) come from a root that begins with **p* rather than **f* results from an important set of regular correspondences between Germanic and other branches of Indo-European, from which it is inferred that a regular sound change **p* > **f* occurred in the common ancestor of the Germanic languages. This is one of a complex set of changes known collectively as Grimm's Law, after the linguist, lexicographer, and folk-tale collector Jacob Grimm, who made an important formulation of this set of changes in 1822.

It is by application of this sort of methodology that we can be certain that some pairs of words, such as English *care* and Latin *cūra* 'care', or Latin *deus* and Greek *theós* 'god', are not related, in spite of their identical meaning and superficial similarity in form. Conversely, some pairs of words which show little formal or semantic similarity, such as English *head* and French *chef* 'leader, boss', can be shown to share a common origin.

In a small but very important set of cases, whole words can be clearly identified as direct reflexes of a single word in proto-Indo-European, rather than as developments from a shared root. For instance, *father* has a wide set of cognates in Germanic, including Old Frisian *feder, fader*, Old Saxon *fadar*, Old High German *fater*, Old Icelandic *faðir*, Gothic *fadar* (although, interestingly, this is a very rare word in Gothic, in which the more usual word for 'father' is *atta*). Unlike in the case of *file*, we can also identify cognate words meaning 'father' in a wide range of languages from other branches of Indo-European, for instance Latin *pater*, ancient Greek πατήρ (*patḗr*), Sanskrit *pitár-*, Early Irish *athir*, Old Persian *pitā*, Tocharian A *pācar*. (Tocharian A and the related Tocharian B are the most easterly Indo-European languages, preserved in documents discovered in western China.) On the basis of these attested word forms, an Indo-European word meaning 'father' of approximately the form **ph₂tér-* is commonly reconstructed (the h_2 in the reconstruction represents a laryngeal sound assumed to have existed in Indo-European, which in this position can be understood as giving rise to the sound /ə/, hence probably /pəˈter/). The various attested forms can all be explained as arising from this same starting point, allowing for what is assumed about sound change in the pre-history of each language, and for assumptions about the morphology of Indo-European. Thus, the initial consonant /f/ in the English word again reflects the Grimm's Law change **p* > **f* in the common ancestor of the Germanic languages. (The history of the medial consonant is rather more complex, involving a further change known as Verner's Law, the discovery of which was itself an important stage in the development of the notion of regular sound change, since it explained a set of apparent exceptions to Grimm's Law.)

Similarly, for 'mother', English *mother* has cognates in West Germanic and North Germanic (not though in Gothic, which has *aiþei*), including: Old Frisian *mōder*, Old Saxon *mōdar*, Old High German *muoter*, Old Icelandic *móðir*. Cognates in other branches of Indo-European include: classical Latin *māter*, ancient Greek *μήτηρ*, Sanskrit *mātar-*, Early Irish *māthir*, Avestan *mātar-*, Tocharian A *mācar*. On the basis of these attested word forms, an Indo-European word meaning 'mother' of approximately the form **máh$_2$ter-* or perhaps **méh$_2$ter-* is commonly reconstructed.

It is almost certainly not accidental that the reconstructed words meaning 'father' and 'mother' have the sequence of sounds *-ter-* in common. This is found also in the reconstructed Indo-European forms assumed to lie ultimately behind English *brother* and *daughter* (but not *sister*, in which the *-t-* is of later origin, perhaps by analogy with the other words). Most scholars are therefore happy to recognize the existence of an element *-ter-* involved in forming words denoting kinship relationships, although opinions differ on the origin of this element and its possible connections with other suffixes in Indo-European. This leaves open the question of what the etymologies of the first elements of *mother* and *father* are. One suggestion is that both words may originate as forms suffixed in *-ter-* on the syllables /ma/ or /pa/ that are typical of infant vocalization, and which are probably reflected by English *mama* and *papa*, as well as forms in a wide variety of languages worldwide. However, there are other viable suggestions to explain the origin of both words.

This discussion has pushed several words back far beyond the limits of the historical record. This is is possible because we have a rich and early historical record for so many Indo-European languages. The historical record for many languages is much less rich, and this can impose severe limits on etymological research (although there have been significant achievements in areas such as the study of proto-Bantu). In addition, there are many languages that cannot be linked with large language families like Indo-European; some languages are (to the best of present knowledge) complete isolates (e.g., in the view of most scholars, Basque or Korean), while many others can only be linked securely with one or two other languages (e.g. Japanese and the related languages of the Ryukyu Islands). Of course, this does not mean that the whole of the lexis of such languages is necessarily unrelated to words found in other languages; the lexis of Japanese, for instance, contains large numbers of loanwords, including a very large contribution from Chinese during the medieval period, and a large recent contribution from English, such as *terebi* 'television' or *depāto* 'department store'. Both of these words show accommodation to the phonological system of Japanese, as well as clipping (i.e. shortening of the word form), which is common in such loanwords. Such words or clipped elements of such words may also form new words in Japanese; for instance the second element of the word *karaoke* is a clipping of *ōkesutara*, borrowed from English *orchestra* (the first element is Japanese *kara* 'empty').

22.5 Words of unknown or uncertain etymology

As already seen, English has a richly documented and well-studied history and belongs to an extended language family many members of which are unusually well documented over a very long history. However, even in English there are many words that defy satisfactory etymological explanation. Some words go back to Old English, but no secure connections can be established with words in other Germanic languages, nor can a donor be identified for a loanword etymology. Some examples (all investigated recently for the new edition of the *Oxford English Dictionary*) include *adze, neap* (tide), *to quake* (which could just be an expressive formation), or (all first attested in late Old English) *plot, privet*, or *dog, hog, pig* (these last three probably bear some relationship to one another, but exactly what is less clear). Some words of unknown etymology first recorded in Middle English include *badge, big, boy, girl, nape, nook, to pore, to pout, prawn*. Some more recent examples include *to prod* (first attested 1535), *quirk* (1565), *prat* (1567), *quandary* (1576), *to puzzle* (*c*.1595), *pimp* (1600), *pun* (1644).[7] For some of these words numerous etymological explanations have been suggested, but none has yet met with general acceptance.

In each of these cases there is relatively little doubt that we are dealing with a single coherent word history, but we are simply unable to explain its ulterior history. A slightly different kind of case is exemplified by *queer*. This is recorded from 1513 in the meaning defined by *OED* as 'strange, odd, peculiar, eccentric', and there is little doubt that most current senses developed from this beginning, including the modern use in the meaning 'homosexual'. Its origin is uncertain; borrowing from German *quer* 'transverse, oblique, crosswise, at right angles' is a possibility, but the semantic correspondence is not exact, and figurative uses of the German word, such as '(of a person) peculiar', are first attested much later than the English word. The interesting further complication in the case of *queer* is that in contemporary English *queer* also occurs in criminals' slang in the meaning 'of coins or banknotes: counterfeit, forged'. This may seem an unsurprising or at least plausible semantic development from 'strange, odd', but the difficulty is that this use (first recorded in 1740) seems to have developed from a meaning 'bad; contemptible, worthless; untrustworthy; disreputable', that is first recorded in 1567, and in early use this always shows spellings of the type *quire*. It therefore seems that in the 16th

[7] The frequency of words beginning with certain initial letters in these lists of examples reflects the fact that they have been drawn from the new edition of the *OED* currently in progress, in which the alphabetical sequence M to R is the largest continuous run of entries so far published.

century there may have been two distinct words, *queer* 'strange, odd, peculiar, eccentric' and (in criminals' slang) *quire* 'bad; contemptible, worthless; untrustworthy; disreputable'. The one may have originated as a variant of the other, but there appears to be no formal overlap in the first century or so of co-existence of the two words. In the late 17th century, *quire* 'bad; contemptible, worthless; untrustworthy; disreputable' begins to appear in the spelling *queer*, suggesting a lowered vowel that is confirmed by the modern pronunciation. This change in form may well be the result of formal association with *queer* 'strange, odd, peculiar, eccentric', on the grounds of similarity of form and semantic proximity (what is odd often being deemed bad, etc.). A very difficult question is whether modern English has one word or two: *quire*, later *queer* 'bad; contemptible, worthless; untrustworthy; disreputable' seems the direct antecedent of *queer* 'of coins or banknotes: counterfeit, forged', but, if association with *queer* 'strange, odd, peculiar, eccentric' is what has caused an irregular change in word form from *quire* to *queer*, can we be certain that the two words have not become completely conflated for modern English speakers? An idiom such as *as queer as a nine bob note* may be construed by some speakers as simply showing the meaning 'peculiar' rather than specifically 'counterfeit'. Certainly, the case is much more difficult than that of *file* 'type of metal tool' and *file* 'set of documents', where the intuition that there are two unrelated meanings, hence homonymy, coincides perfectly with the historical perspective.[8]

The remainder of this chapter will look at some other types of scenario in which careful investigation of word histories by etymological methods presents tensions for the conception of the lexicon as consisting of a set of entirely discrete words with separate histories. By careful application of etymology, it is often possible to detect the grey areas, where lexical split or merger is in progress, either diachronically between different stages in the historical development of a language, or synchronically between different varieties of language.

22.6 Lexical merger and lexical split, and other types of 'messiness' in the histories of words

Proving that lexical merger has occurred can present difficulties for etymological-historical methodology. For instance, Old English has two distinct verbs in the meanings (intransitive) 'to melt, become liquid' and (transitive) 'to cause to melt, to make liquid'. The first is a strong verb, *meltan*, with principal parts: present stem *melt-*, past tense (1st and 3rd person singular) *mealt*, past tense (plural) *multon*, and past participle *gemolten*. The second is a weak verb, of which the infinitive is either *meltan* or

[8] For fuller discussion of this example see Durkin (2009: 216–18).

mieltan in different dialects of Old English, but which has past tense and past participle formed by a dental suffix. The forms of this verb that are actually recorded in Old English typically show syncopation of the dental suffix, e.g. past tense (1st and 3rd person singular) *mielte* and past participle *mielt*, but forms without syncopation of the dental suffix are also found, e.g. past participle *gemælted*. The two words are ultimately developed from the same Germanic base, and are ultimately cognate with words in other branches of Indo-European, the most direct correspondence being with ancient Greek μέλδειν (*méldein*) 'to melt'. In modern English both sets of meanings are realized by a regular, weak verb, *melt*, with past tense and past participle *melted*. (A descendant of the original strong past participle survives, however, in specialized meaning as the adjective *molten* designating liquefied metal or glass.) Modern English *melt* is clearly the descendant of either Old English *meltan* (strong) or *meltan, mieltan* (weak), but describing quite what has happened is a little more difficult. Many verbs that were strong in Old English have switched to showing weak inflections in later English; thus modern English *melt* could in formal terms show the direct descendant of *meltan* (strong), with change in declensional class. On the other hand, many verbs that typically showed syncope of the dental suffix after a stem ending in a dental consonant have become regularized to show final *-ed* in later English; hence modern English *melt* could equally show the direct descendant of *meltan, mieltan* (weak). We could hypothesize that the strong and weak verbs have merged in the later history of English, giving one merged modern English verb *melt* in both transitive and intransitive uses. However, proving that this has happened purely by etymological methodology is difficult: from the data I have presented so far, we may infer from semantic similarity that *melt* in the meanings (intransitive) 'to melt' and (transitive) 'to cause to melt' shows a single polysemous lexeme, but etymological methodology alone does not rule out the alternative scenario where there is a continuous history of two verbs, *melt*[1] (intransitive) 'to melt' and *melt*[2] (transitive) 'to cause to melt' which have simply become homonyms in modern English. Since English has a particularly richly documented history, we can look at what sort of verbal morphology is found in Middle English. Here, as well as uses of weak forms such as *melted* in meanings of the old strong verb *meltan* (intransitive) 'to melt', we also find historically strong forms in transitive meanings, e.g. from Caxton 'Saturne ... malte and fyned gold and metalles'. In fact, the historical evidence when taken all together suggests a general confusion of forms in Middle English and Early Modern English: thus, in a 16th-century text we find 'The Jewes when they molted a golden calfe ... did neuer thinke that to be God', with a past tense form *molted* that shows the weak past tense ending *-ed* but the stem vowel of the old strong past participle, used in a transitive meaning where the weak verb would have been expected historically. Thus the detailed historical data suggests strongly that merger has taken place; but without this level of detail the hypothesis of merger would be harder to support by historical methods alone.[9]

[9] For further discussion of this and of the examples of lexical split discussed later in this section, and for further examples, see Durkin (2009: 79–88).

Close study of word histories from historically well-attested languages suggests that processes of merger are in fact not uncommon. Reduction in the overall level of morphological variety, as shown for instance by the English verb system diachronically, is one common cause, as exemplified by *melt*. Another is where borrowing is found from more than one donor language. For instance, in the Middle English period English was in close contact with both French and Latin. Specifically, in the late Middle English period, English came to be used increasingly as a written language in contexts where either French or Latin or both had previously been used over a long period of time. In this context, many loanwords occur in English that could on formal grounds be from either French or Latin, and which show a complex set of borrowed meanings, which again could be explained by borrowing from either language. Examples include *add, animal, information, problem, public*. In some cases, particular form variants point strongly to input from one language rather than the other, or a particular meaning is found in French but not in Latin, or vice versa. Sometimes a particular meaning is attested earliest in a text that is translated directly from the one language, but it may be found a few years later in a text translated from the other. In most instances, the likeliest scenario seems to be that there has been input from both languages, reflecting multiple instances either of direct word borrowing or of semantic influence on an earlier loan; over time, multiple inputs have coalesced, to give semantically complex, polysemous words in modern English.[10]

Demonstrating that lexical splits have occurred is generally a simpler task for etymological methodology, although pinpointing the precise point at which a split has occurred can be more difficult, especially since fine-grained historical data suggests that splits tend to diffuse gradually through a speaker group. For instance, modern English has two distinct words, *ordinance* and *ordnance*. The first is typically found in the meaning 'an authoritative order', and the second in specialized military meanings such as 'artillery' and 'branch of government service dealing especially with military stores and materials'. Both words show the same starting point, Middle English *ordenance, ordinance, ordnance*, a borrowing from French, showing a wide range of meanings such as 'decision made by a superior', 'ruling', 'arrangement in a certain order', 'provisions', 'legislative decree', 'machinery, engine', 'disposition of troops in battle'. In Middle English the forms with and without a medial vowel could be used in any of these meanings: the formal variation does not pattern significantly with the semantic variation. In course of time, the form without a medial vowel, *ordnance*, became usual in military senses, while the form *ordinance* became usual in general senses. Possibly what we have here is a situation where a pool of variants existed, and speakers in different social groups have selected different forms from within that pool of variants, *ordnance* having been the form that became usual within the military, but *ordinance* in most other groups using this word. Very gradually, as some meanings have fallen out of use and others have come to be used more or less exclusively with one word form or the other, a complete split

[10] On words of this type see Durkin (2002), Durkin (2008), Durkin (2014).

has occurred, with *ordinance* and *ordnance* becoming established as distinct lexemes with different meanings. The time-frame over which this occurred appears to have been very long: the *OED*'s evidence suggests that it is not complete before the 18th century, and even in contemporary English *ordinance* may occasionally be found in the military senses, although in formal use it is likely to be regarded as an error.

Similar splits may also be found that affect only the written form of a word, particularly in modern standard languages with well-established orthographic norms. For instance, modern English *flour* originated as a spelling variant of *flower*; flour was perceived metaphorically as the 'flower' or finer portion of ground meal. The word *flower* is a Middle English borrowing from French, and it is found in the meaning 'flour' already in the 13th century; both meanings still appear under the single spelling *flower* in Johnson's dictionary in 1755, although by this point some other written sources already distinguish clearly between the spellings *flower* and *flour* in the two meanings.

There are, however, instances of lexical split that are much less categorical. One such instance is shown by the modern English reflex(es) of Middle English *poke* 'bag, small sack'. The word survives in this meaning in modern Standard English only in fossilized form in the idiom *a pig in a poke* (referring to something bought or accepted without prior inspection), but it remains in more general use in some regional varieties of English. Various other semantic developments ultimately from the same starting point survive in certain varieties of English. From the meaning 'small bag or pouch worn on the person' the narrowed meaning 'a purse, a wallet, a pocketbook' developed, although this is labelled by *OED* as being restricted to North American criminals' slang; a further metonymic development from this, 'a roll of banknotes; money; a supply or stash of money', is labelled by *OED* as belonging to more general slang use. Metaphorical uses recorded as still current in different varieties of English included (in Scottish English) 'a bag-shaped fishing net, a purse-net', (in Scottish English and in the north of England) 'an oedematous swelling on the neck of a sheep', (in North America, chiefly in whaling) 'a bag or bladder filled with air, used as a buoy or float'. Running alongside this splintering in meaning there are interesting patterns of formal variation: for instance, in Scottish English the form types *pock* and *pouk* occur as well as *poke* (reflecting phonological developments that are familiar from other words of similar shape), although these form variants do not appear to have become associated exclusively with particular meanings. In this instance, we can see that the etymological principle in use in a historical dictionary can effectively group all of this material together under a single dictionary headword *poke*, as showing a single point of origin, without any definitive split into different word forms employed in different meanings. However, what *poke* denotes will differ radically for different speakers of English depending on their membership of different speaker groups, and it is likely that if an individual speaker happens to be familiar with the meanings 'money' and 'a bag or bladder filled with air' he will be very unlikely to perceive any relationship between them, any more than between historically unrelated homonyms such as *file* 'type of metal tool' and *file* 'set of documents'.

22.7 Conclusions

Etymology is an essential tool in tracing the historical origin and development of individual words, and in establishing word histories. Indeed, this could serve as a definition of etymology, broadly conceived.[11] Etymological method depends on an interaction between arguments based on word form and arguments based on word meaning. Regular sound changes are a cornerstone of etymological argument, especially when attempts are made to trace word histories far beyond the limits of the surviving written record. In a historical perspective, how we identify distinct word histories is heavily dependent on the application of etymology. As such, etymology can pose provocative questions about whether we can always identify complex words as coherent entities with a single, discrete history.

[11] On definitions of etymology see Alinei (1995), Durkin (2009).

CHAPTER 23

HOW WORDS AND VOCABULARIES CHANGE

DIRK GEERAERTS

23.1 Introduction: lexical and vocabulary changes

When we talk about words changing, we first of all need to make a distinction between changes to individual words and changes in the vocabulary. ('Vocabulary', in the technical linguistic sense in which we will be using the term in this chapter, refers to the set of words that are available to the speakers of a language.) Our words change when the form or meaning of words taken by themselves undergo transitions, but our words also change when the vocabulary that we have at our disposal develops. Isn't that, though, the same thing? If we know how (and perhaps even why) individual words change, don't we always at the same time deal with changes in the vocabulary? Studying changes in words as separate entities presupposes that the words are already there; if we study the historical development of any particular word in a language, that word is already by definition part of the language. Changes in the total vocabulary, on the other hand, include processes through which *new* words enter the language; vocabulary changes concern changes in the total inventory, in contrast with lexical changes that merely affect entities in the inventory. It follows that taking our perspective at the level of the vocabulary gives us a more encompassing view than taking our perspective at the lexical level (that is to say, at the level of individual words). If we think of the vocabulary as an inventory of form/meaning pairs (i.e. of word forms expressing certain meanings), then the changes that we would most likely study from the lexical point of view are a natural part of what we would want to study from the vocabulary point of view—but not the other way round. If a given word acquires a new meaning, then the vocabulary changes. But if a new word is introduced into the vocabulary, it is obviously not the case that any given word automatically changes its meaning. The vocabulary perspective is therefore the more encompassing one, and it is the one we will adopt here. Before we present a classification of the ways in which vocabularies change, however, a few nuances and further refinements need to be introduced.

In the first place, when we define the vocabulary of a language as an inventory of form–meaning pairs, we tend to assume that meanings are neatly demarcated entities that exist more or less as tangible packages of information. That is a far from accurate image. Rather than to think of them as carriers of clearly distinguishable and clearly identifiable packages of information, it is more appropriate to think of words as having meaning potential, that is, of having the possibility to express a flexibly defined range of meanings when they are put to use in a given context. (See Taylor 2003 for the theoretical issues involved; also Riemer, this volume.) An analogous remark applies to the concept of vocabulary. Describing a vocabulary as an inventory of form–meaning pairs seems to suggest that we are dealing with a list whose members can be enumerated in an exhaustive fashion. If that were the case, the question 'How many words does this language have?' could receive a very precise answer, such as '337,451'. This would be absurd, as a number of considerations show. Suppose we maintain that to count as a word of a language, the word has to be used and understood by all the speakers of the language. Now, one reason why we have dictionaries is precisely because all of us do not understand all the words of the language, even if it is our mother tongue. So, if universal knowledge of a word cannot be the criterion for including it in the vocabulary of a language, could we perhaps say that a word needs to be used by a sufficient number of users of the language, or (lowering our expectations a little bit) that it needs to be recognized and accepted by a sufficient number of users? Then we would need a criterion for determining what 'a sufficient number' involves, and such a criterion is not readily available. It follows that it is something of a simplification and an idealization to talk about 'the vocabulary of a language'. For practical purposes, there are just words that are more or less frequently used, or more or less easily recognized and accepted. Like meanings, vocabularies are entities without clear boundaries.

In the second place, when we think of the vocabulary as an inventory of form–meaning pairs, we could study that inventory from two different points of view—from the point of view of the forms or from the point of view of the meanings. When we adopt a semantic point of view we are primarily interested in language as an instrument of expression. Vocabularies change through the introduction of new words or the introduction of new meanings, and these changes are driven by the fact that language users feel the need to modify the expressive power of the language. But words may also change from a purely formal point of view. When we look at the long-term history of words, the shape of words changes because languages change their pronunciation, and more generally, the shape in which words appear. The French word *main* 'hand' derives from Latin *manus*, and the German word *bieten* 'to offer' is distantly related to Gothic *biudan*. In both cases the shape of the younger words and the system within which they are used (such as the expression of a 1st or 2nd person on a verb, or the distinction between present and past tenses) is the result of long-term changes in the formal make-up of the language. Even though this kind of formal change is also one of the ways in which 'words change', it does not lie within the scope of the present chapter (but see Durkin on Etymology, this volume, for more information on the formal perspective).

Thirdly, we need to introduce some terminology to better distinguish between the focus on the vocabulary and the focus on individual words. The former is an example of what we call an 'onomasiological' perspective in lexicology, the latter an example of a 'semasiological' perspective. (The semasiology/onomasiology pair is a terminological distinction that was introduced in lexical studies by European structuralist semantics in the first half of the 20th century; however, it is not widespread within contemporary linguistic terminology. For more information on the history of lexical semantics, see Geeraerts 2010a.) Without entering into details, we could say that the terms name converse perspectives on word meaning. The semasiological perspective starts from the word and considers the meanings it can express. The basic phenomenon here is polysemy, i.e. the existence of various meanings in the range of application of a word. This is the perspective behind a standard alphabetical dictionary. The onomasiological perspective starts from the meanings to be expressed and considers the various means of expression that are available. Basic phenomena here are synonymy (identity of meaning) and other forms of meaning-based relatedness among words. This is the field of synonym dictionaries and thesauri (see Kay, this volume).

If we now have another look at the way in which words change, we can say two things. First, if we go beyond individual words and take the vocabulary perspective, we are basically taking an onomasiological point of view (because we are interested in changes in the expressive means of the language at large), and if we take the perspective of individual words we are basically taking a semasiological point of view (because we study how the polysemy—or meaning potential—of a given word develops). Second, semasiological change is a form of onomasiological change, because it changes the lexical inventory of expressive means, but not the other way round. This asymmetrical relationship between semasiology and onomasiology now also defines how we will organize the chapter (and that is why we spent some time introducing it). We will first present, in section 23.2, an overview of mechanisms of onomasiological change in the broad sense, and then zoom in, in sections 23.3 and 23.4, on mechanisms of semasiological change. In section 23.5, we shift our focus from the introduction of new words and meanings to the disappearance of words and meanings. The chapter rounds off with an example illustrating the interaction between the various mechanisms surveyed in sections 23.2–23.5.

A more detailed coverage of diachronic lexical semantics than what we can offer here may be found in Ullmann (1957, 1962), Waldron (1967), Sappan (1987), Warren (1992), Geeraerts (1997), Blank (1997), and Fritz (1998). While these works basically continue the traditional prevalence of the semasiological point of view, an onomasiological perspective is found in Grzega (2004) and Tournier (1985). Grygiel and Kleparski (2007) present a comprehensive and instructive overview of the main trends in historical semantics from the 19th century up to the present day. The most recent developments are covered in Winters, Tissari, and Allan (2010) and Allan and Robinson (2011).

23.2 Onomasiological mechanisms: lexicogenesis

If we temporarily ignore the semasiological mechanisms of onomasiological change, the remaining onomasiological mechanisms are essentially what are sometimes called 'lexicogenetic' mechanisms, i.e. procedures for creating new words. Four basic types may be distinguished: morphological word formation, transformation of existing words, pure neologism, and borrowing. (It is worth noting that in this area of lexicology, neither the classification nor the terminology is entirely stabilized. Many alternatives exist, and what follows gives only a broad idea of the relevant phenomena.)

First, new words may be formed by the regular application of morphological rules for word formation (see Booij, this volume). Languages have mechanisms for creating new words through the combination of existing words, or through the combination of existing words and affixes (word-formation elements that cannot occur on their own). In the first case, when words are combined, the process is called 'composition': with *door* and *knob* English can coin the word *doorknob*, with *engine* and *combustion* we get *combustion engine*, and so on. In the second case, when the process is called 'derivation', affixes may be prefixes like *un-* in *unlikely* or *unwise*, or suffixes like *-y* in *shadowy* or *-ness* in *loveliness*.

Crucially, while *unlikely* and *shadowy* are frequent, conventional words, it is important to realize that such mechanisms can be used to form new words on the spot. Take the following Internet example, from a forum discussing contemporary giclée prints: 'I dig the Klimt, too, and the whole thing has a *klimtiness* about it. There's a day to night or birth to death sense.' A stylistic similarity with the paintings of Gustav Klimt triggers the adjective *klimty*, and that is further turned into a noun by adding *-ness*. It is improbable that the ad hoc formation *klimtiness* will become so frequent as to enter the general vocabulary of English, but even so, *klimtiness* is perfectly understandable for speakers of English (provided they have an idea of who Klimt is). Derivational elements like *-y* and *-ness*, in other words, can be used to create words 'on-line'. This is a general point of some importance. When we talk about lexicogenetic mechanisms for creating new words, the implication is not that the new word automatically becomes part of the more or less stable, commonly shared vocabulary, or, as a reflection of that, that it will be automatically incorporated in the standard dictionaries. That will only happen if a sufficient number of people start using the word on a sufficient number of occasions (and lexicographers might differ in their assessment of these criteria); creation is different from conventionalization.

Second, new words may be formed by the transformation of existing words, for instance through clipping (*pro* from *professional*) or blending (*brunch* as a merger of *breakfast* and *lunch*, or Dutch *concullega* 'a colleague who is at the same time a competitor', from *concurrent* 'competitor' and *collega* 'colleague'). Blending of this type is very productive in media language and computer speech: think of words like *docudrama* (*documentary, drama*), *docutainment* (*documentary, entertainment*), *docusoap* (*documentary, soap opera*), *infotainment* (*information, entertainment*), *mockumentary* (*mocking, documentary*), *shockumentary* (*shocking, documentary*) for the former, and *blog* (*web, log*), *emoticon* (*emotion, icon*), *malware* (*malicious, software*), *netiquette* (*internet, etiquette*), *podcast* (*ipod, broadcast*) for the latter. Acronyms, i.e. abbreviations formed by using the initial elements of a compound word or phrase, can also be included here. Examples are *nimby* and *snafu*, derived from *not in my back yard* and *situation normal: all fucked up*. In recent years, the use of initials (the first element of a word) has been very frequent in compounds and blends with the characters *e* for *electronic* and *i* for *internet*: *e-book, e-commerce, e-marketing, e-phone, e-school; ipod, ipad, iphone*. (The way in which the *e* and *i* in these words are pronounced makes clear, incidentally, that the initial element is taken from the spelling of *electronic* and *internet* and not from their pronunciation: the *e* in *e-book* is the written character *e*, with a pronunciation as in *free*, and not the first sound of *electronic*, with a pronunciation as in *bed*.)

A borderline case of transformation (it is often described as a type of word formation rather than transformation) is conversion, when the word class of an item changes without further formal changes. This happens when a verb like *hit* appears as a noun; the process may also involve proper names like *xerox, hoover*, or *google* (these are names of companies, but they are also verbs describing actions associated with those companies' products).

Third, new words may be created out of the blue, without starting from existing words or word formation rules. This type of word creation is sometimes called 'neologism', though the term may also be used in a broad sense, as a name for any type of lexical innovation. To achieve terminological precision, 'pure neologism' may be used in the restricted sense. A well-known example of this process is the scientific term *quark*, as the name for elementary particles in the model of particle physics introduced by Murray Gell-Mann in 1964. Gell-Mann (1994) himself has explained how he got the word from a passage ('Three quarks for Muster Mark!') in James Joyce's *Finnegans Wake*, where it appeared as a nonce word. When we say that pure neologisms are created 'out of the blue', that should be taken with a grain of salt: it does not mean that people coining such a new word have no sources of inspiration at all. When Richard Dawkins (1976) introduced *meme* as a term for ideas and habits that are transmitted culturally rather than biologically, he had Greek words like *mimema* and *mimesis* as a model, and obviously, the biological *gene* also played a role. *Gas* 'steam, vapour, matter in an air-like condition' belongs in the same set. It was invented by the Flemish physician Jan Baptist van Helmont (1579–1644), with explicit reference to the Greek word *chaos* 'empty space' (and possibly with some inspiration from Paracelsus). Onomatopoeia (phonetic imitation) is also one of the sources for pure neologism (see Childs, this volume). Think of *tiki-taka* as the name for the style of football playing developed by FC Barcelona and characterized by fast passings of the ball designed to maximize ball possession. When *tiki-taka* was introduced in Spanish football commentaries it was not a new word, but a metaphorical use of the name of the toy known as *clackers* in English. But originally, as a name for the toy, *tiki-taka* is onomatopoetic: the name imitates the sound that is produced when the two balls that the toy consists of are rhythmically banged against each other by swinging the rope on which they are suspended. In modern languages, pure neologism is a relatively rare process, but if you go back to the origin of language, all root words of a given language family by definition have an etymological origin as pure neologisms.

Fourth, new expressions may be borrowed from other languages (see Grant, this volume). Borrowing competes with morphological word formation for being the most common, most productive lexicogenetic mechanism. It comes in different shapes. Next to straightforward loanwords, we may find less conspicuous forms of borrowings like loan translations, when each of the composite elements of a foreign word or phrase is translated into the receptor language. For instance, Dutch has borrowed the German word *Übermensch* as such, but when *Übermensch* is the model for English *superman*, or when German *Zeitschrift* 'journal, magazine' is transposed into Dutch *tijdschrift*, we have examples of loan translations. Borrowing is particularly interesting from a historical point of view, because it reflects cultural contacts among languages. In the present-day globalized world, English is the prominent source of loanwords for most of the world's languages. But ironically, the vocabulary of English is itself extremely rich in lexical borrowings: just think of the influence of French (*beef, boil, broil, butcher, jail, judge, jury, captain, company, corporal*) as a result of the Norman conquest, or the incorporation of Hindi words (*bungalow, cot, jungle, loot, pajamas, punch, shampoo, thug*) in the colonial era. Loan influences going in two directions are specifically illustrated by processes of borrowing-back: a source language may borrow back a word after it was developed independently by the receptor language. Thus, French borrowed the Dutch word *manneken* 'small person; hence: human doll' in the medieval period, but after it had morphed into French *mannequin* 'life-size human doll, model', 18th-century Dutch borrowed (back) the word *mannequin* (which also entered English as a loanword).

Many loanwords introduce new concepts together with the new words; contemporary languages borrow *computer* from English because the technology originated in the Anglophone world. But loans may also introduce competition for concepts that are already lexicalized in the receptor language. Young people in non-English speaking countries who adopt the currently popular *oh my god* idiom usually do not lack expressions of surprise, awe, or indignation in their mother tongue. Similarly, when *cool* is internationalized as a term of positive evaluation, the reason is surely not that a lexical gap needs to be filled, i.e. that the receptor languages lack terms of positive appreciation. Conversely, languages may also coin native words as an alternative to incoming loans. Afrikaans, for instance, uses *rekenaar* (literally 'calculator') as an alternative for *computer*. Which factors ultimately decide in such situations of onomasiological competition remains understudied, but, as in other areas of lexical research, the ever-increasing availability of large text corpora opens up exciting perspectives for a quantitative study of lexical alternations. (See Zenner, Speelman, and Geeraerts 2012 for an example involving loanwords, and Geeraerts, Grondelaers, and Bakema 1994 for an overall framework for quantitative onomasiology.)

23.3 Semasiological mechanisms: denotational changes

If we now turn our attention to the mechanisms of semasiological change, we first need to introduce a distinction between denotational and non-denotational changes of meaning. The second of these involves changes in the emotive overtones of words; is a word felt as being emotionally positive, negative, or neutral? This is a class of changes that we will deal with in the next section. In the present section, we concentrate on the mechanisms of semantic change that constitute the core of historical semantics, i.e. the mechanisms that shape the development of the descriptive meaning of words, or, as it also known, the 'referential' or 'denotational' meaning—the meaning, that is, through which words can act as categories to describe the world. We will work in two steps. First we present a traditional classification of core mechanisms and then add a few nuances that come from more recent work in the field of diachronic semantics.

The traditional classification of denotational semantic changes includes four basic types: specialization, generalization, metaphor, and metonymy. In the case of semantic *specialization*, the new meaning is a restriction of the old meaning; the new meaning is a subcase of the old. In the case of semantic *generalization*, the reverse holds; the old meaning is a subcase of the new. Classic examples of specialization are *corn* (originally a cover-term for all kinds of grain, now specialized to 'wheat' in England, to 'oats' in Scotland, and to 'maize' in the United States), *starve* (moving from 'to die' to 'to die of hunger'), and *queen* (originally 'wife, woman', now restricted to 'king's wife, or female sovereign'). Examples of generalization are *moon* (primarily the earth's satellite, but extended to any planet's satellite), and French *arriver* (which originally meant 'to reach the river's shore, to embank', but which now signifies 'to reach a destination' in general). Processes of specialization and generalization often have a social background. Specialization regularly originates in specific professional circles. Thus, the Dutch word *drukken* 'to press, to push hard' acquired the specialized meaning 'to print' in the context of the (older) printing workshop. Conversely, generalization may signal the spreading of a term outside of its original, technically restricted domain. The generalization of *arriver* is said to have involved its spread from the language of boatmen and sailors to the general vocabulary.

There is a lot of terminological variation in connection with specialization and generalization. 'Restriction' and 'narrowing' of meaning equal 'specialization', while 'expansion', 'extension', 'schematization', and 'broadening' of meaning equal 'generalization'. In addition, the meanings involved can be said to enter into relations of taxonomical subordination or superordination. In a taxonomy (a tree-like hierarchical classification) of concepts, the specialized meaning is subordinate with regard to the original one, whereas the generalized meaning is superordinate with regard to the original.

Like specialization and generalization, it is convenient and customary to introduce 'metaphor' and 'metonymy' together, even though the relationship is not as close as with the former pair. Metaphor is then said to be based on a relationship of similarity between the old and the new reading, and metonymy on a relationship of contiguity. More needs to be said about this distinction, but we should first introduce some examples. Current computer terminology yields cases of both types of change. The *desktop* of your computer screen, for instance, is not the same as the desktop of your office desk—except that in both cases, it is the space (a literal space in one case, a virtual one in the other) where you position a number of items that you regularly use, or that need attention. The computer desktop, in other words, is not literally a desktop in the original sense, but it has a functional similarity to the original; the computer reading is a metaphorical extension of the original office furniture reading. Functional similarities also underlie metaphorical expressions like *bookmark, clipboard, file, folder, cut,* and *paste. Mouse* is also metaphorically motivated, but here the metaphorical similarity involves shape rather than function. But now consider a statement to the effect that your desktop will keep you busy for the next two weeks, or you ask where your mouse has gone when you are trying to locate the pointer on the screen. In such cases, *desktop* and *mouse* are used metonymically. In the former case, it's not the virtual space as such that is relevant, but the items that are stored there. In the latter case, it's not the mouse as such (the thing that you hold in your hand) that you refer to, but the pointer on the screen that is operated by the mouse. The desktop and the stored items, or the mouse and the pointer, have a relationship of real-world connectedness that is usually captured by the notion 'contiguity'. When, for instance, one drinks a whole bottle, it is not the bottle as such but merely its contents that are consumed: *bottle* can be used to refer to a certain type of container and the (spatially contiguous) contents of that container. When lexical semanticians state that metonymical changes are based on contiguity, contiguity should not be understood in a narrow sense as referring to spatial proximity only, but more broadly as a general term for various associations in the spatial, temporal, or causal domain.

Several additional remarks are due here. In the first place, to get a better grip on metaphor and metonymy (which are by far more frequent in the life of languages than specialization and generalization), recurrent patterns of metonymic and metaphorical extension can be identified. This is achieved by a classification of the target and source concepts involved in the extensions. Thus, the *bottle* example mentioned above exhibits the name of a container (source) being used for its contents (target), a pattern that can be abbreviated as 'container for contents'. Making use of this abbreviated notation, other common types of metonymy are the following: 'a spatial location for what is located there' (*the whole theatre was in tears*); 'a period of time for what happens in that period, for the people who live in that period, or for what is produced in the period' (*the nineteenth century had a nationalist approach to politics*); 'a material for the product made from it' (*a cork*); 'the origin for what originates from it' (*astrakhan, champagne, emmental*); 'an activity or event for its consequences' (when the *blow* you have received hurts, it is not the activity of your adversary that is painful, but the physical effects that it has on your body); 'an attribute for the entity that possesses the attribute' (*majesty* does not only refer to 'royal dignity or status', but also to the sovereign himself); and of course 'part for whole' (*a hired hand*). The relations can often work in the other direction as well. *To fill up the car*, for instance, illustrates a type 'whole for part'—it's obviously only a part of the car that gets filled up.

As far as metaphor is concerned, the increasing popularity of metaphor research in the last two decades has started to fill a gap in the traditional treatments of the subject. The identification of regular patterns of metonymy of the kind just mentioned is quite common in traditional treatises on diachronic semantics, but similar metaphorical patterns were not recognized. With the advent of Lakoff's model of 'conceptual metaphors', however, a finer-grained description of metaphorical patterns has evolved that takes the form of the identification of conceptual metaphors such as AN ARGUMENT IS A JOURNEY, LOVE IS WAR, MORE IS UP, or THEORIES ARE BUILDINGS (see Lakoff and Johnson 1980, and compare Gibbs 2008 for the current state of the art in metaphor research). The latter pattern, for instance, is present in examples like the following: 'Is that the *foundation* for your theory? The theory needs more *support*. The argument is *shaky*. We need some more facts or the argument will *fall* apart. We need to *construct* a strong argument for that. We need to *buttress* the theory with solid arguments. The argument *collapsed*. The theory will *stand* or *fall* on the strength of that argument.'

In the second place, the definition of 'contiguity' is intuitively less obvious than that of similarity: how exactly should a concept like contiguity be understood, given that it is less familiar than similarity? The mutual demarcation of metonymy and metaphor is a subject of an ongoing debate that we will not try to cover in any detail, but we may indicate the two main approaches that are being pursued (see Croft 1993, Dirven 2002, and Peirsman and Geeraerts 2006 for the basic positions in the debate). First, some scholars try to elucidate the notion of metonymy by introducing the concept of 'domain'. Metaphorical similarity exists as a relation that connects entities across different domains of experience. Metonymy, on the other hand, is a relationship that holds between entities in the same 'chunk of experience'. This ties in with another distinction: whereas entities that are similar need not have anything to do with each other objectively (i.e. before the similarity is noticed or apart from its being noticed), entities that are related by contiguity can be said to have something to do with each other in an objective sense; they interact or co-occur in reality, and not just in the mind of the beholder (as in the case of relations based on similarity).

The other approach tries to reconstruct the internal cohesion of the category 'metonymy' by analysing how the less obvious cases of contiguity link up with the clearer ones. Part–whole relations are a clear case—they constitute a core example of metonymy, and it is easy to see how 'contiguity' applies to them. Other regular types of metonymy can then be related to the part–whole pattern when we recognize that the wholes need not be spatial or concrete. Thus, the pattern that we referred to as 'a period of time for what happens in that period, etc.' is intelligible if we recognize that time periods can be seen as containers holding people or events. In a similar way, the pattern 'action for agent' (*government* is the act of governing, but it is also the governing agency) fits into the metonymy category if we recognize that actions and events can be seen as functional wholes containing participants, locations, instruments, and the like.

In the third place, it turns out that not just the definition of contiguity but that of similarity-based metaphor as well is in need of clarification. A definition of metaphor in terms of similarity is in fact deceptively simple. The difficulty may become apparent by considering the shift in meaning of, for instance, a word like *hammer*. In its central reading, a hammer is a tool for striking or hitting consisting of a heavy head of metal, stone, or other hard material, attached to an elongated handle. But then there are other objects that we call *hammer*: the padded wooden parts of a piano that are set in motion by touching the keys and that strike the strings, or the element of a gun or another explosive device that hits the firing pin or the percussion cap, or the outermost of the three small bones that constitute the middle ear of mammals. This list of readings (all of which arose later than the basic tool sense) does not exhaust the polysemy of *hammer*, but in all of the cases mentioned here, the motivating link between the central reading and the derived reading involves a form of similarity—similarity of shape and/or function. But except perhaps for the anatomical reading, these applications of *hammer* would not be called metaphorical; hammers in pianos or guns are certainly not hammers in any figurative sense; they are, quite simply, hammers. Neither, for that matter, would it be correct to explain the shift as a case of generalization. The exact definition of such a broadened meaning would in fact be difficult to determine, because any definition one tries out tends to be either too broad or too narrow. For instance, if it were the case that *hammer* had broadened its meaning to 'elongated instrument for hitting with a reinforced head', such a definition would be too narrow with regard to the anatomical reading (for which the 'reinforced head' part is irrelevant, and which is not really an instrument anyway). At the same time, the definition would be too broad, because a number of medieval weapons for hitting and striking, like clubs, maces, morning stars, and battle axes, would then be included in the definition, i.e. they would erroneously be considered hammers.

This implies that the definition of metaphor will have to be refined by adding, for instance, that metaphor involves figurative similarity, and not just similarity *per se*. At the same time, the set of basic semasiological mechanisms will have to include the concept of changes based on literal similarity in order to account for the kinds of shifts exhibited by *hammer*. This solution will, however, remain largely terminological as long as we do not have a theory of figurativity—a theory, in other words, that allows us to determine when a particular word meaning is (possibly, to a certain degree) figurative or not. In contemporary semantic theory, literal similarities—and more generally, the role played by central senses in structuring the polysemy of lexical items—receive specific attention in so-called prototype-theoretical models of lexical semantics (the prototype being the core reading from which others are derived). (For a prototype conception of meaning in general, see Taylor 2003. The various consequences of prototypicality for diachronic semantics are explored in Geeraerts 1997.)

23.4 Semasiological mechanisms: non-denotational changes

Non-denotational meaning changes may in principle involve any type of non-descriptive meaning. Apart from their descriptive content, words may differ—and may change—on the basis of their emotive value (like carrying a positive or negative overtone) or on the basis of their stylistic value (like being formal or informal), or possibly other dimensions. In actual practice, the types of change discussed in the literature involve emotive meanings. Two major types of emotive meaning change are distinguished. 'Pejorative' change involves a shift towards a (more) negative emotive meaning. 'Ameliorative' change involves a shift towards a (more) positive emotive meaning. Let us consider some examples from Dutch. In older Dutch, *wijf* simply means 'woman' (in a general sense, not even with the specification of marriage, as in contemporary English). In present-day Dutch, however, it is a term of invective, with an impact and range not unlike English *bitch*. *Berucht* originally meant 'famous', for whatever reason; nowadays, it is 'famous for the wrong reasons, infamous'. Similarly, 17th-century authors would use *hoogdravend* to refer to a lofty, exalted style, but for the contemporary speaker of Dutch, *hoogdravend* is merely 'inappropriately elevated, pompous, bombastic'. Examples of change for the good are somewhat more difficult to find, but *moed* illustrates the phenomenon well: it used to mean 'state of mind, character' of whatever type, but it has now upgraded to 'courage, braveness'. *Leuk* (an iconic word in Dutch, as it is the most generally applicable term of positive appraisal) likewise comes from an evaluatively neutral source; like its English cognate *luke(warm)*, it originally meant 'tepid, somewhat warm but not hot'.

Four additional remarks are in order. In the first place, pejorative and ameliorative changes have to be clearly distinguished from devices such as euphemism and hyperbole—the latter are stylistic procedures, not semantic changes to word meaning. In the case of euphemism, people use a word with a less negative overtone instead of the more common, more negative or taboo word. *To pass away* or *to part with this life* are euphemistic expressions for *to die*, just like *lady of the night* and *prostitute* are in contrast with *whore, hooker, harlot, floozy, tramp*. Using *public woman* instead of *whore* does not change the emotive value of either term. On the contrary, it presupposes that one is neutral and the other negative; only in that way can using one be euphemistic and using the other dysphemistic. By comparison, there is a change of emotive value, and hence a true pejorative shift, when a word such as *boor* changes its meaning from the primarily neutral value 'peasant' to the negative meaning 'unmannered man'. The difference can also be expressed in more theoretical terms: whereas pejorative change is a diachronic semasiological process, devices such as euphemism involve onomasiological relations among denotationally synonymous words.

This does not mean, in the second place, that repeated euphemism could not be the cause of a true diachronic change. The euphemistic effect of an expression may, in fact, wear off. The negative evaluation of the referent of the expression then gradually undermines the original euphemistic value of the expression. Thus, in Dutch, the original euphemistic acronym *wc* is now less positively evaluated (i.e. has less euphemistic force) than *toilet*. A similar pattern occurs with other stylistic devices. Specifically, hyperbole involves the exaggerated expression of a negative or positive appreciation of something, such as when something is called *brilliant* when it is just good, or when, conversely, someone's behaviour is called *debilitating* when it is merely unwise. In these cases, the hyperbolic effect presupposes the stronger negative force of a word such as *debilitating* as against *unwise*, or the stronger positive force of *brilliant* as opposed to *good*. However, the repeated use of the hyperbolic expression may erode its force. Thus, *terribly* in expressions like *to be terribly sorry* has gone through an ameliorative shift from 'inspiring terror' to the neutral meaning 'in a high degree'. In a similar way, the frequent stylistic use of *awesome* as an exaggerated term of praise leads to a semasiological shift from 'inspiring awe' to (simply) 'good'.

In the third place, pejorative and ameliorative changes may or may not be accompanied by denotational changes. The shift that leads *boor* from 'peasant, farmer' to 'unmannered man' is simultaneously a shift of denotational and of emotional value. The transition seems impossible, however, without a primary shift that changes the emotive overtones of *boor* without changing the denotation. Rather in the way in which the negative expression *whore* contrasts with the neutral expression *prostitute* (while basically expressing the same denotational content), *boor* was a derogatory denomination for peasants before the negative part of that usage was detached and generalized into 'unmannered person'; the shift in emotive value without a shift in the denotational value is the missing link to get to the eventual change of the denotational value. In this respect, let us also note that the pejorative or ameliorative change may or may not involve the disappearance of the original meaning. *Sensual*, for instance, has undergone a denotational and pejorative change from the neutral meaning 'pertaining to the senses' (*sensual pleasures*) via 'given to the pursuit of the pleasures of the senses' (*a sensual person*) to 'voluptuous, licentious' (*a sensual picture*), but as the examples show, all three readings continue to exist alongside each other.

In the fourth place, because the emotive meaning of words involves the expression of values and evaluations, emotive meanings characteristically reflect the existence of social restrictions, or the way in which a particular social group is stereotypically appreciated (see Burridge, this volume). Not surprisingly, we encounter cases where one group's dissenting appreciation of a particular phenomenon leads to a distinct emotive shift reflecting the difference of opinion. Specifically, it may happen that a term referring negatively to a particular social group is adopted by the members of that group as a positive term of self-identification. In the course of the 20th century, this has happened with *queer* in the meaning 'homosexual', but 17th-century Dutch (to name only one other example) witnessed a similar process when *geus*, originally an invective for the insurgents fighting Spanish rule, was taken over by the insurgents as a term of honour and self-identification.

23.5 Necrolexicology: Vanishing Words and Meanings

All the mechanisms that we have surveyed so far, from both an onomasiological and a semasiological angle, are mechanisms of innovation—mechanisms, in other words, that introduce new meanings or new words. But words and meanings also disappear. Surprisingly, perhaps, vanishing words and meanings have not been studied as extensively in the linguistic literature as emerging words and meanings. By contrast, they receive considerable attention in popular, anecdotally oriented publications on the life of languages; the world of forgotten words and obsolete meanings is a treasure trove for language afficionados.

With regard to the disappearance of meanings, three basic patterns may be identified. The case that most readily comes to mind when we think of meanings lost in time is the situation in which the central reading of a word remains constant, but where one of the derived meanings does not persist. An example is the word *mole*, referring to the small, furry, and near-blind mammal that excavates underground tunnels and holes (and ruins your lawn with the mounds of soil it heaves up in the process). The word has other senses (such as when it refers to a spy infiltrating an enemy organization), but from its appearance in English in the 15th century to the present day, the animal sense has maintained its central position in the structure of the word. In the 17th century, the word also appears with the metaphorical reading 'a person with poor (physical or mental) vision', but this meaning does not persist; the *Oxford English Dictionary* lists quotations from 1616 to 1677, and then the meaning disappears.

Central meanings do not always remain constant, however. The second pattern to be distinguished is one in which the original meaning of a word disappears in the process of leading to a new one—the new meaning takes over the central position and ousts the old one. The *hoogdravend* example mentioned earlier is a case in point. In contemporary Dutch, *hoogdravend* is just 'inappropriately elevated, pompous, bombastic', and the original meaning 'lofty, exalted' has disappeared entirely. This pattern is the one that will raise the most etymological interest. The question 'What is the original meaning of...?' becomes all the more intriguing to the extent that the distance between the present-day meaning and the original meaning increases. Many speakers of English may be surprised to learn that the historically first meaning of *to tell* is 'to count' (even though they are familiar with bank tellers and ATMs, or Automated Teller Machines), and a large majority will be unaware that *thing* originally referred to a meeting, an assembly, or council, specifically of a legal or administrative kind.

The third pattern also involves cases in which the originally central reading largely disappears, but without being replaced by a new dominant meaning. The original meaning may then live on in isolated, specialized contexts. Thus, the English word *nitid* (a loan from Latin) was originally used with the meaning 'bright, shining; polished, glossy' in a variety of contexts, including colours, coloured things, and in a figurative sense people, but for contemporary English, the *Oxford English Dictionary* labels it as 'chiefly botanical', i.e. it is primarily used in a specialized botanical context, referring to the colouring of leaves. The specialized context in which original meanings survive may also be idioms and fixed expressions. In the 17th century, the Dutch word *huik* named a popular type of long hooded cape. That meaning has long been lost, but *huik* is still present (and not easily understood) in the figurative idiom *zijn huik naar de wind hangen*, 'to sail with the wind, to opportunistically adapt one's behaviour or opinions to the circumstances'.

Now that we have an idea of how meanings disappear, the disappearance of words may be described in a lapidary way: words disappear when all their meanings disappear; the evanescence of a word is the limiting case of the eclipse of its meanings. But why would that happen at all? We have mentioned some of the structural configurations that may be involved in the waning of meanings, but why do meanings evaporate? In a very basic sense, there are two crucial mechanisms at work: words (or words in a given meaning) are no longer used because the concept they express is no longer used, and words (or words in a given meaning) are no longer used because the concept they express receives an alternative expression. Or, to put it more simply: a word is no longer used in a certain meaning because the thing in question is forgotten, or because the word as such is no longer fashionable as the expression of that meaning.

The first case is probably the easiest to imagine. The garment meaning of Dutch *huik* is no longer used because the garment in question is no longer in use. Similarly, *marconigram* has disappeared from the English language because radiotelegraphy has been replaced by other forms of wireless communication. One nuance has to be added here: in a historicizing context, words such as these could still be used. If you write a novel about the Low Countries in the 17th century, or a history of wireless communication, words like *huik* and *marconigram* will respectively make perfect sense. If we are to talk about the death of words at all, then, we should be aware that this is a relative notion; at least in some cases words are easy to resuscitate.

Fashion plays a role when the concept to be expressed does not disappear but when there is onomasiological competition for its expression. Earlier in this chapter, we illustrated this process with the rivalry between a borrowed term and a native alternative; if Afrikaans can choose between *computer* and *rekenaar*, or German between *computer* and *Rechner*, or French between *computer* and *ordinateur*, what are the deciding factors that may eventually lead to the disappearance of one of the alternatives? The same question obviously applies to all situations involving onomasiological rivals. Although the mechanisms in question have not yet been studied very systematically in lexicological research, it is a plausible position to take that the same factors are at work here as in other areas of the language—people adapt their linguistic habits (in the case at hand, make certain onomasiological choices) because they want to blend in with a given group or mirror the linguistic behaviour of a role model. These processes of group dynamism, identification, and prestige constitute what we may loosely refer to as 'fashion', but from a linguistic point of view it is more appropriate to refer to them as the sociolinguistic forces behind lexical changes. Similar mechanisms to the ones that sociolinguists identify in the case of, for instance, phonetic variation and change are likely to be relevant for sociolexicology—though the fact that sociolexicology has to come to terms with meaning tends to complicate matters from a methodological point of view (for an analysis of these methodological challenges, see Geeraerts 2010b).

23.6 Beyond mechanisms: interactions

It is imperative, for a good understanding of lexical developments, not to look at isolated processes of change alone, but to investigate how different developments hang together, both semasiologically and onomasiologically. Let us illustrate by having a brief look at the word *smurf*. If we follow the pathways of its development, we will see how even in the short lifespan of a relatively infrequent word, a majority of the mechanisms that we have surveyed play a role, and how, more generally, those mechanisms do not occur in isolation, but rather interact in various ways in the evolution of words and vocabularies.

Smurf was initially a pure neologism, introduced as the Dutch translation of *schtroumpf*, the word that the Belgian cartoonist Peyo chose in order to name the tiny blue creatures around whom he built his French comic strip. *Schtroumpf* itself is also a pure neologism, although it may have been inspired by the German word *Strumpf* 'sock' (doesn't the Phrygian cap worn by the smurfs resemble a sock?). The Dutch 'translation' of *schtroumpf* as *smurf* was taken over in the English translation of the cartoon series, i.e. *smurf* entered the English language as a loan from Dutch. The related Dutch verb *smurfen* appears in English as *to smurf*. Starting from the noun *smurf*, the Dutch verb *smurfen* is an example of morphological derivation (just like the French *schtroumpfer* is a derivation from *schtroumpf*), whereas English *to smurf* is an example of conversion. Semantically, the verbs *schtroumpfer*, *smurfen*, and *to smurf* are special because they are maximally schematic, i.e. their meaning is very general and underspecified. It is a characteristic gimmick of the comic strip that these verbs can basically be used as a prop for any other verb—although, not surprisingly, the vagueness of the verb turns out to be particularly useful when a euphemistic effect needs to be achieved. The noun *smurf* develops semasiologically in ways that are parallel in English and Dutch. In both languages, it can be used outside the context of the original cartoon to refer negatively to an insignificant or somewhat weird, out-of-the-ordinary person. But it can also, less frequently, be used half-jokingly as a term of endearment, for instance when addressing children. In semasiological terms, these are changes based on figurative similarity, and they instantiate common patterns that we can identify as INSIGNIFICANT IS SMALL (when something is *dwarfed*, it is reduced to irrelevance by something more important) and BEAUTIFUL IS SMALL (as when your lover is your *baby*). In English, but not in Dutch, the noun *smurf* also develops a more specific reading in the context of games and Internet interactions. In this context, a smurf is an experienced gamer or forum participant posing as a newcomer. If *smurf* in this reading is then taken over in Dutch, we have an example of borrowing-back and we have come full circle in the history of *smurf*. Complicated? Well, that's just how words smurf, isn't it?

CHAPTER 24

LEXICAL BORROWING

ANTHONY P. GRANT

24.1 Introduction

Copying words from one speech tradition to another (these copied items are generally known as 'loanwords' or 'loans') is taken casually by many educated people, including some linguists, as being the prototype, and also the most widespread and extensively documented form of what happens in contact-induced language change. This lexical accretion process is often referred to as 'borrowing', a heavily contested and rather inaccurate term.

There is much more to contact-induced language change than this alone, as is obvious when one examines more detailed studies of the effects of contact between pairs of languages; see e.g. Sasse (1985) on interaction between Arvanitika (diasporic Tosk Albanian) and Dhimotiki Greek in Attica. Some studies of contact-induced language change show that lexical borrowing by speakers of one language from another is not even very significant in quantitative terms; Aikhenvald (2002) shows that in northwest Amazonia, although speakers of the Arawakan language Tariana experienced considerable structural influence on their language from Tukanoan languages, few words are borrowed from Tukanoan languages into Tariana—local ethnolinguistic ideologies regard the lexicon as emblematic of speech community identity. In this view languages differ in regard to vocabularies rather than structures.

Much of the sizeable theoretical literature, including Haspelmath (2009), Haugen (1950), Lehiste (1987), Thomason (2001), Weinreich (1953), and Winford (2003), starts building theories of contact-induced language change from examination of borrowed lexicon or concentrates on it. The best literature on this topic (including Thomason and Kaufman 1988, with its five-point cumulative scale of borrowing) is inductive, building upon the analysis of numerous case studies from a wide geographical range. Prevailing thought holds that speakers of culturally prestigious or politically powerful languages ('donor languages') bring about changes upon the languages ('recipient languages') used by less powerful populations, with acquisition of labels for previously unfamiliar items

(Haspelmath 2009's *cultural borrowing*) preceding the replacement by borrowed labels of pre-existing labels for familiar concepts ('replacive borrowing' or Haspelmath's 'core borrowing').

All languages for which we have a decent-sized dictionary or more than a few hundred words of lexicon show the effects of ancient or recent borrowing, especially of cultural vocabulary. Apparent exceptions to the universal cumulative ordering of lexical borrowings, from cultural to replacive borrowing in the Thomason–Kaufman borrowing scales (Thomason and Kaufman 1988: 74–6), can often be resolved by further investigation of the language contact history. The large tranche of loans from Norse into English mostly comprises words for which Old English, having equivalents, did not need Norse counterparts; in this case, necessary borrowings seem to precede unnecessary borrowings chronologically. Most of these loans, however, are first principally attested in northern forms of Middle English. Most early Norse loans into Old English refer to phenomena which were new concepts to Anglo-Saxons, such as types of Viking warship or of Norse legal practice. These concepts did not survive the early Middle English period, so the words became obsolete (Burnley 1992). Lost loans are also attested in the French component. For instance, Middle English *terremote* from Latin via French was replaced by the English compound *earthquake*.

Other proposed universals of lexical borrowing turn out to be less robust though still widely relevant. Moravcsik (1978) proposed several, including the proposition that words whose primary sense is verbal are never borrowed. Her own first language, Hungarian, disproves this; Hungarian *ir* 'write' is borrowed from (Turkic) Volga Bulgar, and is cognate with Turkish *yaz(mak)* 'to write'.

24.2 Mechanisms and motivations for lexical borrowing

Borrowing is just one set of techniques among the processes of lexical change.[1] Clark (1982) distinguished 'necessary' and 'unnecessary' borrowings, drawing on data from the Polynesian Outlier language Ifira-Mele (already a heavy and unequal borrower of items from the neighbouring Eastern Oceanic language, the relatively loan-shy South Efate) in its relations with Bislama, French, and English. He noted no borrowings were really 'necessary' because speakers of the language could always find other means of expressing newer concepts.

An original approach to contact linguistics is the work of Frans van Coetsem, especially van Coetsem (2000). This divides the issues into manifestations of two processes. It opposes 'borrowing' to 'imposition', whereby some features of the language of a speech

[1] For more on lexical change, see Geeraerts (this volume).

community which undergoes or has undergone language shift to a more prestigious language are preserved and transmitted. This sort of borrowing is not confined to lexicon, but the submerged language provides a substratum. Examples of 'substratal' elements are loans from British Celtic into Old English (often continued in modern English) with modern reflexes such as *bin* or *crag*, as well as river names, some Celtic, such as *Severn*, and some pre-Celtic, such as *Aire*. Words subsequently borrowed into the language are 'adstratal' elements. The reconstructible lexicon of Proto-Germanic is supposed to have a high percentage (35 per cent or more) of words of non-Indo-European origin (though see Salmons 2004); but since no convincing etymologies have been found for almost all of these 'obscure' items, much of the lexicon of what is generally a well-understood and solidly reconstructed proto-language is opaque and claims of borrowing are factitious—we may assume, but cannot prove, that these words are borrowed. Similarly about 3 per cent of the English lexicon consists of words of mysterious origin, including *boy, girl, dog, jump, pour, ever, prawn*, and *keep*.[2]

Backus (1996) and Heath (1978) proposed that all borrowing is a kind of code-mixing or code-switching. This may be true of borrowings which enter a language in the first generations when some speakers of the two languages can (but need not) be bilingual, but it cannot be taken seriously for linguistic behaviour in subsequent generations. English contains words such as *family* and *ceremony* which are generally taken to derive via Latin from Etruscan, a language which was never known to English speakers. Bilingualism on the part of speakers of the recipient language in the donor language is not a prerequisite. Few speakers of Spanish in the Caribbean in the years following Columbus's voyages there acquired much competence in the Arawakan language Taíno, whose speakers they eventually extirpated, although this did not preclude them from passing a number of Taíno words into Spanish and thence English (examples being *tobacco, canoe, hammock, potato, barbecue*). Bilinguals would presumably have been native speakers of Taíno who had learnt Spanish. French had some prestige in England even before the Norman Conquest (forms of *fever* and *proud* occur in Old English before 1066), but its cultural prestige was combined with overwhelming political power for several centuries afterwards, though French speakers never outnumbered English speakers in England.

We may note the value of the lists drawn up by Morris Swadesh (esp. Swadesh 1955) for investigating distant genealogical relations between languages; the lists serve as a metric of the levels of the vocabulary which are especially (though not completely) immune to replacement by borrowing. The 100-, 200- and 215-item lists are decreasingly borrowing-proof, and this tendency can be demonstrated as being true for language after language (see Table 24.1). The first level in Thomason and Kaufman's schema involves lexical borrowing, first non-basic, latterly also basic items, with tacit assumptions that borrowing of basic items succeeds transfer of non-basic items. Grant (2000, 2003) shows that each act of borrowing into a linguistic system involves 'transfer of

[2] See also Durkin (this volume).

Table 24.1 Rates of borrowing on the cumulative 223-item Swadesh list (see Appendix) for languages with over 60 million speakers, arranged in order of the percentage of their Swadesh list vocabulary consisting of loanwords

0–5%	German, Spanish, Arabic, Mandarin, Wu, Cantonese/Yue, Russian, Italian, Portuguese, Ukrainian, Vietnamese, Korean
5–10%	Javanese, Malay-Indonesian, Turkish
10–15%	French, Japanese, Tamil, Thai-Lao
15–20%	English, Panjabi, Bangla, Marathi, Telugu
>20%	Hindi-Urdu, Swahili

fabric' (i.e. forms with overt phonological forms), 'transfer of pattern' (replication of the syntactic, semantic, or other patterns in which the item is used; cf. Heath 1984 on 'pattern transfer', also known as a 'calque'), and often both. Lexical borrowing always involves transfer of fabric and often transfer of some pattern too. The factors broadly correspond to the issues of 'direct versus indirect diffusion' in Heath (1978), though transfer and pattern do not compete.

Haugen (1950), based on the analysis of American English borrowings into American Swedish and American Norwegian, introduced the concept of 'loanshift'. This refers to a native word whose meaning has changed because of influence from a semantically or phonologically similar word in the donor language. An American Swedish example is *att krossa gatan* 'to cross the street', echoing English *to cross*; Swedish *krossa* means 'to crush' (Glendening 1965). Bright (1953) gives an example from Karuk. The introduced fruit PEAR was named *vírusur* 'bear' because both English words were homophonous to early speakers of Karuk.

Multiple reflexes of a single form often coexist in one language, although only one will be inherited (Sanskrit scholarship calls such forms 'tadbhavas'), while the remainder are borrowed from earlier stages of the same language and retain many or all of their phonological properties ('tatsamas'). Multiple reflexes are also sometimes borrowed into a language. Latin REGĀLIS 'kingly' appears in English in three shapes: *real* (as in 'real tennis'), *royal*, and *regal*. The first is Norman French, the second central French of Paris, the third, taken later, comes directly from Latin. French has itself inherited *royal* and has back-borrowed *régal* from its ancestor Latin. Such back-borrowings, often called *cultismos*, are widespread as Latin loans into Romance languages, identifiable because their forms have not undergone sound changes experienced by directly inherited lexemes. The role of tatsamas must not be underestimated; French has its greatest number of loans from its ancestor Latin, as does Spanish (statistics in Patterson and Urrutibeheity 1975).

Sometimes borrowings coexist with inherited forms, and sometimes they replace inherited forms completely. The compound spatial preposition *in front of* with its French core is more frequent than older *before*, which is increasingly restricted to temporal contexts. *Around* from Norman French has extirpated Old English *ymb* in modern English, and the same is true of *to change* (again from French, out of Late Latin and ultimately from Celtic) against Old English *wixlan*. Sometimes the two or more words coexist as equals, or the inherited word occupies a more marginal role while the loanword has a wider range of senses and uses. *To hurt* is from French, but though we preserve Old English *scathing* and *unscathed, to scathe* is obsolete.

Certain subsets of a language's lexicon may be especially prone to borrowing. This is also the case with lexicons typifying certain registers. Dixon (1990) described the construction of avoidance registers or 'mother-in-law languages' in Australian languages (speech styles used to address relatives who are socially tabooed), some of them being remarkably comprehensive systems, and noted that many 'mother-in-law words' in Dyirbal are everyday words with the same meaning in the nearby language Yidiny, and vice versa, while some others are avoidance style words in both languages.

24.3 Adlexification, supralexification, relexification

Replacement of pre-existing items by words from another language is a form of relexification, a process which is often extensive, though always partial, as no language ever relinquishes all its lexicon. Relexification contrasts with cultural borrowing ('adlexification') insofar as relexification refers to the replacement of a pre-existing label for a concept which the speech community had already recognized and labelled. 'Supralexification' (coined in Hancock 1971: 288) also involves the complication of pre-existing semantic fields through borrowing terms which add to the complexity of the post-borrowing system. Welsh Romani (Sampson 1926) inherited words for BLACK, WHITE, RED from Indic and used a pan-Romani loan from South Slavic for GREEN. It did not preserve the widespread Romani form of South Slavic origin for YELLOW, replacing this with the Welsh loan *melanō* (Welsh *melyn*). It added a word for BLUE, *blūa*, from English (no pan-Romani forms for BLUE are attested although some borrowed forms for BLUE are widespread in Romani varieties). Similarly Welsh *gwyrdd* (from Latin *viridis*) 'green' provided a fresh label for a colour whose territory had hitherto been subsumed between *glas* 'blue, grey' and *llwyd* 'grey, brown' (Palmer 1981).

The contact history of some English canine terms is instructive for several issues in contact-induced language change. Old English used Germanic *hund* (German *Hund*), a word of probable Indo-European vintage, while *docga*, unique to English, is recorded first for Late Old English as a term for 'hunting dog'. Modern English uses *dog*, while the modern reflex of *hund, hound*, remains in more specialized terminology. *Bitch* and *puppy/pup* are of uncertain origin, although they may both originate in French loans which have both undergone semantic shift (*biche* 'doe' and *poupée* 'doll' are suggested as etyma in *OED* online). *Dog* is borrowed by German as *Dogge* 'hunting dog'.

Items referring to taboo or despised matters (including offensive names for groups which the speech community despises) are often borrowed. Hungarian *nemet* 'German' derives from Pannonian Slavic **nemecki* 'German', originating in **nemoj* 'mute' (Benkö and Imre 1972). Haspelmath (2009) regards the borrowing of terms for taboo concepts as one kind of 'therapeutic borrowing'.

24.4 Two cross-linguistic studies of lexical borrowing: Haspelmath and Tadmor (2009) and Brown (1999)

The most comprehensive study of lexical borrowing across a range of languages from different regions is to be found in the collected volume by Haspelmath and Tadmor (2009); this takes data from 41 languages representing every traditionally inhabited continent except North America (though western Asia is thinly represented). Each chapter is written by experts in the language (often native speakers of the languages). The lexical sample is constrained but large, using the equivalents of the 1,460 items of the Loanword Typology Database, itself ultimately deriving from the semantically organized concepts of Buck's (1949) dictionary of synonyms in Indo-European languages. Not all concepts have equivalents in all languages which could be obtained for this study, while in many languages there is more than one equivalent for many concepts. Furthermore, some labels for some concepts in some languages are nonce borrowings from a more powerful or prestigious language. Intra-Swahili borrowings and those from Cushitic languages are not discussed in the Swahili chapter, nor are loans from Jaqi languages including Aymara listed for Imbabura Quechua. Both strata constitute several per cent of the respective lexical samples on top of the recognized loans from other sources.

These provisos conceded, this is still a valuable resource and its findings should not be ignored (see Table 24.2). Loan percentages in the sample range from 62.7 per cent in the south-central Romani variety of Selice, south Slovakia (the majority of these loans derive from Hungarian, though older loans from various languages and newer loan layers from Slovak and Czech are also present) to 1.2 per cent in Mandarin Chinese. At 6 per cent, Old High German, the sole 'old' language in the sample without 'modern world' items, shows a higher proportion of loans (mostly from Latin) than this. Different categories of words have different proportions of loans; Clothing and Grooming averages 39.5 per cent loans, while Sense Perception only has 11.6 per cent loans. 41.0 per cent of the 1,504 English entries on the list are borrowings. Tadmor (2009: 61) shows that although 31.2 per cent of the nouns in the 41 samples are loans, this proportion drops to 15.2 per cent for adjectives and adverbs, and to 14.0 per cent for verbs.

Haspelmath and Tadmor attribute this disparity in loan absorption to the differing social circumstances in which the Selice Romani and Mandarin speech communities operated. The first was semi-itinerant, socially marginalized and with a history of

Table 24.2 Proportion of loans within the 1,460-item dataset and within various levels of the Swadesh list in 20 out of the 41 languages surveyed in Haspelmath and Tadmor (2009), including the six most and six least heavily borrowing languages

Language	No. of items	Loan proportion (%)	100-item Swadesh list	223-item Swadesh list
Selice Romani	1,431	62.7	27	34.6
Tarifiyt Berber	1,526	51.7	17	32
Gurindji	842	45.6	19	40
Romanian	2,137	41.8	9.5	14
English	1,504	41.8	9	15.5
Saramaccan	1,089	38.3	28	39
Japanese	1,975	34.9	17	18
Indonesian	1,942	34.0	9	16
Vietnamese	1,477	29.0	4–5	12.5
Swahili	1,610	27.8	5	8+
Thai	2,063	26.1	8	15
Hausa	1,452	22.2	3	3.5
Dutch	1,513	19.1	2	2
Hawai'ian	1,245	13.6	0	1.4
Seychelles Creole	1,879	10.7	0	2
Otomi	2,158	10.7	1	2.5
Ket	1,030	9.7	0	2.5
Manange	1,009	8.3	0	1.4
Old High German	1,203	5.8	0	0.5
Mandarin Chinese	2,042	1.2	0	1

multilingualism but none of literacy, while the latter speech community had long held political domination over other groups and could access a written language of immense prestige. But this sociologically based explanation may be questioned. Romanian and English (the latter the increasingly dominant world language since the mid-18th century) are also in the top five heavy borrowing languages, while Tarifiyt Berber has borrowed more than half its lexicon in the sample (principally from local and classical forms of Arabic, latterly also from Spanish and French). Most non-internationalist borrowings into English are first recorded between 1000 and 1600; Old English appears to have had fewer than 5 per cent securely identifiable borrowings of any kind in its lexeme stock. Comparing borrowing levels in this sample with those on the Swadesh lists for the various languages in the study, we find that in every case the larger lexical sample contains a higher proportion of loans than the Swadesh lists do for these languages. Work is proceeding on producing similar databases (with 1,600 concepts interrogated including all those in the Loanword Typology Database) for some major languages omitted from the project, and for several others.

Semantic fields especially attractive to loanwords can easily be selected and studied in Haspelmath and Tadmor's collection. They added two fields to Buck's original 22, namely Miscellaneous Function Words (23) and The Modern World (24), and extend Buck's original list from 1,059 items to 1,460. Unsurprisingly, given that the first things to be expressed by loanwords into a language are items which the recipient speech community sees as cultural innovations, The Modern World is the field which contains the highest proportion of loanwords, and this is true of most of the sampled languages. (It is also unsurprising that field 4—The Human Body, whose components and practices are universal across humanity—has one of the lowest loan proportions.) Items such as *kangaroo*, the name for which diffused from *gangurru* 'small black kangaroo' in Queensland's Guugu Yimidhirr language to English (possibly initially via translations of accounts of the 1769 voyage of Captain James Cook) and thereafter to other languages, are expressed by forms of the same loan (based on the English form *kangaroo*) in most languages surveyed.

Haspelmath and Tadmor proposed a 'Leipzig–Jakarta list' from the 100 least-borrowed items on the Loanword Typology Database list, but this has shortcomings as a replacement for the Swadesh list as a means of calibrating inherited or unborrowed items. Had Haspelmath and Tadmor used a different set of 41 languages, the contents of the list would have been different because different words would have remained unborrowed in the sampled languages.

No concept is recorded in the Loanword Typology Database list for which speakers of at least one language have not adopted a borrowed form as the principal or only means of expression. All concepts on the Swadesh list are expressed by borrowings in some language: 16 per cent of such items in the modern English version of the 215-item Swadesh list are borrowings, mostly from Norse or Norman French (compare 0.5 per cent for Icelandic). In some languages whose speech communities have long been multilingual in one or more languages of greater prestige the proportion of loans on the Swadesh list can reach beyond 30 per cent. The Northern Songhay mixed Songhay–Berber language Tadaksahak of Mali draws little more than 50 per cent of its Swadesh list lexicon from Songhay, which accounts for the bulk of the language's productive bound morphology but fewer than 300 of its attested lexical items (Christiansen-Bolli 2010). Brahui, a Dravidian language of Pakistan, preserves even less of its Swadesh list contents and uses even more loans (Bray 1934).

Native North American languages are extensively represented in Brown (1999), which examines the equivalents of 77 mostly post-Columbian referents in almost 200 indigenous languages from throughout the Americas. Again there are data gaps (most notably, equivalents for the term CORIANDER are found only in the southwestern US and in Latin America). Nonetheless, the study illustrates the degree of lexical borrowing in the various languages. Languages whose speakers came into contact with speakers of Spanish or Portuguese have on the whole borrowed more terms for labelling Euroamerican items than those who interacted with speakers of other languages such as French or English. Here again regional factors come into consideration. A large number of Native languages in certain parts of the Americas (Plains and southeastern US, for instance) seem to practise what one might call 'iron rations borrowing': a minimum set of acculturational items is taken over and is then generalized or employed in compounds or composite forms, while other acculturational concepts are expressed by words which have either changed or expanded their original meanings, or else form compounds to express these meanings.

Variation can occur within regions. A Californian language such as Kashaya Pomo uses *kawá:yu, yé:wa, potrí:yu'*, for 'horse, mare, colt', all borrowed from Spanish *caballo, yegua, potrero* respectively, another one such as Washo borrows only *gawá:yu'* 'horse' and builds compounds with it using only inherited elements: *dalá'iŋ dewdéwluwe'* 'female horse' and *dewdéwluwe' ŋá'miŋ* 'young horse' to express female sex, size, or immaturity (Bright 1960). Languages in certain language families seem especially resistant to lexical borrowing, but in some cases borrowing between related languages (e.g. between certain groups of Mayan languages: see Wichmann and Brown 2003) is considerable, while borrowing into Athabaskan languages ranges from fewer than twenty in Chiricahua Apache, taken from Spanish (Hoijer 1939), to several hundred, mostly from Russian, into Alaskan languages. Nearly all the loans are nouns.

24.5 The diachronic value of lexical borrowings

Informed analysis of lexical borrowings often provides investigators with diachronic information not readily available otherwise. For example, Welsh *berem* 'yeast' derives from Old English *beorm*, the etymon of modern regional English *barm*, though Welsh English is non-rhotic[3] (Clive Grey, p.c., 2004). Similarly, in Nicaragua, Miskitu *aras* 'horse', a label for a post-Columbian introduction, is taken from a variety of English which was evidently still rhotic in the late 17th century, and Miskitu Creole English is rhotic (Mark Jamieson, p.c., 2000). Sometimes loanwords are the only evidence of the existence of an unattested language. Holzer (1989) presents terms from an otherwise unattested Indo-European 'Tememaric' language, spoken somewhere in eastern Europe, into Baltic and Slavic languages, while Kaufman (1980) discusses elements of 'Submerged Northern Mayan' in the lexicon of Huastec, also Mayan but showing a different set of sound correspondences from those attested in the borrowed words. Loans

[3] The terms 'rhotic' and 'non-rhotic' apply to accents of English according to whether a post-vocalic 'r', as in *bar* and *barm*, is pronounced. The presence of 'r' in the Welsh word indicates that at the time the word was borrowed, post-vocalic 'r' was pronounced in English.

into Welsh, Cornish, and Breton (sundered from its sister-languages around 500 CE) present evidence for Latin influence on British Celtic which is reflected in its descendants (Elsie 1979).

Wanderwörter—wandering words—often travel far. Walsh (1992) presents a study of *nantu*, a word for 'horse' taken from Kaurna (the ancestral language of Adelaide) which spread to many languages of central Australia and the Northern Territory along well-established trails established by White drovers. Comrie (1981) mentions the case of Greek *nómos* 'law', which passed into Persian *nâma* and thence into several Mongolic languages of Siberia as *nom* 'book'.

Patterns of Kari'na borrowing into Garifuna (Hoff and Taylor 1980) are unusual, as these elements may come from a Kari'na pidgin, which may have had a limited vocabulary confined to the basics necessary for communication. Additionally, the proportion of Kari'na elements in the Garifuna Swadesh list appears to be considerably greater than that in the Garifuna lexicon as a whole.

There has been cross-linguistic work on the borrowing of phrasal adverbs and of subordinating and coordinating conjunctions (Matras 1998; Grant 2012a shows that these do not constitute a borrowing hierarchy), pronouns (Thomason and Everett 2005), copulas and 'have' verbs (Grant 2012b), verbs in general (even as unchangeable elements integrated through the use of light verbs, the usual method in e.g. Yiddish; Wohlgemuth 2009 studies this), numerals (Souag 2007 discusses this for the Berber language family), and even some cases of definite and indefinite articles and adpositions, though these last categories do not seem to have attracted much cross-linguistic literature. Anything with independent status as a word is potentially borrowable, and cases of borrowing and thereafter of productive, unmarked, normative, and quotidian use of all these items can be found in the literature.

Failure to recognize that lexical items are borrowed rather than inherited can lead to faulty subgrouping of languages. Cree absorbed many loans from Ojibwe, leading Bloomfield (1946), who did not recognize them as loans, to create a misguided 'Central Algonquian' grouping which Rhodes (1989) has unravelled.

24.6 Purism and lexical borrowing

We see that not all speech communities are equally open to the absorption of loanwords; they thereby practise forms of linguistic purism. We may distinguish between purism as the result of linguistic engineering—a political act—and purism which is the outcome of speakers of a particular language instinctively relying on inherited or 'native' morphemic resources as the means of encoding previously unfamiliar concepts, thereby creating 'incoinings'. (Some languages such as Estonian have also expanded their lexicon with *ex nihilo* neologisms in addition to incoinings and loanwords: Viitso 1994.) Purism is rarely if ever absolute. Icelandic is an example of purism brought about through language engineering (its ancestral form, Old Norse, absorbed some loans from Goidelic and Latin; Icelandic also has Danish and English loans); Native American languages of the Great Plains, such as Lakhota and Cheyenne, represent the other tendency, as Brown (1999) shows. Icelandic's puristic approach involves both semantic extension of pre-existing words (*simi* 'thread; telephone') and the creation of neologisms from pre-existing morphemes (*tala* 'to count'; *tölva* 'computer': Thráinsson 1994: 188–189). Thomas (1991) discusses linguistic purism, giving especial attention to purism in South Slavic languages (though Thomas wrote before political splits in Serbo-Croat).

Although English has absorbed many words from Norse, Dutch, Greek, French, and Latin (principally since the Norman Conquest), this borrowing has not passed without adverse comment, nor without attempts to arrest these changes. Typical of this is the Inkhorn Debate, the name given to disputes about the fitness of English for use as a language of advanced learning which was waged during much of the 16th century. Neologizers (e.g. Thomas Elyot), archaizers (e.g. Edmund Spenser), and purists (e.g. John Cheke) argued the case for vocabulary expansion by borrowing new terms, retrieval of archaic terms, and creating compound words or by developing new senses of pre-existing terms respectively (Baugh and Cable 1993). The neologizers largely won, though by no means all their coinages remained in use. Shakespeare's comedy *Love's Labour's Lost* guys more extreme tendencies in neologizing and the malapropisms which often ensue in the mouths of less educated speakers. Later attempts at purism in English proved unsuccessful, though some, such as the campaigns waged by the Society for Pure English, have been rather sophisticated linguistically even if *parti pris*. Lexical strata targeted by English purists tend to be the non-Germanic ones; the attempt to erase all loanwords is referred to as 'ultrapurism'. English has no Language Academy corresponding to French's puristic Académie française.

Puristic attitudes coexist with prejudice and linguistic ignorance in many cases because their motivations are generally ideological rather than scholastic. Moghaddam (1963, cited in Jazayery 1983) claimed that Arabic loans in Farsi were actually back-borrowings from Farsi into Arabic and therefore native. Sabino Arana, a native speaker of Spanish, created some erroneously etymologized neologisms for Basque including *Euzkadi* 'Basque Country' (Trask 1997). Mussolini's followers' inept attempts at purism, often expelling Latin-derived words from Italian in favour of some from Germanic and Greek, are mentioned in Kramer (1983).

Attempts to rid Turkish of Arabic and Persian elements which predominated during the Ottoman period and to replace them by neologisms, or by back-borrowings from Old Turkic or from other Turkic languages, are documented in Lewis (1999). The impetus under reformist dictator Kemal Atatürk was ideological (the desire to make Turkey modern, secular, statist, and Western-facing). The success of such moves is mixed at best: Turkish still contains plentiful forms from Persian, Arabic, and increasingly French and English. Successful replacement of a highly unsuitable Arabic script with an essentially phonemic alphabet using Latin letters helped spread literacy to the bulk of the Osmanli Turkish-speaking population. But this movement also led to the bizarre Sun-Language Theory, now mercifully abandoned, which claimed that all words derived from *güneş*, Turkish for 'sun'.

Purism is not confined to written languages or their speakers. Chitimacha, an extinct isolate from Southern Louisiana, never had a written form, but its last speaker once refused to dictate a myth to linguist Morris Swadesh because the speaker forgot the Chitimacha word for 'skunk' (Swadesh 1946). Cuzco Quechua is little used in writing; its speakers have absorbed many Spanish words which had been adapted earlier to Quechua phonology, and it also absorbed many words from Jaqi languages (including Aymara) to which it may owe its distinction between plain, aspirated, and glottalized voiceless stops. The large Spanish element, manifest in Coronel-Medina (2002), which uses English as its matrix language, is almost undetectable in many works on the language with Spanish as matrix language; their dictionaries often omit entries for concepts which are usually or only expressed by Spanish loans.

24.7 Wider consequences of lexical borrowing

Lexical borrowings can be the first step by which a language acquires new structural features. Word boundaries within the donor language are not always recognized (or thereafter respected) by speakers of the recipient language. Spanish (and sometimes English) has absorbed hundreds of Arabic nouns with the definite article obligatorily attached (such as *aldea* 'village'), although in the Middle Ages a knowledge of Arabic must have been widespread among Romance speakers in southern Spain.

Incorporation of borrowings depends upon the structure of the borrowing language. English absorbs loans easily, as its productive inflectional morphology is sparse. Some other languages have special paradigms for borrowed languages (e.g. Romani: Boretzky 1994), which may even largely comprise borrowed morphemes (in Romani's case mostly from Greek).

Nouns usually outnumber verbs in the number of borrowings. Unusually from a cross-linguistic perspective, Mon-Khmer elements in Acehnese (Sidwell 2005) include more non-nouns than nouns, but this case is anomalous. Many languages borrow no verbs; many others, such as Turkish, Yiddish, and Hindi, must with few exceptions (e.g. Yiddish *shmadn* 'to baptize' from Hebrew) conjugate them using auxiliary 'light' verbs. There are several sets of cardinal numerals in many languages of East and Southeast Asia (from Chinese) and some in the Philippines (from Spanish), elsewhere usually from Chinese. Both numeral sets are crucial to full operation as a speaker of said language even among monolinguals, and the borrowed numeral set is usually more comprehensive or extensive than the inherited one.

An example of a heavily borrowing language is Chamorro, which has taken all its cardinal and ordinal numerals directly from Spanish, in addition to borrowing some pronouns (*yo* 'I'), many prepositions (*fuera* 'except for'), several subordinating conjunctions (*mientras* 'while'), numerous adverbs, sometimes with different meanings from

Spanish source forms (*siempre* 'certainly' but Sp. 'always'), several forms of the copulas *ser* and *estar* (*estaba* 'there used to be', *será* 'maybe'), the demonstrative adjective 'this' (*este*), and the indefinite article *un*, a category previously unknown in Chamorro (Topping, Ogo, and Dungca 1975).

Phonological adaptation of loans generally begins with assimilation of borrowings to the recipient language's segmental and phonological system, and such information may make it possible to stratify loans chronologically even from a single donor language (see Clark 1977 on Spanish loans in Sayula Popoluca of Mexico). But a larger battery of loans may introduce whole new sets of phones and indeed new syllabic canons (e.g. complex onsets and codas), and earlier phonotactic constraints may be relaxed. Lake Miwok of central California (Callaghan 1963) absorbed more segments (first from Hill Patwin, later from Spanish, finally from English) than it had previously possessed. New distinctive features may be introduced through their inclusion in loans. Urdu added the feature [+uvular] by borrowing words containing /q/ (*qiilaa* 'fortress') from Persian and Arabic. Nguni languages of southern Africa introduced new airstream mechanisms, such as click consonants, via borrowings from Khoisan languages (Maddieson 1988).

Loanwords may introduce new suprasegmental patterns as well as intonational patterns, which are initially confined to loans, and borrowing may be the cause of tonogenesis. Thurgood (1999) discusses Tsat, an Austronesian language of Hainan Island, China, which absorbed hundreds of words from regional Chinese. This has helped a tonal system similar to that of the local Minnan variety to develop. Borrowed phonemes sometimes leach from loans into native lexicon: Zulu -*hlanu* 'five' contains /ɬ/, absorbed from Khoisan, in an inherited stem (cf. Swahili -*tano* 'five'; Guthrie 1967–71).

Grammatical adaptation of loans varies from one language to the next, and even structural subsets in a single language may behave differently. We note the use of invariant forms in Russian (*kino* 'cinema' from German is neuter and indeclinable, but feminine *mašina* 'car', from French *machine* but with a semantic change specific to Russian, declines regularly for both numbers and all cases; declensions are dealt with in Timberlake 1993). Metanalysis may occur. Swahili *kitabu* 'book' < Arabic *kitaab* is reconstrued as a *ki-/vi-* noun in Swahili; its plural is *kutub* in Arabic but *vitabu* in Swahili. Similarly, English *mudguard* was borrowed as *madigadi*, construed as a plural noun of the extensive *n-/ma-* class and given an analogical singular *digadi* (John Kelly, p.c.). Languages with fluid boundaries between verbal, nominal, and adjectival form-class categories would find it easier to absorb loans quickly and productively as verbs. Through loanwords, speakers of a language may acquire new morphology which can be applied to inherited words; a case in point is the English agentive suffix -*er*, ultimately from Latin -*ārius*.

24.8 Conclusions

We can draw many general and some universal conclusions about lexical borrowing. The first relate to the chronological primacy of cultural over core borrowings, and the robustness of the Swadesh lists as being proportionally more immune to borrowing when compared with the lexicon of a language as a whole. General conclusions relate to the relative ease of borrowability of nouns against verbs and other parts of speech, and the proneness of particular semantic fields to change through borrowing. Furthermore, lexical borrowing provides the gateway for others kinds of contact-induced linguistic change to enter a language.

APPENDIX

223-ITEM SWADESH LIST

1. I 2. you (singular) 3. he 4. we 5. you (plural) 6. they 7. this 8. that 9. here 10. there 11. who 12. what 13. where 14. when 15. how 16. not 17. all 18. many 19. some 20. few 21. other 22. one 23. two 24. three 25. four 26. five 27. big 28. long 29. wide 30. thick 31. heavy 32. small 33. short 34. narrow 35. thin 36. woman 37. man (adult male) 38. man (human being) 39. child 40. wife 41. husband 42. mother 43. father 44. animal 45. fish 46. bird 47. dog 48. louse 49. snake 50. worm 51. tree 52. forest 53. stick 54. fruit 55. seed 56. leaf 57. root 58. bark 59. flower 60. grass 61. rope 62. skin 63. meat 64. blood 65. bone 66. fat (n.) 67. egg 68. horn 69. tail 70. feather 71. hair 72. head 73. ear 74. eye 75. nose 76. mouth 77. tooth 78. tongue 79. fingernail/claw 80. foot 81. leg 82. knee 83. hand 84. wing 85. belly 86. guts 87. neck 88. back 89. breast 90. heart 91. liver 92. drink 93. eat 94. bite 95. suck 96. spit 97. vomit 98. blow 99. breathe 100. laugh 101. see 102. hear 103. know 104. think 105. smell 106. fear 107. sleep 108. live 109. die 110. kill 111. fight 112. hunt 113. hit 114. cut 115. split 116. stab 117. scratch 118. dig 119. swim 120. fly (v.) 121. walk 122. come 123. lie 124. sit 125. stand 126. turn 127. fall 128. give 129. hold 130. squeeze 131. rub 132. wash 133. wipe 134. pull 135. push 136. throw 137. tie 138. sew 139. count 140. say 141. sing 142. play 143. float 144. flow 145. freeze 146. swell 147. sun 148. moon 149. star 150. water 151. rain 152. river 153. lake 154. sea 155. salt 156. stone 157. sand 158. dust 159. earth 160. cloud 161. fog 162. sky 163. wind 164. snow 165. ice 166. smoke 167. fire 168. ashes 169. burn 170. road 171. mountain 172. red 173. green 174. yellow 175. white 176. black 177. night 178. day 179. year 180. warm 181. cold 182. full 183. new 184. old 185. good 186. bad 187. rotten 188. dirty 189. straight 190. round 191. sharp 192. dull 193. smooth 194. wet 195. dry 196. correct 197. near 198. far 199. right 200. left 201. at 202. in 203. with 204. and 205. if 206. because 207. name 208. brother 209. clothing 210. cook 211. cry/weep 212. dance 213. shoot 214. sister 215. spear 216. work 217. six 218. seven 219. eight 220. nine 221. ten 222. twenty 223. hundred

CHAPTER 25

LEXICAL LAYERS

MARGARET E. WINTERS

25.1 Introduction

The lexicon is a complex and multi-faceted component of language which can be parsed in various ways. [1] The meaning of words is, of course, the most basic approach from the point of view of speakers. From a morphosyntactic viewpoint, we inherently have some conceptual sense of grammatical categories—nouns, verbs, adjectives, and so on—even if the labels must be learned in school or, perhaps, not at all. But meaning and grammatical classification are only some of the aspects of the lexicon. Naive speakers, as well as linguists, make judgements as to the register of words, their suitability in various forms of discourse, and the effect the choice may have on the listener/reader. Germane to these judgements are degrees of formality, the distinctiveness of literary and poetic language, the jargons and specialized vocabulary of trades and professions, as well as vocabulary which might identify gender, a social group, or socio-economic status. Intersecting with these grammatical and pragmatic categories are what we might call historical and contact-induced layers, that is, components of the lexicon which arise from significant and often pervasive borrowings from other languages. These are components which may have their own phonological, morphological, semantic, stylistic, and even syntactic and orthographic identity; the layer may, at times, be identified in some way by naive native speakers who recognize that the layer, or sub-lexicon, is somehow different from the core lexicon of their language.

The rest of this introduction discusses the notion of lexical layers and the ways in which they might be considered synchronically and diachronically. Sections 25.2 and 25.3 consider the sources of layers and how they emerge, with examples drawn from a

[1] I appreciate the many suggestions from John Taylor and Geoff Nathan which have very much improved this text. All errors of fact and interpretation, however, are mine.

number of languages, while section 25.4 looks at some broader issues which arise from a study of lexical layers.

25.1.1 Layering and contact

Languages and their lexicons develop in several ways. First, and most fundamentally, a language usually has as its core what it has inherited from earlier stages, as far back in time as we can trace ancestry and origins. English, for example, is a Germanic language, related closely to Dutch, German, and Yiddish, all of which are Western Germanic and stem from an original Western Germanic dialect (see Durkin, this volume). More distantly, it is related to the Scandinavian languages, Swedish, Norwegian, Danish, and Icelandic, all members of the Northern Germanic family. Projected even further back in time is common Germanic. Earlier still is Indo-European, the hypothesized parent language of much of Europe and parts of Asia. The core grammar and lexicon of English is inherited without interruption through these chronological stages.

Genetic inheritance is not the only source of linguistic formation. A second, important aspect is observable through the interactions that languages (or, to be precise, speakers of languages) have with each other. In the lexicon particularly, contact is a powerful force, in great part because it is through contact that languages acquire layers of linguistic units which are not inherited from earlier forms of the language. The next paragraphs briefly review the ways in which this contact may occur, using the terminology developed in the 19th century and still current in diachronic studies, and illustrated by a brief look at the early external history of what eventually becomes French.

In the first century BCE, Celtic tribes flourished in what is now the northern part of France. The Romans conquered that territory, starting in 44 BCE with Julius Caesar's invasion of what was then called Gallia. As they did elsewhere, the Romans settled in Gallia, establishing towns and awarding veterans of their wars with land. Over a period of time the two peoples—and their languages—coexisted, but eventually the Celts were either displaced or assimilated to Roman linguistic and cultural dominance. Before the Celtic language disappeared on what was now Roman territory, however, it had some influence on the Latin spoken there; some 200 French words come from the Celtic of the territory that is now northern France as does part of the French number system.[2] Celtic is called a substratal language (literally 'under layer') since it preexisted in what became Roman territory and influenced Latin before disappearing.

[2] The words refer mostly to local features (*grève* 'sandy shore', *lande* 'heath'), plants (*bouleau* 'birch', *bourdaine* 'black alder', *chêne* 'oak'), wildlife (*alouette* 'lark'), and rural life (*boue* 'mud', *cervoise* 'ale', *charrue* 'plow', *glaise* 'loam'). French, in addition, has a ten-base number system like English (10-19, 20-29, etc.) for the lower numbers but becomes twenty-base under Celtic influence above 60 (60-79, literally sixty-nineteen, 80-99, literally eighty-nineteen). For Celtic and Germanic influence, see Pope (1934).

Contrasting with substratal influence is superstratal influence (literally 'over layer'). Here too the key is contact, although in this case the language which provides lexical influence is one whose speakers arrive in a given territory later than the language being influenced. Again the superstratal language, the one from which borrowing takes place, eventually falls out of use in the territory. To continue with Gallia, in the early part of the Common Era (3rd, 4th, and 5th centuries), Germanic tribes invaded what had become Roman lands. For various reasons, not least the fact that in Roman settlements life was much more comfortable than in their own, these tribes eventually adopted the Latin language, on its way to becoming French. Before disappearing, however, Germanic languages (Frankish in the north, Burgundian, Visigothic further south) contributed to the vocabulary of the Latinate language of Gallia. Words referred to Germanic noble society (*baron, héraut* 'herald', *chambellan* 'chamberlain'), warfare (*heaume* 'helmet', *guerre* 'war'), and seafaring. In addition, the Vikings, who settled parts of what is now eastern England from the 8th to the 11th centuries, furnished, among other technical terms, the French names for the compass points, *nord, sud, est, oust.*

Contact, then, is essential to the notion of stratal influence or layering. While the two terms are not exactly synonymous, they share the notion of borrowings (often extensive) across languages resulting from prolonged contact of peoples speaking them. Where the terms differ is that layering is a wider notion, as will be seen in the varied examples in section 25.2, while stratal influence includes, definitionally, the fact that, after a certain period of co-existence, the source language for borrowing disappears in the territory where the borrowing takes place, irrespective of whether the influence is deemed substratal or superstratal. The next sections expand on the notion of layers, and in particular how they may be viewed as going beyond the traditional strata.

25.1.2 Synchrony, diachrony, and their interaction

Layering is a phenomenon which can be viewed from multiple points of view. The stratal approach reviewed above is diachronic, based, in fact, in early 19th century discussions of 'deep' or geological time (Gould 1987). The most usual understanding of stratal processes is narrower than the full historical process of contact and borrowing which may result in real layers, since stratal influence implies the disappearance of one language after a period of bilingualism and/or intense contact, with the borrowing viewed as unidirectional. But even over time we can study bidirectional lexical borrowing and, as will be seen below, there is no necessity that the source language disappears, even in some limited geographic area. When we turn to the synchronic point of view, studying the results of contract and borrowing at some specific point in time, there are no such restrictions. In some cases, such as 'fashionable' borrowings, there are not even restrictions on the length of contact for the establishment of a layer.

In summary, 'stratum' may be considered subordinate to the notion of 'layer'. While both phenomena arise through prolonged contact between languages and/or dialects, the notion of a stratum is normally restricted to a linguistic layer that influences another language and then, in the territory where the influenced language functions, disappears. 'Layer', on the other hand, refers more broadly to the results of borrowing as a consequence of contact; the two languages/dialects may never have been spoken in the same geographic territory and each may coexist indefinitely among the world's languages.

25.2 Kinds of contact

This section looks at the different kinds of contact which have given rise to layers.

25.2.1 Armed and political conquest

The most obvious kind of contact leading to new lexical layers in a language is the conquest of one linguistic community by another. While conquest may take many forms, we will start with what is arguably the most prototypical: conquest by force leading to occupation of the defeated political entity by the successful invader. Conquerors who occupy a geographic area will impose laws, sometimes social customs, and also language on those they conquer. Linguistic conquest, however, is usually more complex and less complete than one might suppose.

The limiting case is the total linguistic conquest of a region by those invading and occupying the territory. This is, for perhaps obvious reasons, very rare; speakers—particularly adult speakers—do not easily acquire full functionality in a language other than their own, even when recourse to their native language is forbidden. What more often occurs is a change in the language of education, the outcome of much colonialism. In Haiti, for example, Creole is the native and adult language, but, until recently, standard French was the language of instruction, giving rise not so much to the suppression of Creole, but rather to a diglossic situation.

One of the best studied examples of the effect of invasion and occupation concerns the Norman conquest of England in 1066 when Duke William of Normandy defeated King Harold of England (or at least of southeast England) at the battle of Hastings. Duke William (from then on King William of England, known as William the Conqueror) moved his court to England, bringing with it Norman law, judicial courts, education, and a new elite population. His grandson, Henry II of England, subsequently married Eleanor of Aquitaine, a southern French noblewoman (and divorced wife of the King of France), thereby adding another complication to this already complicated linguistic situation. First, Eleanor brought many French lands to her marriage, thus expanding the continental territories ruled by the English king. By all accounts she was devoted to the arts and culture and stimulated enthusiasm on what is now British land for French poetry and, more generally, French courtly society. Historians usually date the end of the Norman/French occupation as 1204, with the ascension to the throne of Eleanor and Henry's son John who was, arguably, an English king.

Before 1204, those who were the most enthusiastic about French culture and language were not the traditional speakers of Anglo-Saxon (the language of those conquered in 1066 and beyond), but rather those imported from the continent to be the judges, teachers, courtiers, and overseers of Anglo-Saxon labour. French was not imposed on these labourers, or even on craftsmen or those belonging to the trading and merchant classes. Society was diglossic with clear class and other social barriers between English and French speakers. Indicative of this division is the fact that some of the earliest works in the French of England meant for the conquered were textbooks of French, intended to help upward climbing individuals (Kibbee 1991).

The situation gradually evolved so that there was a great deal more contact between the languages. The result, as is well known, is that English, although Germanic in basic structure and vocabulary, has a lexicon which is approximately 60 per cent Latinate (van Gelderen 2006: 4), with most of the Latinate elements borrowed from French, either in the centuries immediately following the Conquest or later (especially during the 16th and 17th centuries). While the motivations for borrowing are discussed below (section 25.3), it is worth looking at the range of semantic fields where French culture influenced the language. From the time of the earliest contact, general fields include food, with the much cited contrast between Latinate terms for what one eats and the Germanic animal names (*pork* and *pig*, *beef* and *cow*, *veal* and *calf*); feudalism (*liege, homage, chivalry, peasant*); the nobility (*baron, duke, count, prince, dame, sir*); government (*parliament, government, council, minister, mayor, chancellor*); religion (*abbey, clergy, parish, prayer*); the military (*battalion, dragoon, infantry, cavalry, army, squad, squadron, sergeant, lieutenant, captain, colonel, general, admiral*); and architecture (*aisle, arcade, arch, vault, belfry*). Perhaps even more interesting are what one would think of as basic words like colour terms, although some of these are far from primary and may have been borrowed along with fashion design (*mauve, beige, maroon, blue, orange, violet, vermilion, turquoise, lilac, scarlet*). English uses Latinate/French terms as well for common vegetables and fruits (*cabbage, carrot, nutmeg, quince, lemon, orange, apricot*[3]) and, finally, for certain months of the year (*January, March, May, July, November, December*).

25.2.2 Cultural conquest

Not all contact involves a physical presence of the sort which occurs when one political entity occupies another. There are many examples of what might be called cultural conquest, where lexical items (or whole lexical networks) are used because the culture represented by the words is admired by some segment of the borrowing speakers. French borrowed lexical items in various semantic categories from Italian in the 16th century,

[3] British English probably has more in this category than American English, e.g. *aubergine*, where American English uses *eggplant*, and *mange-touts*, called *sugar snap peas* in American English; both French borrowings date from the 18th century.

not because of political conquest, but through admiration for Italian arts, cuisine, and decoration. Over the centuries there appeared terms related to cuisine (*soufflé, croissant, marmalade, meringue, casserole, mustard, mayonnaise, sauce*) and the arts (*surrealism, cubism, symbolism, art nouveau*). The popularity of things Italian was intensified under the influence of Catherine De Medici (1519–1589), the Italian-born queen of France and regent during the minority of her son, later Charles IX. Terms were brought into French in architecture (*stuc* 'stucco', *grotte* 'grotto'), music (*violin, madrigal, concert*), and cuisine (*artichaut* 'artichoke', *broccoli, sorbet*). Many were also borrowed into English, either from Italian directly or via French.

For a modern example of layering, evolved largely through cultural conquest, we can turn to the Japanese lexicon. Japanese has always been a language which borrowed extensively, with the result that it has long been viewed by its speakers as well as by linguistics as stratified, with a basic layer of native lexical items, borrowings from Chinese—a language which in the past played the role of French and Latin in English (that is, a source of technical and learned forms)—and a further foreign layer (Ito and Mester 1995: 817; Shibatani 1987).

The stratification is mirrored in many aspects of the phonological and morphological system of Japanese. Certain voicing phenomena occur only with native compounds, so that underlying *yudoofu* 'boiled tofu' is *yu* 'hot water' and *tofu,* while *degutʃi* 'exit' is built from *de* 'leave' and *kutʃi* 'mouth'. Other layers do not display this voicing assimilation. On the other hand, units of Chinese origin all contain monosyllabic roots which may only combine with other Sino-Japanese roots (Ito and Mester 1995: 818– 819). The writing system serves as a further marker of layers, in that Japanese has one syllabary for native words, one for foreign words other than Chinese, and widely-used Chinese characters for words borrowed from that language. In addition certain morphological processes serve to preserve these lexical layers as synchronically viable and not simply etymological.

The cultural conquest of the language and the accompanying expansion of the non-Chinese foreign layer began politically in the 20th century with the occupation of Japan by American troops after World War II, and expanded subsequently through the media with the popularity of American culture in that country. Earlier borrowings were also a matter of contact, with Portugal and the Netherlands in the 16th and 17th centuries, bringing to Japanese words like *pan* 'bread' and *koton* 'cotton' from Portuguese,[4] both borrowed with the objects they designate. In the 18th century some borrowings from German also entered Japanese, among them medical terms, since German speakers brought western medicine to this culture. Also among them are *arubaito* 'part-time work' (German *Arbeit* 'work') and *enerugi* 'energy'.

While in the past Chinese was the major source of borrowing, not just of lexical items but also of a counting system and of one of the three Japanese writing systems, English is

[4] Contrary to popular belief, the Japanese for 'thank you', *arigato*, does not come from Portuguese *obrigado*, but is of native origin.

now the dominant influence, although geographically the United States and Great Britain are too far away for geographic contact to be considered a major impetus for borrowing. The semantic fields involved are wide, although a great deal can be subsumed under technology and popular culture, in their various manifestations. Among the technology items are *sutōbu* 'space heater' (English *stove*), *rimōto kontorōru* ('remote control'), usually shortened to *rimokon*, and *wapuro*, from English 'word processor'. Among popular culture terms are *depāto*, shortened from *depātomento sutoa* 'department store', and *oke* (a shortening of 'orchestra') which appears in the compound *karaoke*, with the first half being the native word for 'empty'; the same lexical item appears in *karate* (literally 'empty hand'). The range of English and American influence on Japanese culture can be glimpsed in borrowings such as *hōmu*, from '(train station) platform', *ketto* 'blanket', and *neru* 'flannel'. In each of these cases, the borrowing comes from the last syllable of the English word, *form* (with a sound change [f]>[h] to mask it further), *ket*, and *nel* respectively.

25.2.3 The influence of religion

The interaction of religion with other aspects of culture may also produce layering of the lexicon in a given language. Religions tend to spread without regard for national or linguistic borders and, as a result, become a force for lexical borrowing as part of their being adopted. The spread of Islam brought with it the infiltration of the relevant Classical Arabic lexicon into a large number of unrelated languages, such as Turkish and Bahasa Indonesia, with an expansion not only of the lexicon, but also of the phonemic inventory through the introduction of non-native velar and guttural consonants. The Arabic words have been, for the most part, either nativized or calqued. Another example is the spread of the Orthodox Church in what is now known as the Baltic Sprachbund. In the western part of the later Roman Empire, Christianity took hold via Greece, with the result that Greek lexical influence on Latin extended to a new semantic field. Among the words which entered Latin as Christianity was adopted in the west were *ecclesia* 'church' (cf. English *ecclesiastical*), *diabolus* ' devil' (Latinized from the Greek *diabolos*), *angelus* from Greek *angelos*, literally 'messenger', and *presbyter* 'priest'.

Latin is, from most points of view, no longer a living language in the sense that there are no native speakers. To the extent that it can be said to borrow lexical items, they are limited in semantic field and not necessarily perpetuated from one generation to another; and the same goes, arguably, for ecclesiastical Greek. The situation of other religious languages is more dynamic. If we look at the interaction of Yiddish and Hebrew in the context of Judaism, for example, we find a relationship which is still fluid (see Jacobs 2005: 276–277).

The Hebrew under discussion here is Biblical Hebrew, not the Hebrew of Israel, a revived and modernized language. In most orthodox Jewish communities, Biblical Hebrew is the language of worship, referred to as *loshen khoydesh* 'language of sanctity' while the language of the home, business, and all things secular is some other language. Yiddish, the home language of eastern European Jews (and those in the west more generally), is called, in Yiddish, *mamaloshn*, literally 'mother language'. The distinction is not rigid, however.

There have been translations of religious materials into Yiddish, mostly for the use of women who might not be expected, in orthodox communities, to know Hebrew; there exist as well some commentaries on holy writings and other secondary religious material either written directly in Yiddish or in translation (Fader 2007; Frakes 2004).

As a result of these interactions, a large number of words of Hebrew origin are still entering the Yiddish of orthodox Jews. Some of these lexical items are, of course, directly religious, so that God (whose name cannot be spoken) may be referred to as *hashem*, from Hebrew 'the name', used in Hebrew for the same purpose. Similarly, 'teacher', particularly of sacred subjects, is *lamed* rather than Germanic *lerer*. Other words are borrowed, probably from the discourse of Talmudic study and commentary on the Bible, like *l'moshl* 'for example', which eventually loses its connotation of religious commentary and competes in all aspects of Yiddish with indigenous *tsum bayspil*. Others are expressions taken wholesale into Yiddish, for example *seyfer toyre* 'Torah scroll' or *malokh hamovis*, 'Angel of Death'.

25.2.4 Adstrata

One other kind of borrowing pertains to minority languages (Weinreich 1953). The impetus for the development of a layer in these cases is the influx of lexical items by speakers of one language from another when the borrowing speakers are members of a community of immigrants who, usually for one or two generations, remain speakers of the language of their country of origin. Because the two languages coexist, although not equally as to status or number of speakers, it seems appropriate to use the term 'adstratum'; at least during the period of time during which immigration and settlement take place, the languages coexist in a given geographic location.

Yiddish-speaking immigrants from Eastern Europe settled in the United States, and in particular New York, from the 1870s to World War I. They and their children spoke that language at home, although the second generation learned English at school and often were encouraged to abandon Yiddish for English in order to become 'regular' Americans. Words taken into English from Yiddish are numerous, but there was also the reverse influence. Even native speakers of the first generation, who may never have become fluent in English and were even illiterate in the Roman alphabet (Yiddish being written in a somewhat modified version of the Hebrew alphabet), acquired some words from the wider community surrounding them. Not surprisingly they used English words, or those adapted from English, for objects or concepts acquired in their new homes; examples include *opstairsike(r)* 'person living upstairs in the same building', *boychick* 'a young boy', and *alrightnik* 'a nouveau riche; someone who has prospered'. Perhaps less predictably, they adapted items for which there were Yiddish equivalents; they spoke of the *shtrit* 'street' rather than using *gos* and of the *vinde* 'window' rather than the *fenster*. This kind of borrowing, although defining a specific speech community, tends to be relatively short-lived; with few exceptions, the second generation was bilingual and their children often had no or little knowledge of the immigrant language.

25.2.5 Fashion

Section 25.2.4 addresses one example of a kind of layering which is relatively ephemeral; generational changes often put an end to borrowing, as the borrowing language is no longer used. Another source of this temporary phenomenon is fashion. One need only think of the 18th century influx of French in German and Russian as a mark of education, refinement, and sophistication. Proust's *A la recherche du temps perdu* contains a short scene where the protagonist/narrator is speaking with a woman of fashion who insists on sprinkling her French with English (*le four o'clock* for 'afternoon tea') while the young man keeps protesting that he does not know the language. Young speakers of modern Japanese use English in the same way as Proust's Madame Swan to show they are up-to-date. It is hard to say, though, whether permanent layers are being developed by these bows to fashion or if, in another generation, another language (through its youth culture, perhaps) will become the source of borrowings. We can only judge by looking backward: English definitely has a Latinate layer, entering the language either via French or directly from Latin starting even before the Conquest and continuing up to the present, while Romanian has a Slavic layer through geographic proximity with Slavic-speaking peoples. Like English, Romanian has assimilated most of its borrowings both phonologically and in morphology. Verbs take on Romance endings (*iubesc* 'I love' and *citire* 'reading' have Slavic roots, while the endings, *-esc* and *-ri* respectively, are inheritances from Latin). Even with a conscious attempt to relatinize the Romanian lexicon in the late 18th and 19th centuries through the substitution of French words where Slavic was recognized, Slavic remains a historically very robust layer and includes core items like those cited above and others like *da* 'yes' and *prietem* 'friend' (Mallinson 1988: 415). For both English and Romanian it is easy in retrospect to perceive the emergence and continued existence of a layer. On the other hand, modern Russian does not have anywhere near the French influence it might have retained from what was fashionable two centuries ago, although *etazh* (French *étage* 'floor [of a building]) and *tualet* (French *toilette*) remain as relatively isolated examples.

25.3 The emergence of layers

Borrowing does not always result in the emergence of a lexical layer. The issue, however, is not always clear-cut.

First, in many cases, especially when a language is predisposed to accept non-native (or non-native-like) lexical items, many words are borrowed individually, one by one, often along with items which are new to the culture and therefore need to be named as they are adopted. We can point to French *smoking* 'smoking jacket' (worn in 19th century England) which evolved into 'dinner jacket' for formal wear. As mentioned above, fashion-conscious Parisians took a small meal in the afternoon which they called *le four-o'clock*. The word *pajamas*, from Hindi, came to western culture with this loose, flowing item of clothing, although with a narrowing of meaning; *bungalow* is another, although isolated, borrowing from Hindi. These are culturally interesting examples, but they do not, of themselves, constitute a layer.

Something which comes closer to a genuine synchronic layer is the lexicon of a specific semantic field, borrowed from another language in recognition of the leadership of speakers of that language in some domain. In addition to borrowings from Italian into French in the Renaissance (fine and applied arts and cuisine), and from French into German and Russian in the 18th and 19th centuries (diplomacy, fashion, and the arts), some further examples can be mentioned. To continue the discussion of cooking (note the more up-scale French term *cuisine* in English), a new wave of borrowing from French into English has been occurring in the last decades, under the influence of a blossoming of interest in food and the popularity of cooking shows on television, both in the United States and Britain. Home cooks no longer set ingredients, pots, and utensils out before cooking, but rather prepare their *mise-en-place*. They don't help each other out, but rather someone serves as *sous chef* (literally 'under chef'). A new, vacuum-based form of preparation, especially for fish and vegetables, has become popular recently: cooking *sous-vide* (literally 'under emptiness'). These neologisms have become part of the English borrowing of cooking terms from French which started at least as long ago as the 11th century.

Where borrowing occurs in a specific field, there seems to be greater consciousness of the donor language so that a layer may remain phonologically distinctive despite the integration of the field into the borrowing language. Italian music terms in English are a good example: *allegro, presto, viola, piano, cello,* and *timpani* all end with a full vowel, a relatively rare occurrence in words of Anglo-Saxon origin. In addition, *cello* retains the Italian palatal [tʃ]; compare *cell, circular,* and *cycle,* all borrowed into English (from Latin in the first two cases and Greek in the third) but assimilated to English [s]. Its plural, at least among musicians, may even be the Italian *celli.*

In Germany of the 18th and 19th centuries, certain sciences developed as a field separate from the earlier, inclusive rubric of 'natural philosophy'. Where English and the Romance languages coined terms based on Greek, German speakers preferred to translate the component parts of technical vocabulary one morpheme at a time (a *calque* or loan translation). Examples can be found on the Periodic Table of the Elements and from the technical vocabulary of linguistics (Table 25.1).

Table 25.1 The technical lexicon of German

Greek Compound	German	English
oxus 'sour' + *gennan* 'material'	*Sauerstoff*	*oxygen*
Ydro- 'water'	*Wasserstoff*	hydrogen
helios 'sun'	*Sonnenstoff*	helium
phonos 'sound' + *logos* 'study'	*Lautlehrer*	phonology
morphos 'form'	*Formenlehrer*	morphology

While a technical lexicon is, perhaps, not quite a layer, one could argue that it provides another kind of structured borrowing.

25.4 Layers and their synchronic characteristics

Borrowings can be studied both diachronically and synchronically. The diachronic study is one of progressive adaptation of non-native words to the host language and culture, although not necessarily to the point of full integration. From a synchronic point of view this integration—or lack thereof—is the focus: how the words are pronounced (within or outside of the native phonological inventory), how they substitute semantically for native words or provide nuances of meaning, and how they fit into, and perhaps even influence, the morphological and grammatical structures of the host language.

25.4.1 Phonological consequences

Because English has so thoroughly integrated its Latinate/French borrowings, it is a good place to start. First, we may note some unevenness in the distribution of sounds in the modern language. While we find some words with [θ] which entered English from Greek via French and Latin (*theatre* is a good example), most words containing interdental fricatives are Germanic and include such high frequency words as *the, these, with*, and *they*, the last of which comes from northern Germanic. Some Germanic words respect the complementary distribution of [θ] and [ð] (*breath* and *breathe*), while the words of Greek origin show no such alternation. On the other hand, words with [ʒ] (*leisure, pleasure*)—a relatively rare sound in English—are invariably Latinate, while words with phonemically nasal vowels (*lingerie* and *entourage* are salient examples) are perceived as French, or at least not English.

This phenomenon is observable in other languages as well. French does not have a native [ŋ], but the sound is found in borrowings from English like *smoking* 'dinner jacket' (discussed above), *parking* 'parking lot', *baby-sitting*, and *jogging*. French has also borrowed words with [w] from English (*whiskey, weekend*). Interestingly, many French speakers hesitate with the pronunciation, although nativized words like *ouest* [wɛst]—ultimately Germanic in origin—present no difficulty.

English speakers will identify certain clusters, such as [ʃm] and [ʃl], as non-English in origin; many come from Yiddish, whose source is often recognized for these forms. It would be an overstatement, perhaps, to propose a full Yiddish layer, but words like *shmaltz* 'chicken fat' (and hence anything like a poem or song with verstated sentimentality) and *shlep* 'to carry' (and, by extension, to imply difficulty in carrying or even moving oneself around) have certainly become part of standard English as has a

Yiddish-based expressive habit of showing derision or lack of importance by rhyming a word with a nonce-form starting with [ʃm], such as *fancy-shmancy*.

In terms of prosody, the stress rules for English are notoriously complex, partly because they apply differently to words of Latinate and Germanic origin. Indeed, many aspects of the stress rules in Chomsky and Halle's seminal *Sound Pattern of English* (1968) derive ultimately from the complex interaction of the Germanic and Romance layers of modern English. Germanic roots tend to be shorter than those from French, and are very often monosyllabic (or, if disyllabic, with a schwa in the second syllable, e.g. *apple*), although this may be masked by the Germanic tendency toward affixation and/or compounding. Romance words, on the other hand, may take stress on a variety of syllables, although rarely on the first except in disyllabic words. In this they are reflexes of the Latin stress rule, by which stress falls on the second last syllable if it is heavy, otherwise on the third last syllable, with two-syllable words having initial stress by default. A great deal of the Latinate vocabulary came into English from French, however, where post-stress syllables either were deleted or reduced to [ə] which then became silent. As a result English ends up with many words in this layer with final stress. British English and American differ here on occasion so that, for example, *garage* usually takes initial stress in British English and final stress on the other side of the Atlantic. As mentioned, compounding is a typically Germanic process, and English compounds, even if one or more of their components are Romance, have stress on the first element. Germanic suffixes (*-like, -hood*) do not change the stress, while Romance suffixes such as *-ic* often do (*ecónomy ~ económic, fántasy ~ fantástic,*) usually in association with a change in vowel quality as well.

Other examples of synchronic adaptation (or partial adaptation) are found above in the discussion of the borrowing of English words into Japanese, which are then shortened or compounded in a very native way to the point where they are no longer recognizable as coming from English. In addition, many of these borrowings have been adapted into Japanese in ways which have modified the phonemic—or at least the allophonic—inventory of the language (see Table 25.2; data from Labrune 2012: 98).

Table 25.2 Japanese loan phonology

Japanese	Source/Gloss
famirii	family
tisshu	tissue
tsiiru	German Ziel 'goal'
kwootsu	quartz
vinteeji	vintage
yerusaremu	Jerusalem

In native Japanese phonology, [f] in *famirii* is an allophone of [h] which appears natively only before [u]. In *tisshu* and *tsiiru*, [t] and [ts] are allophones, normally in complementary distribution, with [t] palatalizing before a high front vowel and [ts] occurring only before [u]. The [w] of *kwootsu* is found in native words only before [a] and the [j] of *vinteeji* only before non-high front vowels [a], [u], and [o]. The [v] of this last example is foreign to Japanese.

25.4.2 Speaker awareness

To what extent are native speakers aware of the layering of their language? Words borrowed to show that one is culturally fashionable keep their foreign association; that is their point, after all. In some cases awareness may be brought about by education (not specifically linguistic education). Yiddish speakers frequently know when they encounter Hebrew words because they are, in many cases, at least religiously educated in Hebrew as well. Semantic differentiation helps to perpetuate this consciousness since in some subcultures it is considered close to blasphemy to call a holy book by the Germanic Yiddish term *bukh* instead of the Semitic *seyfer.* Additionally, most Hebrew words retain their original spelling, that is, without symbols for vowels (diacritics are sometimes used as they sometimes are in Hebrew); spelling too therefore clearly marks the origin of this layer. But many other layers disappear in the sense that some borrowed words have become completely assimilated and therefore speakers are no longer able to differentiate by the contributing language; a given lexical item is simply 'English' or 'Japanese' or 'Yiddish'.

In languages like English, where layers may have different stylistic values, we find a kind of (sub)conscious awareness of layering which manifests itself in word choice in formal speech and writing. English abounds in pairs of words, with roughly the same meaning, where one member of the pair is a short, 'plain', Germanic word, the other is a longer, and stylistically more elevated 'fancy' word of Latin/French origin. Examples are legion: *show ~ manifest, done ~ completed, (to) ease ~ facilitate, rise ~ ascend, fall ~ descend, stay ~ remain, handle ~ manipulate, end ~ terminate, beginning ~ commencement*. Another striking feature of English are nouns of Germanic origin which have corresponding adjectives based in Latin. Examples include *land ~ terrestrial, moon ~ lunar, noun ~ nominal, sea ~ marine, milk ~ lactic, brain ~ cerebral, brother ~ fraternal*. Since the Latin-based words tend to be multisyllabic, phonology interacts diachronically with etymology and synchronically with register. While speakers/writers may not know that the 'fancy' words come from French and Latin, they are aware that they carry a particular stylistic value.

25.4.3 Grammatical consequences

Borrowings may have repercussions for the syntax and morphology of a language. We looked above (section 25.2.2) at restrictions in Japanese on the monosyllabic shape of

Table 25.3 Yiddish plural markers

Root origin	Form	Plural marker origin	Plural form
Germanic	bukh 'book'	Germanic	Bikher
	land 'land'		lender
	hant 'hand'		hent
	tajkh 'river'		tajkhn
Romance	delegate 'delegate'	Germanic	delegatn
Slavic	slup 'pole'	Slavic	slupes
Slavic	samovar	Germanic	samovar
Hebrew	seyfer 'religious book'	Hebrew	sforim
Germanic	poyer 'peasant'	Hebrew	poyerim
Greek	doktor 'doctor'	Hebrew	doktorim

the Chinese layer or the clipping within the more modern 'foreign' layer. Yiddish differentiates, for the most part, its noun plural endings so that on the whole this morphological component reflects word origin. However, certain words of German origin take a Hebrew plural marker (*-im*) which has also been extended to isolated borrowings from other languages (Table 25.3).

As a general rule, languages do not borrow verb morphology, but rather bare verbs which are adapted to the borrowing language and assimilated into its inflectional paradigms. Almost without exception, verbs borrowed into English are assimilated to the 'weak' paradigm, whereby past tense and past participle are formed by suffixation of *-ed*. One exception is the verb *strive* (from Old French *estriver*) which forms its past tense by a change in vowel (*strove*) and its past participle by suffixation of *-en* (*striven*). Another is *quit*, from Old French *quitier*, which, like Germanic *cut, put, and set* is unchanged in its paradigm. In terms of present tense inflection, however, the third person singular form of English verbs of any origin are marked by *-s* (the modals, all of Germanic origin, are, of course, exceptional). A parallel case is that the Hebrew basis of a substantial part of the Yiddish lexicon has been adapted to Germanic morphology. Verbs in Yiddish, even of Hebrew origin, take *-t* in the third person, not the zero of Hebrew masculine verb forms or the *-et* of the feminine forms.

Nouns, however, as illustrated by the Yiddish/Hebrew example above, may bring their plurals with them, with the plural morpheme, as a rule, remaining associated with the noun it was attached to upon entering the borrowing language. In English, the *-a* of Greek-based *criteria, phenomena* and of Latin *data* do not extend to Germanic nouns or even to those from French. Most (naive) speakers, however, see these plurals as somehow irregular or may even use them as singulars, but do not,

I suspect, associate them directly with Greek or Latin.[5] Speakers do, however, extend them, so that some nouns of Greek origin are assimilated to the Latin paradigm, and Anglophones will, with some hesitation, suggest *octopi* as the plural of *octopus* and *syllabi* for more than one *syllabus*.

The intermingling of Germanic and Romance elements may be illustrated by the spread of the Latinate suffix -*Vble*. It entered English from French (from Latin -*Vbilis* 'capable of, able to') as the ending of a great number of French-derived adjectives like *legible, comprehensible, edible, potable*. The suffix then spread to the formation of deverbal adjectives of Germanic origin, almost entirely in the form -*able*. In addition to *readable, understandable, eatable*, and *drinkable*, which coexist with their respective Latinate adjectives, we have both *feasible* and *doable*. Even so, the distinction is still apparent, often as a question of register, so that, while *edible* and *eatable* may be interchanged, *potable* and *drinkable* can be differentiated in usage. Selectional restrictions may also apply; most subjects of cognitive perception are *understandable*, while accents and other aspects of oral delivery might more often be judged as (*in*)*comprehensible*. The choice of vowel linking the deverbal stem to the -*ble* suffix is a historical matter and must be learned; Latin used the linking vowel which corresponded to the verb class (conjugation) of the verb in question. The strong tendency in modern English is to use *i* where the word is of Latinate origin and *a* otherwise. The later form is the productive one, so relatively new formations, like *surfable* and *downloadable* are all spelled with *a*; in reality the vowel is reduced to a schwa [ə] in all but the most carefully articulated versions.

Comparatives and superlatives of adjectives come from two sources in English, the Germanic endings -*er*, -*est* (*taller, tallest*) and the Latinate constructions with *more, most* (*more impressive/*impressiver, most impressive/*impressivest*). Although the source of the distribution in English may have started with the differentiated layers, it seems likelier in contemporary English that the distribution of types has to do with the stress pattern or even the simple length of the adjective in question (Hilpert 2008).[6] Even so, the preference for short adjectives to take -*er*/-*est* makes sense historically, since Germanic roots tend to be short (and often monosyllabic). Shorter Romance adjectives were incorporated into this morphosyntactic tendency, so that, for example, most speakers would say *curter* (from French *court* 'short') and *grayer* (French *gris*).

Verbal expressions also reflect the alternation between Germanic and (borrowed) Latinate sources. So-called phrasal verbs, consisting of a verb (usually monosyllabic and

[5] Yiddish, again, may be the exception because so many Yiddish speakers know at least some Hebrew; this may be the explanation of the spread, limited as it is, of the plural -*im* to a few non-Hebraic nouns.

[6] There is a certain amount of hesitation as well. In writing the last sentence, even as I set out this marker of the Latinate layer in English, I was not sure whether *more likely* or *likelier* was more felicitous. I suspect that there has been a certain amount of semantic differentiation here, if in no other way than as a matter of register. There are also playful extensions; I recently heard the self-consciously odd proposal of *excentricer* in place of *more excentric*. There is also the possibility of combining the two constructions; although frowned upon by purists, the double construction is attested in Shakespeare: 'This was the most unkindest cut of all' (Julius Caesar, III.2).

of Germanic origin) and a particle/preposition, may often be paraphrased by one-word Latinate equivalents; *go in* ~ *enter, sail round* ~ *circumnavigate, put up with* ~ *endure, tolerate.*

Other morphosyntactic and even syntactic aspects of English reflect the strength of its Latinate layer. Several examples can be mentioned. First, the *'s* genitive (*Nancy's book*) is Germanic, deriving from the majority of Old English strong declensions, while the *of* possessive is Romance, a calque on the French possessive marker *de* (*the story of my life*) (see Gries and Stefanowitsch 2004 for the distribution of the two forms.) Compounds formed on the Germanic pattern (*table leg*) often contrast with periphrastic constructions, again with *of* (*leg of the table*). The former is probably preferred in the unmarked situation, but a good number of contexts, such as one of contrast (*not the leg of the chair*) call for the Latinate construction. The so-called dative shift alternation (*I gave Mary the book* vs. *I gave the book to Mary*) again reflects the competing resources of English; the first construction is Germanic, the second is Romance. Interestingly, while Germanic verbs, such as *give*, are equally acceptable in both constructions, polysyllabic (Latinate) verbs tend to reject the V NP NP construction; verbs like *donate, explain, demonstrate* seem marginal or even ungrammatical with a non-prepositional dative (?* *We donated the charity some clothes*/**We explained Mary the problem*). Finally, we can mention a curious relic from French legal terminology, whereby an adjective, contrary to the prevailing (Germanic) pattern in English, follows the noun it modifies: *court martial, attorney general, president elect, prince regent.* The plural marker *-s* attaches to the initial item of these expressions: *courts martial.*[7]

25.5 Conclusion

All languages borrow. This chapter has focused on the processes and motivations for relatively large-scale borrowing and on the consequences for the receiving language, especially in those cases where the borrowed items constitute a 'layer', or sub-lexicon derived from a specific source language. These borrowed items may become so fully integrated into the receiving language that they are no longer perceived to be in any way 'foreign'; they are—synchronically—indistinguishable from the rest of the borrowing language. More interesting are those situations where the layer remains identifiable, marked by a distinctive stylistic value, and even exhibiting characteristic phonological, morphological, syntactic, semantic, and orthographic features. English is an especially interesting case, in that the influx of Romance elements into this Germanic language has been so enormous, and has been ongoing for at least a millennium. In many cases, the Germanic and Romance elements have become so intertwined that they can be identified only by experts. In other cases the distinctiveness of the Romance layer

[7] I thank John Taylor for the observations in these last two paragraphs.

is manifest in numerous ways—in stylistic value, in semantic domains, and even in the choice between competing syntactic constructions. Other instances of layering, like the Chinese sub-lexicon of Japanese or the Hebrew sub-lexicon of Yiddish, are somewhat more identifiable as such by naive native speakers of Japanese or Yiddish respectively, and display orthographic peculiarities as well as differentiation in core linguistic components. All these cases—and many more—give rise to linguistic and socio-linguistic phenomena which are quite different in nature and more deeply integrated into the borrowing language than the often random results of sporadic borrowing.

PART V

WORDS IN THE MIND

CHAPTER 26

WORD ASSOCIATIONS

SIMON DE DEYNE AND GERT STORMS

26.1 Introduction

The word association task is one of the most archetypical experiments in psychology. In a typical word association task, a person is asked to write down the first word(s) that spontaneously come to mind after reading a cue word. This straightforward task is referred to as a free association task, since no restrictions are imposed on the type of answers that are produced. In this sense it is different from related procedures such as verbal fluency tasks, in which one must, for example, name as many animals or words beginning with a given letter as possible.

For over a century, psychologists and psychiatrists like Galton (1880) and Bleuler (1911/1950) have been fascinated by the way word associations offer a window on structures and processes in the human mind. Even today, the word association task remains an influential tool in cognitive science for the same reasons.

While the basic experimental paradigm has not changed much, the implications, usage, and understanding of the word association task has changed significantly throughout its history. Many of these changes reflect the evolution of the last decades, such as advances in neuro-imaging and electrophysiological techniques, further theoretical developments in network theory, and the availability of large amounts of data and massive computational power. A first surge in the study of word associations reflected the prevalent behaviourist ideas of the time by focusing on the notion of direct association strength, where associations represented a conditioned language response to a verbal cue. This associative strength reflects the fact that most people give similar responses in a word association task. For example, when they are presented the cue word HAMMER, the associate response NAILS is given by almost half of all participants and with twice the probability of the response WOOD. The notion of strength is still important in explanations of several psychological phenomena such as our ability to recall words from episodic memory. A frequently used paradigm to test how associative strength affects the ease of recall is the cued recall task (for an overview see Nelson, Schreiber, and McEvoy 1992). In this task participants are asked to memorize a list of words and are later asked to recall as many words as possible in response to an associated cue. For example, the success of recalling the studied word CORK when presented with the cue BOTTLE will depend on the associative strength between these words (Nelson and Bajo 1985). Associative strength is also central to semantic priming, a phenomenon where recognizing a target word (e.g. BUTTER) is enhanced by an earlier presented cue word, or prime, that is strongly related (e.g. BREAD) in contrast to a weakly related one (e.g. JAM). In most cases, the target is recognized or named faster, and the magnitude of this effect depends on the strength of the relationship between prime and target; this can be expressed by the number of associates they share (see Lucas 2000 for a detailed discussion).

From the 1960s researchers proposed that the focus on associative strength between isolated word pairs was not suited for the study of the meanings of words. Especially the work by Deese indicated a radical departure from a narrow view on word associations based on strength between single pairs of words (Deese 1965; Szalay and Deese 1978). According to this new approach, the central issue is not the single connection but how the meaning of a word is conveyed by the entire set of connections to the stimulus in a larger network of knowledge. This shifts the focus from stimulus–response properties, such as associative strength between two words, to their response distributions. It offers a way of quantifying how closely related two words are by looking at the commonalities between two words. In this second approach, the words BLOOD and ACCIDENT might not be directly associated, but the overlap of these words with common associations such as WOUND, HURT provides insight into the way they are related. This idea was initially explored in Deese's (1965)[1] factor analytic studies on nouns and adjectives, and inspired many modern approaches to semantic memory that rely on distributional similarity, such as Latent Semantic Analysis (LSA: Landauer and Dumais 1997; Steyvers, Shiffrin, and Nelson 2004) and topic models (Andrews, Vinson, and Vigliocco 2008). These models are founded on the notion that the meaning of a word can be derived from the context in which it is used. Since we are exposed to thousands of words every day, this context is rich, and tracking regularities in language allows us to discover a significant part of the meaning of words. The strength of these models hinges on the massive amounts of information available in co-occurrences in written and spoken language which allows the inference of meaning beyond the contexts in which a word occurs. This way, statistical techniques similar to the factor analytic studies by Deese (1965) allow us to infer that the words COSMONAUT and ASTRONAUT have the same meaning, even though are not strongly associated and rarely co-occur in the same text. If they occur in a sufficiently large number of similar contexts, this is a strong

[1] While an extensive and up-to-date review of the literature on word associations is lacking, the works of Deese (1965) and the review by Cramer (1968) are still relevant. Especially the work by Deese was visionary, as it stresses the importance of the structure of the network of associations rather than the strength of single cue–response pairs, and proposes a method that inspired many distributional lexico-semantic models, influential in the late 1990s.

indication that their meanings are related. In the case of word associations, two words will have a similar meaning not because they are associated, but because they have many associates in common. This approach has been very successful in the study of semantic similarity of words, vocabulary acquisition, and episodic and semantic priming described earlier.

Most recently, the global structure of the network has become a frontier to the field. This approach demonstrates how networks or graphs derived from association data are used to learn about the development of language and the way words are retrieved efficiently. The large networks in which related words are connected show structure that is not apparent by looking at the strength of the connection between pairs of words or the associations they share. One of the key findings is the fact that the mental lexicon is organized as a small world network, where similar words are clumped together and any word can be reached by taking only a few hops in the network (Steyvers and Tenenbaum 2005; De Deyne and Storms 2008b). Such an organization promotes the ease of retrieval of words from the lexicon and makes the network more resilient to damage.

These three lines of research correspond to a shift from local interactions between pairs of words to interactions within a subgraph (meaning derived from distributional measures) and global characteristics of the network (network topology and centrality). These three levels, reflect the microscopic, mesoscopic, and macroscopic structure in the network and represent a recurring theme useful for discussing how recent findings from word associations inform us about structure of the mental lexicon at different scales. Section 26.2 describes the large-scale word association norms that are available. Next, Section 26.3 explains how they are characterized in terms of their semantic content and how different theories account for the variety of associative responses. Not surprisingly, word associations are closely related to the language used in daily life, but there are important points of divergence that are often overlooked. These will be discussed at the end of this section.

When studying the mental lexicon[2] through word associations, we often think of it as a network where nodes are automatically activated through spreading activation. This network-based view helps us to understand many word processing advantages that underlie effects of word frequency and context variability. The last part of this Chapter (Section 26.5) focuses on networks derived from word associations. It starts with a discussion of how a weighted directed network can be constructed as an approximation of the mental lexicon, and considers how empirical findings of various lexical and semantic centrality effects can be explained by such a network. This section closes with a macroscopic view of the network by looking at its global properties, specifically from the perspective of how the network might change and grow over time. Using knowledge about the global network structure, this section ends with a discussion of spreading activation as a mechanism for retrieving information from the network. Especially the surge of interest from

[2] In contrast to other scholars (e.g. Levelt 1992), we focus in this chapter on semantic aspects of the mental lexicon without going into the phonological and morphological properties of words.

network science in other fields including psychology has led to a renewed interest in network approaches to the lexicon. In the final section we speculate on how very recent developments are likely to shape our future understanding of the mental lexicon.

26.2 Word association data sets

Before discussing the theoretical and empirical findings derived from the word association task, a short overview of the availability of norms is in place. While there is a large collection of norms available based both on normal and non-normative populations (cf. Cramer 1968), few studies have attempted to compile a reasonably sized approximation of a semantic network. The largest British English word association databases are the Edinburgh Associative Thesaurus (EAT: Kiss et al. 1973) and the Birkbeck norms (Moss and Older 1996). The EAT associations consist of responses for 8,400 cues collected between 1968 and 1971 from 100 speakers, while the Birkbeck norms include 40–50 responses for a total of 2,646 cues. For American English, the University of South Florida dataset (USF: Nelson, Schreiber, and McEvoy 2004) describes norms based on 5,018 cues collected from the late 1970s onwards and has been used in numerous studies.

Large sets of associations (for more than 1,000 words) have also been collected in languages other than English, including Korean (Jung, Na, and Akama 2010), Japanese (Okamoto and Ishizaki 2001), and Dutch. Currently, the Dutch dataset represents the largest resource publicly available. It consists of 12,000 cues and more than 3 million responses (De Deyne, Navarro, and Storms 2013). In contrast to previous studies in English, it uses a continued rather than discrete procedure, in which each participant gives three associates to every word on a list of cue words. In this study, new cue words are gradually added using a snowballing principle by which, starting from a small seeding set of words, new words are added based on the frequency with which they occur as responses.[3]

26.3 Composition and origins of word associations

While the free association task itself is straightforward, its unconstrained nature makes it difficult at first to grasp what association responses actually tell us about the lexicon. Many accounts hinge on the intuition that word associations reflect our experience with written

[3] At the moment, the same procedure is being used to compile a new English word association dataset. The new study can be accessed at http://www.smallworldofwords.com/ and currently contains associations for 8,000 cue words.

and spoken language in a verbal stimulus–response kind of manner. However, such a view might oversimplify matters. To understand the nature of word association responses, we can investigate the syntactic and semantic properties of the responses. The most obvious observation is that associative responses are far from homogeneous. They include clang responses (BUTTER–BATTER) which indicate a phonological or orthographic relationship and different kinds of semantic relationships such as contrast (MAN–WOMAN, DARK–BRIGHT), coordination (APPLE–PEAR, GREEN–RED), near synonymy (SOUR–TART), and thematically defined relations (HAMMER–NAIL, MOUSE–CHEESE). The responses can also be distinguished according to whether the cue–response relationship is syntagmatic or paradigmatic. In a syntagmatic relationship (SMELLY–CHEESE), cue and response have a different syntactic role in a sentence and can belong to different part-of-speech classes. A syntagmatic relation need not be one that is current in normal speech, as with YELLOW and BANANA. In a paradigmatic relation (CHEESE–SOCKS), the words have the same syntactic function in a sentence.

Differences between responses depend on the individual, on the response position in continued association procedures, and on the characteristics of the cue. Clang responses, for example, often occur faster than semantically related responses, and are quite frequent with second language learners (McCarthy 1990) and patient groups. Paradigmatic responses are the most common type in adults, while children until the age of 9 provide more syntagmatic responses (Nelson 1977). This difference has been explained in terms of increasing word understanding, especially through reading (Cronin 2002). Fig. 26.1 shows the distribution from De Deyne et al. (2008) of syntagmatic vs. paradigmatic responses over various word classes as well as a characterization of their semantic composition. Fig. 26.1(a) illustrates the dominance of paradigmatic responses for nouns and syntagmatic responses (mostly nouns) for adjectives and verbs; Fig. 26.1(b) shows the semantic distribution of the responses. Taxonomic responses include contrast, coordination mentioned

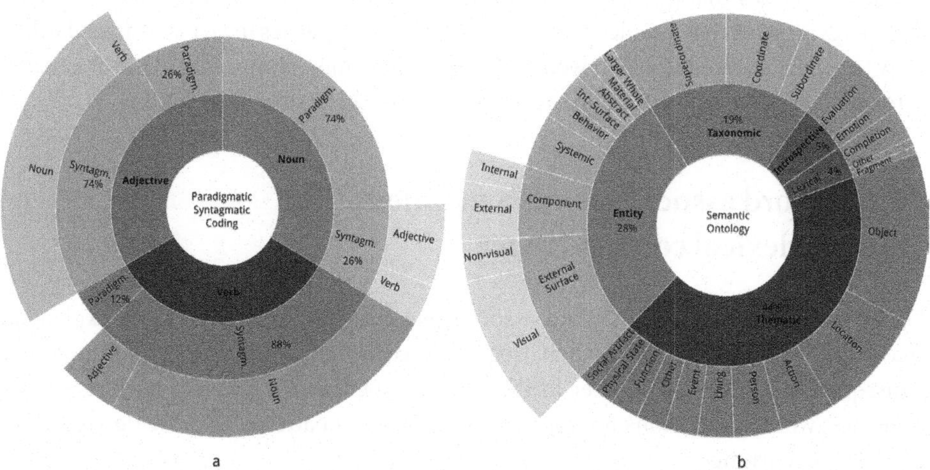

FIG 26.1 (a) Distribution of paradigmatic and syntagmatic responses for adjective, noun, and verb cues; (b) semantic composition of association responses.

earlier, but also superordinate or hypernymy (APPLE–FRUIT) and subordinate or hyponomy (APPLE–JONAGOLD) responses. Entity or meronymy responses correspond to attributes or features that are part of the concept (DOG–TAIL). While both entity and taxonomic responses contribute to what is often understood as the denotation of a word or the semantic content necessary for defining a concept, the most common responses in word association data are those that capture thematic relations, indicating some sort of contiguity in time and space rather than similarity in meaning. Together with introspective judgements such as SUNSET–NICE, thematic responses indicate that the task is very sensitive to the connotation of words. Finally, many non-semantic responses indicate purely lexical information such as compounding (WATER–FALL), idiomatic uses (SOUR–GRAPES), or rhyme (TALK–WALK). Apart from the relative importance derived from response counts, reaction times and the sequence of different responses in continued word association tasks indicate that some types of semantic information are more readily available than other types (Barsalou et al. 2008; De Deyne et al. 2008b). Taxonomic and lexicon information including clang and compounding responses in particular are more readily available than other types of responses. Learning about the types of responses using this qualitative approach offers a first way to refine semantic theories about how the mental lexicon is organized and how it interacts with other types of representation. This will now be discussed.

26.3.1 Theories of semantic memory and word associations

Word associations are part of many models of word processing, but the debate about their origin and role is still ongoing. There are at least two different points of view worth mentioning. According to one, word associations mainly reflect word co-occurrence in language. A second view acknowledges this contribution from language, but proposes that word associations reflect an additional kind of process. This process gives rise to distinct mental properties that go beyond the information captured in written or spoken text. Recent revisions of this idea describe these additional properties in terms of an embodied view (e.g. Barsalou 2008) which would allow a contribution of more thematic or situated sensory-dependent simulations in the process of generating word associations.

26.3.2 Word associations as a manifestation of lexical co-occurrence

One school of thought treats word associations purely as a variable to be explained. According to this view, words that frequently co-occur will become associated and consequently activate each other in the lexicon (Spence and Owens 1990). As a consequence, word associations mirror the same statistical patterns as those derived from lexical co-occurrence.

Studies that compare association response frequencies with predictions from computational models using text co-occurrences show that such a relationship is indeed present (Griffiths and Steyvers 2003; Hahn and Sivley 2011; Wettler, Rapp, and Sedlmeier 2005). This view is also supported by experimental findings where new word associations are added to the lexical network. In a lexical decision task, Schrijnemakers and Raaijmakers (1997) showed that associations initially established in episodic memory by simple co-occurrence activate different semantically related words from those that are already represented in the adult lexicon. However, this might not be the complete story, as results of these studies are far from univocal. The findings from word co-occurrences derived from text invariably report only a moderate correlation with association frequencies. One possible reason for the limited success is the treatment of documents as a 'bag-of-words' in many large-scale co-occurrence models. This 'bag-of-words' term indicates that only the occurrence of a word in a document or paragraph is considered. It ignores other potentially important information such as syntax, word order, or the more abstract mental representations we need to construct when interpreting a sentence (cf. Kintsch 1988). These limitations are confirmed by other empirical findings on how word associations are formed. For example, Prior and Bentin (2003) showed that incidental associations were formed more easily if words were presented in a sentential context than when words were presented as isolated pairs. These findings were interpreted as evidence for the integration of lexical associations during a late stage of processing in which a mental model is constructed and related to existing world knowledge.

Finally, the word association task itself poses different constraints for responses than those in ordinary conversation: they are free from a speaker's intention to communicate some particular conceptual content in a given discourse context. Instead, they are simply the expression of thought (Szalay and Deese 1978). In part, this attempt to approach a language of thought is what makes word associations unique and useful compared to methods based on statistical patterns in spoken and written text.

26.3.3 Dual process and embodied accounts

The heterogeneous character of word association responses and the typical order in which these types are generated highlighted in the previous section suggests the existence of qualitatively different underlying processes or representations. Many theoretical proposals on how people generate word associates draw strongly on dual process accounts. For example, de Groot (1980) proposes that these responses depend on both a fast process for directly connected words and a relatively slow process that makes no use of automatic connections between associated words but which depends on meaningful interpretation of the cue. Along the same lines, Barsalou and colleagues have presented a dual process account that relies on both linguistic and situated simulations (Barsalou et al. 2008; Santos et al. 2011). According to this theory, certain types of information become activated very quickly. This is attributed to distributional properties of language, such as the frequent co-occurrence of words. Other information only becomes available after extended processing, which requires the situated simulation of conceptual properties. Supporting evidence comes from neuro-imaging studies where fMRI measurements showed that during a property generation task and an association task, linguistic areas such as Broca's area became activated during early responses and areas such as the precuneus, which are often associated with mental imagery, became activated during late responses (Simmons et al. 2008).

A final aspect of the mental lexicon that is often overlooked relates to the fact that words like TROUBLE and VACATION and many others differ in terms of valence, i.e. the degree to which they carry a positive or negative connotation. Particularly through word association data, valence is revealed to be an important structural property of the lexicon, as shown in Deese's (1965) work on adjectives. The way modality specific information including emotions affect word associations indicates considerable overlap between the types of semantic properties encoded in a lexico-semantic system and modality-specific representations based on perceptual simulations. This is supported by recent studies showing that purely linguistic context provides enough information to account for findings previously explainable in an embodied account only. These studies show how linguistic co-occurrence data can predict whether a word encodes auditory, olfactory, or visual information (Louwerse and Connell 2011), the location of places on a map (Louwerse and Benesh 2012), or the valence of words (Hutchinson and Louwerse 2012). The fact that different aspects of meaning become encoded in both a lexico-semantic and more sensory-specific system reflects some redundancy, which is not that surprising considering that language reflects the structure of the physical environment. Studying the semantic types of word association responses and the time-course of these responses in word associations offer us the opportunity to study this issue in depth. As noted earlier, the goals of communication and lexicosemantic representation are likely to offer only indirect access to certain semantic properties such as valence while previous work suggests that word associations provide a privileged route to this knowledge.

The conclusion from this review echoes the claims found in the literature on corpus linguistics and associations reviewed by Mollin (2009) and in the domain of lexicalized concepts by McRae, Khalkhali, and Hare (2011), stating that the association task does not reflect authentic language production, but should rather be seen as tapping into the semantic information of the mental lexicon. Such a proposal also aligns with the original ideas of Collins and Loftus (1975), in which the network depends both on semantic similarity and lexical co-occurrence in language. The idea of a network and its intimate connection with word associations has recently experienced a surge of interest. In the following section we will show how the implementation of these ideas in a realistic sized network offers a new perspective on the structure and growth of the mental lexicon.

26.4 Word association networks

The metaphor of the mental lexicon as a web of connected words goes back to the 1960s, when notions of graph or network theory were first applied in the context of word associations (Pollio 1966; Kiss 1968). In contrast to distributed semantic networks, where the meaning of a single word involves multiple processing units (e.g. Plaut et al. 1996), such a network is often constructed as a localist network, where each node in the network corresponds to a word. Apart from word associations, such networks can also be based on other resources such as written text corpora, feature norms, or linguistic expert knowledge (cf. WordNet: Fellbaum 1998, and this volume). In the case of word associations, the network consists of nodes corresponding to cue words and unlabelled links connecting them. The network captures the aggregated responses from numerous people. Given that communication is central to language, one can expect that convergence to a shared underlying network might be beneficial. As such, the mental network represents a cultural artefact accessed by language users with different vocabularies but who share a broadly similar linguistic environment. While this network is still a gross simplification of how words are represented in the brain at the level of the individual, representing our knowledge of words in networks offers advantages of flexibility and interpretability. First of all, networks scale well: we can easily represent the knowledge of tens of thousands of words and the connections between them. Second, networks imply processes that operate on them. One example is spreading activation, discussed in the next section. Third, network links can be directed, weighted, and qualitatively varied. For example, a directed network can account for asymmetry effects in priming, where the prime ENGINE will strongly facilitate processing the target CAR, but not vice versa (e.g. Koriat 1981). It can also explain asymmetry in relatedness judgements for pairs like CHINA–KOREA, where Korea is considered more similar to China than vice versa (Tversky 1977).

There are also disadvantages to approximating the mental lexicon with networks derived from word associations. A first one has to do with the size of the network. If a person responds with an association that was never presented as a cue, little can be inferred about its connectivity in the network, as its node has no outgoing links. Since only words that were presented as cues can be considered, the reliability of network-derived measures depends entirely on the number of cues in the study. To know how many nodes are needed to get a fairly good coverage of the mental lexicon, one can look at estimates of vocabulary size. However, such estimates vary considerably, depending on how words are counted and what is understood as knowing a word: 40,000 is often quoted as the number of words known by the average American high school graduate (Aitchison 2012). A measure of the coverage of the network would be more useful. As reflected by Zipf's law, most words are very rare and a few words occur extremely frequently. If the words in the network are weighted by their token count, a network of 12,000 nodes captures more than 90 per cent of the words encountered in written texts (De Deyne et al. 2012).

A second limitation concerns the absence of weak links in the networks. Most studies use a discrete free association task, meaning that each person generates only a single response per cue. For a cue like TULIP, 69 per cent of the participants respond FLOWER. This illustrates how strong associations mask the presence of weaker ones. In discrete tasks, response frequencies are only reliable for very strong associations, while weaker links are unreliable or missing (Nelson, McEvoy, and Dennis 2000). This absence of weak associations is seen as an important drawback of the association procedure

(Aitchison 2012). It also led to questioning the results of previous findings in mediated priming (e.g. Ratcliff and McKoon 1994), where prime and target are only indirectly related through a mediator (e.g. LION → TIGER → STRIPES; see Fig. 26.2 for an illustration). The difference in reliability between weakly and strongly related words presumably affects a host of other tasks that require access to the mental lexicon. Additional evidence for the missing weak links comes from studies where participants judge the associative strength of word pairs: participants judge pairs to be related, even if they never co-occurred as cues and associates (Maki 2007). Fortunately, this last limitation is mostly practical in nature. Recent studies address this problem by using a continued procedure where each participant provides multiple associates to each cue, covering weak links and increasing the density of the network. As predicted, these weak links are important at a behaviour level, and explain the variability in numerous semantic and word processing tasks (De Deyne, Navarro, and Storms 2013).

26.4.1 Lexical and semantic richness effects in terms of network centrality

One of the best-documented findings in visual word processing concerns differences in the ease of processing certain words over others. These differences are explained by a range of extrinsic variables such as word length, printed word frequency, imageability, the age at which the word is acquired (age of acquisition, or AoA), and context variability. Possible accounts of how these extrinsic factors determine word processing often resort to explanations in terms of connectivity differences between words in a network representation of the lexicon. To date, only a few of these theoretical claims have been directly tested. In the case of word imageability, concrete words are thought to have a different number of connections compared with abstract words (de Groot 1989). For AoA, the word processing advantage for early acquired words can be explained by the incremental acquisition of the lexicon which positions these early-acquired words more centrally in the network than later-acquired words (see De Deyne, Navarro, and Storms 2013). Similar network accounts exist for word frequency, number of dictionary meanings, and context diversity. The distinction between strongly connected words and sparsely connected ones is also framed in a more intrinsic fashion using studies that look at semantic richness effects in word processing (Pexman, Holyk, and Monfils 2003). In these studies, the number of different associates of a cue (i.e. its set size or out-degree) consistently affects the results of various visual word recognition tasks including lexical decision and word-naming reaction times, but also tasks where semantic involvement has been limited or semantic effects have been inconclusive, such as perceptual identification or sentence reading (Duñabeitia, Avilés, and Carreiras 2008). All these accounts share the idea that the structure of the mental lexicon determines how efficiently people can retrieve and produce words.

However, there are many ways to measure network structure which could affect the ease of word processing. Consider the network in Fig. 26.2 that shows the structure

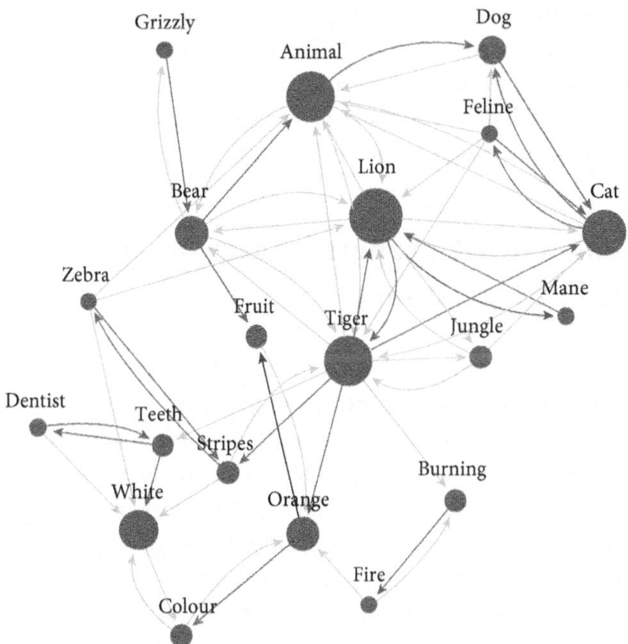

FIG 26.2 Simplified network around the node for TIGER. Nodes with more incoming links (i.e. larger in-degree) are larger. Edges with stronger weights are darker.

around the node TIGER. The importance of the node can be judged by the number of incoming links (less important than LION) or the number of outgoing links (more important than BEAR).

Because simple measures like the number of incoming and outgoing links do not fully exploit the information encoded in the network, more sophisticated measures might provide more detailed answers. A richer index of centrality would be one that also takes into account the structure among the connected nodes such as the degree to which the neighbours of TIGER themselves are connected. Examples of such measures include clustering coefficients, betweenness, and PageRank. Each of these measures goes beyond counting the number of incoming or outgoing links. The clustering coefficient measure is related to in- and out-degree, but is more sophisticated by considering how often the direct neighbours of a node (i.e. the nodes directly connected to it) are connected themselves. Thus, words with strongly interconnected neighbours are considered to be semantically coherent. The neighbours for a word like BANK might reflect a more loose semantic coherence, due to the presence of multiple senses. Other measures like betweenness and PageRank include information of the whole network to determine how central or important a node is in the network structure. Betweenness captures how many times you can encounter a node by traversing paths in the network. PageRank is slightly different in the sense that it is a recursive measure. It detects nodes that are central by taking into account the centrality of the neighbours of a node as well. While no systematic studies have compared multiple tasks and indices, a couple of studies suggest such measures have potential. In these studies, elaborate measures like PageRank capture effects of both semantic processing (De Deyne and Storms 2008b; De Deyne, Navarro, and Storms 2013; Griffiths, Steyvers, and Firl 2007), in which networks are formed based on shared meaning or associations, and phonological processing, using networks where words with similar phonology like CAT–HAT are linked (Vitevitch 2008).

26.4.2 Global network properties, network growth, and spreading activation

While looking at the interconnectedness of a single node or a pair of nodes in the network is useful for studying how central and meaning-related words are, the properties of large-scale networks that become apparent only when this network is studied as a whole. A number of studies (e.g. De Deyne and Storms 2008b; Steyvers and Tenenbaum 2005) have found that, similar to other growing networks, the global structure of word association networks does not have an arbitrary organization but corresponds to a small world structure with on average 3–4 nodes between any two words. Such a structure was also found in a study by Milgram (1967), who reported that any two persons in the United States are separated by on average six other persons who know each other pairwise. A similar structure was found for many other networks, and the chapter on word frequency by Joseph Sorell (this volume) provides a more detailed discussion using examples from text corpora and the World Wide Web.

In addition to short average path lengths, small world networks exhibit small diameters and high clustering. These properties allow efficient word search and retrieval and make the network robust against damage (Steyvers and Tenenbaum 2005). One property of this topology is the presence of a small number of hubs, i.e. nodes with degree values much higher than average. Table 26.1 gives ten examples of hubs for three recent datasets and Fig. 26.3 shows their role in the network as a whole. The rankings in Table 26.1 are very similar, regardless of the measure used (in-degree or PageRank) or the type of network. Although speculative, this might indicate that certain properties are universally more central in the human semantic system. The list of hubs also indicates how word associations reflect psychological or subjective meaning. For instance, if we ignore pronouns and articles but look at the most frequent adjectives and nouns in English and Dutch using the SUBTLEX frequency counts (Brysbaert, New, and Keuleers 2012; Keuleers, Brysbaert, and New 2010), the most important hubs, indicated by word frequency counts, are {GOOD, TIME, MAN, WAY, SORRY, PEOPLE, THING, SIR, LITTLE, NIGHT} in English and {GOOD, MAN, PEOPLE, DAY, WOMAN, TIME, BEAUTIFUL, YEAR, DEATH, LIFE} in Dutch. Despite the fact that words at the high-end spectrum of the frequency distribution tend to be stable, they agree only moderately with respect to which entries of the mental lexicon are considered central. Moreover, a similar pattern of divergence between psychological centrality and linguistic centrality can be observed in the hubs reported by Steyvers and Tenenbaum (2005) for the networks based on Roget's thesaurus

Table 26.1 Hubs in English and Dutch word association networks using in-degree and PageRank centrality measures. The English words are derived from the University of South Florida (USF) norms (Nelson et al. 2004) and a new database under development (SWOW-EN: De Deyne and Storms, in preparation). The Dutch word association norms are taken from De Deyne et al. (2013).

USF		SWOW_EN		Leuven-2012	
In-degree	PageRank	In-degree	PageRank	In-degree	PageRank
money	money	man	money	water	water
car	car	person	food	money	food
water	water	me	water	food	money
food	food	good	love	pain	tasty
bird	bird	strip	word	car	music
tree	dog	black	car	tasty	car
cold	cold	out	music	music	pain
dog	fish	people	time	beautiful	sea
book	tree	control	happy	children	beautiful
Love	book	life	green	school	warm

(Roget 1911): {LIGHT, CUT, HOLD, SET, TURN} or WordNet (Miller 1995): {BREAK, CUT, RUN, MAKE, CLEAR}.

A possible approach to the small world structure of the mental lexicon is to regard such a structure as the manifestation of an underlying growth process, a property shared with other dynamic networks such as networks of scientific collaboration, neural networks, and the World Wide Web (Watts and Strogatz 1998). The most influential account is based on preferential attachment whereby new nodes become connected to the network in proportion to the number of existing connections they have with neighbouring nodes. While this idea works well using an aggregate network, the growth of the mental lexicon in a single individual might require a slightly different attachment scheme. For example, according to the mechanism of preferential acquisition, new nodes might become preferentially attached to other nodes depending on the structure of the learning environment (Hills et al. 2009). Regardless of the differences between these accounts, both are able to predict a number of interesting phenomena. For instance, the network growth model by Steyvers and Tenenbaum (2005) explains how the age at which a word is acquired and its frequency in language independently contribute to the ease with which a word is processed. In addition to large-scale modelling approaches, studies on the development of individual networks in children have shown that small world connectivity is indicative of later vocabulary development, where children with more cohesive and structured networks are more proficient language learners (Beckage, Smith, and Hills 2010).

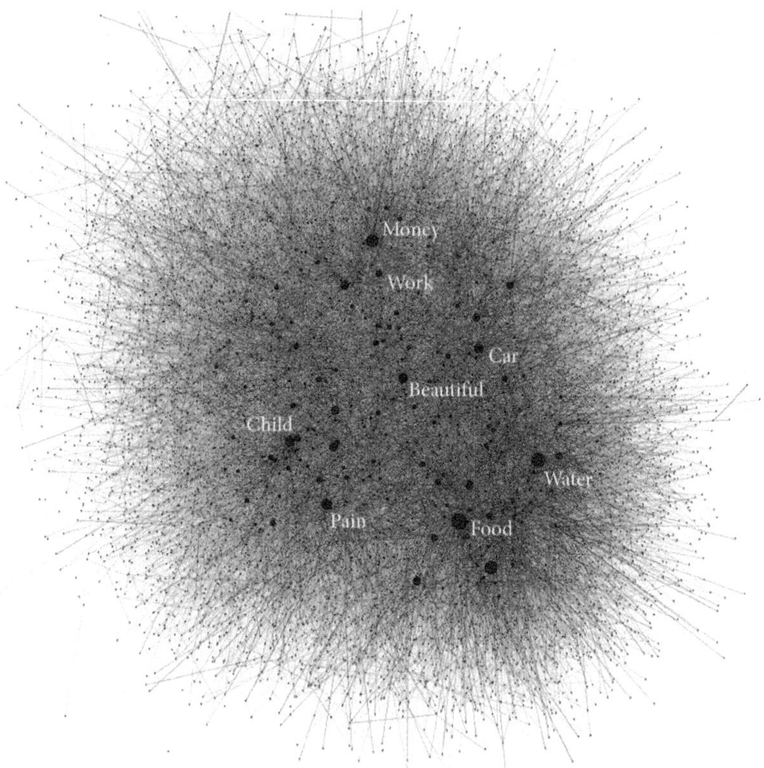

FIG 26.3 Visualization of the Dutch word association lexicon based on the first response for over 12,000 words in the word association task from De Deyne et al. (2012). The size of the nodes indicates the importance of a word in terms of in-degree. A small number of these nodes have an in-degree that is much larger most other nodes. These nodes are considered network hubs and some examples that also occur in Table 26.1 are labelled.

One of the hallmarks of the small world architecture is efficient search due to the short distances in the network and its clustered structure. One way of accessing the mental lexicon is based on the idea of searching a network through a mechanism of spreading activation (Bock and Levelt 1994; Collins and Loftus 1975). When a word represented by a node in the network becomes activated, for instance during reading, connected nodes are also activated. This spreading activation mechanism has been very influential, as it describes a plausible mechanism for searching and retrieving words in the mental lexicon. It explains a whole range of findings including automatic priming (Neely 1977) and the occurrence of hesitation pauses within sentences (Schachter et al. 1994). This activation process is supposed to be largely autonomous and parallel in the sense that lexical retrieval entails automatic access to the meaning of a word. For instance, when participants are presented with ambiguous words, the different senses automatically become activated (Seidenberg et al. 1982).

Spreading activation has also been criticized, since it might be too flexible and unconstrained (Ratcliff and McKoon 1994). Due to the short distances in a small world network, any two words can be reached in fewer than three steps. This would imply that the entire network becomes activated every time activation spreads. Additional assumptions are needed. A first solution assumes that activation decays over distance where distant nodes receive less activation than close ones. In addition, one could also assume that nodes with many links will result in a more diffuse activation. The idea of spreading activation is often implemented as a Markov chain or random walk over the network (e.g. De Deyne et al. 2012; Ramage, Rafferty, and Manning 2009), closely similar in spirit to the PageRank measure introduced earlier. For example, in a study by De Deyne et al. (2012), participants were presented with triads such as CUP, TEACHER, and HAIL that were drawn randomly from a large set of cue words. Many sampled triads were not directly associated. Even when there was no direct association and little semantic overlap, participants showed reliable agreement about which pairs from a triad were most related. The absence of direct association shows an additional effect of the spreading activation mechanism by its ability to enrich the sparse network with additional information derived from indirect links between nodes. While such a model was quite successful in predicting the participants' preferences among the triads, it corroborates the point made by Deese (1965) that valuable information is encoded in the network structure itself, rather than in the single strengths.

26.5 Future directions

The availability of large mental lexicons derived from word associations and the recent developments in graph theory highlight the direction for future research in the field. A first development follows from a better understanding of the growth and evolution of networks. In line with the network growth models described in the previous section, it would be interesting to see how such a network evolves over time, especially in old age, where the few studies available have not been able to sketch out a coherent picture of the ageing lexicon. For example, similar to qualitative changes in children (see the paradigmatic–syntagmatic shift discussed earlier), evidence from Alzheimer patients suggests that a reverse shift towards syntagmatic responses might occur in old age (Baker and Seifert 2001). However, it remains unclear whether this holds for ageing in general. Other studies show a shift away from responses with negative valence in the ageing lexicon. The structure of the network might also explain semantic errors in many degenerative conditions such as aphasia or the findings of hyper-activation of weakly linked words in schizophrenia (e.g. Rossel and David 2006). Moreover, as the web of words is in constant motion whenever new words are added and old ones reinforced, it can be expected that further advances in this field will allow a more dynamic view of the network, which could provide us with better insights into how information becomes activated in a particular context and how the network as a cultural artefact evolves over time.

A related topic is the study of semantic networks at different scales, ranging from a single individual to comparative studies of different cultures and groups of second language learners. A starting point for the latter type of studies was pioneered by Szalay and Deese (1978), who used a continued procedure to compare the relative importance of certain concepts in different cultures.

A second advancement in graph theory is the way large multiplex graphs are modelled. Combined with a dynamic network view, this might inform us how different types of information become activated over time. Such a multiplex network allows us to incorporate labelled edges in the network, similar to the IS-A, HAS-A labels in earlier network accounts (see Collins and Loftus 1975). Identifying these edge-labels might help us to estimate the contribution of different types of information such as thematic, lexical, or perceptual information in a single network.

As is often the case in psychology, perhaps the biggest challenge will lie in further integrating these findings. This will involve integrating the rich research programme on episodic memory using paradigms such as cued recall (e.g. Nelson and Zhang 2000), with advanced semantic and word processing theories and models. In sum, representing the mental lexicon as a vast semantic network has been a useful metaphor for many years and its potential to connect at least some missing bits and pieces deserves the large-scale systematic inquiry that has recently taken place.

CHAPTER 27

ACCESSING WORDS FROM THE MENTAL LEXICON

NIELS O. SCHILLER AND
RINUS G. VERDONSCHOT

27.1 Speech production mechanisms

Producing speech is a seemingly automatic process. We produce speech at a rate of 4–6 syllables per second. On average, words in Germanic languages such as Dutch or English are less than 1.5 syllables in length, which means that speakers of these languages utter about 3–4 words per second (not taking pauses into account). Even a conservative estimate of 3 words per second amounts to more than 5,000 words in a half-hour conversation (something which is not usually considered to be a complicated activity). In reality, however, speaking is one of the most complex forms of skilled serial behaviour, involving the planning of numerous processes (Lashley 1951). To produce speech, we need to translate our intentions into articulatory motor actions in order to set air molecules in motion so that our interlocutors can decode these vibrations into semantic content. There are about 40 muscles involved in movements of the speech apparatus (MacNeilage 2008). These muscles are orchestrated in a fine-grained way, and subtle changes in the positioning of the articulators can have tremendous effects on the auditory perception of the speech signal. MacNeilage (2008) estimates that each second of speech involves about 225 different muscle activations, i.e. one muscle event every 5 milliseconds.

In the last decades, comprehensive models of language production have been developed which describe the details of the speech production process (e.g. Bock and Levelt 1994; Caramazza 1997; Dell 1986; Fromkin 1971; Garrett 1975, 1980; Levelt 1989; Levelt et al. 1999). Among other processes, speaking comprises the encoding of meaning, the selection of words, the retrieval of syntactic features, and the encoding of phonological and phonetic form (for a detailed but concise overview see Griffin and Ferreira 2006). Models of speech production so far cover mostly single-word or single-utterance production, whereas in real conversations speakers construct narratives and engage in dialogues.

Researchers exploring language production generally agree that the encoding of meaning, including conceptual-semantic processing, precedes the encoding of form, including phonological-phonetic processing (or phonological encoding; see Schiller 2006). It is fair to say that there is as yet little agreement regarding the precise flow of information within the speech production system. Some models assume that information flows in a temporally strictly serial (or discrete) manner from conceptual preparation to the initiation of articulation (Bloem and La Heij 2003; Butterworth 1989; Garrett 1980, 1988; Levelt 1989, 1999, 2001; Levelt et al. 1999). More precisely, while semantic concepts activate many lexical candidates, only a single candidate is selected and further encoded at the phonological level (but see Roelofs 2008, who demonstrates that under certain task conditions a limited amount of cascading activation can be observed). The selection of that candidate, i.e. the target lexical item, is dictated by the intention of the speaker.

This process is generally assumed to be *competitive*, i.e. alternative candidates compete for selection. If more candidates are activated (especially when the activation levels of other candidates are high), lexical selection will take longer compared to when there are few competitors (or when competitors' activation is low). The intended candidate will typically have the highest level of activation at a particular point in time, and will therefore be selected. The empirical workhorse for testing the claim of lexical selection by competition has been the Picture–Word Interference paradigm (henceforth PWI; a variant of the Stroop task). In this paradigm, to-be-named pictures are accompanied by superimposed or auditorily presented distractor words (Glaser 1992; Glaser and Düngelhoff 1984; Glaser and Glaser 1989; Posnansky and Rayner 1977; Rosinski et al. 1975). When distractor words are of the same semantic category (picture: BED, distractor: table), it usually takes longer than when they are not (distractor: apple).

Recently, the process of competitive lexical selection has been challenged by an alternative account called the Response Exclusion Hypothesis (REH; Mahon et al. 2007). The REH states that lexical selection does not depend on the number and activation of potential competitors, and that spreading of activation only has a facilitative effect. Instead, selection takes place at a later (post-lexical) stage, namely the stage where production-ready representations enter an output buffer in which they will reside, ready to be pronounced. In the PWI paradigm, the distractor words are assumed to have access to this buffer prior to the picture, and need to be removed before the picture's name can be pronounced. The response buffer is believed to also contain a basic semantic mechanism, which can detect whether or not a distractor word is a suitable response in a particular setting (i.e. the verb 'sleep' is not a suitable response when the task is naming an object but not the action, e.g. 'bed').

Mahon et al. (2007) observed facilitation for the 'bed–sleep' combination, which they attribute to the spreading of activation arising from the activation of these multiple semantic items (bed, sleep) and 'sleep' was not a suitable candidate for production. In contrast, if the distractor were 'table', it would be suitable (or 'response-relevant' in REH terms) when the task is object naming and hence would have an extended stay in the buffer, which would have resulted in a longer naming latency for the 'bed–table' combination. The claims of the REH sparked an intense discussion (e.g. Abdel Rahman and Melinger 2009; Mahon et al. 2012; Spalek et al. 2013; Starreveld et al. 2013) on whether or not lexical selection is by competition (a matter still under debate).

As stated earlier, some models are called *discrete* because they make the claim that the stages of word retrieval or lexical access are operating in strict temporal succession. In contrast, another class of models assumes that the temporal relationship between the stages in speech production is not discrete. Instead, these models assume that processing proceeds in *cascade* or is even *interactive* (Caramaza 1997; Dell 1986, 1988; Humphreys et al. 1988; MacKay 1987; Stemberger 1985). According to cascading and interactive models of lexical access, all lexical candidates activate their phonological forms before any single candidate has been selected as the target item. These models are called *cascaded* or *interactive* because activation of lexical items cascades from higher levels (lexical-semantic) to lower levels (phonological-phonetic), and processing at lower later levels can start as early as possible. Let us illustrate serial and cascaded models of lexical access by using the example of naming the picture of an animal, i.e. a *cow*.

According to discrete theories of lexical access, the picture of a *cow* will activate the concept COW as well as many other concepts belonging to the same category such as *donkey, horse, pig*, etc. via the spreading of activation of a category node (FARM) ANIMAL. Activated concepts automatically activate their corresponding lexical entries—or *lemmas*, in Levelt's terminology. However, following Levelt et al. (1999), 'only selected lemmas will become phonologically activated' because 'it would appear counterproductive to activate the word forms of all active lemmas that are not selected' since 'their activation can only interfere with the morphophonological encoding of the target' (p. 15). Therefore, discrete theories of lexical access predict that the names of category members of the picture, i.e. *donkey, horse, pig*, etc., are not phonologically encoded since they are not selected for production.

Evidence from speech errors (e.g. Garrett 1975, 1980), tip-of-the-tongue states (e.g. Brown and McNeill 1966; Vigliocco et al. 1997), aphasic speakers (Goodglass et al. 1976), and electrophysiological measures (Schmitt et al. 2000; Van Turennout et al. 1997) suggested that lexical-semantic processing generally precedes phonological processing in language production. Here, we will restrict ourselves to discussing behavioural data from studies employing speeded naming paradigms. Probably the best-known empirical evidence for discrete lexical processing is the study by Levelt and collaborators from 1991. In the sixth experiment of this study, participants were asked to name a series of pictures. In about one-third of the trials, an auditory stimulus (a word or a non-word) was presented 73 ms after picture onset. In these cases, participants were requested not to name the picture but to make a lexical decision to the auditory stimulus by pressing one of two buttons. When the stimulus was a word, it belonged to one of the four conditions: identical, semantic, phonological, or unrelated. For instance, when a desk was depicted, the auditory word was *bureau* ('desk') in the identical condition, *stoel* ('chair') in the semantic condition, *stoep* ('pavement') in the phonological condition, and *muts* ('cap') in the unrelated condition. In a previous experiment, a word that was phonologically related (e.g. *buurman* 'neighbour') to the picture (e.g. *bureau* 'desk') yielded a strong phonological facilitation effect in lexical decision, demonstrating the phonological activation of the picture name *bureau*. The phonological condition in the current experiment, however, included a word (i.e. *stoep* 'pavement') that was phonologically related to a semantic alternative, namely *stoel* ('chair'). If semantic alternatives such as *stoel* ('chair') become phonologically activated when seeing *bureau* ('desk'), a phonologically related word like *stoep* should exhibit an effect on lexical decision latencies. The results, however, showed that for words in the phonological condition there was no effect, while there was an effect for the identical and semantic conditions, demonstrating that semantic alternatives were at least partially activated. Levelt et al. (1991) argued on the basis of their results that non-selected semantic alternatives are not phonologically encoded in language production, supporting the discrete processing view.

More evidence in favour of discrete lexical access comes from a seminal study by Schriefers et al. (1990). They asked participants to name a set of pictures (e.g. *bureau* 'desk') and presented auditory distractors at three different stimulus onset asynchronies (SOAs): 150 ms before picture onset (−150 ms), simultaneous with picture onset (0 ms), and 150 ms after picture onset (+150 ms). Semantically related distractors (e.g. *stoel* 'chair') slowed down the naming process relative to an unrelated distractor (e.g. *fles* 'bottle') only at the earliest SOA, while phonologically related distractors (e.g. *buurman* 'neighbour') facilitated picture naming at SOAs 0 ms and +150 ms, but not at the early SOA of −150 ms. The fact that semantic distractors had an effect early in processing whereas phonological distractors exerted a late effect supported the general notion that semantic processing preceded phonological processing (but see Jescheniak and Schriefers 2001 as well as Starreveld 2000 for early phonological effects). However, more important here is the fact that semantic and phonological effects *did not overlap in time*, suggesting that lexical-semantic processing has to be completed before phonological processing can start (but see Damian and Martin 1999, who found overlapping semantic and phonological effects). The findings of Schriefers et al. have been taken to support discrete models, in which lexical access proceeds in two serially ordered stages—retrieval of lexical-semantic representations and retrieval of phonological word forms—which do not affect each other.

The claim about strict temporal seriality between semantic and phonological activation has not remained unquestioned. In contrast to serial theories of lexical access, cascaded theories predict phonological encoding of *cow* as well as of all the category members, i.e. *donkey, horse, pig*, etc. The reason is that there is no principled boundary for the spreading of activation. According to cascaded models, once the lexical level has been activated, there is no principled reason to prevent activation from spreading further to phonological forms of words.

For instance, Dell and O'Seaghdha (1991, 1992) argued that the methodology of Levelt et al. (1991) was not sensitive enough to pick up the phonological activation of multiple lexical candidates because semantic alternatives (e.g. *stoel* 'chair') will only receive a fraction of the activation that the target (e.g. *bureau* 'desk') receives. A word like *stoep* ('pavement'), which is phonologically related to the alternative, *stoel*, will receive even less activation. Therefore, the effect of a mediated prime like *stoep* for *bureau* might be difficult to detect.

To enhance the phonological activation of alternative lexical candidates, Peterson and Savoy (1998) investigated near-synonyms. More specifically, they presented a set of pictures and asked participants to name them. On half of the trials, a word appeared in the middle of the picture after a variable SOA. On these trials, participants were asked not to name the picture, but instead to read aloud the word. Twenty of these word-naming trials occurred with ambiguous pictures, i.e. pictures for which participants could reliably use two different names. An example would be COUCH, for which on average in 84 per cent of the cases the dominant name *couch* is used while the secondary name *sofa* occurred on average in 16 per cent of the cases. The words were either phonologically related to the dominant name (e.g. *count*—COUCH) or to the secondary name (e.g. *soda*—SOFA) or unrelated (e.g. *horse*). The question Peterson and Savoy (1998) were asking was whether or not a priming effect could be obtained for words that were phonologically related to the secondary meaning (e.g. *soda*). Note that discrete and cascaded models of lexical access make different predictions here. Discrete models predict phonological priming only for dominant-related words (e.g. *count*) because most participants would select the dominant name (e.g. *couch*) on most trials. Since non-selected lexical items never become phonologically encoded, no effect for *soda* is predicted. Cascaded models, however, predict priming for both types of word, since even lexical candidates that are ultimately not selected do get phonologically activated. Results showed robust phonological priming effects for both dominant-related and secondary-related words, suggesting that during the lexicalization of a picture, lexical candidates that correspond to the picture's dominant and secondary meaning become activated up to the phonological level.

In a similar study, Jescheniak and Schriefers (1998) replicated the findings by Peterson and Savoy (1998) with a different methodology in German. In their study, again pictures were presented, some of which are ambiguous in German (e.g. *Schäfer–Hirte*; both meaning 'shepherd'), together with auditory distractor words that were phonologically related to the dominant name of the picture (e.g. *Schädel* 'skull') or the secondary name of the picture (e.g. *Hirn* 'brain'). Their results revealed reliable effects, i.e. faster picture-naming latencies, from both types of phonologically related distractor in the picture–word interference task, and supported cascaded processing but not discrete models of lexical access. Levelt et al. (1999) accommodated Peterson and Savoy (1998) as well as Jescheniak and Schriefers (1998) by suggesting that under certain circumstances, multiple appropriate lexical candidates might be selected and phonologically encoded. Near-synonyms such as *couch* and *sofa* would be one such case, sub- and superordinates such as *rose* and *flower* might be another under certain circumstances.

Cutting and Ferreira (1999) also made an attempt to distinguish discrete and cascaded models by using homophone pictures such as BALL. A ball could be a sport utility (ball_{toy}) or a formal dancing event ($\text{ball}_{\text{social event}}$), i.e. two different meanings with maximal phonological overlap. Shortly before the onset of a picture (SOA –150 ms), participants were presented with auditory distractor words that were related to the depicted meaning (e.g. *game*–ball_{toy}) or the non-depicted meaning of the homophone (e.g. *dance*–$\text{ball}_{\text{social event}}$), or unrelated (e.g. *hammer*). Cutting and Ferreira's (1999) question was whether the picture of a toy ball would be named faster in the presence of a distractor word that is related to the non-depicted meaning of the homophonic picture (i.e. 'dance' related to [dance] ball) than in the unrelated condition. Moreover, would naming the same picture at the same SOA be slower in the presence of a distractor word that is related to the depicted meaning (i.e. 'frisbee' related to [toy] ball) compared to the unrelated condition? Their reasoning was that if phonological effects were not observed at the same time as semantic effects, this would be evidence for semantic and phonological processing having different time courses, and a discrete model would be supported. If, on the other hand, phonologically related distractors do affect picture naming at the same time as semantically related distractors, that would be evidence for an overlapping time course of semantic and phonological processing implying cascading processing.

Results revealed that distractors that were related to the non-depicted meaning of the homophonic target picture name facilitated naming relative to the unrelated condition. At the same SOA, semantic interference effects (e.g. *frisbee*–ball_{toy}) were found. Presumably, the distractors that were related to the non-depicted meaning (e.g. *dance*) activated a cohort of meaning-related word forms (including $\text{ball}_{\text{social event}}$), which activated their corresponding lexical representations. These lexical representations in turn activated their corresponding word forms. That way the homophonic word form *ball* receives activation from two sources, i.e. from the selected ball_{toy} and the non-selected $\text{ball}_{\text{social event}}$. Cutting and Ferreira (1999) argued that phonological processing could be affected by semantically processed stimuli even though these stimuli are not semantically similar to the target. The phonological and semantic processing of non-target lexical items under the same timing conditions suggests that semantic and phonological processes operate with overlapping time courses, supporting cascaded models of lexical access. Levelt et al. (1999) suggested an alternative explanation: the distractor word *dance* may co-activate its associate $\text{ball}_{\text{social event}}$ semantically and phonologically in the perceptual network. The word form *ball* in the perceptual network could then directly pre-activate its corresponding word form in the production network, leading to faster naming latencies of the picture of a ball_{toy}.

Using a picture–picture interference paradigm, Morsella and Miozzo (2002) provided more evidence demonstrating that semantically irrelevant stimuli get phonologically encoded. Participants in their study were shown two pictures overlapping each other, one in green and one in red, and were asked to name the green pictures as fast and as accurately as possible. Pictures' names were either unrelated (e.g. $\text{BED}_{\text{green}}$–$\text{HAT}_{\text{red}}$) or phonologically related (e.g. $\text{BED}_{\text{green}}$–$\text{BELL}_{\text{red}}$). Results showed significantly faster naming latencies for the related than for the unrelated pairs in English, but not in Italian, where exactly the same picture pairings were used without the pictures' names being phonologically related. The authors argue that their finding can best be accounted for by cascaded models of lexical access which hold that unselected lexical nodes, i.e. the red distractor picture, activate their phonological representations. Thus, BELL may activate its phonological representation including the segments /b/, /ɛ/, /l/. When the target BED gets phonologically encoded, some of its segments, i.e. /b/ and /ɛ/, were already activated by the distractor and therefore their selection is facilitated, leading ultimately to faster production of the target word. On the whole, their data can be accommodated by cascaded models of lexical access but not by discrete models, which do not assume phonological activation of non-selected candidates. However, one may argue that speakers activate all visible picture names, i.e. the green as well as the red in this case, even though they were only required to name the green object, and that when there was phonological overlap between the picture names, naming times became faster. Navarrete and Costa (2005) replicated and extended the findings of Morsella and Miozzo (2002) in Spanish (but see e.g. Jescheniak et al. 2009 for a failure to replicate Morsella and Miozzo's results).

This overview showed that there is empirical evidence for both positions, i.e. the discrete and the cascaded/interactive theory of lexical access. In fact, these two positions are heavily debated in the literature. What has become clear is that the extreme positions are no longer tenable—instead, propositions such as *limited cascading* have been made (e.g. Roelofs 2008).

27.2 Accessing morphologically complex forms

In this section, we discuss lexical access and encoding of morphologically complex words. Morphologically complex (as opposed to simplex) words are word forms that consist of more than one meaningful sub-unit, i.e. morpheme (see Booij, this volume). Morphologically complex forms can be inflected, derived, or compounded word forms. Inflected forms (e.g. *walks, walked, walking*) belong to the same syntactic word class, while derived forms belong to different syntactic word classes, such as *walker* (a noun derived from the verb *to walk*; someone who walks) or *walkable* (an adjective; something that can be walked).

Compounds are combinations of free morphemes with internal structure. One morpheme determines the compound's syntactic category and usually its semantic class (the so-called *head*: Di Sciullo and Williams 1987; Selkirk 1982). Compounding is in principle a recursive mechanism, i.e. compounded words can be used to create another compound. For example, *snowball* (SNOW + BALL) can be concatenated with FIGHT to form *snowball fight*. Semantically transparent compounds such as *snowball fight* are usually distinguished from semantically opaque compounds, which are not related to the meaning of their constituting morphemes (e.g. *deadline keeping*: Sandra 1990; Zwitserlood 1994).

27.2.1 Representation of complex words

We will discuss how complex word forms are represented in the lexicon and how they are encoded in the process of speech production. For instance, are morphologically complex words represented individually? Full-listing models have made such claims (e.g. Butterworth 1983; 1989). However, agglutinative languages such as Hungarian, where syntactic or semantic functions are expressed by highly productive affixes added to the root morpheme, make full-listing models rather implausible (see Waksler 2000 for additional evidence against full-listing models). Decompositional models suggesting a morpheme-by-morpheme construction, on the other hand, may not be able to account for the experimental evidence alone, either. Instead, a dual-route model including both mechanisms may be favoured (Frauenfelder and Schreuder 1992).

Separate access of morphemes is suggestive of decomposed preparation of compound words (Caramazza et al. 1988; Levelt et al. 1999; Taft and Forster 1976). That is, compounds do not have to be stored and accessed as whole units. This conception is in accordance with linear frequency effects of the constituents but not of the whole compound; higher constituent frequency is associated with shorter naming latencies (e.g. Bien et al. 2005; but see Janssen et al. 2008 for contrasting results in Chinese and English).

The error analysis of aphasic patients' compound production also supports the decompositional view. Misproductions were found to be morpheme-based, i.e. errors such as constituent substitutions decreased with decreasing transparency and increasing frequency of the constituting morphemes (Blanken 2000; see also Badecker 2001; Hittmair-Delazer et al. 1994; but see Bi et al. 2007). Furthermore, some dysgraphic patients show morphological boundary effects in their spelling behaviour (Schiller et al. 2001).

27.2.2 Processing of complex words

There is considerable evidence that morphological structure plays a role in speech production planning (Roelofs 1996, 1998; Zwitserlood 2000). However, Waksler's (2000: 227) statement, that '[w]ords with multiple affixes, different morphological types of affixes, and most of the different affixation processes used in languages have yet to be systematically examined in the production domain', is still true after more than a decade.

The production of words is assumed to be prepared serially. There is much evidence suggesting that phonemes and other phonological components of words are encoded incrementally, from beginning to end (e.g. Meyer 1990, 1991; Schiller 2005, 2006; Wheeldon and Levelt 1995). It has also been suggested that morphologically complex words are prepared incrementally from left to right (Roelofs 1996; Roelofs and Baayen 2002). For instance, Roelofs (1996) compared production latencies of sets of words that were homogeneous regarding their initial syllable (e.g. *bijbel, bijna, bijster*; 'bible', 'almost', 'loss') with sets of words that were heterogeneous (e.g. *bijbel, hersens, nader*;

'bible', 'brain', 'further'). Phonological overlap resulted in a facilitation of 30 ms in homogeneous sets. However, if the initial syllables also constituted morphemes (e.g. BIJ in *bijvak, bijrol, bijnier*; 'subsidiary subject', 'supporting role', 'kidney'), the facilitation was significantly larger; homogeneous sets were now produced 74 ms faster than heterogeneous ones. In contrast, non-initial morphemes in homogeneous sets (e.g. BOOM in *stamboom, spoorboom, hefboom*; 'pedigree', 'barrier', 'lever') did not lead to a significant preparation effect. Roelofs (1996) concluded that morphemes are planning units in the production process, and that language production proceeds incrementally from left to right.

Speech errors sometimes include inflectional and derivational morphemes, e.g. *he liked I would hope you* instead of *he hoped I would like you* or *groupment* instead of *grouping*. There is evidence suggesting that inflectional suffixes, e.g. *-ed*, pattern differently in errors than non-morphemic word endings, supporting a morphological interpretation of inflectional errors (Bybee and Slobin 1982). The existence of naturally occurring derivational errors may be taken as support that roots and derivational affixes are stored separately (Fromkin 1973). In an experimental study, Pillon (1998) reported significantly more stranding errors for morphologically complex words than for monomorphemic control words. However, Pillon did not control for semantic relatedness between the target and error. Therefore, more 'morphological' errors could have occurred for morphologically complex words (such as *troupeau traînard* → *traîneau troupard*) than for monomorphemic words (such as *cadeau bâtard* → *bâteau cadard*) due to the additional semantic relatedness in the former words. Melinger (2003) compared laboratory-induced errors between English prefixed words derived from free stems involving a high degree of semantic relatedness (e.g. *reload–unload*) with words derived from bound roots involving a low degree of semantic relatedness (e.g. *induce–reduce*). She observed more errors in naming prefixed words than control words and, most importantly, no difference in the distribution of errors between free-stem and bound-root prefixed words. Her results demonstrate that morphological errors are more frequent than phonological errors in laboratory-induced paradigms, and that there is no correlation between semantic relatedness ratings and error frequency. These data suggest that morphemes are processed as units by the speech production system, and that the lexical representation of words must include information about their morphological structure.

Zwitserlood et al. (2000) investigated morphological effects in language production by comparing the standard, immediate picture–word interference paradigm with a delayed variant. In the delayed variant, the prime word is read aloud and precedes the overtly named target picture by 7–10 trials. That is, in any trial only one stimulus is presented to the participant; consequently, effects during picture naming are not conflated with the reading of prime words.

Importantly, in the delayed paradigm, picture naming was facilitated by some 30 ms when a morphologically related complex prime word preceded the picture by 7–10 trials (Zwitserlood et al. 2000; see also Feldman 2000). This facilitation could not be explained by semantic or phonological form overlap between prime words and target pictures. When the same pictures were paired with semantic or phonological primes, inhibition and facilitation effects, respectively, were observed in the immediate but not in the delayed variant of the paradigm (Zwitserlood et al. 2000). That is, in contrast to morphological effects, semantic and phonological effects are suggested to be short-lived and not effective after seven or more intervening trials. Subsequent experiments suggested that similar facilitation effects result from a morphological relation of the picture name with derivations and compounds irrespective of the position or the related morpheme (prefix vs. suffix; initial vs. head constituent; Zwitserlood et al. 2002). It was proposed that the facilitation effects arise at the word form level where the morphologically complex words and the pictures activate the same word form representation, whereas the respective representations are distinct at the conceptual and lemma level (Zwitserlood et al. 2000, 2002; Zwitserlood 2004).

Dohmes et al. (2004) compared picture-naming latencies in two sets of German items using the delayed variant of the picture–word interference paradigm (long-lag priming paradigm: Zwitserlood et al. 2000; Feldman 2000). In the first set, picture names (e.g. *Ente* 'duck') were primed by either a semantically transparent or opaque compound (e.g. *Wildente* 'wild duck', and *Zeitungsente,* lit. 'newspaper duck', 'false report'). In the second set, prime words corresponded to semantically transparent compounds (e.g. *Buschrose* 'bush rose') or contained the complete picture name (e.g. *Rose* 'rose') only formally (e.g. *Neurose*, 'neurosis'). In each set, the priming effects were measured relative to an unrelated condition and picture naming latencies were facilitated by about 30–40 ms only for the morphologically primed conditions, but independent of the transparency status (i.e. transparent or opaque).

Koester and Schiller (2008, 2011) replicated Dohmes et al. (2004) in Dutch. Target picture names (e.g. *ekster* 'magpie') were primed by semantically transparent or opaque compounds (e.g. *eksternest* 'magpie nest'; *eksteroog*, lit. 'magpie eye', 'corn/induration of the skin'); a different set of targets (e.g. *jas* 'coat') was primed by semantically transparent compounds (e.g. *jaszak* 'coat pocket') or form-related words containing the complete picture name without being a morpheme (e.g. *jasmijn* 'jasmine'). Compound-picture pairs were selected such that picture names and primes overlapped either in the first or the second morpheme. In a long-lag priming paradigm using the same timing parameters as in Dohmes et al. (2004), significant morphological priming effects of about 30 ms were obtained for both transparent and opaque primes but not for form-related words. Furthermore, there was no statistical difference between transparent and opaque primes.

Koester and Schiller (2008, 2011) argue that their effects cannot be explained by the semantic or phonological relationship between primes and targets because semantic and phonological effects do not survive the distance between prime and target in a long-lag priming paradigm (Feldman 2000; Zwitserlood et al. 2000). The effects are therefore suggested to be due to the morphological relation between prime and target.

Morphological priming effects are extremely robust, even surviving a language switch (Verdonschot et al. 2012). For instance, reading aloud the Dutch compound *tongzoen* ('French kiss') or *landtong* ('finger of land') facilitated the naming of a picture of a *tongue*, even after 7–10 intervening naming trials and even when those intervening trials were in a different language (English in this case). In fact, there was no statistical difference in the magnitude of the effect for intervening trials in the same language as the target or in a different language. Even more recently, Kaczer et al. (submitted) demonstrated that the priming effect still holds when novel compounds were produced, e.g. *appelgezicht* ('apple face'), for naming a target picture of an *apple*. The priming effect for the novel compounds was even stronger than for existing compounds, such as *appelmoes* ('apple sauce'). This was presumably because participants focused even more on the separate constituents than in the case of existing compounds. In a second session, this difference between novel and existing compounds disappeared, presumably because the novel compounds were no longer novel to the participants. However, both novel and existing compounds still yielded a morphological priming effect when compared to unrelated compounds. The ERPs reflected those morphological priming effects in the second session, but were less clear in the first session (Kaczer et al., submitted).

Others have denied a psycholinguistic basis for morphological representations. Rather, morphological effects are supposed to emerge as the result of semantic and word-form processing as well as from their interaction (Joanisse and Seidenberg 1999, 2005; Plaut and Gonnerman 2000). However, if semantic processes influenced the facilitation effects reported by Koester and Schiller (2008; 201, 2011), semantic transparency should have resulted in a difference between transparent and opaque conditions. Specifically, one would expect increased RTs for the production of picture names (e.g. *ekster* 'magpie') primed by transparent (e.g. *eksternest* 'magpie nest') relative to opaque compounds (e.g. *eksteroog* 'corn') due to lexical competition (Glaser and Glaser 1989; Levelt et al. 1999). Importantly, the absence of a difference between the transparent and opaque conditions cannot be explained by a putative phonological effect that overshadowed the semantic one because the transparent and opaque conditions did not differ with regard to their phonological overlap with the picture names. Similarly, if phonological processes influenced the observed effects, form overlap should have resulted in significant facilitation. However, facilitation for naming a target picture (e.g. *jas* 'coat') was only found for morphologically related primes (e.g. *jaszak* 'coat pocket'). In other words, the absence of an effect for mere form-related primes (e.g. *jasmijn* 'jasmine') suggests that the effect for morphologically related primes is not due to phonological overlap because the phonological overlap was the same in both conditions. Moreover, together with the absence of a semantic influence, the semantic relation with the target picture name cannot account for the facilitation for morphologically related primes. Rather, it is suggested that the effects are due to the morphological relation between primes and targets, and that these relations are explicitly represented in the mental lexicon (Badecker 2001; Zwitserlood et al. 2000). Thus, the results from the long-lag priming paradigm in German (Dohmes et al. 2004; Zwitserlood et al. 2000, 2002) and Dutch (Kaczer et al., submitted; Koester and Schiller 2008, 2011; Verdonschot et al. 2012) are consistent with the conception of morphology as being independent of semantics (Aronoff 1994; but see Marslen-Wilson et al. 1994). These findings support decompositional models of (compound) word production. The effect of a morphological relation between compound constituents and picture names suggests that the morphemes are available to the parser and may be planning units in language production (Roelofs 1996; Roelofs and Baayen 2002). Morphologically complex words, at least compounds, do not seem to be stored and prepared as whole-word forms. That is, a full-listing account (e.g. Butterworth 1983) is incompatible whereas full-parsing and dual-route models are compatible with the present data (Badecker 2001; Bien et al. 2005; Blanken 2000; Levelt et al. 1999; Stemberger and MacWhinney 1986; Taft 2004).

27.3 Conclusion

In this chapter we have discussed the way in which words are accessed in our mental lexicon. We have reviewed evidence in favour of discrete models of lexical access as well as cascaded/interactive models, including the response exclusion hypothesis. At the moment, it seems that limited cascading of activation can best account for the experimental findings. We further discussed the lexical representation of, and access to, morphologically complex words. We have seen that a full-form representation of complex words yields many problems. Rather, it seems that we store complex words in terms of their constituting morphemes, and that the morphological relations between words are particularly strong, even surviving a switch to a different language.

CHAPTER 28

THE BILINGUAL LEXICON

JOHN N. WILLIAMS

28.1 Introduction

The essential questions motivating much psycholinguistic research on the bilingual lexicon go back to Weinreich's (1953) classification of different types of bilingualism, which he linked to different acquisition contexts. Drawing on Saussure's distinction between the signifier (word) and the signified (concept), he proposed that the child exposed to two languages from birth represents the two languages in a common, fused system of signifier–signified relations. Words in the two languages access a common conceptual store. Weinreich referred to this as 'compound bilingualism'. In contrast, adults learning a second language store the languages in separate systems of signifier–signified relations leading to 'co-ordinate bilingualism'. Alternatively, the second language is parasitic on the first, and second-language words only activate meaning via their first-language translations following associations between signifiers, known as 'subordinative bilingualism'. Much the same distinctions have driven psycholinguistic research on the bilingual lexicon. Can bilinguals keep the representation and processing of their languages distinct, suggesting a co-ordinate organization? Or is there interaction between their languages in moment-by-moment processing and overlap in underlying representation, suggesting a compound organization? And how does the representation and processing of second-language words change as a function of proficiency and acquisition context? Although not all of the possible combinations of acquisition context, proficiency, and modality (listening, reading, speaking) have been tested, it is already clear that the situation is not quite as Weinreich imagined.

Throughout this chapter the term 'bilingual' will be used very loosely to refer to anyone with knowledge of more than one language. Thus, an 'advanced Dutch-English bilingual' would be someone whose first language (L1) is Dutch and who speaks English as a second (or even third or fourth) language ('L2') to an advanced level. Unless otherwise stated, the research described here has been on people who began to learn their second language after their first, usually in a school context, and who are at an advanced level of proficiency. Typically, the participants are university students, tested either in their home country or while studying abroad.

28.2 Comprehension processes

28.2.1 Recognizing forms

First, consider the simple act of recognizing a spoken word out of context. If you are a co-ordinate bilingual you should behave essentially like a monolingual in each of your languages. When listening to your L1 you will engage your L1 system, and when listening to L2 you will engage your L2 system. But this is not the case. Suppose a Dutch-English bilingual hears the phrase 'click on the desk' in the context of a display containing pictures of a desk, a dustbin lid, a pineapple, and a globe. The experiment is conducted entirely in English. Their eye movements are monitored and reveal they are likely to glance at the dustbin lid before settling on the desk (Weber and Cutler 2004). Monolingual speakers of English are much less likely to do this, so why do the Dutch? The Dutch for 'lid' is *deksel*, so it appears that on hearing the initial /dɛ/ of 'desk' the bilinguals momentarily activate the Dutch word, even though they know that they will only hear English words in the experiment (see also Spivey and Marian 1999, for a similar effect in Russian-English bilinguals). They do not seem to be able to prevent auditory input contacting their Dutch lexicon and affecting where they direct their attention, even though they know that no Dutch words will occur. In fact, what we see here is no more than an extension of the normal processes of parallel activation of multiple lexical candidates, competition, and resolution that occur during monolingual listening (Marslen-Wilson 1989; McClelland and Elman 1986). Whilst all listeners have to resolve competition between similar-sounding words during the recognition process, the bilingual has to deal with competitors from their other language(s) potentially delaying recognition, or at least making recognition more effortful. These results also show that input is being projected to representations in both the current and non-current languages simultaneously. A similar effect can be obtained when the heard word is in the L1 and the competitor comes from a weaker L2, although only when the competitor is a phonologically similar cognate of an L1 word (Blumenfeld and Marian 2007).

Research on visual word recognition points to the same conclusion. If a Dutch-English bilingual is performing a lexical decision task[1] in English, their decisions will be faster than expected for words like TYPE, which are identical to the Dutch word with the same meaning but differ slightly in pronunciation (Dijkstra, Grainger, and van Heuven 1999). Facilitation is even obtained when the cognate is only similarly spelled in the two

[1] In a lexical decision task the participant has to indicate by pressing response keys whether a stimulus (e.g. BLEMP) is an English word or a pseudoword as quickly but as accurately as they can.

languages, such as the English-Dutch pair *flood–vloed* (Dijkstra, Miwa, Brummelhuis, Sappelli, and Baayen 2010). These are true, or near cognates, and the facilitation is assumed to reflect activation of L1 representations during a task that is conducted entirely in the L2. For 'false friends' like RUST (which means 'rest' in Dutch—same form, different meaning) lexical decision times are slower than expected, but only if the list in which they are embedded also contains words from the other language (Dijkstra, Van Jaarsveld, and Ten Brinke 1998; Smits, Martensen, Dijkstra, and Sandra 2006). This is presumably because the form activates different meanings, or alternatively, because different representations of the orthographic word form become active in each language and then have to compete with each other for control of the required response (Dijkstra and Van Heuven 2002). Again, these effects are merely an extension of the normal recognition processes in the monolingual. A written word momentarily activates representations of orthographically similar words from the 'bottom up', and this competition is resolved as more stimulus information arrives (McClelland and Rumelhart 1981). A consequence of this competition between alternatives in the monolingual is that the time to recognize a word is affected by how many similarly spelled words there are in the language—the more such words, the more intense the competition for recognition (Johnson and Pugh 1994). In the bilingual, the number of similarly spelled words in all languages known to the participant is the best predictor of recognition time (van Heuven, Dijkstra, and Grainger 1998). This is an important result because competition between words across languages implies that functionally speaking their lexical representations are contained within the same system. Thus, recognition processes operate in essentially the same way in the monolingual and bilingual; it is just that the bilingual cannot avoid accessing representations in non-current languages.

One may object that these tasks require responses to individual words. What about the more natural situation of hearing or reading words in context? There is evidence that in highly constraining contexts, bilinguals do have language-specific expectations for upcoming words. So a Spanish-English bilingual reads the code-switched word *carta* ('letter') more slowly in *He needed to put a stamp on the carta before he mailed it*, than in the more neutral *Andrea dropped a carta in the mailbox on the corner*, whereas the opposite pattern is found if the critical word is in English (Altarriba, Kroll, Sholl, and Rayner 1996). This suggests that the linguistic context does lead to higher activation of words in the expected language when the context is itself highly constraining. On the other hand, using eye movement tracking during reading sentences in the L2, Libben and Titone (2009) found the typical relatively fast reading of cognates and inhibition of false friends in neutral sentence contexts for highly proficient French-English bilinguals. This shows that merely being embedded in an utterance of the same language does not by itself induce language-selective lexical access. In highly constraining contexts they only found cognate effects in the early stage recognition measures (first fixation time), suggesting that, as in Altarriba *et al.* (1996), when specific predictions can be made, they are language-specific. But in this case they reduce, and do not eliminate, the tendency to access representations in the non-current language. And using a priming methodology on German-English bilinguals, Elston-Güttler *et al.* (2005) found that the word *gift* in 'The woman gave her friend an expensive gift' primed POISON (*gift* means poison in German), showing that the word had activated its German meaning even though this was irrelevant in the context. These latter two studies therefore suggest that even constraining sentence contexts do not necessarily eliminate cognate effects in bilinguals. Elston-Güttler *et al.*'s participants were advanced learners of English tested in Germany, and Libben and Titone's participants were highly proficient French-English bilinguals tested in Montreal, so in both cases the L1 was likely to be used outside of the laboratory, and hence not dormant. Interestingly, in Elston-Güttler *et al.*, if the participants first watched a 20-minute film in their L2 English just before doing the task, then the cognate priming effect disappeared, suggesting that language context can modulate interference from the L1 if it is sufficiently well established. Thus, linguistic context clearly can reduce cognate effects on recognition, just as one would expect from the general interplay of bottom-up and top-down factors that characterizes language processing in general. What is perhaps surprising, though, is that a language context *per se* has little effect unless it is strongly instantiated. Further studies manipulating language context and country of testing are clearly needed.

The above studies show that word forms in current and non-current languages compete with each other during the recognition process. This suggests a compound form of representation, since for words to compete with each other they must be stored within a common system. Models of bilingual word recognition make this assumption explicit: the Bilingual Interactive Activation (BIA) model (Dijkstra and Van Heuven 2002) for visual word recognition, and the Bilingual Model of Lexical Access (BIMOLA) for spoken-word recognition (Grosjean 1997). For languages that share certain graphemes and phonemes, it seems intuitively obvious that the same representations should be utilized, but the deeper claim is that the abstract representations of word forms are also contained in a common system. This compound form of representation appears to apply to late learners, at all levels of proficiency.

28.2.2 From form to meaning: a common conceptual code?

Following Weinreich (1953), one may wonder whether common or separate meanings are accessed by L1 and L2 words. But this question, simple as it may seem, obscures deep questions about what is meant by 'meaning' and what is meant by 'common'. With regard to meaning, do we make a distinction between conceptual structure and lexical meanings—a two-level semantics (Bierwisch and Schreuder 1992; Pavlenko 1999)—or is there simply a one-to-one mapping between concepts and words (Levelt, Roelofs, and Meyer 1999)? Clearly, it would be naive to assume that words in different languages can have exactly the same meanings, or that all meanings are expressible in all languages. For example, Japanese has one word, *ashi*, that refers to the leg and the foot. Clearly, this does not mean that Japanese people cannot conceive of legs and feet as separable concepts (Vigliocco and Vinson 2007). The assumption in bilingual lexicon research is that whereas there exists a common, language-independent conceptual substrate that is accessed by language (and which motivates utterances), there must be language-specific mappings from concepts to words. This does not necessarily mean that lexicalization patterns cannot affect conceptualization (Vigliocco and Filipovic 2004). For example, Pavlenko (1999) argues for a distinction between lexical-semantic representations and concepts, with the former being potentially rapidly acquired, and permitting language-specific conceptual structures to be formed through experience over time. In a different vein, Van Hell and De Groot (1998) propose a distributed feature model, inspired by connectionist approaches to word meaning, in which word forms from different languages map onto a common conceptual code and induce their own language-specific patterns of activation. As a result, words from different languages may share varying numbers of conceptual features. For example, comparisons between word associations in L1 and L2 (Van Hell and De Groot 1998) suggest that there is more overlap between the conceptual codes activated in L1 and L2 by concrete words and cognates than abstract words. In this way, a common code can be combined with language-specific patterns of activation over that code.

Evidence for a common conceptual substrate across languages comes from cross-language semantic priming. Within one language the time to recognize a word, say CHAIR, is facilitated if it is preceded by a semantically related 'prime' word like TABLE (Meyer and Schvaneveldt 1971). The same effect can be obtained reliably across languages, at least when the prime is in the L1 and the target in the L2. For example, for an English-Italian bilingual TABLE will prime SEDIA ('chair') (see Altarriba and Basnight-Brown 2007, for a review). In order to provide convincing evidence of shared underlying meaning such effects have to be automatic, e.g. the result of automatic spreading activation around the conceptual system (Collins and Loftus 1975) and not the result of conscious expectancy strategies (Neely 1977). Bilingual researchers have used a range of techniques to ensure automaticity: tasks that distract attention from the primes (Fox 1996); brief, but still visible primes (Keatley, Spinks, and de Gelder 1994; Tzelgov and Ebenezra 1992); or primes presented so briefly that they are subliminal (Basnight-Brown and Altarriba 2007; Perea, Dunabeitia, and Carreiras 2008; Williams 1994). Cross-language semantic priming effects have been obtained in all cases, suggesting that L1 and L2 words do share components of meaning. Once again, even for late learners and learners at various levels of proficiency we find evidence for compound organization, in the sense that a common conceptual system is shared between languages, although without denying the possibility of language-specific conceptual structures forming within that system.

28.2.3 Accessing meaning from form

Even if we accept that words in all languages ultimately map onto a common conceptual code, there remains the issue of how it is accessed by L2 forms and how this may depend on level of proficiency. One highly influential hypothesis is that at low levels of proficiency L2 words access meaning via their L1 translations, an idea instantiated in the 'Revised Hierarchical Model' of bilingual memory, or RHM (Kroll and Stewart 1994; Kroll, Van Hell, Tokowicz, and Green 2010). To begin with, L2 words have much weaker mappings onto the conceptual system than their L1 translations. So learners use direct lexical connections between L2 words and their L1 translation equivalents enabling them to exploit the strong mapping from L1 words to meaning. This is equivalent to the notion of subordinative bilingualism in the sense that the L2 is parasitic on the L1. With increasing proficiency, learners develop direct mappings from L2 forms to meanings.

There are four main lines of evidence that support the RHM. First, comparisons of picture naming and word translation: at low levels of proficiency, translation from L1 to L2 is faster than naming pictures in L2, whereas at higher proficiency there is no difference (Chen and Leung 1989; Potter, So, Voneckardt, and Feldman 1984). Naming pictures in L2 requires use of direct form–meaning connections, which is problematic at low proficiency, but translation can be achieved by exploiting L1-to-L2 lexical-level connections, and hence is relatively fast. At higher proficiency, both tasks engage the conceptual system and so take about the same time. Second, semantic blocking effects in translation: when naming pictures one after another, response times slow down when items are presented in blocks organized by semantic category, reflecting competition in the concept–form mappings. The same effect occurs when translating words from L1 to L2, suggesting conceptual mediation, but not when translating from L2 to L1, suggesting that the conceptual level is by-passed and lexical-level translation connections are used instead (Kroll and Stewart 1994). Third, form and meaning interference in translation recognition: in this task people are given pairs of words and asked to indicate if they are correct translations. For example, an English-Spanish bilingual might be given pairs like MAN—HAMBRE or MAN—MUJER. The correct response in both cases is 'no', but responses might be relatively slow because HAMBRE is orthographically similar to 'hombre' ('man'), and MUJER means 'woman'. A slow-down in the first case reflects form-level interference and is greater at low than high levels of proficiency, whereas in the second case the interference is meaning-based and is greater at high proficiency (Talamas, Kroll, and Dufour 1999). This pattern of results is consistent with a shift from lexical to conceptually mediated translation, as predicted by the RHM. Fourth, semantic and translation priming effects: whereas there is good evidence for automatic semantic priming from L1 to L2, effects tend to be much weaker or entirely absent in the L2 to L1 direction (Basnight-Brown and Altarriba 2007; Fox 1996; Keatley *et al.* 1994; Silverberg and Samuel 2004; Tzelgov and Ebenezra 1992). Only in highly proficient bilinguals or early acquirers of high proficiency are the semantic priming effects the same size regardless of direction (Perea *et al.* 2008; Silverberg and Samuel 2004). This is consistent with L2 form–meaning mappings being initially relatively weak, as one might expect. In contrast, many of the studies that failed to find L2–L1 semantic priming did find L2–L1 translation priming; e.g., from CHIEN to DOG for an English-French bilingual (Basnight-Brown and Altarriba 2007; Fox 1996; Keatley *et al.* 1994) and L2–L1 translation priming has even been obtained for newly learned words (Altarriba and Knickerbocker 2011; Williams and Cheung 2011). The weakness of L2–L1 semantic priming and relative robustness of

L2–L1 translation priming at anything but very high levels of proficiency is consistent with the RHM.

Although many lines of evidence lend support to the RHM, it is probably an over-simplification to say that all L2 words initially activate meaning only via L1 translations. If translation is achieved purely lexically, then translation times should not be affected by semantic variables. But De Groot and Poot (1997) found that Dutch-English bilinguals translate concrete words more quickly than abstract words in both translation directions and at all levels of proficiency. This points to the involvement of meaning in the translation process. And in translation recognition tasks, meaning-based interference has been found even in low-proficiency bilinguals (Altarriba and Mathis 1997; Sunderman and Kroll 2006). Given the emerging picture from psycholinguistics for high levels of interaction and cross-talk between different codes, it seems unlikely that bilinguals of whatever proficiency would ever rely on a single pathway for accessing meaning from L2 words. It seems more likely that activation traverses multiple pathways, with different degrees of involvement of different pathways according to proficiency and type of word.

In fact, reflexes of translation effects can emerge even at quite high levels of proficiency. Silverberg and Samuel (2004) showed that for early Spanish-English bilinguals BULL facilitated lexical decisions on the Spanish target TORNILLO ('screw'). They argue that this is because BULL activates its meaning directly, which then activates the form of the Spanish translation *toro*, which then facilitates recognition of the form-similar TORNILLO. Thierry and Wu (2007) gave proficient late-learner Chinese-English bilinguals a semantic relatedness judgement test, including English word pairs like *Post-Mail* and *Train-Ham*. Some of the pairs would contain a character repetition when translated into Chinese. For example, the pair *Train-Ham* translates as *Huo Che-Huo Tui* (火车–火腿). Different ERP responses were obtained for items with and without character repetition, suggesting that at an unconscious level the participants were being influenced by the form similarity between the words in their native language. Even though the task was all in English, they were implicitly translating the words into Chinese. Wu and Thierry (2010) provide evidence that, specifically, they were being influenced by the sound of the Chinese translations and not their written forms. Thus, there are reverberating effects around the lexical system at all levels, reflecting interactions between translation equivalents, although whether these necessarily reflect the kinds of translation connections posited by the RHM is not clear.

28.2.4 What meaning is accessed by L2 words?

The research reviewed above intentionally does not address the complexities of form–meaning mappings across languages. The notion of 'translation equivalence' is treated simplistically as items sharing a common meaning. Clearly, this is not the case for many words. For example, a homonym in one language (e.g., *bank* in English) will most likely be translated by different words in another (e.g., in Italian, *banca* for financial bank and *riva* for river bank). One-to-many mappings in meanings across languages slows down both processing and acquisition due to competition between alternative translations (Degani and Tokowicz 2010).

A more subtle problem occurs when L2 words correspond to polysemous meanings of an L1 word. For example, the Chinese word *jie* covers the meanings of both English *lend* and *borrow*, and *wenti* covers the meanings of *problem* and *question*. Jiang (2002) showed that Chinese-English bilinguals rate word pairs like *problem–question* as more highly semantically related (relative to unrelated control pairs) than do English monolinguals, and their response times are faster. Jiang argues that this is because they essentially utilize the L1 meaning of the L2 translation, and are only prevented from rating the words as having an identical meaning by explicit knowledge of their non-equivalence.

It does appear that L1 polysemy continues to colour the interpretation of L2 words, even at high levels of proficiency. In Elston-Güttler and Williams (2008), advanced German-English bilinguals were asked to indicate whether the last word of sentences formed a plausible completion. For a sentence such as 'His shoes were uncomfortable due to a bubble', the time to respond 'Implausible' was slower than for native speakers of English (relative to the plausible sentences). The reason is that the translation equivalent of *bubble* in German is *Blase*, which also means *blister*. *Blase* would not be regarded as a homonym, but rather as a polysemous word that has a broader meaning than the English translation equivalent. Once again, it appears that the L1 meaning influences L2 processing. However, note that in this case the majority of responses were correct. The learners did indicate that the completion was implausible, suggesting that they knew the correct English meaning of the word. Either this is a reflection of explicit knowledge of the correct meanings, or interference is a reflection of residual connections from earlier stages of development, whether lexical level translation connections or connections from L2 form to L1 meaning. In any case, the shadow of L1 meaning appears to be remarkably difficult to shake off.

Given the existence of homonomy and polysemy within all languages, it is more realistic to think in terms of acquisition of senses rather than of a unitary meaning. Whilst learners may indeed assume that words learned as translation equivalents share a common core meaning, they may not assume that all the senses of the word are shared. Kellerman (1979) found that learners' willingness to transfer a particular usage of the L1 Dutch word *breken* ('to break') to the L2 was related to how close it was to the core meaning of the word, as established through multidimensional scaling. For example, 'break a cup' (in Dutch) was rated as being readily translatable into English, whereas 'break a fall' was not; clearly, the former is more representative of the core meaning of *breken*. Thus, the various senses of an L2 word may need to be acquired through experience, not simply copied over from an assumed translation equivalent. Finkbeiner *et al.* (2004) argue that if L2 words are associated with fewer senses than L1 words then this can explain the asymmetry in priming effects noted earlier, i.e. that priming effects tend to be weaker from the L2 to the L1 than vice versa. Indeed, even priming between translations can show this asymmetry when primes are masked and the target task is lexical decision (Finkbeiner *et al.* 2004; Jiang and Forster 2001). If one considers the proportion of the target meaning that overlaps with the prime, an L2 target with few senses will overlap completely with an L1 prime with many senses. But an L1 target with many senses will only partially overlap with an L2 prime with few senses. Thus, acquisition of word meaning over time can be conceived as the accumulation of senses.

Even within a single word sense one might wonder which specific components of meaning are shared between translations, and whether L2 words simply inherit the entire meaning of the L1 sense with which it is associated. Williams (1994) provides evidence that automatic (in this case subliminal) L1 to L2 priming is most reliable for pairs that are semantically similar, e.g. FENCE–HAIE ('hedge' in French), as opposed to merely associated, e.g. NEEDLE–FIL ('thread' in French). De Groot and Nas (1991) also failed to find subliminal cross-language priming for associates. This may suggest that L2 words do not necessarily inherit the conceptual associates of L2 translations, but map onto a more restricted lexical meaning (Pavlenko 1999). This point will be further elaborated below.

28.2.5 How can direct form–meaning connections be acquired?

If acquiring direct form–meaning connections in the L2 is problematic, what can be done to help? There is some evidence that even at the early stages of vocabulary learning, differences in instructional method can have an effect. Comesana *et al.* (2009) showed that meaning interference effects in translation recognition, indicative of direct meaning access, could be obtained after only one session of instruction on novel words, but only if the words were learned with pictures. Perhaps, then, if the instructional technique can avoid reliance on translations, direct mappings to meaning can be acquired more easily. On a larger scale, Linck, Kroll, and Sunderman (2009) found meaning interference effects in translation recognition only for immersion learners, not for classroom learners matched for proficiency. Silverberg and Samuel (2004) only found automatic L2–L1 semantic priming for early learners who had also learned their L2 through immersion. This research points to the role of extensive language experience in real contexts of use for developing strong form–meaning mappings in the L2.

In a laboratory-based study of word learning, Williams and Cheung (2011) examined L3 to L1 semantic priming effects from newly learned words in Chinese-English bilinguals learning French as L3. Recall that previous research has generally shown L2 to L1 semantic priming effects to be weak. In this study, L3 (French) words were first learned with their L2 (English) translations, for example *écureuil* was learned as the translation of *squirrel*. The participants then performed a semantic priming test using the novel L3 (French) words as primes and L1 (Chinese) words as targets. Robust priming of translation targets was obtained, e.g., from *écureuil* to 松鼠('squirrel' in Chinese). Since the French words were never learned with their Chinese translations, this priming is not due to mere repetition of the learning experiences, but presumably reflects a deeper semantic connection. This was confirmed by priming from the French words to Chinese targets that were semantically similar, e.g., between *écureuil* and 松鼠 ('animal'). However, no priming was obtained to targets that were associated but not semantically similar, e.g. between *écureuil* and 果仁 ('nut'). This suggests some restriction on the semantic information that is accessible from words when learned in translation pairs and is reminiscent of the previous priming results of Williams (1994), which also showed a dissociation between priming for semantically similar and associated pairs. In Williams and Cheung (2011), the only learning task that resulted in priming of associates was one in which the novel French words were learned in the context of pictures that actually contained the associate. For example, some of the pictures depicted a squirrel holding a nut. In the subsequent test, *écureuil* primed 果仁 ('nut'). These results suggest an essentially episodic view of word learning (see also Perfetti, Wlotko, and Hart 2005). Novel words may readily map onto the lexical meaning of their translation equivalents, but they may form associations with other concepts only through experience.

Pavlenko (1999) makes a distinction between lexical meanings and the conceptual structures to which they ultimately relate and which provide words with, amongst other things, connotative meaning. She quotes from Eva Hoffman's (1989) book *Lost in Translation: A Life in a New Language*:

> The words I learn now don't stand for things in the same unquestioned way they did in my native tongue. 'River' in Polish was a vital sound, energized with the essence of riverhood, of my rivers, of my being immersed in rivers. 'River' in English is cold—a word without an aura. It has no accumulated associations for me, and it does not give off the radiating haze of connotation. It does not evoke.
>
> (Hoffmann 1989: 106)

Thus, while learners may rapidly learn a mapping between an L2 form and a lexical meaning inherited from an L1 translation (Jiang 2002), only through episodes of actual usage will they acquire the associations between this word meaning and deeper conceptual structures. More needs to be done to explore the impact of learning experiences on the underlying representation of word meaning and to tease apart different aspects of meaning in a more systematic way than is usual in this research.

28.3 Production

The theme running through all of the above comprehension studies is that bilinguals show detectable processing effects due to activation of lexical and semantic representations in the non-current language. Bilinguals do not appear to be able to entirely 'switch off' their other languages, even in situations where only one language appears to be relevant. Perhaps this is not too surprising, since it may be difficult to apply a language filter to determine which pathways an incoming stimulus will traverse. But when it comes to production, apart from code-switching or occasional other-language intrusions

(Poulisse and Bongaerts 1994), bilinguals do generally appear to be able to speak in the intended language, implying that they are able to switch off their other languages. However, psycholinguistic research has revealed that here too activation of representations in the non-concurrent language has a detectable effect.

In the case of visual word recognition, we saw that processing of a word in one language is affected by cognates in other languages. Similar cognate facilitation effects occur in production tasks, such as picture-naming. If an advanced Catalan-Spanish bilingual is asked to name pictures in Spanish, they are faster to do so for cognates like *gato* (*gat* in Catalan—'cat') than for non-cognates like *mesa* (*taula* in Catalan—'table'). The effect can also be obtained when pictures are to be named in the L1, although the effect is smaller (Costa, Caramazza, and Sebastian-Galles 2000). Similar effects on L2 picture-naming have been obtained for Japanese-English bilinguals, where the scripts are very different (Hoshino and Kroll 2008). These results suggest that when a bilingual wants to express a concept in the current language, they cannot avoid activating the phonological form of the word in non-current languages. For cognates, the overlap in phonological representations produces faster responses. Colomé (2001) showed that effects of phonological activation in the non-current language can be detected for non-cognates as well. Highly advanced Catalan-Spanish bilinguals were shown a letter, e.g. m, followed by a picture, e.g. a table. They had to indicate whether the sound of the letter was contained in the name of the picture in Catalan, but without saying the name of the picture aloud. In this case, the correct answer is 'no' because the name of the picture is *taula*. However, the Spanish for table—*mesa*—does contain the target sound, and this makes people slower than for trials where the target sound is in neither the Catalan or Spanish names. Participants seemed to automatically activate the sound of the Spanish translation of the word even though this was completely irrelevant to the task. There is therefore evidence that even in production tasks bilinguals cannot switch off non-current languages.

What about mapping from concepts to words (the reverse of form–meaning mapping in comprehension)? It is known from research on monolinguals that when naming an object there is competition between lexical alternatives (Levelt *et al.* 1999). For example, Wheeldon and Monsell (1994) showed that if a person has just said 'shark' in response to the definition 'Man-eating fish', a few trials later their time to name a picture of a whale will be slower than if they had not recently produced a related word. This effect is not due to problems recognizing the object but to finding its name, i.e., the process of lexicalization. It is assumed that whenever one entertains the concept of a shark, words with similar meanings are also activated to some extent and compete with the intended word for selection (a similar process is more obviously at work in word substitution errors of the kind 'Put it in the oven at a low speed'). Prior production of a potential competitor temporarily increases its activation level, and it interferes with production of the intended word more than usual. This effect shows that concepts are mapped onto words in a competitive process (see also Schriefers, Meyer, and Levelt 1990, for evidence from a picture–word interference pradigm). From a bilingual perspective, one can then ask whether this competition extends to words in the non-current language. There is research to suggest that it does. Using the same paradigm as Wheeldon and Monsell (1994), Lee and Williams (2001) showed that if an English-French bilingual utters 'shark' in response to a definition, a few trials later they will suffer interference in naming a picture of a whale in French as 'baleine' (see also Hermans, Bongaerts, De Bot, and Schreuder 1998, for evidence from a picture–word interference paradigm). This result suggests that words in the non-intended language compete for selection in production with words in the intended language. It is consistent with the research described above showing activation of non-current language words during production, but also provides strong evidence that the relevant representations are contained within the same system. It should be noted though that Costa *et al.* (1999) have claimed that whilst there may be activation of non-current language words, these do not actually compete for selection with words in the intended language. They showed that when a Catalan-Spanish bilingual names a picture of a table in L1 as 'taula' their responses are facilitated if the word *mesa* (which means 'table' in Spanish) is printed on the picture, compared to an unrelated control word. If there really were competition between words in different languages for selection, then a large interference effect from *mesa* would have been expected. Clearly this is a very different, and even less natural, paradigm from that used by Lee and Williams (2001), and possibly behaviour was affected by strong L2 to L1 translation connections, as proposed by the RHM. Or else the ability to avoid competition from other-language words might reflect a change in the language control mechanism at higher levels of proficiency (Costa and Santesteban 2004).

In order to explain competition effects between alternatives during lexical selection, it is usual to appeal to a 'lemma' level of representation that is intermediate between concepts and word forms. This controls the mapping between lexical concepts and forms and is the locus for attaching syntactic information about the word (Levelt *et al.* 1999). For example, lemmas for verbs will be linked to representations indicating whether they are transitive or intransitive or whether they participate in ditransitive and/or prepositional dative constructions. Nouns in certain languages will be linked to representations indicating their grammatical gender. There is evidence that in bilinguals there is an interaction between the syntactic information attached to lemmas in the two languages. For example, Greek-German bilinguals are faster to translate noun phrases (containing a gender-marked adjective followed by a noun) from L1 Greek into L2 German if they have the same grammatical gender in both languages (Salamoura and Williams 2008). Similarly, German-Dutch bilinguals are faster to name pictures in their L2 Dutch if the grammatical gender of the noun is the same in the two languages (Lemhöfer, Spalek, and Schriefers 2008). In the case of argument–structure alternations, Salamoura and Williams (2007) showed that if a Greek-English bilingual uses, say, a double-object dative structure in L1 Greek, then they are relatively likely to reuse that structure subsequently when producing an utterance in L2 English, replicating the usual within-language syntactic priming effect (see also Schoonbaert, Hartsuiker, and Pickering 2007). Cross-language gender and syntactic priming effects can be regarded as reflecting the sharing of syntactic representations associated with lemmas in different languages, and again point to the relevant representations being contained in essentially the same system.

Despite there being activation of lexical representations in the non-current language even during production, people do nevertheless generally speak in the intended language. Obviously, there is some additional control process at work to ensure that the intended language is used. One influential proposal about how this is achieved is through inhibition of the non-current language (Abutalebi and Green 2007; Green 1998). Lexical representations (specifically lemmas in this model) carry language tags that allow words in specific languages to be inhibited according to task demands. Support for this idea comes from the observation that when switching between languages there is a greater cost associated with switching from a weaker L2 to the stronger L1 than vice versa (Lee and Williams 2001; Macnamara, Krautham, and Bolgar 1968; Meuter and Allport 1999). For example, an English-French bilingual might be asked to name two pictures in succession, with the language to be used for each picture indicated by a cue. If the first picture is named in L2 French, the time to name the second picture in L1 English will be slower than if the first picture had also been named in L1 English. This switching cost is much greater than for the comparison between English-French and French-French trial sequences (Lee and Williams 2001). The reason for this is that in order to speak a relatively weak L2, the strong L1 has to be massively inhibited. If the L1 is then required, it takes relatively more time to disinhibit it. But in order to speak the L1 a weak L2 requires hardly any inhibition, and hence, paradoxically, is relatively more available when required. The executive functions that are at work here are not specific to language, but engaged in all task-switching situations (Macnamara *et al.* 1968; Meuter and Allport 1999). The switching cost asymmetry is not found in balanced bilinguals, which according to the inhibitory control account is because both languages require equal amounts of inhibition. Alternatively, it might reflect a greater ability to simply ignore activated lexical representations in the non-current language, implying a change in the control mechanism with increasing proficiency (Costa and Santesteban 2004)

28.4 Conclusion

Bilinguals are unable to simply switch off their non-current languages. Experiment after experiment shows that L1 and L2 lexical representations are simultaneously active during processing in both comprehension and production, leading to various 'cross-talk' effects between the languages. In recognition and production non-current language forms become active, producing cognate facilitation and false-friend interference in recognition tasks. In the mapping between form and meaning in comprehension, the meanings of other-language translations colour the semantic activity produced by L2 words. In the mapping between meaning and form in production, there is activation of other language lemmas. Thus, bilinguals appear to have surprisingly little control over their language systems, particularly in comprehension. To be sure, a control mechanism does exist, and is most evident in production tasks. Exercising this control system to manage their languages may enhance executive functions in bilinguals (Bialystok 2009). The fact that language-independent brain areas for task management have to be recruited implies that language-internal mechanisms for managing the activation of the competing language systems are not sufficient.

But co-activation of a bilingual's language systems does not necessarily tell us anything about their underlying organization. Even if the L1 and L2 lexical representations were contained in distinct systems, as in co-ordinate bilingualism, they could still become simultaneously active in response to linguistic stimuli or communicative intentions. What evidence is there that lexical representations in different languages are actually contained within the same system? This is where direct evidence for competition between representations in different languages is critical because it implies that representations are in some sense contained within the same functional system, or else why would they have to compete with each other? Here we can point to evidence that in the bilingual the orthographic neighbourhood for visual word recognition has to be defined over both L1 and L2, and to cross-language competition effects in word production. Cross-language gender and syntactic priming effects suggest that lemma representations for words in different languages are connected to shared representations of their syntactic properties. Such findings point to a compound representation of lexical knowledge. Whereas Weinreich (1953) thought that this was characteristic of early, simultaneous acquirers, instead we find compound organization even for later learners of second languages.

The compound view is also consistent with neuroimaging work on lexico-semantic processing in bilinguals that shows activation in similar brain areas (specifically left frontal and temporo-parietal cortex) in L1 and L2 across a range of proficiency levels and lexical tasks (for reviews see Abutalebi 2008; Indefrey 2006). This overlap has been observed even for languages as dissimilar as Chinese and English (Chee, Tan, and Thiel 1999). The only differences between L1 and L2 brain activity that do occur are at lower L2 proficiency, where there is additional brain activity in pre-frontal areas, regions known to be associated with domain-general executive functions. This is assumed to reflect the additional control demands required when processes are of low automaticity, and, as discussed above, when the L1 has to be inhibited in order to speak a weaker L2 (Abutalebi 2008).

A somewhat different picture emerges when we consider the mapping between form and meaning in comprehension. Here there is good evidence for a subordinative relationship between L2 and L1, at least in the earlier stages of acquisition; L2 words access meaning via a lexical-level translation connection to the L1, enabling them to exploit the strong mapping between L1 form and meaning. However, it is also clear that all-or-none, system-wide statements of this kind are an oversimplification. Mediated access to meaning is merely a tendency; there is also evidence for direct access even from newly learned words and for a greater semantic involvement in translation for some words rather than others. Simple box-and-arrow models such as the RHM have been useful in allowing researchers to formulate hypotheses about access routes to meaning, but it is now time to move beyond gross distinctions between lexical form and meaning and to address at a finer level of grain the actual content of the semantic and conceptual representations that are accessed by L2 words, how this varies at different levels of proficiency, and perhaps most importantly of all, how it is affected by different learning tasks and environments. After all, the way that lexical knowledge is represented in the mind of the bilingual is a result of learning experiences, and it is through understanding the connection between learning, representation, and processing that this field can have more impact upon teaching practice and language policy.

CHAPTER 29

WORDS AND NEUROPSYCHOLOGICAL DISORDERS

DENNIS TAY

29.1 Introduction

Neuropsychological disorders provide an important perspective on the nature of words and the relationship between language and the human mind. Just as our knowledge of any device is based on how it functions and malfunctions, our understanding of the language faculty is enriched by studying word use of both 'normal' and afflicted individuals. This chapter discusses neuropsychological disorders and word use from two angles. The first recounts the standard perspective of words as targets of pathology, as in the case of language disorders where individuals lose their word-finding ability. A brief introduction to major issues in language disorder research will be followed by a specific discussion of anomia (or nominal aphasia), which impairs the ability to recall names for objects and people. I discuss how the usage of words by afflicted individuals informs not only the construction of theoretical models of language processing but, at a more speculative level, age-old philosophical debates on the nature of proper names. The second angle considers words not as targets, but as signposts of pathology in psychological disorders such as psychogenic seizures and delusional thought. I discuss patients' use of metaphors in interviews and therapy sessions as a specific instance where studies of word use bear clinical implications and potential applications. I conclude by proposing some possible directions for metaphor and corpus research in mental health discourse.

29.2 Defining, classifying, and identifying language disorders

A language disorder is broadly defined as impairment to the comprehension and/or use of spoken, written, and/or other symbol systems, and is characterized by the American Speech-Language-Hearing Association[1] as part of a broader spectrum named communication disorders. The definition and classification of language disorders involve issues such as what exactly the components of a person's language competence are, what it takes for a disorder to be considered exclusively linguistic, its varying degrees of severity, and the existence of clearly identifiable neural or psychological underpinnings (Bishop 1994, 1997). The wide scope of these issues becomes apparent if we admit a broad view of language competence as the ability to produce and understand sounds, words, and sentences in any communicative situation, since any of these aspects can be impacted by a combination of neurobiological, psychological, and social factors (Wahrborg 1991). A way to focus discussion and theorization of language disorders is to look into circumstances and conditions which exclusively impact language ability to a sufficiently severe and persistent extent, and these conditions have come to be known as specific language impairments (SLI). Individuals are generally thought to have SLI if they experience impairment in language without any obvious accompanying impairment such as mental retardation, autism, or neurological damage (Bishop 2006). The converse is also true, in that language-impaired individuals who also experience these other impairments are not normally considered as having SLI (World Health Organization 1992). SLIs are not exclusive to childhood but are most frequently observed in childhood (Leonard 2000), with afflicted children scoring low on comprehension and production tests across different aspects of language such as vocabulary, grammar, and reading. Although robust diagnostic criteria have been proposed and implemented for SLI (Tomblin et al. 1996), some researchers have problematized the notion by suggesting that supposedly language-specific disorders could be a mere part of a larger spectrum of co-occurring disorders involving other non-verbal faculties (Bishop 1994).

Beyond the context of language development and acquisition, language disorders can also occur throughout the lifespan, typically as a consequence of traumatic brain injuries and dementia types such as Alzheimer's (Murdoch et al. 1987; Vinson 2007). The traditional approach in language disorder research has been to establish causal links between damage to specific brain areas and particular language disorders (Benson 1979), as with the well-known Broca's (1865) and Wernicke's (1874) areas, deemed to be responsible respectively for Broca's and Wernicke's aphasia. Since Broca's aphasia is characterized by loss of language production and preservation of language comprehension, and Wernicke's aphasia by loss of comprehension and preservation of production,

[1] www.asha.org

these two aphasia types have become prominent exemplars of the idea that mutually independent language functions are coupled with correspondingly independent neural substrates.

While the traditional approach laid the foundations for modern neuropsychology of language, contemporary neuroimaging research suggests that language abilities are distributed across the brain in complex ways which resist strict localization and which are only beginning to be understood (Hillis 2007; Small 1994). One aspect which crucially remains constant despite paradigm shifts in theory is the need to study the characteristics of language output from the perspective of linguistic categories. We turn to this in the next section with a discussion of anomia and its impact on the function of naming.

29.3 The case of anomia

Anomia, or nominal aphasia, is a common symptom which occurs with many types of language disorder and neurological disease (Laine and Martin 2006). It is characterized by difficulty with recalling names, even those of famous people, family and friends, and everyday objects like food and clothing. Although it seems fairly common for people to experience occasional lapses or 'tip-of-the-tongue' experiences when trying to recall names of things (Brown and McNeill 1966; Jones and Langford 1987), naming difficulties in clinically diagnosed cases are by definition far more severe and persistent. The obvious importance of names in everyday communication has stimulated many theoretical and clinical questions about anomia, not the least of which is whether the particular difficulty with names implies a lexical or conceptual store for names separate from other types of word (Laine and Martin 2006)—an issue which we will shortly revisit.

The clinical assessment of anomia usually requires individuals to provide names of pictured objects, with error patterns and frequencies providing a basis for diagnosis. A popular example is the Boston Naming Test (Kaplan et al. 1983), which consists of 60 line drawings depicting objects increasingly less familiar and thus presumably more difficult to name (e.g. *bed* vs. *abacus*). The controlled emphasis on individual words is preferred over an assessment of spontaneous conversation because word-finding difficulties may be concealed by alternative forms of expression over longer stretches of language, although narrative speech and story-telling tasks are also used because they better reflect everyday communicative situations faced by the subjects (Mayer and Murray 2003; Prins and Bastiaanse 2004). A range of responses can be expected from suspected anomia cases from standard picture-naming tasks. Subjects may first and foremost provide no answer, with typical remarks like *I don't know*, or *I know the answer but I can't say it* (Laine and Martin 2006: 102). Instances of circumlocution are also common, where subjects offer valid descriptions but are unable to produce the required target word (e.g. saying *the mother of my mother* instead of *grandmother*). Another frequent type of error is known as *paraphasia*, commonly subdivided into phonological and semantic paraphasia. Subjects may have trouble pronouncing the target word correctly, and/or may make naming errors which reflect a loss of ability to categorize objects. Some common semantic errors include confusing generic and specific categories (e.g. naming both a car and a bicycle as a vehicle, or naming all vehicles as a car), confusing members from related categories (e.g. calling a television set a computer), or confusing members from unrelated categories (e.g. calling a horse a gun) (Rohrer et al. 2008).

To better appreciate the nature of these errors and make subsequent predictions about language behaviour, researchers construct models which situate them within the overall processes of language comprehension and production. Fig. 29.1 depicts a simplified example of a standard model used by clinicians to theorize the processes involved in naming (see Laine and Martin 2006: 38 for a fuller model). The first step involves the non-linguistic processes of visual analysis and pattern recognition upon seeing an object or picture. The semantic and phonological systems are subsequently accessed to retrieve the pertinent words, meanings, and sounds, before the name of the object or picture is finally produced. As illustrated by Fig. 29.1, one common assumption underlying such models is that the naming process involves functionally independent stages (Laine and Martin 2006: 39), which allows clinicians to investigate questions about naming errors with reference to the interrelationships between stages. For example, are naming errors a result of impairment to the visual (Farah 2004), semantic, or phonological system(s), or the linkages between these? As clinicians identify and categorize individuals based on how the observable characteristics of their symptoms correspond with theoretical models, the models are themselves gradually refined and improved in the face of these characteristics. The most recent models have furthermore capitalized upon advancing computer simulation technology to demonstrate and argue that language comprehension and production involve mutually interconnected and dependent processes, and such models have characterized an ongoing paradigm shift known as connectionism (Bechtel and Abrahamsen 2002).

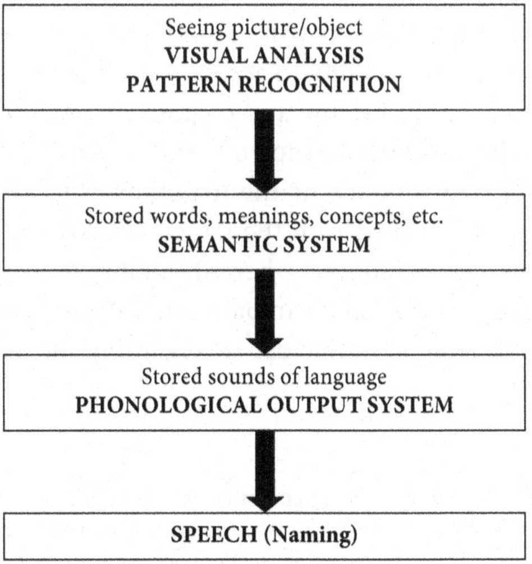

FIG 29.1 A simplified naming model.

I have thus far provided a brief introduction to anomia as a language disorder at the level of words, and the attendant clinical perspectives which aim to understand the language characteristics of afflicted individuals. At this point, we can raise the question whether anomic characteristics might shed any light on longstanding philosophical issues related to the nature of proper names. Since many cultures would consider names to be the primary markers of personal identities (see Blount, this volume), it would be unsurprising for loved ones of anomic individuals to worry that the 'forgetting' of their names is symptomatic of, or will eventually lead to, the forgetting of their identities. This implied association between names and identities has in fact been at the heart of a long philosophical debate over whether *Suzy* and *John* are just meaningless and arbitrarily assigned labels (Kripke 1980; Mills 1843), or whether they are also linked to certain descriptive properties, or knowledge, of the people they refer to (Frege 1892; Russell 1905). Suppose, for instance, that my father's name is John. The former position would contend that there is nothing in the label *John* which contributes to, or is associated with, my knowledge of him. Literary enthusiasts might interpret Shakespeare's 'a rose by any other name would smell as sweet' (*Romeo and Juliet*) as adopting a similar stance. On the other hand, the latter position would argue that the label has a specific meaning for me, and that this meaning is associated with conceptual knowledge of my father's attributes, such as 'the man who raised me'. (For a fuller treatment of these and related issues within linguistics and philosophy, see Anderson 2007, and this volume.)

Results from experimental studies of the naming performance of anomic patients can provide an empirical basis for such philosophical speculations. When framed in experimentally testable terms, the philosophical issue translates to whether one needs to access one's conceptual knowledge about an individual (i.e. the semantic system in Fig. 29.1) before being able to successfully name that individual. If the answer is yes, as implied by the latter position described above, we would expect individuals with cognitive impairment such as that brought about by Alzheimer's disease to experience relative difficulty with proper names, and to exhibit anomic symptoms. If the answer is no, there should not be any remarkable difference in naming performance between individuals who differ only in terms of their ability to access conceptual knowledge. Experiments comparing the performances of healthy and cognitively impaired subjects in providing the names of famous persons have shown that the former group was indeed more successful, and have offered support for the hypothesis that naming requires access to semantic information associated with the target[2] (Delazer et al. 2003; Hodges and Greene 1998). However, rare exceptions where the ability to produce proper names is preserved despite cognitive and semantic impairment (de Bleser 2006; Lyons et al. 2002) suggest that philosophical and scientific debate regarding the nature of proper names

[2] It is worth bearing in mind that naming difficulties could also result from degradation to the phonological system (see Fig. 29.1), rather than just the semantic system (Delazer et al. 2003), something which the aforementioned philosophical debate on the linguistic and conceptual nature of proper names has not been particularly concerned with.

has not yet been fully resolved. It suffices for the present purpose to simply observe how words bear social, philosophical, and scientific implications which are more convergent than might be often assumed.

In the next section, I turn my attention to the reciprocal direction of how linguistic theorization of words can potentially inform clinical research and application. I discuss the case of metaphor use by individuals afflicted with seizures and delusions, where the use of words is not a target of pathology, but rather a potential signpost to it.

29.4 Words as signposts to other disorders: metaphors, seizures, and delusions

In certain psychological conditions where language ability is not normally jeopardized, patterns underlying word use may well be reflective of deeper cognitive phenomena related to the condition(s) in question. Roe and Lachman (2005: 227), for example, suggest that the narratives of patients with schizophrenia or manic depression 'offer a window into the uniqueness of each individual … in conjunction with his or her strengths, weaknesses, wishes, activities, and preferences', with clear implications for diagnosis and treatment. One particular mechanism of word use which has been linked to underlying cognitive processes, and which has captured the attention of both linguists (Lakoff 1993; Lakoff and Johnson 1999) and mental health professionals (Blenkiron 2010; Stott et al. 2010) is metaphor—the mechanism of describing 'something in terms of something else' (Semino 2008: 1). If asked to give examples of metaphors, many people might think of clichés like *my lover is a rose* or *life is a journey* and regard them as aesthetically pleasing at best and redundant at worst for everyday communication. An alternative perspective from the influential Conceptual Metaphor Theory (Lakoff 1993) claims that metaphors are not only pervasive in everyday language but reflect how we *conceptualize* one concept in terms of another. Consider the following two sets of sentences used to describe the notion of anger (Lakoff and Kövecses 1987).

1. He was *boiling* in anger. He *exploded* with anger.
2. He could not *fight off* his anger. He *succumbed* to his anger.

In (1), the words *boiling* and *exploded* as used in the context of describing anger suggest that we can speak of anger in metaphorical terms as some sort of hot fluid. The claim made by Conceptual Metaphor Theory is that we are not just speaking but also actively *reasoning* about anger in terms of our knowledge about hot fluids. For example, we reason that an increase in the temperature and pressure of the hot fluid would suitably describe an increase in the amount of anger, as evidenced by the fact that most people would have little trouble understanding a novel sentence like *she was twenty degrees nearer to boiling point than I was*. Likewise, as seen in words like *fight off* and *succumbed* in (2), we can also speak and reason about anger in terms of a physical opponent to be overcome. In technical terms, concepts understood this way (e.g. anger) are known as target domains, while the concepts used to understand them (e.g. hot fluid) are known as source domains. Metaphoric conceptualization occurs when inferences from source domains are transferred, or mapped, onto target domains (Gentner and Boronat 1992; Lakoff 1993). Evidence for the cognitive import of metaphor has been directly provided by psycholinguistic experiments demonstrating that people do think in a metaphoric manner (Boroditsky 2000; Meier and Robinson 2004; Nayak and Gibbs 1990), and less directly through observations of similar source–target associations in otherwise unrelated languages like English, Mandarin Chinese, and Arabic (Maalej 2004; Yu 1998).

In the mental health context, where the conceptualization and verbal discussion of patients' mental states and life circumstances are of primary significance, the implications of metaphor have not gone unnoticed. Counsellors and psychotherapists have found that metaphors are helpful in building rapport, accessing and symbolizing patient emotions, and initiating change (Blenkiron 2010; Kopp and Craw 1998; Lyddon et al. 2001). Kopp and his associates (Kopp 1995; Kopp and Craw 1998) have provided many examples of how metaphors are used to describe patients' problems, ranging from AIDS to agoraphobia, and the therapeutic breakthroughs thus achieved. Besides playing a role in general communication, metaphors may also contribute to the more specific tasks of diagnosing and understanding patients' conditions. Consider the case of seizure attacks, where clinicians often conduct extensive interviews with patients to better understand the subjective nature of their symptoms and experiences. Interviews have become increasingly important to complement established diagnostic procedures such as electroencephalography (EEG) because they can help distinguish whether the individual's condition is neurological or more psychological in nature (Reuber 2008). Specifically, the symptoms of psychogenic non-epileptic seizures (PNES) resemble those of epileptic seizures, but are triggered by social and/or psychological distress rather than excessive electrical activity in the brain. A recent study of patient interview transcripts (Plug et al. 2009) investigated whether the types of metaphor used by patients to describe their experiences could serve as a marker to differentiate PNES from epileptic cases. Clinicians in the study asked standard open-ended questions such as *tell me about the first/last/worst seizure you can remember*, but were requested to avoid interjecting and influencing patients' responses in any way. It was found that patients who were subsequently confirmed as PNES cases were more likely to metaphorically describe seizure attacks in spatial terms, while patients subsequently confirmed as epileptic cases were more likely to describe seizure attacks as an agent or force. For example, PNES patients speak of being *out of* seizures, *within* seizures, or *going through* seizures, while epileptic patients speak of *fighting* with seizures, and seizures *creeping up* on them and *trying to do things*. The authors suggest that the key difference between these metaphors lies in the extent of agency they ascribe to the epileptic condition. Spatial metaphors imply that seizures are a mere 'passive backdrop' (Plug et al. 2009: 999) to the patient's continued ability to perform everyday actions, but agent/force metaphors may imply that seizures exert a stronger degree of control over the patient's life. Applying Conceptual Metaphor Theory, the differences in the choice of metaphors between these patient groups directly reflect differences in how seizure attacks are subjectively experienced. This would in turn provide valuable and easily accessible diagnostic information to complement EEG tests in distinguishing different patient categories. If clinicians are trained to be sensitive towards distinctive keywords which signal the use of prominent source domains such as spatiality or forces, metaphors could turn out to be useful signposts towards more effective diagnoses of epilepsy.

Another area of mental health in which patients' use of metaphorical words could reveal valuable insights is the case of delusional thought. The American Psychiatric Association (1994: 765) describes delusional thought as the firm belief in a patent falsehood. Examples of delusions include the belief that one is possessed by the devil, or that there are insects feeding on one's body (Rhodes and Jakes 2004). When overtly stated, these propositions are taken as literal by delusional patients but resemble metaphors to non-delusional individuals. Based on the hypothesis that delusional thoughts are the result of a gradual 'fusion' between two conceptual domains, Rhodes and Jakes (2004) outline a theoretical framework for the role of metaphor in the formation and maintenance of delusions. Semi-structured interviews similar to those in Plug et al.'s seizure study were used to elicit (i) patients' descriptions of their delusional thoughts, (ii) recollections of how they were formed, (iii) present experiences related to them, and (iv) problems and goals in the patients' lives. It was found that, in a number of cases, patients' recollected onset of their delusional thoughts involved incidental associations which were drawn and subsequently elaborated between two separate domains. For example, a patient who believed that she was possessed by the devil reported a childhood incident where the nuns in her religious school gave her a disapproving look, at the same time that she happened to be looking at a devil statue and wondering if she was like the devil. She eventually developed auditory hallucinations of the devil's voice and the delusional thought of possession. In Rhodes and Jakes's framework, the formation of her delusion involved moving from thinking A IS LIKE B (*I am like the devil*) to believing that A IS B (*I am possessed by the devil/I am the devil*), and (re)organizing memories and experiences in light of the new conceptual association. Similar to Plug et al.'s study, the underlying assumption is that patients' words reflect the experiences, perceptions, and cognitive schemas which are directly relevant to aspects of their psychological conditions. Linguistic frameworks which guide the systematic analysis of these words could thus make a valuable contribution to clinical practice (Tay 2012, 2013).

29.5 Patient metaphors and corpora

The examples above suggest that probing patient experiences with semi-structured interviews and other elicitation procedures may yield metaphors which offer insights into the particularities of individual conditions. Moving beyond the level of the individual patient, transcribed data from interviews may also provide a basis for building databases or corpora for the analysis of recurrent patterns and themes of metaphor use (Rhodes et al. 2005). One commercially available data source which can be used to build a corpus of psychotherapy transcripts covering different types of mental disorder and treatment approach is the *Counseling and Psychotherapy Transcripts, Client Narratives, and Reference Works* collection published by Alexander Street Press.[3] The collection includes transcripts, reference materials, video re-enactments of therapy sessions, and is mainly intended as an educational resource for mental health professionals. It is, however, also a valuable resource for researchers of mental health discourse who cannot readily collect their own data. The following are some sample research directions with clinical implications which can be investigated with standard corpus techniques:

(i) The source and target domains of metaphors in mental health discourse (e.g. therapy sessions, semi-structured interviews). More specifically, the presence of significant associations between (aspects of) particular disorders and particular source domain keyword(s), which may point towards complementary use of words as diagnostic markers.
(ii) Changes in patterns of metaphor use across time, especially in contexts like counselling and psychotherapy where ideas tend to be revisited and re-negotiated as the sessions progress (Angus and Korman 2002).
(iii) Other possible associations between the properties of metaphorical words (e.g. part of speech, novel vs. conventional, universal vs. culture-specific) and therapeutically relevant variables (e.g. type of disorder, therapeutic function of metaphor). Such associations are useful in identifying which aspects of metaphorical words might be implicated in therapeutic processes, other than their conceptual contents.

The key advantage of the corpus approach is the ability to quickly investigate linguistic forms over large amounts of text, which provides a basis for making generalizations about language use. Any comprehensive attempt to translate linguistic investigation into clinical tools is in fact likely to need to pass some generalizability criteria. Currently, however, metaphor and corpus researchers face the problem that 'conceptual mappings are not linked to particular linguistic forms' (Stefanowitsch and Gries 2006: 1), which makes automatic identification and retrieval of metaphors far from straightforward. While corpora annotated with semantic fields would help in retrieving source/target domains, such a corpus does not appear to be available yet for mental health discourse. Researchers would thus still have to either rely on preconceived lexemes or keywords or simply return to manual investigation of the data. A workable solution is to manually identify metaphorical keywords from a manageable subset of the corpus (e.g. a single

[3] Available at http://alexanderstreet.com/

therapist–patient pair) before subjecting the larger corpus to interrogation (Cameron and Deignan 2003). Another solution is to begin with a keyword analysis (Partington 2003) which may reveal particularly salient words associated with sources or targets. This might be effective for texts which deal exclusively with singular themes such as the nature of delusion in controlled semi-structured interviews, but is less likely to be successful for counselling sessions, where we can expect a diverse range of targets and sources. However, with the rapid development of new research methods and software for both qualitative and quantitative corpus analysis (Kimmel 2012; Stefanowitsch and Gries 2006), research questions of the type discussed above will be answered with increasing breadth, depth, and reliability.

29.6 Conclusion

The study of words, and language in general, profits from a consideration of both normal cases of language use and cases where the language system is afflicted. This chapter has discussed the nature of words as both targets and signposts of pathology in the context of neuropsychological disorders such as anomia, seizures, and delusional thought. With metaphor as an example, the chapter has also explored how patients' words could help us understand more about how they conceptualize and experience their afflictions, which should be a useful complementary tool for mental health professionals.

PART VI

WORDS IN ACQUISITION AND LEARNING

CHAPTER 30

FIRST WORDS

EVE V. CLARK

30.1 Introduction

WHEN do children use their first words? How recognizable are their first words? Can they always be distinguished from babbling? While some children produce a few identifiable words as early as 10 to 12 months of age, others start later and may only produce their first words around 22 to 24 months. The normal range for children beginning to talk covers a wide span, and children typically understand many words before they try to say them themselves (Clark and Hecht 1983; Fenson et al. 1994).

Children tend to favour the sounds most prevalent in their babbling in their first words. And the dividing line between babbling and something intended as a word is not always easy to draw. In addition, the first words children produce are often hard to identify because they have yet to master all the relevant articulatory skills. In their early words, young children typically omit final consonants, liquids, and unstressed syllables; they simplify consonant clusters, and they produce many homophonous forms. All this makes their first words hard to understand (McCune and Vihman 2001; Stoel-Gammon 2011). In addition, children who are just beginning to produce words lack adult-like knowledge of the meanings associated with specific words, another factor that hinders early attempts at communication with language.

In this chapter, I focus on the sources children draw on as they establish meanings for their early words, and on the role of conversational interaction in the acquisition of words and their meanings.

30.2 Conceptual basis for early word meanings

Where do children get their earliest meanings for new words? Can they build on prior conceptual development? Children could make use of existing conceptual categories as a source as they begin to assign (some) meaning to specific word forms (Clark 2004; Slobin 1985). By age 1, they have a notion of object permanence and are familiar with a variety of object categories, action types, and certain spatial relations—what can go into containers, for instance, or on supporting surfaces (Clark 1973). Their conceptual categories of objects offer a basis for word meanings grounded in what children have observed so far in the world around them—preliminary meanings for nouns that designate specific object types. In fact, children rely heavily on shape to identify instances of categories (Baldwin 1989; Gershkoff-Stowe and Smith 2004; Graham and Diesendruck 2010). They also rely on parts and their configurations for the same purpose, and start to learn part terms quite early (Kobayashi 1998; Rakison and Butterworth 1998; Saylor and Sabbagh 2004).

Young children rely on conceptual categories of actions as they start attaching meanings to their first verbs, and consistently use their early verb forms (usually a single form for each verb) for any relevant action type in context, regardless of timing (aspect and tense), gender, person (1st, 2nd, or 3rd), or number (singular, plural) of participants involved (Gathercole, Sebastián, and Soto 1999; Veneziano and Parisse 2010). As a result, because young children begin with conceptual categories of event types, their early verb uses consistently overlap with adult usage (Huttenlocher, Smiley, and Charney 1983).

Children pay attention not only to the presence of objects but also to their disappearance. Once they have established object permanence, they readily map such conceptual categories as non-presence or disappearance onto negative words like *gone* or *no* (Gopnik and Meltzoff 1986). They also appear to rely on a conceptual distinction between 'one' and 'more than one' in their earliest mapping of a notion of number to a linguistic term like English *two*, only later supplanted by the plural morpheme on nouns, in English the plural *-s* (Clark and Nikitina 2009).

Children also seem to build on conceptual categories as they start to assign meanings to prepositions and verbs used for talking about spatial relations. For instance, when given a container such as a plastic glass and a small object, 1-year-olds consistently place the object *in* the container (even when given no instruction to do so). And with a supporting surface and a moveable object, they consistently place the object *on* the surface (Clark 1973; McDonough, Choi, and Mandler 2003).

But the lexical mapping of space and spatial relations differs in different languages; and, not surprisingly, children are also heavily influenced from the start by how the adults around them use each spatial term, so this too 'shapes' their acquisition of the relevant meanings (Choi 2006; Choi et al. 1999). Compare the domains for English *put in* and *put on* with Korean *kkita* 'fit tightly/interlock' shown in Fig. 30.1.

What is important to note here is that children rely on their own experience so far—the categories of objects, actions, and relations they have observed—when they begin to attach meanings to words. But their experience with new words is modulated and further shaped by how adults use those words as they talk with young children.

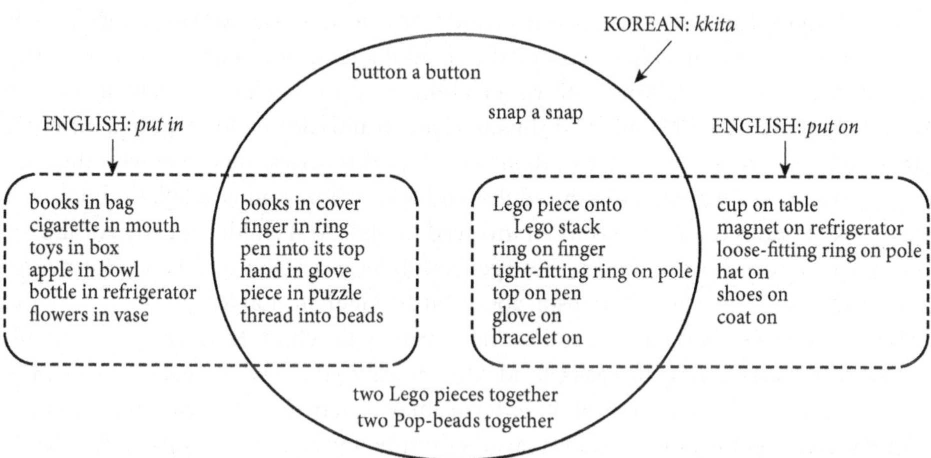

FIG. 30.1 The domains for English *putting in* or *on*, compared to Korean *kkita* 'fit tightly'.

Source: Choi (2006: 211).

30.3 Early nouns and verbs

When children first start to produce words, they produce them one at a time, often with long intervals in between. Production takes effort—both for retrieval and articulation—so children's first words are often not only hard to interpret but also hard to categorize. How can we tell whether a child at the one-word stage is producing a noun or a verb? Often we can't until children start to elaborate their early utterances by adding more words, or by adding grammatical morphemes such as word endings or pronouns, or by doing both of these things. In fact, children's choice of a particular word for picking out an object vs. an action probably depends on the initial context of acquisition. For example, some children latch onto the adult verb *open* as the word to use when opening boxes, pulling pop-beads apart, pulling a chair out from the table, and so on—with a general meaning of 'gain access to'. But others pick up the word *door* instead, for exactly the same range of activities (Griffiths and Atkinson 1978). So one has to exercise caution in identifying members of word classes like 'noun' and 'verb' when children are still using only one word at a time.

Given that caveat, several researchers have observed that children's early vocabularies (up to 100–200 words) tend to contain more adult terms for objects than for actions (Gentner 1982). Gentner ascribed this to a general difference in the complexity of reference: nouns pick out object types that typically involve just one category instance, but verbs pick out event types that require paying attention to an action and its timing as well as to however many participants are relevant in each case (the arguments of each verb). This, she argued, rendered verb meanings in general more complex than the meanings of most nouns for children learning a first language.

In addition to this difference between words for objects and actions in children's early usage, several researchers have observed that adults tend to favour nouns over verbs, overall, when they are talking with young children, for example in American English (Goldfield 1993). Indeed, both child-directed speech and early child usage in a variety of languages show more use of nouns than verbs, but this varies somewhat with the context. For example, English-speaking adults tend to use more nouns in talk to children as they look at books than they do when involved in play. And children's early vocabularies, up to 200 words or so, reflect these general differences (Kauschke and Hofmeister 2002; Kim, McGregor, and Thompson 2000; Tardif, Gelman, and Xu 1999).

But do these observations constitute a 'noun bias' in the child's lexicon? Nouns in children's speech may simply be easier to identify as associated with object referents early on, while the word-class status of other terms may be harder to identify, even later on. Moreover, the proportion of nouns (vs. other terms) rarely exceeds 35 per cent of early vocabularies (in the 50–200 word range), and often amounts to no more than 25 per cent of the child's recognizable words (Bloom, Tinker, and Margulis 1993; Sandhofer, Smith, and Luo 2000). Even more telling is that fact that adults (and their children) vary the proportions of nouns and verbs in their speech depending on the activity they are involved in. Adults consistently produce relatively more nouns when they are looking at books with their young children than when they are playing with toys with them (see Choi 2000, for American English and Korean; Tardif, Shatz, and Naigles 1997, for American English, Italian, and Mandarin). So adults do a lot of object labelling when looking at pictures in books (and hence produce more nouns), while in free play they tend to focus more on activities (hence more verbs).

In addition to this general source of variation, languages differ typologically, such that some require use of continuing nominal or pronominal references for subsequent mentions after the initial introduction of a referent, while other languages have no pronouns at all, and simply rely on the addressee to keep track of what has already been mentioned. The outcome is that some languages make proportionately more use of nouns (e.g. English, French, German) in many utterances while others make proportionately more use of verbs (e.g. Japanese, Korean, Mandarin).

In short, languages differ typologically, and language use among adults differs depending on the context of the talk, with some contexts favouring more noun uses than uses of verbs. Both factors influence how children use the words they produce from the start. In many languages, children may initially produce a slightly higher proportion of nouns than non-nouns, but in languages that favour verbs typologically, this balance quickly shifts as they acquire more vocabulary (Choi 2000).

30.4 Pragmatics of early language use

When parents talk with their young children, they take care either to follow what the child is already attending to, or else to actively establish joint attention with the child on whatever they want to draw the child's attention to (Callahan et al. 2011; Carpenter et al. 1998; Childers et al. 2007; Estigarribia and Clark 2007). Infants attend to adult gaze and follow it from an early age (Morales et al. 2000); they also follow pointing gestures (Morisette, Ricard, and Gouin-Decarie 1995). Indeed, adults rely on both gaze and gesture to capture the young child's attention (Rader and Zukow-Goldring 2010).

Once adult and child are jointly attending to the same event or the same object in context, the adult can go ahead and show it to the child, label it and talk about it, link it to other events or objects already familiar to the child, and so on. That is, joint attention is the starting point for any communicative exchange, whether verbal or non-verbal, the starting point for any kind of cooperative interaction. By starting from joint attention, the participants in any exchange can start from the same point in establishing common ground, and then adding to it as they each contribute to the exchange in progress.

What do adults and children jointly attend to? Typically this is an object or an event at the locus of joint attention, and so physically co-present with speaker and addressee. It may be something that the adult wishes to call attention to, introduce to the child, compare to something else. In each case, by establishing joint attention on it, the adult and child narrow the domain of possible reference for any (adult) speech co-present on such occasions. That is, joint attention is typically accompanied by both physical and conversational co-presence when adults interact with small children. Adults and children talk about the here-and-now, what's in the locus of joint attention. What is important about this is that this effectively eliminates much uncertainty that might otherwise be present about the (adult) speaker's intended reference.

When adults offer children words for unfamiliar objects, in fact, they first establish joint attention with the child, show them the object in question, and then proceed first to label it and then to talk about its various properties, often relating it to things already known that belong in the same conceptual domain (Clark and Estigarribia 2011). Adults thereby make use of physical and conversational co-presence as they label new objects and flag properties that distinguish those objects from near neighbours in the same domain. In this way, they set children up to learn not only the reference but also the sense of new words they encounter.

Two other pragmatic principles play a role from the beginning in language acquisition. The first is *conventionality*—the fact that all the members of a community observe a set of agreements about how their language should be used. These agreements cover vocabulary—which words to use to convey which meanings; constructions—the syntactic combinations used to convey such meanings as causation or transitivity; pronunciation—the sound system governing how to say the words of the language; and the general patterns of usage for a large stock of agreed-on meanings. Conventionality pertains to the generally accepted meaning of a term, but the precise meaning can be negotiated or adjusted to fit specific occasions. This flexibility is part of what makes languages so useful as systems for communication.

Hand-in-hand with conventionality goes the principle of *contrast*, at its most basic the principle that any difference in form signals a difference in meaning (Clark 1987, 1990). Conventionality and contrast together help people maintain a language as a communicative system. Conventions support stable meaning–form links, and contrast tells speakers when to infer that a different meaning is in play from one that might have been expected. For children, recognition of both principles is critical: learning that there is a word for *X* in the language being acquired leads them to actively request words for things, while encountering words that differ from word forms already known licenses added inferences in context about what a new, unfamiliar form might mean. Children observe both principles from early on—perhaps from the start of using language. In particular, contrast appears to play a central role in children's acquisition of new word meanings and their relations to word meanings already known (Clark and Grossman 1998; Diesendruck and Markson 2001).

Conventionality and contrast together serve to keep the neighbouring meanings of different forms distinct—for children, such close neighbours as *sofa* vs. *chair, apple* vs. *pear*, or *van* vs. *truck*, or for adults such terms as *sofa* vs. *couch, painkiller* vs. *analgesic, charitable* vs. *eleemosynary*. The differences in meaning may also be rather subtle, as in the modulations of meaning added by different case endings. Different terms may also mark social contrasts with register differences—formal vs. informal speech (choices of *vous* vs. *tu*, say), speech to an in-group vs. outsiders, speech to children vs. adults, and so on. In some societies, pronunciation and lexical choices may mark social class, and they commonly serve to identify the dialect being spoken. Adult speakers observe these differences as a matter of course; young children observe them and learn how and when to make use of them in the process of acquisition.

30.5 Discerning intentions

At what point do young children successfully identify speaker intentions? How soon do they recognize that, just as people carry out certain physical actions with a goal in mind, they also produce words with a specific goal? Several researchers have explored the ability of 1-year-olds to infer intentions by looking at the circumstances under which the infants will imitate adult actions (Gergely, Bekkering, and Király 2002). The logic is the following: if the adult is perceived to be constrained by having her hands occupied while trying to turn on a light, say, children should not copy the way she actually manages this turning on. But if she turns on the light in some unusual way and could have done so normally, then when asked to imitate, they should copy the way the adult does it. Twelve-month-olds saw either an adult clutching a shawl around her (therefore with hands occupied) and bending forward to touch a button on top of a box with her forehead in order to activate a light, or an adult not holding anything who bent forward to carry out the same action in the same way. The infants were more likely to imitate the adult's action in the second case—where nothing constrained the adult, so the manner of acting had to be deliberate or intended to be done that way—than in the first case, where holding the shawl constrained the adult's options. Indeed, in the first case, infants were more likely to reach out a hand to press the button, as shown in Fig.

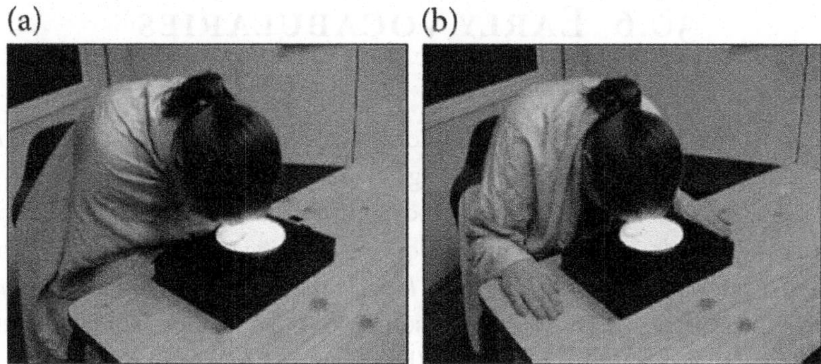

FIG 30.2 Pressing the button with hands occupied (panel a) or with hands free (panel b).

Source: Gergely, Bekkering, and Király (2002: 755); reprinted with permission.

30.2. In short, infants as young as 12 months old can make appropriate inferences about the adult's intentions.

This is important in considering the inferences children can make about adult word use. What do they infer about reference, for example, when an adult produces a word or phrase? Can they identify the intended referents of words addressed to them? Word-learning studies have shown that 2-year-olds are attentive to pragmatic cues that identify either an object or an action as the intended referent of a new word (Tomasello and Akhtar 1995). Moreover, children this age consistently select intentional actions over accidental ones in identifying the referents of new words for actions (Tomasello and Barton 1994). They also attend to speaker intentions about possible relations between two new words, and can successfully identify a superordinate–subordinate or inclusion relation after hearing only one instance of an utterance like 'A *Y* is a kind of *X*', having just learnt what an *X* was (Clark and Grossman 1998). Taken together, these findings strongly suggest that children depend on inferences about communicative intent from early on as they interact with adults talking to them. They appear to understand very early that language is for communicating: adults choose words to express their intentions, just as they choose actions.

One result of this is that even very young children are sensitive to adult repairs. If an adult mis-labels something and then makes a repair, two-year-olds take that repair into account in making further inferences about possible referents of the repaired label compared to the original label (Clark and Grossman 1998). They are also attentive to adult facial expressions of surprise and to non-specific interjections like *oops* or *uh-oh* in word-learning studies, and interpret these appropriately as indicating non-referents when they can't see the speaker's intended target for an unfamiliar label (Tomasello and Barton 1994). Finally, they make spontaneous repairs themselves, correcting their own pronunciations, for example, from as young as age 1. They typically get closer to the adult target the second time around. They correct their own word choices too, and, as they acquire more language, they repair morphological affixes, and also syntactic constructions (see further Clark 1982).

30.6 Early vocabularies

The earliest words children produce fall into similar domains at a point where they can produce around 100–200 words (around age 2). They have some words for the people around them, e.g. *mama, papa, baby* (typically in self-reference); for small moveable objects (e.g. *key, bottle, cup*); for items of clothing (e.g. *shoe, hat, mitten*); for food (e.g. *milk, juice, cheese, apple*); for toys (e.g. *ball, block, book*); for a few animals (e.g. *cat, dog, bird*); for vehicles (e.g. *car, bus, boat*); and some words for routines and activities, such as *upsy-daisy* (being lifted up), *beddie-bye* (being put to bed), *peekaboo* (game), *byebye* (waving goodbye), *up* (get up or down), *open* (request for access), *vroom* (motion of car), and so on (Clark 1995). (See Table 30.1.)

While children's early words can be sorted into groups this way, with very similar groupings observable across languages, this is just the start. Each domain is gradually elaborated as children add further words that belong in each domain and are therefore connected in meaning. For example, over time, children may start with *dog*, then add other animal terms such as *cat, sheep, horse*, and *tiger*, along with words for the kinds of noise each kind of animal makes: *woof-woof* or *bark, miaow, baa, grrr*, or *roar*. They add terms for the young of each kind: *puppy, kitten, lamb, foal, cub*. They link the different animal terms to superordinates like *animal* as well as linking terms like *dog* to more specific subordinates such as *terrier* or *boxer* (Clark 1995). The patterns of development for each domain depend on

Table 30.1 Production: typical first words from 10 to 50, by domain Based on Clark (1979), Nelson (1973), Tardif et al. (2008)

~10 words:	people–*daddy, mommy, Timmy, girl*
	moveable objects–*ball, cracker, cookie*
	places: *house*
	routines: *bye, that*
~30 words:	people: *daddy, mommy, Timmy, Anna, girl, baby*
	animals–*doggie, kitty, duck*
	moveables–*ball, key, clock, top, bottle*
	food–*cracker, cookie, juice, apple*
	places–*drawer, house*
	routines, actions–*up, bye, hi, peek-a-boo, more, all gone, hot, that*
~50 words:	people–*daddy, mommy, Timmy, Anna, Lee, Jan, girl, baby*
	animals–*doggie, kitty, duck, pig, cow*
	moveables–*ball, book, glasses, key, watch, top, light, rock, bottle*
	vehicles–*car, boat*
	clothing–*shoe, sock, hat*
	food–*cracker, cookie, juice, apple, rice, turkey, pea*
	body-parts–*ear, eye, toes*
	places–*drawer, box, house*
	routines, actions–*up, bye, hi, no, peek-a-boo, more, all gone, hot, that*

children's experiences as they grow up. Some children learn many animal terms by age 4, while others become more expert with terms for dinosaurs or cars (Chi and Koeske 1983). Others still may, early on, learn many terms for different kinds of birds or plants. As they get older, children fill in many domains to some degree, but in the end differ considerably in the depth of knowledge that accompanies each domain, just as adults do.

Early vocabulary size and content appears to be quite similar across languages, as judged from data collected for Cantonese, Danish, Dutch, English, French, Hebrew, Italian, Korean, and Mandarin. Researchers have measured similarity in terms of children's early words in both comprehension and production, using very similar versions of the same checklist—the Communicative Development Inventory (CDI)—across languages (Bleses et al. 2008; Bornstein et al. 2004; Brown 1998; Caselli et al. 1999; D'Odorico et al. 2001; Fenson et al. 1994; Kern 2010). However, comprehension scores for some languages appear to be lower early on than for others. For example, in Danish, the phonology of the language appears to present children with a real challenge as they try to identify words in the speech stream, and their scores for comprehension are considerably lower than for children the same age acquiring English (Bleses et al. 2008).

What do children use their first words for? Essentially they add more specific content to their earlier communication of assertions (signalled with pointing gestures) and requests (reaching gestures) (Bates, Camaioni, and Volterra 1975; Bruner 1975; Werner and Kaplan 1963). Their early gestural communications are sometimes accompanied by vocalization of some kind as well, before they manage any recognizable words (Carter 1978; Masur 1983). At this stage, children's gestures, like their earliest words, play an important role in directing adult attention to what is currently of interest to the child, or to what the child actively wants (Golinkoff 1986). The addition of words makes their early gestural communications more specific and so more readily interpretable in context (Kelly 2011; Masur 1983; Olson and Masur 2011).

At what point do young children realize that words can serve communicative needs? While they commonly begin to communicate by relying on gestures, often combined with some kind of vocalization, by the age of one they can readily associate sequences of sounds and words with objects (Woodward and Hoyne 1999). When 1-year-olds are presented with novel objects while the experimenter produces either a word for the object or a sound (from a small noise-maker), they readily associate either one with a new object, but by 1;8, they no longer associate a sound with an object. This suggests that they home in on language as a communicative device with age, as they come to realize that there are conventional, established words for objects, actions, and relations (Clark 1987, 1990; Grosse et al. 2010).

30.7 Lexical packaging

Lexical packaging presents another typological factor in the acquisition of word meanings: different languages 'package' meanings differently in certain domains (see Majid, this volume). One domain that has been studied in some detail is that of position and motion in space. For example, in some languages, motion verbs incorporate information about manner of motion as well motion itself, as in English *stroll* (which can be glossed as 'move on foot in a casual, leisurely manner'), *stride* (move on foot with a purpose), *run* (move fast on foot), and so on, and they place information about direction of motion in satellite particles and adverbs like *up, down, out*, and *away* as in *go up the hill, go off along the edge of the river*, etc.). In other languages, verbs of motion tend to combine information about motion and direction or path, as in Spanish *bajar* 'go down', *entrar* 'go in', *salir* 'go out', and leave manner to optionally added phrases (e.g. *corriendo* 'running', *flotando* 'floating') or simply to be inferred from context (see further Slobin 1996;Talmy 1985).

How do children acquire such verbs? Mastering the intricacies of motion verb meanings takes time, and children acquiring a language like English may rely for some time on general-purpose verbs like *go* for motion or *put* for placement in space (Clark 1978; see also Chenu and Jisa 2006). But children acquiring other languages may adopt very specific verbs (without necessarily having acquired the full meanings) from a very early age. This holds for children learning languages like Tzeltal (Brown 1998) and Tzotzil (de Léon 1999), for example, where the placement verb serves simultaneously as a classifier for the type of object being manipulated, as well as for languages like Hebrew (Armon-Lotem and Berman 2003; Keren-Portnoy 2006) and Korean (Choi and Gopnik 1995; Kim, McGregor, and Thompson 2000). Overall, children attend to adult usage and adopt whatever forms adults favour for specific activity types. The same holds true for children's acquisition of terms for specific object types.

30.8 What is the vocabulary spurt?

In the first six years of life, children acquire an estimated 14,000 words, averaging some nine words a day from age 1 on (Carey 1978). Somewhere between 18 and 22 months, many children give evidence of a rather rapid shift in their rate of word production (Goldfield and Reznick 1990; Rescorla, Mirak, and Singh 2000). Researchers have proposed a variety of explanations, ranging from the advent of a 'naming insight' (that there are words for all the things around one) to conceptual reorganization(s) triggered by the acquisition of the first words, or to the emergence of (new) strategies for acquiring words—for instance, the recognition that word meanings contrast, so each new word encountered must differ in meaning from those already acquired (Clark 1990). But these explanations probably all depend to some extent on yet another factor.

The large individual differences in children's rates of word acquisition depend in part on differences in motor ability. The clarity of children's articulations is important in determining how recognizable any newly acquired words are to the adults around them. Some children take several days or even weeks of attempting a new word before they can produce a recognizable version, while others manage this after only one or two attempts (Clark 1993; Dromi 1987; see also Iverson 2010; Stoel-Gammon 2011; Vihman, DePaolis, and Keren-Portnoy

2009). Moreover, children may not even attempt to produce any combinations of words until they can readily produce single words in a recognizable fashion (Dromi 1986).

Another factor that contributes to individual differences is the amount of speech adults address directly to children early on. The more conversational interaction they participate in before age three, for example, the larger children's vocabularies are upon entry to school. And, already at age 2, those children who are talked to more have larger vocabularies and process familiar words faster than children who have been talked to less (Fernald and Marchman 2011; Hart and Risley 1995).

But does the onset of an increase in children's ability to produce more and more words require a special explanation of its own, or it is simply the statistical outcome of the general learning processes involved in acquiring new words? McMurray (2007) argued convincingly that no special explanation is necessary. Rather, the so-called vocabulary spurt is the natural outcome of steady additions to the child's vocabulary. Acceleration, he pointed out, is to be expected in any system where (a) words are being acquired in parallel and (b) those words differ in difficulty so some are picked up quickly while others take longer. Difficulty itself can be attributed to a range of factors, including phonological complexity, length, frequency, contexts of use, and the child's degree of fine motor skill. Using a statistical model, McMurray demonstrated that, given a Gaussian distribution, the rate of acquisition in production will appear to accelerate over time when there are fewer easy words (those learned early) compared to a larger proportion of harder words overall. In short, the vocabulary spurt or vocabulary explosion in production is a side effect of parallel learning combined with variation in how much time it takes to learn to produce new words.

30.9 Co-occurrence and Collocation

Many of the earliest word combinations children produce tend to be fixed or formulaic in nature, with the same phrases and combinations being used each time with specific target words (Lieven, Pine, and Baldwin 1997). When children hear words in the speech around them, those words tend to occur most frequently or only in one particular combination. For example, some nouns occur with a definite article (*the*) more often than with an indefinite article (*a*); some verbs appear first with particular objects (*drink milk*, *eat bread*), and some nouns with particular adjectives (e.g. *little boy, three blind mice*). That is, with word combinations some collocations are more frequent than others, and certain 'frames' may be much more frequent for some target words than others, e.g. *sit in your chair* vs. *sit in your truck* (Bannard and Matthews 2008).

Frequent sequences, made up of two, three, or four words, appear to be stored together in memory, and so become readily accessed as whole chunks in production (Arnon and Clark 2011). This suggests that children do not simply target isolated words as they are acquiring language; they also attend to the immediate linguistic contexts of words, and store those as well. And as they work on the meanings of unfamiliar words in such frames, the meanings of elements within the frames may also offer clues to new word meanings (Goodman, McDonough, and Brown 1998). For example, terms from the same semantic domain can generally appear in the same syntactic frames.

Where do frames come from? First, adults make frequent use of them as they present young children with new words. They serve to highlight the word at the end of a clause and so draw particular attention to that word in context (Clark 2010; Clark and Estigarribia 2011). Second, as adults interact with young children, they encourage them to contribute too, whether just one word, or more than that, to complete an utterance initiated by the adult. Adult and child effectively share in the construction of utterances that are more complex than those produced by the children on their own. Several researchers have argued that this is the route into syntax for young children. This is where they learn how to combine words into constructions (Scollon 1976; Veneziano, Sinclair, and Berthoud 1990). Furthermore, their ability to produce word combinations depends on vocabulary size: the larger their vocabulary, the earlier they appear to produce word combinations (McGregor, Sheng, and Smith 2005).

30.10 Common Ground and Information Flow

Words help in establishing common ground. With joint attention, adult and child may have common ground in a particular setting, and that narrows the possibilities for what the adult or child is talking about on that occasion. As a result, young children often initiate exchanges even with single-word utterances, picking out a topic in context. And the adult interlocutor follows up, typically ratifying the child's choice of topic, thereby placing it in common ground, and adding some new information for the child to take in. At the same time, the child is still limited by a small vocabulary and lack of skill in retrieving the appropriate words as needed.

Adults help children get going in part by scaffolding, presenting an event already in common ground, an event where the child can insert missing (new) information when the adult pauses and waits, as in the exchange in (1):

(1) Mother: Did you see Philip's bird? Can you tell Herb?
Child (1;6.11): *Head, head, head.*
Mother: What landed on your head?
Child: *Bird.*

Many conversations with very young children consist of just such adult scaffolding, with child 'insertions', and occasional additions of new information, generally by the adult participant. In fact, children often initiate exchanges, even when very young, but they have difficulty contributing new information as the exchange proceeds, as shown in (2):

(2) Child (1;9.7, opening cover of tape-recorder): *Open. Open. Open.*
Adult: Did you open it?
Child (watching tape-recorder): *Open it.*
Adult: Did you open the tape-recorder?
Child (still watching): *Tape-recorder.*

Here the child ratifies (repeats) each piece of information added by the adult, but adds nothing new himself in his later turns (Clark 2007; Veneziano, Sinclair, and Berthoud 1990).

Adults often repeat the information offered by the child in initiating an exchange, but they generally add something more in doing so, as in (2). In this way they can advance the exchange by first acknowledging or ratifying what the child said, and then adding something new to that. This information flow, from given to new within each speaker's turn, follows the pattern of first introducing something, then placing it in common ground (as given), and then adding something new. By age 2, children readily ratify new information offered by others, typically by repeating it. But they take another couple of years or so before they consistently add new information themselves to whatever is already in common ground (Clark and Bernicot 2008; see also McTear 1985; Scollon 1976). While children start to participate in conversational exchanges with their first words, they take several years to learn how to contribute appropriately, not only ratifying what is new from the other speaker, but also contributing new information themselves.

30.11 Adult feedback

As they talk with their children, adults offer feedback about the words they use—how they say them, whether it's the right word for the occasion; about the forms of the words—how they should be said to be understood; and about the constructions used, given the child's apparent intended meaning. When young children over-extend words early on, for example, adults can respond in several ways. They could simply accept the child's usage. They can also reject it (*That's not a dog*), offer a more appropriate label (*That's a cat*), or both correct and offer an alternative in the same utterance (*That's not a dog; it's a cat*). Finally, adults could both provide a new label and add a reason for why it's (more) appropriate (Mervis 1984). Chapman and her colleagues (1986) compared three forms of feedback—acceptance, correction with a replacement term, and correction with some explanation attached—as responses to young children's spontaneous over-extensions between age 1;3 and 1;7. Overall, correction with explanation was the most effective over time: *That's a yo-yo—see the string?*, followed by correction with replacement: *That's not a ball, it's a yo-yo*. This suggests that children take account of the added information about some property of the referent type in dropping their earlier over-extensions of words like *ball*. Interestingly, when parents offer their children new words, they typically also provide information about properties that will help distinguish one category from another, information about parts and properties, and about motion and function (Clark 2007; Clark and Estigarribia 2011).

But adults don't only correct their children when they pick the wrong word. They are constantly monitoring them to make sure they have understood what their children intended to say: they check on pronunciations of words; they check on word choices; they check on morphology—both inflections and free morphemes; and they check on syntactic constructions. In doing this, they reformulate their children's utterances mainly with side-sequences, questions couched in conventional form that present children with the meaning the adult thinks was intended on that occasion. The child can then accept the reformulation, or reject it if the adult misunderstood. (Children reject adult reformulations about 10 per cent of the time.) The importance of such reformulations is that they present children with a conventional way to say *X*, and simultaneously offer them a direct contrast to whatever form the child had just used (Chouinard and Clark 2003). In Western cultures, middle-class adults reformulate up to 60 per cent of child errors of phonology, morphology, lexicon, and syntax from age 1;6 to 3 or 3;6. So, within the natural course of conversation, as adults check up on what their children mean, they simultaneously offer corrective feedback about the conventional way to say things, and they do this so as to contrast the conventional form with the child's error.

30.12 Conclusion

Words are devices for making one's intentions more accessible to others, but to succeed in using words appropriately for this purpose children must learn several things. They must learn first to produce words so they are recognizable to their addressee. They must establish some meaning for each word they produce, and add to these meanings until their uses of each word largely coincide with adult patterns of use. They must learn to access and retrieve the word needed for a specific occasion. They must also go beyond uses of single words alone to produce combinations of words. In doing this, they need to adopt the syntactic constructions licensed by the ambient language. And they need to do all this in order to be able to participate in communicative exchanges using language.

From their first words on, young children appear to adopt words as a tool for communication. Their words clarify the intent associated with such gestures as pointing and reaching, and supplant symbolic gestures taught early on for communicative purposes. In their productions of words, children appear to attend from the start to the same pragmatic factors that adults rely on in *using* language—joint attention, physical co-presence, and conversational co-presence. They also recognize early on that language is conventional—this is what allows people to use language for communication: the users have agreed on what each word generally means within their community.

Children's first words, then, place demands on children: they must learn to say them and to use them to communicate their intentions, and so make clearer what they are interested in and what they want from one occasion to the next.

CHAPTER 31

HOW INFANTS FIND WORDS

KATHARINE GRAF ESTES

31.1 Introduction

To learn what a word means, or to learn how a word functions in sentences, infants must first discover individual words in the continuous stream of speech. For adults, detecting words seems like a trivial problem because they can rapidly use stored knowledge of known words to segment the speech signal. However, when hearing an unfamiliar language, adults encounter the same problem that infants face in their native language. It is difficult to tell where one word ends and the next begins because spoken language does not contain fully reliable acoustic cues to word boundaries. The segmentation problem is even more difficult for infants than for adults because infants lack a priori knowledge that the speech stream consists of individual units, that they must detect these units, then decipher their meanings, and link them together in sentences to extract higher-level structure. Yet before 1 year of age infants begin to find words and to make sense of the words they detect. This crucial achievement sets the stage for further advances in language acquisition. The present chapter addresses the development of infants' ability to segment words. It examines the information that infants use to discover words, as well as the connections between word segmentation and vocabulary acquisition.

A seminal study by Jusczyk and Aslin (1995) provided early evidence that infants can detect words in continuous speech. Jusczyk and Aslin tested 6- and 7.5-month-olds' ability to recognize word forms within fluent speech passages when they had previously heard the words presented in isolation. This series of experiments, and many subsequent word segmentation experiments, used the head-turn preference procedure. In the procedure, infants were first familiarized with a pair of native language (English) words presented in isolation, with pauses between repetitions (e.g. *bike* … *bike* …). During testing, infants heard passages that contained the familiarized target words (e.g. 'The girl rode her big *bike*') and passages that contained novel words ('The *cup* was bright and shiny'). Differences in infants' listening times to the passages indicated whether they detected the familiarized words. To measure listening time, the test passages were played from speakers mounted near blinking lights on the left and right sides of the room. When the infant looked toward a light, a test passage played. When the infant looked away, the passage stopped. Thus, infants controlled the duration of their listening time to the stimuli. Jusczyk and Aslin found that 7.5-month-olds listened longer to the passages with familiarized target words than to passages with novel words. This demonstrates that infants detected the target words within the passages. Six-month-olds did not discriminate the two types of passages, thereby giving no indication that they had detected the target words. Over this brief time window, between 6 months and 7.5 months, infants develop the ability to detect words in continuous speech. Jusczyk and Aslin (1995) also found that 7.5-month-olds could perform the reverse process; when they were first familiarized with words embedded in passages, they listened longer to isolated repetitions of the target words than to novel words. This measure of infants' attention to familiar and novel words has revealed the capabilities and limitations of infant word segmentation. Jusczyk and Aslin's (1995) study provided the foundation for a rich literature exploring the emergence of infants' ability to find words in continuous speech.

31.2 Early use of known words to detect new words

One of the earliest processes that infants use to detect words is quite similar to the primary process that adults use. Given their large lexicons, adults frequently apply top-down knowledge of stored lexical units to segment words, including unfamiliar words (e.g. Marslen-Wilson and Welsh 1978; McClelland and Elman 1986). For known words, boundaries are already well defined. Adults can also readily use the known words surrounding a novel word to identify the new item. Infants lack large vocabularies, but some words are highly frequent in infants' input and may be detected quite early. For example, infants hear many repetitions of their own names and names for their caregivers. Bortfeld et al. (2005) found that 6-month-old infants can recognize their own names as well as the highly familiar word *Mommy* in passages of running speech. Furthermore, they found that infants can take advantage of these early words to detect new words. When infants heard passages containing the familiar word (*Mommy* or the child's own name) followed by a consistent target word (e.g. *Mommy's <u>feet</u>*), they used the familiar word to segment the target word. During testing, infants listened longer to repetitions of target words than to repetitions of novel words. Infants did not show this discrimination pattern when presented with an unfamiliar name preceding the target during familiarization, even if it was phonologically similar to a familiar name (e.g. *Tommy's <u>feet</u>*). The infants required the anchor of a salient, highly familiar word in order to support the discovery of a new word. This study demonstrates that young infants can use stored word knowledge to segment continuous speech. Because of infants' small vocabularies, their use of known words is limited, but the mechanism is consistent with how adults segment speech.

31.3 Learning from words in isolation

Stored word knowledge supports the ability to learn more words. However, infants cannot fully rely on known words to segment speech. How do infants break into the speech signal when they only know a few words? Words produced in isolation may provide novice language learners with a way to start identifying and storing words. When words occur surrounded by silence, the signal is pre-segmented, allowing infants to learn about the word's phonological form without working to extract it from the surrounding context. Brent and Siskind (2001) have proposed that infants acquire an initial vocabulary of words heard in isolation that they subsequently use to detect other words. In support of this argument, Brent and Siskind analysed samples of mothers speaking to their 9- to 15-month-old infants. They found that about 9 per cent of mothers' speech to infants consisted of words in isolation. Importantly, a substantial number of the words in infants' early vocabularies were words that had previously occurred in isolation. Furthermore, the frequency with which a mother produced a given word in isolation reliably predicted the child's ability to produce that word later in development; sheer frequency of exposure was not a reliable predictor of word use. Lew-Williams, Pelucchi, and Saffran (2011) have also provided experimental evidence that hearing words in isolation can help infants to detect words in fluent speech, even when they are listening to an unfamiliar language.

31.4 Detecting words at utterance edges

In addition to words in isolation, words that occur at the beginnings and ends of utterances provide relatively clear word boundary information. One word boundary is available 'for free' because it follows or precedes a pause. There is evidence that the edges of utterance boundaries are particularly useful for infants' word segmentation. Seidl and Johnson (2006) found that 8-month-old infants segmented words at utterance edges more readily than words that occurred in the middle of sentences. The effect was the same for words that occurred utterance-initially or utterance-finally. Seidl and Johnson explained that these findings support the Edge Hypothesis: infants use utterance edges to detect words in fluent speech, therefore words that occur at utterances edges will be easier to segment than completely embedded words. This may occur because of the silences that precede and follow utterances, or because of the strengthening and word lengthening that commonly occur at the beginnings and ends of utterances. There could also be a broad cognitive or perceptual bias to attend to the beginnings and ends of sequences. Many of these facilitative effects could also occur at other types of boundary, such as those that occur at mid-utterance pauses or at intonational phrases (e.g. Nazzi et al. 2000). These possible explanations are not mutually exclusive. There may be a combination of effects driving the facilitation of word segmentation at utterance edges. Regardless of the underlying cause, infants' use of edges has potential to be a powerful cue for detecting words.

However, words in isolation and at the edges of utterances are insufficient to fully support the development of word segmentation skills. Even infant-directed speech primarily consists of continuous sequences that contain multiple words (Brent and Siskind 2001; see also Fernald and Morikawa 1993). Many of the words that infants must learn will not frequently occur at edges, in isolation, or surrounded by highly familiar words. However, there are numerous cues to word boundaries that provide additional support for detecting words. Although none of these cues is fully reliable, they provide probabilistic word boundary indicators that can be combined to facilitate segmentation.

31.5 Stress cues to word boundaries

One source of information for identifying word boundaries is stress patterns. From very early in life, infants are sensitive to prosody (Mehler et al. 1988; Nazzi, Bertoncini, and Mehler 1998). For example, lexical stress is a salient acoustic characteristic of the speech signal, and infants discriminate words with different lexical stress patterns by 2 months of age (Jusczyk and Thompson 1978). Lexical stress provides a strong segmentation cue. For example, most English bisyllabic words follow a trochaic stress pattern in which strong (stressed) syllables precede weak (unstressed) syllables (e.g. BAby). The opposing iambic pattern, in which weak syllables precede strong syllables, occurs in English but is less common (e.g. guiTAR). English-speaking adults use stressed syllables to identify word onsets (Cutler and Norris 1988; McQueen, Norris, and Cutler 1994), and there is evidence that infants do as well (Curtin, Mintz, and Christiansen 2005; Echols, Crowhurst, and Childers 1997; Morgan 1996). Jusczyk, Houston, and Newsome (1999) found that 7.5-month-olds segmented trochaic syllable sequences from fluent speech passages. When presented with iambic sequences, they mis-segmented, interpreting the stressed syllable as the word-initial syllable. By 10.5 months, infants could correctly segment iambic words, possibly by integrating other cues to word boundaries. However, stress has been found to be a particularly powerful word segmentation cue. At around 8–9 months of age and beyond, infants weigh stress cues more heavily than syllable-level patterns (Johnson and Jusczyk 2001; Johnson and Seidl 2009) or phoneme-level word boundary markers (Mattys et al. 1999). Thus, attention to where stressed syllables fall in the speech signal provides important information regarding where words begin and end.

31.6 Statistical cues to word boundaries

In order for infants to use native language stress patterns to detect words, they must be able to determine what the predominant lexical stress patterns are. The same principle holds for other language-specific cues to word boundaries (discussed in more detail below). Infants must know how cues align with word onsets and offsets in order for the information to be useful. This seems to require that infants extract a vocabulary of stored phonological forms and detect the recurrent patterns across them, such as 'English words frequently have stressed first syllables'. Isolated words and words at utterance edges will provide infants with some segmented items, but others must be extracted from continuous speech. One source of information for establishing an initial lexicon of segmented words is based on patterns of sound co-occurrences in the language. Over speech corpora, sound sequences within words occur together more reliably than sound sequences that cross word boundaries (Harris 1955; Swingley 2005). Moreover, young infants, as well as children and adults, are able to detect these patterns of transitional probability cues to word boundaries (Aslin, Saffran, and Newport 1998; Saffran, Aslin, and Newport 1996; Saffran et al. 1997).

To test infants' ability to use transitional probabilities in word segmentation, Saffran et al. (1996) presented 8-month-olds with an artificial language in which the only reliable word boundary cues were the patterns of transitional probabilities within and across words. Within words, the transitional probability from one syllable to the next was perfect (1.0) because these syllables reliably co-occurred. For example, the infants heard fluent speech sequences like *golatu#pabiku#tibudo#daropi*. Within the word *golatu*, the syllable *go* was always followed by *la* and *tu*. However, the syllable *tu* could be followed by any of the three remaining word-onset syllables in the language (*pa, ti, da*). Therefore, the transitional probability from one syllable to the next was lower (.33) across word boundaries. After only 2 minutes of listening to the language, infants demonstrated learning of its structure. During testing, infants discriminated between words from the language and low transitional probability part-word sequences that had crossed word boundaries (e.g. *bu#pabi*), showing longer listening times to the novel part-words. There is recent evidence that infants as young as 5 months can use transitional probability information in statistical word segmentation tasks (Thiessen and Erikson 2013; and perhaps even younger, see Teinonen et al. 2009).

Infants may use transitional probability information to segment words from continuous speech before they have access to other cues (Saffran and Thiessen 2003). It is not necessary to generalize a pattern across vocabulary items (e.g. stressed syllables usually start words) in order to use transitional probability. Rather, it can act as a language-general mechanism that is available before infants have learned word boundary indicators that are specific to their native languages. Thiessen and Saffran (2003) reported that when transitional probability and stress cues were placed in conflict (i.e. when stress occurred on the second syllable of statistically defined words),

7-month-olds weighed the transitional probability patterns more heavily than the stress patterns, but 9-month-olds showed the opposite pattern. Johnson and Jusczyk (2001) and Johnson and Seidl (2009) also found that 9- and 11-month-olds followed stress cues, rather than syllable-transitional probability cues. Thiessen and Saffran (2003, 2007; see also Thiessen and Erickson 2013) have proposed that infants use transitional probability information to acquire a small vocabulary of stored word forms. Based on this vocabulary, they can extract regularities, such as how stressed syllables correlate with word boundaries, as well as other language-specific cues that can be used to detect words in fluent speech. As knowledge of language-specific cues strengthens, reliance on transitional probability may decline.

31.7 Phonotactic cues

In addition to syllable-level probabilities, language-specific phoneme patterns also mark words. The phonotactic patterns of a language include the constraints on the allowable locations and combinations in which phonemes can occur in a given language, as well as the frequency of occurrence of phonemes and phoneme combinations. Phonotactic information can serve as a word boundary cue once infants have learned that some phonemes and phoneme combinations do not occur word-initially or word-finally in their native language. For example, in English, words do not start with the phoneme /ŋ/ (the final consonant in *sing*), and cannot end with the consonant /h/ (the initial consonant in *hat*). English words also do not begin or end with certain consonant clusters. This information can identify word boundaries. For example, if a listener encounters a phoneme sequence such as /bd/, phonotactic information indicates that a word boundary is present because words do not begin or end with /bd/ in English. However, the cluster can occur in continuous speech across a word boundary, as in the phrase *bad boy*. Thus, knowledge of the constraints on phoneme combinations and locations can guide listeners to the correct interpretation of word onsets and offsets.

Adults use phonotactic information in word recognition. McQueen (1998) demonstrated that participants were faster to identify words in fluent speech when the sequences contained phonotactic cues to word boundaries. Mattys and Jusczyk (2001) investigated this process in 9-month-olds. Infants listened to passages of speech that contained target (nonsense) words. One word (e.g. *gaffe*) was embedded in a phonotactic context that supported word segmentation. That is, the phoneme sequences in which the word was embedded formed consonant clusters at the target word onsets and offsets that rarely (or never) occur within native-language (English) words. Rather, the phoneme sequences typically occur across word boundaries. For example, the target word *gaffe* occurred in sentences such as *A spun gaffe heads the list of new inventions*. The sequences /n/–/g/ and /f/–/h/ do not typically occur within English words, and so these consonant sequences indicate likely word boundaries. In contrast, the other word (e.g. *tove*) was embedded in a phonotactic context that did not support word segmentation.

Rather, the phoneme sequences at the onset and the offset of the target word typically occurred within English words. The target word *tove* occurred in sentences such as *A gruff tove knows most forest animals*. The consonant clusters /f/–/t/ and /v/–/n/ can occur at word boundaries, but they also occur within English words, allowing the target word to blend into the surrounding words. In testing, infants heard repetitions of the two target words as well as repetitions of novel words. Compared to the novel words, infants listened longer to the words that had been embedded in the phonotactic contexts that supported segmentation. They did not differentiate the novel words from the words embedded in the poor phonotactic segmentation contexts. This suggests that the infants recognized the words from the good phonotactic segmentation contexts when they were subsequently produced in isolation, but not the words from the poor contexts. Thus, by 9 months of age infants are sensitive to language-specific phoneme patterns, and can use them in word segmentation.

31.8 Allophonic cues

Another type of phonemic word boundary cue present in fluent speech is allophonic variation. Phonemes are realized differently depending on word position. For example, the /t/ produced at word onset is aspirated (*tip* is pronounced [tʰɪp]), but the word-internal /t/ in *stop* is not. Jusczyk, Hohne, and Bauman (1999) tested the sensitivity of 9- and 10.5-month olds to these subtle differences in phoneme realizations as they occur in fluent speech (see also Hohne and Jusczyk 1994). The infants were presented with a two-syllable item that could be produced with two different allophonic variations of the phonemes /t/ and /r/: half of the infants heard *night rates* and half heard *nitrates*. They were also familiarized with an unrelated word (e.g. *hamlet*). During testing, infants heard passages that contained both allophonic variation target words as well as the unrelated words. The 10.5-month-olds listened significantly longer to the alternative variation of the target word; that is, infants exposed to *night rates* treated *nitrates* like an unfamiliar word (and vice versa). The 9-month-olds displayed no difference in listening time. This series of experiments shows that by 10.5-months of age, infants are sensitive to the patterns of allophonic variations that occur within and across words in fluent speech. Therefore, they may be able to use this information to detect words.

31.9 Integrating word boundary markers

The studies reviewed above indicate that there are many cues to word boundaries present in the speech stream. However, none of these cues is fully reliable. A given child will not hear every word produced in isolation, some words will have non-dominant stress patterns, and some will begin with infrequent phoneme sequences that also occur across word boundaries. If an infant relies too strongly on any individual cue, she is in danger of mis-segmenting or failing to segment a substantial portion of her input. However, there is power in integrating multiple probabilistic word boundary indicators. One way that multiple cues can be beneficial is that learners may use the presence of one cue to detect new informative cues. For example, as discussed above, Thiessen and Saffran (2003, 2007) have proposed that infants use transitional probability information to learn about lexical stress. Lew-Williams et al. (2011) found that infants can integrate words in isolation with transitional probability information to facilitate word segmentation. In addition, Sahni, Seidenberg, and Saffran (2010) reported that infants could use a language-general segmentation cue, transitional probability, to discover a novel language-specific cue to word onsets.

Studies examining the integration of word segmentation cues have largely addressed how infants interpret cues when they are placed in conflict (e.g. Johnson and Jusczyk 2001; Thiessen and Saffran 2003; Mattys et al. 1999). However, there is evidence that infants can integrate converging information to detect cohesive sequences in speech. Morgan and Saffran (1995; see also Morgan 1994) presented 6- and 9-month-olds with syllable strings that contained correlated cues; both syllable sequence patterns and rhythmic patterns indicated that the syllables formed a coherent unit. In other conditions, infants heard syllable strings in which the cues conflicted or were unavailable. One cue indicated that the syllables should be grouped together, but the other did not, or no cues were present. The 9-month-olds only displayed evidence of grouping the syllable sequences into cohesive units when both cues were present. They seemed to require the availability of the converging cues to word structure. In contrast, 6-month-olds did not take advantage of the conjunction of the patterns as effectively as the older infants. The ability to integrate word segmentation cues may require developmental time and experience to fully emerge. Studies demonstrating how infants integrate convergent information or use an early segmentation strategy to detect new cues support the idea that the complexity present in the ambient language is important for development. Rather than hindering acquisition, the richness of the linguistic signal may facilitate word segmentation, and language acquisition more broadly (Sahni et al. 2010; Smith and Yu 2008; Yu and Smith 2007).

Computational models also indicate that multiple converging information sources can facilitate word segmentation. For example, Christiansen, Allen, and Seidenberg (1998) designed a connectionist model of word segmentation that was able to reliably identify word boundaries based on a conjunction of cues. The model, a simple recurrent network, was exposed to a corpus of infant-directed speech. The input included information about phonemes, lexical stress patterns, and utterance boundaries. When all sources of information were available, the network could reliably identify word boundaries. However, none of these sources of information alone was sufficient to mark the words. Perruchet and Tillmann (2010) also examined the abilities of computational models and human adults to integrate word boundary cues such as transitional probabilities, the perceived word-likeness of sequences, and the context that emerged when word boundary markers were present for some but not all words. Human participants and the models were better able to detect word-like chunks when multiple cues to word boundary locations were available than when only transitional probability information supported segmentation.

Many computational models have addressed the word segmentation problem (reviewed in Brent 1999). The models differ in characteristics such as the nature of the input, learning algorithms, and how the output of learning is represented (e.g. Frank et al. 2010; Mirman et al. 2010; Monaghan and Christiansen 2010; Perruchet and Tillmann 2010; Räsänen 2011; Rytting, Brew, and Fosler-Lussier 2010). But a common theme in many models is the assumption that in order to process speech, it is necessary to identify individual words in the speech stream. Moreover, young learners must detect words in order to associate meanings with them and to determine how they function in sentences. Swingley's (2005) computational model focused on the effectiveness of infants' word segmentation mechanisms for extracting real words from infant-directed speech. Swingley proposed that infants use clustering strategies to detect coherent sound sequences. The model indicated that regularities present in syllable co-occurrences can support the detection of a substantial number of real words. Swingley proposed that infants use patterns of syllable probabilities to detect statistically cohesive sound sequences that increase in familiarity. The items enter a 'protolexicon' of words that have a representational foundation in memory (Swingley 2005: 118). These stored units may then be available for further linguistic processing, such as being associated with meanings or in tracking syntactic patterns.

31.10 Learning meanings for segmented words

Experimental evidence further strengthens the notion that infants detect and store word forms and then apply those representations to the process of associating forms with meanings during word learning. Swingley (2007) found that 19-month-olds showed stronger learning of object names when the infants first heard the names embedded in speech passages before they acted as object labels. Exposure to the phonological forms led to more precise representations of the labels: infants detected mispronunciations that they failed to detect without prior experience hearing the words in passages. Several recent experiments have probed the connection between word segmentation and word learning by investigating how infants use specific word segmentation cues, such as syllable transitional probabilities, phonotactics, or prosody, to extract words and then apply those units to support linguistic functions.

In one such experiment, Graf Estes et al. (2007) examined infants' ability to detect words using statistical cues, then to use those words as object labels. The 17-month-old infants first participated in a word segmentation task. They listened to an artificial language in which the only cue to word boundaries was the pattern of syllable transitional probabilities within words (high probability) vs. across-word boundaries (low probability), similar to the statistical learning experiments described previously (e.g. Saffran et al. 1996). After listening to the speech stream, they immediately participated in an object-labelling task. For one group of infants, the objects were labelled with words from the artificial language. For the other group of infants, the objects were labelled with low transitional probability sequences that crossed word boundaries or syllable sequences that never occurred together in the speech stream. Graf Estes et al. (2007; see also Graf Estes 2012) found that infants only learned the labels when they had prior opportunity to segment them from the speech stream; they learned the high-probability words as labels, but not the low-probability sequences. Hay et al. (2011) found a similar pattern of results when infants listened to an unfamiliar natural language (English-learning infants presented with Italian). Graf Estes and colleagues have proposed that by tracking statistical regularities, infants segment coherent units that are ready to be associated with meanings.

Graf Estes (2014) also recently found that infants can use native language phonotactic patterns to detect words in fluent speech, and then use the word form representations to facilitate label learning. The infants (14-month-olds) listened to passages in which target words were surrounded by words that produced good phonotactic word boundary contexts or poor word boundary contexts, based on the passages from Mattys and Jusczyk's (2001) original study of phonotactic word segmentation. When infants heard the target words embedded in good word boundary contexts, they learned the words as object labels. When the words were embedded in contexts that did not support segmentation, they failed to learn the labels. They also failed to learn the labels in the absence of any prior exposure to the labels. The results of this experiment indicate that novice word learners, such as 14-month-olds, are able to take advantage of language-specific word segmentation cues, then store those representations until a potential referent is available.

Recently, Shukla, White, and Aslin (2011) presented evidence that even younger infants, 6-month-olds, can use word segmentation cues to detect a new word and associate it with an object. The infants listened to short utterances in an artificial language while watching animated sequences that contained a target object and two unlabelled distractor objects. The target object reliably co-occurred with a bisyllabic sequence that had perfect internal transitional probability (i.e. a word), but was surrounded by syllables that varied. The target object moved during labelling while the distractor objects remained still. During testing, the infants viewed the target and a distractor object and heard the reliable syllable sequence or a syllable sequence that had crossed word boundaries in the artificial language. When they heard the high transitional probability word sequence, infants increased their looking to the target object. They did not increase looking to the target when they heard the across-word sequence. However, this pattern of results only occurred for infants who, during training, heard the word at the end of a prosodic pattern that indicated the end of a phrase. When the word crossed a prosodic phrase boundary during training, the infants did not associate it with the target object (rather, they seemed to map the word to the distractor; see Shukla et al. 2011 for additional details). The prosodic pattern marking the edges of phrases seemed to be crucial for associating the word form and referent. Shukla et al.'s study indicates that even very young infants have the potential to segment linguistic units and associate them with referents. Infants who have only just started to comprehend a few common and salient native language words (Bergelson and Swingley 2012; Tincoff and Jusczyk 1999, 2012) already possess mechanisms for segmenting words from fluent speech and learning the roles that those words play.

Despite the strength of infants' word segmentation abilities, they do not always segment the speech stream correctly. Infants may mis-segment when a word is inconsistent with their expectations about word form characteristics. For example, Jusczyk et al. (1999) reported that infants seemed to segment the sequence *taris* from the phrase *guitar is* because the dominant English stress pattern indicates that the second (stressed) syllable in *guitar* is actually the onset of a word (see also Cutler and Butterfield 1992, for evidence with adults). In other experiments, infants fail to detect words when limited segmentation cues are available (e.g. Johnson and Tyler 2010; Mattys and Jusczyk 2001). There are also classic examples of children's segmentation errors that appear in speech production. A child who is instructed to behave replies, 'I am /heɪv/' (Peters 1983: 43). Children sometimes treat common phrases such as *look at, want to*, and *do it* as single words before eventually decomposing them into their parts (Peters 1985; see also Brown 1973). Such segmentation errors do not occur randomly. Rather, they represent sensible generalizations of word segmentation processes. In the first example above, experience with phrases in which *be* precedes adjectives, such as *be careful* and *be nice*, leads children to parse *behave* as 'be + have' /heɪv/, in which *have* is a new adjective. In other cases, highly frequent exposure to common phrases leads children to interpret them as cohesive units. For example, children may rarely hear *look* when it is not followed by *at*. The input patterns indicate that *look at* is a lexical unit, and children treat it accordingly. Infants and children must accumulate greater experience with the speech signal in order to override these early errors. Given the complexity of the speech signal and the robustness of many word segmentation cues, it is remarkable that children do not display these kinds of mistakes more frequently. Such segmentation errors are notable for what they reveal about how children construct their knowledge of the speech signal.

31.11 Word segmentation and vocabulary development

The studies reviewed above establish that infants possess many tools for finding words in fluent speech. There is also evidence of a close connection between word segmentation and word learning. Infants across a range of ages show superior learning of object labels when they have had prior opportunity to segment those labels from fluent speech (Graf Estes et al. 2007; Hay et al. 2011; Shukla et al. 2011; Swingley 2007). Word segmentation may provide a foundation for vocabulary acquisition. Infants may extract a store of word forms that are not yet associated with meanings. When the opportunity arises, because of increases in experience or cognitive skills, those previously stored word forms could then readily be available to associate with meanings. This prior store of word forms may contribute to why vocabulary development accelerates so dramatically for many children during the second year of life. Infants do not start word learning as blank slates at around 1 year of age. Rather, they have accrued months of experience listening to speech. This exposure leads to the discovery of many individual word forms, as well as to expectations about the phonological and prosodic forms that words are likely to take, thereby facilitating learning of words that are consistent with these patterns (Graf Estes, Edwards, and Saffran 2011).

Word segmentation is a fundamental process in language acquisition. It follows that word segmentation ability should be associated with language acquisition progress. Infants who have difficulty segmenting words from fluent speech may be at a disadvantage in vocabulary development because they do not have stored word forms available to associate with meanings. In addition, they may have difficulty during online sentence processing if they are slow to identify the speaker's referent. Infants who are skilled at word segmentation will have greater opportunities to learn about the meaning, context, and grammatical roles of the words they detect than infants who are not (see a related argument in Fernald, Perfors, and Marchman 2006; Marchman and Fernald 2008).

Newman et al. (2006) reported that children's language abilities can be linked to their segmentation skills in infancy. Infants participated in word segmentation tasks that tested the use of cues such as prosody or phonotactics, or the ability to recognize words across changes in the speaker's gender. In this retrospective study, infants were initially tested between 7.5 and 12 months. At age 2, infants who had larger vocabularies (the top 15 per cent of the sample) were more likely to have shown successful segmentation as infants (as indicated by following the novelty or familiarity preference pattern that was reliably exhibited at the group level) than infants with smaller vocabularies (the bottom 15 per cent of the sample). Children at the high and low ends of vocabulary size differed in their ability to segment words from fluent speech as younger infants.

In a subsequent study, Newman and colleagues (2006) re-tested a subset of the same group of children between 4 and 6 years of age. To examine whether associations between segmentation performance and language skills could be due to general cognitive differences between children who were identified as 'segmenters' versus 'non-segmenters' as infants, the children were tested on measures of linguistic and non-linguistic cognitive abilities. Children who were segmenters as infants had higher scores on languages measures than the non-segmenters, but the two groups did not differ in general intellectual abilities, or non-verbal intelligence. The segmenters had higher scores for both vocabulary and syntax. Thus, Newman et al.'s research supports the idea that early segmentation performance lays a foundation for subsequent language development. Children who have difficulty identifying words in fluent speech may then find it challenging to associate meanings with new words, to learn their grammatical roles, and to combine them with other morphemes to form complete utterances.

Singh, Reznick, and Xuehua (2012) recently reported a longitudinal study examining the association between word segmentation at 7.5 months and vocabulary size at 24 months. Infants were familiarized with a pair of words presented in isolation, then tested on their ability to recognize the words embedded in passages. Infants also participated in a second, more challenging task. They were familiarized with a pair of words, but in testing, one of the words was produced in a different pitch, and the other word was produced in the same pitch as during familiarization. To succeed, infants had to recognize the familiarized word and generalize their representation of the word across acoustic variation. Singh and colleagues found that infants' ability to recognize the target words at 7.5 months (measured as the looking time difference to target words vs. unfamiliar words) was significantly correlated with productive vocabulary size at 24 months. For the simple segmentation task in which the speaker's voice was consistent from familiarization to test, performance was also correlated with general cognitive skills. However, for the complex task that required generalization across voices, performance was associated with vocabulary size, but not general cognitive ability.

The work of Newman and colleagues and Singh and colleagues provides further evidence that early language processing abilities are meaningfully related to later language acquisition progress. Previous studies have demonstrated similar associations in a variety of tasks: the ability to process rapid auditory transitions (Benasich and Tallal 2002), native and non-native phoneme discrimination (e.g. Kuhl et al. 2005; Tsao, Liu, and Kuhl 2004), and speed of lexical access (Fernald and Marchman 2012; Fernald et al. 2006; Marchman and Fernald 2008) in infancy are all associated with later language outcomes. Segmentation ability follows the same pattern. Future research will be necessary to investigate whether infants' attention to particular word segmentation cues (e.g. transitional probability, lexical stress) are also associated with later language skills. The findings from these correlational studies indicate that measures of fundamental language processing abilities, such as word segmentation, have the potential to be extended for practical application. By understanding individual variation in such skills, it may be possible to gain greater understanding of development in children at risk of lasting language impairments.

31.12 Conclusion

For adults, the act of segmenting speech usually occurs automatically. Considering word segmentation from the infant's perspective emphasizes the magnitude of the challenge that word segmentation poses for language processing and acquisition. Despite the complexity of the speech signal and the lack of obvious word boundary markers, infants discover individual words. Before age 1, they are sensitive to many cues to where words begin and end. Infants detect and use language-general cues, such as isolated words, utterance edges, and transitional probabilities. They also learn and apply language-specific cues, such as lexical stress and phonotactics. Although no cue is fully reliable, their convergence is highly informative. Infants' precocious learning mechanisms and speech processing capabilities allow them to access these information sources to pull out individual words from continuous speech—words that can then be associated with meanings and added to the lexicon. Thus, the ability to find words is an essential, fundamental skill in language acquisition.

CHAPTER 32

ROGER BROWN'S 'ORIGINAL WORD GAME'

REESE M. HEITNER

> [P]rior to the time that his language acquisition studies were in full swing, Brown wrote a book, *Words and Things*, that contained a thoughtful assessment of some of the problems facing the language learner, including how to extract meaning from the speech signal. It is instructive to consider some of his intuitions about this process because his reflections occurred prior to the first studies of infant speech perception. Moreover, some of his characterizations of these issues are still right on the mark.
>
> (Jusczyk 1997: 18)

32.1 The Original Word Game

A towering figure within the field of psychology and linguistics, Roger Brown (1925–97) helped to define the new field of developmental psycholinguistics in the years following the cognitive revolution of the late 1950s and 1960s. Through his scholarship and guidance, the field of child language development has matured so that insights issuing from within the psycholinguistic laboratory impact linguistics and psychology more generally—think of Steven Pinker's *The Language Instinct* (1994) or Paul Bloom's *Descartes' Baby* (2004). By contrast, this chapter focuses on Brown's Original Word Game: what was (and wasn't) so 'original', what was unique about Brown's conception of a 'word', and finally how the psycholinguistic 'games' he played in the 1950s could find a new home in the high-tech infant speech laboratory of the 21st century.

The 'Original Word Game' consists of two players—a tutor who knows the language and a player learning the language. The rules are as follows:

> The tutor names things in accordance with the semantic custom of his community. The player forms hypotheses about the categorical nature of the things named.

> He tests his hypotheses by trying to name new things correctly. The tutor compares the player's utterances with his own anticipations of such utterances and, in this way, checks the accuracy of fit between his own categories and those of the player. He improves them by correction. In concrete terms, the tutor says 'dog' whenever a dog appears. The player notes the phonemic equivalence of these utterances, forms a hypothesis about the non-linguistic category that elicits this kind of utterance and then tries naming a few dogs himself.
>
> (Brown 1958a: 194)

Brown was not the first to describe this fundamental building block of language, namely, the word-to-referent relationship. Indeed, Brown himself may have inherited the 'original word game' phrase from his Harvard colleague, Jerome Bruner (1957: 18). Even further back, one can uncover the writings of several historical figures who also provided a brief account of the word-learning process, among them St Augustine, John Locke, Lev Vygotsky, Ludwig Wittgenstein, and, just after Brown, the philosopher W. V. O. Quine. None were professionally trained experimental developmental psycholinguists by today's standards. But neither, strictly speaking, was Brown. And like the brief selections arranged chronologically below for comparison, Brown's Original Word Game presents an idealized and simplified picture of early word learning. But like a caricature, what it loses in detail it can gain in suggestive force.

Saint Augustine (354–430 AD)

Seemingly quoted more than any other non-psychologist or non-linguist is St Augustine's anecdotal reflection on his own early language development. In Book I, Chapter VIII of his *Confessions*, Augustine (398/1961) writes:

> This I remember; and have since observed how I learned to speak. It was not that my elders taught me words (as, soon after, other learning) in any set method; but I, longing by cries and broken accents and various motions of my limbs to express my thoughts, so that I might have my will, and yet unable to express all I willed, or to whom I willed, did myself, by the understanding which Thou, my God, gavest me, practice the sounds in my memory. When they named anything, and as they spoke turned towards it, I saw and remembered that they called what they would point out by the name they uttered. And that they meant this thing and no other was plain from the motion of their body, the natural language, as it were, of all nations, expressed by the countenance, glances of the eye, gestures of the limbs, and tones of the voice, indicating the affections of the mind, as it pursues, possesses, rejects, or shuns. And thus by constantly hearing words, as they occurred in various sentences, I collected gradually for what they stood; and having broken in my mouth to these signs, I thereby gave utterance to my will.

John Locke (1632–1704)

Among Empiricist philosophers of the Enlightenment, John Locke is also remembered for his comments on children's language development. In Book III, Chapter IX, Section 9 of his *Essay Concerning Human Understanding*, Locke (1690/1979) explains:

> For if we will observe how children learn languages, we shall find that, to make them understand what the names of simple ideas or substances stand for, people ordinarily show them the thing whereof they would have them have the idea; and then repeat to them the name that stands for it; as white, sweet, milk, sugar, cat, dog. But as for mixed modes, especially the most material of them, moral words, the sounds are usually learned first; and then, to know what complex ideas they stand for, they are either beholden to the explication of others, or (which happens for the most part) are left to their own observation and industry...

Lev Vygotsky (1896–1934)

Closer to our own era, Vygotsky, like Brown, conducted some experimental language games, so-called 'double stimulation', i.e. word–object sorting tasks consisting of wooden blocks of various shapes, sizes, and colours each marked with a nonsense word. These experiments were designed to document children's 'spontaneous' categorization behaviours, free from the direct influence of the child's 'linguistic milieu'. But Vygotsky's naturalistic observations of children's language development also demonstrated how idiosyncratic thought patterns are channelled in stages by the linguistic forces of the adult community:

> [A] child's use of *quah* to designate first a duck swimming on the pond, then any liquid, including the milk in his bottle; when he happens to see a coin with an eagle on it, the coin is also called a *quah*, and then any round, coinlike object. This is typical of a chain complex—each new object included has some attribute in common with another element, but the attributes undergo endless changes.
>
> (Vygotsky 1934/1986: 127)

> Only the mastery of abstraction, combined with advanced complex thinking, enables the child to progress to the formation of genuine concepts. ... The decisive role in this process, as our experiments have shown, is played by the word, deliberately used to direct all subprocesses of advanced concept formation. (p. 139)
>
> Practical experience also shows that direct teaching of concepts is impossible and fruitless. A teacher who tries to do this usually accomplishes nothing but empty verbalism, a parrotlike repetition of words by the child, simulating a knowledge of the corresponding concepts but actually covering up a vacuum. (p. 150)

Ludwig Wittgenstein (1889–1951)

No overview of language learning would be complete without Wittgenstein's critique. In fact, it is with the same quote from Augustine by which Wittgenstein begins his own remarks in the posthumously published *Philosophical Investigations*. After quoting Augustine, Wittgenstein (1953) complains:

(1) ... These words [of Augustine], it seems to me, give us a particular picture of the essence of human language. It is this: the individual words in language name objects—sentences are combinations of such names.—In this picture of language we find the roots of the following idea: Every word has a meaning. This meaning is correlated with the word. It is the object for which the word stands.

Augustine does not speak of there being any difference between kinds of word. If you describe the learning of language in this way you are, I believe, thinking primarily of nouns like 'table', 'chair', 'bread', and of people's names, and only secondarily of the names of certain actions and properties; and of the remaining kinds of word as something that will take care of itself.

(2) ... Let us imagine a language for which the description given by Augustine is right. The language is meant to serve for communication between a builder A and an assistant B. A is building with building stones: there are blocks, pillars, slabs and beams. B has to pass the stones, and that in the order in which A needs them. For this purpose they use a language consisting of the words 'block', 'pillar', 'slab', 'beam'. A calls them out;—B brings the stone which he has learnt to bring at such-and-such a call.—— Conceive this as a complete primitive language.

(5) ... A child uses such primitive forms of language when it learns to talk. Here the teaching of language is not explanation, but training.

(7) In the practice of the use of language (2) one party calls out the words, the other acts on them. In instruction in the language, the following process will occur: the learner *names* the objects; that is, he utters the word when the teacher points to the stone.—And there will be this still simpler exercise: the pupil repeats the words after the teacher —— both of these being processes resembling language.

We can also think of the whole process of using words in (2) as one of those games by means of which children learn their native language. I will call these games 'language games' and will sometimes speak of a primitive language as a language game.

And the processes of naming the stones and of repeating words after someone might also be called language games. (pp. 2–5)

W. V. O. Quine (1908–2000)

Among philosophers, W. V. O. Quine prominently engaged issues of language. Quine's well-known discussion of 'Gavagai' (published in 1960 soon after Brown's *Words and Things* in an analogously entitled book *Word and Object*) is a philosophical exercise in what Quine called 'radical translation':[1]

> The utterances first and most surely translated in such a case are ones keyed to present events that are conspicuous to the linguist and his informant. A rabbit scurries by, the native says 'Gavagai', and the linguist notes down the sentence 'Rabbit' (or 'Lo, a rabbit') as tentative translation, subject to testing in further cases. The linguist will at first refrain from putting words into his informant's mouth, if only for lack of words to put. When he can, though, the linguist has to supply native sentences for his informant's approval, despite the risk of slanting the data by suggestion. Otherwise he can do little with native terms that have references in common. For, suppose the native language includes sentences S1, S2, and S3, really translatable respectively as 'Animal', 'White', and 'Rabbit'. Stimulus situations always differ, whether relevantly or not; and, just because volunteered responses come singly, the classes of situations under which the native happens to have volunteered S1, S2, and S3, are of course mutually exclusive, despite the hidden actual meanings of the words. How then is the linguist to perceive that the native would have been willing to assent to S1 in all the situations where he happened to volunteer S3, and in some but perhaps not all of the situations where he happened to volunteer S2? Only by taking the initiative and querying combinations of native sentences and stimulus situations so as to narrow down his guesses to his eventual satisfaction.
>
> (Quine 1960: 27–29)

What should we make of these passages? First, Brown's picture of word learning fits comfortably within a general view of early word learning as an ongoing process of coordinated joint attention among a more experienced speaker (teacher, tutor, native, informant), the language, the world, and an observant listener (the learner, pupil, child, investigator). Language effectuates a semantic pairing of words with meanings, and no one denies that children must somehow learn to associate specific word forms with specific meanings. It is just that they must do this for all sorts of words: for nouns less obvious than *dog, duck, slab*, and *rabbit*; for verbs more subtle than *bring, eat*, and *sleep*; for adjectives beyond shape, size, and colour; and for prepositions, pronouns, subordinators, auxiliaries, and determiners, never part of any naming game. We can agree with Bloom (2006) that 'association' is—or at least can be—a benign term while still acknowledging that (i) most words are eventually understood partially and some entirely on the basis of other words, (ii) some words are initially interpreted in light of other words,

[1] Quine's depiction of 'radical translation' recalls the case of the French naturalist Pierre Sonnerat who, it is said, mistakenly interpreted a native's shout *Indri!* ('look!' in Malagasy) as the name of the animal, a lemur, they had spotted. The authenticity of this account, as well as other similar stories surrounding the etymological origins of *kangaroo* and *vasistas* (the French word for transom, or fanlight) has, however, been challenged; see Hacking (1981).

Table 32.1 Roger Brown's 'Original Word Game' in historical context

Issue		Writer: Saint Augustine	John Locke	Lev Vygotsky	Ludwig Wittgenstein	W. V. O. Quine	Roger Brown	Eve Clark	Paul Bloom	Michael Tomasello
Properties of Input?	word-referent contiguity	yes	yes	no	yes	yes	yes	yes	no	no
	ostensive naming	yes	yes	no	yes	yes	yes	yes	no	no
Properties of Learner?	theory of mind	yes	no	no	no	no	no	yes	yes	yes
	hypothesis testing	no	no	no	no	yes	yes	yes	no	no
	independent	yes	yes	no	no	no	no	no	yes	no
	object-centric	no	no	no	yes	yes	yes	no	yes	no
Word Games Support?	object categorization	no	no	yes	no	yes	yes	yes	yes	yes
	speech categorization	no	no	no	no	no	YES	no	no	no

including morphosyntactic suffixes (e.g. past tense *-ed*, plural *-s*), and (iii) words are not always paired with pre-existing concepts. Words can lead children to rethink, refine, or reconfigure meanings, as argued by Nelson (2001) in her response to Bloom (2001).

Second, there are some differences among these writers. Table 32.1 attempts—by forcible compression—to summarize their remarks, supplemented by three additional columns keyed to the more recent research of Eve Clark (Clark 1993, 2009, this volume), Paul Bloom (2000, 2001, 2006), and Michael Tomasello (1998, 2000, 2003). Be forewarned. These issues tend to defy unqualified responses, and simplistic 'yes' and 'no' entries serve to point out the relative importance these word-learning parameters have for these scholars. The table also reflects a narrow reading of these writers. The selected passages are no more exhaustive than Brown's description of the Original Word Game represents the entirety of his thoughts on language development. The reckless ambition embodied in such a compressed table is intended to generate 'talking points' of relative importance rather than 'QED arguments' of foregone conclusion.

Reading down, the left column in Table 32.1 lists a number of word-learning issues. Reading across, each writer is pigeonholed with a 'yes' or 'no' response, and shaded cells serve to highlight some convergent themes and divergent approaches. One common word-learning trope is the intuitive centrality of at least word-referent contiguity and even directly ostensive definitions. Save for Bloom and Tomasello (and Vygotsky), it would seem some form of partially staged metalinguistic input in the form of referent labelling was taken to be an important, perhaps necessary, component of early word learning. Something as minimally scaffolded as just reciting *dog* whenever a dog appears is supposed to occur, according to Brown. Even Wittgenstein, while distancing himself from Augustine's naming, seems to view at least *children's* word learning as some sort of 'primitive language game' consisting of pointing, naming, and repeating. As Clark observes in her contribution to this volume, '[w]hen adults offer children words for unfamiliar objects, in fact, they first establish joint attention with the child, show them the object in question, and then proceed first to label it and then to talk about its various properties' (p. 525). But while fairly common, arguably useful and obviously engaging for both child and caregiver, the significance of such early word learning practices is, according to Bloom (2000), misplaced, and according to Tomasello (2000), misunderstood.

For Bloom, no word-learning support is necessary, because children will learn what they need to learn without any additional input beyond normal adult conversation. Instead of trying to compute physically anchored statistical covariations between words and their referents, children are, argues Bloom, tracking mentally tethered thought bubbles. It is their 'theory of mind' which makes for efficient word learning. If you know what someone is trying to do, if you know what someone is thinking, *if you know what someone means*, it is a lot easier to interpret their words. So while we are perhaps more likely to say *dog* when dogs are present, we also routinely say *dog* when there are no dogs present. For Bloom, then, even if some aspects of everyday conversation (subject to diverse sociolinguistic and cultural norms: see Lieven 1994) do naturally tilt toward metalinguistic labelling when among children, word learning is still more an achievement of mind reading than spatial-temporal word–referent association—and Bloom (2006) credits Augustine with this insight.

For Tomasello, children are not bound by brute word–referent associations either. But not so much because of their superlative mind-reading skills, but because children are *not* trying to learn word–referent associations. Children are learning how to use words as communicative instruments while immersed within a robust context of socially interactive cues which encourage them to take advantage of the communicative power and precision of language. From this social-pragmatic 'usage-based theory of language acquisition' (Tomasello 2003), children do not have problems learning a dictionary because they are instead learning how to live a language (Nelson 2009). In this way, word labelling—and even word understanding itself—is better viewed as a conversational by-product of just trying to make ourselves clear. This is why the 'mini-linguistic lessons' embodied in Brown's Original Word Game can misrepresent children's word learning experiences, and the field would do better to abandon these word–referent 'mapping metaphors,' argues Tomasello (2001: 1120).

Another related point highlighted in Table 32.1 is how efficiently and independently children hit upon intended meanings. It would seem Augustine did it on his own and everything was more or less obvious.[2] But for Brown, early word learning was more a process of trial and error, naturally encouraging some adult intervention. In fact, among these writers, only Quine (and Wittgenstein in later passages) philosophically problematize the interpretation of words more than Brown. Even given the head-start help of 'basic-level' or 'level of utility' naming patterns (as documented by Vygotsky 1934/1986: 143 and Brown 1958b, and subjected to much research since; Malt, this volume), Brown suggests that word meanings still have to be methodically drawn and quartered. So while both physical word–object contiguity and mental communicative-intent psychology can help children pre-empt some errors, adult participation can anticipate, prevent, clarify, and simply correct. This explains Clark's interests in analysing child-directed speech (Clark 2009), in investigating how early word comprehension is far from perfect (Clark 1993) and, in her contribution to this volume, in highlighting the role adult monitoring, restatement, reformulation, and different types of feedback enhance conversational flow and encourage conventional forms. In doing so, she challenges a dismissive attitude toward the linguistic significance of child-directed speech, characteristic of Bloom.

For Bloom, child-directed speech is a sideshow. Maybe helpful but definitely not essential. For him, children's word learning is just too quick and too accurate to await such services. In terms of initial input, manifest meaning, and autonomy, Brown appears to have more in common with his philosophical contemporaries than all of his successors. There are other patterns in Table 32.1. Children's early word learning could favour nouns for a variety of reasons, argues Clark, with some factors tied to the child and the referent (conceptualizing objects vs. actions) and others related to the situational language preferences of adults (reading books vs. playing with toys) and even the language itself (English vs. Japanese; see Clark, this volume). By contrast, Bloom (2000) considers children's noun biases to be the result of a default 'object-centric' interpretation

[2] As pointed out by Eve Clark (p.c.), we have to be a little suspicious about St Augustine's account of his own language learning. Can any of us really remember how we learned our language in infancy?

of the physical world—and children are in this way (as well as others, he argues) just like adults. Moreover, while both Clark and Bloom agree that the so-called 'vocabulary spurt' (typically occurring between 18 and 22 months) could well be a statistical inevitability, Bloom also insists that the phenomena of 'fast mapping' and 'mutual exclusivity' are not peculiar to word learning. For Bloom, neither the child's word learning problems nor the child's word learning solutions are all that unusual.

So while differing in some respects, Bloom and Tomasello eventually converge at a point beyond the word labelling of Brown's Original Word Game. They both reject word-learning accounts based upon salient spatial-temporal contiguity (Smith 2000) for being insufficient, but also reject accounts premised upon linguistically specific word-learning constraints (Golinkoff, Mervis, and Hirsh-Pasek 1994; Markman 1989; Waxman 1999) for being unnecessary. For their part, Hirsh-Pasek et al. (2004) have proposed a hybrid 'emergentist coalition model' whereby different cues and skills (associative, linguistic, and social) play different roles at different times. Perhaps another source of agreement could be found by viewing children's sense of communicative intent as the pragmatic basis for the interlocking inference matrix these proposed word learning constraints and principles try to explain.

Third, acknowledging that word learning requires words and meanings to be linked in accordance with community practice proffers very little. As Waxman (1999) explains,

> If the dubbing ceremony is to be informative at all, the infant must solve a difficult three-part task. First, the infant must parse the relevant word (*tziminche* or *tapir*) from the continuous speech stream; second, the infant must identify the relevant entity(ies) (the tapir) in the scenario; third, the infant must establish a word-to-object mapping between the two. In essence, infants must discover the relevant linguistic units, the relevant conceptual units, and the precise mapping between them. (p. 242)

And developmental psychologists have been hard at work filling in all three parts of this word-learning process in greater detail. Among these researchers was Brown himself.

For unlike Augustine, Locke, Vygotsky, Wittgenstein, and Quine, word learning was not a step along the way to some early 'theory of everything' (Augustine and Locke) or to an understanding of human cognition generally (Vygotsky, Wittgenstein, and Quine). For Brown, word learning deserved its own scholarly space:

> We play this game as long as we continue to extend our vocabularies and that may be as long as we live. However, as adults, the task centers on the formation of the category named. All other aspects of the game have been overlearned to the point of automatic perfection. The child plays with more difficulty because he has all the rudiments to acquire. He must learn to categorize speech itself so that he can identify equivalent and distinctive utterances in what the tutor says. He must learn the motor skills of producing such utterances so that they are recognizable to the tutor. Finally, he, like the adult, must form the referent categories. These part processes are not only analytically separable. They are actually separated in much of the child's earliest learning. In the first two years he is forming conceptions of space,

time, causality, and of the enduring object. These conceptions, so brilliantly studied by Piaget (1929, 1953), are the basic referent categories and they are formed with little assistance from language. At the same time, through babbling and attending to the speech of others, the infant is learning to perceive and to produce speech, though as yet he may have no idea of linguistic reference. When the rudiments have been brought to a certain minimal efficiency they come together in the Original Word Game. We then find that the speech skills have a tremendous potential for assisting the formation of non-linguistic categories. The total list of such categories that a child must learn is a cognitive inventory of his culture. Speech, therefore, is the principal instrument of cognitive socialization.

(Brown 1958b: 194–195)

32.2 Language-specific speech perception: the issue

While others (like Vygotsky and Quine) had also noted the influence words can have on categorization (the penultimate row in Table 32.1), only Brown enjoys a legacy of some fifty years of increasingly sophisticated word games which experimentally confirm how word labels direct children's categorizing behaviour (Kessel 1988; Hall and Waxman 2004). Nevertheless, Brown's vision of a full 'analytic separation' of referent categorization and speech categorization has not yet been realized. But what could this be? It would be the effect that referent categorization (and interpretive meaning generally) can have on the phonemic categorization of words themselves.

Brown was ahead of his time in recognizing that the phonemic categorization of words cannot be taken for granted. Save for some lip-service from Quine,[3] only Brown called our attention to the inherent duality of word-learning games. For in addition to categorizing a world of objects, properties, events, and actions (with and without the help of words), Brown realized that word forms themselves had to be categorized. And this realization was, as the late Peter Jusczyk reminds us in the epigraph to this chapter, indeed novel. For Brown, '[t]he important research question is to discover how the child learns to categorize speech in terms of phonemic attributes' (1958a: 203). Continuing, Brown explains: 'A child born into an English speaking community must learn to attend to the difference between voiceless [p] and voiced [b] but to ignore the difference between aspirate [pʰ] and non-aspirate [p]. Generally, he must learn to notice phonemic contrasts but may ignore those that are not phonemic' (p. 203).

[3] In a casual aside, Quine (1960) notes: 'Incidentally I shall here ignore phonematic analysis (§18), early though it would come in our field linguist's enterprise; for it does not affect the philosophical point I want to make' (p. 28). In two related articles (Heitner 2005, 2006), I argue that this neglect does, however, destabilize some of Quine's philosophical positions.

How does the child do this? How are allophonic differences recognized as phonemically equivalent?[4] We are still not entirely sure. But Brown should be at least credited with uncovering an experimentally untapped solution: allophonic speech categorization, like object categorization, could itself be a by-product of an ongoing 'word game' process. Perhaps some aspects of phonemic speech perception are partially bootstrapped from some budding appreciation of some word meanings. After all, the one-to-one connection between words and referents is really a many-to-many relation between *types* of word token and *types* of referent. Allophonic word-tokens are grouped into phonological classes just as much as referent tokens are grouped into ontological classes. And if children can use words to guide object categorization, perhaps the inverse is also true. Maybe infants can use object categorization to guide the phonemic categorization of speech. At least that is the idea (Heitner 2004). But it is not really my idea. It was Roger Brown's. And it is his intuition—that some aspects of speech perception may, in part, be underwritten by a hint of interpretive semantics—which is the signature contribution of his Original Word Game. (It also represents an oblique acknowledgement of the semantic basis of phonemic categorization, touching on an old debate which consumed much of the pre-generative distributional or taxonomic linguistics of the 1940s and 1950s (Heitner 2005), and which Brown addresses in chapter 1 of *Words and Things*.[5])

Complementing the claim that the categorization of our world is rarely conducted in a linguistic vacuum, but is mediated by socially transmitted word labels (in addition, of course, to the more directly accessible features of shape, material, function, etc.), is the claim that speech forms are not categorized in an interpretive vacuum either. In addition to relying on the bottom-up, phonetically accessible features of similarity and phonotactic distribution, infants may also phonemically categorize words, at least in part, through a top-down reliance on some socially transmitted information in the form of what objects, properties, activities, and events the word tokens are actually associated with. In short, if one word implies one referent, and two words imply two

[4] Allophonic variation is not the only source of speech variability. Differences in speech production due to age, gender, accent, speaking rate, and immediate linguistic context, must also be routinely accommodated (Johnson 2005).

[5] In 'The Analysis of Speech' (the first chapter of *Words and Things*) Brown asks, 'What part does linguistic meaning play in the procedure for determining phonemes' (1958a: 32)? According to Brown, when phonemically categorizing phones from scratch, reliance on meaning is neither avoidable nor deplorable. Likewise, in the preface to the 1968 paperbound printing of *Words and Things*, Brown concedes, 'The perception of speech has turned out to be a still more remarkable accomplishment than Chapter 1 represents it as being. Evidently, we do not proceed in a pedestrian linear fashion identifying each vowel and consonant in its turn but rather only sample acoustic data drawing on our knowledge of grammar and meaning to make up the rest' (pp. iii–iv). Together, these remarks represent a potential trifecta of semantically influenced phonology: (i) in terms of theoretical analysis, Brown argues that phonology is sensitive to semantics, (ii) in terms of psycholinguistic processing, Brown acknowledges that phonology is sensitive to semantics, and (iii) in terms of early development, I suspect Brown would not be surprised if phonology was sensitive to semantics.

referents, then two referents should imply two words, and one referent only one word. More generally, an expectation to pair one word with one meaning could help infants identify phonemic word types among phonetic word tokens. In fact, Brown accidentally noticed the possibility of this cyclical bootstrapping symmetry while playing one of his word games.

32.3 Language-specific speech perception: the game

In an overlooked section of 'The Original Word Game' chapter of *Words and Things*, Brown described a series of word game experiments which show 'Speech Categories Operating as a Guide to Referent Categories' (the title of the section). In these experiments, Brown experimentally manipulated the phonemic categorization of speech so as to demonstrate the effect that phonemic speech perception has on the categorization of objects. Almost by accident, he also demonstrated the inverse effect: object categorization influencing the phonemic categorization of speech. Here is how he did it.

Brown started with a set of 85 Munsell colour chips, equally spaced across a carefully graded spectrum of hues, with saturation and brightness held constant. In the context of a word–object pairing game, the tutor selected eight chips, distinguishable only by seven equally spaced perceptible gaps in hue. Each chip was randomly presented one at a time to a subject and named by a single nonsense one-syllable word. Once all eight chips had been named, the subject was asked to group the eight chips in accordance with the verbal practices of the tutor.

Simple enough, but the words Brown used in these experiments were as carefully selected as the Munsell chips. The eight nonsense syllables were constructed according to a carefully graded phonetic spectrum of vowels and vowel lengthening. Non-randomly arranged and including repetitions, the words were [ma] [ma] [mo] [mo] [ma:] [ma:] [mo:] [mo:]. While the phones [a] (the vowel in the American pronunciation of *not*) and [o] (the vowel in the word *note*) are phonemically contrastive in English, vowel lengthening, denoted by [:], is not. As predicted, the subjects (fifteen Harvard students) generally classified the eight chips into two categories. After all, these speakers heard only *two* words ('ma' and 'mo'), and given the uniform colour spacing between the chips, there was little reason to impose any other categorical scheme on the eight objects. The non-phonemic discrepancies of vowel lengthening were dismissed as incidental variation.

Now Brown brought in the Navaho subjects. When he conducted the same experiment with the same eight Munsell chips with the same eight word tokens, the Navaho subjects grouped the eight chips according to the number of words they heard. But the Navaho subjects could no more assume the differences in vowel length did not indicate a different word than the English-speaking subjects could assume such phonetic differences did make a difference. Vowel lengthening is phonemically contrastive in Navaho, so the eight chips were grouped into four categories. Clearly, speech perception could affect object categorization. How could it not? If words generally mean what they do via a one-to-one correspondence between word forms and word meanings, then if one perceives one word, one will naturally expect one category; two words, two categories, and so on. Indeed, the effect of linguistic labelling on object categorization has since become a focus of developmental psycholinguistic research (for toddlers, see Gelman and Coley 1990; Gelman et al. 2000; Hall et al. 2008; Waxman and Markow 1995; for infants, see Fulkerson and Waxman 2007).

This is not to say that the Harvard undergrads could not also be encouraged to group the coloured chips into four categories, like the Navaho. With some corrective feedback, the Harvard subjects learned to attend to differences in vowel lengthening. Brown reports that many of the subjects had indeed 'noticed' the vowel lengthening of some of the words. But rather than acting on this distinction, they had dismissed it as unintentional and insignificant, prompting Brown (1958a) to credit his subjects with 'no better statement of the cognitive status of non-phonemic variations' (p. 215). Brown had cleverly identified the invisible power of the phonemic ear.

Invisible but not invincible, for Brown had one more move to make. Fifteen new English-speaking subjects were recruited for a slightly different experiment. Rather than sample and label eight equally spaced Munsell chips, Brown chose coloured chips where the perceptual gaps among some were greatly exaggerated. The gaps which separated chips named with and without vowel lengthening—[ma] vs. [maː], [mo] vs. [moː]—were *four* times as great as the perceptual gaps separating the chips named with the [a] vowel vs. the [o] vowel. By biasing the perceptual grouping of the chips, Brown wondered if the subjects could be prompted into violating their own phonemic expectations. Given enough referent-based support to group the eight chips into four (rather than two) categories, would these English-speaking subjects be willing to treat [ma] and [maː], [mo], and [moː], as different words?

Yes and no. According to Brown, only two of the subjects grouped the eight chips into four categories in one trial. Four other subjects eventually learned to group the chips into four categories after a second naming trial. Yet six subjects remained unconvinced, stubbornly refusing to believe, as Brown (1958a) put it, 'that a difference in vowel length could make two words different and so signal a categorical distinction in the non-linguistic world' (p. 215).

But Brown's conclusion is characteristically charming. The mere fact that *any* of the English-speaking subjects could be experimentally pushed to recategorize native speech forms—in only one trial—was significant. As Brown (1958a) excitedly concluded: 'This result demonstrates a facet of the Word Game that we have not yet discussed. It is evidently possible for non-linguistic reality to serve as a guide to the categorization of speech. The isomorphic relationship can be useful in either direction. An inescapable visual difference leads us to look for a speech difference' (p. 216).

32.4 Language-specific speech perception: the problem

How is this related to phonological development, and in particular to infant speech perception? Perhaps a visual *similarity* among objects (or identity of interpretive meaning generally) could lead infants to 'look for'—or better, create—allophonic speech *equivalences*. If phonologically hardened adults—after years of native language experience, but with the right support—could be referentially pressured into recategorizing word tokens, then perhaps infants are also susceptible to this effect. Arguably even more so, for two reasons. First, young infants have yet to fully commit to any specific phonological system. Second, the process of language-specific phonological specialization actually requires infants to recategorize a variety of phonetic distinctions.

But unlike Brown's subjects, infants are not in the business of increasing their sensitivity to phonetic distinctions. Just the opposite. A variety of now-standard experiments in infant speech perception indicate that neonates are innately prepared to discriminate among most, if not all, phonetic speech distinctions (Jusczyk 1997; Kuhl and Meltzoff 1997; Werker and Pegg 1992). 'By and large,' Jusczyk (1985) concludes, 'these studies indicate that infants are capable of discriminating virtually every type of phonetic contrast that they have been tested on' (p. 205), suggesting that infants are 'universal phoneticists', biologically endowed to perceive all possible phonetic distinctions.

Over the course of the first year, then, the developmental process of language-specific infant speech perception generally entails losses of perceptual sensitivity rather than gains (Werker 1989). At issue, however, are the mechanisms supporting this winnowing process of selective perceptual attrition. On one hand, this transition appears to be directly related to the infant's linguistic exposure, including the language-specific allophonic patterns phonotactically distributed in the ambient speech (Jusczyk 1997; Jusczyk and Aslin 1995), which could be—and apparently are—tracked by infants (Peperkamp and Dupoux 2002; Maye, Werker, and Gerken 2002; Yoshida et al. 2010). (Their sensitivity to allophonic regularities also seems to help infants detect word boundaries and extract words from the speech stream; Graf Estes, this volume.) On the other hand, this phonetic exposure to and statistical analysis of the language may not be sufficient to account for the full range of infant allophonic speech perception. Rather, some minimal interpretive experience with the language may also be in play, or even necessary, to explain infants' selective perceptual desensitivity. In addition to hearing an acoustic speech stream, infants may be listening for meaningful words (Jusczyk 1997: 252, n. 3).

In fact, accounts of phonological development that implicitly assume or explicitly argue that language-specific speech perception can develop in an interpretive vacuum are arguably incomplete for purely logical reasons (in addition to some psychological concerns[6]). To see why, consider the fact that two languages may draw upon similar phonetic resources but nevertheless instantiate different phonological systems. The same pair of phones, e.g. [p] and [pʰ], can create phonemically contrastive minimal pairs in one language, say Hindi, but merely allophonically related pronunciations of the same word in another, like English. (The English word *soap*, for instance, is subject to free variation or dialectical patterns. Either [p] or [pʰ] is used to pronounce the final consonant—evidence of their phonemic equivalence.) In fact, the only feature that may distinguish such cross-classified phones is that they are semantically contrastive in one language but not in another. In this way, free allophonic variation presents a *logical* challenge to the establishment of language-specific phonemic speech categories because it undermines the well-behaved phonotactic regularities of complementary allophonic distribution (Heitner 1999).[7] As Jusczyk (1997) points out, 'It is not enough to know which sounds appear in one's native language; one also has to discover which differences among these sounds are relevant for conveying distinctions in meaning' (p. 9). How, then, do infants do it?

32.5 Language-specific speech perception: the experiment

While some researchers have speculated about the role of interpretive semantic cues in partially underwriting language-specific speech perception in infancy (Jusczyk 1985; Kuhl et al. 1992; Macnamara 1982; Vihman 1996; Walley 1993; Werker and Tees 1984), Brown's Original Word Game provides the experimental playbook by which to test if infant speech perception is indeed sensitive to semantic information. One reason: if naming obviously contrived objects (like Brown's coloured chips) can prod adults to unnaturally increase their phonetic discrimination, perhaps infants, who are already naturally predisposed to collapse allophonic distinctions, can be experimentally encouraged to do so through the manipulative naming of some referential props.

[6] Some infant research speaks to this 'learning language in a vacuum' issue. Kuhl, Tsao, and Liu (2003) conclude that changes in phonetic discrimination among 9- to 10-month infants are not the result of mere linguistic exposure. Rather, phonetic discrimination evolves as the result of linguistic exposure within a normal environment of human interaction. Whether this human interaction is just normal people doing and saying normal things, or also includes an infant's natural ambition to interpret speech for meaning, however, was not tested. Interestingly, Kuhl's results are consistent with Baldwin, Markman, Bill, Desjardins, Irwin, and Tidball (1996), who report that infants do not learn word-to-object pairings when novel objects are named through a disembodied loudspeaker. It would seem that the Original Word Game requires the social interaction of real human players.

[7] Such conflicting phonologies may or may not also present a very practical problem for simultaneous bilingual infants. For recent studies, see Albareda-Castellot, Pons, and Sebastián-Gallés (2011).

How would such a Brown-inspired word game experiment work? If some aspects of phonemic speech perception are related to some incipient awareness of what people are actually talking about, then insofar as two allophonically related word tokens are repeatedly used to refer to the same referent, infants would be referentially cued to ignore a phonetic distinction and treat the word tokens as phonemically equivalent. By contrast, when these same two word tokens are consistently used to refer to two different referents, infants would be referentially cued to retain speech discrimination of the phonetic distinction. By systematically associating two phonetically similar word tokens with either (a) the same (type of) object to encourage phonetic assimilation, or (b) two different (types of) objects to sustain phonetic discrimination, infant speech perception could be—at least under these idealized and simplified word game conditions—susceptible to what classically trained perceptual psychologists would recognize as an example of laboratory-induced 'acquired equivalence' (Lawrence 1949). In this way, if differences in speech discrimination are observed between infant groups, then it would seem that the variable of non-linguistic reality can indeed influence speech perception, just as Roger Brown suggested some fifty years ago.

32.6 The original word game: back to the future

After all, we know Brown thought (save homonyms) that 'invariance in speech signals some invariance outside of speech, some referent invariance' (1958a: 227). Would he not also agree that invariance among referents would be reflected in some 'speech invariance' (save for synonyms and co-referring names)? And might not this phonological expectation prompt infants, as Brown put it, to 'ignore those [phonetic distinctions] that are not phonemic' (1958a: 203)? A one-to-one pairing between (types of) words and (types of) referents allows bootstrapping not only from language to categorization, but from categorization to phonemic speech classification.

Perhaps infants who have yet to reach their first birthday are blind to this sort of word game information. And even if not blind, they might still be unable to exploit this type of word–object cross-modal pairing due to some sort of processing bottleneck (Pater, Stager, and Werker 2004; Werker and Yeung 2005). In any event, even if these cross-modal pairings might theoretically affect infant speech perception, the word–object associations are arguably only precursors to full-blown word learning. In terms of C. S. Peirce's (1894/1998) typology of signs, human word learning requires more than just an indexical recognition of cross-modal timing (like Pavlov's salivating dogs). Real word learning soon entails a symbolic appreciation of meaning (as part of a linguistic system). It is the difference between an associative 'goes with' relation vs. a semantic 'stands for' interpretation (Werker et al. 1998). Fortunately, for the experiment to work, it matters little how infants represent these word–object relations, how they conceive of the experimental props, and what types of learning support are necessary (e.g. moving rather than static objects, see Gogate, Walker-Andrews, and Bahrick 2001). All they have to do is treat some objects as the same, others as different, and cross-modally pair these same/different objects to some (allophonically related) speech tokens. And some recent research by Werker and her colleagues is exquisitely suggestive.

Yeung and Werker (2009) and Werker, Yeung, and Yoshida (2012) report that they succeeded in manipulating infant speech perception by cross-modally associating visual cues with phonetic word labels. Very much in the spirit of Brown's word games, an experimental group of 9-month-old English-learning infants was presented with two phonetically distinct syllable word tokens cross-modally paired with two distinct visual cues: [d̪a] (with a dental alveolar stop) was consistently paired with a moving video picture of one object while [ɖa] (with a retroflex alveolar stop) was paired with a moving video picture of a different object.

In this experiment, 9-month-old English-learning infants were chosen because, at this age, the infants already demonstrate a perceptual desensitivity to non-phonemic phones like [d̪] and [ɖ]. However, their perceptual window may still be open enough for targeted manipulation. Could the infants be experimentally trained to recover their lost speech sensitivity on the basis of associative visual cues? Yes. Results indicated that—unlike two control groups which either received no training or were subjected to inconsistent pairings between words and objects—the experimental infants regained their perceptual discrimination of this non-phonemic distinction.

So, when given a good reason to *increase* their perceptual discrimination (phonetically distinct words associated with two different referents), 9-month-old infants are quick to respond. And the inverse? When given analogous reasons to *decrease* their perceptual discrimination (phonetically distinct words associated with the same referent due to naturally occurring allophonic variation), infants are likely also to respond (see the discussion section in Yueng and Werker 2009: 241).

The upshot? Whereas words are exploited 'as lures for cognition' (Brown 1958a) or 'as invitations to form categories' (Waxman 1999) by adults, children, and even toddlers in order to learn more about their world, younger infants are not yet positioned to fully exert this sort of linguistic leverage. Rather, they are more likely to exploit a naive understanding of basic physical objects (Spelke 1994) and basic human intentions (Gergely 2003) to first learn as much as they can about their language. An opportunistically sequenced cyclical bootstrapping strategy of leaning on some interpretive cues to inform *word* categorization and then also leaning on words to inform *world* categorization is not circular. It is smart—potentially yet another example of the 'fox-like' (Maratsos and Deák 1995) nature of children's language acquisition. In a sense, infants have the linguistic motive, the social opportunity, and perhaps the cognitive means to use some interpretive cues as a developmental mechanism supporting language-specific phonemic speech perception. If only Brown could be there to play this round of his Original Word Game—and catch them in the act.

Acknowledgements

Without endorsing all the views and conclusions presented here, this chapter has benefited from improvements suggested by Eve Clark and Katherine Nelson, Distinguished Professor Emerita of Psychology at the Graduate Center of the City University of New York. Thanks also to John R. Taylor for his editorial revisions along the way.

CHAPTER 33

WHICH WORDS DO YOU NEED?

PAUL NATION

33.1 Introduction

One of the most striking features of words and word use can be seen if we turn a text into a word list which shows us the frequencies of the words in the text. The first thing we notice is that a small number of words like *the*, *of*, and *is* occur very frequently. These words make up a very large proportion of the text: *the* typically accounts for 7 per cent of the words in a written text, which means that on average every 14th word is *the*. Another noticeable feature is that very many of the different words occur only once. So, we have a small group of very frequent words and a large group of infrequent words. A less noticeable but very important feature of such a frequency list is that if we draw a graph of the frequency-ranked list, with frequency figures on the vertical axis and each word from the most frequent to the least frequent on the horizontal axis, we get a quickly falling and flattening smooth curve. The smooth regular pattern of the curve is an indication that there is a formula that describes it, and this formula is called Zipf's law after the psycholinguist George Zipf (1935) who first described it (see Sorell, this volume). The formula says that Rank multiplied by Frequency gives the same answer (a constant) for each word on the list. So, if the first-ranked word *the* occurs 70 times in a 1,000-word text, the second-ranked word (*of*) will occur 35 times ($2 \times 35 = 70$), the third-ranked word will occur around 23 times ($3 \times 23 \approx 70$), the fourth word around 17 times ($4 \times 17 \approx 70$), and so on. Zipf's law does not always work well, especially with lower-frequency words, but it is a reasonably useful description of the distribution of vocabulary in a text.

Since a relatively small number of different words accounts for a very large proportion of the running words in a text, researchers interested in the teaching and learning of languages have seen the value of developing lists of those very useful words so that learners can get the greatest benefit from their early vocabulary learning. If we look at the vocabulary of a novel, for example, knowing the most frequent 100 words will mean that you are familiar with 50 per cent of the running words. If you know the most frequent 1,000 words, you will be familiar with over 80 per cent of the running words, and if you know 2,000 words, you will be familiar with close to 90 per cent (including proper names). To get these percentage coverage figures, it is not enough to know any 1,000 words or any 2,000 words—they need to be the generally most frequent 1,000 or 2,000 words. Thus developing word lists of the most useful words has been seen as an excellent contribution to planning a good vocabulary-learning programme.

33.2 Making word lists

There are three important decisions to make when constructing a word list. The first concerns the reasons for making the list, a topic we return to in a moment. The second involves the kinds of text that will be used as a source of the words. Will the corpus of texts be a written corpus or a spoken corpus or a mixture of both? If it is a mixture of both, what will be the proportions of spoken and written texts? If it is a corpus of spoken texts, will it include scripted speech as in movies and television programmes? Will it include formal speaking as in university lectures, radio broadcasts, and parliamentary debates? The nature of the corpus strongly determines the nature of the list resulting from it. The third major decision is the unit of counting. The most basic unit of counting is the word type. A word type is largely distinguished by its form. Any change in the form will result in a different type. The words *book* and *books* are two different word types, as are *walk* and *walking*. In some word counts (Carroll, Davies, and Richman, 1971), capitalization resulted in different word types. So *book*, *Book*, and *BOOK* were counted as three different word types. Typically, however, capitalization is not used as a distinguishing feature unless there is a very strong reason to do so. Once learners know the inflectional system of English, there seems to be little sense in distinguishing words that differ only by the addition of an inflection.

A word list, then, might consist of lemmas. A lemma is a headword and its inflected forms which are all the same part of speech (Leech, Rayson, and Wilson 2001). *Walk*, *walks*, *walking*, and *walked* are all members of the same lemma—the verb *walk*. Note that *walk* (the noun) and its plural form, *walks*, would be members of a different lemma. There is some debate about what to include in a lemma. Should contracted forms like *n't* be included? Should alternative spellings like *labor* and *labour* be included?

A third unit of counting is the word family (Bauer and Nation 1993). A word family consists of a headword and its closely related inflected and derived forms. *Friend*, *friends*, *friendly*, *unfriendly*, *friendless*, *friendship*, and *befriend* are all members of the same word family. Bauer and Nation set up several levels of word families based on the spoken and written regularity of the affixes, their frequency, and their productivity. Using such a list it is possible to define the level of word families by listing the permitted affixes.

The decision on which unit of counting to use (the word type, the lemma, or the word family) will depend on the purposes for making a list. If the list is being made for productive purposes, i.e. for speaking or for writing, then the word type or the lemma is probably the best choice because knowing how to use one member of the word family does not mean that you know how to use the other members (Vermeer 2004). If the list is being made for receptive purposes, i.e. for listening or for reading, then the word family at a level appropriate for the proficiency of the learners is the best choice. It is important to stress that word families are intended for receptive purposes, i.e. for listening and reading. This is because the assumption that lies behind word families is that knowing one or more members of the family makes the others reasonably comprehensible with the help of spoken or written context. They are *not* intended for productive purposes—speaking or writing—because knowing one member of the family does not make it likely that learners could produce other members of the family with the correct affixes and in appropriate contexts. The advantages of word families are that there is evidence that they are psychologically real (Bertram, Laine, and Virkkala 2000; Nagy et al. 1989), and both common sense and experience shows that language users have few difficulties in coping with them in listening and reading. A disadvantage is that learners at different proficiency levels may require different levels of word families to match their current knowledge of affixes. A further disadvantage is that the connection between some family members may not be obvious (e.g. *swim–swimmingly*). In these cases, the words would need to be placed in different families.

Word families have come in for some unwarranted criticism. Research on foreign language learners' knowledge of affixes (Schmitt and Meara 1997; Schmitt and Zimmerman 2002) has focused on productive use of affixes which requires much greater knowledge than receptive interpretation. Word families have also been criticized for having a mixture of high-and low-frequency members. So, of course, do lemmas, but the relative frequency of members is irrelevant. The essential condition for lemma and word family membership is close form and meaning relationships.

To judge whether items should belong to the same word family, we should look for an etymological relationship, transparency and regularity of form and meaning relationships among the family members, and the absence of extra meaning that goes beyond the meaning of the parts (affixes and stems).

33.3 Native speakers and second- or foreign-language learners

When deciding what words to focus on for vocabulary growth, it is important to distinguish between native speakers and learners of English as a second or foreign language. On average, young native speakers of English increase their vocabulary size at the rate of around 1,000 word families a year from the age of about 2 or 3 years. The rule of thumb for estimating young native speakers' vocabulary size, then, is to take their age in years minus two and multiply by 1,000. Thus a 6-year-old is on average likely to have a vocabulary size of around 4,000 word families (Biemiller and Slonim 2001) and a 13-year-old around 11,000 word families (Coxhead, Nation, and Sim 2015), while a graduate student is likely to know around 20,000 word families (Coxhead, Nation, and Sim 2015). There is, of course, a large variation between speakers of the same age. Biemiller (2005) found that by the end of grade 6, vocabulary sizes ranged from 7,000 to over 13,000 word families. Even poor readers with lower vocabulary sizes still know several thousand words and are able to make substantial additions to their vocabulary each year, so that 13-year-olds with the lower ranges of vocabulary size still know at least 7,000 word families.

Non-native speakers who from an early age have lived in a country where English is used as the main language are likely to increase their vocabulary size at the same rate as native speakers, and to have comparable vocabulary sizes.

Many non-native speakers who live in countries where English is a foreign language may have rather small vocabulary sizes of 2,000 words or fewer in spite of having studied English for several years (Milton 2009; Nurweni and Read 1999). Others may have more respectable vocabulary sizes (Nguyen and Nation 2011), and it is important that teachers and course designers test the vocabulary sizes of their target learners to see what they know (Beglar 2010; Nation and Beglar 2007).

Corpus-based research on spoken and written texts shows that learners need a vocabulary size of between 6,000 and 9,000 words in order to cope with unsimplified spoken and written input (Adolphs and Schmitt 2003; Nation 2006; Webb and Rodgers 2009a, 2009b). This vocabulary size plus proper nouns is needed to reach 98 per cent coverage of the tokens in unsimplified texts, leaving 2 per cent to be inferred from context, looked up, or ignored. Because many non-native speakers of English have vocabulary sizes which are well short of this goal, planning for vocabulary learning is an important part of a well-designed language course.

Because vocabulary size is such a critical component of language use (Perfetti and Hart 2001, 2002), a planned approach to vocabulary development has many benefits for learners.

33.4 Vocabulary levels

A widely used way of planning for vocabulary learning is to divide vocabulary into various levels, typically in a sequenced series of levels based largely but not exclusively on frequency of occurrence and the range of use of the words. Most of these levels are of significance only for non-native speakers of English, because by the time they are teenagers, native speakers are well beyond the limits of high-frequency and mid-frequency words.

33.4.1 High-frequency words

High-frequency words are those with the highest frequency and widest range across a variety of different kinds of text. That is, they are words that occur in all kinds of use of the language, both spoken and written, formal and informal. The classic list of such words for learners of English as a foreign language is Michael West's list of 2,000 headwords, *A General Service List of English Words* (West 1953). This list has been criticized for its age, and there is no doubt that recently frequent words like *e-mail, internet, television*, and *computer* should be included. Research has shown that any changes to the 2,000-word list, though worthwhile, are likely to be rather small (Nation and Hwang 1995). There has also been a suggestion that the high-frequency words should number 3,000 rather than 2,000 (Schmitt and Schmitt 2014). Nation (2001a) looked at various reasons why the list should be around 2,000 words, but ultimately it is a somewhat arbitrary decision where high-frequency words end and mid- or low-frequency words begin.

Most of the function words of English occur within the first 2,000 words, but these words, like *a, the, of, because, one, two, under*, consist of 176 word families and so account for only a small proportion of the different word families in the first 2,000 words of English (Nation 2001b: 206). However, they make up a very large proportion of text coverage—in most texts around 47 per cent of the running word tokens.

The General Service List was designed as a list of words primarily for reading. It is likely that there is value in having separate lists of high-frequency spoken words and high-frequency written words. This distinction is incorporated in the frequency markings of the *Longman Dictionary of Contemporary English* and agrees with Biber and Conrad's (2009) view of the major distinction between the different kinds of English texts. Certainly, the most frequent content words in spoken texts differ from those in written texts (McCarthy and Carter 1997).

The General Service List is not solely based on word frequency. When making the list, West (1953: ix–x) considered several other factors, including (1) ease or difficulty of learning, (2) necessity (a word was included if it was the only way of expressing an important idea), (3) cover (words were excluded even if they were frequent if there were other high-frequency words which could easily replace them), (4) stylistic level (highly formal and highly colloquial words were excluded), and (5) emotional and intensive words (such words were excluded). It is likely that when West developed the list he was also trialling it by writing graded readers, and that this trialling resulted in changes to the list. It is also noteworthy that the first version of the list (the Interim Report on Vocabulary Selection) was published in 1936 and arose out of a sponsored conference in 1934. Word lists based solely on frequency data are unlikely to be completely satisfactory for pedagogical purposes.

33.4.2 Mid-frequency words

Schmitt and Schmitt (2014) distinguish mid-frequency from low-frequency words. Mid-frequency words are those which are not high-frequency words but occur within the most frequent 9,000 words of English. Because Schmitt and Schmitt see the high-frequency words as a list of 3,000 words, their mid-frequency words are those from the fourth 1,000 to the ninth 1,000 inclusive. A major justification for distinguishing mid-frequency from low-frequency words is that knowledge of the high- and mid-frequency words would give learners close to 98 per cent coverage of most kinds of texts. This level of coverage, where there is only one unknown word in every 50 running words, typically allows unassisted comprehension of unsimplified texts (Hu and Nation 2000; Schmitt, Jiang, and Grabe 2011).

The most available lists of mid-frequency words are those that accompany the Range program, which can be downloaded from Paul Nation's website.[1] The same lists are used in the VocabProfiler programs on Tom Cobb's website, the Compleat Lexical Tutor.[2]

Mid-frequency words are a sensible learning goal for learners who already know the high-frequency words and do not have special academic purposes in reading.

33.4.3 Academic words

If learners have special academic purposes in mind, there is a list of very useful words which provide a respectable amount of text coverage (around 10%) across a wide range of academic disciplines. This list is the Academic Word List (Coxhead 2000) and consists of 570 word families, divided into 10 sub-lists according to their frequency and range in academic texts. The Academic Word List assumes knowledge of the words in the General Service List and builds on that. If the General Service List is taken as a list of high-frequency words, then the words in the Academic Word List are all from the mid-frequency word level. While the Academic Word List provides around 10 per cent coverage of academic texts, it provides less than 2 per cent coverage of novels and around 4 per cent coverage of newspapers. Learning the words on the Academic Word List is an excellent way of quickly gaining access to the vocabulary needed to read academic texts. Here are some words from the Academic Word List: *abstract, adjust, circumstantial, coherent, differentiate, empirical, furthermore, innovation, major, overlap, phenomenon, protocol, refine, schedule, thesis, virtual, whereas*. Over 90 per cent of these words came to English from French, Latin, or Greek. They are mainly formal words that are used not only for the ideas that they communicate but also for the serious tone that they add to the writing. There are several websites and published texts which are designed to help the learning of words from the Academic Word List.

Learning the words from the Academic Word List is the obvious next step for learners who know the high-frequency words and who need to study through the medium of English. Corson's (1997) work on the lexical bar suggests that learning words from the Academic Word List may be more difficult than learning the high-frequency words, because they tend to be multisyllabic and involve the use of prefixes and suffixes. This generalization, however, is unlikely to be true for learners who speak Romance languages like French, Spanish, or Italian, because a very large proportion of the words in

[1] http://www.victoria.ac.nz/lals/about/staff/paul-nation

[2] http://www.lextutor.ca/

the Academic Word List are cognate with words in those languages. For example, just over 80 per cent of the words in the Academic Word List have words of related form and meaning in Spanish.

The words in the Academic Word List need to be learnt both receptively and productively. Learners with academic purposes in mind need not only to be able to recognize these words in reading and listening but also to produce them in speaking and writing.

The Academic Word List was made by creating a corpus of almost four million words of academic texts from four major divisions of Humanities, Science, Commerce, and Law, and within each major division there were seven subject disciplines, making a total of twenty-eight. To get into the Academic Word List, a word had to occur in all four major divisions, and in at least fifteen of the twenty-eight subdivisions. Words in the General Service List were automatically excluded.

The Science Word List (Coxhead and Hirsh 2007) is an extension of the Academic Word List, and includes 314 word families that are not in the General Service List and not in the Academic Word List, but which occur frequently across a range of science subjects. It includes words like *absorb, bacteria, degrade, membrane, nucleus*. This list provides around 4 per cent coverage of science texts, which is excellent coverage for such a small group of words at this level.

33.4.4 Low-frequency words

The three levels of high-frequency, mid-frequency, and low-frequency words are mutually exclusive. The high-frequency words consist of the first 2,000 or 3,000 words of English. The mid-frequency words consist of the 3rd or 4th 1,000 words through to the 9th 1,000 words of English. The low-frequency words include all those from the 10th 1,000 onwards. When setting up word lists, it makes sense to set up separate lists of proper nouns, transparent compounds, marginal words (*ummm, ah, gosh, wow*), and abbreviations. This is done partly on the assumption that these words involve a different kind of learning burden. For example, before we read a text we would not expect to have to know the names of characters and places in the text. This is information that we pick up during our reading.

How many low-frequency words are there? This is not an easy question to answer, and certainly cannot be answered by accepting statements of dictionary-makers about the number of words in their dictionaries. We cannot accept these statements, first, because they are often not the result of serious counting but are produced for publicity purposes to help the sale of the dictionaries. Secondly, the criteria for making such a count are typically not explained. For example, if the dictionary lists the inflected forms of the headword next to the headword, are these counted as separate words or not? In addition, many entries in very comprehensive dictionaries are actually phrases like *managed care, salivary gland*, and *stick figure*, where the meaning of the whole is clearly related to the meaning of the parts.

Vocabulary size is seen as being an important indicator of reading skill and the readiness to benefit from academic study. However, it would be going too far to suggest that schools should focus on vocabulary growth with the aim of avoiding educational inequality (see e.g. Hirsh 2013). Vocabulary size affects reading comprehension, but it is also a result of substantial reading and wider world knowledge. It is likely that focusing on reading and subject-matter study will have greater educational benefits than focusing simply on vocabulary.

33.4.5 Technical words

Many low-frequency words are technical words in a particular subject area. Medicine, for example, has a very large technical vocabulary consisting of thousands of words. Because of its history, many of these words come from Greek. Botany and zoology also have very large technical vocabularies. Subject areas like applied linguistics, geography, and psychology probably have smaller technical vocabularies of between 1,000 and 2,000 words. If multi-word phrases are also included, then this increases the size of the technical vocabularies.

Learning the technical vocabulary of the particular subject area is naturally an important goal for anyone studying in that subject area. Technical vocabulary can make up somewhere between 20 per cent and 30 per cent of the tokens in a technical text (Chung and Nation 2004). This means that somewhere between one word in every five and one word in every three, will be a technical word in a technical text.

Technical words can be high-frequency, mid-frequency, or low-frequency words. In medicine, for example, words like *body, head, cough,* and *cold* can be considered as technical words, because they occur very frequently within that subject area and are closely related in meaning to the knowledge of that subject area. We tend to think of technical words as those which are unlikely to be known by someone who does not work within that area, but in some technical fields most of the technical vocabulary is also relatively well known outside of that field.

The best way to decide which words are technical or not is to consult an expert in the field, asking questions like these. Is this word closely related to the subject matter of your field? If someone saw this word, would they typically associate it with your field? Do you need to use this word a lot within your field? (See L'Homme, this volume.) A faster but slightly less accurate way is to compare the frequency of words within a technical field with their frequency in a large corpus which does not include any texts from that particular technical field. Words that occur only within the technical field and not in the general corpus are highly likely to be technical words. Words that occur with a much higher frequency in the technical field than in the general corpus are also highly likely to be technical words (Chung and Nation 2004).

Technical vocabulary needs to be learnt while learners study within a particular subject area. Learning the subject matter is to a large degree learning the vocabulary. It does not make sense to try to study the technical vocabulary of a subject area before actually studying the subject.

Many areas of our daily life involve some kind of technical vocabulary. There is a technical vocabulary of cooking, a technical vocabulary of computing, and a technical vocabulary of gardening. Learning technical vocabulary is one of the most important ways that a native speaker's vocabulary grows once they know the first 10,000 or so words of the language. To truly measure someone's vocabulary size, we would also need to measure the size of their technical vocabularies. This is one of the major challenges in vocabulary size testing.

We have looked at the three major levels of vocabulary: high-frequency vocabulary, mid-frequency vocabulary, and low-frequency vocabulary. We have also looked at three special types of vocabulary: general academic words, science words, and technical vocabulary. While general academic words occur mainly within the mid-frequency vocabulary, technical vocabulary can come from all three of the major levels.

33.5 Uses of word lists

The major use of word lists is for research purposes, and this research can inform language teaching and learning. Thorndike and Lorge's (1944) early research on English word lists helped the design of basic word lists for foreign-language teaching (West 1953) and aided the development of vocabulary tests. In addition, it provided a basis for the analysis of English vocabulary (Stauffer 1942; Thorndike 1941) and the analysis of texts. More recent word lists (Kucera and Francis 1967) have provided frequency data for psychological experiments involving reaction time and lexical storage. Let us look first at the use of word lists for testing.

33.5.1 Word lists and vocabulary testing

One of the least researched areas in applied linguistics is vocabulary size testing. One of the major reasons for the poor research in this area has been a lack of readily available word lists to use as a basis for drawing up a sample of words to test. Thorndike (1924) was aware of the methodological problems, but his article describing these was not widely known and as a result researchers using dictionary-based samples of words wildly overestimated native speakers' vocabulary sizes. It is likely that one of the motivations that drove Thorndike to develop his word lists was the value of frequency-based word lists as a source of data for developing a vocabulary test. Certainly, he used his word lists to make an early test of vocabulary size. More recently, the Vocabulary Size Test (Beglar 2010; Nation and Beglar 2007) was able to be developed because substantial word family lists based on a large corpus could be used as a source for representative samples of words to go into the test. Being able to use carefully designed word lists avoids the major sampling problems faced by those who used dictionary-based samples.

33.5.2 Word lists and text coverage

Word lists have been used as a way of setting goals for foreign- and second-language learners. Some studies (Adolphs and Schmitt 2003; Bongers 1947; Webb and Rodgers 2009b) compared texts to word lists to see how much vocabulary, and what vocabulary, learners of English as a foreign language would need to know in order to be able to read without a great deal of external assistance. Such studies look at text coverage, i.e. what proportion of the tokens in a text or collection of texts is covered by particular word lists. An important question which arises in such studies is the minimum amount of text coverage that is needed for a learner to be able to read a text without the help of dictionaries or some other support. Hu and Nation's (2000) research suggested that this should be around 98 per cent. This means that for unassisted reading, only two words per 100 tokens should be unfamiliar to the reader, equivalent to roughly one unknown word in every five lines. More recent research (Schmitt, Jiang, and Grabe 2011) suggests that there is probably not one coverage threshold but that the larger vocabulary size a learner has, the better it will be for reading. However, a vocabulary size which provides close to 98 per cent coverage is certainly a desired goal.

Word list-based research looking at the relationship between vocabulary size and text coverage (Nation 2006) shows that for 98 per cent coverage of novels a vocabulary size of around 9,000 words is needed. For reading newspapers with 98 per cent coverage, a vocabulary size of 8,000 words is needed. This slightly smaller vocabulary size is because in such calculations proper nouns are assumed to be known words, and proper nouns provide higher text coverage in newspapers than they do in novels. For less formal uses of the language such as taking part in conversation or watching movies, a vocabulary size of around 6,000 words provides 98 per cent coverage.

This text coverage research has been one of the motivations for distinguishing mid-frequency vocabulary, because high-frequency vocabulary and mid-frequency vocabulary include what most users of the language would need for dealing with non-technical reading.

Text coverage research has also been used as the primary justification for developing word lists like the Academic Word List and the Science Word List. Such word lists provide good coverage of academic and science texts. Similarly, research on technical words and their text coverage has shown that technical vocabulary makes up a very large proportion of the words in any technical text (Chung and Nation 2004).

One danger in interpreting such research is that text coverage is often wrongly associated with comprehension. 98 per cent coverage of a text is not the same as 98 per cent comprehension of a text. In the research by Hu and Nation (2000), adequate comprehension was defined as around 80 per cent as measured by multiple-choice and recall tests.

Another danger is that 98 per cent coverage is seen as covering most of the vocabulary in the text. From the point of view of tokens, this is largely true, but from the point of view of word types or word families, it is certainly not true. For example, in an average novel of around 100,000 tokens, 2 per cent of the tokens will consist of around 2,000 words and although some of these words will be repeated, there are likely to be well over 1,000 different word families which are not covered by the first 9,000 words and which are not proper nouns. This means that someone with a vocabulary size of 9,000 words reading such a novel will still face a very large number of unknown word families.

The availability of word lists and of computer programs which use them to analyse texts has greatly increased our knowledge of what vocabulary learners of English need to know and how much they need to know.

33.5.3 Word lists and the deliberate teaching and learning of vocabulary

An attractive feature of word lists is that they can show what needs to be learnt. This may then be an encouragement for teachers to teach vocabulary and for learners to learn from word lists. Let us look first at vocabulary teaching.

Native speakers of English do not require special deliberate attention to vocabulary except for word recognition when they are learning to read and for technical vocabulary when they study. The vast majority of native-speaker vocabulary growth occurs through listening and reading rather than through direct instruction (Nagy and Herman 1985). There is value in encouraging native speakers to become interested in words and in learning word-part analysis techniques and useful word parts, but these are not essential to normal vocabulary growth. As we saw in section 33.3, native speakers have large enough vocabularies to easily handle the leisure reading that they choose to do, although they may need a little vocabulary help (but not much) with more technical reading. For most native speakers, vocabulary size is not a major issue in the reading that they typically do.

For non-native speakers of English, however, there is great value in planning for vocabulary growth (see Boers, this volume), and word lists can play an important role in this planning. Direct instruction of vocabulary by a teacher is really only feasible for the high-frequency words of the language. This is a small enough group of words to justify such teaching time. The creation of the Academic Word List and the Science Word List is a way of increasing the number of high-frequency words that could be deliberately taught for learners who have special purposes. Beyond this, the deliberate teaching of vocabulary to learners of English as a foreign or second language is not an efficient use of classroom time, and learners are best encouraged to take control of their own deliberate vocabulary learning and to rely on substantial listening and reading for vocabulary growth.

In addition, research on vocabulary teaching and on working through vocabulary exercises shows that such activity is likely to result in well under half of the words actually being learnt. For evidence of this, see the vocabulary learning outcomes of the research on the involvement load hypothesis (Folse 2006; Hulstijn and Laufer 2001; Keating 2008; Kim 2008b) and on vocabulary notebooks (Walters and Bozkurt 2009). The deliberate teaching of vocabulary is neither efficient nor highly effective, and there are better alternatives.

The deliberate learning of vocabulary, on the other hand, needs to be encouraged, particularly among learners of English as a foreign language (see Boers, this volume). This deliberate learning, however, needs to be seen in the wider context of a well-balanced course. A well-balanced language course contains four strands which have equal amounts of time devoted to them—meaning-focused input, meaning-focused output, language-focused learning, and fluency development (Nation 2007; Nation and Yamamoto 2012). The deliberate learning of vocabulary makes up only part of the language-focused learning strand. This means that only a small proportion of the course time should be given to such learning, and that a very large proportion of the course time (the input, output, and fluency development strands) should be given to meaning-focused incidental learning.

Word lists can be an important source of vocabulary for deliberate learning. Ideally, the lists themselves should not be used for finding words to learn but should be used as a way of checking that the words that the learner has chosen to learn are at the most appropriate level for them. This means that foreign-language learners should know their vocabulary size and what level of vocabulary they should be focusing on. Barker (2007) presents a useful set of guidelines for training learners in choosing what words to learn.

One of the main arguments made against using word lists as a source of words to learn is that they encourage learning out of context. There is no experimental research which shows that learning words in context is superior to learning words out of context, and there is plenty of research which shows that decontextualized learning is highly effective (Elgort 2011; Nation 2001b: 296–316).

33.5.4 Word lists and reaction-time studies

Frequency-based word lists play an important role in studies that look at the storage and accessibility of vocabulary. For example, several studies have examined whether the idea of the word family is psychologically real (Bertram, Laine, and Virkkala 2000; Nagy et al. 1989). Basically, the methodology of such studies involves seeing if learners' speed of response to a word is more affected by the frequency of the word type itself or by the total frequency of the family that the word fits into. The research shows that for receptive use the total frequency of the word family is the best predictor of reaction time. To carry out such studies, reliable frequency figures are needed for the types and word families. This returns us to a problem that we looked at in the beginning of this chapter—the representativeness of the corpus. Brysbaert and New (2009) found that both corpus size and the nature of the corpus had marked effects on the quality of the frequency figures. For high-frequency words, a corpus of 1 million tokens was sufficient. For low-frequency words, a corpus of over 30 million tokens was needed. The availability of very large diverse corpora means that the frequency figures for low-frequency words can now be more discriminating. Brysbaert and New also found that word lists based on a spoken-language corpus (movies) provided more useful frequency figures to relate to reaction times than lists based on a written corpus.

33.5.5 Word lists and research on word parts

The availability of word lists has meant that it is easier to do research on word parts taking account of the usefulness of the words that they occur in. Stauffer (1942) and Bock (1948) used Thorndike and Lorge's list to find the most useful prefixes in English. Nagy and Anderson (1984) used the word list made for the *American Heritage Dictionary* to estimate the size of word families. Wei (2012) used the British National Corpus word family lists to see how many words from the 3rd 1,000 to 10th 1,000 could be accessed by word stems contained in the first 2,000 words of English. The most productive stem was *-posit-/-pos-*, found in the high-frequency word *position* (Wei and Nation 2013). This stem provided access to 21 lower-frequency words. In total, around 2,000 mid-frequency words could be accessed by stems contained in the first 2,000 words. When learning lower-frequency words, relating already known words is a useful mnemonic device.

33.5.6 Word lists and curriculum design

Frequency-based word lists have been extremely important in the development of one of the most useful resources for vocabulary learning and foreign language development—graded readers. Graded readers are texts which are written within a controlled vocabulary so that learners of English as a foreign language can read with ease and enjoyment right from the early stages of language learning. Michael West, who was largely responsible for the development of the General Service List, was also the developer of the first series of graded readers, the New Method Supplementary Readers, published by Longman. Now, every major English Language Teaching publisher has its own series of graded readers typically involving five or six stages from a few hundred words to around 3,000. Unfortunately, very few of these publishers now make their word lists readily available to teachers or curriculum developers; partly as a result of this, each publisher has its own set of carefully guarded graded word lists. This means that course designers must also develop their own word lists if they wish to take a systematic approach to vocabulary development within a course.

There are surprisingly few language courses which claim to pay special attention to vocabulary by basing the progression of their course on well-designed word lists. This may be because of the strong grammar focus of most courses.

The ready availability of powerful computers, large and varied corpora, and flexible software has meant that it is now easier than ever to create word lists. Fortunately, the availability of the tools has also been accompanied by research into how these tools are best used (Nation and Webb 2011; Schmitt 2010), and the principles of corpus linguistics have an important role to play in word list research. There is no ultimate word list. The best word list is the one which is most suited to the purpose for which it is being used, and when the purpose changes, the list will also need to change.

CHAPTER 34

WORDS IN SECOND LANGUAGE LEARNING AND TEACHING

FRANK BOERS

34.1 Introduction

SUCCESSFUL learning of a second language (by which we mean a second, third, or nth language) is strongly associated with vocabulary learning. Learners' scores on vocabulary tests have been found to be reliable predictors of general proficiency, regarding both language production (Iwashita et al. 2008) and comprehension (Qian 1999; Schmitt, Jiang, and Grabe 2011; Staehr 2009). Such findings confirm Wilkins' (1972: 111) famous statement that 'while without grammar little can be conveyed, without vocabulary nothing can be conveyed'.

Second-language vocabulary learning is a daunting task. There are a great many words to be learned if one wishes to be able to cope unaided with authentic discourse in the second language. There is also a lot to be learned about any given word. Knowing a word includes knowledge about the contexts in which the word is typically used: knowing *tummy* includes knowledge that this word (instead of *stomach*) is often used by children or by adults addressing children. Word knowledge also means appreciation of the different senses or functions that a single word form can have: predators *catch* prey, people *catch* a train and can also *catch* a cold. Knowledge of a word thus entails knowledge of which other words it habitually co-occurs with. *A pretty woman* sounds fine, but *a pretty man* sounds odd. As Firth (1957: 11) famously stated, 'You shall know a word by the company it keeps.' Further, knowledge of a word involves its pronunciation (witness often-mispronounced words such as *debt* and *gauge* by learners of English, and the problem that English-speaking learners of French have with words spelled with *u* such as *tu*, *plus*, and *chutte*), as well as its spelling (*exercises* in English but *exercices* in French) and its grammar (e.g. English *information* does not have a plural form, cf. French *informations).*

Given the magnitude of the vocabulary-learning task, it is not surprising that applied linguists have proposed ways of prioritizing segments of vocabulary for learning. As this is an area that is described in detail in Nation, we will here only briefly reiterate the gist of those proposals. The remainder of the chapter will be devoted to ways of helping learners to expand their vocabularies.

34.2 Prioritization

It is undeniable that some words are of more practical use than others. *Run* can be used to describe more events of self-propelled motion than, say, *jog* or *sprint*. In addition, the word is used with extended meanings in phrases such as *running water* and *running a business*, where *jogging* or *sprinting* would not fit. While it stands to reason that language learners are best served by learning high-utility words first, it is hard to gauge degrees of usefulness directly. However, it is possible to gauge the general utility of a word indirectly by investigating the frequency with which it is used, and by checking whether its usage is confined to specialized discourse. Such an exercise has become increasingly feasible in recent times thanks to the availability of electronically searchable language corpora.

Corpus-based frequency data are an invaluable source of information for second-language vocabulary pedagogy. First, inclusion of frequency information in learners' dictionaries can help dictionary users appreciate the relative importance of the words they look up. Second, frequency data can inform the design of tests for vocabulary size (Nation and Beglar 2007; Schmitt, Schmitt, and Clapham 2001). Third, since frequency information is an indirect way of gauging the relative utility of words, it can help teachers and materials designers make sure that learners are given ample opportunities for acquiring words that are known to be most useful in the early stages of their learning. For example, Schmitt and Schmitt (2012) propose that priority in (English) vocabulary instruction should be given to the 3,000 most frequent words—or, rather, the 3,000 most frequent 'word families' (i.e. lemmas, their derivations, and their inflected forms).

Yet knowledge of those 3,000 word families is usually far from sufficient for adequate text comprehension (Hu and Nation 2000; Laufer 1989; Laufer and Ravenhorst-Kalovski 2010; Schmitt, Jiang, and Grabe 2011). Several thousand more words need to be known (at least receptively) for a learner to cope independently with a variety of authentic text genres (Nation, 2006). Implementing the frequency principle to decide which words merit prioritization beyond the 3,000 highest-frequency words is impracticable, however, because the corpus frequency of words drops drastically and then levels off beyond the high-frequency words (Zipf 1949). In any case, the vocabulary-learning demand is such that it cannot possibly be met through classroom instruction alone. Vocabulary uptake from exposure to second-language text outside the classroom is addressed in the next section.

34.3 Vocabulary Acquisition as a By-Product of Message-Focused Communication

People normally focus on the content of a message rather than its precise wording. New words do tend to receive some attention (Godfroid, Boers, and Housen 2013) and they may leave some trace in memory; but this is typically a very superficial trace that will quickly erode unless the same word is soon encountered and attended to again. When re-encountered, the form of the word may gradually become familiar, and given sufficient numbers of encounters in semantically transparent contexts, its meaning may also gradually emerge to the learner (Webb 2007a). This cumulative, incremental word learning as a by-product of primarily message-focused activities is often called 'incidental' learning (as opposed to 'intentional' learning).

The vast majority of studies on incidental vocabulary learning to date have investigated uptake from reading (Cho and Krashen 1994; Horst, Cobb, and Meara 1998; Paribakth and Wesche 1999; Pigada and Schmitt 2006; Waring and Takaki 2003), and of necessity it is that body of research that informs the following discussion. It needs to be borne in mind, however, that findings from reading studies may not be generalizable to vocabulary acquisition as a by-product from listening (Vidal 2003), where the learner cannot give pause to unfamiliar words as the flow of input continues, or as a by-product from face-to-face interaction (Newton 1995).

How often a word needs to be encountered during reading for durable word knowledge to develop depends on a multitude of factors, but there is general agreement among vocabulary researchers that it will usually take a lot of encounters. The more optimistic estimates range from between six and ten, provided these occur within a short span of time (Cobb 2007; Waring and Nation 2004). The problem is that, beyond the high-frequency vocabulary bands, it is improbable that a second-language learner will stumble on the same word time and again, and with interludes short enough to prevent erosion of memory traces, even if they were to read extensively in the second language every day. By its very nature, vocabulary that is infrequent does not lend itself well to learning from exposure alone.

Apart from the long intervals between encounters, several more obstacles can hinder incidental vocabulary learning (Laufer 2003). First, it cannot be taken for granted that learners realize that they do not understand a word. Due to phonological or orthographic similarities, they may mistake a new word for one they are familiar with. They may mistake *adopt* for *adapt*, *prize* for *price*, and *scarred* for *scared*. In the case of homonyms and polysemous words, they may mistake an unfamiliar usage for one they know. *Thick* employed to mean 'stupid' may be misinterpreted as the opposite of *thin*. The learner's mother tongue may have words that look like the second-language word but do not share its meaning. These deceptive cognates are often referred to as 'false friends'.

This is the case with *thick* from the perspective of a Dutch speaker, because Dutch *dik* (which resembles *thick*) means 'big', not 'stupid'. Again, this may lead learners to overestimate their comprehension. A French-speaking learner of English may wrongly assume that *actually* means 'at the moment', because that is the meaning of French *actuellement*. An English-speaking learner of French may wrongly assume that *éventuellement* means 'in the end', while it means 'perhaps'. An English-speaking learner of German may not realize that German *Gift* refers to poison, not to a present. An English-speaking learner of Dutch may mistake *fabriek* (factory) for fabric. A French-speaking learner of English may misinterpret *I envy you* as 'I fancy you', because of the meaning of *envie* in French. A Dutch reader who encounters the word *transpire* in an English text may assume this means 'to sweat', because that is the meaning of Dutch *transpireren*. Interestingly, experimental psycholinguistics research shows that, even after the learner has acquired the appropriate meaning of second-language words that have deceptive cognates in their mother tongue, the latter will still tend to be co-activated in the learner's mind during second-language processing. (See Williams, this volume.)

The second factor that can affect the chances of a learner giving pause to a new word is the importance of that word for overall text comprehension. Even if the learner does realize or suspect that she does not comprehend a given word, comprehension of this word may not be perceived as crucial to comprehending the text passage as a whole. Especially if one is carried away by the content or story line of a text, one may ignore unfamiliar words.

Another explanation for the slow pace of word learning from extensive reading is that the precise meaning of a new word can only begin to emerge if the word is encountered in contexts that are rich in semantic clues and if the learner makes effective use of those clues (Webb 2008). Studies on guessing from context caution that new words are not always accompanied by revelatory hints at their meaning—and in cases where a learner starts off with a wrong first assumption (possibly due to the aforementioned deceptive lookalikes) counter-evidence is often ignored (Laufer and Sim 1985; Nassaji 2003).

These kinds of obstacles put second-language learners at a disadvantage in comparison to first-language learners, for at least three reasons. First, the amount of exposure to the first language is far greater. From birth, a child is immersed virtually every waking hour in the language to be acquired. One that arrives in a new linguistic community, say, at the age of 7 has already missed out on many thousands of hours of 'minable' input, and the amount of exposure when a language is learned in a school context is minute in comparison to L1 acquisition. Second, the language that caregivers use to young children is very repetitive. When an adult learns a second language, she is likely to be exposed to messages about a greater diversity of subjects and thus with less repetition of the same words. Third, first-language vocabulary acquisition is naturally less susceptible to interference from other words than second-language vocabulary acquisition. By the time the second language learning venture begins, the learner may already have labels in L1 for most things, and this has the potential to impede acquisition of the L2 labels (Ellis 2008). In the following sections we look at interventions intended to help second-language learners overcome these disadvantages in comparison to first-language acquirers.

34.4 Manipulating texts to enhance vocabulary uptake

In order for readers to make good use of contextual clues to infer the meaning of an unknown word, they need to comprehend the text passage in which the unknown word occurs. A first way of removing obstacles to successful guessing from context is thus to provide reading materials made up largely of familiar words, so that the meaning of the unfamiliar words stands a good chance of being inferred adequately. That is part of the rationale behind simplified, or graded readers. These are texts (often adaptations of well-known novels or short stories) meant for learners at particular levels of proficiency and made up of words that are believed to be within those learners' reach. Apart from instilling a liking for extensive reading in the second language, fostering reading fluency, and engendering intuitions about the usage patterns of half-familiar words (such as their grammatical behaviour and the words they tend to co-occur with), such texts are intended to provide opportunities for smooth vocabulary expansion because any unknown words are likely to be met in accessible contexts (Nation and Deweerdt 2001). The question remains, of course, whether readers whose text comprehension is not hindered by the occasional unknown word will effectively give much attention to that word—and attention is widely believed to be a prerequisite for intake (Schmidt 2001).

An additional proposal for enhancing learning from context has been to teach learners guessing-from-context strategies. This typically involves steps such as identifying the part of speech of the word (e.g. as a noun or verb), using grammar cues (such as word order or inflection) to infer semantic roles, and analysing the broader context. Recognizing affixes (e.g. *anti-* in *antidote*, *-less* in *homeless*) can also help, although ambiguity cannot be ruled out. While the prefix *in-* will often denote something negative (*inaccurate, inadequate, invalid*), it does not in *invaluable*. While *pre-* can generally be taken to mean 'before', that interpretation would not help in understanding *predator*. A learner might even interpret *predator* as someone who woos a potential partner before asking them out for a date. Good readers tend to be good at using guessing strategies, and so it seems worth raising learners' awareness of such strategies (Fukkink and de Glopper 1998), although the real effect of this awareness-raising on actual second-language vocabulary learning is under-researched. The connection between reading comprehension and effective use of contextual clues may be a bit of a chicken-and-egg question: do you get better at comprehending texts because you learn to make good use of contextual information, or do you get better at mining contexts because you comprehend them well? In any case, no matter how well versed one may be in mining contextual clues, there is no guarantee (a) that all unknown words will be subjected to guessing-from-context attempts and (b) that such attempts will lead to the correct interpretation of the word.

To enhance the chances of words being attended to, words of interest are sometimes typographically highlighted (i.e. underlined, bolded, or italicized) (Paribakth and Weshe, 1997; Han, Park, and Combs 2008). To increase the likelihood that learners attach the correct meanings to word forms, glosses of the words' meanings may be provided (De Ridder, 2002; Ko, 2012; Kost, Fost, and Lenzini, 1999; Watanabe 1997). Giving students practice in using dictionaries must be a worthwhile investment of time, too, as inefficient use is quite common (Laufer 2011; Laufer and Hill 2000). While such interventions are certainly beneficial for text comprehension purposes, the extent to which they also foster long-term vocabulary retention is a matter of debate (Hulstijn, Hollander, and Greidanus 1996; Petchka 2010).

According to Hulstijn and Laufer (2001), the likelihood of vocabulary uptake from exposure is greatest if the learner feels a genuine need to find out about a word, invests effort into looking for the desired information, and thoroughly evaluates whether the information (e.g. a dictionary definition) truly satisfies the need that triggered the search. The evaluation stage is likely to be particularly important for retention (Keating 2008). The relatively disappointing retention rates that have been reported in some of the glossing studies may be explained by the observation that look-ups during reading typically serve the purpose of resolving text comprehension questions rather than intentional word learning (Hulstijn 1993). Once the learner feels text comprehension is ensured, she may turn her attention to what follows in the text rather than engaging any further with the characteristics of the word. As a result, it can take many consecutive look-ups before the word begins to be retained in memory (Peters et al. 2009).

An additional motivational factor that can hinder retention pertains to words whose meanings can also be expressed by means which the learner has already mastered (Ellis 2008; Webb 2007b). For instance, a learner may not experience strong motivation to add *exhausted* or *knackered* to her repertoire when she feels capable of expressing more or less the same notion with the familiar expression *very tired*. This motivational factor—in concert with the frequency factor—helps explain why many learners' vocabulary growth reaches a plateau after the high-frequency bands are mastered, especially when it comes to vocabulary for active usage.

Announcing that a vocabulary test will follow a reading task seems to stimulate retention (Peters 2012). This, however, changes the purpose of the reading task from message-focused activity to deliberate vocabulary-focused study, which we turn to next.

34.5 Deliberate vocabulary learning

If it is hard to attend simultaneously to the content of a text and the precise wording that is used to convey that content, then language learners will be well served by processing the same text at least twice. Once the content of the text is familiar, attention can be turned more easily to the way this content is expressed, and this naturally includes the use of vocabulary. The vocabulary thus becomes a subject of study in its own right. This is known as intentional or deliberate learning. Complementing message-focused activities by vocabulary-focused activities accelerates second-language vocabulary growth considerably (Ekhert and Tavakoli 2012; Laufer and Roitblat-Rozovski 2011).

Intentional vocabulary learning entails efforts to store target words in long-term memory. A number of word memorization techniques are listed below. First, however, it is useful to sketch some theories of memory for language that have been particularly influential in second-language vocabulary research; this will help clarify the merits of the techniques.

Let's start with models that emphasize the importance of rehearsal mechanisms. According to Baddeley (1997), repetition (e.g. overt articulation) of a new word is crucial for the word to be temporarily held in working memory, a prerequisite for entry into long-term memory. Rehearsal is pertinent also after the word has crossed the threshold to long-term memory. Intervals between repetitions need to be small enough in the beginning to avoid decay of the memory trace, and gradually made longer as the risk of attrition decreases (Pimsleur 1967). This is known as 'expanded spacing' or 'expanded rehearsal', a principle harking back to the work of Ebbinghaus (1885). Retrieval practice in keeping with this principle is advocated by Nation (2001), who advises learners to create packs of flashcards (with the target word on one side and a cue for retrieval—usually the L1 translation—on the other) for retrieval practice.

The mental operations that a learner performs when engaging with a new word will influence the durability of memory traces, and will thus influence the amount of practice required for its entrenchment in long-term memory. 'Levels of Processing' theory (Craik and Lockhart 1972; Craik and Tulving 1975) holds that 'deep', elaborate processing of words generates more durable memory traces than superficial rote learning. Retention is fostered by the creation of rich associations with the meaning of the word. Also worth mentioning is 'Dual Coding' theory (Paivio and Desrochers 1979), which emphasizes the importance of concreteness of meaning for ease of learning. Concrete meanings (e.g. the meaning of *horse*) can be visualized more readily than abstract meanings (e.g. the meaning of *faith*), and that makes the former easier to remember. It is therefore proposed that coding words in a 'dual' fashion, i.e. in association with an image, is beneficial, since memory of this image may provide a pathway for retrieval of the word itself. Recent studies inspired by Dual Coding theory show that also words with abstract meanings can be made more memorable if visuals can be found that illustrate these meanings (Farley, Ramonda, and Liu, 2012). Abstract uses of words (e.g. *embarking on a project; a kneejerk reaction*) can be made more imageable and thus memorable by making learners aware of their primary, concrete uses (*embarking on a ship; the uncontrolled jerking response of your leg when the GP taps the knee with a small hammer*) (Boers 2000a, 2000b, 2001). Given that imagery is by definition connected to the semantics of the word, Dual Coding may be situated within the Levels of Processing approach, as both give precedence to meaning over word form to make vocabulary memorable.

According to 'Transfer Appropriate Processing' theory (Morris, Bransford, and Franks 1977), the effectiveness of any mnemonic technique needs to be gauged relative to the learning goal. According to this model, meaning-focused processing will result first and foremost in strong memory traces about the meaning of a word, whereas a focus on the orthographic and/or phonological features of a word is required to ensure accurate recall of those features. As we shall see below, a focus on word form can also vary in terms of 'depth' of processing—a point that has meanwhile been acknowledged also within the Levels of Processing framework (Lockhart and Craik 1990). Processing that is transfer-appropriate is congruent with the purpose that the acquired knowledge is intended to serve. In other words, the method of learning will determine the nature of the resulting knowledge representation. For example, comprehension activities will result first and foremost in receptive word knowledge, while it takes output activities to stimulate productive knowledge (Joe 1998). Another example is the use of visuals as a mnemonic aid. This will promote retention of the meaning of new words rather than their precise phonological/orthographic form (Boers et al. 2009).

Finding positive evidence for the effectiveness of an instructional method will be contingent to some degree upon whether the test format is congruent with the type of learning that is promoted by the instructional method. The benefits of semantic elaboration will be attested in tests that measure knowledge of word meaning; but to do well on tests that require (re-)production of the target words, learners will benefit from an instructional method that also stimulates engagement with the form of those words. One of the proponents of Transfer Appropriate Processing in second-language vocabulary research is Barcroft (2002, 2003). The multifaceted nature of vocabulary knowledge is also a reason why vocabulary testing should employ diverse measures (Laufer et al. 2004; Webb 2005). Given the multifaceted nature of vocabulary knowledge, it is also to be expected that a combination of learning strategies will be required for a learner to obtain comprehensive knowledge of a word. What follows is a non-exhaustive list of memorization techniques, tentatively grouped according to whether they orient the learner's attention primarily to the form of words, to their meaning, or to both.

Simple form-oriented memorization techniques are saying the word repeatedly out loud or writing it down. Learners may also retain the stress pattern and pronunciation of a word from singing along with a song or from reciting poetry. Creating rhymes with a new target word is another option to remind oneself of the pronunciation of the target (e.g. creating a rhyme with *room* will help entrench the pronunciation of *tomb*). That words are often remembered quite spontaneously in combination with a mnemonically helpful co-text is illustrated by the mutual cueing effect for some people of *See you later* and *alligator*. A certain amount of metalinguistic awareness may provide additional pathways for engagement with word forms. For example, learners can be made aware of formal features that have mnemonic potential, such as alliteration (e.g. in *skyscraper* and in *tiptoe*). They may be alerted to inconsistencies between spelling and pronunciation (e.g. the unpronounced 'b' in *tomb*), be referred to analogues for this pattern (e.g. *bomb* and *climb*), and may perhaps even be encouraged to think about the reasons behind the pattern (e.g. articulatory ease motivating language change) as a pathway for elaboration.

Meaning-oriented memorization techniques are typically of the 'paired-associate' type, and include learning the L1 translation equivalent of the L2 word (if there is one), defining the meaning of the word (e.g. *lukewarm* is located on a scale between cold and warm), comparing near-synonyms (e.g. *truck* vs. *lorry*), categorizing the word (e.g. a *cardigan* is an item of clothing), drawing the object that word refers to or one that the word can easily be related to (e.g. drawing a cactus to illustrate the adjective *prickly*), matching the word with a picture of its referent, conjuring up a mental image of the concept denoted by the word, and enacting the meaning of the word (e.g. making a fist when learning the meaning of *squeeze*). The direction of the association in all these cases is from the L2 word to an elucidation of its meaning (e.g. an L1 counterpart). This direction of paired-associate learning has been found to engender primarily receptive knowledge, i.e. the ability to recognize or retrieve the meaning of the L2 words when the L2 words are given, whereas the reversed direction—which we turn to below—is more conducive to productive knowledge, i.e. retrieval of the L2 words when primed by a meaning cue (Webb 2009).

Among memorization techniques intended to stimulate engagement with the form as well as the meaning of new words are output activities where the learner practises a new word in a new context, for instance by inventing a sentence or scenario to insert the word in—this requires not only embedding the word in a context that fits its meaning but also accurate recollection of the pronunciation and/or spelling of the word. As already mentioned, paired-associate learning where the L2 word is retrieved on the basis of a meaning prime provides practice in retrieval of word form, too. Common primes for retrieval are L1 translation equivalents, pictures, and L2 synonyms. At a more metalinguistic level, learners may benefit also from evaluating whether the form of a given word matches its meaning (Deconinck, Boers, and Eyckmans 2010; Kantartzis, Kita, and Imai 2011). There is a certain amount of iconicity or sound symbolism in language such that some words seem better candidates than others to express a given notion (Nuckolls 1999; Nygaard, Cook, and Nanny 2009; Ramachandran and Hubbard 2001). *Bombastic* sounds bigger than *mini*. The /sw/ onset that is shared by *sweep, swish, swivel, swirl, swing*, and *swoop* seems to evoke the particular kind of movement that is part of the meaning of these words (Bloomfield 1933; Parault and Schwanenflugel 2006). Iconicity can be exploited also at the level of written representation of the word, especially in languages that use logographic script (e.g. Chinese) containing pictographic traces (Shen 2010).

In the case of transparent compounds (*armchair, rainbow, counterevidence*), learners may contemplate how the different word parts contribute to the overall meaning, and by doing so attend to the makeup of the word as well as its meaning. In addition, learners may conjure up images that reflect both the makeup and the meaning of such words. In the case of *skyscraper*, the learner can imagine a tall building scraping against the sky. The meaning and form of *tiptoe* may be associated with a visual of a cartoon character walking on the tips of his toes. There is some evidence that pointing out the original meanings of parts of words can aid retention (Corson 1997). Awareness that the Latin-origin *precede* consists of *pre* ('before') and a reduction of *cedere* ('go') may render the word more concrete. Informing learners that *window* was originally a compound consisting of 'wind' and 'eye' may incite some cognitive engagement with the word that can help entrench it in memory.

A recurring recommendation in the literature is to connect new words with already acquired knowledge (Sokmen 1997). This is straightforward when *cognates* (i.e. words that are similar in form and meaning) are available in the learner's mother tongue or another language that the learner is familiar with. An English-speaking learner of French can use her knowledge of the cognate *vehicle* to retrieve the French word *véhicule*. According to Hall (2002), learners are naturally inclined to tie new words to potential cognates (also see Williams, this volume). The availability of cognates will depend on the degree of relatedness of the familiar and the target language. For example, English and Dutch both belong to the Germanic language family and thus have a lot in common. Many cognates may also be available if one language has strongly influenced the other. English has borrowed a large proportion of its vocabulary from French, for instance. Another example is the abundance of English loanwords in Japanese (Daulton 2008). At the same time, it must be borne in mind that the pronunciation of loanwords may in some cases be so far removed from the acoustic properties of the original word that recognition of cognate status cannot be taken for granted.

Paired-associate learning with already familiar words (such as words in the mother tongue) can be stretched beyond cognates in the strict sense of the word. When a target word shows sufficient acoustic or orthographic overlap with a familiar word, then the latter may possibly be turned into a paired associate of the target word (and thus serve as a retrieval cue) if a meaning-relation between them can somehow be created. For example, the word *leopard* may be paired with *jeopardy* because of formal resemblance and because knowledge that a leopard is a dangerous animal provides a link with the meaning of *jeopardy* ('dangerous'). Thanks to this type of association, many more L1 words than genuine cognates may become available as potential associates for L2 target words. Dutch *puntje* ('sharp end') can be associated with English *puncture* through a mental scene where a sharp object has punctured a tyre. Similarly, Dutch *bleek* ('pale') can serve as a retrieval cue for English *bleach*, thanks to the partial phonological overlap and because we know that bleach turns fabrics pale. This memorization technique has become known as the Keyword Method (Atkinson 1975). It is a memorization technique that relies on mental imagery and is thus in keeping with Dual Coding theory. The technique can be stretched so as to create keywords whose link with the target word meaning requires a fair degree of imagination. For example, an English-speaking learner of Dutch may try to use *tree* as a keyword for the retrieval of *trui* ('jumper') via an image of a tree that is wearing a jumper. One of the advantages claimed for the Keyword Method is that it can even render words with abstract meanings imageable (and thus more memorable) by virtue of a link with a concrete-meaning keyword. A French- or Dutch-speaking learner might use a mental picture of people applauding a hero and cheering *Bravo!* to help retain the meaning and form of the English word *brave*. An English-speaking learner of Dutch may try to remember Dutch *vrolijk* (merry) by mentally picturing merrily *frolicking* chimpanzees. Still, target words with abstract meanings do not seem to lend themselves as well to the technique as words with concrete meanings (Shapiro and Waters 2005).

The Keyword Method has been put to the test in dozens of studies. It has been assessed favourably in many of them (Avila and Sadoski 1996; Brown and Perry 1991; Moore, and Surber 1992; Pressley, Levin, and Delaney 1982; Pressley et al. 1982), but also found not to be particularly beneficial for long-term retention (Wang and Thomas 1995) and in some cases actually found *less* effective than rote learning (Barcroft, Sommers, and Sunderman 2011; Campos, Gonzales, and Amor 2003). It seems that the effectiveness of the technique can be dampened by many factors, most notably the quality of the keyword. If the form of the keyword is not sufficiently similar to that of the target, then it cannot much help retrieval of the target form. It follows that if the learner's L1 is quite different from the target language at the level of script and sound, the chances of finding useful keywords will be rather slim. Another variable is whether the keyword and the association with the target word are suggested by the teacher or if the learners themselves are encouraged to generate a suitable keyword (Campos, Amor, and Gonzalez 2004). In the former case, there is perhaps a greater risk that the learner finds the association too far-fetched to be memorable (Sagarra and Alba, 2006).

A crucial question is whether the learner is prepared to try out a new memorization technique in the first place, especially if it is a technique that is quite effortful—remembering not just the target word but also its associated keyword and the image that links the two. Especially more mature learners may prefer to stick with other learning techniques that they have grown used to and that they feel work well for them. Worth mentioning also is that mnemonic techniques, which pave longish mnemonic routes for the retrieval of the target words, are likely to slow down retrieval speed. More generally, it must be clear that the rich associations fostered by some of the memorization techniques outlined in this section engender knowledge representations that are different from those that would emerge if the words were learned incrementally and incidentally through repeated exposure in natural discourse, which is the way the bulk of vocabulary in the mother tongue is acquired.

It must be clear from the above that a large number of techniques and strategies exists to foster retention of words, but also that the action radius of each is confined in terms of the kind of words that lend themselves to it, the facet of word knowledge that is engendered, and the type of learner who is likely to embrace the proposed technique. Diverse techniques and strategies complement one another, and research indeed shows that successful language learners report taking more and more diverse initiatives to expand their vocabularies than do less successful learners (Fan 2003; Gu and Johnson 1996). Again, there may a chicken-and-egg question here: do learners become more proficient because they use a wide range of strategies, or are proficient learners in a better position to make use of strategies thanks to their level of proficiency? After all, with increasing proficiency comes an increasing potential for successful guessing from context and for associating new words with already known ones. Many pedagogy-oriented second-language vocabulary researchers pin hopes on the benefits of strategy instruction to accelerate learners' independent vocabulary learning (Grenfell and Harris 1999; Nation 2001), but it is not easy to find evidence of such benefits, because growth in a learner's vocabulary need not be causally related to an increase in the number of strategies that a learner reports using after strategy instruction.

34.6 Hard words and words made harder

Some words appear harder to commit to memory than others. As already mentioned in connection with Dual Coding theory, words with abstract meanings tend to be harder to remember than words with concrete meanings (Walker and Hulme 1999), probably because concrete meanings more readily call up mental images than abstract ones (Hamilton and Rajaram 2001). Learning will also be harder if a word refers to a concept that the learner is unfamiliar with and that has no L1 counterpart (Jiang 2002), such as culture-specific concepts.

The entrenchment of the precise meaning and use of a word may also be hindered by interference from semantic neighbours, such as *plate* competing with *dish* and *course; speak* competing with *talk, tell*, and *say; house* competing with *home*. The confusability of word meanings is enhanced if two words are phonologically (and/or orthographically) similar (e.g. *exhausting* and *exhaustive* in English, *accrocher* and *raccrocher* in French). As mentioned before, this kind of interference can also stem from the learner's mother tongue, as when deceptive cognates are activated along with the target word (see Williams, this volume, on co-activation of L1 and L2). For instance, a Dutch-speaking learner of German may find it hard to divorce the meaning of German *Meer* (sea) from the meaning the same word form has in Dutch (lake). When it comes to memorizing spelling of new words, confusion is known to be caused by phonological/orthographic neighbours (e.g. *break* vs. *brake; steal* vs. *steel; lead* vs. *led; vain* vs. *vein*) and co-activation of counterparts in the L1 (e.g. English *photographer* vs. Dutch *fotograaf*).

A combination of both semantic and phonological neighbourhood effects can be expected to be particularly troublesome. A classic example is the degree of mnemonic effort many people need to invest to distinguish the meanings of *stalactite* and *stalagmite* even in their mother tongue. Imagine, then, a beginning learner of English asked to learn a set of semantically related words, such as words for fruits: *apple, orange, grapefruit, lemon, pear, melon, grapes, peach, apricot, plum*, and *pineapple*. Unless most of these words are already known, the learner will face the challenge of avoiding cross-associations from one word meaning to the next. There will be a considerable risk of confusion with *lemon* and *melon*, for example. It is not difficult to see how some of the other words in the list are susceptible to the same kind of confusion. In the same vein, presenting a learner with a set of new words for pieces of clothing including both *shirt* and *skirt* may well increase the likelihood of these two words getting interchanged. It therefore looks as though hard words can be made even harder if teaching and learning methods are not chosen judiciously.

In fact, there is a substantial body of experimental evidence to suggest that asking learners to memorize sets of new words that belong to the same category (e.g. parts of a house or emotional states), that have opposite meanings (e.g. *cheap* vs. *expensive; plummet* vs. *soar*), or that are confusable due to formal resemblances (e.g. *rise* vs. *raise; terrific* vs. *terrible; interesting* vs. *interested*) makes learning particularly challenging (Erten and Tekin 2008; Finkbeiner and Nicol 2003; Tinkham 1997; Waring 1997). Although evidence of this kind has been available for a long time (Higa 1963), it seems not to have made much of an impact on the way target vocabulary is commonly presented in mainstream textbooks, despite attempts to offer clear pedagogical guidelines distilled from the research findings. Nation (2000) advises teachers and materials writers to allow time for one word (say, *lemon*) to settle down in the learner's memory before introducing a potentially intrusive neighbour (say, *melon*). This more gradual expansion of domain-related vocabulary would be fostered also through engagement (possibly by applying one or more of the aforementioned memorization techniques) with target words as they are encountered in discourse. This selective, 'as-the-opportunity-presents-itself' stance would naturally avoid crowding the learner's mind with semantically and/or formally confusable words. It would also be more akin to naturalistic first-language vocabulary acquisition; parents do not typically sit down with their toddlers one morning to run them through an exhaustive inventory of furniture terms.

34.7 Beyond single words

Given the title and theme of this volume, we have deliberately focused on questions about learning *words* in a second language. However, vocabulary learning also involves developing mastery of a multitude of multi-word items, such as *by and large, on the other hand, turn up, give in, pull it off, over the top, on the ropes, out of the blue, under the weather, brain drain, credit crunch, left high and dry, red herring, break even, follow suit, and so on and so forth*. The meaning of many of these multi-word items transcends the meanings of the words they consist of to a degree where learners fail to adequately interpret the expression even though they are familiar with the words as single items (Boers, Eyckmans, and Stengers 2007; Martinez and Murphy 2011). Native speakers (including language teachers) are seldom aware of the semantic opacity of the idiomatic expressions they use. It may therefore be helpful for a monolingual English reader of this text to consider one or two phrasal expressions in another language in order to appreciate the obstacles for interpretation that a second language learner faces when it comes to phrasal vocabulary. French *sans doute* literally translates as 'without doubt', yet its meaning is 'perhaps'. (To express certainty in French, one would need to say *sans aucun doute*, 'without *any* doubt'.) The Dutch expression *de kogel is door de kerk* translates literally as 'the bullet is through the church', but it is hard to imagine a learner of Dutch independently figuring out its meaning ('an important decision has been made'). Yet learners stand to gain a lot from including phrasal expressions in their vocabulary-learning efforts. For one thing, corpus studies have revealed that language abounds with phrasal vocabulary (Moon 1998; Sinclair 1991). For another, studies have shown strong correlations between learners' mastery of multi-word items and their scores on general proficiency tests (Boers et al. 2006; Dai and Ding 2010).

As with single words, mastery of a multi-word item involves many facets of knowledge (Nation and Webb 2011: 190), including formal constraints (*Let's play it by ear* sounds fine, but *Let's play it by* the *ear* is odd) and usage restrictions (one would not expect to find a phrase like *a real pain in the neck* in an academic article). What this means, of course, is that the magnitude of the vocabulary learning task—daunting as it is even if 'only' single words are considered—is much greater than has been suggested so far in this chapter.

Recognition of this phrasal dimension of vocabulary and the challenges it poses for second-language learners is by no means new (Palmer 1925), but interest in it has picked up very quickly since the 1990s. Among the influential 'early' books intended to raise teachers' awareness of the importance of phrasal vocabulary are Willis (1990), Nattinger and Decarrico (1992), and Lewis (1993). Research on L2 phrasal vocabulary has since followed the trail laid by the explorers of L2 word learning. First, attempts have been made to identify phrasal expressions that should receive priority in learning and teaching by virtue of their high frequency of use (and thus presumably their high utility) as attested in general language corpora (Martinez and Schmitt 2012) or in corpora representing specific discourse genres (Liu 2012; Simpson-Vlach and Ellis 2010). Second, studies have been conducted to gauge the pace of (incidental) acquisition of phrasal expressions as a by-product of message-focused engagement with the target language, under conditions where the input texts are manipulated to draw the learner's attention to the target expressions, or as a result of deliberate learning (see Boers and Lindstromberg 2012 for a review). Third, impediments to the acquisition of L2 phrasal vocabulary have been identified that are reminiscent of those found to hamper L2 word acquisition, including interference from the mother tongue (Laufer and Waldman 2011; Nesselhauf 2003). Fourth, techniques for helping learners commit multi-word items to memory have been proposed and tested (see Boers and Lindstromberg 2009 for a review). Finally, researchers have cautioned against studying confusable items together because this increases the risk of confusion actually taking place (Boers et al. 2014; Webb and Kagimoto 2011).

34.8 Conclusion

Second-language vocabulary learning is a mammoth task. One important proposal has been to downsize the task by prioritizing high-frequency words. As we have seen, the problem is that beyond the highest-frequency word, it becomes increasingly hard to decide which words merit prioritization over others. The task is further complicated by the fact that many words have multiple uses and figure in phrasal expressions that are targets for learning in their own right.

One has to be hopeful that a fair amount of vocabulary acquisition will occur as a result of learners' engagement with samples of the target language outside the language course. Given the generally slow and incremental nature of incidental vocabulary acquisition, this requires substantial amounts of exposure to and/or interaction in the target language. Various ways of accelerating vocabulary uptake from L2 texts have been proposed, including training in strategies such as guessing from context and manipulating texts with a view to drawing learners' attention to selected words and phrases. After noticing new (uses of) words, these new items still need to be committed to long-term memory. This can happen through repeated encounters, through output activities, and by applying validated memorization techniques. Although the latter can be helpful, most have a confined action radius, in terms of the kinds of item that lend themselves well to the particular technique, the kinds of learner who find the technique useful, and the facet of word knowledge that the technique fosters. It is therefore the judicious use of mutually complementary techniques and interventions that is likely to be pedagogically most beneficial.

PART VII

NAMES

CHAPTER 35

NAMES

JOHN M. ANDERSON

35.1 Introduction

Names are a rather special kind of word, to the extent that they have even sometimes been denied the status of 'word', or indeed of being a part of language (e.g. Strawson 1950). Certainly, people often identify with their name, revealed by such metaphors as that in *making a name for oneself*; or they may resent it. And names are more generally a matter of concern and of familiarity than other words, and this can lead to their developing in different ways from these other words (e.g. Morpurgo-Davies 2000): their phonological development, for instance, may be retarded or accelerated. Given that the origin of individual names, when this can be established, is typically in other words, this difference is most obvious when we compare the history of a name with its cognate common word. For instance, Colman (1992: 59) observes, concerning an Old English name element, that '[t]he development of the name element cognate with *æðele* "noble", ... represented by the forms <ÆÐEL>, ÆGEL>, <ÆIEL>, <ÆL>, illustrates a phonological change not attested for the related common word'.

Names have indeed often been regarded as magical, for instance as helping fulfil or at least encourage what the name-giver wishes for the named: *Modesty*, *Prudence*. Consider Smith-Bannister on naming traditions in early modern England: 'Children were named and supposed to act accordingly' (1997: 13). Because of such 'magic', different naming traditions encourage or eschew the giving to children of the names of gods or saints, or names based on words with religious associations (say *Concepción*). Extreme examples of this are Puritan names such as that based on *If-Christ-had-not-died-for-you-you-had-been-damned-barebone* (Bowman 1932: 91). Particular significance has commonly been attributed to names.

However, the 'meaning' of names, in common usage, corresponds to the sense of the common word cognate (which may belong to another language). This 'meaning' is often culturally salient in a range of different ways. For instance, names and their etymology have enjoyed, particularly in the Middle Ages and Renaissance, an important place in biblical and other scholarly exegesis (Robinson 1993: part IV). More mundanely, there is much popular concern, in English-speaking communities, for instance, with the 'meaning' of names, particularly when a name is being selected. And, particularly in non-literate cultures, name-giving and name-using may have a range of social functions, including serving, if the name reflects the circumstances of the name-giving, as reminders of history (cf. Duke 2005: §3.5, on various African linguistic communities).

This chapter is concerned with the place of names, if any, in the lexicon, and how this relates to name-giving. I shall also deal more generally with ideas concerning the grammar of names, and its relationship to their interpretation. This latter is not usually to be identified with their etymological 'meaning'. I shall look particularly at the status of names as a part of speech, and how this category, whatever its status, differs from other categories. For the moment, what I understand by 'name' is a member of the set of words that conform to the syntactic behaviour of *Mary*, *John*, etc. and *London*, *Snaefell*, etc. And a part of speech is typically composed of a set of minimal lexical items (words) that share a prototypical class-meaning and distribution. I shall focus on the prototypical name, the personal name, though I shall conclude by indicating something of their relationship to other names, such as the place names just illustrated.

35.2 Names and parts of speech

The status of at least some of the parts of speech has often been controversial. Quite apart from the general question of the cardinality of the sets of parts of speech to be found in different languages, and thus the universality of at least some of them, views concerning the hierarchization of distinctions in the parts of speech has varied. Certain notionally and distributionally distinctive sets of words have been assigned to parts of speech subordinate to some other.

For instance, in one tradition, once widespread, 'nouns' include 'nouns substantive' and 'nouns adjective'. Gildersleeve and Lodge (1895: §16), for instance, distinguish the following parts of speech: 'Noun (Substantive and Adjective), the Pronoun, the Verb, and the Particles (Adverb, Preposition, and Conjunction)'. This identification of 'substantive' and 'adjective' as 'nouns' depends in large part on the similarities in inflection found in some languages, notably the classical languages. But another factor seems to be that substantives and adjectives, in English, for instance, are also often syntactically inter-convertible. Thus, nouns may readily occur in attributive position, the place in structure most obviously fulfilled by adjectives, as in (1a):

(1) a. the iron box
b. the poor

And adjectives can occur in the position most characteristic of nouns, as illustrated by (1b). One traditional way of looking at this is the assumption that the members of a part of speech may be converted, lexically, into another. Notionally, the difference between noun and adjective—between entity-denoting and quality-denoting—is easily bridged, perhaps favouring conversion.

But the same kind of notional affinity can be discerned between some verbs and some adjectives, particular those denoting states, as illustrated by the pairs such as those in (2):

(2) a. Mary knows that.
    b. Mary is aware of that.

And, of course, adjectives can be converted to verbs, as in (3a):

(3) a. Fenella has finally tidied her room.
    b. Sukie is very excited.

And states that result from processes are often expressed by adjectives based on a process verb, as in (3b). Indeed, different parts of speech in general participate in such relationships of derivation and conversion.

Most recent discussions of adjectives accept their status as a distinct part of speech, though typically with a rather schizophrenic distribution, divided between attribution and predication. Predication is characteristic of verbs; attribution is associated with nominal structure. Related to this, the adjective is also of a complex notional character with different aspects which are shared with non-prototypical nouns and verbs. And it has been suggested that it is this complexity of meaning and distribution—this markedness—that underlies the non-universality of adjectives as a part of speech. Adjectives, at least, may constitute a distinct part of speech in many languages, but cross-linguistically the set of parts of speech is not uniformly constituted in this and other ways.

I have cited the status of adjectives and offered a brief allusion to the history of views on this status, in order to highlight the rather different history of the study of names—often labelled 'proper names', or 'proper nouns'. A variety of views have been put forward concerning how names differ from (other) words or specifically from (other) nouns. And the bracketing and the disjunction in the preceding sentence indicate three of the contrasting views that might be taken on the most fundamental issue concerning the grammatical status of names, their relation to the categorization involved in the idea of part of speech. These views involve different answers to the questions: are names different from all other words in some way? Do they belong to the same part of speech as nouns? Are they indeed a kind of noun? I shall refer here to names vs. nouns, without at this point pre-judging the relationship between the classes.

However, the history of discussion of names has, with few exceptions, been based on the assumption that they are a sub-type of a larger class, labelled as 'noun' or 'name' or 'substantive', a class among whose members we can distinguish 'common nouns/names' and 'proper nouns/names'. Consider again Gildersleeve and Lodge (1895: §16): 'The *Substantive* gives a name: **vir**, *a man*; **Cocles**, *Cocles*; **dōnum**, *a gift*'. Again, in Latin the morphology might support this view. But, in English also, according to the influential grammar of Lindley Murray (1795: 23), '[a] substantive or noun is the name of anything that exists, or of which we have any notion, as, man, virtue, London, etc.'. And there has recently tended to predominate in the grammatical and lexical literature the positing of a part of speech 'noun', of which, according to Cobbett (1823: §40), '[t]here are two [branches]; for Nouns are some of them PROPER and some COMMON'. The grammar of names and their classification are more complex and interesting than all of this suggests, however. This emerges when we ask the question: to what extent is the grammar of names less distinct from that of nouns than that of adjectives is?

35.3 The meaning of names

Nevertheless, let us begin by looking at the basis for this near-consensus on the grammatical status of names. This consensus among linguists, and others, is apparently shared among languages themselves, which mostly lack the facility for simple differentiation offered in English by the two words 'noun' and 'name'. And in English usage of these terms is extremely varied. In particular, 'name' is often applied to what are seen as words for basic-level categories (such as 'bird names'). Such observations suggest that there is a perceived relationship between words like *Cocles* or *Mary* and words like *vir* or *boy*. However, there is a similar perceived relationship between names/nouns and pronouns, revealed in, for instance, the punning whereby 'mi' is 'a name I call myself'. Gildersleeve and Lodge (1895: §16), however, and Cobbett (1823: §17), as well as many others, regard 'pronoun' as a separate part of speech. But an opposing view is offered by, for example, Huddleston (1988: 24): 'we shall subclassify nouns as common nouns, proper nouns or pronouns' (cf. Halliday (1994: §6.6). Whatever the status of the connection between noun, name, and pronoun, awareness of it partly accounts for why there has been such resistance to, or at least lack of interest in, alternative views of the grammatical status of names.

Before we look further into this status and the basis of the noun–name–pronoun connection, I want to contrast the consensus on syntactic categorization with the controversial semantics of names. There is a long history in philosophical literature, in particular, of concern with names; and indeed the 'common' vs. 'proper' distinction is based on a Latinization of Greek philosophical terms describing the universal vs. particular signification of nouns vs. names. The major controversy concerning the semantics of names concerns what sense, if any, is to be attributed to them. I understand 'sense' along the lines of the three-way distinction of Lyons (1977: ch.7) among sense, denotation, and reference (see too Anderson 2007: §3.2). The sense of (in the first instance) a lexical item is language-internal; it is the semantic value of the item in relation to other items in the linguistic system; and it is independent of particular context. Denotation is also context free, but it is not purely language-internal; it is the perceived relation between an item and those phenomena that it can appropriately be attributed to. Reference is contextually determined: it is the relation between elements in an utterance and the particulars that they invoke.

Disagreement on the semantics of names came into sharp focus in Mill (1843 [1919]) and reactions to it. Mill (1843 [1919]: 21) declares:

> Proper names are not connotative; they denote the individuals that are called by them; but they do not indicate or imply any attributes as belonging to those individuals. When we name a child by the name of Paul, or a dog by the name Caesar, these names are simply marks used to enable those individuals to be made subjects of discourse.

In terms of the terminology just introduced above, I take Mill's 'denotation' to be reference, and the absence of 'connotation' with names as reflecting lack of sense, and I understand 'denotation' according to the usage of Lyons (1977).

Mill relates his analysis to the failure of names to show predicativity, so that (4a) is only equative and not predicative:

(4) a. The one who left is John.
    b. John is the one who left.
    c. John is a postman.

Referentially equated expressions are, in an appropriate context, reversible, as in (4b). Contrast (4c), where the post-copular expression is normally predicative. This immediately distinguishes names from nouns (and adjectives)—but not from pronouns. The name in (4) is also definite in its reference, as are personal pronouns and some determiners. I shall pursue below the grammatical significance of this grouping. But let us proceed here with concern for the sense of nouns and names.

Lyons (1977: 221), in pursuing Mill's viewpoint, argues that the fact that it is 'possible to infer, with a very good chance of being right, that from an utterance like *My friend John came to see me on Monday* that the friend who came to see me was male ... does not force us to say that "John" and "male" are semantically related in the way that "man" or "boy" and "male" are'. The relation between 'John' and 'male' reflects merely a cultural convention. But all such associations are 'conventional', according to Anderson (2007: §5.4). So that in various contexts, particularly certain work environments, the conventional association between 'boy' and 'young', for instance, may be flouted. These conventions are all equally linguistic. Anderson argues that names do have 'minimal sense'—essentially distinctions in gender in a wide sense, including, for instance, place vs. person.

However, a more fundamental objection to Mill's characterization of names has come from those who, like Searle (1958, 1969: §7.2) and Kripke (1981), argue that 'proper names are shorthand definite descriptions' (Searle 1969: 165); they are associated with a 'descriptive backing'. Searle, for instance, cites sentence types where such 'descriptive backing' is necessarily involved. Thus, the equative in (5a) can be said to convey information in a way that (5b) does not:

(5) a. Hesperus is Phosphorus.
 b. Hesperus is Hesperus.

Anderson (2007: §5.3), however, observes that in (5a) what is signalled linguistically is the identity of reference that is associated with all equatives—such as those in (4)—which is superfluous in the case of (5b), unless emphatic. On his account, the only information conveyed by (5a) is that the names refer to the same entity, just as the descriptions in (6) do:

(6) The rabbit over there is the one I saw yesterday.

In neither case is there appeal to a change in the sense of a linguistic item. The most obvious intended effect of the utterance (5a), if it is thought to come as news to the interlocutor, is that whatever encyclopaedic information is tagged to the entities identified by the names *Hesperus* and *Phosphorus* should be associated with a single entity. Names, like other words, accrue encyclopaedic (and indeed indexical) information concerning what they signify (by respectively identification and denotation). But how this relates to sense is not straightforward.

35.4 Names and nouns

Much of the discussion of names by grammarians, as well as philosophers, is again focused on the semantics of names; and is, indeed, heavily influenced by the philosophical debate. Thus, for example, Jespersen (1924: 66) ranges himself with 'descriptivists' like Searle and their insistence on 'descriptive backing' for names, while Lyons (1977: 220) criticizes Jespersen's arguments from a Millian 'lack-of-connotation' standpoint. Other avowed Millians include Ullman (1951 [1957]) and, more recently, Coates (2009). However, linguists, particularly of course onomasts, give greater recognition to the variety of types of names other than personal names. And they have paid much more attention to the range of grammatical properties that might be attributed to names, while for the most part not questioning the view of the name as a kind of noun. Gary-Prieur (1994: 223) announces '... je rejoins le point de vue de la grammaire traditionelle, qui présente N[om]p[ropre] et N[om]c[ommun] comme deux categories lexicales subdivisant celle du nom' (see too Sloat 1969). Indeed, some have doubted that there can be a clear separation between noun and name (Jespersen 1924: 169); noun vs. name is not a difference 'of kind but of degree' (Pulgram 1954: 42). One might interpret van Langendonck's (2005, 2007) notion of a 'proprial lemma' as an attempt to make explicit a restricted version of some such view.

On the other hand, a body of work attempts to throw into doubt the integration of names into a linguistic system (e.g. in Lass 1973: 395), or at least their status as essentially parts of speech (see e.g. Coates 2005, 2006). For Coates 'proper names' are associated with the onymic 'mode of referring'—essentially denotation-free reference—and the grammatical category of 'proper noun' is merely an epiphenomenal development. But pursuit of such a view comes up against ineluctable evidence for the distinctive participation of names in the syntax, morphology, and phonology of a language (e.g. Anderson 2007: especially p. 159; see too Colman 2006: 141–142). And 'proper names' that are allegedly not 'proper nouns' are interpretable, as described below, as expressions converted to names. Similarly, Gary-Prieur's (1994: 243) claim that '... un nom proper peut apparaître dans toutes les distributions caractéristiques du nom *à l'intérieur du S[yntagme] N[ominal]*' depends on continuing to treat as names nouns which have been converted from a name base and have thereby acquired denotation.

Moreover, if one adopts the name-as-noun assumption, it proves difficult to come up with a grammatical characterization of what exactly names share with nouns and of what kind of noun they might be. See, for example, Sweet (1891: §164; Schipsbye 1970; Seppänen 1974). Despite this, Bloomfield (1933: 205) and others point to the rejection in English and other languages of pluralization and of an accompanying determiner, especially articles, despite, or perhaps because of, the acknowledged definiteness of the names we have encountered here so far. But this cannot be generalized: there are not only languages that lack articles and plural marking on nouns but also others where the equivalents of the instances of name that we have looked at are regularly accompanied by an article. The problem is not satisfactorily resolved by suggesting that names in English are preceded by 'a zero allomorph of the definite article' (Sloat 1969), or that they undergo an equally controversial and over-powerful syntactic 'movement' to an 'empty' category (Longobardi 1994, 2001).

In some languages, such as Māori, the article with names is a dedicated marker of a name in certain positions (e.g. Biggs 1969), but in others, such as the Mexican isolate Seri (Marlett 2008), it is in common between names and nouns. For the latter, compare the equative sentence, marked as such by the equative copula (EQ), with a pre-copular noun marked with a following definite article in (7a), with the expression immediately preceding the equative copula in (7b):

(7) a. Hipiix hiif quij haa ha.
this.one my.nose the EQ DEC
('This is my nose')

b. Hipiix Juan quih haa ha.
this.one Juan the EQ DEC
('This is Juan')

The name in this expression is followed by the same definite article. The DEC element marks a declarative. Particularly in Seri, this serves to group names and (definite) nouns together. And in inflected languages names typically share at least part of their declensional system with nouns—but also with pronouns and adjectives. This sharing may extend to derivational processes, particularly diminutives. And all this may be a further indication of a close connection between names and other categories including nouns. And there are further indications.

We now come back to the historical and sometimes contemporary sources of names. Laying aside, in particular, lall names, those based on baby-talk or imitation thereof, it appears that, where a history can be established, names originate in common words, where nouns are perhaps the most fertile source cross-linguistically (cf. Hilka's list of sources summarized in Pulgram 1954: 9). This ignores much variation between languages associated with the different functions of giving names, so that, for example, 'most Mohawk proper names referring to persons and places are verbs' (Mithun 1984: 46).

And we should note also, as concerns the connection between noun and name, a further consequence of common inflectional morphology. A partially shared inflectional system can allow differentiation between etymologically related nouns and names in terms of a difference in declensional class. Thus the Old English name *Brorda* is declined according to the 'weak' declension, whereas the cognate noun *brord* ('prick, lance') is declined 'strong' (Colman 2014: 254). All of this reinforces my previous observations that there is some intimate connection between names and nouns—and between them and pronouns. However, Anderson (2007) maintains that their syntactic behaviour does not seem to support a grammatical equation of name and noun, and—as we shall see in section 35.8—this correlates with their different relationship with entities.

35.5 Names, pronouns, and determiners

The basic distribution of names is quite unlike that of nouns. We have seen that names are normally not predicative; in this they resemble pronouns, but not 'common nouns'. And, as non-predicatives, their distribution is that of noun phrases—or rather determiner phrases—again like definite pronouns in particular. Lyons (1977: 214–215) groups together 'proper names', 'personal and demonstrative pronouns', and 'descriptive noun phrases' as the three main classes of 'referring expressions'. All three expressions in (8) are understood as making definite reference to an individual:

(8) a. Bill
 b. he
 c. the customer (who came this morning)

The amount of description necessary in (8c) to make an identification of the individual varies according to context, but the noun on its own does not refer: it no doubt helps in identifying the referent, but it does not refer in the absence of *the*. *Bill* and *he* in (8a) and (8b) respectively may require more or less context for identification, but they can refer in the absence of linguistic description.

Customer on its own denotes the set of entities to which the term *customer* may appropriately be applied. Compare Lyons (1977: 208): '[p]hrases like "the cow", "John's cow", or "those three cows over there" may be used to refer to individuals, whether singly or in groups, but the word "cow" alone cannot'. Nouns in English must be part of a definite determiner phrase if definite reference to individuals is to be made; whereas names and personal and demonstrative pronouns are lexically definite. A syntactic difference associated with this is the typical absence of restrictive attributives with names and personal pronouns. In these terms, the phrase containing *Tracies* in (9a) is not a simple name, but the name is the base for conversion to a noun (see e.g. Allerton 1987; Anderson 2007: §6.2):

(9) a. the three Tracies in my class

b. Δen ksero enan Pavlo
   not know-1 a Paul

Tracies in (9a) is marked out as a noun not just by the presence of *the*, very unusual with personal names in English, and also by the presence of the numeral and plural inflection, but also by the presence of a restrictive attributive. Similarly, the name in the Greek sentence in (9b) has been so converted, as signalled by the preceding indefinite. Names in Greek, like those in Seri, are typically preceded by a definite article.

This conclusion concerning the lexical definiteness of names in English and many other languages, together with other considerations, leads Anderson (2007: ch. 8) to suggest that the instances of names (and pronouns) we have been looking at are categorially complex. Specifically, names are converted lexically into definite determiners. In doing so, the name satisfies the valency of the determiner, which, as a functional category, normally requires a complement; in this case the complementation is internal. If we adapt the simple notation of Anderson (2011), we can represent this as in (10a), and represent the relation between article and noun in (8c) as in (10b):

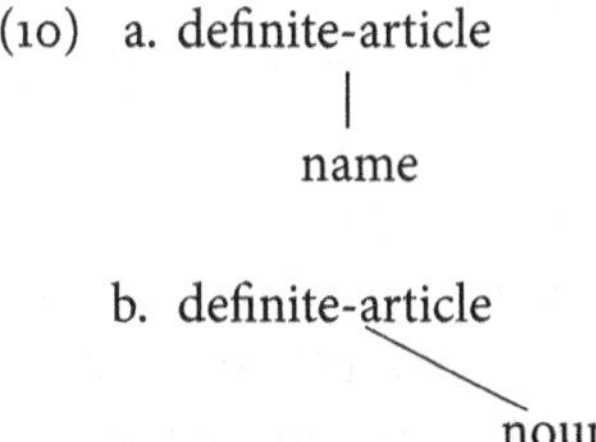

The lines are dependency arcs, headed at the upper ends. In (10b) we have a syntactic dependency, where the two categories differ in linear position; in (10a) there is lexical dependency, where the realization of the categories coincides. In both cases, it is the head that determines the syntactic distribution of the expression. The name converted to a determiner in (10a) depends on the kinds of categories that determiners depend on, notably prepositions.

In the same way we can indicate the conversion in (8) as in (11a):

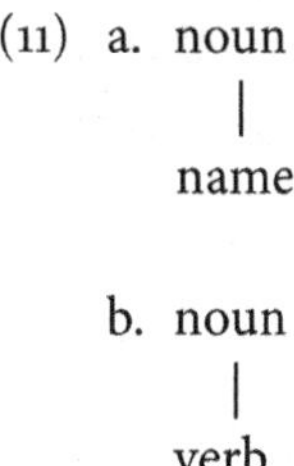

b. noun
|
verb

The converted name is thus enabled to display the properties alluded to above that are associated with nouns. In this instance the name does not satisfy the valency of the noun, since nouns, not being functional, do not require to be complemented. Indeed, the prototypical noun does not take any complement. The name might be said to be lexically attributed to the noun. We have a similar situation with verbs converted to nouns, such as *cook*—as is represented in (11b).

35.6 Names in vocatives and nomination

The complexity attributed to the name in (4), as represented in (10a), receives some justification from the fact that, as Lyons (1977: §7.5) observes, there are circumstances in which names do not serve the function of definite reference. In the first place there is what Lyons calls 'the vocative function' (1977: 217), where they are 'being used to attract the attention of the person being called or summoned'. The vocative may occur by itself, or as part of an utterance, as in (12a) and (12b) respectively:

(12) a. Bill!
b. Come and help, Bill!
c. Pedro, ¿áz intáho?
Pedro, what did.you see.s/he/it/them
('Pedro, what did you see')

Lyons (1977: 217) describes the function of the names in examples such as (12) as 'quasi-referential'. Definite reference, however, is associated with arguments in a predication, as in (13a): or its presence is parasitic thereon, as in the response in (13b):

(13) a. The office despatched the letter on the Tuesday.
b. When did the office despatch the letter? On the Tuesday.

Bill is not an argument in (12a), nor is its presence necessarily a response to a previous utterance. Anderson (2007: §8.4) suggests that even in (12b) the vocative introduces a distinct act of speech from the request or order preceding; the name has not undergone the conversion resulting in (10a). Significantly, in Seri the article that accompanies the name in (7b) is lacking in (12c). Similarly, the class-prefix associated with referential use of nouns and names in Zulu is lacking in vocatives (Doke 1943: §§643–646).

Lyons (1977: 217–219) distinguishes from both 'referential function' and 'vocative function' the function of names in 'nominations', which term he defines as follows (1977: 217): 'by saying that X nominates some person as John we shall mean that X assigns the name "John" to that person'. And he goes on to distinguish between 'didactic' and 'performative' nomination as in (14a) vs. (14b):

(14) a. He is called William.
b. I name this child William.
c. I'm going to call you Bill (to distinguish you from my brother, and because we're friends)
d. «Pancho» mpah.
Pancho s/he.is.called

Sentence (14a) is appropriate when a name has already been given for the first time; it is for the speaker given information that is being transmitted. But in (14b), the name is being given for the first time, as at a baptism—though, depending on the culture, there may be a succession of 'baptisms', formal or informal, as in (14b) vs. (14c).

Whatever the structure of these sentences, they do not involve reference as described above. Again in Seri the name in (14d) is not accompanied by a definite article. *William* in (14a–b) does not refer to an individual, but to itself. It is only when such nominations have occurred that the name is associated with an individual. The name can then be used to refer to an individual or be used as a term of address to that individual, because by virtue of nomination it identifies an individual. Anderson (2007: §8.3) describes this as involving activation of the name: the name and its association with an individual is now part of the lexicon. Many languages have an onomasticon of inactive names, though in different communities the contents of the onomasticon may be more or less strictly regulated, and their common-word sources may be more or less direct, more or less transparent. Colman (2014), for instance, provides a detailed examination of what regulates the contents of the Old English onomasticon. Inactive names can have only self-reference, as in the metalinguistic comment of (15a):

(15) a. 'Sacheverell' is an unusual name.
b. 'Haustellum' is an unusual noun/word.
c. 'Hypnagogic' is an unusual adjective/word.

Examples (15b–c) illustrate similar metalinguistic expressions involving 'common words'. The identificatory function that nomination confers means that the name can be converted to a definite determiner and be used to refer, or be converted to a vocative, which, as indicated above, Anderson (2007: §8.4) interprets as a grammaticalized speech act.

Thus, on this analysis, in most instances of use of a name in most languages it is a complex part of speech, involving a converted structure with a name base and a categorially distinct head. Similarly, along the same lines, the verb in (16a) is complex in this way, unlike the unconverted verb in (16b):

(16) a. John leaves on Tuesday.
b. John may leave on Tuesday.

In (16a) the verb has been converted to the finiteness category that we find expressed independently in (16b). Some words are inherently complex rather than as the result of conversion (or morphological derivation). Thus many adverbs have an inherent structure headed by the equivalent of a locative preposition that governs a deictic pronominal element. This accounts for the distribution of, say, *here* or *now*, which is that of a prepositional phrase, and for the deictic role otherwise associated with some pronouns and determiners.

However, Anderson (2007) proposes that the name that is the base for the conversion in (10b) singles out a distinct part of speech, with distinctive syntactic and lexical properties, and it appears unconverted in the onomasticon and in nominations. This was also recognized by some of the Stoics, who can be interpreted as having made a grammatical distinction, not merely a semantic one, between 'name' and 'noun' (Householder 1995). But, as we have seen, the consensus on the status of names is quite other.

35.7 Names and identification

The identification provided by an active name is distinct from denotation: the latter is associated with a set of entities sharing certain characteristics; but a name is more or less arbitrarily identified with a name-holder, whatever the motivations of the name-giver. Once given, a name is in principle independent of such motivations. On the other hand, we as speakers accumulate encyclopaedic information associated with a named person or place—instances of the entity-types most commonly given names. And though we know that most names, particularly personal names, are not uniquely identifying out of context, we don't normally expect all the people we know who share a personal name to also share distinguishing properties—that is, to share a denotation.

Of course, given the ultimate source of names in common words, often nouns, there is most obviously disagreement concerning noun vs. name status in the case of particular uniquely-identifying/denoting items. Thus Sørensen (1958: 168) claims: An entity like 'the Channel' is an appellative ['common noun']—not a proper name; for we can ask 'what C(c)hannel' and answer 'the channel between England and France' The fact that we use a capital letter when 'the channel' is short for 'the channel between England and France' does not affect the grammatical description of 'the Channel'. The use of a capital letter is a mere convention of speech economy.

Anderson (2007: 191–192) suggests that Sørensen's 'convention' is 'effectively an admission that *the Channel* is used as a name; it is institutionalized as such' (see too Allerton 1987: §1). Indeed, a speaker of British English at least would find Sørensen's question 'what C(c)hannel'—or indeed 'which C(c)hannel?'—rather strange, unless some stretch of water other than *the Channel* had been introduced as a *channel*. A figurative relation between name and its noun base makes this even more apparent in the case of *la Manche*—or *Isthmos*, until the name became the base for a reconversion.

Anderson (1977: 192) argues that we need to recognize antonomasia, whereby a noun or an expression containing a noun (including its sense) may be converted to a name. Given the definiteness of activated names, retention of the article in such as *the Channel* is unsurprising, and indeed its invariance supports identification of the name. Just like the conversion in (11b), that in (17) retains the sense and denotation of the base—though these may be obscured for various reasons, and retained as encyclopaedic information associated with the entity the name identifies:

(11) a. noun
|
name

b. noun
|
verb

(17) name
|
(the) noun

Conversely, some (11a) conversions involve not simply a noun denoting those entities sharing a name, as in (9a), but conversion of encyclopaedic information concerning the individual identified by a name:

(9) a. the three Tracies in my class

The latter is illustrated by *a virgil* and the like, or the conversion of *the Sun* to *sun*. Anderson (2007: §9.2.3) notes also morphologically marked name-based derivations involving various derived parts of speech such as *sodomy/sodomite/sodomize* or *Byronic*. Retention or not by the derivative of the initial capital of the onymic base seems to correlate with degree of familiarity with the source and with its status as such.

35.8 Names as 'entitatives'

The most obvious grammatical connection between non-vocative active names and some instances of nouns is dependency on a definite determiner, as spelled out obviously in languages like Seri, or Greek. Recall Seri (7):

(7) a. Hipiix hiif quij haa ha.
this.one my.nose the EQ DEC
('This is my nose')

b. Hipiix Juan quih haa ha.
this.one Juan the EQ DEC
('This is Juan')

Greek is similar, so that, as we have seen, the presence of an indefinite before the name instead of the definite article *o* makes rather a salient marker of conversion:

(9) b. Δen ksero enan Pavlo.
not know-1 a Paul

In languages without a syntactically distinct definite article, such as Latin, definiteness is a lexical property which, in the case of nouns, may be reflected in word order. The definiteness of names in English is lexical—as it is with generic plural nouns, such as the subject in (18a):

(18) a. Horses are lovely animals.

b. Ta aloɣa ine orea zoa.
the horses are lovely animals

Compare the Greek equivalent in (18b) (from Holton et al. 1997: 279)—which is ambiguous between a generic and a non-generic reading.

But nouns are only contingently dependent on definiteness, while with non-vocative active names it is essential. And it is the same with deictic pronouns, personal and demonstrative. And both names and these pronouns enable identification of a referent without recourse to description or textual co-reference. According to Anderson 2007: ch. 8), this is because both classes contribute inherent identificatory substance to the definite head determiner: names are identified, indexed, with a particular individual—or set of individuals—in the lexicon, and personal and demonstrative pronouns rely on an act of deixis, or differentiation by mode of participation by the referent in the speech act. In English something like (10a) is appropriate as a characterization of both active non-vocative names and deictic pronouns:

(10) a. definite-article
|
name

But pronouns also differ in being inherently complex in the way (10a) indicates, whereas names are only derivatively definite determiners. Such pronouns are, as it were, defective, or, more positively, temporary names, linked to a particular discourse context: we can distinguish, if you like, between permanently indexed names and deictic names. If something like the preceding is appropriate, then names are much more closely connected with pronouns than nouns.

And this is emphatically confirmed by the failure of both names and pronouns to occur predicatively and to resist attributives, as well as being made syntactically attributive. They are thus, as we have seen, clearly differentiated in their grammar from nouns. The difference is a reflection of the difference between identification and denotation. Predicativity is associated with 'contentive' parts of speech such as verb, noun, and adjective; these are parts of speech which, unlike names and pronouns, may be associated with a wide variety of detailed denotational requirements and distinctions. However, equally, names and pronouns are not 'functional' categories like determiners, simple prepositions, or finiteness, which are highly relational: the 'function' of the latter is to bind structures together. Names and pronouns link intralinguistically only by co-reference.

In this respect, names and pronouns resemble prototypical nouns, such as *pig*, *stone*, or *mud*, in their non-relationality. And this property is argued by Anderson (2007: §8.2) to be a consequence of the fundamental notional value that does connect them and accounts for their perceived relatedness: their status as what he calls 'entitatives'. They identify phenomena perceived as entities: nouns denote classes of entities; names and deictic pronouns identify individuals. However, the very different way in which they relate to entities underlies the discrepancy in grammatical status between nouns on the one hand and names and pronouns on the other. In these terms, nouns can be thought of as 'names' that are provided with the abstraction of denotation in place of simple identification—as having undergone 'contentivization'.

35.9 Types of Name

What precedes is devoted almost entirely to personal names, anthroponyms, names given to individual people by nomination. The names are drawn from a source that may be a standard onomasticon listing names and information associated with them.

These are what Allerton calls 'pure names' (1987: 67–9). But selection of name may (also) be determined by ancestry (as with Greek propatronymics and promatronymics) or they may be drawn from (combinations of) a designated set of common words (as in Seminole—Lévi-Strauss 1966: 182–183) or common words associated with the context of the nomination (as described for African languages by Duke 2005) or from some mixture of these and other conventions. Duke (2005: §§3.2.2.1, 3.4), following Nübling (2000), lists the properties of the 'ideal proper name': 'precise identification', 'brevity', 'ease of memorization', and 'formal marking of onomastic status'. Different languages prioritize one or other of these, and Duke illustrates that they can be in conflict.

Other names applied to individual people—patronymics, family names, tribal names, and others—are associated with genealogy (like the selection of propatronymic personal names), rather than selection from an onomasticon. As active names these can typically behave grammatically like personal names, alone or in combination with the personal name, though possible combinations are language-particular in terms of selection and sequence. In many languages surnames, or family names, are largely based on place names, on personal names (such as patronymics), on nouns denoting occupation, and on nicknames (e.g. Dolan 1972).

Personal names often have hypocoristic alternatives, and individuals may acquire nicknames of different sorts; these may supplement or serve as alternatives to the formally given name (Anderson 2007: §4.2.2). And individuals may be given a succession of names marking stages in their maturity or social relationship, as in Ilongot (Rosaldo 1984). There is obviously much more to say about personal names, including non-core varieties such as 'pro-names' of address such as *mate*, *pal*, Scottish *Jimmy*, and titles that can in certain circumstances usurp the status of personal name (*nanny*, *madame*). 'Personal' names can also be given to pets: typically dogs, cats, cage-birds, cars, boats, homes, as well as, perhaps less 'personally', to works of art; less 'personal' still are the names given to ships and other vehicles of mass transportation, or, in another respect, those given to corporations. This observation is edging us into non-personal names. And I want now to conclude with a glance at some of the other types of name and their grammatical properties, without any intention of attempting to establish a proper typology.

Along with personal names, traditionally the most studied sub-class of name are place names, toponyms. Names are assigned to topographically and socially salient places: areas of sea and land, particularly politically relevant areas, mountains, rivers, settlements, and the like. When names are first given to places their source is usually more transparent than with many nominations with personal names, whether it is a description (*Newtown*, *Sweetwater*) or based on another name (*Georgia*) or a combination of these (*Dartmouth*). And with toponyms there scarcely needs to be recourse to an onomasticon as opposed to a gazetteer, whose contents are not typically used in assigning a name, unless the intention is to establish ethnic and other links by 'transporting' a known name, with or without the addition of *New* or the like. However, quite complex cultural factors can determine the assignment of place names, as demonstrated by some of the contributions to Tooker (1984).

In sharing with personal names the function of identification, place names also share most of their basic syntax. But, as with the plural use of family names in English (*the Browns*), some toponyms identify individual groups (*the Pyrenees*), and, like them, they usually take a definite article. However, with place names the article is part of the name, and the plural name doesn't appear in the singular without an article, whereas *the Browns* involves a family-identifying name converted to a plural name—so we can have not only *one of the Browns* but also *Brown*, the latter as a simple name. Other properties correlating with the semantics of toponyms are the inclusion of orientational terms (*East*, *Upper*), and, of course, their typical inclusion in locational expressions (*at* ..., *in* ..., etc.). However, there is a vast literature on place names in different languages, and it is not my intention to show any disrespect towards all this scholarship by pretending to do more here than advertising the existence of place names (just in case that might be necessary).

Even just mentioning some other names types serves to take us further away from what I have taken to be the prototypicality of the personal name; and this is revealed in the typical occurrence of these non-prototypical names as noun conversions rather than simple names. Thus, product names (from detergents to computer software) identify individual varieties of a type of product, and as such are often readily converted into mass or count nouns which in acts of reference help identify the referent, as in (*Pour in some Bisto*, *She drives a Panda*). And number names, active names converted from numeral determiners such as those in *one/two/three/four (of the) animal(s)*, inherit their sense from the numerals. They constitute distinct members of a series; and as such they have a very distinctive syntax (*Two and two make four*, etc.). Such series also characterize chronological names, chrononyms, but typically these are limited series that recur, as with the names of days of the week. In some languages these names are (at least in part) numeral-derived, as in Greek *Triti* 'Tuesday'—cf. *tritos* 'third': this is patently derived from the hierarchical adjectival (ordinal) form of the numeral. Such names typically occur as deictics (*I'll come (on) Tuesday*) or as nouns (as in (13)); and there are dedicated deictic-name amalgams in the series *Tomorrow/Today/Yesterday*.

CHAPTER 36

PERSONAL NAMES

BENJAMIN BLOUNT

36.1 Introduction

Paradoxes abound on the topic of personal names in the English-speaking world. Everyone has at least two of them, typically three, sometimes more. Personal names have special qualities. Their bearers guard them carefully, making sure that their names are used in culturally appropriate ways. The misuse or mispronunciation of a person's name usually elicits a correction, followed by an apology by the offending person. Strangers are not to use them without a proper introduction. While most people keep them for a lifetime, names can be dropped, added, or altered, an indication that they no longer reflect the bearer correctly or appropriately. People are aware also that their names each carry different significance, that the surname is a family name, that the first or given name is the one most used and informal, and that the second or middle name may be slighted altogether, or in some cases used in lieu of the first name. In a fundamental sense, a name is equated to the individual. A name is a person's social, cultural, and legal identity.

Despite the known importance of personal names—specifically their universality, lifetime association, social significance, and official and legal qualities—they elicit relatively little interest in their own right, as names. They are seldom topics of comment or discussion, unless they have unusual properties, as, for example, when a person has the same given and surname. A literary example can be seen in Ken Follett's recent book, *The Fall of Giants* (2010), in which one character, William Williams, was known as Billy Twice.

Even among linguists, onomastics—the study of personal names—is generally seen as marginal to other interests (see the chapter by Anderson in this volume). The well-known lexicographer John Algeo sees personal names as essentially devices useful only for reference or address, devoid of social, psychological, or cultural importance (1985: 142). Other linguists, however, view personal names in broader terms, and insist that their study include social and historical factors (Allerton 1987; Lieberson 1984;

Tooker 1984). A large literature, in fact, exists on social and historical aspects of personal names. An account of 100 years of social science contributions to the study of personal names, for instance, was published more than a quarter of a century ago (Lawson 1984).

The relative indifference to names beyond their referencing function is all the more remarkable in the light of knowledge that names can be made, acclaimed, broken, disgraced, or ruined. Personal names can be seen as proxies of the people who bear them, and through actions and behaviour the names, as proxies, can become famous, infamous, successful, or notorious—essentially any of the conditions which individuals create or find themselves in as they move through life. Personal names can track social change and social status and thus must be a part of social and cultural systems. While family names are inherited, an individual's given and middle names can also be selected in honour of other people, usually someone who is a relative or a famous person. Other factors are present such as the considerations that go into selection of names given to infants. Personal names can link individuals into social histories, locally within the family and more broadly within society, both reflective of underlying systems of knowledge, even if awareness of those systems is marginal or superficial. Personal names are parts of social, cultural, and historical systems.

This chapter attempts to contribute to a theory of personal names by underlining the role of culture in an understanding of personal names. The knowledge that individuals have of personal names, outlined above, is cultural, but it is only a part of a more complete account. Individuals know primarily about how personal names are to be used or employed, but even much of that knowledge tends to operate out of awareness, a property of cultural cognitive systems (Blount 2014). A proper theory of personal names needs to make knowledge and information about them, i.e. culture, visible. In addition, if a theory of personal names is to be developed, knowledge about personal names as systems is necessary, as is knowledge of how the systems came into being.

A comparative perspective is needed also to bring into relief the larger systemic picture of what personal names are and what their place in society is. The following will identify and examine characteristics of personal naming systems that are basic and common, identifying at the same time variations across societies in regard to those themes. The framework for presentation and discussion was developed by the author for research projects on personal naming systems. Those included a thorough survey of the literature on naming systems of American Indians, of African societies, and of the world's foraging societies, to the extent that information was available on them. The framework utilized below was informed by those studies, which range across the world's inhabited continents and across all stages of livelihood types, from foraging to pastoralism, horticulture, agriculture, and industrialization.[1]

[1] A sizeable and growing body of literature exists on non-European personal naming systems: Agyekum 2006; Akinnaso 1983; Alia 2007; Anderson 1984; Antoun 1968; Asante 1991; Bamberger 1974; Beidleman 1974; Bregenzer 1968; Brewer 1981; Draper and Haney 2006; Eder 1975; Ekpo 1978; Guemple 1965; Herbert 1995; Kimenyi 1978; Koopman 2002; Marlett 2008; Middleton 1961; Mohome 1972; Pongweni 1983; Price and Price 1972; Ramos 1974; Roth 2008; Ryan 1981; Stewart 1993; Bean 1980; Dousset 1997; and Tonkin 1980, among many others.

This chapter first addresses basic properties of personal naming systems, followed by illustrations of those properties focused on cultural practices surrounding the assignment of names to children at birth. The discussions draw mainly from English but in comparison with non-European societies, especially the Luo of Kenya, among whom the author lived and studied for two years (Blount 1972). Attention will be given to historical aspects of English-language personal naming systems, including sources of names and changes in their use and frequency through time.

36.2 Basic properties of personal naming systems

Personal names always have the property of individuation. They serve to single out, to point to the individual who bears the name in question. In all societies, every member receives at least one personal name, a name that belongs to the recipient and that distinguishes him or her from other members of the society. In the historically earliest naming systems only one name was assigned, but as individuation became more difficult due to population growth and to the same name being assigned to more than one individual, other names were added. In English, these included descriptors (*Big John, Ivan the Terrible*), nicknames (*Bear, Blondie*), and eventually surnames and middle names. The underlying principle is that each person is entitled to being individuated.

A second fundamental property of personal names is that they categorize their bearers. The most obvious case is through inheritance of a surname or family name. All individuals who receive a surname at birth are members of the category indicated by the name. Names are also recognized as culturally appropriate, and the assignment of a name or names to a child places the child in a societal group bearing the culture in question.

Personal names are used in all societies for both reference and address. All uses of personal names, however, highlight the fact that the name is a proxy for the person. A name belongs to its bearer and is equated with the person. In all societies, individuals can be assigned, or can choose, a new name. If an individual's persona changes, then the conditions arise for a name change. Childhood names, for instance, may be replaced when a person outgrows childhood—a widespread feature of naming systems around the world (Alford 1988). The critical point is that the relationship between a person and a name goes far beyond mere labelling. The name and the person become synonymous socially, the name 'standing in' for the person.

36.3 Birth names

All societies assign personal names to children, but there are sharp cultural differences in many aspects. Most societies give names to infants at or soon after birth, but among many societies naming is delayed. The Inca of Peru and the Maasai of East Africa delayed naming until a child was 1 year old, while in Korean society names were given after 100 days (Alford 1988: 34–35). The rationale was to not give a name until there was some assurance that the individual would survive early childhood. Among the Luo of Kenya, a baby girl is assigned names three days after she is born and a baby boy's names are given on the fourth day. According to the Luo, infant girls are hardier than infant boys, and boys are given the extra day to survive prior to naming. In some societies, naming occurred only after a child demonstrated some observable accomplishment which revealed its persona. The Zuni of the southwestern US give names to infants when they begin to crawl, and the Buganda of East Africa assign names when children are weaned, typically around the age of 3 years (Alford 1988: 36). What seems to underlie these practices is an effort to give children names once they survive early infancy and have an opportunity to become a person. Personhood, or persona, is what matters.

36.3.1 Types of name given to children

Societies differ in terms of the number and types of names given to newborns. The common practice among Euro-American groups is to assign at least three names. Although the names individually and collectively differentiate a child, they each serve different referential and social roles. The name that is expected to carry the major referential load is the so-called given, personal, or Christian name. The family name, also called the last or surname, is considered to be more formal than the other two and assigns a child to a recognized kinship unit. In European societies, the unit is typically a family. In other societies, the kinship-unit name is a lineage or clan name, traced typically through the male line of descent, or less commonly through the female line.

There are several cultural variations in the form of kinship-unit names. Among some societies that have family names, the order of names is family name, middle name, and personal name. The pattern is most commonly found in East Asia, in particular among Chinese and Koreans. The late and famous Chinese statesman, *Chou en Lai*, belonged to the *Chou* family/lineage and his given name was *Lai*. Another pattern is found in Spanish-speaking countries, where double surnames can be given, the first reflecting the male line through the father and the second the female line through the mother. Someone named *Garcia-Quijano* (or *Garcia y Quijano*) would have membership in the two kinship lines. Yet another system can be found in societies where the child is given a surname that includes the father's name with a suffix indicating whether the child is a daughter, *Sigurdadóttir*, or son, *Sigurdason* (examples from Icelandic).

Even greater variety can be found in societies that have lineage or clan names assigned to children. One pattern is similar to that found in societies with family names; each child receives the same surname as all members of the family, although the referential scope is not the family or even household unit but a larger social group. In some instances, each child is given a different kinship-unit name, but it is recognized by other members of the society as specific to the given kinship unit. The Luo of Kenya can serve as a good example. When Luo infants are named, on the third or fourth day of life, they are given at least three names (Blount 1993). One name is related to circumstances relative to the birth. In times of famine, a child might be given the name *Ladhri* 'famine'. Similarly, a child born during the time of Kenyan independence from Britain might be given the Swahili name *Uhuru* 'freedom', or a child might be named after the first president of Kenya, *Kenyatta*. The given name might also refer to the time of day when a child is born, for instance *Okinyi* 'morning' or *Otieno* 'night'. The circumstances of the birth itself might be a name source. A large infant at birth might be given the name *Odongo* 'big, large', and one who has undergone a breech birth might be called *Obama*, from the verb *bamo* 'to turn, rotate, or twist'. The practice of giving a child a name related to current surroundings is widespread in Africa, including among the Zulu in southern Africa (Suzman 1994).

Luo children are also given a second name, which typically links them with their mother's kin group—a means of extending kin relations that anthropologists call complementary filiation. Similar cultural practices are found in many societies, including the southern part of the United States. A common pattern there is for a child's middle name to be complementary linking a child to the parental lineage not reflected in the surname, especially for girls, whose middle name would reflect the mother's line. Middle names in Chinese and Korean may show the same pattern.

An especially interesting aspect of Luo naming practices is that they consider a child's most important name to be the lineage or clan name, the third name given to infants. The name is inherited from an ancestor and it can be selected in a number of ways. The preferred way is for a grandmother or another elderly female relative to have a dream about a relative who will be, by definition, ancestral to the child. The dream is thought to reveal the wish of that ancestor for the child to be named after him or her. Of particular interest is that the name is known by only a small number of close adult relatives; it is thought to be too important and powerful to be widely known, much less used to refer to or to address the child. In fact, children do not even know that they have the name until they are old enough to be responsible with it. It may seem strange that the most important name is not broadly known or used publicly in childhood. As a proxy for the persona, however, the name needs to be protected, especially in view of the fact that infants and children are especially vulnerable to disease and other life-threatening events.

A second aspect of restricting the ancestral name of Luo children until their early teens is that it further validates the selfhood of the children. Relaxation or removal of restrictions on knowledge and use of the name socially ratifies the individual as a responsible member of society. An interesting parallel can be found among the Cuna people of Panama, where children are not actually given names until their early teens, on the same grounds as the relaxation of restrictions among the Luo. Cuna children are given names only when they reach an age where they can be responsible citizens. Until that point, they are called by nicknames or terms simply meaning 'girl' or 'boy' (Alford 1988: 36). The transition from childhood to early adulthood, incidentally, is marked by ritual in many societies, although name changes do not always occur.

36.3.2 Sources of birth names

While the kinship-unit name is automatically inherited, the first or given name is typically chosen from the names of relatives, friends, and important personages, or increasingly from lists of available names published in books or online. Middle names, as discussed, may be from maternal lines, or they may be for aesthetic purposes, to produce along with the given and kinship-unit name a name-set that avoids disharmony and patterns that are peculiar or difficult. Three multisyllabic names in a row, for example, are less common than other patterns. Single-syllable middle names in particular may be chosen to help with the 'flow' of the names, i.e. essentially for aesthetic or euphonic reasons (see Whissell 2001, and her chapter in this volume; also Hebert and Harper 1995; Levine and Willis 1994).

When the project on personal naming practices of Native American societies began, I soon realized that I could not rely on Anglo-American naming conventions. Implicit assumptions and understandings had to be made explicit. As noted, the terms 'first or given name or Christian name' and 'last name, surname, or family name' are culturally specific to only some societies. The term 'kinship-unit name' can replace the latter and works well, but with the necessary understanding that what matters is reference or linkage to a kinship category. The category of 'first or given name or Christian name' is more problematic. Of course, many of the world's societies are not Christian. 'First name' likewise has limited application, given that in some societies names are in reverse order to those in English. 'Given name' can apply to all of the names assigned to a child. In the effort to be more culture-free, I use the term 'primary identity name' to refer to the chosen (non-inherited) 'given name', but that is only slightly better. In some cases 'primary identity names' can be inherited, as when an individual is named fully after an ancestor, as in Robert Smith, Jr. 'Primary identity name', however, is the name which is most commonly used in reference or to address an individual, for example *John* and *Mary* in English, and *Odier* 'midnight' and *Akinyi* 'morning' in Luo. Perhaps the best strategy is to recognize that cultural variation in assignment of names across societies is widespread, but that distinctions between assigned primary identity names and inherited kinship-unit names are present in most societies.

Several other aspects of birth names require at least brief consideration. One of these is who has the authority to choose an infant's name. In European societies, it is typically the mother, father, or mother and father together. Other members of kinship and friendship networks, however, may play a role. Grandparents in particular may make suggestions, recommendations, or in some cases demands about which names are chosen. Final approval may be voiced by the parents, but that does not mean that they alone select the identity names. In other societies, especially in preindustrial ones, the locus of authority is very different. In fact parents are often excluded from the process. Among North American Indians two patterns were common. One pattern was that a grandparent selected the name or names, other pattern being that a name specialist in the society made the choices. An advantage of the latter, as seen by the members of the society, is that the specialist would have depth and breadth of knowledge both about the history and place of a family within the broader society and about the broader society itself. A name could be chosen strategically, with a view toward societal placement of an individual beneficial to all involved.

36.3.3 Open and fixed personal naming systems

A further aspect about how names are chosen is whether there is an open system in which considerable latitude exists in name choice, or whether the system is fixed and constraints are much stronger. In actuality there are no totally open systems: cultural constraints always apply, but in fixed systems names may be much more limited. The choice of names may be determined not only by what is culturally acceptable but by other factors such as order of birth, gender, religion, or even by legal mandates. An example of an open system would be the United States, generally speaking, where parents can choose virtually any noun as the identity name for a child, although some governmental limitations apply, for example, to expletives and to numerals (Hanks and Hodges 2007). Still, the majority of personal names are selected from established inventories, but the system is becoming more open through time. Preferred identity names for males have shown a remarkable stability for at least a century, but in recent years there has been a considerable shift toward names that reflect the importance of appeal and popularity, a process that historically has been a characteristic of preferred female names. *John*, for example, was among the top five names assigned to male infants in the English-speaking world for at least a century. It usually occupied the top spot, but by 2001 it had fallen to number 21, replaced by the top five names *Michael, Jacob, Matthew, Nicholas*, and *Christopher* (US Census 2001). Female names have always shown more variability. *Mary, Elizabeth, Rachel*, and *Katherine* have been high on lists of preferred names for much of the past century, but in 2001 the top five names were *Hannah, Emily, Sarah, Madison*, and *Brianna. Mary* had fallen to number 81, *Elizabeth* to 10, *Rachel* to 31, and *Katherine* to 14.

An example of a fixed system is Iceland. Like Germany, Denmark, and Finland, Iceland has a governmentally approved list of names for males and females. The Icelandic Personal Names Register contains a list of 1,712 male names and 1,853 female names. The names are all culturally Icelandic, conforming with Icelandic canons of grammar and pronunciation. Only the names on the list can be used for Icelandic citizens. Icelandic first (identity) names have major importance in the naming system, given that surnames (kinship-unit names) follow patronymic rules. A surname is thus a child's father's first name with the suffix *-dóttir* or *-son/sen* attached. Telephone directories list individuals by their first names, not surnames. As occasionally happens, parents want to name a child by a name not on the list, but they face difficult odds. In a recent case, a non-approved name for a newborn girl was mistakenly allowed at birth. It was later discovered that the name on the girl's official documents was the Icelandic word for girl, *Stulka*. An appeal to have the original name accepted was denied, on grounds that the birth name was from a noun that takes a masculine article and was thus not suited to be a female name.

Gender distinctions in personal names are almost universal, though not all the names assigned to children require gender distinction. In the vast majority of cases, however, gender distinctions are maintained. Of all the kinds of information that personal names carry, gender is in fact foremost (Alford 1988: 67). The distinction may be maintained by cultural convention, as in English, but in some societies names are distinguished by morphological features. In Luo, again, an O-prefix makes a name male, whereas an A-prefix renders a name female. Inherited lineage (kinship-unit) names may, however, override the differentiation. A female named after a male relative will have the O-prefix; similarly, a male named after a female relative will have an A-prefix. Interviews with Luo adults with cross-gender lineage names revealed that they did not personally like their names, but they nonetheless recognized their importance. In English, a number of names can be either female or male: *Meredith, Sydney, Morgan, Andrea,* and *Jordan,* among others. A recent phenomenon has been first names derived from surnames, names which can be for either females or males. Examples include *Taylor, Cameron,* and *Riley.* Genderless names constitute only a very small percentage of the total number of personal names, and none has ever attained widespread popularity. A number of names have the same pronunciation but are differentiated by spelling, for example *Brook* (male) and *Brooke* (female), and similarly for *Francis* and *Frances, Robin* and *Robyn.*

36.3.4 Religious sources for identity names in English

Where do personal identity names come from? For the most part, names are not created anew, although there are exceptions, as in recent African-American names. Rather, they are chosen from extant cultural inventories. Icelandic names come from pre-established lists, but the names came at some point in their history from other sources.

The blockbuster source of first or identity names in English is the Bible. Taking the 2001 US Census information as the baseline, three of the top ten female names are biblical: *Hannah* (number 1), *Sarah* (3), and *Elizabeth* (10), as are six of the top ten names for males: *Michael* (1), *Jacob* (2), *Matthew* (3), *Joseph* (6), *Zachary* (7), and *Joshua* (8); two others are from historically later religious sources, *Nicholas* (4) and *Christopher* (5). The larger percentage of male biblical names suggests that male names reflect a deeper historical conservatism than do female names, where popularity appears to play a greater role. The historical record bears out the conservatism vs. popularity contrast even beyond religious considerations. Table 36.1 shows the 10 most popular first names for females in the United States in 25–30-year increments from 1870 to 2001.

A total of 37 different names are found in the listings. Only one, *Elizabeth,* appears in five of the six lists. *Mary* and *Catherine/Katherine* each appears in four of them, *Margaret, Helen, Alice, Ruth,* and *Dorothy* are each in two of the lists, and the other 29 appear only once. Of the 29, 19 appear in the last three time periods. Only *Elizabeth, Mary,* and *Catherine* span the period of 131 years. The patterns for males are different, as

Table 36.1 Top ten first names for females in the United States, 1870–2001

1870	1900	1925	1950	1975	2001
Mary	Mary	Mary	Mary	Jennifer	Hannah
Anna	Ruth	Barbara	Susan	Amy	Emily
Elizabeth	Helen	Dorothy	Deborah	Sarah	Sarah
Emma	Margaret	Betty	Linda	Michelle	Madison
Alice	Elizabeth	Ruth	Patricia	Kimberly	Brianna
Edith	Dorothy	Margaret	Barbara	Heather	Kaylee
Florence	Catherine	Helen	Nancy	Rebecca	Kaitlyn
May	Mildred	Elizabeth	Catherine	Catherine	Hailey
Helen	Francis	Jean	Karen	Kelly	Alexis
Katherine	Alice	Ann(e)	Carol(e)	Elizabeth	Elizabeth

Source: U.S. Census, 2001

shown in Table 36.2. A total of 25 different names appear. Two names, *John* and *James*, are present in five of the six lists, *William, Joseph, Michael*, and *Robert* are present in four of the lists, *George* and *Thomas* are found in three of the lists, *Charles, Christopher*, and *David* are present in two lists, and fourteen names appear only once. Ten of those 14 appear in the last three time periods. Comparison of the records indicates that (1) there are more different female than male names; (2) both male and female names show greater variability in the past half century than in the previous one; (3) more male than female names are of biblical or religious origin.

A finer-grained record than the 25-year increments in Tables 36.1 and 36.2 would show that individual names may be highly popular for several years and then sink from a high rank to a lower one. The website of the US Social Security Administration contains a list of the top five names for female and male names in the last 100 years.[2] *Emily* was the top name for females from 1996 to 2007, *Jennifer* was top from 1970 to 1984, and *Mary* was first from 1912 to 1946 and again from 1953 to 1961, having been replaced in the interim by *Linda*. For males, *Jacob* has held the number one rank from 1999 through 2012, and *Michael* held the top spot from 1954 to 1959 and again from 1961 to 1998, with *David* at number one for 1960. In fact, *John, Robert, James, Michael*, and *Jacob* collectively held the top rank for the entire century except for *David* in 1960. This again attests to the conservatism in selection of male first names and the important of religious sources. Of the female names which hold the top spot for all but the past four years—*Mary, Jennifer, Emily, Lisa*, and *Linda*—Mary is the only one with religious origins.

[2] http://www.ssa.gov/oact/babynames/top5names.html

Table 36.2 Top ten first names for males in the United States, 1870–2001

1870	1900	1925	1950	1975	2001
William	John	Robert	John	Michael	Michael
John	William	John	Robert	Jason	Jacob
Charles	Charles	William	James	Matthew	Matthew
Harry	Robert	James	Michael	Brian	Nicholas
James	Joseph	David	David	Christopher	Christopher
George	James	Richard	Steven	David	Joseph
Frank	George	George	William	John	Zachary
Robert	Samuel	Donald	Richard	James	Joshua
Joseph	Thomas	Joseph	Thomas	Jeffrey	Andrew
Thomas	Arthur	Edward	Mark	Daniel	William

Source: U.S. Census, 2001

Hebrew is the source of many of the religious names, Latin secondarily. Although specific patterns of selection might differ in native English-speaking areas in the US, the United Kingdom, Canada, Australia, and New Zealand, the sources and names are similar. The original distribution derives, of course, from the United Kingdom. Space is not available to trace the distributions and regional differences, but the important point is that the names and their patterns are very old, attesting to the stability of a personal naming system across large areas of the earth.

36.4 Surnames in English

Surnames in English are inherited, as codified by law. Where did they come from and when did they begin to appear? Surnames did not exist in England prior to 1100 AD, but emerged over the next few centuries, in particular from 1250 to 1450 (Bowman 1932; Redmonds 2002) and continuing into the 18th century (Smith-Bannister 1997). Prior to the appearance of surnames, individuals had a given, identity name, many of them of religious origin. The vast majority of people lived in rural areas and made their livings locally. If further individuation was needed, descriptive names or nicknames could be applied, so that there might be a *John* and a *Big John* and even a *Little John*. Place of residence or origin could be used, such as *Mary of Dover* or *Elizabeth of Brighton*. The names of famous and powerful individuals especially reflected individual traits or origins, as *Richard the Lionhearted, William the Conqueror, Katherine of Aragon*, or *Mary Queen of Scots*. Yet another possibility was occupation, such as *Thomas the baker* or *Emma the seamstress* (Dolan 1972).

The reason why the English began to adopt surnames may have been a burgeoning population and the need to better individuate residents, but more likely it was due to the appearance of poll taxes. Property taxes had been required as payments to government, but the need for further taxes led to the imposition of taxes on individuals, a poll tax. When individuals needed to pay taxes, a better method of distinguishing them for record-keeping became necessary, and the introduction of surnames for that purpose was a logical step to take. Especially important English poll taxes were exacted in 1377, 1379, and 1381 (Fenwick 1998), although taxes had been imposed more than 100 years earlier. Surnames were created largely by formalizing the descriptive first and given names (Reaney 1991). *Mary of Dover* thus would become *Mary Dover*, and *Thomas the baker* would become *Thomas Baker*.

The majority of surnames were created from one of four sources. The first was from patronymic surnames, which consisted of the father's first name plus a suffix or prefix to denote surname status. In England that often took the form of the suffix *-son* plus the father's name, to give *Johnson, Watson, Wilson, Danielson*, and so forth. This system, however, did not create a patronymic system. Once a name like *Robertson* was created, it became the surname, and children of that and subsequent generations had the surname *Robertson*. Not all patronymic names had the suffix *-son*; the father's name could be used without modification, or it could have an *-s* suffix, to produce *Richards* or *Collins*. A second common means to create surnames was to use a person's occupation or titular position as the surname, producing *Smith* (blacksmith), *Cook, Wainwright* (barrel maker), and *Chapman* (shopkeeper). A third type of surname is topographical, and derives from the place or type of location where a person resided. Matthew who lived by the river would become *Matthew River*, Anna who lived on a hill would become *Anna Hill*. Barbara who lived in Eaton would become *Barbara Eaton*. The fourth type came from descriptions of behavioural or physical traits that had been used as adjectives to individuate people. Thus *White, Good, Long, Meek*, and *Wise*, among many others, became surnames.[3]

Surnames arose to further individuate their bearers, and they serve well in that regard. A common perception, however, is that a person's first name serves the greatest functional role in differentiating them and that the surname is secondary. In one sense that is correct; the first name is the identity name, the one that is proxy for the person and that has the most usage. Surnames categorize people, whereas each person has their own first name. In lists of personal names, however, there will be more different surnames than there will be first names. That is a consequence of the conservatism of first names; parents tend to select established names again and again, each generation. A list may contain several individuals named *Michael, Jacob, Elizabeth*, or *Emily*, but each is likely to have a different surname. Outside of family, relatives, and friends, surnames individuate to a greater degree than do first names.

[3] See http://www.forebears.co.uk/surnames.

36.5 Name changes

The addition of surnames in medieval Europe represents a type of name change. Any given individual had a newly official name assigned, providing a new status as taxpayer and at the same time further individuating the person. Name changes, whatever their type, typically indicate a change in status or position. As individuals move through life, their positions in society change. Some changes are inevitable, like moving from infancy to childhood to adulthood. Even those changes, however, are overlaid with culture, defining when one period ends and another begins. Other changes are more specifically social, including marriage, parenthood, and advancement in social position and status, through whatever means. Not all changes in life conditions merit name changes, but name changes can occur in all societies. In the industrialized world, the most common name change is for a woman at marriage to take the surname of her husband, although that prescription is undergoing change. Individuals can also change their own names, legally, for a variety of reasons. Dislike of the personal name is one. Another is related to social promotion, common among individuals who have or want to become popular, an example being performers. The famous US boxer *Cassius Clay* became *Muhammad Ali* when he adopted Islam. The late US cowboy movie star *John Wayne* was originally *Marion Morrison*. A change, however, need not be toward simplification. The singer *Engelbert Humperdinck* was originally *Arnold George Dorsey*.

Richard Alford (1988: 86) noted in his cross-cultural study of name changes that changes are more common in small and less complex societies and in societies in which individuals tend to have unique names. The correlation makes sense, given that these name changes are less likely to cause social or kin-group dislocation. One name is substituted for another, and the name change itself may be the salient aspect of newly self-ascribed status. In many small-scale societies, individuals can simply announce that they no longer want to be called *X* but *Y*, and their wishes are typically granted, barring conflict with cultural convention. Throughout a person's lifetime, name change may occur several times, but in each case the name represents the person and serves society through individuation and membership categorization.

Changes in terms of address can also occur as an individual moves through life stages through the assignment of descriptive nicknames or terms of endearment. The latter are associated, of course, with personal or intimate relationships. Nicknames typically occur within special social groups, as among teenage friends or members of athletic teams, most commonly during adolescence (see the chapter in this volume by Kennedy). Alford (1988: 82) found that nicknames usually are one of four types, based on physical or behavioural abnormalities, occupation, and place of origin. In terms of usage, they signal emergent or achieved identity, as opposed to ascribed or assigned identity, thus complementing the roles of assigned names. Nicknames are more likely to be less common that assigned names, and thus they individuate to a greater extent and carry significant social weight. The origin of the term 'nickname' indicates its complementary status. According to the *Oxford English Dictionary* (online), the word *ekename* 'additional name' was derived from Old English *eaca* 'an increase', and has been in use since the 14th century.

36.6 Summing up and a further consideration of origins

In this survey of personal naming practices, several major points have been presented. These include:

- Personal naming is universal. All societies have names which members recognize as characteristic of the society, and all societal members are given at least one of the names.
- Personal naming systems have histories which include social and cultural properties.
- Personal names serve in reference and address to individuate members of society, distinguishing them from other members.
- Personal names categorize individuals as belonging to multiple social and cultural units, including the society itself, kinship units within the society (family, lineage, clan), and, in most societies, gender.
- Core cultural properties of personal naming systems can be seen in societal practices of assigning names at birth or relatively soon thereafter.
- Cultural variation exists in terms of who has the right to assign birth names, with the nuclear family carrying the responsibility in industrial societies, while smaller-scale societies tend to invest the right in grandparents or recognized name specialists.
- Appropriate birth names have multiple sources, subject to societal constraints and cultural convention, specifically kinship groups and a repertoire of acceptable personal identity names.
- Societies can be characterized as having comparatively open or fixed sources of personal names. In open systems, virtually any culturally recognized name can be assigned to children, as in the US, but in closed systems, names have to be selected from pre-established lists, as in Iceland.
- Open systems of naming have flexible rules, but favoured or preferred names occur with high frequency and can be stable across many generations.
- Gender is the most widely occurring feature of personal names cross-culturally, with virtually all societies differentiating names of that basis.
- In Anglo societies, assignment of male names is typically more constrained and conservative in comparison with female names, perhaps indicating preference for greater stability in names associated with family lines and tradition.

- Surnames arose in Europe in the Middle Ages, along with increased population but especially with record-keeping associated with poll taxes. The major sources for selection of surnames were from already-present individuating descriptive names, specifically individual traits, family line, place of origin, and occupation.
- Name changes occur in all societies but more frequently in smaller, less complex societies. A name change reflects a change in a person's status or position in life.
- Nicknames are literally 'additional names', usually assigned by one's peers in close social groups during adolescence, and may individuate to a greater extent than assigned names.

The following section extends the discussion of individuation, name uniqueness, and the name as equating to persona. The information derives from a third project of the author's, a compilation and comparison of personal names from the historically earliest and technologically simplest societies, those who survived by foraging for food, typically through a combination of gathering wild food, hunting, and fishing.

At first glance, it might seem that naming systems of foragers would have little to tell us about the systems found among industrialized societies. The latter involve more elements and are more complex, like other aspects of large-scale societies. The opposite, however, is true. As in biology, where much can be learned about contemporary, complex species by focusing on earlier, less complex ones, foraging people's naming systems can shed light on aspects of naming that may be harder to see in contemporary societies.

The sample of foraging societies was limited to those for which sufficient information was available in the literature, and includes groups who existed from the late 19th century through much of the 20th century. They represent only a small percentage of foraging societies if the entire period of prehistory is included, given that foraging was a way of life for humans for at least 100,000 years, and probably much longer. Still, the sample of 26 societies shows remarkable similarities, even though they are from different continents. The true origins of the shared features will almost certainly never be known, but the extent of similarities suggests that there was a naming system that was stable for very long periods of time.

The sample includes one society from Asia, one from Australia, three from Africa, four from South America, and 17 from North America (see Table 36.3).

Comparisons were made across 15 categories, but only the categories most relevant to the present discussion are included here: Identity Names; Maximal Individuation; (Named) After Ancestor; Multiple Names; Nicknames; Tekyonyms; (Name) Prohibited after Death; Marriage Name; and Family Name. Tabulations of those features by society are shown in Table 36.4.

Some features were found to be present in all societies, although other features were not reported in the literature and thus could not be counted. An account is provided below.

Table 36.3 Foraging societies: names, locations, areas, and regions

Society/Band	Location	Area	Region
Aranda	Old World	Australia	Desert/Outback
!Kung San	Old World	Africa	Kalahari
Kua San	Old World	Africa	Kalahari
=Kade San	Old World	Africa	Kalahari
Ainu	Old World	Asia	Northern
Gosiute	New World	North America	Great Basin
Paiute	New World	North America	Great Basin
Blackfeet	New World	North America	High Plains
Cree	New World	North America	High Plains
Crow	New World	North America	High Plains
Gros Ventre	New World	North America	High Plains
Arapaho	New World	North America	Central Plains
Comanche	New World	North America	Central Plains
Dakota	New World	North America	Central Plains
Hidatsa	New World	North America	Central Plains
Kiowa	New World	North America	Central Plains
Oglala	New World	North America	Central Plains
Omaha	New World	North America	Central Plains
Pawnee	New World	North America	Central Plains
Pomo	New World	North America	California
Yakima	New World	North America	California
Yokut	New World	North America	California
Jivaro	New World	South America	Amazon Basin
Kayapo	New World	South America	Amazon Basin
Sanuma	New World	South America	Amazon Basin
Sirono	New World	South America	Amazon Basin

- ***Identity Name.*** In all societies, each member of a band (the social group) had one name that served as primary identification, through reference or address. That pattern continues to the present time, although of course individuals in contemporary society have more than one name.
- ***Maximal Individuation.*** This feature refers to instances in which all individuals in a band have unique names. Names simply could not be given to more than one person and no two people could have the same name. Individuation was maximized. Twenty-one of the 26 foraging societies showed this feature. It was not present in

Table 36.4 Features of forager personal naming systems

Society	ID Name	Max Ind.	Mult-Names	Nick-Names	Tekno nyms	Prohib-Death	Constr-Usage	Family Names	Marry-Names	Title/Status
Aranda	+	+	+	+	+	+	+	–	–	–
!Kung San	+	–	+	+	+	+	+	–	–	–
Kua San	+	+	+	+	o	+	+	–	–	–
=Kade San	+	+	+	+	+	+	+	–	–	–
Ainu	+	+	+	+	+	+	+	–	–	–
Gosiute	+	+	+	+	+	+	+	–	–	–
Paiute	+	+	+	+	+	+	+	–	–	–
Blackfeet	+	+	+	+	o	+	+	–	–	–
Cree	+	+	+	+	o	+	+	–	–	–
Crow	+	+	+	+	o	+	+	–	–	–
Gros Ventre	+	+	+	+	+	+	+	–	–	–
Arapaho	+	+	+	+	o	+	+	–	–	–
Comanche	+	+	+	+	+	+	+	–	–	–
Dakota	+	+	+	+	o	o	+	–	–	–
Hidatsa	+	+	+	+	+	+	+	–	–	–
Kiowa	+	+	+	+	o	+	+	–	–	–
Oglala	+	+	+	+	o	o	+	–	–	–
Omaha	+	+	+	+	+	+	+	–	–	–
Pawnee	+	+	+	+	+	+	+	–	–	–
Pomo	+	o	+	+	o	+	+	–	–	–
Yakima	+	–	+	+	+	+	+	–	–	–
Yokut	+	–	+	+	+	+	+	–	–	–
Jivaro	+	+	+	+	o	o	+	–	–	–
Kayapo	+	+	+	+	+	+	+	–	–	–
Sanuma	+	o	+	+	o	o	+	–	–	–
Siriono	+	+	+	+	+	+	+	–	–	–
TOTALS	26 +	21 + 3 – 2 o	26 +	26 +	15 + 11 o	22 + 4 o	26 +	26 –	26 –	26 –

+ = reported present; – = reported absent; o = not reported

three of them, and no information was available for two of them. Although the suite of names by which individuals in present-day societies are known contributes to individuation, the process is not maximal.

- ***Multiple Names.*** All 26 of the societies had this feature, but the names were in addition to each individual's identity name. They included nicknames and teknonyms. The latter is the use of kin-terms for reference and address, e.g. father-of-X, daughter-of-Y. The same pattern exists in present-day societies (but see the two items below).
- ***Nicknames.*** These were used in all 26 of the groups, and appear to be a universal feature of naming.
- ***Teknonyms.*** The use of teknonyms occurred in all of the societies for which information was available, 15 altogether. The 11 omissions in the literature may have been due to failure to recognize them as names. In contemporary society, teknonyms are used for reference (*Mary's mother, Bob's brother*), though rarely as forms of address.
- ***Prohibited after Death.*** This feature refers to a prohibition that will likely strike many readers as strange, but it is a near-universal in foraging societies. Only four of the 26 foraging societies were not reported to have this feature. 'Prohibited after Death' means that a deceased person's name may not be used in reference, ever. The use would be considered to be a serious, even dangerous breach of social convention. The explanation is that a use of the name invokes the person, calling up the person, who is no longer alive. It is one of the strongest, if not the strongest, equation of a name with the person. The taboo was so strong that in some bands words that were similar to and invocative of a name could no longer be used. Circumlocution or replacement was necessary, or the word's pronunciation had to be changed in order to reduce its resemblance to the actual name. Among the Trukese in the South Pacific, if a deceased person's name was the same as the word for a common object, the object had to be given a new name after the bearer's death (Alford 1988: 116). The Guarani of Paraguay entrusted the invention of replacement names to elderly women. In his book on the 'magic' of names, Edward Clodd (1968) noted that the Guarani word for 'jaguar' had to be changed three times in seven years. Name restrictions and taboos thus could be important sources of lexical change. The prohibition on use of a deceased person's name has been lost in contemporary naming systems, perhaps due to the lessening of individuation, the non-uniqueness of most given names, and the association of names with property (Alford 1988: 117).
- ***Constraints on Usage.*** All 26 of the societies showed presence of this feature. The reference is to preferred avoidance of the use of an identity name, especially in address. As in prohibition after death, the use of an individual's name invoked the person—a social liberty that was avoided unless there was a close relationship with the person. Use of the name was too dangerous; it was the individual's persona, invoked only with care. This meant that teknonyms were frequently used, given that they were considered to be honorific, foregrounding kinship

> over individualism. Avoidance of the social use of an identity name is common among small-scale societies. In English-speaking societies, the use of first names is socially appropriate only when a proper introduction has been made (a 'baptism', in Kripke's terminology, 1972). It seems safe to say that the avoidance is still present in all societies, but an exclusionary rule can be used, a social introduction that removes the restriction by simply 'knowing the person'.

The picture that emerges is that individuation was a feature of personal naming systems from the outset, but it was not a simple differentiation of one member of a band from another. Rather, it was taken seriously, to the point that people tried to avoid use of the name, given that its use exercised power over its bearer. In addition, the name simply could not be used after its bearer's death, for the same reason: namely, that it invoked the persona and thus the person. Nicknames were also universally present in foraging societies, but like identity names, they were surrounded by strong prescriptive rules governing use. Teknonyms were common and undoubtedly eased the social burden for reference and address in light of prohibitions and avoidances. Except for prohibition of use of a deceased person's name and the use of teknonyms, all of these properties are still present in societies today, although relaxed in constraints and social importance.

Lastly, if the features Marriage Name (change of name at marriage), Family Names, and Status/Title Names are considered, all of which are absent in all of the 26 societies (Table 36.4), a rationale is present for their appearance in more technologically advanced societies. The presence of those features is an indication of the importance of families and family names in social and economic systems that emphasize property, property rights, and associated wealth. Maximally individuating names and equating them with the person were reduced in order to accommodate these new concerns. The introduction of family names shifted the equation partially from individuation to categorization.

CHAPTER 37

PLACE AND OTHER NAMES

CAROLE HOUGH

37.1 Introduction

The term 'place name' (or 'toponym') literally refers to the name of a place, ranging from Alaska, the largest state in the USA, to Llanwrtud Wells in Wales, Britain's smallest town. However, the branch of name studies that deals with place names ('toponomastics') also encompasses the names of natural features such as bodies of water, mountains, and forests, as well as those of man-made structures such as buildings, bridges, and roads. All such names evolved to help human societies to function more efficiently by imposing order on their surroundings, so the naming principles are to some extent similar.

In general the oldest names are those of major landscape features: islands, rivers, and mountains. The youngest are those of streets in new housing estates. It is customary to distinguish between so-called 'major names'—those that would appear on a road atlas, such as the names of cities, towns, and rivers—and so-called 'minor names' that would only appear on a detailed local map, such as the names of streets, buildings, and small landscape features. Traditional scholarship has tended to focus on the former, as they are often the earliest and have the most evidential value for the study of historical languages and peoples. However, a growing awareness of the importance of minor names as evidence for local history, dialectology, and culture has led in recent years to a more inclusive approach.

One of the longest established research projects is the English Place-Name Survey (EPNS), a systematic county-by-county analysis of the place names of England.[1] This

[1] Many of the examples within this chapter are from volumes of the English Place-Name Survey. Others are from Ekwall (1960), Everett-Heath (2005), Mills (2003), and Room (2006). Among excellent online sources are *Ainmean-Àite na h-Alba (AÀA)/Gaelic Place-Names of Scotland* http://www.gaelicplacenames.org/index.php, *Archif Melville Richards Placename Database* http://www.e-gymraeg.co.uk/enwaulleoedd/amr/, *Bunachar Logainmneacha na hÉireann/Placenames Database of Ireland*, http://www.logainm.ie/, *History and Hidden Meanings of Britain's Brilliant Place Names from Ordnance Survey* http://www.ordnancesurvey.co.uk/oswebsite/freefun/didyouknow/placenames/, *Names in Denmark* http://names.ku.dk/, and *Placenames NI* http://www.placenamesni.org/.

has been in progress since the 1920s and has served as a model for other national surveys. The emphasis is on identifying the etymological origin of each name by tracing it back through time. The resulting collections of early spellings are also utilized in the study of diachronic language development. This approach is primarily historical and philological, revealing the languages spoken in different areas and at different periods through close examination of successive strata of name giving. An alternative approach that has come to prominence since the late 20th century draws on sociolinguistics, focusing on the synchronic study of name use within communities and the implications for language planning.[2]

37.2 Settlement names

37.2.1 Languages

The prototypical place name is the name of a human settlement. In the Western world, these are generally towns, cities, and villages, many of which have been in existence for a thousand years or more. In England, some 13,400 settlements were recorded in Domesday Book (1086), mostly with names created during the Anglo-Saxon period from Old English or Old Norse. Many of these names have survived to the present day, although their origins tend to have been obscured by linguistic changes.[3] Few place names appear to survive from the Celtic language spoken in southern Britain prior to the arrival of the Anglo-Saxons around the 5th century AD, and variously known as British, Brittonic, or Proto-Welsh.[4] The neighbouring countries of Scotland and

[2] Developments in this area are outlined by Rose-Redwood, Alderman, and Azaryahu (2010).

[3] Exeter appears in Domesday Book as <Execestre> ('Roman town on the River Exe'), reflecting a derivation from OE *ceaster* 'Roman town', and Domesday's <Snotingeham> shows that Nottingham ('homestead of Snot's family') contains an Anglo-Saxon personal name *Snot*. The loss of initial <s> is generally attributed to Norman influence. The same explanation was at one time offered for the changes affecting Exeter and Cambridge, but these are now believed to reflect standard processes of dissimilation in English. Unfortunately Domesday itself is often unreliable. Cambridge appears as <Cantebrigie>, obscuring the river name reflected in an 8th-century spelling <Grontabricc> ('bridge over the River Granta'), and Derby already appears in its modern form, whereas a 10th-century spelling <Deoraby> more clearly reflects an origin from ON *djúr-bȳ* 'deer farmstead'. For many of England's place names, Domesday Book is the earliest record, and must be treated with caution. For the names of other parts of the British Isles, extant sources are often much later, and correspondingly problematic.

[4] The reasons for this have been much discussed. Since names can be used without understanding of semantic meaning, they are easily taken over by incoming settlers, and hence the names of many areas represent a palimpsest of the different languages spoken through time. The scarcity of pre-Anglo-Saxon place names in England has led name scholars to conclude that the Britons themselves were wiped out, despite archaeological and historical evidence to the contrary (see e.g. Higham 2007). I have argued elsewhere that the informational content of place names was more relevant during the Middle Ages than in later periods, making it less likely for names to be transferred between speakers of mutually unintelligible Celtic and Germanic languages (Hough 2012).

Wales, where the Anglo-Saxon settlements were later or less extensive, have a much higher proportion of place names from the Celtic languages. The historical varieties known as Cumbric and Pictish are found in the south and northeast of Scotland respectively, while Gaelic names are common throughout Scotland, and Welsh names throughout Wales. So too Cornish names predominate in the county of Cornwall in the far southwest of England, where Cornish continued to be spoken until the 18th century.

Names from these different varieties of Celtic are related both to each other and to those in other parts of the Celtic world, particularly Ireland, the Isle of Man, and Brittany. Indeed, the P-Celtic (or 'Gallo-Brittonic') languages Breton, British, Cornish, Cumbric, Pictish, and Welsh may more appropriately be regarded as a dialect continuum, representing a single language spoken across much of the mainland of Britain from pre-Roman times until the arrival of the Anglo-Saxons. The Q-Celtic (or 'Goidelic') languages Old Irish, Scottish Gaelic, and Manx represent the other main branch of Common Celtic, and again form closely similar names. So too, Germanic place names often have cognate forms in Old English and Old Norse, making it difficult to differentiate the two languages in areas of the British Isles where both were spoken. Like their Celtic predecessors, the Anglo-Saxons reached Britain from mainland Europe, as did various later groups of Scandinavian incomers, and hence there are close links with names in the continental homelands of Denmark, Germany, and Norway. Moreover, since naming patterns appear to have been established even before the Indo-European language family subdivided into branches such as Celtic and Germanic, underlying similarities unite apparently unrelated groups of place names throughout Europe and beyond.

37.2.2 Structures

Most place names are descriptive in some way, and the two main kinds of settlement name within the Indo-European languages describe the natural or built environment. The former appear to be the earliest type created by Germanic settlers in different areas, and are also characteristic of the Celts. The term designating the feature described is known as the defining element or 'generic'. This can stand alone, as in Cwm in Wales from Welsh *cwm* 'valley', Holme in England from Old Norse (ON) *holmr* 'island, water-meadow', Perth in Scotland from Pictish **pert* 'copse', and Wick in England from Old English (OE) *wīc* 'specialized farm'. Most names, however, are compound, adding a descriptive term known as the qualifying element or 'specific' to give names such as Cwm-yr-Eglwys 'valley of the church', Durham 'hill island' (referring to a peninsula), Larbert 'half copse', and Shapwick 'sheep farm'. In general, the defining element precedes the qualifier in place names from the Celtic languages (except those pre-dating the 6th century), but follows it in place names from the Germanic languages. The defining element of Llanwrtud is Welsh *llan* 'church', while the qualifier is a personal name *Gwrtud*: 'church of Gwrtud'. English *well* refers to a mineral well, and differentiates the small spa town of Llanwrtud Wells from neighbouring Llanwrtud. Semantically parallel to Llanwrtud is Alvechurch 'Ælfgyth's church' in England, with a feminine personal name *Ælfgyth* qualifying OE *cirice* 'church', but here the element order is Germanic. A common factor is that the main stress falls on the qualifier, so pronunciation often helps to differentiate between Celtic and Germanic formations: Llanˈwrtud, ˈAlvechurch.

Names describing the settlement itself are known as 'habitative'; those describing its surroundings as 'topographical'. The most common habitative generic in English place names is OE *tūn* 'farmstead, village, manor'. This gives rise to hundreds of names including many occurrences each of Kingston 'king's manor', Middleton 'middle farmstead', and Norton 'north village'. Recurring names such as these are often further differentiated by a later element or 'affix' referring to location or ownership, as with Kingston upon Hull, Middleton on the Wolds, and King's Norton. Similar in meaning to OE *tūn* is ON *bȳ* 'farmstead, village'. Names such as Derby 'deer farmstead', Grimsby 'Grímr's farmstead', and Wetherby 'wether-sheep farmstead' are particularly characteristic of the Danelaw, the area of eastern England allocated to the Danes following the Viking invasions of the 9th century. Map 1 shows place names from ON *bȳ* on the mainland of Britain represented in the Ordnance Survey 1:50,000 Gazetteer, with the heaviest concentration in northeast England. By contrast, Map 2 shows the high incidence in Wales of place names containing Welsh *llan*, while Map 3 shows the smaller number but wider distribution of place names from the topographical generic *aber* 'river-mouth, confluence' found in the P-Celtic languages of both northern and southern Britain.[5]

Other common habitative generics include OE *burh* 'stronghold' and OE *hām* 'homestead'. These are found in some of the earliest names created by the Anglo-Saxon settlers, including Bamburgh 'Bebbe's stronghold', Chobham '*Ceabba's homestead', Dagenham '*Dæcca's homstead', and Egham 'Ecga's homestead'.[6] Also early is OE *ceaster* 'old fortification', found in the names of Roman towns such as Chester. The qualifying element is often the original Romano-British name, as in Dorchester, Manchester, and Rochester. The most common topographical element in English place names is OE *lēah*. This identifies areas of ancient woodland, but has a range of meanings referring chronologically to the woodland itself, clearings in woodland, and pasture land. Recurrent compounds include Langley 'long wood', Shirley 'bright clearing', and Shipley 'sheep pasture'. Different modern forms often develop from a single origin: OE *hēah lēah* 'high wood or clearing' gives rise to Healaugh, Healey, Heeley, and Highleigh.

[5] I am grateful to Ellen Bramwell and Daria Izdebska for assistance with the preparation of the maps.

[6] Early types of name have been identified on the basis of factors such as proximity to sites with archaeological evidence for early Anglo-Saxon settlement, and occurrence in early written sources. These approaches are taken respectively in Cox (1973) and Cox (1976).

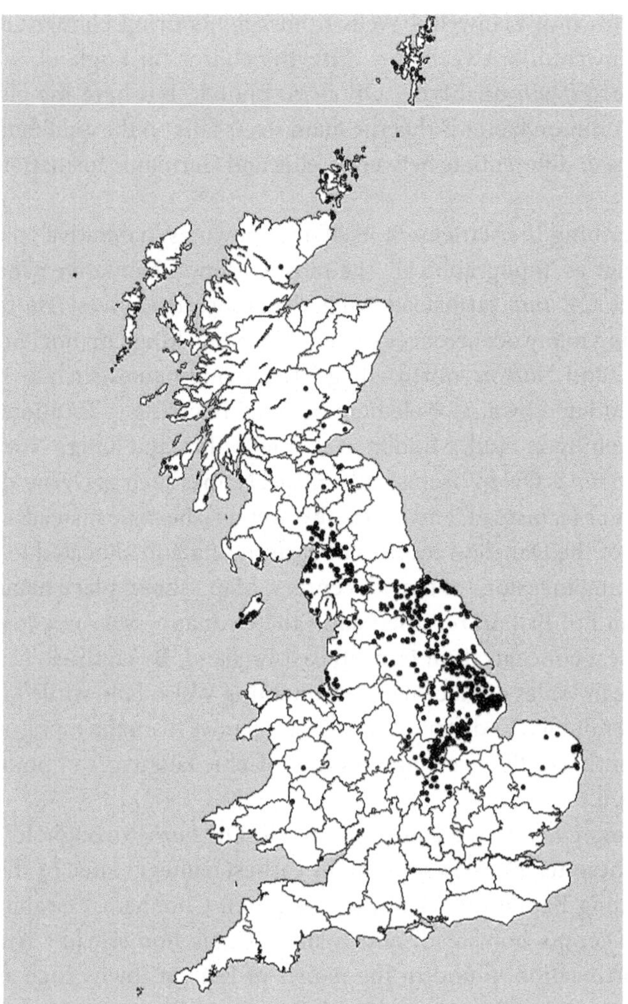

MAP 1 Place names from ON *bȳ* 'farmstead, village'. The map was created using GenMap UK software and contains Ordnance Survey data © Crown copyright and database right 2013.

Similar formations are found in place names from other European languages. ON *holmr* is the generic of Stockholm 'pole island' in Sweden and other names in Scandinavia,[7] while ON *bȳ* is the generic of many names in Denmark including Sæby 'village by the sea or lake', Gammelby 'old village', and Nørreby 'north village'—the equivalent of Norton in England. Cognates of OE *lēah* occur as generics in names such as Venlo 'wood by a marsh' in The Netherlands and Waterloo 'sacred wood by water'

[7] The meaning of the compound 'pole island' is uncertain, but may refer to the mooring poles of the maritime city.

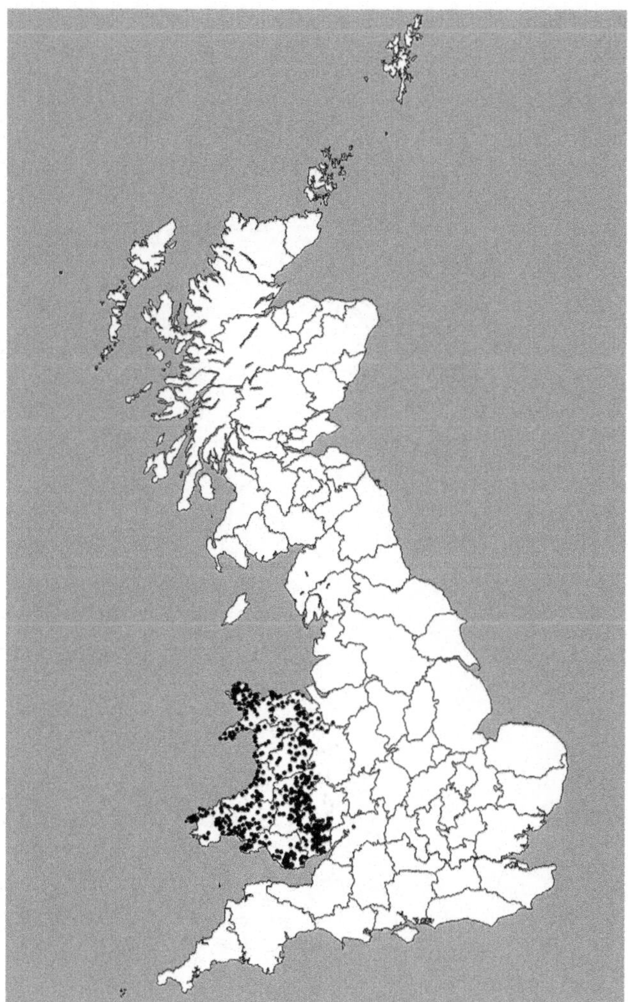

MAP 2 Place names from Welsh *llan* 'church'. The Map was created using GenMap UK software and contains Ordnance Survey data © Crown copyright and database right 2013.

in Belgium; cognates of OE *hēah* occur as qualifiers in names such as Hanover 'high bank' in Germany and Hátún 'high farm' in Iceland. ON *tún*, the generic of Hátún, is cognate with OE *tūn* and impossible to distinguish from it in areas of Scandinavian settlement in England, especially where the qualifiers are Scandinavian personal names. Examples such as Flixton 'Flik's farm' and Kedleston 'Ketill's farm' are common within the Danelaw, and might in theory represent new formations from ON *tún*. However, as a high proportion are attached to attractive sites unlikely to have been previously unoccupied, they are believed to represent existing formations from OE *tūn*, with the original

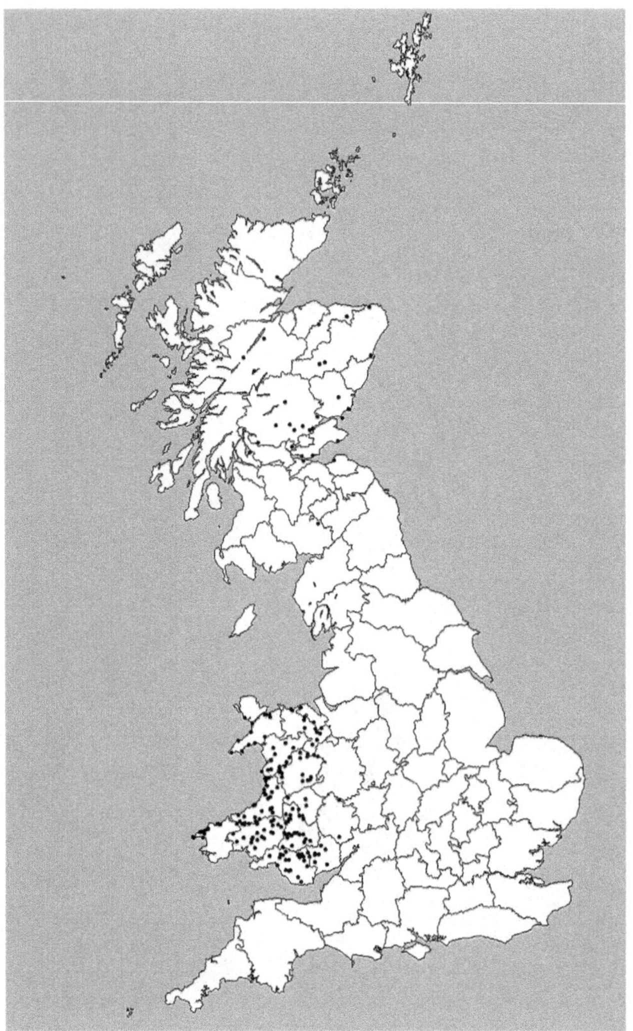

MAP 3 Place names from P-Celtic *aber* 'river-mouth, confluence'. The map was created using GenMap UK software and contains Ordnance Survey data © Crown copyright and database right 2013.

qualifiers replaced by the names of the Danish overlords who took over the farms in the first phase of Viking settlement.[8]

Other places are named after inhabitants, as with Jarrow 'fen people' and Ripon 'Hrype tribe' in England. This type is relatively rare except in the names of districts and countries. Wales 'Britons, foreigners' is the name given by the Anglo-Saxons to their

[8] A chronology of Danish settlement names in England was established by Cameron (1965, 1970, 1971) on the basis of features such as attractiveness of site, combinations with Danish or English elements, and grammatical and phonological patterns.

Celtic neighbours, while the Welsh name for the country is *Cymru* 'people from the same region, kinsmen'. As Owen (2012: 98) observes, '**Cymru** talks of inclusion and kinship, **Wales** talks of exclusion and difference'. It is more common for qualifying elements to refer to minority groups, as in Swaffham 'homestead of the Swabians' from OE *hām* 'homestead', and Walton 'village of the Britons'. Both are found within areas of predominantly Anglo-Saxon settlement. Paible in the Hebrides, Paplay and Papley in Orkney, Papil in Shetland, and Papýli in Iceland are all Old Norse names meaning 'settlement of *papar*', apparently referring to Celtic priests or monks encountered by the incoming Scandinavians and named from a term related etymologically to the word *pope*.[9]

Non-descriptive names are less common in Britain and continental Europe than in other parts of the world, where naming traditions encompass allusions to mythological or historical events. Examples include the Tibetan name Darjeeling 'land of the thunderbolt' in India, referring to the thunderbolt of the Hindu god Indra, and the Māori name Whakatane 'act like a man' in New Zealand, referring to a woman who retrieved a canoe drifting out to sea. Sometimes known as 'incident names', they are also characteristic of names given by European explorers. The name of the state of Texas may derive from an incident where a Spanish explorer was greeted by native Americans with the word *techas* 'friends'.[10]

Even descriptive names do not necessarily describe the location they now designate. Whereas the recurrent names mentioned above were generally each created independently to describe a similar location, settlers in a new area often reuse familiar names for nostalgic or territorial reasons. Many names were transplanted in this way by European immigrants to the African, American, and Australian continents. New Hanover in South Africa was named after Hanover in Germany by German settlers, the place name Derby in the US state of Connecticut was transferred from England, and the place name Perth in Australia was transferred from Scotland. Other names are commemorative, based on the names of people. Washington, the capital of the USA, was named after George Washington, the first President. Melbourne, the capital of the state of Victoria in Australia, was named after William Lamb, 2nd Viscount Melbourne, and Victoria itself was named after Queen Victoria. Pretoria, now the administrative capital of South Africa, was named after a Boer statesman, Andries Pretorius. Bloemfontein, the judicial capital, may have been named after a local farmer, Jan Bloem. What these all have in common is that they were bestowed as a deliberate naming act. The majority of descriptive names, on the other hand, evolve from *ad hoc* expressions, which gradually become fixed over the course of time. In this respect, non-descriptive names have more in common with the personal names discussed in Blount (this volume), while descriptive names have more in common with surnames.

[9] These names have been much discussed, and are the subject of ongoing research (Crawford 2002; Ahronson 2007).

[10] The tradition is widely reported, but unverifiable.

37.2.3 Morphology

Place names are grammatically interesting. Some include the definite article, as with Cwm-yr-Eglwys in Wales, La Coruña 'the column' in Spain, and Las Vegas 'the meadows' in the USA. Others include a preposition, as with Kingston upon Hull and Middleton on the Wolds in England. Place names from inflected languages often preserve the locative case, which had merged with the dative in Old English and other Germanic languages. Whereas the name Healey and its variants derives from OE *hēah lēah* 'high wood or clearing', the dative form *hēan lēage* results in Handley, Hanley, and Henley. Canterbury, recorded in the early 9th century as <to Cantuarabyrg>, contains the same defining element as Bamburgh, but in the dative form *byrig* 'stronghold of the people of Kent'. Similarly, Ripon appears in Domesday Book as <Ripum>, with the dative plural <um> inflection.

Many qualifiers appear in the genitive case, sometimes but not always indicating possession. Derby is first recorded in the 10th century as <Deoraby>, with the medial <a> representing a genitive plural inflection also seen in <Cantuarabyrg>. The genitive singular often survives as medial <s> in place names such as Grimsby 'Grímr's farmstead' and Kingston 'king's manor'.

A distinctive group of names comprises a qualifier only, often with a genitive inflection implying an omitted generic. Examples include St Andrews in Scotland '(place with the shrine of) St Andrew', St Ives in Cornwall '(church dedicated to) St Ya', and St Dogmaels in Wales '(church dedicated to) St Dogmael'. Some names of this type in North America result from their discovery by European explorers on the feast day of the respective saint. Into this category falls St John's in Canada, although the place name St Andrews in Canada and New Zealand was transferred from Scotland.

The recorded history of many names does not begin until centuries after they were created, and in some instances an original generic may have dropped out. St Weonards in England 'church of St Gwennarth' is first recorded *c.*1130 as <Lann Sant Guainerth>, from a generic cognate with Welsh *llan*, and other such formations may have a similar history. The tendency for place names to be shortened is common throughout the world. Shanghai, Chinese for 'by the sea', is first recorded as <Shanghaizhen>, with the generic *zhèn* meaning 'garrison post'. Los Angeles 'the angels' in California is a reduced form of the Spanish phrase *el pueblo de la reyna de los angeles* 'the town of the queen of the angels'—now often further abbreviated to the initials LA. Māori place names are famously long, and are usually contracted: the full name of Whakatane is *Me Whakatane au i au* 'I shall act like a man'.

37.2.4 Analogy

One of the problems with name studies is that established types of formations tend to attract others to them, leading to false (or 'folk') etymologies. Another St Ives in Dorset is first recorded in the 12th century as <Iuez> '(place overgrown with) ivy', but later gained the word *Saint* by analogy with the Cornish and other names. Similarly, defining elements are highly repetitive. The generic *llan* 'church' occurs in over 300 Welsh place names (see Map 2), but has also influenced the development of at least a dozen others. Sometimes *llan* replaces an earlier *nant* 'valley, stream', as in Llancarfan (<nant carban> 1136–54 '(place by the) valley of Carfan') and Llantarnam (<Nant Thirnon> 1179 'valley of (the stream) Teyrnon'), while Llangwathan (<luin guaidan> 1136–54 'Gwaiddan's grove') shows 'the more familiar *llan* substituted for *llwyn* "grove"' (Owen and Morgan 2007: 222, 280, 262). The qualifying element of Aberford in England (<Ædburford> 1176 'Eadburh's ford') is a feminine personal name OE *Ēadburh*, but has developed by analogy with P-Celtic *aber* 'river-mouth, confluence' (see Map 3), perhaps helped along by the watery connotations of the generic OE *ford* 'ford'. Similarly, the common habitative generic OE *hām* 'homestead' has affected the development of Durham, originally from ON *holmr* and recorded in the 11th century as <Dunholm>.

In other instances, the desire to make sense of names whose original meaning has been obscured leads them to develop along non-standard lines. Swansea, on the coast of Wales (<Swensi> *c.*1140), derives from a Scandinavian personal name with ON *ey* 'Sveinn's island'. Its modern form, however, has developed by analogy with the words *swan* and *sea*.

37.2.5 Name changes

The age of a name does not necessarily reflect the age of the settlement to which it refers. Many settlements have been renamed, or partially renamed, sometimes more than once. Before the discovery of the mineral well in the 18th century, Llanwrtud Wells was known as *Pont Rhydferan* 'bridge at the ford of the short share-land'. Derby replaced the Old English name *Northworthy* 'north enclosure' following the Danish invasions of England. It is not uncommon for places to have more than one name in different languages. Some become obsolete, but others remain in use alongside each other. The earlier Gaelic name of St Andrews was *Kilrimont* 'church of the royal hill', the Welsh name of St Dogmaels is *Llandudoch* 'church of (St) Tydoch', and the Welsh name of Swansea is *Abertawe* 'mouth of the river Tawe'.

Early forms of descriptive names often show instability until a particular combination of qualifier and generic becomes fixed. In some occurrences of Kingston, the qualifier fluctuates between OE *cyninges* 'king's' and OE *cyne* 'royal', the two versions 'king's manor' and 'royal manor' being synonymous. Generic variation also occurs, and has been discussed by Ekwall (1962, 1964) and Taylor (1997).[11] Such instability is less common with commemorative and other types of bestowed name, but here there is often competition between rival formations by different claimants. In the USA, present-day

[11] Taylor (1997) argues that variation between different habitative generics may reflect differences in the status or function of a place at different times.

New York was successively named New Amsterdam, New York, and New Orange (after the Prince of Orange) during alternating periods of Dutch and British rule, while New Orleans was named Nouvelle Orléans by its French founders (after the Duc d'Orléans), but anglicized when it was sold to the United States in 1803. Many of the commemorative names bestowed during the period of British and European colonialization replaced indigenous names, some of which are gradually being reinstated. In other instances, existing names were simply adapted to fit the phonetic structures of incoming languages. Canberra, the capital of Australia, appears to be from a word meaning 'meeting place' in the aboriginal Ngunnawai language. Toronto in Canada may have the same meaning in the Huron language,[12] and Alaska is from an Aleut word variously translated as 'great land', 'mainland', or 'peninsula'.

37.2.6 Onomastic geography

The geographical distribution of names from different languages and of different types throws light on population movement and settlement patterns. Parallels with names in Denmark and Norway have been used to identify areas of Danish and Norwegian settlement in the British Isles; parallels with names in Ireland to trace the route taken by Gaelic-speaking Scots in Scotland; and parallels with areas of West Germanic settlement in mainland Europe to locate the continental origins of the Anglo-Saxons. The repetitive nature of name formations facilitates comparative analysis, making it possible to identify toponymic isoglosses by mapping recurrent generics. In northeast Scotland, the incidence of over 300 place names from Pictish **pett* 'piece of land' defines the area inhabited by Picts prior to the takeover of the Pictish kingdom by Gaels in the 9th century. In eastern England, the extent of Danish settlement is defined by names from ON *bȳ* (see Map 1). Perhaps most strikingly, the whole of Estonia can be divided into linguistic regions on the basis of name suffixes (Päll 2012).

The nationalities of colonists during the European Age of Exploration is similarly reflected in surviving place names. The occurrence of Spanish *San(ta)* 'saint' in names such as San Diego, San Francisco, San José, Santa Barbara, and Santa Rosa identifies areas of Spanish settlement in the USA (particularly California); and the presence of Scottish settlers in what is now Harare, Zimbabwe, is revealed by transferred names from Scotland such as St Andrews Park, Strathaven, and Braeside.[13]

The evidence is not always clear-cut, however, and some aspects remain controversial. There has been much discussion regarding the dating of the English *bȳ*-names, some of which contain post-Conquest personal names suggesting that the generic may have been productive in England long after the period of Danish colonization.[14] The most thorough

[12] An alternative derivation is from an Iroquois term meaning 'poles in the water'.

[13] These derive respectively from the name of the patron saint of Scotland, Gaelic *srath-avon* 'valley of the (River) Avon', and Scots *braeside* 'hillside'.

[14] Alternatively, these personal names may have replaced the original qualifiers, as with the Danish–English *tūn* names discussed above.

recent discussion considers it likely that the majority of such names were indeed created by speakers of Old Norse before the 11th century, but concludes that further research is needed before the matter can be regarded as settled (Abrams and Parsons 2004). The issue of the Anglo-Saxon homelands has also recently been reopened. Following the account given by the 8th-century historian Bede, the Anglo-Saxons are generally thought to have come to Britain over the North Sea from areas now comprising northern Germany and southern Denmark. On the basis of correspondences between ancient place name elements in England and on the continent, however, Udolph (2012) challenges this model and argues that the route was across the English Channel from parts of northern Germany, the Netherlands, and Flanders.

This type of evidence also has chronological implications. As well as defining the extent of Danish settlement in England, the occurrence of ON *bȳ* in the Danelaw and in other areas invaded by the Vikings, such as Normandy, establishes that the generic was in use during the Viking Age, and helps to provide dating parameters for *bȳ*-names in Denmark. Again, however, there are controversial issues. It remains uncertain to what extent spatial distribution is related to chronology. Through a series of maps plotting the distribution of the Scandinavian generics *staðir* 'farm', *setr* 'dwelling', and *bólstaðr* 'secondary farm' in northern Scotland, Nicolaisen argued that the more limited geographical range of *staðir* indicated an early phase of settlement, with *setr* and *bólstaðr* revealing 'a gradual progressive spreading of settlement in this order' (1976: 76). This position has not been widely accepted, and is modified in the latest edition of Nicolaisen's book (2001: xviii–xix). Name evidence is cumulative, and as place name surveys advance, material may come to light that casts doubt on previous theories. The limited distribution of place names from Gaelic *sliabh* in southwest Scotland has long been taken to reflect an early stage of settlement, but this conclusion is challenged by the identification of other *sliabh*- names in different parts of the country (Nicolaisen 2007; Taylor 2007).

37.2.7 Early vocabulary

As has already been seen, some place names contain terms unrecorded in written sources. The Pictish language is largely unknown except from inscriptions and names, so terms such as **pert* 'copse' and **pett* 'piece of land' can only be reconstructed from this range of evidence. Unattested cognates of Welsh *llan* occur in names from other P-Celtic languages: indeed, about 50 parishes in Cornwall are named from Cornish **lann* 'church-site'.

For many languages, including earlier stages and varieties of English, the written record is incomplete, and names preserve additional information. Since most names originate in speech, the colloquial register is particularly well represented: this is significant for the study of languages that are mainly spoken rather than written, such as Scots (Scott 2008). In some instances, the meaning can be worked out from the context; in others, by comparison with cognates in other European languages. English place names such as Wreighill and Wreighburn combine an unattested OE **wearg* with topographical generics found elsewhere with animal names. Comparison with cognates such as ON *vargr* 'wolf' suggests a similar meaning for the Old English term. Again, the evidence is cumulative, and interpretation of a group of place names may be revised as further instances come to light. The qualifier of topographical names such as Purbeck and Purley was formerly taken to be OE *pur* 'bittern, snipe'. However, an occurrence in the Scottish name Pusk, with the habitative generic OE *wīc* 'specialized farm', indicated a type of farm animal, and the names are now thought to derive from the etymon of English dialect *pur* 'male lamb'.

Comparison of recurring generics also makes it possible to pinpoint semantic meaning more accurately. In a series of ground-breaking studies culminating in their 2000 book, Gelling and Cole undertook an analysis of Old English topographical generics in relation to the landscape features described. This revealed that the topographical vocabulary of Old English was more finely discriminating than that of later stages of English, with precise terms for features that would later be subsumed under broader headings. As regards different types of valley, a *botm* was flat and easily flooded, a *byden* was deep, a *canne* had steep sides, a *cumb* was short and broad, and a *hop* was remote and enclosed, while *denu* was the standard term for a main valley. Similarly with terms for woodland: *bearu* designated a small wood, *fyrth* was scrubland on the edge of forest, *grāf* was a coppiced wood, *hyrst* was a wooded hill, and *wudu* was used for large stretches of woodland. Most of Gelling and Cole's research was based on fieldwork, but key evidence was also provided by qualifying elements. The majority of qualifiers found in combination with *holt* 'wood' are terms for individual species of tree, and this helps to define the generic as 'single-species wood'.

An important caveat, however, is that name elements are not identical to vocabulary words, and name evidence is not directly applicable to other areas of language. A number of factors lead to names developing differently from lexis. These include their characteristically compound structure, and the tendency to associate them with similar-sounding words. Moreover, recent research has highlighted significant differences between toponymic and lexical uses of terminology. Just as the Indo-European languages split off from each other and developed separately, so too the toponymicon split off from the lexicon at an early stage and has continued to develop separately up to the present day (Hough 2010). Problems relating to the reconstruction of unattested vocabulary are discussed by contributors to Elmevik and Strandberg (2010) in relation to the languages of Austria, Denmark, Germany, Iceland, Norway, and Sweden, and in connection not only with settlement names but with the other types of name that will be considered more briefly in the rest of this chapter.

37.3 Names of natural features

37.3.1 Island names

Islands tend to be the first features encountered and named by explorers and migrants, and hence their names are among the earliest given by different groups of speakers, from the pre-Celtic incomers to the British Isles and continental Europe to the European explorers of the African, American, and Australian continents. In the Northern Isles of Scotland, where the names are overwhelmingly of Scandinavian origin, the only names taken to pre-date the Scandinavian settlements of *c*.800 are the island names Fetlar, Unst, and Yell. Others such as Papa Stour and Papa Westray again refer to the communities of Celtic ecclesiastics who were already there when the Scandinavians arrived.

Like settlement names, many island names are compounds. Unsurprisingly, the generic is often a word for 'island', as with ON *ey* in Alderney, Guernsey, and Stronsay, and more recent formations such as the commemorative name Prince Edward Island in Canada and the incident name Easter Island in the Pacific, discovered by a Dutch explorer on Easter Day 1722.

Some of the earliest names, however, refer to a quality with a suffix, and this morphology can help to identify prehistoric formations. Sometimes referred to as 'primary naming', the stratum is datable to the early Indo-European period when the suffixes were productive, as opposed to 'secondary naming' based on words in the lexicon. In the Hebrides, Iona (<Ioua> *c*.700) appears to be a secondary name '(place of) yew trees' from Old Irish, whereas Mull (<Malaios> *c*.150) may be a primary name 'lofty (one)', and is pre-Celtic.

37.3.2 Water names

Again, names of major water features tend to have a high survival rate, representing one of the earliest naming strata. As with island names, suffixed formations are particularly early. Among the most ancient river names in Britain are the Ayr in Scotland and the Don in England, cognate respectively with the Aar in Belgium, the Ahr in Germany, and the Ara in Spain, and with the Danube (with cognate names in the nine countries it flows through), the Don in Russia, and the Donwy in Wales. It is no coincidence that they are paralleled in different parts of Britain and Europe. One aspect of the early toponymicon mentioned above was a river-naming system in use across continental Europe and Britain during the prehistoric period. Sometimes referred to as 'Old European hydronymy', there has been much debate as to whether this ancient river-naming system represents an Indo-European or non-Indo-European language. Whereas Vennemann (1994) argues for the latter, an Indo-European origin is strongly supported by Kitson (1996). Subsequent research into river names and other ancient toponyms has found little evidence for non-Indo-European roots (e.g. Særheim 2012).

The names of smaller rivers and streams tend to be later, but still preserve important evidence. Nicolaisen (1980: 37) points out that the complementary distribution of the generics *brook*, *creek*, and *lick* in the United States reflect 'different lexical choices for the naming of streams in American English'.

37.3.3 Hill names

In comparison to the names of islands and rivers, hill names have received little attention, although their potential as evidence for language and history is illustrated by

Drummond's (2007) study of hill names in Scotland. Again, the names of major hills and mountains tend to be more ancient than those of smaller features. One focus of current research is the longevity of hill names in comparison to other types of names. Contrasting results pertain to different areas, possibly due to differences in local conditions. Whereas Ainiala (1997) found that in southern Finland, hill names survived relatively well, Drummond (2009) found that in southern Scotland, they were more likely to be replaced than settlement names and other toponyms.

37.4 Names of man-made structures

37.4.1 Building names

With exceptions such as Cox's (1994) study of English inn names, building names have been relatively neglected by traditional scholarship, but have come to prominence as part of the focus on urban toponymy within the 'critical toponymies' school. An inclusive approach to the study of inner-city areas, encompassing the names of churches, cinemas, hotels, houses, parks, pubs, railway stations, restaurants, schools, shops, theatres, and so on, can provide insights into past and present community identity, as illustrated by Sandst's (2015) study of names in the Nørrebro district of Copenhagen.[15]

37.4.2 Road names

Research into road and street names has two main foci. One is historical. In England, the earliest roads date back to Roman times, as with Fosse Way and Watling Street, and some medieval towns have street names from the Anglo-Saxon period. As with settlement names, the geographical scatter of common generics can throw light on settlement patterns. In England, early street names from ON *gata* 'road' characterize urbanized areas within the Danelaw, whereas OE *strǣt* 'Roman road' is more common in Anglo-Saxon towns. Again, however, the evidence must be handled with care, and Fellows-Jensen (2010) argues that only if the qualifying element is also Danish can the name be regarded as Scandinavian rather than as an analogical formation following the pattern of the early *gata* names.

A more recent focus of research is into contemporary patterns of street naming as part of the construction of community identity. Several of the contributions to Berg and Vuolteenaho (2009) are on this theme, forming part of the 'critical toponymies'

[15] A summary of the study appeared as the February 2013 Feature of the Month on the website www.onomastics.co.uk, under the title 'Semantically related names: cities-within-cities'.

approach mentioned above, while Sandst (2015) discusses the use of semantically related street names to create a cohesive unit within one area of Nørrebro.

37.5 Conclusion

It will be clear that there are two major differences between place names and the personal names discussed in Blount (this volume). First, although some place names are transferred, they are not taken from a name pool, as with personal names, but created to identify the place. There is therefore a more direct connection between the name and its referent. Secondly, whereas the referent of a personal name is a human being, the referent of a place name is more fuzzy. A name such as Chicago, the Lake District, or Poland may have a prototypical core—an area which everyone would agree is encompassed by the name—but on the edges of the area there would be less certainty as to how far the name extends.

In other respects, however, the different kinds of name have much in common. Whereas place names more than personal names reflect interaction between human beings and the natural environment, all names are strongly influenced by the social environment. Both at their point of origin and in their later development, they reflect the structures and priorities of the cultures to which they belong. Modern scholarship has begun to adapt techniques from sociolinguistics in order to investigate uses of names at the present day, and this in turn is shedding new light on the creation and evolution of names in the past.

A sociolinguistic approach lends itself particularly to the analysis of names in oral circulation. Field names, formerly an integral part of life within farming communities, are now rapidly falling out of use and fading from living memory, so there is some urgency to the task of recording them. Burns (forthcoming) reports on a study of such names in northeast Scotland, where the Doric dialect is spoken. Techniques such as participant observation and semi-structured interviews not only proved effective as a means of collecting the data but revealed additional information on processes of name changes. Among them were instances of code-switching between dialects, variant forms of a single name within conversations, fluctuation in the use or non-use of definite articles, lack of standardized spellings, and attempts to explain opaque names by constructing folk etymologies. All have a bearing on issues discussed in a historical context earlier in this chapter. Like much of the work directed towards the development of socio-onomastic methodologies in other areas of name studies, Burns's paper is based on a doctoral project. It offers an exciting glimpse of the rich vein of new research being opened up by the next generation of scholars.

CHAPTER 38

NICKNAMES

ROBERT KENNEDY

38.1 Introduction

NICKNAMES hold a special place within naming practices, and their study within onomastics reflects this. From a formal perspective they are notable for their structural tendencies, whether phonological, morphological, or syntactic (Anderson 2003; de Klerk and Bosch 1996, 1997; Kennedy and Zamuner 2006; McCarthy and Prince 1986), and from a sociological perspective, their intricacies of appropriateness and usage are complex and varied (Dorian 1970; Lawson 1973; Leslie and Skipper 1990; Morgan et al. 1979; Phillips 1990; Wierzbicka 1992).

Although theories of the sociolinguistics of nickname usage have been advanced (Leslie and Skipper 1990; Morgan et al. 1979; Wierzbicka 1992), empirical study of nicknames tends to focus upon their usage within a specific setting or subculture (Adams 2008; Crozier 2004; de Klerk and Bosch 1996; Dorian 1970; Kennedy and Zamuner 2006; Phillips 1990; Skipper and Leslie 1988; Skipper 1986; Skipper 1990; Zaitzow et al. 1997), so a more general picture of nicknames does not always emerge from such research. This chapter thus provides an overview of structural and sociolinguistic properties of nicknames, framing them as a special kind of name and therefore as a special kind of noun phrase.

Some preliminary concerns warrant comment, as they represent recurrent themes in nickname analysis. Notably, because of variation in form and usage, not all researchers agree on a single definition for the phenomenon. In this chapter, a form will be considered a nickname if it is a proper noun bearing reference to some individual and differing (even minimally) from the formal name associated with the same individual.[1] In

[1] The term originates from middle English *eke-name*, where *eke* relates to an addition or augmentation. An *ekename* was thus an extra name; the initial *n* was transferred to the word *nickname* via metanalysis from the indefinite article.

addition, I will reserve the term 'referent' for the individual named by a nickname (other researchers may use 'recipient' or 'nicknamee' for the same notion). I will use 'coiner' for the individual(s) who create nicknames, and 'user' for those who use them in speech and writing.

This chapter is organized as follows: section 38.2 provides a working definition of nicknames and highlights their primary characteristics, while section 38.3 establishes some functionally determined first-order subtypes. The remainder of the chapter uses these subtypes to frame a description of structural and sociolinguistic properties of nicknames. Sections 38.4 and 38.5 examine the grammatical and structural properties of nicknames, and section 38.6 focuses on semantic aspects. Section 38.7 outlines how nickname formation and usage is sensitive to sociolinguistic dimensions, and section 38.8 deals with some remaining issues and provides a summary.

38.2 Definition and Characteristics

There is among studies of nicknames a variety of definitions, ranging in inclusiveness and reflecting the variation we see along dimensions of form, content, and function. Other terminology has emerged for specific subtypes of nickname. For example, briefer nicknames are often called 'hypocoristics' and include subtypes like 'petnames', 'callnames', and 'bynames'. On the other hand, terms to indicate more elaborate nicknames include 'descriptive phrases' and 'monikers' (Maurer and Futrell 1982; Zaitzow et al. 1997).

In form, nicknames vary in size, rhythm, and phonemic composition; they range from truncated and recurrent monosyllables and disyllables such as *Tom* or *Sally* to longer specialized phrases such as *The Iron Horse* or *The Sultan of Swat*.[2] Within the shortest types of hypocoristics, forms may range in how closely derived they are. Some nicknames are derived predictably via truncation and suffixation, such as *Martin* → *Marty* or *Abigail* → *Abby*, while others are associated with common forenames but with a standard and unpredictable phonological change, such as *William* → *Bill* or *Margaret* → *Peg*.

In content, nicknames vary by whether they are derivative of given names or surnames, such as the preceding hypocoristic examples, or are arrived at via some more creative process. Morgan et al. (1979) provide some terminology to express this difference: derived nicknames have an internal source (i.e. within the referent's formal name), while creative nicknames have an external source. While phrasal nicknames

[2] Following Skipper (1990) I consider any article *the* which appears in conjunction with a phrasal nickname to be part of it, and I italicize it to reflect this. Moreover, phrasal nicknames seem typically to receive title capitalization in texts, whereby all content words are capitalized but prepositions and articles are not. Across narratives, however, there is variation as to whether an initial article is to be capitalized; here, I capitalize initial words.

are typically externally derived, hypocoristics may also be creative, such as *Lefty* for any left-handed person, *Mookie* (for the professional baseball player William Wilson), or *Tiger* (for the professional hockey player Dave Williams). Morgan et al. (1979) and Skipper (1986, 1990) limit 'nickname' to externally derived productions and exclude internally derived forms.

In function, nicknames vary in their usage as reference, address, or both. Furthermore, some nicknames are used among members of some definable community—a school, workplace, or settlement—while others are used by members of the general public for famous referents, such as athletes, politicians, performers, and other celebrities. Allen (1983) and Abel (2004) situate this as a dimension of distance between coiners or users and the referent, but distance and publicness are not coextensive. For example, a possible distant nicknaming scenario would be soldiers nicknaming their general (Abel 2004), which is not equivalent to a press-given public nickname for a celebrity.

Beyond phonological form, nicknames may be noted for properties of informality and intimacy. Nevertheless, none of these is necessary as a component of our working definition. First, while nicknames may necessarily be informal in their usage, such informality could be argued to follow directly from their being structurally distinct from a formal name. If a formal name is one that is used in formal contexts—settings such as schools, houses of worship, and government offices—then the nickname emerges only in other less formal contexts.

Second, nicknames are not inherently intimate or friendly. This is clearly the case for nicknames used by the general public in reference to celebrities. Moreover, in some cases the content of the nickname is disparaging—an unlikely result except where the referent and user are not emotionally close or the referent is unaware of the usage.

This is not to imply that properties of intimacy, formality, creativity, reference, or address are not of import in the study of nicknames. Indeed, they are important features for classifying nicknames, but it is crucial not to rely on them as definitive characteristics for all nicknames. We may thus settle upon the definition repeated below, which is the most inclusive possible conception of the nickname, and includes internal derivations, even simple truncations, as objects of analysis.

(1) Nickname: a proper noun that bears reference to some individual and which differs (even minimally) in structure from the formal name associated with the same individual.

This is the conception adopted by de Klerk and Bosch (1996), Holland (1990), Kennedy and Zamuner (2006), and Zaitzow et al. (1997), among others. Holland (1990) expresses a compelling philosophical point in favour of the more inclusive approach—that shortened forms ought not to be excluded from study if the users themselves consider them to be nicknames. De Klerk and Bosch (1996, 1997) and Kennedy and Zamuner (2006) also note that interesting empirical trends in the structural and sociolinguistic aspects of nicknames emerge even within the subset of internally derived forms.

A summary of dimensions along which nicknames vary is given in (2).

(2) Summary of dimensions

Dimension	Values	
Referential usage	address	reference
Phrasality	hypocoristic	phrasal, Homeric
Derivedness	internal	external, creative, coined
Affect	affection	disparagement
Publicness	common	public
Distance	close, intimate	distant

Because of the many ways in which nicknames may vary in form and function, it would at first glance seem that little in the way of principled generalization can made among them. Nevertheless, these dimensions interact with each other; nicknames of reference are less constrained in size than nicknames of address, while derisive nicknames are less likely than positive nicknames to be used as address. Moreover, sociolinguistic dimensions also interact with each of these; for example, form, function, and content may each differ by the gender of the coiner and recipient and by the social structure of the community. As a consequence, some clear patterns emerge once we sort nicknames along phonological, morphosyntactic, and sociolinguistic dimensions.

The remainder of this chapter will survey the structural, referential, and sociolinguistic properties of forms which match this definition. Within the widely encompassing domain of nicknames as defined in (1), items may vary by whether they are (a) referential or vocative, (b) constrained or phrasal, (c) internally or externally derived, (d) positive or negative in connotation, among other dimensions. These dimensions are interrelated, though none of them is equivalent to any other.

38.3 Primary subtypes: phrasality, derivedness, and reference

Before diving into the structural and sociolinguistic properties of nicknames, let us return to the dimensions articulated in (2) and identify phrasality, derivedness, and referential usage as primary subcategories. This will help us sort out some variation in form and usage in later sections.

38.3.1 Phrasality

Nicknames vary in their phrasality. At one end of this dimension are hypocoristics—single-word forms, usually one or two syllables in length. Examples of typical internally derived hypocoristics and their formal forename sources are provided below for female (3a) and male names (3b). Note that hypocoristics may also be derived from surnames in a similar manner, as in (3c).

(3)	*Formal name*	*hypocoristic*
a.	Susan	Sue
	Jennifer	Jenny
	Sarah	Sally
	Margaret	Peg
	Jessica	Jess
	Abigail	Abby
	Barbara	Barb
b	John	Jack
	James	Jim
	Robert	Bob
	Henry, Harold	Harry
	Peter	Pete
	Martin	Marty
c.	Smith	Smitty
	Jones	Jonesie
	McDonald	Mac (or any surname in *Mc-* or *Mac-*)
	Murray	Muzz
	Cooper	Coop

At the other end of the same dimension are phrasal nicknames—multi-word structures built from two or more roots, possibly also with some additional functional elements such as articles or prepositions. Such forms are potentially more elaborate and descriptive, and may be more likely in written text or scripted oral narrative than in spontaneous speech. Kennedy and Zamuner (2006) suggest the term 'Homeric nicknames' for these phrasal structures, in recognition of their similarity in form and function to the epithets used for characters in the epic poetry of Homer, such as *civilizer of men* (for Athena) and *the swift-footed one* (for Achilles). Like Homer's epithets, modern Homeric nicknames are recurrent descriptive structures that identify particular individuals and are used as an alternative form of reference for them. Examples of Homeric nicknames are readily found for celebrities, politicians, and athletes:

(4)

Formal name	*Homeric nickname*
Frank Sinatra	Old Blue Eyes
Jean Harlow	The Blonde Bombshell
Lou Gehrig	The Iron Horse
Babe Ruth	The Sultan of Swat
Wayne Gretzky	The Great One

38.3.2 Derivedness

Independently of phrasality, a spectrum of likeness is observable, ranging from internally derived forms, relatively unchanged from their sources, to those that differ slightly, such as *Bill* for *William*, to externally derived forms that are completely unrelated in form and either share semantics with the source name (such as *Dutch* for *Holland*) or describe traits of the referent (such as *Red* for a red-haired person). Notably, both hypocoristics and Homeric nicknames may be externally derived.

The fame of the recipient is independent of both phrasality and derivedness; celebrity nicknames that fall within the range of derived or descriptive hypocoristics are not unusual (5). These are found in both the British and North American press.

(5)

Formal name	*Hypocoristic*
Diana Spencer	Di
Sarah Ferguson	Fergie
Madonna	Madge
Margaret Thatcher	Maggie
Michael Jackson	Jacko
David Beckham	Becks
Prince William	Wills
Daniel Alfredsson	Alfie
Daniel Ovechkin	Ovie
Shaquille O'Neal	Shaq
Bruce Springsteen	The Boss
Maurice Richard	Rocket

38.3.3 Reference

A separate dimension along which nicknames vary is their referential usage. A simple but inaccurate assumption is that any nickname can be used as 2nd person address and as 3rd person reference, but this is not always the case.

Some nicknames may only be used as reference but not address; this tends to be the case for many phrasal Homeric names. Athlete nicknames like *The Iron Horse* or *The Great One*, for example, would be suitable descriptions in a sports narrative or broadcast but not as a means of addressing the referent directly. Some hypocoristics would also be unsuitable as address if they are disparaging (Dickey 1997; Dorian 1970). Other nicknames may only be used as forms of address, as seen in intrafamilial petnames such as *sweetie* or *love*.

38.4 Morphosyntactic properties

Regardless of their phrasality and derivedness, a set of common morphosyntactic properties of all nicknames may be observed (Carroll 1983; Coates 2006; Hockett 1958; Pierini 2008; Van Langendonck 2007). Some of these are typical of noun phrases generally, while others are typical of proper names in particular. For example, as noun phrases, nicknames are replaceable as a whole by other noun phrases or pronouns, may serve as an argument of a verb, as subject, object, or oblique, and may be used as vocatives (Anderson 2003, 2007).

Like other proper names, nicknames refer to individual entities (Carroll 1983; Coates 2006; Hockett 1958; Lyons 1977; Pierini 2008; Van Langendonck 2007), although, as with other names, the same form may apply to more than one entity. Anderson (2003) argues that names are determinative and neither definite nor indefinite, though they may be derivatively definite; the same may be presumed to apply to nicknames. Moreover, this property is independent of the presence of a definite article.

In fact, the occurrence of a definite article is sensitive to the nickname type and its context (Anderson 2003, 2007; Tse 2004). In referential contexts, definite articles may appear with Homeric and hypocoristic forms, and nicknames may be classified by whether they require or resist definite articles. For example, *The Sultan of Swat* is a phrasal nickname which requires an article in referential usage, while *Old Blue Eyes* forbids it (6a). In address contexts, definite articles do not occur in any nickname, even those that have articles in 3rd person reference (6b), analogous to bare titles such as *doctor, captain*, or *duke*.

(6) *Forms in reference and address*

	a. Reference	b. Address
Phrasal:	*(The) Sultan of Swat	(*The) Sultan of Swat
	(*The) Old Blue Eyes	(*The) Old Blue Eyes
Hypocoristic	(The) Rocket	(*The) Rocket
	*(The) Boss	(*The) Boss
Title:	*(the) Captain	(*the) Captain

38.4.1 Historical perspective on phrasal nicknames

The syntactic properties of phrasal nicknames in particular allow for some hypothesizing regarding the impetus for their historical emergence. American sports narrative of the early 20th century is replete with descriptive referring expressions to denote the participants in events such as baseball games. A notable phenomenon of the era is for writers to use co-referential phrases in contexts where pronouns or repeated surnames would suffice. Thus, game summaries of the time would use a formal name for the first mention of a particular referent, but subsequent narrative would use alternative means of reference; recurrent nicknames and novel constructions were both used in this manner. The example in (7) illustrates Babe Ruth being referred to with a nickname in this style.

(7) Some dopesters contend that every ball game has its psychological moment, and Ruth certainly seized upon the all-important time to make his only hit of the game. While the Sultan of Swat had been dormant in the early innings, his brother Yanks were the same. (*New York Times*, 28 June 1920)

Such back reference is not limited to nicknames, but other types of back-referencing are not as uniquely identifying. For example, in the same narrative, the pitcher Al Russell receives the less unique back-reference *the Red Sox hurler*.

(8) In the eighth Babe got so familiar with Russell and his projectile that he shook a ball game out of Al's clutches and turned it over to the Yankees. The Red Sox hurler, who apparently had his old team all measured for a trimming, saw his bubble vision of triumph burst when Babe spanked a ball against the exit gate in right centre.[3]

In another summary from the same era, the Brooklyn pitcher Nap Rucker is given the back-reference *the old southpaw*.

> Nap Rucker, another aged citizen, was the big hero of the occasion as far as the Brooklyn fans were concerned. The old southpaw is a portly party now, but for the sake of old times and all that he went out on the mound and threw slow balls that the Yanks couldn't hit at all.
>
> (*NYT*, 11 April 1922)

It seems that the phrasal nickname, at least for professional athletes, owes its origins to the demands of good narrative description. In a game summary, a large number

[3] As an aside, it may be of interest to note that the *New York Times* used what now might be regarded as the British spelling *centre*. It would seem that the spellings *centre* and *center* were in competition in the US at the time.

of participants are named. Repetition of each participant's name is avoided, but the usual device for doing so—by use of a pronoun—itself could be awkwardly repetitive as well as ambiguous in such a highly populated story. Thus, the writer uses multiple phrases for the same individual; an individual's phrasal nickname may appear as one of these referring expressions, but notably about no more frequently than the formal name itself.

As an example of multiple structures applied to an individual referent, another game summary is framed around the effort of the Red Sox pitcher Jack Quinn (*NYT*, 23 June 1922). Quinn is alternately referred to as *Old Jack Quinn, the veteran Polish flinger, the portly old Boston pitcher*, and *the old-timer*, alongside simple pronominal back-reference. Within the same piece, the Red Sox themselves are called *the red-hosed clan of Duffy, the Fenway Fusileers*, and *the Duffy crew*, while the Yankees are called *the Yanks, the American League champions, the champs, the locals, the visitors*, and *the Huggins clan*. The absence of capitalization in such forms suggests the author considered these novel forms rather than recurrent nickname structures.

Florid description within sports narrative of that era is typical of baseball narrative in American news publications, but not of British publications such as *The Times* describing association or rugby football. Skipper (1985) links the baseball narrative style to the contemporary emergence of folk heroics in American literature.

Such descriptive devices survive in modern sports narrative in various forms, including the heavy noun phrase as identified by Ferguson (1983) and the substitute noun phrase as identified by Kennedy and Zamuner (2006). The substitute noun phrase is a phenomenon marked by recurrence of the same structure, but falling short of attaching to a unique individual as an established nickname. Kennedy and Zamuner (2006) characterize this structural type as a convenient trope whereby the same structure may be used recurrently for different individuals; for example *the enigmatic Russian* and *the big Slovak* are both recurrent structures used by modern hockey writers, but neither structure is reserved for any particular individual. The substitute NP is a special case of Ferguson's more general category of the heavy noun phrase, which is truly a collection of complex noun phrases with a range of internal structures, such as adjacent appositives, lengthy adjective chains, and prepositional adjuncts.

38.5 Structural properties

Any generalizations in form we see for nicknames are easier to illustrate among hypocoristics than among Homeric structures, since the former are more constrained in size and segment composition than the latter. Nevertheless, even where discussing such restrictions, some structural tendencies are observable in Homeric forms that are analogous to those of hypocoristics.

38.5.1 Internally derived truncations

The primary device by which derived hypocoristics are drawn from formal forenames or surnames is to truncate to a form one or two syllables in length (9), where the second syllable is produced by means of a vocalic suffix or augmentation. Some truncations seem to require the augmentation, as in *Martin* → *Marty*, while some resist it, as in *Allan* → *Al*.

(9)	*Formal name*	*Truncation*	*Truncation + augment*
	Edward	Ed	Eddie
	Robert	Rob	Robby
	Martin	–	Marty
	Allan	Al	–
	Susan	Sue	Susie
	Christine	Chris	Christy

Moreover, the size of the target is relevant, not the amount of removed material. Three-syllable names truncate to single syllables rather than to disyllables; thus *Christopher* truncates to *Chris* not *Christoph*, and *Jennifer* truncates to *Jen* or *Jenny* but not *Jennif*.

Where formal names themselves are monosyllabic, they are untruncatable and some alteration or augmentation must be used. Thus hypocoristics for *John* and *Jane* require augmentation, as in *Johnny* and *Janie*.

The example of *John* evokes the case of additional alterations, as it has the alternative hypocoristic *Jack*. A small set of given names in English have some such segmental change in addition to or in lieu of truncation, as in *James* → *Jim*, *William* → *Bill*, *Robert* → *Bob*, *Dorothy* → *Dot* or *Dolly*, *Mary* → *Molly*, *Elizabeth* → *Betsy*, and *Margaret* → *Peggy*.

38.5.2 Types of augmentation

By far the most common nickname ending is vocalic [i], expressed in writing with numerous alternative spellings such as *-y*, *-ie*, and *-i*. Other endings are also observed, notably *-o* and *-er* (in non-rhotic accents, [ə]), as well as the consonantal form *-s* (which assimilates in voicing to the preceding segment). Nevertheless, the prevalence of [i] over other endings recurs in the hypocorisms reported by Phillips (1990) and Kennedy and Zamuner (2006).

The inclusion of a nickname ending is influenced by other linguistic and sociolinguistic factors. A common finding is that vocalic endings generally are more typical of female and/or more intimately known referents (de Klerk and Bosch 1996; Phillips 1990), though the endings *-o* and *-er* are more likely among male nicknames.

38.5.3 Phonemic effects

There are also some emergent effects of phoneme type upon nickname structure. De Klerk and Bosch (1997) show that certain phonemes are more likely than others within hypocoristics; for example, voiced plosives are more frequent as initial consonants in male hypocoristics, while nasals, liquids, and voiceless plosives are more frequent initial consonants in female hypocoristics.

Among nicknames for professional hockey players, Kennedy and Zamuner (2006) find that vocalic endings are more likely if a truncation ends in a single voiced consonant or in consonant sequence. This tendency affects the syllable structure of the hypocorism, reflecting cross-linguistic tendencies which favour voiced consonants in intervocalic position but voiceless ones word-finally. Thus, vocalic suffixes occur in forms with voiced consonants such as *Phillips* → *Philly*, *Nabokov* → *Nabby*, and *Ovechkin* → *Ovie*, but monosyllables are used for forms terminating with voiceless consonants such as *Popovic* → *Pop*, *Afinagenov* → *Af*, and *Yashin* → *Yash*. Where the truncation yields a consonant sequence, vocalic suffixes tend to emerge, as in *Alfredsson* → *Alfie*, *Anderson* → *Andy*, unless the second consonant is an alveolar sibilant, as in *Gretzky* → *Grets*.

Where truncation is evident, the remaining portion typically must be able to stand alone as a phonologically licit monosyllable, even if a vocalic suffix would save any stranded consonants. For example, *rugby* truncates to *rugger*, not *rugber* (see McCarthy and Prince 1986 for discussion).

38.5.4 Underived or coined hypocoristics

Outside of strictly derived truncations, length restriction still appears to be relevant. Indeed, a subset of nickname forms is observable which are just as restricted in size length as derived truncations, but are semantically driven like Homeric forms. Kennedy and Zamuner (2006) call such forms 'suppletives' (analogous to suppletive morphology), and identify them specifically as underived hypocoristics.

Many externally derived hypocorisms are monosyllabic or disyllabic, with the second syllable bearing no stress and containing one of the allowable endings. Interestingly, Kennedy and Zamuner (2006) find parallel phonemic effects for internally and externally derived hypocoristics: there is a tendency for monosyllabic external forms to end in voiceless consonants, as in *Doc* or *Gump*, and for disyllabic forms to contain medial voiced consonants, as in *Bullet* or *Tiger*. Nevertheless, unlike internally derived forms, external forms may allow one of a limited set of consonants to close the second syllable (e.g. [t, m, n, l, d]). A similar trend is observable among the externally derived forms reported by de Klerk and Bosch (1996).

Poetic devices such as alliteration and rhyme may also be seen to operate within Homeric nickname coinage, both in the link between formal name and nickname and among the components of a multi-word Homeric nickname.

38.5.5 Other hypocorisms

Several other types of internally derived structures are observable within hypocorisms, including initialisms, reduplication, and wordplay associations. Initialisms typically use the names of the first letters of the spelled form of the referent's forename and surname, though just one initial is possible as well. A previously unreported fact about initialisms is their tendency to receive primary stress on the final syllable (which is generally true of longer initialisms), unless the two initials are identical (as in *CC*) or the second initial is *J* (as in *CJ*).

A small set of public celebrity nicknames combine a forename initial with a truncation of the surname, seen for athletes such as Alex Rodriguez (*A-Rod*) and performers such as Jennifer Lopez (*J-Lo*) and Kristen Stewart (*K-Stew*). Forms that combine forename and surname truncations, such as *Cujo* for Curtis Joseph or *ScarJo* for Scarlett Johansson, are also found.

Reduplication may be seen among internally and externally derived forms, for example *Boomboom* for the hockey player Bernard Geoffrion. Other difficult-to-classify forms include segment substitutions that change the name to a different word, such as *toad* for *Todd*. Such forms appear to combine the shared phonemic structure of internal derivations with the semantic aspect of external forms.

38.6 Semantic and sociolinguistic content in nicknames

As Adams (2009: 82) succinctly puts it, in the semantic tradition spanning Frege to Searle, names themselves have little semantic content. Yet not only do nicknames share the same reference as the formal name of their referents, they either have an added sense (even if the added value is simply a degree of informality) or a different sense from their corresponding formal names. Moreover, externally derived nicknames do have semantic content. The type of content can vary widely but is commonly based in metonymic associations with the referent, alluding to their physical or behavioural traits or to their characteristic activities (Dorian 1970; de Klerk and Bosch 1996, 1997; Leslie and Skipper 1990; McDowell 1981; Van Langendonck 1983; Zaitzow et al. 1997).

Abel (2004), Kennedy and Zamuner (2006), Skipper (1990), and Wilson and Skipper (1990) note nicknames based on the referent's place-of-origin (e.g. *Buck* as in *Buckeye* for Ulysses S. Grant, an Ohioan) or ethnic associations (e.g. *Dutch* for people of Dutch or German descent), as well as wordplay based on the presumed semantic component of the referent's formal name. Abel (2004), Dorian (1970), and Kennedy and Zamuner (2006) also describe second-order assignations, whereby a referent inherits someone else's nickname by virtue of sharing some trait or background with that individual (e.g., *Chico* and *King* being passed from one hockey player to another).

38.7 Sociolinguistic properties

The descriptive semantic component of a nickname is closely tied to the sociolinguistic and pragmatic aspects of its usage; nicknames reflect social roles and represent affective associations (Morgan et al. 1979; Wierzbicka 1992). Indeed, much research on nicknaming practices reveals some recurrent themes regarding the gender, power differential, and degree of closeness of the coiners and referents. In particular, the gender of the referent influences the type of semantic content that tends to emerge in nicknames, while the personal distance and the relative power of the coiner and referent affect the tone and appropriateness of the form. These sociolinguistic effects may be tied together through the linkage of informality and the extent of appropriateness for a speaker to use a particular informal structure in the presence of its referent.

38.7.1 Affect, closeness, and power

Nicknames often evoke additional layers of social relationship and hierarchy, for example, by encoding identity, judgement, assessment, or evaluation that peers may make in relation to their nickname targets. The nickname's mark of identity is not just for the referent; knowledge of nicknames constitutes knowledge of in-group norms. Thus, nickname usage identifies the user as much as the referent. In fact, this secondary indexicality of the nickname is more consistently present than its first-order indexation, since nicknames are always known to users but not always to the referents; in such a circumstance, the in-group knowledge is also restricted just to the users. Indexation of any kind suggests that nickname usage marks solidarity among users. Gasque (1994) documents this for 1950s-era college students, and Skipper (1986) for coalminers.

Nicknames also invoke either positive affect such as affection or approval or negative affect such as pejoration or disparagement (de Klerk and Bosch 1996; Dickey 1997; Dorian 1970; Phillips 1990). Moreover, a seemingly pejorative name could be used ironically to indicate solidarity.

Where user and referent know each other, the nickname signifies a degree of familiarity (de Klerk and Bosch 1996; Dorian 1970; Phillips 1990). Among more distant relationships nicknames may still encode some affection or solidarity with the referent, especially if there is a positive connotation to the name. This can be seen in many of Abel's Civil War examples, such as *Old Rock* or *Old Reliable*. In fact, usage of nicknames for Civil War generals in modern writings attempts to capitalize on the solidarity aspect of nicknames; an author evokes intimacy with the (past) world of the subject, in a sense adding authenticity to the narrative. Conversely, disparaging nicknames in distant relationships encode negative evaluations, and may either highlight the distance or encode some resentment of the power differential.

Power is a recurrent theme for the sociolinguistics of nicknaming (Abel 2004; Adams 2008; Crozier 2004). In close relationships, even positively connoted nicknames belie the relatively greater power the coiner has over the referent (Phillips 1990). Power is more obviously in play in cases of negative, unwelcome nicknames assigned to unwilling referents. Adams (2009) highlights nicknames as markers of assessment and power differential, evident even in simple examples from *Peanuts* such as *Pig Pen* and *Chuck*.

We may thus view the disparaging behind-the-back nickname as a means of balancing or reclaiming power from a disliked authority figure, at least psychologically for the user. Examples from Abel's Civil War data like *Crazy Tom* and from Crozier's schoolteacher data like *Dragon* or *Death Breath* illustrate this. Adams (2008) uses the power component to offer a critical analysis of former US president G. W. Bush's nicknaming practices (e.g. *Landslide* for Tony Blair, *Dino* for Jean Chrétien, *Frazier* for Dianne Feinstein), arguing that they represent his conflation of executive power and state authority.

38.7.2 Contextual appropriateness

Both positive and negative types of nickname are beset by constraints of appropriateness, restricting the contexts in which they may be used. The informal component of the nickname suggests they are to be avoided in formal or legal contexts as either address or reference. Pejoratives, because of their negative intent, would be more observable as address and not reference, but not inherently so. Dickey (1997) includes nickname usage in a larger context of name-usage practices in academic settings; users may use different forms for the same referent as a function of social setting, with disparaging forms (e.g. *The Fish*) possible only in the absence of the referent or the referent's equals.

Dorian (1970) describes a particularly unique scenario where affect, identity, appropriateness, and basic reference intersect. Within a small Scottish village in which only a limited set of formal forenames and surnames are available, a large body of bynames emerges in part to provide additional referential distinctiveness; some bynames are internally derived while others are external. In addition to the typical external sources of content, Dorian also finds derisive nicknames like *Johnny Lassie* or *Sputie* as well as nonsensical forms, some of which are nonetheless disparaging, as in *Fildie* and *Nogie*, while others are more neutral, such as *Bebban* and *Dodgey*.[4]

Generally, users would use offensive bynames only among those who share a similar evaluation of the referent, in part out of solidarity. Yet the intricacies of appropriateness are more nuanced: 'a friend and contemporary can use this kind of byname to the individual's face with impunity, where the same usage from a younger man or recent acquaintance would be resented' (Dorian 1970: 313).

[4] While *Dodgey* probably has a negative connotation for many readers, Dorian reports it as a neutral form.

38.7.3 Gender effects

Much research indicates reliable trends whereby variation in semantic and structural subtypes is linked to the gender of the recipient and the coiner. Phillips (1990) finds gender differences in the source of coinage and semantic content of nicknames, and links them to sex role stereotypes. Notably, more females than males receive nicknames from their fathers; creative male nicknames typically convey potency or activity (e.g. *Wild Bill, Dave Atlas*), while female ones invoke personal or physical evaluation (e.g. *Braceface, Sweetie, Munchkin*). Also, females are more likely to receive external nicknames, while males are more likely to have derived names, and surname-derived nicknames are more likely among males than females. In structural terms, males are more likely to have nicknames with the vocalic endings *-o* or *-er*, while females are more likely to have nicknames ending in [iː].

To test whether these gender differences would fade in specific contexts, Zaitzow et al. (1997) survey the forms and sources of nicknames for incarcerated female felons. The prison setting is one in which nicknaming could be rampant because of the power and solidarity relationships that emerge within prison societies, while the unmixed, all-female nature of the community provides a potential locus for the male-driven component of coinage to be absent. Surprisingly, female felon nicknames pattern more like the general population than anything unique to the prison population. Female nicknames still tend to be coined by family members, not from prison peers; only about one third are internally derived (e.g. *Cindy, JJ, Marty, Sinbad* for 'bad Cindy'); and among the externally derived remainder, nicknames tend to reflect appearance and attitude rather than deeds (e.g. *Pebbles, Slim Goodie, Flaca, Sunshine*).

De Klerk and Bosch (1996, 1997) uncover a range of effects, such as differences in the frequency of phoneme type within female and male nicknames. Unlike Phillips (1990), they find more derived forms among females (e.g. *Trini* from *Catriona* and *Furry* from *Jennifer*), as well as more suffixes, but more nicknames based on physical traits among males (e.g. *Fatboy, Mosquito*). Interestingly, they find no difference between males and females in the rate of usage, in whether the nicknames were known to the referent, or in the distribution of positive and negative nicknames. Males and females also differ in their research by the coiners and semantic types of their nicknames, as well as whether they consider derived truncations to count as nicknames.

That female and male nicknames have different tendencies of phonological probability is not surprising, given independent findings of phonotactic effects in forenames themselves; for example, Cutler et al. (1990) find different frequencies of vowels in female and male forenames. Cassidy et al. (1999) show that speakers may infer the referent's gender from a variety of phonological properties of a given name, such as stress pattern, number of syllables, and the nature of the final phoneme. Slater and Feinman (1985) note a relationship between phoneme frequency and sex in both names and nicknames.

38.7.4 Folk linguistic beliefs

The question of whether internally derived forms should count empirically as nicknames reappears in several other ways. First, de Klerk and Bosch (1996) note it as a gender effect, where internally derived forms are considered nicknames more often for females than for males. Second, it illustrates a notable set of folk linguistic beliefs about what counts as a 'good' nickname.

Kennedy and Zamuner (2006) provide a short survey of journalistic literature on nicknaming practices, uncovering some strongly held and recurrent folk linguistic beliefs about 'good' and 'bad' nicknaming practices. Nicknames are held in higher esteem if they are original, phrasal, semantically contentful, and employ some sort of poetic device such as rhyming or alliteration. Nicknames which merely use truncation or which evoke modern pop culture phenomena or concepts are less favoured.

38.8 Discussion

Curiously, much of the descriptive content of nicknames informs the study of the emergence of formal surnames themselves. Studies of the emergence of surnames locate similar semantic sources to what is seen for externally derived nicknames (Hiller 2000; Paffard 1980). Paffard (1980: 35) even argues that some surnames originate from nicknames, such as *Mallory* for an unlucky person, *Peacock* for someone vain, and *Wolfe* for someone savage; surnames that refer to dark hair (e.g. *Moore, Browne, Morris*) or ruddy complexions (e.g. *Reade, Russell*) may similarly be of nickname origin.

Nickname-like structures are apparent in other contexts. A notable feature of Australian and New Zealand English is the relatively high frequency of hypocorisms for common nouns (Bardsley 2003, 2010; Bardsley and Simpson 2009; Huddleston and Pullum 2002: 1636; Kiesling 2006; Simpson 2001; Wierzbicka 1984, 1986). Some Australian examples include *hospo* (hospitality worker), *cozzie* (swim costume), *journo* (journalist), and *rego* (car registration), while New Zealand examples include *sparky* (electrician), *chippy* (carpenter, or fish and chip shop), *postie* (postman), and *boatie* (hobby sailor). Such forms share the formative properties and informal connotation of nicknames, but their reference and definiteness are more aligned with other common nouns than with proper names.

38.8.1 Toponymic nicknames

Some of the structural and syntactic properties of personal nicknames are reflected in the nicknames used for geopolitical toponyms, such as names for towns, cities, states, and provinces. Examples of Homeric nicknames for cities are common, such as *the*

Big Apple (New York), *the City of Angels* (Los Angeles), *the Emerald City* (Seattle), *the Big Easy* (New Orleans), *the City of Brotherly Love* (Philadelphia), or *the Old Pueblo* (Tucson). Homeric names for American states are so conventionalized that each state has an official one, such as *The Golden State, The Empire State,* and *The Sunshine State.* Hypocoristics are also common, including initialisms such as *TO* (for Toronto), *LA* (Los Angeles), and *DC* (District of Columbia), and truncations such as *Philly* (Philadelphia) and *Indy* (Indianapolis).

Intricacies of usage are paralleled here as well. Some cities have disparaging nicknames, such as *La-La-Land* (Los Angeles) or *The Big Smoke* (Toronto, among others). Others have forms which, while not clearly disparaging, are nonetheless not used by their own residents, such as *Beantown* (Boston) or *Frisco* and *San Fran* (San Francisco).

Even the dimension of reference and address may arise for toponymic nicknames. While it may seem odd that a toponym be used for anything but reference, there are contexts in which an individual may be addressing the full population of a city or state via radio or television broadcast. In such cases, the speaker may address their audience with the toponym or toponymic nickname. Moreover, if the speaker uses a toponymic Homeric nickname, and that nickname usually has a definite article, the article is dropped from the address usage, as in the imaginable *Good morning, Big Apple.*

38.8.2 Nicknaming in other languages

The study of nicknames and their usage has by no means been restricted to English nicknames, and a survey of research on nicknames in other languages reveals some common cross-linguistic themes. For example, there is a recurrent reliance on physical, behavioural, cultural, and familial traits in the semantic patterns of their coinage, as evidenced in Chinese (Ebbherhard 1970; Kehl 1971), Irish (Breen 1982), Ningbo (Ruan 2008), Romanian (Firica 2007a, 2007b), Russian (Superanskaya 2003), Serbo-Croatian (Cilas Simpraga 2006; Simunovic 2003; Vidovic 2010), Tumbuka (Moyo 2002), Yoruba (Adetunji 2010), Zinacantan (Collier and Bricker 1970), and Zulu (Molefe 2001; Turner 2004).

Likewise, some research focuses on emergent phonological patterns within nickname forms; often their structural properties are revealing of a language's phonological system more generally. This has been argued for Dutch (Geeraerts 2002), German (Fery 1997; Gruter 2002; Ito and Mester 1997), Icelandic (Willson 2008), Italian (Floricic 2007), Quechua (Toliver 2008), and Serbo-Croatian (Cilas Simpraga 2006).

The notion of nicknames serving functions of brevity and disambiguation is also widely attested, as seen in Egyptian Arabic (Antoun 1968), Icelandic (Hale 1981), Irish (Breen 1982), Panamanian Creole (Aceto 2002), Portuguese (Fucilla 1979), Saami (Anderson 1984), Serbo-Croatian (Vidovic 2010), Scottish Gaelic (Dorian 1970), and Spanish (Barrett 1978; Brandes 1973, 1975; Gilmore 1982).

Still other research investigates sociolinguistic aspects of nicknaming practices, noting their interaction with identity, power, and community membership, as in Chinese (Ebberhard 1970; Kehl 1981; Wong 2007), Italian (Cohen 1977), Panamanian Creole (Aceto 2002), Scottish Gaelic (Dorian 1970), Sesotho (Akindele 2008), Spanish (Brandes 1973, 1975), Xhosa (de Klerk 2002), and Zulu (Molefe 2001). In addition, some research focuses on how nicknames encode affection or disparagement, as in Chinese (Wong 2007), German (Ehlers 2009; Koss 2006), Irish (Breen 1982; Lele 2009), Kuwaiti Arabic (Haggan 2008; Yassin 1978), Quechua (Toliver 2008), Saramaka (Price and Price 1972), Serbo-Croatian (Lewis 2011), Spanish (Brandes 1973, 1975; Gilmore 1982), Scottish Gaelic (Dorian 1970), Tzintzuntan (Foster 1964), Xhosa (de Klerk 2002), Yoruba (Adetunji 2010), and Zulu (Ndimande-Hlongwa 2010). Gender-based differences in form and content are also common, as seen in Kuwaiti Arabic (Haggan 2008), Ningbo (Ruan 2008), Spanish (Fernandez Juncal 2008), Tumbuka (Moyo 2002), and Zulu (Turner 2004).

Moreover, the notion of the nickname as a historical source for surnames is noted in numerous languages, such as Basque (Salaberri Zaratiegi 2009), Hungarian (Goicu 2008), Iberian Jews (Ferreira 2007), Romanian (Firica 2007a, 2007b), Portuguese (Fucilla 1979), and Spanish (Boullon 2007; Fucilla 1978). Some studies of nicknames analyse their form and content within the context of a language's naming practices more generally: Akindele (2008) for Sesotho, Dinic (2009) and Pujic (2009) for Serbo-Croatian, Koopman (2009) for Zulu, Van Langendonck (2001) for Dutch and Flemish, and Zinkevicius (2009) for Lithuanian.

In short, given the wide variety of languages and cultures represented in the preceding overview, it would be fair to presume that any culture in which nicknaming practices are distinct from other formal naming practices probably also has intricate structural, semantic, sociolinguistic, and affective patterns observable in their usage.

38.8.3 Summary

Whether the object of study is the nickname of an individual person or a hypocorism of a place name or common noun, we have seen numerous recurrent structural and grammatical characteristics of nicknames, independently of their derivedness and phrasality. Alongside these internal characteristics, we have seen that nicknames carry an element of informality, and their potential semantic content allows for some interesting sociolinguistic effects of gender, power, and appropriateness to emerge.

The centrality of truncation to the derivation of hypocoristics, and of the parallel size restriction among externally derived forms, suggests that alongside informality, brevity is a primary goal of nickname formation. Even Homeric nicknames seem to respect a functional limit on their length, having a tendency not to include more than two content or root morphemes. Inverse to the degree of phonemic overlap between the nickname and its derivational source is the degree of creativity in the nickname form. Thus, nickname formation is subject to a pair of competing operative demands. On the one hand, nickname usage is driven by a goal of brevity, seen most clearly in derived truncations and the similarly brief externally derived hypocoristics. On the other hand, nickname usage is driven by a goal of creativity and uniqueness, a conflicting demand which favours longer descriptive expressions over shorter ones.

CHAPTER 39

CHOOSING A NAME

How Name-Givers' Feelings Influence Their Selections

CYNTHIA WHISSELL

39.1 NAMES

THE act of naming involves a name-giver, a name, and a person, animal, or object to be named. This chapter will focus on name-givers and on the feelings that influence the names they give. Names belong to the class of proper nouns, which is a subclass of nouns in general. Nouns such as *dog* are used to label groups of objects, while proper nouns such as *Rover* are bestowed on individual dogs. Although common nouns such as *cat* and *dog* and familiar proper names such as *Toronto* or *London* are fixed within a language, names assigned to individuals are a matter of choice. Because of this freedom, name-givers can give expression to their own expectations, hopes, and feelings within a name. Names are continually being chosen for new babies, for new pets, and even for inanimate objects such as boats and cars. Many people select their own nicknames and their own 'handles' or working names in gaming and blogging spheres. Some go so far as to legally change their names to ones they regard as more suitable.

Name choice is not a matter of labelling alone. If it were, any distinct set of letters and numbers could serve as a label. This idea is vigorously rejected by Patrick McGoohan's character, Number 6, in the British television series *The Prisoner*. Number 6's existential cry 'I am not a number, I am a free man' continues to echo in cyberspace forty years after the series' demise. In a similar vein, the character Data (from the series *Star Trek: The Next Generation*) objected to having his name pronounced in the British way [dɑːtə] rather than American way [deɪtə]: 'one is my name, the other is not.' Far from being mere labels, names are meaningful, and naming is a meaningful act accomplished by name-givers. This conclusion is supported by the rituals associated with name-giving and the enshrinement of name-giving practices in many different cultures (see Blount, this volume). One important accompaniment of name-giving is emotion, and emotions or feelings frequently influence the names that people choose and assign.

39.2 Parental choice

Parental name-givers are not always free to choose their child's name because of constraints associated with the traditional practices of their cultures (Lieberson 1984; Rossi 1965; Sigurd and Tayanin 2008). Members of some cultures (e.g. the Akan of Ghana: Agyekum 2006) name children according to the day of the week on which they are born, and members of others (e.g. the Balinese and Japanese: Ryō 1992) according to their birth order. Name-givers of the Laotian Kammu culture represent events of local import in their children's names (Sigurd and Tayanin 2008), and some Indian parents give babies 'crazy crooked' names such as Cowdung in order to discourage bad luck (Fuller 1965). In Islamic cultures, commonly used names such as Malik (king), Noor (light), and Aziz (mighty) reflect the attributes of Allah (www.faizani.com/articles/names.html). Chinese names must be demonstrably 'auspicious' for the individual to whom they are being assigned (Edwards 2006); this is because names are 'identifiers,' 'representations of personality,' and 'emblems of parents' expectations' (Xiaoyan 1996: iii).

English-speaking parents in Western cultures are relatively unconstrained in their name choices. The two main traditions that influence them involve the importance of kin names (those of parents, grandparents, uncles, aunts, etc.) and of names associated with popular and religious figures (such as film stars and saints). Although public opinion and popularity do not have the strength of tradition, they still influence naming preferences. Popular figures produce 'name bumps' such as the one seen recently for the name Barack. According to US Social Security Administration data, Barack rose from 12,535th in popularity in the US in 2007 to 2409th in 2008, the year that Barack Obama was elected president. The name Adolf experienced a similar bump in Germany around 1933, when Hitler was much admired, though the popularity of the name had declined drastically by 1944 (Wolffsohn and Brechenmacher 2001). Clark Gable's first name was unusually fashionable from the mid-1920s to the mid 1940s, the years of the actor's greatest renown, and the name Elvis has been steadily increasing in popularity since the mid-1950s. Similar trends are illustrated in Fig. 39.1, which shows a pronounced bump for the name Franklin in the 1930s and 1940s, when FDR (Franklin Delano Roosevelt) was the US President and in Fig. 39.2, which shows a bump for the name Angelina in the 2000s, when Angelina Jolie was a popular actress.

The main argument of this chapter rests on name-givers' freedom to express their feelings, whether their current state of mind or their future expectations for the name-recipient, as part of the name-selection process. Name-givers might select names for artistic or aesthetic reasons (Levine and Willis 1994) or because names are associated with power and fame, as illustrated immediately above. To the extent that

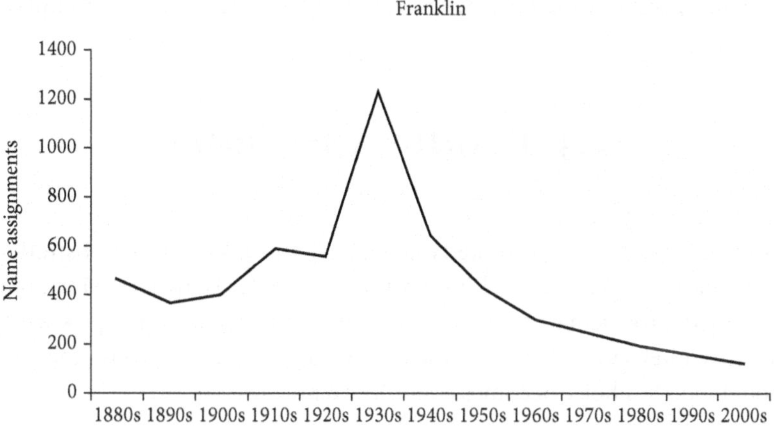

FIG. 39.1 A name bump in the 1930s and 1940s for the name Franklin, based on US Social Security data and the Baby Name Voyager website (http://babynamewizard.com/voyager)

Note: The Baby Name Voyager is an online resource which uses US Social Security data to track name popularity across time, and displays graphic information for individual names on demand. It indicates that most names are associated with a popularity peak, followed by a decline in popularity.

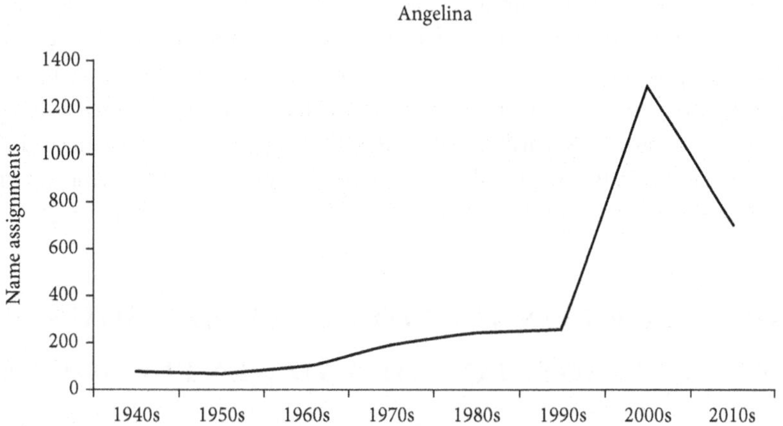

FIG. 39.2 A name bump in the 2000s for the name Angelina, based on US Social Security data and the Baby Name Voyager website (http://babynamewizard.com/voyager)

name-givers are constrained in their choices, they may be prevented from expressing their feelings. Yet even under constraint, name-givers may still exercise choice. For example, given that a kin name is to be used, parents might be able to select from among several kin names; there will also be a choice among several popular names. As well, variants or diminutives of kin names may be adopted rather than the names themselves (Sigurd and Tayanin 2008); moreover, kin naming decreases sharply with birth order (Rossi 1965). Although name-givers' feelings about the person or object they are naming are not the only determinant of name choice, they do influence the selection of names.

39.3 Fairies and trolls

How do feelings become incorporated into names? The following demonstration develops the first part of an answer to this question. The reader is invited to imagine a computer game with three female fairies and three male trolls in it, and to pick which of the following six names should belong to the fairies and which to the trolls. If the names are spoken out loud, the choice becomes easier. The names are:

Leethay, Dergun, Koorvo, Eflil, Reptic, Mimlu

Most English-speakers choose Leethay, Eflil, and Mimlu as fairy-names and Dergun, Koorvo, and Reptic as troll-names, even though the usual clues to name gender such as length (women's names are on average longer than men's) or a final [iː], [ə], or [ɑː] (common endings for women's names) are not available in the name set. Moreover, these made-up names do not sound much like any well-known English names. What is there in the names themselves to suggest that they should belong to a fairy and not to a troll (or vice versa)? The answer lies in name sounds and in the feelings that they represent and convey. There are many [l] and [m] consonants in the fairy names. Such consonants convey feelings of pleasantness and gentleness. In contrast, there are several harsh consonants such as [d], [g], [k], and [r] in the troll names. Regarding the vowels, the long [iː] in first syllable of Leethay is gentle, while the [uː] in the first syllable of Koorvo is tough. Feelings become incorporated into names by means of sound choices because sounds are connected to feelings.

39.4 The connection between sounds and feelings: tough and gentle sounds

The feelings assigned to the various sounds described above were not drawn out of a hat at random, nor are they merely a matter of opinion. There is strong statistical evidence for the connection between sounds and feelings (Whissell 1999, 2000); theories of emotion focusing on facial expression can be employed to explain the connection. The statistical evidence rests on samples of thousands of words with feelings attached to them. These feelings were identified by people who were asked about their reactions to the words. When words were compared in terms of the sounds they included, some sounds, such as [l] and [m], were clearly seen to occur more often in words which people saw as gentle and pleasant (e.g. *love, mommy*), while other sounds, such as [k], [r], [g], and [d], were just as clearly biased in their tendency to appear more often in words with powerful negative emotional associations (e.g. *grudge, dark*). The tie between sound inclusion and word emotionality is probabilistic, not absolute. Not every word including [k] sounds is tied to negative feelings and not every word including [l] has warm and fuzzy associations: *cookie* and *kill* are two obvious counterexamples. When one considers the English language as a whole, however, [k] sounds appear more often in words with nasty or unpleasant implications, and [l] sounds in words with lovely or pleasant ones.

The emotional character of sounds is illustrated in summary form in Fig. 39.3, where various sounds are shown around the rim of a circle. Sounds closest to one another, such as [ʃ], [r], and [t], are emotionally similar, and sounds across the circle from one another are most different, e.g. [ɛ], [m], and [l] in comparison to [ʃ], [r], and [t]. Tough and gentle sounds are located in the neighbourhood of each of the Tough and Gentle labels in the figure. Thus, the negative emotional associations of [k], [r], [g], and [d] are illustrated by their closeness to the Tough label, and the positive associations of [l], [m], and [iː] by their closeness to the Gentle label.

The sound signals characteristic of word sounds are important in establishing the theoretical sound–feeling tie, as are the muscles in the face, mouth, and throat that people use when they speak. Different sounds that people make when speaking aloud have different characteristics. For example, plosive consonants such as [g] or [k] are noisier than liquid consonants such as [l] or nasal consonants such as [m]. Noisier sounds are more energetic and less soothing. As well, people use different mouth postures and facial expressions when they enunciate different sounds. There is a good reason why photographers ask their sitters to say *cheese* rather than *gouda* just before a shot is taken. Saying *cheese*, especially in an exaggerated way where the middle [iː] sound is elongated, produces a smile. Saying *gouda*, on the other hand, results in a rather odd, and not particularly amiable, facial expression. Emphasizing the [uː] in the centre of *gouda* (or

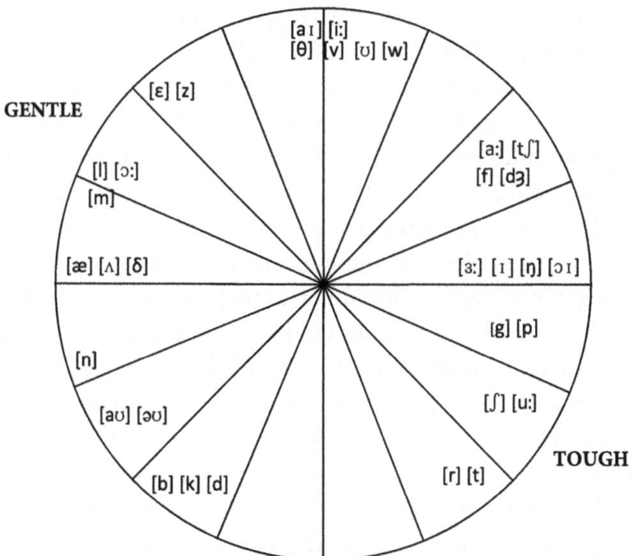

FIG. 39.3 The emotional character of name sounds. Sounds close to one another in the circle are emotionally similar, sounds across the circle from one another are emotionally opposite, and sounds closer to the Tough or Gentle label have that emotional character.

at the end of *shoo*) produces an off-putting face with an outwardly puckered mouth. In the system of sound–feeling associations developed by Whissell (2000) and employed throughout this chapter, 'smiling' [iː] is therefore classified as a gentle sound while 'off-putting' [uː] is classified as a tough sound.

Tough and gentle sounds are used in the analysis of names further below. The tough category includes many of the plosives, e.g. [k], [p], [t], [g], as well as [r], [ʃ], and [ŋ]. The gentle category includes [l], [m], [θ], [z] and the vowels [iː] and [ɛ]. The enunciation of tough sounds involves relatively abrupt and stiff movements, while the enunciation of gentle ones involves a more relaxed facial and vocal apparatus.

Additional sound–feeling connections are exemplified by the enunciation of *alone* and *yuck! Alone* produces the slack mouth and the jaw-sag typical of sadness, while *yuck!* makes the gorge rise and might even generate the wrinkled nose and slightly protruding tongue characteristic of disgust. *Yuck* forms an interesting contrast to *yummy*: both begin with the phonemes [j] and [ʌ] which are neither definitively tough nor gentle, but the words end very differently: the expression of distaste ends with [k], a tough sound, and the appetitive expression with [m] and [iː], which are gentle ones. The important role that facial muscles play in emotion has been stressed by Paul Ekman (Ekman and Friesen 2003). Ekman based his theory on Darwin's pioneering work of 1873 *The Expression of the Emotions in Man and Animals* (Hess and Thibault 2009). According to Ekman, people both consciously and unconsciously employ their faces to experience as well as express emotions. Because of the doubly adaptive function of the face (experience/expression), anything that makes a person smile (such as saying *cheese*) would probably encourage that person to be happy, and anything that makes a person's face sad (such as saying *alone*) would promote a sense of sadness. Strack, Martin, and Stepper (1988) have shown that simply holding a pencil between one's teeth (which uses some of the same muscles as smiling) leads to a greater appreciation of humour than holding the pencil in one's lips (which inhibits the use of smiling muscles).

The motor theory of speech perception points to the importance of the muscular experience in our understanding of spoken language (Liberman and Mattingly 1985). According to the motor theory, our knowledge of the muscle movements involved in enunciating words is just as important to our understanding of them as are the sound signals produced by the movements. Sound and emotion overlap in their use of the same facial and throat muscles, and these muscles are fundamental to the experience and expression of emotion and to the enunciation of sounds. In order for the argument connecting sound to emotions or feelings to be valid, emotions need not be forced by facial expressions or sound enunciations; they can be merely suggested by them, with the suggestion originating from the muscles of the face and throat and their movements.

The connection between facial expression, emotion, and sound is evident in *visimes*, the basic visual units of facial expression characterizing speech. The name highlights the fact that visemes are the *vis*ible equivalent of phon*emes*. Visimes are expressed on a speaker's face, primarily in the area of the lips, and they are important both for lip-reading and for the creation of realistic animated characters. Sample animation-based visemes developed by the company Annosoft can be found at

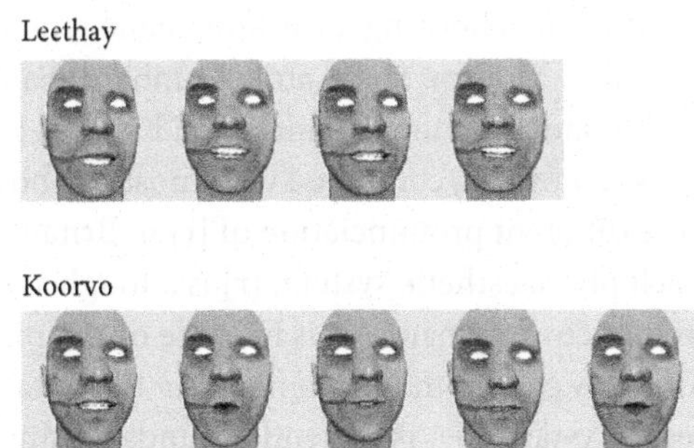

FIG. 39.4 Animation-based visemes for the names *Leethey* ([l], [iː], [θ], [eɪ]) and *Koorvo* ([k], [uː], [r], [v], [əʊ] (created by Annosoft, cited with permission)

http://www.annosoft.com/docs/Visemes12.html. These basic visimes were used to represent freeze-frame shots of the face of a generic speaker speaking the names of Leethay and Koorvo (Fig. 39.4). *Leethay* visemes are appreciably smilier or happier in expression than *Koorvo* visemes, and potentially more welcoming as well.

39.5 Different ways of identifying the feelings in sounds

The phonaesthetic system used here to describe the feelings that sounds promote relies entirely on statistical evidence (Whissell 1999, 2000). Other researchers have used different but overlapping classification systems for phonaesthetics. Fónagy (1991) and Jakobson and Waugh (1979), for example, spent a good deal of time discussing the feelings associated with specific sounds such as [r] and [l]. Crystal (1995), also employing a statistical methodology, offered a series of criteria to describe words that sound beautiful. The overlap between systems becomes evident when sounds classified according to different systems are assigned similar emotional characteristics: [r] is classified as an active and nasty sound and [l] as a soft and gentle one by Fónagy, by Jakobson and Waugh, and by the system used here. This is especially impressive in view of the fact that Fónagy's data were based in part on speakers of French and Hungarian, while Jakobson and Waugh's examples came from German, French, and English, among other languages. Crystal's criterion of the inclusion of [l] and [m] sounds in beautiful words chimes with the presence of both these sounds in the 'gentle' category of this system. Moreover, this system assigns more pleasant emotions to front consonants rather than back ones, just as Crystal did.

In *By Hook or by Crook*, Crystal (2007: 157) addressed the phonaesthetics of names, noting that male actors choosing a working name 'tend to go for hard-sounding "plosive" consonants such as k and g': examples include Cary Grant and Douglas Fairbanks.

On the other hand, female actors choosing a working name tend to favour [m] and [l] sounds: examples are Marilyn Monroe and Carole Lombard. Famous cowboys of the past tended to select notably short and tough names (e.g. Kit, Tex, Buck). Crystal considered the name Roy Rogers 'a bit weak, compared with most cowboy names' (p. 157): this is probably because of the different pronunciation of [r] in Britain and North America. According to the Whissell phonaesthetic system, [r] is a tough sound, and Roy Rogers qualifies as a suitably tough cowboy name. It is because of the phonaesthetics of their names that we would probably choose the Lamonian over the Gatak denizens of an alien planet as potential allies (Crystal 2007: 158); gentle sounds dominate in the first name, tough sounds in the second.

Crystal (1995) analysed around 100 words which lexicographers, writers, and members of the public claimed to be 'beautiful' (none of the words were names), and identified 10 contributing factors. A beautiful word should preferably:

- consist of at least three syllables;
- have stress on the first syllable;
- contain an [m];
- contain an [l];
- make use of other common consonants, such as [s] and [n];
- not use low-frequency consonants, such as [ʃ] and [tʃ], [p] and [g];
- have consonants with different manners of articulation, i.e. the consonants should be a mix of fricatives, plosives, nasals, etc.;
- have vowels which are short rather than long, e.g. [ɪ] rather than [iː], [ʌ] rather than [a:];
- have vowels pronounced in the front rather than the back of the vocal apparatus, e.g. [iː], [ɛ], and [æ], at least at the beginning of the word;
- should begin with low rather than high vowels, e.g. [æ] and [a:] rather than [ɪ] and [ʊ].

The overlap between Crystal's system and the one employed in this study is not total, but the degree of agreement between these two and other systems, a form of triangulation, validates the phonaesthetic approach.

39.6 Boys and girls

My boy, Bill! He'll be tall and as tough as a tree, will Bill
Like a tree he'll grow, with his head held high
And his feet planted firm on the ground
And you won't see nobody dare to try
To boss him or toss him around!...

A kid with ribbons in her hair! A kind o' sweet and petite...
My little girl, pink and white as peaches and cream is she
My little girl, is half again as bright
As girls are meant to be!
Dozens of boys pursue her
Many a likely lad does what he can to woo her...

(lyrics from *Carousel*, 'Soliloquy', Rodgers and Hammerstein)

One of the most important distinctions that parents make as name-givers is related to the sex/gender of the child they are naming. Most cultures embrace a system of stereotypes related to gender, and in Western society this system involves the association of toughness with men and gentleness with women. The association is exemplified by the above lyrics and by a nursery rhyme attributed to Britain's poet laureate Robert Southey which affirms that boys are made of 'snigs (eels) and snails and puppy dogs' tails' while little girls are made of 'sugar and spice and all things nice.' If parents associate feelings of toughness with boys and feelings of gentleness with girls, they will assign their children names which reflect these feelings. In terms of the phonaesthetic scoring system developed by the author, this means that names assigned to boys will contain more tough sounds, while names assigned to girls will include more gentle ones.

A study of 5.5 million names from a US census sample confirmed these predictions in every respect (Whissell 2001b). Boys' names were more like the troll names introduced above, while girls' names were more like the fairy names. Names such as Derek, Gilbert, Adrian, and Christopher contain notably active and tough sounds while names such as Emily, Hannah, Isabella, and Lily contain more gentle and pleasant ones. Using only the feelings tied to name sounds and no other name details it was possible for a computer program to correctly guess, 80 per cent of the time, whether the name-holder was a male or a female. This finding confirms the importance of the emotional information encoded in names. Furthermore, when some made-up names such as Meja, Neelee, Rohmekehn, and Guhr were included in a task where volunteers were asked to rate the masculinity of the name, it was again evident that names with tougher sounds, such as [r] and [g]— the last two names—were judged as more masculine than names with gentler sounds, such as [i] and [l]—the first two (Whissell 2001a).

According to US data, androgynous names such as Taylor and Ashley (used at appreciable rates for both men and women) follow the feminine rather than the masculine pattern for sound feelings—they tend to be gentle rather than tough (Whissell 2001b). Historically, androgynous names go through a three-step process where they are used first for men, later for women as well as men, and finally mainly for women (Lieberson, Dumais, and Baumann 2000). Parents are likely to avoid giving their sons names identified as androgynous. Social Security data used by the Baby Name Voyager suggest that Leslie has arrived at the final stage of this three-part process and is now generally regarded in the US as a girl's name.

Other differences between boys' and girls' names include length (girls' are longer), name ending (long [iː] and [ə] endings are more common in girls' names), name variability (one is likely to encounter more distinct name types in a group of 100 girls than in a group of 100 boys), and stress pattern (stress is earlier in boys' names). Differences between boys' and girls' names are described and discussed by various authors including Barry and Harper (1995), Slater and Feinman (1985), Lieberson and Bell (1992), Cassidy, Kelly, and Sharoni (1999), Hough (2000), and Whissell (2001a, 2001b).

39.7 Then and now

	Boys	Girls
1940	James, John, Robert	Mary, Barbara, Patricia
1970	Michael, James, David	Jennifer, Lisa, Kimberly
2000	Jacob, Michael, Matthew	Emily, Hannah, Madison

(Most Popular US Names: http://www.ssa.gov/oact/babynames/)

Name popularity fluctuates, and names popular in one generation tend to be less popular in the next. A person's age can often be estimated from his or her name, with a Mildred or a Donald being almost certainly older than 70 and a Madison or a Noah younger than 20 (in 2013). Fig. 39.5 displays the popularity of Mildred, whose use peaked in the early 1900s, and Madison, whose use peaked in the early 2000s,

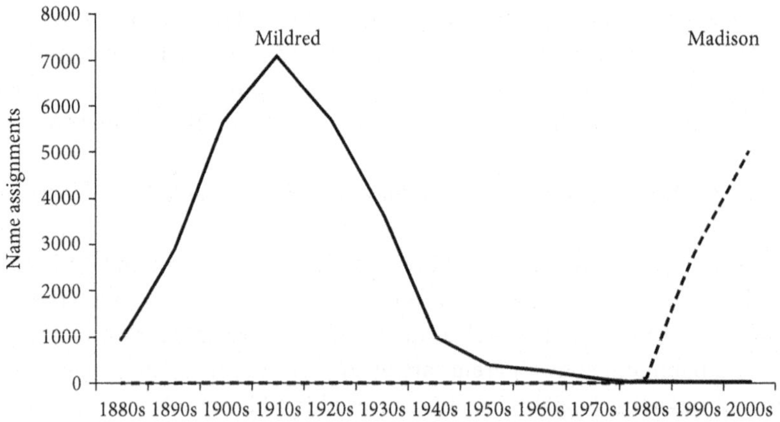

FIG. 39.5 Changes in name popularity over time: *Mildred* (solid line) and *Madison* (dotted line) peak 100 years apart (based on US Social Security data and the Baby Name Voyager).

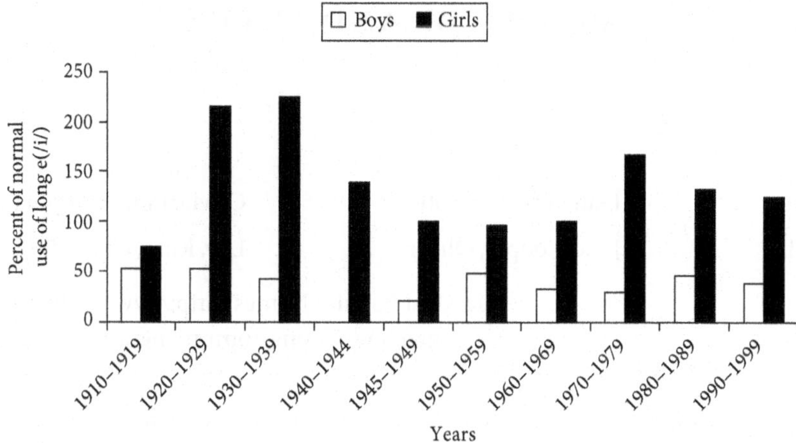

FIG. 39.6 The use of gentle long [iː] in boys' and girls' names during the 20th century (Whissell 2003a).

one century later. Boys' names are less changeable in terms of popularity than girls' names. In the examples at the head of this section, at least one boys' name remained popular over each 30 year time-span; the same was not true for girls' names.

When the sound make-up of names changes, the emotions associated with names also change, often in ways related to social and historical events. This can be seen in Fig. 39.6, which depicts the use of long [iː], a gentle sound, in the names chosen by name-givers of the 20th century. The data come from US Social Security applications and include the ten most popular boys' and girls' names for each year (http://www.ssa.gov/oact/babynames/; Whissell 2003a). The dark bars represent girls' names and the lighter bars boys' names, with taller bars indicating a greater use of long [iː]. As expected, girls' names include more [iː] sounds than boys' names, and there are historical fluctuations in both sets of names. Popular boys' names chosen by parents during the challenging days of the Second World War (1940–44) were toughened up; they included absolutely no gentle [iː] sounds. The use of [iː] sounds in girl's names decreased at this same time, and remained low for the following two decades.

Girls' names included the most [iː] sounds in the 1920s and 1930s, when women's suffrage had been newly achieved, and in the 1970s, when women's rights to abortion became recognized in the US in the famous Supreme Court case of *Roe* vs *Wade*. Within the 20th century, peaks in the gentleness of names chosen by name-givers seem to be associated with successes in the women's rights movement (for girls' names) and the absence of war (for boys'). Another study (Whissell 2006c) has shown that the use of tough and gentle sounds in names is related to the introduction of the birth control pill (when boys' names become tougher and girls' names less so), to inflation (when girls' names become less tough), and to economic depression (when girls' names become tougher and boys' less tough in a surprising reversal), as well as to war. The examples show that emotions engendered by large-scale historical events significantly affect name-givers' feelings and became encoded in their children's names.

39.8 Here and there

	Boys	Girls
Canada	Liam, Ethan, Jacob	Olivia, Emma, Sophia
Australia	Jack, Cooper, Oliver	Lily, Ruby, Charlotte

2012 Most Popular Names (http://www.babycenter.ca/pregnancy/naming/top10namesaroundtheworld/)

Even predominantly English names are not always equally popular in all English-speaking countries. This is illustrated by the sample of Canadian and Australian favourites listed above. There are also differences in name popularity within a single country. In the US in 2010, the three most popular boys' names in Alabama were William, James, and John, and in California Jacob, Daniel, and Anthony (Social Security data). For girls, popular names were Emma, Isabella, and Madison in Alabama, and Isabella, Sophia, and Emily in California. There is minimal overlap across states: Isabella is the only name amongst the top three in both. A study of US popular names after the 2000 presidential election, which had generated a good deal of talk about 'red states' and 'blue states,' indicated that there were several geographic trends in the use of long [iː] in popular names (Whissell 2006b). A move towards the southern states was associated with an increase in the use of [iː] in girls' names and a move toward the western states was associated with greater use of [iː] in both boys' and girls' names. Parents from 'red' states won by Bush in 2000 gave their children more stereotypically masculine and feminine names than parents from 'blue' states won by Gore. The toughest names for both boys and girls were assigned by New England parents. Historical and cultural differences among groups of English-speakers are phonaesthetically embodied in name choices (Whissell 2006b).

39.9 Names and nicknames

Alexander: Al, Alex, Alec, Sandy, Zander, Sandor, Sacha
Elizabeth: Liz, Lizzy, Lisa, Beth, Betty, Liza, Eliza

It will surprise no one to learn that nicknames, which are often bestowed as a sign of affection, are generally shorter than actual names.[2] They are also easier to pronounce.

[2] For more on nicknames, see Kennedy, this volume.

The last is because they include more sounds mastered earlier by English-speaking children. Women's nicknames are most easily pronounced, followed by men's nicknames, women's names, and men's names (Whissell 2003b). In addition, nicknames incorporate more pleasant and gentle sounds than full names for both men and women. One reason for this is the [iː] ending characteristic of so many nicknames (Nicky, Billy, Jenny, Peggy). Crystal (1993) noted the distinctly masculine characteristics of the nickname Bob. *Bob* is easy for children to pronounce because its repeated consonant, [b], is mastered early (Whissell 2003b). Phonaesthetically, [b] is an unpleasant sound and the central vowel of the name is active and cheerful. *Bob* is therefore a prototypical masculine nickname, both in terms of the phonaesthetic system employed here and in terms of Crystal's criteria. De Klerk and Bosch (1997) argue for the importance of phonaesthetics in the assignment of nicknames, and point to the positive social intent of name-givers as a main concomitant of this assignment. They also note the choice of gentler sounds (in this case, consonants) for women's nicknames and harsher ones for men's. *Bob* is therefore a prototypical masculine nickname, both in terms of the phonaesthetic system employed here and in terms of Crystal's criteria.[3]

39.10 Cats and dogs

Cats Fairy Mouse, Lady Phylida, Maebellyne
Dogs Rajah, Razzmatazz, Gargoyle

Emotion (usually affection) is also involved in the names that pet owners assign to their pets. Such names are often creatively constructed (e.g. Fuzzmuzz, Blueprint, and the examples above) and they tend to be longer than people's names. Interestingly, cats' names are more like women's names and dog's names like men's, regardless of the pet's sex. According to the author's phonaesthetic system, cats' names are gentler and dogs' names tougher (Whissell 2006a). This suggests that cats as a group are viewed as more 'feminine' pets than dogs, which are considered more 'masculine' by name-givers. Many web sites offer long lists of pet names for scrutiny, some of them even classifying the names in terms of sex as well as type of pet (e.g. http://www.petnames.net/). Pets' names in general are easier to pronounce than people's names because they include sounds mastered earlier by children.

[3] The character Kate, in the television program Blackadder, relies on the name *Bob* to establish her masculinity (http://www.youtube.com/watch?v=BLTR8qYWJbQ). After having been hired by Blackadder while masquerading as a young man, Kate mistakenly introduces herself as 'Kate.' Blackadder questions whether this 'isn't a bit of a girl's name?' to which Kate replies 'Oh, it's, um, short for Bob.'

39.11 Black and White

	Boys	Girls
Distinctively Black Names	Deshawn, DeAndre, Marquis	Imani, Ebony, Shanice
Distinctively White Names	Jake, Connor, Tanner	Molly, Amy, Claire

(Levitt and Dubner 2005)

Names vary according to both the race and the social class of name-givers (Lieberson 1984; Lieberson and Bell 1992). Fryer and Levitt (2004) reported a dramatic change in Californian naming patterns which took place during the late 1960s and early 1970s. They associate the change with the way in which the Black Power movement instilled pride for distinctiveness in the African American population. Before the watershed, names given to Black and White children had been rather similar, but after it they became quite different, as in the examples above. In *Freakonomics*, Levitt and Dubner (2005) provide a list of the most distinctively White and most distinctively Black names in California. Table 39.1 shows the percentage of tough and gentle sounds in distinctively Black and distinctively White men's and women's names (Whissell 2000). There were 80 names in all, 20 in each of the four groups.

In keeping with stereotypes discussed previously, White men's names contain the most tough and the fewest gentle sounds, while White women's names contain fewer tough sounds and the most gentle ones. Black names fall in between these two extremes, with Black men's names containing as many tough sounds as White men's names but more gentle ones, and Black women's names containing few tough or gentle sounds. Black names were longer than White names by roughly one sound. These patterns support the description of White men's names as 'toughest', White

Table 39.1 Phonaesthetic differences in distinctively Black and White names

Group	Gender	%* Gentle	% Tough	Phonaesthetic description
Black	Men	26	37	Tough + Gentle
	Women	20	26	Blandest
White	Men	16	38	Toughest
	Women	35	30	Gentlest

* The % of all sounds in the group of names that fit the emotional category

women's as 'gentlest', Black men's as 'tough and gentle' (i.e. both), and Black women's as 'bland' (i.e. neither). Men's names are tougher than women's within each racial group.

Although some Black name-givers buck the trend in the use of distinctively Black names, those who follow it tended to be of lower socioeconomic status so that, over time, distinctively Black names became indicators of low status. Such names were not related to a lack of success once class implications had been controlled by mathematical adjustment (Fryer and Levitt 2004). The majority of Black name-givers are mothers, and it is these mothers' emotions that are reflected in their children's names. Black mothers' name choices suggest that they wish their sons to be both strong and loving (tough and gentle), which is an easy wish to understand. It is not clear why mothers' choices for Black girls' names are so bland; perhaps the emotions in Black girls' names are meant to be inconspicuous, inoffensive, or 'average', and to avoid calling attention to the person named.

Even when new naming trends arise, such as the ones described above for distinctively Black names, name-givers encode emotional information in the sound patterns of the names they choose.

39.12 Names of fictional characters

Harlequin Heroes	Juan-Varo, Max, Sam, Massimo, Ryland, Nick
Harlequin Heroines	Ava, Kayla, Angela, Lydia, Lucy, Blair

(Harlequin Romance series advertisement, May 2012)

Authors of fiction are concerned with the naming of their characters. The BabyNames.com web site has a section on Tips for Writers, and there is even a site (www.obsidianbookshelf.com/html/fantasycharacternames.html) dedicated to the naming of fantasy fiction characters. David Lodge discusses the importance of name selection in chapter 8 of *The Art of Fiction* (1992). Lodge, who emphasizes the importance of meaning in fictional name choices, attributes a coarse masculinity to the name of one of his characters—Vic Wilcox—because of its word associations (victor, cock). From the phonaesthetic perspective, this name employs many phonemes located in the tough or stereotypically masculine region of Fig. 39.3. As well, by Crystal's (1993) criteria, the first name is also short and punchy, and therefore typically masculine.

In an article on naming from an online magazine for writers (www.fictionfactor.com/guests/name.html), Cynthia VanRooy points out that 'names are magic' and that their sound and rhythm are 'paramount' so that 'time and angst' are appropriately spent in identifying names that will 'sing on the page'. Most of the examples VanRooy cites in her article are from romance fiction. The names at the head of this section were also sampled from romance fiction. These names were scored in terms of their inclusion of gentle and tough sounds; there were 1.67 gentle sounds for every tough sound in heroines' names, and only 0.9 in heroes' names. Heroines' names were predominantly gentle while heroes' names were not. These names display the pattern for gender differences described in section 39.6.

Naming was important to many of the major figures in English literature. Shakespeare's comedic characters had descriptively meaningful names (Kökeritz 1950: 240). According to her name, Mrs Quickly (perhaps pronounced, suggestively, Quick-lie) might have been brisk, or easy, or both (Kökeritz 1950: 242). Gordon (1917: 4) bewailed the degradation of meaningful naming in English literature, and pointed to Charles Dickens as the last author to employ the 'descriptive nomenclature' so characteristic of Smollett and Goldsmith. The three authors created characters such as the overly humble and cadaverous Uriah Heep (*David Copperfield*), the noble young dupe Lord Verisoft (*Nicholas Nickleby*), Hugh Strap, the barber's apprentice (*Roderick Random*), and the idealized country vicar Dr Primrose (*The Vicar of Wakefield*), and, of course, Ebenezer Scrooge (*A Christmas Carol*). The earliest English novel, *The Pilgrim's Progress*, provides an extreme instance of descriptive naming. John Bunyan's characters include Christian (the protagonist in search of salvation), Mr Worldly Wiseman (a provider of bad advice to Christian), and Messers Legality and Civility (who rely on the Law rather than the Gospel).

39.13 Creative and unusual names

Creative spelling
Mikaela: Mikayla, Mikala, Mikalah
Brittany: Brittaney, Brittny, Britany, Brittainy, Brittni, Britney, Britni

Invented Names
Girls': Ataina, Cassima, Eilonwy, Ihrin, Kaydee, Lisbil, Makyla, Milenko, Quinella, Taejah
Boys': Auron, Deveron, Flaco, Jerec, Kremonoth, Lite, Pokadowa, Rupaic, Trendon, Xref

(Made-up baby names from www.just-think-it.com/sbn/madeup-m.htm)

Some parents value creativity in naming. If they are hesitant to take the plunge into using totally invented names, they might vary the spelling of existing names. In the examples at the head of this section, the standard spelling of a name has been identified by its early appearance and greater popularity in the Baby Name Voyager. Alternative spellings appear later and less frequently. Alternative spellings seldom impact on the phonetic makeup of a name, and parents using them can claim simultaneous credit for both uniqueness and connectedness: their child is different, but not too different.

A similar half-way measure involves the joining of names, for example the use Bobbyjo or Lizann as first names.

Some parents give their children totally invented names, or at least very unusual ones such as Zyr (an actual boy's name) or Chavez (an actual girl's name; Levine and Willis 1994). Examples from a web site which claims to offer hundreds of thousands of unique names are provided at the head of this section. Although what the site offers as 'made-up names' are not entirely made up (the name Eilonwy belongs to a female fictional character, and Shamrock, a suggested male name, is not made up), they are definitely unusual. The names shown above were analysed in terms of their use of tough and gentle sounds. Female names had 0.87 gentle sounds for every tough one, and male names had 0.55. Although these values are different from those in the previous section, the expected male/female difference (with female names favouring gentle sounds more than male names) is also present in the made-up names.

Parents giving their children totally unique names are taking a risk: uniqueness can be interpreted as creativity but it can also be interpreted as 'differentness' or 'not belonging'. Several studies have addressed stereotypical perceptions of people with unusual names. Although some researchers report positive responses to such names, the majority of studies point to negative stereotypes. Levine and Willis (1994) noted that actual people bearing unusual names were rated, on the basis of their names alone, as being less successful, less cheerful, less healthy, and less moral than those bearing common names. The authors also pointed out that unusual names were most often used by lower-income Black parents for girls. The mother was the chief naming parent for this group, which was distinguished by low socioeconomic and minority status. When parents were asked about their reasons for choosing a name for their child, most of them cited kinship naming or aesthetic reasons (a liking for the name); none mentioned possible future consequences to their children. Names were not chosen because they 'sounded successful' or could promote success later in a child's life. The father in the Shel Silverstein song sung by Johnny Cash ('A Boy Named Sue') would have been a standout in the set of parents interviewed in this study; he anticipated negative reactions to the unusual (and gender-inappropriate) name he had given his son, and foresaw that these reactions would produce a tough kid who was able to defend himself. Levine and Willis's findings give rise to an interesting question: in parents' minds, is naming about the child or about the parent? Not only did parents not name their child with future consequences in mind, but the data show that they seldom considered the match between the name they chose and their child.

39.14 What's in a name?

The title for this concluding section comes from Shakespeare's *Romeo and Juliet* (Act 2, Scene 2, line 43). It is part of Juliet's diatribe on the *un*-importance of names—especially the names Montague and Capulet—though most current users employ it in attempts to establish their importance. Most of us are convinced that there is something in names, so that Juliet's question is asked and answered, again and again, in many different ways. It is much in evidence on the web: Google Canada offers more than 36 million sites in response to the prompt 'What's in a name?' and these include baby naming sites, trademark sites, sites dealing with names in chemistry and biology, and numerological sites for both humans and pets. Research has shown that people's names convey information about characteristics such as ethical caring (trustworthiness, sincerity), popular fun (outgoingness, humour), success (ambition, confidence), and gender (masculinity or femininity; Mehrabian 2001).

What *is* in a name? At the micro-level, there are several distinguishing characteristics such as length, stress pattern, and phonetic make-up. The expression of kinship patterns, cultural practices, name stereotypes, and creativity are evident at the macro-level. Names also encode and convey emotional (aesthetic) messages by means of their component visimes and phonemes. When name-givers choose a name, they tend to choose one whose shapes and sounds reflect their feelings.

PART VIII

FUN WITH WORDS

CHAPTER 40

FUNNY WORDS

Verbal Humour

VICTOR RASKIN

PREAMBLE

THIS chapter snuck into this Handbook on false pretence. Its real title is 'Verbal Humour': this is what the editor solicited and the author delivered. Having noticed that all the other chapters have the word 'word' in their titles, he (that would be me, Victor Raskin) cheated by demoting the real title into the subtitle and putting the word 'word(s)' as the second word in the totally—well, almost totally—fictitious title. You see, there are practically no funny words: words are funny when put together into sentences and texts. Most of what follows applies to short joke texts, typically to short canned (Fry 1963: see an elaboration below) jokes, those that are produced from (usually faulty) memory and often follow a phrase like, *Have you heard the one about . . . ?*

Growing up in the USSR, once a major producer of humour, as a native speaker of Soviet Russian, now frozen and half-forgotten, I found the name of the Georgian town Tziplakakia enormously funny. *Kakia* does not have to be explained to anybody who speaks an Indo-European language and is 'regular' or takes Metamusil: *cacare* in Latin has nothing to do with cocoa, even though there is at least one joke that explicitly relates (IOUJ-1: here and elsewhere, it stands for 'I owe you a joke that you will find in a later section') chocolate to defecation. *Tzip*, rapidly repeated, is the Russian come-hither sound to chickens (mostly, not chicks) when you spread the feed for them: it is definitely redundant communication—they would run towards you no matter what you say, including reciting Hölderlin in German or keeping silent. The elegant French definite article *la* elevates this *Come here, you chicken shit!* message to an impossibly high social status, making the total truly hilarious. Or not.

Speaking of elevated social status, an obscenity occurring in a speech from a high pulpit (think, a pre-Francis pope) often constitutes a pretty low-level joke, so the word may be mistaken for a funny one but it is only the inappropriate context that makes it so. No philosopher or thinker to date has had much to say on words that are funny per se—except for Max Eastman (1936), a man of many trades, who seriously believed that the sound [k] was funny, and who knows, in those tough post-Depression, pre-war, Stalin's purges times, this may have been the only thing that was funny and affordable—except perhaps for their hairstyles and fashions.

40.1 Introduction

In computer science, which is not funny at all, there is a concept of NP-complete, where NP stands for 'nondeterministic polynomial' (to defeat the disclaimer above, each of these two words is funny enough but together, they rate somewhere between ROFL and LMAO). NP-complete computational decision problems are, roughly, those of which Wikipedia cheerfully states, 'the time required to solve even moderately sized versions of many of these problems can easily reach into the billions or trillions of years, using any amount of computing power available today' (2012). In artificial intelligence (AI), a loosely similar complexity for AI problems is referred to as AI-complete, thus extending the *-complete* term to other areas.

By an even looser metaphorical extension—rather than in a direct application (see Raskin 1985: ch. 2 for a discussion of the difference)—UH-complete problems would be those whose full solution includes complete knowledge of 'us humans' (UH), which are very hard to achieve for (you guessed it) us humans. These include the complete definition and cognition of life, love, language, meaning, and indeed humans. As a human activity, a mode of communication, a particular form of language, whose meaning differs from casual, non-humorous forms, the problem of defining, comprehending, and representing/describing humour is UH-complete many times over, which means it is still UH-complete, as per this important-looking formula:

$$\text{UH-complete} \times N = \text{UH-complete}$$

where N is any number, integer or not so much, positive or not quite, real or essentially dubious.

40.2 Attempts at definition of verbal humour

Let us jump ahead by announcing that there is no universally accepted definition of humour and remind ourselves that, similarly, there is no definition of life, love, human, etc. To those who tend to dismiss disciplines without strict definitions as 'soft', 'amorphous', 'mushy', etc., a gentle reminder is due that in mathematical logic, easily the most formal and rigorously defined and formulated discipline among the hard sciences and this author's 'native tongue', such basic concepts as proposition and truth/falsity cannot be defined either, just as the truthfulness of the axioms has to be assumed rather than proven.

Mindful of that, Raskin (1985) produced this 'precise' definition of the humour act, similar to Searle's (1969) definitions of speech acts, which some trusting souls were moved to take and quote seriously:

$$HU(S,H,ST,E,P,SI,SO) = X,$$

where X = F or X = U, standing for FUNNY and UNFUNNY, respectively.

It is a formula, right, so it must be true. Let us see what this piece of formalized wisdom actually says. A humour act (HU), it professes with fake formal profundity, depends on a certain speaker (S) and hearer (H)—more generally, producer and consumer, or sender and recipient. It insists, therefore, on human participation, thus slyly implying that, if a frog in a swamp slips on a banana peel and mutates, as frogs are prone to do, hilarious as this inherently is, it is not humour because no human produces or perceives it—exactly as in the notorious case of the noise of a falling tree in a people-less forest. Crucially contributing to humour is the stimulus (ST), which is, for us, essentially a short text. Then, there is experience (E) and psychology (P), followed by the situation of the joke (SI) and then the society (SO) in which the humour act occurs (SO). Any questions? Yes, whose experience and psychology, for instance? Fair enough, here is a more detailed formula from Raskin (1985):

$$VJ\left(S,H,T,E_s,E_h,E_{s,h},P_s,P_h,SI,SO_{s,h}\right) = F$$

This formula has indexed parameters: E_s, E_h, $E_{s,h}$, P_s, P_h and attributes the experiential parameters to the speaker, hearer, and joint speaker–hearer experiences, and the psychological parameter, separately, to the speaker and hearer. It also explicitly replaces an abstract stimulus with text because what is being defined is a verbal joke (VJ).

Is it not, actually, true that all of these parameters do define each occurrence of humour? If so, humour should be defined, probably, as the set of all humorous events or, more narrowly, of all verbal jokes. The problem is that we do not know how to account for any experiential parameter, let alone for the psychology and sociology in which the humour act or a verbal joke occurs. In fact, an independent definition of humour would have helped to define those much more complex parameters. In other words, this formulaic chicanery has the cognitive content of another, much simpler formula, HU = X, where X stands for all the parameters defining humour. This degenerate (in a strict, non-funny mathematical sense—and yes, there is a hilarious real-life anecdote about that as well! IOUJ-2)—formula has the advantage of not missing a single parameter.

40.3 Quasi-theories of humour

So, short of arriving at a substantive definition, we have been telling things about humour—just as, trying to capture the concept of love, at least in its romantic sense, we have been writing and reading a lot of novels. Here is what an influential thinker on literary humour included in the list of what we laugh at:

> We laugh at absurdity; we laugh at deformity. We laugh at a bottle nose in a caricature; at a stuffed figure of an alderman in a pantomime, and the tale of Slaukenbergius. A dwarf standing by a giant makes a contemptible figure enough. Rosinante and Dapple are laughable from contrast, as their masters from the same principle make two for a pair. We laugh at the dress of foreigners, and they at ours. Three chimneysweepers meeting three Chinese at Lincoln's Inn Fields, they laughed at one another till they were ready to drop down. Country people laugh at a person because they never saw him before. Any one dressed in the height of the fashion, or quite out of it, is equally an object of ridicule. One rich source of the ludicrous is distress with which we cannot sympathize from its absurdity or insignificance. It is hard to hinder children from laughing at a stammerer, at a negro, at a drunken man, or even at a madman. We laugh at mischief. We laugh at what we do not believe. We say that an argument or an assertion that is very absurd, is quite ludicrous. We laugh to show our satisfaction with ourselves, or our contempt for those about us, or to conceal our envy or our ignorance. We laugh at fools, and at those who pretend to be wise—at extreme simplicity, awkwardness, hypocrisy, and affectation.
>
> (Hazlitt 1903: 8–9)

Many things can be said about the validity or coverage of this list, but we will touch on that in the theory section. What is interesting here is the confusion of humour with laughter—or rather merging them into the same category. Hazlitt is one of the earliest examples of this recurring phenomenon but certainly not the last—see, for instance, the much publicized and quickly forgotten Provine (2001). Yet Ruch's (1995) definitive verdict, in an experiment designed by the real master, was that humour appreciation and laughter are divorced from each other in the humour consumers' minds. Of course, besides humour perception not expressing itself in laughter, there is the realization that people also laugh when tickled, embarrassed, being friendly, having a good time, suffering from a medical condition called 'pseudo-bulbar palsy', or for whatever other reason unrelated to humour.

Back to the 'magic' formula. When an earlier version was first published in Raskin (1979), it came with an emphatic disclaimer that it provided only an appearance of a definition. Nevertheless, over the years I have often found myself quoted positively on that definition as if it were meaningful. Another non-definition, also cautioned against right there, was the 'Co-operative Principle of Humour', fashioned after the Gricean Co-operative Principle of Bona Fide Communication:

Co-operative Principle of Bona Fide Communication:

(i) Maxim of Quantity: Give exactly as much information as required.
(ii) Maxim of Quality: Say only what you believe to be true.
(iii) Maxim of Relation: Be relevant.
(iv) Maxim of Manner: Be succinct. (cf. Grice 1975: 45–7)

Now for the deceptively convincing 'Co-operative Principle of Humour':

(i) Maxim of Quantity: Give exactly as much information as is necessary for the joke.
(ii) Maxim of Quality: Say only what is compatible with the world of the joke.
(iii) Maxim of Relation: Say only what is relevant to the joke.
(iv) Maxim of Manner: Tell the joke efficiently.

There is no end of problems with that principle but, on the most generously trusting interpretation of it, it may teach us how to tell a joke but not what a joke is. The maxims of quantity, relation, and manner are effectively the same as for bona fide communication. The full formulation of those would include something like 'for the situation', as in 'give exactly as much information as required for the situation'. If the situation is telling a joke, the maxims are automatically narrowed down to what the second list presents. The maxim of quality is different because it releases the speaker from an obligation to be true to the real world, accepting instead the world of the joke, with its three-legged chickens that nobody can catch, genies from bottles that mess up the wishes, etc. This maxim follows, in fact, the same principle of 'willing suspension of disbelief' that Coleridge formulated 200 years ago, talking about poetry and fiction (Coleridge 1817). But even with this pearl of wisdom inside it, the co-operative principle falls short of telling us anything about humour.

There are, however, quite a few readers and even researchers who appreciate non-essentialist, associative attempts to circumscribe rather than to actually define humour. In a recent, as usual brilliant presidential address, Elliott Oring (2011a) compared humour to art. We just saw above that jokes shared with fiction and poetry the need for the suspension of disbelief. Since the mid-1980s, publishers have treated individual jokes as copyrighted, even though their length hardly ever exceeds the 250-word limit that an academic book is allowed to quote from a single source without paying royalties. In that, jokes are now treated as a finished product, just like Dorothy Parker's short poem, 'Men seldom make passes at girls who wear glasses'. But what is the purchase in comparing or equating humour to art? One would understand the reductionist approach: explaining X in terms of Y if Y is well defined and/or is easier to understand. But if anything, art in general is more complex than humour, so accepting this thesis, which is easy, will send us this message, that whatever humour is—and we are not saying what it is—it is as complicated as any art form.

Since at least Keith-Spiegel (1972) and, I am afraid, strongly but unintentionally propagated by Raskin (1985), humour researchers have referred to three major groups of theories: superiority, release, and incongruity. The superiority/aggression/hostility theory maintains that all humour is based on humans' pleasure at others' misfortunes that the observers themselves do not experience. This view of humour was shared by the classics in Greece and Rome and practised to perfection by Cicero, who used it to represent his targets as deformed, subnormal, devoid of mind and honour. Later, Hobbes (1651) became the strongest proponent of that kind of humour. It had increasingly fewer proponents in the last century, and there are hardly any current humour researchers who advocate this view, but this does not at all mean that there is no such humour: in fact, much of the low humour on the web is of a hostile nature. It is sometimes claimed that young children also start with hostile humour and then graduate out of it.

The view of humour as release was first proposed by Spencer (1860) but is mostly associated with Freud, who maintained that humour offered a welcome release from the yoke of reality and its hardwired logic. Absurd humour may come to mind here but Freud's own sense of humour did not go much higher than German puns about bodily functions. Well, three-legged chickens, intergalactic travels, and other non-real elements in humour may also come under release. Freud's indirect pictorial humour may have been closer to absurdity when he interpreted a society lady's persistent dream of a Fedora hat as evidence that her husband had impressive genitals.

It is much harder to dismiss the incongruity theories which dominate the current view of humour, and again, Raskin (1985) and the later iterations of the linguistic theory of humour have contributed to it in spite of my persistent denial of anything but politeness towards incongruity. Usually first associated with Kant (1790), incongruity treats humour as a surprising juxtaposition of two different situations in a way that sort of makes sense but not really. Incongruity was elevated to an almost scientific status by massive psychological experiments measuring subjects' response to incongruity and its resolution (see e.g. Shultz 1976). My idea of opposing scripts in a joke has also been seen as support for incongruity, and my explicit opposition to this identification fell on deaf atheoretical ears. I have nothing against incongruity per se—I just maintain that my theory is neutral to all of these theoretical claims because they are all partial: not all jokes are aggressive and even fewer are based on release/liberation, and incongruity theories make a much lesser cognitive claim than the linguistic theories of humour to which I have contributed.

Elliott Oring (2011b) mounted a very well-thought-out attack against the second iteration of the linguistic theory of humour (Attardo and Raskin 1991) and its partial confirmation in a massive opportunistic psychological experiment (Ruch et al. 1993). I responded (Raskin 2011), with enormous respect and profuse compliments, that his attack was brilliant and all wrong—and matched it with equally strong arguments. However, my main target was his alternative theory of appropriate incongruity: a text is funny when it displays appropriate incongruity, and appropriate incongruity materializes in a joke. The lack of an independent definition of appropriate inconguity does not present a problem to Oring as it unfortunately does to anyone whose parents did not protect them carefully from the yoke of mathematics and logic.

This circularity, apparently not offensive to certain kinds of researcher, including those with otherwise solid repuations, also characterizes the briefly famous 'theory of benign violations', masterfully propagated by a recent trade book (McGraw and Warner 2014). A joke, according to this view, involves a benign violation: a clear violation of logic or of law takes place but it is not scary. What this short-lived theory, joining the equally well-advertised and forgotten Provine (2001) and Hurley et al. (2011)—cf. Raskin (2014)—shares with all the above theories, often of much more select pedigrees, is that they are loose and partial: there are jokes that are aggressive, liberating, involving benign violation, and many that are not. Besides, even more ruinously, there are texts that are all of the above and yet are not jokes and not intended as such. In scientific terms, that would be tantamount to saying that two plus two makes four sometimes but quite often not, or that a physical object without support will most likely fall to the ground unless it does not. This is not what real theory is like. What is it like?

40.4 Real theory

Since this is all supposed to be about the word, let us look at a pretty decent description of the possible senses of the word *theory* (it is not a funny word except perhaps as in *I have a theory why Nicole left Jason*—big deal, as if there were no universal explanation, especially if you look at the hunk she went to from Jason). The sense in which the word is used in the parentheses is number 7, and this is also pretty much the actual sense in which it is used in quasi-theories which purport to fall under the definitive first sense. Senses 3, 5, and 6 are actually unnecessary, all overlapping with senses 2, 1, and 2 again, respectively.

1. A coherent group of tested general propositions, commonly regarded as correct, that can be used as principles of explanation and prediction for a class of phenomena: Einstein's theory of relativity. Synonyms: principle, law, doctrine.
2. A proposed explanation whose status is still conjectural and subject to experimentation, in contrast to well-established propositions that are regarded as reporting matters of actual fact. Synonyms: idea, notion, hypothesis, postulate. Antonyms: practice, verification, corroboration, substantiation.
3. In mathematics, a body of principles, theorems, or the like, belonging to one subject: number theory.
4. The branch of a science or art that deals with its principles or methods, as distinguished from its practice: music theory.
5. A particular conception or view of something to be done or of the method of doing it; a system of rules or principles: conflicting theories of how children best learn to read.
6. Contemplation or speculation: the theory that there is life on other planets.
7. Guess or conjecture: My theory is that he never stops to think words have consequences (dictionary.com, 2014).

Other dictionaries (for instance, the one built into this Apple computer) add something like 'general principles independent of the phenomenon explained' to sense 1, the most serious definition of *theory*, and it is this part of the definition which is violated, to me not benignly, by those appropriate incongruities and benign violations in the previous section.

One would think that the structure of a theory should be developed in the philosophy of science but, funnily enough, it is not: obsessing instead about matters like empirical verification or lack thereof in physics—as if physics were still reigning supreme among sciences rather than being in a state of total and rather funny collapse—I am clearly laughing at the misfortune of others here.

So, over a decade ago, I insisted, much to my co-author's chagrin, on including a heavy 'philosophy of science' chapter to Nirenburg and Raskin (2004: ch. 2). It was written in desperation: for reasons outlined both above and below as well as some others, a theory needed to be built, and the philosophy of science which, one would think, should have developed a set of recommendations on how to do it right, had been—and has been—completely silent on the subject. So I proceeded with an imaginary DIY kit. Some of the results still hold; others have been revised, updated, and upgraded.

I still believe in the theory-methodology-results triple. Theory determines the format of the results and it licenses methodologies for obtaining these results. Theory also enables and ensures optimization, scalability, extent of generalization, bias detection, evaluation, standardization, reusability, and last but not least, explanation hypotheses.

Every theory includes at least these six components:

- body of the theory: set of explanatory and predictive statements about its purview—pretty much according to the first dictionary sense of *theory* quoted above;
- purview: the phenomena that the theory takes on itself to deal with, or what it is the theory of;
- premises: the implicit axiomatic statements that the theory takes for granted—these are not stated clearly by many theories and cause most misunderstanding;
- goals: the final results of the successful formulation of a theory;
- methods of falsification: the clearly stated hypothetical situation which would prove the theory wrong, a counterexample—we follow here Popper's (1972) view that a hypothesis that is unfalsifiable in principle is not only not a theory but is actually a faith;
- methods of justification/evaluation: a set of statements on how to check the veracity of the body statements and, wherever possible, on how to compare the theory to its competition, if any.

Of all of these components, the body is the most obvious or at least the most visible, while the premises are very rarely stated, explicated, discussed, or defended—because they are 'obvious' to a community of scholars. This neglect leads to narrow, partisan approaches that are rarely scalable or reusable. Also, somewhere between falsification and evaluation, there is the issue of empirical verification, often by visual observation, that philosophy of science is interested in to the point of obsession, mostly excluding non-physics theories from consideration. I consider it a very sane and productive principle of verification the way Susan Haack (1993) proposed to combine empirical observation of what is observable with the coherence of the rest that is unobservable—and most is not.

A well-developed, mature, self-aware, and therefore usable theory is characterized by all the properties below—it must be and actually is:

- adequate, if it provides an accurate account of all the phenomena in its purview;
- effective, if it comes with a methodology for its implementation;
- formal, if it submits itself to logical rules, irrespective of whether it does or does not use a specific formalism—confusing formality with formalism is one of the worst and unfortunately most common offences in discussing a formal theory;
- constructive, if that implementation can be completed in finite time;
- decidable, if there is an algorithm for its implementation in principle;
- computable, if this algorithm can actually be implemented;
- explicit, if it is fully aware of all of its components and provides a full account of each of them.

Let us see how this piece of metatheory applies to a theory of humour. Since it has only been applied (Raskin 2012a, 2012b) to the Script-based Semantic Theory of Humour (SSTH)–General Theory of Verbal Humour (GTVH)–Ontological Semantic Theory of Humour (OSTH) dynasty of linguistic theories (Raskin 1985; Attardo and Raskin 1991; Raskin et al. 2009; see also Raskin 2012a, 2012b), let us look there. The components that these theories share have been:

- body: the main hypothesis that the text of a (potential) joke is compatible, in full or in part, with two opposing scripts;
- purview: textual humour, most easily applicable to short canned jokes;
- premises: mostly that a text can be recognized as humour-carrying in the process of normal linguistic-semantic analysis within a certain approach and understood the way humans do;
- goals: mostly to account for how each joke works, which amounts to understanding it the way people do and going beyond that to a full explanation, the way people don't;
- falsification: a joke that is not based on overlapping and opposed scripts—not yet produced, it appears; and
- justification: see Ruch et al. (1993) on a successful psychological experiment that bore out most of the GTVH claims.

The body, the main hypothesis of SSTH, is perhaps the most cited piece of wisdom in current humour research, and because it deals with the juxtaposition, as it were, of two opposed scripts, it is seen, to no consequence or effect, as an incongruity type of theory. GTVH, Salvatore Attardo's and my General Theory of Verbal Humour, makes the script opposition and the text of the joke into two of the six knowledge resources of the body of the theory, namely, the logical mechanism, situation, target, and the narrative structure, as per the following descriptions (Raskin et al. 2009):

- language: the actual textual artefact, whether spoken, written, mimed, gestured, expressed through dress, etc., with all the choices at the relevant levels of linguistic analysis, e.g. syntax, phonology;
- narrative strategy: the overall textual genre, e.g. riddle, conversational retort, humourous short story (cf. Attardo 1994);
- target: the optional, usually stereotypical, butt of the joke;
- situation: the scriptually evoked situation that forms the backdrop of the joke;
- logical mechanism: the (situationally) false, pseudological reasoning that playfully masks the oppositeness and seems to resolve the incongruity presented by it;
- script opposition: the juxtaposition of two different scripts.

The latest version in this family of linguistic theories of humour, reported in that article, is finally delivering what the original SSTH posited as a conditional: it would work when a real formal theory of linguistic semantics is developed. The Ontological Semantic Theory of Humour (OSTH) is based on (you guessed it) Ontological Semantic Technology (OST), which provides meaning representation of sufficient coverage to account for humour. Moreover, while in SSTH it was stipulated that the scripts were to be discovered in the process of normal semantic analysis, and the opposition types were extra—well, in OST, they no longer are.

What sets the linguistic theories of humour apart from quasi-theories is that the former but definitely not the latter present a set of necessary and, most importantly, sufficient conditions for a text to be (at least potentially) funny; moreover, the linguistic theories are fully explicitly self-aware of all of their ingredients. The quasi-theories can only manage partial and not always valid necessary conditions; they are also implicit, loosely described, and trivially falsifiable.

In fact, the linguistic theory of humour is so well formulated now that it can serve as an adequate basis for computational humour. Computational humour deals with the computer's ability to detect and to generate humour. Introduced by me on a stupid bet as my contribution to Raskin and Attardo (1994), it inspired a large group of computer scientists to build a number of toy systems that generated jokes. When in a couple of years I attempted to expose these games as pretty useless both for artificial intelligence and insights into humour, Stock (1996) salvaged the initiative with his talk of its uses for edutainment. These days, computers are increasingly used as partners in communication with humans, e.g. as computer friends to shut-in single patients; and their ability to tell a joke from serious communication is essential, as is the human ability to be emulated to insert a joke into a conversation. Both law enforcement and industry are increasingly interested in analysing social networks (I know this is not funny!), and with the amount of humour, irony, and sarcasm there, the computers that must be used in analysis must understand what is serious and what is not. Well, obviously, to understand that, they must understand what the texts mean, and our current predominantly machine-learning based attempts to handle that without understanding text would be funny if they weren't so sad.

Related to computational humour is the issue of computational creativity. While human creativity is not well defined, scholars from various disciplines are looking at the computer's ability to produce something other than what it is programmed to do; and an area that many scholars address is creativity in humour. Most jokes are not terribly creative, following a template, a pattern, or sometimes just a convenient ready-made pun. But the ones that are innovative are a good test case to try and have the computer reproduce.

40.5 Jokes

Well, those readers who have survived the heavy theory section deserve some relief. After delivering on the two joke IOUs issued earlier, we will talk about various aspects and types of jokes. Massive examples of jokes, including the barely printable ones, can be found in my 1985 *Semantic Mechanisms of Humor*. A messy taxonomy of humour, where topics, methods, and everything else, is mixed together was produced years ago by Arthur Asa Berger (1999), and it comes to you without any endorsement.

IOUJ-1: A peasant boy is dying to get his girlfriend to have sex with him. A more experienced friend advises him to give her a lot of chocolates, and so he does. He buys several chocolate bars and starts feeding them to her one after another on their next date. As he urges her to have more he keeps asking her if she is feeling anything. After denying that for a while, she blushingly confesses that she is beginning to feel something. 'What?' he asks in great excitement. 'I think I need to shit,' she says.

IOUJ-2: A young mathematician—let's call him W—received an apparent offprint. There was no cover letter in the envelope, and the text was in Japanese that he did not know, but several times throughout the Japanese text, he saw 'W. degenerate' in Latin characters. He spent the following several weeks learning to read Japanese, and when he was proficient enough he figured out something he could have gotten long before from just knowing what the article was about: he had discovered and discussed a new function named after him, and 'W. degenerate' referred to its value on the zero argument, 'degenerate W. function', as per mathematical terminology. Nothing personal!

The scripts opposed in these unremarkable jokes are the desire to have sex versus the desire to defecate, in the first joke, and W. insulted in a way totally inappropriate for a mathematical article and W. uninsulted because the offending expression was part of a legitimate terminological expression. The first opposition is sort of vulgar, and the second is boring—and so are the jokes. The nature and quality of the opposition is a decisive factor in the quality of the joke. The primitive pun in the next joke renders it, well, primitive: 'He is a man of letters: he works at the Post Office' (Esar 1961). How about this one: 'What's the difference between the sparrow? There is no difference between the sparrow: both sides of the sparrow are completely identical, especially the left one.' This joke is hard to get for most hearers who are not used to absurd jokes. It is one of the most sophisticated jokes I have ever heard. Its path runs something like:

- difference between the sparrow and??: no bail-out → have to make your own two out of one → divide the one you have into two → halves
- 'identical halves': no work
- 'especially the left': no possible interpretation → absurd → funny

People vary as to how hard they are prepared to work on getting a joke, and they give up earlier or later if the going is too hard. It is pretty hard in the case of the sparrow joke. There is a relation also between the length of the joke and the difficulty of getting it. Catering to the least refined tastes in humour, authors often retell short jokes as long 'tall tales'. There are standard recipes for presenting jokes, such as the triple structure: 'The first man ... The second man ... And the third man [delivers the punch line]'. 'Gobi desert canoe club', once Salvatore Attardo's favourite joke, puzzles some hearers by its brevity. Others are puzzled by imperfect puns, such as, 'Why did the cookie cry?—Because its mother was a wafer so long'.

All of the examples above are 'canned' jokes (Fry 1963). The opposite category is situational humour: witticisms produced on the fly and rarely reproducible: 'You should have been there.' I mentioned at the very beginning that words by themselves are hardly ever funny. Nevertheless, a word out of place ruins a joke. Verbal humour is delivered beyond the constraints of a short joke. There are funny short stories and novels, film comedies, and sitcoms—but it is probably fair to conclude that the word plays a much more visible role in short canned jokes.

The words are structured into sentences in any language: syntax takes care of that, and since Chomsky (at least in the mid-1950s through to the mid-1960s, his genius years) syntax has been treated as a very tightly woven mathematical structure that takes a considerable and highly sophisticated effort to explicate and which the native speaker easily uses without any effort. Sentences are organized into paragraphs and those into whole texts much more loosely and not exclusively linguistically: other rules, such as culture-specific rhetorical rules govern coherence and cohesiveness. Thus, the topic-sentence-first in a paragraph, topic-paragraph-first in a text rule of American writing never fails to amuse and/or irritate a continental European who is taught to organize a text chronologically.

Canned jokes possess an additional structure on top of all that, and this is why they are somewhat easier to structure and compute than non-humorous 'open text'. A joke has a set-up, which normally introduces the first, misleading script, a punchline that triggers the switch to the second opposed script, and retroactively, as it were, the elements of the second script are surreptitiously sprinkled over the setup. These elements are obviously present in all the joke examples above, but they were made famous by the notorious joke that my *Semantic Mechanisms of Humor* stuffed down everybody's throat. It continues to travel from one piece of humour research to another, and it would be inappropriate to finish this opus without quoting it:

> 'Is the *doctor* at home?' the *patient* asked in his *bronchial* whisper. 'No,' the *doctor's* young and pretty wife *whispered* back. '**Come right in**!'

The italicized words are from the first misleading script, the doctor–patient one. After it is defeated by the boldfaced punchline, the hearer/reader backtracks and realizes that the underlined words were inserted in the setup that actually belong to the second script of adultery, apparently misled by the patient's whisper, which indicates the loss of voice due to an illness in the first script and intimacy in the second. The incurable romantic of the bored wife invited a man in because her husband was not in—a cue which makes no sense medically (well, if successful, the encounter may lead to medical problems of a different kind, and speaking of medicine, the whisper should be pharyngeal, not bronchial—but nobody can use the correct medical term in a joke and live!).

So you see, this is not about funny words, except that it is/was. There are no funny words per se. In fact, Per Se is one of the most expensive *prix fixe* restaurants in the world, so expensive that even New Yorkers don't laugh . . . Tziplakakia!

CHAPTER 41

WORD PUZZLES

HENK J. VERKUYL

41.1 Introduction

WORD puzzles generally use letters as their basic elements rather than sound units. This raises the question (section 41.2) of what counts as a word for the purpose of word puzzles. While linguists generally use a combination of phonological, syntactic, and semantic criteria for identifying words, word puzzles rely on orthographic conventions. Section 41.3 discusses three elements determining what counts as a word puzzle: retrieval of lexical and encyclopedic knowledge, ingenuity in dealing with word forms, and the sense of beauty as part of the search of perfection. In section 41.4, three forms of puzzling are discussed in some detail: flats, forms, and crosswords. The ground will then have been prepared for a detailed comparison of cryptic crosswords in English and Dutch (section 41.5). This comparison reveals that the English convention of writing compound words with an internal space has consequences for the way in which English speakers deal with the notion of word, while the Dutch convention of writing compounds as one word also determines the way they look at words. This contrast has led to enormous differences in the way Dutch and English speakers do their word puzzling.[1,2]

[1] I would like to thank my former colleague Piet Verhoeff for letting me profit from his uncommon expertise in solving both English and Dutch cryptic crosswords; also Ray Nickerson for his stimulating remarks on an earlier version.

[2] The *OED* defines *English* as 'the language of England, now widely used in many varieties throughout the world'. The term will be used in this wide sense, but there are also many instances in which it is to be understood more narrowly. Most of the crossword examples discussed in this chapter, including those taken from Greeff (2003), are by setters who work for British newspapers.

41.2 What counts as a word (in puzzling)?

41.2.1 Word and morpheme

A third of the way into the last century, Bloomfield (1933: 178) gave his famous definition of a word as a 'minimal free form': a word is the smallest linguistic unit able to be used 'on its own'. The definition can lead to tricky questions, such as whether or not the determiners *an* and *the* in *an apple* and *the apple* are words. To circumvent problems such as these, linguists tended to work with the notion of morpheme, understood as the smallest unit able to carry meaning.

A morpheme consists of phonemes, defined as the smallest segmental sound units capable of making a meaning distinction. The focus on morphemes and phonemes had the effect of detaching linguistic units from their written appearance: how a word was spelled was of no significance. English could have been written in Georgian rather than Roman letters; it would have been the same language and would have sounded just the same. In 1929, Turkish changed from using Arabic script to Roman script, and still remained Turkish.

Nowadays linguists are more willing to take wordhood as a theoretical concept. Even so, when morphologists (not 'wordists') do so, they see a word as a layered complex of phonological, syntactic, and semantic characteristics (see, among many others, Allwood et al. 2010; Booij 2007; Jackendoff 2002; Spencer 1991). Taking a word as a three-layered theoretical construct, however, ignores the fact that speakers of English are likely to think of the word *black* as having five letters rather than the four phonemes /b/, /l/, /æ/, and /k/. In their judgement about what counts as the basic units for carrying meaning, they take into account this fourth layer of their knowledge about words, namely the orthographic system. This conforms with the popular definition of a word as an uninterrupted sequence of letters surrounded by spaces (or punctuation marks). Puzzle-makers do not ask for phonemes but for letters. The notion of a word puzzle is therefore firmly based in the orthographic conventions of a particular language. In the mental lexicon, the orthography of a word is an important factor in the knowledge speakers have of a word, and (as just mentioned) the orthographic information may even be more salient than phonological information.

41.2.2 Compounding

At this point it is necessary to take compounding into account. The English word *rivermouth* is composed of the two words *river* and *mouth*. Dutch has the same procedure: *rivier* and *mond* come together to make *riviermond*. However, there is an important difference between the two languages. In English, the preferred option is to write the components of the compound as separate words: *river mouth*, the orthographic form *rivermouth* being somewhat unusual. In Dutch, the convention is to write the compound without an internal space. French goes even further in this respect than English, as we can see in Table 41.1.

Table 41.1 Compounding in English, Dutch, and French

English	Dutch	French
river basin	stroomgebied	bassin fluvial
river mouth	riviermond	embouchure
blood group	bloedgroep	groupe sanguin
bloodstain	bloedvlek	tache de sang
city hall	stadhuis	hôtel de ville
cityscape	stadsgezicht	vue de la ville
concert hall	concertgebouw	salle de concert
sign language	gebarentaal	langage gestuel
crossword puzzle	kruiswoordraadsel	mots croisés
fine-tooth comb	stofkam	peigne fin
road hog	wegpiraat	fou du volant

There has been an intensive discussion about the word status of the examples like those in this table. With respect to the English column, it is generally agreed that a compound word—spaced or not—is a word and not a phrase, not least because the qualifying word lacks a determiner. In French, however, the situation is more complex; some of the examples do contain a determiner in the modifying part: *fou <u>du</u> volant, vue de <u>la</u> ville*. In Dutch and German, compounding results in just one word, written without internal spaces. If there is an exhibition (in Dutch: *tentoonstelling*) of tents (in Dutch: plural *tenten*), then the Dutch have a *tentententoonstelling*; if this exhibition concerns oxygen tents (in Dutch: plural *zuurstoftenten*), then they are able to stage a *zuurstoftententententoonstelling*. And so on. Nowadays, however, most Dutch speakers use English as their second reading language; because of this there is an increasing tendency to follow the English orthographic convention and to insert a word space.

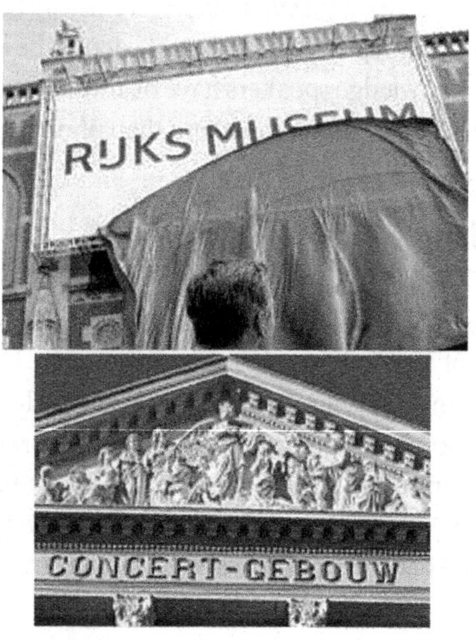

This trend no doubt explains the indignation and strong disapproval expressed in 2012 by the Dutch Foundation for Spotting Incorrect Spacing (no joke!) when a designer created a new logo for the Rijksmuseum (National Gallery) in Amsterdam in which she separated RIJKS and MUSEUM by a space. Here the old genitive *s* clearly occupies the space that would occur between the compounding elements *rijk* and *museum*, with the *s* serving as a linking element. Words with *rijks-* as their first element therefore need to be written as one word. In letters to the editors of daily newspapers one often finds indignation expressed about the decline of the Dutch language, manifest whenever dailies write *bloed groep* 'blood group' and *kruiswoord raadsel* 'crossword puzzle'. Mostly, these reactions are in the context of resistance to the penetration of English into Dutch. In the Rijksmuseum case, though, it was seen as an incorrect use of the language. It did not help very much when the designer was supported by a commissioner who pointed out that in 1865 the architect Cuypers had RIJKS MUSEUM engraved on one of the pillars in the way shown on the upper picture on p. 704. It is interesting to see that at that time people were uncertain about how to spell new compounds. On the tympanum of the Concertgebouw in Amsterdam, built in the same period, one can still read CONCERT-GEBOUW. In the Dutch spelling system, the hyphen has the function of connecting two words until such time as their status as a compound has become sufficiently familiar so that it can be spelled as one word.[3] Nowadays, both *Rijksmuseum* and *Concertgebouw* have reached the status of being spelled without any space, and this practice will no doubt be maintained until the influence of English spelling conventions becomes too great to resist.

In spite of uncertainty about whether or not compounds count as one word, English puzzle-setters generally identify the basic unit of the crossword puzzle as the orthographic word, offset by spaces. That is, for obtaining the answer:

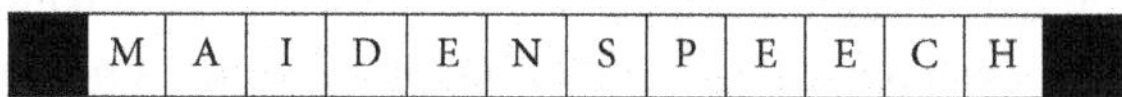

they give a Clue *C* = *Each MP needs one composed* (6,6) rather than taking the answer as a word consisting of twelve letters. The signal (6,6) is used to indicate that the comma stands for a space separating two words of six letters each which happen to form a compound. (We may note in passing that this clue contains an anagram spread over the three underlined words, the missing 'i' being provided by *needs one*.) American setters have fewer scruples; in the above example, Shortz (2006) would not give the (6,6) information at all.

This section has focused on the first part of the compound *word puzzle*. In the following section we discuss what goes into the notion of a puzzle.

[3] A similar trend is of course operative in English. As new compounds become more frequent, they sometimes come to be written either with a hyphen or as one word without a space. Even so, the option of writing compounds without a space generally remains available.

41.3 What counts as puzzling (in word puzzling)?

41.3.1 Knowledge

There are crossword puzzles which mainly focus on knowledge. The clue *Capital of Iran* leads to the answer TEHRAN. The problem here is to get to this piece of encyclopedic knowledge by consulting one's memory and, if one does not succeed, by consulting puzzle dictionaries or internet sites. Puzzles of this kind do not require ingenuity, yet they fall under the heading of word puzzles, in this case because the clue asks for a proper name with six letters. A game often played during long car journeys is geographical chaining. With TEHRAN as the starting point, the first link could be NAIROBI, the second ISLAMABAD, the third DENVER, and so on. Here the players are guided by the implicit clue *Capital of.* ... In this way, parents may extend their children's general knowledge (or their own) in all sorts of encyclopedic domains such as names of towns, rivers, musical instruments, or historical personages.

Knowledge is also the only guide in getting from the clue *a long low sound expressing discomfort* (4) to the right answer, MOAN. In this case, puzzlers have to access the right-hand side of their mental dictionary entry for *moan*, something in the nature of 'a noise expressing discomfort due to physical or mental suffering or sexual pleasure often in the form of a long, low sound', in order to get to the headword *moan*. The basic idea of a puzzle of this kind is that the clue gives sufficient information from the definition in order for the puzzler to arrive at the appropriate headword.

In a regular dictionary the headword (H) *hypothermal* is explained in terms of a definition (D) in which descriptions such as 'not very hot', 'tepid', 'lukewarm' are likely to appear. Looking up the headword *tepid*, however, one does not find 'hypothermal' as an explaining term in the definition but rather something like 'only slightly warm, almost cold', 'lukewarm'. Similarly, *lukewarm* might be defined as 'barely or moderately warm', 'tepid'. If ≥ stands for 'more difficult or at the same level of difficulty', H ≥ D represents the way in which a regular dictionary relates H to D. H is explained in terms which are easier than H, or in terms which are equal in difficulty. Puzzle dictionaries are quite different in that they have a D ≤ H relation, where D is (part of) the clue and H is the answer. In a puzzle dictionary—in fact, a kind of reverse semantic dictionary—the entry

lukewarm tepid (5), hypothermal (11)

has this structure, where, in terms of difficulty, *lukewarm* = *tepid* and *lukewarm* < *hypothermal*. 'Difficulty' may be taken here as pertaining to specialized vocabulary that can be seen as technical, professional, learned, elitist, and so on. One may also understand 'difficult' as equivalent to 'less common.' Sometimes, the clue simply counts as a synonym of the answer, as in the case of the clue *wealthy* requiring the answer PROSPEROUS. In most cases, however, the clue is a hyponym or has an even weaker semantic relation with the answer, as in the pair *hang around*–WAIT.

This form of puzzling is often considered a mere pastime (read: waste of time). In order to counter this reproach, puzzlers may point out that they see it as a way for people to keep their vocabulary up to date or even to extend it. They have support from cognitive scientists who maintain that mental activities fostered by this kind of puzzle do indeed appear to contribute to keeping the brain in good working order under the rubric: 'If you don't use it you lose it' (Hall et al. 2009; Keijzer 2011; Nickerson 1977).

41.3.2 Ingenuity

Ingenuity comes in as soon as structure is involved. Word forms are structured entities, so there may be a relation between the structure of the clue and the structure of the answer. For example, a puzzle-maker may invent the clue *Large bay with a distorted sort of long low sound* (4). Here the solution depends on the D-to-H strategy discussed above. First, a large bay, or a large area of sea partially enclosed by land, can be called a gulf. Second, the description 'long low sound' should be sufficient to evoke the headword *moan*. The next step is suggested by the word *distorted* and involves mapping the collection of letters in *moan* onto another collection of letters, in *Oman*. This connection is partly dependent on encyclopedic knowledge because one has to know that there exists a Gulf of Oman. The phrase *large bay* in the clue justifies the transformation of *moan* into its anagram OMAN.

There is more to ingenuity than moving letters around. Consider the clue *This country joins two countries diametrically opposed* (7). Here the idea is to piece together two proper names in a way suggested by the clue in order to get a new proper name consisting of seven letters. One has to find two countries diametrically opposed, which is quite difficult given that there are nearly 200 countries in the world. In order to prevent loss of interest, the setter may therefore decide to give some more information by rephrasing the clue as *This European country joins two Asian countries diametrically opposed* (7). That should enable the puzzler to find the answer ROMANIA, which contains both *Iran* and *Oman* and joins them together in an acceptable way. Here ingenuity goes hand in hand with geographical knowledge.

The qualification 'in an acceptable way' raises a crucial issue: both *Iran* and *Oman* have an *n* but one does not find two *n*s in *Romania*. The join has an overlap, whereas Oman and Iran are discrete. It is precisely on this point that we see that the *OED* definition of puzzle—'a game, toy, or problem designed to test ingenuity or knowledge'—lacks an important element, namely that the solution should invoke the sense of beauty. Beauty is for many puzzlers the decisive factor. It raises questions like: Is it pleasing to join two words of four letters into a complex of seven letters by suppressing an *n*? Is the join of OMAN and IRAN comparable to the telescoping of two parts of a drainpipe (allowing the suppression of an *n*) or does it require strict adjacency (with no suppression)? A choice between these options is guided by a sense of beauty: drainpipe aesthetics, which allows the smuggling away of a redundant *n*, may be considered a weakness, whereas strictness may be regarded as being closer to the Platonic ideal.

41.3.3 The sense of beauty

There can be no doubt about the sort of beauty under consideration: it is Platonic in the pure philosophical sense, predominantly because in puzzling there is not only a tendency for a perfect match between clue and answer but also a need to match an answer with an ideal immaterial form.

To illustrate how closely the search for beauty is connected with puzzling, consider the following true story. In the basement of our former house, the cupboard built below the flight of stairs going up to the main floor had a moisture problem due to lack of ventilation. As the door of the cupboard already had some holes in it, the logical step was to bore some more holes in the stairway. Freehand. Over-confidence is not always a good guide, so the result in (a) was ugly. It should, of course, have been what is shown in (b). This figure fails to be the ideal form itself because a representation has all the limitations of concreteness. This would become obvious if, for example, the picture was enlarged up to the level of pixels. Underlying the representations (a) and (b), however, there is an abstract complex of measures and proportions determining the beauty of a structure in which three dots are located in a box: (b) is clearly much closer to the Ideal Form than (a).

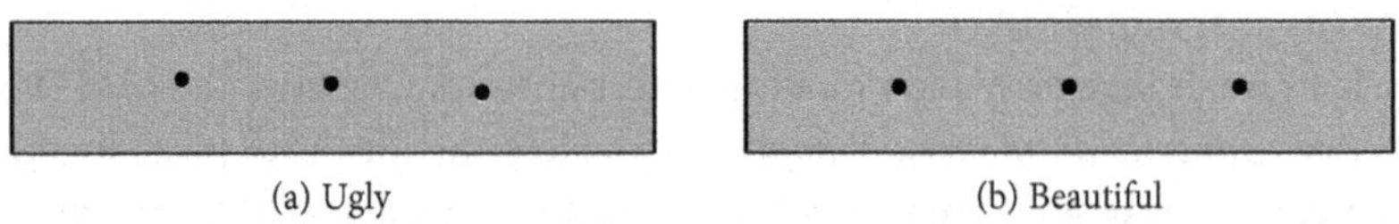

(a) Ugly (b) Beautiful

Although pictures do not have anything to do with clues and answers in word puzzles, they demonstrate the close connection between the sense of beauty and the sense of perfectness. At a certain level of ingenuity, clue and answer need to form a perfect pair. This puts heavy constraints on puzzle-makers, as we shall see. We now have three guides to puzzling: knowledge, ingenuity, and beauty. These three together will lead us through the domain of word puzzles.

41.4 Flats, forms, and crosswords

For linguists the domain of word puzzling is fascinating because of the important role of elementary mathematical operations underlying the activities of the puzzlers, such as permutation, deletion, addition, substitution, reversal, joining, splitting, and many other formal operations. One has to take that literally: these are operations on word *forms*, rather than on word meanings. Certainly, meaning does play a role but very much in the way in which it is taken in the Chomskyan generative theory: as a secondary touchstone for syntax. This can be demonstrated briefly with the help of some examples taken from the website of a prominent American puzzle organization, the National Puzzle League (NPL), founded on 4 July 1883. In the 130 years of its existence the NPL has collected more than seventy different types of word puzzles. Their principal distinction is quite useful in its simplicity:

1. Flat. A flat has one dimension: the answer is a single sequence of letters forming a word in some specific way relating to the clue.
2. Form. A form is two-dimensional and presumes a crossing of words.

Flats will play an important role in the present chapter, forms to a lesser degree, because the crossword, being a form in virtue of its two dimensions, has more or less freed itself from this category and so is being treated as a category of its own.

Forms in the NLP sense are essentially all sorts of geometric figures made up of words. The Right Pyramidal Windmill is just one of the many sorts of crossings in a certain prescribed mathematical figure. In the triangles the horizontal words cross with the vertical words, whereas the edges of the wings are formed by *street gangs* and by the expression *coming apart at the seams.*

RIGHT PYRAMIDAL WINDMILL

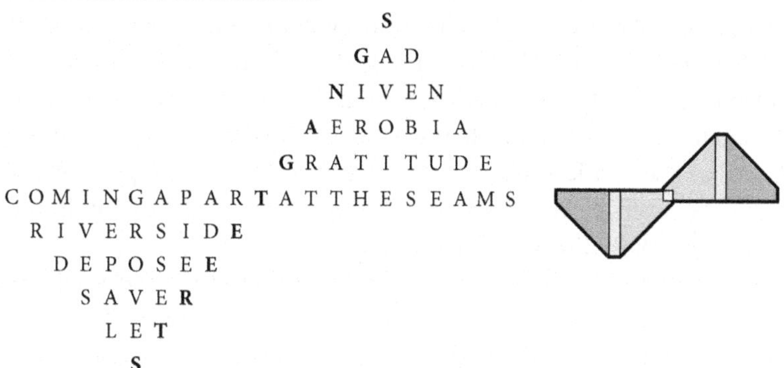

Flats presume the mathematical operations mentioned above. As they also play an important role in crossword puzzles, it is necessary to pay attention to some of their properties. Flats presume an almost insane inclination to play with word forms, taking them apart or making them belong to a structured set.[4] The restrictions on these

[4] Another manifestation of this sort of formal insanity is writing a meaningful story with the restriction that only one vowel may be used (the so-called *A*-story, *E*-story, etc.), or writing a postcard with a meaningful text consisting of only the first 13 letters of the alphabet. Or collecting palindromes in an attempt to pay tribute to symmetry in language forms. And so on. Battus (1981) is an impressive collection of different sorts of formal obsession. It was certainly inspired by Oulipo, the French Workshop for potential literature founded in 1960 by Raymond Queneau and others. Oulipo products include poems in which all the words have the same number of letters, or a novel (*La disparition* by Georges Perec) in which the vowel *e* does not appear, or a text in which each word *n* is one letter longer than *n-1*, etc.

operations are, however, essential: they provide the sense of beauty discussed earlier. A famous example of a structured deletion set is the following sequence:

startling—starling—staring—string—sting—sing—sin—in—n

Nothing in the word *startling* itself reveals the relationship with the other seven words in the sequence. The one-letter-deletion relation is present as part of our knowledge of English words stored in our mental lexicon. The sequence is amusing, and taken by itself it shows, to a certain degree, a glimmer of beauty. On seeing the eight words thus connected, real puzzlers will ask whether the sequence would be more perfect if it contained only nouns, or only verbs, or if just one and the same vowel were to be allowed. And, of course, they will collect the deleted letters by construing the set {t, l, a, r, t, g, s, i, n} in order to see whether words can be formed from this set which have to do with the sequence. Then, suddenly, they will experience beauty, because as soon as the letters form the word *startling*, it gives sense to an otherwise accidental sequence. No drainpipe aesthetics. But real puzzlers, however satisfied by this result, will also continue by raising the question: is this indeed the most pleasing sequence that can be made? Questions like these all boil down to an attempt to find aesthetically satisfying restrictions on the rules of the game. This is a purely Platonic way of thinking about perfectness, and as such is an organizing principle in word puzzling. (Linguists also share this affection for the beauty of restrictions in the rules they construct.)

An anagram is a flat involving the rearrangement of letters. *Beneath Chopin* (3,5,5) becomes THE PIANO BENCH. This example shows how important semantics may be as a complementary asset of the clue. The venom shown by the word play on *Wasilla*, the small Alaskan town which is home to the American Tea Party leader Sarah Palin—ALL I SAW—also has a semantic base. In this case we have to do with a special subcategory of the anagram: the reversal. An even stronger form of reversal is the palindrome, as in the NLP example DRAW PUPIL'S LIP UPWARD.

The above examples clarify the notion of flat, but they also serve as an introduction to what has become an essential part of the English cryptic crossword. The clue–answer pairs of these cryptic crosswords are generally flats. As a consequence, the English crossword is to be seen as a game playing with word forms rather than with word meanings.

41.5 Comparing the English and the Dutch crossword

This section is not an introduction to the English or Dutch crossword. There are many good introductions on how to solve cryptic crosswords.[5] Yet it is necessary here to say

[5] For the ingredients and history of the English crossword, see Amende (2001), Arnott (1981), Danesi (2002), Greeff (2003), Greer (2001), Macnutt (2001), Shortz (2006), and Skinner (1993). For the Dutch crossword, see Verschuyl (2004, 2005).

something about the history of word puzzling in the two countries, although many of the books mentioned in the footnote to this paragraph give historical information. What justifies the comparison of the English and Dutch styling of the crossword is that it sheds light on how deep the effects of certain orthographic conventions are on the notion of the word in the mental lexicon. This can be shown by reviewing in detail the semantic relations between a clue *C* and its answer *A* and the way these are handled in English and in Dutch.

41.5.1 Some history

Crossword puzzling has been popular in Britain and the Netherlands since the 1920s, but the two countries share a warming-up period before the advent of the crossword proper. Newspapers played an important role in popularizing all sorts of word puzzling, there being no puzzle magazines at the time. The majority of puzzles were flats: anagrams, charades, reversals, containers, and the like, mostly aimed at children. At the beginning of the last century, the liberal Dutch newspaper *Algemeen Handelsblad* started a special children's section on its back page called *Below the Line*, edited by Dr. Linkerhoek ('Dr Left Corner'). Children (and their parents) were entertained with language games of the sort just discussed, but also with curious slips of the tongue, amusing examples of misunderstanding, little stories and poems. The puzzle section did not appear out of the blue; at the end of the 19th century several newspapers already had sections with puzzles having a high pedagogical content. The letter puzzle in Table 41.2, for convenience transposed here into English, is quite typical of the period. The answers to the six clues are HORSE, DEAR, SHORE, SHED, HISS, and RAID, giving the solution HORSERADISH. Here, the need to spell correctly is combined with general knowledge and the basic principle of cryptography—the representation of letters by ciphers.

The Filler can be seen as a prelude to the development of forms, i.e. the two-dimensional puzzle (see Table 41.3). Only one vertical column intersects meaningfully with the horizontal lines.

Table 41.2 Letter puzzle

The whole has 11 letters and is a plant of the cabbage family	
1 2 6 10 5	animal
8 5 7 6	utterance of surprise
4 1 2 3 5	going on it from the boat may cause wet feet
10 1 5 8	small building for storage
11 9 4 10	make the sound of the 19th letter
6 7 9 8	sudden attack

Table 41.3 Filler

The middle column forms the name of an English politician

Broad silk necktie	A	S	**C**	O	T
Operetta composer	L	E	**H**	A	R
Lean and hagard because of suffering	G	A	**U**	N	T
Opera by Bellini	N	O	**R**	M	A
Person who competes in a race	R	A	**C**	E	R
Very pale with shock, fear, or illness	A	S	**H**	E	N
Animate object as distinct from a living being	T	H	**I**	N	G
Exclamation used as a greeting	H	E	**L**	L	O
Extended exchange of strokes	R	A	**L**	L	Y

On 19 December 1913, two days before Arthur Wynne published the first ever crossword puzzle in the *New York World* newspaper, the daily *Algemeen Handelsblad* published the puzzle shown in Fig. 41.1. This is very close to what was introduced by Wynne because here words are indeed crossing. The clues were given in the form of instructions going from one outside letter to the other: *Put letters in the little squares, so that you can read from* A–B: is lighted on festive occasions [LAMPION]; C–D: a magnificent building [KASTEEL (= castle)]; D–A: used by a wagoner to guide his horse [LEIDSEL (= rein)]; C–B: every girl loves to have them in her hair [KRULLEN (= curls)]; E–F: the word that is missing in: *The little thing walked… into the school alone* [PARMANTIG (=jauntily)]; G–H: is found at the bottom of a doorway [DREMPEL (= threshold)]. It is remarkable that the answers C–D, D–A, and C–B are reversed. The Dutch word corresponding to the English *castle* is *kasteel*, not **leetsak*. This sort of reversal does not normally occur in crosswords. This turns out after all not to be the first crossword, because essential for the crossword is, of course, that

A				E				B
	L	A	M	P	I	O	N	
	E			A			E	
	S			R			L	
G	D	R	E	M	P	E	L	H
	I			A			U	
	E			N			R	
	L	E	E	T	S	A	K	
D				F				C

FIG. 41.1 Proto-crossword puzzling.

given a vertical-horizontal crossing of words, adjacent rows and columns also cross. The four gaps hide a check failure.

Summarizing, one can observe that in the tradition of word puzzling at the end of the 19th and the first quarter of the 20th century, there is an increasing tendency to move from flats to forms. One may see this as a development preparing the ground for adult puzzles. Given the increased complexity of the task, crosswords appeared to be more suitable for adults than for children; in general, word puzzles for children should not take too long to solve.

41.5.2 Diverging developments

The English cryptic crossword has a high degree of flatness, in the sense that all the tricks characterizing this form of word puzzling are an essential part of what gives the English crossword its unique character. The development of the crossword in the Netherlands has focused less on flatness. This does not mean that there has been no interest in it.[6] But the Dutch lack of interest in flatness as an essential ingredient for crosswords certainly has to do with the crucial linguistic difference between the English and the Dutch crossword described in section 41.5.3.

The crossword as a form of word-puzzling made its entry in Britain in 1922. The first Dutch crossword appeared on 12 January 1925, introduced by Dr. Linkerhoek in the *Algemeen Handelsblad*. It began as a children's game but within a week it had invaded the adult world. It instantly became a hit, and practically all the dailies and weeklies started to offer crosswords (with enormous prizes) for adults. The Dutch crossword became a knowledge game at the same time that English crossword-setters were popularizing the cryptic crossword. In the late 1920s and the 1930s the English crossword developed into a game with heavy emphasis on ingenuity and beauty. The setters E. P. Powers (Torquemada), A. F. Ritchie (Afrit), and D. S. Macnutt (Ximenes) are generally considered to be the ones who established the rules determining the level of ingenuity and the criteria for beauty. In view of the discussion in section 41.3.3 about Platonic beauty, these rules constrain the game aesthetically by determining what constitutes a pleasing clue–answer pair. Meanwhile, the Dutch crossword developed into a pedagogical game centred around lexical and encyclopedic knowledge. At first sight, this difference can be explained in terms of cultural differences between the two peoples, but the story turns out to be more complex than that.

On 12 February 1949, a left-wing highbrow Dutch weekly *De Groene* ('The Green') suddenly introduced a new type of crossword called the *cryptogram* under the

[6] In 1981, the mathematician and linguist Hugo Brandt Corstius produced his brilliant book *Opperlandse taal- en letterkunde* (lit. 'Upperlandic linguistics and literature') which is unrivalled in its study of all aspects of flatness. It is still very popular (witness its extended reprint in 2002), and it certainly contributed to the decision to award to Brandt Corstius the highest literary prize in the Netherlands in 1987. So there is a good appreciation in Holland for the sense of beauty in flats.

label: 'Finally the crossword puzzle has become adult.' This clearly was an attempt to transplant the English cryptic crossword as a new, more sophisticated variant of the existing knowledge-based crossword which was (and still is) popular in Holland. The enthusiastic explanation of the new puzzle form in *De Groene* reads like an introduction to the English cryptic crossword. Newspapers followed suit, and so for a couple of years the Dutch and English cryptic crosswords resembled each other quite closely.

However, the Dutch cryptogram gradually began to distinguish itself from its English counterpart by becoming more and more semantics-based. The difference turns out to be determined not only culturally but also linguistically, and is possibly due to the leading setter of the 1950s and the following decades, H. A. Scheltes (1921–1987). He started with anagrams and other tricks familiar from the basic stock of English cryptic techniques, but quite soon moved on to open up the domain of compounds for the cryptic crossword. As a by-product the answers started to increase in length, because a compound may occur as part of a larger compound written as one orthographic word. This increase in complexity and length continued in later decades, and at present is one of the hallmarks of the Dutch cryptogram. This process made it possible for the cryptic crossword to become more and more semantic. The explanation is quite straightforward: one-word compounds allow for more independent relations between parts of the clue and parts of the answer than is the case with simple words.

41.5.3 Cryptogrammar

Whatever the differences between the English and Dutch cryptic crosswords, there is one thing they have in common: a semantic relation between the clue *C* and the answer *A*. Without it, the game would be impossible. We have already noted that there is a certain directionality in this relation, from D(efinition) to H(eadword), as discussed in section 41.3.1. This relation implies that the more general D term in *C* should lead to a more specific or at least a synonymous H term in *A*. The pair *C* = *Alternative number first by a singer* (5)—*A* = TENOR fulfils this requirement because the set of alternatives contains options expressed by words like *or, dilemma, possibility, choice*, etc., and because *ten* is included in the set of numbers, not the reverse.

In logical semantics, it is quite usual to treat meanings as sets (pictured by circles). For example, the set of tenors is properly included in the set of singers, so this inclusion relation can be used to relate the meaning of the noun *tenor* to the meaning of the noun *singer. Tenor* is a hyponym of *singer*—as long as the inclusion relation between the set of tenors and the set of singers is taken to hold. Not all meaning relations are based on inclusion, but the use of circles makes it possible to deal with that fact too, as we shall see shortly. They also make it possible to chart the four possible logical semantic relations which can exist between words.

41.5.4 Semantic relations between clue and answer

Verschuyl (2004) proposed representing the semantic relation between clue and answers as an I (represented pictorially as a vertical straight line), with the clue *C* on top of the I and the answer *A* at the bottom. This I connects the clue and answer on the basis of four logically possible relations between the circles A and C, shown in Fig. 41.2. The circles represent what falls under the meanings of *A* and *C* and their intersection contains information about what is shared by them. Thus, Fig. 41.2a represents a situation in which *C* is synonymous with *A*, as in the pair *C* = *shut* and *A* = CLOSE. The synonymy relation holds if and only if all things that shut also close, and conversely if all things that are closed are also shut. It is generally assumed that it is practically impossible to find two perfect synonyms (see Fellbaum, this volume). This is presumably why the *OED* hedges the definition of a synonym as a word having exactly the same or nearly the same meaning as another word.

The relation in Fig. 41.2b is that of inclusion. *Accountant* is a hyponym of *human* (as long as there are no robots doing the job; in that case, there would be members of A outside C, which would make Fig. 41.2c the proper semantic relation between the two words). In a dictionary, proper inclusion constitutes the stable semantic relation between a Headword H and the general term in the definition D: a chair is a seat which . . ., a puzzle is a game which . . ., an accountant is a person who . . ., etc. They all fit the scheme: an A is a C, where *A* is the hyponym of *C* and *C* is a hyperonym of *A*. Hyponymy is an important means for providing structure in the mental lexicon by making it possible to get from more specific to more general information. The full meaning of a word *A* can be understood as the set of circles $C_1, C_2, \ldots, C_n$ containing A.

The best term to label the overlap in Fig. 41.2c seems to be *contingency*, in the philosophical sense of something being a fact without having to be so. Many accountants are certified, that is, they are officially recognized as meeting some expertness criterion. But there are also accountants who are not certified. This excludes *certified* from being a hyperonym of *accountant*, which makes the semantic relation weaker than the one in Fig. 41.2b. If certification is mandatory in a country, the pair *certified* and *accountant* would fall under Fig. 41.2b as in the case of *university graduate* and *holder of a doctorate*. In many contingency relations, the position of circle A is not fixed with respect to C

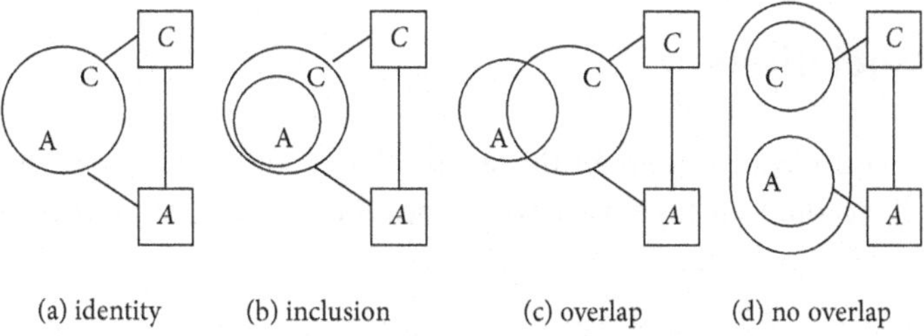

FIG. 41.2 Four logical possibilities of relating lexical meaning.

and so one can see the intersection as varying between containing nearly all and nearly no members of A. If one were to move the circle A in Fig. 41.2c more to the left up to the point where say, 95 per cent of A is outside C, the semantic relation would become very weak. This could apply, for example, to the pair *freckled-black-haired*, as opposed to *freckled-red-haired*, where the intersection would be larger. On the other hand, if there are situations in which *shut* and *close* are not really synonyms and the pair $C = shut$ and $A =$ CLOSE would have, say, a 95 per cent, overlap, then Fig. 41.2c also applies, but with a tendency to ignore the 5 per cent so as to land either in Fig. 41.2a or in Fig. 41.2b. We will see that Fig. 41.2c is an interesting category in word puzzling.

Moving circle A out of C in Fig. 41.2c could continue up to the point where the intersection between A and C is the empty set. This yields the situation pictured in Fig. 41.2d. It covers pairs like *girl–boy, dog–cat*, but also *chair–dog, centaur–amazon, yes–no, pedal–bike*, etc. Given this enumeration, Fig. 41.2d would become a heterogeneous garbage can. The first step to remedy this deficiency is to place an oval O in (d) providing a superset standing for a property that connects A and C in some way: *girl* and *boy* are in opposition given a proper domain in which this opposition holds. This could be a binary opposition as in the case of *male* vs. *female* (with O = sex), or *girl* vs. *boy* (with O = young human beings). In this way, Fig. 41.2d can cover various kinds of complementarity relation such as negation, contrast, or contradiction.

We still face the question of how to deal with non-complementary pairs like *pedal–bike, weather–cheerful, Friday–fish*. At this point it should be observed that the circles in Fig. 41.2 pertain to sets and sets contain elements that can be counted. The relation between *loaf* and *bread* cannot be captured as a hyponymy relation because the word *bread* is a mass noun. (The relation, instead, is one of meronymy; see Fellbaum, this volume.) Furthermore, sets contain elements of the same ontological kind. This makes it impossible to have Fridays and fishes as members of the same set.

There are two possible ways of solving this problem. One is to appeal to the part-of relation (*pedal–bike, loaf–bread, nose–body*) and to construct a set of relations parallel to those in Fig. 41.2.[7] The other is to keep Fig. 41.2 and ask how it can deal with associations which play such an important role in retrieving knowledge stored in the mental lexicon. We will see that this second option renders the first unnecessary, and also that it contributes to our understanding of one of the essential ingredients of the English cryptic crossword, namely, associations.

41.5.5 Associations

Consider the connections between the words *Friday* and *fish, school* and *cane, bible* and *church*. To account for them we have to appeal to associations rather than to stable

[7] The part-of relation has received a lot of attention in psycholinguistics following Miller and Johnson-Laird (1976) (see e.g. Margolis and Laurence 1999), as well as in logical semantics (e.g. the study of mereological structure in Link 1998).

semantic relations of the type displayed in Fig. 41.2a and 41.2b. Strictly speaking, they should all fall under Fig. 41.2d, because their intersection is the empty set. But, as said earlier, it is not even possible for the pair *Friday–fish* to fall under Fig. 41.2d because *Friday* denotes a set of abstract temporal units and the set of fishes contains concrete objects.

If we look for an appropriate oval set O containing both items, we need to find a common factor which puts them fully or partly in O. A plausible commonality is a set C of situations in which Fridays occur and situations in which fish occurs, so that a comparison between A and C can be made at the same level of abstraction. In this particular case, these could be situations in which it is Friday and situations in which fish occurs on the menu. If it turns out that fish is eaten only on Fridays, Fig. 41.2b would apply, but as soon as fish is eaten on other days than Friday, we find ourselves with the situation in Fig. 41.2c. When the Catholic Church used to be a more dominant force in ruling the daily life of families, the association between Friday and fish was much stronger than it is nowadays; the intersection between A and C was much larger. To take another example: Dutch speakers have a quite strong association between the football club Ajax and the colours red and white. The set containing football clubs and the set containing the colours red and white are too different for them to have a possible overlap. So the next step is to think of situations in which one obtains information about Ajax (by watching matches, by reading about them, and so on) and situations in which the combination of red and white is being experienced. In this way, we end up once again with Fig. 41.2c. The strength of the association in Holland is determined by the dominant position of the club in football competitions, an evident counterforce being that in away matches the players are not allowed to wear their red and white colours.[8]

This account rests on the same foundation as the theory of generalized quantification, which analyses the contribution of determiners and adverbials to sentence meaning. Thus the meaning of *all* can be seen in terms of connecting a set A with another set C, so that all members of A are fully contained in C (*All Advocates are Clever*), whereas the meaning of *some* indicates that the intersection of A and C in Fig. 41.2c contains at least some members (*Some Advocates are Clever*). Similarly, the meanings of *always* and *sometimes* can be understood in terms of the intersection of sets of situations. *Practically none* is a determiner which tells us that the intersection between A and C is nearly empty apart from negligibly few elements. And so on. For the study of the linguistic nature of associations, the theory of generalized quantification turns out to be quite relevant to Fig. 41.2c.[9]

[8] The construal of sets of situations brings the analysis of lexical meaning into the domain of what is known as event semantics, with its study of quantification over eventualities. There is an abundant philosophical, logical, and linguistic literature on this topic. See e.g. Bach (1981), Barwise and Perry (1983), Davidson (1980), Landman (2000), Lasersohn (1995).

[9] There is a huge literature on generalized quantification. See e.g. Barwise and Cooper (1981), van Benthem and ter Meulen (1984), van Benthem and Westerståhl (1995), Peters and Westerståhl (2006).

The notion of association is flexible enough to capture the relation between the count noun *loaf* and the mass noun *bread*. The situations in which we use the word *loaf* overlap with the situations in which the word *bread* is relevant. However, there are situations in which loaves are not bread and situations in which there is bread without there being loaves. The intersection of the two sets of situations again matches Fig. 41.2c. The configuration in Fig. 41.2d also turns out to be the first step in capturing a part-of relation. Birds have limbs, so a limb is part of a bird. This provides a strong associative oval, as it also does with *pedal* and *bike*, and with *treadler* and *organ*. It is clear that the set of limbs is disjoint from the set of birds, but in some way the oval part-of relation has much in common with the hyponymy relation in Fig. 41.2b or with the overlap relation in Fig. 41.2c: it provides strong ties between two words given the construal of situations. The fact that always when one sees a tiger one sees stripes makes it possible to consider striped as a semantic property of the noun *tiger*. Due to the intersection of sets of situations in which one sees tigers and in which one sees stripes, this relation has the same sort of strength as the hyponymy relation between two sets of countable entities.

Summarizing, it seems that for connecting the meanings of two words in a language one can appeal to the set of situations in which the referent of one word occurs and the set of situations in which the second word can apply. This also determines the logical consequences of the relation. One may not conclude from a situation in which someone is whistling that this is tuneful. This will be the case only in some situations. Associations evoked by puzzle makers are legitimized by what puzzlers have experienced in real-life situations as connections obeying one of the configurations in Fig. 41.2. In this respect, the present logical-semantic analysis ties in with psycholinguistic research into word association, semantic priming, and lexical retrieval (De Deyne and Storms, this volume; Neely 1977; Nickerson 2011).

41.5.6 Cryptotypes

In the preceding section, the relation between a clue *C* and its answer *A* was pictorially taken as an I. As soon as there are two I's in a clue–answer pair, there are four logical possibilities for connecting them, as shown in Fig. 41.3. The first is the H-type (where the dashed line stands for the connection between two compounding elements). An example is the pair *C* = *principal route* (7); *A* = HEADWAY. Here there is an I-connection between *principal* and *head* and a second I-connection between *route* and *way*. For another example, we could split the *A* PECCABLE into PEC and CABLE and construct a complex clue *C* in which the chest muscle denoted by *pec(toral)* is associated with the strength expressed by *cable*. Another one is: *C* = *Circle an island* (4); *A* = OMAN. It is also easy to recognize the pair *C* = *Alternative number; A* = TENOR as an instance of the H-type. In Dutch, this is a very popular type of *C–A* pair. One of Scheltes's nicest examples was *C* = *Er is een Brit teveel* (lit. 'There is one Briton too many'); *A* = OVERSCHOT 'surplus.' Dutch *over* means '(There is) too many' while *Schot* is the Dutch word for *Scot*.

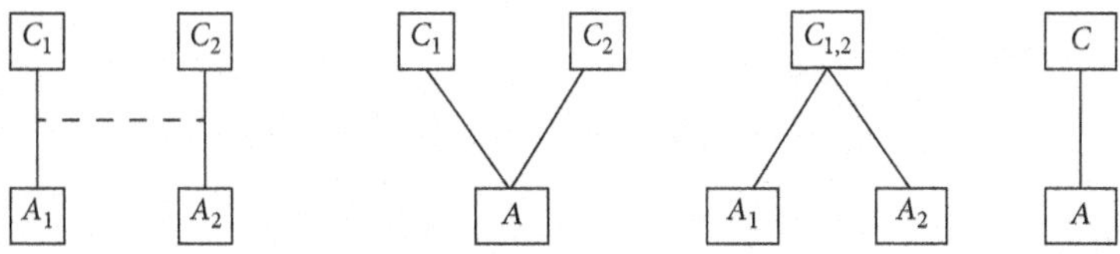

FIG. 41.3 Four logical possibilities of connecting two I's.

If there is a Briton too many, there is automatically a surplus. This makes it a better clue than *Circle an island* because Oman has to do neither with an island nor with a circle.

The second type in Fig. 41.3 is the V-type. For English we have: C = *Tuneful American painter* (8); A = WHISTLER, or *Summing up to 18* (5); A = SIGMA. In the latter case, *sigma* is to be identified both as the 18th letter of the Greek alphabet and as the mathematical summation sign. For Dutch we have C = *Vogelmest* (lit. 'bird's manure') (4); A = GIER 'vulture' or 'slurries'. The V-type is based on the ambiguity of A. Dutch *gier* means 'vulture,' which according to (1b) leads to C_1 *vogel* 'bird'; *gier* also means 'manure', which in Dutch leads to the hyperonym *mest* in C_2.

The third type in Fig. 41.3 is the A-type. It is the reverse of the V-type. However, recall that in word puzzling there is the Definition-to-Head-order, which means that the answer is in most cases a hyponym of the clue or at best a synonym. The direction from C to A is from general to specific. So the A-type is an unnatural one and it hardly occurs. This is also the reason why Fig. 41.2 does not consider the situation in which C is a subset of A. A possible instantiation in English would be C = *key* (6,4); A = *master plot* on the basis of (near-)synonymy. In Dutch the clue could be *gier* and the answer *vogelmest*. As has been pointed out, this doesn't work well because of the wrong direction from Head to Definition. The fourth type in Fig. 41.3 is a simple I.

With I as a basic building block, a simple H and a simple V may combine into a 2:1-type, as shown (in simplified form) in Fig. 41.4: C = *doubly evil sailor;* A = SINBAD. In C it is easy to recognize the H: *evil* has an I-relation to *sin* and (doubly!) *evil* has an I-relation to *bad*. From *sailor* there is one I connecting C to SINBAD, the well-known sailor in the Arabian fairy tale. The complex type consisting of three I-relations between Clue and Answer can be seen as an H with its right arm functioning as the left arm of a V with a 2:1 structure.[10]

A more linguistic example is C = *Listen to a number makes more confident;* A = HEARTEN. *Hear ten* forms an H and *Makes more confident* is connected to the answer as an I constituting the right arm of V. The clue C = *XI ay 100* occurring in Balfour (2004), a fascinating book about how important it is for immigrants to master crossword puzzling as a part of their assimilation, is a 1:2-type. The clue part *XI* leads to the number 11 which is the number of players in a football team (in this particular case the well-known English major league club *Everton*), the part *ay* occurs in the expression

[10] Verschuyl (2004) provides a type-logical grammar for the recursion involved; it is possible to extend the complex types H and V into more complex types by simply adding a basic type I.

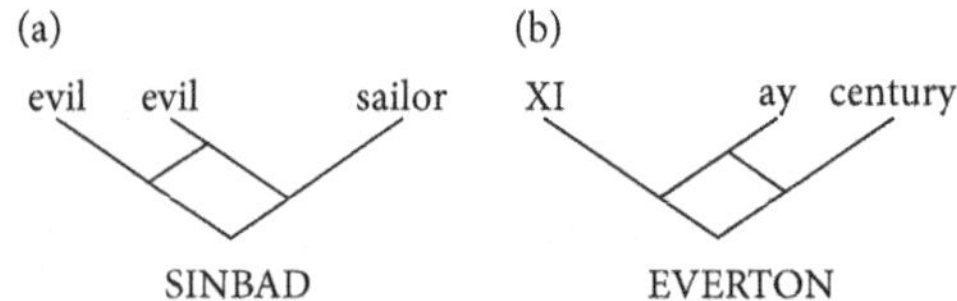

FIG. 41.4 Two complex types: (a) 2:1 and (b) 1:2.

For EVER *and ay*, and in cricket 100 stands for a century. A century scored is often referred to as a TON. In this way, the answer is composed on the basis of the I-pairing *XI*–EVERTON and the H-pairing *ay* + *100*—EVER+TON.

At this point it should be observed that on the typology given so far, English *C–A* relations do not deviate very much from those in Dutch. But if we now introduce as a factor the complexity of an answer, the way is open for more complex relations. The 2:3 type is a typically Dutch one. *C* = *Daar liggen de spruitjes te slapen* (10) (lit: 'There lie the sprouts to sleep'); *A* = GROENTEBED (lit: VEGETABLE BED or GREEN IN BED). The left arm of V has a binary split: *de spruitjes* + *daar liggen te slapen* = GROENTE + BED, whereas its right arm is parsed as: *Daar* + *de spruitjes* + *liggen te slapen* corresponds to TE + GROEN + BED. Another very nice one is: *C* = *Zij vermaken anderen daar met blunders* (9); A = ERFLATERS 'testators.' In Dutch, the unambiguous word *erflater* is composed of *erf* (from the verb *erven* 'inherit') and *later* (from the verb *laten* 'bequeath, let'). In its plural form *erflaters* allows for another parsing into *er* 'there' and *flaters*, which is the plural form of *flater* 'blunder.' Hence the task in *C* = *They amuse others there with blunders*. But the Dutch verb *vermaken* is ambiguous: it means 'amuse, entertain,' but also 'bequeath.' Here we are at the heart of what makes the Dutch cryptic crossword cryptic, with the possibilities offered by compounding, puns, and different parsings being important semantic instruments.

Verschuyl (2005) randomly sampled a large number of crossword diagrams made by different setters for both English and Dutch. For English, the average word length of *A* in Gilbert (1993), Skinner (1993), Greer (2001), and Greeff (2003) is around five letters. The same applies to American crosswords (e.g. Shortz 2006), and to the French cryptic 'mots croisés.' For Dutch, by contrast, diagrams set by the most important weeklies and dailies (most of them presenting cryptic crosswords just once a week as opposed to the simple crosswords which appear daily) have a much higher average length. At present, the average word length of Dutch cryptic crosswords has nearly doubled as compared with the average in 1950/1960, which was then comparable with the current average of the English, American, and French answers: between 5 and 6 letters per word. It is not unusual to have one-word answers in Dutch consisting of more than 15 letters. They often contain a pun, as in *C* = *Paris & Helena; A* = SCHAAKLIEFHEBBERS. The Dutch verb *schaken* is ambiguous between 'play chess' and 'abduct.' If you know that Paris abducted Helen and that they were lovers, then in *schaakliefhebbers* 'chess lovers' the ambiguity of *schaken* appears unexpectedly in the compound. Or in: *C* = *Het onderscheid tussen goud, zilver en brons* 'the difference between gold, silver and bronze'; *A* = PRIJSVERSCHIL 'difference in price.' Dutch *prijs* is ambiguous between English *price* and *prize*. The compound *A*, however, is normally used without this ambiguity, but given *C* it suddenly appears to the puzzle-solver as a possible but highly unusual use of the compound.

41.5.7 The real difference

Fig. 41.3 contains straight lines because they fit Figs 41.2a and 41.2b. In that sense, they meet the requirements of the Platonic ideal forms. However, Platonic beauty suffers from the menace of predictability and boredom. The empirical fact is that some people prefer associations to stable semantic relations between words. It is also a fact that there are really nice examples of associative clue–answer pairs, illustrated in Fig. 41.5. The H-type suffers from a weak semantic relation between *aarzeling* 'hesitation' and *twee* 'two', whereas the Dutch word *strijd* 'battle' denotes a sort of fighting (*gevecht*). Indeed, it is certainly permitted in English to connect the word *hesitation* with *double* or *two*, but semantically the relation between clue and answer falls under Fig. 41.2c.

The dots between *flat* and *raft* express the weak form of the relation displayed in Fig. 41.2c: the situations in which one experiences flats overlap hardly at all with situations in which rafts occur. The semantic relation between *raft* and *float(er)* is more stable. Other examples of dot-relations are the left arm of the 2:1 V-type consisting of the *C* = *Keep in office* and *A* = RE-ELECT. In both arms of the V there is only a weak association in the pairs *keep*-RE and *office*-ELECT.

The 2:1-type at the right side in Fig. 41.5 is helpful for understanding an essential feature of the English crossword: the mixing of object language and metalanguage. *Hat* and *pipe* are used in the language to talk about hats and pipes. Italics indicate that we are talking about the words *hat* and *pipe*. Setters do not make the distinction, in order to mislead. This brings up the semantic relation in Fig. 41.2d; there is no overlap between the set of hats H and the set HL = {a,h,t} of letters forming the word *hat*. The same applies to the set P of pipes and the set PL = {e, i, p} of letters from which the word *pipe* is constructed. One has to ignore the difference between a set S and its name *S* and construe a set HL + PL which is identical to the set of letters making up a hyponym for 'things that can be found in a cemetery'.

For non-linguists, this formulation is a horror, but it reflects precisely what is happening. The identity relation involves the metalinguistic level. In *Rat must emerge from the rock layer* the clue presents *Rat must* (misleadingly) in the object language, but in fact it

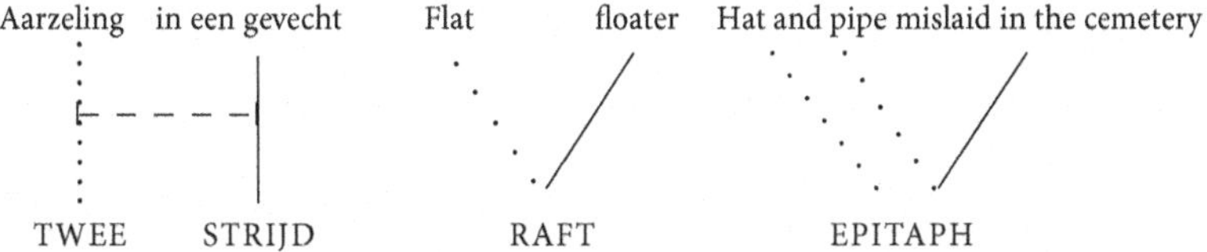

FIG. 41.5 Weak semantic relations.

is an anagram of the *A* = STRATUM at the metalevel. Identity is found in the (meagre) semantics of the metalinguistic level in which two word forms in *C* are identical to one word form in *A*, their meaning relation being reduced to having exactly the same number of letters. At the metalevel, the proper noun *New York* can be seen as identical to *NY*. The same holds for the relation between *C* = ... one ... and the letter *I* in the pair *C* = *One fled the country; A* = IRAN. This metalinguistic relation between word forms falls under Fig. 41.2a under the label of (form-)identity.

In summary, we can see what English-speaking crossword puzzlers do. Constrained by the ideal of one spaceless word per answer, they have a preference for (dotted) associations. The Dutch are more interested in complex semantic I-relations matching Fig. 41.2a and 41.2b, puns, and unexpected reparsing included.

41.6 Conclusion

From a linguistic point of view, it seems possible to explain some of the differences between cryptic crossword puzzling in the two languages with different orthographic conventions. One can see that the notion of a word in English-speaking countries is heavily influenced by the written appearance of words as surrounded by spaces. English speakers know that a compound counts as a word, but they react differently. One telling example is that when Nickerson (2011) made a list of English palindromes he reached the number of 66. But they are all simplex words in the sense that they do not have internal spacing or hyphens. A list of palindromes in Dutch would include considerably more items because compounds like *parterretrap* 'ground floor staircase' and *parterreserretrap* 'ground floor veranda staircase' are taken as one unspaced word.

In terms of the four options in Fig. 41.2, one could say that the English crossword puzzle operates in the two right-hand configurations Fig. 41.2c and 41.2d, whereas the Dutch counterpart is more open to inclusion and identity as the determining relations. This is why the H-type and the V-type have manifested themselves in the Dutch way of crossword puzzling, because the way compounds are taken in Dutch facilitates not only the simple H- and V-types but also the more complex types in Fig. 41.4.

A FINAL WORD

CHAPTER 42

WHY ARE WE SO SURE WE KNOW WHAT A WORD IS?

ALISON WRAY

42.1 Introduction: the troublesome notion of 'word'

JULIEN (2006: 617) comments that there is something strange at the heart of our conception of 'word'.[1] Despite Hockett's (1987: 3) reassurance that 'everybody knows what a word is', it has proved extraordinarily difficult for linguists to settle on descriptions and definitions that pin it down entirely satisfactorily. In this chapter I want to explore why that is, and what seems to be happening to the notion of word in current linguistics.

It is not that we should be particularly concerned with definitions *per se*, because one can know something without being able to alight on a complete definition of it (cf. Wray 2002, 2008a, 2009). But definitions cannot be entirely dodged. In many contexts where it is important to understand what has been claimed or discovered in relation to language, the devil will be in the detail of what someone actually meant when they referred to something as a word.

My primary aim is to examine whether the word is difficult to pin down because it is inherently vague or only because we look at it in a manner that makes it seem so. When an entity defies easy description or definition, it may mean that there is not much to grasp hold of, or that there is too much to take in. I will develop the case for the word being an inherently vague phenomenon, one that looks more solid and more clear-cut

[1] I am grateful to Dick Hudson, Peter Matthews, and John Taylor for gracious and constructive comments on a previous draft of this chapter. I have no doubt left in many things that they might wish I had removed, and failed to add details they felt important. Nevertheless I believe that the revised version has benefited in significant ways from their insights.

than it is because of the domination of a strong prototype (the noun) and of a cultural practice (writing).

42.1.1 Why does it matter what the word is?

There are several reasons why it matters that we understand what the word is. Within linguistics itself there is naturally a requirement that beliefs and assumptions are refreshed in the light of new evidence and theories. More broadly, ideas about wordness that people deploy in their various domains of activity can heavily impact on what they are able to achieve. In foreign language teaching, for instance, if teacher and students believe that languages can be learned by memorizing lists of words and then combining them using grammatical rules, that belief will influence how they go about their respective tasks and how success in learning is measured. For example, a standard way of assessing second-language proficiency is to estimate a learner's vocabulary size. Such measures do have value—vocabulary size does tend to increase with proficiency, and one will normally manage a lot better if one knows a lot of words and not much grammar than the other way round. But there is more to learning a language than learning the words. It is deceptively easy to compile lists of vocabulary for memorization as isolated units, and renownedly difficult to combine the items idiomatically later (Pawley and Syder 1983; Wray 2002). Curiously, though, while language-teaching materials focused on supporting the learning of larger units than words have been available for more than twenty years (e.g. Lewis 1993; Willis 1990), there remains a strong sense for most teachers and learners that the word is the core unit of language. Could this perception be at least part of the explanation for the difficulties that adults typically face in mastering a new language?

The nature of the word is of importance in clinical contexts too. In the diagnosis of acquired communication disorders such as aphasia and Alzheimer's disease, language is often a primary source of the clinician's information about a person's condition. Clinical tests of language are constructed on the basis of the beliefs and assumptions of the designer—ones that may not be entirely in keeping with the latest accounts of language. Thus, Balota and Yap (2006: 649) state, 'Research at the word level is particularly tractable and revealing as words are well-defined units that can be analysed and processed at various levels.' Yet, as this chapter will demonstrate, words are anything but well defined. In addition, it is commonplace for tests of language disability to elicit responses composed of a single (orthographic) word, e.g. through naming tasks. It is not that such tests don't measure anything useful, for they clearly do. However, characteristically, little is asked about how a person's responses in such tests correspond to the rather different challenges of real interaction (Wray 2008b). Elements of language tested in isolation inform us primarily about only those elements—in isolation. Yet, as we shall see, words are so far from isolated in real use that some linguists have challenged their capacity to be defined autonomously at all.

A further issue in diagnostic tests regards the selection of particular types of word as representative. For entirely understandable reasons, it is easier to construct a test around the meanings of concrete nouns and action verbs than around items with more abstract meanings, or words like *of* and *the*. What status, then, do the latter have, and how generalizable to them are findings using the former? Later, it will be proposed that there is a clear reason why concrete nouns and verbs are selected for tests, and that there are indeed important sacrifices in modelling linguistic capacity only on what can be done with such words.

42.1.2 Doubt about the reliability of 'word' as a concept

In the comparative linguistic domain, assumptions about the universality of wordhood crumble almost as soon as they are tested beyond the narrow domain of European languages (Dixon and Aikhenvald 2002a). Even the very idea that all languages have words has been questioned (p. 32) and 'it appears that only some languages actually have a lexeme with the meaning 'word' (p. 2)—though see Goddard's chapter (this volume) for discussion of that assertion. But even in the context of a single language like English, there is a problem with what a word is: the definition required for operating in one domain is different from that in another. It is mysterious that quite so much trouble should be caused by taking a different viewpoint on what, one might have supposed, was the same thing in the end.

We shall see that there are further complications too, and it may seem that John Sinclair's view—that 'the word is not the principal unit of meaning in a language' (Sinclair 2010: 37) or even that 'the word alone is not a unit of language' (Lew 2010: 757)—is inescapable. But if so, what of Hockett? Is he not right as well? We patently *do* feel that we know what a word is. So where do those powerful intuitions about the word come from? As Sapir (1921: 35) put it, 'What, then, is the objective criterion of the word? The speaker and hearer feel the word, let us grant, but how shall we justify their feeling?'

42.2 What happens when we try to pin down the concept 'word'?

Linguists, in trying to capture and account for observations relating to the domains of meaning, pronunciation, and grammar, as well as the cognitive processing of words, have solved the problem of definition by focusing on the particular element that concerns them. Trask (2004)[2] itemizes ten or more word-like units that linguists describe,

[2] Although it is an informal piece published only (as far as I know) on the internet, Trask's is a deliberate choice for the present purpose, being an accessible attempt by a linguist of standing to explain the different ways in which words can be defined. Others also cover this matter, including Dixon and Aikhenvald (2002a), Julien (2006), and Hanks (2013), all much-cited in this chapter, though comprehensive sets of definitions seem surprisingly rare, with a tendency, rather, for analysts to define only the unit relevant to their interests. My purpose in examining the types collectively is to note where

of which a subset, largely comprising his main categories, will form the basis of some discussion here.[3]

The ***orthographic word***, the unit we write with a space either side, is intrinsically the easiest to identify and work with, notwithstanding a few uncertainties around hyphenation.[4] As will become clear, it is a powerful player in the overall definition of word, even though the location of written word boundaries is not entirely regular, and carries with it some measure of historical baggage. The ***phonological word*** is demarcated in terms of features like the number or location of stresses, vowel harmony, phonological configurations reliably associated with the start or end of the unit, and so on (see Hildebrandt, this volume). A number of orthographic words therefore will not count as phonological words (e.g. unstressed articles and prepositions—see 'clitics' below). The phonological word is a more troublesome category than the orthographic word. For one thing, speech is far less stable than writing. For another, in continuous speech, each instantiation will be a little different from the last. And although words in isolation have rather different features from those they have within longer utterances, it will be tempting to characterize phonological words outwith a usage context. As a result, there is a risk that the phonological word becomes contaminated by features more appropriately attributed to the orthographic word pronounced.

Trask defines the ***lexical item*** (or ***lexeme***) as 'an abstract unit of the lexicon (vocabulary) of a language, with a more or less discernible meaning or function'. Being abstract, 'it must be represented in speech or writing by one of the possibly several forms it can assume for grammatical purposes' (p. 3). By 'various forms' he means at least the immediate set of inflected realizations of the lexeme, such as singular and plural and the various tenses of a verb and cases of a (pro)noun or adjective. By calling the lexical item 'a word in the sense in which a dictionary contains words' (p. 3),[5] Trask seems, though, to exclude the wider word family, the 'group ... of words which share the same root and are semantically related, e.g. *vision, visualize, visual, visually,*

there are potential issues around the boundaries that do not surface when definitions are distributed in this way.

[3] Trask begins by stating that there are 4 main definitions of word, but the paper goes on to list them under 9 main headings, perhaps due to an error in the use of sub-headings. My best interpretation is that he intended the following 4 as main types: orthographic, phonological, lexical items, and short forms, with lexical items subdivided into: citation forms, grammatical word-forms, inflections and derivations, multi-part and discontinuous words, content words, grammatical words (i.e. function words—see note 6), and clitics. Since my own aim is not taxonomic, I have homed in on the types of most interest to the present discussion, ignoring short forms entirely and drawing out grammatical word forms and clitics for special mention.

[4] When searching for text computationally, one has to remember that punctuation marks are also markers of word-ends. However, with the exception of the hyphen, which blurs the word boundary question in any case, punctuation marks are followed by a space. Thus, although one will not want to count the punctuation mark as part of the word, it also need not be viewed as an alternative marker of the word boundary.

[5] In his 2007 manuscripts, Sinclair had abandoned the term 'lexical item' 'because it is associated with dictionaries rather than structures' (Cheng et al. 2009).

visualization' (Pellicer-Sánchez 2013: 6128; see also Nation's chapter, this volume, on word families.).

There has been extensive discussion over the years about how highly inflecting languages like Latin, and, even more so, agglutinating languages like Turkish and Zulu, should be captured in descriptions of the lexical item, since the set of potential forms will proliferate well beyond what any dictionary could list, leaving the boundary between what is lexis and what is grammar difficult to locate (cf. Jackendoff 2002). The answer is probably different for the descriptive linguist than it is for the psycholinguist. Models of processing are tied into models of how grammar operates on lexis in practice, with emergent models of grammar, like Construction Grammar (Goldberg 2003, 2006), rendering it possible that not all of the theoretically allowable realizations of a lexical item have equal status. Some may be completely lexicalized forms in their own right, some may be privileged frames into which a limited number of variations can be inserted, while others will need to be constructed from scratch (Wray 2002: 268–269). The basis on which these different configurations arise will be that of precedent in input (i.e. frequency) linked with function, salience, etc.—the same principles that privilege some multi-word strings as lexical items in their own right (Wray 2002, 2008). For one study arguing this in the context of Turkish, see Durrant (2013).

Trask's ***grammatical wordform***, 'one of the several forms that may be assumed by a lexical item for grammatical purposes' (p. 4), is the unit that most linguists term the 'grammatical word':[6] 'an entity that is located between morphemes and phrases in the structural hierarchy' (Julien 2006: 618) and that 'shows independent distribution and internal cohesion' (p. 623). The other type of particular importance in Trask's inventory is the ***clitic***, which 'leans' phonologically on another item. It is 'an item which represents a lexical item and a grammatical wordform but which does not make a phonological word by itself' (Trask 2004: 8). Examples include function words like infinitive *to* and reduced forms like *n't* in English and 'fused' words like *du* (*de* + *le*) and *aux* (*à* + *les*) in French. There are reasons both to view the clitic as word-like, and not to (see later). The trouble that clitics cause for analysts is well exemplified in the discussions in Dixon and Aikhenvald's (2002b) collection, including Matthews' (2002: 275) admission that '"clitic" is the [unit] that leaves me most confused.' Julien (2006: 622) states, 'the question of whether clitics are words or not does not have a definite answer.'

Trask does not consider those phonological entities that mark hesitation (e.g. *er, um*), physical reflexes (e.g. *oops, ouch*), and emotional expressions (e.g. *uh-huh, uh-uh, ah-hah, oo-er*). These items are language-specific and context-sensitive, so it is clear that

[6] Trask does use the term 'grammatical word' too, but, like various others, including Hunston (2008: 272), means by it the 'small words' or function words, which have 'little or no identifiable meaning, but . . . one or more grammatical functions' (p. 4). In a nutshell, his 'grammatical words' and 'content words' jointly constitute the set of his 'grammatical wordforms.' For clarity, I will use the term 'function word' when referring to Trask's 'grammatical word.'

they are culturally transmitted. There are also predictable patterns to their usage. Yet they are in some ways peculiar, relative to other word types:[7]

- they are resistant to paraphrasing;
- they are phonologically autonomous, can be surrounded by pauses, and can bear stress (hence are phonological words);
- on the other hand, their phonetic realizations can be quite variable (within limits);
- although their distribution is not unrestricted, they do not fall into any of the main grammatical classes and do not enter into syntactic relations with other items;
- they lack fully conventionalized spelling;
- the emotional expressions, though not the hesitation ones, can carry very distinctive intonational patterns.

Trask also does not mention swearwords (cf. Burridge, this volume). We can recognize two basic motivations for using swearwords. For many people they are simply part of the general vocabulary, taking on a role similar to that of fillers and pronominals, as well as nouns, verbs, and adjectives. Here, swearing is essentially a social choice, tied to identity, power, and attitude (Jay 2000: 146ff.). Swearwords as vocabulary add little to our understanding of the nature of the word because they are just additional examples of existing categories. But their use as spontaneous expressions of emotion pushes the boundaries of the definition of the word, for they occupy a grey zone in terms of their core nature and their usage. Since swearing is a noticeable feature of some post-brain damage conditions and some developmental disorders, such as Tourette's syndrome, many researchers have proposed that swearing is a reflex normally subject to an inhibitory mechanism but impeded in these conditions. Since the mid-19th century there has also been a theory that swearwords are a product of cortical and subcortical structures in the right hemisphere of the brain (Jay 2000: 41).

Where does this plethora of descriptions of the word leave us? In the context of description itself there is really no problem with simply acknowledging that words individually and collectively have different characteristics that are more or less relevant to the different tasks that we might undertake. But there is, nevertheless, some sort of hierarchy to them when it comes to explaining our intuitions about what a word is. It will be proposed below that some features draw our eye more than others, and that it is not always easy to tell just why that is the case. Moreover, some interesting puzzles arise at the interface of the different techniques now available for tracking the nature and behaviour of words.

42.3 Our intuition about the word

Which of the types of word described above is closest to what we intuitively consider to be a word, and why? Trask's 'lexical item' is the most abstract and all-encompassing

[7] I am grateful to John Taylor for the observations that follow.

word-like unit in the externalized language. If we combine his definition with Jackendoff's (2002: 30)—'an item stored in the lexicon, i.e. in long-term memory'[8] —can we infer that it is this entity, whether social or mental, that underlies our intuition about what a word is? If so, we might wonder why it is realized differently across phonology, grammar, and semantics. In proposing his own conception of what the lexicon contains, Jackendoff (2002: 30) acknowledges that the lexical item does not map consistently onto any of the other unit types outlined above: 'lexical items may be bigger or smaller than grammatical words; not all grammatical words are lexical items; more controversially, there are rather complex lexical items that contain no phonological material.'[9]

Our intuition, if based on the lexical item, would, then, have to accommodate in some way the complexity of its relationship with our phonological, grammatical, and orthographic observations. The result would be that our intuitions were themselves made complex. Yet they seem relatively simple. So, should we perhaps look elsewhere for an explanation of our intuitions?

Some have supposed that it is the grammatical wordform that lies at the heart of our intuition (Julien 2006: 619), this being the unit that is manipulated to create new utterances. In contrast, the phonological word is generally viewed as a rather unlikely candidate, on account of its failure reliably to map onto grammar and semantics: 'if a string of linguistic elements can be identified as a phonological word, it cannot be concluded from this fact that the same string is also a word in any nonphonological sense' (Julien 2006: 618). Yet one might equally argue that the units that speakers naturally demarcate in their continuous output must be deeply rooted in core linguistic knowledge, even if not directly available to explicit intuitive insights.

42.3.1 Orthography and intuition

Meanwhile, according to Bloomfield (1933: 178),

> The analysis of linguistic forms into words is familiar to us because we have the custom of leaving spaces between words in our writing and printing. People who have

[8] As noted, Trask offers 'lexeme' as an alternative term for 'lexical item'. Julien (2006) defines 'lexeme' as 'an entry in the speaker's mental lexicon', thus completing the circle. Nevertheless, it is not unproblematic to assume that an entity abstracted by the linguist from the externalized, observable language across users is the same thing as the internal representation of elements of that language in an individual's mind. Furthermore, the 'lexeme' is, for some, much more extensive in scope—the anchor for a set of grammatical words (e.g. *sing, singer, singable, song, songster*) that might, for example, conveniently be listed and learned together by a second language student. But what a native speaker knows about the distributions of those members belies any easy relationship in processing between each instantiation and its formal lexical root.

[9] This last assertion arises from his contention that the lexicon contains constructions that can range from completely lexicalized forms, through frames of lexical material with gaps for variable inserted material, to entirely abstract frames with no lexical material at all (p. 51). (However, see the discussion of 'Is the Pope a catholic?' sentences in Wray 2002: 32f, where it is argued that it is the individual examples that are stored in memory, not the abstract frame.)

> not learned to read and write have some difficulty when, by any chance, they are called upon to make word-divisions.

Bloomfield's observation suggests that orthography plays a significant role in pinning down the word. But in that case, how were word divisions determined in the first place (Taylor 2012: 33)? What patterns of word division would be observed in a language written down for the first time, or from the pen of an illiterate person?[10] Past cases of the transition to writing may not be all that helpful here. In long-established written languages, convention and fossilization will by now have occluded any original rationale. Meanwhile, languages first written down under the influence of a colonial or other external agent, as so many have been, may reflect more the assumptions and practices of the instigator than local intuitions. For example, Dixon and Aikhenvald (2002a: 8) observe that, under the respective influence of the English and Dutch, some members of the Bantu language family are written disjunctively—that is, with white spaces between morphemes—while others are written conjunctively—with morphemes joined into larger units, even though 'there is no inherent grammatical difference between these languages'.

The first attempt to write down a language—if not influenced by other factors—would not of course take place in a context of knowing no word boundaries at all, for language acquisition would be impossible without the identification of a larger number of independent units that end up coinciding with the orthographic word. Other elements of wordhood might be supplementing that knowledge. Indeed, it could be that grammatical and phonological words, along with the lexical item, jointly contribute to an intuition about where to place the white spaces. Orthographic words could emerge from the ways in which these properties coincide. Hall (1999: 2) notes that there is certainly a relationship between phonological words (pwords) and grammatical words: 'There is ... near unanimity in the literature that pword boundaries—unlike those of syllables and feet—must align with morpho(syntactic) boundaries.' Dixon and Aikhenvald (2002a: 30) extend

[10] It is often asserted that Latin and Greek were first written without word divisions and that this indicates the superficiality of any claim of a deep link between our intuition about wordness and the influence of orthography (since one would not want to suggest that Classical writers did not know what words were). However, in both cases, the practice of *scriptio continua* succeeded rather than preceded word division (Wingo 1972: 132; Nagy 2009: 420; Saenger 1997: 9–10). Nagy proposes that *scriptio continua* was adopted because written texts were intended to support oral presentation, which required fluent production—word breaks tending to undermine this. In other words, texts were expected to be rehearsed and thus highly familiar to the performer, making the written version only an aide-memoire rather than a primary source. Although it is cognitively more difficult to read a text if the words are run together, Nagy argues that this was not an issue until silent reading became a dominant cultural practice, along with the shift to a reliance on the written text as a resource in its own right. Saenger (1997) makes a direct connection between orthographic practices and how a given culture uses written texts in relation to oral ones: 'the ancient world did not possess the desire, characteristic of the modern age, to make reading easier and swifter because the advantages that modern readers perceive as accruing from ease of reading were seldom viewed as advantages by the ancients. These include the effective retrieval of information in reference consultation, the ability to read with minimum difficulty a great many technical, logical, and scientific texts, and the greater diffusion of literacy throughout all social strata of the population' (p. 11).

this observation. A language inserts orthographical word boundaries neither consistently at the boundaries of phonological words nor at those of grammatical words, but rather at the points where the two coincide. Thus, a phonological word will constitute an orthographic word where it contains one or more grammatical word. Where a grammatical word contains one or more phonological words, the orthographic boundaries will be drawn around that.

How might this claim be tested? Suppose someone knew how to form the letters in their language, but had never seen written many of the phonological forms they wished to write down. When they attempted to write them, would they, as Dixon and Aikhenvald suggest, home in on the coincidence of boundaries between phonological and grammatical units? Letters written by 19th-century semi-literate petitioners (Fairman 2000, 2002, 2003, 2006) and by French children (Guillaume 1927/73) at first sight suggest so. Fairman finds *taket* for *take it* while Guillaume reports *aidi* for *ai dit*, *cecerai* for *ce serait*, and *semy* for *s'est mis*. However, semi-literate writers seem at least as likely to add boundaries *within* grammatical words as to delay them until the coincidence of a termination of phonological and grammatical words. Thus, from Fairman's collection, *in form* for *inform*, *a gree* for *agree*, *de terminashon* for *determination*, *a nuf* for *enough*; and from Guillaume's, *a ses* for *assez*, *a bitant* for *habitant*, and *dé colle* for *d'école*. However, this may not in fact be evidence countering Dixon and Aikhenvald's suggestion. Rather, it may simply be that one or more other factors also play a role in determining word boundaries. Two contradirectional dynamics may be in action: a tendency to operate with larger grammatical words than linguists customarily assume, leading to only sparse orthographic word divisions, and a tendency to then break them up for some other reason than the location of a phonological and grammatical boundary.

The first part of this process, the inclination to write longer units, would come about because of the way people who have not seen their language written down—or at least not often or extensively—identify and work with their grammatical words. In emergent grammar models, the operating units in the language do not have to be conceived as the smallest *possible* elements—those which could not be further divided and reconstructed using a productive rule—but only as the smallest *useful and recurrent* elements. Construction Grammar (e.g. Goldberg 2003, 2006), for instance, allows for quite complex mixtures of lexical and abstract material in a productive frame. If these constructions constitute, for a given speaker, the grammatical words of the language, there will be many instances where several orthographic words contribute to one grammatical word.[11]

If Dixon and Aikhenvald are right about the orthographic word boundaries being located at the coincidence of phonological and grammatical word boundaries, then having longer grammatical words will result in use of fewer word boundaries—as we saw with the first examples from Fairman and Guillaume.

[11] Compare Sinclair (2010: 38), 'I will follow my usual practice here and use the term *lexical item* for any configuration of text which has a distinct sense, whether it consists of one or more words and whether or not those words are contiguous.'

However, the second dynamic would now come into play, and prevent the semi-literate writer from entirely tolerating grapheme strings that represented these long, underanalysed constructions. Semi-literate writers have by definition had some literacy education, and their exposure to the written language will, in the cases of English or French at least, have tended to be predominantly letters, syllables, and monosyllabic orthographic words (Fairman 2000, 2003). This would instil a sense of unease about allowing a string of graphemes to go on too long before a word break was inserted. Where, then, should one be added, if, as Dixon and Aikhenvald suggest, the natural place would be only at the end of the grammatical word? The decisions would not be random, but predicated on previous experience—detaching from the body of the grammatical word some portion that the writer had experience of separating, whether as a separate word or as a syllable once written alone for practice (thus, in the examples above, *a gree, a nuf, in form, a bitant, a ses, de, dé*).[12]

In the course of developing full literacy, increased familiarity with the written forms would draw the orthographical presentation ever closer to convention, and the power of standard orthography may be such that any intuitions about wordness deriving from internal processing would soon be heavily influenced, if not overridden, by experience with language on the page. Once there are established orthographic words, they are liable to become a source rather than just an expression of knowledge. As Dąbrowska (2009) points out, from about the age of 10, children's primary source of new vocabulary is written texts. This means that orthographic information is part of the initial encoding in much word learning in literate societies.

42.3.2 The influence of orthography on linguistic analysis

Linguists are not immune from the influence of orthography either, which may be why it is not uncommon to find circularity in comments about the relationship between written words and other wordlike units. Huang and Xue (2012: 494) observe:

> That a word is an intuitive unit shared in many languages seems to be borne out with alphabetical writing systems of the world. Most alphabetical writing systems incorporate a convention to mark the boundary of a word.

Sapir (1921: 34) comes rather close to this difficulty too, in his assertion that:

> the naïve Indian, quite unaccustomed to the concept of the written word, has nevertheless no serious difficulty in dictating a text to the linguistic student word by word . . . he can readily isolate the words as such, repeating them as units.

[12] In another context, something similar was observed. A novice learner of Welsh who memorized chunks as part of a performance for television was most vulnerable to errors in her reproduction at those points in the sequence where her input experience had included alternative continuations from that locus (Wray 2004).

Though he notes the refusal on the informant's part to isolate grammatical units with no meaning, he does not entirely avoid the problem of how the linguistic student could *know* independently that the dictated units are words, as opposed to defining as words the units that he is given to write down. Dixon and Aikhenvald (2002a: 7–8) direct a similar criticism at Pike's definition of the word as 'the smallest unit arrived at for some particular language as the most convenient type of grammatical entity to separate by spaces', for:

> [this part of] his definition is circular—spaces are written around a grammatical word and a grammatical word is what is felt to be appropriately written between spaces; that is, no explicit criterion for 'grammatical word' is provided.[13]

A different kind of manifestation of the power of the orthographic word is observed in Bloomfield's (1933: 179) argument for the status of *the* as a separate word. Even though it cannot occur without a noun, he notes that it falls into paradigm with *this* and *that* in *this thing, that thing, the thing.* Since *this* and *that* can 'occur freely as sentences' in their own right (e.g. *What would you like? That.*), he concludes that *the* must have the same status as a word, even though it cannot so appear. Bloomfield seems to take it that *this* and *that* each constitute a single word with two different linguistic functions, as pronoun and determiner, rather than treating the pronoun and the determiner as separate homophonous and homographic words. Had the determiners happened to be spelled, say, *thes* and *thet*, it might have been easier for him to recognize that *the* shares properties only with them and not with the pronouns—much as we hold *of* and *off* very separately in our intuition, despite a historical closeness that did not see them fully differentiated in spelling until the 17th century. Bloomfield, on account of his failure to distinguish between two different items, struggles to reconcile their different qualifications for wordhood, and would also presumably have found it difficult to account for just what sort of grammatical or semantic unit this *this/that/the* set was. Emergent grammar theories avoid this sort of problem, by allowing the use to which a unit is put to dictate how it is defined semantically and grammatically (Smith, this volume).

According to Julien (2006: 619), 'we need criteria for wordhood that are independent of our theory of how morphology and syntax work and interact and independent of our ideas of how words ought to behave'. However, whether the written form is independent enough is questionable.

If orthography plays a role in demonstrating, and perhaps also influencing, the intuitive notion of the word, this still does not mean that it does more than assist intuition in navigating, by various means, a fundamental problem with what the word really is.

[13] Rankin et al. (2002: 198), on the other hand, defend their use of intuitive wordhood as the starting point for how they model a language grammar: 'The process of selecting some data that strike us intuitively as words and then seeing if we can account for things on that basis is certainly a case of iterative hypothesis refinement, but it is not circular.'

Orthographic practices encourage and perpetuate the expectation of clear and replicable boundaries between words. But perhaps they only fool us into believing that writing depicts what we already know, when in fact they are defining and marshalling aspects of a less tangible knowledge. Suppose the notion of word were inherently vague—too vague for us to feel comfortable about. How would theory handle that?

42.4 The vagueness of wordhood

In this section I want to consider what it would look like, from the point of view of linguistic description and theory, if wordhood were fundamentally vague.[14] I shall propose that the different purposes for which words and their behaviour are described interact to give the impression of greater clarity and certainty about wordhood than any one of them could engender alone.

Matthews (2002: 275) suggests that 'a sentence may consist not wholly of words; but in part of "words" and also in part of "clitics", which are not words.' He challenges the idealized view of language, that 'sentences can be divided exhaustively into words and words exhaustively into roots and affixes' (p. 279). He depicts the clitic as a kind of dustbin category, 'liable to be applied wherever we have any kind of difficulty... in saying that a form is unequivocally a word; or unequivocally an affix' (p. 279).

I will develop a case for how this might be so. To do so, it will be necessary to examine from several different angles how vagueness becomes disguised. We have seen already how different aspects of the word, highlighted in different types of linguistic analysis—phonological, grammatical, semantic—are not easily compatible, but are superficially reconciled to the satisfaction of our intuition by overlaying the orthographic word as the arbiter of wordhood. Now, in examining a parallel division of the conceptual space—what language itself is, vs. what linguistic description is for—we shall see how the tendency to overlook certain differences in purpose and agenda in linguistic research has allowed vague features of wordhood to be overwritten by a type of clarity derived from another domain. Again, it is the orthographic word that dominates, though less directly.

[14] Here I do not mean the fuzziness that arises from trying to characterize in simple terms something that is complex. Dick Hudson (p.c.) has argued that the reason the word can be hard to define is that we operate on the basis of a prototype, from which individual instances may deviate to a greater or lesser degree (see sections 42.1 and 42.6). The entire set of words will fully share rather few characteristics, but the members all belong to the category of word by virtue of possessing some of them. Thus, 'Words strike me as splendidly identifiable, thanks to a whole bundle of properties that tend (strongly) to combine: word stress, meaning, syntax, morphology, and (of course) orthography.' My argument here is not at odds with Hudson's view, so much as focused on a slightly different issue. My interest is in the eligibility of words to be reliably ascribed certain properties, rather than whether any given word has a particular set or subset of them.

But is it really plausible to contemplate inherent vagueness for something as intuitively solid as the word? Our intellectual culture has been changing towards a greater tolerance of uncertainty (van Deemter 2010). We have had the cultural shock of the wave-particle duality in quantum physics, and complexity (or chaos) theory has influenced a number of scientific domains, including applied linguistics (Beckner et al. 2009; Ellis 2013; Larsen-Freeman and Cameron 2008). Perhaps in part as a result, research into wordhood has, as we have seen, begun to engage with how to navigate elements of vagueness. There seems nowadays to be less focus than once there was on the quest for one or more 'true' definitions of the word lurking somewhere under the confusion, waiting to be found. We can discern more readiness to see the fuzziness of the word concept as fundamental and inescapable. We are perhaps moving into an era where we will not need to satisfy a desire for complete certainty about where the word starts and stops.

42.4.1 The company words keep

We can track this change over some quarter-century at least, and it can be attributed in large measure to the impact of the corpus as a tool for exploring language. Many assumptions about what words do and what they mean have been fundamentally challenged by the evidence from large corpora. Distributional patterns have emerged that it is difficult to predict or explain using a standard model of language as a set of words combined by a small number of replicable rules.

There are at least two non-alignments between these patterns and the rule-based generative models. One is that the latter predict as grammatically possible a wide range of sentences that are not actually attested and that sound wrong to a native speaker. We don't say **it's third past seven* even though we do say *it's quarter past seven* and *it's half past seven*, and 20 minutes is a recognized fraction of the hour (Pawley and Syder 1983). The other is that the examples that are attested in the language contain much more semantic nuance than can be explained by viewing the individual grammatical words as free agents. The words seem to affect each other, in terms of both meaning and mutual distribution. Sometimes one item determines which of a range of meanings of another is intended, as in *bullet hole, bullet point, bullet train*. Often the combination of words has a meaning of its own that is not a reliable amalgamation of the components at all, e.g. *no fear, at all, for good*.

As a result, Sinclair (1987) challenged the assumption that we normally operate an 'open choice principle' when constructing our output—that is, that we build it entirely out of individual (grammatical) words and morphemes. Although he does allow for language to be constructed and decoded in this way, he considers it to be the exception. His alternative parallels the one already acknowledged in relation to constructing words out of morphemes according to replicable rules—although *hardly* is a valid word of English, it is not derived from *hard* in the same way as *easily* is derived from *easy*.

Sinclair proposes that we prefer, in managing linguistic input and output, to work with units larger than single grammatical words[15] (the 'idiom principle'):

> a language user has available to him or her a large number of semi-preconstructed phrases that constitute single choices, even though they might appear to be analysable into segments.
>
> (Sinclair 1987: 320)

This view leads him to downgrade the word as a operant, venturing that 'the lexical item is characteristically phrasal, although it can be realized as a single word' (Sinclair 2004: 122).

Since Sinclair's proposal, Firth's (1957: 11) much-quoted adage, 'you shall know a word by the company it keeps', has been significantly extended through examinations of the more subtle features of collocation and the logical corollaries of these observations. For instance, Cheng et al. (2006, 2009) have used concgrams to broaden the location parameters for counting co-occurrence. Concgrams are 'instances of co-occurring words irrespective of whether or not they are contiguous, and irrespective of whether or not they are in the same sequential order' (Cheng et al. 2009: 237). On another tack, Mollet, Wray, and Fitzpatrick (2011) experimented with tracking the collocates of an orthographic word's collocates, better to understand how the presence or absence of word C affects word A's co-occurrence with word B.

However, the more language is examined from these angles, the more a paradox is revealed. As described in the next sections, the paradox has two elements. The first is that the very methods demonstrating the interdependency of words, and hence raising questions about how clear-cut a word can be in its own right, are fundamentally reliant on the orthographic word as the unit of investigation. The second part of the paradox derives from the first. If the word cannot be reliably defined as a replicable unit, how can one apply frequency measures to examine a word's distributional behaviour? This dual paradox in turn generates a logical problem that cuts to the heart of how corpus evidence is interpreted. The problem can be solved—but not without imposing one or another pragmatic agenda, and not without completing the circle (whether vicious or virtuous) whereby each type of evidence shores up the other.

42.4.2 The orthographic word as a unit in research

Grefenstette (2010) views it as highly detrimental to modern linguistic research that computational linguistics has been, since its inception, so heavily influenced by print dictionaries. It has meant that research approaches remain constrained by

[15] However, under the idiom principle, there is a discussion to have about whether the components of a multi-word string really are grammatical words. The outcome depends on how one models the grammar of the language.

the dominance of single-word inventories, even though it is increasingly clear that multi-word bases are needed. Specifically, the research has been bound to proceed from orthographic word to structure:

> [The] essentially word-based approach to language led to the development of computational parsers also based on words. Individual words (space-separated tokens) are often ambiguous, both syntactically and semantically. This problem has led to much research in computational linguistics, from part of speech tagging to Word Sense Disambiguation.
>
> (Grefenstette 2010: 3)

As a result, Grefenstette argues, analysts inevitably tend to develop research questions that assume the orthographic word as a unit, and models of language will consequently struggle fully to shake off its influence.

Sinclair navigates the basic problem quite well, by allowing the word to be nothing more than an orthographical form of no interest. For example, he refers to the word space in the middle of *of course* as 'intrusive' and 'structurally bogus', since

> this phrase operates effectively as a single word ... The *of* in *of course* is not the preposition *of* that is found in grammar books ... Similarly, *course* is not the count noun that dictionaries mention; its meaning is not a property of the word, but of the phrase.
>
> (Sinclair 1987: 321)

But while few now would question Sinclair's judgement in relation to such evidently holistic phrases, orthographic wordhood still tends to run through descriptions of less fixed associations. All accounts based on corpus-based frequency are anchored into what orthographic words do, even if they then proceed to argue that the words are co-selected or joined together.

42.4.3 What frequency measures signify

One of the most useful but most compromising elements of word-based corpus research is the ease and reliability with which individual orthographic words can be counted. In order to say anything of value about the frequency of a phenomenon, it is obviously vital to be satisfied that one is counting examples of the same thing. But what is 'the same'? Is it enough that two orthographic forms look identical for them to be treated as examples of a single form? It is well-recognized that homographs, e.g. (river) *bank* vs. (high street) *bank*, are difficult for computers to separate out. But they are only a fraction of the potential problem. There are two particular challenges that arise besides obvious homographs and the highly polysemous items whose different senses, although in some way related, have quite different distributions and associations within and across parts of speech. One is whether some orthographic words are, other than on the page, so invisible that they should not be counted. The other is that we never truly encounter the same word twice.

42.4.3.1 *Invisible words*

If two orthographic words co-occur frequently in text, should we conceive of them as independent agents, co-selected, or as a single unit that has not been divided? The answer may not be the same for all such pairings, but, returning to the earlier example, Sinclair argues that the two orthographic words in *of course* should not be viewed as separate words. We only conceive of them as *of* and *course* because they are written as two orthographic units, and perhaps because we feel we can figure out a historical origin based on two grammatical words that have fused (Bybee 2010)—compare, for example, French *aujourd'hui* (today) from *au jour de* [*hui* < Latin *hodie*]. It is important to recognize that such information is not directly relevant to understanding the nature of the item in the modern language. Ontogeny does not have to recapitulate phylogeny, and so we do not need to suppose that the knowledge of a living speaker captures the historical provenance of an item, unless education supply that information.

If, as Sinclair suggests, *of course* is not, for the contemporary language user, composed of *of* and *course* any more than *cupboard* is composed of *cup* and *board*, it follows that when tracking the incidence of *of* and *course* as independent items of choice under the control of the language user, their occurrences within this phrase should be excluded. Since many of the orthographic words affected by such a decision are highly frequent, there will be an inevitable impact on the frequency profiles of the language's lexicon. There are many thousands of multi-word expressions that might be argued to fall into the same category as *of course*. Excluding occurrences of orthographically separated words within all of them would have a massive impact on the patterns observed across a corpus.[16]

So much for the principle, but is there evidence that *of* and *course* are indeed invisible? One source is the speed at which words within such an expression are recognized, relative to when they operate more independently. Sosa and MacFarlane (2002: 233–234) report:

> Reaction time to *of* in the highest frequency collocations was significantly slower than in the less frequent collocations, indicating holistic storage for the frequent collocations and therefore impeded access to *of* as an independent word.

[16] The point here is that while there is clearly a linguistic rationale for considering the *of* in *of course* to share characteristics with the *of* in *one of them* (whereas there is no such rationale for counting the *of* in *official*), there would probably be more appetite for recognizing that *of course* occupies an intermediate position between the other two, were it not for the operational convenience of automatic searching conventions, based on the location of spaces. Excluding phrases like *of course* from corpus searches is not an easy thing to achieve. Either one has to decide that the frequency of the pairing is itself a rationale for exclusion (which would make it impossible to research collocational frequency on a neutral basis) or one must construct an enormous stop list of the expressions that, for some reason independent of frequency, are judged to fall into the category that should be excluded. Knowing where to draw the line is a major challenge (Wray 2002, 2008, 2009).

Insofar as corpus counts are considered a proxy for the individual's encounters with language (on which topic see later), it would also be reasonable to look for evidence in the awareness of the native speaker. If we asked a native speaker to comment on the meaning or occurrence of the word *course*, would its participation in the expression *of course* contribute to the response? Sinclair (1987: 323) suggests not. Considering where native speakers derive their sense of the core meaning of a word from, he proposes: 'A likely hypothesis is that the 'core' meaning is the most frequent independent sense.' Another kind of evidence comes from speakers' 'blindness' to the internal composition of an expression when using it. In a US court case featuring the term *coon ass* (Wray and Staczek 2005), the user of the expression claimed not to have noticed that it contained a racially offensive word.

An additional source of evidence comes from first and childhood second-language acquisition. It seems that many if not most multi-word expressions are first acquired whole, or least in sizeable chunks. Peters (1983) was one of the first to propose that children start large and progressively segment their input, rather than looking for small units and learning how to build them up. Wray (2002) assembles evidence from a number of studies indicating that children adopt large chunks of input material and break them down only if and when they need to. For instance, she reports Ellen, at 1 year 9 months, using the expression ['taipə'kɒpə'kɒpi] (copied from her mother's *time for a cup of coffee*) as her means of requesting a biscuit. Dąbrowska and Lieven (2005) used longitudinal datasets to examine the output of two children when aged 2–3. This output was compared with the input they received from their mothers. The analysis showed that although the children were producing novel output, it was constructed from chunks of input that they had heard, which were combined or modified using only one or two operations (chaining, insertion). As the children got older, more operations could be used, and their internalized knowledge appeared to be increasingly abstract, in that some lexical material within multi-word strings was replaced by gaps that enabled the insertion of a wider range of alternative items.

According to Construction Grammar—the model adopted by Dąbrowska and Lieven—native speaker adults are still working with such partly-lexicalized–partly-abstract frames, which suggests that the child does not ever break them down entirely, to the point where there would be full flexibility for substitution. Construction Grammar attributes patterns to verbs, such that not only *give* [someone] *a good talking to* but also *give* [someone] [something] derive their form from input that has been only partly broken down to the abstract level. Thus Dąbrowska and Lieven (2005: 447) show how one child derives the frame *get [thing] ready* from the following input from the mother:

MOTHER: shall we get you ready to go out?
MOTHER: well we're go-ing to <get the eh> [//] get the room ready, aren't we?
MOTHER: well we're just about to get Cinderella ready for the ball.

We do not need to suppose that the child will ever have broken the frame down any further, even though both *get* and *ready* do have independent existences, because it is a frame that carries a meaning-related function in its own right (Wray 2002).

42.4.3.2 *Never the same word twice*

> At the individual level, every instance of language use changes an idiolect's internal organization.
>
> (Ellis 2013: 1879)

At the culmination of a lifetime's work exploring the patterns into which orthographic words fall, Sinclair opted for the idea that one never really encounters the same word twice (Cheng et al. 2009). Much as we easily recognize that *red* cannot have the same meaning in *red paint* and *red hair*, since paint the colour of red hair would not be called 'red', so Sinclair extends this idea to a much wider set of words. His 'meaning shift unit' (MSU), which term was to replace 'collocation', focuses attention on the notion that 'each new combination of words generates a shift in meaning, even if this is only relatively subtle, compared with other possible combinations involving one or more of the words' (Cheng et al. 2009: 237).

Were we to adopt Sinclair's position, we would claim that *hard work* has dedicated meaning, and *hard labour* has a sufficiently different meaning for us not to be allowed to view *hard* in each case as more than a homophone—though characterizing the occurrences in terms of their difference leaves us with a problem with regard to their evident semantic and formal similarity. It also seems, particularly in the light of his earlier observation about *of course*, that *hard* as a separate item might not be fully relied on to contribute to the meaning of *hard work* (though it need not be seen as quite as bleached as *of* and *course*). The distinctive meaning of *hard work* is determined by its contexts and cotexts[17] of use. Cheng et al. (2009), whose concgrams enable them to accommodate as the same MSU both *hard ... work* and *work ... hard*, point out that the cotext is what will enable us to differentiate two different MSUs for *back ... flat*, so we don't confuse *flat on [one's] back* with *back to [one's] flat*.

It will not end there. If cotext is contributing to the meaning of an MSU, then each cotext can affect the meaning differently. When I select *hard work* on one occasion, it could have a different meaning from when I select it on another occasion, because of what I've already said or what someone else has said. (The context will also play a role—study or physical labour, for instance.) Cotext can be tracked computationally, but it is not limited to a defined window in a corpus program. My selection of *hard work* is influenced by the wider cotext of my life—all the things I have heard before—and my personal construal of the conceptual boundary within which an activity is reasonably defined as 'hard work'. My suite of influences on the meaning of this MSU will be different from anyone else's and different from my own ten years ago or ten years hence.

Taken to its logical conclusion, could this mean that it is not just other instances of *hard* that are irrelevant to understanding an instance of *hard work*, but also other instances of *hard work*? Each usage (including, but not only, each pronunciation) will be slightly different. A collection of instances of *hard work*, even gathered from a corpus of

[17] 'Cotext' is a term used by Sinclair (e.g. 2004: 30, 131–48) to refer to the text surrounding an item of interest, without implying anything about the discourse level (as 'context' does).

just my linguistic activity, let alone from a standard corpus with so many different voices and genres, will not be tracking recurrent instances of one event, but the coincidence of superficially similar events.

This is an interesting position for Sinclair to end up in. A major source of his evidence for language patterns is the corpus. Yet any corpus-based count is founded on the formal similarity of orthographic forms, whether single words or word strings, and is severely limited in its capacity to take into account anything in the cotext or context beyond collocation at a fairly basic level. Where earlier the problem was in counting invisible words, now it seems that nothing can really be counted at all. How can this be squared with our obvious ability to notice that occurrences of a given lexical item are, for all their differences, also instances of the same thing? A solution comes from recent proposals offered by Taylor (2012) in relation to the mental lexicon, and from Lachs, McMichael, and Pisoni (2000) and Port (2007, 2010) for phonological representations of language. All of them focus on the brain's capacity to store a vast amount of episodic information. Lachs et al. (2000) view the mental lexicon as:

> an integrated, functionally-identical subsection of a larger, more general memory system, in which all experience with speech is encoded and preserved in a detail-rich, complex and multidimensional representation. (p. 164)

Just as humans are able to retain rich episodic traces of life experiences, so they also retain the wealth of auditory information contained in spoken input—a proposal that Lachs et al. claim 'present[s] serious challenges to traditional views of speech perception, in which the process of abstraction plays a major role' (p. 150).

In similar vein, Taylor considers that the capacity to retain complex memories of speech events means that our knowledge of any given lexical item is extremely rich:

> Speakers are exquisitely sensitive to the language that they encounter, noting the uses of words, their collocations and their syntactic environments, the constructions and their special semantics and conditions of use, as well.
>
> (Taylor 2012: 283–4)

Does this imply, then, that we do not notice and abstract the patterns in input, and do not construct a systematic knowledge of how the language works? It does not, for 'experience with speech is *encoded* in memory' (Taylor 2012: 286), not just stored in it. However, the information encoded is not a simple abstraction but rather a rich account of its particular patterns of use:

> Thus, a word encountered in a linguistic exchange will be remembered along numerous dimensions, including, among others, (a) its immediate lexical environment, (b) the containing syntactic construction and its semantic-pragmatic value, and (c) its pronunciation, indexed with respect to characteristics of the speaker and the communicative exchange.
>
> (Taylor 2012: 286)

These detailed traces of the individual speech events are drawn upon to create an exemplar-based model for future production and comprehension. The exemplar model of lexical knowledge is tolerant of high levels of complexity, and will not require that any particular element be loosened from its context unless there is a reason to do so. In mastering a linguistic system on the basis of input, we engage with what is similar across speech events, but also retain a wealth of information about what is different.

Although this approach to modelling language does solve the problem that Sinclair's proposal raises, it does so at a high price, for it forces a breach between two ways of conceptualizing language. Lachs et al., Port, and Taylor are focused on the individual's internal knowledge of the language, amassed from all of those complex exemplars. Two people may well not have the same representations of a given lexical item, because they have not encountered identical input. This non-alignment doesn't matter in a fundamentally psycholinguistic model, because it is of no consequence that person A's experience of a given item cannot be amalgamated with person B's. But Sinclair's evidence is from corpora. In a corpus-focused account of language, the output of many people is indeed amalgamated, in the expectation that it offers a rough and ready account of the average individual's input. The difficulty is that, as we have seen, the nature of corpus data, combined with the mechanisms by which it can be interrogated, cannot capture the rich data that the individual is able to process. In the past, when it was assumed that the individual, like the computer, was filtering out most of the speech-event-specific detail, the impact of this difference was less marked. But if individuals construct their knowledge of language precisely on the amalgamation of that detail, then the evidence from current corpus research is much less satisfactory as a proxy for the individual's input.

Corpus linguistics has not, traditionally, been tasked to model the internal knowledge of the speaker/hearer.[18] The need to address how the two relate is, however, a corollary of Sinclair's proposal about the MSU, for, while his observations and claims are anchored in corpus linguistics, the MSU drives him inexorably towards approximating the individual's knowledge. On examination, we find that the gulf between the individuals' internalized language and the community's externalized language is, here, as wide as it could be. The individual speaker's exemplars are not directly reflected in anything that corpora can easily capture at the moment.

As Port (2010: 53) makes clear, this situation need not obviate entirely the exercise of *identifying* generic profiles: 'generalizations—the patterns that are shared by the speech of a community—comprise categories all right.' However, 'they exist only as statistical regularities at the level of the community.' Therefore, we have to be sure not to extrapolate from externalized patterns back to what is represented in any given individual's head.

[18] On the other hand, corpus evidence is very often used by those investigating psycholinguistic questions. For example, researchers who want to compare the response of informants to different types of linguistic input (such as formulaic vs. non-formulaic word strings) will typically select their stimuli on the basis of frequency patterns in corpora.

Yet, once again, we cannot really avoid doing so. Corpus data are the best evidence we have for the nature of the linguistic environment from which we develop our internal knowledge of our language(s). There clearly are relationships between the two, and if we are to understand the nature and provenance of linguistic intuition, we cannot ignore the role of the external pool of language that we, and corpora, tap into.

42.5 Where individual knowledge and the external language meet

A recurrent theme of this chapter has been the undeniable fact that we have very strong intuitions—gleaned from our linguistic experience, one assumes—about what the patterns are in the language 'out there'.[19] If, as suggested above, these patterns are both vague and highly complex, again we must ask how we are anchoring that intuitive certainty. We have seen that at least some measure of intuition may well be culturally rather than psychologically determined—imposed by education, literacy, and convention.

One account of lexical knowledge that ties together intuition, corpus evidence, and the vagueness of the word is Hanks's (2013) norms and exploitations model. In the face of evidence that individual occurrences of a given lexical item are always slightly different from any previous occurrence, he proposes that meaning is anchored into a norm, extrapolated from experience, and on the basis of which future uses, both canonical and metaphorical and/or creative, can be interpreted. A norm will underpin a strong intuition about the word's meaning and indeed its status as a unit at all. Hanks quotes a passage from a Julian Barnes novel that includes the clause, *I hazarded various Stuartesque destinations* (p. 13) and shows how, in its context, *hazarded* can be understood to mean *guessed* while *Stuartesque* is a creative form derived from a pattern in which the ending indicates an association with the referent (Stuart), 'typically in respect of certain noticeable or even eccentric or bizarre characteristics' (p. 15). In both cases, the words can be interpreted with reference to clear prototypical usages.

In the light of the previous discussion, three important things must be noted about Hanks' approach. First, he invokes corpus data as the analyst's source of evidence about normal usage (Hanks 2013: 91–92), demonstrating that his purpose is to describe the externalized language rather than the individual speaker's knowledge (though he would presumably not deny the relationship between the two—see Fig. 42.1 below). Secondly, he focuses on orthographic words as the basic unit of analysis, even though he is far from averse to the notion that many lexical items contain more than one orthographic

[19] In this section, I do not refer to individual, or internal, language as I-language and externalized language as E-language, because I do not mean to capture and imply the purposes and assumptions that are associated with these terms within the Chomskyan framework.

word (pp. 50ff.). Thirdly, norms apply most obviously to content words. Function words like *of* and *to*, and indeed adverbs, are invoked as components of the linguistic environment in which nouns and verbs occur, rather than having a strong norm entry in their own right (though presumably there is no reason why they cannot have one if it can be extrapolated from its uses).

What we appear to see, in juxtaposing Hanks's and Sinclair's accounts of language, is two sides of a coin. Where Hanks is modelling the socially shared language, Sinclair is bound to model the user's internal knowledge. Where Hanks accounts primarily for content words, which have a strong semantic identity that can be mapped onto a norm, Sinclair's model is most powerful with the 'small words', such as function words (*of, to*, etc.) and delexicalized verbs (e.g. *take* in *take up, take into account*), which are the ones that have least independence. Could it be that these two factors are linked? It would mean that content words have greater distinctiveness in the shared language of a community than they do in the mind of the individual user. If this were so, how could it come about? What is happening in the language as a shared resource that is different from what happens in the mind of each person involved in the sharing? And how does it relate to intuition?

I want to suggest that there is indeed something going on here, and that it entails an external, social rationalization of the inherent vagueness of language in the mind. Fig. 42.1 demonstrates the mechanism by which our individual knowledge, and hence our intuition about language, is influenced by the cultural norms of the dictionary and orthography. Each of these four elements has its own level of vagueness.

In Fig. 42.1, *individual knowledge* of the word (1) is fundamentally vague in the ways outlined above with reference to the proposals of Taylor, Lachs et al., and Port, because it is a rich extrapolation from language in use (process a). The ensuing behaviour of speakers (process b) creates an instability in the *external language* (2) as described by Sinclair, but one that is moderated by the influence of dictionaries and the conventions of writing on individuals' output (h, i); as outlined earlier, intuition is heavily influenced by education and literacy. The *corpus-based dictionary* (3) is itself somewhat unstable, in that the source data are variable (c). Corpora are typically used as a means of approximating the experience of the individual, but, as noted earlier, patterns observed in a multi-genre, multi-speaker/writer corpus are not directly representative of the experience of any given individual:

> Language is emergent at ... two distinctive but interdependent levels: an idiolect is emergent from an individual's language use through social interactions with other individuals in the communal language, while a communal language is emergent as the result of the interaction of the idiolects.
>
> (Ellis 2013: 1878)

In interpreting the inexactitudes of the corpus for dictionary use, the entries are stabilized by convention (d) and by the intuition of the lexicographer (f), who can

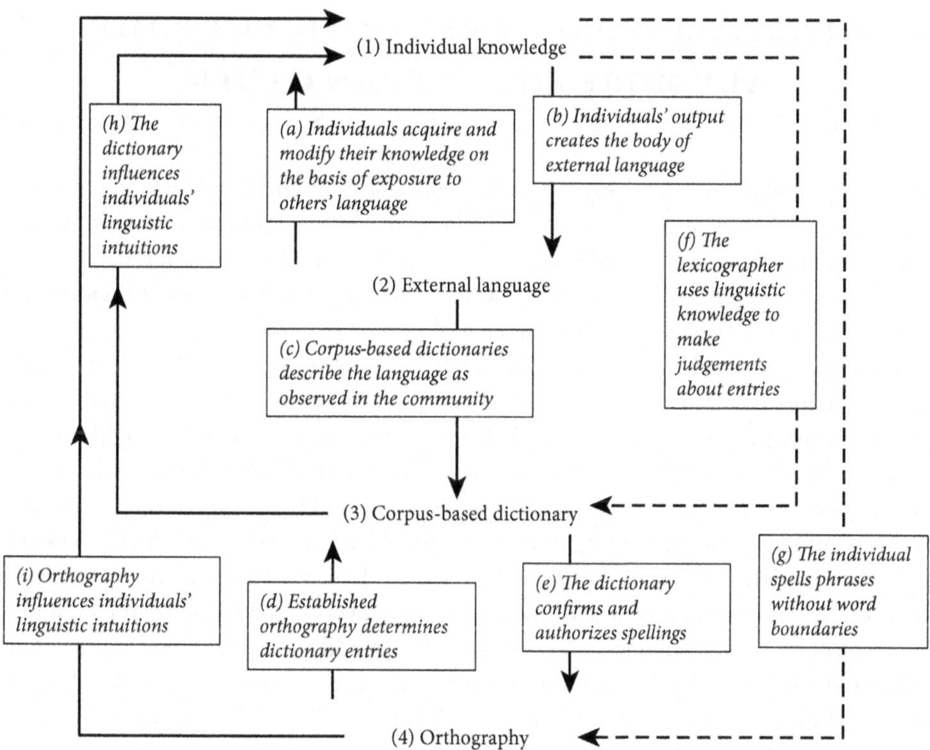

FIG. 42.1 The symbiosis of mental, social, and cultural factors in defining linguistic knowledge.

differentiate between plausible patterns in the language and erratic ones. The *orthography* (4) is most stable of all, being marshalled by dictionary entries (e) and the full force of literacy education. But it is influenced to a small extent by the behaviour of individuals (g) who may, in particular, remove written word boundaries within single lexical items (e.g. *alot, atall, aswell*: Wray 1996), with gradual influence on practices which then feed into the dictionary (e.g. *alright, into, cannot*).

What Hanks' model does in the context of this set of relationships is to reap evidence from the external language to offer dictionary-like accounts of meaning that reflect the individual's intuition about the core meaning of a lexical item. But where do those norms come from? We can see from Fig. 42.1 that they could be derived from the individual's linguistic knowledge, as extrapolated from patterns observed in the external language. But they could also be influenced, at least, by the orthography into an expectation that words are discrete and replicable and/or by the dictionary into an expectation that words have core meanings, as they do in dictionaries.

With this last point in mind, and referring back also to the earlier observation regarding the relative status of the content word and function word in the models of Hanks and Sinclair, we can now turn to consider the most radical possibility of all, regarding the vagueness of wordhood.

42.6 All words are equal, but some are more equal than others

Hijacking Hanks' norm and exploitation idea for a moment, it is worth considering whether our notion of the word as a reliable entity is itself founded on a prototype. Suppose that language is overall rather vague and ill-defined in terms of reliable word-hood, but that we have a strong norm of 'word'—a clear sense of what a really good word looks like, and use that as a point of reference.

The prototype word, the norm, would surely be content-rich. An old trick in the linguistics lecture theatre is to ask students to shout out examples of words. Invariably, they offer exclusively nouns or, if they do stray from nouns, it is no further than highly visualizable verbs (that therefore often have a nominal counterpart, such as *run*, or an associated gesture or sign, such as *like*), or adjectives associated with objects, such as *big* and *red*. It would be rather surprising to hear—other than from a student who foresaw the point being made—words like *of*, *perhaps*, or *or*. Students are surprised that, in racking their brains for examples of words, they apparently overlooked what are in fact highly frequent items in the language, and ones that they readily accept as being words when presented with them. Such items are, as suggested earlier, somewhat invisible when we are looking for examples of 'good' words. For further evidence of the noun as clear prototype, see Heitner's (this volume) quotations from St Augustine, John Locke, Vygotsky, Wittgenstein, and Quine, in which the process of language acquisition is entirely characterized in terms of learning how to name things.

Were the prototype to be narrowed down further than the noun generally, we might home in on concrete nouns, since our initial encounters with language are so rich in them. Clark (this volume) notes that child-directed speech in the United States contains a great many nouns, particularly when the adult is engaged in joint attention with the child over a book. That is, the adult draws attention to objects, and names or describes them. Of course, not all cultures pay this sort of direct attention to children's word learning. However, the labelling of physical objects is surely a universal component of what children learn to do. According to Graf Estes (this volume), infants are looking for cues that will enable them to manipulate language effectively and to that end, '[they] require the anchor of a salient, highly familiar word in order to support the discovery of a new word' (p. 537).

If children were to develop a strong norm of wordhood based on the concrete noun, what would happen as they continued to master the language as a whole? Emergent models[20] suggest that the child might not need to isolate all the grammatical words of

[20] The fundamental principle of emergent grammar is that we accumulate our knowledge of what can be, and normally is, done in our language on the basis of stochastically tracking patterns in our input (Ellis 2013). The raw frequency of occurrences interfaces with other navigational elements, such as salience, contextual associations, and recency, to build a complex, ever-shifting memory imprint that can be used to interpret further instances and to construct one's own output.

the language in order to use it effectively. The pre-literate child—as indeed the illiterate adult—certainly would have a sense of the word, but it would not run with equal force through the entire language. Concrete nouns are at the extreme edge of language forms, in being associated with physical objects that can be organized into sets with easily perceptible characteristics.

Thus some items would be recognized as definitely words—linguistic units associated with, particularly, physical items. Others would be somewhat analogous with the prototype, representing abstract concepts perhaps, or physical action. Verbs, while possessing a strong semantic content, are also associated with a grammatical pattern that sustains a meaning in its own right (Hunston and Francis 2000), but that nevertheless tends to make it difficult to separate the verb from certain of its collocates:

> When doing fieldwork on a previously undescribed language one may—in some cases—felicitously cite a noun and ask about its meaning and use. But it is bad practice to do the same for a verb. One should always include at least minimal information about core arguments, asking about 'she hit him' rather than just about 'hit'. A noun generally names a type of object and may be used just for this; but a verb describes an action or state which requires a number of participants and these should be specified.
>
> (Dixon and Aikhenvald 2002a: 33)

But at the far end of the continuum there would also be massive retinue of less well-defined forms, not cut clearly into words. This would include partly lexicalized frames with gaps in them (e.g. *the __-er the __-er*) and various bits and pieces with roles rather difficult to pin down out of context, such as particles like *up* in *wash up* and *dress up*.

The most robust of the lexical categories are undoubtedly noun and verb:

> Once we leave the relatively safe territory of nouns and verbs, classification of words into parts of speech becomes increasingly problematic ... It also turns out that many of the most frequently used words do not easily fit into any of the standard categories.
>
> (Taylor 2012: 46–47)

Taylor's observation, which relates to how linguists classify language, may be no less true of how users organize their knowledge. Yet, in a literate community, even these most tricky items would be designated as word or not-word by convention—a convention that may throw up many anomalies (compare *out of* and *into*). Not surprisingly, someone without confident command of the conventions, such as the semi-literate writers cited earlier, could struggle at times to guess where the boundaries should go. But for those who have mastered literacy, the orthographic identity given to these shadowy items would reinforce the intuition that the entire language was constructed out of words, even if some orthographic words did not attract any of the other accoutrements of wordhood. In this way, literacy would impose extensive constraints on our capacity to recognize the boundaries of what (else) a word can be (Logan 2004).

42.7 Conclusion

If human languages had no words, we might by now have noticed that our attempt to divide languages into them was fruitless. If human languages were entirely made up of words, we might expect that our taxonomies would be tidier than they are. Emergent grammar models suggest—without necessarily explicitly stating—that we don't need to see the entirety of a language as divided up into neat word-sized packages, any more than we need to divide up a landscape entirely into objects as discernible as windmills and cottages. There is a lot of other 'stuff' in a landscape. It contextualizes and helps us interpret the clearly delineated items, but cannot be reduced to just a set of such items.

So it may be that much of language is not really words at all. As Matthews (2002: 273) observes, 'there are many general concepts that should not be generalised beyond the point at which their application is illuminating'. Without doubt a plausible account of what humans know in knowing language must include an awareness of recombinable parts. But it does not follow that all the recombinable parts are the same size—some might be complex configurations comprising many orthographic words. Nor does it follow that just because nouns can be singled out as individual lexical items, and verbs too—albeit with their constructional entourage—that the entire language must be isolatable and definable in that way.

Perhaps, then, words are just the bits that fall off when you shake the utterance. It may be only the belief in the universal discreteness of words that has perpetuated the quest to pin down every bit of a language into words. Our theoretical models have, until recently, required such exactness. Now that we have models more tolerant of underspecification, variation, and inherent vagueness, the word may find it occupies a lesser place.

References

Aarts, B. (2007). *Syntactic Gradience: The Nature of Grammatical Indeterminacy*. Oxford: Oxford University Press.

Abdel Rahman, R., and Melinger, A. (2009). Semantic context effects in language production: a swinging lexical network proposal and a review. *Language and Cognitive Processes* 24: 713–34.

Abel, E. L. (2004). Nicknames of American Civil War generals. *Names* 52: 243–85.

Abrams, L., and Parsons, D. N. (2004). Place-names and the history of Scandinavian settlement in England. In J. Hines, A. Lane, and M. Redknap (eds), *Land, Sea and Home*: Settlement in the Viking Period. Leeds: Maney, 379–431.

Abutalebi, J. (2008). Neural aspects of second language representation and language control. *Acta Psychologica* 128: 466–78.

Abutalebi, J., and Green, D. (2007). Bilingual language production: the neurocognition of language representation and control. *Journal of Neurolinguistics* 20: 242–75.

Académie française (1694). *Le Dictionnaire de l'Académie française*. Paris: Coignard & Coignard.

Accademia della Crusca (1612). *Vocabolario degli Accademici della Crusca*. Venice: Accademia della Crusca.

Aceto, M. (2002). Ethnic personal names and multiple identities in Anglophone Caribbean speech communities in Latin America. *Language in Society* 31: 577–608.

Ackema, P., and Neeleman, A. (2002). Syntactic atomicity. *Journal of Comparative Germanic Syntax* 6: 93–128.

Ackema, P., and Neeleman, A. (2004). *Beyond Morphology: Interface Conditions on Word Formation*. Oxford: Oxford University Press.

Ackema, P., and Neeleman, A. (2007). Morphology ≠ Syntax. In G. Ramchand and C. Reiss (eds), *The Oxford Handbook of Linguistic Interfaces*. Oxford: Oxford University Press, 325–52.

Ackema, P., and Neeleman, A. (2010). The role of syntax and morphology in compounding. In S. Scalise and I. Vogel (eds), *Cross Disciplinary Issues in Compounding*. Amsterdam: Benjamins, 21–36.

Ackerman, F., and Stump, G. T. (2004). Paradigms and periphrastic expression: a study in realization based lexicalism. In L. Sadler and A. Spencer (eds), *Projecting Morphology*. Stanford, Calif.: CSLI, 111–58.

Ackerman, F., Stump, G. T., and Webelhuth, G. (2011). Lexicalism, periphrasis and implicative morphology. In B. Borsley and K. Borjars (eds), *Non-Transformational Theories of Grammar*. Oxford: Blackwell, 325–58.

Adamczik, K. (ed.) (1995). *Textsorten—Texttypologie: eine kommentierte Bibliographie*. Münster: Nodus.

Adams, H. (1907). The grammar of science. In *The Education of Henry Adams*, ch. 31. Boston: Houghton Mifflin.

Adams, M. (2008). Power, politeness and the pragmatics of nicknames. *Names* 57: 81–91.

Adams, M. (2009). Nicknames, interpellation, and Dubya's theory of the state. *Names* 56: 206–20.

Adams, W. L. (2008). Hangman, spare that word: the English purge their language. Time (World), 3 October.

Adetunji, A. (2010). Nicknaming soccer players: the case of Nigerian supporters of English Premier League club sides. *California Linguistic Notes* 35.

Adolphs, S., and Schmitt, N. (2003). Lexical coverage of spoken discourse. *Applied Linguistics* 24(4): 425–38.

Agyekum, K. (2006). The sociolinguistics of Akan personal names. *Nordic Journal of African Studies* 15(2): 206–35.

Ahronson, K. (2007). *Viking-Age Communities: Pap-Names and Papar in the Hebridean Islands.* Oxford: ArchaeoPress.

Aikhenvald, A. Y. (2002a). *Language Contact in Amazonia.* Cambridge: Cambridge University Press.

Aikhenvald, A. Y. (2002b). Typological parameters for the study of clitics, with special reference to Tariana. In R. M. W. Dixon and A. Y. Aikhenvald (eds), *Word: A Cross-Linguistic Typology.* Cambridge: Cambridge University Press, 42–78.

Ainiala, T. (1997). On perpetuation, demise and change in place-names. In R. Liisa Pitkänen and K. Mallat (eds), *You Name It: Perspectives on Onomastic Research.* Helsinki: Finnish Literature Society, 106–15.

Aitchison, J. (2000). *Language Change: Progress or Decay.* Cambridge: Cambridge University Press.

Aitchison, J. (2012). *Words in the Mind: An Introduction to the Mental Lexicon.* Chichester: Wiley.

Akindele, D. F. (2008). Sesotho address forms. *Linguistik Online* 34: 3–15.

Akinnaso, F. N. (1983). Yoruba traditional names and the transmission of cultural knowledge. *Names* 31: 139–58.

Akita, K., Imai, M., Saji, N., Kantartzis, K., and Kita, S. (2011). Mimetic vowel harmony in Japanese. In P. Sells and B. Frellesvig (eds), *Japanese/Korean Linguistics.* Stanford, Calif.: CSLI, 1–15.

Albareda-Castellot, B., Pons, F., and Sebastián-Gallés, N. (2011). The acquisition of phonetic categories in bilingual infants: new data from an anticipatory eye movement paradigm. *Developmental Science* 14: 395–401.

Albert, R., Jeong, H., and Barabási, A.-L. (1999). The diameter of the WWW. *Nature* 401(6749): 130–31.

Alford, H. (2005). Not a word. *New Yorker*, 29 August.

Alford, R. D. (1988). *Naming and Identity: A Cross-Cultural Study of Personal Naming Practices.* New Haven, Conn.: HRAF Press.

Algeo, J. (1985). Is a theory of names possible? *Names* 33: 136–44.

Alia, V. (2007). *Names & Nunavut: Culture and Identity in the Inuit Homeland.* New York: Berghahn Books.

Alinei, M. (1995). Thirty-five definitions of etymology: or, etymology revisited. In W. Winter (ed.), *On Languages and Language: The Presidential Addresses of the 1991 Meeting of the Societas Linguistica Europaea.* Berlin: Mouton de Gruyter, 1–26.

Allan, K. (1977). Classifiers. *Language* 53(2): 285–311.

Allan, K. (1986). *Linguistic Meaning.* 2 vols. London: Routledge & Kegan Paul.

Allan, K., and Burridge, K. (1991). *Euphemism and Dysphemism: Language Used as Shield and Weapon.* New York: Oxford University Press.

Allan, K., and Burridge, K. (2006). *Forbidden Words: Taboo and the Censoring of Language.* Cambridge: Cambridge University Press.

Allan, K., and Robinson, J. A. (eds) (2011). *Current Methods in Historical Semantics.* Berlin: Mouton de Gruyter.

Allen, I. L. (1983). Personal names that became ethnic epithets. *Names* 31: 307–17.

Allerton, D. J. (1987). The linguistic and sociolinguistic status of proper names. *Journal of Pragmatics* 11: 61–92.

Allwood, J., Hendrikse, A., and Ahlsén, E. (2010). Words and alternative basic units for linguistic analysis. In P. J. Henrichsen (ed.), *Linguistic Theory and Raw Sound.* Copenhagen Studies in Language 40: 9–26.

Alpher, B. (1994). Yir-Yoront ideophones. In L. Hinton, C. Nicholson, and J. J. Ohala (eds), *Sound Symbolism.* Cambridge: Cambridge University Press, 161–77.

Alpher, B., and Nash, D. (1999). Lexical replacement and cognate equilibrium in Australia. *Australian Journal of Linguistics* 19(1): 5–56.

Alsina, A. (2009). The prepositional passive as structure sharing. In M. Butt and T. Holloway King (eds), *Proceedings of the LFG09 Conference.* Stanford, Calif.: CSLI. <http://csli-publications.stanford.edu/>.

Altarriba, J., and Basnight-Brown, D. M. (2007). Methodological considerations in performing semantic- and translation-priming experiments across languages. *Behavior Research Methods* 39: 1–18.

Altarriba, J., and Knickerbocker, H. (2011). Acquiring second language vocabulary through the use of images and words. In P. Trofimovich and K. McDonough (eds), *Applying Priming Methods to L2 Learning, Teaching and Research.* Amsterdam: Benjamins, 21–48.

Altarriba, J., Kroll, J., Sholl, A., and Rayner, K. (1996). The influence of lexical and conceptual constraints on reading mixed-language sentences: evidence from eye fixations and reading times. *Memory and Cognition* 24: 477–92.

Altarriba, J., and Mathis, K. M. (1997). Conceptual and lexical development in second language acquisition. *Journal of Memory and Language* 36: 550–68.

Altmann, G. (1978). Towards a theory of language. *Glottometrika* 1: 1–25.

Altmann, G. (1980). Prolegomena to Menzerath's Law. *Glottometrika* 2: 1–10.

Altmann, G. (1983). H. Arens' 'Verborgene Ordnung' und das Menzerathsche Gesetz. In M. Faust et al. (eds), *Allgemeine Sprachwissenschaft, Sprachtypologie und Textlinguistik: Festschrift für P. Hartmann.* Tübingen: Narr, 31–9.

Altmann, G. (1993). Science and linguistics. In R. Köhler and B. B. Rieger (eds), *Contributions to Quantitative Linguistics.* Dordrecht: Kluwer Academic, 3–10.

Altmann, G. (2013). Aspects of word length. In R. Köhler and G. Altmann (eds), *Issues in Quantitative Linguistics* 3. Lüdenscheid: RAM, 23–38.

Altmann, G., and Schwibbe, M. (1989). *Das Menzerathsche Gesetz in informationsverarbeitenden Systemen.* Hildesheim: Olms.

Amanuma, Y. (1974). *Giongo Gitaigo Jiten* [A Dictionary of Onomatopoeic and Ideophonic Expressions]. Tokyo: Tokyodo.

Ameel, E., Malt, B. C., and Storms, G. (2008). Object naming and later lexical development: from baby bottle to beer bottle. *Journal of Memory and Language* 58: 262–85.

Ameel, E., Storms, G., Malt, B. C., and Sloman, S. A. (2005). How bilinguals solve the naming problem. *Journal of Memory and Language* 53: 60–80.

Ameka, F. (ed.) (1992). Special issue on 'interjections'. *Journal of Pragmatics* 18(2/3).

Ameka, F. K. (1994). Areal conversational routines and cross-cultural communication in a multilingual society. In H. Pürschel (ed.), *Intercultural Communication*. Bern: Lang, 441–69.

Ameka, F. K. (2001). Ideophones and the nature of the adjective word class in Ewe. In F. K. Erhard Voeltz and C. Kilian-Hatz (eds), *Ideophones*. Amsterdam: Benjamins, 25–48.

Ameka, F. K. (2009). Access rituals in West African communities: an ethnopragmatic perspective. In G. Senft and E. B. Basso (eds), *Ritual Communication*. New York: Berg, 127–52.

Ameka, F. K., and Breedveld, A. O. (2004). Areal cultural scripts for social interaction in West African communities. *Intercultural Pragmatics* 1(2): 167–87.

Amende, C. (2001). *The Crossword Obsession: The History and Lore of the World's Most Popular Pastime*. Darby, Penn.: Diane Publications. Repr. 2002, New York: Berkley Books.

American Heritage Dictionary of the English Language, The (1969). 5th edn 2011. Boston: Houghton Mifflin.

Ammermann, S. (2001). Zur Wortlängenverteilung in deutschen Briefen über einen Zeitraum von 500 Jahren. In K.-H. Best (ed.), *Häufigkeitsverteilungen in Texten*. Göttingen: Peust & Gutschmidt 59–91.

Amstad, T. (1978). Wie verständlich sind unsere Zeitungen. Dissertation, University of Zürich.

Andersen, E. S. (1978). Lexical universals of body-part terminology. In J. H. Greenberg, C. A. Ferguson, and E. A. Moravcsik (eds), *Universals of Human Language*, vol. 3. Stanford, Calif.: Stanford University Press, 335–68.

Anderson, J. M. (2003). On the structure of names. *Folia Linguistica* 37: 347–98.

Anderson, J. M. (2007). *The Grammar of Names*. Oxford: Oxford University Press.

Anderson, J. M. (2011). Referentiality and the noun. *Hermes* 47: 13–29.

Anderson, M. (1984). Proper names, naming, and labeling in Saami. *Anthropological Linguistics* 26: 186–201.

Anderson, S. (1977). On mechanisms by which languages become ergative. In C. Li (ed.), *Mechanisms of Syntactic Change*. Austin: University of Texas Press, 317–63.

Anderson, S. R. (1982). Where's morphology? *Linguistic Inquiry* 13: 571–612.

Anderson, S. R. (1992). *A-morphous Morphology*. Cambridge: Cambridge University Press.

Anderson, S. R. (2000). Some lexicalist remarks on incorporation phenomena. *Studia Grammatica* 45: 123–42.

Anderson, S. R. (2001). Lexicalism, incorporated (or incorporation, lexicalized). Proceedings of the 36th Annual Meeting of the Chicago Linguistics Society, 13–34.

Anderson, S. R. (2005). *Aspects of the Theory of Clitics*. Oxford: Oxford University Press.

Andrews, M., Vinson, D., and Vigliocco, G. (2008). Inferring a probabilistic model of semantic memory from word association norms. In B. C. Love, K. McRae, and V. M. Sloutsky (eds), *Proceedings of the 30th Annual Conference of the Cognitive Science Society*. Austin, Tex.: Cognitive Science Society, 1941–6.

Angus, L. E., and Korman, Y. (2002). A metaphor theme analysis: conflicts, coherence and change in brief psychotherapy. In S. R. Fussell (ed.), *The Verbal Communication of Emotions: Interdisciplinary Perspectives*. Mahwah, NJ: Erlbaum, 151–65.

Anon. (n.d.). International Commission on Zoological Nomenclature. In Wikipedia <http://en.wikipedia.org/wiki/International_Code_of_Zoological_Nomenclature>. Accessed 28 August 2012.

Annamalai, E. (1968). Onomatopoeic resistance to sound change in Dravidian. In B. Krishnamurti (ed.), *Studies in Indian Linguistics*. Poona: Center for Advanced Study in Linguistics, 15–19.

Anthony, L. (2011). AntConc (3.2.4w) [computer software]. Retrieved from <http://www.antlab.sci.waseda.ac.jp/software.html>.

Antić, G., Grzybek, P., and Stadlober, E. (2005). Mathematical aspects and modifications of Fucks' generalized Poisson distribution. In R. Köhler, G. Altmann, and R. G. Piotrovski (eds), *Quantitative Linguistik/Quantitative Linguistics: Ein Internationales Handbuch/An International Handbook*. Berlin: de Gruyter, 158–80.

Antoun, R. T. (1968). On the significance of names in an Arab village. *Ethnology* 7: 158–70.

Aoki, H. (1994). Symbolism in Nez Perce. In L. Hinton, J. Nichols, and J. J. Ohala (eds), *Sound Symbolism*. Cambridge: Cambridge University Press, 15–39.

APA (1994). *Diagnostic and Statistical Manual of Mental Health Disorders*, 4th edn. Washington, DC: American Psychiatric Association.

Apresjan, J. (1976). Regular polysemy. *Linguistics* 142: 5–32.

Apresjan, J. (2000). *Systematic Lexicography*, trans. K. Windle. Oxford: Oxford University Press.

Arens, H. (1965). *Verborgene Ordnung: die Beziehungen zwischen Satzlänge und Wortlänge in deutscher Erzählprosa vom Barock bis heute*. Düsseldorf: Schwann.

Armon-Lotem, S., and Berman, R. A. (2003). The emergence of grammar: early verbs and beyond. *Journal of Child Language* 30: 845–77.

Arnon, I., and Clark, E. V. (2011). Why *Brush your teeth* is better than *Teeth*: children's word production is facilitated in familiar sentence-frames. *Language Learning and Development* 7: 107–29.

Arnot, M. (1981). *What's Gnu? A History of the Crossword Puzzle*. New York: Vintage.

Aronoff, M. (1976). *Word Formation in Generative Grammar*. Cambridge, Mass.: MIT Press.

Aronoff, M. (1994). *Morphology by Itself: Stems and Inflectional Classes*. Cambridge, Mass.: MIT Press.

Aronoff, M., Meir, I., and Sandler, W. (2005). The paradox of sign language morphology. *Language* 81(2): 301–44.

Arthur, J. M. (2003). *The Default Country: A Lexical Cartography of Twentieth-Century Australia*. Sydney: University of NSW Press.

Asante, M. K. (1991). *The Book of African Names*. Trenton, NJ: Africa World Press.

Aslin, R. N., Saffran, J. R., and Newport, E. L. (1998). Computation of conditional probability statistics by 8-month-old infants. *Psychological Science* 9(4): 321–4.

Asudeh, A., and Mikkelsen, L. H. (2000). Incorporation in Danish: implications for interfaces. In R. Cann, C. Grover, and P. Miller (eds), *Grammatical Interfaces in HPSG*. Stanford, Calif.: CSLI.

Atkinson, R. C. (1975). Mnemotechnics in second-language learning. *American Psychologist* 30: 821–6.

Atoda, T., and Hoshino, K. (1995). *Giongo gitaigo tsukaikata jiten* [Usage Dictionary of Sound/Manner Mimetics]. Tokyo: Sotakusha.

Attardo, S. (1994). *Linguistic Theories of Humor*. Berlin: Mouton de Gruyter.

Attardo, S., and Raskin, V. (1991). Script theory revis(it)ed: joke similarity and joke representation model. *Humor: International Journal of Humor Research* 4(3–4): 293–347.

Augustine, St (398/1961). *The Confessions of Saint Augustine*. New York: Random House.

Augustine, St (1950). *The Greatness of the Soul. The Teacher*, trans. Joseph M. Colleran. Westminster, London: Newman.

Austin, J. L. (1961). *Philosophical Papers*. Oxford: Clarendon Press.

Austin, P. K., and Sallabank, J. (eds) (2011). *The Cambridge Handbook of Endangered Languages*. Cambridge: Cambridge University Press.

Avila, E., and Sadoski, M. (1996). Exploring new applications of the keyword method to acquire English vocabulary. *Language Learning* 50: 385–412.

Awoyale, Y. (1983–84). On the semantic fields of Yoruba ideophones. *Journal of the Linguistic Association of Nigeria* 2: 11–22.

Awoyale, Y. (1988). On the non-concatenative morphology of Yoruba ideophones. Paper delivered at the 19th African Linguistics Conference, Boston University.

Awoyale, Y. (2000). The phonological structure of Yoruba ideophones. In H. Ekkehard Wolff and O. D. Gensler (eds), *Proceedings of the 2nd World Congress of African Linguistics (Leipzig 1997)*, 293–309. Cologne: Köppe.

Ayer, A. (1971[1946]). *Language, Truth and Logic*. Harmondsworth: Penguin.

Azad, K. (2007). Demystifying the natural logarithm (ln). Retrieved from <http://betterexplained.com/articles/demystifying-the-natural-logarithm-ln/>.

Bach, E. (1981). The algebra of events. *Linguistics and Philosophy* 9: 5–16.

Backus, A. M. (1996). *Two in One: Bilingual Speech of Turkish Immigrants in the Netherlands*. Tilburg: Tilburg University Press.

Bacon, F. (1605). *The Advancement of Learning*. London: Henrie Tomes.

Badecker, W. (2001). Lexical composition and the production of compounds: evidence from errors in naming. *Language and Cognitive Processes* 16: 337–66.

Baddeley, A. (1997). *Human Memory: Theory and Practice*. Hove: Psychology Press.

Baerman, M., Brown, D., and Corbett, G. G. (2005). *The Syntax–Morphology Interface: A Study of Syncretism*. Cambridge: Cambridge University Press.

Baerman, M., Corbett, G. G., and Brown, D. (eds) (2007). *Deponency and Morphological Mismatches*. Oxford: Oxford University Press.

Bailey, N. (1721). *An Universal Etymological English Dictionary*. London: Nathan Bailey.

Bak, P. (1996). *How Nature Works: The Science of Self-Organized Criticality*. New York: Copernicus Press.

Baker, B., and Harvey, M. (2010). Complex predicate formation. In M. Amberber, B. Baker, and M. Harvey (eds), *Complex Predicates: Cross-linguistic Perspectives on Event structure*. Cambridge: Cambridge University Press, 13–47.

Baker, M. C. (1988). *Incorporation: A Theory of Grammatical Function Changing*. Chicago: University of Chicago Press.

Baker, M. C. (1996). *The Polysynthesis Parameter*. New York: Oxford University Press.

Baker, M. (2003). *Lexical Categories: Verbs, Nouns and Adjectives*. Cambridge: Cambridge University Press.

Baker, M. C. (2009). Is head movement still needed for noun incorporation? The case of Mapudungun. *Lingua* 119: 148–65.

Baker, M. K., and Seifert, L. S. (2001). Syntagmatic-paradigmatic reversal in Alzheimer-type dementia. *Clinical Gerontologist* 23: 65–79.

Baldwin, D. A. (1989). Priorities in children's expectations about object label reference: form over color. *Child Development* 60: 1291–1306.

Baldwin, D., Markman, E., Bill, B., Desjardins, R., Irwin, J., and Tidball, G. (1996). Infants' reliance on a social criterion for establishing word-object relations. *Child Development* 67: 3135–53.

Balfour, S. (2004[2003]). *Pretty Girl in Crimson Rose (8): A Memoir of Love, Exile and Crosswords*. Amsterdam: Atlantic Books.

Balota, D., and Yap, M. (2006). Word recognition, written. In K. Brown (ed.), *Encyclopedia of Language and Linguistics*, 2nd edn, vol. 13. Oxford: Elsevier, 649–54.

Baltin, M., and Postal, P. (1996). More on reanalysis hypothesis. *Linguistic Inquiry* 27: 127–45.

Bamberger, J. (1974). Naming and the transmission of status in a central Brazilian society. *Ethnology* 13: 363–78.

Bammesberger, A. (1984). *English Etymology*. Heidelberg: Winter.

Bannard, C., and Matthews, D. (2008). Stored word sequences in language learning. *Psychological Science* 19: 241–8.

Barabási, A.-L. (2003). *Linked: How Everything Is Connected to Everything Else and What It Means*. New York: Plume.

Barabási, A.-L., and Albert, R. (1999). Emergence of scaling in random networks. *Science* 286: 509–12. Retrieved from <http://arxiv.org/pdf/cond-mat/9910332v1.pdf>.

Barcroft, J. (2002). Semantic and structural elaboration in L2 lexical acquisition. *Language Learning* 52: 323–63.

Barcroft, J. (2003). Effects of questions about word meaning during L2 Spanish lexical learning. *Modern Language Journal* 87: 546–61.

Barcroft, J., Sommers, M. S., and Sunderman, G. (2011). Some costs of fooling Mother Nature: a priming study on the Keyword Method and the quality of developing L2 lexical representations. In P. Trofimovich and K. McDonough (eds), *Applying Priming Methods to L2 Learning, Teaching and Research*. Amsterdam: Benjamins, 49–72.

Bardsley, D. (2003). The rural New Zealand English lexicon 1842–2002. Ph.D thesis, Victoria University of Wellington.

Bardsley, D. (2010). The increasing use of hypocoristics in New Zealand English. *New Zealand English Journal* 24: 55–65.

Bardsley, D., and Simpson, J. (2009). Hypocoristics in New Zealand and Australian English. In P. Peters, P. Collins, and A. Smith (eds), *Comparative Studies in Australian and New Zealand English: Grammar and Beyond*. Amsterdam: Benjamins, 49–73.

Barker, D. (2007). A personalized approach to analyzing 'cost' and 'benefit' in vocabulary selection. *System* 35: 523–33.

Baroni, M., and Evert, S. (2006). The zipfR package for lexical statistics: a tutorial introduction. [Technical report.] Universities of Bologna and Osnabrück. Retrieved from <http://zipfr.r-forge.r-project.org/>.

Barr, D. J., and Keysar, B. (2002). Anchoring comprehension in linguistic precedents. *Journal of Memory and Language* 46: 391–418.

Barrett, R. A. (1978). Village modernization and changing nicknaming practices in northern Spain. *Journal of Anthropological Research* 34: 92–108.

Barrett, R. (2012). *Ideophones and (Non-)arbitrariness in the K'iche' Poetry of Humberto Ak'abal*. Portland, Ore.: Linguistic Society of America.

Barsalou, L. (1999). Perceptual symbol systems. *Behavioral and Brain Sciences* 22: 577–660.

Barsalou, L. (2008a). Grounded cognition. *Annual Review of Psychology* 59: 617–45.

Barsalou, L. W. (2008b). Grounding symbolic operations in the brain's modal systems. In G. R. Sermin and E. R. Smith (eds), *Embodied Grounding: Social, Cognitive, Affective, and Neuroscientific Approaches*. New York: Cambridge University Press, 9–42.

Barsalou, L. W., Santos, A., Simmons, W. K., and Wilson, C. D. (2008). Language and simulation in conceptual processing. In M. De Vega, A. M. Glenberg, and A. C. Graesser (eds), *Symbols, Embodiment, and Meaning*. Oxford: Oxford University Press, 245–83.

Barwise, J., and Cooper, R. (1981). Generalized quantifiers and natural language. *Linguistics and Philosophy* 4: 159–219.

Barwise, J., and Perry, J. (1983). *Situations and Attitudes*. Cambridge, Mass.: MIT Press.

Basnight-Brown, D. M., and Altarriba, J. (2007). Differences in semantic and translation priming across languages: the role of language direction and language dominance. *Memory and Cognition* 35: 953–65.

Bates, E., Camaioni, L., and Volterra, V. (1975). The acquisition of performatives prior to speech. *Merrill-Palmer Quarterly* 21: 205–26.

Battus [Hugo Brandt Corstius] (1981). *Opperlandse taal- en letterkunde*. Amsterdam: Em. Querido. Repr. 2002.

Bauer, L., and Nation, I. S. P. (1993). Word families. *International Journal of Lexicography* 6(4): 253–79.

Baugh, A. C., and Cable, T. (1993). *A History of the English Language*. London: Routledge.

Bean, S. (1980). Ethnology and the study of proper names. *Anthropological Linguistics* 22(7): 305–16.

Bechtel, W., and Abrahamsen, A. (2002). *Connectionism and the Mind: Parallel Processing, Dynamics, and Evolution in Networks*, 2nd edn. Malden, Mass.: Blackwell.

Beck, D. (2008). Ideophones, adverbs, and predicate qualification in Upper Necaxa Totonac. *International Journal of American Linguistics* 74(1): 1–46.

Beckage, N. L., Smith, L., and Hills, T. (2010). Semantic network connectivity is related to vocabulary growth rate in children. In S. Ohlsson and R. Catrambone (eds), *Proceedings of the 32th Annual Conference of the Cognitive Science Society*, 2769–74. Austin, Tex.: Cognitive Science Society.

Beckner, C., Blythe, R., Bybee, J., Christiansen, M., Croft, W., Ellis, N. C., Holland, J, Ke, J., Larsen-Freeman, D., and Schoenemann, T. (2009). Language is a complex adaptive system: position paper. *Language Learning* 59: 1–26.

Beglar, D. (2010). A Rasch-based validation of the Vocabulary Size Test. *Language Testing* 27(1): 101–18.

Beidleman, T. O. (1974). Kuguru names and naming. *Journal of Anthropological Research* 30: 281–93.

Béjoint, H. (2010). *The Lexicography of English*. Oxford: Oxford University Press.

Bell, A., Brenier, J. M., Gregory, M., Girand, C., and Jurafsky, D. (2009). Predictability effects on durations of content and function words in conversational English. *Journal of Memory and Language* 60: 92–111.

Benasich, A. A., and Tallal, P. (2002). Infant discrimination of rapid auditory cues predicts later language impairment. *Behavioural Brain Research* 136(1): 31–49.

Benkö, L., and Imre, S. (1972). *The Hungarian Language*. Budapest: Akadémiai Kiadó.

Bennett, T., Grossberg, L., and Morris, M. (eds) (2005). *New Keywords: A Revised Vocabulary of Culture and Society*. Oxford: Blackwell.

Benson, F. D. (1979). *Aphasia, Alexia and Agraphia*. New York: Churchill Livingstone.

Beretta, A., Fiorentino, R., and Poeppel, D. (2005). The effects of homonymy and polysemy on lexical access: an MEG study. *Cognitive Brain Research* 24: 57–65.

Berg, L. D., and Vuolteenaho, J. (eds) (2009). *Critical Toponymies: The Contested Politics of Place Naming*. Farnham: Ashgate.

Bergelson, E., and Swingley, D. (2012). At 6–9 months, human infants know the meanings of many common nouns. *PNAS: Proceedings of the National Academy of Sciences of the United States of America* 109(9): 3253–8.

Bergen, B. K. (2004). The psychological reality of phonaesthemes. *Language* 80(2): 290–311.

Berger, A. A. (1999). *An Anatomy of Humour*. New York: Transaction.

Berkeley, B. (1965[1710]). *The Principles of Human Knowledge*. In D. M. Armstrong (ed.), *Berkeley's Philosophical Writings*. New York: Collier Macmillan, 41–128.

Berlin, B. (1992). *Ethnobiological Classification: Principles of Categorization of Plants and Animals in Traditional Societies*. Princeton, NJ: Princeton University Press.

Berlin, B. (1994). Evidence for pervasive synesthetic sound symbolism in ethnozoological nomenclature. In L. Hinton, J. Nichols, and J. J. Ohala (eds), *Sound Symbolism*. Cambridge: Cambridge University Press, 76–93.

Berlin, B. (2004). Tapir and squirrel: further nomenclatural meanderings toward a universal sound-symbolic bestiary. In G. Sanga and G. Ortalli (eds), *Nature Knowledge: Ethnoscience, Cognition, and Utility*. Oxford: Berghahn, 119–27.

Berlin, B., and Kay, P. (1969). *Basic Color Terms: Their Universality and Evolution*. Berkeley: University of California Press.

Berlin, B., and O'Neill, J. P. (1981). The pervasiveness of onomatopoeia in Aguaruna and Huambisa bird names. *Journal of Ethnobiology* 1(2): 238–61.

Bertram, R., Laine, M., and Virkkala, M. (2000). The role of derivational morphology in vocabulary acquisition: get by with a little help from my morpheme friends. *Scandinavian Journal of Psychology* 41(4): 287–96.

Berwick, R., and Chomsky, N. (2011). The biolinguistic program: the current state of its evolution. In A. M. Di Sciullo and C. Boeckx (eds), *The Biolinguistic Enterprise: New Perspectives on the Evolution and Nature of the Human Language Faculty*. Oxford: Oxford University Press, 19–41.

Besemeres, M., and Wierzbicka, A. (eds) (2007). *Translating Lives: Living with Two Languages and Cultures*. St Lucia: University of Queensland Press.

Best, K.-H. (2005). Wortlängen. In R. Köhler, G. Altmann, and R. G. Piotrovski (eds), *Quantitative Linguistik/Quantitative Linguistics: Ein Internationales Handbuch/An International Handbook*. Berlin: de Gruyter, 260–73.

Bhat, D. N. S. (1994). *The Adjectival Category*. Amsterdam: Benjamins.

Bi, Y., Han, Z., and Shu, H. (2007). Compound frequency effect in word production: evidence from anomia. *Brain and Language*, 103: 55–6.

Bialystok, E. (2009). Bilingualism: the good, the bad, and the indifferent. *Bilingualism: Language and Cognition* 12: 3–11.

Biber, D. (1988). *Variation Across Speech and Writing*. Cambridge: Cambridge University Press.

Biber, D. (1995). *Dimensions of Cross-linguistic Variation: A Cross-linguistic Comparison*. Cambridge: Cambridge University Press.

Biber, D., and Conrad, S. (2009). *Register, Genre, and Style*. Cambridge: Cambridge University Press.

Biber, D., Conrad, S., Reppen, R., Byrd, P., and Helt, M. (2002). Speaking and writing in the university: a multi-dimensional comparison. *TESOL Quarterly* 36: 9–48.

Biber, D., Johansson, S., Leech, G., Conrad, S., and Finegan, E. (1999). *Longman Grammar of Spoken and Written English*. Harlow: Longman.

Bickel, B. (1998). Rhythm and feet in Belhare morphology. Rutgers Optimality Archive, <http://roa.rutgers.edu>.

Bickel, B. (2011). Absolute and statistical universals. In P. Colm Hogan (ed.), *The Cambridge Encyclopedia of the Language Sciences*. Cambridge: Cambridge University Press, 77–9.

Bickel, B., Gaenszle, M., Lieven, E., Paudyal, N. P., Rai, Ichchha Purna, R., Manoj, R., Novel, K., and Stoll, S. (2007). Free prefix ordering in Chintang. *Language* 83(1): 43–73.

Bickel, B., Hildebrandt, K. A., and Schiering, R. (2009). The distribution of phonological word domains: a probabilistic typology. In J. Grijzenhout and B. Kabak (eds), *Phonological Domains: Universals and Deviations*. Berlin: Mouton de Gruyter, 47–75.

Bickerton, D. (2009). *Adam's Tongue: How Humans Made Language, How Language Made Humans*. New York: Hill a& Wang.

Biederman, I. (1987). Recognition-by-components: a theory of human image understanding. *Psychological Review* 94(2): 115–47.

Biemiller, A. (2005). Size and sequence in vocabulary development. In E. H. Hiebert and M. L. Kamil (eds), *Teaching and Learning Vocabulary: Bringing Research into Practice*. Mahwah, NJ: Erlbaum, 223–42.

Biemiller, A., and Slonim, N. (2001). Estimating root word vocabulary growth in normative and advantaged populations: evidence for a common sequence of vocabulary acquisition. *Journal of Educational Psychology* 93(3): 498–520.

Bien, H., Levelt, W. J. M., and Baayen, R. H. (2005). Frequency effects in compound production. *Proceedings of the National Academy of Sciences* 102: 17876–81.

Bierwisch, M., and Schreuder, R. (1992). From concepts to lexical items. *Cognition* 42: 23–60.

Biggam, C. P. (2012). *The Semantics of Colour: A Historical Approach*. Cambridge: Cambridge University Press.

Biggs, B. (1969). *Let's Learn Maori: A Guide to the Study of the Maori Language*. Wellington: Reed.

Bishop, D. V. (1994). Is specific language impairment a valid diagnostic category? Genetic and psycholinguistic evidence. *Philosophical Transactions of the Royal Society of London, series B: Biological Sciences* 346(1315): 105–11.

Bishop, D. V. (1997). *Uncommon Understanding: Development and Disorders of Language Comprehension in Children*. Hove: Psychology Press.

Bishop, D. V. (2006). What causes specific language impairment in children? *Current Directions in Psychological Science* 15(5): 217–21.

Bishop, R. G. (1984). Consonant play in lexical sets in northern Totonac. *SIL Mexico Working Papers* 5: 24–31.

Black, H. C., Garner, B., et al. (1891). *Black's Law Dictionary*. St Paul, Minn.: West. 9th edn 2009.

Black, W., Elkateb. S., Rodriguez, H., Alkhalifa, M., Vossen, P., Pease, A., Bertran, M., and Fellbaum, C. (2006). The Arabic WordNet Project. In *Proceedings of the Conference on Lexical Resources in the European Community* (Genoa).

Blake, B. J. (2001). *Case*. Cambridge: Cambridge University Press.

Blank, A. (1997). *Prinzipien des lexikalischen Bedeutungswandels am Beispiel der romanischen Sprachen*. Tübingen: Niemeyer.

Blanken, G. (2000). The production of nominal compounds in aphasia. *Brain and Language* 74: 84–102.

Blenkiron, P. (2010). *Stories and Analogies in Cognitive Behaviour Therapy*. Chichester: Wiley.

Bleses, D., Vach, W., Slott, M., Wehberg, S., Thomsen, P., Madsen, T. O., and Basbøll, H. (2008). Early vocabulary development in Danish and other languages: A CDI comparison. *Journal of Child Language* 35: 619–50.

Bleuler, E. (1911/1950). *Dementia Praecox or the Group of Schizophrenias*. New York: International Universities Press.

Bloem, I., and La Heij, W. (2003). Semantic facilitation and semantic interference in word translation: implications for models of lexical access in language production. *Journal of Memory and Language* 48: 468–88.

Bloom, L., Tinker, E., and Margulis, C. (1993). The words children learn: evidence against a noun bias in early vocabularies. *Cognitive Development* 8: 431–50.

Bloom, P. (2000). *How Children Learn the Meaning of Words*. Cambridge, Mass.: MIT Press.

Bloom, P. (2001). Précis of *How Children Learn the Meaning of Words*. *Behavioral and Brain Science* 24: 1095–1103.

Bloom, P. (2004). *Descartes' Baby*. New York: Basic Books.

Bloom, P. (2006). Word learning and theory of mind. In W. E. Mann (ed.), *Augustine's Confessions: Critical Essays*. Lanham, Md.: Rowman & Littlefield, 17–29.

Bloomfield, L. (1933). *Language*. New York: Holt, Rinehart, & Winston.

Bloomfield, L. (1946). Algonquian. In H. Hoijer and C. Osgood (eds), *Linguistic Structures of Native America*. New York: Viking Fund Publications in Anthropology, 85–129.

Blount, B. G. (1972). Aspects of Luo socialization. *Language in Society* 1: 236–48.

Blount, B. G. (1993). Luo personal names: reference and meaning. In S. Mufwene and L. Moshi (eds), *Topics in African Linguistics*. Washington, DC: American University Press, 131–40.

Blount, B. G. (2014). Situating cultural models in history and cognition. In M. Yamaguchi, D. Tay, and B. Blount (eds), *Language, Culture, and Cognition in the 21st Century: The Intersection of Cognitive Linguistics and Cognitive Anthropology*. London: Palgrave Macmillan.

Blumenfeld, H. K., and Marian, V. (2007). Constraints on parallel activation in bilingual spoken language processing: examining proficiency and lexical status using eye-tracking. *Language and Cognitive Processes* 22: 1–28.

Boas, F. (1934). *Geographical Names of the Kwakiutl Indians*. New York: Columbia University Press.

Bochkarev, V. V., Shevlykova, A. V., and Solovyev, V. D. (2012). Average word length dynamics as indicator of cultural changes in society. <http://arxiv.org/abs/1208.6109>.

Bock, C. (1948). Prefixes and suffixes. *Classical Journal* 44: 132–33.

Bock, J. K. (1986). Syntactic persistence in language production. *Cognitive Psychology* 18: 355–87.

Bock, J. K., and Griffin, Z. M. (2000). The persistence of structural priming: transient activation or implicit learning? *Journal of Experimental Psychology: General* 129: 177–92.

Bock, K., and Levelt, W. (1994). Language production: grammatical encoding. In M. A. Grenssbacher (ed.), *Handbook of Psycholinguistics*. San Diego, Calif.: Academic Press, 954–84.

Boeckx, C. (2011). Some reflections on Darwin's problem in the context of Cartesian biolinguistics. In A. M. Di Sciullo and C. Boeckx (eds), *The Biolinguistic Enterprise: New Perspectives on the Evolution and Nature of the Human Language Faculty*. Oxford: Oxford University Press, 42–64.

Boers, F. (2000a). Metaphor awareness and vocabulary retention. *Applied Linguistics* 21: 553–71.

Boers, F. (2000b). Enhancing metaphoric awareness in specialized reading. *English for Specific Purposes* 19: 137–47.

Boers, F. (2001). Remembering figurative idioms by hypothesising about their origin. *Prospect* 16: 35–43.

Boers, F. (2011). Cognitive semantic ways of teaching figurative phrases: an assessment. *Review of Cognitive Linguistics* 9(1): 227–61.

Boers, F., Demecheleer, M., Coxhead, A., and Webb, S. (2014). Gauging the effects of exercises on verb–noun collocations. *Language Teaching Research* 18(1): 54–74.

Boers, F., Eyckmans, J., Kappel, J., Stengers, H., and Demecheleer, H. (2006). Formulaic sequences and perceived oral proficiency: putting a lexical approach to the test. *Language Teaching Research* 10: 245–61.

Boers, F., Eyckmans, J., and Stengers, H. (2007). Presenting figurative idioms with a touch of etymology: more than mere mnemonics? *Language Teaching Research* 11: 43–62.

Boers, F., and Lindstromberg, S. (2009). *Optimizing a Lexical Approach to Instructed Second Language Acquisition*. Basingstoke: Palgrave Macmillan.

Boers, F., and Lindstromberg, S. (2012). Experimental and intervention studies on formulaic sequences in a second language. *Annual Review of Applied Linguistics* 32: 83–110.

Boers, F., Piquer Píriz, A. M, Stengers, H., and Eyckmans, J. (2009). Does pictorial elucidation foster recollection of idioms? *Language Teaching Research* 13: 367–82.

Bolinger, D. L. (1940). Word affinities. *American Speech* 15: 62–73.

Bolinger, D. L. (1948). On defining the morpheme. *Word* 4: 18–23.

Bolinger, D. L. (1950a). Rime, assonance, and morpheme analysis. *Word* 6: 117–36.

Bolinger, D. L. (1950b). Shivaree and the phonestheme. *American Speech* 25: 134–5.

Bolinger, D. L. (1963). The uniqueness of the word. *Lingua* 12: 113–36.

Bolinger, D. L. (1965). *Forms of English.* Cambridge, Mass.: Harvard University Press.

Bolinger, D. (1971). *The Phrasal Verb in English.* Cambridge, Mass.: Harvard University Press.

Bonami, O., and Boyé, G. (2007). French pronominal clitics and the design of paradigm function morphology. In G. Booij, B. Fradin, A. Ralli, and S. Scalise (eds), *Online Proceedings of the Fifth Mediterranean Morphology Meeting,* 291–322. <http://mmm.lingue.unibo.it>.

Bongers, H. (1947). *The History and Principles of Vocabulary Control.* Wocopi: Woerden.

Booij, G. (1996). Inherent versus contextual inflection and the Split Morphology Hypothesis. In G. Booij and J. van Marle (eds), *Yearbook of Morphology* 1995. Dordrecht/Boston: Kluwer, 1–16.

Booij, G. (1999). *The Phonology of Dutch.* Oxford: Oxford University Press.

Booij, G. (2007). *The Grammar of Words: An Introduction to Linguistic Morphology,* 2nd edn. Oxford: Oxford University Press.

Booij, G. (2010). *Construction Morphology.* Oxford: Oxford University Press.

Booij, G. (2012). *The Grammar of Words,* 3rd edn. Oxford: Oxford University Press.

Booij, G., Lehmann, C., and Mugdan, J. (eds) (2000/2004). *Morphologie: ein internationales Handbuch zur Flexion und Wortbildung/Morphology: A Handbook on Inflection and Word Formation.* Berlin: de Gruyter.

Boretzky, N. (1994). *Romani: Grammatik des Kalderaš-Dialekts mit Texten und Glossar.* Berlin: Harrassowitz.

Bornstein, M. H., Cote, L. R., Maital, S., Painter, K., Park, S.-Y., Pascual, L., Pêcheux, M.-G., Ruel, J., Venuti, P., and Vyt, A. (2004). Cross-linguistic analysis of vocabulary in young children: Spanish, Dutch, French, Hebrew, Italian, Korean, and American English. *Child Development* 75: 1115–39.

Boroditsky, L. (2000). Metaphoric structuring: understanding time through spatial metaphors. *Cognition* 75: 1–28.

Bortfeld, H., Morgan, J. L., Golinkoff, R. M., and Rathbun, K. (2005). Mommy and me: familiar names help launch babies into speech-stream segmentation. *Psychological Science* 16(4): 298–304.

Boullon, A. (2007). An approach to the linguistic configuration of surnames in Galicia. *Verba* 34: 285–309.

Brandes, S. H. (1973). Social structure and in personal relations in Navanogal, Spain. *American Anthropologist* 75: 750–65.

Brandes, S. H. (1975). The structural and demographic implication of nicknames in Navabnogal, Spain. *American Ethnologist* 2: 139–48.

Breen, R. (1982). Naming practices in western Ireland. *Man* 17: 701–13.

Brent, M. R. (1999). Speech segmentation and word discovery: a computational perspective. *Trends in Cognitive Sciences* 3(8): 294–301.

Bourigault, D., and Slodzian, M. (1999). Pour une terminologie textuelle. *Terminologies nouvelles* 19: 29–32.

Bowdler, T. (1818/1843). *The Family Shakspeare: In Ten Volumes; in which Nothing is Added to the Original Text; But Those Words and Expressions are Omitted which Cannot with Propriety be Read Aloud in a Family*, vol. 1: *The Comedies*, 3rd edn. London: Longman, Hurst, Rees, Orme, & Brown.

Bowman, W. D. (1932). *The Story of Surnames*. London: Routledge.

Boyd-Graber, J., Fellbaum, C., Osherson, D., and Schapire, R. (2006). Adding dense, weighted connections to WordNet. In *Proceedings of the Third Global WordNet Meeting* (Jeju Island, Korea).

Bray, D. de S. (1934). *The Brahui Language, II and III*. Delhi: Manager of Publications.

Bregenzer, J. (1968). Naming practices in South America. *Journal of the Minnesota Academy of Sciences* 35: 47–50.

Brennan, S. E., and Clark, H. H. (1996). Conceptual pacts and lexical choice in conversation. *Journal of Experimental Psychology: Learning, Memory, and Cognition* 22: 1482–93.

Brent, M. R., and Siskind, J. M. (2001). The role of exposure to isolated words in early vocabulary development. *Cognition* 81(2): B33–B44.

Brentari, D. (1998). *A Prosodic Model of Sign Language Phonology*. Cambridge, MA: MIT Press.

Bresnan, J. (1978). A realistic transformational grammar. In M. Halle, J. Bresnan, and G. A. Miller (eds), *Linguistic Theory and Psychological Reality*. Cambridge, Mass.: MIT Press, 1–59.

Bresnan, J. (1982). The passive in lexical theory. In J. Bresnan (ed.), *The Mental Representation of Grammatical Relations*. Cambridge, Mass.: MIT Press, 3–86.

Bresnan, J. (2001). *Lexical-Functional Syntax*. Oxford: Blackwell.

Brewer, C. (2007). *Treasure-House of the Language: The Living OED*. New Haven, Conn.: Yale University Press.

Brewer, E. C., et al. (1870). *Brewer's Dictionary of Phrase and Fable*. London: Cassell, Fetter, & Galpin. 18th edn, Edinburgh: Chambers, 2009.

Brewer, J. D. (1981). Bimanese personal names: meaning and use. *Ethnology* 20: 203–15.

Bright, W. O. (1952). Lexical acculturation in Karok. *International Journal of American Linguistics* 18: 73–82.

Bright, W. O. (1960). Animals of acculturation in California Indian languages. *University of California Publications in Linguistics* 4: 215–46.

Brinton, L. J., and Traugott, E. C. (2005). *Lexicalization and Language Change*. Cambridge: Cambridge University Press.

Broca, P. (1865). Du siège de la faculté du langage articulé. *Bulletins de la Société d'anthropologie* 6: 337.

Bromhead, H. (2009). *The Reign of Truth and Faith: Epistemic Expressions in 16th and 17th Century English*. Berlin: Mouton de Gruyter.

Bromhead, H. (2011). Ethnogeographical categories in English and Pitjantjatjara/Yankunytjatjara. *Language Sciences* 33(1): 58–75.

Bromhead, H. (2013). Mountains, rivers, billabongs: ethnogeographical categorization in cross-linguistic perspective. Ph.D thesis, Australian National University.

Brophy, J., and Partridge, E. (1931). *Songs and Slang of the British Soldier: 1914–1918*, 3rd edn. London: Routledge & Kegan Paul.

Brown, C. H. (1976). General principles of human anatomical partonomy and speculations on the growth of partonomic nomenclature. *American Ethnologist* 3(3): 400–24.

Brown, C. H. (1999). *Lexical Acculturation in Native American Languages*. Oxford: Oxford University Press.

Brown, C. H. (2008). Hand and arm. In M. Haspelmath, M. Dryer, D. Gil, and B. Comrie (eds), *The World Atlas of Language Structures Online*. Munich: Max Planck Digital Library. <http://wals.info>.

Brown, D., and Chumakina, M. (2012). What there might be and what there is: an introduction to canonical typology. In D. Brown, M. Chumakina, and G. G. Corbett (eds), *Canonical Morphology and Syntax*. Oxford: Oxford University Press, 1–19.

Brown, D., Chumakina, M., Corbett, G., Popova, G., and Spencer, A. (2012). Defining 'periphrasis': key notions. *Morphology* 22: 233–75.

Brown, D., and Hippisley, A. (2012). *Network Morphology: A Defaults Based Theory of Word Structure*. Cambridge: Cambridge University Press.

Brown, P. (1998). Children's first verbs in Tzeltal: evidence for an early verb category. *Linguistics* 36: 713–53.

Brown, P. (2007). 'She had just cut/broken off her head': cutting and breaking verbs in Tzeltal. *Cognitive Linguistics* 18: 319–30.

Brown, R. (1958a). How shall a thing be called? *Psychological Review* 65: 14–21.

Brown, R. (1958b). *Words and Things*. New York: Free Press.

Brown, R. (1973). *A First Language: The Early Stages*. Cambridge, Mass.: Harvard University Press.

Brown, R., and McNeill, D. (1966). The 'tip of the tongue' phenomenon. *Journal of Verbal Learning and Verbal Behavior* 5: 325–37.

Brown, T. S., and Perry, F. L. (1991). A comparison of three learning strategies for ESL vocabulary acquisition. *TESOL Quarterly* 25: 655–70.

Bruening, B. (2012). Word formation is syntactic: adjectival passives in English. To appear in *Natural Language and Linguistic Theory*. Downloaded 15 Feb. 2013 from <http://udel.edu/~bruening/Downloads/AdjectivalPass3.pdf>.

Bruner, J. (1957/2006). Going beyond the information given. In *Search of Pedagogy: The Selected Works of Jerome S. Bruner*, vol. 1. New York: Routledge, 7–23.

Bruner, J. S. (1975). The ontogenesis of speech acts. *Journal of Child Language* 2: 1–20.

Brysbaert, M., and New, B. (2009). Moving beyond Kucera and Francis: a critical evaluation of current word frequency norms and the introduction of a new and improved word frequency measure for American English. *Behavior Research Methods* 41(4): 977–90.

Brysbaert, M., New, B., and Keuleers, E. (2012). Adding part-of-speech information to the SUBTLEX-US word frequencies. *Behavior Research Methods* 1(7): 991–7.

Buccino, G., Riggio, L., Melli, G., Binkofski, F., Gallese, V., and Rizzolatti, G. (2005). Listening to action related sentences modulates the activity of the motor system: a combined TMS and behavioral study. *Cognitive Brain Research* 24: 355–63.

Buchanan, M. (2002). *Nexus: Small Worlds and the Groundbreaking Science of Networks*. New York: Norton.

Buchi, E. (2016). Etymological dictionaries. In P. Durkin (ed.), *The Oxford Handbook of Lexicography*. Oxford: Oxford University Press, 338–49.

Buck, C. D. (1988[1949]). *A Dictionary of Selected Synonyms in the Principal Indo-European Languages*. Chicago: University of Chicago Press.

Buendía, M., and Faber, P. (2012). EcoLexicon: algo más que un tesauro sobre el medio ambiente. In J. L. Martí Ferriol and A. Muñoz Miquel (eds), *Estudios de traducción e interpretación: entornos de especialidad*, vol. 2. Castelló: Publicaciones de la Universitat Jaume I.

Burchfield, R. (1972). Four-letter words and the OED. *Times Literary Supplement* 13 (October).

Burchfield, R. W. (1972–86). *Oxford English Dictionary Supplement*. Oxford: Clarendon Press.

Burchfield, R. (1989). *Unlocking the English Language*. London: Faber & Faber.

Burenhult, N. (2006). Body part terms in Jahai. *Language Sciences* 28(2–3): 162–80.

Burenhult, N., and Levinson, S. C. (2008). Language and landscape: a cross-linguistic perspective. *Language Sciences* 30(2–3): 135–50.

Burenhult, N., and Majid, A. (2011). Olfaction in Aslian ideology and language. *The Senses and Society* 6(1): 19–29.

Burger, H. G. (1984). *The Wordtree.* Merriam, Kans.: Wordtree.

Burgess, A. (1992). *A Mouthful of Air*, ch. 10. London: Hutchinson.

Burnley, D. (1992). Lexis and semantics. In R. M. Hogg (ed.), *The Cambridge History of the English Language*, vol. 2. Cambridge: Cambridge University Press, 409–99.

Burns, A. (forthcoming). Change and progress: a socio-onomastic study of field-names in Aberdeenshire. *Names.*

Burridge, K. (1993). Evidence for taboo and euphemism in Early Dutch. In T. Dutton, M. Ross, and D. Tryon (eds), *The Language Game: Papers in Memory of Donald C. Laycock.* Canberra: Pacific Linguistics, 81–94.

Burridge, K. (2012). Euphemism and language change. Lexis, E-Journal in English Lexicology, 65–92. <http://lexis.univ-lyon3.fr/spip.php?article179]>.

Butler, S. (1670s). Satire upon the imperfection and abuse of human learning. Reprinted in *The Poetical Works of Samuel Butler*, vol. 2 (London: Pickering, 1835), 233.

Butterworth, B. (1983). Lexical representation. In B. E. Butterworth (ed.), *Language Production*, vol. 2. Cambridge, Mass.: Academic Press, 257–94.

Butterworth, B. (1989). Lexical access in speech production. In W. Marslen-Wilson (ed.), *Lexical Representation and Process.* Cambridge, Mass.: MIT Press, 108–35.

Bybee, J. (2006). Language change and universals. In R. Mairal and J. Gil (eds), *Linguistic Universals.* Cambridge: Cambridge University Press, 179–94.

Bybee, J. (2007). *Frequency of Use and the Organization of Language.* New York: Oxford University Press.

Bybee, J. (2010). *Language, Usage and Cognition.* New York: Cambridge University Press.

Bybee, J., and Slobin, D. (1982). Rules and schemas in the development and use of English past tense. *Language* 59: 251–70.

Byrd, R. J., Calzolari, N., Chodorow, M., Klavans, J., Neff, M., and Rizk, O. (1987). Tools and methods for computational lexicology. *Computational Linguistics* 13(3–4): 219–40.

Byron, L. (1819–24). *Don Juan*, canto 3, stanza 88. London: Murray.

Cabré, M. T. (2003). Theories of terminology: their description, prescription and evaluation. *Terminology* 9(2): 163–200.

Cacciari, C., and Tabossi, P. (eds) (1993). *Idioms: Processing, Structure, and Interpretation.* Hillsdale, NJ: Erlbaum.

Callaghan, C. A. (1963). *Lake Miwok Dictionary.* Berkeley: University of California Press.

Callahan, T., Moll, H., Rakoczy, H., Warneken, F., Liszkowski, U., Behne, T., and Tomasello, M. (2011). Early social cognition in three cultural contexts. *Monographs of the Society for Research in Child Development* 76(299). Bethesda, Md.

Cameron, A., et al. (1986–). *The Dictionary of Old English.* Toronto: Institute of Medieval Studies.

Cameron, K. (1965). *Scandinavian Settlement in the Territory of the Five Boroughs: The Place-Name Evidence.* Nottingham: University of Nottingham. Repr. in K. Cameron (ed.), *Place-Name Evidence for the Anglo-Saxon Invasion and Scandinavian Settlements* (Nottingham: English Place-Name Society, 1975), 115–38.

Cameron, K. (1970). Scandinavian settlement in the territory of the Five Boroughs: the place-name evidence. Part II: Place-names in *thorp. Mediaeval Scandinavia* 3: 35–49.

Reprinted in K. Cameron (ed.), *Place-Name Evidence for the Anglo-Saxon Invasion and Scandinavian Settlements* (Nottingham: English Place-Name Society, 1975), 139–56.

Cameron, K. (1971). Scandinavian settlement in the territory of the Five Boroughs: the place-name evidence. Part III: The Grimston-hybrids. In P. Clemoes and K. Hughes (eds), *England Before the Conquest: Studies in Primary Sources Presented to Dorothy Whitelock*. Cambridge: Cambridge University Press. Reprinted in K. Cameron (ed.), *Place-Name Evidence for the Anglo-Saxon Invasion and Scandinavian Settlements* (Nottingham: English Place-Name Society, 1975), 147–63.

Cameron, K. (ed.) (1975). *Place-Name Evidence for the Anglo-Saxon Invasion and Scandinavian Settlements*. Nottingham: English Place-Name Society.

Cameron, L., and Deignan, A. (2003). Combining large and small corpora to investigate tuning devices around metaphor in spoken discourse. *Metaphor and Symbol* 18(3): 149–60.

Campos, A., Amor, A., and Gonzalez, M. A. (2003). Limitations of the mnemonic-keyword method. *Journal of General Psychology* 130: 399–413.

Campos, A., Amor, A., and Gonzalez, M. A. (2004). The importance of the keyword-generation method in keyword mnemonics. *Experimental Psychology* 51: 125–31.

Caramazza, A. (1997). How many levels of processing are there in lexical access? *Cognitive Neuropsychology* 14: 177–208.

Caramazza, A., Laudanna, A., and Romani, C. (1988). Lexical access and inflectional morphology. *Cognition* 28: 297–332.

Carbaugh, D. (2005). *Cultures in Conversation*. Mahwah, NJ: Erlbaum.

Carbaugh, D., Berry, M., and Nurmikari-Berry, M. (2006). Coding personhood through cultural terms and practices: silence and quietude as a Finnish 'natural way of being'. *Journal of Language and Social Psychology* 25(3): 203–20.

Carey, S. (1978). The child as word learner. In J. Bresnan, G. Miller, and M. Halle (eds), *Linguistic Theory and Psychological Reality*. Cambridge, Mass.: MIT Press, 264–93.

Carey, S. (1988). Lexical development: the Rockefeller years. In B. Hirst (ed.), *The Making of Cognitive Science: Essays in Honor of George A. Miller*. Cambridge: Cambridge University Press, 197–209.

Carnie, A. (2013). *Syntax: A Generative Introduction*, 3rd edn. Oxford: Blackwell.

Carpenter, M., Nagel, K., and Tomasello, M. (1998). Social cognition, joint attention, and communicative competence from 9–15 months. *Monographs of the Society for Research in Child Development* 63(255). Bethesda, Md.

Carroll, J. B., Davies, P., and Richman, B. (1971). *The American Heritage Word Frequency Book*. New York: Houghton Mifflin.

Carroll, J. M. (1983). Toward a functional theory of names and naming. *Linguistics* 21: 341–71.

Carstairs-McCarthy, A. (1999). *The Origins of Complex Language: An Inquiry into the Evolutionary Origins of Sentences, Syllables, and Truth*. Oxford: Oxford University Press.

Carstairs-McCarthy, A. (2005). The evolutionary origin of morphology. In M. Tallerman (ed.), *Language Origins: Perspectives on Evolution*. Oxford: Oxford University Press, 435–41.

Carter, A. L. (1978). From sensori-motor vocalizations to words: a case study of the evolution of attention-directing communication in the second year. In A. Lock (ed.), *Action, Gesture, and Symbol: The Emergence of Language*. London: Academic Press, 309–49.

Carter, R. (1976). Some constraints on possible words. *Semantikos* 1: 27–66.

Caselli, C., Casadio, P., and Bates, E. (1999). A comparison of the transition from first words to grammar in English and Italian. *Journal of Child Language* 26: 69–111.

Casey, P. J. (1992). A re-examination of the roles of typicality and category dominance in verifying category membership. *Journal of Experimental Psychology: Learning, Memory, and Cognition* 12: 257–67.

Cassidy, F. G., and Hall, J. H. (1985–2011). *Dictionary of American Regional English*. Cambridge, Mass.: Belknap Press of Harvard University Press.

Cassidy, K. W., Kelly, M. H., and Sharoni, L. J. (1999). Inferring gender from name phonology. *Journal of Experimental Psychology: General* 128: 1–20.

Cawdrey, R. (1604). *A Table Alphabeticall, conteyning and teaching the true writing and vnderstanding of hard usuall English wordes*. London: Edmund Weaver.

Cawdrey, R. (1997[1604]). *A Table Alphabeticall, Conteyning and Teaching the True Writing, and Understanding of Hard Usuall English Words*, ed. R. E. Siemens. Toronto: University of Toronto Library.

Chamberlain, A. F. (1903). Primitive taste-words. *American Journal of Psychology* 14: 146–53.

Chapman, K. L., Leonard, L. B., and Mervis, C. B. (1986). The effect of feedback on young children's inappropriate word usage. *Journal of Child Language* 13: 101–17.

Chappell, H., and McGregor, W. (eds) (1996). *The Grammar of Inalienability: A Typological Perspective on Body Part Terms and the Part–Whole Relation*. Berlin: Mouton de Gruyter.

Chebanov, S. G. (1947). On conformity of language structures within the Indo-European family to Poisson's Law. In *Comptes rendus (Doklady) de l'Académie des sciences de l'URSS* 55(2): 99–102.

Chee, M. W. L., Tan, E. W. L., and Thiel, T. (1999). Mandarin and English single word processing studied with functional magnetic resonance imaging. *Journal of Neuroscience* 19: 3050–56.

Chen, H., and Leung, Y. (1989). Patterns of lexical processing in a nonnative language. *Journal of Experimental Psychology: Learning, Memory, and Cognition* 15: 316–25.

Cheney, D., and Seyforth, R. (1990). *How Monkeys See the World*. Chicago: University of Chicago Press.

Cheng, W., Greaves, C., Sinclair, J. M., and Warren, M. (2009). Uncovering the extent of the phraseological tendency: towards a systematic analysis of concgrams. *Applied Linguistics* 30(2): 236–52.

Cheng, W., Greaves, C., and Warren, M. (2006). From n-gram to skipgram to concgram. *International Journal of Corpus Linguistics* 11(4): 411–33.

Chenu, F., and Jisa, H. (2006). Caused motion constructions and semantic generality in early acquisition of French. In E. V. Clark and B. F. Kelly (eds), *Constructions in Acquisition*. Stanford, Calif.: CSLI, 233–61.

Chi, M. T. H., and Koeske, R. D. (1983). Network representation of a child's dinosaur knowledge. *Developmental Psychology* 19: 29–39.

Childers, J. B., Vaughan, J., and Burquest, D. A. (2007). Joint attention and word learning in Ngas-speaking toddlers in Nigeria. *Journal of Child Language* 33: 199–225.

Childs, G. T. (1989). Where do ideophones come from? *Studies in the Linguistic Sciences* 19: 57–78.

Childs, G. T. (1994). African ideophones. In L. Hinton, J. Nichols, and J. J. Ohala (eds), *Sound Symbolism*. Cambridge: Cambridge University Press, 247–79.

Childs, G. T. (2011). *A Grammar of Mani*. Berlin: de Gruyter.

Cho, K., and Krashen, S. (1994). Acquisition of vocabulary from the Sweet Valley Kids series: adult ESL acquisition. *Journal of Reading* 37: 662–7.

Choi, S. (2000). Caregiver input in English and Korean: use of nouns and verbs in book-reading and toy-play contexts. *Journal of Child Language* 27: 69–96.

Choi, S. (2006). Influence of language-specific input on spatial cognition: categories of containment. *First Language* 26: 207–32.

Choi, S., and Gopnik, A. (1995). Early acquisition of verbs in Korean: a cross-linguistic study. *Journal of Child Language* 22: 497–529.

Choi, S., McDonough, L., Bowerman, M., and Mandler, J. M. (1999). Early sensitivity to language-specific spatial categories in English and Korean. *Cognitive Development* 14: 241–68.

Chomsky, N. (1957). *Syntactic Structures*. The Hague: Mouton.

Chomsky, N. (1970). Remarks on nominalization. In R. Jacobs and P. Rosenbaum (eds), *Readings in English Transformational Grammar*. Waltham, Mass.: Ginn, 184–221.

Chomsky, N. (1995). *The Minimalist Program*. Cambridge, Mass.: MIT Press.

Chomsky, N. (2000). *New Horizons in the Study of Language and Mind*. Cambridge: Cambridge University Press.

Chomsky, N. (2007). Of minds and language. *Biolinguistics* 1: 1009–27.

Chomsky, N., and Halle, M. (1968). *The Sound Pattern of English*. Cambridge, Mass.: MIT Press.

Chouinard, M. M., and Clark, E. V. (2003). Adult reformulations of child errors as negative evidence. *Journal of Child Language* 30: 637–69.

Christiansen, M. H., Allen, J., and Seidenberg, M. S. (1998). Learning to segment speech using multiple cues: a connectionist model. *Language and Cognitive Processes* 13(2–3): 221–68.

Christiansen-Bolli, R. (2010). *A Grammar of Tadaksahak, a Berberised Songhay Language*. Cologne: Köppe.

Christophe, V. (1998). *Les émotions: tour d'horizon des principales théories*. Villeneuve-d'Ascq: Presses universitaires du Septentrion.

Chung, T. M., and Nation, P. (2004). Identifying technical vocabulary. *System* 32(2): 251–63.

Church, K., and Hanks, P. (1990). Word association norms, mutual information and lexicography. *Computational Linguistics* 16(1): 22–9.

Ciccotosto, N. (1991). Sound symbolism in natural languages. Thesis, University of Florida.

Ciccotosto, N. (1995). *Sound Symbolism in Natural Languages*. Ann Arbor, Mich.: University Microfilms.

Cilas Simpraga, A. (2006). Family nicknames in Promina. *Folia Onomastica Croatica* 15: 39–69.

Clackson, J. (2007). *Indo-European Linguistics: An Introduction*. Cambridge: Cambridge University Press.

Claridge, G. (2005). Simplification in graded readers: measuring the authenticity of graded text. *Reading in a Foreign Language* 17(2). <http://nflrc.hawaii.edu/rfl/october2005/claridge/claridge.html>.

Clark, E. V. (1973). Non-linguistic strategies in the acquisition of meaning. *Cognition* 2: 161–82.

Clark, E. V. (1978). Strategies for communicating. *Child Development* 49: 953–9.

Clark, E. V. (1979). Building a vocabulary: words for objects, actions, and relations. In P. Fletcher and M. Garman (eds), *Language Acquisition: Studies in Language Development*. Cambridge: Cambridge University Press, 149–60.

Clark, E. V. (1982). Language change during language acquisition. In M. E. Lamb and A. L. Brown (eds), *Advances in Developmental Psychology*, vol. 2. Hillsdale, NJ: Erlbaum, 171–95.

Clark, E. V. (1987). The principle of contrast: a constraint on language acquisition. In B. MacWhinney (ed.), *Mechanisms of Language Acquisition*. Hillsdale, NJ: Erlbaum, 1–33.

Clark, E. V. (1990). On the pragmatics of contrast. *Journal of Child Language* 17: 417–31.

Clark, E. V. (1993). *The Lexicon in Acquisition*. Cambridge: Cambridge University Press.

Clark, E. V. (1995). Language acquisition: the lexicon and syntax. In J. L. Miller and P. D. Eimas (eds), *Handbook of Perception and Cognition* 2nd edn, vol. 11: *Speech, Language, and Communication*. New York: Academic Press, 303–37.

Clark, E. V. (2004). How language acquisition builds on cognitive development. *Trends in Cognitive Sciences* 8: 472–8.

Clark, E. V. (2007). Young children's uptake of new words in conversation. *Language in Society* 36: 157–82.

Clark, E. (2009). *First Language Acquisition*, 2nd edn. Cambridge: Cambridge University Press.

Clark, E. V. (2010). Adult offer, word-class, and child uptake in early lexical acquisition. *First Language* 30: 250–69.

Clark, E. V., and Bernicot, J. (2008). Repetition as ratification: how parents and children place information in common ground. *Journal of Child Language* 35: 349–71.

Clark, E., and Clark, H. (1979). When nouns surface as verbs. *Language* 55: 767–811.

Clark, E. V., and Estigarribia, B. (2011). Using speech and gesture to inform young children about unfamiliar word meanings. *Gesture* 11(1): 1–23.

Clark, E. V., and Grossman, J. B. (1998). Pragmatic directions and children's word learning. *Journal of Child Language* 25: 1–18.

Clark, E. V., and Hecht, B. F. (1983). Comprehension, production, and language acquisition. *Annual Review of Psychology* 34: 325–49.

Clark, E. V., and Nikitina, T. V. (2009). One vs. more than one: antecedents to plural marking in early language acquisition. *Linguistics* 47: 103–39.

Clark, H. H. (1991). Words, the world, and their possibilities. In G. Lockhead and J. Pomerantz (eds), *The Perception of Structure*. Washington, DC: APA, 263–77.

Clark, H. H., and Carlson, T. B. (1981). Context for comprehension. In J. Long and A. Baddeley (eds), *Attention and Performance*, vol. 9. Hillsdale, NJ: Erlbaum, 313–30.

Clark, H. H., and Clark, E. V. (1977). *Psychology and Language: An Introduction to Psycholinguistics*. New York: Harcourt Brace Jovanovich.

Clark, H. H., and Marshall, C. R. (1981). Definite reference and mutual knowledge. In A. K. Joshi, B. Webber, and I. Sag (eds), *Elements of Discourse Understanding*. Cambridge: Cambridge University Press, 10–63.

Clark, H. H., and Wilkes-Gibbs, D. (1986). Referring as a collaborative process. *Cognition* 22: 1–39.

Clark, L. (1977). Phonological acculturation in Sayula Popoluca. *International Journal of American Linguistics* 43: 128–38.

Clark, R. (1982). 'Necessary' and 'unnecessary' borrowing. In A. Halim (ed.), *Papers from the Third International Conference on Austronesian Linguistics*, vol. 3: *Accent on Variety*. Canberra: Australian National University, 137–43.

Clements, G. N. (1990). The role of the sonority cycle in core syllabification. In J. Kingston and M. E. Beckman (eds), *Papers in Laboratory Phonology 1: Between the Grammar and Physics of Speech*. Cambridge: Cambridge University Press, 283–333.

Clodd, E. (1968). *Magic in Names*. Detroit: Singing Tree Press.

Coates, R. (2005). A new theory of properhood. In E. Brylla and M. Wahlberg (eds), *Proceedings of the 21st Congress of Onomastic Sciences, Uppsala, 19–24 August* 2002, vol. 1, 124–37.

Coates, R. (2006). Properhood. *Language* 82: 356–82.

Coates, R. (2009). A strictly Millian approach to the definition of the proper name. *Mind and Language* 24: 433–44.

Cobb, T. (2007). Computing the vocabulary demands of L2 reading. *Language Learning and Technology* 12: 38–63.

Cobbett, W. (1823). *A Grammar of the English Language, in a Series of Letters, Intended for the Use of Schools and of Young Persons in General; but more especially for the Use of Soldiers, Sailors,*

Apprentices, and Plough-boys. London. (Edited, with an introduction, by R. Burchfield, Oxford University Press, Oxford 1984).

Cohen, E. N. (1977). Nicknames, social boundaries, and community in an Italian village. *International Journal of Contemporary Sociology* 14: 102–13.

Collier, G. A., and Bricker, V. R. (1970). Nicknames and social structure in Zinacantan. *American Anthropologist* 72: 289–302.

Coleman, L., and Kay, P. (1981). Prototype semantics: the English word *lie*. *Language* 57: 26–44.

Coleridge, S. T. (1817). *Biographia Literaria.* London: Rest Fenner.

Collins, A. M., and Loftus, E. F. (1975). A spreading-activation theory of semantic processing. *Psychological Review* 82: 407–28.

Collins, A. M., and Quillian, M. R. (1969). Retrieval time from semantic memory. *Journal of Verbal Learning and Verbal Behavior* 8(2): 240–47.

Collins, C. (2005). A smuggling approach to the passive in English. *Syntax* 8: 81–120.

Colman, F. (1992). *Money Talks: Reconstructing Old English.* Berlin: Mouton de Gruyter.

Colman, F. (2006). Review article. In E. Brylla and M. Wahlberg (eds), *Proceedings of the 21st International Congress of Onomastic Sciences, Uppsala, August 19–24 2002*, vol. 1, Uppsala Språk- och folkminnesinstitutet 2005. *Nomina* 29: 133–46.

Colman, F. (2014). *The Grammar of Names in Anglo-Saxon England: The Linguistics and Culture of the Old English Onomasticon.* Oxford: Oxford University Press.

Colomé, A. (2001). Lexical activation in bilinguals' speech production: language-specific or language-independent? *Journal of Memory and Language* 45: 721–36.

Comesana, M., Perea, M., Pineiro, A., and Fraga, I. (2009). Vocabulary teaching strategies and conceptual representations of words in L2 in children: Evidence with novice learners. *Journal of Experimental Child Psychology* 104: 22–33.

Comrie, B. (1981a). *The Languages of the Soviet Union.* Cambridge: Cambridge University Press.

Comrie, B. (1981b). *Language Universals and Linguistic Typology.* Oxford: Blackwell.

Comrie, B. (1992). Before complexity. In J. A. Hawkins and A. Gell-Mann (eds), *The Evolution of Human Language.* Redwood City, Calif.: Addison-Wesley, 193–211.

Comrie, B., and Kuteva, T. (2005). The evolution of grammatical structures and 'functional need'. In M. Tallerman (ed.), *Language Origins: Perspectives on Evolution.* Oxford: Oxford University Press, 185–206.

Condamines, A. (1993). Un exemple d'utilisation de connaissances de sémantique lexicale: acquisition semi-automatique d'un vocabulaire de spécialité. *Cahiers de lexicologie* 62: 25–65.

Conklin, H. C. (1955). Hanunóo color categories. *Southwestern Journal of Anthropology* 11(4): 339–44.

Conklin, H. C. (1973). Review: color categorization. *American Anthropologist* 75(4): 931–42.

Connelly, N. G. (2005). *Nomenclature of Inorganic Chemistry: IUPAC Recommendations.* London: Royal Society of Chemistry.

Considine, J. (2008). *Dictionaries in Early Modern Europe: Lexicography and the Making of Heritage.* Cambridge: Cambridge University Press.

Conrad, J. (1911). *Under Western Eyes*, Prologue. Repr. 2003, New York: Dover.

Cook, J. (1967). *The Journals of Captain James Cook*, vol. 3: *The Voyage of the Resolution and Discovery* 1776–1780, ed. from the original MSS by J. C. Beaglehole. Cambridge: Cambridge University Press for the Hakluyt Society.

Cooper, D. (1986). *Metaphor.* Oxford: Basil Blackwell.

Cooper, W. E., and Ross, J. R. (1975). Word order. In R. E. Grossman, L. J. San, and J. J. Vance (eds), *Papers from the Parasession on Functionalism.* Chicago: Chicago Linguistic Society, 63–111.

Corbett, G. G. (2000). *Number*. Cambridge: Cambridge University Press.

Corbett, G. G. (2007). Canonical typology, suppletion, and possible words. *Language* 83(1): 8–42.

Corbett, G. G. (2012). *Features*. Cambridge: Cambridge University Press.

Corbyn, C. A. (1854/1970). *Sydney Revels (the Eighteen-Fifties) of Bacchus, Cupid and Momus; being choice and humorous selections from scenes at the Sydney Police Office and other public places, during the last three years*. Presented by Cyril Pearl. Sydney: Ure Smith.

Cordella, M. (2004). *The Dynamic Consultations: A Discourse Analytical Study of Doctor–Patient Communication*. Amsterdam: Benjamins.

Coronel-Median, S. (2002). *Quechua Phrasebook*. Sydney: Lonely Planet.

Corson, D. J. (1997). The learning and use of academic English words. *Language Learning* 47(4): 671–718.

Cortese, M. J., and Khanna, M. M. (2007). Age of acquisition predicts naming and lexical-decision performance above and beyond 22 other predictor variables: an analysis of 2,342 words. *Quarterly Journal of Experimental Psychology* 60: 1072–82.

Costa, A., Miozzo, M., and Caramazza, A. (1999). Lexical selection in bilinguals: do words in the bilingual's two languages compete for selection? *Journal of Memory and Language* 41: 365–397.

Costa, A., and Santesteban, M. (2004). Lexical access in bilingual speech production: evidence from language switching in highly proficient bilinguals and L2 learners. *Journal of Memory and Language* 50: 491–511.

Costa, A., Caramazza, A., and Sebastian-Galles, N. (2000). The cognate facilitation effect: implications for models of lexical access. *Journal of Experimental Psychology: Learning, Memory, and Cognition* 26: 1283–96.

Cowie, A. P. (1998). *Phraseology: Theory, Analysis, and Applications*. Oxford: Oxford University Press.

Cox, B. (1973). The significance of the distribution of English place-names in *-hām* in the Midlands and East Anglia. *Journal of the English Place-Name Society* 5: 15–73. Repr. in K. Cameron (ed.), *Place-Name Evidence for the Anglo-Saxon Invasion and Scandinavian Settlements* (Nottingham: English Place-Name Society, 1975), 55–98.

Cox, B. (1976). The place-names of the earliest English records. *Journal of the English Place-Name Society* 8: 12–66.

Cox, B. (1994). *English Inn and Tavern Names*. Nottingham: Centre for English Name Studies.

Coxhead, A. (2000). A new academic word list. *TESOL Quarterly* 34(2): 213–38.

Coxhead, A., and Hirsh, D. (2007). A pilot science-specific word list. *Revue française de linguistique appliquée* 12(2): 65–78.

Coxhead, A., Nation, I. S. P., and Sim, D. (2015). Creating and trialling six forms of the Vocabulary Size Test. *TESOLANZ Journal* 22: 13–26.

Courtenay, K. (1976). Ideophones defined as a phonological class: the case of Yoruba. *Studies in African Linguistics*, supplement 6: 13–26.

Cowie, A. P. (1998). *Phraseology: Theory, Analysis, and Applications*. Oxford: Oxford University Press.

Crabb, G. (1916[1816]). *English Synonymes Explained*. London: Routledge.

Craigie, W. A., et al. (1937–2002). *A Dictionary of the Older Scottish Tongue: From the Twelfth Century to the End of the Seventeenth*. Chicago: University of Chicago Press/ Aberdeen: Aberdeen University Press/London: Oxford University Press.

Craik, F. I. M., and Lockhart, R. S. (1972). Levels of processing: a framework for memory research. *Journal of Verbal Learning and Verbal Behavior* 11: 671–84.

Craik, F. I. M., and Tulving, E. (1975). Depth of processing and the retention of words in episodic memory. *Journal of Experimental Psychology: General* 104: 268–94.

Cramer, I. (2005). Das Menzerathsche Gesetz. In R. Köhler, G. Altmann, and R. G. Piotrowski (eds), *Quantitative Linguistik/Quantitative Linguistics: Ein Internationales Handbuch/An International Handbook*. Berlin: de Gruyter, 650–88.

Cramer, P. (1968). *Word Association*. New York: Academic Press.

Crawford, B. (2002). *The Papar in the North Atlantic: Environment and History*. St Andrews: Committee for Dark Age Studies, University of St Andrews.

Croft, W. (1993). The role of domains in the interpretation of metaphors and metonymies. *Cognitive Linguistics* 4: 335–70.

Croft, W. (2001). *Radical Construction Grammar: Syntactic Theory in Typological Perspective*. Oxford: Oxford University Press.

Croft, W. (2007). Beyond Aristotle and gradience: a reply to Aarts. *Studies in Language* 31: 409–30.

Croft, W. (2010). Pragmatic functions, semantic classes, and lexical categories. *Linguistics* 48: 787–96.

Cronin, V. S. (2002). The syntagmatic–paradigmatic shift and reading development. *Journal of Child Language* 29: 189–204.

Cross-linguistic Database for Deponency. <www.smg.surrey.ac.uk/deponency/>.

Crothers, J., and Shibatani, M. (1977). Issues in the description of Turkish vowel harmony. In R. M. Vago (ed.), *Issues in Vowel Harmony*. Amsterdam: Benjamins, 63–88.

Crozier, R. (2004). Recollections of schoolteachers' nicknames. *Names* 52: 83–99.

Cruse, A. D. (1986). *Lexical Semantics*. Cambridge: Cambridge University Press.

Crystal, D. (1967/2004). English word classes. In B. Aarts, D. Denison, E. Keizer, and G. Popova (eds), *Fuzzy Grammar: A Reader*. Oxford: Oxford University Press, 191–211.

Crystal, D. (1987). How many words. *English Today* 12: 11–4.

Crystal, D. (1993). What's in a Name, Bob? *English Today* 9(4): 53–4.

Crystal, D. (1995). Phonaesthetically speaking. *English Today* 11(2): 8–12.

Crystal, D. (1998). *Language Play*. London: Penguin/Chicago: Chicago University Press.

Crystal, D. (2000). *Language Death*. Cambridge: Cambridge University Press.

Crystal, D. (2003). *English as a Global Language*, 2nd edn. Cambridge: Cambridge University Press.

Crystal, D. (2005). *By Hook or By Crook: A Journey In Search of English*. New York: Overlook Press.

Crystal, D. (2006). *Words, Words, Words*, ch. 4. Oxford: Oxford University Press.

Crystal, D. (2010). *The Cambridge Encyclopedia of Language*, 3rd edn. Cambridge: Cambridge University Press.

Crystal, D. (2011). *The Story of English in 100 Words*. London: Profile.

Culicover, P. W. (1999). *Syntactic Nuts: Hard Cases, Syntactic Theory, and Language Acquisition*. Oxford: Oxford University Press.

Curtin, S., Mintz, T. H., and Christiansen, M. H. (2005). Stress changes the representational landscape: evidence from word segmentation. *Cognition* 96(3): 233–62.

Cutler, A., and Butterfield, S. (1992). Rhythmic cues to speech segmentation: evidence from juncture misperception. *Journal of Memory and Language* 31(2): 218–36.

Cutler, A., McQueen, J., and Robinson, K. (1990). Elizabeth and John: sound patterns of men's and women's names. *Journal of Linguistics* 20: 471–82.

Cutler, A., and Norris, D. (1988). The role of strong syllables in segmentation for lexical access. *Journal of Experimental Psychology: Human Perception and Performance* 14(1): 113–21.

Cutting, J. C., and Ferreira, V. S. (1999). Semantic and phonological information flow in the production lexicon. *Journal of Experimental Psychology: Learning, Memory, and Cognition* 25: 318–44.

Czaykowska-Higgins, E. (1998). The morphological and phonological constituent structure of words in Moses-Columbia Salish (Nxa'amxcín). In E. Czaykowska-Higgins and M. Dale Kinkade (eds), *Salish Languages and Linguistics: Theoretical and Descriptive Perspectives*. Berlin: Mouton de Gruyter, 153–95.

Dąbrowska, E. (2009). Words as constructions. In V. Evans and S. Pourcel (eds), *New Directions in Cognitive Linguistics*. Amsterdam: Benjamins, 201–23.

Dąbrowska, E., and Lieven, E. (2005). Towards a lexically specific grammar of children's question constructions. *Cognitive Linguistics* 16(3): 437–74.

Dai, Z., and Ding, Y. (2010). Effectiveness of text memorization in EFL learning of Chinese students. In D. Wood (ed.), *Perspectives on Formulaic Language: Acquisition and Communication*. New York: Continuum, 71–87.

Daille, B., Habert B., Jacquemin C. and Royauté J. (1996). Empirical observation of term variations and principles for their description. *Terminology* 3(2): 197–257.

Daly, L. (1967). *Contributions to a History of Alphabetization in Antiquity and the Middle Ages*. Brussels: Latomus.

Damasio, A. (1994). *Descartes' Error: Emotion, Reason and the Human Brain*. New York: Putnam.

Damasio, A. (2000). *The Feeling of What Happens*. London: Random House.

Damian, M. F., and Martin, R. C. (1999). Semantic and phonological codes interact in single word production. *Journal of Experimental Psychology: Learning, Memory, and Cognition* 25: 345–61.

Danesi, M. (2002). *The Puzzle Instinct: The Meaning of Puzzles in Human Life*. Bloomington: Indiana University Press.

Dascal, M. (1987). *Leibniz: Language, Signs and Thought*. Amsterdam: J. Benjamins.

Daulton, F. E. (2008). *Japan's Built-In Lexicon of English-Based Loanwords*. Clevedon: Multilingual Matters.

Davidson, D. (1980). *Essays on Actions and Events*. Oxford: Clarendon Press. 3rd edn 1985.

Dawkins, R. (1976). *The Selfish Gene*. Oxford: Oxford University Press.

Deacon, T. W. (2003). Universal grammar and semiotic constraints. In M. Christiansen and S. Kirby (eds), *Language Evolution*. Oxford: Oxford University Press, 111–39.

de Bleser, R. (2006). A linguist's view on progressive anomia: evidence for Delbrück (1886) in modern neurolinguistic research. *Cortex* 42: 805–10.

de Boinod, A. J. (2006). *The Meaning of Tingo and Other Extraordinary Words from Around the World*. New York: Penguin Press.

Deconinck, J., Boers, F., and Eyckmans, J. (2010). Helping learners engage with L2 words: the form–meaning fit. *AILA Review* 23: 95–114.

De Deyne, S., Navarro, D. J., Perfors, A., and Storms, G. (2012). Strong structure in weak semantic similarity: a graph based account. In N. Miyaki, D. Peebles, and R. P. Cooper (eds), *Proceedings of the 34th Annual Conference of the Cognitive Science Society*. Austin, Tex.: Cognitive Science Society, 1464–9.

De Deyne, S., Navarro, D., and Storms, G. (2013). Better explanations of lexical and semantic cognition using networks derived from continued rather than single-word associations. *Behavior Research Methods* 45(2): 480–98.

De Deyne, S., and Storms, G. (2008a). Word associations: network and semantic properties. *Behavior Research Methods* 40: 213–31.

De Deyne, S., and Storms, G. (2008b). Word associations: norms for 1,424 Dutch words in a continuous task. *Behavior Research Methods* 40: 198–205.

De Deyne, S., and Storms, G. (in preparation). Continued word association norms in English.

Deese, J. (1965). *The Structure of Associations in Language and Thought*. Baltimore, Md.: The John Hopkins Press.

Degani, T., and Tokowicz, N. (2010). Ambiguous words are harder to learn. *Bilingualism: Language and Cognition* 13: 299–314.

de Groot, A. M. B. (1980). *Mondelinge woordassociatienormen: 100 woordassociaties op 460 Nederlandse zelfstandige naamwoorden* [Oral word association norms: 100 word associations to 460 Dutch nouns]. Lisse: Swets & Zeitlinger.

de Groot, A. M. B. (1989). Representational aspects of word imageability and word frequency as assessed through word associations. *Journal of Experimental Psychology* 15: 824–45.

de Groot, A. M. B., and Nas, G. L. J. (1991). Lexical representation of cognates and noncognates in compound bilinguals. *Journal of Memory and Language* 30: 90–123.

de Groot, A. M. B., and Poot, R. (1997). Word translation at three levels of proficiency in a second language: the ubiquitous involvement of conceptual memory. *Language Learning* 47: 215–64.

de Klerk, V. (2002). Xhosa nicknames for Whites: a double-edged sword. *Nomina Africana* 16: 146–63.

de Klerk, V., and Bosch, B. (1996). Nicknames as sex-role stereotypes. *Sex Roles* 35: 525–41.

de Klerk, V., and Bosch, B. (1997). The sound patterns of English nicknames. *Language Sciences* 19: 289–301.

Delazer, M., Semenza, C., Reiner, M., Hofer, R., and Benke, T. (2003). Anomia for people names in DAT: evidence for semantic and post-semantic impairments. *Neuropsychologia* 41(12): 1593–8.

De Léon, L. (1999). Verbs in Tzotzil early syntactic development. *International Journal of Bilingualism* 3: 219–40.

Dell, G. S. (1986). A spreading-activation theory of retrieval in sentence production. *Psychological Review* 93: 283–321.

Dell, G. S. (1988). The retrieval of phonological forms in production: tests of predictions from a connectionist model. *Journal of Memory and Language* 27: 124–42.

Dell, G. S., Oppenheim, G. M., and Kittredge, A. K. (2008). Saying the right word at the right time: syntagmatic and paradigmatic interference in sentence production. *Language and Cognitive Processes* 23(4): 583–608.

Dell, G. S., and O'Seaghdha, P. G. (1991). Mediated and convergent lexical priming in language production: a comment on Levelt et al. (1991). *Psychological Review* 98: 604–14.

Dell, G. S., and O'Seaghdha, P. G. (1992). Stages of lexical access in language production. *Cognition* 42: 287–314.

Demuth, K. (2006). Crosslinguistic perspectives on the development of prosodic words. *Language and Speech* 49(2): 129–35.

Demuth, K., Culbertson, J., and Alter, J. (2006). Word-minimality, epenthesis and coda licensing in the early acquisition of English. *Language and Speech* 29(2): 137–74.

De Ridder, I. (2002). Visible or invisible links: does the highlighting of hyperlinks affect incidental vocabulary learning, text comprehension and the reading process? *Language Learning and Technology* 6: 123–46.

de Saussure, F. (1948[1916]). *Cours de linguistique générale*. Paris: Payot. Repr. 1979.

Diccionario de la lengua española (1780). Madrid: Real academia española.

Dick, P. K. (1986). How to build a universe that doesn't fall apart two days later. In *I Hope I Shall Arrive Soon*. London: Gollancz.

Dickey, E. (1997). Forms of address and terms of reference. *Journal of Linguistics* 33: 255–74.

Dickinson, E. (*c*.1862–86). *Complete Poems*, no. 1212. Boston: Little Brown.

Diesendruck, G., and Markson, L. (2001). Children's avoidance of lexical overlap: Apragmatic account. *Developmental Psychology* 37: 630–41.

Diffloth, G. (1972). Notes on expressive meaning. In P. M. Peranteau, J. N. Levy, and G. C. Phares (eds), *Papers from the Eighth Regional Meeting, Chicago Linguistic Society*. Chicago: Chicago Linguistic Society, 440–47.

Diffloth, G. (1976). Expressives in Semai. In P. N. Jenner, L. C. Thompson, and S. Starosta (eds), *Austroasiatic Studies*, pt 1. Honolulu: University Press of Hawai'i, 249–64.

Diffloth, G. (1994). i: big, a: small. In L. Hinton, J. Nichols, and J. J. Ohala (eds), *Sound Symbolism*. Cambridge: Cambridge University Press, 107–14.

Dijkstra, T., and Van Heuven, W. J. B. (2002). The architecture of the bilingual word recognition system: from identification to decision. *Bilingualism: Language and Cognition* 5: 175–97.

Dijkstra, T., Grainger, J., and van Heuven, W. J. B. (1999). Recognition of cognates and interlingual homographs: the neglected role of phonology. *Journal of Memory and Language* 41: 496–518.

Dijkstra, T., Miwa, K., Brummelhuis, B., Sappelli, M., and Baayen, H. (2010). How cross-language similarity and task demands affect cognate recognition. *Journal of Memory and Language* 62: 284–301.

Dijkstra, T., van Jaarsveld, H., and Ten Brinke, S. (1998). Interlingual homograph recognition: effects of task demands and language intermixing. *Bilingualism: Language and Cognition* 1: 51–66.

Dimitrova-Vulchanova, M., and Martinez, L. (2013). A basic level for the encoding of biological motion. In C. Paradis, J. Hudson, and U. Magnusson (eds), *The Construal of Spatial Meaning: Windows into Conceptual Space*. Oxford: Oxford University Press, 144–68.

Dingemanse, M. (2011a). Ezra Pound among the Mawu: ideophones and iconicity in Siwu. In P. Michelucci, O. Fischer, and C. Ljungberg (eds), *Semblance and Signification*. Amsterdam: Benjamins, 39–54.

Dingemanse, M. (2011b). *The Meaning and Use of Ideophones in Siwu*. Nijmegen: Max Planck Institute for Psycholinguistics.

Dingemanse, M. (2011c). Ideophones and the aesthetics of everyday language in a West-African society. *The Senses and Society* 6(1): 77–85.

Dingemanse, M. (2012). Advances in the cross-linguistic study of ideophones. *Language and Linguistics Compass* 6(10): 654–72.

Dingemanse, M., and Majid, A. (2012). The semantic structure of sensory vocabulary in an African language. In N. Miyake, D. Peebles, and R. P. Cooper (eds), *Proceedings of the 34th Annual Conference of the Cognitive Science Society*. Austin, Tex.: Cognitive Science Society 300–5.

Dinic, J. (2009). The anthroponymy of Grliska River Basin. *Onomatoloski Prilozi—Srpska Akademija Nauka i Umetnosti* 19–20: 621–739.

Dirven, R. (2002). Metonymy and metaphor: different mental strategies of conceptualisation. In R. Dirven and R. Pörings (eds), *Metaphor and Metonymy in Comparison and Contrast*. Berlin: Mouton de Gruyter, 75–111.

Di Sciullo, A. M., and Boeckx, C. (eds), *The Biolinguistic Enterprise: New Perspectives on the Evolution and Nature of the Human Language Faculty*. Oxford: Oxford University Press.

Di Sciullo, A. M., and Williams, E. (1987). *On the Definition of Word*. Cambridge, Mass.: MIT Press.

Dixon, R. M. W. (1972). *The Dyirbal Language of North Queensland* (Cambridge Studies in Linguistics, 9). Cambridge: Cambridge University Press.

Dixon, R. M. W. (1977a). *A Grammar of Yidiny*. Cambridge: Cambridge University Press.

Dixon, R. M. W. (1977b). Some phonological rules in Yidiny. *Linguistic Inquiry* 8: 1–34.

Dixon, R. M. W. (1980). *The Languages of Australia*. Cambridge: Cambridge University Press.

Dixon, R. M. W. (1990). The origin of 'mother-in-law vocabulary' in two Australian languages. *Anthropological Linguistics* 32(1/2): 1–56.

Dixon, R. M. W., and Aikhenvald, A. Y. (2002a). Word: a typological framework. In R. M. W. Dixon and A. Aikhenvald (eds), *Word: A Cross-Linguistic Typology*. Cambridge: Cambridge University Press, 1–41.

Dixon, R. M. W., and Aikhenvald, A. (2002b). *Word: A Cross-Linguistic Typology*. Cambridge: Cambridge University Press.

Dixon, T. M. (2003). *From Passions to Emotions: The Creation of a Psychological Category*. Cambridge: Cambridge University Press.

Dixon, T. M. (2008). *The Invention of Altruism: Making Moral Meanings in Victorian Britain*. Oxford: Oxford University Press.

Djao, W. (2003). *Being Chinese: Voices from the Diaspora*. Tucson: University of Arizona Press.

D'Odorico, L., Carubbi, S., Salerni, N., and Calvo, V. (2001). Vocabulary development in Italian children: a longitudinal evaluation of quantitative and qualitative aspects. *Journal of Child Language* 28: 351–72.

Dohmes, P., Zwitserlood, P., and Bölte, J. (2004). The impact of semantic transparency of morphologically complex words on picture naming. *Brain and Language* 90: 203–12.

Doke, C. M. (1943). *Textbook of Zulu Grammar*, 3rd edn. London: Longmans, Green.

Dolan, J. R. (1972). *English Ancestral Names: The Evolution of the Surname from Medieval Occupations*. New York: Clarkson N. Potter.

Dolscheid, S., Shayan, S., Majid, A., and Casasanto, D. (2013). The thickness of musical pitch: psychophysical evidence for linguistic relativity. *Psychological Science* 24(5): 613–21.

Donohue, M. (2003). The tonal system of Skou, New Guinea. In S. Kaji (ed.), *Proceedings of the Symposium Cross-linguistic Studies of Tonal Phenomena: Historical Development, Phonetics of Tone, and Descriptive Studies*. Tokyo: Tokyo University of Foreign Studies, 329–55.

Donohue, M. (2008). Complex predicates and bipartite stems in Skou. *Studies in Language* 32(2): 279–335.

Dorian, N. C. (1970). A substitute name system in the Scottish Highlands. *American Anthropologist* 72: 303–19.

Douglas, M. (1966). *Purity and Danger: An Analysis of Concepts of Pollution and Taboo*. London: Routledge & Kegan Paul.

Dousset, L. (1997). Naming and personal names of Ngaatjajarra-speaking people, Western Desert: some questions related to research. *Australian Aboriginal Studies* 2: 50–54.

Downing, L. (1999). Prosodic stem ≠ prosodic word in Bantu. In T. A. Hall and U. Kleinhenz (eds), *Studies on the Phonological Word*. Amsterdam: Benjamins, 73–98.

Downing, L. J., and Stiebels, B. (2012). Iconicity. In J. Trommer (ed.), *The Morphology and Phonology of Exponence*. Oxford: Oxford University Press, 379–426.

Draper, P., and Haney, C. (2006). Patrilateral bias among a traditionally egalitarian people: Ju/Hoansi naming practice. *Ethnology* 44(3): 243–59.

Dromi, E. (1987). *Early Lexical Development*. Cambridge: Cambridge University Press.

Drummond, P. (2007). *Scottish Hill Names: The Origin and Meaning of the Names of Scotland's Hills and Mountains*. [Glasgow:] Scottish Mountaineering Trust.

Drummond, P. (2009). Place-name losses and changes: a study in Peeblesshire. A comparative study of hill-names and other toponyms. *Nomina* 32: 5–17.

Ducrot, O. (1973). *Qu'est-ce que le structuralisme? Le structuralisme en linguistique*. Paris: Seuil.

Duden = *Vollständiges orthographisches Wörterbuch der deutschen Sprache* (1880). Leipzig: Konrad Duden.

Duke, J. (2005). African anthroponyms and structural principles of the 'ideal' name. In E. Brylla and M. Wahlberg (eds), *Proceedings of the 21st Congress of Onomastic Sciences, Uppsala 19–24 August 2002*, vol. 1, 138–50.

Duñabeitia, J. A., Avilés, A., and Carreiras, M. (2008). NoA's ark: influence of the number of associates in visual word recognition. *Psychonomic Bulletin & Review* 15(6): 1072–7.

Durbin, M. (1973). Sound symbolism in the Mayan language family. In M. S. Edmonson (ed.), *Meaning in Mayan Languages: Ethnolinguistic Studies*. The Hague: Mouton, 23–49.

Durkin, P. (2002). 'Mixed' etymologies of Middle English items in *OED3*: some questions of methodology and policy. *Dictionaries: The Journal of the Dictionary Society of North America* 23: 142–55.

Durkin, P. (2008). Latin loanwords of the early modern period: how often did French act as an intermediary? In R. Dury, M. Gotti, and M. Dossena (eds), *Selected Papers from the Fourteenth International Conference on English Historical Linguistics*, vol. 2: Lexical and Semantic Change. Amsterdam: Benjamins, 185–202.

Durkin, P. (2009). *The Oxford Guide to Etymology*. Oxford: Oxford University Press.

Durkin, P. (2014). *Borrowed Words: A History of Loanwords in English*. Oxford: Oxford University Press.

Durkin, P. (ed.) (2016). *The Oxford Handbook of Lexicography*. Oxford: Oxford University Press.

Durrant, P. (2013). Formulaicity in an agglutinating language: the case of Turkish. *Corpus Linguistics and Linguistic Theory* 9(1): 1–38.

Durst, U. (2001). Why Germans don't feel 'anger'. In J. Harkins and A. Wierzbicka (eds), *Emotions in Crosslinguistic Perspective*. Berlin: Mouton de Gruyter, 119–52.

Dury, P. (1999). Étude comparative et diachronique des concepts ecosystem et écosystème. *Meta* 44(3): 485–99.

Dyen, I. (1963). Lexicostatistically determined borrowing and taboo. *Language* 39(1): 60–6.

Eastman, M. (1936). *Enjoyment of Laughter*. New York: Simon & Schuster.

Ebbinghaus, H. (1885). *Über das Gedachtnis: Untersuchungen zur experimentellen Psychologie*. Leipzig: Duncker & Humblot. [English translation (1913): *Memory. A Contribution to Experimental Psychology*. New York: Teachers College, Columbia University.]

Eberhard, W. (1970). A note on Chinese nicknames. In W. Eberhard (ed.), *Studies in Chinese Folklore and Related Essays*. Bloomington: Indiana University Press.

Echols, C. H. (1993). A perceptually based model of children's earliest productions. *Cognition* 46: 245–96.

Echols, C. H. (1996). A role for stress in early speech segmentation. In J. L. Morgan and K. Demuth (eds), *Signal to Syntax: Bootstrapping From Speech to Grammar in Early Acquisition*. Mahwah, NJ: Erlbaum, 151–70.

Echols, C. H., Crowhurst, M. J., and Childers, J. B. (1997). The perception of rhythmic units in speech by infants and adults. *Journal of Memory and Language* 36(2): 202–25.

Echols, C. H., and Newport, E. L. (1992). The role of stress and position in determining first words. *Language Acquisition* 2: 189–220.

Eder, J. F. (1975). Naming practices and the definition of affines among the Batik of the Philippines. *Ethnology* 14(1): 59–70.

Edwards, R. (2006). What's in a name? Chinese learners and the practice of adopting 'English' names. *Language, Culture, and Curriculum* 19(1): 90–103.

Ehlers, K.-H. (2009). Forms of address in elementary school: on children's address form usage in Germany. *Zeitschrift für germanistische Linguistik* 37: 315–38.

Ehri, L. C., and Wilce, L. S. (1980). The influence of orthography on readers' conceptualization of the phonemic structure of words. *Applied Psycholinguistics* 1: 371–85.

Eitan, Z., and Timmers, R. (2010). Beethoven's last piano sonata and those who follow crocodiles: cross-domain mappings of auditory pitch in a musical context. *Cognition* 114(3): 405–22.

Ekhert, J., and Tavakoli, P. (2012). The effects of word exposure frequency and elaboration of word processing on incidental L2 vocabulary acquisition through reading. *Language Teaching Research* 16: 227–52.

Ekman, P., and Friesen, W. V. (2003). *Unmasking the Face*. Los Altos, Calif.: Malor Books.

Ekpo, M. U. (1978). Structure in Ibibio names. *Names* 26: 271–84.

Ekwall, E. (1960). *The Concise Oxford Dictionary of English Place-Names*, 4th edn. Oxford: Clarendon Press.

Ekwall, E. (1962). Variation and change in English place-names. *Vetenskaps-Societetens i Lund Årsbok* 3: 49.

Ekwall, E. (1964). Some cases of variation and change in English place-names. In *English Studies Presented to R. W. Zandvoort on the Occasion of his Seventieth Birthday.* Supplement to *English Studies* 45: 44–9.

Elderton, W. P. (1949). A few statistics on the length of English words. *Journal of the Royal Statistical Society, series A, General* 112: 436–45.

Elenbaas, N. (1999). A unified account of binary and ternary stress: considerations from Sentani and Finnish. Ph.D dissertation. University of Utrecht.

Elgort, I. (2011). Deliberate learning and vocabulary acquisition in a second language. *Language Learning* 61(2): 367–413.

Eliot, T. S. (1944). Little Gidding; East Coker. In *Four Quartets*. London: Faber & Faber.

Ellis, N. C. (2008). Usage-based and form-focused language acquisition: the associative learning of constructions, learned-attention, and the limited L2 endstate. In P. Robinson and N. Ellis (eds), *Handbook of Cognitive Linguistics and Second Language Acquisition*. London: Routledge, 372–405.

Ellis, N. C. (2013). Emergentism. In C. Chapelle (ed.), *Encyclopedia of Applied Linguistics*, vol. 3. Oxford: Wiley-Blackwell, 1873–82.

Elman, J. L. (2005). Connectionist models of cognitive development: where next? *Trends in Cognitive Sciences* 9(3): 111–17.

Elmevik, L., and Strandberg, S. (eds) (2010). *Probleme der Rekonstruktion untergegangener Wörter aus alten Eigennamen: Akten eines internationalen Symposiums in Uppsala 7–9, April 2010*. Uppsala: Swedish Science Press.

Elsie, R. W. (1979). A synchronic and diachronic analysis of genetic relationships in the basic vocabulary of Brittonic Celtic. Ph.D dissertation, Rheinische Friedrich-Wilhelms-Universität zu Bonn.

Elston-Güttler, K., and Williams, J. N. (2008). L1 polysemy affects L2 meaning interpretation: evidence for L1 concepts active during L2 reading. *Second Language Research* 24: 167–87.

Elston-Güttler, K. E., Gunter, T. C., and Kotz, S. A. (2005). Zooming into L2: Global language context and adjustment affect processing of interlingual homographs in sentences. *Cognitive Brain Research* 25: 57–70.

Elyot, Sir T. (1538). *The Dictionary of Syr Thomas Elyot, Knyght*. London: Thomas Berthelet.

Embick, D., and Marantz, A. (2008). Architecture and blocking. *Linguistic Inquiry* 39: 1–53.

Embick, D., and Noyer, R. (2007). Distributed morphology and the syntax/morphology interface. In G. Ramchand and C. Reiss (eds), *The Oxford Handbook of Linguistic Interfaces*. Oxford: Oxford University Press, 289–324.

Emerson, R. W. (1844). The poet. In *Essays: Second Series*. Boston: Munroe.

Emmott, C. (1997). *Narrative Comprehension: A Discourse Perspective*. Oxford: Oxford University Press.

Enfield, N. J. (2002). *Ethnosyntax: Explorations in Grammar and Culture*. Oxford: Oxford University Press.

Enfield, N. J. (2011). Taste in two tongues: a Southeast Asian study of semantic convergence. *The Senses and Society* 6(1): 30–37.

Enfield, N. J., and Levinson, S.C. (eds) (2006). *Roots of Human Sociality: Culture, Congnition and Interaction*. Oxford: Berg.

English Place-Name Survey (1924–). Cambridge and Nottingham: English Place-Name Society.

Erten, İ. H., and Tekin, M. (2008). Effects on vocabulary acquisition of presenting new words in semantic sets versus semantically unrelated sets. *System* 36: 407–22.

Estigarribia, B., and Clark, E. V. (2007). Getting and maintaining attention in talk to young children. *Journal of Child Language* 34: 799–814.

Erman, B., and Warren, B. (2000). The idiom principle and the open choice principle. *Text* 20(1): 29–62.

Esar, E. (1961). *Humorous English*. New York: Horizon.

Estienne, R. (1643). *Dictionarium, seu Latinæ Linguæ Thesaurus*. Paris: Robert Estienne.

Estopà, R. (2001). Les unités de signification spécialisées élargissant l'objet du travail en terminologie. *Terminology* 7(2): 217–37.

Estoup, J.-B. (1916). *Les gammes sténographiques*. Paris: Institut sténographique de France.

Evans, N. (2010). *Dying Words: Endangered Languages and What They Have to Tell Us*. Oxford: Wiley-Blackwell.

Evans, N. (2011). Semantic typology. In J. J. Song (ed.), *The Oxford Handbook of Linguistic Topology*. Oxford: Oxford University Press, 504–33.

Evans, N., and Levinson, S. C. (2009). The myth of language universals: language diversity and its importance for cognitive science. *Behavioral and Brain Sciences* 32: 429–92.

Evans, V., and Green, M. (2006). *Cognitive Linguistics: An Introduction*. Edinburgh University Press.

Evans-Pritchard, E. E. (1934). Imagery in Ngok Dinka cattle-names. *Bulletin of the School of Oriental Studies* 7(3): 623–28.

Everett, D. L. (2005). Cultural constraints on grammar and cognition in Pirahã: another look at the design features of human language. *Current Anthropology* 46: 621–46.

Everett-Heath, J. (2005). *The Concise Dictionary of World Place-Names*. Oxford: Oxford University Press.

Fader, A. (2007). Reclaiming sacred sparks: linguistic syncretism and gendered language shift among Hasidic Jews in New York. *Journal of Linguistic Anthropology* 17(1): 1–22.

Fairman, T. (2000). English pauper letters 1800–34, and the English language. In D. Barton and N. Hall (eds), *Letter Writing as a Social Practice*. Amsterdam: Benjamins, 63–82.

Fairman, T. (2002). 'Riting these fu lines': English overseers' correspondence 1800–1835. *Verslagen en Mededelingen (Koninklijke Academic voor Nederlandse Taal-en Letterkunde)* 3: 557–73.

Fairman, T. (2003). Letters of the English labouring classes and the English language 1800–34. In M. Dossena and C. Jones (eds), *Insights into Late Modern English*. Bern: Lang, 265–82.

Fairman, T. (2006). Words in English Record Office documents in the early 1800s. In M. Kytö, M. Rydén, and E. Smitterberg (eds), *Nineteenth-Century English: Stability and Change*. Cambridge: Cambridge University Press, 56–88.

Faloutsos, M., Faloutsos, P., and Faloutsos, C. (1999). On power–law relationships of the Internet topology. <http://www.cis.upenn.edu/~mkearns/teaching/NetworkedLife/power-internet.pdf>.

Fan, F., Grzybek, P., and Altmann, G. (2010). Dynamics of word length in sentence. *Glottometrics* 20: 70–109.

Fan, M. Y. (2003). Frequency of use, perceived usefulness, and actual usefulness of second language vocabulary strategies: a study of Hong Kong learners. *Modern Language Journal* 87: 222–41.

Farah, M. J. (2004). *Visual Agnosia*, 2nd edn. Cambridge, Mass.: MIT Press.

Farley, A. P., Ramonda, K., and Liu, X. (2012). The concreteness effect and the bilingual lexicon: the impact of visual attachment on meaning recall of abstract L2 words. *Language Teaching Research* 16: 449–66.

Felber, H. (1984). *Terminology Manual*. Paris: Unesco and Infoterm.

Feld, S. (1982). *Sound and Sentiment: Birds, Weeping, Poetics, and Song in Kaluli Expression*. Philadelphia: University of Pennsylvania Press.

Feldman, L. B. (2000). Are morphological effects distinguishable from the effects of shared meaning and shared form? *Journal of Experimental Psychology: Learning, Memory and Cognition* 26: 1431–44.

Fellbaum, C. (1990). The English verb lexicon as a semantic net. *International Journal of Lexicography* 3/4: 278–301.

Fellbaum, C. (ed.) (1998). *WordNet: An Electronic Lexical Database*. Cambridge, Mass.: MIT Press.

Fellbaum, C. (2000). Autotroponymy. In Y. Ravin and C. Leacock (eds), *Polysemy*. Cambridge: Cambridge University Press, 52–67.

Fellbaum, C. (2002). The semantics of troponymy. In R. Green, S. H. Myang, and C. Bean (eds), *The Semantics of Relationships: An Interdisciplinary Perspective*. Dordrecht: Kluwer, 23–34.

Fellbaum, C. (2013). Purpose verbs. In J. Pustejovsky, P. Bouillon, H. Isahara, K. Kanzaki, and C. Lee (eds), *Recent Trends in Generative Lexicon Theory*. Berlin: Springer, 371–84.

Fellbaum, C., and Chaffin, R. (1990). Some principles of the organization of the verb lexicon. In *Proceedings of the 12th Annual Conference of the Cognitive Science Society*. Hillsdale, NJ: Erlbaum, 420–8.

Fellbaum, C., and Mathieu, Y. Y. (2011). A corpus-based examination of scalar verbs of emotion. In *Proceedings of Cognition, Emotion, Communication* (Nicosia).

Fellbaum, C., and Miller, G. A. (2003). Morphosemantic links in WordNet. *Traitement automatique des langues* 44(2): 69–80.

Fellbaum, C., Osherson, A., and Clark, P. E. (2007/9). Putting semantics into WordNet's morphosemantic links. In *Proceedings of the Third Language and Technology Conference* (Poznán, Oct. 2007). Repr. in Z. Vetulani and H. Uszkoreit (eds), *Responding to Information Society Challenges: New Advances in Human Language Technologies*. Berlin: Springer, 350–8.

Fellbaum, C., and Vossen, P. (2012). The challenge of multilingual WordNets. *Lexical Resources and Evaluation* 46: 313–26.

Fellows-Jensen, G. (2010). Place-names as evidence for urban settlements in Britain in the Viking period. In J. Sheehan and D. Ó Corráin (eds), *The Viking Age: Ireland and the West*. Dublin: Four Courts Press, 89–96.

Fenk-Oczlon, G. (1989). Word frequency and word order in freezes. *Linguistics* 27: 517–56.

Fenson, L., Dale, P. S., Reznick, J. S, Bates, E., Thal, D. J., and Pethick, S. (1994). Variability in early communicative development. *Monographs of the Society for Research in Child Development* 59. Bethesda, Md.

Fenwick, C. C. (1998). *The Poll Taxes of 13771379, and 1381*. 3 vols. Oxford: Oxford University Press.

Ferguson, C. (1983). Sports announcer talk: syntactic aspects of register variation. *Language in Society* 12: 153–72.

Fernald, A., and Marchman, V. A. (2011). Causes and consequences of variability in early language learning. In I. Arnon and E. V. Clark (eds), *Experience, Variation, and Generalization: Learning a First Language*. Amsterdam: Benjamins, 181–202.

Fernald, A., and Marchman, V. A. (2012). Individual differences in lexical processing at 18 months predict vocabulary growth in typically developing and late-talking toddlers. *Child Development* 83(1): 203–22.

Fernald, A., and Morikawa, H. (1993). Common themes and cultural variations in Japanese and American mothers' speech to infants. *Child Development* 64(3): 637–56.

Fernald, A., Perfors, A., and Marchman, V. A. (2006). Picking up speed in understanding: speech processing efficiency and vocabulary growth across the 2nd year. *Developmental Psychology* 42(1): 98–116.

Fernandez Juncal, C. (2008). Sociolinguistic patterns in onomastics. *Revista española de lingüística* 38: 5–20.

Fernando, C. (1996). *Idioms and Idiomaticity*. Oxford: Oxford University Press.

Ferreira, V. G. (2007). Seven surnames of Jews from the Iberian Peninsula. *Names* 55: 473–80.

Ferrer-i-Cancho, R., and Elevåg, B. (2010). Random texts do not exhibit the real Zipf's law-like rank distribution. *PLoS ONE* 5(3): 10. doi:10.1371/journal.pone.0009411.

Ferrer-i-Cancho, R., and Solé, R. V. (2001a). The small world of human language. *Proceedings of The Royal Society of London, series B: Biological Sciences* 268(1482): 2261–65.

Ferrer-i-Cancho, R., and Solé, R. V. (2001b). Two regimes in the frequency of words and the origins of complex lexicons: Zipf's law revisited. *Journal of Quantitative Linguistics* 8(3): 165–73.

Ferris, C. (1993). *The Meaning of Syntax: A Study in the Adjectives of English*. London: Longman.

Féry, C. (1997). Uni und Studis: die besten Wörter des Deutschen. *Linguistische Berichte* 172: 461–90.

Fillmore, C., Kay, P., and O'Connor, M. C. (1988). Regularity and idiomaticity in grammatical constructions: the case of *let alone*. *Language* 64(3): 501–38.

Finkbeiner, M., Forster, K., Nicol, J., and Nakamura, K. (2004). The role of polysemy in masked semantic and translation priming. *Journal of Memory and Language* 51: 1–22.

Finkbeiner, M., and Nicol, J. (2003). Semantic category effects in second language word learning. *Applied Psycholinguistics* 24: 369–83.

Firica, C. (2007a). Nicknames and bynames in Oltenia today. *Studia Romanica et Anglica Zagrabiensia* 52: 109–34.

Firica, C. (2007b). Romanian onomastics: theoretical problems concerning the anthroponymic categories of nicknames and bynames. *Studia Romanica et Anglica Zagrabiensia* 52: 215–57.

Firth, J. R. (1930). *Speech*. London: Benn. (Reprinted in J. R. Firth, *The Tongues of Men and Speech* Oxford: Oxford University Press, 1964).

Firth, J. R. (1935). The use and distribution of certain English sounds. *English Studies* 17: 2–12.

Firth, J. R. (1957a). A synopsis of linguistic theory 1930–1955. In F. Palmer (ed.) *Selected Papers of J. R. Firth 1952–59*. London: Longman, 168–205.

Firth, J. R. (1957b). General linguistics and descriptive grammar. In *Papers in Linguistics 1934–1965*. Oxford: Oxford University Press, 216–28.

Firth, J. R. (1957c). *Papers in Linguistics 1934–1951*. London: Oxford University Press.

Flesch, R. (1948). A new readability yardstick. *Journal of Applied Psychology* 32(3): 221–33.

Floricic, F. (2007). Observations on consonant gemination in Italian hypocoristics, pt 2. *Archivio glottologico italiano* 92: 129–78.

Fodor, J. (1980). Methodological solipsism considered as a research strategy in cognitive science. *Behavioral and Brain Sciences* 3: 63–73.

Fodor, J. A. (1981). *Representations: Philosophical Essays on the Foundations of Cognitive Science*. Cambridge, Mass.: MIT Press.

Fodor, J. (1998). *Concepts: Where Cognitive Science Went Wrong*. Oxford: Oxford University Press.

Foley, W. A. (1991). *The Yimas Language of New Guinea*. Stanford, Calif.: Stanford University Press.

Follett, K. (2010). *Fall of Giants*. New York: Penguin.

Folse, K. (2006). The effect of type of written exercise on L2 vocabulary retention. *TESOL Quarterly* 40(2): 273–93.

Fónagy, I. (1991). *La vive voix: essays de psycho-phonétique*. Paris: Payot.

Forsyth, M. (2011). *The Etymologicon*. London: Icon.

Fortis, J.-M. (1996). La notion de langage mental: problèmes récurrents de quelques théories anciennes et contemporaines. *Histoire épistémologie langage* 18: 75–101.

Fortson, B. W. (2009). *Indo-European Language and Culture: An Introduction*, 2nd edn. Oxford: Blackwell.

Foster, G. M. (1964). Speech forms and perception of social distance in a Spanish speaking Mexican village. *Southwestern Journal of Anthropology* 20: 107–22.

Fox, E. (1996). Cross-language priming from ignored words: evidence for a common representational system in bilinguals. *Journal of Memory and Language* 35: 353–70.

Frakes, J. C. (2004). *Early Yiddish Texts 1100–1750 with Introduction and Commentary*. Oxford: Oxford University Press.

Francis, G. (1993). A corpus-driven approach to grammar: principles, methods and examples. In M. Baker, G. Francis, and E. Tognini-Bonelli (eds), *Text and Technology: In Honour of J. Sinclair*. Amsterdam: Benjamins, 137–56.

Frank, M. C., Goldwater, S., Griffiths, T. L., and Tenenbaum, J. B. (2010). Modeling human performance in statistical word segmentation. *Cognition* 117(2): 107–25.

Fraser, B. (1970). Idioms within a transformational grammar. *Foundations of Language* 6(1): 22–42.

Frauenfelder, U. H., and Schreuder, R. (1992). Constraining psycholinguistic models of morphological processing and representation: the role of productivity. In G. Booij and J. van Marle (eds), *Yearbook of Morphology 1991*. Dordrecht: Foris, 165–83.

Frazer, Sir J. G. (1911). *The Golden Bough, part 11: Taboo and the Perils of the Soul*, 3rd edn. London: Macmillan.

Frege, G. (1892). Über Sinn und Bedeutung. *Zeitschrift fur Philosophie und philosophische Kritik* 100: 25–50.

Frege, G. (1986[1892]). On sense and nominatum. In A. P. M. ich (ed.), *The Philosophy of Language*. New York: Oxford University Press, 186–98.

Friedin, R. (1975). The analysis of passives. *Language* 51: 385–405.

Friedl, A. (2006). Untersuchungen zur Texttypologie im Russischen anhand von 609 Texten in 13 Textsorten. Master's thesis, Graz University.

Fritz, G. (1998). *Historische Semantik*. Stuttgart: Metzler.

Fromkin, V. A. (1971). The non-anomalous nature of anomalous utterances. *Language* 47: 27–52.
Fromkin, V. A. (1973). *Speech Errors as Linguistic Evidence*. The Hague: Mouton.
Fry, W. F., Jr (1963). *Sweet Madness*. Palo Alto, Calif.: Pacific Books.
Fryer, R. G., and Levitt, S. D. (2004). The causes and consequences of distinctively Black names. *Quarterly Journal of Economics* 119: 767–805.
Fucilla, J. G. (1978). Spanish nicknames as surnames. *Names* 26: 139–76.
Fucilla, J. G. (1979). Portuguese nicknames as surnames. *Names* 27: 73–105.
Fucks, W. (1956). Mathematical theory of word formation. In C. Cherry (ed.), *Information Theory*. New York: Academic Press, 154–70.
Fukkink, R. G., and de Glopper, K. (1998). Effects of instruction in deriving word meaning from context: a meta-analysis. *Review of Educational Research* 68: 450–69.
Fulkerson, A., and Waxman, S. (2007). Words (but not tones) facilitate object categorization: evidence from 6- and 12-month-olds. *Cognition* 105: 218–28.
Fuller, M. (1965). 'The naming of names' in Indian folk belief. *Asian Folklore Studies* 24(1): 63–79.
Gallahorn, G. E. (1971). The use of taboo words by psychiatric ward personnel. *Psychiatry* 34(3): 309–21.
Galton, F. (1880). Psychometric experiments. *Brain* 2: 149–62.
Ganeri, A. (2002). *Perishing Poles*. New York: Scholastic.
Gangemi, A., Guarino, N., Masolo, C., Oltramari, A., and Schneider, L. (2002). Sweetening ontologies with DOLCE. In *Knowledge Engineering and Knowledge Management: Ontologies and the Semantic Web*. Heidelberg: Springer, 166–81.
Garrett, M. F. (1975). The analysis of sentence production. In G. H. Bower (ed.), *The Psychology of Learning and Motivation*, vol. 9. San Diego, Calif.: Academic Press, 133–77.
Garrett, M. F. (1980). Levels of processing in sentence production. In B. Butterworth (ed.), *Language Production: Speech and Talk*, vol. 1. New York: Academic Press, 177–220.
Garrett, M. F. (1988). Processes in language production. In E. F. J. Newmeyer (ed.), *Language: Psychological and Biological Aspects*. Cambridge: Cambridge University Press, 69–96.
Gary-Prieur, M. N. (1994). *Grammaire du nom propre*. Paris: Presses universitaires de France.
Gasque, T. J. (1994). Looking back to Beaver and the Head: male college nicknames in the 1950's. *Names* 42: 121–32.
Gathercole, V. C. M., Sebastián, E., and Soto, P. (1999). The early acquisition of Spanish verbal morphology: across-the-board or piecemeal knowledge? *International Journal of Bilingualism* 3: 133–82.
Gaudin, F. (2003). *Socioterminologie: une approche sociolinguistique de la terminologie*. Brussels: Duculot.
Gazdar, G., Klein, E., Pullum, G. K., and Sag, I. (1985). *Generalized Phrase Structure Grammar*. Oxford: Blackwell.
Geeraerts, D. (1993). Vagueness's puzzles, polysemy's vagaries. *Cognitive Linguistics* 4: 223–72.
Geeraerts, D. (1997). *Diachronic Prototype Semantics: A Contribution to Historical Lexicology*. Oxford: Clarendon Press.
Geeraerts, D. (2010a). *Theories of Lexical Semantics*. Oxford: Oxford University Press.
Geeraerts, D. (2010b). Lexical variation in space. In P. Auer and J. E. Schmidt (eds), *Language in Space: An International Handbook of Linguistic Variation*, vol. 1: *Theories and Methods*. Berlin: Mouton de Gruyter, 821–37.

Geeraerts, D., Grondelaers, S., and Bakema, P. (1994). *The Structure of Lexical Variation: Meaning, Naming, and Context.* Berlin: Mouton de Gruyter.

Geeraerts, G. (2002). Folk name-giving in Averbode and Okselaar. *Naamkunde* 34: 5–55.

Geertz, C. (1973). *The Interpretation of Cultures.* New York: Basic Books.

Geertz, C. (1983). *Local Knowledge.* New York: Basic Books.

Gelling, M., and Cole, A. (2000). *The Landscape of Place-Names.* Stamford: Shaun Tyas.

Gell-Mann, M. (1994). *The Quark and the Jaguar: Adventures in the Simple and the Complex.* Cambridge, Mass.: Abacus

Gelman, S., and Coley, J. (1990). The importance of knowing a dodo is a bird: categories and inferences in 2-year-old children. *Developmental Psychology* 26: 796–804.

Gelman, S., Hollander, M., Star, J., and Heyman, G. (2000). The role of language in the construction of kinds. *Psychology of Learning and Motivation* 39: 201–63.

Gentner, D. (1982). Why nouns are learned before verbs: linguistic relativity versus natural partitioning. In S. A. Kuczaj (ed.), *Language Development*, vol. 2: *Language, Thought, and Culture.* Hillsdale, NJ: Erlbaum, 301–34.

Gentner, D., and Boronat, C. B. (1992). Metaphor as mapping. Paper presented at the Workshop on Metaphor, Tel Aviv.

Gergely, G. (2003). The development of teleological versus mentalizing observational learning strategies in infancy. *Bulletin of the Menninger Clinic* 67: 113–31.

Gergely, G., Bekkering, H., and Király, I. (2002). Rational imitation in preverbal infants. *Nature* 415: 755–6.

Gerlach, R. (1982). Zur Überprüfung des Menzerath'schen Gesetzes im Bereich der Morphologie. *Glottometrika* 4 (Bochum: Brockmeyer), 95–102.

Gershkoff-Stowe, L., and Smith, L. B. (2004). Shape and the first hundred nouns. *Child Development* 75: 1098–114.

Gibbs, R. W. (1985). On the process of understanding idioms. *Journal of Psycholinguistic Research* 14(5): 465–72.

Gibbs, R. W. (1986). Skating on thin ice: literal meaning and understanding idioms in conversation. *Discourse Processes* 9: 17–30.

Gibbs, R. W. (1995). Idiomaticity and human cognition. In M. Everaert, E. van der Linden, A. Schenk, and R. Schreuder (eds), *Idioms: Structural and Psychological Perspectives.* Hillsdale, NJ: Erlbaum, 97–116.

Gibbs, R. W. (2007). Idiomaticity and formulaic language. In D. Geeraerts and H. Cuyckens (eds), *Handbook of Cognitive Linguistics.* Oxford: Oxford University Press, 697–725.

Gibbs, R. W. (ed.) (2008). *The Cambridge Handbook of Metaphor and Thought.* Cambridge: Cambridge University Press.

Gibbs, R. W., and Van Orden, G. (2012). Pragmatic choice in conversation. *Topics in Cognitive Science* 4: 7–20.

Giegerich, H. J. (2009). Compounding and lexicalism. In R. Lieber and P. Stekauer (eds), *The Oxford Handbook of Compounding.* Oxford: Oxford University Press, 178–200.

Gilbert, V. (1993). *How to Crack the Cryptic Crossword.* London: Pan Books in association with The Daily Telegraph.

Gildersleeve, B. L., and Lodge, G. (1895). *Gildersleeve's Latin Grammar*, 3rd edn. London: Macmillan.

Gilmore, D. D. (1982). Some notes on community nicknaming in Spain. *Man* 17: 686–700.

Gisborne, N. (2008). Dependencies are constructions. In G. Trousdale and N. Gisborne (eds), *Constructional Approaches to English Grammar.* Berlin: Mouton de Gruyter, 219–55.

Gisborne, N. (2010). *The Event Structure of Perception Verbs.* Oxford: Oxford University Press.

Givón, T. (1984). *Syntax: A Functional-Typological Introduction.* Amsterdam: Benjamins.

Givón, T. (1989). The linguistic code and the iconicity of grammar. In *Mind, Code, and Context: Essays in Pragmatics.* Hillsdale, NJ: Erlbaum, 69–125.

Givón, T. (1995). *Functionalism and Grammar.* Amsterdam: Benjamins.

Givón, T. (2010). The adaptive approach to grammar. In B. Heine and H. Narrog (eds), *The Oxford Handbook of Linguistic Analysis.* Oxford: Oxford University Press, 27–50.

Gladkova, A. (2007). Universal and language-specific aspects of 'propositional attitudes': Russian vs. English. In A. C. Schalley and D. Khlentzos (eds), *Mental States*, vol. 2: *Language and Cognitive Structure.* Amsterdam: Benjamins, 61–83.

Gladkova, A. (2008). Tolerance: new and traditional values in Russian in comparison with English. In C. Goddard (ed.), *Cross-linguistic Semantics.* Amsterdam: Benjamins, 301–29.

Gladkova, A. (2010). *Russkaja kul'turnaja semantika: emocii, cennosti, zhiznennye ustanovki* [Russian cultural semantics: emotions, values, attitudes]. Moscow: Languages of Slavonic Cultures.

Gladkova, A. (2013). 'Intimate' talk in Russian: human relationships and folk psychotherapy. *Semantics and/in Social Cognition, special issue of Australian Journal of Linguistics* 33(3): 322–44.

Glaser, W. R. (1992). Picture naming. *Cognition* 42: 61–105.

Glaser, W. R., and Düngelhoff, F.-J. (1984). The time course of picture–word interference. *Journal of Experimental Psychology: Human Perception and Performance* 10: 640–54.

Glaser, W. R., and Glaser, M. O. (1989). Context effects in Stroop-like word and picture processing. *Journal of Experimental Psychology: General*, 118: 13–42.

Gleick, J. (2011). *The Information: A History, a Theory, a Flood.* New York: Pantheon.

Gleitman, L. R., Cassidy, K., Nappa, R., Papafragou, A., and Trueswell, J. R. (2005). Hard words. *Language Learning and Development* 1: 23–64.

Gleitman, L., and Papafragou, A. (2005). Language and thought. In K. J. Holyoak and R. G. Morrison (eds), *The Cambridge Handbook of Thinking and Reasoning.* Cambridge: Cambridge University Press, 633–62.

Glendening, P. J. T. (1965). *Teach Yourself to Learn a Language.* London: English Universities Press.

Goatly, A. (1997). *The Language of Metaphors.* London: Routledge.

Goatly, A. (2007). *Washing the Brain: Metaphor and Hidden Ideology.* Amsterdam: Benjamins.

Goddard, C. (1992). Traditional Yankunytjatjara ways of speaking: a semantic perspective. *Australian Journal of Linguistics* 12(1): 93–122.

Goddard, C. (1996a). The 'social emotions' of Malay (Bahasa Melayu). *Ethos* 24(3): 426–64.

Goddard, C. (1996b). *Pitjantjatjara/Yankunytjatjara to English Dictionary*, revised 2nd edn. Alice Springs: IAD Press.

Goddard, C. (2001a). Lexico-semantic universals: a critical overview. *Linguistic Typology* 5(1): 1–66.

Goddard, C. (2001b). *Sabar, ikhlas, setia*: patient, sincere, loyal? A contrastive semantic study of some 'virtues' in Malay and English. *Journal of Pragmatics* 33: 653–81.

Goddard, C. (2001c). *Hati*: a key word in the Malay vocabulary of emotion. In J. Harkins and A. Wierzbicka (eds), *Emotions in Crosslinguistic Perspective.* Berlin: Mouton de Gruyter, 171–200.

Goddard, C. (2004). Speech-acts, values and cultural scripts: a study in Malay ethnopragmatics. In R. Cribb (ed.), Asia Examined: Proceedings of the 15th Biennial Conference of the ASAA 2004, Canberra, Australia. Canberra: Asian Studies Association of Australia and Research School of Pacific and Asian Studies, Australian National University. <http://coombs.anu.edu.au/SpecialProj/ASAA/biennial-conference/2004/Goddard-C-ASAA2004).pdf>.

Goddard, C. (ed.) (2006). *Ethnopragmatics: Understanding Discourse in Cultural Context.* Berlin: Mouton de Gruyter.

Goddard, C. (2008). Contrastive semantics and cultural psychology: English *heart* vs. Malay *hati.* In F. Sharifian, R. Dirven, N. Yu, and S. Niemeier (eds), *Culture, Body, and Language: Conceptualizations of Internal Body Organs across Cultures and Languages.* Berlin: Mouton de Gruyter, 75–102.

Goddard, C. (2009). The conceptual semantics of numbers and counting: an NSM analysis. *Functions of Language* 16(2): 193–224.

Goddard, C. (2011a). *Semantic Analysis: A Practical Introduction*, revised 2nd edn. Oxford: Oxford University Press.

Goddard, C. (2011b). The lexical semantics of 'language' (with special reference to 'words'). *Language Sciences* 33(1): 40–57.

Goddard, C. (2012). 'Early interactions' in Australian English, American English, and English English: cultural differences and cultural scripts. *Journal of Pragmatics* 44: 1038–50.

Goddard, C. (2013). Semantics and/in social cognition. Introduction to special issue of *Australian Journal of Linguistics* 33(3): 245–56.

Goddard, C., and Wierzbicka, A. (eds) (2002). *Meaning and Universal Grammar: Theory and Empirical Findings.* 2 vols. Amsterdam: Benjamins.

Goddard, C., and Wierzbicka, A. (2004). *Cultural Scripts.* Special issue of *Intercultural Pragmatics* 1(2).

Goddard, C., and Wierzbicka, A. (2009). Contrastive semantics of physical activity verbs: 'cutting' and 'chopping' in English, Polish, and Japanese. *Language Sciences* 31: 60–96.

Goddard, C., and Wierzbicka, A. (2014a). *Words and Meanings: Lexical Semantics across Domains, Languages and Cultures.* Oxford: Oxford University Press.

Goddard, C., and Wierzbicka, A. (2014b). Semantic fieldwork and lexical universals. *Studies in Language* 38(1): 80–127.

Godfroid, A., Boers, F., and Housen, A. (2013). An eye for words: gauging the role of attention in L2 vocabulary acquisition by means of eye-tracking. *Studies in Second Language Acquisition* 35(3): 483–517.

Goedemans, R. W. N., van der Hulst, H. G., and Visch, E. A. M. (1996). *Stress Patterns of the World, pt. 1: Background.* The Hague: Holland Academic Graphics.

Gogate, L., Walker-Andrews, A., and Bahrick, L. (2001). Intersensory origins of word comprehension: an ecological-dynamic systems view. *Developmental Science* 4: 1–37.

Goicu, V. (2008). Family names based on nicknames from the Beius area. *Limba romana* 57: 527–36.

Goldberg, A. (2003). Constructions: a new theoretical approach to language. *Trends in Cognitive Sciences* 7(5): 219–24.

Goldberg, A. (2006). *Constructions at Work: The Nature of Generalization in Language.* Oxford: Oxford University Press.

Goldfield, B. A. (1993). Noun bias in maternal speech to one-year-olds. *Journal of Child Language* 20: 85–99.

Goldfield, B. A., and Reznick, S. (1990). Early lexical acquisition, rate, content, and the vocabulary spurt. *Journal of Child Language* 11: 171–83.

Goldin-Meadow, S. (2007). The challenge: some properties of language can be learned without linguistic input. *Linguistic Review* 24(4): 417–21.

Goldsmith, J. (1976). *Autosegmental Phonology.* Bloomington: Indiana University Press.

Golinkoff, R. M. (1986). 'I beg your pardon?': the preverbal negotiation of failed messages. *Journal of Child Language* 13: 455–76.

Golinkoff, R., Mervis, C., and Hirsh-Pasek, K. (1994). Early object labels: the case for a developmental lexical principles framework. *Journal of Child Language* 21: 125–55.

Gomi, T. (1989). *An Illustrated Dictionary of Japanese Onomatopoeic Expressions*, trans. J. Turrent. Tokyo: Japan Times.

Goodglass, H., Kaplan, E., Weintraub, S., and Ackerman, N. (1976). The 'tip-of-the-tongue' phenomenon in aphasia. *Cortex* 12: 145–53.

Goodman, J. C., McDonough, L., and Brown, N. B. (1998). The role of semantic context and memory in the acquisition of novel nouns. *Child Development* 69: 1330–44.

Gopnik, A., and Meltzoff, A. (1986). Relations between semantic and cognitive development in the one-word stage: the specificity hypothesis. *Child Development* 57: 1040–53.

Gordon, E. H. (1917). The name of characters in the works of Charles Dickens. *University of Nebraska Studies in Language, Literature, and Criticism* 1, paper 5: 3–35.

Goudswaard, N. (2005). *The Begak (Ida'an) Language of Sabah*. Utrecht: LOT.

Gould, S. J. (1987). *Time's Arrow, Time's Cycle*. Cambridge, Mass.: Harvard University Press.

Gould, S. J., and Lewontin, R. C. (1979). The spandrels of St Marco and the Panglossian paradigm: a critique of the adaptationist programme. *Proceedings of the Royal Society of London* 205: 281–8.

Gove, P. B. (1961). *Webster's Third New International Dictionary of the English Language*. Springfield, Mass.: Merriam-Webster.

Graf Estes, K. (2012). Infants generalize representations of statistically segmented words. *Frontiers in Psychology* 3. doi: 10.3389/fpsyg.2012.00447.

Graf Estes, K. (2014). Learning builds on learning: infants' use of native language sound patterns to learn words. *Journal of Experimental Child Psychology* 26: 313–27.

Graf Estes, K., Edwards, J., and Saffran, J. R. (2011). Phonotactic constraints on infant word learning. *Infancy* 16(2): 180–97.

Graf Estes, K., Evans, J. L., Alibali, M. W., and Saffran, J. R. (2007). Can infants map meaning to newly segmented words? Statistical segmentation and word learning. *Psychological Science* 18(3): 254–60.

Graham, S. A., and Diesendruck, G. (2010). Fifteen-month-old infants attend to shape over other perceptual properties in an induction task. *Cognitive Development* 25: 111–23.

Grant, A. P. (2000). Fabric, pattern, shift and diffusion: what Oregon Penutian can tell historical linguists. Paper presented at Hokan-Penutian Conference, University of California, Berkeley (June).

Grant, A. P. (2003). Review of Ruth King, *The Lexical Basis of Grammatical Borrowing: A Prince Edward Island Case Study*. *Word* 54: 251–6.

Grant, A. P. (2012a). Processes of grammaticalisation and 'borrowing the unborrowable': contact-induced change and the integration and grammaticalisation of borrowed terms for some core grammatical construction types. In B. Wiemer, B. Wälchli, and B. Hansen (eds), *Grammatical Replication and Borrowability in Language Contact*. Berlin: de Gruyter, 191–232.

Grant, A. P. (2012b). Contact, convergence and conjunctions: a cross-linguistic study of borrowing correlations among certain kinds of dependent clause markers. In I. Léglise and C. Chamoreau (eds), *The Interplay of Variation and Change in Contact Settings: Morphosyntactic Studies*. Berlin: Mouton de Gruyter, 191–233.

Grant, W., and Murison, D. D. (1927–76). *The Scottish National Dictionary*. Edinburgh: Scottish National Dictionary Association.

Greeff, F. (2003). *The Hidden Code of Cryptic Crosswords: Hero Stands Among Them Anonymously.* Slough: Foulsham.

Green, A. (1995). The prosodic structure of Burmese: a constraint-based approach. *Working Papers of the Cornell Phonetics Laboratory* 10: 67–96.

Green, D. W. (1998). Mental control of the bilingual lexico-semantic system. *Bilingualism: Language and Cognition* 1: 67–81.

Green, J. (1943). *Journal*, 4 May. Paris: Plon.

Green, J. (1996). *Chasing the Sun: Dictionary-Makers and the Dictionaries They Made.* London: Jonathan Cape.

Green, J. (2012). The Altyerre story: 'suffering badly by translation'. *Australian Journal of Anthropology* 23(2): 158–78.

Greenberg, J. (1963). Some universals of grammar, with particular reference to the order of meaningful elements. In J. Greenberg (ed.), *Universals of Language.* Cambridge, Mass.: MIT Press, 73–113.

Greenberg, J. (1969). Some methods of dynamic comparison in linguistics. In J. Puhvel (ed.), *Substance and Structure of Language.* Berkeley: University of California Press, 147–203.

Greenberg, J. (1978). How does a language acquire gender markers? In J. Greenberg, C. A. Ferguson, and E. Moravcsik (eds), *Universals of Human Language.* Stanford, Calif.: Stanford University Press, 47–82.

Greenberg, J., Osgood, C. E., and Jenkins, J. J. (1963). Memorandum concerning language universals. In J. H. Greenberg (ed.), *Universals of Language.* Cambridge, Mass.: MIT Press, xv–xxvii.

Greenberg, S., and Sapir, J. D. (1978). Acoustic correlates of 'big' and 'thin' in Kujamutay. *Proceedings of the Annual Meeting of the Berkeley Linguistics Society* 4: 293–310.

Greer, B. (2001). *How to Do the Times Crossword.* London: HarperCollins.

Grefenstette, G. (2010). Estimating the number of concepts. In G.-M. de Schryver (ed.), *A Way with Words: Recent Advances in Lexical Theory and Analysis.* Kampala: Menha, 143–56.

Grenfell, M., and Harris, V. (1999). *Modern Languages and Learning Strategies: In Theory and Practice.* London: Routledge.

Greswell, W. P. (1833). *A View of the Early Parisian Greek Press, Including the Lives of the Stephani*, 2nd edn. Oxford: S. Collingwood.

Grice, H. P. (1975). Logic and conversation. In P. Cole and J. L. Morgan (eds), *Speech Acts.* New York: Academic Press, 41–58.

Grice, P. (1975). Logic and conversation. In P. Cole and J. Morgan (eds), *Speech Acts.* New York: Academic Press, 41–58. Reprinted in H. P. Grice (ed.), *Studies in the Way of Words* (Cambridge, Mass.: Harvard University Press, 1989), 22–40.

Gries, S. T., and Stefanowitsch, A. (2004). Extending collostructional analysis: a corpus-based perspective on 'alternations'. *International Journal of Corpus Linguistics* 9: 97–129.

Griffin, J. (1985). Euphemisms in Greece and Rome. In D. J. Enright (ed.), *Fair of Speech: The Uses of Euphemism.* Oxford: Oxford University Press, 32–43.

Griffin, Z. M., and Bock, J. K. (1998). Constraint, word frequency, and the relationship between lexical processing levels in spoken word production. *Journal of Memory and Language* 38: 313–38.

Griffin, Z. M., and Ferreira, V. S. (2006). Properties of spoken language production. In M. J. Traxler and M. A. Gernsbacher (eds), *Handbook of Psycholinguistics*, 2nd edn. Amsterdam: Elsevier, 21–59.

Griffiths, P. D., and Atkinson, M. (1978). A 'door' to verbs. In N. Waterson and C. Snow (eds), *The Development of Communication*. London: Wiley, 311–19.

Griffiths, T. L., Steyvers, M., and Firl, A. (2003). Prediction and semantic association. In S. Becker, S. Thrun, and K. Obermayer (eds), *Advances in Neural Information Processing Systems 15*. Cambridge, Mass.: MIT Press, 11–18.

Griffiths, T. L., Steyvers, M., and Firl, A. (2007). Google and the mind: predicting fluency with PageRank. *Psychological Science* 18: 1069–76.

Griffiths, T. L., Steyvers, M., and Tenenbaum, J. (2007). Topics in semantic representation. *Psychological Review* 114: 211–44.

Grimm, J., Grimm, W., et al. (1838–1961). *Deutsches Wörterbuch*. Leipzig: Hirzel.

Grosjean, F. (1997). Processing mixed language: issues, findings, and models. In A. M. B. De Groot and J. F. Nas (eds), *Tutorials in Bilingualism: Psycholinguistic Perspectives*. Mahwah, NJ: Erlbaum, 225–54.

Gross, D., Fischer, U., and Miller, G. A. (1989). The organization of adjectival meanings. *Journal of Memory and Language* 28: 92–106.

Gross, M. (1994). Constructing lexicon-grammars. In B. Atkins and A. Zampolli (eds), *Computational Approaches to the Lexicon*. Oxford: Clarendon Press, 213–63.

Grosse, G., Behne, T., Carpenter, M., and Tomasello, M. (2010). Infants communicate in order to be understood. *Developmental Psychology* 46: 1710–22.

Grotjahn, R. (1982). Ein statistisches Modell für die Verteilung der Wortlänge. *Zeitschrift für Sprachwissenschaft* 1: 44–75.

Grotjahn, R., and Altmann, G. (1993). Modeling the distribution of word length: some methodological problems. In R. Köhler and B. B. Rieger (eds), *Contributions to Quantitative Linguistics*. Dordrecht: Kluwer, 141–53.

Gruter, T. (2002). Why Thomas is 'Tomu' and Markus 'Kusu': an OT account of hypocoristics in Bernese Swiss German. *McGill Working Papers in Linguistics/Cahiers linguistiques de McGill* 16: 65–94.

Grygiel, M., and Kleparski, G. A. (2007). *Main Trends in Historical Semantics*. Rzeszów: Wydawnictwo Uniwersytetu Rzeszowskiego.

Grzega, J. (2004). *Bezeichnungswandel: Wie, Warum, Wozu? Ein Beitrag zur englischen und allgemeinen Onomasiologie*. Heidelberg: Winter.

Grzybek, P. (2006). History and methodology of word length studies: the state of the art. In P. Grzybek (ed.), *Contributions to the Science of Text and Language: Word Length Studies and Related Issues*. Dordrecht: Springer, 15–90.

Grzybek, P. (2007). On the systematic and system-based study of grapheme frequencies: a re-analysis of German letter frequencies. *Glottometrics* 15: 82–91.

Grzybek, P. (2010). Text difficulty and the Arens–Altmann Law. In P. Grzybek, E. Kelih, and J. Mačutek (eds), *Text and Language: Structures, Functions, Interrelations, Quantitative Perspectives*. Vienna: Praesens, 57–70.

Grzybek, P. (2013a). Homogeneity and heterogeneity within language(s) and text(s): theory and practice of word length modeling. In R. Köhler and G. Altmann (eds), *Issues in Quantitative Linguistics 3*. Lüdenscheid: RAM, 66–99.

Grzybek, P. (2013b). The emergence of stylometry: prolegomena to the history of term and concept. In K. Kroó and P. Torop (eds), *Studies in 19th Century Literature*. Budapest: L'Harmattan, 58-75.

Grzybek, P. (2013c). Arens–Altmann Law. In R. Köhler, P. Grzybek, and S. Naumann (eds), *Formale und Quantitative Linguistik*. Berlin: de Gruyter.

Grzybek, P. (2013d). Empirische Textwissenschaft: Prosarhythmus im ersten Drittel des 20. Jahrhunderts als historisch-systematische Fallstudie. In A. Hansen-Löve, B. Obermayr, and G. Witte (eds), *Form und Wirkung: Phänomenologische und empirische Kunstwissenschaft in der Sowjetunion der 1920er Jahre*. Munich: Fink 427–55.

Grzybek, P. (2013e). Samoreguliatsiia v tekste (na primere ritmicheskikh protsessov v proze). In I. A. Pil'shchikov (ed.), *Sluchainost' i nepredskazuemost' v istorii kul'tury*. Tallinn: Acta Universitatis Tallinniensis, 78–115.

Grzybek, P., and Altmann, G. (2002). Oscillation in the frequency–length relationship. *Glottometrics* 6: 97–107.

Grzybek, P., and Kelih, E. (2005). Häufigkeiten von Wortlängen und Wortlängenpaaren: Unte rsuchungen am Beispiel russischer Texte von Viktor Pelevin. In E. Binder, W. Stadler, and H. Weinberger (eds), *Zeit–Ort–Erinnerung: Slawistische Erkundungen aus sprach-, literatur- und kulturwissenschaftlicher Perspektive*. Innsbruck: Institut für Sprachen und Literaturen der Universität Innsbruck, 395–407.

Grzybek, P., and Kelih, E. (2006). Empirische Textsemiotik und quantitative Text-Typologie. In J. Bernard, J. Fikfak, and P. Grzybek (eds), *Text & Reality/ Text & Wirklichkeit*. Ljubljana: ZRC, 95–120.

Grzybek, P., Kelih, E., and Stadlober, E. (2009). Slavic letter frequencies: a common discrete model and regular parameter behavior? In R. Köhler (ed.), *Issues in Quantitative Linguistics*. Lüdenscheid: RAM, 17–33.

Grzybek, P., and Stadlober, E. (2007). Do we have problems with Arens' Law? A new look at the sentence–word relation. In P. Grzybek and R. Köhler (eds), *Exact Methods in the Study of Language and Text: Dedicated to G. Altmann on the Occasion of his 75th Birthday*. Berlin: Mouton de Gruyter, 205–17.

Grzybek, P., Stadlober, E., and Kelih, E. (2007). The relationship of word length and sentence length: the inter-textual perspective. In R. Decker and H.-J. Lenz (eds), *Advances in Data Analysis*. Berlin: Springer, 611–18.

Grzybek, P., Stadlober, E., Kelih, E., and Antić, G. (2005). Quantitative text typology: the impact of word length. In C. Weihs and W. Gaul (eds), *Classification: The Ubiquitous Challenge*. Heidelberg: Springer, 53–64.

Gu, P. Y., and Johnson R. K. (1996). Vocabulary learning strategies and language learning outcomes. *Language Learning* 46: 643–79.

Guarino, N., Oberle, D., and Staab, S. (2009). What is an ontology? In S. Staab and R. Studer (eds), *Handbook on Ontologies*, 2nd edn. Heidelberg: Springer.

Guemple, D. L. (1965). Saunik: name sharing as a factor governing Eskimo kinship terms. *Ethnology* 4: 323–55.

Guillaume, P. (1973[1927]). First stages of sentence formation in children's speech. In C. A. Ferguson and D. I. Slobin (eds), *Studies in Child Language Development*. New York: Holt, Rinehart & Winston, 522–41.

Güldemann, T. (2008). *Quotative Indexes in African Languages: A Synchronic and Diachronic Survey*. Berlin: Mouton de Gruyter.

Guthrie, M. (1967–71). *Comparative Bantu I–IV*. Farnborough: Gregg International.

Haack, S. (1993). *Evidence and Inquiry: Towards Reconstruction in Epistemology*. Oxford: Blackwell.

Habib, S. (2011a). Angels can cross cultural boundaries. *RASK, International Journal of Language and Communication* 34: 49–75.

Habib, S. (2011b). Ghosts, fairies, elves, and nymphs: towards a semantic template for non-human being concepts. *Australian Journal of Linguistics* 31: 411–43.

Hacking, I. (1981). Was there ever a radical mistranslation? *Analysis* 41: 171–5.

Haggan, M. (2008). Nicknames of Kuwaiti teenagers. *Names* 56: 81–94.

Hagoort, P., Hald, L., Bastiaansen, M., and Petersson, K. M. (2004). Integration of word meaning and world knowledge in language comprehension. *Science* 304(5669): 438–41.

Hahn, L., and Sivley, R. (2011). Entropy, semantic relatedness and proximity. *Behavior Research Methods* 43: 746–60.

Haiman, J. (1985). *Natural Syntax: Iconicity and Erosion*. Cambridge: Cambridge University Press.

Hale, C. S. (1981). Modern Icelandic personal bynames. *Scandinavian Studies* 53: 115–46.

Hall, C. B., Lipton, R. B., Sliwinski, M., Katz, M. J., Derby, C. A., and Verghese, J. (2009). Cognitive activities delay onset of memory decline in persons who develop dementia. *Neurology* 73(5): 356–61.

Hall, C. J. (2002). The automatic cognate form assumption: evidence of the parasitic model of vocabulary development. *International Review of Applied Linguistics* 40: 69–87.

Hall, D., Corrigall, K., Rhemtulla, M., Donegan, E., and Xu, F. (2008). Infants' use of lexical-category-to-meaning links in object individuation. *Child Development* 79: 1432–43.

Hall, D., and Waxman, S. (eds). (2004). *Weaving a Lexicon*. Cambridge, Mass.: MIT Press.

Hall, T. A. (1999a). The phonological word: a review. In T. A. Hall and U. Kleinhenz (eds), *Studies on the Phonological Word*. Amsterdam: Benjamins, 1–22.

Hall, T. A. (1999b). Phonotactics and the prosodic structure of German. In T. A. Hall and U. Kleinhenz (eds), *Studies on the Phonological Word*. Amsterdam: Benjamins, 99–132.

Hall, T. A., and Hildebrandt, K. A. (2008). Phonological and morphological domains in Kyirong. *Linguistics* 46(2): 215–48.

Hall, T. A., Hildebrandt, K. A., and Bickel, B. (2008). Introduction: theory and typology of the word. *Linguistics* 46(2): 183–92.

Halle, M. (1973). Prolegomena to a theory of word formation. *Linguistic Inquiry* 4: 3–16.

Halle, M., and Marantz, A. (1993). Distributed morphology and the pieces of inflection. In K. Hale and S. J. Keyser (eds), *The View From Building 20*. Cambridge, Mass.: MIT Press, 111–76.

Halliday, M. A. K. (1982). How is a text like a clause? In S. Allen (ed.), *Text Processing: Proceedings of Nobel Symposium 51*. Stockholm: Almquist & Wiksell, 209–39.

Halliday, M. A. K. (1994). *An Introduction to Functional Grammar*, 2nd edn. London: Arnold.

Halliday, M. A. K. (2005). *Studies in English Language*. London: Continuum.

Halliday, M. A. K., and Hasan, R. (1976). *Cohesion in English*. London: Longman.

Hallig, R., and von Wartburg, W. (1952). *Begriffssystem als Grundlage für die Lexikographie: Versuch eines Ordnungsschemas*. Berlin: Akademie.

Hamilton, M., and Rajaram, S. (2001). The concreteness effect in implicit and explicit memory tests. *Journal of Memory and Language* 44: 96–117.

Hampton, J. A. (1997). Associative and similarity-based processes in categorization decisions. *Memory & Cognition* 25: 625–40.

Han, Z., Park, E., and Combs, C. (2008). Textual enhancement of input: issues and possibilities. *Applied Linguistics* 29: 597–618.

Hancock, I. F. (1971). A provisional comparison of the English-derived Atlantic creoles. In D. H. Hymes (ed.), *Pidginization and Creolization of Language*. Cambridge: Cambridge University Press, 287–91.

Handy, C. (1991). *The Age of Unreason*. London: Random House.

Hanks, P. (2013). *Lexical Analysis: Norms and Exploitations*. Cambridge, Mass.: MIT Press.
Hanks, P., Hardcastle, K., and Hodges, F. (2007). *A Dictionary of First Names*, 2nd edn. Oxford: Oxford University Press.
Hanser, S. F., Doyle, L. R., McCowan, B., and Jenkins, J. M. (2004). Information theory applied to animal communication systems and its possible application to SETI. In R. P. Norris and F. H. Stootman (eds), *Bioastronomy 2002: Life Among the Stars*. San Francisco, Calif.: Astronomical Society of the Pacific, 514–18.
Hanson, K., and Kiparsky, P. (1996). A parametric theory of poetic meter. *Language* 72: 287–335.
Hanyu Da Cidian (1992). Shanghai: Hanyu Da Cidian Chubanshe.
Hardin, C. L., and Maffi, L. (eds) (1997). *Color Categories in Thought and Language*. Cambridge: Cambridge University Press.
Harris, C. L., Ayçiçegi, A., and Gleason, J. B. (2003). Taboo words and reprimands elicit greater autonomic reactivity in a first language than in a second language. *Applied Psycholinguistics* 24: 561–79.
Harris, R., and Taylor, T. J. (1997). *Landmarks in Linguistic Thought: The Western Tradition from Socrates to Saussure*. London: Routledge.
Harris, Z. S. (1955). From phoneme to morpheme. *Language* 31: 190–222.
Harrison, K. D. (2004). South Siberian sound symbolism. In E. J. Vajda (ed.), *Languages and Prehistory of Central Siberia*. Amsterdam: Benjamins, 199–214.
Hart, B., and Risley, T. R. (1995). *Meaningful Differences in the Everyday Experience of Young American Children*. Baltimore, Md.: Brookes.
Hartley, R. V. L. (1928). Transmission of information. *Bell System Technical Journal* 7(3): 535–63.
Haspelmath, M. (1993). *A Grammar of Lezgian*. Berlin: Mouton de Gruyter.
Haspelmath, M. (1999). Optimality and diachronic adaptation. *Zeitschrift für Sprachwissenschaft* 18: 180–205.
Haspelmath, M. (2009a). An empirical test of the agglutination hypothesis. In E. Magni, S. Scalise, and A. Bisetto (eds), *Universals of Language Today*. Dordrecht: Springer, 13–29.
Haspelmath, M. (2009b). Lexical borrowing: concepts and issues. In M. Haspelmath and U. Tadmor (eds), *Loanwords in the World's Languages: A Comparative Study*. Berlin: Mouton de Gruyter, 35–54.
Haspelmath, M. (2011). The indeterminacy of the word and the nature of morphology and syntax. *Folia Linguistica* 45(1): 31–80.
Haspelmath, M., Dryer, M. S., Gil, D., and Comrie, B. (eds). (2005). *The World Atlas of Language Structures*. Oxford: Oxford University Press.
Haspelmath, M., and Sims, A. D. (2010). *Understanding Morphology*. London: Hodder Education.
Haspelmath, M., and Tadmor, U. (eds) (2009). *Loanwords in the World's Languages: A Comparative Study*. Berlin: Mouton de Gruyter.
Haugen, E. (1950). The analysis of linguistic borrowing. *Language* 26: 210–31.
Hauk, O., Davis, M. H., Kherif, F., and Pulvermüller, F. (2008). Imagery or meaning? Evidence for a semantic origin of category-specific brain activity in metabolic imaging. *European Journal of Neuroscience* 27: 1856–66.
Hauser, M. D., Chomsky, N., and Fitch, W. T. (2002). The faculty of language: what is it, who has it, and how did it evolve? *Science* 298: 1569–79.
Hauser, M. D., and Fitch, T. (2003). What are the uniquely human components of the language faculty? In M. H. Christiansen and S. Kirby (eds), *Language Evolution*. Oxford: Oxford University Press, 158–81.

Hay, J., Pelucchi, B., Graf Estes, K., and Saffran, J. R. (2011). Linking sounds to meanings: Infant statistical learning in a natural language. *Cognitive Psychology* 63: 93–106.

Hazlitt, W. (1903). Letters on the English comic writers, Lecture I: On wit and humour. In *Collected Works*, vol 8. London: Dent, 5–30.

Hearst, M. (1992). Automatic acquisition of hyponyms from large text corpora. In Proceedings of the Fourteenth International Conference on Computational Linguistics, Nantes.

Heath, J. (1978). *Linguistic Diffusion in Arnhem Land*. Canberra, ACT: AIAS.

Heath, J. (1984). Language contact and language change. *Annual Review of Anthropology* 13: 367–84.

Hebert, B. III, and Harper, A. S. (1995). Increased choice of female phonetic attributes in first names. *Sex Roles* 32(11/12): 809–19.

Heine, B. (1997). *Cognitive Foundations of Grammar*. New York: Oxford University Press.

Heitner, R. (1999). Revisiting Roger Brown's 'Original Word Game': an experimental approach to the pseudo-semantic basis of language-specific speech perception in late infancy. In U. Priss (ed.), *Proceedings of the 10th Annual Midwest Artificial Intelligence and Cognitive Science Conference*. Menlo Park, Calif.: AAAI Press, 50–5.

Heitner, R. (2004). The cyclical ontogeny of ontology: an integrated developmental account of speech and object categorization. *Philosophical Psychology* 17: 45–57.

Heitner, R. (2005). An odd couple: Chomsky and Quine on the phoneme. *Language Sciences* 27: 1–30.

Heitner, R. (2006). From a phono-logical point of view: neutralizing Quine's argument against analyticity. *Synthese* 150: 15–39.

Henderson, J. (2002). The word in Eastern/Central Arrernte. In R. M. W. Dixon and A. Y. Aikhenvald (eds), *Word: A Cross-Linguistic Typology*. Cambridge: Cambridge University Press, 100–124.

Henri, F. (2010). A constraint-based approach to verbal constructions in Mauritian: morphological, syntactic and discursive aspects. Dissertation, University of Mauritius and University of Paris Diderot–Paris 7.

Henry, A. (1995). *Belfast English and Standard English*. New York: Oxford University Press.

Herbert, R. K. (1995). The sociolinguistics of personal names: two South African case studies. *South African Journal of African Languages* 15(1): 1–8.

Hermans, D., Bongaerts, T., De Bot, K., and Schreuder, R. (1998). Producing words in a foreign language: can speakers prevent interference from their first language? *Bilingualism: Language and Cognition* 1: 213–29.

Hess, U., and Thibault, P. (2009). Darwin and emotion expression. *American Psychologist* 64: 120–8.

Higa, M. (1963). Interference effects of intralist word relationship in verbal learning. *Journal of Verbal Learning and Verbal Behavior* 2: 170–5.

Higham, N. (ed.) (2007). *Britons in Anglo-Saxon England*. Woodbridge: Boydell.

Hildebrandt, K. A. (2005). A phonetic analysis of Manange segmental and suprasegmental properties. *Linguistics of the Tibeto-Burman Area* 28(1): 1–36.

Hildebrandt, K. A. (2007). Prosodic and grammatical domains in Limbu. *Himalayan Linguistics* 8: 1–34.

Hiller, U. (2000). British family names: their history, their meaning. *Praxis des neusprachlichen Unterrichts* 47: 428–31.

Hillis, A. E. (2007). Aphasia: progress in the last quarter of a century. *Neurology* 69: 200–13.

Hills, T. T., Maouene, M., Maouene, J., Sheya, A., and Smith, L. (2009). Longitudinal analysis of early semantic networks: preferential attachment or preferential acquisition? *Psychological Science* 20: 729–39.

Hilpert, M. (2008). The English comparative: language structure and language use. *English Language and Linguistics* 12: 395–417.

Hinton, L., Nichols, J., and Ohala, J. J. (1994a). Introduction: sound-symbolic processes. In L. Hinton, J. Nichols, and J. J. Ohala (eds), *Sound Symbolism*. Cambridge: Cambridge University Press, 1–12.

Hinton, L., Nichols, J., and Ohala, J. J. (eds) (1994b). *Sound Symbolism*. Cambridge: Cambridge University Press.

Hinton, L., Nichols, J., and Ohala, J. J. (eds) (2006). *Sound Symbolism*, 2nd edn. Cambridge: Cambridge University Press.

Hippisley, A., Chumakina, M., Corbett, G. G., and Brown, D. (2004). Suppletion: frequency, categories and distribution of stems. *Studies in Language* 28(2): 389–421.

Hirsh, E. D. (2013). A wealth of words. *City Journal* 23(1): <www.city-journal.org/2013/23_1_vocabulary.html>.

Hirsh-Pasek, K., Golinkoff, R., Hennon, E., and Maguire, M. (2004). Theories at the frontier of developmental psychology. In G. Hall and S. Waxman (eds), *Weaving a Lexicon*. Cambridge, Mass.: MIT Press, 173–204.

Hirst, G. (2009). Ontology and the lexicon. In S. Staab and R. Studer (eds), *Handbook on Ontologies*, 2nd edn. Heidelberg: Springer.

Hittmair-Delazer, M., Andree, B., Semenza, C., De Bleser, R., and Benke, T. (1994). Naming by German compounds. *Journal of Neurolinguistics* 8: 27–41.

Ho, D. Y. F. (1996). Filial piety and its psychological consequences. In M. H. Bond (ed.), *The Handbook of Chinese Psychology*. Hong Kong: Oxford University Press, 155–65.

Hobbes, T. (1651). *Leviathan*. London: Crooke. Facsimile edn, Oxford: Clarendon Press, 1909.

Hock, H. H., and Joseph, B. D. (1996). *Language History, Language Change, and Language Relationship: An Introduction to Historical and Comparative Linguistics*. Berlin: Mouton de Gruyter.

Hockett, C. F. (1958). *A Course in Modern Linguistics*. New York: Macmillan.

Hockett, C. (1963). The problem of universals in language. In J. Greenberg (ed.), *Universals of Language*. Cambridge, Mass.: MIT Press, 1–29.

Hockett, C. F. (1982[1960]). The origin of speech. In W. S.-Y. Wang (ed.), *Human Communication: Language and Its Psychobiological Bases*. New York: Freeman, 4–12.

Hockett, C. (1987). *Refurbishing our Foundations: Elementary Linguistics from an Advanced Point of View*. Amsterdam: Benjamins.

Hodges, J. R., and Greene, J. D. W. (1998). Knowing about people and naming them: can Alzheimer's disease patients do one without the other? *Quarterly Journal of Experimental Psychology, section A: Human Experimental Psychology* 51(1): 121–34.

Hoey, M. (2005). *Lexical Priming: A New Theory of Words and Language*. London: Routledge.

Hoey, M., Mahlberg M., Stubbs, M., and Teubert, W. (2007). *Text, Discourse and Corpora: Theory and Analysis*. London: Continuum.

Hoffer, E. (1954). *The Passionate State of Mind*. New York: Harper, 98.

Hoffman, D. D., and Richards, W. A. (1984). Parts of recognition. *Cognition* 18(1–3): 65–96.

Hoffman, E. (1989). *Lost in Translation: A Life in a New Language*. New York: Penguin Books.

Hohenberger, A. (2008). The word in sign language. *Linguistics* 46(2): 249–308.

Hohne, E. A., and Jusczyk, P. W. (1994). Two-month-old infants' sensitivity to allophonic differences. *Perception and Psychophysics* 56(6): 613–23.

Hoijer, H. (1939). Chiricahua loan-words from Spanish. *Language* 15: 110–15.

Holland, T. J. (1990). The many faces of nicknames. *Names* 38: 255–72.

Holmes, Sr, O. W. (1858). *The Autocrat of the Breakfast Table*, Boston: Phillips, Sampson, ch. 5.

Holton, D., Mackridge, P., and Philippaki-Warburton, I. (1997). *Greek: A Comprehensive Grammar of the Modern Language*. London: Routledge.

Holzer, G. (1989). *Entlehnungen aus einer bisher unbekannten indogermanischen Sprache im Urslavischen und Urbaltischen*. Vienna: ÖAW.

Holzknecht, S. (1988). Word taboo and its implications for language change in the Markham family of languages, PNG. *Language and Linguistics in Melanesia* 18: 43–69.

Hombert, J. -M. (1992). *Terminologie des odeurs dans quelques langues du Gabon*. Pholia.

Hood, T. (1827). *Hero and Leander*, stanza 41.

Hopper, P. J., and Traugott, E. C. (2003). *Grammaticalization*. Cambridge: Cambridge University Press.

Horn, L. (1989). Morphology, pragmatics and the un-verb. In K. deJong and Y. No (eds), *Proceedings from the Sixth Eastern State Conference on Linguistics*. Columbus, OH, 93–103.

Horst, M., Cobb, T., and Meara, P. (1998). Beyond a clockwork orange: acquiring second language vocabulary through reading. *Reading in a Foreign Language* 11: 207–23.

Horton, W. S., and Gerrig, R. J. (2005). Conversational common ground and memory processes in language production. *Discourse Processes* 40: 1–35.

Horton, W. S., and Slaten, D. G. (2012). Anticipating who will say what: the influence of speaker-specific memory associations on reference resolution. *Memory and Cognition* 40: 113–26.

Hoshino, N., and Kroll, J. F. (2008). Cognate effects in picture naming: does cross-language activation survive a change of script? *Cognition* 106: 501–11.

Hough, C. (2000). Towards an explanation of phonetic differentiation in masculine and feminine first names. *Journal of Linguistics* 36(1): 1–11.

Hough, C. (2010). *Toponymicon and Lexicon in North-West Europe: 'Ever-Changing Connection'.* Cambridge: University of Cambridge, Department of Anglo-Saxon, Norse and Celtic.

Hough, C. (2012). Celts in Scandinavian Scotland and Anglo-Saxon England: place-names and language contact reconsidered. In M. Stenroos, M. Mäkinen, and I. Særheim (eds), *Language Contact and Development around the North Sea*. Amsterdam: Benjamins, 3–22.

Householder, F. W. (1946). On the problem of sound and meaning: an English phonestheme. *Word* 2: 83–4.

Householder, F. W. (1995). Aristotle and the Stoics on language. In E. F. K. Koerner and R. E. Asher (eds), *Concise History of the Language Sciences*. London: Pergamon/Elsevier, 93–9.

Howarth, P. A. (1996). *Phraseology in English Academic Writing*. Tübingen: Niemeyer.

Hu, M., and Nation, I. S. P. (2000). Vocabulary density and reading comprehension. *Reading in a Foreign Language* 13(1): 403–30.

Huang, C.-R., and Xue, N. (2012). Words without boundaries: computational approaches to Chinese word segmentation. *Language and Linguistics Compass* 6(8): 494–505.

Huddleston, R. (1984). *Introduction to the Grammar of English*. Cambridge: Cambridge University Press.

Huddleston, R. D. (1988). *English Grammar: An Outline*. Cambridge: Cambridge University Press.

Huddleston, R. (2002). Clause type and illocutionary force. In R. Huddleston and G. Pullum, *The Cambridge Grammar of the English Language*. Cambridge: Cambridge University Press, 851–945.

Huddleston, R., Payne, J., and Peterson, P. (2002). Coordination and supplementation. In R. Huddleston and G. Pullum, *The Cambridge Grammar of the English Language*. Cambridge: Cambridge University Press, 1273–1364.

Huddleston, R., and Pullum, G. K. (2002a). *The Cambridge Grammar of the English Language*. Cambridge: Cambridge University Press.

Huddleston, R., and Pullum, G. (2002b). Preliminaries. In R. Huddleston and G. Pullum, *The Cambridge Grammar of the English Language*. Cambridge: Cambridge University Press, 1–42.

Hudson, R. (1990). *English Word Grammar*. Oxford: Blackwell.

Hudson, R. (2000). Grammar without functional categories. In R. D. Borsley (ed.), *The Nature and Function of Syntactic Categories*. San Diego, Calif.: Academic Press, 7–35.

Hudson, R. (2001). Clitics in word grammar. *UCL Working Papers in Linguistics* 13: 243–97.

Hudson, R. (2003). Gerunds without phrase structure. *Natural Language and Linguistic Theory* 21: 579–615.

Hudson, R. (2007). *Language Networks: The New Word Grammar*. Oxford: Oxford University Press.

Hughes, G. (1991). *Swearing: A Social History of Foul Language, Oaths and Profanity in English*. Oxford: Blackwell.

Hughes, G. (2006). *An Encyclopedia of Swearing: The Social History of Oaths, Profanity, Foul Language, and Ethnic Slurs in the English-Speaking World*. New York: Sharpe.

Hulstijn, J. H. (1993). When do foreign language learners look up the meaning of unfamiliar words? The influence of task and learner variables. *Modern Language Journal* 77: 139–47.

Hulstijn, J. H., Hollander, M., and Greidanus, T. (1996). Incidental vocabulary learning by advanced foreign language students: the influence of marginal glosses, dictionary use, and reoccurrence of unknown words. *Modern Language Journal* 80: 327–39.

Hulstijn, J., and Laufer, B. (2001). Empirical evidence for the involvement load hypothesis in vocabulary acquisition. *Language Learning* 51(3): 539–58.

Humphreys, G. W., Riddoch, M. J., and Quinlan, P. T. (1988). Cascade processes in picture identification. *Cognitive Neuropsychology* 5: 67–103.

Hunston, S. (2008). Starting with the small words. *International Journal of Corpus Linguistics* 13(3): 271–295.

Hunston, S., and Francis, G. (2000). *Pattern Grammar: A Corpus-Driven Approach to the Lexical Grammar of English*. Amsterdam: Benjamins.

Hurford, J. (2002). The roles of expression and representation in language evolution. In A. Wray (ed.), *The Transition to Language*. Oxford: Oxford University Press, 311–34.

Hurley, M. M., Dennett, D. C., and Adams, R. B. (2011). *Inside Jokes: Using Humor to Reverse-Engineer the Mind*. Cambridge, Mass.: MIT Press.

Hüsken, W. N. (1987). *Noyt Meerder Vreucht*. Deventer: Sub Rosa.

Hutchinson, S., and Louwerse, M. M. (2012). The upbeat of language: linguistic context and perceptual simulation predict processing valence words. In N. Miyake, D. Peebles, and R. P. Cooper (eds), *Proceedings of the 34th Annual Conference of the Cognitive Science Society*. Austin, Tex.: Cognitive Science Society, 1709–14.

Huttenlocher, J., Smiley, P., and Charney, R. (1983). Emergence of action categories in the child: evidence from verb meanings. *Psychological Review* 90: 72–93.

Huxley, A. (1937). *The Olive Tree*. London: Chatto & Windus.

Hyman, L. M. (2008). Directional asymmetries in the morphology and phonology of words, with special reference to Bantu. *Linguistics* 46: 309–50.

Hyman, L. M., Katamba, F., and Walusimbi, L. (1987). Luganda and the strict layer hypothesis. *Phonology Yearbook* 4: 87–108.

Hymes, D. H. (1964). *Language in Culture and Society: A Reader in Linguistics and Anthropology*. New York: Harper & Row.

Idström, A., and Piirainen, E. (eds) (2012). *Endangered Metaphors*. Amsterdam: Benjamins.

Imai, M., Kita, S., Nagumo, M., and Okadad, H. (2008). Sound symbolism facilitates early verb learning. *Cognition* 108(1): 54–65.

Indefrey, P. (2006). A meta-analysis of hemodynamic studies on first and second language processing: which suggested differences can we trust and what do they mean? *Language Learning* 56: 279–304.

Inkelas, S. (1993). Nimboran position class morphology. *Natural Language and Linguistic Theory* 11: 559–624.

Inkelas, S. (1989). Prosodic constituency in the lexicon. Ph.D dissertation, Stanford University.

Inkelas, S., and Zec, D. (1995). Syntax–phonology interface. In J. A. Goldsmith (ed.), *The Handbook of Phonological Theory*. Oxford: Blackwell, 535–49.

International Commission on Zoological Nomenclature (2000). International Code of Zoological Nomenclature 4th edn. <http://www.nhm.ac.uk/hosted-sites/iczn/code/>.

Ito, J., and Mester, A. (1992). *Weak Layering and Word Binarity*. Santa Cruz, Calif.: Linguistic Research Center, Cowell College.

Ito, J., and Mester, A. (1995). Japanese phonology. In J. Goldsmith (ed.), *The Handbook of Phonological Theory*. Oxford: Oxford University Press, 816–38.

Ito, J., and Mester, A. (1997). Sympathy Theory and German truncations. In V. Miglio and B. Morén (eds), *Proceedings of the Hopkins Optimality Workshop/Maryland Mayfest 1997*. University of Maryland Working Papers in Linguistics 5: 117–39.

Ito, J., and Mester, A. (2003). Weak layering and word binarity. In T. Honma, M. Okazaki, T. Tabata, and S. Tanaka (eds), *A New Century of Phonology and Phonological Theory: A Festschrift for Professor Shosuke Haraguchi on the Occasion of His Sixtieth Birthday*. Tokyo: Kaitakusha, 26–65.

Ito, J., and Mester, A. (2009). The extended prosodic word. In J. Grijzenhout and B. Kabak (eds), *Phonological Domains: Universals and Deviations*. Berlin: Mouton de Gruyter, 135–94.

Iverson, J. (2010). Developing language in a developing body: the relationship between motor development and language development. *Journal of Child Language* 37: 229–61.

Iwashita, N., Brown, A., McNamara, T., and O'Hagan, S. (2008). Assessed levels of second language speaking proficiency: how distinct? *Applied Linguistics* 29: 24–49.

Jackendoff, R. (1983). *Semantics and Cognition*. Cambridge, Mass.: MIT Press.

Jackendoff, R. (1989). What is a concept, that a person may grasp it? *Mind and Language* 4: 68–102.

Jackendoff, R. (1995). The boundaries of the lexicon. In M. Everaert, E.-J. van der Linden, A. Schenk, and R. Schreuder (eds), *Idioms: Structural and Psychological Perspectives*. Hillsdale, NJ: Erlbaum, 133–65.

Jackendoff, R. (1996). Semantics and cognition. In S. Lappin (ed.), *The Handbook of Contemporary Semantic Theory*. Oxford: Blackwell, 539–59.

Jackendoff, R. (2002a). *Foundations of Language: Brain, Meaning, Evolution*. Oxford: Oxford University Press.

Jackendoff, R. (2002b). What's in the lexicon? In S. Nooteboom, F. Weerman, and F. Wijnen (eds), *Storage and Computation in the Language Faculty*. Dordrecht: Kluwer, 23–58.

Jackendoff, R. (2010). *Meaning and the Lexicon: The Parallel Architecture*. Oxford: Oxford University Press.

Jackendoff, R. (2011). What is the human language faculty? Two views. *Language* 87: 586–624.

Jacobs, N. (2005). *Yiddish: A Linguistic Introduction*. Cambridge: Cambridge University Press.

Jacquemin, C. (2001). *Spotting and Discovering Terms through Natural Language Processing*. Cambridge, Mass.: MIT Press.

Jaeggli, O. (1982). *Topics in Romance Syntax*. Dordrecht: Foris.

Jakobson, R., Fant, C. G. M., and Halle, M. (1952). *Preliminaries to Speech Analysis*. Cambridge, Mass.: MIT Press.

Jakobson, R., and Waugh, L. R. (1979). *The Sound Shape of Language*. Bloomington: Indiana University Press.

Jakubíček, M., Kilgarriff, A., Kovář, V., Rychlý, P., and Suchomel, V. (2013). The TenTen Corpus Family. Presened at the International Conference on Corpus Linguistics, Lancaster.

Janssen, N., Bi, Y., and Caramazza, A. (2008). A tale of two frequencies: determining the speed of lexical access in Mandarin Chinese and English compounds. *Language and Cognitive Processes* 23: 1191–223.

Janssen, N., and Caramazza, A. (2009). Grammatical and phonological influences on word order. *Psychological Science* 20(10): 1262–8.

Jay, T. (2000). *Why We Curse: A Neuro-psycho-social Theory of Speech*. Philadelphia: Benjamins.

Jazayery, M. A. (1983). The modernization of the Persian vocabulary and language reform in Iran. In I. Fodor and C. Hagège (eds), *Language Reform: History and Future*, vol. 2. Hamburg: Buske, 241–67.

Jescheniak, J. D., Oppermann, F., Hantsch, A., Wagner, V., Mädebach, A., and Schriefers, H. (2009). Do perceived context pictures automatically activate their phonological code? *Experimental Psychology* 56: 56–65.

Jescheniak, J. D., and Schriefers, H. (2001). Priming effects from phonologically related distractors in picture–word interference. *Quarterly Journal of Experimental Psychology* 54A: 371–82.

Jespersen, O. (1905/1962). *Growth and Structure of the English Language*. Oxford: Blackwell.

Jespersen, O. (1922a). *Language: Its Nature, Development, and Origin*. London: Allen & Unwin.

Jespersen, O. (1922b). Symbolic value of the vowel i. *Phonologica* 1: 283–303.

Jespersen, O. (1924). *The Philosophy of Grammar*. London: George Allen & Unwin.

Jewell, E. J., Abate, F., and McKean, E. (2001). *The New Oxford American Dictionary*. Oxford: Oxford University Press.

Jiang, N. (2002). Form–meaning mapping in vocabulary acquisition in a second language. *Studies in Second Language Acquisition* 24: 617–37.

Jiang, N., and Forster, K. I. (2001). Cross-language priming asymmetries in lexical decision and episodic recognition. *Journal of Memory and Language* 44: 32–51.

Joanisse, M. F., and Seidenberg, M. S. (1999). Impairments in verb morphology after brain injury: a connectionist model. *Proceedings of the National Academy of Sciences* 96: 7592–7.

Joanisse, M. F., and Seidenberg, M. S. (2005). Imaging the past: neural activation in frontal and temporal regions during regular and irregular past-tense processing. *Cognitive, Affective and Behavioral Neuroscience* 5: 282–96.

Joe, A. (1998). What effects do text-based tasks promoting generation have on incidental vocabulary acquisition? *Applied Linguistics* 19: 357–77.

Johnson, E. K., and Jusczyk, P. W. (2001). Word segmentation by 8-month-olds: when speech cues count more than statistics. *Journal of Memory and Language* 44(4): 548–67.

Johnson, E. K., and Seidl, A. H. (2009). At 11 months, prosody still outranks statistics. *Developmental Science* 12(1): 131–41.

Johnson, E. K., and Tyler, M. D. (2010). Testing the limits of statistical learning for word segmentation. *Developmental Science* 13(2): 339–45.

Johnson, K. (2005). Speaker normalization in speech perception. In D. Pisoni and R. Remez (eds), *The Handbook of Speech Perception*. Oxford: Blackwell, 363–89.

Johnson, N. F., and Pugh, K. R. (1994). A cohort model of visual word recognition. *Cognitive Psychology* 26: 240–346.

Johnson, S. (1755). *A Dictionary of the English Language*. London: J. & P. Knapton

Johnson, S. (1791). In J. Boswell, *The Life of Samuel Johnson*, ch. 47.

Johnson, S. (2008). Plan of a dictionary of the English language. In T. Fontenelle (ed.), *Practical Lexicography: A Reader.* Oxford: Oxford University Press, 19–30.

Jones, H. G., and Langford, S. (1987). Phonological blocking in the tip-of-the-tongue state. *Cognition* 26: 115–22.

Joseph, B. (2002). The word in Modern Greek. In R. M. W. Dixon and A. Y. Aikhenvald (eds), *Word: A Cross-Linguistic Typology*. Cambridge: Cambridge University Press, 243–65.

Julien, M. (2006). Word. In K. Brown (ed.), *Encyclopedia of Language and Linguistics*, 2nd edn, vol. 13. Oxford: Elsevier, 617–24.

Jung, J., Na, L., and Akama, H. (2010). Network analysis of Korean word associations. In *Proceedings of the NAACL HLT 2010 First Workshop on Computational Neurolinguistics*, 27–35. Association for Computational Linguistics.

Jusczyk, P. (1985). On characterizing the development of speech perception. In J. Mehler and R. Fox (eds), *Neonate Cognition: Beyond the Blooming, Buzzing Confusion*. Hillsdale, NJ: Erlbaum, 199–230.

Jusczyk, P. (1997). *The Discovery of Spoken Language*. Cambridge, Mass.: MIT Press.

Jusczyk, P. W., and Aslin, R. N. (1995). Infants' detection of the sound patterns of words in fluent speech. *Cognitive Psychology* 29(1): 1–23.

Jusczyk, P. W., Hohne, E. A., and Bauman, A. (1999). Infant's sensitivity to allophonic cues for word segmentation. *Perception and Psychophysics* 61(8): 1465–76.

Jusczyk, P. W., Houston, D. M., and Newsome, M. (1999). The beginnings of word segmentation in English-learning infants. *Cognitive Psychology* 39(3–4): 159–207.

Jusczyk, P. W., and Thompson, E. (1978). Perception of a phonetic contrast in multisyllabic utterances by 2-month-old infants. *Perception and Psychophysics* 23(2): 105–9.

Justeson, J., and Katz, S. (1995). Co-occurrences of antonymous adjectives and their contexts. *Computational Linguistics* 17(1): 1–19.

Kabak, B., and Revithiadou, A. (2009). An interface approach to prosodic word recursion. In J. Grijzenhout and B. Kabak (eds), *Phonological Domains: Universals and Deviations*. Berlin: Mouton de Gruyter, 105–34.

Kaczer, L., Timmer, K., and Schiller, N. O. (in preparation). Long-lag priming effects of novel and existing compounds on naming familiar objects reflect memory consolidation processes: a combined behavioral and ERP study.

Kakehi, H., Tamori, I., and Schourup, L. (1996). *Dictionary of Iconic Expressions in Japanese*. Berlin: Mouton.

Kamp, H., and Reyle, U. (1993). *From Discourse to Logic*. Dordrecht: Kluwer.

Kant, I. (1790). *Kritik der Urteilskraft*. Berlin: Lagarde. English translation by J. H. Bernard: *Critique of Judgment* (New York: Hafner, 1951).

Kantartzis, K., Kita, S., and Imai, M. (2011). Japanese sound symbolism facilitates word learning in English speaking children. *Cognitive Science* 35: 626–30.

Kaplan, E., Goodglass, H., and Weintraub, S. (1983). *Boston Naming Test*. Philadelphia: Lea & Febiger.

Katriel, T. (1986). *Talking Straight: Dugri Speech in Israeli Sabra Culture*. Cambridge: Cambridge University Press.

Katz, J. J. (1973). Compositionality, idiomaticity, and lexical substitution. In S. Anderson and P. Kiparsky (eds), *A Festschrift for Morris Halle*. New York: Holt, Rinehart, and Winston, 357–76.

Katz, J. J., and Postal, P. M. (1963). Semantic interpretation of idioms and sentences containing them. *MIT Research Laboratory of Electronics Quarterly Progress Report* 70: 275–82.

Kaufman, T. (1980). Pre-Columbian borrowing involving Huastec. In K. Klar, M. Langdon, and S. Silver (eds), *American Indian and Indoeuropean Studies for Madison S. Beeler*. The Hague: Mouton, 107–14.

Kaufman, T. (1986). Symbolism and change in the sound system of Huastec. In *Conference on Sound Symbolism* (16–18 Jan). Berkeley, Calif.

Kaufman, T. (1994). Symbolism and change in the sound system of Huastec. In L. Hinton, J. Nichols, and J. J. Ohala (eds), *Sound Symbolism*. Cambridge: Cambridge University Press, 63–75.

Kauschke, C., and Hofmeister, C. (2002). Early lexical growth in German: a study on vocabulary growth and vocabulary composition during the second and third year of life. *Journal of Child Language* 29: 735–57.

Kay, C., Roberts, J., Samuels, M., and Wotherspoon, I. (2009). *Historical Thesaurus of the Oxford English Dictionary*. Oxford: Oxford University Press.

Kay, P., Berlin, B., Maffi, L., and Merrifield, W. (1997). Color naming across languages. In C. L. Hardin and L. Maffi (eds), *Color Categories in Thought and Language*. Cambridge: Cambridge University Press, 21–58.

Kay, P., Berlin, B., Maffi, L., Merrifield, W. R., and Cook, R. (2009). *The World Color Survey*. Stanford, Calif.: CSLI.

Kay, P., and McDaniel, C. K. (1978). The linguistic significance of the meanings of basic color terms. *Language* 54(3): 610–46.

Kay, P., and Regier, T. (2003). Resolving the question of color naming universals. *Proceedings of the National Academy of Sciences of the United States of America* 100(15): 9085–9.

Kayne, R. S. (1969). The transformational cycle in French syntax. Doctoral dissertation, MIT.

Kayne, R. S. (1975). *French Syntax: The Transformational Cycle*. Cambridge, Mass.: MIT Press.

Kayne, R. S. (1991). Romance clitics, verb movement and PRO. *Linguistic Inquiry* 22: 647–86.

Keating, G. (2008). Task effectiveness and word learning in a second language: the involvement load hypothesis on trial. *Language Teaching Research* 12(3): 365–86.

Keatley, C. W., Spinks, J. A., and de Gelder, B. (1994). Asymmetrical cross-language priming effects. *Memory and Cognition* 22: 70–84.

Keesing, R. (1984). Rethinking mana. *Journal of Anthropological Research* 40: 137–56.

Keesing, R. M., and Fifi'i, J. (1969). Kwaio word tabooing in its cultural context. *Journal of the Polynesian Society* 78: 154–77.

Kehl, F. (1971). Chinese nicknaming behavior: a sociolinguistic pilot study. *Journal of Oriental Studies* 9: 149–72.

Keil, F. (1989). *Concepts, Kinds, and Cognitive Development*. Cambridge, Mass.: MIT Press.

Keijzer, M. C. J. (2011). Language reversion versus general cognitive decline: towards a new taxonomy of language change in elderly bilingual immigrants. In M. S. Schmid and W. Lowie (eds), *Modeling Bilingualism: From Structure to Chaos*. Amsterdam: Benjamins, 221–32.

Keith-Spiegel, P. (1972). Early conceptions of humor: varieties and issues. In J. H. Goldstein and P. E. McGhee (eds), *Psychology of Humor*. New York: Academic Press, 3–39.

Kelih, E. (2008). Phoneminventar–Wortlänge: einige grundsätzliche Überlegungen. Aktual'ni problemy hermans'koï filolohiï. *Chernivtsi: Knihi* 21: 25–9.

Kelih, E. (2010). Wortlänge und Vokal- Konsonantenhäufigkeit: Evidenz aus slowenischen, makedonischen, tschechischen und russischen Paralleltexten. *Anzeiger für Slavische Philologie* 36: 7–27.

Kelih, E. (2012). Systematic interrelations between grapheme frequencies and the word length: empirical evidence from Slovene. *Journal of Quantitative Linguistics* 19(3): 205–31.

Kelih, E., Antić, G., Grzybek, P., and Stadlober, E. (2005). Classification of author and/or genre? The impact of word length. In C. Weihs and W. Gaul (eds), *Classification: The Ubiquitous Challenge*. Heidelberg: Springer 498–505.

Kellerman, E. (1979). Transfer and non-transfer: where we are now. *Studies in Second Language Acquisition* 2: 37–57.

Kelly, B. F. (2011). A new look at redundancy in children's word and gesture combinations. In I. Arnon and E. V. Clark (eds), *Experience, Variation, and Generalization: Learning a First Language*. Amsterdam: Benjamins, 75–89.

Kelly, M. H. (1992). Using sound to solve syntactic problems: the role of phonology in grammatical category assignments. *Psychological Review* 99: 349–64.

Kemmerer, D. (2006). Action verbs, argument structure constructions and the mirror neuron system. In M. A. Arbib (ed.), *Action to Language via the Mirror Neuron System*. Cambridge: Cambridge University Press, 347–73.

Kennedy, R., and Zamuner, T. (2006). Nicknames and the lexicon of sports. *American Speech* 81: 387–422.

Keren-Portnoy, T. (2006). Facilitation and practice in verb acquisition. *Journal of Child Language* 33: 487–518.

Kern, S. (2010). Les premiers mots du jeune enfant français: analyse quantitative et qualitative du vocabulaire réceptif et productif des deux premières années de vie. *Rééducation orthophonique* 244: 149–65.

Kessel, F. (ed.) (1988). *The Development of Language and Language Researchers: Essays in Honor of Roger Brown*. Hillsdale, NJ: Erlbaum.

Keuleers, E., Brysbaert, M., and New, B. (2010). SUBTLEX-NL: a new frequency measure for Dutch words based on film subtitles. *Behavior Research Methods* 42: 643–50.

Keuleers, E., Lacey, P., Rastle, K., and Brysbaert, M. (2012). The British Lexicon Project: lexical decision data for 28,730 monosyllabic and disyllabic English words. *Behavior Research Methods* 44: 287–304.

Kibbee, D. (1991). *For to Speke Frenche Trewly: The French Language in England 1000–1600*. Amsterdam: Benjamins.

Kibrik, A. E. (1977). *Opyt strukturnogo opisanija arčinskogo jazyka, II: Taksonomičeskaja grammatika*. Moscow: Izdatel'stvo Moskovskogo universiteta.

Kiesling, S. F. (2006). English in Australia and New Zealand. In B. B. Kachru, Y. Kachru, and C. L. Nelson (eds), *The Handbook of World Englishes*. Malden, Mass.: Blackwell, 74–89.

Kilian-Hatz, C. (2001). Ideophones from Baka and Kxoe. In F. K. Erhard Voeltz and C. Kilian-Hatz (eds), *Ideophones*. Amsterdam: Benjamins, 155–63.

Kim, M., McGregor, K. K., and Thompson, C. K. (2000). Early lexical development in English- and Korean-speaking children: language-general and language-specific patterns. *Journal of Child Language* 27: 225–54.

Kim, Y. (2008b). The role of task-induced involvement and learner proficiency in L2 vocabulary acquisition. *Language Learning* 58(2): 285–325.

Kimenyi, A. (1978). Aspects of naming in Kinyarwanda. *Anthropological Linguistics* 20: 258–71.

Kimmel, M. (2012). Optimizing the analysis of metaphor in discourse: how to make the most of qualitative software and find a good research design. *Review of Cognitive Linguistics* 10(1): 1–48.

Kintsch, W. (1988). The role of knowledge in discourse comprehension: a construction-integration model. *Psychological Review* 95: 163–82.

Kiparsky, P. (2008). Universals constrain change; change results in typological generalizations. In J. Good (ed.), *Language Universals and Language Change*. Oxford: Oxford University Press, 23–53.

Kirkpatrick, A. (2007). *World Englishes: Implications for International Communication and English Language Teaching*. Cambridge: Cambridge University Press.

Kiss, G. R. (1968). Words, associations and networks. *Journal of Verbal Learning and Verbal Behavior* 7: 707–13.

Kiss, G. R., Armstrong, C., Milroy, R., and Piper, J. (1973). An associative thesaurus of English and its computer analysis. In A. Aitken, R. Bailey, and N. Hamilton-Smith (eds), *The Computer and Literacy Studies*. Edinburgh: Edinburgh University Press, 153–65.

Kita, S. (1997). Two-dimensional semantic analysis of Japanese mimetics. *Linguistics* 35: 379–415.

Kita, S. (ed.) (2003). *Pointing: Where Language, Culture, and Cognition Meet*. Mahwah, NJ: Erlbaum.

Kitson, P. R. (1996). British and European river-names. *Transactions of the Philological Society* 94: 73–118.

Klamer, M. (2002). Semantically motivated lexical patterns: a study of Dutch and Kambera expressives. *Language* 78(2): 258–86.

Klaus, A., Yu, S., and Plenz, D. (2011). Statistical analyses support power law distributions found in neuronal avalanches. *PLoS ONE* 6(5): e19779; doi:10.1371/journal.pone.0019779.

Klepousniotou, E. (2002). The processing of lexical ambiguity: homonymy and polysemy in the mental lexicon. *Brain and Language* 81: 205–23.

Ko, M. H. (2012). Glossing and second language vocabulary learning. *TESOL Quarterly* 46: 56–79.

Kobayashi, H. (1998). How 2-year-old children learn novel part names of unfamiliar objects. *Cognition* 68: B41–B51.

Koester, D., and Schiller, N. O. (2008). Morphological priming in overt language production: electrophysiological evidence from Dutch. *NeuroImage* 42: 1622–30.

Koester, D., and Schiller, N. O. (2011). The functional neuroanatomy of morphology in language production. *NeuroImage* 55: 732–41.

Koestler, A. (1964). Originality, emphasis, economy. *The Act of Creation*, ch. 3. London: Hutchinson.

Köhler, R. (1986). *Zur linguistischen Synergetik: Struktur und Dynamik der Lexik*. Bochum: Brockmeyer.

Köhler, R. (1999). Der Zusammenhang zwischen Lexemlänge und Polysemie im Maori. In J. Genzor and S. Ondrejovič (eds), *Pange lingua*. Bratislava: Veda, 27–34.

Köhler, R. (2005). Synergetic linguistics. In R. Köhler, G. Altmann, and R. G. Piotrovski (eds), *Quantitative Linguistik: ein Internationales Handbuch?/ Quantitative Linguistics: An International Handbook*. Berlin: de Gruyter, 760–74.

Köhler, R. (2006). The frequency distribution of the lengths of length sequences. In J. Genzor and M. Bucková (eds), *Favete Linguis: Studies in Honour of Viktor Krupa*. Bratislava: Academic Press, 142–52.

Köhler, R. (2008). Sequences of linguistic quantities: report on a new unit of investigation. *Glottotheory* 1(1): 115–19.

Köhler, R. (2012). *Quantitative Syntax Analysis*. Berlin: de Gruyter.

Köhler, R., and Naumann, S. (2008). Quantitative text analysis using L-, F- and T-segments. In B. Preisach et al. (eds), *Data Analysis: Machine Learning and Applications*. Berlin: Springer, 637–46.

Köhler, W. (1929). *Gestalt Psychology*. New York: Liveright.

Kökeritz, H. (1950). Punning names in Shakespeare. *Modern Language Notes* 65(4): 240–3.

Koopman, A. (2002). *Zulu Names*. Pietermaritzburg: University of Natal Press.

Koopman, A. (2009). Uniqueness in the Zulu anthroponymic system. *Onoma* 44: 69–91.

Kopp, R. R. (1995). *Metaphor Therapy: Using Client-Generated Metaphors in Psychotherapy*. New York: Brunnel/Mazel.

Kopp, R. R., and Craw, M. J. (1998). Metaphoric language, metaphoric cognition, and cognitive therapy. *Psychotherapy* 35(3): 306–11.

Koriat, A. (1981). Semantic facilitation in lexical decision as a function of prime-target association. *Memory & Cognition* 9: 587–98.

Koskela, A. (2016). Identification of homonyms in different types of dictionaries. In P. Durkin (ed.), *The Oxford handbook of Lexicography*. Oxford: Oxford University Press, 457–71.

Koss, G. (2006). Nicknames: variation and internal differentiation in a linguistic field. *Beiträge zur Namenforschung* 41: 1–12.

Kost, C. R, Fost, P., and Lenzini, J. J. (1999). Textual and pictorial glosses: effectiveness of incidental vocabulary growth when reading in a foreign language. *Foreign Language Annals* 32(1): 89–92.

Kövecses, Z. (2000). *Metaphor and Emotion*. Cambridge: Cambridge University Press.

Kövecses, Z. (2002). *Metaphor: A Practical Introduction*. Oxford: Oxford University Press.

Kövecses, Z., and Szabó, P. (1996). Idioms: a view from cognitive semantics. *Applied Linguistics* 17(3): 326–55.

Kramer, J. (1983). Language planning in Italy. In I. Fodor and C. Hagège (eds), *Language Reform: History and Future*, vol. 2. Hamburg: Buske, 301–16.

Kripke, S. (1972). Naming and necessity. In D. Davidson and G. Harman (eds), *Semantics of Natural Language*. New York: Humanities Press, 253–355.

Kripke, S. (1980). *Naming and Necessity*. Oxford: Blackwell.

Kripke, S. (1981[1972]). *Names and Necessity*. Oxford: Blackwell.

Kroeber, A. L. (1909). Noun incorporation in American languages. XVI Internationaler Amerikanisten-Kongress, Vienna, 569–76.

Kroll, J. F., and Stewart, E. (1994). Category interference in translation and picture naming: evidence for asymmetric connections between bilingual memory representations. *Journal of Memory and Language* 33: 149–74.

Kroll, J. F., Van Hell, J. G., Tokowicz, N., and Green, D. W. (2010). The revised hierarchical model: a critical review and assessment. *Bilingualism: Language and Cognition* 13: 373–81.

Kucera, H., and Francis, W. N. (1967). *A Computational Analysis of Present-Day American English*. Providence, RI: Brown University Press.

Kuhl, P. K., Conboy, B. T., Padden, D., Nelson, T., and Pruitt, J. (2005). Early speech perception and later language development: Implications for the 'critical period'. *Language Learning and Development* 1(3–4): 237–64.

Kuhl, P., and Meltzoff, A. (1997). Evolution, nativism and learning in the development of language and speech. In M. Gopnik (ed.), *The Inheritance and Innateness of Grammars*. New York: Oxford University Press, 7–44.

Kuhl, P., Tsao, F., and Liu, H. (2003). Foreign-language experience in infancy: effects of short-term exposure and social interaction on phonetic learning. *Proceedings of the National Academy of Science* 100: 9096–101.

Kuhl, P., Williams, K., Lacerda, F., Stevens, K., and Lindblom, B. (1992). Linguistic experience alters phonetic perception in infants by 6 months of age. *Science* 255: 606–8.

Kunene, D. P. (2001). Speaking the act: the ideophone as linguistic rebel. In F. K. Erhard Voeltz and C. Kilian-Hatz (eds), *Ideophones*. Amsterdam: Benjamins, 183–91.

Kumar, R., Raghavan, P., Rajagopalan, S., and Tomkins, A. (1999). Trawling the Web for emerging cyber-communities. *Computer Networks* 31: 1481–93.

Kurath, H., et al. (1952–2001). *Middle English Dictionary*. Ann Arbor: University of Michigan Press.

Kutsch Lojenga, C. (1994). *Ngiti, A Central-Sudanic Language of Zaire*. Cologne: Köppe.

Kwiatkowski, P. (1992). The phonology of onomatopoeia: a Polish–English contrastive study. Thesis, Nicholas Copernicus University.

Kyd, T. (c.1589). *The Spanish Tragedy*, II.i.108.

Labrune, L. (2012). *The Phonology of Japanese*. Oxford: Oxford University Press.

Lachs, L., McMichael, K., and Pisoni, D. B. (2000). Speech perception and implicit memory: evidence for detailed episodic encoding of phonetic events. Research on Spoken Language Processing, Progress Report no. 24. Bloomington: Indiana University.

Laeng, B., Brennan, T., Elden, Å., Paulsen, H. G., Banerjee, A., and Lipton, R. (2007). Latitude-of-birth and season-of-birth effects on human color vision in the Arctic. *Vision Research* 47: 1595–1607.

Lahti, K. (2012). *Ideophones in Vladimir Mayakovsky's work*. Portland, Ore.: Linguistic Society of America.

Laine, M., and Martin, N. (2006). *Anomia: Theoretical and Clinical Aspects*. New York: Psychology Press.

Lakoff, G. (1987). *Women, Fire and Dangerous Things: What Categories Reveal About the Mind*. Chicago: University of Chicago Press.

Lakoff, G. (1993). The contemporary theory of metaphor. In A. Ortony (ed.), *Metaphor and Thought*, 2nd edn. Cambridge: Cambridge University Press, 202–51.

Lakoff, G., and Johnson, M. (1980). *Metaphors We Live By*. Chicago: University of Chicago Press.

Lakoff, G., and Johnson, M. (1999). *Philosophy in the Flesh: The Embodied Mind and its Challenges to Western Thought*. New York: Basic Books.

Lakoff, G., and Kövecses, Z. (1987). The cognitive model of anger inherent in American English. In D. Holland and N. Quinn (eds), *Cultural Models in Language and Thought*. Cambridge: Cambridge University Press, 195–221.

Lakoff, R. T. (2000). *The Language War*. Berkeley: University of California Press.

Lamp, F. J. (1979). *African Art of the West Atlantic Coast: Transition in Form and Content*. New York: L. Kahan Gallery.

Lamp, F. J. (1986). The art of the Baga: a preliminary inquiry. *African Arts* 19: 2.

Landau, S. I. (2001). *Dictionaries: The Art and Craft of Lexicography*. Cambridge: Cambridge University Press.

Landman, F. (2000). *Events and Plurality*. Dordrecht: Kluwer Academic.

Langacker, R. (1987). *The Foundations of Cognitive Grammar*, vol. 1: *Theoretical Prerequisites*. Stanford, Calif.: Stanford University Press.

Lanham, L. W. (1960). The comparative phonology of Nguni. Thesis, University of the Witwatersrand.

Lapointe, S. G. (1980). A theory of grammatical agreement. Doctoral dissertation, University of Massachusetts at Amherst.

LaPolla, R. J. (1994). An experimental investigation into phonetic symbolism as it relates to Mandarin Chinese. In L. Hinton, J. Nichols, and J. J. Ohala (eds), *Sound Symbolism*. Cambridge: Cambridge University Press, 130–47.

Larsen-Freeman, D., and Cameron, L. (2008). *Complex Systems and Applied Linguistics*. Oxford: Oxford University Press.

Lasersohn, P. S. (1995). *Plurality, Conjunction and Events*. Dordrecht: Kluwer.

Lashley, K. S. (1951). The problem of serial order in behavior. In L. A. Jeffress (ed.), *Cerebral Mechanisms in Behavior*. New York: Wiley, 112–31.

Lass, R. (1973). Review of P. H. Reaney, *The Origins of English Surnames*. Foundations of Language 9: 392–402.

Lass, R. (1999). Phonology and morphology. In R. Lass (ed.), *The Cambridge History of the English Language, vol. 3: 1476–1776*. Cambridge: Cambridge University Press, 56–186.

Laufer, B. (1989). What percentage of text lexis is necessary is essential for comprehension? In C. Lauren and M. Nordman (eds), *Special Language: From Humans Thinking to Thinking Machines*. Clevedon: Multilingual Matters, 316–23.

Laufer, B. (2003). Vocabulary acquisition in a second language: do learners really acquire most vocabulary by reading? *Canadian Modern Language Review* 59: 565–85.

Laufer, B. (2011). The contribution of dictionary use to the production and retention of collocations in a second language. *International Journal of Lexicography* 24: 29–49.

Laufer, B., Elder, C., Hill, K., and Congdon, P. (2004). Size and strength: do we need both to measure vocabulary knowledge? *Language Testing* 21: 202–27.

Laufer, B., and Hill, M. (2000). What lexical information do L2 learners select in a CALL dictionary and how does it affect word retention? *Language Learning and Technology* 3: 58–76.

Laufer, B., and Ravenhorst-Kalovski, G. C. (2010). Lexical threshold revisited: lexical coverage, learners' vocabulary size and reading comprehension. *Reading in a Foreign Language* 22: 56–70.

Laufer, B., and Sim, D. D. (1985). Taking the easy way out: non-use and misuse of clues in EFL reading. *English Teaching Forum* 23: 7–10.

Laufer, B., and Waldman, T. (2011). Verb–noun collocations in second language writing: a corpus analysis of learners' English. *Language Learning* 61: 647–72.

Laurence, S., and Margolis, E. (1999). Concepts and cognitive science. In E. Margolis and S. Laurence (eds), *Concepts: Core Readings*. Cambridge, Mass.: MIT Press, 3–82.

Laver, J. (1994). *Principles of Phonetics*. Cambridge: Cambridge University Press.

Lawrence, D. (1949). Acquired distinctiveness of cues: transfer between discriminations on the basis of familiarity of the stimulus. *Journal of Experimental Psychology* 39: 770–84.

Lawson, E. D. (1973). Men's first names, nicknames, and short names: a semantic differential analysis. *Names* 21: 22–7.

Lawson, E. D. (1984). Personal names: 100 years of social science contributions. *Names* 32(1): 45–74.

Lea, D. (2008). *The Oxford Learner's Thesaurus*. Oxford: Oxford University Press.

Lee, M.-W., and Williams, J. N. (2001). Lexical access in spoken word production by bilinguals: evidence from the semantic competitor priming paradigm. *Bilingualism: Language and Cognition* 4: 233–48.

Leech, G., and Li, L. (1995). Indeterminacy between noun phrases and adjective phrases as complements of the English verb. In B. Aarts and C. F. Meyer (eds), *The Verb in Contemporary English*. Cambridge: Cambridge University Press, 183–202.

Leech, G., Rayson, P., and Wilson, A. (2001). *Word Frequencies in Written and Spoken English*. Harlow: Longman.

Le Guen, O. (2011). Materiality vs. expressivity: the use of sensory vocabulary in Yucatec Maya. *The Senses and Society* 6(1): 117–25.

Lehiste, I. (1987). *Lectures on Language Contact*. Cambridge, Mass.: MIT Press.

Lehmann, C. (2004). Interlinear morphemic glossing. In G. Booij, C. Lehmann, and J. Mugdan (eds), *Morphologie: ein internationales Handbuch zur Flexion und Wortbildung/Morphology: A Handbook on Inflection and Word Formation*. Berlin: de Gruyter, 1834–57.

Lehrberger, J. (2003). Automatic translation and the concept of sublanguage. In S. Nirenburg, H. Somers, and Y. Wilks (eds), *Readings in Machine Translation*. Boston, Mass.: MIT Press, 207–20.

Lele, V. (2009). 'It's not really a nickname, it's a method': local names, state intimates, and kinship register in the Irish Gaeltacht. *Journal of Linguistic Anthropology* 19: 101–16.

Lemhöfer, K., Spalek, K., and Schriefers, H. (2008). Cross-language effects of grammatical gender in bilingual word recognition and production. *Journal of Memory and Language* 59: 312–30.

Leonard, L. B. (2000). *Children with Specific Language Impairment*. Boston, Mass.: MIT Press.

Lepschy G. C. (1971). *A Survey of Structural Linguistics*. London: Faber & Faber.

Lerat, P. (2002). Qu'est-ce que le verbe spécialisé? Le cas du droit. *Cahiers de lexicologie* 80: 201–11.

LeRoux, J., Moropa, K., Bosch, S., and Fellbaum, C. (2008). Introducing the African Languages Wordnet. (2008). In A. Tanács, D. Csendes, V. Vincze, C. Fellbaum, and P. Vossen (eds), *Proceedings of The Fourth Global WordNet Conference*. Szeged: University of Szeged, Dept of Informatics, 269–80.

Leslie, P. L., and Skipper, J. K. (1990). Toward a theory of nicknames: a case for socio-onomastics. *Names* 38: 273–82.

Levelt, W. J. M. (1989). *Speaking: From Intention to Articulation*lation. Cambridge, Mass.: MIT Press.

Levelt, W. J. M. (1992). Accessing words in speech production: stages, processes and representations. *Cognition* 42: 1–22.

Levelt, W. J. M. (1999). Models of word production. *Trends in Cognitive Sciences* 3: 223–332.

Levelt, W. J. M. (2001). Spoken word production: a theory of lexical access. *Proceedings of the National Academy of Sciences* 98: 13464–71.

Levelt, W. J. M., Roelofs, A., and Meyer, A. S. (1999). A theory of lexical access in speech production. *Behavioral and Brain Sciences* 22: 1–75.

Levelt, W. J. M., Schriefers, H., Vorberg, D., Meyer, A., Pechmann, T., and Havinga, J. (1991). The time course of lexical access in speech production: a study of picture naming. *Psychological Review* 98: 122–42.

Levin, B. (1993). *Verb Classes and Alternations*. Chicago: University of Chicago Press.

Levin, B., and Rappaport, M. (1986). The formation of adjectival passives. Linguistic Inquiry 17: 623–61.

Levine, M. B., and Willis, F. N. (1994). Public reactions to unusual names. *Journal of Social Psychology* 134(5): 561–68.

Levinson, S. C. (2000). Yélî Dnye and the theory of basic color terms. *Journal of Linguistic Anthropology* 10(1): 3–55.

Levinson, S. C. (2007). 'Cut' and 'break' verbs in Yélî Dnye, the Papuan language of Rossel Island. *Cognitive Linguistics* 18(2): 207–17.

Levisen, C. (2012). *Cultural Semantics and Social Cognition: A Case Study of the Danish Universe of Meaning.* Berlin: Mouton de Gruyter.

Levisen, C. (2013). On pigs and people: the porcine semantics of Danish interaction and social cognition. In C. Goddard (ed.), *Semantics and/in Social Cognition.* Special issue of *Australian Journal of Linguistics* 33(3): 344–64.

Levisen, C. (forthcoming). The cognitive semantics of *kastom*: areal semantics and the evolution of sociality concepts in Melanesian creoles.

Lévi-Strauss, C. (1966). *The Savage Mind.* Chicago: University of Chicago Press. (Translated from *La penséé sauvage*, Paris, Plon, 1962).

Levitt, S. D., and Dubner, S. J. (2005). *Freakonomics: A Rogue Economist Explores the Hidden Side of Everything.* New York: HarperCollins.

Levy, P. (1987). *Fonología del totonaco de Papantla.* Mexico City: UNAM.

Lew, R. (2010). Review of de Schryver (ed.), *A Way with Words. Lexikos* 20: 757–59.

Lewis, A. P. (2011). Hvar's campanilism-stereotypes and collective nicknames on the island of Hvar. *Studia Ethnologica Croatica* 23: 215–37.

Lewis, C. S. (1952). *Out of the Silent Planet.* London: Pan.

Lewis, C. S. (1960). *Studies in Words.* Cambridge: Cambridge University Press.

Lewis, G. (1999). *The Turkish Language Reform.* Oxford: Oxford University Press.

Lewis, M. (1993). *The Lexical Approach.* Hove: Teacher Training.

Lew-Williams, C., Pelucchi, B., and Saffran, J. R. (2011). Isolated words enhance statistical language learning in infancy. *Developmental Science* 14(6): 1323–9.

L'Homme, M. C. (1998). Le statut du verbe en langue de spécialité et sa description lexicographique. *Cahiers de lexicologie* 73(2): 61–84.

L'Homme, M. C. (2012). Le verbe terminologique: un portrait de travaux récents. In F. Neveu et al. (eds), *Actes du 3e Congrès mondial de linguistique française*, Lyon: EDP Sciences.

L'Homme, M. C., and Bernier-Colborne, G. (2012). Terms as labels for concepts, terms as lexical units. *Applied Ontology*, special issue: 'Ontologies and Terminologies: Continuum or Dichotomy'.

Li, W. (1992). Random texts exhibit Zipf's-law-like word frequency distribution. *IEEE Transactions on Information Theory* 38(6): 1842–45.

Libben, M. R., and Titone, D. A. (2009). Bilingual lexical access in context: evidence from eye movements during reading. *Journal of Experimental Psychology: Learning, Memory, and Cognition* 35: 381–90.

Liberman, A. (2005). *Word Origins And How We Know Them: Etymology for Everyone.* Oxford: Oxford University Press.

Liberman, M. (2011). Real trends in word and sentence length. <http://languagelog.ldc.upenn.edu/nll/?p=3534>.

Lieber, R., and Scalise, S. (2007). The lexical integrity hypothesis in a new theoretical universe. In G. Booij et al. (eds), *On-line proceedings of the Fifth Mediterranean Morphology Meeting, Fréjus 15–18 Sept. 2005*, University of Bologna. <http://mmm.lingue.unibo.it/>.

Lieber, R., and Štekauer, P. (2009). *The Oxford Handbook of Compounding*. Oxford: Oxford University Press.

Lieberman, A. M., and Mattingly, I. G. (1985). The motor theory of speech perception revised. *Cognition* 21(1): 1–36.

Lieberson, S. (1984). What's in a name?… some sociolinguistic possibilities. *International Journal of the Sociology of Language* 45: 77–88.

Lieberson, S., and Bell, E. O. (1992). Children's first names: an empirical study of social taste. *American Journal of Sociology* 98(3): 511–54.

Lieberson, S., Dumais, S., and Baumann, S. (2000). The instability of androgynous names: the symbolic maintenance of gender boundaries. *American Journal of Sociology* 105(5): 1249–87.

Lieven, E. (1994). Crosslinguistic and crosscultural aspects of language addressed to children. In C. Gallaway and B. Richards (eds), *Input and Interaction in Language Acquisition*. Cambridge: Cambridge University Press, 56–73.

Lieven, E. V. M., Pine, J. M., and Baldwin, G. (1997). Lexically-based learning and early grammatical development. *Journal of Child Language* 24: 187–219.

Linck, J. A., Kroll, J. F., and Sunderman, G. (2009). Losing access to the native language while immersed in a second language: evidence for the role of inhibition in second-language learning. *Psychological Science* 20: 1507–15.

Lindner, S. (1981). A lexico-semantic analysis of English verb particle constructions with OUT and UP. Ph.D dissertation, University of California, San Diego.

Lindsey, D. T., and Brown, A. M. (2002). Color naming and the phototoxic effects of sunlight on the eye. *Psychological Science* 13(6): 506–12.

Lindstromberg, S. (2010). *English Prepositions Explained*. Amsterdam: Benjamins.

Link, G. (1998). *Algebraic Semantics for Natural Language*. Stanford, Calif.: CSLI.

Liu, D. (2012). The most frequently-used multiword constructions in academic written English: a multi-corpus study. *English for Specific Purposes* 31: 25–35.

Lleó, C. (2003). Prosodic licensing of coda in the acquisition of Spanish. *Probus* 15: 257–81.

Lleó, C. (2006). The acquisition of prosodic word structures in Spanish by monolingual and Spanish-German bilingual children. *Language and Speech* 49(2): 205–29.

Lleó, C., and Arias, J. (2009). The role of weight-by-position in the prosodic development of Spanish and German. In J. Grijzenhout and B. Kabak (eds), *Phonological Domains: Universals and Deviations*. Berlin: Mouton de Gruyter, 221–47.

Locke, J. (1979[1690]). *An Essay Concerning Human Understanding*. New York: Oxford University Press.

Lockhart, R. S., and Craik, F. I. G. (1990). Levels of processing: a retrospective commentary on a framework for memory research. *Canadian Journal of Psychology* 44: 87–112.

Lodge, D. (1992). *The Art of Fiction*. New York: Penguin.

Lødrup, H. (1991). The Norwegian pseudo passive as structure sharing. *Working Papers in Scandinavian Syntax* 47: 118–29.

Loftus, E. F., and Palmer, J. C. (1974). Reconstruction of automobile destruction: an example of the interaction between language and memory. *Journal of Verbal Learning and Verbal Behavior* 13: 585–9.

Logan, R. K. (2004). *The Alphabet Effect: A Media Ecology Understanding of the Making of Western Civilisation*. Cresskill, NJ: New Hampton Press.

Longobardi, G. (1994). Reference and proper names. *Linguistic Inquiry* 25: 609–66.

Longobardi, G. (2001). The structure of DPs. In M. Baltin and C. Collins (eds), *The Handbook of Contemporary Syntactic Theory*. Oxford: Blackwell, 562–603.

Lorente, M. (2002). Verbos y discurso especializado. *Estudios de lingüística española (ELiEs)* 16.

Louwerse, M. M., and Benesh, N. (2012). Representing spatial structure through maps and language: Lord of the Rings encodes the spatial structure of Middle Earth. *Cognitive Science* 36: 1556–69.

Louwerse, M., and Connell, L. (2011). A taste of words: linguistic context and perceptual simulation predict the modality of words. *Cognitive Science* 35: 381–98.

Lowe, P., and Pike, J. (1990). *Jilji: Life in the Great Sandy Desert.* Broome, WA: Magabala Books.

Lucas, M. (2000). Semantic priming without association: a meta-analytic review. *Psychonomic Bulletin & Review* 7: 618–30.

Lucy, J. A. (1997). The linguistics of 'color'. In C. L. Hardin and M. Luisa (eds), *Color Categories in Thought and Language*. Cambridge: Cambridge University Press, 320–46.

Lutz, C. A. (1988). *Unnatural Emotions: Everyday Sentiments on a Micronesian Atoll and their Challenge to Western Theory*. Chicago: University of Chicago Press.

Lyddon, W. J., Clay, A. L., and Sparks, C. L. (2001). Metaphor and change in counselling. *Journal of Counseling and Development* 79(3): 269–74.

Lyons, F., Hanley, J. R., and Kay, J. (2002). Anomia for common names and geographical names with preserved retrieval of names of people: a semantic memory disorder. *Cortex* 38: 23–35.

Lyons, J. (1968). *Introduction to Theoretical Linguistics*. Cambridge: Cambridge University Press.

Lyons, J. (1977). *Semantics*. 2 vols. Cambridge: Cambridge University Press.

Lyons, J. (1995). *Linguistic Semantics*. Cambridge: Cambridge University Press.

Maalej, Z. (2004). Figurative language in anger expressions in Tunisian Arabic: an extended view of embodiment. *Metaphor and Symbol* 19: 51–75.

McArthur, T. (ed.) (1981). *The Longman Lexicon of Contemporary English*. Harlow: Longman.

McCarthy, J. J. (1985). *Formal Problems in Semitic Phonology and Morphology*. New York: Garland.

McCarthy, J., and Prince, A. (1986). Prosodic morphology. Technical Report 32, Rutgers University Center for Cognitive Science 1996. Available at: <http://works.bePress.com/john_j_mccarthy/54>.

McCarthy, M. (1990). *Vocabulary*. Oxford: Oxford University Press.

McCarthy, M., and Carter, R. (1997). Written and spoken vocabulary. In N. Schmitt and M. McCarthy (eds), *Vocabulary: Description, Acquisition and Pedagogy*. Cambridge: Cambridge University Press, 20–39.

McCawley, J. D. (1998, 2nd edn.). *The Syntactic Phenomena of English*. Chicago: Chicago University Press.

McClelland, J. L., and Elman, J. L. (1986). The TRACE model of speech perception. *Cognitive Psychology* 18(1): 1–86.

McClelland, J. L., and Rumelhart, D. E. (1981). An interactive activation model of context effects in letter perception, pt 1: An account of the basic findings. *Psychological Review* 88: 375–407.

McCowan, B., Doyle, L. R., and Hanser, S. F. (1999). Quantitative tools for comparing animal communication systems: information theory applied to bottlenose dolphin whistle repertoires. *Animal Behaviour* 57: 409–19.

McCowan, B., Doyle, L. R., and Hanser, S. F. (2002). Using information theory to assess the diversity, complexity, and development of communicative repertoires. *Journal of Comparative Psychology* 116: 166–72.

McCune, L., and Vihman, M. M. (2001). Early phonetic and lexical development: a productivity approach. *Journal of Speech, Language, and Hearing Research* 44: 670–84.

Macdonald, D. (1962). The string untuned. *New Yorker*, 10 March.

McDowell, J. H. (1981). Toward a semiotics of nicknaming: the Kamsá example. *Journal of American Folklore* 94: 1–18.

McDonough, L., Choi, S., and Mandler, J. M. (2003). Understanding spatial relations: Flexible infants, lexical adults. *Cognitive Psychology* 46: 229–59.

McGlaughlin, F. (2004). Is there an adjective class in Wolof? In R. M. W. Dixon and A. Y. Aikhenvald (eds), *Adjective Classes: A Cross-linguistic Typology*. Oxford: Oxford University Press, 242–62.

McGraw, P., and Warner, J. (2014). *The Humor Code: A Global Search for What Makes Things Funny*. New York: Simon & Schuster.

McGregor, K. K., Sheng, L., and Smith, B. (2005). The precocious two-year-old: status of the lexicon and links to grammar. *Journal of Child Language* 32: 563–85.

McGregor, W. B. (1986). Sound symbolism in Kuniyanti. MS.

McGregor, W. B. (1996). Sound symbolism in Gooniyandi: a language of Western Australia. *Word* 47: 339–64.

McGregor, W. B. (2001). Ideophones as the source of verbs in Northern Australian languages. In F. K. Erhard Voeltz and C. Kilian-Hatz (eds), *Ideophones*. Amsterdam: Benjamins, 205–22.

MacKay, C. J. (1999). *A Grammar of Misantla Totanac*. Salt Lake City: University of Utah Press.

MacKay, D. G. (1987). *The Organization of Perception and Action: A Theory for Language and Other Cognitive Skills*. New York: Springer.

MacKay, D. G., Shafto, M., and Taylor, J. K. (2004). Relations between emotion, memory, and attention: evidence from taboo Stroop, lexical decision, and immediate memory tasks. *Memory and Cognition* 32: 474–88.

McMahon, D. M. (2006). *Happiness: A History*. New York: Atlantic Monthly Press.

McMurray, B. (2007). Defusing the childhood vocabulary explosion. *Science* 317: 631.

Macnamara, J. (1982). *Names for Things: A Study of Human Learning*. Cambridge, Mass.: MIT Press.

Macnamara, J., Krautham, M., and Bolgar, M. (1968). Language switching in bilinguals as a function of stimulus and response uncertainty. *Journal of Experimental Psychology* 78: 208–15.

MacNeilage, P. (1998). Evolution of the mechanisms of language output: comparative neurobiology of vocal and manual communication. In J. Hurford, M. Studdert-Kennedy, and C. Knight (eds), *Approaches to the Evolution of Language*. Cambridge: Cambridge University Press, 221–41.

MacNeilage, P. F. (2008). *The Origin of Speech*. Oxford: Oxford University Press.

Macnutt, D. (2001). *Ximenes on the Art of the Crossword*. Claverley: Swallowtail Books.

McQueen, J. M. (1998). Segmentation of continuous speech using phonotactics. *Journal of Memory and Language* 39(1): 21–46.

McQueen, J. M., Norris, D., and Cutler, A. (1994). Competition in spoken word recognition: spotting words in other words. *Journal of Experimental Psychology: Learning, Memory, and Cognition* 20(3): 621–38.

McQuown, N. A. (1990). *Grámatica de la lengua totonaca* (Coatepec, Sierra Norte de Puebla). Mexico City: UNAM.

McRae, K., Khalkhali, S., and Hare, M. (2011). Semantic and associative relations: examining a tenuous dichotomy. In V. Reyna, S. Chapman, M. Dougherty, and J. Confrey (eds), *The*

Adolescent Brain: Learning, Reasoning, and Decision Making. Washington, DC: American Psychological Association.

McTear, M. (1985). *Children's Conversation*. Oxford: Blackwell.

MacWhinney, B., Keenan, J. M., and Reinke, P. (1982). The role of arousal in memory for conversation. *Memory and Cognition* 10: 308–17.

McWhorter, J. H. (2011). *Linguistic Simplicity and Complexity: Why Do Languages Undress?* Berlin: Mouton de Gruyter.

Maddieson, I. (1988). Borrowed sounds. In J. A. Fishman, A. Tabouret-Keller, M. Clyne, B. Krishnamurti, and M. Abdulaziz (eds), *The Fergusionian Impact: In Honour of Charles A. Ferguson on the Occasion of his 65th Birthday*. New York: Mouton de Gruyter, 1–16.

Maduka, O. N. (1983–84). Igbo ideophones and the lexicon. *Journal of the Linguistic Association of Nigeria* 2: 23–9.

Maduka, O. N. (1988). Size and shape ideophones in Nembe: a phonosemantic analysis. *Studies in African Linguistics* 18: 93–113.

Maduka-Durenze, O. N. (2001). Phonesemantic hierarchies. In F. K. Erhard Voeltz and C. Kilian-Hatz (eds), *Ideophones*. Amsterdam: Benjamins, 193–204.

Mahon, B. Z., Costa, A., Peterson, R., Vargas, K., and Caramazza, A. (2007). Lexical selection is not by competition: a reinterpretation of semantic interference and facilitation effects in the picture–word interference paradigm. *Journal of Experimental Psychology: Learning, Memory, and Cognition* 33: 503–35.

Mahon, B. Z., Garcea, F. E., and Navarrete, E. (2012). Picture–word interference and the response exclusion hypothesis: a response to Mulatti and Coltheart. *Cortex* 48: 373–7.

Majid, A. (2006). Body part categorisation in Punjabi. *Language Sciences* 28(2–3): 241–61.

Majid, A. (2010). Words for parts of the body. In B. C. Malt and P. Wolff (eds), *Words and the Mind: How Words Capture Human Experience*. New York: Oxford University Press, 58–71.

Majid, A., Bowerman, M., Van Staden, M., and Boster, J. S. (2007). The semantic categories of cutting and breaking events: a crosslinguistic perspective. *Cognitive Linguistics* 18: 133–52.

Majid, A., Enfield, N. J., and van Staden, M. (eds). (2006). Parts of the body: cross-linguistic categorisation. Special issue, *Language Sciences* 28(2–3).

Majid, A., Gullberg, M., van Staden, M., and Bowerman, M. (2007). How similar are semantic categories in closely related languages? A comparison of cutting and breaking in four Germanic languages. *Cognitive Linguistics* 18: 179–94.

Maki, W. S. (2007). Judgments of associative memory. *Cognitive Psychology* 54: 319–53.

Makkai, A. (1972). *Idiom Structure in English*. The Hague: Mouton.

Malinowski, B. (1935). The language of magic and gardening. In *Coral Gardens and Their Magic*, II, pt 4, div. 5. London: Routledge.

Malkiel, Y. (1975). *Etymological Dictionaries: A Tentative Typology*. Chicago: University of Chicago Press.

Malkiel, Y. (1993). *Etymology*. Cambridge: Cambridge University Press.

Mallinson, G. (1988). Rumanian. In M. Harris and N. Vincent (eds) *The Romance Languages*. Oxford: Oxford University Press, 391–419.

Mallory, J. P., and Adams, D. Q. (2006). *The Oxford Introduction to Proto-Indo-European and the Proto-Indo-European World*. Oxford: Oxford University Press.

Malouf, R. (2000[1998]). *Mixed Categories and the Hierarchical Lexicon*. Stanford, Calif.: CSLI.

Malt, B. C. (2013). Context sensitivity and insensitivity in object naming. *Language and Cognition* 5: 81–97.

Malt, B. C., Gennari, S., Imai, M., Ameel, E., Tsuda, N., and Majid, A. (2008). Talking about walking: biomechanics and the language of locomotion. *Psychological Science* 19: 232–40.

Malt, B. C., Gennari, S., Imai, M., Ameel, E., Saji, N., and Majid, A. (2014). Human locomotion across languages: constraints on moving and meaning. *Journal of Memory and Language*. 74: 107–23

Malt, B. C., Li, P., Pavlenko, A., Zhu, H., and Ameel, E. (2015). Bidirectional lexical interaction in late immersed mandarin-English bilinguals. *Journal of Memory and Language* 82: 86–104.

Malt, B. C. and Majid, A. (2013). How thought is mapped into words. *WIREs Cognitive Science* 4: 583–97.

Malt, B. C., and Sloman, S. A. (2004). Conversation and convention: enduring influences on name choice for common objects. *Memory and Cognition* 32: 1346–54.

Malt, B. C., and Sloman, S. A. (2007). Category essence or essentially pragmatic? Creator's intention in naming and what's really what. *Cognition* 105: 615–48.

Malt, B. C., Sloman, S. A., Gennari, S., Shi, M., and Wang, Y. (1999). Knowing versus naming: similarity and the linguistic categorization of artifacts. *Journal of Memory and Language* 40(2): 230–62.

Malt, B. C., and Wolff, P. (eds) (2010). *Words and the Mind: How Words Capture Human Experience*. New York: Oxford University Press.

Mandelbrot, B. (1953). An informational theory of the statistical structure of language. In W. Jackson (ed.), *Symposium on Applications of Communications Theory*. London: Butterworths, 486–500.

Mandelbrot, B. (1982). *The Fractal Geometry of Nature*. New York: Freeman.

Mann, T. (1924). *The Magic Mountain*, trans. H. T. Lowe-Porter, ch. 6. Berlin: Fischer.

Maratsos, M., and Deák, G. (1995). Hedgehogs, foxes and the acquisition of verb meaning. In M. Tomasello and W. Merriman (eds), *Beyond Names for Things: Young Children's Acquisition of Verbs*. Hillsdale, NJ: Erlbaum, 377–404.

Marchman, V. A., and Fernald, A. (2008). Speed of word recognition and vocabulary knowledge in infancy predict cognitive and language outcomes in later childhood. *Developmental Science* 11(3): F9–F16.

Margolis, E., and Laurence, S. (eds) (1999). *Concepts: Core Readings*. Cambridge, Mass.: MIT Press.

Markman, E. (1989). *Categorization and Naming in Children*. Cambridge, Mass.: MIT Press.

Markman, E. M., and Wachtel, G. F. (1988). Children's use of mutual exclusivity to constrain the meanings of words. *Cognitive Psychology* 20: 121–57.

Marlett, S. (2008). The form and function of names in Seri. *International Journal of American Linguistics* 74: 47–82.

Marr, D. (1982). *Vision: A Computational Investigation into the Human Representation and Processing of Visual Information*. San Francisco, Calif.: Freeman.

Marslen-Wilson, W. (1989). Access and integration: projecting sound onto meaning. In W. Marslen-Wilson (ed.), *Lexical Representation and Process*. Cambridge, Mass.: MIT Press, 3–24.

Marslen-Wilson, W., Tyler, L. K., Waksler, R., and Older, L. (1994). Morphology and meaning in the English mental lexicon. *Psychological Review* 101: 3–33.

Marslen-Wilson, W. D., and Welsh, A. (1978). Processing interactions and lexical access during word recognition in continuous speech. *Cognitive Psychology* 10(1): 29–63.

Martinez, R., and Murphy, V. A. (2011). Effect of frequency and idiomaticity on second language reading comprehension. *TESOL Quarterly* 45: 267–90.

Martinez, R., and Schmitt, N. (2012). A phrasal expressions list. *Applied Linguistics* 33: 299–320.
Marttila, A. (2011). *A Cross-Linguistic Study of Lexical Iconicity and its Manifestation in Bird Names*. Munich: Lincom.
Masur, E. F. (1983). Gestural development, dual-directional signaling, and the transition to words. *Journal of Psycholinguistic Research* 12: 93–109.
Matan, A., and Carey, S. (2001). Developmental changes within the core of artifact concepts. *Cognition* 78: 1–26.
Matisoff, J. A. (1973). *The Grammar of Lahu*. Berkeley: University of California Press.
Matisoff, J. A. (2004). Areal semantics: is there such a thing? In A. Saxena (ed.), *Himalayan Languages, Past and Present*. Berlin: de Gruyter, 347–93.
Matras, Y. (1998). Utterance modifiers and universals of grammatical borrowing. *Linguistics* 36: 181–231.
Matthews, P. H. (1991). *Morphology*. Cambridge: Cambridge University Press.
Matthews, P. H. (2002). What can we conclude? In R. M. W. Dixon and A. Y. Aikhenvald (eds), *Word: A Cross-linguistic Typology*. Cambridge: Cambridge University Press, 266–81.
Mattys, S. L., and Jusczyk, P. W. (2001). Phonotactic cues for segmentation of fluent speech by infants. *Cognition* 78(2): 91–121.
Mattys, S. L., Jusczyk, P. W., Luce, P. A., and Morgan, J. L. (1999). Phonotactic and prosodic effects on word segmentation in infants. *Cognitive Psychology* 38(4): 465–94.
Maurer, D. W., and Futrell, A. W. (1982). Criminal monikers. *American Speech* 57: 243–55.
Maurer, D., and Mondloch, C. J. (2006). The infant as synaesthetic? In Y. Munakata and M. Johnson (eds), *Processes of Change in Brain and Cognitive Development*. Oxford: Oxford University Press, 449–71.
Maye, J., Werker, J., and Gerken, L. (2002). Infant sensitivity to distributional information can affect phonetic discrimination. *Cognition* 82: B101–B111.
Mayer, J. F., and Murray, L. L. (2003). Functional measures of naming in aphasia: word retrieval in confrontation naming versus connected speech. *Aphasiology* 17(5): 481–97.
Mazaudon, M. (2004). On tone in Tamang and neighbouring languages: synchrony and diachrony. In S. Kaji (ed.), *Proceedings of the Symposium Cross-Linguistic Studies of Tonal Phenomena*. Tokyo: ILCAA, Tokyo University of Foreign Studies, 79–96.
Mazaudon, M. (2012). Paths to tone in the Tamang branch of Tibeto-Burman (Nepal). In G. de Vogalaer and G. Seiler (eds), *The Dialect Laboratory: Dialects as a Testing Ground for Theories of Language Change*. Amsterdam: Benjamins, 139–77.
Medin D. L., and Schaffer, M. M. (1978). Context theory of classification learning. *Psychological Review* 85: 207–38.
Mehler, J., Jusczyk, P., Lambertz, G., Halsted, N., Bertoncini, J., and Amiel-Tison, C. (1988). A precursor of language acquisition in young infants. *Cognition* 29(2): 143–78.
Mehrabian, A. (2001). Characteristics attributed to individuals on the basis of first names. *Genetic, Social, and General Psychology Monographs* 127(1): 59–88.
Meier, B. P., and Robinson, M. D. (2004). Why the sunny side is up: associations between affect and vertical position. *Psychological Science* 15(4): 243–7.
Mel'čuk, I. A. (1989). Semantic primitives from the viewpoint of the Meaning–Text Linguistic Theory. *Quaderni di semantica* 10(1): 65–102.
Mel'čuk, I. A. (2012). *Semantics: From Meaning to Text*. Amsterdam: Benjamins.
Melinger, A. (2003). Morphological structure in the lexical representation of prefixed words: evidence from speech errors. *Language and Cognitive Processes* 18: 335–62.

Mendenhall, T. C. (1887). The characteristic curves of composition. *Science* 9(214): 237–46.

Mendoza, M. (2007). Derivational resources in P'urhepecha: morphological complexity and verb formation. *Acta Linguistica Hungarica* 54(2): 157–72.

Menzerath, P. (1954). *Die Architektonik des deutschen Wortschatzes*. Bonn: Dümmler.

Menzerath, P., and de Oleza, J. M. (1928). *Spanische Lautdauer: Eine experimentelle Untersuchung*. Berlin: de Gruyter.

Mervis, C. B. (1984). Early lexical development: the contributions of mother and child. In C. Sophian (ed.), *Origins of Cognitive Skills*. Hillsdale, NJ: Erlbaum, 339–70.

Mervis, C. B. (1987). Child-basic object categories and early lexical development. In U. Neisser (ed.), *Concepts and Conceptual Development: Ecological and Intellectual Factors in Categorization*. New York: Cambridge University Press, 201–33.

Meunier, F., and Granger, S. (eds) (2008). *Phraseology in Foreign Language Learning and Teaching*. Amsterdam: Benjamins.

Meuter, R. F. I., and Allport, A. (1999). Bilingual language switching in naming: Asymmetrical costs of language selection. *Journal of Memory and Language* 40: 25–40.

Meyer, A. S. (1990). The time course of phonological encoding in language production: the encoding of successive syllables of a word. *Journal of Memory and Language* 29: 524–45.

Meyer, A. S. (1991). The time course of phonological encoding in language production: phonological coding inside a syllable. *Journal of Memory and Language* 30: 69–89.

Meyer, D. E., and Schvaneveldt, R. W. (1971). Facilitation in recognizing pairs of words: evidence of a dependence between retrieval operations. *Journal of Experimental Psychology* 90: 227–34.

Meyer, D. E., and Schvanefeldt, R. W. (1976). Meaning, memory structure and mental processes. *Science* 192: 27–33.

Meyer, M. (1982). *Logique, Langage, Argumentation*. Paris: Classiques Hachette.

Middleton, J. (1961). The social significance of Lugbara personal names. *Uganda Journal* 25: 34–42.

Mieder, W. (2004). *Proverbs: A Handbook*. Westport, Conn.: Greenwood Press.

Milgram, S. (1967). The small world problem. *Psychology Today* 2: 60–7.

Miller, G. A. (1957). Some effects of intermittent silence. *American Journal of Psychology* 70(2): 311–14.

Miller, G. A. (1967). *The Psychology of Communication*. New York: Basic Books.

Miller, G. A. (1991). *The Science of Words*. New York: Scientific American Library.

Miller, G. A. (1995a). WordNet: a lexical database for English. *Communications of the ACM* 38: 39–41.

Miller, G. A. (1995b). WordNet: an on-line lexical database. *International Journal of Lexicography* 3(4) (special issue).

Miller, G. A., Beckwith, R., Fellbaum, C., Gross, D., and Miller, K. (1990). Introduction to WordNet: an on-line lexical database. *International Journal of Lexicography* 3/4: 235–44. Reprinted in T. Fontenelle (ed.), *Practical Lexicography*. Oxford: Oxford University Press, 327–34.

Miller, G. A., and Fellbaum, C. (1991). Semantic networks of English. In B. Levin and S. Pinker (eds), *Cognition*, special issue, 197–229. Reprinted in B. Levin and S. Pinker (eds), *Lexical and Conceptual Semantics*. Oxford: Blackwell, 197–229.

Miller, G. A., and Hristea, F. (2006). WordNet nouns: classes and instances. *Computational Linguistics* 32(1): 1–3.

Miller, G. A., and Johnson-Laird, P. N. (1976). *Language and Perception*. Cambridge: Cambridge University Press.

Miller, K. (1998). Modifiers in WordNet. In C. Fellbaum (ed.), *WordNet: An Electronic Lexical Database*. Cambridge, Mass.: MIT Press, 47–67.

Miller, P. (1992). Clitics and constituents in Phrase Structure Grammar. Doctoral dissertation, Utrecht University.

Miller, P., and Sag, I. (1997). French clitic movement without clitics or movement. *Natural Language and Linguistic Theory* 15: 573–639.

Mill, J. S. (1919[1843]). *A System of Logic*, 9th edn. London: Longmans.

Mills, A. D. (2003). *A Dictionary of British Place-Names*. Oxford: Oxford University Press.

Millwood-Hargrave, A. (2000). *Delete Expletives?* London: Advertising Standards Authority, British Broadcasting Corporation, Broadcasting Standards Commission, Independent Television Commission.

Miral, R., and Gil, J. (2006). A first look at universals. In R. Mairal and J. Gil (eds), *Linguistic Universals*. Cambridge: Cambridge University Press, 1–45.

Mirman, D., Graf Estes, K., and Magnuson, J. S. (2010). Computational modeling of statistical learning: effects of transitional probability versus frequency and links to word learning. *Infancy* 15(5): 471–86.

Mitchell, M. (2009). *Complexity: A Guided Tour*. New York: Oxford University Press.

Mithun, M. (1982). The synchronic and diachronic behavior of plops, squeaks, croaks, sighs, and moans. *International Journal of American Linguistics* 48(1): 49–58.

Mithun, M. (1984a). Principles of naming in Mohawk. In E. Tooker (ed) *Naming Systems*. Washington DC: American Ethnological Society, 40–54.

Mithun, M. (1984b). The evolution of noun incorporation. *Language* 60: 847–94.

Mithun, M. (1986). On the nature of noun incorporation. *Language* 62: 32–7.

Mithun, M. (1999). *The Languages of Native North America*. Cambridge: Cambridge University Press.

Mithun, M. (2000). Incorporation. In G. Booij, C. Lehmann, and J. Mugdan (eds), *Morphologie: ein internationales Handbuch zur Flexion und Wortbildung/Morphology: A Handbook on Inflection and Word Formation*. Berlin: de Gruyter, 916–28.

Mithun, M., and Corbett, G. G. (1999). The effect of noun incorporation on argument structure. In L. Mereu (ed.), *The Boundaries of Morphology and Syntax*. Amsterdam: Benjamins, 49–71.

Moghaddam, M. (1963). *Āyandeh-ye zabān-e Farsi*. Tehran: Iraj Afshar.

Mohome, P. M. (1972). Naming in Sesutho: its cultural and linguistic basis. *Names* 30: 171–85.

Mok, W. E. (1993). Bibliography on sound symbolism. *University of Hawai'i Working Papers in Linguistics* 25: 77–120.

Mok, W. E. (2001). Chinese sound symbolism: a phonological perspective. Thesis, University of Hawai'i.

Molefe, L. (2001). Onomastic aspects of Zulu nicknames with special reference to source and functionality. Doctoral dissertation, University of South Africa, Pretoria.

Mollet, E., Wray, A., and Fitzpatrick, T. (2011). Accessing second-order collocation through lexical co-occurrence networks. In T. Herbst, P. Uhrig, and S. Schüller (eds), *Chunks in Corpus Linguistics and Cognitive Linguistics: In Honour of John Sinclair*. Berlin: Mouton de Gruyter, 87–121.

Mollin, S. (2009). Combining corpus linguistics and psychological data on word co-occurrence: corpus collocates versus word associations. *Corpus Linguistics and Linguistic Theory* 5: 175–200.

Monaghan, P., and Christiansen, M. H. (2006). Why form–meaning mappings are not entirely arbitrary in language. In *Proceedings of the 28th Annual Conference of the Cognitive Science Society*. Mahwah, NJ: Erlbaum, 1838–43.

Monaghan, P., and Christiansen, M. H. (2010). Words in puddles of sound: modelling psycholinguistic effects in speech segmentation. *Journal of Child Language* 37(3): 545–64.

Monaghan, P., Mattock, K., and Walker, P. (2012). The role of sound symbolism in language learning. *Journal of Experimental Psychology: Learning, Memory, and Cognition* 38(5): 1152–64.

Montemurro, M. A. (2001). Beyond the Zipf–Mandelbrot law in quantitative linguistics. *Physica A* 300: 567–78.

Montiel-Ponsada, E., Aguado, G., Gómez-Pérez, A., and Peters, W. (2010). Enriching ontologies with multilingual information. *Natural Language Engineering* 17(3): 283–309.

Moon, R. (1998). *Fixed Expressions and Idioms in English: A Corpus-Based Approach*. Oxford: Oxford University Press.

Moon, R. (2008). Conventionalized as-similes in English: a problem case. *International Journal of Corpus Linguistics* 13(1): 3–37.

Moore, J. L., and Surber, J. R. (1992). Effects of context and keyword methods on second language vocabulary acquisition. *Contemporary Educational Psychology* 17: 286–92.

Morales, M., Mundy, P., Delgado, C. E. F., Yale, M., Messinger, D., Neal, R., and Schwartz, H. K. (2000). Responding to joint attention across the 6- through 24-month a period and early language acquisition. *Journal of Applied Developmental Psychology* 21: 283–98.

Moravcsik, E. A. (1978). Language contact. In J. H. Greenberg, C. A. Ferguson, and E. A. Moravcsik (eds), *Universals of Human Language*. Stanford, Calif.: Stanford University Press, 93–123.

Morgan, J. L. (1994). Converging measures of speech segmentation in preverbal infants. *Infant Behavior and Development* 17(4): 389–403.

Morgan, J. L. (1996). A rhythmic bias in preverbal speech segmentation. *Journal of Memory and Language* 35(5): 666–88.

Morgan, J., O'Neill, C., and Harré, R. (1979). *Nicknames: Their Origins and Social Consequence*. London: Routledge & Kegan Paul.

Morgan, J. L., and Saffran, J. R. (1995). Emerging integration of sequential and suprasegmental information in preverbal speech segmentation. *Child Development* 66(4): 911–36.

Morisette, P., Ricard, M., and Gouin-Decarie, T. (1995). Joint visual attention and pointing in infancy: a longitudinal study of comprehension. *British Journal of Developmental Psychology* 13: 163–75.

Morpurgo-Davies, A. (2000). Greek personal names and linguistic continuity. In S. Hornblower and E. Matthews (eds), *Greek Personal Names: Their Value as Evidence*. Oxford: Oxford University Press, 13–39.

Morris, C. D., Bransford, J. D., and Franks, J. J. (1977). Levels of processing versus transfer appropriate processing. *Journal of Verbal Learning and Verbal Behavior* 16: 519–33.

Morsella, E., and Miozzo, M. (2002). Evidence for a cascade model of lexical access in speech production. *Journal of Experimental Psychology: Learning, Memory, and Cognition* 28(3): 555–63.

Morton, H. C. (1995). *The Story of Webster's Third: Philip Gove's Controversial Dictionary and its Critics*. Cambridge: Cambridge University Press.

Moss, H., and Older, L. (1996). *Birkbeck Word Association Norms*. Hove: Psychology Press.

Moyo, T. (2002). Aspects of nicknames among the Tumbuka. *Names* 50: 191–200.

Mugglestone, L. (2005). *Lost For Words: The Hidden History of the* Oxford English Dictionary. New Haven, Conn.: Yale University Press.

Müller, M. (1861). The theoretical stage, and the origin of language. *Lectures on the Science of Language, 9*. New York: Scribner's.

Murdoch, B. E., et al. (1987). Language disorders in dementia of the Alzheimer type. *Brain and Language* 31(1): 122–37.

Murphy, G. (1996). On metaphoric representation. *Cognition* 60: 173–204.

Murphy, G. L. (2004). *The Big Book of Concepts*. Cambridge, Mass.: MIT Press.

Murphy, G. L., and Brownell, H. H. (1985). Category differentiation in object recognition: typicality constraints on the basic category advantage. *Journal of Experimental Psychology: Learning, Memory, and Cognition* 11: 70–84.

Murray, J. A. H., et al. (1884–1928). *A New English Dictionary on Historical Principles*. Oxford: Clarendon Press. Later issued as the *Oxford English Dictionary*.

Murray, L. (1795). *English Grammar, Adapted to the Different Classes of Learners*. (Reprinted Menston: Scolar Press, 1968).

Myers, C. S. (1904). The taste-names of primitive peoples. *British Journal of Psychology* 1: 117–26.

Myung J., Blumstein S. E., and Sedivy J. C. (2006). Playing on the typewriter, typing on the piano: manipulation knowledge of objects. *Cognition* 98: 223–43.

Nagy, G. (2009). Performance and text in ancient Greece. In G. Boys-Stones, B. Graziosi, and P. Vasunia (eds), *Oxford Handbook of Hellenic Studies*. Oxford: Oxford University Press, 417–31.

Nagy, W. E., and Anderson, R. C. (1984). How many words are there in printed school English? *Reading Research Quarterly* 19(3): 304–30.

Nagy, W. E., Anderson, R., Schommer, M., Scott, J. A., and Stallman, A. (1989). Morphological families in the internal lexicon. *Reading Research Quarterly* 24(3): 263–82.

Nagy, W. E., and Herman, P. A. (1985). Incidental vs. instructional approaches to increasing reading vocabulary. *Educational Perspectives* 23: 16–21.

Nänny, M., and Fischer, O. (eds) (1999). *Form Miming Meaning: Iconicity in Language and Literature*. Amsterdam: Benjamins.

Narrog, H., and Heine, B. (eds) (2011). *The Oxford Handbook of Grammaticalization*. Oxford: Oxford University Press.

Nash, D. (1986). *Topics in Warlpiri Grammar*. New York: Garland.

Nassaji, H. (2003). L2 vocabulary learning from context: strategies, knowledge sources, and their relationship with success in L2 lexical inferencing. *TESOL Quarterly* 37: 645–70.

Nation, I. S. P. (2000). Learning vocabulary in lexical sets: dangers and guidelines. *TESOL Journal* 9: 6–10.

Nation, I. S. P. (2001a). How many high frequency words are there in English? In M. Gill, A. Johnson, L. Koski, R. Sell, and B. Warvik (eds), *Language, Learning, and Literature: Studies Presented to Håkan Ringbom*. Åbo: Åbo Akademi University, 167–81.

Nation, I. S. P. (2001b). *Learning Vocabulary in Another Language*. Cambridge: Cambridge University Press.

Nation, I. S. P. (2006). How large a vocabulary is needed for reading and listening? *Canadian Modern Language Review* 63(1): 59–82.

Nation, I. S. P. (2007). The four strands. *Innovation in Language Learning and Teaching* 1(1): 1–12.

Nation, I. S. P., and Beglar, D. (2007). A vocabulary size test. *Language Teacher* 31: 9–13.

Nation, I. S. P., and Deweerdt, J. P. (2001). A defence of simplification. *Prospect* 16: 55–67.

Nation, I. S. P., and Heatly, A. (2002). Range: a program for the analysis of vocabulary in texts. Computer software. <http://www.vuw.ac.nz/lals/staff/paul-nation/nation.aspx>.

Nation, I. S. P., and Hwang, K. (1995). Where would general service vocabulary stop and special purposes vocabulary begin? *System* 23(1): 35–41.

Nation, I. S. P., and Webb, S. (2011). *Researching and Analyzing Vocabulary*. Boston, Mass.: Heinle Cengage Learning.

Nation, I. S. P., and Yamamoto, A. (2012). Applying the four strands to language learning. *International Journal of Innovation in English Language Teaching and Research* 1(2): 167–81.

Nation, P., and Beglar, D. (2007). A vocabulary size test. *Language Teacher* 31(7): 9–13.

Nattinger, J. R., and DeCarrico, J. S. (1992). *Lexical Phrases and Language Teaching*. Oxford: Oxford University Press.

Navarrete, E., and Costa, A. (2005). Phonological activation of ignored pictures: further evidence for a cascade model of lexical access. *Journal of Memory and Language* 53: 359–77.

Nayak, N. P., and Gibbs, R. W. (1990). Conceptual knowledge in the interpretation of idioms. *Journal of Experimental Psychology: General* 119(3): 315–30.

Nazzi, T., Bertoncini, J., and Mehler, J. (1998). Language discrimination by newborns: toward an understanding of the role of rhythm. *Journal of Experimental Psychology: Human Perception and Performance* 24(3): 756–66.

Nazzi, T., Kemler Nelson, D. G., Jusczyk, P. W., and Jusczyk, A. M. (2000). Six-month-olds' detection of clauses embedded in continuous speech: effects of prosodic well-formedness. *Infancy* 1(1): 123–47.

Ndimande-Hlongwa, N. (2010). Nicknames of South African soccer teams and players as symbols of approbation in a multilingual and multicultural country. *South African Journal of African Languages* 30: 88–97.

Neely, J. H. (1976). Semantic priming and retrieval from lexical memory: evidence for facilitatory and inhibitory processes. *Memory & Cognition* 4(5): 648–54.

Neely, J. H. (1977). Semantic priming and retrieval from lexical memory: roles of inhibitionless spreading activation and limited capacity attention. *Journal of Experimental Psychology: General* 106: 226–54.

Neely, J. H. (1991). Semantic priming effects in visual word recognition: a selective review of current findings and theories. In D. Besner and G. U. Humphreys (eds), *Basic Processing in Reading: Visual Word Recognition*. Hillsdale, NJ: Erlbaum, 264–336.

Nelson, D. L., and Bajo, M. T. (1985). Prior knowledge and cued recall: category size and dominance. *American Journal of Psychology* 4: 503–17.

Nelson, D. L., McEvoy, C., and Dennis, S. (2000). What is free association and what does it measure? *Memory & Cognition* 28: 887–9.

Nelson, D. L., McEvoy, C., and Schreiber, T. (1990). Encoding context and retrieval conditions as determinants of the effects of natural category size. *Journal of Experimental Psychology: Learning, Memory, and Cognition* 16: 31–41.

Nelson, D. L., McEvoy, C., and Schreiber, T. (2004). The University of South Florida free association, rhyme, and word fragment norms. *Behavior Research Methods, Instruments, and Computers* 36: 402–7.

Nelson, D. L., Schreiber, T. A., and McEvoy, C. L. (1992). Processing implicit and explicit representations. *Psychological Review* 99: 322–48.

Nelson, D. L., and Zhang, N. (2000). The ties that bind what is known to the recall of what is new. *Psychonomic Bulletin & Review* 7: 604–17.

Nelson, K. (1973). Structure and strategy in learning to talk. *Monographs of the Society for Research in Child Development* 38(149).

Nelson, K. (1977). The syntagmatic-paradigmatic shift revisited: a review of research and theory. *Psychological Bulletin* 84: 93.

Nelson, K. (2001). The name game updated. *Behavioral and Brain Science* 24: 1114.

Nelson, K. (2009). Wittgenstein and contemporary theories of word learning. *New Ideas in Psychology* 27: 275–87.

Nespor, M., and Vogel, I. (2007[1986]). *Prosodic Phonology*. Berlin: Mouton de Gruyter.

Nesselhauf, N. (2003). The use of collocations by advanced learners of English and some implications for teaching. *Applied Linguistics* 24: 223–42.

Nesselhauf, N. (2005). *Collocations in a Learner Corpus*. Amsterdam: Benjamins.

Nettle, D. (1995). Segmental inventory size, word length, and communicative efficiency. *Linguistics* 33: 359–68.

Nevins, A. (2009). On formal universals in phonology. *Behavioral and Brain Sciences* 32(5): 461–2.

Newman, R., Ratner, N. B., Jusczyk, A. M., Jusczyk, P. W., and Dow, K. A. (2006). Infants' early ability to segment the conversational speech signal predicts later language development: a retrospective analysis. *Developmental Psychology* 42(4): 643–55.

Newman, S. (1967). Yokuts. *Lingua* 17: 182–99.

Newmeyer, F. J. (1993). Iconicity and generative grammar. *Language* 68: 756–96.

Newton, J. (1995). Task-based interaction and incidental vocabulary learning: a case study. *Second Language Research* 11: 159–77.

New York Times (1920). Young man named Ruth saves game. 28 June, p. 18.

New York Times (1922a). Jack Quinn uses Yankees harshly. 23 June, p. 20.

New York Times (1922b). Yanks make clean sweep in Brooklyn. 11 April, p. 24.

Nguyen, L. T. C., and Nation, I. S. P. (2011). A bilingual vocabulary size test of English for Vietnamese learners. *RELC Journal* 42(1): 86–99.

Nhàn, N. T. (1984). The syllabeme and patterns of word formation in Vietnamese. Ph.D dissertation, New York University.

Nichols, J. (1971). Diminutive sound symbolism in western North America. *Language* 47: 826–48.

Nickerson, R. S. (1977). Crossword puzzles and lexical memory. *Attention and Performance* 6: 699–718.

Nickerson, R. S. (2011). Five down, absquatulated: crossword puzzle clues to how the mind works. *Psychonomic Bulletin Review* 18: 217–41.

Nicolaisen, W. F. H. (1976/2001). *Scottish Place-Names: Their Study and Significance*. London: Batsford/Edinburgh: Birlinn.

Nicolaisen, W. F. H. (1980). Onomastic dialects. *American Speech* 55: 36–45.

Nicolaisen, W. F. H. (2007). Gaelic *sliabh* revisited. In S. Arbuthnot and K. Hollo (eds), *Fil súil nglais: A Grey Eye Looks Back*. A Festschrift in Honour of Colm Ó Baoll. Ceann Drochaid: Clann Tuirc, 175–86.

Niemikorpi, A. (1991). Suomen kielen sanaston dynamiikkan. *Acta Wasaensia* 26(2). Vaasa: Vaasan yliopisto.

Niemikorpi, A. (1997). Equilibrium of words in the Finnish Frequency Dictionary. *Journal of Quantitative Linguistics* 4(1–3): 190–96.

Ninio, A. (2006a). *Language and the Learning Curve: A New Theory of Syntactic Development*. New York: Oxford University Press.

Ninio, A. (2006b). Kernel vocabulary and Zipf's law in maternal input to syntactic development. In D. Bamman, T. Magnitskaia, and C. Zaller (eds), *BUCLD 30: Proceedings of the 30th Annual Boston University Conference on Language Development*. Somerville, Mass.: Cascadilla Press, 423–31.

Nirenburg, S., and Raskin, V. (2004). *Ontological Semantics*. Cambridge, Mass.: MIT Press.

Noonan, P. (1990). *What I Saw at the Revolution*, ch. 5. New York: Random House.

Norde, M., Lenz, A., and Beijering, K. (2013). Current trends in grammaticalization research. *Language Sciences* 36: 1–160.

Nordlinger, R., and Sadler, L. (2004). Nominal tense in crosslinguistic perspective. *Language* 80: 776–806.

Nosofsky R. M. (1986). Attention, similarity, and the identification–categorization relationship. *Journal of Experimental Psychology: General* 115: 39–57.

Noss, P. A. (1975). The ideophone: a linguistic and literary device in Gbaya and Sango with reference to Zande. In S. H. Hurreiz and H. Bell (eds), *Directions in Sudanese Linguistics and Folklore*. Khartoum: Khartoum University Press, 142–52.

Noss, P. A. (1985). The ideophone in Gbaya syntax. In G. J. Dimmendaal (ed.), *Current Approaches to African Linguistics* 3. Dordrecht: Foris, 241–55.

Nübling, D. (2000). Auf der Suche nach dem idealen Eignenname. *Beiträge zur Namenforschung* 35: 275–301.

Nuckolls, J. B. (1996). *Sounds Like Life: Sound-Symbolic Grammar, Performance and Cognition in Pastaza Quechua*. Oxford: Oxford University Press.

Nuckolls, J. B. (1999). The case for sound symbolism. *Annual Review of Anthropology* 28: 225–52.

Nunberg, G., Sag, I. A., and Wasow, T. (1994). Idioms. *Language* 70(3): 491–538.

Nurweni, A., and Read, J. (1999). The English vocabulary knowledge of Indonesian university students. *English for Specific Purposes* 18(2): 161–75.

Nygaard, L. C., Cook, A. E., and Nanny, L. L. (2009). Sound to meaning correspondences facilitate word learning. *Cognition* 112: 181–6.

Oakeshott-Taylor, J. (1984). Phonetic factors in word order. *Phonetica* 41: 226–37.

Ochs, E., and Schieffelin, B. (1989). Language has a heart. *Text* 9: 7–25.

Oda, H. (2000). An embodied semantic mechanism for mimetic words in Japanese. Thesis, Indiana University.

Odden, D. (1996). *The Phonology and Morphology of Kimatuumbi*. Oxford: Clarendon Press.

Ohala, J. J. (1983). Cross-language use of pitch: an ethological view. *Phonetica* 40: 1–18.

Ohala, J. J. (1984). An ethological perspective on common cross-language utilization of Fo of voice. *Phonetica* 41: 1–16.

Ohala, J. J. (1994). The frequency code underlies the sound-symbolic use of voice pitch. In L. Hinton, J. Nichols, and J. J. Ohala (eds), *Sound Symbolism*. Cambridge: Cambridge University Press, 325–47.

Okamoto, J., and Ishizaki, S. (2001). Associative concept dictionary and its comparison with electronic concept dictionaries. In PACLING2001: 4th Conference of the Pacific Association for Computational Linguistics, 214–20.

Olausson, L., and Sangster, C. (2006). *Oxford BBC Guide to Pronunciation*. Oxford: Oxford University Press.

Olawsky, K. J. (2002). What is a word in Dagbani? In R. M. W. Dixon and A. Y. Aikhenvald (eds), *Word: A Cross-Linguistic Typology*. Cambridge: Cambridge University Press, 205–26.

Oller, J., and Wiltshire, A. (1997). Towards a semiotic theory of affect. In S. Niemeier and R. Dirven (eds), *The Language of Emotions*. Amsterdam: Benjamins, 33–54.

Olson, D. R. (1970). Language and thought: aspects of a cognitive theory of semantics. *Psychological Review* 77: 257–73.

Olson, J., and Masur, E. F. (2011). Infants' gestures influence mothers' provision of object, action, and internal state labels. *Journal of Child Language* 38: 1028–54.

Ong, W. J. (1982). *Orality and Literacy: The Technologizing of the Word*. London: Methuen.

Onions, C. T. (1966). *The Oxford Dictionary of English Etymology*. Oxford: Oxford University Press.

Ono, H. (1984). *Nichiei Gion Gitaigo Katsuyo Jiten* [A Practical Guide to Japanese–English Onomatopoeia and Mimesis]. Tokyo: Hokuseido.

Oring, E. (2011a). Humor is art. Presidential address, International Society for Humor Studies, Boston University.

Oring, E. (2011b). Parsing the joke: the General Theory of Verbal Humor and appropriate ambiguity. *Humor: International Journal of Humor Research* 24(2): 203–22.

Orlov, J. K. (1982). Linguostatistik: Aufstellung von Sprachnormen oder Analyse des Redeprozesses? (Die Antinomie 'Sprache–Rede' in der statistischen Linguistik). In J. K. Orlov, M. G. Boroda, and I. Š. Nadarejšvili, *Sprache, Text, Kunst: Quantitative Analysen*. Bochum: Brockmeyer, 1–55.

Ortony, C., Clore, G., and Foss, M. (1987). The referential structure of the affective lexicon. *Cognitive Science* 11: 341–64.

Osborne, C. R. (1974). *The Tiwi Language*. Canberra: Australian Institute of Aboriginal Studies.

Oxford English Dictionary. Oxford: Clarendon Press, 1933. Reissued version of *A New English Dictionary on Historical Principles*, by J. A. H. Murray, H. Bradley, W. A. Craigie, and C. T. Onions, with a one-volume supplement by W. A. Craigie and C. T. Onions. 2nd edn 1989, by J. A. Simpson, E. S. C. Weiner, et al. 3rd edn and *OED Online* (2000–), by J. A. Simpson, E. S. C. Weiner, et al.

Owen, H. W. (2012). Cymru: place-names in Wales. In M. Gunn (ed.), *Logainmneacha: Place-Names*. Dublin: Everson Gunn Teoranta, 70–105.

Owen, H. W., and Morgan, R. (2007). *Dictionary of the Place-Names of Wales*. Handysul: Gomer Press.

Pace-Sigge, M. (2013). *Lexical Priming in Spoken English Usage*. London: Palgrave Macmillan.

Packard, J. (2000). *The Morphology of Chinese: A Linguistic and Cognitive Approach*. Cambridge: Cambridge University Press.

Paffard, M. (1980). The fascination of a name. *Use of English* 32: 33–40.

Page, L., Brin, S., Motwani, R., and Winograd, T. (1998). The PageRank citation ranking: bringing order to the web. Technical report, Computer Science Department, Stanford University.

Paivio, A., and Desrochers, A. (1979). Effects of an imagery mnemonic on second language recall and comprehension. *Canadian Journal of Psychology* 33: 17–28.

Palermo, D. S., and Jenkins, J. J. (1964). *Word Association Norms: Grade School Through College*. Minneapolis: University of Minnesota Press.

Päll, P. (2012). Observations on the geographical distribution of toponymic endings in Estonia. *Eesti ja soome-ugri keeleteaduse ajakiri: Journal of Estonian and Finno-Ugric Linguistics* 3: 155–72.

Palmer, F. (1981). *Semantics*. Cambridge: Cambridge University Press.

Palmer, G. B., and Nicodemus, L. (1985). Coeur d'Alene exceptions to proposed universals of anatomical nomenclature. *American Ethnologist* 12(2): 341–59.

Palmer, H. E. (1925). Conversation. Repr. in R. C. Smith (ed.), *The Writings of Harold E. Palmer: An Overview* (Tokyo: Hon-no-Tomosha, 1999), 185–91.

Parault, S. J., and Parkinson, M. (2008). Sound-symbolic word learning in the middle grades. *Contemporary Educational Psychology* 33(4): 647–71.

Parault, S. J., and Schwanenflugel, P. J. (2006). Sound-symbolism: a piece in the puzzle of word learning. *Journal of Psycholinguistic Research* 35(4): 329–51.

Paribakth, T. S., and Weshe, M. (1997). Vocabulary enhancement activities and reading for meaning in second language vocabulary acquisition. In J. Coady and T. Huckin (eds), *Second Language Vocabulary Acquisition: A Rationale for Pedagogy*. Cambridge: Cambridge University Press, 174–99.

Paribakth, T. S., and Weshe, M. (1999). Reading and 'incidental' L2 vocabulary acquisition: an introspective study of lexical inferencing. *Studies in Second Language Acquisition* 21: 195–224.

Parsons, T. (1990). *Events in the Semantics of English*. Cambridge, Mass.: MIT Press.

Partington, A. (1998). *Patterns and Meanings: Using Corpora for English Language Research and Teaching*. Amsterdam: Benjamins.

Partington, A. (2003). *The Linguistics of Political Argument: Spin-Doctor and the Wolf-Pack at the White House*. London: Routledge.

Pater, J., Stager, C., and Werker, J. (2004). The perceptual acquisition of phonological contrasts. *Language* 80: 384–402.

Patterson, W. T., and Urrutibeheity, H. (1975). *The Lexical Structure of Spanish*. The Hague: Mouton.

Pavlenko, A. (1999). New approaches to concepts in bilingual memory. *Bilingualism: Language and Cognition* 2: 209–30.

Pavlenko, A., and Malt, B. C. (2011). Kitchen Russian: cross-linguistic differences and first-language object naming by Russian–English bilinguals. *Bilingualism: Language and Cognition* 14: 19–45.

Pawley, A., and Syder, F. H. (1983). Two puzzles for linguistic theory: nativelike selection and nativelike fluency. In J. C. Richards and R. W. Schmidt (eds), *Language and Communication*. New York: Longman, 191–226.

Payack, P. J. J. (2008). *A Million Words and Counting*. New York: Citadel.

Pearsall, J., and Hanks, P. (1998). *The New Oxford Dictionary of English*. Oxford: Oxford University Press. Later edns as *The Oxford Dictionary of English*.

Pearson, J. (1998). *Terms in Context*. Amsterdam: Benjamins.

Peeters, B. (2000). 'S'engager' vs 'to show restraint': linguistic and cultural relativity in discourse management. In S. Niemeier and R. Dirven (eds), *Evidence for Linguistic Relativity*. Amsterdam: Benjamins, 193–222.

Peeters, B. (ed.) (2006). *Semantic Primes and Universal Grammar: Evidence from the Romance Languages*. Amsterdam: Benjamins.

Peeters, B. (2013). *Râler, râleur, râlite*: discours, langue et valeurs culturelles. In C. Claudel, P. von Münchow, M. Pordeus, F. Pugnière-Saavedra, and G. Tréguer-Felten (eds), *Cultures, discours, langues: nouveaux abordages*. Limoges: Lambert-Lucas, 117–41.

Peeters, B. Ah méfiance, quand tu tiens la France ... *Cahiers de praxématique* [Online], 60: 2013. <http://praxematique.revues.org/3872>.

Peirce, C. (1894/1998). What is a sign? In Peirce Edition Project (eds), *The Essential Peirce: Selected Philosophical Writings, vol. 2: 1893–1913*. Bloomington: Indiana University Press, 4–10.

Peirce, C. S. (1935). *The Collected Papers of Charles S. Peirce*, vol. 2. Cambridge, Mass: Harvard University Press.

Peirce, C. S. (1955). Logic as semiotic: the theory of signs. In J. Bucler (ed.), *Philosophical Writings of Peirce*. New York: Dover, 99–119.

Peirsman, Y., and Geeraerts, D. (2006). Metonymy as a prototypical category. *Cognitive Linguistics* 17: 269–316.

Pellicer-Sánchez, A. (2013). Vocabulary and reading. In C. Chapelle (ed.), *Encyclopedia of Applied Linguistics*, vol. 10. Oxford: Wiley-Blackwell, 6127–33.

Peperkamp, S. (1996). On the prosodic representation of clitics. In U. Kleinhenz (ed.), *Interfaces in Phonology*. Berlin: Akademie, 102–27.

Peperkamp, S., and Dupoux, E. (2002). Coping with phonological variation in early lexical acquisition. In I. Lasser (ed.), *The Process of Language Acquisition*. Frankfurt: Lang, 359–85.

Perea, M., Dunabeitia, J. A., and Carreiras, M. (2008). Masked associative/semantic priming effects across languages with highly proficient bilinguals. *Journal of Memory and Language* 58: 916–30.

Perfetti, C. A., Wlotko, E. W., and Hart, L. A. (2005). Word learning and individual differences in word learning reflected in event-related potentials. *Journal of Experimental Psychology: Learning Memory and Cognition* 31: 1281–92.

Perlmutter, D. M. (1970). Surface structure constraints in syntax. *Linguistic Inquiry* 1: 187–255.

Perrin, N. (1992). *Dr. Bowdler's Legacy: A History of Expurgated Books in English and America*. Boston: Godine.

Perruchet, P., and Tillmann, B. (2010). Exploiting multiple sources of information in learning an artificial language: human data and modeling. *Cognitive Science* 34(2): 255–85.

Pesmen, D. (2000). *Russia and Soul: An Exploration*. Ithaca, NY: Cornell University Press.

Petchka, K. (2010). Input enhancement, noticing, and incidental vocabulary acquisition. *Asian EFL Journal* 13: 228–55.

Peters, A. M. (1983). *The Units of Language Acquisition*. Cambridge: Cambridge University Press.

Peters, A. M. (1985). Language segmentation: operating principles for the perception and analysis of language. In D. I. Slobin (ed.), *The Cross-Linguistic Study of Language Acquisition*. Hillsdale, NJ: Erlbaum, 1029–67.

Peters, A. M. (1986). Language segmentation: operating principles for the perception and analysis of language. In D. I. Slobin (ed.), *The Cross-Linguistic Study of Language Acquisition*. Hillsdale, NJ: Erlbaum.

Peters, E. (2012). Learning German formulaic sequences: the effect of two attention-drawing techniques. *Language Learning Journal* 40: 65–79.

Peters, E., Hulstijn, J. H., Sercu, L., and Lutjeharms, M. (2009). Learning L2 German vocabulary through reading: the effect of three enhancement techniques compared. *Language Learning* 59: 113–51.

Peters, S., and Westerståhl, D. (2006). *Quantifiers in Language and Logic*. Oxford: Oxford University Press.

Peterson, R. R., and Savoy, P. (1998). Lexical selection and phonological encoding during language production: evidence for cascaded processing. *Journal of Experimental Psychology: Learning, Memory, and Cognition* 24(3): 539–57.

Pexman, P., Holyk, G., and Monfils, M. (2003). Number-of-features effects in semantic processing. *Memory & Cognition* 3: 842–55.

Philippaki-Warburton, I., and Spyropoulos, V. (1999). On the boundaries of inflection and syntax: Greek pronominal clitics and particles. *Yearbook of Morphology 1998*: 45–72.

Philipsen, G., and Carbaugh, D. (1986). A bibliography of fieldwork in the ethnography of communication. *Language in Society* 15: 387–98.

Phillips, B. (1990). Nicknames and sex role stereotypes. *Sex Roles* 23: 281–89.

Piaget, J. (1929). *The Child's Conception of the World*. New York: Harcourt, Brace.

Piaget, J. (1953). *The Origin of Intelligence in the Child*. London: Routledge.

Pierini, P. (2008). Opening a Pandora's box: proper names in English phraseology. *Linguistik Online* 36: 43–58.

Pierrehumbert, J. (2001). Exemplar dynamics: word frequency, lenition and contrast. In J. Bybee and P. Hopper (eds), *Frequency and the Emergence of Linguistic Structure*. Amsterdam: Benjamins, 137–58.

Pigada, M., and Schmitt, N (2006). Vocabulary acquisition from extensive reading: a case study. *Reading in a Foreign Language* 18: 1–28.

Piirainen, E. (2012). *Widespread Idioms in Europe and Beyond: Toward a Lexicon of Common Figurative Units*. Frankfurt am Main: Lang.

Pike, K. L. (1947). *The Intonation of American English*. Ann Arbor: University of Michigan Press.

Pike, K. L. (1959). Language as particle, wave and field. *Texas Quarterly* 2(2): 37–54.

Pillon, A. (1998). Morpheme units in speech production: evidence from laboratory-induced verbal slips. *Language and Cognitive Processes* 13: 465–98.

Pimsleur, P. (1967). A memory schedule. *Modern Language Journal* 51: 73–5.

Pinker, S. (1989). *Learnability and Cognition: The Acquisition of Argument Structure*. Cambridge, Mass.: MIT Press.

Pinker, S. (1994). *The Language Instinct*. New York: HarperCollins.

Pinker, S. (1997). *How the Mind Works*. New York: Norton.

Pinker, S. (2007). *The Stuff of Thought: Language as a Window into Human Nature*. New York: Penguin.

Pinker, S., and Bloom, P. (1990). Natural language and natural selection. *Behavioral and Brain Sciences* 13(4): 707–27.

Pinker, S., and Jackendoff, R. (2005). The faculty of language: what's special about it? *Cognition* 95: 201–36.

Piozzi, H. L. (1968[1794). *British Synonymy; or, An Attempt at Regulating the Choice of Words in Familiar Conversation*. Menston: Scolar Press.

Plank, F. (1984). 24 grundsätzliche Bemerkungen zur Wortarten-Frage. *Leuvense Bijdragen* 73: 489–520.

Plath, S. (1965). Words. In *Ariel*. London: HarperCollins.

Plaut, D. C., and Gonnerman, L. M. (2000). Are non-semantic morphological effects incompatible with a distributed connectionist approach to lexical processing? *Language and Cognitive Processes* 15: 445–85.

Plaut, D., McClelland, J., Seidenberg, M., and Patterson, K. (1996). Understanding normal and impaired word reading: computational principles in quasi-regular domains. *Psychological Review* 103: 56–115.

Plug, L., Sharrack, B., and Reuber, M. (2009). Seizure metaphors differ in patients' accounts of epileptic and psychogenic nonepileptic seizures. *Epilepsia* 50(5): 994–1000.

Plungian, V. A. (2001). Agglutination and flection. In M. Haspelmath, E. König, W. Oestericher, and W. Raible (eds), *Language Typology and Language Universals: An International Handbook*, vol. 1. Berlin: de Gruyter, 669–77.

Pollio, H. R. (1966). *The Structural Basis of Word Association Behavior*. The Hague: Mouton.

Pope, M. K. (1934). *From Latin to Modern French*. Manchester: Manchester University Press.

Popescu, I.-I., Altmann, G., Grzybek, P., Jayaram, B. D., Köhler, R., Krupa, V., Mačutek, J., Pustet, R., Uhlířová, L., and Vidya, M. N. (2009). *Word Frequency Studies*. Berlin: Mouton de Gruyter.

Popescu, I.-I., Naumann, S., Kelih, E., Rovenchak, A., Sanada, H., Overbeck, A., et al. (2013). Word length: aspects and languages. In R. Köhler and G. Altmann (eds), *Issues in Quantitative Linguistics* 3. Lüdenscheid: RAM, 224–81.

Pollard, C., and Sag, I. A. (1992). Anaphors in English and the scope of binding theory. *Linguistic Inquiry* 23: 261–303.

Pollard, C., and Sag, I. A. (1994). *Head-Driven Phrase Structure Grammar*. Chicago: University of Chicago Press.

Pongweni, A. J. C. (1983). *What's in a Name? A Study of Shona Nomenclature*. Gweru, Zimbabwe: Mambo Press.

Popper, K. R. (1972). *Objective Knowledge: An Evolutionary Approach*. Oxford: Clarendon.

Port, R. F. (2007). How are words stored in memory? Beyond phones and phonemes. *New Ideas in Psychology* 25: 143–70.

Port, R. F. (2010). Rich memory and distributed phonology. *Language Sciences* 32: 43–55.

Posnansky, C. J., and Rayner, K. (1977). Visual-feature and response components in a picture-word interference task with beginning and skilled readers. *Journal of Experimental Child Psychology* 24: 440–60.

Post, M. (2009). The phonology and grammar of Galo 'words': a case study in benign disunity. *Studies in Language* 33(4): 934–74.

Postal, P. M. (1979). *Some Syntactic Rules in Mohawk*. New York: Garland.

Postal, P. M. (1985). *Studies of Passive Clauses*. Stony Brook: SUNY Press.

Postal, P. M. (1996). A glance at French pseudopassives. In C. Burgess, K. Dziwirek, and D. B. Gerdts (eds), *Grammatical Relations: Theoretical Approaches to Empirical Questions*. Stanford, Calif.: CSLI.

Potkay, A. (2007). *A Story of Joy: From the Bible to Late Romanticism*. Cambridge: Cambridge University Press.

Potter, M. C., So, K. F., Voneckardt, B., and Feldman, L. B. (1984). Lexical and conceptual representation in beginning and proficient bilinguals. *Journal of Verbal Learning and Verbal Behavior* 23: 23–38.

Potts, C. (2007). The expressive dimension. *Theoretical Linguistics* 33: 165–98.

Poulisse, N., and Bongaerts, T. (1994). First language use in second language production. *Applied Linguistics* 15: 36–57.

Premack, D., and Woodruff, G. (1978). Does the chimpanzee have a theory of mind? *Behavioral and Brain Sciences* 4: 515–26.

Pressley, M., Levin, J. R., and Delaney, H. D. (1982). The mnemonic keyword method. *Review of Educational Research* 52: 61–91.

Pressley, M., Levin, J. R., Kuiper, N., Bryant, S., and Michener, S. (1982). Mnemonic versus nonmnemonic vocabulary-learning strategies: additional comparisons. *Journal of Educational Psychology* 74: 693–707.

Price, R., and Price, S. (1972). Saramaka onomastics: an Afro-American naming system. *Ethnology* 11: 341–57.

Priestley, C. (2013). Social categories, shared experience, reciprocity and endangered meanings: examples from Koromu (PNG). In C. Goddard (ed.), *Semantics and/in Social Cognition*. Special issue of *Australian Journal of Linguistics* 33(3): 257–81.

Prieto, P. (2006). The relevance of metrical information in early prosodic word acquisition: a comparison of Catalan and Spanish. *Language and Speech* 49(2): 231–59.

Prince, A., and Smolensky, P. (1993). *Optimality Theory: Constraint Interaction in Generative Grammar*. New Brunswick, NJ: Rutgers University Center for Cognitive Science Technical Report 2.

Prins, R., and Bastiaanse, R. (2004). Analysing the spontaneous speech of aphasic speakers. *Aphasiology* 18(12): 1075–91.

Prinz, J. J. (2002). *Furnishing the Mind: Concepts and their Perceptual Basis*. Cambridge, Mass.: MIT Press.

Prinz, J. (2004). *Gut Reactions*. Cambridge, Mass.: MIT Press.

Prior, A., and Bentin, S. (2003). Incidental formation of episodic associations: the importance of sentential context. *Memory & Cognition* 31(2): 306–16.

Provine, R. R. (2001). *Laughter: A Scientific Investigation*. Harmondsworth: Penguin.

Pujic, S. (2009). The onomastics of Pridvorci near Trebinje. *Onomatoloski Prilozi—Srpska Akademija Nauka i Umetnosti* 19–20: 523–620.

Pulgram, E. (1954). *Theory of Names*. Berkeley, Calif.: American Name Society.

Pullum, G. K. (2011). The passive in English. Language Log post 24 Jan. 2011. Downloaded 12 Mar. 2013 from <http://languagelog.ldc.upenn.edu/nll/?p=2922>.

Pullum, G., and Huddleston, R. (2002a). Negation. In R. Huddleston and G. Pullum, *The Cambridge Grammar of the English Language*. Cambridge: Cambridge University Press, 785–849.

Pullum, G., and Huddleston, R. (2002b). Adjectives and adverbs. In R. Huddleston and G. Pullum, *The Cambridge Grammar of the English Language*. Cambridge: Cambridge University Press, 525–96.

Pulvermüller, F. (2005). Brain mechanisms linking language and action. *Nature Reviews Neuroscience* 6: 576–82.

Pustejovsky, J. (1991). The syntax of event structure. *Cognition* 41: 47–81.

Pustejovsky, J. (1995). *The Generative Lexicon*. Cambridge, Mass.: MIT Press.

Qian, D. D. (1999). Assessing the roles of depth and breadth of knowledge in reading comprehension. *Canadian Modern Language Review* 56: 282–308.

Quine, W. V. O. (1960). *Word and Object*. Cambridge, Mass.: MIT Press.

Quirk, R. (1982). *Style and Communication in the English Language*. London: Arnold.

Rader, N. de V., and Zukow-Goldring, P. (2010). How the hands control attention during early word learning. *Gesture* 10(2–3): 203–22.

Raffelsiefen, R. (1999). Diagnostics for prosodic words revisited. In T. A. Hall and U. Kleinhenz (eds), *Studies on the Phonological Word*. Amsterdam: Benjamins, 133–201.

Rakison, D. H., and Butterworth, G. E. (1998). Infants' use of object parts in early categorization. *Developmental Psychology* 34: 49–62.

Ramachandran, V. S., and Hubbard, E. M. (2001). Synaesthesia: a window into perception, thought, and language. *Journal of Consciousness Studies* 8: 3–34.

Ramage, D., Rafferty, A., and Manning, C. (2009). Random walks for text similarity. *Proceedings of the 2009 Workshop on Graph-Based Methods for Natural Language Processing*. Singapore: SunTEC, 23–32.

Ramos, A. R. (1974). How the Sanuma acquire their names. *Ethnology* 13: 171–85.

Rankin, R., Boyle, J., Graczyk, R., and Koontz, J. (2002). A synchronic and diachronic perspective on 'word' in Siouan. In R. M. W. Dixon and A. Y. Aikhenvald (eds), *Word: A Cross-linguistic Typology*. Cambridge: Cambridge University Press, 180–204.

Rapp, D. N., and Samuel, A. G. (2002). A reason to rhyme: phonological and semantic influences on lexical access. *Journal of Experimental Psychology: Learning, Memory, and Cognition* 28(3): 564–71.

Räsänen, O. (2011). A computational model of word segmentation from continuous speech using transitional probabilities of atomic acoustic events. *Cognition* 120(2): 149–76.

Raskin, V. (1979). Semantic mechanisms of humor. In C. Chiarello et al. (eds), *Proceedings of the Fifth Annual Meeting of the Berkeley Linguistics Society*. Berkeley: BLS, 325–35.

Raskin, V. (1985). *Semantic Mechanisms of Humor.* Dordrecht: Reidel.

Raskin, V. (2011). On Oring on GTVH. *Humor: International Journal of Humor Research* 24(2): 223–31.

Raskin, V. (2012a). A little metatheory: thoughts on what a theory of computational humor should look like. *AAAI Artificial Intelligence of Humor Symposium Technical Report.* Arlington, Va.: AAAI.

Raskin, V. (2012b). Humor theory's purview: what is reasonable to expect from a theory of humor. Plenary address, ISHS '12: International Conference on Humor Research, Jagellonian University, Cracow.

Raskin, V. (2014). Review of *Inside Jokes: Using Humor to Reverse Engineer the Mind*, by M. M. Hurley, D. C. Dennett, and R. B. Adams, Jr. *European Journal of Humor Research* 1(3): 1.

Raskin, V., and Attardo, S. (1994). Non-literalness and non-bona-fide in language: approaches to formal and computational treatments of humor. *Pragmatics & Cognition* 2(1): 31–69.

Raskin, V., Hempelmann, C. F., and Taylor, J. M. (2009). How to understand and assess a theory: the evolution of the SSTH into the GTVH and now into the OSTH. *Journal of Literary Theory* 3(2): 285–312.

Rastier, F. (2009). *Sémantique interprétative*, 3rd edn. Paris: Presses universitaires de France.

Ratcliff, R., and McKoon, G. (1994). Retrieving information from memory: spreading-activation theories versus compound-cue theories. *Psychological Review* 101: 177–84.

Ratliff, M. (1992). *Meaningful Tone: A Study of Tonal Morphology in Compounds, Form Classes, and Expressive Phrases in White Hmong.* DeKalb, Ill.: Center for Southeast Asian Studies.

Ravitch, D. (2004). *The Language Police: How Pressure Groups Restrict what Students Learn.* New York: Vintage.

Rawls, J. (2001). *Justice as Fairness: A Restatement.* Harvard, Mass.: Harvard University Press.

Ray, S. H. (1926). *A Comparative Study of the Melanesian Island Languages.* Cambridge: Cambridge University Press.

Reaney, P. H. (1991). *A Dictionary of English Surnames.* London: Routledge.

Reddy, M. (1993). The conduit metaphor: a case of frame conflict in our language about language. In A. Ortony (ed.), *Metaphor and Thought*, 2nd edn. Cambridge: Cambridge University Press, 284–324.

Redmonds, G. (2002). The English Poll Taxes, 1377–81. <http://www.american ancestors.org/the-english-poll-taxes-1377–1381/>.

Regier, T., and Kay, P. (2004). Color naming and sunlight: commentary on Lindsey and Brown (2002). *Psychological Science* 15(4): 289–90.

Regier, T., Kay, P., and Cook, R. S. (2005). Focal colors are universal after all. *Proceedings of the National Academy of Sciences of the United States of America* 102(23): 8386–91.

Regier, T., Kay, P., and Khetarpal, N. (2007). Color naming reflects optimal partitions of color space. *Proceedings of the National Academy of Sciences of the United States of America* 104(4): 1436–41.

Renard, J. (1988). *Journal*, November (trans. L. Bogan and E. Roget). Portland, Ore.: Tin House Books.

Renouf, A. (1986). Lexical resolution. In W. Meijs (ed.), *Corpus Linguistics and Beyond: The Proceedings of the 7th International Conference of English Language Research on Computerised Corpora.* Amsterdam: Rodopi, 121–31.

Rescorla, L., Mirak, J., and Singh, L. (2000). Vocabulary growth in late talkers: lexical development from 2;0 to 3;0. *Journal of Child Language* 27: 293–311.

Reuber, M. (2008). Psychogenic nonepileptic seizures: answers and questions. *Epilepsy and Behavior* 12: 622–35.

Rey, A. (1995). *Essays on Definitions*. Amsterdam: Benjamins.

Rey, G. (1998). Concepts. In E. Craig (ed.), *Routledge Encyclopedia of Philosophy*, vol. 2. London: Routledge, 505–17.

Rheingold, H. (1988). *They Have a Word for It: A Lighthearted Lexicon of Untranslatable Words and Phrases*. New York: Tarcher; distributed by St. Martin's Press.

Rhodes, J. E., and Jakes, S. (2004). The contribution of metaphor and metonymy to delusions. *Psychology and Psychotherapy: Theory, Research and Practice* 77(1): 1–17.

Rhodes, J. E., Jakes, S., and Robinson, J. (2005). A qualitative analysis of delusional content. *Journal of Mental Health* 14(4): 383–98.

Rhodes, R. (1989). The Cree connection. Paper read at the 28th Algonquian Conference. Washington, DC, October.

Rhodes, R. A. (1994). Aural images. In L. Hinton, J. Nichols, and J. J. Ohala (eds), *Sound Symbolism*. Cambridge: Cambridge University Press, 276–92.

Rhodes, R. A., and Lawler, J. M. (1981). Athematic metaphors. In R. Hendrick, C. Masek, and M. F. Miller (eds), *Papers from the Seventeenth Regional Meeting of the Chicago Linguistic Society*. Chicago: Chicago Linguistic Society, 318–42.

Rice, K. (2000). *Morpheme Order and Semantic Scope: Word Formation in the Athapaskan Verb*. Cambridge: Cambridge University Press.

Riemer, N. (2005). *The Semantics of Polysemy: Reading Meaning in English and Warlpiri*. Berlin: Mouton.

Riemer, N. (2006). Reductive paraphrase and meaning: a critique of Wierzbickian semantics. *Linguistics and Philosophy* 29(3): 347–79.

Riemer, N. (2010). *Introducing Semantics*. Cambridge: Cambridge University Press.

Riemer, N. (2013). Conceptualist semantics: explanatory power, scope and uniqueness. *Language Sciences* 35 1–19.

Rivas, A. M. (1977). A theory of clitics. Doctoral dissertation, MIT.

Roberson, D. (2005). Color categories are culturally diverse in cognition as well as in language. *Cross-Cultural Research* 39(1): 56–71.

Roberson, D., Davies, I., and Davidoff, J. (2000). Color categories are not universal: replications and new evidence from a stone-age culture. *Journal of Experimental Psychology: General* 129(3): 369–98.

Roberts, J., and Kay, C., with Grundy, L. (eds) (2000). *A Thesaurus of Old English* 2nd edn. London: King's College/Amsterdam: Rodopi.

Robinson, F. C. (1993). *The Tomb of Beowulf and other essays on Old English*. Oxford: Blackwell.

Roe, D., and Lachman, M. (2005). The subjective experience of people with severe mental illness: a potentially crucial piece of the puzzle. *Israel Journal of Psychiatry and Related Sciences* 42(4): 223–30.

Roediger, H., and Neely, J. (1982). Retrieval blocks in episodic and semantic memory. *Canadian Journal of Psychology* 36: 213–42.

Roelofs, A. (1996). Serial order in planning the production of successive morphemes of a word. *Journal of Memory and Language* 35: 854–76.

Roelofs, A. (1998). Rightward incrementality in encoding simple phrasal forms in speech production: verb–particle combinations. *Journal of Experimental Psychology: Learning, Memory and Cognition* 24: 904–21.

Roelofs, A. (2008). Tracing attention and the activation flow in spoken word planning using eye movements. *Journal of Experimental Psychology: Learning, Memory, and Cognition* 34: 353–68.

Roelofs, A., and Baayen, H. (2002). Morphology by itself in planning the production of spoken words. *Psychonomic Bulletin and Review* 9: 132–8.

Roget's International Thesaurus (1992[1852]). 5th edn, ed. R. L. Chapman. New York: HarperCollins.

Roget's Thesaurus of English Words and Phrases (2002[1852]). 150th anniversary edition, ed. G. W. Davidson. London: Penguin.

Rohrer, J. D., Knight, W. D., Warren, J. E., Fox, N. C., Rossor, M. N., and Warren, J. D. (2008). Word-finding difficulty: a clinical analysis of the progressive aphasias. *Brain* 131: 8–38.

Room, A. (2006). *Placenames of the World: Origins and Meanings of the Names for 6,600 Countries, Cities, Territories, Natural Features and Historic Sites*, 2nd edn. Jefferson, NC: Macfarland.

Rosaldo, M. Z. (1980). *Knowledge and Passion: Ilongot Notions of Self and Social Life*. Cambridge, Mass.: Cambridge University Press.

Rosaldo, R. (1984). Ilongot naming: the play of associations. In E. Tooker (ed.), *Naming Systems*. Washington, DC: American Ethnological Society, 11–24.

Rosch, E. (1978). Principles of categorization. In E. Rosch and B. Lloyd (eds), *Cognition and Categorization*. Hillsdale, NJ: Erlbaum, 27–48.

Rosch, E., and Mervis, C. (1975). Family resemblances: studies in the internal structure of categories. *Cognitive Psychology* 7: 573–605.

Rosch, E., Mervis, C. B., Gray, W., Jason, D., and Boyes-Braem, P. (1976). Basic objects in natural categories. *Cognitive Psychology* 8: 382–439.

Rosen, S. T. (1989). Two types of noun incorporation: a lexical analysis. *Language* 65: 294–317.

Rosenthal, P. (2005). *Words and Values*. New York: Oxford University Press.

Rose-Redwood, R., Alderman, D., and Azaryahu, M. (2010). Geographies of toponymic inscription: new directions in critical place-name studies. *Progress in Human Geography* 34: 453–70.

Rosinski, R. R., Golinkoff, R. M., and Kukish, K. S. (1975). Automatic semantic processing in a picture–word interference task. *Child Development* 46: 247–53.

Ross, H. E. (1960). Patterns of swearing. *Discovery* 21: 479–81.

Rossell, S. L., and David, A. S. (2006). Are semantic deficits in schizophrenia due to problems with access or storage? *Schizophrenia Research* 82: 121–34.

Rossi, A. S. (1965). Naming children in middle-class families. *American Sociological Review* 30(4): 499–513.

Roth, C. F. (2008). *Becoming Tsimshian: The Social Life of Names*. Seattle: University of Washington Press.

Ruan, G. (2008). Personal nicknames in Ningbo dialect. *Wuhan Daxue Xuebao/Wuhan University Journal* 61: 319–24.

Rubino, C. (2001). Iconic morphology and word formation in Ilocano. In F. K. Erhard Voeltz and C. Kilian-Hatz (eds), *Ideophones*. Amsterdam: Benjamins, 303–20.

Ruch, W. (1995). Will the real relationship between facial expression and affective experience please stand up: the case of exhilaration. *Cognition and Emotion* 9(1): 33–58.

Ruch, W., Attardo, S., and Raskin, V. (1993). Toward an empirical verification of the General Theory of Verbal Humor. *Humor: International Journal of Humor Research* 6(2): 123–36.

Ruhl, C. (1979). Alleged idioms with *hit*. In W. Wölck and P. L. Garvin (eds), *The Fifth LACUS Forum*. Columbia, SC: Hornbeam Press, 93–107.

Ruhl, C. (1989). *On Monosemy: A Study in Linguistic Semantics*. Albany, NY: SUNY.

Rundell, M. (2005). *Macmillan Phrasal Verbs Plus Dictionary*. London: Macmillan.

Russell, B. (1905). On denoting. *Mind* 14: 479–93.

Ryan, P. (1981). An introduction to Hausa personal nomenclature. *Names* 29: 139–64.

Rybicki, J. (2012). The great mystery of the (almost) invisible translator: stylometry in translation. In M. P. Oakes and M. Ji (eds), *Quantitative Methods in Corpus-Based Translation Studies: A Practical Guide to Descriptive Translation Research*. Amsterdam: Benjamins, 231–48.

Ryō, O. (1992). Some problems concerning personal names. *Senri Ethnological Studies* 34: 23–37.

Rytting, C. A., Brew, C., and Fosler-Lussier, E. (2010). Segmenting words from natural speech: subsegmental variation in segmental cues. *Journal of Child Language* 37(3): 513–43.

Sadock, J. M. (1980). Noun incorporation in Greenlandic: a case of syntactic word-formation. *Language* 57: 300–319.

Sadock, J. M. (1985). Autolexical syntax: a theory of noun incorporation and similar phenomena. *Natural Language and Linguistic Theory* 3: 379–441.

Sadock, J. M. (1991). *Autolexical Syntax: A Theory of Parallel Grammatical Representations*. Chicago: University of Chicago Press.

Saenger, P. (1997). *Space Between Words: The Origins of Silent Reading*. Stanford, Calif.: Stanford University Press.

Særheim, I. (2012). Ancient toponyms in south-west Norway: origin and formation. In M. Stenroos, M. Mäkinen, and I. Særheim (eds), *Language Contact and Development around the North Sea*. Amsterdam: Benjamins, 53–66.

Saffran, J. R., Aslin, R. N., and Newport, E. L. (1996). Statistical learning by 8-month-old infants. *Science* 274(5294): 1926–8.

Saffran, J. R., Newport, E. L., Aslin, R. N., and Tunick, R. A. (1997). Incidental language learning: listening (and learning) out of the corner of your ear. *Psychological Science* 8(2): 101–5.

Sagarra, N., and Alba, M. (2006). The key is in the keyword: L2 vocabulary learning methods with beginning learners of Spanish. *Modern Language Journal* 90: 228–43.

Sager, J. C. (1990). *A Practical Course in Terminology Processing*. Amsterdam: Benjamins.

Sager, J. C., Dungworth, D., and McDonald, P. F. (1980). *English Special Languages: Principles and Practice in Science and Technology*. Wiesbaden: Brandstetter.

Sahni, S. D., Seidenberg, M. S., and Saffran, J. R. (2010). Connecting cues: overlapping regularities support cue discovery in infancy. *Child Development* 81(3): 727–36.

Salaberri Zaratiegi, P. (2009). Euskal deituren jatorria eta etxe izengoitiak. *Anuario del Seminario de filologia vasca 'Julio de Urquijo'* 43(1–2): 819–30.

Salamoura, A., and Williams, J. N. (2007). Processing verb argument structure across languages: evidence for shared representations in the bilingual lexicon. *Applied Psycholinguistics* 28: 627–60.

Salamoura, A., and Williams, J. N. (2008). The representation of grammatical gender in the bilingual lexicon: evidence from Greek and German. *Bilingualism: Language and Cognition* 10: 257–75.

Salim, H. (2012). Collocation and other relationships in translations of the Qur'an: a corpus-based application of lexical priming theory to a unique theological text. Ph.D dissertation, University of Liverpool.

Salmons, J. (2004). How (non-)Indo-European is the Germanic lexicon? And what does that mean? In I. Hyvärinen, P. Kallio, and J. Korhonen (eds), *Etymologie, Entlehnungen und Entwicklungen: Festschrift für Jorma Koivulehto zum 70. Geburtstag*. Helsinki: Société Néophilologique, 311–21.

Samarin, W. J. (1965). Perspective on African ideophones. *African Studies* 24: 117–21.

Samarin, W. J. (1971). Survey of Bantu ideophones. *African Language Studies* 12: 130–68.

Samarin, W. J. (1979). Simplification, pidginization, and language change. In I. F. Hancock (ed.), *Readings in Creole Studies*. Ghent: Story-Scientia, 55–68.

Sampson, J. (1926). *The Dialect of the Gypsies of Wales*. Oxford: Clarendon Press.

Sandhofer, C. M., Smith, L. B., and Luo, J. (2000). Counting nouns and verbs in the input: differential frequencies, differential kinds of learning? *Journal of Child Language* 27: 561–85.

Sandler, W. (1999). Cliticization and prosodic words in a sign language. In T. A. Hall and U. Kleinhenz (eds), *Studies on the Phonological Word*. Amsterdam: Benjamins, 223–54.

Sandra, D. (1990). On the representation and processing of compound words: automatic access to constituent morphemes does not occur. *Quarterly Journal of Experimental Psychology* 42A: 529–67.

Sandst, L. (2015). By rum grænse: et forstudium of sproglige byer-i-byen [City space borders: a preliminary study of linguistic cities-within-cities]. NORNA-Rapporter 91(2): 199–217.

Sanford, A. J. (2002). Context, attention and depth of focussing during interpretation. *Mind and Language* 17: 188–206.

Santos, A., Chaigneau, S. E., Simmons, W. K., and Barsalou, L. W. (2011). Property generation reflects word association and situated simulation. *Language and Cognition* 3: 83–119.

Sapir, E. (1911). The problem of noun incorporation in American languages. *American Anthropologist* 13: 250–82.

Sapir, E. (1921). *Language: An Introduction to the Study of Speech*. New York: Harcourt Brace.

Sappan, R. (1987). *The Rhetorical-Logical Classification of Semantic Changes*. Braunton: Merlin.

Sasse, H.-J. (1985). Sprachkontakt und Sprachwandel: die Gräzisierung der albanischen Mundarten Griechenlands. *Papiere zur Linguistik* 32(1): 37–95.

Sauer, H. (2009). Glosses, glossaries, and dictionaries in the medieval period. In A. P. Cowie (ed.), *The Oxford History of English Lexicography, vol. 1: General-Purpose Dictionaries*. Oxford: Clarendon Press, 17–40.

Saunders, B. A. C., and van Brakel, J. (2002). The trajectory of color. *Perspectives on Science* 10(3): 302–55.

Savage-Rumbaugh, S., and Lewin, R. (1994). *Kanzi: The Ape at the Brink of the Human Mind*. New York: Wiley.

Saylor, M. M., and Sabbagh, M. A. (2004). Different kinds of information affect word learning in the preschool years: the case of part-term learning. *Child Development* 75: 395–408.

Scannell, J. W. (1997). Determining cortical landscapes. *Nature* 386: 452.

Scarborough, D. L., Cortese, C., and Scarborough, H. S. (1977). Frequency and repetition effects in lexical memory. *Journal of Experimental Psychology: Human Perception and Performance* 3(1): 117–34.

Schachter, S., Rauscher, F., Christenfeld, N., and Crone, K. T. (1994). The vocabularies of academia. *Psychological Science* 5: 37–41.

Schäfer, J. (1980). *Documentation in the OED: Shakespeare and Nashe as Test Cases*. Oxford: Clarendon Press.

Schegloff, E. A., Jefferson, G., and Sacks, H. (1977). The preference for self-correction in the organization of repair in conversation. *Language* 52: 361–82.

Schiering, R., Bickel, B., and Hildebrandt, K. A. (2010). The prosodic word is not universal, but emergent. *Journal of Linguistics* 46: 657–709.

Schiller, N. O. (2005). Verbal self-monitoring. In A. Cutler (ed.), *Twenty-First Century Psycholinguistics: Four Cornerstones*. Mahwah, NJ: Erlbaum, 245–61.

Schiller, N. O. (2006). Phonology in the production of words. In K. Brown (ed.), *Encyclopedia of Language and Linguistics*. Amsterdam: Elsevier, 545–53.

Schiller, N. O., Greenhall, J. A., Shelton, J. R., and Caramazza, A. (2001). Serial order effects in spelling errors: evidence from two dysgraphic patients. *Neurocase* 7: 1–14.

Schilling-Estes, N. (2007). Sociolinguistic fieldwork. In R. Bayley and C. Lucas (eds), *Sociolinguistic Theory: Theories, Methods, and Applications*. Cambridge: Cambridge University Press, 165–89.

Schipsbye, K. (1970). *A Modern English Grammar, with an Appendix on Semantically Related Prepositions*, 2nd edn. London: Oxford University Press.

Schmidt, R. W. (2001). Attention. In P. Robinson (ed.), *Cognition and Second Language Instruction*. Cambridge: Cambridge University Press, 3–32.

Schmitt, B. M., Münte, T. F., and Kutas, M. (2000). Electrophysiological estimates of the time course of semantic and phonological encoding during implicit picture naming. *Psychophysiology* 37: 473–84.

Schmitt, N. (ed.) (2004). *Formulaic Sequences*. Amsterdam: Benjamins.

Schmitt, N. (2010). *Researching Vocabulary: A Vocabulary Research Manual*. Basingstoke: Palgrave Macmillan.

Schmitt, N., Jiang, X., and Grabe, W. (2011). The percentage of words known in a text and reading comprehension. *Modern Language Journal* 95(1): 26–43.

Schmitt, N., and Meara, P. (1997). Researching vocabulary through a word knowledge framework: word associations and verbal suffixes. *Studies in Second Language Acquisition* 19: 17–36.

Schmitt, N., and Schmitt, D. (2014). A reassessment of frequency and vocabulary size in L2 vocabulary teaching. *Language Teaching* 47(4): 484–503.

Schmitt, N., Schmitt, D., and Clapham, C. (2001). Developing and exploring the behaviour of two new versions of the Vocabulary Levels Test. *Language Testing* 18: 55–88.

Schmitt, N., and Zimmerman, C. (2002). Derivative word forms: what do learners know? *TESOL Quarterly* 36(2): 145–71.

Schoonbaert, S., Hartsuiker, R. J., and Pickering, M. J. (2007). The representation of lexical and syntactic information in bilinguals: evidence from syntactic priming. *Journal of Memory and Language* 56: 153–71.

Schrauf, R. W. (2009). Longitudinal designs in studies of multilingualism. In K. de Bot and R. W. Schrauf (eds), *Language Development over the Lifespan*. New York: Routledge, 245–70.

Schriefers, H., Meyer, A., and Levelt, W. J. M. (1990). Exploring the time course of lexical access in language production: picture–word interference studies. *Journal of Memory and Language* 29: 86–102.

Schrijnemakers, J., and Raaijmakers, J. (1997). Adding new word associations to semantic memory: evidence for two interactive learning components. *Acta Psychologica* 96: 103–32.

Schulam, P., and Fellbaum, C. (2010). Automatically determining the semantic gradation of German adjectives. In Proceedings of KONVENS, Saarbrücken.

Schultze-Berndt, E. (2001). Ideophone-like characteristics of uninflected predicates in Jaminjung (Australia). In F. K. Erhard Voeltz and C. Kilian-Hatz (eds), *Ideophones*. Amsterdam: Benjamins, 355–73.

Scollon, R. (1976). *Conversations with a One-Year-Old*. Honolulu: University of Hawai'i Press.

Scott, M. (2008). Words, names and culture: place-names and the Scots language. *Journal of Scottish Name Studies* 2: 85–98.

Scott, M. (2013). *WordSmith Tools 6.0*. Oxford: Oxford University Press.

Scutt, J. A. (2002). Vilifying women on the football field. <http://www.philcleary.com.au/afl_racism_football_scutt.htm>.

Searle, J. R. (1958). Proper names. *Mind* 67: 166–71.

Searle, J. R. (1969). *Speech Acts*. Cambridge: Cambridge University Press.

Seebold, E. (1981). *Etymologie: eine Einführung am Beispiel der deutschen Sprache*. Munich: Beck.

Seidenberg, M. S., Tanenhaus, M. K., Leiman, J. M., and Bienkowski, M. (1982). Automatic access of the meanings of ambiguous words in context: some limitations of knowledge-based processing. *Cognitive Psychology* 14: 489–537.

Seidl, A., and Johnson, E. K. (2006). Infant word segmentation revisited: edge alignment facilitates target extraction. *Developmental Science* 9(6): 565–73.

Seiter, W. J. (1980). *Studies in Niuean Syntax*. New York: Garland.

Selkirk, E. O. (1978). On prosodic structure and its relation to syntactic structure. In T. Fretheim (ed.), *Nordic Prosody II*. Trondheim: TAPIR, 111–40.

Selkirk, E. O. (1980a). The role of prosodic categories in English word stress. *Linguistic Inquiry* 11: 563–605.

Selkirk, E. O. (1980b). Prosodic domains in phonology: Sanskrit revisited. In M. Aronoff and M.-L. Kean (eds), *Juncture: A Collection of Original Papers*. Saratoga: Anma Libri, 107–29.

Selkirk, E. O. (1982). *The Syntax of Words*. Cambridge, Mass.: MIT Press.

Selkirk, E. O. (1984). *Phonology and Syntax: The Relation Between Sound and Structure*. Cambridge, Mass.: MIT Press.

Selkirk, E. O. (1996). The prosodic structure of function words. In J. L. Morgan and K. Demuth (eds), *Signal to Syntax: Bootstrapping From Speech to Grammar in Early Acquisition*. Mahwah, NJ: Erlbaum, 187–213.

Semino, E. (2008). *Metaphor in Discourse*. Cambridge: Cambridge University Press.

Seppänen, A. (1974). *Proper Names in English: A Study in Semantics and Syntax*. Tampere: Department of English Philology, University of Tampere.

Seuren, P. (1998). *Western Linguistics: An Historical Introduction*. Oxford: Blackwell.

Seuren, P. (2009). *Language in Cognition*. Oxford: Oxford University Press.

Shannon, C. E. (1948). A mathematical theory of communication. *Bell System Technical Journal* 27: 379–423, 623–56.

Shannon, C. E. (1951). Prediction and entropy of printed English. *Bell System Technical Journal* 30: 50–64.

Shapiro, A. M., and Waters, D. L. (2005). An investigation of the cognitive processes underlying the keyword method in foreign vocabulary learning. *Language Teaching Research* 9: 129–46.

Sharifian, F. (2011). *Cultural Conceptualisations and Language: Theoretical Framework and Applications*. Amsterdam: Benjamins.

Sharifian, F., Dirven, R., Yu, N., and Neiemier, S. (eds) (2008). *Culture, Body, and Language: Conceptualizations of Internal Body Organs across Cultures and Languages*. Berlin: Mouton de Gruyter.

Shayan, S., Ozturk, O., and Sicoli, M. A. (2011). The thickness of pitch: crossmodal metaphors in Farsi, Turkish, and Zapotec. *The Senses and Society* 6(1): 96–105.

Sheidlower, J. (2009). *The F-Word*, 3rd edn. Oxford: Oxford University Press.

Sheinman, V., Fellbaum, C., Julien, I., Schulam, P. F., and Tokunaga, T. (2013). Large, huge or gigantic? Identifying and encoding intensity relations among adjectives. *Lexical Resources and Evaluation* 47(3): 797–818.

Sheinman, V., and Togunaga, T. (2009). AdjScales: visualizing differences between adjectives for language learners. *IEICE Transactions* 92-D(8) 1542–50.

Shen, H. H. (2010). Imagery and verbal coding approaches in Chinese vocabulary instruction. *Language Teaching Research* 14: 485–99.

Shepard, R. N., and Cooper, L. A. (1992). Representation of colors in the blind, color-blind, and normally sighted. *Psychological Science* 3(2): 97–104.

Sherzer, J. (1976). *An Areal-Typological Study of American Indian Languages North of Mexico*. Amsterdam: North-Holland.

Shew, W. L., Yang, H., Yu, S., Roy, R., and Plenz, D. (2011). Information capacity and transmission are maximized in balanced cortical networks with neuronal avalanches. *Journal of Neuroscience* 31(1): 55–63.

Shibatani, M. (1987). Japanese. In B. Comrie (ed.), *The World's Major Languages*. Oxford: Oxford University Press, 855–80.

Shi-xu and Feng-Bing (2013). Contemporary Chinese communication made understandable: a cultural psychological perspective. *Culture & Psychology* 19(1): 3–19.

Shmelev, A. (2012a). Možno li ponjat' russkuju kul'turu čerez klučerez ključevye slova russkogo jazyka? In A. Zalizniak, I. Levontina, and A. Shmelev, *Ključevye idei russkoj jazykovoj kartiny mira* [Key ideas of the Russian linguistic picture of the world]. Moscow: Jazyki slavjanskoj kul'tury.

Shmelev, A. (2012b). Russkij vzgljad na 'zapadnye' koncepty: jazykovje dannye. In A. Zalizniak, I. Levontina, and A. Shmelev, *Ključevye idei russkoj jazykovoj kartiny mira* [Key ideas of the Russian linguistic picture of the world]. Moscow: Jazyki slavjanskoj kul'tury, 395–409.

Shortz, W. (ed.) (2006). *The New York Times Little Black (and White) Book of Crosswords*. New York: St. Martin's Press.

Shukla, M., White, K. S., and Aslin, R. N. (2011). Prosody guides the rapid mapping of auditory word forms onto visual objects in 6-mo-old infants. *PNAS: Proceedings of the National Academy of Sciences of the United States of America* 108(15): 6038–43.

Shultz, T. R. (1976). A cognitive-developmental analysis of humor. In A. J. Chapman and H. C. Foot (eds), *Humor and Laughter: Theory, Research and Applications*. London: Wiley, 11–36.

Shweder, R. A. (1991). *Thinking Through Cultures: Expeditions in Cultural Psychology*. Cambridge, Mass.: Harvard University Press.

Shweder, R. A. (2004). Deconstructing the emotions for the sake of comparative research. In A. S. R. Manstead, N. Frijda, and A. Fischer (eds), *Feelings and Emotions: The Amsterdam Symposium*. Cambridge: Cambridge University Press, 81–97.

Shweder, R. A., Haidt, J., Horton, R., and Joseph, C. (2008). The cultural psychology of the emotions: ancient and renewed. In M. D. Lewis, J. M. Haviland-Jones, and L. Feldman Barrett (eds), *Handbook of Emotions*, 3rd edn. New York: Guilford Press, 409–27.

Sicoli, M. A. (2010). Shifting voices with participant roles: voice qualities and speech registers in Mesoamerica. *Language in Society* 39(4): 521–53.

Sidwell, P. (2005). Acehnese and the Aceh-Chamic language family. In A. P. Grant and P. Sidwell (eds), *Chamic and Beyond: Studies in Mainland Austronesian Languages*. Canberra, ACT: Pacific Linguistics, 211–31.

Siegel, D. (1974). Topics in English morphology. Ph.D dissertation, MIT.

Sigurd, B., and Tayanin, D. (2008). Creativity and tradition in baby naming. *Lund University Department of Linguistics Working Papers* 53: 133–44.

Silverberg, S., and Samuel, A. G. (2004). The effect of age of second language acquisition on the representation and processing of second language words. *Journal of Memory and Language* 51: 381–98.

Silverstein, M. (1994). Relative motivation in derivational and indexical sound symbolism of Wasco-Wishram Chinookan. In L. Hinton, J. Nichols, and J. J. Ohala (eds), *Sound Symbolism*. Cambridge: Cambridge University Press, 40–60.

Simmons, W., Hamann, S., Harenski, C., Hu, X., and Barsalou, L. (2008). fMRI evidence for word association and situated simulation in conceptual processing. *Journal of Physiology* (Paris) 102: 106–19.

Simon, H. (1955). On a class of skew distribution functions. *Biometrika* 42(3/4): 425–40.

Simons, G. F. (1982). Word taboo and comparative Austronesian linguistics. In A. Halim, L. Carrington, and S. A. Wurm (eds), *Papers from the Third International Conference on Austronesian Linguistics*, vol. 3. Canberra: Pacific Linguistics, 157–226.

Simpson, J. (2001). Hypocoristics of place names. In D. Blair and P. Collins (eds), *English in Australia*. Amsterdam: Benjamins, 89–112.

Simpson-Vlach, R., and Ellis, N. C. (2010). An academic formulas list: new methods in phraseology research. *Applied Linguistics* 31: 487–512.

Simunovic, P. (2003). Nicknames in Croatian. *GOVOR: Casopis za fonetiku* 20(1–2): 421–29.

Sinclair, J. M. (1987). *Collocation: a progress report*. In R. Steele and T. Threadgold (eds), *Essays in Honour of M. Halliday*. Amsterdam: Benjamins, 319–31.

Sinclair, J. M. (1991). *Corpus, Concordance, Collocation*. Oxford: Oxford University Press.

Sinclair, J. M. (1999). The lexical item. In E. Weigand (ed.), *Contrastive Lexical Semantics*. Amsterdam: Benjamins, 1–24.

Sinclair, J. M. (2003). *Reading Concordances*. Harlow: Pearson Longman.

Sinclair, J. M. (2004). *Trust the Text: Language, Corpus and Discourse*. London: Routledge.

Sinclair, J. M. (2005). Corpus and text: basic principles. In M. Wynne (ed.), *Developing Linguistic Corpora: a Guide to Good Practice*. Oxford: Oxbow Books, 1–16.

Sinclair, J. M. (2010). Defining the definiendum. In G.-M. de Schryver (ed.), *A Way with Words: Recent Advances in Lexical Theory and Analysis*. Kampala: Menha, 37–47.

Sinclair, J. M. and Moon, R. (eds) (1989). *Collins Cobuild Dictionary of Phrasal Verbs*. Glasgow: Collins.

Sinclair, J. M. et al. (1987). *Collins COBUILD English Language Dictionary*. London: Collins. 6th edn 2008.

Singh, L., Reznick, J. S., and Xuehua, L. (2012). Infant word segmentation and childhood vocabulary development: a longitudinal analysis. *Developmental Science* 15(4): 482–95.

Sitwell, O. (1949). *Laughter in the Next Room*, ch. 7. London: Macmillan.

Skinner, D. (2012). *The Story of Ain't: America, its Language, and the Most Controversial Dictionary Ever Published*. New York: HarperCollins.

Skinner, K. (1993). *How to Solve Cryptic Crosswords*. Kingswood: Elliot Rightway.

Skipper, J. (1985). Nicknames, folk heroes, and assimilation: Black league baseball players 1894–1950. *Journal of Sport Behavior* 89: 100–114.

Skipper, J. (1986). Nicknames, coal miners, and group solidarity. *Names* 34: 134–45.

Skipper, J. (1990). Placenames used as nicknames: a study of major league baseball players. *Names* 38: 1–20.

Skipper, J. K., and Leslie, P. L. (1988). Women, nicknames, and blues singers. *Names* 36: 193–202.

Slater, A. S., and Feinman, S. (1985). Gender and the phonology of North American first names. *Sex Roles* 13(7/8): 429–40.

Sloat, C. (1969). Proper names in English. *Language* 45: 26–30.

Slobin, D. I. (1985). Crosslinguistic evidence for the language-making capacity. In D. I. Slobin (ed.), *The Crosslinguistic Study of Language Acquisition*, vol. 2: *Theoretical Issues*. Hillsdale, NJ: Erlbaum, 1157–256.

Slobin, D. I. (1996). Two ways to travel: verbs of motion in English and Spanish. In M. S. Shibatani and S. A. Thompson (eds), *Grammatical Constructions: Their Form and Meaning*. Oxford: Clarendon Press, 195–220.

Small, S. L. (1994). Connectionist networks and language disorders. *Journal of Communication Disorders* 27: 305–23.

Smith, L. (2000). Learning how to learn words: an associative crane. In R. Golinkoff and K. Hirsh-Pasek (eds), *Becoming a Word Learner: A Debate on Lexical Acquisition*. New York: Oxford University Press.

Smith, L., and Yu, C. (2008). Infants rapidly learn word-referent mappings via cross-situational statistics. *Cognition* 106(3): 1558–68.

Smith, M. C. (2010). Lexical categories and pragmatic functions. *Linguistics* 48: 717–77.

Smith, M. C. (2011). Multiple property models of lexical categories. *Linguistics* 49: 1–51.

Smith-Bannister, S. (1997). *Names and Naming Patterns in England 1538–1700*. Oxford: Oxford University Press.

Smith-Stark, T. C. (1974). The plurality split. In M. W. L. Galy, R. A. Fox, and A. Brucks (eds), *Proceedings of the 10th Annual Meeting of the Chicago Linguistic Society*. Chicago: CLS 657–71.

Smits, E., Martensen, H., Dijkstra, T., and Sandra, D. (2006). Naming interlingual homographs: variable competition and the role of the decision system. *Bilingualism: Language and Cognition* 9: 281–97.

Smyth, H. W.(1956). *Greek Grammar*, revised edn by G. M. Messing. Cambridge, Mass.: Harvard University Press.

Smythe Kung, S. (2005). Sound symbolism and expressive language in Huehuetla Tepehua. MS, University of Texas.

Snell-Hornby, M. (1986). The bilingual dictionary: victim of its own tradition? In R. R. K. Hartmann (ed.), *The History of Lexicography*. Amsterdam: Benjamins, 207–18.

Snow, R., Jurafsky, D., and Ng, A. (2006). Semantic taxonomy induction from heterogenous evidence. In Proceedings of COLING/ACL, Sydney.

Soanes, C., and Stevenson, A. (2003). *The Oxford Dictionary of English*. 2nd edn of Pearsall and Hanks, *The New Oxford Dictionary of English*.

Soanes, C., and Stevenson, A. (eds) (2008). *Concise Oxford English Dictionary*, 11th edn, revised. Oxford: Oxford University Press.

Sokmen, A. J. (1997). Current trends in teaching second language vocabulary. In N. Schmitt and M. McCarthy (eds), *Vocabulary: Description, Acquisition and Pedagogy*. Cambridge: Cambridge University Press, 237–57.

Solan, L. (1993). When judges use the dictionary. *American Speech* 68(1): 50–7.

Sorell, C. J. (2013). A study of issues and techniques for creating core vocabulary lists for English as an International Language. Doctoral dissertation, Victoria University of Wellington.

Sørensen, H. S. (1958). *Word Classes in Modern English, with Special Reference to Names, and with an Introductory Theory of Grammar, Meaning and Reference*. Copenhagen: G. E. C. Gad.

Sosa, A. V., and MacFarlane, J. (2002). Evidence for frequency-based constituents in the mental lexicon: collocations involving of. *Brain and Language* 83: 227–36.

Souag, L. (2007). The typology of number borrowing in Berber. In N. Hilton, R. Arscott, K. Barden, A. Krishna, S. Shah, and M. Zellers (eds), *CamLing 2007: Proceedings of the Fifth University of Cambridge Postgraduate Conference in Language Research*. Cambridge: Cambridge Institute of Language Research, 237–44.

Spalek, K., Damian, M. F., and Bölte, J. (2013). Is lexical selection in spoken word production competitive? Introduction to the special issue on lexical competition in language production. *Language and Cognitive Processes* 28: 597–614.

Spelke, E. (1994). Initial knowledge: six suggestions. *Cognition* 50: 431–45.

Spence, D., and Owens, K. (1990). Lexical co-occurrence and association strength. *Journal of Psycholinguistics* 19: 317–30.

Spencer, A. (1991). *Morphological Theory: An Introduction to Word Structure in Generative Grammar*. Oxford: Blackwell.

Spencer, A. (1995). Incorporation in Chukchi. *Language* 71: 439–89.

Spencer, A. (2000). Morphology and syntax. In G. Booij, C. Lehmann, and J. Mugdan (eds), *Morphologie: ein internationales Handbuch zur Flexion und Wortbildung/Morphology: A Handbook on Inflection and Word Formation*. Berlin: Mouton de Gruyter, 312–35.

Spencer, A. (2004). Morphology: an overview of central concepts. In L. Sadler and A. Spencer (eds), *Projecting Morphology*. Stanford, Calif.: CSLI, 67–110.

Spencer, A. (2006). Morphological universals. In R. Mairal and J. Gil (eds), *Linguistic Universals*. Cambridge: Cambridge University Press, 101–29.

Spencer, A., and Luis, A. (2012). *Clitics: An Introduction*. Cambridge: Cambridge University Press.

Spencer, A., and Zwicky, A. (eds) (1998). *The Handbook of Morphology*. Oxford: Blackwell.

Spencer, H. (1860). Physiology of laughter. *Macmillan's Magazine*. Reprinted in *Essays, Scientific, Political and Speculative*, vol. 2 New York: Appleton, 1891, 452–66.

Sperber, D., and Orri, G. (2010). A pragmatic perspective on the evolution of language. In R. Larson, V. Déprez, and H. Yamakido (eds), *The Evolution of Human Language: Biolinguistic Perspectives*. Cambridge: Cambridge University Press, 124–32.

Spevack, M. (ed.) (1993). *A Shakespeare Thesaurus*. Hildesheim: Olms.

Spivey, M. J., and Marian, V. (1999). Cross talk between native and second languages: partial activation of an irrelevant lexicon. *Psychological Science* 10: 281–4.

Sportiche, D. (1996). Clitic constructions. In J. Rooryck and L. Zaring (eds), *Phrase Structure and the Lexicon*. Bloomington: IULC Press, 213–76.

Staehr, L. S. (2009). Vocabulary knowledge and advanced listening comprehension in English as a foreign language. *Studies in Second Language Acquisition* 31: 577–607.

Stainton, R. J. (2006). Meaning and reference: some Chomskian themes. In E. Lepore and B. C. Smith (eds), *The Oxford Handbook of Philosophy of Language*. Oxford: Oxford University Press, 913–40.

Stark, L. R. (1969). The lexical structure of Quechua body parts. *Anthropological Linguistics* 11(1): 1–15.

Starreveld, P. A. (2000). On the interpretation of onsets of auditory context effects in word production. *Journal of Memory and Language* 42: 497–525.

Starreveld, P. A., La Heij, W., and Verdonschot, R. G. (2013). Time course analysis of the effects of distractor frequency and categorical relatedness in picture naming: an evaluation of the response exclusion account. *Language and Cognitive Processes* 28: 633–54.

Stauffer, R. G. (1942). A study of prefixes in the Thorndike list to establish a list of prefixes that should be taught in the elementary school. *Journal of Educational Research* 35(6): 453–58.

Stefanowitsch, A., and Gries, S. T. (eds) (2006). *Corpus-Based Approaches to Metaphor and Metonymy*. Berlin: Mouton de Gruyter.

Stein, J. (1966). *The Random House Dictionary of the English Language*. New York: Random House.

Steiner, G. (1967). The retreat from the word. In *Language and Silence*. New Haven, Conn.: Yale University Press, 25–6.

Štekauer, P., Valera, S., and Körtvélyessy, L. (2012). *Word-Formation in the World's Languages*. Cambridge: Cambridge University Press.

Stemberger, J. P. (1985). An interactive activation model of language production. In A. Ellis (ed.), *Progress in the Psychology of Language*. Mahwah, NJ: Erlbaum, 143–86.

Stemberger, J. P., and MacWhinney, B. (1986). Frequency and the lexical storage of regularly inflected forms. *Memory and Cognition* 14: 17–26.

Stenroos, M., Mäkinen, M., and Særheim, I. (eds) (2012). *Language Contact and Development around the North Sea*. Amsterdam: Benjamins.

Stevenson, C. L. (1937). The emotive meaning of ethical terms. *Mind* 46: 14–31.

Stewart, J. (1993). *African Names: Names from the African Continent for Children and Adults*. New York: Citadel Press.

Steyvers, M., Shiffrin, R. M., and Nelson, D. L. (2004). Word association spaces for predicting semantic similarity effects in episodic memory. In A. F. Healy (ed.), *Experimental Cognitive Psychology and its Applications*. Washington, DC: American Psychological Association, 237–49.

Steyvers, M., and Tenenbaum, J. B. (2005). The large-scale structure of semantic networks: statistical analyses and a model of semantic growth. *Cognitive Science* 29: 41–78.

Stock, O. (1996). Password Swordfish: verbal humor in the interface. In J. Hulstijn and A. Nijholt (eds), *Proceedings of the International Workshop on Computational Humor (TWLT 12)* (University of Twente, Enschede), 1–8.

Stoel-Gammon, C. (2011). Relationships between lexical and phonological development in young children. *Journal of Child Language* 38: 1–34.

Storms, G., De Boeck, P., and Ruts, W. (2000). Prototype and exemplar-based information in natural language categories. *Journal of Memory and Language* 42: 51–73.

Stott, R., Mansell, W., Salkovskis, P., Lavender, A., and Cartwright-Hatton, S. (2010). *Oxford Guide to Metaphors in CBT: Building Cognitive Bridges*. Oxford: Oxford University Press.

Strack, F., M., Leonard, L., and Stepper, S. (1988). Inhibiting and facilitating conditions of the human smile: a nonobtrusive test of the facial feedback hypothesis. *Journal of Personality and Social Psychology* 54(5): 768–77.

Strauss, U., Grzybek, P., and Altmann, G. (2006). Word length and word frequency. In P. Grzybek (ed.), *Contributions to the Science of Text and Language: Word Length Studies and Related Issues*. Dordrecht: Springer, 277–95.

Strawson, P. F. (1950). On referring. *Mind* 59: 320–44.

Stubbs, M. (2002). *Words and Phrases: Corpus Studies of Lexical Semantics*. London: Blackwell.

Stukova, N. P. (2011). The role of formulaic language in the creation of grammar. Doctoral dissertation, University of New Mexico.

Stump, G. N. (2001). *Inflectional Morphology: A Theory of Paradigm Structure*. Cambridge: Cambridge University Press.

Sunderman, G., and Kroll, J. F. (2006). First language activation during second language lexical processing: an investigation of lexical form, meaning, and grammatical class. *Studies in Second Language Acquisition* 28: 387–422.

Superanskaya, A. V. (2003). Contemporary Russian nicknames. *Folia onomastica croatica* 12–13: 485–98.

Suzman, S. M. (1994). Names as pointers: Zulu personal naming practices. *Language in Society* 23(2): 253–72.

Svorou, S. (1994). *The Grammar of Space: Typological Studies in Language*. Amsterdam: Benjamins.

Swadesh, M. (1946). Chitimacha. In C. Osgood and H. Hoijer (eds), *Linguistic Structures of Native America*. New York: Wenner-Gren, 345–62.

Swadesh, M. (1955). Towards greater accuracy in lexico-statistical dating. *International Journal of American Linguistics* 21: 121–37.

Swanson, R. A., and Witkowski, S. (1977). Hopi ethnoanatomy: a comparative treatment. *Proceedings of the American Philosophical Society* 121(4): 320–37.

Sweet, H. (1891). *A New English Grammar*, vol. 1. Oxford: Oxford University Press.

Swingley, D. (2005). Statistical clustering and the contents of the infant vocabulary. *Cognitive Psychology* 50(1): 86–132.

Swingley, D. (2007). Lexical exposure and word-form encoding in 1.5-year-olds. *Developmental Psychology* 43(2): 454–64.

Szalay, L. B., and Deese, J. (1978). *Subjective Meaning and Culture*. Mahwah, NJ: Erlbaum.

Szpyra, J. (1989). *The Phonology–Morphology Interface*. London: Routledge.

Szymanek, B. (2010). *A Panorama of Polish Word-Formation*. Lublin: Wydawnictwo KUL.

Tabul-Lavy, G. (2012). Intra-word inconsistency in apraxic Hebrew-speaking children. *Clinical Linguistics and Phonetics* 26(6): 502–17.

Tadmor, U. (2009). Loanwords in the world's languages: findings and results. In M. Haspelmath and U. Tadmor (eds), *Loanwords in the World's Languages: A Comparative Study*. Berlin: Mouton de Gruyter, 55–75.

Taft, M. (2004). Morphological decomposition and the reverse base frequency effect. *Quarterly Journal of Experimental Psychology* 57A: 745–65.

Taft, M., and Forster, K. I. (1976). Lexical storage and retrieval of polymorphemic and polysyllabic words. *Journal of Verbal Learning and Verbal Behavior* 15: 607–20.

Talamas, A., Kroll, J. F., and Dufour, R. (1999). From form to meaning: stages in the acquisition of second-language vocabulary. *Bilingualism: Language and Cognition* 2: 45–58.

Talmy, L. (1985). Lexicalization patterns: semantic structure in lexical forms. In T. Shopen (ed.), *Language Typology and Syntactic Description*, vol. 3: *Grammatical Categories and the Lexicon*. Cambridge: Cambridge University Press, 57–149.

Tanaka, J. W., and Taylor, M. (1991). Object categories and expertise: is the basic level in the eye of the beholder? *Cognitive Psychology* 23: 457–82.

Tardif, T., Fletcher, P., Liang, W., Zhang, Z., Kaciroti, N., and Marchman, V. A. (2008). Baby's first 10 words. *Developmental Psychology* 44: 929–38.

Tardif, T., Gelman, S. A., and Xu, F. (1999). Putting the 'noun bias' in context: a comparison of Mandarin and English. *Child Development* 70: 620–35.

Tardif, T., Shatz, M., and Naigles, L. (1997). Caregiver speech and children's use of nouns versus verbs: a comparison of English, Italian, and Mandarin. *Journal of Child Language* 24: 535–65.

Tay, D. (2012). Applying the notion of metaphor types to enhance counseling protocols. *Journal of Counseling and Development* 90(2): 142–9.

Tay, D. (2013). *Metaphor in Psychotherapy: A Descriptive and Prescriptive Analysis*. Amsterdam: Benjamins.

Taylor, D. M., and Hoff, B. J. (1980). The linguistic repertory of the Island Carib in the seventeenth century: the men's language—a Carib pidgin? *International Journal of American Linguistics* 46: 301–12.

Taylor, J. R. (2003). *Linguistic Categorization*, 3rd edn. New York: Oxford University Press.

Taylor, J. R. (2012). *The Mental Corpus: How Language is Represented in the Mind*. Oxford: Oxford University Press.

Taylor, S. (1997). Generic-element variation, with special reference to eastern Scotland. *Nomina* 20: 5–22.

Taylor, S. (2007). *Sliabh* in Scottish place-names: its meaning and chronology. *Journal of Scottish Name Studies* 1: 99–136.

Teinonen, T., Fellman, V., Näätänen, R., Alku, P., and Huotilainen, M. (2009). Statistical language learning in neonates revealed by event-related brain potentials. *BMC Neuroscience* 10. doi: 10.1186/1471-2202-10-21.

Temmerman, R. (2000). *Towards New Ways of Terminological Description: The Sociocognitive Approach*. Amsterdam: Benjamins.

Tennyson, A., L. (1850). *In Memoriam A.H.H.*, canto 5.

Termium Plus® <http://termiumplus.gc.ca/> Accessed 29 August 2012.

Terrill, A. (2006). Body part terms in Lavukaleve, a Papuan language of the Solomon Islands. *Language Sciences* 28(2–3): 304–22.

Thesaurus Linguae Latinae (1894–). Leipzig: Teubner.

Thierry, G., and Wu, Y. J. (2007). Brain potentials reveal unconscious translation during foreign-language comprehension. *Proceedings of the National Academy of Sciences of the United States of America* 104: 12530–35.

Thiessen, E. D., and Erickson, L. C. (2013). Discovering words in fluent speech: the contribution of two kinds of statistical information. *Frontiers in Psychology* 3. doi: 10.3389/fpsyg.2012.00590.

Thiessen, E. D., and Saffran, J. R. (2003). When cues collide: use of stress and statistical cues to word boundaries by 7- to 9-month-old infants. *Developmental Psychology* 39(4): 706–16.

Thiessen, E. D., and Saffran, J. R. (2007). Learning to learn: infants' acquisition of stress-based strategies for word segmentation. *Language Learning and Development* 3(1): 73–100.

Thomas, D. D. (1962). On defining the 'word' in Vietnamese. *Văn-Hóa Nguyệt-San* 11: 519–23.

Thomas, D. (1961). Poetic manifesto. *Texas Quarterly* 4(4): 47.

Thomas, G. (1991). *Linguistic Purism*. London: Longman.

Thomason, S. G. (2001). *Language Contact: An Introduction*. Washington, DC: Georgetown University Press.

Thomason, S. G., and Everett, D. L. (2005). Pronoun borrowing. *Proceedings of the Berkeley Linguistics Society* 27: 301–15.

Thomason, S. G., and Kaufman, T. (1988). *Language Contact, Creolization and Genetic Linguistics*. Berkeley: University of California Press.

Thompson, L. C. (1965). *A Vietnamese Grammar*. Seattle: University of Washington Press.

Thoreau, H. (1854). Reading. In *Walden*. Boston: Ticknor & Fields.

Thorndike, E. L. (1924). The vocabularies of school pupils. In J. C. Bell (ed.), *Contributions to Education*. New York: World Book Co., 69–76.

Thorndike, E. L. (1941). *The Teaching of English*. New York: Teachers College, Columbia University.

Thorndike, E. L., and Lorge, I. (1944). *The Teacher's Word Book of 30,000 Words*. New York: Teachers College, Columbia University.

Thráinsson, H. (1994). Icelandic. In E. König and J. van der Auwera (eds), *The Germanic Languages*. London: Routledge, 142–89.

Thurgood, G. (1999). *From Ancient Cham to Modern Dialects: Two Thousand Years of Language Contact and Change: With an Appendix of Chamic Reconstructions and Loanwords*. Honolulu: University of Hawai'i Press.

Tiee, H. H. (1986). *A Reference Grammar of Chinese Sentences.* Tucson: University of Arizona Press.

Timberlake, A. (1993). Russian. In B. Comrie and G. G. Corbett (eds), *The Slavonic Languages.* London: Routledge, 827–86.

Tincoff, R., and Jusczyk, P. W. (1999). Some beginnings of word comprehension in 6-month-olds. *Psychological Science* 10(2): 172–5.

Tincoff, R., and Jusczyk, P. W. (2012). Six-month-olds comprehend words that refer to parts of the body. *Infancy* 17(4): 432–44.

Tinkham, T. (1997). The effects of semantic and thematic clustering on the learning of second language vocabulary. *Second Language Research* 13: 138–63.

Toliver, R. H. (2008). Borrowing processes and the affect phenomenon in Quechua nicknames. *Serie Linguistica Peruana* 55: 49–73.

Tomasello, M. (1998). Reference: intending that others jointly attend. *Pragmatics and Cognition* 6: 219–34.

Tomasello, M. (2000a). The social-pragmatic theory of word learning. *Pragmatics* 10: 401–14.

Tomasello, M. (ed.) (2000b). Primate cognition. *Cognitive Science* 3.

Tomasello, M. (2001). Could we please lose the mapping metaphor, please? *Behavioral and Brain Science* 24: 1119–20.

Tomasello, M. (2003). *Constructing a Language: A Usage-Based Theory of Language Acquisition.* Cambridge, Mass.: Harvard University Press.

Tomasello, M., and Akhtar, N. (1995). Two-year-olds use pragmatic cues to differentiate reference to objects and actions. *Cognitive Development* 10: 201–24.

Tomasello, M., and Barton, M. E. (1994). Learning words in nonostensive contexts. *Developmental Psychology* 30: 639–50.

Tomblin, J. B., Records, N. L., and Zhang, X. (1996). A system for the diagnosis of specific language impairment in kindergarten children. *Journal of Speech, Language, and Hearing Research* 39(6): 1284–94.

Tonkin, E. (1980). Jealousy names, civilized names: anthroponomy of the Jlao Kru of Liberia. *Man* 15: 653–64.

Tooker, E. (ed.) (1984). *Naming Systems.* Washington, DC: American Ethnological Society.

Topping, D., Ogo, P., and Dungca, B. (1975). *Chamorro–English Dictionary.* Honolulu: University of Hawai'i Press.

Tournier, J. (1985). *Introduction descriptive à la lexicogénétique de l'anglais contemporain.* Paris/Genva: Champion/Slatkine.

Trask, L. (2004). What is a word? University of Sussex Working Papers in Linguistics and English Language. <https://www.sussex.ac.uk/webteam/gateway/file.php?name=essay---what-is-a-word.pdf&site=1>.

Trask, R. L. (1997). *The History of Basque.* London: Routledge.

Travis, C. E. (2006). The communicative realization of *confianza* and *calor humano* in Colombian Spanish. In C. Goddard (ed.), *Ethnopragmatics: Understanding Discourse in Cultural Context.* Berlin: Mouton de Gruyter, 199–230.

Trier, J. (1931). *Der Deutsche Wortschatz im Sinnbezirk des Verstandes.* Heidelberg: Winter.

Tsao, F. M., Liu, H. M., and Kuhl, P. K. (2004). Speech perception in infancy predicts language development in the second year of life: a longitudinal study. *Child Development* 75(4): 1067–84.

Tse, G. Y. W. (2004). A grammatical study of personal names in present-day English, with special reference to the usage of the definite article. *English Studies* 3: 241–59.

Tsur, R. (1992). *What Makes Sound Patterns Expressive? The Poetic Mode of Speech Expression*. Durham, NC: Duke University Press.

Tsur, R. (2012). *Playing by Ear and the Tip of the Tongue: Precategorial Information in Poetry*. Amsterdam: Benjamins.

Tufvesson, S. (2011). Analogy-making in the Semai sensory world. *The Senses and Society* 6(1): 86–95.

Tuggy, D. (1993). Ambiguity, polysemy, and vagueness, *Cognitive Linguistics* 4: 273–90.

Tuldava, J. (1993a). Measuring text difficulty. In G. Altmann (ed.), *Glottometrika* 14: 69–81.

Tuldava, J. (1993b). The statistical structure of a text and its readability. In L. Hřebíček and G. Altmann (eds), *Quantitative Text Analysis*. Trier: WVT, 215–27.

Turner, N. (2004). Female nicknaming practices amongst the Zulu. *Nomina Africana* 18(1–2): 1–17.

Turton, D. (1980). There's no such beast: cattle and color naming among the Mursi. *Man* 15(2): 320–38.

Tversky, A. (1977). Features of similarity. *Psychological Review* 84: 327–52.

Tzelgov, J., and Ebenezra, S. (1992). Components of the between-language semantic priming effect. *European Journal of Cognitive Psychology* 4: 253–72.

Udolph, J. (2012). The colonisation of England by Germanic tribes on the basis of place-names. In M. Stenroos, M. Mäkinen, and I. Særheim (eds), *Language Contact and Development around the North Sea*. Amsterdam: Benjamins, 23–51.

Uhlířová, L. (1997a). O vztahu mezi délkou slova a jeho polohou ve větě. *Slovo a slovesnost* 58: 174–84.

Uhlířová, L. (1997b). Length vs. order: word length and clause length from the perspective of word order. *Journal of Quantitative Linguistics* 4(1–3): 266–75.

Ullman, S. (1951). *The Principles of Semantics*. Oxford: Blackwell.

Ullmann, S. (1957). *The Principles of Semantics*, 2nd edn. Oxford/Glasgow: Blackwell/Jackson.

Ullmann, S. (1962). *Semantics: An Introduction to the Science of Meaning*. Oxford: Blackwell.

van Benthem, J., and ter Meulen, A. (eds) (1984). *Generalized Quantifiers: Theory and Applications*. Dordrecht: Foris.

van Benthem, J., and Westerståhl, D. (1995). Directions in generalized quantifier theory. *Synthese Library* 55: 389–419.

van Coetsem, F. (2000). *A General and Unified Theory of the Transmission Process in Language Contact*. Heidelberg: Winter.

van Deemter, K. (2010). *Not Exactly: In Praise of Vagueness*. Oxford: Oxford University Press.

van der Hulst, H. (ed.) (1999). *Word Prosodic Systems in the Languages of Europe*. Berlin: Mouton de Gruyter.

van der Hulst, H., Goedemans, R. W. N., and van Zanten, E. (eds) (2010). *A Survey of Word Accentual Patterns in the Languages of the World*. Berlin: Mouton de Gruyter.

van Driem, G. (1987). *A Grammar of Limbu*. Berlin: Mouton de Gruyter.

van Gelderen, E. (2006). *A History of the English Language*. Amsterdam: Benjamins.

van Hell, J. G., and de Groot, A. M. B. (1998). Conceptual representation in bilingual memory: effects of concreteness and cognate status in word association. *Bilingualism: Language and Cognition* 1: 193–211.

van Heuven, W. J. B., Dijkstra, T., and Grainger, J. (1998). Orthographic neighborhood effects in bilingual word recognition. *Journal of Memory and Language* 39: 458–83.

van Langendonck, W. (1983). Socio-onomastic properties of by-names. In A. J. L. Sinclair (ed.), *G. S. Nienaber: 'n Huldeblyk*. Bellville: UWC Press, 34–62.

van Langendonck, W. (2001). Bynames within the personal name system. *Nomina Africana* 15(1–2): 203–11.
van Langendonck, W. (2005). Proper names and proprial lemmas. In E. Brylla and M. Wahlberg (eds), *Proceedings of the 21st International Congress of Onomastic Sciences, Uppsala, 19–24 August 2002*, vol. 1, 315–23.
van Langendonck, W. (2007). *Theory and Typology of Proper Names*. Berlin: Mouton de Gruyter.
van Oostendorp, M., Ewen, C. J., Hume, E., and Rice, K. (eds) (2011). *The Blackwell Companion to Phonology*. Oxford: Blackwell.
van Rooyen, C. S., Taljaard, P. C. and Davey, A. S. (1976; revised June 1980). *Zulu (course book)*. Pretoria: UNISA.
van Staden, M. (2006). The body and its parts in Tidore, a Papuan language of Eastern Indonesia. *Language Sciences* 28(2–3): 323–43.
van Turennout, M., Hagoort, P., and Brown, C. M. (1997). Electrophysiological evidence on the time course of semantic and phonological processes in speech production. *Journal of Experimental Psychology: Learning, Memory, and Cognition* 23: 787–806.
Veale, T. (2012). *Exploding the Creativity Myth*. London: Bloomsbury.
Veneziano, E., and Parisse, C. (2010). The acquisition of early verbs in French: assessing the role of conversation and of child-directed speech. *First Language* 30: 287–311.
Veneziano, E., Sinclair, H., and Berthoud, J. (1990). From one word to two words: repetition patterns on the way to structured speech. *Journal of Child Language* 17: 633–50.
Vennemann, T. (1994). Linguistic reconstruction in the context of European prehistory. *Transactions of the Philological Society* 92: 215–84.
Verdonschot, R. G., Middelburg, R., Lensink, S. E., and Schiller, N. O. (2012). Morphological priming survives a language switch. *Cognition* 124: 343–9.
Vermeer, A. (2004). The relation between lexical richness and vocabulary size in Dutch L1 and L2 children. In P. Bogaards and B. Laufer (eds), *Vocabulary in a Second Language: Selection, Acquisition, and Testing*. Amsterdam: Benjamins, 173–89.
Verschueren, J. (1999). *Understanding Pragmatics*. London: Arnold.
Verschuyl, H. J. (2004[1988]). Cryptogrammatica: Het cryptogram als taalspel [= Cryptogrammar: the cryptic crossword as a language game], 6th edn. Utrecht: Kosmos-Z&K Uitgevers.
Verschuyl, H. J. (2005). *Het geheim van de puzzle: Geschiedenis van het puzzelen in Nederland [= The secret of the puzzle: history of puzzling in the Netherlands]*. Utrecht: Kosmos-Z&K Uitgevers.
Vidal, K. (2003). Academic listening: a source of vocabulary acquisition? *Applied Linguistics* 24: 56–89.
Vidovic, D. (2010). Family nicknames in Pucisca on the island of Brac. *Rasprave Instituta za Hrvatski Jezik i Jezikoslovlje* 36: 345–67.
Vigario, M., Freitas, M. J., and Fróta, S. (2006). Grammar and frequency effects in the acquisition of prosodic words in European Portuguese. *Language and Speech* 49(2): 175–203.
Vigliocco, G., Antonini, T., and Garrett, M. F. (1997). Grammatical gender is on the tip of Italian tongues. *Psychological Science* 8: 314–17.
Vigliocco, G., and Filipovic, L. (2004). From mind in the mouth to language in the mind. *Trends in Cognitive Sciences* 8: 5–7.
Vigliocco, G., and Vinson, D. P. (2007). Semantic representation. In G. Gaskell (ed.), *The Oxford Handbook of Psycholinguistics*. Oxford: Oxford University Press, 195–215.

Vigliocco, G., Vinson, D. P., Lewis, W., and Garrett, M. F. (2004). Representing the meanings of object and action words: the featural and unitary semantic space hypothesis. *Cognitive Psychology* 48: 422–88.

Vihman, M. (1996). *Phonological Development: The Origins of Language in the Child.* New York: Blackwell.

Vihman, M. M., DePaolis, R. A., and Keren-Portnoy, T. (2009). A dynamic systems approach to babbling and words. In E. Bavin (ed.), *Handbook of Child Language.* Cambridge: Cambridge University Press, 163–82.

Viitso, T.-R. (1998). Estonian. In D. Abondolo (ed.), *The Uralic Languages.* London: Routledge, 115–48.

Vinson, B. P. (2007). *Language Disorders Across the Lifespan*, 2nd edn. Clifton Park, NY: Thomson Delmar Learning.

Vitevitch, M. S. (2008). What can graph theory tell us about word learning and lexical retrieval? *Journal of Speech Language and Hearing Research* 51: 408–22.

Voeltz, F. K. E., and Kilian-Hatz, C. (eds) (2001). *Ideophones.* Amsterdam: Benjamins.

Vogel, I. (1990). The clitic group in prosodic phonology. In J. Mascaró and M. Nespor (eds), *Grammar in Progress: GLOW Essays for Hank van Riemsdijk.* Dordrecht: Foris, 447–54.

Vogel, I. (2009). The status of the clitic group. In J. Grijzenhout and B. Kabak (eds), *Phonological Domains: Universals and Deviations.* Berlin: Mouton de Gruyter, 15–46.

von Staden, P. M. S. (1977). Some remarks on ideophones in Zulu. *African Studies* 36: 195–224.

Vossen, P. (ed.) (1998). *EuroWordNet: A Multilingual Database with Lexical Semantic Networks.* Dordrecht: Kluwer.

Vossen. P., and Fellbaum, C. (2009). Universals and idiosyncrasies in multilingual wordnets. In H. Boas (ed.), *Multilingual Lexical Resources.* Berlin: de Gruyter, 319–45.

Vydrin, V. (1989). Reflection of the nominal classification in Manden and South-Western Mande languages: the connection category. *Zeitschrift für Phonetik, Sprachwissenschaft und Kommunikationsforschungen* 42(1): 91–101.

Vydrin,V. (2001). *Esquisse contrastive du kagoro (Manding).* Cologne: Köppe.

Vydrin, V. (2002). Areal and genetic features in West Mande and South Mande phonology: in what sense did the Mande languages evolve? In H. Ekkehard Wolff (ed.), *Areal Phenomena in West Africa*, special issue of *Journal of West African Languages* 30(2): 113–25.

Vygotsky, L. (1934/1986). *Thought and Language.* Cambridge, Mass.: MIT Press.

Wahrborg, P. (1991). *Assessment and Management of Emotional and Psychosocial Reactions to Brain Damage and Aphasia.* San Diego, Calif.: Singular Publishing Group.

Waksler, R. (2000). Morphological systems and structure in language production. In L. R. Wheeldon (ed.), *Aspects of Language Production.* Hove: Psychology Press, 227–47.

Waldron, R. A. (1967). *Sense and Sense Development.* London: Deutsch.

Walker, I., and Hulme, C. (1999). Concrete words are easier to recall than abstract words: evidence for a semantic contribution to short-term serial recall. *Journal of Experimental Psychology: Learning, Memory, and Cognition* 25: 1256–71.

Walley, A. (1993). More developmental research is needed. *Journal of Phonetics* 21: 171–6.

Walsh, M. (1992). A nagging problem in Australian lexical history. In T. Dutton, M. Ross, and D. Tryon (eds), *The Language Game: Papers in Memory of Donald C. Laycock.* Canberra, ACT: Pacific Linguistics, 507–19.

Walters, J., and Bozkurt, N. (2009). The effect of keeping vocabulary notebooks on vocabulary acquisition. *Language Teaching Research* 13(4): 403–23.

Wang, A. Y., and Thomas, M. H. (1995). Effects of keyword on long-term retention: help or hindrance? *American Psychology* 87: 468–75.

Waring, R. (1997). The negative effects of learning words in semantic sets: a replication. *System* 25: 261–74.

Waring, R., and Nation, I. S. P. (2004). Second language reading and incidental learning. *Angles on the English Speaking World* 4: 11–23.

Waring, R., and Takaki, M. (2003). At what rate do learners learn and retain new vocabulary from reading a graded reader? *Reading in a Foreign Language* 15: 130–63.

Warren, B. (1992). *Sense Developments: A Contrastive Study of the Development of Slang Senses and Novel Standard Senses in English.* Stockholm: Almqvist & Wiksell.

Wasow, T. (1977). Transformations and the lexicon. In P. Culicover, T. Wasow, and J. Bresnan (eds), *Formal Syntax.* New York: Academic Press, 327–60.

Watanabe, Y. (1997). Input, intake, and retention: effects of increased processing on incidental learning of foreign language vocabulary. *Studies in Second Language Acquisition* 19: 287–307.

Waters, S. (2012). 'It's rude to VP': the cultural semantics of rudeness. *Journal of Pragmatics* 44: 1051–62.

Waterson, N. (1956). Some aspects of the phonology of the nominal forms of the Turkish word. *Bulletin of the School of Oriental and African Studies* 18: 378–91.

Watts, D. J., and Strogatz, S. H. (1998). Collective dynamics of 'small-world' networks. *Nature* 393: 440–2.

Waugh, E. (1950). In Harvey Breit: Talk with two writers. *New York Times*, 19 November.

Waxman, S. (1999). The dubbing ceremony revisited: object naming and categorization in infancy and early childhood. In D. Medin and S. Atran (eds), *Folkbiology.* Cambridge, Mass.: MIT Press, 233–84.

Waxman, S., and Markow, D. (1995). Words as invitations to form categories: evidence from 12- to 13-month-old infants. *Cognitive Psychology* 29: 257–302.

Webb, S. (2005). Receptive and productive vocabulary learning: the effects of reading and writing on word knowledge. *Studies in Second Language Acquisition* 27: 33–52.

Webb, S. (2007a). The effects of repetition on vocabulary knowledge. *Applied Linguistics* 28: 46–65.

Webb, S. (2007b). The effects of synonymy on vocabulary learning. *Reading in a Foreign Language* 19: 120–36.

Webb, S. (2008). The effects of context on incidental vocabulary learning. *Reading in a Foreign Language* 20: 232–45.

Webb, S. (2009). The effects of pre-learning vocabulary on reading comprehension and writing. *Canadian Modern Language Review* 65: 441–70.

Webb, S., and Kagimoto, E. (2011). Learning collocations: do the number of collocates, position of the node word, and synonymy affect learning? *Applied Linguistics* 32: 259–76.

Webb, S., and Rodgers, M. P. H. (2009a). The lexical coverage of movies. *Applied Linguistics* 30(3): 407–27.

Webb, S., and Rodgers, M. P. H. (2009b). The vocabulary demands of television programs. *Language Learning* 59(2): 335–66.

Weber, A., and Cutler, A. (2004). Lexical competition in non-native spoken-word recognition. *Journal of Memory and Language* 50: 1–25.

Webster, A. K. (2012). *Rex Lee Jim's 'Mouse that Sucked': On Iconicity, Interwoven-ness, and Ideophones in Contemporary Navajo Poetry.* Portland, Ore.: Linguistic Society of America.

Webster, N. (1783). *The American Spelling Book*. Boston.
Webster, N. (1828). *An American Dictionary of the English Language*. New York: S. Converse.
Wei, Z., and Nation, P. (2013). The word part technique: a very useful vocabulary teaching technique. *Modern English Teacher* 22(1): 12–16.
Weinreich, U. (1953). *Languages in Contact: Findings and Problems*. The Hague: Mouton.
Weinreich, U. (1969). Problems in the analysis of idioms. In J. Puhvel (ed.), *Substance and Structure of Language*. Berkeley, Calif.: University of California Press, 23–81.
Wei Zheng, (2012). *Word Roots in English: Learning English Words through Form and Meaning Similarity*. Wellington: Victoria University of Wellington.
Wei Zheng, and Nation, P. (2013). The word part technique: a very useful vocabulary teaching technique. *Modern English Teacher* 22(1): 12–16.
Wells, H. G. (1901). The First Men in the Moon. <http://www.gutenberg.org/ebooks/1013>.
Werker, J. (1989). Becoming a native listener. *American Scientist* 77: 54–9.
Werker, J., Cohen, L., Lloyd, V., Casasola, M., and Stager, C. (1998). Acquisition of word–object associations by 14-month-old infants. *Developmental Psychology* 34: 1289–309.
Werker, J., and Pegg, J. (1992). Infant speech perception and phonological acquisition. In C. Ferguson, L. Menn, and C. Stoel-Gammon (eds), *Phonological Development: Models, Research, Implications*. Timonium, Md.: York Press, 285–311.
Werker, J., and Tees, R. (1984). Cross-language speech perception: evidence for perceptual reorganization during the first year of life. *Infant Behavior and Development* 7: 49–63.
Werker, J., and Yeung, H. (2005). Infant speech perception bootstraps word learning. *Trends in Cognitive Science* 9: 519–27.
Werker, J., Yeung, H., and Yoshida, K. (2012). How do infants become experts at native-speech perception? *Current Directions in Psychological Science* 21(4) 221–6.
Werner, H., and Kaplan, B. (1963). *Symbol Formation*. New York: Wiley.
Wernicke, C. (1874). *Der Aphasische Symptomenkomplex: Eine Psychologische Studie auf Anatomischer Basis*. Breslau: Cohn & Welgert.
Wescott, R. W. (1973). Tonal icons in Bini. *Studies in African Linguistics* 4(2): 197–205.
West, M. (1953). *A General Service List of English Words*. London: Longman, Green.
Wettler, M., Rapp, R., and Sedlmeier, P. (2005). Free word association corresponds to contiguities between words in texts. *Journal of Quantitative Linguistics* 12: 111–22.
Wheeldon, L. R., and Levelt, W. J. M. (1995). Monitoring the time course of phonological encoding. *Journal of Memory and Language* 34: 311–34.
Wheeldon, L. R., and Monsell, S. (1994). Inhibition of spoken word production by priming a semantic competitor. *Journal of Memory and Language* 33: 332–56.
Whissell, C. (1999). Phonosymbolism and the emotional nature of sounds: evidence of preferential use of particular phonemes in text of differing emotional tone. *Perceptual and Motor Skills* 89: 19–48.
Whissell, C. (2000). Phonoemotional profiling: a description of the emotional flavour of English texts on the basis of the phonemes employed in them. *Perceptual and Motor Skills* 91: 617–48.
Whissell, C. (2001a). Sound and emotion in given names. *Names* 49(2): 97–120.
Whissell, C. (2001b). Cues to referent gender in randomly constructed names. *Perceptual and Motor Skills* 93: 856–8.
Whissell, C. (2003a). The emotional symbolism of two English e-sounds: /i/ as in 'cheap' is pleasant and /ɪ/ as in 'chip' is active. *Perceptual and Motor Skills* 96: 149–65.
Whissell, C. (2003b). Pronounceability: a measure of language samples based on children's mastery of the phonemes employed in them. *Perceptual and Motor Skills* 96: 748–54.

Whissell, C. (2006a). Emotion in the sounds of pets' names. *Perceptual and Motor Skills* 102: 121–4.

Whissell, C. (2006b). Geographical and political predictors of emotion in the sounds of favourite baby names. *Perceptual and Motor Skills* 102: 105–8.

Whissell, C. (2006c). Historical and socioeconomic predictors of the emotional associations of sounds in popular names. *Perceptual and Motor Skills* 103: 451–6.

Wichmann, S., and Brown, C. H. (2003). Contact among some Mayan languages: inferences from loanwords. *Anthropological Linguistics* 45(1): 57–93.

Wichmann, S., Rama, T., and Holman, E. W. (2011). Phonological diversity, word length, and population sizes across languages: the ASJP evidence. *Linguistic Typology* 15(2): 177–97.

Wierzbicka, A. (1984). Diminutives and depreciatives: semantic representation for derivational categories. *Quaderni di semantica* 5: 123–30.

Wierzbicka, A. (1986). Does language reflect culture? Evidence from Australian English. *Language in Society* 15: 349–74.

Wierzbicka, A. (1990). Antitotalitarian language in Poland: some mechanisms of linguistic self-defense. *Language in Society* 19: 1–59.

Wierzbicka, A. (1992). *Semantics, Culture and Cognition: Universal Human Concepts in Culture-Specific Configurations*. New York: Oxford University Press.

Wierzbicka, A. (1996). *Semantics: Primes and Universals*. Oxford: Oxford University Press.

Wierzbicka, A. (1997). *Understanding Cultures Through Their Key Words: English, Russian, Polish, German, Japanese*. New York: Oxford University Press.

Wierzbicka, A. (1999). *Emotions Across Language and Cultures: Diversity and Universals*. Cambridge: Cambridge University Press.

Wierzbicka, A. (2003). *Cross-Cultural Pragmatics: The Semantics of Social Interaction*, 2nd edn. Berlin: Mouton de Gruyter.

Wierzbicka, A. (2005). There are no 'colour universals', but there are universals of visual semantics. *Anthropological Linguistics* 47(2): 217–44.

Wierzbicka, A. (2006a). *English: Meaning and Culture*. New York: Oxford University Press.

Wierzbicka, A. (2006b). Anglo scripts against 'putting pressure' on other people and their linguistic manifestations. In C. Goddard (ed.), *Ethnopragmatics: Understanding Discourse in Cultural Context*. Berlin: Mouton de Gruyter, 31–63.

Wierzbicka, A. (2007). Bodies and their parts: an NSM approach to semantic typology. *Language Sciences* 29(1): 14–65.

Wierzbicka, A. (2008a). Why there are no 'colour universals' in language and thought. *Journal of the Royal Anthropological Institute* 14(2): 407–25.

Wierzbicka, A. (2008b). A conceptual basis for intercultural pragmatics and world-wide understanding. In M. Pütz and J. Neff-van Aertselaer (eds), *Developing Contrastive Pragmatics: Interlanguage and Cross-cultural Perspectives*. Berlin: Mouton de Gruyter, 33–46.

Wierzbicka, A. (2010a). *Experience, Evidence and Sense: The Hidden Cultural Legacy of English*. New York: Oxford University Press.

Wierzbicka, A. (2010b). 'Story': an English cultural keyword and a key interpretive tool of Anglo culture. *Narrative Inquiry* 20(1): 153–81.

Wierzbicka, A. (2011). Defining 'the humanities'. *Humanities Australia* 2: 53–61.

Wierzbicka, A. (2012). 'Advice' in English and in Russian: a contrastive and cross-cultural perspective. In H. Limberg and M. A. Locher (eds), *Advice in Discourse*. Amsterdam: Benjamins, 309–32.

Wierzbicka, A. (2013). Translatability and the scripting of other peoples' souls. *Australian Journal of Anthropology* 24(1): 1–22.

Wierzbicka, A. (2014a). *Imprisoned in English: The Hazards of English as a Default Language.* New York: Oxford University Press.

Wierzbicka, A. (2014b). Can there be common knowledge without a common language? English 'duty' vs. German 'Pflicht'. *Common Knowledge* 21(1): 141–71.

Wikipedia (2005). Nomenclature of inorganic chemistry.

Wikipedia (2012). NP-Complete. <http://www.wikipedia.org/wiki/NP-complete>.

Wilbur, R. (1987). In E. Kastor, 'Richard Wilbur survives the poet laureate initiation'. *Los Angeles Times*, 13 October.

Wilde, O. (1891). The critic as artist. In *Intentions*. New York: Dodd & Mead.

Wilkins, D. (1972). *Linguistics in Language Teaching*. London: Arnold.

Wilkins, J. (1968[1668]). *An Essay towards a Real Character, and a Philosophical Language.* Menston: Scolar Press.

Williams, E. (1981). On the notions 'lexically related' and 'head of a word'. *Linguistic Inquiry* 12: 245–74.

Williams, J. N. (1994). The relationship between word meanings in the first and second language: Evidence for a common, but restricted, semantic code. *European Journal of Cognitive Psychology* 6: 195–220.

Williams, J. N., and Cheung, A. (2011). Using priming to explore early word learning. In P. Trofimovich and K. McDonough (eds), *Applying Priming Methods to L2 Learning, Teaching and Research: Insights from Psycholinguistics.* Amsterdam: Benjamins, 73–103.

Williams, R. (1976). *Keywords: A Vocabulary of Culture and Society*. London: Croom Helm.

Willis, D. (1990). *The Lexical Syllabus: A New Approach to Language Teaching.* London: Collins ELT.

Willson, K. J. (2008). Icelandic nicknames. Doctoral dissertation, University of California, Berkeley.

Wilson, B. S., and Skipper, J. K. (1990). Nicknames and women professional baseball players. *Names* 38: 305–22.

Wimmer, G., and Altmann, G. (1996). The theory of word length: some results and generalizations. *Glottometrika 15: Issues in General Linguistic Theory and the Theory of Word Length.* Trier: WVT, 112–33.

Wimmer, G., and Altmann, G. (1999). *Thesaurus of Univariate Discrete Probability Distributions.* Essen: Stamm.

Wimmer, G., and Altmann, G. (2005). Unified derivation of some linguistic laws. In R. Köhler, G. Altmann, and R. G. Piotrovski (eds), *Quantitative Linguistik: ein Internationales Handbuch/ Quantitative Linguistics: An International Handbook.* Berlin: de Gruyter, 791–807.

Wimmer, G., and Altmann, G. (2006). Towards a unified derivation of some linguistic laws. In P. Grzybek (ed.), *Contributions to the Science of Text and Language: Word Length Studies and Related Issues.* Dordrecht: Springer, 329–37.

Wimmer, G., Köhler, R., Grotjahn, R., and Altmann, G. (1994). Towards a theory of word length distribution. *Journal of Quantitative Linguistics* 1(1): 98–106.

Winford, D. (2003). *An Introduction to Contact Linguistics*. London: Arnold.

Wingo, E. O. (1972). *Latin Punctuation in the Classical Age.* The Hague: de Gruyter.

Winston, M. E., Chaffin, R., and Herrmann, D. (1987). A taxonomy of part–whole relations. *Cognitive Science* 11: 417–44.

Winters, M. E., Tissari, H., and Allan, K. (eds) (2010). *Historical Cognitive Linguistics.* Berlin: Mouton de Gruyter.

Witkowski, S. R., and Brown, C. H. (1985). Climate, clothing, and body-part nomenclature. *Ethnology* 24(3): 197–214.

Wittgenstein, L. (1953). *Philosophical Investigations*. Oxford: Basil Blackwell.

Wnuk, E., and Majid, A. (2012). Olfaction in a hunter-gatherer society: insights from language and culture. In *Proceedings of the 34th Annual Conference of the Cognitive Science Society*. Austin, Tex.: Cognitive Science Society, 1155–60.

Wohlgemuth, J. (2009). *A Typology of Verbal Borrowing*. Berlin: Mouton.

Wolffsohn, M., and Brechenmacher, T. (2001). Nomen est omen: the selection of first names as an indicator of public opinion in the past. *International Journal of Public Opinion Research* 13(2): 116–39.

Wong, J. (2006a). Contextualizing aunty in Singaporean English. *World Englishes* 25(3–4): 451–66.

Wong, J. (2006b). Social hierarchy in the 'speech culture' of Singapore. In C. Goddard (ed.), *Ethnopragmatics: Understanding Discourse in Cultural Context*. Berlin: Mouton de Gruyter, 99–126.

Wong, S. Y. J. (2007). Nicknames in Hong Kong and England: forms, functions, and their relation to personal names and other forms of address. Doctoral dissertation, Open University.

Woodbury, H. (1975). Onondaga noun incorporation: some notes on the interdependence of syntax and semantics. *International Journal of American Linguistics* 41: 10–20.

Woodward, A. L., and Hoyne, K. L. (1999). Infants' learning about words and sounds in relation to objects. *Child Development* 70: 65–77.

Woordenboek der Nederlandsche Taal (1863–1998). Leiden: Instituut voor Nederlandse Lexicologie.

World Health Organization (1992). *The ICD-10 Classification for Mental and Behavioural Disorders: Diagnostic Criteria For Research*. Geneva: WHO.

Wordnik (2008–). <www.wordnik.com>.

Wray, A. (1996). The occurrence of 'occurance' and 'alot' of other things 'aswell': patterns of errors in undergraduate English. In G. Blue and R. Mitchell (eds), *Language and Education*. Clevedon: Multilingual Matters, 94–106.

Wray, A. (2002a). *Formulaic Language and the Lexicon*. Cambridge: Cambridge University Press.

Wray, A. (2002b). Dual processing in protolanguage: performance without competence. In A. Wray (ed.), *The Transition to Language*. Oxford: Oxford University Press, 113–37.

Wray, A. (2004). 'Here's one I prepared earlier': formulaic language learning on television. In N. Schmitt (ed.), *Formulaic Sequences: Acquisition, Processing and Use*. Amsterdam: Benjamins, 249–68.

Wray, A. (2008a). *Formulaic Language: Pushing the Boundaries*. Oxford: Oxford University Press.

Wray, A. (2008b). Formulaic sequences and language disorders. In M. Ball, M. Perkins, N. Müller, and S. Howard (eds), *Handbook of Clinical Linguistics*. Oxford: Blackwell, 184–97.

Wray, A. (2009). Identifying formulaic language: persistent challenges and new opportunities. In R. Corrigan, E. Moravcsik, M. Oulali, and K. Wheatley (eds), *Formulaic Language*, vol. 1: *Structure, Distribution, Historical Change: Typological Studies in Language*. Amsterdam: Benjamins, 27–51.

Wray, A., and Staczek, J. J. (2005). One word or two? Psycholinguistic and sociolinguistic interpretations of meaning in a civil court case. *International Journal of Speech, Language and the Law* 12(1): 1–18.

Wright, E. (1939). *Gadsby*. Laurel, NY: Lightyear Press.

Wright, J. (1898–1905). *The English Dialect Dictionary*. Oxford: Clarendon Press.

Wu, Y. J., and Thierry, G. (2010). Chinese–English bilinguals reading English hear Chinese. *Journal of Neuroscience* 30: 7646–51.

Wulff, S. (2008). *Rethinking Idiomaticity: A Usage-Based Approach*. London: Continuum.

Wurm, S. A. (1970). Austronesian and the vocabulary of languages of the Reef and Santa Cruz Islands: a preliminary approach. In S. A. Wurm and D. C. Laycock (eds), *Pacific Linguistic Studies in Honour of Arthur Capell*. Canberra: Pacific Linguistics, 467–553.

Wüster, U. (1979). *Einführung in die allgemeine Terminologielehre und terminologische Lexikographie*. Vienna: Springer.

Wyld, H. C. (1920/1936). *A History of Modern Colloquial English*. Oxford: Blackwell.

Xiaoyan, L. (1996). *Best Chinese Names: Your Guide to Auspicious Names*. Singapore: Asiapac.

Yassin, M. A. F. (1978). Personal names of address in Kuwaiti Arabic. *Anthropological Linguistics* 20: 53–63.

Ye, Z. (2004). Chinese categorization of interpersonal relationships and the cultural logic of Chinese social interaction: an indigenous perspective. *Intercultural Pragmatics* 1(2): 211–30.

Ye, Z. (2013). Understanding the conceptual basis of the 'old friend' formulas in Chinese social interaction and foreign diplomacy: a cultural script approach. In C. Goddard (ed.), *Semantics and/in Social Cognition*. Special issue of *Australian Journal of Linguistics* 33(3): 366–86.

Yeung, H., and Werker, J. (2009). Learning words' sounds before learning how words sound: 9-month-olds use distinct objects as cues to categorize speech information. *Cognition* 113: 234–43.

Yong, H., and Peng, J. (2008). *Chinese Lexicography: A History from 1046 BC to AD 1911*. Oxford: Oxford University Press.

Yoon, K.-J. (2004). Not just words: Korean social models and the use of honorifics. *Intercultural Pragmatics* 1(2): 189–210.

Yoshida, K., Pons, F., Maye, J., and Werker, J. (2010). Distributional phonetic learning at 10 months of age. *Infancy* 15: 420–33.

Yu, C., and Smith, L. B. (2007). Rapid word learning under uncertainty via cross-situational statistics. *Psychological Science* 18(5): 414–20.

Yu, N. (1998). *The Contemporary Theory of Metaphor: A Perspective from Chinese*. Amsterdam: Benjamins.

Zaitzow, B. H., Skipper, J. K., and Bryant, C. (1997). Nicknames of female felons. *Names* 45: 83–100.

Zec, D. (1988). Sonority constraints on prosodic structure. Ph.D dissertation, Stanford University.

Zenner, E., Speelman, D., and Geeraerts, D. (2012). Cognitive sociolinguistics meets loanword research: measuring variation in the success of anglicisms in Dutch. *Cognitive Linguistics* 23: 749–92.

Zeshan, U. (2002). Towards a notion of 'word' in sign languages. In R. M. W. Dixon and A. Y. Aikhenvald (eds), *Word: A Cross-Linguistic Typology*. Cambridge: Cambridge University Press, 153–79.

Zinkevicius, Z. (2009). Interaction of Lithuanian personal names. *Baltistica* 44: 125–34.

Zipf, G. K. (1935). *The Psycho-Biology of Language*. Cambridge, Mass.: MIT Press. Reprinted 1965.

Zipf, G. (1949). *Human Behavior and the Principle of Least Effort: An Introduction to Human Ecology*. New York: Hafner.

Zörnig, P. (2013a). Distances between words of equal length in a text. In R. Köhler and G. Altmann (eds), *Issues in Quantitative Linguistics* 3. Lüdenscheid: RAM, 117–29.

Zörnig, P. (2013b). A continuous model for the distances between coextensive words in a text. *Glottometrics* 25: 54–68.

Zwicky, A. M. (1977). *On Clitics*. Bloomington: Indiana University Linguistics Club.

Zwicky, A. (1992). Some choices in the theory of morphology. In R. Levine (ed.), *Formal Grammar: Theory and Implementation*. Oxford: Oxford University Press, 327–71.

Zwicky, A. M. (1995). What is a clitic? In J. Nevis, B. Joseph, D. Wanner, and A. M. Zwicky (eds), *Clitics: A Comprehensive Bibliography 1892–1991*. Amsterdam: Benjamins.

Zwicky, A. M., and Pullum, G. K. (1983). Cliticization vs. inflection: English *n't*. *Language* 59: 502–13.

Zwitserlood, P. (1994). The role of semantic transparency in the processing and representation of Dutch compounds. *Language and Cognitive Processes* 9: 341–68.

Zwitserlood, P. (2004). Sublexical and morphological information in speech processing. *Brain and Language* 90: 368–77.

Zwitserlood, P., Bölte, J., and Dohmes, P. (2000). Morphological effects on speech production: evidence from picture naming. *Language and Cognitive Processes* 15: 563–91.

Zwitserlood, P., Bölte, J., and Dohmes, P. (2002). Where and how morphologically complex words interplay with naming pictures. *Brain and Language* 81: 358–67.

Index of Languages

Subject Index

OXFORD HANDBOOKS IN LINGUISTICS

THE OXFORD HANDBOOK OF APPLIED LINGUISTICS
Second edition
Edited by Robert B. Kaplan

THE OXFORD HANDBOOK OF ARABIC LINGUISTICS
Edited by Jonathan Owens

THE OXFORD HANDBOOK OF CASE
Edited by Andrej Malchukov and Andrew Spencer

THE OXFORD HANDBOOK OF COGNITIVE LINGUISTICS
Edited by Dirk Geeraerts and Hubert Cuyckens

THE OXFORD HANDBOOK OF COMPARATIVE SYNTAX
Edited by Guglielmo Cinque and Richard S. Kayne

THE OXFORD HANDBOOK OF COMPOSITIONALITY
Edited by Markus Werning, Wolfram Hinzen, and Edouard Machery

THE OXFORD HANDBOOK OF COMPOUNDING
Edited by Rochelle Lieber and Pavol Štekauer

THE OXFORD HANDBOOK OF COMPUTATIONAL LINGUISTICS
Edited by Ruslan Mitkov

THE OXFORD HANDBOOK OF CONSTRUCTION GRAMMAR
Edited by Thomas Hoffman and Graeme Trousdale

THE OXFORD HANDBOOK OF CORPUS PHONOLOGY
Edited by Jacques Durand, Ulrike Gut, and Gjert Kristoffersen

THE OXFORD HANDBOOK OF DERIVATIONAL MORPHOLOGY
Edited by Rochelle Lieber and Pavol Štekauer

THE OXFORD HANDBOOK OF GRAMMATICALIZATION
Edited by Heiko Narrog and Bernd Heine

THE OXFORD HANDBOOK OF HISTORICAL PHONOLOGY
Edited by Patrick Honeybone and Joseph Salmons

THE OXFORD HANDBOOK OF THE HISTORY OF ENGLISH
Edited by Terttu Nevalainen and Elizabeth Closs Traugott

THE OXFORD HANDBOOK OF THE HISTORY OF LINGUISTICS

Edited by Keith Allan

THE OXFORD HANDBOOK OF INFLECTION

Edited by Matthew Baerman

THE OXFORD HANDBOOK OF JAPANESE LINGUISTICS

Edited by Shigeru Miyagawa and Mamoru Saito

THE OXFORD HANDBOOK OF LABORATORY PHONOLOGY

Edited by Abigail C. Cohn, Cécile Fougeron, and Marie Hoffman

THE OXFORD HANDBOOK OF LANGUAGE AND LAW

Edited by Peter Tiersma and Lawrence M. Solan

THE OXFORD HANDBOOK OF LANGUAGE EVOLUTION

Edited by Maggie Tallerman and Kathleen Gibson

THE OXFORD HANDBOOK OF LINGUISTIC ANALYSIS

Second edition

Edited by Bernd Heine and Heiko Narrog

THE OXFORD HANDBOOK OF LINGUISTIC FIELDWORK

Edited by Nicholas Thieberger

THE OXFORD HANDBOOK OF LINGUISTIC INTERFACES

Edited by Gillian Ramchand and Charles Reiss

THE OXFORD HANDBOOK OF LINGUISTIC MINIMALISM

Edited by Cedric Boeckx

THE OXFORD HANDBOOK OF LINGUISTIC TYPOLOGY

Edited by Jae Jung Song

THE OXFORD HANDBOOK OF SOCIOLINGUISTICS

Edited by Robert Bayley, Richard Cameron, and Ceil Lucas

THE OXFORD HANDBOOK OF TENSE AND ASPECT

Edited by Robert I. Binnick

THE OXFORD HANDBOOK OF THE WORD

Edited by John R. Taylor

THE OXFORD HANDBOOK OF TRANSLATION STUDIES

Edited by Kirsten Malmkjaer and Kevin Windle

Lightning Source UK Ltd.
Milton Keynes UK
UKOW07f1953210817
307615UK00003B/7/P

9 780198 808633